THE DEATH OF
AMERICAN
VIRTUE

ALSO BY KEN GORMLEY

ARCHIBALD COX
Conscience of a Nation

THE DEATH OF
AMERICAN
VIRTUE

———

CLINTON *vs.* STARR

KEN GORMLEY

BROADWAY PAPERBACKS NEW YORK

To my wife, Laura,
my best friend always, who supported this project for nine years
as I trekked into the salt mines.

And to our children—Carolyn, Luke, Rebecca, and Maddy—
who brought joy to the author's study.

This book was destined to have many pages because each word
represents a small expression of my love for them.

CONTENTS

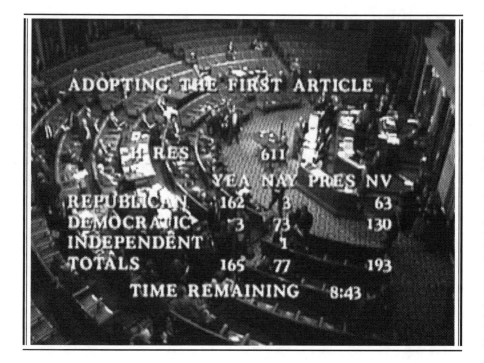

ADOPTING THE FIRST ARTICLE

	YEA	NAY	PRES	NV
REPUBLICAN	162	3		63
DEMOCRATIC	3	73		130
INDEPENDENT		1		
TOTALS	165	77		193

TIME REMAINING   8:43

PRELUDE

COLLISION IN
THE CAPITOL

CHAPTER 1

The Impeachment Vote

I t was an unusual day for a vote that might extinguish a presidency.

Congress rarely did official business on Saturdays, let alone just before the Christmas holiday. But on this morning—December 19, 1998—with a chilly rain pelting the dome of the Capitol, lights were blazing in every office on the House of Representatives side. Fax machines spewed out confidential messages. President Bill Clinton had just launched a surprise attack in the Persian Gulf against Iraqi dictator Saddam Hussein, prompting cries of "Wag the Dog!" by angry Republicans. Now, after a day's postponement out of deference to military troops, the appointed hour had arrived.

Henry Hyde, distinguished Republican from Illinois, strode to the wooden lectern. He was wearing a dark blue suit and red tie befitting the seriousness of the occasion. As chairman of the powerful House Judiciary Committee, the white-maned Congressman Hyde had been responsible for drafting all four articles of impeachment against the forty-second president: Article I accused William Jefferson Clinton of lying to a federal grand jury in connection with the Monica Lewinsky affair; Article II charged him with lying under oath in the sexual harassment lawsuit filed by Paula Jones, an Arkansas employee when Clinton was governor; Article III alleged obstruction of justice and subornation of perjury; Article IV alleged a general "misuse and abuse" of Clinton's high office.

Chairman Hyde would remember this as a "somber, somber" day. The Republicans, herded into line by Majority Whip Tom DeLay, were optimistic that they could push through at least one article. Yet, as Hyde would admit five years later to the day, seated in his suburban Chicago office surrounded by a career's worth of political memorabilia, he felt that he had a "tiger by the tail." He had no idea what would happen when he wrestled that tiger to the ground, or which combatant would survive the struggle.

A strange unease gripped the House chamber. Pornographer Larry Flynt, publisher of *Hustler* magazine, had just run a full-page ad in the *Washington Post* offering a million-dollar bounty for information leading to "evidence of illicit sexual relations" involving members of Congress, especially prominent Republicans. Flynt had dubbed the Starr Report "more depraved and scandalous" than any act Bill Clinton had committed. Now the pornographer had set out to expose the "hypocrisy" of this impeachment drive. As the seventy-four-year-old Hyde stepped to the microphone, he cursed how things had taken such an ugly turn.

It was bad enough that Hyde himself had recently been the victim of an attack by the liberal Internet publication *Salon.* That magazine had revealed that Hyde had engaged in an adulterous affair with a hairdresser named Cherie Snodgrass in 1965, back when Hyde was forty-one years old. Now, thirty-three years later, with his wife Jeanne dead of breast cancer and his four grown children raising children of their own, Hyde had been forced to confess his "youthful indiscretions," the most humiliating experience of his four decades in public life.

In this city infested with political vipers, it seemed that no politician was safe. A day earlier, Flynt's offer of blood money had ensnared Hyde's colleague, Representative Bob Livingston (a Republican from Louisiana), the man slated to replace Newt Gingrich as Speaker of the House in the wake of the disastrous midterm elections in November. Capitol Hill's *Roll Call* now reported that Livingston had engaged in a host of extramarital liaisons—with a female judge in Louisiana, with a lobbyist, and with a member of his own staff. Representative Livingston had tried to blunt the attack, calling Flynt a "bottom feeder." To this, Flynt replied smugly, "Well, that's right. But look what I found when I got down there." Everywhere one turned, there appeared to be destruction, carnage, bodies littered across the road. On this historic Saturday morning, Henry Hyde was still determined to do his constitutional duty.

Democrats and Republicans took turns at the microphone, alternately defending and excoriating President Bill Clinton. Chairman Hyde yielded two minutes of time to his friend, Speaker designate Bob Livingston. What Livingston would say, under these odd circumstances, Hyde had no idea.

"You know," Hyde whispered to Livingston as he brushed past him stiffly, "these things blow over."

Speaker pro tem Ray LaHood (R-Ill.), a huge American flag draped behind him, wielded the gavel like a railroad man prepared to pound steel ties into the track. He pronounced somberly: "Proceed." Livingston arranged his typed remarks on the lectern. Tall, thin, silver-haired, and famous for his unflappable demeanor, Bob Livingston was a model of congressional comportment. Today there was something ill at ease about his appearance.

"Mr. Speaker," he began. The time was 9:45 A.M.

Livingston had completed writing out this statement the previous night in a fit of insomnia, wrestling with demons that this Clinton madness had unleashed. He wore a dark pin-striped suit and a Christmas tie; the latter conveyed not a hint of yuletide cheer. "We are all pawns on the chessboard," Livingston read through his bifocals, "and we are playing our parts in a drama that is neither fiction nor unimportant."

Those who knew Bob Livingston recognized that there was something strange about his delivery. The normally strong and confident fifty-five-year-old lawyer from New Orleans was fiddling with his fingers and straightening his tie. "I will vote to impeach the president of the United States and ask that his case be considered by the United States Senate," said the Speaker designate. He touched the microphone nervously, as if reaching for some fixed object to steady him.

"To the president I would say: Sir, you have done great damage to this nation over this past year." Livingston's hands flew out of control, making gestures and pointing as if out of sync with his speech. "You, sir, may *resign* your post."

The Democrats erupted into boos, hisses, and catcalls.

Livingston's face became pinched and defiant. He had been stewing over this segment of the speech ever since that vile pornographer Larry Flynt had "outed" him. The previous day, he had ripped up the draft into a hundred pieces. "It just needs a kicker," he had said to his secretary, Raine Simpson, his eyes puffy with exhaustion. "It needs a better ending."

At two or three in the morning, Congressman Livingston had awakened in a cold sweat, lying beside his wife, Bonnie, his faithful mate of thirty years. At that god-awful hour it had struck him like a fiery bolt: "I realized what the ending was going to be," he recalled years later.

Bob Livingston now stared at the sea of angry Democratic colleagues, raising his hand like a policeman to halt them.

"*You* resign!" they shouted back, unfazed by the Speaker designate's quivering hand. "*You* resign!"

Speaker pro tem LaHood pounded his gavel. He bellowed over the melee, "The House will be in order!"

Livingston waited for a lull. Then he delivered the punch line with a loud and defiant voice: "And I can only challenge *him* [President Clinton] in such fashion if I am willing to heed my *own* words." There came a scattering of gasps. The House fell into silence, as if members suddenly recognized what was about to happen.

"To my colleagues, my friends, and most especially my wife and family," Livingston said, delivering his own eulogy, "I have hurt you all deeply, and I beg your forgiveness."

The congressman's hands shook as he gripped the sheet of paper. "I must set the example that I hope *President Clinton* will follow. Mr. Speaker . . . I shall vacate my seat and ask my governor to call a special election to take my place."

Pandemonium now erupted on both sides of the aisle, like an earthquake shaking the foundations of a city. Livingston spoke over the din: "I thank my wife most especially for standing by me. I love her very much."

As his final declamation in the well of Congress, the dishonored representative declared, "God bless America."

Livingston grabbed his sheaf of papers, looking like a man who had just walked into the mouth of hell. Members stood up, uncertain how to handle the news. They burst into spontaneous applause that filled the House chamber like the roar in the Roman Colosseum after a dozen lions had been unleashed. Democrats and Republicans pounded their hands together, giving ovations for wholly different reasons. Journalists scribbled frantically on notepads, preparing urgent news releases to inform the world that one of the most powerful congressmen had just resigned and had dared President Clinton to do the same.

Chairman Henry Hyde slumped back in his chair, absorbing this latest bombshell with a sense of deep sorrow. He later recalled, "I wished he had stuck it out. . . . I'd have liked to see an honest show of hands of members who had had the same experience [of marital infidelity]." Said Hyde, with undisguised bitterness, "I felt it was an unnecessary waste of a good member."

David Schippers, chief counsel to the Judiciary Committee and close ally of Hyde's, stood at the rear of the hall in a state of shock. He walked over, draped his arm around Bob Livingston, and told him, "I hope to God you'll be back."

Schippers perceived, suddenly, that the Democrats "were acting disgraceful." He could hear them laughing. "They were taking pleasure in our discomfiture," he later said. Within the Republican caucus, a new strain of anger was bubbling up. "We felt that Clinton was behind it all," said Schippers. "That was his mode of operation."

Democratic representative José Serrano of New York, who had taken over the microphone, only incensed Republicans further by declaring, "My constituents don't hate Bill Clinton. They love him and pray for him at this moment. . . . The bullies get theirs, and you're going to get yours too!"

Democratic leader Dick Gephardt hustled out of the cloakroom and offered an olive branch, urging Livingston, for the good of the American people, to reconsider his resignation and calling upon both parties to end the "politics of personal destruction." The Republicans weren't buying it. They were convinced that Clinton and his political operatives were behind the Democratic leader's insincere expression of sympathy. "I somehow think of Aesop's fable about the crocodile tears," Robert Livingston later said.

Order was finally restored, long enough for members of Congress to vote on the impeachment question. Two counts passed with solid majorities—those relating to Clinton's lying in front of the grand jury and his obstruction of justice. Two articles failed—those relating to Clinton's lying in the Paula Jones deposition and his general abuse of high office. The vote was strictly along party lines.

David Schippers turned to a Republican staffer and gasped, "My God, they have just impeached the president of the United States!"

As pandemonium erupted, members of Congress took refuge in the restrooms as reporters flooded into the halls. One of Bob Livingston's fellow Republicans, looking shell-shocked, told a reporter, "This has not been a rational day."

Years later, after building a successful international lobbying firm and leaving this nightmare behind him, Robert Livingston would reconstruct his decision to resign: "I stood up and resigned my job in an effort to convince the president of the United States that he had done wrong." Livingston's voice turned hard, almost icy: "I wanted him *gone*. I wanted him *impeached*. I wanted him to be shown for the liar under oath that he was when he was president of the United States and [that] he violated his oath of office to the United States of America." To accomplish this, Livingston said, he was prepared to "take the heat."

President Clinton would later disavow any participation in the "outing" of Representative Livingston by Larry Flynt, or in the chaotic events that brought down Bob Livingston. "I knew nothing about it," Clinton said, sitting calmly at his home in Chappaqua, New York. Although Clinton had "always liked" Livingston as a political acquaintance, he was disappointed at how Livingston had "rah-rahed along with Gingrich and DeLay on the impeachment." Livingston's fall from grace in his own personal sex scandal, as Clinton saw it, was "just one more example of [the Republicans'] hypocrisy." The former president continued: "The interesting thing was, Larry Flynt turned out to be a better guy than Ken Starr. I mean basically, the story was that Mrs. Livingston went to him and pleaded with him not to release any more of the details. And [he agreed to that after] Livingston resigned from Congress."

Clinton also scoffed at the assertion that Livingston's resignation was driven by some sort of moral reawakening. The president's intelligence from behind enemy lines indicated that the Republican leadership "came to [Livingston] and said he would have to quit, *not* because they were upset about what he did, but because he was standing in the way of my impeachment."

Chairman Hyde walked back through the marble halls of Congress on that cold Saturday in December, somberly contemplating what a Senate trial might look like. This had been "a heavy day," Hyde would admit, reflecting upon the weekend when he garnered enough votes to impeach the president of the United

States. Glancing at the chilly rain pelting against the windows of the now empty Capitol, the representative from Illinois knew that the days ahead would be even heavier.

———

In Arkansas, time momentarily stood still. Christmas shoppers in downtown Little Rock paused on the streets. Supporters and detractors of Bill Clinton alike froze in their tracks, absorbing the news: The House of Representatives had voted to impeach the first native son of Arkansas ever to occupy the White House.

The day in Little Rock was gray and chilly. A cold front, moving east with light showers, kept temperatures hovering below fifty degrees. Over municipal buildings, red, blue, and white state flags of Arkansas snapped in the breeze. The *Arkansas Democrat-Gazette* had already begun printing Sunday papers bearing the black headline "Impeached." Salvation Army volunteers along West Markham Street held their bells silent. The Rose Law Firm, where First Lady Hillary Rodham Clinton had launched her legal career before moving to Washington, seemed to be paralyzed as if hit by an ice storm. Festive holly wreaths adorning the wooden doors hung like flora stricken by a killing frost. A dozen Mercedes in the parking lot sat idle, as if their batteries had unexpectedly died. Inside the redbrick building, lawyers sat frozen in front of portable television sets, watching replays of the vote tally.

The latest reports from Washington cut in over sound systems of downtown department stores, momentarily interrupting Elvis Presley's "Blue Christmas," a sacred anthem in Little Rock. Elvis was still king in this Southern town; yet even Elvis had to take a backseat today to the shocking news being broadcast from Washington.

Bill Clinton's closest friends were numb from disbelief.

Skip Rutherford, who had cast one of Arkansas's electoral votes during Clinton's triumphant victory of 1992, drove home from his downtown Little Rock office, collapsed in front of the television in his den, and refused to take calls. In this same room, Rutherford had answered a barrage of media calls the night his friend Vince Foster had committed suicide in 1993—after Vince had gone to Washington to help Bill and Hillary make a difference. Now all Rutherford had the strength to do was watch a flickering *Walton Family Christmas Special,* one of his childhood favorites about an honest mountain family that struggled through hard times in the Depression. He watched for hours, with the telephone wire yanked out of the wall, until sleep extinguished this bad dream.

Joe Purvis, who had attended kindergarten with Clinton in the little town of Hope, back when Bill Clinton's name was still "Billy Blythe" and their mothers had pushed them on swings together, was traveling to Washington to attend a

White House Christmas party. Purvis and his wife, Susan, caught the news while changing planes in Cincinnati. The couple looked at each other in horror. Purvis whispered, "My God. . . ." The burly Purvis was big enough to pick Clinton up and throw him into the nearest river, and he felt like doing it now. Among other things, Bill had lied to his face, by flat-out denying the affair with Monica Lewinsky.

Yet the real culprit, Purvis felt, was not Bill Clinton. Whatever had happened with this young intern "was really no one's business but Bill's and Monica Lewinsky's and Hillary's." In Purvis's mind, the true villain here was Kenneth Starr, the Whitewater independent counsel run amok. "I was appalled that Mr. Starr would issue this report that bordered on voyeurism," he would explain, "trying to get a minute description of every sordid little detail of an encounter. Then printing it up . . . and Congress publishing the thing and putting it on the Internet and turning it loose. Talk about obscenity."

Purvis believed there was another group of bad guys—the extremists leading the Republican Congress, who had decided to press impeachment at all costs. They had proclaimed: "We don't give a damn what the American people have said [in rebuffing the Republicans in the November elections]. We want impeachment, and we're going to do it." They were hell-bent on killing Bill Clinton's presidency, regardless of the destruction it rained down on the country.

Arkansas Supreme Court Justice David Newbern had known the Clintons since his days teaching at University of Arkansas Law School, back when Bill and Hillary had arrived in Fayetteville as young professors. Then-Governor Clinton had appointed him to the Court of Appeals in 1978. Now, on the verge of retirement from the state's highest court, he owed a great debt of gratitude to Bill. Sitting with his wife, Carolyn, in the kitchen of their home in the Hillcrest neighborhood of Little Rock, Newbern couldn't shake several disturbing images from his head. Mostly, he was thinking about "the promise Bill Clinton had as a young person."

He was also thinking, specifically, about Hillary. A picture of Bill and Hillary, at the time they had just joined the law faculty at Fayetteville, flashed into his mind: One Sunday afternoon, the Clintons had attended a reception at the Newberns' home on a tree-lined street off College Avenue. The senior professor had been standing on the porch with Hillary when he caught her stealing a glance across the street at a quaint home with a For Sale sign posted. The expression on Hillary's face seemed to indicate that she "was thinking about the life they were about to lead [once Bill got into politics] and the life that they *could* lead if they wanted to just settle down. Stay there in Fayetteville—which is preposterous when you stop to think about it, given what occurred after that." Yet as Newbern watched the impeachment votes recorded on his television screen on this Saturday in December, "it just struck me how different their lives would have been" if Bill and Hillary had told each other, "Let's forget all this political stuff and become law professors, real law professors, and stay here." As news commentators droned on about the impeachment, the image of Hillary staring wistfully at an old house in Fayetteville haunted him. The thought that Newbern couldn't chase out of his mind was, Had Bill Clinton's successes been worth the costs to him and his family?

In Hot Springs, the town where Clinton had grown up, one of his mother's best friends sat in her house on Lake Hamilton, praying that she would not be overcome by anger. Marge Mitchell had known Bill since he was a boy; he had spent a hundred summer days drinking lemonade on her back porch. Bill's mother—Virginia Clinton Kelley—had married her fourth husband, Dick, in Marge's living room. They were like family; Bill was like a son. No matter how much Marge asked God to allow her to understand this crisis far away in Washington, she could not escape a dark conclusion: "They were out to destroy [Bill]," she said. "Whitewater didn't get him, and they picked up something here" in the form of the Monica Lewinsky affair. "It was just politics of pure personal destruction," she said.

Part of it, she believed, had been caused by a "resentment" harbored by people who could not accept that "a small-town boy from a small state" like Arkansas had ascended to the presidency. Although Marge would not deny that Bill "probably made some mistakes," these were personal in nature. They had nothing to do with his duties as president of the greatest country in the free world; Bill had done "a magnificent job" when it came to serving as chief executive. As Marge saw it, any personal shortcomings were for a higher authority to judge. "Gosh, this has been going on since Adam and Eve," she said. "I think the American people have forgiven him. I know the Lord has forgiven him."

Just to be safe, Marge and some of Virginia's closest friends, who had met regularly for lunch as part of a group called the Birthday Club, began praying to Saint Jude, the patron saint of hopeless and impossible causes.

In the towering Ozark Mountains, far removed from Little Rock and Hot Springs, another woman was praying fervently that this demon would pass, for different reasons. Betsey Wright had first met Bill Clinton when they were working on George McGovern's 1972 campaign for president, cutting their political teeth together in Texas. For seven years during Clinton's governorship, Wright had served as his chief of staff and had run three of Clinton's gubernatorial campaigns. She had been in charge of dealing with "bimbo eruptions," including the messy Gennifer Flowers scandal, during the presidential race of 1992. Wright had jumped off the Clinton merry-go-round, completely burned out, after the carousel had packed up and moved to Washington. She had tried to establish an anonymous existence for herself in the most remote northwest corner of Arkansas alongside Beaver Lake. But the impeachment vote had now sent Wright into a psychological tailspin.

The biggest source of shame was that she had *believed* so many of Bill's denials about "other women" over the years. She had passed these fibs and excuses along to the gullible public. "So I just felt so lied to," Wright would say. Now she was haunted by the fact that "I had lied to the country on his behalf."

The Lewinsky affair and the Starr Report had literally pushed her over the edge. "I was a basket case," Wright confided. "I went into a depression. I had to go see the doctor about getting antidepressants. It was awful. . . . There wasn't anything I could do. And I was so angry at Bill. The anger was killing me. I did eventually work through the ability to separate out his policies and performance as president from his personal behavior. And that was very good for me, and very healthy for me. I stopped being ashamed of the role I played in getting him there, because I think he did a good job as president and with his policies. Then I merely had to work through the anger at him. And I had to deal with [the question] 'What is forgiveness?' He was out of the White House before I got rid of my anger."

In response to those who predicted Clinton would be forced to resign after the House voted to impeach him, Wright would laugh at their inanity. "God, they don't know him. The guy doesn't resign. He doesn't give up. He fights to the bitter end." She could see into the future, on that cold Saturday in December. She knew that "it would be a lot messier than that."

Wright was filled with an equal measure of anger and contempt for the Republican-driven House of Representatives and for Independent Counsel Ken Starr, who had brought the country to this horrible day: "It was like a tornado that was out of control. And there is no way to control a tornado. It had been on that path for some time. . . . You kept hoping that something was left from the wreckage of it."

In Texas, just one state away, other folks were worrying about the personal toll on Independent Counsel Ken Starr, whose investigation of the Whitewater scandal and the Monica Lewinsky affair had triggered the impeachment vote. In San Antonio, where Starr had grown up in a tiny white house that had been a World War II army barracks before it had been hauled up the road and deposited in a cow pasture, there was a palpable sense of sadness. In this quiet town—where Vannie Starr had raised her family to understand right from wrong and where "Willie" Starr had worked as a preacher on weekends and as a barber during the week—the world now appeared topsy-turvy. Those who had watched young Ken Starr grow up in a hardworking Christian family knew that he was scrupulously honest and dedicated to the truth. The ugly caricatures of Ken Starr whipped up by the national media, during this investigation of a corrupt president, seemed downright sinful.

Liz Green, who had lived next to the Starrs since the early 1960s, felt the whole picture was warped. "I just believe he [Ken] was anointed to do the job he did," she said, standing in her front yard clutching a rake. "Some people say Ken was wrong and Clinton was the best president we ever had. It's sad to hear that. It's as if good is evil and evil is good."

Kathleen Cavoli, who had attended Sam Houston High School several years behind Ken Starr in the early 1960s, felt that Ken was only doing his job, as distasteful as this whole seamy sex scandal might be. "I mean, it was proven that he [President Clinton] had lied under oath," Cavoli said. "If he [Clinton] had been forthright in the beginning, taken care of business with his family first, and then just come out and said that this is what had happened instead of kicking and screaming all the way," she added, there would have been no need to hire a special prosecutor. As far as Cavoli was concerned, it was Bill Clinton *himself* who deserved blame for this entire impeachment mess.

Ken Starr, for his part, tried to stay as far away from the impeachment disaster as possible. Taking refuge in his split-level home in McLean, Virginia, where he and his wife, Alice, had raised their family, Starr sat in the small TV room and watched the House impeachment vote in silence.

"None of this was a victory for Ken," Alice later reflected. "He had never looked at it that way."

Alice herself would admit to experiencing an odd sense of relief as she watched the impeachment votes tallied. She remembered feeling, "I think the House gets it, that this is a serious matter. . . . And it isn't just about sex in the White House, and it isn't a private matter. It happened in the Oval Office, and he [President Clinton] lied before Congress, he lied to his cabinet members, and he lied in a court of law in grand jury testimony."

Ken Starr discussed none of these impressions with his wife. "I had very little to say or offer," he would later admit. "So it was just a quiet time of watching. I don't think I was much of a companion [for Alice]. I was just observing what I knew was something historic." Starr did not gloat with his independent counsel prosecutorial team. He did not drive into Washington to join in a celebration with Republicans in the capital. It was comforting to know that the House had taken his much-maligned report seriously. Beyond that, Starr had mixed emotions as the votes were tallied.

On one hand, Starr believed that the president had cooked his own goose and needed to take responsibility for the mess in which the country now found itself. "How cruelly ironic," the independent counsel said later, "that all of this could have been avoided if the president had settled this [Paula Jones] case." Still, Starr did not believe this was "a cause for celebration and joy and so forth." He would reflect: "It was a time that everyone should just repair to their own offices and thoughts and, if they were so inclined, to pray and hope that the nation would come through this okay."

Sitting in his TV room watching the House of Representatives adjourn in chaos, the former independent counsel would identify his overriding emotion as one of puzzlement and frustration. He asked himself: "Why did all of this have to happen? Why did we get to where we are? This is all so unnecessary."

———

MONICA Lewinsky, now twenty-five years old, whose sexual affair with Clinton during her stint as a White House intern had somehow entwined itself with the Paula Jones case and with Ken Starr's Whitewater investigation, was still reeling from the trauma. Holed up in an apartment in the Westwood section of Los Angeles, close to her father's home, Lewinsky reacted with a mixture of "shock and fear" to Congress's vote. She wasn't consciously processing that this was the second time a president had been impeached by the House of Representatives in American history. "When you're a part of something," she said, "you don't think of it in historical terms." Mostly, Lewinsky felt "apprehensive" about where this impeachment mud slide might lead next. "Because there was this disconnect between the fact that everybody in the country—or it seemed most people in the country—didn't want this to happen. And yet, somehow, Congress was going ahead and impeaching him. So, I found that to be very frustrating. And on a personal note, I didn't know what the implications were going to be for me."

Paula Jones, whose civil lawsuit had ensnared Bill Clinton, experienced a wholly different set of emotions. Watching television with her then-husband, Steve, in their small beachfront condominium in California, Jones felt disbelief mixed with exhilaration. The former Arkansas state employee, who had filed a lawsuit charging then-Governor Clinton with making lewd sexual advances toward her during a conference held at the Excelsior Hotel, was unable to speak. "I was so numb to the whole thing," Jones would say with her heavy Arkansas drawl. "My mom would call me and say sometimes, 'Paula, it just seems like a dream. That you're the one who got this all going'—and this and that." In Jones's opinion, the action Congress was taking was both justified and necessary for the country. "I did. Because I saw what kind of man was in office. Absolutely, for history. And hopefully, they won't be electing people who have rumors in their past by the time they get elected. Because usually they're true [the rumors], most of the time."

Jones knew that Bill Clinton, if removed as president, could end up back in

Arkansas, where he might haunt her and her family. Yet Jones was prepared to face that risk, for the sake of seeing him booted out of office. "I thought he was going to be gone," she said, sipping a Diet Coke. "I was excited about that. I thought he was going to be out of the White House."

Susan McDougal, having spent eighteen months in federal prisons for criminal contempt after refusing to answer questions propounded by Ken Starr's prosecutors, was prepared to return to jail rather than aid and abet this presidential witch hunt. For McDougal, the pictures appearing on the television screen as the impeachment proceedings steamed forward evoked images of malevolence and depravity. "I started watching the House Republicans and knowing that so much of what they were saying had been woven by David Hale and [ex-husband] Jim McDougal. And it just—it made me sick. It appeared to me that it was evil. That Henry Hyde was evil."

Susan McDougal had never viewed herself as a central player in the White-water business deal. Yet here she was, a convicted felon whose life had been wrecked and who had been housed in penitentiaries in seven states along with "rats and roaches." Her father had suffered a stroke while she was in jail; her mother had endured multiple heart bypasses. Her former husband, Jim McDougal, had lost his real estate fortune and had met his end in federal prison in Texas, suffering from bipolar disorder and dying a pauper's death in solitary confinement. Every person who had been swept into this maelstrom, it seemed, was faced with ruination, including President Clinton himself. The sole cause of this catastrophe, she believed, was Ken Starr.

"I think he's a horrible man," Susan McDougal said. "I think he's Satan. I really do believe that he is an incarnate evil because he is so bland and because he is so uncaring of what devastations happened under his watch, whether or not he himself had anything to do with it. It was wrought by his hand. And I can't forgive it, that Jim McDougal died naked on a floor begging for his medicine and begging the OIC [Office of the Independent Counsel] to help him after they promised to put him in a medical facility. In fact, I can't talk of [Jim] McDougal hardly without crying that he sold his soul to them and they cared so little for [him] while they talked about Christianity. It makes me physically sick."

Susan McDougal would never be shaken from her belief that this endless parade of scandals and investigations was driven by a fervent desire—on the part of extremist Republicans (especially Ken Starr)—to destroy Bill Clinton personally and everything his administration stood for, regardless of whom they crushed in the process. On that dark Saturday in December, it all seemed to fall into place with frightening efficacy.

The Reverend Tony Campolo, a Baptist minister who had counseled Clinton after the president confessed to an adulterous affair with Monica Lewinsky, had spent the afternoon holding a prayer session with the president in his private study inside the White House. After the vote in the House of Representatives, the minister emerged and told reporters: "I think he [President Clinton] is tired. He's very upbeat and confident that things will work out, but he's very tired."

CHAPTER

2

———

BILL CLINTON AND KEN STARR

Former President Bill Clinton, seated in a Philadelphia hotel suite shortly after recovering from quadruple-bypass heart surgery in 2004, was remarkably calm and reflective in discussing the scandals that engulfed him in the White House. When Ken Starr's name was mentioned, however, his eyes flashed with anger.

"I always thought I understood him," said Clinton. "I mean, we had similar childhoods, in a way." Although Starr's background was "more fundamentalist" than Clinton's, their origins could be traced to similar Southern roots. From the first time Starr had visited the White House to take his deposition in the Whitewater matters, the former president recalled having grave doubts "whether he [Starr] was looking for the truth as opposed to looking for a way to use this vast apparatus of power he had to find that Hillary or I had done something wrong."

Several things about Ken Starr caused the president to be wary, from that first meeting. Clinton knew that Starr had appeared on PBS's *MacNeil/Lehrer NewsHour* just months before his appointment as independent counsel, openly advocating that the president could be sued civilly in the *Paula Jones* case. This punctured any pretense in Clinton's mind that Starr was a neutral prosecutor. Second, the president knew that Starr had grown up in the "hard-scrabbled" part of North Texas, where the religious right had first planted its seeds, and then attended Harding College in central Arkansas for two years. Everyone from Arkansas, Clinton said, lifting his eyebrows, knew what "Harding" stood for at that time: "Well, it was an ultraconservative Church of Christ school that in the fifties had a president who was a leading, militant anti-Communist. And was rather well known in those super anti-Communist circles around America." The Church of Christ believed in "the saving grace of baptism" and was "steeped in the New Testament teachings of Jesus." While serving as governor, Bill Clinton had established positive relationships with Harding and had used his good offices to benefit that institution. Yet as soon as he moved to Washington, he knew that some Arkansans who grew up in this tradition of "extreme conservatism" saw the Clinton presidency as a threat to their religious and moral well-being.

Said Clinton: "I grew up around a lot of people like this. They were always most comfortable when they had an enemy. So if you're asking, 'What did that Harding background mean to me?' it was basically conservative fundamentalist and more comfortable in any political setting where there was an enemy."

Looking unusually gaunt after his heart surgery, Clinton pushed aside a *New York Times* crossword puzzle and conjured up a vision of his first meeting with Ken Starr during the inception of the Whitewater investigation. "He was a smart man," the president said of his nemesis. "He knew the whole thing was a huge lie," said Clinton, his face reddening. "And I looked at him and I thought, you know, this fellow just thinks he's doing the Lord's work. And he's got the power and he's going to use it."

Bill Clinton and Ken Starr, two men who would engender intense, polar opposite feelings among the American public, in reality embodied flip sides of the same life story. Both had been born into Southern families of modest means—the word *poor* would not be an exaggeration in either case. Both had been born within a month of each other, a few hundred miles apart. Both seemed destined for great things. Yet both men had deep beliefs and strong ambitions that, in the last decade of the twentieth century, steered them into a collision course that produced disastrous consequences for themselves, and for those surrounding them.

———

BILL Clinton had entered the world on August 19, 1946, a steamy hot day in Hope, Arkansas, a town abutting the Texarkana border. The name recorded on the boy's official birth record—William Jefferson Blythe III—had been his sole inheritance from a restless traveling-salesman father who had died three months earlier in a freak automobile accident. The unglamorous truth, forever part of his life story, was that "Billy" Blythe's father had skidded off the highway during a rainstorm and drowned in a drainage ditch. As a result, Billy's mother was the dominant figure in his life.

Virginia Cassidy Blythe, the daughter of an ice deliveryman from Hope, was a woman who possessed uncommon gregariousness and drive that would one day serve her son well. Virginia was determined to give young Billy every tool necessary to succeed, despite her status as a twenty-year-old widowed mother. She put herself through school to become a nurse anesthetist. She married a car dealer,

Roger Clinton, and moved to Hot Springs in 1950. She bought Billy his first Bible and signed him up for the Park Place Baptist Church choir, to balance out the more worldly extracurricular activities available in Hot Springs.

Virginia Clinton Kelley would marry four men over the course of her lifetime—one of them (Roger Clinton) twice. She was strong, opinionated, loving, comical, and sentimental. Virginia drank Chivas Regal, bet on ponies, loved nightclubs, and applied heavy layers of makeup each morning: a quintessential Hot Springs woman. She continued to play a major role in Bill's life, even after his star rose as the leading political figure in Arkansas and he made the leap at age forty-six that no other son of that tiny Southern state had ever made—to the White House. Although she died in 1994 of breast cancer—far too young, her friends would lament, for such a high-spirited woman—they would agree that it was probably for the better. If she had been around to witness the dogged pursuit of her son by that despicable special prosecutor, said her friends, Virginia probably would have gone after Ken Starr and stuffed that report where it would cause him as much pain as it had caused Bill.

———

KENNETH Winston Starr was born a month before Bill Clinton, on July 21, 1946, in Vernon, Texas—just a short ride from the Arkansas border. His father, William D. "Willie" Starr, a minister in the Church of Christ denomination, traced his roots back to Texas pioneer days. The elder Starr preached in Thalia, an area near the Red River dominated by wheat fields and cow pastures. To make ends meet, he had supplemented his part-time ministerial duties with the worldly trade of barbering. This unusual combination led Willie Starr to move his family to San Antonio, a town that included more churches and additional heads of hair to cut and thus provided sustenance to the family both spiritually and materially. Ken Starr grew up in San Antonio in the 1950s, a happy, earnest, and deeply religious boy. The elder Starr passed along to his son a love of scriptures, an occasional urge to cut hair, and an unwavering (some would say unyielding) moral compass.

Like Bill Clinton, Ken Starr was indelibly shaped by a strong and self-reliant mother. However, the indulgent Hot Springs resort life, which had energized Clinton's mother, was the antithesis of the Southern life that Vannie Starr endorsed. Vannie worked tirelessly on the home front, canning vegetables from the garden, making homemade jam, and shelling pecans. She cooked hearty meals that consisted of chicken or roast and a mess of vegetables—mostly okra, purple-hull peas, corn, cabbage—"all the good vegetables" that had sustained Willie Starr as a young man on the farms of East Texas. Vannie Starr tended to their small white house, gave her husband inexhaustible support, and made sure there was time set aside each night for reading Bible stories to the three children.

Although Willie Starr would die of a heart attack in 1989, never hearing the word Whitewater or the name Monica Lewinsky, Vannie Starr would live to the ripe age of ninety-one. She was still residing in the family house in San Antonio when *National Enquirer* reporters began snooping around for quotes about her son Ken, the nation's most famous (or infamous) special prosecutor. Until her last days, however, Vannie was convinced that her son was acting morally and properly in investigating a president plagued with scandal. It was not Ken's fault, she believed firmly, that he had been roped into pursuing a president who did not know the difference between truth and lies, righteousness and sin.

———

BILL Clinton attended college at Georgetown from 1964 to 1968, attracted by the lure of foreign service and government work. He was elected to student government, excelled in the U.S. Constitution and Law course taught by Walter I. Giles, and earned a job on Capitol Hill as a clerk to J. William Fulbright, prominent U.S. senator from Arkansas.

Ken Starr likewise entered college in the fall of 1964, staying closer to home at Harding College in Searcy, Arkansas, just sixty miles north of Little Rock. By his junior year, after being elected class representative and excelling scholastically, Starr had been smitten by the urge for new intellectual challenges and was dreaming of a career in the diplomatic corps or foreign service. So Starr packed up his boxes and moved to George Washington University in Washington, D.C., just a few miles from where Bill Clinton was making his mark. An earnest student with a boundless capacity for work, Starr sought out a job on Capitol Hill, clerking for the conservative Congressman Bob Price from the Panhandle of Texas. Here, he worked late into the night, proud to have a parking spot and thrilled to have late-night access to books in the Library of Congress. Starr was enthralled with learning, especially when it came to comprehending how the intricate American system of government functioned. One day, he decided, he might like to do government work.

Bill Clinton spent two years in England as a Rhodes scholar at Oxford. He was haunted, during this time, by personal conflicts involving his moral views concerning the Vietnam War, and shared these concerns with those he trusted back home, including his mother's close friend Marge Mitchell. After receiving a draft notice, signing up for the graduate ROTC program in Arkansas, receiving a deferment, having the deferment withdrawn yet still managing to avoid being drafted—a series of moves that later caused some commentators to label him a draft dodger—Clinton returned to the states to attend Yale Law School in 1970.

Ken Starr spent a year in the State Department as his own way of sorting out the turmoil of Vietnam. From there, Starr won a full fellowship to Brown University to pursue a Ph.D. in political science. While working on the fellowship, he became enamored with constitutional law, so he packed up his car and moved to Duke Law School in August 1970. It was the same year Clinton was moving into a house on Long Island Sound to begin Yale Law School.

As he settled into legal studies at Duke, Starr had just tied the knot with Alice Mendell, a petite, poised New Yorker with a degree from Swarthmore College, whom he had met two years earlier while attending a Harvard summer school class. Clinton—although he did not yet know it—was likewise in the process of meeting his future wife, sharing late-night conversations at Yale with a frizzy-haired young woman named Hillary Rodham. This Wellesley graduate with hippie-style glasses was very much Clinton's intellectual equal. She also shared his taste for politics.

After law school graduation, Clinton returned home to Arkansas, married Hillary (who bucked Southern tradition by keeping her Rodham surname), and soared to the top of his new profession. After an unsuccessful run for Congress, Clinton was elected state attorney general in Arkansas and soon became at the age of thirty-two the youngest governor in the country, taking the oath of office in 1978.

Starr earned a clerkship on the Supreme Court with Chief Justice Warren Burger, practiced law at a top firm in Los Angeles, worked as counselor to Attorney General William French Smith in the Reagan administration, and then was appointed (at age thirty-seven) to serve as judge on the U.S. Court of Appeals for the D.C. Circuit, the youngest person ever named to that court. Several years later, President George H. W. Bush tapped Starr to serve as solicitor general of the United States, the top lawyer representing the government in the Supreme Court. In his early forties, Starr had already moved to the pinnacle of the legal profession. It was not uncommon for solicitors general to earn seats on the nation's highest court. Starr, aware of that history, permitted a flame of hope and ambition to burn inside him. One day, he daydreamed in moments of solitude, he might be considered for this supreme honor.

Starr's dream was temporarily thrown off track when Bill Clinton, only forty-six, unexpectedly defeated President Bush in the election of 1992. As the festivities of the inaugural parade dispersed, Starr stepped down as solicitor general and returned to private practice in Washington, joining the prestigious Kirkland & Ellis firm, whose glittering windows provided a bird's-eye view of the White House, where President Clinton had just taken up residence.

Those who knew Bill Clinton and Ken Starr most intimately and who watched them rise up from humble roots and ascend to the highest peaks of their respective professions did not see ruthless partisans or monsters with horns sprouting from their heads. To the contrary, they observed brilliant, thoughtful, empathetic leaders whose true qualities somehow became blurred by an ugly scandal that came to bind them together at the ankles.

Although most of the world watching the Clinton-Starr saga unfold viewed the characters as good or evil, wearing black hats or white hats, President Bill Clinton and Independent Counsel Ken Starr—a closer look at the historical record reveals—had far more in common than most Americans, including Clinton and Starr themselves, would ever choose to admit.

———

THE Bill Clinton whom Marge Mitchell had known since he was seven years old seemed destined to leave an indelible mark on the world, with an asterisk next to his name indicating "American success story." After his mother, Virginia, married Roger Clinton, the family bought a house in Hot Springs on Park Avenue, above the resort area where steaming hot mineral springs and bathhouses and nightclubs and casinos established a pulsating, thriving livelihood for the town. Marge and Virginia had become fast friends in 1953 after meeting in a hospital delivery room; Marge was a nurse, Virginia a nurse anesthetist. From then on, they had called each other "Sister" and watched each other's children like their own. On days off, they fished for crappie together in nearby lakes. Together, the two ladies immersed themselves in the busy Hot Springs life of the 1950s, working and juggling the challenges of young motherhood. As Marge would describe the future President Bill Clinton: "He just was always a fine little fellow, well-behaved, had great manners, 'yes, ma'am, no, ma'am.' And he was, you know, always a friendly sort. He liked to shoot basketball goals and so, you know, he'd come home from school and start shooting basketball goals."

Young Billy Blythe, who soon changed his name to Bill Clinton, displayed a natural love of learning. "He was an avid reader early," recalled Marge, "and he was reading, studying, you know, went to his room before dinner. And he would come out always happy." Standing on the back deck of her home on Lake Hamilton, where Clinton had frequently "flopped" as a teenager, Marge was prepared to stick up for Bill any chance she got. She would lower her voice and add, "Now, you know, I don't need to go into the facts that there were some problems in that household, but, you know, as a kid, it did not seem ever to bother him."

Clinton's high school Latin teacher, Elizabeth Buck, age ninety-seven, would echo those sentiments. "I always knew him to be a gentleman," she said, seated in a wheelchair at a nursing home outside Hot Springs. Young Bill Clinton, she said, had an unusually inquisitive mind. "I told him when I taught third-year Latin that we were going to hold court against Cataline [the man accused of plotting to kill

Cicero in order to subvert the Roman empire]. Clinton volunteered, 'Miss Buck, let me be the lawyer.' " The teacher warned him, "Don't you know you have a lost case before you start?" He said, "I'll work real hard if you'll just let me be the lawyer." She said, "Well, go to it." Miss Buck recalled with a grin that on the day he gave his speech for Cataline, all the boys and girls yelled, "Bravo, bravo, bravo!" Bill Clinton, it seemed, was born to do great things on a bigger stage.

Paul Root, Clinton's history teacher at Hot Springs High, recalled a child prodigy with curly brown hair and a razor-sharp mind. "He liked world history," remembered Root. "That's not one of the favorite subjects of most students, but he liked it. And he was good." When discussions turned to international matters, Bill Clinton was already "well acquainted with Europe" and dominated class-room discussions. Before long, said Root, young Clinton was already inquiring "about the possibilities of being in some kind of government service related to foreign affairs."

Natural empathy was one thing that stood out about Bill Clinton as he came of age. David "Paul" Leopoulos, one of Clinton's best childhood friends in Hot Springs, remembered Bill as a boy with an uncommonly well-developed sense of solicitude toward others. Leopoulos would never forget one November day when Clinton dragged home a boy whom he had met at the bus stop. Virginia Clinton asked, "Who's this?" Bill whispered to his mother, "Well, we were talking, and his parents are divorced; he's not going to have any Thanksgiving dinner. Can he have dinner with us?" It was an attribute that Leopoulos saw on display over and over. In early adulthood, when Leopoulos's mother was stabbed to death at her Hot Springs antique shop while Clinton was away at Oxford, Bill immediately bought Leopoulos a plane ticket to England so that they could grieve together. When Leopoulos got married, Clinton traveled over a thousand miles to stand in his wedding.

Another quality that defined Clinton was his personal magnetism. Even at the earliest stages of his political career, he seemed able to convey his passionate be-liefs using simple, compelling words. Ernie Dumas, state capital reporter for the *Arkansas Gazette*, remembered the first time he met candidate Bill Clinton. It was during the 1974 primary season, when Clinton was making his first run for polit-ical office seeking to represent Arkansas's Third Congressional District. Dumas was dispatched to cover the Pope County Democratic Women's Rally, the first major political event of the season. There, all the Democratic candidates engaged in an "old-time speaking affair" in a big gymnasium. The scene was one of pan-demonium. Recalled Dumas: "I remember that there were hundreds and hun-dreds of people filling this place and everybody drinking Cokes, and they were serving hot dogs, and there was just this din." One candidate after another stood up to give his perfunctory speech, with nobody "paying them much attention."

When the baby-faced Bill Clinton was introduced, Dumas would recall, "nobody was paying much attention." Clinton stepped up and began his allotted two-minute talk. Then, as Dumas would tell the story, "for some reason, there was just a quiet settled over the place, just a hush soon after he began to speak. And everybody kind of hushed up and listened. And he had this voice that kind of carried and people paid attention to what he had to say." Clinton spoke no longer than his allocated 120 seconds. Yet somehow he received a standing ovation. As Dumas recalled, "I looked at my notes and I thought, 'He didn't say a damn thing.' There wasn't a word—there was nothing there worth quoting. But it was a few beautiful sentences and ordinary thoughts" that captivated those crammed into the auditorium.

Dumas witnessed that scene repeat itself across the state. Old union loyalists and party stalwarts began "passing hats and raising money for [Clinton]." The result was that newcomer Bill Clinton came close to beating incumbent John Paul Hammerschmidt in the 1974 race for Congress.

Justice David Newbern, even before going on the court in Arkansas, witnessed a similar charisma on display from the moment Clinton became governor. Newbern recalled attending a country music concert featuring an attractive female country superstar at the Robinson Auditorium in Little Rock. When Clinton walked onstage to present the singer with an "Arkansas Travelers" certificate, making her an honorary daughter of the state, the woman "almost swooned." As Newbern observed it, the attractive singer came to the microphone and made remarks about "what a wonderfully handsome governor we had" and was "practically falling at his feet." Although it was an amusing sight to behold, Newbern emphasized that this was an integral piece of Clinton's political persona: "That's something that people have to realize about Bill. . . . What we [have called] a character flaw was not a one-way situation. I mean, women just fell all over him. It was just a phenomenon to watch."

From the start, Clinton also had an uncanny ability to forge a bond with African American voters. Judge L. T. Simes II understood why this was so: Simes had grown up picking cotton in Helena, Arkansas, at a time when the Mississippi Delta of Arkansas was predominantly segregated and inhospitable toward African Americans. He had attended law school in Fayetteville when "wonderboy Clinton" was a young professor. Simes immediately took note that Clinton, unlike most of the stodgy "old-boy" professors, treated black students with the utmost fairness and respect in the classroom. After becoming governor, Clinton bucked the system by appointing highly qualified blacks to key positions in state government. Simes himself became the first African American to serve as chairman of the Arkansas Soil and Water Commission. Although Clinton paid dearly, in political terms, for eschewing the prevailing culture by appointing blacks, that didn't slow him down. During the governor's 1980 reelection campaign, Clinton brought Simes along to a country club in an elite section of eastern Arkansas, where segregation was still firmly entrenched. Notwithstanding the "redneck" audience, Clinton began uttering jaw-dropping declarations about the ugliness of racial prejudice, as Simes tugged at his jacket and pleaded, "Don't do that, Bill. . . . I'm only worth one vote, don't do it for me." Clinton was defeated by Frank White that fall, which required him to vacate the governor's mansion for two years. Still, as Simes and Clinton cried together early that morning after his concession speech, Clinton told Simes not to worry. "We'll be back," he said. "We're not going to let the people down."

Simes would conclude, a hitch of emotion in his voice, "I really believe that Bill Clinton was born to be president." He steadied his composure and added, "In the Bible, it talks about a slave becoming king. Bill's daddy was not a Rockefeller. He didn't come in with any wealth. He had a middle-class mother, a single family woman. It was fate. He was destined."

How then did this uncommonly talented political leader become ensnared in an ugly sex scandal that nearly wrecked his presidency? Clinton's closest friends would all point their fingers at the same man—an overzealous prosecutor named Ken Starr.

As a Christian woman, Nancy Adkins, a co-member of the "Birthday Club" with Virginia Clinton Kelley, couldn't find the right adjective to describe Starr. She confessed, "I've never said I hated anybody, but, believe me, I really think I hate him. God forgive me for saying that, but it's the truth."

Clinton's stepfather, Dick Kelley, settling back in a chair inside his lake cottage where he and Bill Clinton's mother had lived until her death in 1994, gripped his cane and spoke measuredly about the independent prosecutor who had led the investigations against his stepson. "You can't put in there what I think of Starr," Kelley said. "My vocabulary pulls up some dandies." At age eighty-nine, Dick Kelley considered himself a forgiving man. Yet when it came to Starr, he was not prepared to forgive and forget. "No. I haven't forgiven him. They ought to put him in jail and keep him there," Kelley stated. If there were any silver lining to this otherwise dismal story, it was that Virginia had died before witnessing the absolute worst of it. "Ken Starr was lucky she wasn't around," he said, tapping his cane.

———

BEFORE heading the investigation that nearly toppled a presidency, Kenneth Winston Starr had borne none of the markings of a controversial figure. For those who knew him growing up in rural Texas, he would seem like the last person in the world who might be assigned to investigate perjury linked to a national sex scandal. To the contrary, Starr seemed like a person born to do good deeds, to conquer all challenges through hard work and humility, and to win admiration for his absolute decency.

Billie Jeayne Reynolds, Ken's older sister by sixteen years, lived a quiet life as a teacher in Kingwood, Texas, where she avoided the limelight and dodged reporters hunting for Ken Starr's kinfolk. Speaking in a soft voice, she remembered a well-mannered, dimpled little brother with rosy cheeks, who returned happily from school each day and then buckled down to do his homework. "Ken was never pushed, but somehow he just always wanted to do his best," Billie Jeayne recalled. With his older brother, Jerry, he purchased a barbering license and assisted his father to keep the family solvent. Their mother, Vannie, would tell reporters searching for clues about the now-infamous special prosecutor: "He polished his shoes every night, and his daddy's shoes, just sitting down on the floor in front of the TV." An idle mind was the devil's playground; the Starr family believed in hard work to suppress temptation.

As a child, Ken Starr listened attentively as his father rehearsed Sunday sermons under a shade tree in their backyard. As he grew older, Ken kept his own favorite verses of scripture on note cards in his shirt pocket, to read during spare minutes as an opportunity for silent reflection. Religion, according to Billie Jeayne, was always a central force in Ken Starr's life. "Oh, it played a very important role," she said. "I suppose it started [with his] being carried to church when he was three weeks old."

Roberta Mahan, Ken's homeroom teacher at Sam Houston High School, remembered a cherubic boy who was president of his senior class and who worked diligently as a writer and photographer for the school newspaper (the *Raven*) and yearbook (the *Cherokee*). "He was deeply involved in everything," she recalled. "He had a lot of curiosity, he was very intelligent, he wore glasses and looked the part, he was very affable, very well liked by all of the other students."

High school friend Sam Millsap, who himself went on to pursue a career in law, described Starr as uncommonly mature for his age. "He was one of those guys who seemed to be 40 years old from the time they were born," Millsap told a reporter for the *San Antonio Express-News* in 1998. "He was always apart from the rest of the gang, and he was comfortable with that. I never thought that was weird, probably because I was dorky also."

Among his peers, there was a general assumption that Ken Starr would rise to the top, making a name for himself, although few would have imagined that his career path would have taken this particular twist. The junior yearbook in 1963 contained a photo of Starr with a caption: "Kenneth Starr, 'heap big boss man'" of the class. "Ken himself thought he was going to be a preacher," said Miss Mahan. "And I think the other students did, too, knowing that his father was a preacher, and that he was a serious-minded student and that he was religious. He was a moral-type person."

According to high school friend Alan Reaves, Ken was "probably the most conservative of all the kids." Although Starr was a Democrat, he naturally gravitated to the conservative side of the party. Still, Starr admired many public servants regardless of party affiliation. In 1963, he joined a group of student council members making the trek to see President John F. Kennedy at Brooks Air Force Base. Although JFK was too liberal for him politically, Starr couldn't wait to see Kennedy in the flesh. The group from Sam Houston High got close enough to see the handsome president from a distance—a great thrill. The next day, when news reached Sam Houston High that President Kennedy had been assassinated in Dallas, Starr was devastated. "To think that it all happened in Texas," recalled Reaves, "made it all the more horrible." Starr composed a somber editorial for the school newspaper: "Now, as we begin to pick up the pieces and to remold our lives, we have the seldom presented opportunity to [reflect]. For once, instead of worrying about a football game or a date, we suddenly begin to wonder what life is all about."

After enrolling at Harding College, where his brother Jerry taught, Ken Starr stood out as a serious, cheerful, smart, gregarious, free-thinking student. Lou Butterfield bunked with Starr during freshman year and remained a friend for life. As Butterfield told reporters years later, his thin roommate from Texas "had the manners of a country gentleman when he was eighteen years old." In terms of dress and physical appearance, Starr resembled many of his male counterparts at Harding of that era. "He didn't have long hair. It wasn't over his ears," recalled Butterfield, who later returned to Harding as a communications professor. Although beefy sideburns were in vogue in the 1960s, "neither of us had long sideburns. He was fairly conservative. I don't know what else to say about that."

Starr joined Lambda Sigma, an alternative to fraternities and sororities at Harding, and played flag football and basketball. "He was not an outstanding athlete. But few of us were," chuckled Butterfield. During sophomore year, Ken was chosen "club beau" for the Delta Chi Omega girls' club, a "huge honor on campus." The person selected was "someone [the young women] thought would have a good attitude, represent their club well," attending all their big functions with them, including "their banquets and their hayrides."

Harding was initially a good fit for Starr, incorporating many of the building blocks that came to define his adult life. His freshman yearbook included a prominent picture of Harding's president pointing to a pyramid that had written at its foundation, FUNDAMENTAL BELIEF IN GOD. Above that was situated a block that represented THE UNITED STATES CONSTITUTION, and atop that a smaller block, THE AMERICAN WAY OF LIFE: OUR FREEDOM, with an American flag flying at the pinnacle.

As Butterfield would explain the significance of religion in Ken Starr's daily existence, it was always a matter of "choice" for him: "In my life, I have never heard Ken swear. Not one bad word. And some people go, 'Well, he's a prude.' That just wasn't it. Obviously, he didn't smoke or drink or any of those things. A good time on Friday night was not going to Little Rock and getting drunk."

Starr busied himself with a host of other activities. His older brother, Jerry, preached for the Friendship Church of Christ thirty miles away. Ken liked to assist; he would "wait on the Lord's table and pray, lead sing and that kind of stuff," recalled Butterfield.

As a reporter-editor for the student newspaper, Starr wrote regular columns under the breezy heading "Starr Dust." In one column, he reminded fellow students to live by the Golden Rule, admonishing: "Record players blaring at full volume or serenading fellow students with strains of Beatle songs at 1:00 A.M. are examples of our inconsideration for others."

Above all, Ken Starr was known for his scrupulous honesty. In the summers, he earned money to pay tuition by selling Bibles for the Southwestern Company, working alongside Lou Butterfield, who was the company's field manager. Together they drove around the Midwest, principally in rural areas of Ohio, selling family Bibles, Bible concordances, Bible dictionaries, and Bible storybooks. Recalled Butterfield: "Country selling was nice back then. Because people didn't have a lot of salesmen knock on their door. And we didn't do any of the lying. We didn't go up and say, 'I'm taking a survey.'" Folks in rural areas considered it good manners to invite guests in. Starr thrived on this work. Rather than rushing from house to house, he spent time visiting each family, just because he enjoyed people. Frequently, he sold Bibles to eighteen out of twenty families on whose doors he knocked, generating three hundred or four hundred dollars in profit a week, astronomical at the time. "Ken was very good," Butterfield would recall. "He was so personable and so likable."

Starr's integrity was already on display, even at this formative stage of adulthood. In the Bible peddling business, high sales and maintaining eighty-hour workweeks often led to a handsome prize from the Southwestern Company, such as "a really nice suit" or a glittering wristwatch. Yet the summer after sophomore year, Starr gave up his potential bonuses to take a full week off. He did not believe in fibbing to his bosses—so he snitched on himself. Butterfield warned him, "It's going to mess you up, Starr. Because you won't get your watch. You won't get your prizes. You'll lose all your prizes." Starr replied, "I just have to go. And I'll just promise you I'll come back next Monday and I'll work as hard as I ever have." He used the time to drive home to Texas, so that he could seek advice from his old teacher, Miss Mahan. He was feeling constricted by the educational opportunities at a small rural school like Harding. Miss Mahan told him, "Ken, you have the intelligence, you have the ability, you have the background. You need to go where the action is."

Starr returned to sell more Bibles, having decided to attend George Washington University in Washington, D.C., a thrilling prospect. He told his roommate, "I'm going to go as far as I can."

Yet his ambition never seemed to dull his shining qualities. When he met Alice Jean Mendell, the daughter of a successful real estate developer from Mamaroneck, New York, he won over this petite, dark-haired beauty by sheer "niceness." She was Jewish, not a fundamentalist Christian of the sort who had populated Starr's life at Harding. "I had never met a Texan before," Alice would later recall. But this skinny Southerner was extraordinarily friendly, interested in current events. She liked that he carried around a checklist of great classics to read, including *Anna Karenina* and other books that he had never been exposed to in high school. Starr, it seemed, was excited about life itself. "He was the nicest person I've ever met," Alice would say four decades later with a smile.

As a wave of rebellion swept college campuses during the late 1960s, Starr was the antithesis of a hippie. "He never wore bell-bottoms," recalled Alice. Ken preferred long pants—usually straight-legged blue jeans—and wore short-sleeved shirts, no matter what the weather.

From the day they were married, he was the picture of attentiveness, a perfect Southern gentleman. Alice would never forget the afternoon that they tied the knot in August 1970, in a simple ceremony held at her parents' home. Ken drove off gallantly with his bride in their blue Volkswagen Bug, through the pouring rain, to embark on their honeymoon in the Poconos. When they arrived at their romantic destination—Split Rock Lodge—the building had burned to the ground and its remains were still "smoldering." The newlyweds were forced to book a room at a nearby Holiday Inn, hardly the love nest they had envisioned. Even so, Alice was impressed that her husband was able to view this disaster as a positive omen. Ken told her "if we make it through this, we'll probably have a very strong marriage." Alice laughed at the memory, adding: "Which we have."

Ken Starr, having advanced swiftly in the legal profession, treasured the flexibility that came with being a federal appeals judge in Washington. It gave him the ability to coach his children's soccer teams, teach Sunday school, and remain active in church. "This was genuinely great living, and I was very fortunate indeed and blessed to be able to have this kind of opportunity," he later said.

So when Attorney General Dick Thornburg called Starr personally after George H. W. Bush was elected president, and asked him to resign his lifetime judicial post to serve as solicitor general, it caused him great anguish. Judge

Starr said no to the offer, twice. Finally, General Thornburg summoned Starr to his office and declared that "it was his judgment and speaking on behalf of the president that I should be the administration's solicitor general." There was also a strong insinuation, although no promise, that the Bush administration would put him on the short list for a Supreme Court appointment. After discussing his plight with Alice, Judge Starr called Thornburg back and said respectfully, "Mr. Attorney General, I have decided to accept the offer."

With that, Starr placed the phone down and walked into his judge's chambers, where he "bawled like a baby." In this wood-paneled room filled with U.S. Reports, where he had typed out hundreds of opinions on his computer and immersed himself in the rule of law in many complex yet wondrous cases, Judge Kenneth W. Starr believed he had found the ideal life. Years later he would confide, "I didn't want to leave that court. But I did try very much not to—like Lot of biblical times—to look back, but to keep looking forward."

Ironically, Starr was mindful that accepting this position as solicitor general might hurt, rather than enhance, his chances of ever being appointed to the Supreme Court. No matter how sterling a lawyer's won-loss record as solicitor general, a high-profile position like this could become a "lightning rod," especially in modern times. Yet Starr still accepted the post as solicitor general.

"I am very blessed to have a sense of Providence in life," he said. "And so, I viewed this as entirely entrusted to decision makers that the future was not in my hands. My job was to try to do the very best that I could."

It was that same sense of obligation to public service, and Providence, that led Starr to accept the invitation to become Whitewater independent counsel six years later.

———

By this time, in the summer of 1994, when Ken Starr embarked on a new challenge as Whitewater independent counsel, he would never imagine that a sizable chunk of the American public would one day view him as a Clinton hater and a Republican apparatchik. Alice Starr would say of stories that painted her husband as a political zealot out to get the president: "We don't run around in a circle of any vast right-wing conspirators. We never have. We have dear friends (both Democrats and Republicans), almost all of whom are family friends whom we know from the children's schools or from church or whatever. But neither of us are into a right-wing conspiracy and never have been. And Ken never, ever met with people who conspired about anything."

Indeed, even after her family endured death threats, after U.S. Marshals shadowed the children to school, and after unrelenting public criticism, Alice said that her husband never lost his sense of obligation to complete his job:

"Well, I mean, there was just a huge stress and strain on Ken. He couldn't bring this home. He had to leave it at the office. He worked seven days a week, twelve hours a day, and he was frustrated." Alice summed up the scandal that seemed to have no endpoint: "The whole thing was unpleasant. For him to have to be the person who has to be the prosecutor investigating a president in these kinds of circumstances—Whitewater was one thing. . . . But the Monica Lewinsky scandal, boy, he sure didn't want that. Didn't ask for that. And in hindsight, he tells me that he never would have taken it on had he known what it entailed."

Nor did Alice see her husband as a "Clinton hater" who was out to topple the president. "Never hated him, because he doesn't know him other than the few times he's met him where he's been cooperative, likable, agreeable. You know, the fact that he [Clinton] was probably lying on several occasions, well, that's Ken's job to bring the facts out, they come out where they may. But his job wasn't to hate him or try to convict him. His job was to bring out the facts. He did do that and didn't relish his job at all. It's really the worst job he's ever, ever had."

William Jefferson Clinton and Kenneth W. Starr, two unusually talented Southerners who grew up in modest circumstances, each with ambitions to rise to great heights in public service, were born of the same time and place in American history. The story of how their paths collided so forcefully, dividing the country into warring factions, is the story of how politics and law combined and exploded like gasoline touched by a torch.

Of course, Clinton and Starr would never have crossed paths in American history if not for the activities of an eccentric real estate developer who made his mark in the late 1970s, purchasing investment property along the scenic White River. In that remote venue, the developer constructed a grand vision that included sharing the fruits of his business genius with a few of his special political friends, including Bill and Hillary Clinton.

That man's name was James Bert McDougal.

PART ONE

—————

ARKANSAS
MISCHIEF

CHAPTER 3

BREATHTAKING "WHITEWATER"

L ittle Rock occupies the intersection of two worlds in Arkansas, as if God sketched a neat map before creating this town connecting the rich alluvial country of the Mississippi Delta—where cotton and rice are cash crops—and the rocky, remote terrain of the highlands, which slip into the Ouachita National Forest and the desolate reaches of eastern Oklahoma.

If one were to divide the state of Arkansas diagonally, drawing a line from the northeast corner near the Missouri border to the southwest point at Texarkana, the town of Little Rock would appear smack in the middle. Settled by the Quapaw Indians and white explorers who valued its location flanking the Arkansas River, this charming Southern town (named for a distinctive rock that jutted out and guided travelers up the river) became the capital of the territory of Arkansas in 1820. When the state was admitted to the Union in 1836, Little Rock was the natural choice for its capital. It sealed together two divergent halves of topography, interlocking two otherwise dissimilar types of inhabitants and ways of life.

It was here that Jim McDougal established his base of operations, with grand plans to achieve wealth and roaring success. Later accounts, after the Whitewater scandal broke in the national press, would tend to describe him as "crazy" or "manic" or "drug-induced." But the McDougal who orchestrated land deals and navigated the dual world of Arkansas business and politics during the 1970s was an infinitely more complex—and more interesting—figure than those later depictions would imply.

McDougal's psychological records at the federal prison in Fort Worth, Texas, where he would be housed for nearly a year until his sudden death in 1998, would describe him as a fifty-seven-year-old white male "who has served two months of a 36 month sentence for conspiracy." The intake forms recorded: "He noted he has no family to speak of and no one with whom he maintains contact." Documents also revealed that before his final decline in prison, McDougal was on a regular diet of psychotropic medication, taking sixty milligrams of Prozac per day for depression and "29 mg. of Buspar per day for anxiety."

But this portrait of a broken man would not accurately reflect the early life of

James Bert McDougal. At the time of his birth in the tiny town of Bradford in northeastern Arkansas in 1940, his parents were running the town's general store, where they were, in his mind's eye, "the original American Gothic couple in both appearance and in demeanor." Leo and Lorene McDougal had earned the reputation among local country folk as pillars of the 800-person community. Enthralled at an early age by politics, a young Jim McDougal had listened to speeches of Franklin Delano Roosevelt on long-playing records, memorizing the words and even "mimic[king] the voice and articulation." He was youth director for the Arkansas Democrats for Kennedy during the 1960 election. This propelled him into a job on the staff of the Senate Rackets Committee, chaired by Senator John L. McClellan in Washington.

Although he rarely chose to speak of this episode of his life later, McDougal had been briefly married in 1970 to one Delores Winston Lieberman, who worked for Arkansas Congressman Wilbur Mills. When the couple was quickly divorced after Delores was hospitalized as a manic depressive, Jim fell apart. McDougal himself had been a card-carrying member of Alcoholics Anonymous since age twenty-seven. In his own AA self-portrait composed during his initial prosecution for bank fraud in 1990 (he penned the essay under the pseudonym "Bert," his middle name inherited from his favorite uncle), McDougal would describe a young man who had started drinking at age fifteen. "The very first time I tried alcohol," he wrote, "I drank until I went into a mental black-out." By the time he was twenty-one, by his own account, he was "a chronic severe alcoholic who had flunked out of four universities and been hospitalized repeatedly for treatment of alcoholism." By the age of twenty-four, now working in Washington, "the combination of pills and whiskey had rendered me unable to hold that or any other job." For three years, "I was drunk daily, or in a treatment program sobering up so I could drink some more." On his twenty-seventh birthday, McDougal was released from hospital care for the eighth time. It was then that he decided to supplement his intake of whiskey and vodka with a dose of Bible study and religion. After a three-week drinking binge, during which he became emaciated and broke, McDougal finally hit a brick wall. "Unshaven, dirty, wearing a torn shirt," Jim McDougal wrote of himself, "I went to see an attorney friend and asked him to get me permanently committed to the state mental institution, so that I could stop hurting myself and all the people I loved." That friend immediately sent McDougal to Alcoholics Anonymous. Here, McDougal turned himself around. By 1968, he had secured a job in Senator J. William Fulbright's office, where he thrived as a senior aide to the distinguished senator from Arkansas.

Eventually, McDougal was running Fulbright's Little Rock office. When Fulbright unexpectedly lost his reelection bid to Dale Bumpers in 1974, McDougal fell into a funk; yet, he rebounded quickly, finding a new vocation—dabbling in real estate. He also taught in the political science department at Ouachita Baptist University in Arkadelphia (even though he had not yet finished his own bachelor's or master's degrees) at the invitation of the department chairman—Bob Riley—the man who brought him together with Bill Clinton.

Riley was revered all over Arkansas for his integrity and grit. This decorated war hero wore a trademark black patch over his left eye, covering an empty socket that he had earned during the assault on Guam in World War II after he had thrown himself on a gun turret to protect his fellow marines. Still partially blind, Riley had surmounted a life's worth of obstacles. He not only ran the political science department at this Baptist university—just across the football field from his home—but was also elected lieutenant governor in the early 1970s and then served a brief stint as acting governor in 1975, hiring McDougal as his executive secretary. Riley and his wife, Claudia, took McDougal under their wing and assured him that he could turn his own life around if he willed himself to do it.

In the summer of 1975, at age thirty-five, McDougal was ready to do that. Walking across the tiny Ouachita campus, he spotted a young student who was doing secretarial work in the political science department, and invited her to lunch. Susan Henley, a Latin scholarship student from the paper mill town of Camden, just south of Arkadelphia, was flattered by the interest. Even then, Susan was struck by the eccentric, charming qualities of this Southern gentleman fifteen years her senior. She remembered that he wore expensive Bally shoes. "I don't think they even sold Bally shoes in Arkansas at that time," she recalled. She also noted that the shoes had holes in the bottom. Jim McDougal would at times appear wearing a Ralph Lauren suit, "but it would have a torn lapel or something." Susan explained with a distant smile, "And it interested me that a mind that would love these beautiful things but then would not care so much to keep it perfect. And, again, it was sort of like Jim, sort of the way he was."

The Jim McDougal who courted the young coed was tall and thin, with a birdlike face that looked almost comical. "He had the best sense of humor," recalled Susan. "He was very profane, though, and going to a Christian school and raised in the Baptist church and, you know, only having gone out with ministers in my life, his profanity was unimaginable." At the same time, this older man with a wicked-sharp tongue "was very funny. Just really very funny." One afternoon, Susan locked herself out of the office, so Jim kicked open the door and ushered her inside. He seemed to relish the opportunity to prove that he was a gentleman.

There was also, however, a dark side that McDougal worked hard to keep under wraps. He kept the alcohol demon in check by swearing off liquor, smoking three packs of cigarettes a day, drinking coffee constantly, and attending AA meetings. Susan saw few hints of the brooding, troubled side of Jim during their courtship. He seemed energized, outgoing. Jim took his new date boating on DeGray Lake, floating around with the Rileys for an afternoon on their pontoon boat. Claudia Riley instantly approved of Jim's choice. She recalled Susan as a "shy" and "private" person who was also "a drop-dead gorgeous woman." Claudia enjoyed Susan's quick wit and her sweet innocence. As Susan sunned herself in her black bathing suit, Jim asked where she had gotten her "curves." Susan replied, "They just showed up." Claudia smiled and winked at Jim: This one was a keeper.

Because politics always seemed destined to be part of his life, Jim made sure that he included Susan in his periodic political forays. It was in this fashion that she came to meet candidate Bill Clinton, during her senior year of college.

Claudia and Bob Riley already knew young Bill Clinton. He would regularly "flop" at the Riley house in Arkadelphia, dropping in to engage in political banter and to learn at the feet of the lieutenant governor. "He seemed to admire my husband's courage," explained Claudia Riley. "And he did a lot of things [later] to try to bring recognition to my husband."

There was an additional connection that brought Clinton and McDougal into the same orbit. Clinton, as a Georgetown student, had served as an intern for Senator Fulbright on the Senate Foreign Relations Committee staff. Then he was hired to drive a car for Fulbright during his 1968 Senate campaign. (McDougal eventually had to assign the student to another job, because Clinton distracted the senator with his incessant political chatter.) From the beginning, McDougal and Clinton had trod in the same political circles. So it was perfectly natural that when Clinton decided to make a run for attorney general in the fall of 1975, he would utilize his contacts at Ouachita Baptist University—including the Rileys and McDougal—to garner help.

Susan Henley, who was enrolled in a public speaking class at Henderson State University next door, received a last-minute call one day from Jim, saying, "Clinton is coming over—he wants to have some sort of gathering. The forward guy just called me, and they don't have anybody. It looks like it's going to be a total flop. Is there anything you can do?"

Susan arranged for her entire class to attend the speech. She would never forget that day, watching the candidate with thick, wavy brown hair work the crowd. She recalled that Clinton was "a big, raw-boned, hammy kind of guy." He was "kind of pudgy" with "kind of a pudgy face." He had "both qualities of openness and yet focused intensity, which is kind of a contrast. . . . He could give you the sense that you were the only person in the world." Susan could tell that Clinton took a shine to McDougal. "He seemed to defer to Jim—in my eyes, Jim was very knowledgeable and much more sophisticated and Clinton was looking up to Jim and asking his advice and that sort of thing. It made an impression because at the time I was, you know, falling in love with Jim and we were talking about getting engaged. And Clinton seemed like a nice enough person, but in contrast to McDougal, he was very young and very inexperienced."

The next thing she knew, Clinton hit them both up for contributions. "He asked Jim for money, and Jim gave him a check [equaling the legal limit of $1,500]. And then he asked me for money, and I was a student." So Clinton turned to Jim and said, "Well, you could do that for her, couldn't you?" Susan would remember: "I was just shocked."

The true nature of the McDougal-Clinton relationship would ultimately be lost in the freakish portraits of Jim McDougal painted during the Whitewater scandal. In truth, McDougal and Clinton were two smart men who genuinely liked each other. Some accounts would later ascribe to Bill and Hillary Clinton a hatred or disdain for the quirky real estate investor. Some went so far as to implicate the Clintons, years later, in Jim McDougal's mysterious death in prison. Yet these dark references were at odds with the true history. Remembered Susan, "I never saw them that Bill Clinton didn't pick Jim up literally off his feet," giving McDougal a bear hug. Clinton seemed to get a kick out of the balding real estate man's irreverent wit. Susan McDougal would say of her ex-husband, smiling at the memory, "He was very in the moment, which is, you know, what Clinton enjoyed."

There was also a shared taste for the aphrodisiac of political life. As Susan would explain, "Bill Clinton had always been a kind of a husky, little fat kid, I guess, with not just a whole lot of money and no fancy cars, no stuff, and suddenly he's running for office, he's got a campaign staff, women are starting to respond to him, and McDougal loved that. McDougal fed into that, you know, like 'Who's the flavor of the month?' you know."

At the same time, both men had become serious about marriage. In September of 1975, Clinton had invited McDougal to attend an engagement party at which he was introducing his fiancée from Yale Law School, Hillary Rodham. Clinton was throwing the party in Hot Springs for friends who could not make the voyage to Fayetteville. McDougal was thrilled to attend with Susan in tow. As the guests swirled around, Susan was surprised when Clinton walked up to her, slid his arm around her waist, and razzed her: "I hear you're going to be a child bride." To which she replied, "I don't know anything about that." Susan was stunned by the subtext: Jim had evidently told Clinton he was going to ask her to marry him. For Susan, it was an exciting, fast-paced time.

If Clinton was tickled that McDougal was marrying someone half his age, Susan was no less surprised at Clinton's choice of a mate. "Hillary was very different from the Arkansas cheerleader type, you know, pretty-faced girl that Bill had always been with before," Susan would later say. She wore "great big glasses, and, you know, the vest, frizzy hair, very plain." By Arkansas standards, Hillary cut a "radical" appearance. Explained Susan: "She would not be everyone's cup of tea. She wasn't your stereotypical Southern beauty, for sure, and those were the kinds of girls that Bill had always dated. And also girls who were very sure of themselves socially, you know, girls who could carry off any situation, and certainly that took Hillary years to be able to do in Arkansas." Yet both Susan and Jim were a bit "weird" themselves; they had no problem connecting with Hillary. Jim, in particular, seemed enthralled by Clinton's smart, intellectual bride-to-be, who had worked on the congressional impeachment staff during the Watergate scandal. Hillary Rodham seemed like an interesting match, Jim said, for an up-and-coming Arkansas politician like his good friend Bill Clinton.

Bill and Hillary were married on October 11, 1975, in Fayetteville. Seven months later, Jim and Susan were married in a small ceremony outside Little Rock, at the couple's new "love nest" in the country. Officiating was Bob Riley, an ordained Baptist minister, who memorized the entire ceremony to compensate for his blindness. In attendance were many of Arkansas's political rising stars: Bill and Hillary Clinton; Jim Guy Tucker, a close friend of McDougal's who was now running for Congress; and other luminaries. Susan wore a traditional white wedding dress and carried a single long-stemmed rose. Jim, who had grown big sideburns for the ceremony, wore a mint green Yves Saint Laurent suit with flared pants. The couple's new "love nest" was actually a converted goat shed that Jim had purchased for five thousand dollars and fixed up for an additional twenty thousand, painting it yellow just for fun.

Jim McDougal also surprised his bride by announcing that they were going into the real estate business together.

———

THE drive north from Little Rock, along Highway 65, where Jim McDougal would discover the property that would later land him in jail, provided unsurpassed scenic beauty. After leaving the modest skyscrapers of the city behind and crossing the banks of the Arkansas River, a traveler would enter the foothills of the Ozarks, climbing up through Conway, Bee Branch, and then the town of Clinton. The Ozarks, because they are older than the Rockies, are much gentler in slope, providing ample opportunities for spectacular views. Scattered thickets of ponderosa pines rise up in patches. At higher altitudes, the road is flanked by majestic oaks, sycamores, ash, maples, sweet gums, and hickories. In the spring, Queen Anne's lace and other wildflowers form a colorful carpet along the two-lane highway. An occasional chicken house (for brooding) or strawberry farm occupies a niche in the rocky terrain. Hogs can be spotted on the hillsides, rooting for food. For the most part, however, God created this stretch to remain unsullied by human hands.

That was the attraction for James B. McDougal. He planned to construct an elite politicians' getaway in this remote yet beautiful piece of his home state.

Bill Clinton, when he was first approached by McDougal in 1978 about investing in a piece of property whose name would one day become synonymous with scandal, viewed it as a nonevent. When Clinton first moved to Little Rock and won the election for state attorney general, he and Hillary had invested in a small real estate project that McDougal had put together. "I made a little money," remembered the former president of the initial land deal, "not much money, because I didn't have much to invest. And it seems that it was a pittance now by today's standards, but it was nice, you know, because I was only making twenty-six thousand dollars a year as attorney general."

At this time in the 1970s, investors were raking in money hand over fist in Arkansas land development. Interest rates were kept under control by Arkansas law, land was cheap, and population growth in the cities spurred a huge demand. Clinton explained the lure of the Ozarks: "In the mountains, you had all these retirees who wanted to come down from the Middle West, who wanted a warmer place to retire but still a place with four seasons." Unless economic conditions changed abruptly, Clinton believed, "it seemed as if it was almost impossible to lose money doing it."

So when Jim McDougal came to Bill and Hillary Clinton and asked them to become partners in the Whitewater venture, it seemed like a no-lose venture. "He expected, Jim did, that when we subdivided the land and, you know, put in the roads and did all the things that were necessary and sold the lots, that installment payments on the lots would more than cover our note at the bank and eventually we'd turn quite a profit," said Clinton. "And I think that it would have happened, but for what happened in the late seventies in America, when there was this explosion of interest rates." All of a sudden, it was near impossible for average folks to afford "an extra lot in the Ozark Mountains." Within several years, Whitewater and everything else McDougal touched had gone belly-up.

Then-Governor Clinton never imagined that this investment would turn into a scandal that would imperil his political existence. Indeed, he found such a scenario "inherently improbable," since his dealings with the McDougals were minimal and both he and Hillary eventually "lost money on the land deal."

Even after he was elected president, Clinton viewed the reincarnated Whitewater controversy, and the appointment of a special prosecutor to investigate it, as much ado about nothing. "I had the lowest net worth of any president in modern history," he said. "Everybody who knew anything about me knew I wouldn't take a nickel to see the cow jump over the moon. They knew that whatever else was wrong with me, that I was scrupulously financially honest. And, you know, it was never real. It was all about the narcotic of scandal."

THE real estate development that Jim and Susan McDougal would christen in the summer of 1978 was scratched out of the mountains in the northernmost quadrant of Arkansas, near the remote towns of Flippin, Cotter, and Buffalo City. As Susan McDougal would later tell the FBI, she had obtained her real estate license shortly after she married Jim, helping her husband launch a little business in Little Rock that he dubbed McDougal & Associates. The property near Flippin represented Jim's first big investment. In this isolated area overlooking the limestone bluffs of the White River, McDougal saw his chance to solidify a name for himself among the movers and shakers of Arkansas. The breathtaking views of the river, the world-class rainbow and cutthroat trout dancing through the clear waters, and the picturesque vistas that abounded from this perch atop the Ozark Mountains all made it a perfect destination for professionals just three hours away in Little Rock. It would become a year-round retreat for the wealthy and influential business and political elite of Arkansas. And what better place to start, in gathering up investors, than with the presumptive new governor—Attorney General Bill Clinton—and his well-connected wife, Hillary Rodham?

Susan McDougal would tell the story two decades later: "There were people who would go fishing up there, and there was a landing strip, and he had this idea in his mind that everybody was going to be big buddies and they were all going to go up there." Susan said, smiling faintly, "He'd get an idea in his mind, and he would build a fantasy around it."

After Jim McDougal had lost his job when Senator Fulbright was unexpectedly defeated in the election of 1974, he had splurged by buying an expensive green Mercedes. On a jaunt to the mountains with Susan hanging her arm out the window enjoying the drive, McDougal had pulled over impulsively at a little real estate office in Flippin identified as Ozark Realty Co. This small business, run by local notable Chris Wade, was housed in a cabin that "looked like a cigar shop," recalled Susan. It was a single room, with Wade's wife manning the desk and children running pell-mell around the office. Wade, who would later plead guilty to federal charges of bankruptcy fraud and submitting false loan applications, was a gregarious man with reddish hair and a complexion that was "almost see-through." On that mild winter Saturday in 1978, he was pleased to see a balding man wearing a nice-looking suit and aviator glasses, and an attractive younger woman in bell-bottoms and a tank top, enter his office.

On the spot, Jim McDougal hired Wade to carve up twelve hundred acres that he had just purchased in Marion County. He authorized Wade to sell them off as smaller parcels for $500 down, with modest payments of $75 or $100 a month. In McDougal's master plan, this would fulfill the dreams of countless common people who wanted a little piece of land to build an inexpensive home or cabin but who couldn't afford to buy it outright.

After just six months, the project hauled in a profit of over $100,000.

That summer, the McDougals returned to Ozark Realty as if called back by a divine voice. In fact, the voice on the telephone was not that of God, but of Chris Wade, who reported that he knew of a hot *new* real estate prospect. Wade volunteered to drive the couple over rough roads to a 230-acre tract overlooking the river near Cotter, formerly called the Ranchettes development. This property had just been put up for sale by a company that had gone belly-up. On this day, as the threesome bumped over dirt roads to their destination, the development would take on a new name that would eventually become synonymous with scandal.

Recalled Susan McDougal: "We drove up, and Jim, you know, bought all of the necessary clothing, the boots and the little vest with the pockets." The group slogged ahead, with McDougal wielding a scythe to clear away brush made thick by heavy summer rain, using the other hand to slap away "dog-pecker gnats." When the trio reached the precipice of the property, they took in a breathtaking view: steep limestone bluffs; a handsome hardwood forest framed against a blue sky; small green herons swooping down from their nests; the dramatic slope down to the river, where fishermen in canoes and johnboats were pulling up trophy-sized smallmouths and goggle-eyed perch—the sweetest-tasting fish one could fry up in peanut oil. A velvety mist drifted over the river as if signaling an extraspecial omen.

The three figures gazed down on the White River, which ran fast with water so clear they imagined they could drink it. The sparkling water was just "hitting the rocks and spraying up, and it was just beautiful," recalled Susan. "And I said, 'God, that, you know, looks like white water,'" meaning white-water rapids. Jim expressed confidence that he could get financing to purchase the property. On the spot, he commissioned Wade to resell off the land in parcels and deputized Susan to handle the work of producing brochures that marketed this new recreational mecca.

They decided to call it the White Water Estates.

"We must have been there at the height of the rain," Susan would later observe. "Because I went later, and it looked like a dirty mud puddle."

———

BILL and Hillary Clinton were perfect candidates to share in the opportunity created by this spectacular new investment. Bill was a popular state attorney general. It was public knowledge he had his eye on the governor's mansion. Hillary was a lawyer at the prestigious Rose Law Firm. Already, they were one of the most powerful couples in the state. The Clintons knew Jim McDougal; they liked his quick wit and grandiloquent style. They had already entrusted him with a small five-acre real estate investment—at Saltillo Heights outside Little Rock—on the recommendation of their common mentor, former Senator Fulbright. It was a venture that had yielded a tidy profit of $1,150 for the Clintons. It was no secret that the couple needed to supplement Bill's modest attorney general's salary, if they were going to start a family and gear up for a run for the governor's mansion. They welcomed such opportunities.

In confidential responses to interrogatories issued by the Resolution Trust Corporation in 1995, Bill and Hillary Clinton would explain the whys and hows of the transaction that had turned into an investor's nightmare. President Clinton would tell the RTC investigators: "As a native Arkansan who had spent time all over the state, I had a general knowledge that there were many profitable land investments in the northern part of the state in the 1970's and that there appeared to be a market for vacation and retirement real estate in northern Arkansas, an area of great natural beauty." As an added bonus, he considered Jim McDougal "a political supporter," having first met McDougal between 1966 and 1968, when they both worked for Senator Fulbright. Said Clinton: "I considered him a friend."

It could not be disputed that the Whitewater investment was a tiny blip on the radar screen of Bill and Hillary Clinton when it occurred. They were so preoccupied, in the mid-1970s, with making a name for themselves in Arkansas politics that they barely gave it a thought. This particular deal was consummated in a twenty-minute exchange at the Black-eyed Pea restaurant, famous for its chicken fried steak and fried dill pickles.

It was a cozy eatery just down the hill from the fashionable Hillcrest neighborhood where Bill and Hillary had recently moved into a yellow, modified Victorian house, a step up from the little brick bungalow on L Street, where they had lived when Bill was first elected attorney general. Jim and Susan McDougal had slid into a wooden booth with the Clintons to enjoy Sunday dinner. With its red checkered tablecloths and aromas of Southern cooking, the restaurant was a perfect spot for Little Rock's prominent citizens to break bread. After McDougal enthusiastically described the new property he and Susan were planning to purchase along the White River, he advised the aspiring governor: "You'll want to go in with us on this." McDougal even volunteered to allow the Clintons to borrow the purchase price with little or no money down; he would be happy to include them as partners in this sweet deal. The Whitewater investment, McDougal said, turning to face Hillary, would provide a nice "nest egg" that they could sock away for college tuition, once babies started arriving.

As Susan would later recall the get-together, there was nothing approximating a "serious business discussion." Rather, "it was just like an investment that a friend was going to take care of." In fact, Clinton himself seemed utterly disengaged when it came to this and other business matters. As Susan would note, laughing, "Jim used to say that Bill's eyes rolled back in his head when he would talk to him about money." When Jim decided to talk seriously about financial matters, he inevitably turned to Hillary. But on this Sunday in the Black-eyed Pea, even Hillary inquired little about details. It sounded like a fun, low-risk investment in a hot new recreational spot in their own home state. Before dessert was finished, the Clintons shook hands with the real estate entrepreneur. A high-riding Jim McDougal promised to call the bank in Flippin, where Chris Wade was a founder and director, to work out the appropriate financial arrangements.

The closing on Whitewater took place on August 2, 1978, at 10:00 A.M. Or at least the McDougals closed on the deal; the Clintons did not bother driving up to Flippin. The $203,000 purchase price was secured by a mortgage loan for which all of the new owners—including Bill and Hillary—were jointly and severally liable. The Citizens Bank and Trust Co. of Flippin advanced the lion's share, just over $182,000. It was a healthy loan for such a small institution, but the risk seemed minimal. The bank's loan officers and directors—like everyone else—assumed that Bill Clinton was a shoo-in to become governor. The Clintons planned to build a vacation home on Lot 7, overlooking the spot where the White River met Crooked Creek. The rest of the parcels, the bank officers figured, would go like hotcakes to investors who wanted to rub elbows with the First Family of Arkansas.

Unbeknownst to the loan officer, the 10 percent down payment was funded with a second $20,000 loan from Union Bank of Little Rock, arranged through the maneuvering of Jim McDougal. A simple two-page warranty deed was executed, with the proper tax stamps affixed to it. Through this casual process, the Clintons became co-owners of the Whitewater estates, without ever seeing the property and without ever expending a penny in cash.

Bill Clinton, as much as he didn't give a hoot about money, knew that it was a necessary commodity if he was going to get elected to higher political office. He also knew that he needed it to make mortgage payments and to put children through good schools. Hillary was already fretting about their financial security; elected office, for all of its reward and excitement, would do no more than cover the basics. Nest eggs were important, even for aspiring young politicians. Real estate was one of the few investments a person in public office could make without risking obvious conflicts of interest.

And so the Whitewater investment was finalized, as easily as rolling off a log. If the Clintons believed that they were committing any potential sin, it was that they hoped to gain too much for too little. For a couple sitting at the epicenter of the fast-paced political world of Arkansas in the late 1970s, this seemed like a small transgression.

Handsome maps of the "Whitewater estates" showed a parcel shaped like a ski boot, carved into forty-two separate lots for sale. A yellowed copy of the first advertising brochure, which Susan McDougal had kept in a box for twenty-five years until she disposed of her Whitewater-related papers to put an end to the nightmare, described a pristine piece of property that resembled the stuff of fairy tales. In her own neat printing, Susan had told friends and potential investors about the uncommon beauty of Whitewater, interspersing throughout the text dazzling photos: "Talk about beautiful sights . . . clear water and magnificent Autumn colors. It's a little too cool to swim now (although the trout love it) but come summer, you'll find me floating in the middle."

Bill Clinton won a smashing victory in his campaign for governor in the fall of 1978, garnering 63 percent of the vote. At age thirty-two, he was installed as the youngest governor in the nation. Bill and Hillary, as they daydreamed of setting up a nursery in the governor's mansion, imagined that Whitewater might produce a modest amount of useful extra income.

CHAPTER

4

—·—

McDougal Paints the Town

As with many of Jim McDougal's projects, the reality of the Whitewater investment did not match the grandiose pictures formulated in the architect's head. Flippin, a town that was so small (as locals said) "you could blow through it like grits through a dwarf," was hardly a hot tourist destination. It was located in a dry county, without a single spot to buy beer. The town had few amenities other than one Dairy Queen and a roadside store that sold Confederate flags.

By far the biggest problem with Whitewater was its location. Gene Lyons, a writer who covered the unlikely scandal and owned a fishing camp a short canoe float away, explained that the property was simply located on the wrong side of the river. During the frequent "toad-strangling storms" that bloated the tributary and caused it to flood over, it was impossible to reach the property. Moreover, the parcel was "in the middle of nowhere." Explained Lyons: "Had Whitewater been located on the Baxter County side of the White River, prospective buyers would have been afforded the same views and the same terrific trout fishing without quite the same isolation. Nor would it have required an hour's round trip to buy a six-pack."

There was another aspect of the Whitewater failure that had nothing to do with its jinxed location. For years, usury laws in Arkansas had limited interest rates to 10 percent. Just as Whitewater was revving up in the early 1980s, these caps were removed by constitutional amendment, as the nation sunk into a recession. Interest rates now soared to match those in the rest of the country. As Susan McDougal would explain the worsening dilemma: "We were selling paper at ten, and our loan was at twenty-three, and it turned us upside down." Soon, Whitewater was "losing money at every turn."

Still, Jim McDougal wasn't about to confess error. His strategy was to start "doing more real estate things, putting that money back into [Whitewater] to try to keep it propped up so it wouldn't be a failure, because we had our friends and it was embarrassing to admit that it was a total failure and had lost money." To Susan, her husband was becoming Rube Goldberg. "If one thing wouldn't work to fix something, he'd do seven. And they'd all be convoluted and interrelated, but none of them would work. Like, 'Let's get Hillary to build this house up there.' Well, we're already losing money, you know. Nobody's wanting to buy land there. The economy's in a terrible place, so we're going to spend more money, you know, to do these things." One of Jim's stock phrases was "You've got to stanch the flow of blood."

In the end, the Whitewater scandal, as the press dubbed it, really had little to do with the ill-fated Whitewater property that the Clintons had partnered with the McDougals to purchase in 1978. Rather, it dealt with a series of business ventures that Jim McDougal had leaped into with reckless abandon—most relating to a bank called Madison Guaranty Savings and Loan—in order to rescue himself from the Whitewater fiasco. These unorthodox enterprises soon revealed the darker side of McDougal's personality. Eventually, his mania would reach full bloom when he went for broke by defrauding the federal government.

Hospital records would later confirm that McDougal began coming unglued just as Bill Clinton's career in politics began soaring. Clinton was sworn in as governor in January 1979, beginning a string of electoral victories that would make him the longest-tenured chief executive in Arkansas history. Already, the Whitewater project was beginning to sink into a pool of red ink, although McDougal hid this fact from his fellow investors. To take his mind off the distressing state of his business affairs, McDougal accepted a position in Governor Clinton's administration as an "economic advisor," with a fancy title, an office in the capitol, but little pay.

The day Jim walked into the house and announced that he was going to work at the governor's office was the moment Susan realized that her husband suffered from psychological problems far more serious than impulsiveness. Nearly a thousand people had purchased lots in their real estate ventures. People were "sending in their payments" and deadlines had to be met; "I mean, it was a legal business, it was an accounting business, it was a development business." Despite the precarious state of his business operations that seemed to be blinking "danger!" in all directions, Jim dropped everything and went off to work in the capitol, leaving his wife to sort out the mess. Susan recalled: "I mean, if a man ever did *not* need to go to work at the governor's office for almost no money and spend all of his time there when he had all this stuff going on and we had no staff, it was Jim McDougal."

As Susan lay crying in bed, Jim's response was simply "Don't worry, baby." He added, "I'll always just be a phone call away."

Jim soon began coming home and chastising his wife for being such a "downer." Susan finally decided "what the hell," throwing her own business cares to the wind. She got out of bed, "got dressed and started having fun," dressing provocatively and looking the part of the young in-crowd that had taken over the governor's office in Little Rock, typing correspondence for Jim and joining the orbit of those surrounding the young, handsome governor. Recalled Susan: "And we let the business go to hell, and that was the first manic phase. And everything went to hell pretty quickly. And then we bought the Bank of Kingston on top of that."

No matter how topsy-turvy his life, Jim McDougal was always on the lookout for new conquests. As he and Susan were driving up Highway 23 to a Razorbacks football game in Fayetteville one dazzling fall weekend, Jim spotted an old bank for sale in Madison County. Instantly, he decided that a new business opportunity was beckoning him. Jim told Susan, "Poor people never get loans." He waxed philosophical: "Money is controlled by people who never want to lend money to poor people. They only lend money to other rich people. So we can make a difference by getting this bank and loaning [money] to people with good ideas, and, you know, people who ordinarily are left out of the flow of things." McDougal saw this old brick bank in Kingston as the realization of a lifelong dream. In his early twenties, he had made a failed effort to organize a bank in his hometown of Bradford, as a sort of "people's movement." Governor Orval Faubus had stood in the way of this enterprise. Now McDougal's moment had arrived.

Already tired of the tedious work in the governor's office and of Hillary Rodham's "controlling" style whenever she appeared on the scene, McDougal ditched his job in the state capitol. He purchased 42 percent of the stock of the Kingston bank, becoming chairman of the board and renaming the seventy-year-old institution Madison Bank and Trust Co. of Kingston in honor of America's fourth president, James Madison, because he, like McDougal himself, was a "man of the people." Political rising star Jim Guy Tucker and former Senator Fulbright each invested a small piece of the $700,000 purchase price. In a letter sent from his Washington office, Fulbright seemed simultaneously effusive, cautious, and jocular:

> Dear Jim,
>
> I enclose the proxy statement. When did you change the name of the Bank? My shares are Bank of Kingston!
>
> Your statement is remarkable, assuming those loans of over $4 million are sound! Which of course I do assume. . . .
>
> I am sorry to hear about the gout. I understand it can be very painful and may make you grumpy, which of course may be appropriate for a banker.

Susan recalled, with a faint smile on her face, "We went into Kingston, and we painted every building in the city. For free. We would go to [businesses] and say, 'Would you like [us] to paint your building?' We had an elephant that came to the opening. We had a hot-air balloon. For the people. For the people there, because Jim loved them. . . . He was P. T. Barnum. Really."

Jim felt passionately about this and every other high-soaring project. "He wept over the president of the bank retiring and gave this beautiful speech about this man having given his life," recalled Susan. For Jim McDougal, the American way was a thing of beauty. He had grown up watching his parents, Leo and Lorene McDougal, loan money to good and honest folks in their little general store, being "paid back with love and respect." As Susan would say gently of the husband who later divorced her, who testified in a fashion that convicted both of them at trial, and who died in prison owing millions of dollars to the feds: "There was a side of Jim that only a few of us really knew, that was the epitome of all goodness."

Claudia Riley would add, as an impartial observer who knew Jim McDougal as well as any other person in the world: "Jim did not give a damn about making money. It was the quest. It was the game. It was the play."

————

In its first year, Madison Bank's assets more than doubled, soaring from $1.5 million to $3.6 million. With interest rates rising and certificates of deposit earning 15 percent interest, ordinary customers and farmers were socking away money into CDs. Hippies growing marijuana in the Ozark Mountains were investing bundles in the bank. Yet these new economic forces were also wreaking havoc on Whitewater. Renovations and marketing gimmicks at the bank in Kingston had

gobbled up any profits on the Whitewater venture. The loan McDougal had finagled to make the down payment for Whitewater was coming due. So he solved
the problem by borrowing funds from other sources. Susan McDougal explained that Jim was "too ashamed to admit that it didn't work. We had to keep
taking our personal funds and propping it up." Hillary Rodham Clinton would
later tell Resolution Trust Corporation (RTC) investigators, in sworn statements
signed in 1995, that the Whitewater project seemed to click along smoothly and
that Jim McDougal gave every indication that it was a booming success. She told
the investigators: "There were many years in which the McDougals did not ask for
a contribution. . . . We expected the project to be essentially self-financing when
the requisite number of lots had been sold."

In an effort to spur sales even further, Jim McDougal encouraged Hillary to
finance a two-bedroom, prefab "model home" on the Whitewater property, for a
mere $28,000. Her credit was rock solid; she was a successful lawyer at the Rose
Law Firm. Chelsea Clinton had been born in February 1980—McDougal reminded Hillary that "Whitewater will pay for Chelsea's college." With this
incentive, "Hillary's house" was built on empty land, further entwining the
Clintons in the project. As Mrs. Clinton would later explain to the RTC investigators: "McDougal believed that the placement of a model home on one of the
lots would be helpful to the marketing of the project. . . . I expected Lot 13, for
which I became owner of record, to be sold quickly."

When Bill Clinton lost his first bid for reelection as governor in the 1980
election—getting trounced by Republican Frank White—the Clintons suddenly
needed cash, as Bill prepared to launch a bid to reclaim his office. McDougal's
own debt, meanwhile, was skyrocketing. Yet he did everything possible to keep
the Clintons and other friend-investors from knowing that his financial pyramid
was teetering on the verge of collapse.

Senator Fulbright inquired by letter in early 1982:

> *Dear Jim:*
>
> *How is business in Madison County? You may not have noticed, but
> we are having a depression in Washington. Bill Clinton tells me he is a
> candidate (again). How do you evaluate the situation?*
> *All the best.*

Fulbright added a handwritten postscript: "Give Susan a kiss for me."

Around this time, Jim hatched a plan to rescue his unstable financial empire
by buying the Woodruff County Savings & Loan, which sat just across the river
from his hometown of Bradford, and doubling his risk. "It's gone bankrupt," he
told Susan in announcing the availability of the S&L, "and we could buy it for
less than what you'd pay for a Buick." In fact, the purchase price was considerably

more than that. Yet McDougal was on a roll. Savings and loan associations had recently been deregulated by the federal government, meaning the rules for borrowing and lending were more flexible than ever. For someone who had a voracious appetite for speculative ventures, the S&L business was like a "candy store."

An FBI report of an interview with Susan McDougal at the time of her husband's first prosecution in 1989 commented on the McDougals' business skills: "Neither she [n]or her husband was proficient at running a financial institution." So the couple used the S&L as a clearinghouse, branching out into real estate ventures including resorts and condos, while saddling the federal government with the risk of loss. Jim McDougal rechristened the new enterprise Madison Guaranty Savings and Loan, an entity that would quickly balloon in size, largely due to questionable dealings.

It was shortly after this move that he announced that he was running for Congress.

—————

JIM McDougal's brief foray into politics in 1982 represented the height of his willingness to roll the dice on multiple high-risk ventures. With Democrats nationally seeking to regain their toehold in Congress, McDougal decided to take a shot at unseating the longtime Republican incumbent, Representative John Paul Hammerschmidt, the same man who had beaten young Bill Clinton in 1974.

With hair slicked over his bald pate and wearing aviator glasses, button-down Izod shirt, and tie undone at the collar, the self-styled "country banker" plunged into the race. The *Arkansas Gazette* declared Jim McDougal the "unmistakable" choice among Democrats, and he swept to victory in the primary. Bill Clinton, now ostensibly practicing law at the firm of Wright, Lindsey & Jennings in Little Rock, was fighting to regain the governor's mansion. He had knocked out McDougal's good friend Jim Guy Tucker in the primary. Now McDougal stumped for Clinton out on the hustings, loving every minute of it.

Candidate McDougal railed against President Ronald Reagan; he energized audiences by calling for pay increases for social security recipients; he extolled the virtues of New Deal liberalism. He delivered old FDR speeches verbatim, having memorized them from his LP records as a boy. He even tried to make up for his own lack of commercial appeal with down-home charm. He would poke fun at himself by saying that a handsome politician like Bill Clinton "could appear on television and win a thousand votes with a single smile." But when he [McDougal] appeared on the tube, viewers complained, "Isn't it time for *The Dukes of Hazzard*?"

In the previous year, Jim and Susan's marriage had hit rock bottom. As the pressure from shaky business ventures mounted, they had drifted into voluntary separation and a nonexistent sex life. Now Susan found herself smitten anew by candidate McDougal. "I fell in love with him all over again," she said softly.

McDougal's collection of press clippings from the race, which he would leave behind in a mildewed box after he died, pictured him at the fourth annual rodeo parade in Ouachita County on July 30 with an array of sixteen-year-old "Rodeo Sweetheart" contestants posing beside him. He delivered a "fiery" speech at the Arlington Hotel in Hot Springs. Joining McDougal on the dais was candidate Bill Clinton, proudly holding his eighteen-month-old daughter, Chelsea, wearing a polka-dot sunsuit. McDougal also shared the stage with Hillary Clinton—who now went by her husband's last name, a concession to politics—at the spanking new Democratic headquarters in Pope County, leading a cheer for Bill to become the next governor. Joan Mondale, wife of former Vice President Walter Mondale, even campaigned for McDougal. In the local paper, Mrs. Mondale was pictured at the Berryville Airport standing next to a stunningly attractive Susan McDougal, who was dressed in a billowy white blouse and elegant black skirt that showed off her shapely legs, the proud wife of the candidate.

On election night, McDougal was trounced by Hammerschmidt. He garnered a paltry 34 percent of the vote, a poor showing for an Arkansas Democrat. At this same time, a big loan went bad at the bank in Kingston, sending McDougal into the first of many depressions that required hospitalization.

McDougal's personal papers later revealed that during this period, he started to believe that there was a conspiracy by his political rivals to bring him down. After bank examiners appeared to investigate irregularities, he wrote to his lawyer: "In October at the crucial time in the campaign, they arrived [at Madison Bank & Trust in Kingston] but they weren't the regular examiners. They were a special team of examiners. They stayed the entire month of October making it almost impossible to campaign." Increasingly, McDougal was coming to believe that the world was out to get him. The bank examiners, for their part, left with notepads recording more questions than answers.

Bill Clinton handily won another term as governor. He still viewed McDougal as a friend, but the two men had only infrequent interaction. Increasingly, it was clear that McDougal was suffering from problems that were hampering his judgment. Sitting in his New York home, President Clinton later described McDougal with a sigh of nostalgia, his voice growing softer: "Oh, I loved [Jim]—we had so much fun in the late sixties and early seventies. Working on politics, debating these issues, you know, trying to help Senator Fulbright until he was defeated." Clinton remembered candidate McDougal, in the happy time before McDougal's world collapsed, as a good speechmaker "in an old-fashioned way." Contrary to

THE DEATH OF AMERICAN VIRTUE

later media accounts that portrayed McDougal as a raving lunatic, Clinton remembered a period when McDougal was on top of the world. "He was bright, you know, truly bright," said Clinton. "He just—he suffered from mental illness." By the early 1980s, Clinton recalled, it was increasingly evident that McDougal "had delusions of grandeur, I think, which got him into a lot of the financial trouble he was in."

———

DETERMINED to return to the central orbit of Arkansas's business world, McDougal transferred the principal office of his Madison Guaranty S&L to an abandoned laundry building in the Quapaw Quarter section of Little Rock. Located on South Main Street, the building sat in a blighted area filled with abandoned structures in a "derelict" state.

McDougal loved the location, smack in the middle of a poor black population in need of access to banks. The area was filled with "winos and porn houses." What better place for economic revitalization? McDougal later explained proudly to an Associated Press reporter, in interview notes that survived McDougal's death: "That's where they were grinding people down. No other bank would go down to that part of Main Street. Nobody'd go there but the blacks, but I did." The location was also ideal because it abutted a stately old section of Little Rock filled with grand homes, a few blocks from the governor's mansion. This put McDougal within striking distance of the political power base of the state. McDougal poured money into renovating the building in a trendy Art Deco style that won design awards for its splendor. He built himself a glass-encased office/boardroom, which was perched atop the old laundry boiler. The motif inside included polished brass fixtures, solid ebony floors, and a magnificent stained-glass sculpture. Outside, Jim and Susan shocked traditionalists in Little Rock's business community by painting the building a funky purple-pink.

McDougal used "creative financing" to grow the business of the S&L. One smashing success was the Maple Creek Farms development twelve miles south of Little Rock, a twelve-hundred-acre parcel that he began selling in five-acre parcels for fifteen thousand dollars a pop as an alternative to crowded city life. As McDougal liked to put it, it was "like a snow-cone franchise on a summer day." Susan took charge of the advertising and public relations. In a television commercial that soon became famous among locals, Susan was filmed riding a white stallion through the woods, wearing extra-short cutoffs and boots, extolling the virtues of Maple Creek: "Just a twelve-minute drive from downtown Little Rock," she purred in a sultry Southern voice. Susan McDougal became an instant celebrity and a local sex goddess. Sales boomed.

Maple Creek emboldened Jim to take a daring plunge into a land investment thousands of miles away. He purchased twelve hundred acres on Campobello Island off the coast of Maine, where Franklin Roosevelt had spent his childhood summers. McDougal persuaded Jim Guy Tucker, who now did legal work for Madison Guaranty, to join in the $1.6 million deal. He also solicited seed money from Sheffield Nelson, a prominent businessman and leader of the state Republican Party. McDougal later bragged: "We were selling lots with fifty feet of ocean frontage like hotcakes."

In a move that would complicate life unalterably for the Clintons, Hillary Clinton and the Rose Law Firm were retained to handle legal work for Madison. Jim McDougal would later insist that Governor Clinton one day jogged by the Madison offices, several blocks from the governor's mansion, plopped down in McDougal's new leather chair, and urged him to throw some business Hillary's way. Although Bill Clinton would neither affirm nor deny the conversation, pleading "no recollection" of the visit, McDougal claimed he distinctly remembered Clinton's leaving a big sweat stain on his new leather chair. Documents confirmed that McDougal thereafter paid a two-thousand-dollar-a-month retainer to the Rose Law Firm for work that Hillary and her fellow lawyers undertook on various Madison-related deals.

Jim was now hiring employees by the dozens at the S&L, many of them with no banking experience. A former armed guard was promoted to loan officer. Individuals going through the Alcoholics Anonymous program were given well-paying jobs, because Jim wanted to do his part for sobriety. Three of Susan's brothers, along with other relatives, began earning royal commissions at Madison. Bonuses were doled out like lollipops. Jaguars and Bentleys were lined up like a sparkling fleet in the employee parking lot. *Arkansas* magazine listed Madison as one of the "fastest-growing financial institutions in the South."

Jim McDougal was even beginning to look the part of a cutting-edge business guru, wearing contact lenses, Gap jeans, and a toupee. Everyone seemed to want a piece of the action. But Susan was concerned. She told Jim, "I don't like [these] people; they're really worrying me. I think we're going too fast." She wanted to sell Madison Guaranty and "move back to the country." Susan reminded Jim that they had started out living in a goat shed; those had been happy days. She reminded him of an inside joke they had shared as newlyweds, telling him, "We'll move to the country, and we'll just pull our blue jeans up." The S&L could be sold. They could start over.

But Jim moved forward at a breakneck pace, using Madison Guaranty Savings and Loan and its subsidiaries to fuel a dozen real estate ventures. Senator Fulbright sent a letter to the Madison offices in Little Rock, a touch of worry in the note:

Dear Jim:

You do move fast. What is the Madison Financial Corporation? Is it related to the Madison County Bank, etc.? Have you moved to Little Rock and what is the situation with the Bank [in Kingston]?

With his physical and mental health deteriorating from the stress, Jim Mc-Dougal would increasingly see his misfortunes through a lens of paranoia. For one, he came to believe (according to his own later account) that Susan and Bill Clinton were having an affair. He directly confronted Susan about his suspicions, disbelieving her denial. Second, the bank examiners continued to hound him, and he assumed the worst in their motives. They were going to "close the Savings and Loan," and "keep me from filing as a candidate for Congress."

By spring of 1985, Susan McDougal had begun a relationship with a Madison employee, Pat Harris, to whom she had confided about the dysfunctional state of her marriage. Now she decided to spend the summer with Harris in Dallas to sort out her life. As Susan recalled with an uncomfortable laugh, "Jim helped me pack my things into the car and gleefully sent me off. He said I had become. . . . a downer. I wasn't fun anymore." By this point, she recalled, Jim McDougal was in "full manic bloom."

In November 1985, the *Yellville Mountain Echo,* a local newspaper near Flippin, published a list of delinquent taxpayers. The list included Whitewater Development Corporation. Governor Clinton personally called Jim and Susan (the latter of whom had returned from Dallas and had rented her own apartment) and told them this was unacceptable—the press was insinuating that the governor hadn't paid his taxes. What were they going to do to rectify the situation? Jim replied sarcastically, "If it's not going to work, why don't you guys just get out of it?" To this, Bill replied, "Sounds good to me. Why don't you run it past Hillary?"

Jim McDougal secretly hoped to get the Clintons out of the Whitewater deal. He wanted to take the tax losses from this belly-up corporation and offset profits from a new $550,000 investment in property he had just purchased from International Paper to stop some of the hemorrhaging. As he looked at it, the Clintons hadn't paid a nickel out of their own pockets. They didn't need the losses. "By God," McDougal later said, "this needed to get done."

So Jim asked Susan to "run the papers" over to Hillary. Susan dutifully drove to the Rose Law Firm, thinking this was a simple, amicable parting among business partners. When Susan handed over the document to Hillary for her signature, the First Lady of Arkansas "looked at the document as if it were a snake." As Susan interpreted the body language, Mrs. Clinton "had a great deal of respect for people who were highly educated and she could be quite charming and effervescent with them, but she didn't waste herself on fools, and I pretty much believe that's how she had me tagged." Hillary threw the document on the desk. Susan retrieved it, feeling sick to her stomach. It was evident that Jim had not called in advance; Hillary still didn't believe that Whitewater was going broke. "I mean, to have been sent off by McDougal on this fool's errand, I was just stunned."

As soon as Susan returned to the Madison Guaranty office, Jim ranted, "All these years of our paying for them . . . and now Hillary is annoyed with *me?*" His face turned beet red as he spat out the words: "Well, f—— them."

Hillary may not have been convinced that Whitewater had gone bust, but she had deduced for the first time that McDougal's business empire was on shaky footing. So in July 1986, Mrs. Clinton took a step toward extricating herself and Bill from the morass by returning a batch of files and Madison's monthly retainer check of two thousand dollars to McDougal. In a cover note designed to protect her flank, Mrs. Clinton stated that the Rose Law Firm's representation "has been for isolated matters and has not been continuous or significant." She now declined to accept any further prepayment of legal fees.

Hillary Clinton also sent a blind carbon copy of that letter to Vince Foster, a close friend and partner at the firm, whom she had enlisted to help clean up the McDougal-inspired messes.

Jim McDougal, in the meantime, was still trying to rehabilitate himself. He asked Susan to stop by his new makeshift office on property he had dubbed the Castle Grande project. He said, "Baby, I've found a piece of land that's going to make us more money than Maple Creek." The new project, to be called Lowrance Heights, would be Susan's ticket to freedom. As Jim told her, "It's obvious that our marriage has failed. It's obvious that you want to be on your own, so why don't you buy this piece of land and develop it and make your own money instead of being a drag on society?" McDougal said he knew someone who might be able to help. That person was a former municipal judge named David Hale.

Hale operated a business called Capital Management Services, which had been authorized by the federal government to loan money to companies operated by women and minorities. Susan's tiny advertising agency, Jim explained, would surely qualify for a loan. The money could be used to pay off the last $25,000 debt on Whitewater, getting rid of that headache and the Clintons to boot. As Susan later reconstructed this conversation for the benefit of federal prosecutors, Jim told her, "I have arranged the financing and I will help you with it. I've talked to this man [David Hale]." McDougal narrowed his eyes and added, "It will be a way for you to be a good person and not, you know, be begging to me all the time."

Susan replied sarcastically, "Sure, of course, oh, God, yes. Anything not to be a drag on society. Anything to be a good person."

Several weeks later, Jim called Susan to tell her everything was set. She recalled, "I was to go by David Hale's office the next day, sign the loan papers, pick up a check for three hundred thousand dollars, and bring it back to Jim." In a brief visit that would become the centerpiece of her own criminal prosecution, Susan kept that date with Hale at his shabby one-person office located in the Pulaski Bank. She remembered Hale as a short, pudgy man who was "very obsequious." He appeared to be a quintessential "good ol' boy," who "didn't look the part [of a banker], but he tried to play the part." Having just finished a tennis lesson, Susan dropped by Hale's office wearing a short tennis dress. She engaged in the requisite chitchat, signed several loan papers, and accepted a check made out to "Susan McDougal d/b/a Master Marketing" in the amount of $300,000. Susan recalled, "I made some comments about how easy this was and laughed about how we should do it again sometime. I then left the office and headed downtown to Madison to give Jim the check."

The whole transaction lasted about ten minutes.

By July 1986, the Federal Home Loan Bank Board examiners announced that the McDougals' S&L would have to be shut down or put into receivership due to insolvency. Jim McDougal would later rant that the examiners were "storm troopers" and this was "a pure damn political undertaking." Yet there was now a mountain of evidence that his S&L had engaged in irregularities. The *Arkansas Gazette* ran a story headlined "Madison Has Shakeup." Jim and Susan were booted out as officers and directors. The team of examiners for the first time hinted at possible criminal conduct.

Increasingly, Jim McDougal was suffering from dizziness, blurred vision, and blackouts. As Susan described the state of affairs, Jim was "very, very sick and I [was] literally getting him out of bed and washing him and feeding him and taking care of him. He [was] almost incoherent." During one of Susan's home-care visits, Jim jumped up and bolted down the second-floor fire escape, climbing down to the blistering hot pavement below, where he went into convulsions and collapsed. Susan telephoned Jim Guy Tucker, Jim's friend and sometime lawyer, who sped over to assist in the emergency. By the time he arrived, Tucker recalled, "Jim was clearly out of his mind with a seizure and incoherent." McDougal was taken by stretcher to Baptist Hospital, where a doctor determined that he was afflicted with blocked carotid arteries and had suffered a stroke. A psychiatrist— summoned to evaluate McDougal's erratic behavior—formally diagnosed the patient as manic-depressive.

Susan recalled, "I got him out of the hospital and got him into a place where he was safe. And I would go and take care of him every day and then go home my own self to an apartment. Then the bank of Flippin called, and Jim wasn't even able to cope with it at all. He wasn't talking." Susan had begun seeing a psychiatrist as well. She was attending Al-Anon meetings for family members dragged down by alcoholics. Her marriage with Jim, for all purposes, had disintegrated.

"It was in this climate," wrote Jim McDougal for his lawyer in the midst of his first criminal prosecution, ". . . that I finally had a complete collapse and was forced to leave the savings and loan and was unable to return."

———

BILL and Hillary Clinton, going about their day-to-day lives of governing Arkansas and practicing law, respectively, were largely oblivious to McDougal's tailspin. Susan kept the impending collapse of Jim's house of cards hushed up: "I was so scared to tell the Clintons because, you know, I'd have felt disloyal to Jim."

When the bank in Flippin agreed to collect the Whitewater notes and apply these payments against the mortgage, to break even, Susan was ecstatic. She called the First Lady of Arkansas and told her things were getting back on track. Susan recalled: "God, I was so grateful. So gleeful I called down to the [governor's] mansion and I said, 'Oh, I've got it all worked out, you know, at the bank. But they need your financials, you know, to put in their loan file.'" To Susan's shock, Hillary began "cross-examining" her about Whitewater sales and income. The First Lady seemed unwilling to turn over the Clintons' financials without "more information than that." Why should she take Susan's word that Whitewater was losing money? She wanted documentation before "turning over their own private financials."

So Susan "packed up every single document having to do with Whitewater, every single piece of paper, because Jim wasn't able to even look at it. He wasn't talking, he wasn't walking, he wasn't bathing himself, he wasn't eating." She dumped the papers into a large box filled with everything she could find relating to Whitewater, and asked her brother to drop it off at the governor's mansion. Hillary could have her wish—the Clintons could deal with this mess.

"And I left," said Susan McDougal. "I went to California almost right after that."

The Clintons might have been rid of this nightmare if they had left the Mc-Dougals' papers in the cardboard box, allowing the corporation to die a natural death. Yet Hillary Clinton was determined to be a thorough lawyer and a responsible investor, protecting her own assets. She mailed Susan McDougal a power of attorney in California, and another one to Jim McDougal. The papers would "authorize me to act on your behalf with respect to matters concerning Whitewater Development Corporation." In a cover letter, dated November 1988, Mrs. Clinton stated that she hoped to "get all that behind us by the end of the year." Susan dutifully signed the papers and called Jim the next day, saying, "Well, I did the power of attorney." She was proud of herself "for actually getting something done."

Jim roared back into the phone, "I can't believe you're so stupid, you'll sign anything. You didn't even ask me!" He berated Susan, repeating, "How could you be so stupid? Do you think this woman is your *friend*? Do you think they're trying to *help* you?" Susan answered, "Yes, I did, I thought so."

Jim snapped back, "I'm broke, and I don't have anything, and I would like to use that to buy a piece of land and to start over again. And she knows that very well. Now you have given her your power of attorney."

So Susan hung up the phone and called Hillary Clinton back at the governor's mansion. Her voice trembling, she told Hillary, "Listen . . . I truly believe that Jim should have that vehicle because he has nothing and you have everything. . . . I mean, the inequity of [how Jim is living] and how the two of you are living in and of itself demands that Jim should have this."

Hillary replied curtly, "I won't be talked to in that manner."

Susan shot back, "I'm telling you right now if it comes down to you signing my name to something that takes that away from Jim when he is, you know, struggling to feed himself, that I won't have anything to do with it."

On this acrimonious note, Hillary Clinton and Susan McDougal ended their conversation. When it came to the power of attorney, Susan "never heard from [the Clintons] again." But this incident gave Jim McDougal a reason to hate his old friends Bill and Hillary with a newfound intensity.

CHAPTER

5

SEEDS OF SCANDAL

The Whitewater/Madison Guaranty debacle was the rare scandal that, like a cat, lived multiple lives. The first was born in the autumn of 1989, when Jim McDougal was indicted—along with Susan's two brothers, David and James Henley—on eight felony counts of bank fraud and misapplication of funds. The federal charges involved suspect transactions related to the old industrial park south of Little Rock that McDougal had dubbed Castle Grande. It was adjacent to a thousand landlocked acres that he had already purchased from International Paper.

McDougal had picked up the Castle Grande property for a song—$1.75

million—with a goal of subdividing it to build the area's first microbrewery on the site, a trendy new amenity. In fact, with Madison Guaranty stretched beyond its limits, he was devising a plan to swiftly resell the property at inflated prices, to create the appearance that Madison's net worth had risen by $3 million. This was Mc-Dougal's quick fix to keep the S&L from sinking into insolvency.

Castle Grande and its companion deals would eventually surface as part of a broader criminal scheme that reached far beyond the McDougals. Ultimately, the list of those tangled up in this complex scam would read like a Who's Who of some of Arkansas's most prominent business and political luminaries. Hillary Clinton would be the subject of a draft indictment relating to her legal work on this project, even though that indictment was never issued and remains locked up in a Washington archive.

For now, in the fall of 1989, U.S. Attorney Charles Banks began investigating only one narrow aspect of the Castle Grande investment. A thick report, prepared by special counsel investigating Madison's transactions, dubbed "the Borod & Huggins Report," found that "numerous tracts of land were sold or 'flipped' at inflated values" in order to generate "paper profits" that allowed McDougal to receive jacked-up compensation. On top of "numerous regulatory violations," there were "apparent criminal violations" as well.

Senator J. William Fulbright had suffered a serious stroke in 1988 and was still recovering in Washington. In this enfeebled state and now a witness to potential crimes, he wrote a letter summarizing his dealings with McDougal for the federal bank examiners. Fulbright explained despondently: "As I told you, Jim has gone to California and will not respond in any way. Apparently, he has had a nervous breakdown and simply given up. [Madison] Guaranty is now suing him and foreclosing on his house in Little Rock. . . . So it is a sad tale of misplaced trust, but I expect you have encountered it before."

During his arraignment in front of a United States Magistrate in Little Rock, Jim McDougal, now forty-nine, declared that he had "no assets whatsoever." He had been unemployed for over three years. He was subsisting on social security disability payments of $560 per month, living rent-free in the Rileys' trailer-cottage in Arkadelphia.

McDougal still insisted, in letters to his lawyer, that he was being persecuted for political reasons. Yet there is scant evidence that politics played any role in the first prosecution of McDougal. As McDougal's own lawyer, Sam Heuer, later admitted, "[It was] the documents. They smelled to high heaven."

Indeed, the U.S. attorney in Little Rock who brought McDougal to trial in May 1990 was the antithesis of a partisan operative. A Republican appointed by President Reagan, Charles Banks was a no-nonsense prosecutor who saw the

McDougal case as a cut-and-dried white-collar fraud prosecution. Savings and loan associations were going bust at an alarming rate across the United States. McDougal's "cooking of the books" at Madison, Banks concluded, involved "fairly blatant violations of federal law." The public needed to see that the United States attorney's office meant business.

Sam Heuer, McDougal's court-appointed lawyer, took a stab at pleading insanity on his client's behalf; this motion failed. So McDougal took the stand in his own defense and beat the prosecutors. Invoking his humble roots and insisting that he was neither a fat-cat banker nor a crook, McDougal seemed to have a "spellbinding effect" on the jurors. The jury foreman told a reporter, as they exited the courthouse having acquitted McDougal and his partners: "If they [the bank examiners] had left 'em alone, they'd have *really* made some money!"

Out of the many people tried in 247 S&L prosecutions in the United States in 1990, Jim McDougal and Susan's brothers were the only defendants to escape conviction. Charles Banks was sure beyond a reasonable doubt that McDougal was guilty—yet the jury had spoken. The case was closed. The prosecution of Jim McDougal, as far as U.S. Attorney Banks was concerned, was over.

Susan McDougal by now had relocated to California, starting a new life with Patrick Harris, who was preparing to attend law school, and working as a personal assistant to a former starlet named Nancy Mehta—now the wealthy wife of a famous symphony conductor. Jim McDougal had returned to the little trailer-cottage on the Rileys' property in Arkadelphia, penniless and increasingly beset by emotional, psychological, and financial woes. As Susan observed the plight of her estranged husband, the criminal prosecution was "not even the thing that hurt the most." The hardest thing for McDougal to accept was that he had been publicly declared a failure. "His sense of himself was just gone," Susan recalled.

McDougal, holed up in Arkadelphia, sunk deeper into a depression. On rare occasions, he would drag himself off to Little Rock to visit Jim Guy Tucker and his wife—two of his last remaining friends. The Tuckers' young daughters were among the few people who still treated him like a respectable human being. On one visit, tears nearly came to McDougal's eyes when the girls walked into the family room with eyes sparkling and asked, "Do you have peppermints?" Jim always enjoyed handing out peppermints to people he liked. McDougal had grinned and pulled out two wrapped mints from his stash; he seemed to understand that there were few admirers left. There were few such moments of mental relief.

Susan recalled this period: "He was taking lithium, and the lithium was having a horrible effect of making him very sluggish and depressed and fat and unlike himself. And so he'd go off the lithium, and he discovered Prozac, and he would take twelve a day. And, you know, he was bouncing off walls and he was very bitter toward the Clintons because he felt that they all believed him guilty." Whenever Jim talked to Susan in California, he would go into a tirade, shouting, "If the shoe had been on the other foot, you know, we would not have believed them guilty! We would have supported them; we would have been there for them!"

A single phone call solidified Jim's hatred toward his old friends the Clintons. Near the end of the trial, Susan had called Bill Clinton and told him, "Jim's mother's very sick. One thing you could do that would be lovely, she loves you so much, is to call Lorene and say a word because she's so sick." Bill Clinton answered, "I'll do it right now."

Lorene McDougal did receive a call from the governor. Worried sick about her son, she asked Bill directly, "Would you get Jim a job?" She implored the governor, "If Jim could get work, he would be okay." Clinton replied, "Yes, I think so." This answer brought tears to Lorene McDougal's eyes. She immediately called her son with the good news: Bill Clinton, she said, had in mind "an important job" for Jim. His "reputation [would] be restored."

A day or two after the jury acquitted Jim, the phone rang in the Riley home. It was Governor Clinton, asking for Jim. As Claudia Riley would recall that unforgettable episode: "Jim was living in the house with us at that time as we had nursed him—we continued nursing him back to health." When Claudia handed Jim the phone, he was beaming from ear to ear. He "had been longing for communication from Bill Clinton." He was also excited because there had been the promise of "some kind of employment that went along with this."

Jim listened as Clinton congratulated him on his acquittal. Then, as Claudia Riley remembered vividly, Jim's face turned pale. It was evident that "somebody else had got on the line." It was Hillary Clinton. Hillary and Bill now spoke as one, reminding Jim that they "had incurred $3,000 in expenses since taking over the Whitewater records" and asking if Jim "could reimburse them." According to Claudia Riley, who watched the scene from the living room, "Jim visibly crumbled. I had been standing there in the room, and he absolutely slumped and then he hung up very quickly. He came in here and he sat in a chair by the window, and he never uttered another word that day and that night and for days."

Susan later explained that the disrespect shown to Jim's mother, as she was dying, made McDougal forever bitter: "Jim could never forgive that Lorene got her hopes up and then got them dashed like that. . . . That was really the start of the terrible hatred."

Then in early October 1991, the other shoe dropped. Bill Clinton announced that he was running for president.

I<small>F</small> William Jefferson Clinton, in the fullness of 1992, had not become a serious contender for the presidency of the United States, it is likely that the rest of the world would never have heard the name Jim McDougal or the word Whitewater.

Betsey Wright, Governor Clinton's longtime chief of staff, had written off the Whitewater fiasco as a nonissue. In filling out Clinton's annual disclosure forms, the governor's staffers had dutifully listed Whitewater as an investment. By 1992, however, they believed the Clintons were completely "out of it," free and clear of the McDougals. When Wright discovered that the Clintons had never fully extricated themselves from the Whitewater mess, the staff decided that this demon had to be exorcised. The principal problem was not Whitewater itself—this had lost money for the Clintons and was viewed as nothing more than an albatross around their necks. Rather, the new worry was that "Jim McDougal was a friend of Bill Clinton's and had been on his staff." The concern was that "there was an association." The Clinton campaign knew this sort of linkage could create issues. "We all viewed Jim as a fairly sick, unbalanced person," Wright explained.

Although the essence of the Whitewater story had been rattling around in the local Arkansas papers for years, it had been relegated to old news. It only got legs again, bringing an unexpected scandal to life, because of a story that appeared in the New York Times in March 1992, written by journalist Jeff Gerth.

Former President Bill Clinton would later reflect on the Gerth article and the sweeping investigation it triggered, saying with an air of disbelief, "I mean, you really got to hand it to the Republicans and the New York Times and the Washington Post. It's the first time in history we ever had a major investigation of a guy over an S&L he didn't borrow money from and the land deal he lost money on." Clinton added, "And they turned that into a seventy-million-dollar criminal investigation that wrecked the lives of countless people. I mean, it's quite a tribute to the ability of the Republicans to make sure their own misdeeds aren't investigated and [to] make something out of thin air, and to sucker punch the great institutions of the country, including the [news media] who were supporting it. . . . I mean, it was amazing."

Yet for Jim McDougal, there was a simpler reason why Whitewater came back to life. He later wrote in his memoir, from inside a prison cell: "The Whitewater case unfolded because I wanted Bill Clinton to feel my pain." Jim also had a few bones to pick with newly elected Lieutenant Governor Jim Guy Tucker, whom he was certain had ripped him off for $59,000 in promissory notes from his deceased mother, representing "the last vestige of worth in my family's estates." Now it was payback time.

Sheffield Nelson was an ideal person to broker this story to the national media. He was more than happy to oblige Jim McDougal. Nelson had lost to Bill Clinton in the bitterly fought gubernatorial contest of 1990; he had a score to settle. He was also co-chair of the Republican Party in Arkansas, which put him in a good position to enlist help. One person whom Nelson immediately turned to was Larry Nichols, an offbeat former state employee (and sometime mercenary soldier in Nicaragua) who had sued Clinton during the 1990 campaign, claiming that he was wrongfully fired from his job. Nichols had been the person to first unleash the "bimbo" stories against Clinton, convening a press conference on the state capitol steps and listing five women with whom Clinton allegedly had affairs, including the sexy blond lounge singer Gennifer Flowers. At the time, this had sent shock waves through the Clinton gubernatorial campaign organization. As Nichols himself later acknowledged with pride: "I knew sex sells. . . . I figured I'd pop in with a lawsuit." Now, Sheffield Nelson was joining forces with Nichols to get anti-Clinton stories fed into the national media.

Records contained in the files maintained by McDougal's own lawyer confirm that these efforts were successful. One transcript in those files reveals that Nelson called Jim McDougal to his office (without contacting McDougal's attorney), tape-recorded the conversation, and openly fished for damaging information relating to Bill and Hillary Clinton, Lieutenant Governor Jim Guy Tucker, and other political foes. At one point in the conversation, Nelson specifically told McDougal that the *Times* reporter Jeff Gerth would be calling to ask McDougal questions about Whitewater and that Gerth would want to know "what you're sayin'" that might implicate the Clintons.

Soon afterward, McDougal was meeting with Gerth at the Western Sizzlin in Arkadelphia—McDougal's favorite hangout—telling his story to Gerth and turning over his remaining papers relating to the Clintons and Whitewater.

Jeff Gerth's article appeared on the front page of the *New York Times* on March 8, 1992—a crucial moment in the presidential campaign—just two days before the Super Tuesday primaries in six Southern states. In a piece titled "Clintons Joined S&L Operator in an Ozark Real-Estate Venture," Gerth became the first journalist in the national press corps to bite on the Clinton-McDougal bait. Although the details of the *Times* story were somewhat sketchy, laden down with inconclusive facts and figures, the clear implication was that the Clintons might have engaged in inappropriate business dealings with McDougal while Clinton was governor, and that certain Whitewater records might have "disappeared." (McDougal later admitted that he burned some of the papers after his 1990 trial.)

Both the transcript of the conversation between Sheffield Nelson and Jim McDougal and the Gerth article that appeared shortly thereafter are significant for what they did *not* reveal—namely, statements by McDougal that would suggest any serious wrongdoing by Bill or Hillary Clinton. At this moment in his topsy-turvy life, McDougal had no obvious motive for lying, especially to help the Clintons. His criminal prosecution, he believed, was over. He was feeling emotionally wounded and angry toward the Clintons. He had no apparent reason to protect them, especially after his run-ins with Hillary and the devastating phone call from Bill when his mother was on her deathbed. Even in that context, nothing in the surreptitiously recorded conversation with Sheffield Nelson or in the interview with Jeff Gerth contained any of the blockbuster allegations of criminal conduct, relating to Bill or Hillary Clinton—allegations that McDougal would later unleash after he was convicted.

It was hardly surprising, in retrospect, that the national media would dig into a story that featured shady business dealings between a broken Arkansas businessman living in a trailer in Arkadelphia—who had recently raised an insanity defense in an S&L criminal prosecution—and his former partner, who happened to be running for president of the United States.

Yet media scrutiny alone did not transform Whitewater into a Frankenstein monster. In part, the Clinton campaign itself contributed to creating this nightmare by issuing a series of hasty public statements denying Gerth's account and giving its own adamant version of Whitewater-related events, locking Bill and Hillary Clinton into a story from which they would have trouble extricating themselves, like politicians snagged on barbed wire. Yet the Clintons' foes, too, helped to resurrect those ghosts of Arkansas past. In large measure, the Whitewater story rose from the dead and nearly derailed Bill Clinton's candidacy, because of certain strange events that were set into motion on the eve of the November elections.

———

In early September 1992, as the presidential campaign was galloping into the home stretch, Governor Bill Clinton took a surprise lead over incumbent President George H. W. Bush. As this unexpected turnabout occurred, U.S. Attorney Charles Banks received an unexpected "referral" from Jean Lewis, an investigator from the Tulsa-based Resolution Trust Company. RTC was a federal agency created by Congress to sort out the S&L mess; it was empowered to recommend prosecutions to the FBI and federal law enforcement officials in appropriate cases. In this case, Banks could not disguise his surprise when his first assistant placed the referral on his desk: It related to Madison Guaranty Savings and Loan. That case against McDougal had been lost and closed out three years earlier. Oddly enough, the new referral named as "potential witnesses" Bill Clinton, Hillary Clinton, and Lieutenant Governor Jim Guy Tucker.

Recalled Banks: "I didn't like the smell of it the minute it came in the door. Because it came with a sense of urgency and came from a source that I did not recognize."

Banks, a card-carrying Republican, stood to gain both personally and professionally if George H. W. Bush was reelected. Bush had already nominated Banks for a seat on the federal bench. That appointment was currently held up in the Senate, pending the results of the election. Bush's reelection would virtually clinch his confirmation. Yet Banks did not cotton to the notion of using the criminal justice system to meddle with presidential elections. Banks had lost the first McDougal case fair and square; he was not in the habit of retrying cases and throwing in prominent political figures as shark bait. The U.S. attorney was especially concerned that if a criminal investigation was commenced, even as a "favor" to RTC, the details would be swiftly leaked to the media. The *Arkansas Democrat-Gazette* employed two astute federal beat reporters who would sniff out this case within minutes of a grand jury's being impaneled. Banks had no desire to be used as a political pawn or to throw the election into pandemonium. "I did not want to be responsible for any type of leak that would suggest that he [Clinton] was guilty of a crime," said Banks, "or being the target of a grand jury investigation, before we even knew what the hell was going on." As Banks sized up the situation, the "climate right then was politically very, very highly charged with passion. I mean, we had a major race going on here for the presidency of the United States. And then here this comes in."

A few days after the referral, Banks's first assistant walked back into his boss's office and said, "I've got a woman on the phone from RTC." The first assistant wiped his forehead. "Man," he continued, "she's really pressuring me and the office. What are we going to do about this?" Such a call was highly unusual. As Banks said, "Here is an agency that historically took its damn good time about their work." Now all of a sudden, the RTC people were demanding "get your butt up, take this thing down to the grand jury, and get it started!" Banks's thinking was, "First, this referral is weak. And second, why didn't we get the referral in the first McDougal trial? Why not all the pressure back then? What the hell now is so important?"

After five such calls from Jean Lewis in the RTC office, the Arkansas U.S. attorney finally lost his cool. He would later explain: "I was born at night, but not *last* night. It didn't take me long to figure out why somebody is really interested in trying to get this out here and get this rolling, and get this going before this presidential election is over with."

Banks got on the phone and shouted at the pestering RTC official, "Not me! I'm not going to use this office that way. If the President [Bush] goes down, he goes down. That's just the way it's going to have to be.'"

Later accounts confirm that Sheffield Nelson had been one conduit carrying the Whitewater story to federal authorities. Moreover, records establish that the Bush Justice Department contacted FBI headquarters in Washington to verify that such a case existed and that it involved the Clintons. The machinery was being set in motion to derail candidate Bill Clinton by using Jim McDougal's questionable business dealings to knock the Clinton Express off its tracks.

On October 16, Charles Banks wrote a sharply worded letter to the special agent in charge of the FBI's Little Rock office. He noted that although the allegations against Jim McDougal might have some superficial appeal, "combined with Mr. McDougal's previous acquittal, his present mental state along with no prospect of recovering lost monies from the institution," there was absolutely no reason to recommend a prosecution. Banks went on to castigate his fellow federal officials, contending that "lapse of time [and] the insistence for urgency in this case appears to suggest an intentional or unintentional attempt to intervene into the political process," which "amounts to prosecutorial misconduct and violates the most basic fundamental rule of Department of Justice policy."

The Little Rock office of the FBI sent an urgent teletype to bureau headquarters in Washington, warning them that U.S. Attorney Banks felt strongly that "the alleged involvement of the Clintons in the wrongdoing was implausible, and he was not inclined to authorize an investigation." Indeed, Banks made it clear that he would resign if forced to abuse his power in this fashion. He would reflect a decade later: "I agree there are a lot of things about [Bill Clinton] that I can totally do without, and I never approved of him when he was president. But to use the grand jury to get him politically, if that's the practical effect of what you're going to do, that's not my way of thinking."

President Clinton would later commend Banks's forceful stand on the eve of the 1992 election: "He played it straight. He was an old-fashioned Republican. It wasn't ideology or theology with him; it was based on the evidence. . . . In retrospect, it was a courageous decision by him." The former president cleared his throat and added, referring to the RTC officials who dredged up the McDougal case as a means to come after him, "They just sailed on, you know. It was morally and legally wrong, but nothing happened to them."

And so the Whitewater scandal flared up in the waning days of the presidential election of 1992, cooling off quickly because a Republican U.S. attorney refused to touch it. Yet that glowing spark was fanned back to a flame soon enough.

———

As President-elect Bill Clinton and his wife were packing up their boxes in the Arkansas governor's mansion and preparing for the move east to Washington, they resolved to clean up the last debris of the Whitewater mess. Jim Blair, a family friend and attorney, had scheduled a trip to Arkansas to handle that closing of the books. In an odd twist of fate, the Little Rock airport was fogged in that day.

So Hillary's partner and close friend at the Rose Law Firm who had handled much of the Whitewater paperwork during the campaign—Vince Foster—was summoned by the Clintons to wrap up the failed venture.

As Governor Clinton was celebrating Christmas with his family in Little Rock and preparing to take the oath of office as the forty-second president of the United States, Foster carried the paperwork in his briefcase to Sam Heuer's office. Here, fourteen years after the ill-fated Whitewater deal was consummated, the Clintons transferred all their interests in the company to Jim McDougal. Heuer insisted that there be consideration for the transfer, so he "loaned" McDougal a thousand dollars to pay for the property, a sum that a Clinton representative advanced to Heuer. It was a loan that McDougal never intended to (and never did) repay. In a gesture designed to thumb his nose at Bill and Hillary Clinton, Jim McDougal ground down Foster on a few points, insisting that the Clintons be required to file tax returns in ninety days and thereafter return all the Whitewater corporate records.

With the bargain finalized, sole ownership of Whitewater passed to James B. McDougal. Foster heaved a sigh of relief, pleased to have this monkey off his clients' backs. He returned to the Rose Law Firm, handing the bulky brown folder to his secretary and scribbling an internal memo to the Whitewater Development file dated December 30, 1992.

In that document, which turned out to reflect a tragically premature proclamation of victory, Foster declared that the Whitewater matter was "closed for good."

CHAPTER

6

———

DEATH SONG IN THE WEST WING

Three lawyers who had worked alongside Hillary Rodham Clinton at the Rose Law Firm accompanied President Bill Clinton to Washington, occupying key posts in the new administration. Each of these three men—Vince Foster, Webster Hubbell, and William Kennedy III—was trusted implicitly by the president-elect and the incoming First Lady. Each of them, because of his close bond with Hillary at the Rose firm, had played some silent role in trying to clean up the Whitewater mess before and after the election. Vince Foster had assembled lists of facts relating to the disastrous Whitewater investment, to shape responses for the campaign team after the Jeff Gerth story reignited that issue. Webb Hubbell had joined Foster in poring over the documents. His principal job was addressing "allegations of conflicts" and coming up with "a response to questions that Gerth submitted to the campaign—a list of questions involving not only Whitewater, but Hillary's representation of Madison." Bill Kennedy, the managing partner of the firm, had pulled the corporate records together to figure out how to remove Hillary from the deal, once it became evident that "McDougal was losing it."

Many inside the new Clinton White House quickly came to believe that enemies of the First Family placed targets on the backs of these three Rose Law Firm allies of Hillary from the start of the administration. Whether it was the work of enemies, or fate, each of them was ultimately broken by the move to Washington.

One of them, six months to the day after William Jefferson Clinton's inauguration, would be dead.

———

BERNIE Nussbaum, a wiry, intense, balding lawyer from New York with big ears and hair that puffed up from the sides of his head, was an unlikely figure to be part of the Arkansas migration to Washington. With his tailored suits and unmistakable New York accent, Nussbaum did not look or sound like someone comfortable hanging out in a Southern barbecue pit. Yet he had known Hillary since she had worked for him, as a young attorney on the House Watergate Committee staff, during the tail end of the Nixon presidency. This was back when Hillary wore long hair and 1970s-style Coke-bottle glasses, and Bernie had *some* hair, he liked to joke. All those years ago, Hillary had told Bernie that her fiancé, Bill Clinton, would one day become president. Two decades later, she had a new mailing address in Washington to confirm her prediction.

Bernie now sat with Hillary and President-elect Bill Clinton in the family room of the Arkansas governor's mansion, the smell of pine needles and excitement in the air. Christmas was just a few weeks away; transition planning was in high gear. The Clinton-Gore ticket had won a comfortable victory in November. Now, to the victors belonged the spoils. Key advisers had to be assembled to build the skeleton of a new Clinton administration that would take over power in Washington. Sitting in soft chairs, Bill, Hillary, and Bernie talked about the crucial role that the White House counsel—the chief lawyer for the president—would play in the new administration.

Bernie spoke in a blaring New York voice that at times sounded as if he were talking through a bullhorn. He emphasized that "the last four [elected] presidents had these scandals to deal with." Nixon had endured Watergate. Carter had faced the inquiry dealing with his family peanut warehouse. Reagan and Bush had confronted the Iran-Contra scandal. Bernie told the president-elect, with sufficient volume to make his point, "A lot of legal issues have turned into political problems. You need a counsel to prevent these legal things from blowing up and turning into major political problems."

Nussbaum was not thinking of any particular scandal at the moment. He had given quick advice to the Clinton political team, when Gennifer Flowers told a tabloid that she had engaged in a twelve-year extramarital affair with Governor Clinton. That story had nearly derailed the Clinton campaign. The politicos in the Clinton inner sanctum had consulted Bernie: Should they hire private investigators and try to prove Flowers was lying? Bernie told them to cool it; avoid provocation. "We didn't know if she was telling the truth, or exaggerating," he would later explain. Either way, Bernie felt strongly, "she shouldn't be attacked. She shouldn't be investigated."

That had been sound advice. Although some on the periphery of the Clinton campaign, including celebrity private eye Anthony Pellicano, were later accused of trailing Flowers and trying to discredit her, candidate Clinton himself had dodged a bullet. The Clinton team had come to trust Bernie's judgment.

On this night in the governor's mansion, Bernie was relaxed. In his mind, squalls like the Gennifer Flowers flap were over. He was simply reminding the president-elect that his White House counsel would have to be "smart and tough-minded"; in this brave new world, political assassins lurked everywhere. The White House counsel would have to prevent potential scandals from bubbling up in the first place. Clinton seemed impressed. He joked with the potential appointee, seated between himself and Hillary, "Who will you represent if we need to get divorced?" The three of them laughed. "I'll represent the one with more money," Bernie said, chuckling loudly. It was nice to be among friends.

The next morning, Bill Clinton telephoned Bernie Nussbaum and asked him to serve as his White House counsel.

In reality, it was a package deal. Along with Nussbaum, Clinton had already tapped Vincent Foster to serve as deputy White House counsel. Foster had grown up with Bill in Hope, Arkansas; they had attended kindergarten together. Foster had become friends with Hillary when they worked together on Legal Aid Society projects in the late 1970s and had become Hillary's mentor at the Rose Law Firm. He was a lawyer's lawyer with an impeccable reputation. Both Clintons could take him into their confidences and trust him fully.

The two counselors felt an "instant bonding." Nussbaum was fifty-six years old and a seasoned lawyer. He would later describe the dynamic between himself and his youthful deputy: "He [Foster] was a tall, good-looking, and WASPY person. I was short, non-WASPY." Their personalities were completely different— Nussbaum was loud and brash; Foster was proper and reserved. Yet they both had extensive corporate litigation experience and were cut from the same lawyerly cloth. "We liked each other and trusted each other from the start," remembered Nussbaum, his voice softening.

Nussbaum and Foster were immediately assigned the task of "vetting" President-elect Clinton's appointees who would need to go through the grueling Senate confirmation process. Because the two men, unlike other high-level appointees, were not subject to congressional approval, they decided to vet themselves. Amid unpacked boxes in the empty West Wing offices, Nussbaum and Foster asked each other, "What's the worst thing they can say about me?" For Nussbaum, it was that "I was a corporate lawyer. Representing big companies. I had no feelings for the people." Of course, Nussbaum believed this criticism was silly; he had grown up on the Lower East Side of Manhattan to a family of Polish-Jewish immigrants with a grandfather who ran a shoe repair shop and a father who was a working-class labor organizer. He would refute these verbal attacks when they arose. Now it was the younger man's turn. Foster told Nussbaum, "They're going to say I'm very close to Hillary. They're going to say I was having an affair with Hillary." That rumor had already danced around Arkansas during the presidential election. It would surely flip up its petticoat again. Nussbaum was silent for a moment. He looked Foster straight in the eye and asked, "Did you?" Foster replied softly: "No. I did not." Nussbaum raised his hand and brought the topic to a close. He declared, "Let them say what they want." If crass rumors like this bubbled up in any fashion, the White House team would address them in a dignified fashion.

Years later, Nussbaum reflected on this moment in his New York law office: "I believe that Vince was telling the truth." It was evident that Hillary and Vince were "very close friends." At firm retreats, friends noted that they often walked off together, absorbed in deep conversations. She had a lot of "trust and reliance in him," said Nussbaum. As they began working in the White House together, Vince "helped Hillary on health care. He also handled the personal financial papers for the Clintons." From the start, they were "close professional colleagues." At the same time, Nussbaum insisted, "I saw no indication of any [intimate] relationship." In assessing Foster's denial that he ever had an affair with Hillary Clinton, Nussbaum said quietly, "I have no way of telling for sure, but I believe him."

Those who knew Vince Foster described him as "a man of honesty and integrity," widely respected "for his intelligence and judgment." Bernie Nussbaum witnessed those traits with his own eyes. Yet the job clearly weighed on Foster. Perhaps due to his heightened sense of Southern propriety, Foster seemed uneasy in this new dog-eat-dog environment. "I would describe him as uncomfortable," said Nussbaum. "I have never said that before." He paused. "Yes, uncomfortable."

Although Foster "came in on a high," he was quickly thrown off balance when the political assaults began so quickly and intensely. First, there were fireworks over the failed attempts by the White House to appoint Zoe Baird, and then Kimba Wood, as attorney general. Both of these women were forced to withdraw as nominees because of "nanny problems." (Baird had failed to pay social security taxes for her live-in nanny. Wood had paid taxes, but her nanny was an illegal alien, which created "perception" problems.) There was also the debacle involving Lani Guinier, an African American law professor who had been a classmate of the Clintons at Yale Law School. The White House announced that Guinier would head up the Civil Rights Division of the Justice Department, but her name was abruptly withdrawn due to the controversial nature of some of her writings. The Clinton team was barely out of the starting gate, and it was already taking a drubbing by the press. Political naysayers were clucking that this pack of Arkansas hillbillies couldn't run a country and chew gum at the same time.

Bernie Nussbaum had been involved in Democratic politics most of his life. He knew that Clinton would be subjected to rough treatment by certain angry Republicans who viewed him as an "illegitimate" leader and as an "accidental president." Yet the intensity of the assault was startling, even to those expecting it. Nussbaum explained, "Even Washington pros were surprised at the level of the attack. It started from day one. That made Vince uncomfortable. I was less affected by it. I was used to big fights. I had been involved in major tender offer battles. I said to myself, 'Okay, this is action at the highest level. We will worry about the judgment of history.' " He added, "But Vince was less comfortable. The Travel Office scandal increased that discomfort."

The Travel Office tussle, now a relatively obscure footnote in the history of the Clinton presidency, occurred in May 1993, just four months after Bill Clinton took office. This tempest in a teapot flowed from the new administration's assessment that the White House Travel Office—charged with handling domestic and overseas travel for the national press corps accompanying the president—was awash in mismanagement and bad business practices. Some of the ugliest stories involved embezzlement and accepting kickbacks. Vince Foster assigned Bill Kennedy, now an associate in the White House counsel's office, to investigate the matter. Independent auditors from Peat Marwick dug into the Travel Office's accounting records and found "gross mismanagement." After ordering the FBI to commence a criminal probe, the Clinton White House fired seven employees of that tiny office. Much of the business was slated to be transferred, temporarily, to a Little Rock travel agency run by a distant relative of President Clinton's. There was talk that Clinton friend Harry Thomason and other campaign backers wanted a piece of the action. The First Lady, according to press reports, was up to her elbows in the house-cleaning.

Assertions now began flying that the Clintons and their Arkansas cronies were trying to dispense jobs to kinfolk back home in the hills of Little Rock, and ginning up criminal allegations to do it. Bernie Nussbaum later explained that the White House had inadvertently stirred up a hornet's nest. "People in the Travel Office were doing many inappropriate things, but their patrons were the press. How naive we were." The Travel Office, it turned out, "arranged for trips, and did favors for reporters," even deciding on foreign trips whether the press corps "could bring liquor, furs, and rugs back into this country." Taking on the Travel Office was like taking on the media's sugar daddy.

Bill Kennedy, who led the investigation, personally took a beating in the press. Those closest to Bill and Hillary Clinton, especially their inner circle from Arkansas, believed there were political factors driving the attack.

Hillary Clinton was trying to carve out an unprecedented role as a First Lady, leading the charge on health care reform and further infuriating the Clintons' detractors. Kennedy would later explain: "Some of this stuff was aimed at [Hillary's] health care task force. Some of it was aimed at, you know, 'How dare they bring Arkansans up here and stick them in the White House.' " Some of it, however, was "pure palpable hatred of the Clintons. It started and it never quit."

The FBI submitted a report critical of the White House's handling of the Travel Office matter, forcing the Clinton White House to issue mild reprimands of its own officials, concluding that Travel Office employees "should have been placed on administrative leave rather than fired." It was an embarrassing episode for the fledgling administration.

The Travel Office flap blew over soon enough. But Foster appeared visibly shaken by the dressing-down that his office took—especially because he believed that he and his colleagues had acted honorably and legitimately in every way. "He was depressed not only by the attacks," Nussbaum would recall, "but by our weakness in response to these attacks."

The White House Counsel's Office took a pounding in other areas. The invention and proliferation of cable television had created a twenty-four-hour news cycle that was eating them alive. Suddenly, Foster was being forced to handle stories that "Hillary [was] throwing lamps at the Secret Service" and speculation about likely Supreme Court nominees and a hundred never-ending issues for which the press was demanding comment "in thirty minutes."

Before long, Foster—like many of those in the inner sanctum of the White House—was becoming "beat down, used up," and subjected to tremendous pressure.

—◆—

VINCENT W. Foster, Jr., had come to Washington as a close personal friend of the president and First Lady, which guaranteed him direct access to the Oval Office and a strong position within the administration. Still, he had instant qualms about whether this move was a healthy one, from his family's perspective. Foster's nickname in high school had been "Pencil." He was tall and thin— he "weighed maybe a hundred and fifty pounds dripping wet"—and had a natural studious bent. Foster had graduated first in his class at University of Arkansas Law School in Fayetteville; he had made partner in two years in one of Arkansas's most prestigious firms. Foster was a handsome man whose "mouth curled up" and whose eyes squinted to give him distinct "feline features," causing women to whisper that he looked like the actor Robert Wagner. Through hard work at the Rose Law Firm, Foster had emerged as a leader at the firm, poised to become the next president of the Arkansas Bar Association. He had serious doubts, from the start, that he should chuck all this to go to Washington with the Clintons.

Joe Purvis, who had attended kindergarten with Vince Foster and Billy Blythe in Hope, saw signs of Vince's creeping anxiety early on. He recalled sitting in a restaurant in Little Rock in December 1992, just before the Clinton caravan left for Washington. After midnight, Vince and Lisa Foster waltzed in, having attended a late-night dinner party. Lisa had obviously had "a little something to drink" and made a beeline for Purvis's table, oblivious to the fact that he was seated with an NBC correspondent. Lisa blurted out in rather "salty terms" that "by God, Vince had decided to chuck it all and was going to the White House, and she was miffed and p.o.'d at him and really couldn't believe that he was giving up their life there in Little Rock to take a job in D.C." Vince spotted the reporter and quickly steered Lisa away from the table, so that his wife's expletive-filled commentary would not appear in the next day's national news. Yet the decision to move to Washington, which entailed shelving a successful law practice, dragging his wife away from the home and neighborhood she loved, uprooting a son during his senior year of high school, and jumping into a cauldron of boiling oil in a city known for its unkind treatment of outsiders, was one that gnawed at Foster from the moment he said yes.

When an unflattering *Wall Street Journal* editorial titled "Who Is Vince Foster?" ran in mid-June, this sent a jolt through him. The short but distinctly negative piece, containing a silhouette of Vince's head with a question mark inside it, was prompted by Foster's declining to supply a photograph to the paper, in conjunction with its series of editorials about Rose Law Firm partners now working in the White House. It went on to accuse Foster of playing footloose with the law in his failure to turn over documents relating to Hillary Clinton's nascent health care task force, and suggested that he would face stiff penalties if he ignored a court order to do so. The paper editorialized: "Does it take a $50,000-a-day fine to get this mule's attention?" As Joe Purvis would say, that article was particularly painful "because Vince read the *Wall Street Journal* every day." Now, people around the world, Foster fretted, would see that story as they drank their morning cups of coffee and think that he was an "unscrupulous shyster with questionable ethics." To make matters worse, a follow-up editorial in the *Journal* criticized the new administration for being too slow in finding a replacement for FBI Director William Sessions, suggesting that Foster was "largely to blame."

On May 8, Vince had been selected to deliver the commencement address at his law school alma mater in Fayetteville—a distinct honor. Yet those present would recall that Foster looked uncharacteristically "tired and humorless." Foster's sister, Sheila Anthony, would recall that her brother's voice was "unnaturally strained and tense" during his commencement speech, which troubled her.

In addressing the graduates, Foster spoke somberly: "There is no victory, no advantage, no fee, no favor which is worth even a blemish on your reputation for intellect and integrity." He urged the law graduates to spend as much time as possible with their children. "God only allows us so many opportunities with our children to read a story, go fishing, play catch, say our prayers together," he said with flat affect into the microphone. "Try not to miss a one of them. The office can wait. It will still be there when your children are gone."

One faculty member that day recalled leaning over and whispering to the professor next to him that it was "the most depressing graduation speech I had ever heard, both in content and manner. . . . I didn't realize it until later, but it was, in retrospect, a farewell."

In early June, five months after he had moved to Washington, Foster called Purvis at home in Little Rock. Purvis would recall with clarity: "It was very apparent in talking to him that he sounded depressed. He sounded tired and exhausted." Purvis told Foster, invoking a Southern colloquialism, "Why don't you just tell the president and Hillary that D.C. isn't your lollipop?" Purvis prodded gently, "You'll be welcomed back into the Rose Law Firm, back into the bar here in Little Rock, and nobody'd think any worse of you."

But Foster responded in a subdued tone that he didn't think this was an option. He told his friend that he would be written off as a "dismal failure" if he "couldn't cut it in Washington." He would also feel as if he were "letting down the two best friends he had in Bill and Hillary." Right now, they needed him to assist in selecting a new Supreme Court justice. They counted on his advice on other high-level appointments. This work would literally help define the Clintons' place in history. There was no way, Vince said, for him to walk away from this duty. Every night as he walked out of the White House at ten o'clock, "I get outside that gate and look back, and I see the White House lighted up," he told Purvis in a halting voice. That image haunted Foster even as he went to bed: It reminded him that there was a limitless amount of crucial work waiting for him, the next day and the day after that.

Foster had called from inside his office in the West Wing of the White House, where he was putting in yet another weekend of work. Purvis recalled, "He felt like there was absolutely no way that he could leave that situation and come home. And I really do think he felt trapped."

———

JULY 20, 1993, started out as "the best day we had [ever] had," in the estimation of Bernie Nussbaum. It was six months to the day since Bill Clinton had been sworn in as president. At a morning ceremony in the Rose Garden, President Clinton had announced the appointment of former federal judge Louis Freeh to head the FBI, a nomination that produced enthusiastic bipartisan cheers. The Senate was holding hearings to consider the president's nomination of Ruth Bader Ginsburg as the next associate justice on the Supreme Court—things seemed to be going marvelously.

Not everything, however, was as it appeared. Vince Foster had walked from the Rose Garden back to his office with a stiff stride. Just a day earlier, Foster's assistant had noticed that he had posted three letters using his own stamps. He had left them for mail pickup, an unusual occurrence. One letter was addressed to Foster's mother in Hope, Arkansas. Another was addressed to an insurance company.

White House Counsel Bernie Nussbaum posed for a few photos and returned to his own office, clicking on his minitelevision to watch C-SPAN's broadcast of the morning Senate hearings relating to Judge Ruth Ginsburg. Nussbaum was buoyed by the senators' questions: They seemed like soft pitches down the middle. Unlike prior confirmation hearings that had sparked ugly partisan debate, like those involving Robert Bork and Clarence Thomas, this one had all the earmarks of "a lovefest."

Foster walked into Nussbaum's office in the West Wing, allowing his eyes to glance at the screen, as Nussbaum declared, "We hit two home runs today." He noticed that Foster "seemed distracted." Foster barely reacted to the good news relating to their dual victories. Bernie stood up and put on his suit jacket, determined to savor the moment. He announced, "I'm going out to lunch."

It was the last time Bernie Nussbaum would ever see Vince Foster alive.

An administrative assistant named Linda Tripp, a holdover from the Bush administration, occupied a station outside the two men's offices. Just after noon,

Tripp brought Foster a lunch tray from the White House mess hall. Her boss had requested his usual. Tripp added some M&M's to the tray, knowing that Foster enjoyed this special treat. He ate his meal, which consisted of a cheeseburger, french fries, a Coke, and a few of the tiny chocolate candies. All the while, he glanced at a newspaper. Tripp recalled, during later questioning by federal authorities, that the White House lawyer appeared to be unusually preoccupied. Three times that morning, he had traded phone calls with his friend Bill Kennedy. They never connected. When Foster walked out of his office at approximately 1 P.M., carrying his suit coat but no briefcase, he mentioned to Tripp that there were still some M&M's on the tray—she was welcome to eat them. Foster's last words were, "I'll be back."

Ten years later, having returned to his law firm in New York as a hard-nosed litigator, Bernie Nussbaum looked back on that bright July afternoon with a hitch in his voice: "To this day, it's a sad story. We lost [Vince]. Lost him. He went and killed himself. It was ten years ago. . . . Such a sad thing."

THE day was hot, with temperatures climbing to ninety degrees. In midafternoon, according to official reports, Vince Foster drove his gray 1989 Honda Accord bearing Arkansas license plates to Fort Marcy Park in Fairfax County, Virginia. The park was just off the George Washington Memorial Parkway along the Potomac River, less than seven miles from the White House. Fort Marcy had been constructed as a Civil War fortification to guard Washington against Confederate attacks. It was now operated by the National Park Service as a place for travelers to make pit stops along the parkway, and to enjoy picnics in this beautiful historic setting. Here, atop a small hill with a Civil War cannon in the background, Foster sat down, cocked an antique .38-caliber revolver that had belonged to his father, jammed the four-inch barrel toward the back of his throat, and fired a single bullet into his mouth.

A confidential witness identified in official reports only as "CW" had parked his van in the parking lot and walked into the park, searching for a discreet place to urinate. CW came across what he believed, at first, was a mound of trash. He then realized he had stumbled upon a dead body, the right side stained with blood. The confidential witness jumped back into his van and drove 2.75 miles to the parkway headquarters, where he reported the body to two National Park Service employees, who quickly dialed 911. The time was 5:59 P.M. When U.S. Park Police and rescue personnel arrived on the scene three minutes later, they found Vincent W. Foster, Jr., wearing dress pants and a white button-down shirt, lying dead on the ground just north of the Civil War cannon, two hundred yards from the parking area nearest to the Chain Bridge Road exit. He was positioned on a slant, his head tilted upward, his hair still neatly combed, his legs pointing downward. A pager marked "WHCS" was still attached to his belt. It had been turned off to prevent incoming messages. A pair of glasses, later determined to be Foster's, were found thirteen feet below his body at the bottom of the embankment. Blood, still not completely dry, had flowed from the right side of his face and nostril onto the dirt. Flies had already located the corpse and were gathering in the hot afternoon. The gun was lodged in Foster's right hand—although the body was partially obscured by summer foliage. A gunshot-residue-like material was evident on the thumb and index finger of the corpse, on that same hand.

On the front passenger seat of Foster's car, a black suit jacket was neatly folded. On top of it was Vince's blue silk tie bearing a design of swans. Under the suit coat was a White House identification badge with Foster's name and photo on it. Inside Foster's wallet, in his suit coat, police found $292 in cash, assorted credit cards, and a piece of paper listing the names of the three psychiatrists whom his sister had recommended a few days earlier, but whom he had never reached.

The official autopsy report stated that Foster had died of a gunshot wound with an entrance point approximately 7½ inches from the top of his head. Dr. James Beyer, deputy chief medical examiner of Virginia, who conducted the autopsy with U.S. Park Police in attendance, had observed a "tannish brown indentation" across the back of Foster's right thumb, indicating the place where the thumb had pressed against the trigger guard. Beyer declared that the cause of death was a "self-inflicted" gunshot wound. The autopsy stated that there was no indication of a struggle, nor of foul play. Nor was there any other evidence indicating that anyone other than Foster himself "put a gun in his mouth and pull[ed] the trigger."

THE Secret Service was notified of the death by park police at 8:30 P.M. President Clinton at that time was in the White House library, filming an interview for *Larry King Live.* To complicate an already bad scene, the president had just agreed to stay on the show for an extra half hour. A Secret Service agent stepped forward and briefed Chief of Staff Thomas "Mack" McLarty, who was standing in the wings. McLarty choked back tears. He, too, had grown up with Vince and Bill Clinton in Hope. This seemed impossible.

McLarty issued instructions to the show's producers that no calls should be patched through to Larry King—nothing that might reveal the news about Foster. President Clinton was on live television; that would be a disaster. Next, McLarty ducked into a room and called the First Lady, who had flown to Little Rock to keep her mother company. Hillary's father had just passed away in April; it was a tough time for the Rodham family. As soon as McLarty got Hillary on the line and relayed the news, the First Lady choked out the words, "I can't believe it's true," and then broke down sobbing. McLarty waited for a commercial break and walked onto the television set. He announced, "We have to conclude this interview." President Clinton tried to keep going—but McLarty took him by the arm and steered him upstairs to the living quarters. Here, McLarty sat Clinton down in a chair and told him, "Mr. President, Vince Foster has committed suicide." President Clinton fought back tears. He formulated several questions, asking whether Hillary had been notified, and then broke down crying.

Clinton himself remembered that horrible night, struggling to find suitable words: "First of all, it was really bad for [Hillary] because she was home. And she couldn't, you know, go with me to see Lisa [Vince's wife] and the kids. It was really tough. I mean, I think she felt bereft being apart from us. You know, Vince had been her best friend at the law firm, he had helped me in the attorney general's race, he had encouraged the Rose Law Firm to hire Hillary, and they were both in the litigation section. They were close. They worked on cases together. They were really good friends. And she loved him. Just like I did. We thought he was great, and, you know, Lisa taught Chelsea to swim. We had been at their home together. We were all very close, and it was truly awful. And I felt so bad for Hillary because she was down there tending to her family business and . . ."

In Arkansas, the night was rainy and windy. Thunderstorms had knocked out the power in some sections of Little Rock. The First Lady, staying at her mother's home in the Hillcrest neighborhood, withdrew into a state of shock. President Clinton called his own mother, Virginia Clinton Kelley, in Hot Springs. Together, they wept. "Every man has his breaking point," Virginia said to her son, attempting to keep him strong. "We just don't know where it is."

Skip Rutherford, one of the Clinton's closest friends and advisers, had turned down an offer to join the migration to Washington. He lived only a few blocks away from the Fosters' home in Little Rock. As lightning flashed across the sky, he received a call from Mack McLarty in the White House. Rutherford had been watching the president on *Larry King Live;* he needled Mack—why had they cut short the second hour when Clinton was on such a good— McLarty cut him off. "Skip, will you listen to me?" he said, his voice all business. "Vince Foster is dead."

There was only time to convey basic details. McLarty would move the president out to the Foster home with the help of a Secret Service detail. He told Rutherford, whose experience was in public relations, "Your phone is going to start ringing off the wall in the next thirty minutes. I want you to be prepared."

As soon as McLarty hung up, Rutherford readied himself for the onslaught. The only person at home with him was his nine-year-old daughter, Mary. He set Mary up at the kitchen table with a bottle of Coke and a piece of paper on which he had printed out words to recite. The script read: "My dad is on the phone, and he will call you back when he gets a chance. May I have your number?" Dressed in pajamas, Mary Rutherford understood that something bad had happened. As sheets of rain blew against the kitchen window and thunder rumbled ominously, she asked, "Daddy, what's wrong?" He answered calmly, "Vince Foster apparently just killed himself. . . . I'm going to need your help because it's going to get real busy. You just tell them you are Mary Rutherford and your dad's on the phone and he will call you back just as soon as he gets the chance."

Five minutes later, the calls began in a surge that lasted all night and long into the week.

———

PRESIDENT Clinton could still picture that night vividly, as if it were the worst nightmare of his life. Two things flashed through his mind, as the Secret Service agents in the Presidential Protection Division made arrangements to transport him to Georgetown, where the Fosters lived. First, he had just realized the previous day "how depressed Vince was about the criticisms we were getting . . . and the way he personally was being treated. Especially in the *Wall Street Journal* editorial pages." Learning how upset Vince was had troubled Clinton. "I sometimes forgot that a lot of people who were working for me had not been through the political rough-and-tumble I had been through. And they actually thought if any newspaper in the country editorialized against them that everybody in America read it and believed it."

Foster had seemed so distressed, the president had called his friend the previous night, trying to coax him to come to the White House theater to watch a movie. On occasion, they had relaxed like that together, "especially if Lisa and Hillary were doing something else." The president did his best to sell the idea to Vince. "I loved being with him, and I wanted him to come back to the White House and watch a movie with me. But he said he was home, and he thought he ought to stay with Lisa."

The president had next tried to reassure his friend: "Vince, you can't pay any attention to the *Wall Street Journal* editorial page. You know they're not for us. Anybody that believes what they write on their editorial page is already against us." He explained the politics of the situation, telling Vince in a soft drawl, "They're not going to hurt your reputation. You've got to understand they think they're an arm of the right-wing Republican party. It's their business to beat us."

On the other end of the phone, the president could hear that Vince "tried to laugh about it." But he could tell that his friend "just didn't believe it."

Now, as the president sat with Mack McLarty in the living quarters of the White House digesting the news, his mind raced over these facts. "And so I really was kicking myself for not knowing about it sooner and not picking it up sooner and not reaching out to him [Vince] sooner," Clinton later said. "Wondering if he'd still be alive if he had come to the movies that night with me. You know the whole thing. It was awful."

"And I was thinking about us being little kids together."

———

BERNIE Nussbaum, who had received a call from the White House communications director, raced over to his office in the West Wing. He was present when President Clinton emerged from the residence, trying to pull himself together. "When he came down, he was in shock," recalled Nussbaum. "He was functioning, but in shock."

The president set out with Secret Service agents in a secure Chevy Suburban van and two unmarked cars, headed for the Foster home in Georgetown. Lisa Foster and her family needed support from friends on this night, he insisted. They were in a foreign place, so far removed from Little Rock. The vehicles raced through sleeping traffic lights, traversing the northwest quadrant of the district.

At the Foster home, a rented three-story townhouse, Lisa Foster already had been notified of her husband's death by park police. She was being questioned by criminal investigators, who were asking whether Vince owned guns. Lisa was becoming increasingly agitated and distraught. On the living room couch, she was being consoled by Vince's two sisters and their close friends from Arkansas— Associate Attorney General Webster Hubbell and his wife, Suzy.

As this was occurring, Bill Kennedy undertook the grim task of visiting the Fairfax County hospital to identify Foster's body. A number of Arkansas friends had called to insist that "somebody that knew him and cared ought to go see." Somebody needed to "make absolutely certain" it was Vince. So Kennedy "took that upon myself." Speaking for the first time about this trip to the medical examiner's office, Kennedy would say years later that it was like moving, step by step, in slow motion, through a frightening movie.

Kennedy arrived at the facility in Virginia and produced his White House identification badge. The medical examiner's personnel exchanged a few words, then politely told him that the body had been declared off-limits. Federal investigators were swarming all over the scene; they had issued instructions to keep all visitors out. Kennedy pushed the staffers in white coats aside. He announced in a loud voice with an unmistakable Arkansas accent that he was going to view Vince Foster's body, permission or no permission.

The facility, Kennedy recalled, was "not what you would normally see in the movies as a morgue." It was clean, almost homey, even at this late hour. The decor was "very tasteful." The doctors were considerate of Kennedy's situation.

They could tell he was more than just a big shot with a White House badge; it was obvious he was a close friend of the decedent. They arranged to move Foster's body from the room in which they had been conducting the autopsy to "a place where they could pull a curtain back" so that Kennedy "could look through a window" in a setting of privacy.

Through the glass, Kennedy inspected his friend's body, forcing back an urge to gag. Foster was still dressed in his work clothes. The gunshot wound, Kennedy observed, was clearly evident in his friend's head, where the bullet had exited. Kennedy stared through the window, "absolutely devastated." He later recalled, "I went to the hospital hoping they were wrong. The rational part of me knew that the chance of that was infinitesimal." Now, as he stared at the body of his Arkansas friend, "I was almost reduced to a basket case."

Police and federal investigators were gathering in every corner of the facility. The medical examiner personnel held them back, giving Kennedy a few final minutes alone. As he stood there, Kennedy could not bring himself to formulate a single word, as a farewell. "This was a different-animal-type thing," he recalled, his voice becoming emotionless. Kennedy took a final look at Vince, tried to think of a garbled prayer, then left the hospital silently, walking out into the hot night.

At the Foster home, when Kennedy arrived, the scene was one of absolute "chaos." Webb Hubbell and his wife were huddled around Lisa, trying to console her. Kennedy informed the family that he had driven to the morgue and viewed the body. "It's Vince," he said flatly. He recalled that Lisa "was messed up pretty much." She was unable to articulate a response.

The moment President Clinton arrived, the din became almost deafening. Although Kennedy knew that Clinton's decision to drive out to see the family was the spontaneous act of a grief-stricken friend, he also observed that Clinton's presence "added measurably to the chaos." This small Georgetown neighborhood was now swarming with Secret Service agents, District of Columbia police, and reporters who had trailed the black van from the White House gate. The journalists, drinking coffee to stay awake, were outside talking loudly and waiting to snap photos of the grieving president and his Arkansas assemblage.

Inside, friends and family were mouthing the same words: "What happened? How could Vince do this?" As Kennedy recalled, there was an "incredible bubble of conversation." It only became more impenetrable as the room became more packed. Close friends, tears streaking their faces, tried to reach Lisa and the children to share words of sympathy—but the surging crowd made this impossible.

President Clinton appeared tired and puffy-eyed. Those present assessed that "he had been crying." The president searched out Lisa and embraced her as the White House bodyguards shooed pestering investigators away. Clinton put his arm around Bill Kennedy, almost in a daze, and whispered softly, "Do you have any idea why?"

Kennedy could tell that Foster's death had shaken Clinton to the core. "He is the ultimate politician," Kennedy said candidly. "So you have to know him well. But he was extremely distraught over this."

Kennedy had already spoken to Hillary by phone, to make sure she was all right. The First Lady was "in tears," almost unable to pull herself together. Kennedy later quietly summed up the impact on the Clintons: "They're human beings. They brought Vince to Washington." Both Bill and Hillary, he said, were beating themselves up and repeating over and over, "Why didn't I see this? Why didn't I notice he was in trouble?"

President Clinton asked Kennedy if he would ride back in the van to the White House so they could keep each other company. Kennedy thanked Clinton, but declined. The image of Vince lying on a cold table in the morgue was still eating away at his mind. He needed to be alone.

Said Kennedy, twelve years later, after having returned to law practice in Arkansas and never quite getting over this ordeal in Washington, "It's still hard to talk about to this day. I know it happened. And I know [Vince] is dead. I still have an unyielding disbelief that, one, he's gone and, two, how he went. I've had to deal with that. He was a great guy . . ." Kennedy stopped, unable to say more. Until he added one final thought. "Probably the greatest tragedy of Clinton's time in office," he said, recalling the scandals and other destructive forces plaguing the Clinton administration, "was Vince."

CHAPTER

7

—◆—

CONSPIRACY THEORIES

That night, back at the White House, Bernie Nussbaum agonized over the next step. Advisers and staff arrived at the West Wing like silent sparrows, summoned by the death of one of their own. "People were stunned, in shock," Nussbaum would remember. Patsy Thomasson, who worked for the White House management office, and Maggie Williams, the

First Lady's chief of staff, had gone to Foster's office. When Nussbaum arrived at 10:45 P.M., the light was on, eerily, as if Foster might be coming back to his desk for late night work. When Nussbaum entered, Thomasson was seated in Foster's desk chair, Williams on his sofa. Both women were crying. They had been looking to see if Foster had left behind anything that would provide a clue to this unthinkable act. As Nussbaum remembered it, "They looked in the trash and other places. . . . We were there maybe ten minutes. I joined them, and we did a cursory look for a suicide note." Finding none, they lingered long enough to speak emotionally "about Vince and what a tragedy this was." The three of them then returned to their stations to make more phone calls. White House records indicate that Williams spoke with the First Lady in Arkansas by telephone, before and after she entered Foster's office.

After waking up his entire staff to convey the terrible news, Nussbaum locked the door leading into the White House suite of offices and went home. He later remembered that surreal night: "I could only sleep for a few hours. The phone rang. I bolted up. It was about six o'clock in the morning. It was Lisa [Foster]. She wasn't crying. She seemed calm."

Lisa asked, as if in a trance, "Bernie, I just want to understand something. Did you fire Vince?" Apparently, this rumor had already begun to circulate, along with dozens of other bizarre reports. Nussbaum answered, "Of course not, Lisa. I'd never do that. I'd never want to do that." He added gently, "You know how much admiration I had for Vince."

Lisa replied serenely, "I thought so. I knew it didn't happen. I just wanted you to tell me you didn't fire him."

As Nussbaum remembered the dreamlike conversation, Lisa "spoke in a sweet, calm voice. She was obviously still in shock. . . . She just wanted to satisfy herself."

———

WHEN Bernie Nussbaum returned to the White House the following morning, the staff was still in a collective state of disbelief. One distraught secretary, Betsy Pond, had gone into Foster's office at 7:01 A.M. to straighten up. She wanted it to "look nice when people came to see it." Executive secretary Linda Tripp later testified that Pond had told her she was "looking for a note" in Foster's office. Pond denied ever saying this to Tripp and passed a polygraph test corroborating her denial. An air of suspicion was already settling over the scene. Nussbaum realized that there might be questions about who did what in Foster's office, yet it did not yet occur to him that the room should be sealed. As he would later testify before a Senate Committee investigating Foster's death: "It was not a crime scene. Vince did not die there. One does not typically seal the workplace of a person who commits suicide." To quell rumors, Bernie asked a Secret Service agent to post himself outside Foster's office to watch ingress and egress.

Later that afternoon, President Clinton drifted unannounced into the White House counsel's suite. He and Nussbaum walked past the Secret Service sentry, entering the office to look around. Clinton stopped abruptly; he picked up a framed photo from the early 1950s of Miss Mary's kindergarten class in Hope, Arkansas. It showed a five-year-old Vince Foster standing beside a five-year-old Billy Blythe. Carrying that photo into Bernie's office, Clinton sat down and reminisced about his boyhood experiences with Vince, wiping away tears. The photo was then returned to Foster's office. According to Nussbaum's sworn testimony: "Nothing else was removed from Vince's office that day."

Nussbaum finally met with representatives of the U.S. Park Police and the Justice Department, agreeing to allow those officials to conduct interviews and scour Foster's office the following day, "to search more thoroughly for a suicide note, or similar such document." He also authorized the installation of a lock on Foster's office door to prevent any more unauthorized visits.

It was Nussbaum's belated sealing of Vince Foster's office, his handling of documents, and the carrying away of boxes contained in that office that would trigger the first of many accusations of a possible cover-up, and efforts to link Foster's death with Whitewater.

———

BERNIE Nussbaum was all in favor of cooperation. Yet he was adamantly opposed to permitting law enforcement officials—even those from Clinton's own Justice Department—to rummage, at will, through sensitive documents in the inner sanctum of the White House. With FBI agents gathered around him in Vince Foster's office, Nussbaum personally examined each file, looking for a suicide note, evidence of extortion, or clues to Foster's death. As he reviewed each folder, he orally described its contents to the agents. Any files that were potentially of interest to the FBI were set aside, so they could be copied by the White House and delivered to the Justice Department.

Tempers occasionally flared as Nussbaum called out the general content of papers while FBI agents strained to peek over his shoulder. No suicide or extortion note was found. The search did turn up, however, several boxes of the Clintons' personal files, most relating to investments, taxes, and other financial matters, including the Clintons' Whitewater papers. Foster had been in the process of completing financial disclosure statements and filing tax returns, all of which required these documents. As Nussbaum would later explain to a Senate committee investigating the matter: "It is proper, and indeed traditional, for the White House Counsel's office to assist in this function." Since these files had nothing to do with governmental business—they belonged to the Clintons—he felt strongly that they remained "personal files, which had to be returned." The files included one designated "HRC Financial" containing Hillary Rodham Clinton's financial papers; one called "Clinton Financial Statements"; one relating to the Clintons' income taxes; and one marked "Whitewater Development." Altogether, they constituted a box or two.

The agents looked uncomfortable when Nussbaum declared his intention to return these files to their owners. Yet the FBI did not voice an objection. Nussbaum asked Maggie Williams, the First Lady's chief of staff, to arrange to transfer these documents to the Clintons' personal quarters. He told Williams that the Clintons "would probably want to send the files to Williams & Connolly," the Washington law firm that represented the couple on private, nongovernmental matters.

At 7:25 that evening, the cardboard boxes were carted away by an intern to the third-floor White House residence. Carolyn Huber, special assistant to the president and director of personal correspondence, unlocked a closet and placed the boxes inside. "They were sent to the residence," Nussbaum would later testify, "because it was late in the day, and we were leaving for the funeral in Arkansas early the next morning."

There were also batches of files that contained Vince Foster's own personal records. These were identified for the benefit of the FBI agents and turned over to the Fosters' attorney, James Hamilton, who was present during the search. "I made the transfer," said Nussbaum, "right on the spot." When Nussbaum returned home that evening, Deputy Attorney General Philip Heymann telephoned him after learning about this unusual process. The ordinarily avuncular Heymann exploded: "Bernie, are you hiding something? Is there some horrible secret here that you're hiding?"

Standing before the Senate committee charged with investigating Vince Foster's death, a year later, Nussbaum would vigorously defend his actions in Foster's office that night. "It was my duty as a lawyer, and as White House Counsel, to protect client confidences, including highly sensitive government documents in that office," he said. It was also his duty to ensure that personal files belonging to the Fosters and Clintons went to their respective lawyers. "Every document the investigative authorities [FBI] asked for was given to them," he said.

As to the assertion that there was some nefarious plan to spirit away documents that might implicate the Clintons in the Whitewater scandal, Nussbaum termed this pure poppycock. In Nussbaum's mind, Whitewater was a dead issue. He told the senators: "The Whitewater matter—which subsequently became the focus of so much attention—was not on our minds, or even in our consciousness, in July 1993. Whitewater had absolutely nothing to do with how documents were handled in the White House following Vince Foster's death."

Several years later, when missing Whitewater documents subpoenaed by Independent Counsel Ken Starr suddenly reappeared on a table in the First Family's residence, questions would resurface about the shuttling around of documents in the aftermath of Foster's death. These questions would continue to hang like a pall over the Clinton White House—or at least over those members of the original Clinton team who were still remaining.

————

THE funeral service for Vincent Foster, Jr., took place at St. Andrews Cathedral, the hub of the Catholic diocese in Little Rock. Although Vince had been raised a Presbyterian, Lisa was a devout Roman Catholic—she insisted on a proper Mass, suicide or not. Bill Kennedy, who flew home with the president on Air Force One, served as a pallbearer. He would never forget "stepping out in the sunshine" and helping to carry Foster's coffin down the steps of the cathedral. Hundreds of lawyers and dignitaries and Arkansas mourners stared at the procession, asking themselves in silence, "What caused him to do this?" Kennedy had known for years that Foster had suffered from some form of depression. But why had it suddenly overpowered him? "No one ever knows why somebody does that," Kennedy quietly reflected. "People get to a place where white is black and black is white. Somehow, they manage to convince themselves the world would be a better place if they're not in it." Once he moved away from home, the problem had apparently multiplied in Foster's mind a hundredfold. "I think that here in Little Rock, Vince could deal with his sickness because he could get away and recoup and come back," said Kennedy. "But there [in Washington] you couldn't get away. It never stopped."

A cortege of nearly a hundred cars followed the hearse and the presidential limousine as they transported the Fosters and the First Family to Hope, where Vince was to be buried in his family cemetery plot. The state police had blocked off Interstate 30 going south; onlookers lined bridges across the interstate wherever they could catch a glimpse of the somber procession. In Hope, the crowds swelled to the size of a huge athletic event. One journalist who was known to be particularly anti-Clinton elbowed his way to the front to capture footage of the distraught faces inside the presidential limousine. Joe Purvis, who had grown up in this town with both Vince and Bill Clinton, cursed aloud, "You hypocritical jerk." He would later growl, "I'm kind of sorry I didn't rip the camera out of his hand and punch him out." Purvis and others close to the Fosters and Clintons were incensed that journalists and rubberneckers seemed to forget that the president and First Lady had just "lost one of their best friends in the entire world."

While the media was stirring up stories and hypotheses about the strange death of his childhood friend, Purvis could not help but think about a poem he had memorized in junior high school: "Richard Cory," published in 1897 by Edwin Arlington Robinson. It was about "the fellow who seemingly had everything in the world, was the leader in the town and lived in the biggest house, had everything in the world." It ended with this final line: "And Richard Cory, one calm summer night, went home and put a bullet through his head."

Said Purvis: "Just as that poem ended with an unanswerable question, certainly Vince's suicide left questions."

———

ON the Monday after the funeral, a White House assistant paged Bernie Nussbaum to advise him of an unexpected development. As this assistant had packed up Foster's personal items to ship to his family, scraps of paper had fallen out of Foster's seemingly empty briefcase. In all, there were twenty-eight tiny scraps of yellow paper, containing handwriting that appeared to be Foster's. Nussbaum hurried back to the office. When he pieced the scraps together, the mosaic revealed a list of "things that were troubling [Foster]." The thoughts Vince had scribbled down, in his own hand, included these:

> I made mistakes from ignorance, inexperience and overwork
> I did not knowingly violate any law or standard of conduct
> No one in the White House, to my knowledge, violated any law or standard of conduct, including any action in the travel office. There was no intent to benefit any individual or specific group.

Foster had continued in a hurried scrawl:

> The public will never believe the innocence of the Clintons and their loyal staff
> The WSJ editors lie without consequence
> I was not meant for the job or the spotlight of public life in Washington. Here ruining people is considered sport.

Nussbaum knew that he had an obligation to turn over this evidence to the Justice Department. But he felt that out of decency, the letter should first be shared with the president and First Lady, then shown to Lisa Foster. Otherwise, the press would flash this presuicide note on the evening news before the Clintons and Foster's family had even seen it.

Hillary's office, just ten feet away from his own in the West Wing, was open. The light was on. Nussbaum walked in and spoke gently to the First Lady, who was seated at her desk. "Hillary," he said, "we found [some] scraps of paper. It is a list of things that were bothering Vince. I think you should see them." She followed Nussbaum to his office and began reading the note. Finally, Hillary dropped her eyes. "Bernie," she said, turning away, "I can't deal with this. Do whatever you want."

Nussbaum recalled, "She was depressed. I think she was in bed a lot of this time. She's a tough, strong person. But it was a very gut-wrenching time. Her father had died just a few months earlier. It was a tough scene for her to take."

Next, Bernie contacted Lisa Foster's lawyer to say that he had found something "that Lisa needs to see." Lisa was just returning from Little Rock that night. She would take a detour before returning home.

At 6:00 P.M., Mrs. Foster drove from the airport to the White House, her first visit there since her husband's death. She sat on the sofa, as Bernie shook the pieces of paper from an envelope and spread them across his desk. Lisa did not seem surprised, as she read aloud her husband's scrawl. "He was writing down things that bothered him," she said. Vince was famous for putting his thoughts on paper, she explained. He was doing this openly, just days before his death. Lisa thanked Nussbaum for showing her the note. It was fine, she said, for him to turn over Vince's scribblings to the federal authorities.

The next day, after the president had returned from a quick trip to Chicago, Nussbaum walked into the Oval Office, where President Clinton was seated at his desk, his face still somber from the funeral. Bernie said, "Vince left some sort of note, or list. Do you want to take a look at it? I'm going to turn it over, but I'd like you to see it." President Clinton looked up. He fixed his jaw. "I don't want to look at it, Bernie," he said. "Do whatever is right."

When the note was finally handed over to Attorney General Janet Reno—who in turn directed Nussbaum to turn it over to the U.S. Park Police—the attorney general had only one comment: "Why did you wait twenty-four hours?"

The Justice Department was "thoroughly suspicious" about the timing and circumstances surrounding the removal of documents. Moreover, telephone records later turned over to the Senate committee investigating Whitewater, chaired by Senator Alfonse D'Amato, a New York Republican, would reveal that there was a flurry of phone calls from Hillary Clinton to Washington the night of Vince's death. From her mother's home in Little Rock, the First Lady called her chief of staff, Maggie Williams, for sixteen minutes; an unlisted "trunk line" in the White House for ten minutes; her assistant Carolyn Huber for four minutes; her lawyer friend and confidant Susan Thomases in New York for twenty minutes (Thomases had played a key role in Whitewater damage control during the presidential campaign); and President Clinton in the White House residence at 1:09 A.M. for thirteen minutes.

While Mrs. Clinton and the other participants in these White House calls would later insist that they had "commiserated [with] each other" about Vince's death and did not discuss the papers in his office, it all seemed too doubtful.

Phone records and sworn testimony given to the Senate later confirmed that Mrs. Clinton and her advisers (Thomases and Williams) had actively taken part "in formulating the procedure for reviewing documents in Mr. Foster's office" and directly or circuitously passed along their plan to Bernie Nussbaum. Perhaps most puzzling, a uniformed Secret Service agent recalled seeing Williams leaving Foster's suite of offices at 10:42 P.M. the night of Foster's death, after Nussbaum arrived on the scene. Officer Henry P. O'Neill would testify that Williams was "carrying what I would describe . . . as folders," which were "3 to 5 inches" in thickness. Although Williams denied removing any documents that night—and passed a polygraph test to that effect—the Secret Service officer had a "clear recollection" of these events and was "certain that he saw Ms. Williams remove the documents."

The Justice Department lawyers did not presume that there was anything "terrible" in the papers taken away from Foster's office that would implicate the Clintons in criminal wrongdoing. Rather, they surmised there was something that posed a political danger to the First Family. Perhaps Foster had investigated allegations of a sexual affair involving Bill Clinton during the campaign; perhaps some other documents containing embarrassing material were mixed in with the papers. Whatever the reason, Justice Department officials could not help concluding that the White House was "overreacting to the fear of scandals."

As conspiracy theories and doubts about the circumstances surrounding Foster's death continued to multiply, the government struggled to reach closure on the matter. On August 10, 1993, three weeks after the autopsy, the U.S. Park Police, accompanied by top Justice Department officials, held a press conference. The park police announced that they had completed their inquiry into the death of Vincent W. Foster, Jr. According to Chief Robert Langston, the indisputable cause of death was suicide: "Mr. Foster was anxious about his work, and he was distressed to the degree that he took his own life."

IT was the ultimate irony that the Foster suicide helped to revive the Whitewater scandal—since this was the last thing Vince Foster would have intended, if his mind had been clear enough to assess the consequences. Author James Stewart, who wrote about Whitewater and the Foster suicide in Blood Sport, his authoritative book on these events, would later sit in his New York office and state, "It brought it all back. I mean, if Vince Foster hadn't killed himself, it would have all gone away." The story now had all the ingredients of a bestseller, he explained. "The press loves a mystery. If you want to keep them out in full hue and cry, sustain the mystery. And then if you really want to add fuel to the fire, act like you're trying to prevent the actual truth from coming out. This had all of those elements, plus a dead body."

The suicide of a senior White House official so close to both the president and the First Lady had few parallels in American history. James Forrestal, an aide to President Harry S. Truman, had jumped out a sixteenth-floor hall window at the Bethesda Naval Hospital in 1949, after having been ousted as secretary of defense. This sparked a brief investigation that never fully satisfied some conspiracy theorists. But the Vince Foster death was an altogether different beast. It seemed to bring out of the woodwork an unprecedented swarm of doubting Thomases and accusers, who possessed a morbid curiosity for suicide, drama, political intrigue, and skulduggery.

On July 22, the *Wall Street Journal* published a piece titled "A Washington Death." The paper noted: "We had our disagreements with Mr. Foster during his short term in Washington, but we do not think that in death he deserves to disappear into a cloud of mystery." The newspaper concluded that if Foster was truly driven to take his life out of personal despair, then "a serious investigation should share this conclusion so that he can be appropriately mourned." For the first time, the same newspaper that haunted Vince Foster during his life now called for the appointment of a special prosecutor to get to the bottom of his death.

Self-appointed experts began questioning every aspect of the case: Why wasn't there more blood around Foster's body? Why was the gun still in Foster's hand? Why did nobody hear the shot, including people at the residence of the Saudi Arabian ambassador nearby? Why were there no gunpowder burns inside Foster's mouth? Why did the so-called confidential witness not see a gun in Foster's hand when he first observed the body? And why was no bullet found? Rumors being disseminated on the radio talk shows and in the tabloids ranged from sinister to outlandish. They included assertions that the Clintons and other White House operatives had murdered Foster; tales of secret Swiss bank accounts and drug-smuggling sponsored by the CIA; reports of a "safe house" hideaway in Virginia where Foster was engaging in trysts with girlfriends; and rampant speculation that Foster had been having a clandestine love affair with Hillary Clinton—an affair that had gone awry and had led him to blow his brains out.

If any aspect of the Foster death left a deep scar on the president and First Lady, it was the circulation of these grotesque rumors. Said President Clinton, years later, attempting to contain his anger, "I heard a lot of the right-wing talk show people . . . and all the sleazy stuff they said." He clenched a fist. "They didn't give a rip that he [Foster] had killed himself or that his family was miserable or that they could break the hearts [of Foster's friends and family]. It was just another weapon to slug us with, to dehumanize us with."

The hysteria surrounding the death of one of his best childhood friends, President Clinton said, was an "enlightening experience": "Because I realized I was up against a group of people who, while they claim they have great values and worship God, in fact worship power. And that they would do or say anything, and that they really thought that we were illegitimate occupiers of their natural throne in Washington, D.C., and that anything they said or did against any of us was okay."

Sitting back in the chair at his kitchen table in Chappaqua, President Clinton closed his eyes for a moment, then regained his composure: "You know, I was heartbroken by Vince's death, and I spoke at his funeral and I visited his grave not long ago when I was home. I think about him all the time. But the way they treated the aftermath, the way those people treated his family and Hillary and all of us who were involved in it, it only steeled my resolve to endure this. I thought, 'My country doesn't belong in the hands of people who think like this. This is not human. This has nothing to do with conservative or liberal or Republican or Democrat. This is way beyond the pale if people think that this kind of behavior is legitimate.' And I just said, 'I'm going to take a deep breath and go back to work.' "

In fact, Bill Clinton might have succeeded in going back to work, leaving behind the heartbreaking Vince Foster episode for the rest of his presidency, were it not for several unforeseen developments. A month after Vince's death, a municipal judge, David Hale, was indicted in Arkansas, charged with defrauding the Small Business Association. Some of the transactions for which federal authorities were pursuing Hale involved Jim McDougal. Now Hale suddenly appeared on television news shows, stating that he could prove Bill Clinton had participated in the bogus deals if prosecutors would only cut a deal with him.

Jim McDougal, whose behavior was becoming even more bizarre, emerged from the trailer-cottage on the Riley property to grant interviews scoffing at Hale's allegations. The ornery McDougal almost defied federal prosecutors to indict him again on the Whitewater/Madison Guaranty referrals, which had lain dormant since the 1992 election. He would welcome the opportunity, McDougal growled, to prove Hale was a bold-faced liar.

Another event jostled the dormant scandal back to life. During the fall of 1993, the *Los Angeles Times* was busily working on a story involving rumors that then-Governor Bill Clinton had engaged in various extramarital affairs facilitated by former Arkansas state troopers. Some of those troopers and bodyguards—the *L.A. Times* was reporting—were now coming forward, purportedly for money, to tell tales of driving Governor Clinton to and from clandestine meetings with females and arranging for "dates" whenever the governor spotted women who struck his fancy.

As Bernie Nussbaum would explain the ugly turn of events: "All of a sudden, people started connecting things that were not connectable: Vince [Foster], Whitewater, Clinton having affairs."

By the early days of 1994, allegations of scandal had burst into full bloom, like a garden suddenly flowering with a dozen dark-colored, scary, potentially poisonous species, all unrelated. From this cross-pollination of tainted blossoms, an unexpected political scandal that threatened the existence of the Clinton presidency slowly emerged.

CHAPTER

8

THE SPECIAL PROSECUTOR

Virginia Clinton Kelley, mother of the president, was used to watching strangers take potshots at her son. But she didn't appreciate the relentless drubbing that Bill was taking over the Whitewater nonsense. By late 1993, Virginia Kelley was sick with cancer, her usual exuberance subdued. She was living her life one day at a time with Dick Kelley, her fourth and final husband, at their little white cottage on Bayside Road, which was situated on a peaceful lake in Hot Springs. Virginia still applied heavy makeup each morning, fussing with the white streak that accentuated her black hair—her trademark. She still enjoyed going to the horse races and sipping an evening drink with Dick, indulging in Hot Springs life. But she tired more easily. These nasty goings-on in Washington caused her to worry about Bill, wearing her down even further.

The death of Vince Foster had been a serious blow for the whole family. Virginia had known Vince since he was a little boy back in Hope. In recent years, she and Dick had even retained Foster as their own attorney. Just a week before he died, they had visited with Foster in Washington to attend to some "personal legal matters." His suicide was like losing a son for Virginia, Dick recalled. "Oh, my goodness, when that happened to Vince—she was so broken up."

Now with a fresh batch of stories about Whitewater, Jim McDougal, and Madison Guaranty being ginned up in the press, these attacks on Bill were taking their toll on Virginia. Years later, Dick Kelley sat in front of the cottage's stone fireplace, a cane in hand and photos of the whole Clinton family on the wall behind him. He closed his eyes and said in a quiet drawl, "Well, she didn't believe a thing in the world they said about Whitewater. That was clean as a hound's tooth. There wasn't anything wrong there. But it upset her mightily because they'd just keep hammering on him."

By early January 1994, the "Troopergate" story had just been broken in the news. The war cry was growing louder for an independent counsel to investigate Bill and Hillary. Virginia had just returned from a trip to Las Vegas, where she had attended a concert by Barbra Streisand, her new pal from White House galas. It had been a wonderful trip, but more exhausting than usual.

Late in the afternoon of January 5, Virginia came home and settled into her favorite chair. Dick remembered the sequence of events on this evening vividly. "She drinks Scotch," he said. "So I fixed her a drink. And I said, 'Babe, I'm sorry.' I said, 'You don't feel good.' Virginia answered, 'No, I don't.'" Her appetite had been vanishing. Dick hurried into the kitchen and fixed some soup to soothe her. His wife barely touched it. "So I'm sitting over in this chair," he recalled, pointing to the corner of his den, "and she's sitting over here and she began to tremble." Dick placed a call to Virginia's oncologist, who instructed him to give his wife "a couple tablespoons full of Benadryl and put her to bed," a remedy that would, hopefully, stop the shaking. Wiping back a tear, Dick said, "So that's what we did."

Before she went to bed, Virginia called her son the president. Her body was still trembling after taking the medicine. Yet she did her best to sound chipper, talking about the wonderful shows she had seen in Las Vegas. After that brief phone call to check in on Bill, Virginia turned in early. But Dick sensed something was wrong and had trouble falling asleep.

"Well, I got up about one o'clock," he recounted quietly. "I woke up and I just reached over, and Virginia felt cold. And I said 'Oh, my goodness.' So then—I could tell that she was gone. I called the doctor, and of course, he came right out. And then the coroner came out, and the ambulances came out and all that. They said—this is probably one-thirty in the morning—they said she'd died around midnight."

As his wife's body was being transported to the local funeral home, Dick walked to the phone and dialed a special number that he kept in his wallet for emergencies—the president's direct number in the family residence of the White House. Remembering that night, the eighty-nine-year-old Kelley sat back in his chair and said, "I have never had such an experience in my life as when I had to call Bill at [two] o'clock in the morning to tell him that his mother had passed away. This was really tough."

The president flew to Hot Springs with Hillary and Chelsea for a one-night visitation at the tiny lake cottage. Close friends, including Barbra Streisand, flocked to Arkansas for a funeral service at the Hot Springs Convention Center, which was overflowing with three thousand mourners. Reverend John Miles, who presided over the funeral, told the assemblage: "Virginia was like a rubber ball; the harder life put her down, the higher she bounced."

President Clinton, tears welling up in his eyes, rode in the procession of black cars as his mother's casket was transported to the tiny cemetery in Hope, across the street from where she had grown up as a child, a short distance from the plot where Vince Foster had been laid to rest months earlier. The president was scheduled to attend a European summit to discuss expanding the North Atlantic Treaty Organization (NATO) to include Central European nations, an appointment he could not cancel. As Dick Kelley hugged his stepson good-bye, the older man could see deep pain in Bill's eyes.

A decade later, gazing at an oil painting of Virginia on the wall above his fireplace, a gift from a local Arkansas artist, Dick observed: "Bill loved her very, very, very much." He cleared his throat and added, "Bill was so busy with this other business that he really never had time to grieve over his mother's death."

Even as the dirt was being shoveled on Virginia's grave in Hope, the calls for a Whitewater special prosecutor were growing louder. Senate Minority Leader Bob Dole of Kansas, a likely Republican candidate for president in 1996, declared that the Whitewater/Madison scandal "cries out more than ever now for an independent counsel."

At his NATO meetings in Europe, the president flashed anger and frustration when reporters encircled him, peppering him with questions about Whitewater. A peeved Clinton switched off an NBC News reporter's microphone, snapping, "You had your two questions." CBS News anchor Dan Rather, reporting from Moscow, pronounced that "a cloud has followed Mr. Clinton this entire trip."

The night of January 11, Clinton's advisers gathered in the Oval Office. An exhausted president joined the discussion from Prague, at 2:00 A.M. his time. The Washington group huddled around a speakerphone to rehash the pros and cons of having the White House request that Attorney General Janet Reno appoint a special prosecutor to defuse the situation. Hillary and Bernie Nussbaum vehemently opposed this plan. Nussbaum blared into the phone, "If we allow this, it will be a knife in the heart of this presidency. Nothing happened with Whitewater. But the investigation will range all over. Who knows what's happened in Arkansas over the past twenty years?"

George Stephanopoulos, a senior adviser on policy and strategy, cut off Nussbaum, arguing that Reno should appoint a special prosecutor and be done with it. In his view, "this will be over in six months." The Republican Congress was likely to reauthorize the independent counsel law, anyway. If Reno beat the legislators to the punch and appointed her own special counsel with impeccable credentials, that person could remain in place after the law kicked back into effect. How was the administration supposed to move forward with key initiatives like health care reform, Stephanopoulos asked, moving closer to the phone, if Whitewater kept dominating the national news?

Nussbaum "went bananas" at this logic, thinking back on his experiences during Watergate. "You could appoint *me* independent counsel," he shouted into the speakerphone, meaning it would still be a disaster. "If I was the 'good Bernie,'" he said, "I would take three years, turning over every piece of information to protect myself. If the 'bad Bernie' took over, I would look under every rock, twist and distort, try to distract you. Even the good Bernie will keep going three or four years. A bad Bernie will last forever."

President Clinton, half exhausted in Prague, lost his cool. "You're telling me I can't do it, Bernie, but I'm being killed!" he yelled back into the phone. "I'm going to press conferences here in Europe and Whitewater is all they want to know about. I can't take it."

"Turn over every piece of paper to Congress," Bernie replied. "The president and the First Lady should go to Capitol Hill and answer any questions they want, for as long as they want." Some White House aides in the room gasped—had Nussbaum gone completely bonkers? Turn over everything to Congress and march up to Capitol Hill? That was suicide!

Hillary Clinton stood up. They had vented enough for one night, she said. The president would have to absorb the information and make a decision. "I'll sleep on it," President Clinton said, sounding unusually weary and distant.

———

THE next morning, Hillary walked into Nussbaum's office in the West Wing. She slipped her arm around her old mentor as if to console a soldier who had been wounded fighting for a noble cause. The president, she said, had decided to appoint an independent counsel to get this monkey off his back. "He feels he has no choice," Mrs. Clinton replied soberly.

Bernie looked at the First Lady with sadness in his baggy eyes. "Hillary," he said, "this is a great tragedy."

Looking back on it with the benefit of ten years' hindsight, President Clinton would describe his decision to appoint an independent counsel as one of the greatest miscalculations of his entire presidency. He had expected that the investigation would last "maybe two years, three at most." He had also believed that it would allow him to rid himself of this Whitewater bugaboo. Both of those assumptions, he confessed, proved to be wildly off the mark.

"I mean, I knew Janet Reno would probably appoint a Republican because we were Democrats," Clinton said, explaining his thought processes. "I knew Hillary and I hadn't done anything. I mean, the worst that could happen is we would be bankrupt. We didn't have any money when we got [to the White House], so they'd take what little we had and, you know, they'd be happy."

He was prepared to take it on the chin so that he could go back to being president. Yet he underestimated, Clinton said, the fact that the American media was hungering for a political scandal as big and spectacular as Watergate. Now a collection of Arkansas desperadoes had stepped forward—including David Hale and Jim McDougal—who were dishing up the sensational story they wanted.

"There is no way to minimize in those early days the extent to which the mainstream news coverage was totally polluted by whatever David Hale and those other guys were telling [reporters]," the former president said, shaking his head. "And by [the media's] own desperate desire to restore their own greatness by finding another scandal.

"It wasn't about the truth. But I was so naive, I went along with it."

Bernie Nussbaum, reflecting on that day when he followed orders by delivering the letter to Attorney General Reno requesting that she appoint a special prosecutor, gazed out over the New York skyline from his Manhattan law office and said that if he could have one minute back in his professional career, he would return to 1994 and commit insubordination by refusing to sign that letter.

"At that time, Monica Lewinsky was a junior in college," he explained. "What a shame." Nussbaum leaned back in his chair and stared at the ceiling. "If he [Clinton] didn't do that and didn't appoint a special prosecutor, whatever happened with Lewinsky would have happened in private, as it did with every other president."

This ill-considered decision, he said, "changed the course of history."

———

THE independent counsel law, enacted by Congress in the aftermath of Watergate, had been a response to the infamous Saturday Night Massacre, when President Richard Nixon had fired special prosecutor Archibald Cox in an effort to abort the Watergate investigation. When President Jimmy Carter signed the bill in 1978, it was viewed as a step toward good government and restoring the faith of the public. By the late 1980s and early 1990s, Republicans in Congress (who had detested the statute from the start) were smarting from what they perceived to be abuses of the law by Democrats. In their view, the Iran-Contra investigation headed by Lawrence Walsh was a blatant political attack aimed at President

Ronald Reagan and Vice President George H. W. Bush. Stung by these experiences, the Republican-dominated Congress had allowed the statute to lapse before the presidential election in 1992. Now, with a Democrat in the White House, it was payback time.

President Clinton had campaigned in favor of reauthorizing the law; it was politically awkward for him to resist it. Attorney General Reno, wary of being caught in the political cross fire, threw up her hands and agreed to search for an independent counsel—it had to be someone with impeccable nonpartisan credentials whom neither political party could accuse of rigging the investigation.

Reno quickly zeroed in on Robert B. Fiske, Jr., a lean, gravelly voiced sixty-three-year-old lawyer from New York. Fiske had first been appointed U.S. Attorney in Manhattan by President Gerald Ford, a Republican, yet he had been retained by President Jimmy Carter (a Democrat) because of the lawyer's reputation for integrity. The New York prosecutor had handled hundreds of high-profile criminal cases. Now a partner in the prestigious Davis Polk firm in New York, his hair turned silvery, and his professional résumé glittering from top to bottom, Fiske was a quintessential lawyer's lawyer.

Deputy Attorney General Phil Heymann, who had worked alongside special prosecutor Archibald Cox during Watergate, assembled a list with a handful of additional names: Warren Rudman (a former Republican senator from New Hampshire), Dan Webb (a former U.S. attorney from Chicago), Donald B. Ayer (who had served as deputy attorney general in the Bush administration), and President Bush's former solicitor general—Ken Starr.

A number of accounts would later suggest that Starr had been one of Attorney General Reno's "finalists" for the Whitewater special counsel position. This portrayal was not exactly accurate. Heymann did include Starr on his initial list and contacted Starr to determine his level of interest. Yet Heymann would later divulge that he had scratched Starr's name from contention almost immediately. He made several discreet inquiries and was advised that Starr would be a problematic selection. "I was told that he [Starr] was honorable and certainly very capable," Heymann would explain, "but that he didn't know anything about prosecution and would therefore . . . have to pick prosecutors who he would rely on to a great extent." Moreover, Starr's likely advisers "were thought to be Republican fanatics, not balanced, mainline prosecutors." Heymann concluded, "I couldn't imagine why I would risk a highly partisan investigation."

So Heymann killed the idea of appointing Starr before it ever got out of the gate. Jo Ann Harris, who headed the Criminal Division and assisted Heymann in the selection process, seconded this decision. She felt that a former judge like Ken Starr was the worst possible candidate for an independent counsel appointment. Judges tended to mediate cases instead of conducting investigations and making tough decisions in the trenches like true prosecutors. Starr completely lacked any experience in this line of work. "As much as I like Ken Starr as a person," Harris would later confess, "I just wrote him off."

Robert Fiske, on the other hand, was "as highly regarded a prosecutor personally as there was in the country." He was a moderate Republican who had voted for George Bush in 1992, which was extra frosting on the cake—it meant that people "wouldn't say it was a Democratic fix."

On Wednesday, January 19, 1994, as Washington recovered from a crippling ice storm, Robert Fiske exited a cab and slid, unnoticed, into the Justice Department building. Upstairs, Janet Reno's top advisers whisked him into a conference room, handing him a draft charter that spelled out his prosecutorial power and telling him to "mark it up" however he wished. Fiske sat alone, scratching notes on a yellow legal pad, until he finalized a document that would give him broad authority to investigate Whitewater, Madison Guaranty, David Hale's Capital Management Services, and a swath of related subjects.

Standing behind her desk, in her magnificent attorney general's conference room, Janet Reno stood taller than Fiske by several inches. Neither lawyer was known for being particularly garrulous. Reno read over the proposed charter, with Fiske's handwritten notations. "Are you satisfied that you have all the authority and all the independence that you need?" she asked. The New York lawyer replied, "Yes, I am." Reno handed the charter back to him and said, "Well, you're not going to talk to me again until this is all over."

On Thursday, January 20, Attorney General Reno braved the icy streets and building shutdowns to announce Fiske's appointment, telling the bundled-up reporters that she had searched for someone who would be "the epitome of what a prosecutor should be," and that Robert Fiske "fits that description to a 't.'" Reno blew warmth onto her hands, then concluded: "I expect him to report to the American people, and I do not expect to monitor him."

The White House reaction to Fiske's appointment was guardedly optimistic. President Clinton would later say that he had checked out Fiske's credentials and was satisfied: "All I wanted was a career prosecutor who didn't presume I was a local ax murderer, but was just trying to find the truth." Clinton realized that Republican partisans might try to stretch out the work of this special prosecutor, but how much harm could they really do? Clinton's thought was, "Well, maybe they'll drag it out through 1996, but it will be over."

Among Republicans, Fiske's appointment prompted universal praise. Former U.S. Attorney General Dick Thornburg, who had served in the Bush administration, lauded Fiske as a "first-rate lawyer" and a "solid performer." Representative Jim Leach (R-Iowa), one of Congress's most vociferous advocates of an aggressive Whitewater investigation, told the New York Times: "The Attorney

General has made a quality appointment, an individual of appropriate background and integrity."

This view, however, would change soon enough.

———

THREE days after his appointment, Robert Fiske took an indefinite leave from his law firm and caught a plane to Little Rock. Julie O'Sullivan, who had worked with Fiske at Davis Polk and was now serving as an assistant U.S. attorney in Manhattan, was granted an immediate leave to assist the new Whitewater independent counsel.

Fiske selected space in Two Financial Center in a nondescript, wooded area of West Little Rock, the same brick and darkened-glass building that housed the FBI. Days later, O'Sullivan was driving to a Staples office supply and then stopping at a local hardware store to pick out doorknobs with cheap locks. She later said with a chuckle, "It seemed we would probably need some security."

In that unobtrusive fashion, Robert Fiske left his family behind in Darien, Connecticut, moving to Arkansas to work long days and nights, seven days a week, in a drab building surrounded by magnolias and towering pines. How long he would stay on this remote assignment was uncertain. Fiske's principal goal was to complete the investigation swiftly, because this case created "a question mark about the president." Any such cloud over the White House, he believed, was not good for the country. For Fiske, moving to Little Rock was one way to make sure he was not distracted from the task at hand. "It made it very easy to work long hours," he explained, "because there wasn't anything else to do."

There was no shortage of lawyers signing up to work alongside the highly respected New York lawyer. Rusty Hardin, a Houston trial lawyer who had won over a hundred felony convictions as a district attorney in Harris County, Texas, was impressed with the nonpartisan nature of Fiske's operation. "It really wasn't a liberal/moderate/conservative dichotomy," he said.

Fiske and his prosecutors were soon organizing their work into several distinct criminal matters: First, they were investigating David Hale's recent allegations in the press, in which he claimed that President Bill Clinton was directly linked to Jim McDougal's shady business deals. They also examined a fresh batch of criminal referrals that potentially implicated Jim McDougal, Susan McDougal, and Governor Jim Guy Tucker in an S&L fraud. They also commenced a formal reinvestigation of the death of Vince Foster, to address rampant rumors that still swirled around that tragedy.

Robert Fiske accomplished a great deal as he toiled around the clock on these matters during the winter and spring of 1994. Yet historians would never have the chance to assign a final grade to his work. This was due to forces that swept in so quickly they surprised even Fiske himself.

Whitewater quickly morphed into a melodrama featuring powerful political figures, big money, con artists, murder, allegations of sexual indiscretions, and charges of scandal leveled directly against the president and First Lady of the United States. Combined with an exotic Southern backdrop, set in the environs of Arkansas hitherto unknown to the now-enthralled American public, this national drama played itself out in ways that Robert Fiske never could have imagined— even if he had remained on the job long enough to witness it.

CHAPTER

9

DAVID HALE VISITS JUSTICE JIM

David Hale, a pudgy, smooth-talking former municipal judge and businessman from Little Rock, was known for skating along the edge of the law and propriety. Max Brantley, the *Arkansas Times* editor who covered the Whitewater story, would later put it even less charitably, describing Hale as "a paranoid liar and embezzler." Larry Jagley, the prosecuting attorney for the Sixth Judicial District of Arkansas, who once prosecuted Hale for bilking money from a burial insurance company that served poor and elderly African American families in the delta of southeast Arkansas, sized up Hale: "He is a grifter. He couldn't crawl straight as a child. Continued his crooked way." The Arkansas prosecutor paused, then said, "He's just a crook. Plain and simple, that's all he is."

One major aspect of Fiske's investigation related to Hale's activities running Capital Management Services, a company ostensibly built to lend money to minority-owned businesses. The FBI had raided Hale's office on the same day, in a haunting coincidence, that Vince Foster had killed himself. (Some conspiracy theorists hypothesized that Foster knew about the impending raid and feared it might turn up more damning evidence relating to the Clintons.)

In September 1993, a federal grand jury had returned a four-count indictment against Hale, charging him with defrauding the federal Small Business Administration (SBA) of nearly $900,000 and unearthing a new political scandal in Arkansas.

It was in this highly charged atmosphere that Hale began telling journalists that Jim McDougal and then-Governor Bill Clinton had pressured him into giving a $300,000 loan to Master Marketing, Susan McDougal's advertising company. Some of the proceeds of this loan, Hale started whispering to reporters, were specifically earmarked to go into the failed Whitewater deal in an attempt to salvage it. In return for that bogus deal, the McDougals allegedly would loan Hale $825,000 from Madison Guaranty so that he could leverage another $1 million from the SBA and reap a huge profit.

In footage of an NBC interview with David Hale dated November 6, never aired in full but later subpoenaed by Jim McDougal's lawyers for trial, Hale was filmed sitting in front of a row of law books, wearing a black suit and red-striped tie. Hale admitted to engaging in shady business deals, at which point the interviewer pressed for details:

Q: Who brought about your downfall in your view? Yourself . . . ?
HALE: Myself . . .
Q: Would you consider it was a criminal conspiracy, a scheme to defraud federal regulators? And were there others involved?
HALE: Yes, sir.
Q: Who were they?

Hale stared into the camera, blinking with as much sincerity as he could muster before replying: "Then setting [sic] Governor Bill Clinton, James Mc-Dougal, then the owner of Madison Savings and Loan, and Jim Guy Tucker . . . the present Governor of Arkansas."

Hale's early appearances pointing the finger at the Clintons and others, research now confirms, was accomplished with the direct assistance of "Justice Jim" Johnson, an unabashed Clinton enemy. A former judge on the Arkansas Supreme Court and a colorful political creature who spoke in Southern colloquialisms, Justice Jim lived north of Little Rock in Conway and was a white-haired relic of the segregationist South. Bill Clinton's rise to power in his home state irked Justice Jim, so he vowed to do something about it.

Johnson was born in 1924, when segregation was still thriving in Arkansas. He had served as the local coordinator for then-Governor Strom Thurmond's campaign in 1948, when the South Carolina governor ran for president on the "states' rights" ticket. Johnson rose in the ranks of old-time Southern Democrats in Arkansas politics. He made a "hell of a showing" in the 1955 governor's race against popular incumbent Orval Faubus, largely by promoting the Johnson Amendment, which would have rewritten the Arkansas Constitution to invalidate the U.S. Supreme Court's decision in *Brown v. Board of Education,* preventing public schools from becoming integrated in Arkansas. (Although the Johnson Amendment passed overwhelmingly, the federal courts swiftly struck it down as unconstitutional.)

Johnson also served as editor of *Arkansas Faith,* a newsletter published by the White Citizens' Council. In one issue, he penned a column declaring that "the South will never accept integration, be it immediate or gradual." Another issue, during his tenure as editor in the spring of 1956, published photos of black men kissing white women and warned of "mongrelization." A cartoon in the April 1956 newsletter depicted Arkansas Governor Faubus taking a meat cleaver to segregation underneath the caption: "This will please the niggers and confuse the White Folks!"

After his election to the state senate, Johnson played a leading role in attempting to block African American students from attending Central High School in Little Rock, during the infamous standoff between Governor Faubus and President Dwight D. Eisenhower—a standoff that caused President Eisenhower to dispatch the National Guard to Arkansas. Johnson went on to win a seat on the Arkansas Supreme Court in 1958 with the open support of the Ku Klux Klan, a seat that he held for eight years. (Although Johnson later denied having the formal support of the KKK, he freely admitted, "Surely to God they voted for me.") After a failed run for governor in 1966, Johnson gradually bolted from the Democratic Party, crawled under the Republican tent in Arkansas, and grew to abhor the likes of young Bill Clinton.

Johnson later admitted that he found Clinton to be "a charmer" from the first moment the two of them met. Yet he didn't cotton to Democrats who supported the ultraliberal George McGovern in 1972 (as Clinton had), and he didn't appreciate these younger Arkansas Democrats who were driving the old conservative guard out. As Justice Jim later explained, the die-hard "states' rights" Democrats like him were the ones who had "recaptured the South" after the Civil War and attempted to restore whatever "dignity was left." By the time Bill Clinton entered the scene in Arkansas politics during the late 1970s and 1980s, Johnson felt that the "left-wingers" had wrecked the party. Traitors like Clinton, he believed, had "put together their coalitions of the blacks and leftists and labor and other special interests," and then tacked on "the gays and school-teachers," which "really stole our home base."

Johnson would reflect years later, with both humor and anger punctuating his voice, that he—and other like-minded Southern Democrats—had been forced to take refuge in the Republican Party against their will. "It's not that we are Republicans," he said. "We just didn't have anywhere else to go when the sons of bitches threw us out."

And so Justice Jim Johnson was plenty happy to come to the assistance of his younger friend, David Hale, when Hale appeared at Johnson's farm "absolutely terrified," confiding that he was about to be indicted by the federal authorities. Johnson knew and liked Hale's family. They were a "very sagacious political people" from Yell County. "They play a brand of politics up there that Tammany Hall could study for a while," said Johnson with a chuckle. Hale's older brother had helped Johnson in an early campaign. Johnson would confess, "I was very fond of him and their daddy and the whole family."

David Hale was the consummate Little Rock wheeler and dealer. A short, anemic, hail-fellow-well-met, he loved rubbing elbows with the political and business elite of Arkansas. Hale was onetime national president of the Jaycees, a position that gave him a Rolodex full of contacts. He was a devout Baptist. He was part owner of the Dogpatch U.S.A. amusement park in the Ozark Mountain town of Eureka Springs, before it went belly-up. He was a lawyer and a "judge" on the Little Rock small claims court that handled traffic tickets and other minor violations, giving him local political swat. Hale was also a financier who dispensed loans to small businesses while earning a handsome profit for himself. Now his life of skating on the edge had caught up with him.

Johnson's farm, dubbed "White Haven" as a tribute to the glory days of segregationism, was not the sort of place a person visited by happenstance. As he recalled Hale's unexpected visit, the ashen municipal judge drove up and confided that he was in trouble with the federal authorities. Johnson asked, "What are they indicting you for? What's the charge?" Hale replied, "Conspiring to defraud the government." Johnson asked, "Who else has been indicted in this conspiracy?" Hale replied, "Only me." So Justice Jim immediately devised a legal theory: "Well . . . if you're being indicted for conspiring to defraud, then you've got to have some *conspirators*."

Hale squinted. This was an interesting point. Hale scratched his chin and said that "Clinton had leaned on him" in doing some of the illegal deals. Hale thought some more and told the judge that "Clinton and his gang was a part of it. Those that ran with him." Justice Jim later noted: "And the boy [Hale] had no reason to try to bullshit me."

For Johnson, any opportunity to poke a stick in Bill Clinton's eye was a welcome one. The judge had worked tirelessly behind the scenes during the congressional campaign of 1980 to see Clinton defeated by neophyte Frank White. Johnson had manned the phones and called ward leaders in every precinct of Arkansas, whipping them into a frenzy to bring out the troops for Ronald Reagan and then adding, "By the way, this White boy is going to beat Clinton. He is really catching fire." Johnson chuckled as he recalled the tactic. "Until the day he died, he [Frank White] never knew really how he won."

The white-haired judge also granted interviews for *Slick Willie: Why America Cannot Trust Bill Clinton,* a book authored by Floyd G. Brown during the election of 1992. This eye-popping tome assembled the most outrageous and salacious tales about Clinton in one volume, openly attempting to derail Clinton's run for the presidency.

Part of what Justice Jim disliked about Clinton, truth be told, was the younger man's Hot Springs roots. For Johnson, Hot Springs was "like the manure pile in a barnyard. You just pile it over there, and you know it's over there and you don't want it." With its gambling and drinking and horse racing and mineral baths, Hot Springs represented entertainment with a raunchy twist. "Everybody was in on it in Hot Springs," he would quip. "The natives, they'd entertain the tourists and if it felt good, do it, and they didn't have a lot of second thoughts about the morality of the situation they grew up in." As Johnson saw it, there existed a "Hot Springs state of thought" that thoroughly repulsed him. He recalled that during his state senate days, a legislator from Hot Springs had once found out how he planned to vote on an issue and promptly "sold my vote" to an opponent. When Johnson confronted him, the colleague apologized up and down. "But within an hour, he would have sold my vote again if he could," Johnson said. "That's the Hot Springs state of thought." In Johnson's eyes, Bill Clinton possessed that attribute in spades.

The judge harbored an even more personal grudge. When Clinton was governor, Johnson had asked for a tiny favor, requesting that the governor appoint one of his protégés to a vacancy on the local chancery court. Despite "a faithful promise" from Clinton that the appointment would be made, the favor was never delivered. Stung by that memory, the judge would reflect, "This gave me a lesson to go ahead and express my convictions against Clinton every opportunity I had."

One particularly ripe opportunity had presented itself during the presidential election of 1992. Johnson had pounced on a chance to dredge up letters relating to Clinton's "draft-dodging" Oxford days. Johnson made no bones about calling Clinton a "queer-mongering, whore-happening adulterer; a baby-killing, draft-dodging, dope-tolerating, lying, two-faced, treasonist activist." Johnson had been appalled by Clinton's infamous letter to Colonel Eugene Holmes, in which Clinton suggested that he was morally opposed to the Vietnam War and used this excuse to slide out of the draft. So the judge searched out Colonel Holmes, who had retired to the outer reaches of Arkansas, asking the colonel to write a letter indicating his own contempt for what young Bill Clinton had done to avoid serving his country. Johnson passed along that letter to editor Wesley Pruden at the ultraconservative *Washington Times*, which immediately published the story. That effort briefly blew up in Clinton's face during the campaign, but fizzled out before it did permanent damage.

Now, two years later, with David Hale at his doorstep, Justice Jim dusted off this maneuver from the Colonel Holmes playbook, again contacting his friend Pruden to ask if any major media would be interested in Hale's story. As the judge later recounted with pride, "I retraced those footsteps that I had used in trying to stir up some publicity over that damn [ROTC] letter." Again, it paid dividends; the paper happily published Hale's startling account.

The judge also urged Hale to contact Cliff Jackson, an attorney in Hot Springs—a fellow Clinton enemy who had spent time with Clinton at Oxford and had grown to despise him. Lately, Jackson was making a name for himself by disseminating a story about then-Governor Clinton's purported misuse of Arkansas state troopers to arrange sexual trysts. Jackson, said the retired judge, had good media contacts. Although Johnson considered Jackson "a peculiar duck" who liked to "fly his own boat," they could use Jackson to Hale's advantage. Years later, Johnson described Jackson's tenacity: "Cliff will work vigorously like a hog rooting under the gate to get into the act. He was flexing his little muscles trying to make himself prominent, maybe for some federal appointment later on. He was a smart boy." Johnson was also willing to contact Sheffield Nelson, head of the Arkansas Republican Party and longtime foe of Bill Clinton. Through this combined effort, they could surely get Hale's allegations pumped into the national media.

As usual, Johnson hit pay dirt. The Hale story was swiftly picked up by the *Washington Post*, the *New York Times*, the *Los Angeles Times*, and other major publications. For Justice Jim, it was the least he could do for a friend. Even if Hale were guilty, "damn it, he oughtn't to have to carry the whole load." As the judge told Hale, the key was to go public in a big way. "If the whole ship goes down," he theorized, "these people [including Bill Clinton] will have to come to your rescue."

"I've got a back room here," he added. "If you and your family want to move in, come on." So David Hale moved to the Johnson farm, turning his fate over to the judge's experienced hands.

President Bill Clinton, looking back on these events after Hale had pleaded guilty to multiple felonies and assumed a new identity in Louisiana, felt it was abundantly clear why Hale had suddenly implicated him. "Oh, he was trying to save his backside," said Clinton. "And I think he figured out that he could probably get a better deal if he made it a bigger story." Clinton would note that it was his administration's own SBA that uncovered Hale's misdeeds. "What he did was the biggest rip-off in the history of the Small Business Administration. And so, you know, he began spending a lot of time with Jim Johnson and others, and all of a sudden he had me involved in this, with these crazy stories, none of which were true."

One of the first pitches Hale made, with Johnson's wise counsel, was to the U.S. attorney in Arkansas. Paula Casey had been appointed to this top federal prosecutorial post by Clinton. Hale and his team sensed a whiff of a conflict here. Their first line of attack was to have Hale's attorney set up an appointment with Casey and promise that if she allowed the municipal judge to plead to a "simple misdemeanor," his client would "give us a lot of information" and even "wear a wire."

Casey found the whole proposal ludicrous. She would later say, "Wear a wire to do what?" The whole country knew Hale was under investigation. "I mean, the very notion that we were going to send David Hale to the West Wing, you know, to the Oval Office, wearing a wire," and that the president would incriminate himself, "was just silly."

Yet Hale was crying "conflict of interest!" He had also convinced Jeff Gerth from the *New York Times* to take his side. So Casey recused herself and the entire U.S. attorneys' office in Arkansas.

Reflecting on Hale's successful maneuver to knock her off the case she said, "I have absolutely no respect for [Hale]. I think that he was willing to do anything that he could possibly do to avoid the consequences of his own misconduct. He didn't want to go to prison. I don't blame him. I wouldn't want to go there, either, but I didn't embezzle from the FDIC." She sized it up: "There was nothing honorable about his original conduct. And there was nothing honorable about the way he dealt with it afterwards."

It was through this sequence of events—by which U.S. Attorney Paula Casey was forced to bow out of the entire Hale prosecution—that Independent Counsel Robert Fiske took over the case.

————

FISKE'S book of business had continued to grow. In addition to the original Whitewater/Madison case that centered on a bogus $825,000 loan, the Fiske team also investigated whether Governor Jim Guy Tucker had engaged in tax fraud in buying and reselling a cable television company. They also dug into whether the Clinton White House engaged in improper contacts with the Department of Treasury seeking to thwart the Resolution Trust Corporation's (RTC's) referrals relating to Whitewater and Madison.

Fiske and his lawyers erred on the side of caution, turning away anything that was not directly linked to their original charter. Prosecutor Bill Duffey, who oversaw the Little Rock office, recalled that whenever a potential new matter came in the door, Fiske would say, "Let's go back and see where this fits within our statement of jurisdiction." Lawyers were admonished to keep a copy of the jurisdictional charter in their desks, to make sure that the office did not get sidetracked. Fiske lived by the creed that "sticking to the core jurisdictional charge [Whitewater/Madison Guaranty] and completing our work in a timely manner was more important than taking jurisdiction of a case that was only tangentially related, if related at all." The Justice Department, he felt, was better suited to handle these peripheral matters.

The most significant add-on that Fiske did agree to accept related to Webster Hubbell. The Hubbell scandal had blown wide open in early March 1994, stunning both the White House and the Arkansas legal community. Hubbell had been one of Hillary's closest partners at the Rose Law Firm. He was a personal friend and confidant who regularly golfed and smoked cigars with the president. The six-foot-five, three-hundred-pound "gentle giant" had been a beloved Arkansas Razorbacks football player. He had also been mayor of Little Rock, chief justice of the state supreme court, member of the Arkansas code of ethics commission, and all-around good ol' boy who had moved to Washington and made Arkansans proud. Now Hubbell had been caught red-handed with his hand in the firm's cookie jar. The third-highest-ranking official in the Clinton administration's Justice Department was facing serious jail time.

Hubbell would later say, after serving eighteen months in a federal prison, "I can give you reasons and rationalizations for what was going on in my mind. But there are no valid excuses."

In mid-March, Hubbell faxed a letter of resignation to President Clinton, writing that "the distractions on me at this time will interfere with my service to the country and the president's agenda." In fact, the game was over. As new evidence trickled out, it became evident that Hubbell had bilked his own clients and the Rose Law Firm of nearly a half million dollars, improperly racking up charges for restaurant bills, vacations, gasoline, furs, and lingerie. The *Arkansas Democrat-Gazette* reported that Rose Law Firm partners were seeking stiff sanctions from the Arkansas Supreme Court's Committee on Professional Conduct.

Not only was Hubbell's abrupt resignation a "personal setback" to President and Mrs. Clinton, it could not have come at a worse time. Bernie Nussbaum, still under fire for his handling of the Vince Foster matter, was now immersed in a new flap over whether White House lawyers had improperly contacted the Treasury Department in an effort to derail the RTC investigation of Madison Guaranty and the McDougals. Nussbaum tendered his forced resignation as White House counsel rather than serve as a lightning rod for further attacks on the Clintons. Now Nussbaum, Vince Foster, and Hubbell were all gone, knocking out three of the Clintons' closest friends and staunchest allies. To further inflame the situation, reports surfaced that members of the Rose Law Firm were shredding documents relating to Whitewater, in an effort to destroy incriminating evidence. For an administration already under siege, the Hubbell revelations amounted to sand thrown in the Clinton team's eyes.

Years later, President Clinton sat in his study in Chappaqua, a finger pressed tightly against his face. "Well," he said, "it was a sad day for me personally, because he [Webb] had told me and Hillary both he hadn't done anything wrong. And, you know, he made a terrible mistake in coming to Washington. He wound up being punished probably several times over what would have happened to him if he had stayed in Arkansas—it [the embezzlement] would have come out, and he'd have had to deal with it in the normal way people would have." Shifting his eyes to stare out the window, Clinton added, "I was stunned. And I think everybody I knew was stunned."

Bill Kennedy, who had served as managing partner at the Rose Law Firm before relocating to the White House, was "absolutely devastated" by the revelation of Hubbell's double life. Not only had Hubbell betrayed the trust of every partner in the firm, but he had recklessly dragged the president and First Lady into the mess. The fact that Hubbell had left Little Rock to become associate attorney general of the United States, when he knew "he'd stolen a whole lot of money from clients of this firm," was simply mind-boggling.

Yet Kennedy and others who were victims of Hubbell's thievery were equally angry at how political enemies had manipulated the story. After all, the Clintons, personally, had been victims of Hubbell's scam; Hillary's share of partnership profits had been stolen. Yet someone had leaked the story to the media, managing to get the inquiry funneled to Robert Fiske rather than to the Arkansas Supreme Court's Disciplinary Board or to the local authorities, where it belonged. "Somebody leaked it at the firm," Kennedy would later say. "Some rat bastard went to the press." In Kennedy's view, it was wholly "inappropriate" to inject an independent counsel into the equation. "There's no national crime here," he said. "There's no federal involvement."

But the Office of the Independent Counsel (OIC) did get involved, first subpoenaing Webb Hubbell's bills relating to Madison, and then digging deeper into the scam by which Hubbell had ripped off his partners and clients. Attorney General Reno formally expanded Robert Fiske's jurisdiction to include this new blockbuster criminal matter, determined to keep the Justice Department (where Hubbell had been third in command) out of the mess.

———

It was in the context of the sudden uproar involving the Hubbell case that the dormant conspiracy theories relating to the death of Vince Foster resurrected themselves, now reaching a deafening pitch. The *New York Post* raised questions about how "little blood loss" there was at the Fort Marcy Park scene, intimating that Foster's death had occurred elsewhere. Christopher Ruddy, a journalist who wrote about Foster for the Greensburg (Pa.) *Tribune-Review*—a paper owned by staunchly conservative millionaire Richard Mellon Scaife—churned out articles raising questions about strange carpet fibers on Foster's clothes; the pistol in Foster's hand; the discovery of Foster's eyeglasses more than a dozen feet from his body; and other suspicious factors. Televangelist Pat Robertson asked his *700 Club* program viewers: "Suicide or murder? That's the ominous question surfacing in the Whitewater swell of controversy concerning Vincent Foster's mysterious death." The *New York Post* picked up on that thread of innuendo, reporting that Foster had shared a "secret apartment hideaway" in Virginia with Clinton intimates and hinting that he had been sneaking off with Hillary to engage in an affair there. These reports reached a crescendo with the shocking story aired by conservative radio talk-show host Rush Limbaugh, who announced that a media source "claims that Vince Foster was murdered in an apartment owned by Hillary Clinton."

Joe Purvis, the burly childhood friend of Vince Foster and Bill Clinton, later said of Rush Limbaugh's broadcast: "It was absolutely repulsive, you know, the way he slammed [Vince's] reputation, an excellent man's reputation," with this "seamy slime that he just made up." Purvis said he wanted to shout at Limbaugh and other conservative rumormongers: "For the love of God, leave the family, leave the man alone. Let his family grieve and come to terms with this, you know, with this horrible tragedy."

Contributing to the incessant rumors was the fact that Vince Foster's personal attorney in Washington, James Hamilton, invoked the attorney-client privilege to prevent the Office of Independent Counsel from obtaining key documents belonging to the decedent. Specifically, Hamilton would not release notes of his lawyer-client conversations with Foster, nine days before Foster's death. These handwritten notes remained locked in Hamilton's office safe. What was in them? skeptics asked. Would they reveal secrets concerning Foster's strange death?

Robert Fiske set up a satellite office in Washington, pledging to complete a definitive report concerning the Foster death. He also promised to examine the removal of documents in Foster's office by White House officials the night after Foster's death, and to determine if there had been any irregularities in handling those papers.

In June, Fiske contacted the Clintons' personal attorney, David Kendall, working out a plan to interview the president and First Lady. The questioning would take place at the White House in a quiet fashion, under oath, with questions limited to the Washington aspects of the investigation. The testimony could then be read to the grand jury, in lieu of a formal appearance by the president and First Lady before that body. In this way, Fiske explained, the dignity of the office could be maintained.

President Clinton would later say of his experience responding to questions posed by the independent counsel: "He could have me there every day if he had wanted to. I just wanted [it done]. I wanted to get this thing over with and hope that I had $3.50 left in the bank when my legal bills were paid."

On Sunday afternoon, June 12, Independent Counsel Robert Fiske reported quietly to the side gate of the White House. He was accompanied by prosecutor Rod Lankler, who specialized in homicides and headed up the Foster investigation, and a single court reporter. The press knew nothing of the meeting.

President Clinton's closed-door session took place in the Treaty Room and lasted over two hours. The First Lady occupied the hot seat for an equal amount of time. Fiske and Lankler questioned the Clintons about the death of Vince Foster and Treasury Department contacts relating to the RTC referrals. Both interviews were uneventful.

Fiske would later state that the witnesses were straightforward. "I don't think they were having the time of their life," he said. "Or that this was something that they would have loved to do. But they certainly were cooperative, yes." When it came to the matter of Foster's death, this seemed to be an especially painful subject for the Clintons to revisit. "Yes, I think it was," Fiske said. After asking the uncomfortable questions, however, Fiske found nothing to implicate the Clintons in any regard. At the conclusion of the closed-door sessions, the parties walked away with a sense of mutual respect.

These signals of cooperation between the independent counsel and the White House, however, were not greeted with applause in all quarters. The conservative wing of his own Republican Party was now viewing Fiske as a traitor.

One big demerit was earned when Fiske tried to shut down the congressional Whitewater hearings. Republican Representative James A. Leach of Iowa, senior member of the House Banking Committee, accused Fiske of insubordination for attempting to put the hearings on ice. Congressman Leach—who had ardently supported Fiske's appointment—now castigated the independent counsel for suggesting that congressional hearings "would pose a severe risk to the integrity of [the independent counsel] investigation." Leach declared: "I am concerned that your public lobbying of Congress [to shut down the hearings] has the effect of sending a chilling precedent for Congressional oversight and a fatuous pretext for the majority party which controls the machinery of Congress to delay, defer, or avoid its Constitutional responsibilities."

Senator Bob Dole (R-Kans.), the presumptive Republican challenger to President Bill Clinton in 1996, likewise chastised the special prosecutor for cozying up to the Clinton White House. Yet Fiske held his ground. He continued to oppose "congressional hearings on *any* aspect of the Whitewater affair" until he completed the criminal probe. There was precedent for this position. During Watergate, special prosecutor Archibald Cox had fought mightily to block Senator Sam Ervin's Senate Watergate Committee from holding and televising hearings, because these might taint his case against John Dean and other defendants. Cox had gone so far as to gather up his evidence against Dean and lock it in a safe, so that he could segregate his own criminal case from information derived from Dean's public testimony in Congress. Otherwise, the blurring of Cox's own evidence with the public testimony might wreck his prosecution. Robert Fiske, like Cox, believed that good independent counsels should stay as far away from Congress as humanly possible.

Consequently, many Republicans were beginning to view Fiske as an apostate.

The final nail was pounded into the coffin when Fiske announced that he was wrapping up portions of his criminal probe within six months of his appointment. On Thursday, June 30, Fiske rode the Metroliner from New York to Washington, filing two reports. In one, Fiske cleared the White House with respect to the Treasury Office flap, reporting that no crimes had been committed. In the second, more noteworthy document, he concurred with the Fairfax County medical examiner and park police that Vince Foster had "committed suicide by firing a bullet from a .38 revolver into his mouth. The evidence overwhelmingly supports this conclusion, and there is no evidence to the contrary." Fiske also concluded: "We found no evidence that issues involving Whitewater, or other personal legal matters of the president or Mrs. Clinton were a factor in Foster's suicide."

The Clintons felt vindicated. White House Counsel Lloyd Cutler issued a statement: "We hope these rumor mongers . . . will now leave the Foster family in peace."

Yet the reaction to the dual Fiske reports, in certain quarters, was one of outrage. Senator Lauch Faircloth (R-N.C.), one of Fiske's most ardent critics, took to the Senate floor in June and decried the special prosecutor's investigation as a "coverup." He declared that further hearings were needed to clean up "a whole web of intrigue that has collectively come to be known as Whitewater." Faircloth also publicly rebuked Fiske for issuing his reports, suggesting that they were both premature and flawed. The senator wrote directly to Attorney General Reno on July 1, calling Fiske "unfit for the job."

Looking back on the outcry to Fiske's work in the summer of 1994, President

Clinton expressed incredulity. "It wasn't like he [Fiske] deserved the Congressional Medal of Honor or something. He just did what he was supposed to do with the facts," said the former president. "And, God, the way the Republicans went nuts—Lauch Faircloth and all those right-wing Republicans and the media people."

Clinton believed that his critics were particularly incensed because, once he was foolish enough to agree to an independent counsel, he and Hillary were "supposed to be hung from the highest tree. The truth could not be allowed to get in the way. The facts were completely irrelevant." The hysterical reaction to Fiske's Vince Foster report was proof enough. "Because it wasn't even a complicated case. I mean it was just a no-brainer, a lay-down. Everybody else had concluded it was a suicide. There was no compelling evidence to the contrary. And they were mad."

President Clinton took a deep breath before finishing his thought: "I only began to come to grips with the magnitude of what I was up against when I realized that the facts of Whitewater and all were utterly irrelevant. That's basically why they had to get rid of Fiske. I mean, he, Fiske, was actually doing his job. He was going to find out if I'd stolen any money or broken any laws or done anything I shouldn't have done. He was actually going to do his job."

———

As Robert Fiske swiftly lost favor with the Republican power base that had lauded his appointment, Congress marched forward, reauthorizing the independent counsel law by a three-to-one margin. Republicans who had spent decades fighting the law in the wake of Watergate and Iran-Contra now found an ironic satisfaction in supporting it: What was good for the goose, after all, was good for the gander.

White House Counsel Lloyd Cutler told President Clinton to take a deep breath and remain calm. All would be fine. "No court would ever get rid of an independent Republican like Fiske and put someone else in," Cutler assured the president. Assuming the independent counsel statute was signed back into law, it was inconceivable that Attorney General Reno would recommend anyone other than Fiske to continue the work. On June 30, Clinton affixed his signature to the independent counsel reauthorization bill—as he had pledged to do during his 1992 campaign—calling it "a foundation stone for the trust between the government and our citizens."

That same day, Attorney General Janet Reno wrote to the special three-judge court that oversaw independent counsel investigations, formally requesting that Fiske be reappointed under the revived statute. Criminal Division Chief Jo Ann Harris assumed this was a pro forma matter. The entire Justice Department believed that Fiske was bulletproof. His "reputation for integrity and competence" was so stellar that Congress had even included a provision in the statute specifically permitting the reappointment of Fiske. Harris said, "It certainly never crossed my mind that the court would not understand, for a whole lot of reasons, that the best thing they could do was just appoint Fiske and let it go on. I think she [Reno] felt the same way."

But many surprises awaited those who wagered on the outcome of this particular presidential scandal.

PART TWO

PURSUING THE

PRESIDENT

PAULA CORBIN JONES

In January 1994, just as a second wave of tremors from Vince Foster's death shook the White House and stirred the Whitewater pot, a new threat to the Clinton presidency emerged. At the time, it seemed like a mere nuisance. It came in the form of an article in a hot new conservative magazine, the *American Spectator*, written by a young muckraker named David Brock.

The *Spectator* story possessed a far-out tabloid quality even when it first appeared on the newsstands. On the cover was featured a cartoon that depicted Bill Clinton sneaking out of the governor's mansion at night carrying his shoes, with the provocative title "His Cheatin' Heart." The inside headline read: "Bill's Arkansas bodyguards tell the story the press missed." What followed was akin to a thirteen-page racy novelette about Governor Clinton's secret sexual exploits with dozens of women, mostly unnamed. This was accompanied by an account of Hillary's wild, screaming, door-kicking tirades when she caught Bill on the prowl. In a titillating and irreverent twist, Brock's article also asserted that Hillary was "intimately involved with the late Vincent Foster." The conservative journalist reported that Hillary and Vince had been seen by troopers "embracing and open-mouth kissing." The story even asserted that Foster, famous for his sober Presbyterian bearing, had on one occasion "squeezed [Hillary's] rear end" and "put his hand over one of Hillary's breasts," winking as he gave a thumbs-up sign to Trooper Larry Patterson. Hillary, the story recounted in bodice-ripping prose, "just stood there cooing 'Oh Vince, Oh Vince!' "

Brock's article also described eyebrow-raising locker-room talk between Governor Clinton and his troopers. The future president purportedly told Trooper Patterson that "he had researched the subject in the Bible and oral sex isn't considered adultery."

The *Spectator* article ushered in a new scandal that the tabloids swiftly dubbed "Troopergate." It delighted some commentators, while appalling others. As columnist Richard Harwood wrote in the *Washington Post:* "We keep dishing the dirt because that's what readers want. The media are about as likely to abandon the weather report as to abandon sex." The Troopergate story seemed to sink to new lows. Some troopers who had given interviews to Brock openly admitted that they had attempted to broker a six-figure deal for a tell-all book about Clinton filled with "rumors" and stories from the guard shack at the governor's mansion. To make matters even stranger, lawyer Cliff Jackson (a known anti-Clinton soldier) was acting as the troopers' agent, adding an odor of rotten eggs to the story.

Years later, Brock concluded that much information provided to him by the troopers was unreliable: "Their motivation, I mean, up front from the beginning was to sell a book, to sell an article, to get on TV, all of those things. So it was a moneymaking proposition. There was no question in my mind about that. It made me nervous all the way through." Indeed, Brock later disclosed that he learned two of the troopers were compensated $6,700 each after the piece was published, by a conservative fund-raiser, despite express assurances to Brock that they would not be paid to share their accounts.

The Troopergate story proved to be short-lived. Even the press abandoned it after the troopers admitted they had accepted cash for their interviews. Yet one relatively innocuous passage of Brock's article, appearing in a tiny paragraph on page 26, would rise up from the ashes to threaten the entire Clinton presidency. This three-inch passage reported that a young woman identified only as "Paula" had caught the eye of Governor Clinton at an event held at the Excelsior Hotel in Little Rock. According to Brock's passing reference to the incident, Clinton had instructed an unnamed trooper to "tell her how attractive the governor thought she was," and then to "take her to a room in the hotel" to meet Governor Clinton. The trooper approached the woman, passed along the governor's invitation, and escorted her to the private suite. The brief paragraph ended succinctly: "After her encounter with Clinton, which lasted no more than an hour as the trooper stood by in the hall, the trooper said Paula told him she was available to be Clinton's regular girlfriend if he so desired."

Brock was no stranger to conservative political mud-slinging. He had authored *The Real Anita Hill* in the spring of 1993, a book that was aimed at shredding the reputation of the African American law professor who had testified against Supreme Court nominee Clarence Thomas and who had told the Senate that Thomas had sexually harassed her while she was a young lawyer with the Equal Employment Opportunity Commission. The Anita Hill book project, funded by the *Spectator* and prominent conservative foundations, had earned the admiration of that magazine's publisher, R. Emmett Tyrrell, Jr., who hired Brock to embark on this new assignment.

Tyrrell recalled that Brock was enthusiastic about making a name for himself and that the journalist went so far as to leave a message on his own answering machine, stating: "I'm not here; I'm out to get the president." It was largely happenstance, Tyrrell later said, that Brock made himself world famous with his

Troopergate story. The *Spectator* had never intended to include the name "Paula" in the story; it had a policy against identifying names of alleged victims of sexual misconduct. "It was an accident. An editorial mistake," said Tyrrell. "There never would have been a lawsuit if we hadn't erroneously left her name in the piece."

The Brock article that appeared in the January issue of *Spectator* could have easily faded into obscurity after selling a few thousand copies. Yet the perfect storm was beginning to gather. It was far beyond any horizon that the Clinton advisers in the White House could have seen, even with their powerful spyglasses. Several fluky facts contributed to this tsunami that was about to hit with violent force. One was that Paula Corbin, the woman identified as "Paula" in the article, was engaged to be married to one Stephen Jones at the time of her alleged tryst with the governor in the Excelsior Hotel; they had married in December 1991. This meant that Stephen and Paula were husband and wife at the time the titillating *Spectator* story came out. Another factor was that Steve Jones, a thirty-three-year-old Northwest Airlines ticket agent in Little Rock, was growing increasingly frustrated with his life in Arkansas. An aspiring movie actor, he had played a bit part as Elvis Presley's ghost in the 1989 film *Mystery Train,* which had flopped. He was feeling trapped in small-town America. He was also a man with a volatile temper and despised Bill Clinton. Steve, learning of the *Spectator* article through Paula's sisters, had become enraged. Finally, Bill Clinton had become president, making an otherwise dubious case more enticing to attorneys who, in the real world of deciding how to spend precious time, would probably not have touched it.

Due to the convergence of these unusual forces, Paula Corbin Jones took the action she took next: She contacted a small-time Little Rock lawyer named Danny Traylor and asked to set up an appointment.

———

PAULA Jones, seated in an Italian restaurant in North Little Rock years after the case had been settled, sipped a Diet Coke and relived some of these unpleasant memories with her good friend Debra Ballentine. Having become internationally famous (or infamous) for her role in these events, having posed unclothed for *Penthouse* magazine, having divorced Stephen Jones, having reached celebrity status, and then having receded back into relative anonymity in Cabot, Arkansas, Jones insisted that her case had nothing to do with making money or trying to embarrass President Clinton to weaken him politically. "He'd embarrassed hisself [sic] by doing what he did," she said. "And it has nothing to do with me, or my attorneys and what they were doing. They were doing their jobs. And he [Clinton] just messed up. And he was getting caught. And a lot of people wanted to say, 'Well, they're dragging the president through the mud.' He drug his own self through the mud, by doing what he did."

Settling back to munch on fried provolone sticks dipped in ranch dressing—a compromise lunch that was unhealthy but sufficiently small in quantity—Jones recalled the events of 1994 with mixed emotions. Granted, she had achieved a sort of celebrity status: For this interview session in 2001, she was dressed in a low-cut lime green top and was wearing hoop earrings. Her face was decidedly pretty, revealing no signs of the plastic surgery that had softened the contours of her once aquiline nose. She was surprisingly petite (5 feet 2½ inches in bare feet). She appeared comfortable speaking into microphones. Yet none of her fifteen (or maybe thirty) minutes of fame, she made clear, was worth the hell she had endured in trying to extract justice from President Bill Clinton.

The attorney with whom Paula Jones initially consulted in the winter of 1994 was the last person one would have expected to file a sexual harassment suit against the most powerful man in the United States. Daniel Murray Traylor was a likable solo practitioner, an offbeat character who frequently described himself as a "yellow dog Democrat," meaning a person who would vote for a yellow dog providing it was a Democrat. Traylor was hardly known for handling high-profile cases. He was a real estate lawyer who dabbled in divorces and "whatever came in the door." His office was furnished with knickknacks befitting a secondhand curiosity shop. These included a psychedelic peace sign from the 1960s; a lighted "Jesus head" with butterfly wings around it, which had once belonged to his grandmother circa 1920; and an eclectic assortment of Civil War memorabilia (including a picture of his great-grandpa Traylor, who had fought as a Confederate soldier with General Nathaniel Bedford Forrest).

Traylor was a lawyer who wore large plastic glasses and who probably should have been born in a different era; but God had plopped him down in Little Rock in the latter half of the twentieth century, where he carried out his trade. The thirty-eight-year-old Traylor would find himself thrust into this date with destiny only because he had handled divorce work for a woman named Debra Ballentine, who (as fate would have it) was Paula Jones's best friend.

Ballentine had been the person who first spotted the article in the *Spectator*, and had insisted that Jones redeem her good name. Specifically, Ballentine had told Paula—who had moved to California in mid-1993 with her husband, Steve, and their new baby—that she needed to correct the scurrilous notion that Paula had been a willing participant in a sexual fling with that skirt-chaser Bill Clinton.

Swirling a glass of iced tea, Ballentine recalled how she had pressed Jones to take the story to the authorities or to go public with it from the start. Jones had waved the notion off with embarrassment, instructing her friend, "Never talk about it again." When the Gennifer Flowers story blew up during the presidential campaign of 1992, Ballentine had pushed harder, insisting, "Now's a good time to let people know what happened to you." But Jones had been adamant. "No, no, no," she had repeated. "I don't ever want anybody to know." According to Ballentine, it was only because God had intervened in the form of David Brock's story that Bill Clinton was ensnared. "If it hadn't come out in the *American Spectator*," she said, "to this day, no one would ever know."

The *Spectator* story led to a phone call from Ballentine to Traylor on January 13, 1994. Traylor remembered the precise date, because it happened to be his birthday. As he prepared to cut out early for a birthday celebration and cake, Ballentine briefed her former divorce lawyer on the tabloid article. She said that the woman "Paula" mentioned in the story was her friend, now married and the mother of a little boy. She added that the report of the Clinton incident "had been the cause of marital problems for [Paula], and embarrassment, and she was upset." Ballentine drew upon her own good standing as a former paying client and asked Traylor if he "would meet with the woman to see if there was a legal wrong."

Traylor agreed to call Jones in the next few days, at his earliest convenience. At the time, he did not consider it a priority.

Paula Corbin Jones did not exactly fit the profile of a client whom lawyers would be clamoring to represent. Born in 1966 in the slow-moving town of Lonoke, Arkansas, she had lived a life that until this point had been entirely unremarkable. Her high school English teacher, Judy King, would tell *People* magazine that Paula "was not an exceptional student." King added, "But the world's made up of people who are average." Paula's father, Bobby Gene Corbin, had been a lay Nazarene preacher who earned a living laboring at a local clothing factory. Her mother, Delmer, hemmed dresses out of fabric scraps her husband brought home to make sure that their three girls were properly clothed. When Paula's father died unexpectedly of a heart attack in 1985—he was stricken while playing the piano at church—the life of the Corbin girls changed dramatically. Among other things, the strict Christian rules of the household eased up. One classmate of Paula's told *People*: "The day he died, boy, those skirts went up ten inches."

After the family home burned to the ground in 1986, Delmer Corbin's two youngest daughters, Lydia and Paula, moved into a trailer with Paula's sister Charlotte Corbin Brown and her husband, Mark. During this period of experimenting with men, Paula eventually met Steve Jones and moved in with him in a "two-bedroom saltbox home" in Valonia, just north of Little Rock. She told her coworkers proudly, in describing Steve, that he looked "just like Elvis." Paula had been working a series of part-time and clerical positions. In March 1991, she landed a job as a documents examiner at the Arkansas Industrial Development Commission (AIDC). It was in this position that her fateful encounter with Governor Bill Clinton took place.

Traylor scheduled a meeting with the potential new client a week after her call, because Jones was flying home to visit her family in Little Rock. With Debbie

Ballentine at her side to provide moral support, Jones met in Traylor's modest law office near the courthouse, where Traylor was pouring his fifth cup of coffee for the day. Here, Jones would recount a story that made Traylor's glasses slide down on his nose as he listened. In 1991, then-Governor Clinton, she told him, had made lewd and unwanted sexual advances toward her at the AIDC conference at the Excelsior Hotel and had solicited oral sex from her. As Traylor recalled the question that immediately popped into his mind as Jones shared her version of events was, "So what do you (as a lawyer) do with that? What would Jesus do? I'm not sure." Traylor did some quick legal research, enough to conclude that "it appeared to me that the woman had a cause of action, perhaps a colorable cause of action, against various persons: the troopers . . . probably Bill Clinton." There might also be a claim against the *Spectator,* he surmised, for printing a false or libelous story.

At the same time, Traylor was frank with Jones. He told her, "I ain't tough enough to sue the president of the United States for something like this. . . . I just ain't got it in me. I'm a Democrat, and I voted for Bill Clinton numerous times." Moreover, Traylor brainstormed out loud, even if the allegations were true, what could the president realistically do here? Any effort to settle the case would be "hampered and constrained by the politics" of the situation. Bill Clinton was now "leader of the free world." The president could certainly issue a public statement that Jones had not engaged in an inappropriate liaison with him at the Excelsior Hotel, if that would help to settle down her husband. But a colossal settlement most likely wasn't in the cards. "Realistically," Traylor told his would-be client, "what we could accomplish would be to get public or private apologies from the parties involved and have your legal fees paid by these people." The real question in the back of Traylor's mind was "How am I going to get paid for all this?"

Paula Jones, Danny Traylor would later confess, was not someone he would expect to be the subject of the president's amorous advances. "I never quite frankly found Miss Jones to be attractive," Traylor said. As he met with Jones in his office, he observed that "she needed some nose and teeth work." Yet he found the new client straightforward and credible. He had done his "due diligence," questioning Debbie Ballentine and a second friend, Pam Blackard, both of whom had both corroborated key details of Jones's encounter with Clinton. He was satisfied that the story checked out.

Traylor was equally satisfied that Jones had no ulterior motive other than to correct the record. "Paula had told me," Traylor recalled, that all she wanted "would be something that would clear her name, particularly with reference to her husband and her family." Traylor warned the twenty-seven-year-old that he would not participate in any effort to turn this into a salacious money-making venture. He lectured Jones that there would doubtless be offers from "skin mag-azines" and other sycophants interested in profiting from a potentially juicy scandal. Traylor told the frizzy-haired young woman, "If you're interested in *Playboy* or *Penthouse* or the notoriety or doing political damage to somebody, I ain't your guy. I ain't interested in it."

Jones replied that she had no plan to reap such tawdry benefits from the suit. First, she told Traylor, she was "a nice Christian girl." Moreover, she simply wanted to make clear that she "didn't know what oral sex was, and that wasn't in her repertoire." Traylor rapidly paced around his desk, gulping down coffee and listening to his new potential client carefully. Clearing up this bogus story, it seemed, was *very* important to Jones. She reiterated, in her charming but squeaky voice, that her husband, Stephen, had not taken it well. "It caused a lot of problems" for their marriage, she told the real estate lawyer. "All I want is the salvation of our marriage and my family, and I want the world to know that I'm not a girl that does that kind of thing."

———

THE story that Paula Jones related to Danny Traylor in his law office in January 1994 was essentially the same story that she would repeat for the next four years, after she had become the most famous plaintiff in America.

As Jones would later retell the events in her sworn deposition, she had be-gun work for the Arkansas Industrial Development Commission in March 1991 as a "purchasing assistant," performing odd jobs and filling in as a courier. At this time, her name was Paula Corbin and she was twenty-four years old; she was earning $6.35 per hour, or $10,270 per year. Her employment file indicated that she had applied for the job with modest qualifications, having majored in "exec-utive secretarial" studies at the soon-defunct Capitol City Junior College, before dropping out eight months later. She had worked at a shoe store, at Dillard's department store, at a pest control company, and at a television-and-appliance rental place, never moving beyond low-paying positions. Although her hand-written application listed her typing speed at fifty-five words per minute (after making allowance for errors), the test administered by the state listed her cor-rected speed as twenty-four words per minute. In the space blocked off for the names of references "who are not related to you, and who have knowledge of your work qualifications," Paula Corbin listed her sister Lydia Cathey and friends Debbie Vickers (Ballentine) and Pam Blackard—all of whom would later be-come witnesses in the near-bizarre events involving Governor Clinton.

Paula Corbin received marginal to average performance reviews as an em-ployee at AIDC. Her employment records reveal that she successfully completed two seminars: Stress Management, and Grammar and Usage. She was given periodic assignments as a courier, delivering documents to a variety of government buildings, including the governor's office. At the time that she was asked to work the desk at the AIDC Governor's Quality Conference at the Excelsior Hotel in Little Rock, in May 1991, Paula had held the job less than two months and was still considered a probationary employee.

According to the account that Jones would eventually give under oath, she was working the AIDC registration desk on this day with her friend and coworker, Pam Blackard, when Governor Bill Clinton emerged from the ballroom, having just finished giving a speech. He was now working the crowd. Clinton was then forty-four years old and serving his fifth term as the state's governor. He was also notorious in Razorback territory as a ladies' man and attracted quite a following. As Jones recalled the events, Trooper Danny Ferguson had "come over just to chat or something and he said he was the governor's bodyguard." Jones said, " 'Well, let's see your gun,' or whatever." Smiling, Ferguson "pulled back his coat and he showed us his gun that he was carrying." The trooper reportedly told Jones, "The governor said you make his knees knock."

Later, according to Jones, the bodyguard "come to hand me a note and tell me that the governor wanted to meet with me." On the note was printed a four-digit number. Ferguson told the young employee that Governor Clinton "wants to meet with you in this room number."

Jones would later say she wondered, "What for? What does he want to meet with me for?" She added, "I was excited, though."

The two women caucused. Blackard told her coworker, "Good, maybe we can get a better job." She agreed to watch the desk while Jones went up to the governor's room, but she told Jones not to stay too long. She "didn't want to get in trouble" and didn't want to have to do any explaining. So Jones quickly walked over to the trooper who "escorted me up and around the corner and up the elevator."

The hotel room door to which Ferguson pointed was partly ajar. Governor Clinton, according to Jones's account, immediately greeted her and ushered her into the large suite. She recalled that the room contained "a couch and a couple of wingback chairs and like those vanity tables with flowers on it and it had mirrors and stuff." As soon as she walked in, she recalled, Clinton "seemed like he was loosening his tie with one hand and he acted like he had known me for years. You know. Right off the bat. And I had never met the guy in my life."

The governor said, "I'm Bill Clinton." Jones stated that she replied, " 'I'm Paula Corbin' or whatever."

She began engaging in chitchat, volunteering that she was a new employee for AIDC, which caused the governor to perk up. He drawled that Dave Herrington—her boss—was a good friend. In fact, said Clinton, he had "appointed [Dave] to that job." They ended up standing near the window, where there was "a pretty view up there, because it was really high up." Here, the governor allegedly made his first pass at Paula Corbin. In her words, as they were "talking about the job or whatever," Clinton suddenly began "pulling me over like he has done this a million times and grabs me and pulls me over to him to the windowsill and tries to kiss me and just didn't ask me or nothing.

"I was just really shocked. And I pulled away. . . . I said, 'No.' I said, 'What are you doing?' "

Jones would later testify that she was scared because she knew there was "a state trooper sitting outside the door with a gun." It was disputed, however, whether Trooper Ferguson was anywhere nearby.

What followed, according to her account, was something akin to a game of musical chairs with a raunchy twist. Paula moved to another seat and tried to "ignore what he had just done," attempting to change the subject. "And I was talking to him about Hillary," Jones recalled. She complimented the governor about Hillary's work with kids' causes, and "on how she was really good with children." At this point, she said, Clinton made his second pass at her.

Jones would testify: "He come [sic] over by the wingback chair close to where I was at. Then it's like he wasn't even paying attention to what I was saying to him. Then he goes, 'Oh, I love the way your hair flows down your back.' " In other recountings of the story, Jones added that Governor Clinton commented, "I love your curves."

Jones would insist that she attempted to steer the eager governor back to idle chitchat. This was unsuccessful. Instead, "Governor Clinton pulled me over to him while he was leaning up against the wingback chair and he took his hands and was running them up my culottes." Jones testified that Clinton started "kissing me on the neck, you know, and trying to kiss me on the lips and I wouldn't let him. And then I backed up. I said, 'Stop it. You know. I'm not this kind of girl.' " Next, Jones said, she ran over to the couch. "I thought, What am I going to do? I was trying to collect my thoughts."

It was here on the couch, after more small talk about Hillary's work with needy children, that Clinton made his ultimate advance. According to Jones's sworn testimony, Governor Clinton "come over there, pulled his pants down, sat down and . . ." She would add editorial comment: "I can see the look on his face right now. He asked me, 'Would you kiss it for me?' " Jones would add, "I mean, it was disgusting."

Jones would insist that she didn't miss a beat in replying: "No. I'm not that kind of girl." At that point, she jumped up and told the governor, "I'm going to get in trouble. I've got to be going. I've got to get back to my registration desk."

Clinton allegedly replied, "Well, I don't want to make you do anything you don't want to do."

As she hustled toward the door, Jones said, it was obvious that Governor Clinton was "embarrassed" that things had not gone as planned. Jones would testify that Clinton looked flushed "because I had rejected him." She went on: "And he was pulling up his pants. And he said, 'Well. If you have any trouble, you have Dave Herrington call me immediately.' "

In Jones's version of events, as she made a beeline out the door, she observed Trooper Ferguson waiting directly outside the suite. "I said nothing to him and he said nothing to me," she insisted. She then returned downstairs to her work station.

This account of her quick exit turned out to be dramatically at odds with the sworn testimony of Trooper Danny Ferguson, who flatly contradicted Jones's testimony on several key points.

One fact, however, was not in dispute: The entire sequence of events had spanned only ten or fifteen minutes.

———

ONE of the principal witnesses corroborating Jones was her coworker. Pam Blackard, who considered herself a friend of Paula's yet had no particular motive to lie, would recall Paula walking down the corridor toward her, after Paula returned from her meeting with Bill Clinton upstairs in the hotel room. "From far off I could tell there was something different," Blackard would state under oath. "She was—she just looked different." Blackard also recalled that Paula "was out of breath." Pam asked, "What's wrong?" After sitting down for a minute, Paula answered calmly, "You are not going to believe what happened." Paula went on to recount that after she had walked into the hotel room, "he [Governor Clinton] pulled her to him and . . . I believe he hugged her and gave her a kiss." After that, Paula said, she sat down "and immediately his hand went up her leg and toward her thigh. And she pushed away." Beyond that, Blackard acknowledged, "I'm not sure what happened."

According to Blackard's recollection of their conversation, there was no mention of Clinton exposing himself. Nor was there a specific mention of the governor asking Paula to engage in a sexual act. Yet she did recall that Paula had said, "There's more. It's just too upsetting."

When Pam asked her coworker, "Was he like mean to you?" Paula answered, "No, his mannerism was kind of just calm."

In terms of Paula's demeanor, as she packed up to go home after the Governor's Quality Conference that afternoon, Blackard would testify that Jones was "not crying. Just upset." As they walked out to their cars, Paula was "quiet. Real quiet." Paula said, "Please don't tell anybody." She went on, "I can't believe he asked me up there and immediately started to do that."

During this period, Paula's best friend, Debbie Ballentine, was working at an engineering firm in Little Rock. According to Ballentine's testimony, she received a call from the switchboard operator at approximately 4:00 that afternoon, informing her that Paula Corbin wanted to see her in the lobby. Ballentine recalled: "I could tell something was wrong because she was crying. I also knew something was wrong because she wouldn't show up at my office unannounced." The two women ducked outside to a courtyard for privacy. Here, Paula spoke in a rapid voice and poured out her story of the encounter with Governor Clinton. When Paula got to the part about the governor dropping his pants, Ballentine interjected, "He asked you to do *what?*" Paula replied, "Debbie, he asked me to suck his [expletive deleted]." Ballentine said, "You've got to be kidding!"

Ballentine was incredulous. She waved a finger and chastised her friend: "Why did you go up there, Paula? You know how he is. You know he's got a reputation for being a womanizer." Paula retorted, becoming emotional, "No, I did *not* know that." Ballentine then told Paula that she should notify her boss or go to the police. But Paula became "adamant." She told Ballentine, "I'm just going to forget about it. Please, don't ever tell anyone what happened."

Two days later, Paula recounted a similar story to her sister, Lydia Ruthene Cathey. According to Cathey's testimony, Paula stopped by her home after work and initiated a sister-to-sister talk in one of the bedrooms. Cathey would later testify: "We sat down [on the bed]. She was bawling, she was squalling and everything. She was upset. I asked her what was wrong. And that's when she told me that she went up to Bill Clinton's room. Which Danny Ferguson had took her up there. And she got up there and he [Clinton] was flirty."

Cathey recalled, "She cried most of the time we was in there. And I just kind of cried with her because I felt sorry for her. Because she felt like dirt. She felt like trash. And 'What's people going to think of me?'" Cathey tried to comfort her sister by saying, "I'm sure he's not going to go say nothing. Just let it slide. Just let it go. Just forget about it. You didn't do anything wrong."

Several significant discrepancies soon became apparent, however, between Jones's version of events and that of Trooper Danny Ferguson, who would eventually be named as a codefendant in the lawsuit. Ferguson's rendition cast Jones in a less-than-blameless light.

According to Ferguson's sworn testimony, he was the only trooper assigned to the governor's security detail that day. As Clinton munched on a doughnut, Ferguson spotted Paula Corbin working at a registration desk, recognizing her as a person who occasionally dropped off packages at the governor's office. The trooper sauntered over as the two young ladies "were kind of giggling about the governor's pants being too short. She [Paula] said that she thought he [Clinton] was good-looking, had sexy hair, wanted me to tell him that." According to Trooper Ferguson, Paula giggled that "she'd like to meet [the Governor]." Ferguson meandered his way back to his boss and mentioned this overture. Clinton glanced over at Paula Corbin and invoked one of his favorite lines, telling Ferguson: "She's got that 'come-hither' look." After chatting with reporters for a while, Governor Clinton excused himself by saying that he was "expecting a call from the White House," and told the bodyguard "to go to the car, get his briefcase because his phone messages were in there, and to get a room."

Trooper Ferguson procured a room key from the manager, who provided a suite gratis for the governor's use. After Clinton settled in, the governor told the trooper that if Paula Corbin "wanted to meet him" then "she can come up." So Ferguson rode the elevator back downstairs and handed Paula the room number to Clinton's suite.

According to Ferguson's sworn testimony, Paula initially said she "wasn't sure she could break away from the desk." Ferguson replied in good humor, "It's no big deal. I'll just tell the governor." But several minutes later, Paula Corbin appeared around the corner at the bank of elevators where Ferguson was stationed. He asked, "How did you get away?" Paula answered with a grin that she had told her supervisor "that she wasn't feeling well, that she needed to go to the bathroom." Ferguson asked, "Do you want me to walk up with you?"

Paula answered, "Yeah."

Together, they rode the elevator to the eighth floor. When they exited, Ferguson pointed toward the room, leaving Paula to introduce herself to the governor. According to the trooper's version of events, "I immediately turned and went back downstairs to the second floor where the governor told me to wait."

In a key departure from Paula's account, Trooper Ferguson would testify that he was not guarding the door of Clinton's hotel room, nor was he present when she exited. Rather, he stated emphatically, fifteen or twenty minutes later, Corbin returned to the second floor, where he had maintained his post close to the elevators. "She was smiling," the bodyguard testified. She also "asked me if the governor had any girlfriends." Paula then stated "that she would be his girlfriend."

Ferguson went on to testify that Paula had "asked for a piece of paper and a pen and wrote down her home number and told [him] to give it to Governor Clinton." The young woman told the trooper that she was "living with her boyfriend and that if the boyfriend answered, Governor Clinton should either hang up or say that he had a wrong number."

Ferguson stated that a few minutes later, he rode the elevator upstairs to notify the governor that it was time to leave for a photo op at the mansion. On the subject of Paula Corbin, Governor Clinton told the bodyguard, "She came up here, and nothing happened." At that point, the trooper testified, the two men departed for the governor's mansion.

President Clinton's own account of the alleged encounter sheds little light on the truth of what transpired in the Excelsior Hotel. In fact, Clinton maintained that he had no specific recollection of meeting with Paula Corbin at the conference in the Excelsior Hotel that day. In a telling nondenial, the president would not rule out that he might have met the long-haired, curvaceous state employee that day. During his deposition in the *Jones* case in early 1998—a legal proceeding that nearly lost him his presidency—Clinton would give only a sketchy version of the facts. Under questioning by his own attorney, Robert Bennett, the president responded as follows:

> Q: Mr. President, did you ever make any sexual advances towards Paula Jones?
>
> A: No, I did not.
>
> Q: Did you ever expose yourself to Paula Jones?
>
> A: No, I did not. . . .
>
> Q: Now, Mr. President, you've stated earlier in your testimony that you do not recall with any specificity the May 8th, 1991, conference at the Excelsior; is that correct?
>
> A: That's correct.
>
> Q: If that is true, sir, how can you be sure that you did not do these things which are alleged in Ms. Jones' complaint?
>
> A: Because, Mr. Bennett, in my lifetime I've never sexually harassed a woman, and I've never done what she accused me of doing. I didn't do it then, because I never have, and I wouldn't.

Years later, at home in Chappaqua, chewing on an unlit cigar, the former president would still become angry revisiting this chapter of his life. In dismissing those Sunday morning quarterbacks (including Ken Starr) who would later maintain that he should have 'fessed up, apologized, and taken his lumps rather than letting the Jones allegations balloon into a federal case, Clinton would respond: "I wasn't going to apologize for something I didn't do. She said she wanted her name cleared. I did that from the moment the thing surfaced. I said she didn't do anything wrong, and I didn't sexually harass her. The whole story's not true. If she was worried about the lies of the *American Spectator,* she would have gone after the *American Spectator* instead of getting in bed with them. So this was never what this was about."

Whatever the true and complete story of what went on in the Excelsior

Hotel suite—known only to Bill Clinton and Paula Corbin Jones—it was clear that Clinton became unusually defensive and incensed whenever he was forced to talk about Jones and her lawsuit. "From the beginning," he said, setting his cigar down so that he did not chew it to pieces, "I'm not sure this thing was really level. Although I have no idea what was going through her mind."

Paula Jones's account of her encounter with then-Governor Bill Clinton, from the moment she went public with it, created a messy he-said/she-said battle. It provided perfect grist for a rumor mill that was already churning forward with stories about the offbeat McDougals and Vince Foster's mysterious death.

In this case, there was plenty more to come.

CHAPTER

11

—————

DANNY TRAYLOR: "CAN WE SETTLE FOR FIVE THOUSAND DOLLARS?"

Danny Traylor's office files indicate that shortly after he met with Paula Jones and agreed to take her case, he visited the Little Rock Public Library and photocopied David Brock's *American Spectator* article. Rather than purchase the actual magazine from the newsstand, he wanted to keep out-of-pocket costs to a minimum.

Traylor also began assembling legal research on possible claims Jones might file. His research papers reveal that he copied pages from legal form books to help draft a simple complaint, as if handling a slip-and-fall case. He highlighted Arkansas cases allowing recovery for "emotional distress," for "outrage" (an obscure legal claim involving "injury to plaintiff's emotional well-being"), plus a chunk of the Arkansas Civil Rights Act of 1993, which included remedies for sex discrimination.

Traylor also invested in sufficient postage stamps to write to the National Organization of Women, from which he received a "Legal Resource Kit" with the label "Sex Discrimination and Sexual Harassment." The kit summarized the federal law regarding gender discrimination in the employment setting.

Danny Traylor also took steps to contact the Clinton White House. Traylor had worked as a page for Senator Fulbright. His father, Bob Traylor, had served two terms in the Arkansas state legislature (where he had come to know, of all people, Jim McDougal). The thirty-eight-year-old Traylor knew enough about politics to know that this case could turn into a raging house fire if nobody doused water on it early enough.

So Danny Traylor arranged to meet with George Cook, a prominent Little Rock businessman with close ties to the Clinton White House, at a nearby watering hole. Seated in a dark booth with a beer in front of him, Traylor did not mince words: "So I laid it out to George that 'here's the situation: this woman is pissed off, and I believe that she has a lawsuit against Bill Clinton and Trooper Ferguson. And I've told her that she's got a lawsuit and that I can't do it, but if I can't, there are lawyers out there that will.'"

"It seems to me," Traylor continued, "that the woman's biggest bitch is not so much with Clinton at this time. It's with [Trooper] Ferguson. Shooting his mouth off." As Traylor saw it, there existed a nice window of opportunity here. "This would be an opportunity for the White House to come to the rescue of this poor woman's honor. If Clinton could say, yes, I met with Paula and nothing happened," and if Paula Jones could say, "No, nothing happened," then the rest of the details could be "finessed." Traylor offered his professional opinion that the case could be quickly settled "on a legal and politically ethical-type basis." He was confident, from speaking with Jones, that his client would embrace such a compromise.

Although later accounts of this barroom meeting would suggest that twenty-five thousand dollars was the magic number Traylor was looking for, Traylor himself would insist that his expectations were much lower. "My recollection is the number was five," he said, correcting the record. "I had been messing around with this thing for about two weeks or so. I hadn't spent a whole lot of time on it, but I had spent a little time and the number that came to my mind was five thousand dollars." He was prepared to pay himself about a thousand dollars for his time and aggravation, then give the rest to Jones and put the case to rest. "I thought that I could get in and out of this thing and make my client happy, accommodate or mediate a claim with the president of the United States for five thousand bucks and get on to something else," he recalled.

George Cook would later sign an affidavit stating that Traylor had threatened to "embarrass [Clinton] publicly" if he didn't cough up a hefty settlement. Cook also alleged that Traylor stated that "it would help if President Clinton would get Paula a job out in California," or perhaps find an acting job for Steve Jones in Hollywood, to which Cook had allegedly replied, "That would be illegal."

Yet Traylor would dismiss as "bullshit" such stories that he had tried to blackmail the president. Rather, he declared in his own defense, he was simply describing the facts of Jones's situation: "She's gone to California; her husband works for the airline; they live in Long Beach; they've got one baby; he envisions himself as some type of actor, he's been in some crummy . . . movies; Paula is presently a housewife; she has these skills. You take that information, and you run with it.

"I mean, this woman has got a lawsuit, and it might be a nuisance lawsuit, but it's a lawsuit," he told George. "It was a sexual discrimination/harassment–type thing. It's dirty and messy and ain't my kind of action," but there would be depositions and public allegations that would not be good for the president. He concluded, "You need to get the message up there to very high circles."

Two days later, George Cook called Traylor and said there was nothing he could do. He added, according to Traylor's account, "We're way up in the polls; this can't hurt us." Cook would dispute this version of the story, stating in a sworn affidavit that he told Traylor, "It was a preposterous claim and he [Traylor] should not expect to get any money." No matter how it transpired, not even a nickel was offered by the White House to settle the case.

Years later, having relocated his law office to an apartment building on a side street in Little Rock, Traylor expressed everlasting sorrow that the *Jones* case had not been nipped in the bud before it wreaked havoc. Seated at his oak desk with big band music playing in the background and a breeze blowing in from a propped-open door, he said, "Once this genie got out of the bottle, there was no putting it back in."

Traylor knew that the case was a "tough" one to win, especially because it would be difficult to prove damages. At the same time, he could see danger lights blinking for the White House. "I wish that I had been more forceful in try-ing to describe to that camp up there that this is a bad business, bad juju on this one," Traylor said, his voice tight from too many cups of coffee. "That this is a case, number one. And, number two, it needs to settle. But in the end, it turned into a billion-dollar industry, with lawyers and talk shows."

Traylor rocked back in his chair, coffee mug in hand, reflecting on his own role in the events that followed: "I'm sorry that he [Clinton] was apparently distracted by all of this mess. And that he incurred these huge legal fees and damaged his family life, and put the country through all of this. It's bad, bad business."

With a sigh of resignation he concluded: "I didn't do it. But I probably ought to share some responsibility for it, I guess."

———

THE immediate consequence of the White House's refusal to do business with Danny Traylor was that Paula and Steve Jones got even more ticked off. They were bumping up against a three-year statute of limitations for filing a lawsuit. To further complicate matters, it became evident that Steve Jones loathed Bill Clinton for a hundred reasons, some rational, some not, making Traylor's job even more difficult.

Paula Jones kept calling her lawyer from California and complaining, "We have done what you suggested, Traylor, which is to try to evoke an apology from these people that had done me dirty. Now what are we going to do?" Like any good lawyer, Traylor finally responded, "Let's try something else."

What Traylor did was to call Cliff Jackson, the aforementioned archenemy of Bill Clinton's. Traylor had read in the papers that Jackson was representing the troopers who had blown the whistle on Clinton's alleged marital infidelities, so he figured it was worth a shot.

Years later, having settled into a rustic law office alongside a lake in Hot Springs, a collection of Cato Indian arrowheads (once belonging to his father) adorning the wall, Clifford Jackson expressed no regret about having waded into the Clinton fray. The gangling lawyer, whose smile unveiled an unusually large set of teeth, had come to believe it was his destiny. Draping a long arm across the couch, Jackson reflected on his unusual relationship with Bill Clinton, starting with the days they had played basketball together while at Oxford. "He and I are diametrically opposite personality types," Jackson said. "I say what I mean. I mean what I say. Bill Clinton never says what he means. He never means what he says. Or alternatively, he may mean what he says at the moment, but he won't mean it tomorrow, or the next moment. It is hard to trust people who are like that."

So fierce was Jackson's dislike for his former friend Bill Clinton that he and Sheffield Nelson had formed the Alliance for Re-Birth of the Independent America (ARIA) to warn the entire nation about Clinton. This group had gone to work the day Clinton announced his candidacy for presidency, running a full-page ad in the *Arkansas Democrat* and then taking its message to a national audience, using the catchy phrase "Please Governor Clinton, don't do to America what you've done [to] Arkansas."

After the Clintons moved into the White House, Jackson had written several vitriolic letters to both Bill and Hillary. In one, he implored the president to change his misguided ways: "It is much more fundamental than mere sex. I am talking about your fundamental nature—seemingly inbred and long-polished—and your casual willingness to deceive, to exploit and to manipulate in order to attain personal and political power. I am talking about your willingness to compromise principle until there is no longer any principle left to compromise."

It was this same Cliff Jackson whom Danny Traylor decided to call, in search of legal guidance with respect to Paula Jones's new case.

Jackson offered to do even better—he would provide a "national audience for the airing of Miss Jones' complaints." Luckily, he told Traylor, the troopers were scheduled to hold a big press conference in Washington in a couple of weeks. This was a perfect "forum" for Jones to unmask Clinton in public.

Jackson helped Traylor put together a press packet. He also assisted Traylor in drawing up a fee agreement, covering book deals, movie rights, and a host of sundries that went far beyond an ordinary lawyer-client arrangement. It also contained an odd clause, drafted by Jackson himself, by which Jones promised not to accept any "hush money, jobs or other inducements from Bill Clinton, his supporters or anyone else to cease and desist in her present effort to bring her unique information and perspective to the attention of the American people."

Hoping to head off the matter before it got any stranger, on February 11, 1994, Traylor composed a letter on his one-man law office stationery. Addressed simply to "The President," the letter was faxed to the White House before the scheduled conference:

> Dear Sir:
>
> I represent Ms. Paula Jones. Ms. Jones complains of your conduct at a meeting with her in a private room at the Excelsior Hotel, Little Rock. . . . Today Ms. Jones will characterize your conduct as the equivalent of on-the-job sexual harassment but will refrain from an explicit description as to afford you an opportunity to publicly apologize and take responsibility for your actions.

Traylor told the president that his client had been "defamed" and that "you have personal knowledge that would discredit Trooper Ferguson's account and restore Ms. Jones to her good reputation." He concluded as if in forewarning: "She is requesting that you publicly do so."

Later that same day, Jones and her tiny entourage assembled in Washington at the annual convention of the Conservative Political Action Conference (CPAC). The weather was a nasty mixture of snow and sleet. The audience was decidedly anti-Clinton and rambunctious. Recalled Traylor of the surreal CPAC experience: "I started feeling kind of uneasy about this whole thing, I was wondering what the f—— am I doing? But I had made this commitment, and we're here, and we'll go ahead and give it our best shot."

The transcript of the Jones press conference reveals a freewheeling assemblage that was nearly comical at times. Even Traylor would later admit: "You know, the subject matter lends itself to levity. So there was some of that."

Cliff Jackson, serving as emcee, first announced the launching of the Troopergate Whistle-Blowers Fund to help pay for the legal defense of the Arkansas troopers. Next, he turned the microphone over to Traylor. The Little Rock lawyer issued a disclaimer, "I'm not a political animal as such," but quickly warmed to the CPAC crowd. Traylor told the noisy audience that at the airport, he had picked up a magazine that contained a question on the cover: "Are All Men Pigs?" When he had posed that question to Paula Jones, his client had replied, "Most men aren't really that bad, but there is a good dose of 'oink' in a whole lot of them."

After that brief effort at stand-up comedy, Traylor shifted to a stream-of-consciousness soliloquy about children in third-world countries "fighting over neck bones with dogs." He then declared in a burst of political oratory, "We've got Bosnia. We've got a health care crisis! Mr. President, this is something that shouldn't occupy your energy and your attention. I would encourage you to come forth. Tell the American people what the truth of the matter is. If you've made a mistake, the American people will forgive you, but please come forward. Clear Mrs. Jones' good name! And let's get on with the business of state."

With that introduction completed, the crowd was ready to hear from Jones herself. Dressed in a dark outfit trimmed with golden buttons, she took the stage looking like a deer caught in the headlights of an eighteen-wheeler. Steve Jones, wearing a double-breasted suit with a white handkerchief wedged in his pocket, stood next to his wife with a tight, angry face. The scene quickly became unwieldy. A tape recorder captured the moment, as Paula Jones told a condensed version of her story, and reporters pumped out questions:

> REPORTER: Did he ask you to have sex with him? Yes or no? Did he ask you to have sex with him?
> MS. JONES: [After hesitating]. A type of sex, yes. . . .
> TRAYLOR: I am going to talk to Paula right now and ask her to give you kind of a blow-by-blow account [laughter from the audience] of what transpired in the room. . . .
> REPORTER: A question, that uh, I don't know how quite to say it. Did the governor ask you to perform fellatio?
> PAULA JONES: Excuse me??
> REPORTER: Fellatio?

After a long pause, Cliff Jackson cut in: "Thank you, I will be available outside the room in just a few minutes if you have any questions."

Most accounts of the Paula Jones case would later blame President Clinton and the White House for failing to settle the case immediately before it irreparably damaged his presidency. Yet this revisionist viewpoint failed to take into account the context of the Jones case rollout. The unveiling of Paula

Jones's claim at a CPAC convention with Cliff Jackson acting as master of ceremonies certainly did not give it an aura of seriousness and legitimacy.

Years later, Traylor admitted that he had exercised poor judgment in selecting this particular venue to go public with Jones's charges. "Being seen as allied with Cliff Jackson . . . that was probably, in light of retrospect, unwise." If he were to do it over, Traylor said, he would have stayed away from overt political enemies of President Clinton, since this did nothing to "facilitate a settlement." He further expressed dismay that Cliff Jackson "kind of suckered me in."

The public and media reaction to Paula Jones's maiden appearance at the Washington CPAC convention was underwhelming. Most of the national papers, if they covered the story at all, buried it in their inside sections. The *New York Times* ran a short, 250-word article about the CPAC event, but failed to even mention Jones by name. The *Arkansas Democrat-Gazette* ran a larger front-page story, but it contained only a sprinkling of details concerning Jones's allegations. The *Washington Post* made a brief reference to Jones's allegations as "yet another ascension of Mount Bimbo."

"They butchered us pretty quickly," admitted Traylor. "So we didn't get much traction, right out of the gate."

The conservative media watchdog group Accuracy in Media took out a $14,000 ad in the *Washington Times,* posing the question WHO IS PAULA JONES AND WHY IS THE POST SUPPRESSING HER CHARGE OF SEXUAL HARASSMENT? The ad went on to assert that *Washington Post* reporter Michael Isikoff had been suspended for "insubordination" because he had "protested the editors' refusal to report the Paula Jones story fully." R. Emmett Tyrrell, Jr., editor of the *American Spectator* and the man who had launched the Troopergate story, commented that he was "amazed that journalists have been so cowardly" in failing to treat Jones's allegations as serious news.

Michael Isikoff had indeed been tussling with his editors at the *Post* over publishing the Jones story. A short, wiry journalist known for his boundless nervous energy and his healthy-sized ego, Isikoff wasn't about to let this story get away. After meeting with Jones in Arkansas, he had the gut feeling that her account was believable. Isikoff groaned that *Post* editors were being too cautious, holding him back from publishing a blockbuster piece that readers deserved to see. At Jackson's urging, Traylor promised to give Isikoff an "exclusive" if he ran with the story. "Izzy," as Traylor affectionately called him, hadn't published a word yet. Paula and Steve Jones were "getting itchy." Paula had exposed her story to the world, and nobody seemed to be biting.

So Traylor began "putting out the word," from coast to coast, that he was ready to dump the Jones case and put it up for grabs. "By this time I was, quite frankly, getting tired of the thing," he recalled. "The phone would ring off the hook. People wanting this, that, and the other." Traylor ran a one-man law practice; he had to make a living to put bread on his family's table. The question that began to dominate his thoughts was "Who am I going to pawn this thing off on?"

Two unlikely lawyers whom Traylor contacted as potential pawnees were Gerry Spence, the famous cowboy-booted trial lawyer from Wyoming, and Anita Hill, the African American law professor from Oklahoma who had testified against Clarence Thomas during his confirmation hearings. Neither famous lawyer answered Traylor's letter.

Some lawyers "volunteered to help" on condition that "they could not go public." Among these were Richard Porter and Jerome Marcus, two former classmates at the University of Chicago Law School, now attorneys in Chicago and Philadelphia, respectively. These men, whom Isikoff would later dub "the elves," shared common jurisprudential philosophies as members of the conservative Federalist Society. They offered to strategize and draft legal documents for Traylor as long as it was done surreptitiously.

Danny Traylor drank coffee nonstop and went into a self-imposed "news blackout." Even as he struggled to ditch this clunker, however, other events in Washington began converging to create a ripe environment for Paula Jones's lawsuit. The *American Political Report* ran a piece in March 1994, indicating that 49 percent of the public now believed that "Whitewater was a serious matter requiring a full-scale federal investigation." That publication also reported that the brewing scandals dealing with Whitewater/Madison Guaranty, Vince Foster's death, and "Troopergate" were "beginning to knit together in voters' minds."

For the first time, a segment of the public began to respond positively to Jones's story. A letter dated April 7 from "A Friend" was sent to Jones: "Dear Ms. Jones, I urge you to file a lawsuit against Bill Clinton before the statute of limitations expires on May 8th. This man is a liar, a cheat, a fraud, and a hypocrite who needs to be exposed for what he is to the American people. . . . God go with you."

Several events helped God along, sealing Paula Jones's date with destiny. First, the White House had recently hired Washington criminal superlawyer Robert Bennett to assist with President Clinton's damage-control efforts and to deal with the media; now the Jones matter was added to Bennett's portfolio, giving the case an instant aura of legitimacy. Bennett's appearance in turn gave Isikoff's editors the hook they needed to publish his story about the Jones allegations on the front page of the *Washington Post*. Finally, Traylor received a call from two Virginia lawyers who expressed a willingness to work on the case, with no money up front. "It seemed to me that they were my kind of guys," Traylor said. Suddenly, a new synergy seemed to be building up.

"Then the whole damn thing busted loose," Traylor said.

Traylor had copied a few sample complaints from the "Fright, Shock or Mental Disturbance" section of a legal form book. Jerome Marcus, the invisible "elf" in Philadelphia, faxed him a more polished draft complaint from his home, so it could not be traced to his law office. As the clock ticked toward the May 8 statute of limitations deadline, Traylor was still "feeling isolated." On May 3, he completed the papers necessary to file a complaint in federal court, affixing the cover sheet and typing the amount "$3 million" in the box listing the damages demanded. He also drafted a one-page press release, hoping this might prod the White House to offer a few thousand dollars to make this nuisance case go away. Traylor's telephone records show a series of calls, to and from Jerome Marcus and Richard Porter, as the moment of truth arrived.

Just to be safe, Traylor faxed his draft complaint to the two Virginia lawyers—Gil Davis and Joe Cammarata—scribbling a note, "FYI, Review, Comment. Please call to discuss." Just as Traylor was preparing to walk across the street to file his papers in the courthouse, Cammarata called from along a side road in Virginia. He said, "We're still headed your way, Traylor." Cammarata added that they had perused the draft complaint and that, with all due respect, it "would not withstand court scrutiny for fifteen minutes."

Traylor stared out his seventeenth-floor window in the First Commercial Bank building. A horde of journalists had amassed outside on the street. He explained his predicament to the Virginia lawyer—he had let the cat out of the bag to a few local reporters. So what does he do now? he asked. These newspaper folks wanted a story. Cammarata asked Traylor, "Don't you feel a little sick? Don't you feel a little ill?" Gil Davis chimed in, "Cancel the damn press conference. . . . We'll be there tomorrow."

Gil Davis was a big man accustomed to big cases. He had grown up in Waterloo, Iowa, before attending University of Virginia Law School. As an assistant U.S. attorney in Eastern Virginia, Davis had prosecuted one of the first aircraft hijacking cases in the country. In private practice, he had racked up a $40 million verdict for a poor Kentucky coal miner against a subsidiary of Bethlehem Steel. The case had given Davis the financial freedom to take on cases that tickled his fancy.

Davis was an unabashed Republican; he had pictures of his idol Ronald Reagan hanging on his office wall. He did not particularly like Bill Clinton, because of "integrity questions." Yet Davis was a respectable lawyer who did not allow politics to get in the way of professional duties. Even though the "elves" had secretly enlisted him through a friend, Davis was his own man.

Joe Cammarata, a young, thin, quick-talking Italian American from Brooklyn, shared space in Davis's office. A lawyer and certified public accountant, he had worked for the Department of Justice's Tax Division during the Reagan administration. Now he was a Republican, but he had grown up in the Democratic world of Brooklyn and understood how the political game was played. He also enjoyed the thrill of unconventional tactics making this a dream case.

Davis and Cammarata stayed up all night drafting a new complaint to replace Danny Traylor's shaky effort. Near midnight, they sent their law clerk to the local 7-Eleven to pick up a newspaper and snacks. It was a lucky trip: Michael Isikoff's first story about Paula Jones and her detailed allegations against the president appeared on the front page of the *Washington Post*'s early edition. Years later, the Virginia lawyers revealed that they cherry-picked from Isikoff's article, drawing upon the facts in that story about Paula Jones's X-rated charges against Bill Clinton to draft a more fulsome four-count complaint.

After catching a few winks and throwing clothes into an overnight bag, they boarded a plane for Arkansas. In Danny Traylor's office, on Wednesday, May 4, the Virginia lawyers met with Paula Jones for the first time. She appeared to be a simple Southern gal and wore a flower in her hair. She was accompanied by her mother, Delmer Corbin, a plain-dressed, God-fearing woman who reminded Davis of the folks he had represented in Appalachia.

Davis sized up Jones as "sweet, and a bit naive." After listening to her for an hour, he concluded that "she did have a meritorious claim, her motives were pure, and she was only interested in her own reputation."

Davis was intrigued that—according to the morning papers—the White House had assigned big-shot criminal defense lawyer Bob Bennett, a recent addition to Clinton's team, to squash Jones's lawsuit. Bennett had represented the likes of Defense Secretary Caspar Weinberger in the Iran-Contra scandal. Davis thought to himself, "Well, if there's enough smoke that they think they need to crush this little girl, I wonder if there isn't a fire." So the next day, Davis settled into Traylor's chair, put his feet up on Traylor's desk, and dialed Bob Bennett's number in Washington.

The two men had both been in the U.S. attorney's office during earlier stages of their careers; they were professional friends. After exchanging pleasantries, Davis broke the news that he was now representing Paula Jones. Bennett answered loudly, "Oh, that's too bad." The Washington superlawyer stated that he had discussed these allegations with President Clinton "for hours and hours." The president had assured him "that he doesn't even remember [Jones], let alone anything going on." Bennett admonished Davis, "You just need to remember that he's the president, and he'll be very credible on this issue—and I'm persuaded, having really grilled him on it."

At this point, Davis swiveled in Traylor's chair and asked himself, Was it time to drop the first bomb? During the course of the lawyers' private meetings with Jones, she had volunteered that when Governor Clinton exposed himself, she had observed that his penis was unusually "crooked." Upon further questioning, Jones recalled that she had joked with Debbie Ballentine that it made her think of "the leaning Tower of Pisa," and Jones even drew a picture for the lawyers. Cammarata had nudged Davis and whispered that this could be their ace in the hole. There had been a recent story in the national press about a young boy who had alleged that he had been molested by pop star Michael Jackson; the boy had won a $15 million settlement after his lawyers disclosed that he could identify a "distinguishing feature" of Jackson's genitalia.

Davis now rocked back in the chair and drawled into the phone, "Well, what if I told you that she can identify certain distinguishing characteristics in his genital area?" There was dead silence. Finally, Bennett boomed, "Goddamn it! Here we are lawyers, and we have honorable work to do, and now we're talking about litigation over the president's penis! Where's the dignity in that work?"

Bennett lobbed back his own grenade. "Well, you know . . . I've not seen them, but I understand there's some nude pictures of [Jones] out there." This was an interesting factoid, as Davis sized it up. It meant that the White House had already begun doing its opposition research.

"We're not paying any money," Bennett declared.

"We're not asking for any," Davis replied. "We want a statement by [the president] that will redeem her reputation, that she was not sexually involved with him on an initial meeting or ever."

Said Bennett, "Maybe we can do something there."

Everyone in the room seemed to want to end the case "then and there," especially Paula Jones, who said little except to pipe up that she wanted her good name back. The goal of the Virginia lawyers was simple: "Get some statement from the president she did nothing wrong, she's not that kind of person, apologize, move on. Period. No money. Nothing."

Around lunchtime, Bennett called to tell his Virginia opponents that he could get authority from the president to settle. Davis asked, "Well, where is he? Is he available to you?" Bennett replied, "Yes, he's in the room."

Davis put his hand over the receiver and mouthed the words "He's in the room." The group in Traylor's office, including Jones, instantly fell silent. Cammarata said to himself, "Wow, now we're going to be negotiating directly with the president of the United States. This is pretty good."

Bennett had reviewed the proposed language that the Virginia lawyers had faxed him—he cautioned that the wording might have to be massaged. But they were in the right ballpark. When Bennett volunteered that White House Press Secretary Dee Dee Myers would be the ideal person to read the statement, Davis cut in: "That's a nonstarter, Bob." President Clinton was "the only one that can do it, if it's going to get the attention it deserves to redeem her reputation."

Bennett said, "Hold on." There was another pause. Bennett came back on the phone and said, "Yes, he'll do it."

Cammarata repeated in a whisper, "Wow, this is pretty good."

The Jones lawyers next insisted on including a "tolling agreement" that would suspend the statute of limitations for six months, holding the case open to ensure that the White House did not "trash" Jones once the settlement was signed. They feared that the Clinton team might allow the president to read his statement of quasi contrition and then unleash "political hacks" to malign Jones.

Bennett's tone became subdued. This was a "deal killer," he said. If the case could be breathed back to life any time someone asserted that the White House was "smearing" Jones, the president would be a sitting duck for a half year—an eternity in the life of a politician. There was no way to control what *others* might do to pin the blame on Clinton and to wreak political havoc.

It was already after 4:00. The clerk's office was set to close at 5:00. Davis said he had no alternative but to file the complaint. Bennett interjected: "Look, don't do that, Gil. I know you have a duty to your client. But you owe the president every courtesy you can give him consistent with your duty."

Davis scratched his head. He was a lifelong student of the American Constitution and revered its principles. Bennett was right, he whispered. The president was entitled to every consideration. They would wait one day–just in case a deal could be worked out.

Two factors hastened the collapse of negotiations. One was the arrival of Steve Jones, who had just touched down from California and was acting like a "tough guy," exhibiting an unusually "fiery attitude about Bill Clinton." This became instantly problematic for the Virginia lawyers.

The second person who blew apart any chance of settlement was Paula's sister, Charlotte Corbin Brown. That night, as the Jones group weighed its options, Brown appeared with her husband, Mark, on local television and mocked Paula's story. Looking directly into the camera, Charlotte stated that she had discussed the whole Clinton hoopla with Paula over Christmas, and that it all revolved around a fat settlement. "Whichever way it went," said Charlotte, "she smelled money." Watching her sister on television, Paula broke down crying.

Just as the Jones group was recovering from this blow, a CNN program cited "unnamed White House sources" as saying that Paula Jones had not filed a claim because "she didn't have a case." The Virginia lawyers jumped up in unison, shouting, "White House sources?"

Cammarata turned to Davis and said, "We've got to file."

The feeling of distrust was mutual. In the White House, Bob Bennett and the rest of the president's team were certain that the Jones camp had "leaked a draft complaint," including the grotesque allegation about a "distinguishing characteristic." If this was meant to be a "good faith" step toward settlement, Bennett told himself, it seemed like a perverse way to do it.

Years later, Bennett would conclude that a "good faith" settlement had never really been in the cards. Seated in his Washington office, he said, "Dollar signs were always there. She [Paula Jones] would sell her story, write a book, et cetera." Working out a plan to clear Paula's "good name," he believed, was just empty talk—especially after Steve Jones got into the picture. "My own gut tells me," he said, "that her husband very much pushed it."

Whatever the explanation, even as the two camps talked settlement, both sides were moving into battle mode.

After the CNN broadcast, Paula remained silent. She was holding her knees, as if in a fetal position. She still "didn't want to file." At the same time, Steve Jones was angrier. According to Davis, Paula's husband "was very defensive of her and he was very strong about wanting to pursue the matter in court."

Paula began crying.

Finally, she wiped a tear off her cheek, pushed the frizzy hair out of her eyes, and said, "Okay, I'll file."

———

THE twenty-page complaint against William Jefferson Clinton and Trooper Danny Ferguson, consisting of four counts, was a stretch by any legal standards. Paula Jones had long since missed the deadline for filing a federal sexual harassment claim under Title VII of the civil rights law—the strongest basis for this sort of employment-related lawsuit. The state law tort claims for emotional distress and defamation were more plausible—but the Virginia lawyers wanted to stay out of Arkansas state courts, where judges and juries were likely to be strongly pro-Clinton. Instead, they had piggybacked the state claims onto two weak federal civil rights claims, hoping to patch together a complaint that survived a motion to dismiss. As long as they could get in front of a federal jury in Arkansas, they felt, it was worth taking a roll of the dice.

The amount of money demanded by Paula Jones—$700,000—was a number that had been plucked out of the sky by Davis and Cammarata. The $3 million figure that Danny Traylor had originally planned to demand seemed far too high; it would make the lawsuit look like "a publicity stunt." They needed some peg on which to hang their monetary claim, so they decided on $100,000 for each compensatory count, and $75,000 for each punitive damage claim, producing a grand total of $700,000. As Cammarata later explained, the key consideration was, "How much is going to pass the laugh test?"

The next morning, complaint in hand, the Virginia lawyers took a circuitous route to the courthouse, through an alley. They had called the clerk's office and arranged to enter the building through a rear door, to bypass the throng of reporters. For Cammarata, it was an incredible moment: Here they were, two "ordinary lawyers" walking over to the federal courthouse to file a complaint against the president. None of the media knew what Cammarata and Davis looked like, so they were able to walk through the line of media folk "like Moses parting the Dead Sea."

The courthouse, a five-story limestone edifice built in 1932, was a grand tribute to the Depression-era federal buildings program. Constructed along the same axis as the state capitol building where Bill Clinton had presided as governor, the historic courthouse featured Art Deco light standards and floors made of shiny brown-and-white marble and polychrome tiles, over which Paula Jones's new lawyers now walked briskly.

They took an elevator to the clerk's office on the fourth floor, paid their filing fee, and made sure the document was stamped with the correct date: May 6, 1994. The clerk assigned the case randomly and scribbled down that it would be handled by "U.S. District Judge Susan Webber Wright." By now, reporters had figured out that these were the long-awaited Jones lawyers. Journalists jumped into the elevator with Davis and Cammarata, shouting questions and jamming lenses into their faces. For fun, Cammarata handed one lucky reporter a spare copy of the complaint and said with a mischievous Brooklyn grin, "Read paragraph twenty-two"—it was the paragraph dealing with the alleged "distinguishing characteristic." The journalists scrambled back to their offices in the capitol, pumping out news stories that swiftly moved across the wire services.

Looking back on that fateful day, Cammarata believed that the White House overplayed its hand. Above all, he said, it was a huge mistake for the White House to name Bob Bennett so early. "You name a Babe Ruth, a slugger, before the game starts?" From the opponents' perspective, it was like announcing, "I'm here to kill you. I'm here to lop your head off!" For aggressive litigators like Davis and Cammarata, this amounted to a call to battle.

Davis and Cammarata exited the federal courthouse. Outside, the temperature had already soared to eighty-two degrees. A thick humidity hung in the air like setting gelatin, a typical May day in Arkansas. As their client watched from Danny Traylor's office seventeen stories above them, the Virginia lawyers read a brief statement.

"I do not seek publicity in this matter," they stated on behalf of Jones. "I want a jury of ordinary citizens in Arkansas to look at the facts in this case and to decide who is telling the truth."

ONE piece of fascinating scandal history that remained buried in Gil Davis's files in the basement of his Virginia law office, until years later, related to the fact that Ken Starr was one of the first lawyers Davis contacted for help on the *Jones* case. "Elf" Jerome Marcus had faxed a confidential note to Davis, first suggesting that Jones's lawyers should utilize the talents of Ronald Rotunda, a leading constitutional scholar with an increasingly conservative bent who taught at University of Illinois Law School: "Because [Rotunda's] background is from the left, unlike (for example) Judge Bork or even Ken Starr, I think it would be wonderful to have Professor Rotunda argue on Paula's behalf." Marcus added, tongue-in-cheek: "Of course, if the ACLU is willing to come in, I would think that would be best; but I'm not holding my breath."

Davis decided to pick up the phone and contact Ken Starr. Starr was now a partner at Kirkland & Ellis in Washington. One of the elves with whom Davis had already dealt, Richard Porter, was a member of Starr's firm in its Chicago office. Starr's credentials spoke for themselves. He was a former solicitor general in a Republican administration, not to mention a leading expert on constitutional law. Davis and Cammarata had ordered a transcript of his appearance on the *MacNeil/Lehrer NewsHour* in late May, debating Georgetown law professor Susan Low Bloch and White House Counsel Lloyd Cutler; on this national program, Starr had masterfully argued that the president was not immune from civil suit in the *Jones* matter. So they left a message at Starr's Washington office, hoping that he would return the call.

That same night, while the two lawyers were working in a hotel room, the phone rang. Cammarata picked it up. To his amazement, Ken Starr was on the other end. Cammarata handed the phone to Gil and murmured, "Judge Starr is on the phone, talk to him." After a twenty-minute conversation, followed by additional discussions in ensuing days to discuss presidential power cases, it became clear that Starr was prepared to play some role in the case. "And I think he actually wanted to come in as an amicus," that is, a friend of the court, Davis would recall. Starr would take the position that there was "no Presidential immunity." Yet he made clear that he was not getting into this due to any "personal views" about Paula Jones or Bill Clinton. "He was only interested in the legal matter," said Davis.

Starr, it turned out, was also consulting with a conservative women's group called the Independent Women's Forum, which included prominent female conservative luminaries whom Starr considered friends, about the possibility of filing an amicus brief in the *Jones* case. At the same time, Starr was also consulting with Whitewater independent counsel, Robert Fiske, about filing an amicus curiae brief in the *Jones* case on behalf of the Office of Independent Counsel.

Davis's billing records reveal that he spoke with Starr four and a half hours during the month of June, in six separate conversations. Davis marked down $775 worth of billable time on his time sheets, relating to these conferences. He also reached out to a young lawyer named Paul Rosenzweig, at the urging of Jerome Marcus and Richard Porter. The two elves had been classmates of Rosenzweig at the University of Chicago Law School. In a memo to the *Jones* file dated June 16, Davis wrote that Porter had recommended Rosenzweig, then practicing law in Washington, "as a person who can do some research and help us on the questions we need to have help on." Davis sent at least one batch of material to Rosenzweig; Davis later confirmed that he consulted briefly with Rosenzweig after the elves made the introduction.

This became a sticky subject because Rosenzweig was later hired as one of Starr's principal lawyers; it was Rosenzweig who would be used by those same elves with whom he had attended law school to steer Linda Tripp to Starr's office.

At the time, however, none of the players could have imagined that there would be any connection between Paula Jones's lawsuit and the criminal investigation being run by Robert Fiske and his Office of the Independent Counsel.

Those two matters, it seemed, had absolutely nothing in common.

CHAPTER

12

THREE JUDGES IN BLACK

As Robert Fiske would later explain, he had an indirect interest in the *Jones* case because it might tie in to his Whitewater/Madison Guaranty investigation, as a matter of legal precedent. If the Office of the Independent Counsel (OIC) found any liability on Clinton's part and wanted to go after money damages and restitution, Fiske's lawyers would face the question of whether the president was immune from civil liability—the same question that would be decided by the *Jones* case. When Fiske contacted Ken Starr in the summer of 1994, Fiske first asked the well-known constitutional lawyer "whether we [OIC] should do it." The second question was, "If so, would *he* do it?" Starr replied "yes" on both counts. As a constitutional matter, Starr felt strongly that President Clinton was subject to suit in the *Jones* case. In terms of his own availability, it sounded like a stimulating assignment. He was prepared to handle the OIC brief in the Supreme Court. Fiske and Starr quietly agreed to set up a meeting to discuss this undertaking.

That meeting, for reasons that neither man could have ever anticipated, would never take place.

On the afternoon of August 5, 1994, Robert Fiske was in an airport in Florida when his beeper went off. He walked to a pay phone and dialed his office in Washington. Mark Stein, one of the prosecutors, blurted out, "You were just replaced by Ken Starr."

In Arkansas, the weather was oppressively hot. A FedEx delivery man walked sluggishly into Two Financial Center in Little Rock, requesting a signature on a package. Suddenly, word swept through the office that all lawyers were to report to the OIC conference room. There was a sense that "something was wrong."

The mood in the independent counsel's office, after the news was delivered, turned into one of shock. Said prosecutor Dennis McInerney, "All we thought about was Bob. And how unbelievably unfair this was. And how unfortunate for the country." Julie O'Sullivan, the first lawyer Fiske had hired, was unable to speak. Besides being "a terrific lawyer," Robert Fiske was "a really decent human being." This was cruel and morally outrageous. As lawyers remained frozen in their chairs, O'Sullivan recalled that a new emotion surfaced. "There was a really deep sense of—I can't capture it. I have to say, anger."

Gabrielle Wolohojian, who had transplanted herself from Boston to Little Rock to work on the new tax case involving Governor Jim Guy Tucker, felt suddenly adrift. "I was in an alien landscape—and by that I mean Arkansas itself.... It was sort of like being sent to sleep-away camp," Wolohojian said a decade later, breaking her self-imposed silence regarding that period of her career. "It was all extremely interesting, but you were very far from home. And it had a sense of surreality." Now, the world in Little Rock suddenly seemed even stranger. On a more practical level, there was the question "What should we do?"

Some prosecutors announced on the spot that they were resigning. Others were too stunned to put together an action plan. They all agreed on one thing: "We needed to close the office." It was unclear what authority those hired by Fiske possessed, in the wake of this regime change. "And so, we decided that we needed to secure the offices. Close them and have everyone leave." They would preserve the status quo "until we got instructions."

In Washington, Janet Reno's Justice Department was equally stunned. Jo Ann Harris, chief of the Criminal Division, recalled experiencing a jolt of shock and disbelief when she learned of the court's order. "It certainly never crossed my mind that the court would not understand, for a whole lot of reasons, that the best thing they could do was just appoint Fiske and let it go on," she would say. "I could not believe that they would do anything so stupid."

Harris rode the elevator to the fifth floor, where she delivered the news to Janet Reno. The attorney general stood behind her desk and "sort of fix[ed] her jaw."

Reno certainly knew there was no guarantee that the three-judge panel would reappoint Fiske. Yet this particular selection threw her for a loop. Of Ken Starr, Reno would later say, "To my knowledge, he had limited experience in investigating and pursuing [criminal] investigations. That was my concern."

The OIC lawyers and staff stationed in Little Rock fled the locked building and gravitated to the garden apartment complex on Sam Peck Road, where most of them had made their home in this foreign land. They carried with them food and drinks, commencing a subdued party that resembled a wake. Julie O'Sullivan and Gabrielle Wolohojian, both women in their thirties, partook in a few libations and impulsively decided, "We're going to the Ozarks. We're going to see Arkansas. The hell with this." As Wolohojian explained it, "No one really knew what we should be doing, because we didn't know if, in fact, we had jobs anymore." As a result, she said, "Julie and I decided to take a road trip, rather aimlessly, with plenty of cigarettes in the back of the car. And headed off."

———

THE three-judge panel that oversaw independent counsel investigations, a curious court unknown except to a tiny colony of lawyers, judges, and journalists who navigated within this arcane world, was suddenly thrust into the national spotlight. For seven and a half years, its presiding judge, appointed by Chief Justice William H. Rehnquist, had been Judge George A. MacKinnon of the U.S. Court of Appeals for the District of Columbia. A conservative jurist who had stubbornly refused to be drawn into politics, MacKinnon followed a simple creed in selecting prosecutors to serve under the independent counsel law: Attorneys with strong ties within the Washington Beltway—*of either party*— were generally excluded from consideration. Regardless of good intentions, MacKinnon felt, anyone who moved in national political circles or anywhere near its orbit presented an unnecessary risk as a special prosecutor.

In the fall of 1992, just weeks before Governor Bill Clinton defeated President George H. W. Bush in the November elections, Chief Justice Rehnquist made a quiet move that would forever reshape history. He replaced the elderly

Judge MacKinnon with Judge David B. Sentelle, a fifty-one-year-old federal appeals judge in Washington known for his strong Southern, conservative Republican roots. Rehnquist also added Judge Joseph T. Sneed (age seventy-four) from the Ninth Circuit Court of Appeals in San Francisco, who was even more conservative than Sentelle. The lone Democrat on the panel was seventy-six-year-old Judge John D. Butzner, Jr., from Richmond, a senior judge who had been appointed to the federal appeals court by President Johnson.

Years later, crippled from a stroke and unable to speak except in brief utterances of yes and no, yet still mentally sharp, Judge Butzner would sit in his wheelchair in a skilled nursing facility in Virginia. Here, he confirmed that he had strongly opposed the replacement of Robert Fiske with Kenneth Starr, during secret discussions among the three judges during the summer of 1994. His papers, previously under seal but now housed in an archive at the University of Virginia, bear out the judge's unusual version of events.

As early as November 1992, immediately after Bill Clinton had won the right to move into the White House, Judge Sentelle had circulated a list of eleven "potential Independent Counsel," even before there existed a case to investigate. Sentelle also circulated, via confidential fax, a typed list of prospective candidates that numbered nearly eighty. He had distilled this list down from a larger collection of names that he kept under lock and key.

It had been the practice of the special court, dating back to Judge MacKinnon's tenure, to maintain a "Talent Book" that listed the names and biographies of attorneys who might be candidates for independent counsel assignments. This Talent Book was kept in a safe in the federal courthouse, reserved for the eyes of those jurists allowed to view these restricted documents. As Judge Sentelle himself later described this confidential book, in a rare written response to interview questions: "It was a huge looseleaf ring binder from which pages were regularly withdrawn and new pages added." As judges suggested or vetoed names in consultation with an informal network of advisers, the list would take on a new shape and content. Input came from "anyone who wished to submit it or anyone we could think of to ask." For Sentelle, the criteria for inclusion in the Talent Book, while nowhere spelled out in print, amounted to a basic formula: If a person "seemed to have the qualifications of being an ethical attorney of good experience and broad reputation, with experience relevant to public integrity and/or investigation, that name went in the book."

By July 18, 1994, with Whitewater bubbling up in the news and Attorney General Reno's formal request for appointment of an independent counsel having been filed with the special court, Judge Sentelle now circulated a revised list of forty-one names. For the first time, this list included Kenneth W. Starr in the number thirty-six slot. It also listed Theodore Olson, a close friend of Ken Starr and a leading conservative lawyer in Washington.

Judge Sentelle understood it was best to pick one's fights carefully. He scratched out the name of Ted Olson, stating in a confidential memo to his fellow judges: "Although I have the highest regard for Theodore Olson (No. 29) I am not sure that he is a top candidate for this post. He has spent so long attacking the constitutionality of the Independent Counsel (law)"—losing a challenge in the Supreme Court—"that it might give a bad appearance if we asked him to be one."

By July 20, Judge Sentelle had reached a short list of five leading candidates. Sentelle was particularly keen on his former colleague, Judge Ken Starr. He wrote in a confidential transmission to his fellow jurists: "Starr is a former Judge of this Circuit, and a former Solicitor General, with universal respect around the federal and Washington bars and I think the country at large. He was the consensus choice of the Senate and its adversary as the Special Master to review the Packwood diaries. Although he does not have direct prosecutorial experience, his 7 year stint as counselor to the U.S. Attorney General should give him good experience to supervise investigations and any necessary prosecutions that might result."

The senior Judge Butzner, a Southern Democrat who had spent his career scrupulously avoiding politics, was unpersuaded by this logic. In a respectful but strongly worded internal memo dated July 25, the senior judge wrote to Sentelle and Sneed: "Looking over our candidates, I have serious doubts that we should replace Mr. Fiske unless we can find someone who is well known and who will have the full confidence of the public as well as the President's supporters, and the President's critics. I realize this is a pretty stringent requirement, but unless we meet it we will have no principled reason to appoint a substitute for Mr. Fiske." Butzner went on to implore his two colleagues to "reconsider" replacing Fiske at all.

When it came, specifically, to Ken Starr, Butzner expressed serious misgivings. Seated in his wheelchair years later, his white hair combed neatly, Butzner would make clear that he had concerns on two counts: First, he worried that Starr was a Washington insider. Second, he believed Starr was actively involved in politics and was a political partisan. "Both," said the retired judge firmly, gripping the bar of his wheelchair. His wife, Viola "Pete" Butzner, recalled that her husband had worried aloud at home, insisting that the panel should adhere to Judge MacKinnon's rule of excluding all candidates with political connections inside the Beltway. "He was opposed to taking anyone from the Washington area," she said. "But he was overruled by the other two [judges]."

Days later, Judge Sentelle transmitted a second memo to his colleagues, informing them that prominent attorneys William Webster and Warren B. Rudman had withdrawn their names from consideration. Sentelle now decided to move forward with Starr; he had telephoned Starr and confirmed that he was still interested. Sentelle wrote to tell his colleagues: "I have arranged for an interview with Ken Starr in my chambers on Monday, August 1, 1994 at 1:00."

Around the capital, conservative Republicans and their allies were turning up the heat in opposition to reappointing Robert Fiske. Floyd G. Brown, chairman of the conservative watchdog group Citizens United, wrote directly to the three-judge panel on August 3, railing against Fiske for his report on the death of Vince Foster and asserting that a multitude of "discrepancies" needed to be examined by a fresh, untainted independent counsel.

The newsletter *Clinton Watch,* published by Citizens United, declared in a headline: "The report released by Special Counsel Robert Fiske may not be worth the paper it's printed on." Fiske, the conservative newsletter charged, "has steam-rolled over a significant number of inconsistencies" in the Foster death matter. He was doing nothing but "trying to protect Bill Clinton" and his "liberal agenda."

Most media accounts that would seek to explain the surprise termination of Fiske, and his replacement by Starr, would assume that Judge Sentelle was the prime mover behind Starr's appointment. Certainly, Sentelle was a fan of Starr's. Both were Southerners, both of them had been mentored by the great conservative jurist Robert Bork. Both were anchor tenants of the conservative lawyers' confrere, the Federalist Society. They had served on the federal appeals court together.

Yet Senior Judge Joseph Sneed in San Francisco, it turned out, championed Starr's appointment and pushed the hardest, for reasons the press would never detect. A strong conservative who had worked in the Nixon Justice Department, Sneed had served from 1971 through 1973 as tax professor and dean at Duke Law School. There, one of his star students had been an earnest young man named Kenneth Winston Starr. Sneed, speaking from his San Francisco judicial chambers, where he still reported to work after turning eighty, would later reflect that Starr had made a brilliant impression on him. "Just personally, I really like him, and he was smart," said Sneed. He also appreciated the fact that Starr hailed from Texas. Sneed's own great-granddaddy had been a preacher who settled in Calvert, Texas, and then struck it rich in oil. The Ninth Circuit judge would later joke that Starr's Texas roots boosted his credentials as independent counsel. "Yes, that's true," the elderly judge chuckled. "That's not a negative."

Ken Starr, forty-eight years old with a perpetually youthful smile, was summoned to the fifth floor of the U.S. Courthouse in Washington for an informal meeting with the three-judge panel. Starr's chambers had been in this building when he sat on the Court of Appeals. It was comfortable terrain. Now he settled into a chair in Judge Sentelle's private office, one of the best spots in the building for watching presidential inaugural parades. With Judges Sentelle and Butzner seated on a black leather couch, the three men had a perfect view of the Capitol dome rising up on the Hill. (Because of his advanced age and shaky health, Judge Sneed participated by speakerphone from San Francisco.) Sentelle, who wore large aviator glasses and sported fat, graying sideburns, settled back comfortably, his big Stetson hat parked on a nearby table. Here, the walls and shelves displayed all of the badges and symbols of Southern conservatism. These included a Federalist Society certificate confirming that Sentelle was a charter member, a personally inscribed photo of his mentor Judge Robert Bork, and a beautiful cane hand-carved by a North Carolina Freemason. (Senate Democrats had tried to block Sentelle's confirmation because of his membership in that group; this cane was a reminder by Southern friends that Sentelle and his backers had prevailed.) The old desk in the center of the room held special significance to this particular judge, so it occupied a place of prominence: It had been Judge Bork's when he had sat on the court of appeals in the 1980s.

After pleasantries were exchanged, Judge Sentelle made clear that the meeting's content would remain confidential. The judges discussed "the importance and sensitivity of the investigation" that Starr might be asked to undertake. They also inquired about any possible conflicts of interest. Starr piped up that he had conducted a preliminary "conflict check" at his law firm; there were no skeletons in his closet. The jurists grilled Starr—like any other would-be independent counsel—to ferret out potential problems. "We actually cross-examined [him] pretty thoroughly," Sentelle would later state under oath before the Senate Governmental Affairs Committee.

Ken Starr appeared to be squeaky clean. He knew little about the Whitewater case; he had followed it only sporadically in the papers. A top-notch attorney with a national reputation, he was nevertheless willing to interrupt his lucrative law practice to respond to this new call to public service.

There was no tipoff whether the judges were "trending [his] way." Yet it was clear from the serious nature of the discussion that Ken Starr's name was at the top of a very short list.

That night, Starr drove to his home in McLean, Virginia, and discussed the possible appointment with his wife, Alice. Her reaction was immediately negative: "She thought it was unwise to take it," Starr would later admit. Alice pointed out that he was doing fabulously well in private practice. He was teaching and juggling other responsibilities. Her feeling was, "You're settling into things. Why disrupt that?"

Alice had no doubt that Ken would do a fine, impartial job. "Ken is so fair that the kids never wanted him to be an umpire at their softball and baseball games, because he would always go for the other side," she said, her eyes conveying a gentle humor. He had no preconception of whether "Bill Clinton was guilty or not guilty of what was happening in Arkansas." She concluded, the brightness vanishing from her eyes: "My problem was, taking on a job like that is a no-win situation."

On August 4, Judge Sentelle circulated an incomplete form to his colleagues, spelling out the terms of appointment for an independent counsel. A blank space remained for the name of the appointee. He wrote: "I will have it ready to fill in the blanks should we decide on an appointee on Friday or Monday." The next day, August 5, the four-page order was filed with the clerk of courts; this time, the name "Kenneth W. Starr" had been inserted.

Judge Butzner, the senior judge from Richmond, had been overruled.

Judge Sentelle's brief opinion, ostensibly written for a unanimous court, indicated that because President Clinton's own attorney general had appointed Fiske, it was better for the special court to appoint someone "not affiliated with the incumbent administration." This was not meant to be a negative reflection on Fiske personally. Rather, Fiske had been "compromised" by the fact that he was appointed by Janet Reno, who reported directly to the Clinton White House.

The opinion was signed by all three judges on the special court. In truth, however, there was a lone dissenter, never revealed to the public or to the press. Judge John Butzner, upset and still adamantly opposed to Starr's appointment, agreed to join the opinion only after losing the vote. His papers confirm that he fought the appointment to the end. Wishing to protect the court from being splattered with mud in this messy political terrain, the gentlemanly Butzner signed the opinion and kept quiet.

The reaction in the White House was a loud, collective groan, as if the administration had just taken a punch in the gut. As President Clinton boarded a helicopter to spend the night at his Camp David retreat, a reporter asked him what he thought of Starr's appointment. The president appeared "shell-shocked" and declined to answer the question.

Away from the cameras and microphones, however, President Clinton was not at all sanguine about the selection. He would later say, "They did whatever they could to rig the game. That's what they did. And you had five former presidents of the American Bar Association saying it was inappropriate. He [Starr] obviously had no business being involved in this case. He was clearly biased, and he clearly had never had any prosecutorial experience. But he was a good guy to direct the hunt."

For Clinton, the purpose of the investigation was now clear as crystal. "You know," he said, stroking his chin, "after Starr came in, there was no pretext about what he and all of his supporters were doing. I felt they were Wile E. Coyote in the pack and I was the Road Runner. And the chase was on."

Judge Sentelle would later express shock and dismay that the appointment of a distinguished public servant like Ken Starr would generate such intense political assaults. "Oddly, but perhaps not surprisingly," said Sentelle, "within less than 24 hours after we announced his appointment to investigate President Clinton, various persons connected with the Clinton organization were making just such attacks."

Judge Sentelle also later insisted that the special court's decision to appoint Starr was unassailable, because it was "unanimous" and thus the product of bipartisan consensus on the court. Yet this was not fully accurate. Judge Butzner's papers and his own statements confirm that he opposed the Starr appointment vigorously. As Butzner would write to Judge Sentelle, several years later, after Chief Justice Rehnquist relieved him of his duties on the special court: "I think we differed only once—the appointment of Mr. Starr. But in the end, I decided, as you will recall, to concur. A dissent on this question would have been perceived as politicizing the court."

President Clinton would himself assert that the makeup of the three-judge panel was no coincidence. "You know," he said, "Sentelle was appointed by Chief Justice Rehnquist, who's a very shrewd man and knew exactly what he was doing when he named him [Sentelle] to that panel." As Clinton saw it, Judge Sentelle was exactly what the Republicans wanted, especially those who despised him most. "They're on a crusade," he said. "God has ordained them to crush the infidels. That's the way they look at it. So it's unfortunate when the rules of evidence, the rule of law, the facts, don't conform to what they want to do."

"Ken Starr was their errand boy," the former president said, folding up a pair of half-glasses and smacking them against his palm. "And he danced to their tune, just as hard as he could dance."

———

DAYS after the surprise announcement, Bob Fiske and Ken Starr, dressed in dark business suits, gathered with OIC attorneys in their cramped Little Rock office. The goal was to lay out a transition plan and hopefully to avoid a stampede.

Fiske had worked with Starr over the years and respected him—he had even tried to recruit Starr to his law firm after Starr stepped down as solicitor general. Now, Fiske's goal was simple. "I wanted there to be a minimum amount of disruption," he would later say.

A palpable tension gripped the meeting room. As Fiske introduced his successor with gracious remarks, Starr returned the kind words, waxing eloquent about the gentlemanly Fiske. At one point during the awkward session, Starr in his affable style placed one hand on Fiske's knee and said, "I love this man." There was a collective gasp. Recalled Bill Duffey, "And it just struck people as peculiar."

Julie O'Sullivan, seated across from the two independent counsels, perceived that part of the unhappy reaction was due to the fishy-smelling circumstances. Many staffers knew that Fiske had recently approached Starr about working on an amicus brief in the *Paula Jones* case. Now Starr had been sneaking around talking to the special court, right under Fiske's nose? "And the sort of sense was that, 'Well, if you love him so much, you know, why did you take his job?'"

Starr seemed startled that so many OIC prosecutors were talking about quitting. He pleaded with the lawyers: "Please give me the consideration of at least thinking about it. Or allowing me to talk to you individually about it." Their faces remained blank. Rusty Hardin, the hard-charging Texas trial attorney who had been recruited by Fiske to try the David Hale case, said the scene resembled "a Brown & Root safety convention." Nobody was smiling. In plain Texas terms, it came down to this: "You know, you've taken away Daddy, man."

O'Sullivan saw it as unfortunate all the way around. "Ken Starr did his best in a bad situation," she said. Under these circumstances, however, it wasn't good enough.

Before Ken Starr caught a flight en route to a family beach vacation, Bob Fiske gave him two direct pieces of advice: "One, I told him he should move down here [to Arkansas], both for appearance reasons, and because it's the only way to get the job done. Two, I told him to get someone very experienced in criminal prosecutions to help him, since he did not have that background."

Years later, Fiske would say with a hitch of disapproval: "He agreed to the second, but not to the first."

———

THE transition from Robert Fiske to Ken Starr might have produced fewer sparks if another firecracker had not exploded. On August 12, the *Washington Post* disclosed that just before Fiske was canned, Judge Sentelle had lunched in the Capitol with Senators Lauch Faircloth and Jesse Helms, both Republicans from North Carolina who had been vocal opponents of reappointing Fiske. With the revelation of the "clandestine" Sentelle lunch, all hell broke loose.

The political connections between these three men only heightened the suspicions of home-cooking. Sentelle had grown up in North Carolina, where Helms had been his political mentor; it was Helms who had sponsored Sentelle for appointments to the federal district court and the court of appeals. Faircloth, a wealthy hog farmer from rural North Carolina, had been friendly with the judge back when Sentelle was a local Republican Party chairman. An unidentified witness now told *Post* reporters that Faircloth and Sentelle had been engaged in an "animated" discussion while waiting for the tram underneath the Capitol complex. Rumors swirled around that another witness had heard the men discussing the replacement of Fiske at lunch in the Senate dining room.

Judge Sentelle suspended his usual rule of declining interviews with the media and wrote a sharp retort to the *Post* reporter, denying any impropriety. He noted that both Faircloth and Helms were "old friends" with whom he socialized on occasion. At their lunch in the Senate dining room, Sentelle insisted, most of the conversation had revolved around "prostate difficulties," combined with "western hats, boots, and my relatives in Texas." Judge Sentelle insisted: "To the best of my recollection nothing in these discussions concerned independent counsel matters."

As the "Sentelle lunch" story exploded in the national press, five former presidents of the American Bar Association declared that the lunch "[gave] rise to the appearance of impropriety." Thirty-six Democratic members of Congress wrote to Sentelle decrying his meeting with the Republican senators and calling for Starr's "immediate resignation."

The truth concerning the now-infamous Sentelle lunch with Senators Faircloth and Helms remains one of the unresolved mysteries of the Whitewater saga. Evidence confirms that *Washington Post* reporters had located at least one source who observed the three men engaged in an animated discussion in the bowels of the Capitol, en route to lunch. One prosecutor in the Office of Independent Counsel, himself a Republican, recalled receiving a phone call from a reporter working on the story. This journalist indicated that "a confidential source"—identified as a lobbyist—"had been on a little railway underneath the Capitol complex" and had overheard the conversation between Faircloth and Sentelle. Moreover, "the lobbyist had told [the reporter] in background that they were talking about getting rid of Fiske." Another OIC prosecutor confirmed that he or she had received a call from the *Post* repeating that information and indicating that the confidential source was trustworthy.

In response to a series of written questions years later, Judge Sentelle would address these charges forcefully: "Neither Faircloth nor Helms ever attempted to influence me or to the best of my knowledge any other member of this or any other court in any way, manner, or means. Not only did neither one of them ever specifically suggest Ken Starr, neither of them knew Ken Starr from Adam's off ox." Sentelle added: "We did not discuss Fiske, Starr, or any other matter related to the independent counsel, unless there was some casual mention of whether we had appointed one or not."

Under oath before a Senate committee in 1999 he stated: "There is no vast right-wing conspiracy out to get anybody, and if there was one, we would not meet in the Senate dining room. We would do it by telephone or in secret somewhere. If we were that nefarious, we are not that dumb."

Even Judge Butzner, who vigorously opposed the appointment of Starr, believed that the uproar over the Sentelle lunch amounted to constructing a mountain out of a molehill. At the same time, Butzner remained distressed by other problems, which seemed to mount by the day. Democratic Senator Carl Levin of Michigan—who headed the subcommittee overseeing independent-counsel matters—wrote to the three-judge court on August 12 charging that Starr "lacks the necessary independence." Among other things, Senator Levin pointed to the fact that Starr had appeared on the *MacNeil/Lehrer NewsHour* just months earlier, taking the public position that the president could be sued civilly in a sexual harassment lawsuit such as the *Jones* case.

On his own copy of Senator Levin's letter, Butzner underlined these charges of partisanship against the appointee. He scribbled on that portion of the letter, which was later preserved in his private papers: "Mr. Starr did not mention this at our interview. Nor did he comment on a brief in the Paula Jones case [referring to news reports that Starr had consulted with a conservative women's group about filing an amicus brief in the *Jones* litigation]."

Butzner continued to believe that the entire decision to replace Fiske with Starr was ill considered. Straightening his thick glasses, then pushing away the oxygen tube that lay against his yellow sweater, the white-haired retired judge sat up in his wheelchair and uttered a clear, unambiguous statement, the only full sentence he would muster during this interview session. He said, slowly and emphatically, "I was against Starr, from start to finish."

KEN STARR: SPECIAL PROSECUTOR

As Ken Starr's Office of Independent Counsel got under way—just two months after Starr had consulted with Gil Davis about the *Paula Jones* case—President Clinton blamed himself and the Democrats in Congress, in equal measure, for allowing the expired independent counsel law to rise from the grave and wreak havoc on his presidency. His own Democratic Party, he lamented, "always wanted to look purer than Caesar's wife." Admitted Clinton, "I was as guilty as anybody else. I signed [the law]. We forgot that this whole independent-counsel thing was an overreaction to President Nixon's firing of Archibald Cox. And that in truth, the system worked there. Nixon wound up with an independent counsel. That worked. It worked its way through the system."

In hindsight, the president admitted, reviving this "legal monstrosity" was a horrible blunder for which he paid a steep price. "You have to go all the way back to the early days of [the republic] to find politics as personally venomous as they were in my presidency," he said. "And the Framers would not have been surprised at all at the conduct of Starr and his aides. They thought anybody given unaccountable power would abuse it."

Ken Starr, as he settled into his role as independent counsel, did not view himself as an out-of-control ogre with a partisan political agenda. He later expressed deep disappointment that Clinton would assail him, in such a personal fashion, when he was simply doing his job. Sitting on a couch in his home in McLean, Virginia, after the trauma of the Clinton investigation had subsided, Starr noted that his staff consisted of top-notch professionals, "some of whom had voted for President Clinton." He hastily added, "I came to find out. I never asked about politics in interviews." According to Starr, his overriding goal as Whitewater independent counsel "was to re-create a microcosm of the Justice Department . . . complete with procedural safeguards to guard against the abuse of power."

In order to remain doubly sure that his office acted with zero partisan influence, Starr noted, every decision was subject to "review by the participation of and by [ethics adviser] Sam Dash, which I think was a useful outside check." Dash, a hero of Watergate and a prominent Democrat, was the antithesis of a Republican activist. Starr would counter, in responding to President Clinton's charges that his office had misused its power, that "an assault on the professionalism of the investigation is an assault on the professionalism and reputation of the late Sam Dash."

Starr's first important move as independent counsel was to recruit a new legal team to oversee both the Arkansas and the Washington phases of the investigation. Aware of his own lack of prosecutorial experience, he wanted to compensate by assembling lawyers with a deep reservoir of talent. As his first step, he appointed Hickman Ewing, Jr. (whom Bob Fiske had recommended as a possible hire), to take over the Little Rock office.

Ewing, a former federal prosecutor from Memphis with an easy Southern drawl, had two decades' worth of experience trying white-collar crime and corruption cases. Famous in Tennessee for his photographic memory and his ability to captivate juries with spellbinding orations, Ewing was everything Ken Starr wanted in branding OIC with his own signature.

At age fifty-three, Ewing had moved into private practice after spending the bulk of his career as a federal prosecutor. He had served for eight years during the Reagan presidency as U.S. attorney in Memphis, until he was tossed out in 1988 due to Republican infighting, an experience that had left professional scars on him. A Vietnam veteran who had served as an officer on a navy swift-boat, Ewing had been forever haunted by the fact that his alcoholic father, Hickman Ewing, Sr., had landed in prison for stealing public funds. Once a legendary high school football and basketball coach, the senior Ewing had been elected as Shelby County court clerk, later pleading guilty to embezzlement. He served eighteen months in prison and was stripped of his state citizenship, having been "rendered infamous" under Tennessee law. The family's home was burned to the ground. It was a "devastating" time for Hickman, Jr.

It was also what made him predisposed to handling—and winning—the toughest and ugliest public corruption cases. As U.S. attorney in Memphis, Ewing had become "one of the South's winningest lawmen." He had brought down a governor, ten sheriffs, a few state legislators, a Memphis State basketball coach, and a handful of moonshiners. During this period, Ewing came to embrace, openly, a fundamentalist Christian life. In 1980 he published a law review article titled "Combating Official Corruption by All Available Means," summarizing his own philosophy as a prosecutor by pointing to the Old Testament's First Book of Samuel as a warning against public corruption: "And his sons walked not in his ways, but turned aside after lucre, and took bribes, and perverted judgment."

A state senator who spent two years in prison after being convicted by Ewing said, "If you were the president of the United States, or anyone else that Mr. Ewing was pursuing, I'd say you're in great danger." Before long, Ewing's reputation took on a new dimension: He came to symbolize "Exhibit A" for those who viewed Starr's office as a group of anti-Clinton prosecutorial zealots.

Ken Starr arranged to meet with Hick Ewing at the Sweet Pea Buffet (pronounced "boofay," in proper Southern dialect) in the tiny Arkansas town of Brinkley. This spot was midway between Nashville and Little Rock, a propitious place to determine if they shared any common ground. As Ewing recalled the meeting: "We had lots of chicken and vegetables and barbecue and talked for about three hours and got acquainted." Before they drove back to their respective home bases that night, Starr had offered Ewing a job "looking at everything" within the Whitewater orbit. For starters, Ewing would be "debriefing Webster Hubbell with an eye toward a plea deal."

Ken Starr was impressed with Ewing's strong record of pursuing public corruption. Starr also felt a special kinship with this Memphis lawman because Ewing was an unapologetic Christian who did not park his beliefs at the doorstep when he reported to work. Shortly after Ewing was hired, he was seated at breakfast with Starr at the Waffle House in West Little Rock. The wiry prosecutor removed a pen and sketched out a game plan for the Whitewater investigation on the back of his menu. At Starr's request, Georgetown law professor Sam Dash had addressed the lawyers in Little Rock about ethics and prosecutorial techniques. Ewing now reflected on the serious task that lay before them. When it came to President and Mrs. Clinton, his candid view was, "Personally, I don't think much of their politics, but again, I'm not a political-type person." Ewing was concerned about making sure that both Clintons were forthcoming. "I prayed for them all the time," he later explained. "I prayed that the truth would come out. I want[ed] to find out what happened."

In sketching out an investigative plan for the Whitewater/Madison case, Ewing told his boss over breakfast, "Look, the way I pray is—it's no mystery to God what happened to Vince Foster or what Bill did or what Hillary did. I pray that He'll give us wisdom and disclose to us as much as we can handle in the plan of things."

Folding up the rough plan contained on Ewing's menu, the two men agreed that their overriding duty, in the months (or years) ahead, was to push over every rock in looking for the truth.

———

STARR'S second major appointment in Little Rock was Jackie Bennett, a towering six-foot-three man who grew up in a blue-collar family outside Indianapolis
and then moved to the river town of Madison, Indiana, to attend Hanover College. Bennett played tight end on the football team, excelled at Indiana University
Law School, clerked for several judges, and prosecuted criminals in the U.S.
Attorney's Office near home. He then caught the bug to move beyond the world
of railroads and metal works, accepting an offer to join the Public Integrity Section of the Justice Department in Washington, a huge honor for a small-town boy
from Indiana. Bennett's feeling was, "DOJ can show me the world."

The newly formed Public Integrity Section, born of the Watergate era,
when American citizens had developed a distrust for elected officials, was a perfect fit for Bennett. Originally a Democrat, he had switched his registration to
Republican when he became disillusioned with the wishy-washy policies of the
Carter administration. Now, moving to Washington in the midst of the transition from the Reagan to the Bush presidencies, Bennett felt at home. He saw
himself, above all, as a federal prosecutor who put criminals behind bars without
regard to political affiliation. Bennett had prosecuted Senator David Duren-
berger of Minnesota, a Republican who had used public tax dollars to pay the
mortgage on a condo and then submitted false vouchers, and convicted Texas
Democratic Congressman Albert Bustamante on racketeering and bribery
charges. For this last effort, Bennett received a prestigious John Marshall Award,
bestowed by President Clinton's newly appointed attorney general, Janet Reno.

In his soul, Bennett believed that Public Integrity prosecutors were a distinctive breed. "We prided ourselves on being the storm troopers who had to sort
of parachute into a political hot spot," he said, spelling out his job description.
Based on their grit and nonpolitical orientation, lawyers in Public Integrity
were entrusted to handle the most sensitive cases, an assignment that he loved.

Outwardly gruff but inwardly gentle, Bennett disarmed opponents with his
blunt style. Speaking years after the Whitewater and Lewinsky cases had left
scars on his psyche, Bennett freely admitted that he had grown to become dis-
enchanted with the Public Integrity Section after the Clinton crowd took over.
During the Reagan and Bush years, Bennett felt, there had been a "different tone
in Washington," at least "at a moral level." He had now become "soured" by his
belief that cases were being prosecuted or declined more often according to politics, once the Clinton people took over. Never one to mince words, Bennett acknowledged that he believed that President Bill Clinton was making Justice
Department appointments who were "gaming it," who were "affecting the process in an improper way" based on politics.

Leaning forward at his executive desk at an Indianapolis law firm, after the Starr investigations had receded into history, Bennett said, "I point back to Bill Clinton for that. I think that the fish rotted from the head down. I think he set the tone."

So when Ken Starr offered to rescue him from this purgatory, Bennett leaped at the chance. Starr drove Bennett from the Little Rock airport to the OIC offices, on a snowy January day in 1995, pointing out the beautiful Arkansas scenery and confiding, for Bennett's ears only, that he hoped to have the whole case "wrapped up by year's end." As Bennett would reconstruct that conversation later, "I mean, he wasn't blowing smoke. I think he honestly thought that could happen."

To those who would later accuse Starr's prosecutors of prolonging the Whitewater/Madison investigation because of political bias, Bennett would respond: "Look, a lot of people would like to make the case—let's get right to it—that Ken Starr staffed his office with a bunch of right-wingers who were determined to take him [Clinton] down," said Bennett. "And I'm probably not a good argument in rebuttal."

Yet Bennett said that deep in his heart, he did not believe that "any personal views that I had of Bill Clinton" affected his ability to remain neutral, at least initially.

Indeed, he would later share an anecdote: He had attended the inaugural parade of Clinton in 1993 with friends who had reserved a choice spot on the balcony of the FBI offices looking over Pennsylvania Avenue. On that day, Bennett had felt a positive sense of energy. "Politically, George [H. W.] Bush wasn't my kind of president," he confessed in a deep baritone. Bush seemed "feckless" and uninspiring. "I wasn't passionate about him. And this new guy, Clinton— Boy, he's talented, he's smart. He's performing [well] in the debates." Bennett's assessment as he watched the pomp and festivities of the inaugural parade was, "The better guy won. That's how I viewed it."

Not until he battled the Clinton White House during the Whitewater and Monica Lewinsky ordeals did Bennett irrevocably change his mind.

His eyes becoming steely, Bennett said, "I formed judgments, I'm not going to deny that. I came to think, 'This is a corrupt person.' It took me a while to get to that point. And I will go to my grave believing it fervently; I'd bet my house on it." He summed up his views of the president, whom he would pursue unsuccessfully for five years: "This guy is the most corrupt political figure, in my view, we've ever had. . . . That's him. That's who he is. That's who he's been all along, in my view."

———

As Ken Starr took over the reins as Whitewater independent counsel, it was obvious that he approached the job in ways that dramatically differed from his predecessor. Robert Fiske's parting advice to Starr about moving to Little Rock had been a nonsubtle hint about working full-time as independent counsel. For Fiske it "was an all-consuming job." Additionally, there would be "appearance problems" if one was caught moonlighting in the practice of law when one was supposed to be heading an investigation of this magnitude. Fiske later explained his philosophy: "The only reason an independent counsel is appointed is because there are public allegations against the president. These need to be resolved quickly one way or the other. The president should not be under an unresolved cloud any longer than absolutely necessary."

Ken Starr, however, had always been a multitasker. "The whole structure of the independent counsel statute was that this was a part-time [position]," he explained, "in the sense that you did not leave your law firm. That was expressly contemplated in the statute." Starr had only recently joined the Kirkland & Ellis firm in Washington, and he helped build its appellate section. During the interview with the three-judge panel that appointed him, he had explicitly stated that he was not prepared to abandon the firm. If the judges had said that he had to resign from his law practice, Starr said, "it would have been a very different decision for me."

Nor did Starr believe that he was shirking his duties. He rented an apartment at the Shadow Lake complex in Little Rock to maintain a presence amid his Arkansas staff. He also tirelessly churned out work on planes and in cabs. When he sneaked off for weekends with the family, Alice would usually drive so that Ken could sit in the passenger seat, marking up briefs or sketching out oral arguments on tablets.

When he was in Washington, Starr would schedule meetings at the Kirkland firm in the mornings and then head over to the OIC office on Pennsylvania Avenue for the rest of the day. In Arkansas, he did the bulk of his private work at night. "So I continued to practice law as best I could while at the same time giving [OIC work] top priority," he explained. "And the hours would reflect that. The hours devoted to the OIC eclipse the hours that I was devoting to [law practice at] Kirkland."

The small group of holdover OIC prosecutors, who had previously labored alongside Robert Fiske shoulder-to-shoulder, saw a dramatic change the moment Starr took over. None of them viewed Starr as a right-wing nut. Nor did they see him as a Christian extremist or as a political zealot. Yet most worried that he was a former appellate judge, with no prosecutorial experience, who had spread himself too thin with other commitments as he worked on the investigation in slow motion, on a less-than-full-time basis, losing gobs of time.

Bill Duffey, the senior lawyer in the Little Rock office who had functioned as its de facto deputy under Fiske, was later quick to praise Starr for his "deep academic interest in legal issues." Still, Duffey and his fellow prosecutors with decades' worth of experience in criminal investigations were startled by the new independent counsel's lack of preparedness for the job. He recalled being floored when Judge Starr quizzed him about how to assess a "certain witness's trustworthiness." When Duffey gave his appraisal of whether the witness was lying through his teeth, Starr asked in awe, "Well, how can you tell that?" The new independent counsel seemed to be an academic fish out of water. Although Starr seemed earnest and well intentioned, Duffey observed that the line prosecutors had to regularly coach the new boss "to help him interpret the facts that were being developed."

For OIC lawyer Gabrielle Wolohojian, the starkest difference between Starr and Fiske was that Starr "wasn't physically present as much." When Fiske was in charge, prosecutors could ask him about subpoenas or witnesses at any time of the day or night. He was virtually nailed to his desk and would instantly give them expert guidance based on decades of experience as a federal prosecutor. Starr, on the other hand, floated in and out of the office and reached most major decisions by seeking consensus from the group. He was a "big-picture-type" guy, a pleasant father figure who tended to revert to his judicial role and seek out the "collective judgment" of staffers in order to compensate for his own lack of experience. Getting concrete action accomplished in the Starr office often required a "cycle" of a week or two. Prosecutors needed to arrange a sit-down when their new boss was in town or set up conference calls, so that Starr could vet the issue with his whole staff.

The difference between Fiske and Starr was "a bit too stark for many people on the staff," noted one former OIC prosecutor. As this lawyer with Republican credentials observed it, Starr was a product of a "pretty bookish environment," whereas most OIC prosecutors had come from the rough-and-tumble world of criminal prosecutions. They handled blood and guts on a daily basis and didn't have time to deal with academic exercises. Summing it up as gently as possible, this former prosecutor would say that he would "hire [Starr] in an instant to represent me in the court of appeals," but not to run a major criminal investigation. He would explain, requesting not to be identified: "I wouldn't try to do brain surgery, either."

The holdover lawyers also believed there was another problem with switching leaders in midstream. Duffey lamented, "It was just harder to get people to leave their practices or to leave their government jobs, to come into an investigation a year after it started." Hundreds of impressive résumés were flooding into the office. But they were no longer top draft choices. Duffey, who coordinated interviews at that time, found it "shocking" that many would-be prosecutors openly announced that they wanted a job because they had a "political [predisposition]" and were itching to do battle with President Clinton.

Still, OIC prosecutors gave Ken Starr high marks for working to avoid hiring overt partisans. Mark Tuohey, a veteran of the Jimmy Carter Justice Department whom Starr hired to head up the Washington office, said that any time he scratched an applicant off the list because he determined the person was "politically motivated," Starr backed him up completely. As Tuohey later said, "It was very professionally conducted in the front office."

Yet some staffers worried that new hires with strong anti-Clinton views were slipping through the cracks, largely because Starr was "tone deaf." Moreover, there was a concern that they were settling for "second-tier" lawyers to fill vacancies. Many of Fiske's most highly qualified hires had quietly made the exodus back to their pre-Whitewater careers. The OIC operation was slowly restocked with a new brand of prosecutors, many of whom were young, aggressive, and untested.

Some prosecutors, especially those who had uprooted their families to move to Little Rock, were miffed that Starr was still living in Northern Virginia and commuting to Arkansas. They became downright "irritated" when Starr announced that he was jetting off to teach a course at New York University School of Law before he had even celebrated his first anniversary as independent counsel. They became even more distressed when their boss announced that he was taking three weeks off to teach a summer course at Pepperdine University School of Law in Malibu, California. Nobody doubted that Starr had a "huge capacity for work." There was no question that he toiled away at his multiple occupations every night and weekend. Still, he couldn't walk into a phone booth and turn into Superman. As several top OIC prosecutors saw it, although their boss might be "thinking about" Whitewater while he was in distant cities, his "absence and our inability to interact with him" had the impact of "slow[ing] us down."

"I had no idea how much time he was spending [elsewhere]," said Wolohojian. "I only could tell how much time he was spending in our office. And I didn't consider it to be sufficient."

Picking up their families and moving to Arkansas while putting their "real" legal careers on hold, many staffers believed, created a powerful incentive to "wrap [the case] up and go home." Starr had insulated himself from that incentive by clinging to his toehold in Washington. Like the fabled turtle who resolved to win the race at a quarter-mile an hour, the most consistent criticism of Ken Starr did not relate to lack of honorable intentions. Rather, it related to lack of speed.

As Bill Duffey would sum it up, "I have always said that, if he [Ken Starr] had done it full time, we would have been at the point of [wrapping up the investigation] when the Monica Lewinsky thing came up." This in turn would have caused the attorney general to appoint "a different independent counsel" to investigate that explosive matter.

"Which, I think, would have led to a totally different result."

———

KEN Starr tried to compensate for his handicaps by signing up Sam Dash as an ethics adviser on a contract basis. Dash was a legend in Democratic circles, having served with distinction as chief counsel to the Senate Watergate Committee. An expert in white-collar crime and legal ethics, Dash had also helped to draft the independent counsel statute. If Starr wanted a face that represented nonpartisanship and objectivity, he could not have done any better than Sam Dash's.

Dash, for his part, saw this as a ripe opportunity to ensure that the independent counsel statute fulfilled its original, noble purpose. Dash later explained that he accepted this assignment enthusiastically because he wanted to keep the independent counsel statute from being unfairly tarnished. "There was criticism of Lawrence Walsh in Iran-Contra," said Dash years later, "but I thought that most of it was unfair. And I wanted to play a role to make sure that, in this particular case, since it was a highly political, controversial matter involving the president and Whitewater and the Madison Bank and all those things, that perhaps—by my presence as an ombudsman—I would be able to do something to help the statute be correctly implemented."

Sam Dash had big ears, a blaring Philadelphia voice, and a propensity for telling it straight. Signing him was viewed as a major coup for the Starr operation. But the two men did not always see eye-to-eye. Dash would often needle Starr and his deputies, saying, "The only thing that Whitewater has in common with Watergate is the word 'water.'" This joke usually did not produce smiles. "I think that Ken and some of his staff took offense at that," Dash said. "And their view was that I was sort of playing it down . . . that I was trying to demean his investigation. That was not my purpose." His point was that although Whitewater/Madison fell within the orbit of the statute, this did not make it the case of the century.

For one, none of the Whitewater or Madison dealings had anything to do with Bill Clinton's conduct as president. Nor did they even involve traditional federal issues.

Still, Dash felt he could do some good by keeping the investigation on an even keel. He would receive letters and phone calls at his law school office, berating him: "You ought to be ashamed of yourself. How would you work with that monster Ken Starr?" Dash would reply to these critics: "You're wrong. He [Ken] basically is a man of integrity and a decent person."

Dash still defended his former boss, even after he had quit Starr's employ and returned to the quietude of academia: "It may be that he was not the right person to have taken it in the first place. But that's not the point. I think Ken is dedicated to public service, and, unfortunately, got hurt by it."

———

THE daily functioning of Starr's office was professional and diligent. Most decisions were made only after convening meetings—sometimes with the whole staff—and allowing every prosecutor to provide input. It was, said Mark Tuohey, "a very collegial, collaborative style." Staffers observed no sign of hostility by Starr toward the Clintons. To the contrary, the new independent counsel displayed an old-fashioned reverence for the presidency. "I think that Ken was respectful of the office of the presidency and of the First Lady," said Tuohey, who ran the Washington office. "When certain facts came out on matters that suggested that there might be an involvement of one or more of the Clintons, Ken was always of the view that that had to be looked at very, very thoroughly and vetted thoroughly because you're talking about the office of the presidency." On a day-to-day basis, he said, "I didn't detect partisanship on Ken's part at all."

Moreover, popular fiction notwithstanding, Starr's office did not begin each meeting with a prayer. "We never did that—not one time—with any kind of meeting," said Hickman Ewing. He acknowledged that there was an element of respect given to Starr, in view of his religious background. Prosecutors and staffers "restrained themselves as far as profanity and other things if he was present," admitted Ewing, himself a lay minister. "This was simply because you knew where he was coming from and out of respect you toned it down." But this was not, he insisted, a religious revival tent.

Jackie Bennett, then stationed in Little Rock, acknowledged that Starr's style of running a prosecutor's office could be frustrating. "Everything [involved] spending time in meetings and talking and talking and talking. And I think even Ken would tell you, we probably did a little too much of that from time to time." Meetings could last three to eight hours, depending on the topic. Bennett described Starr's approach: "He's assimilating it. And that's probably not time that's all that badly spent. It was frustrating to us. It was expensive. It wasn't an efficient thing to do. But it wasn't foolish."

Most important, for Bennett, was Starr's unassailable judgment. "I can't think of any decisions on substantive issues that Ken got wrong. I'd be hard pressed to say, 'This was a mistake. This was a major mistake.'"

Moreover, Bennett marveled at Starr's remarkable capacity to produce. "I got on airplanes with him and had seen how the guy works," Bennett said. "On a leg between Washington and St. Louis, he would pull out a draft court of appeals brief, and he would sit there and mark it up and make it really sing. Now, that's what lawyers do."

Even Sam Dash, an expert in the field of complex criminal investigations, would dismiss as bunk portrayals of Starr as a bumbling, worthless independent counsel. "Ken worked almost twenty-four hours a day. I don't remember an important issue where Ken wasn't present, either physically or on the phone," Dash said, defending his former boss. It was clear that Starr was the person responsible for making "the ultimate decisions." But his management style "was that of a judge, rather than of a U.S. attorney." This meant that, as a rule, "he listened and decided issues like a mediator."

Whatever shortcomings Starr may have had as a prosecutor, Dash insisted that Ken Starr was not somebody who was asleep at the wheel: "He was not an absent independent counsel."

—————

As Whitewater prosecutor, Starr was not the diabolic Clinton-slayer that some (including Bill Clinton) would later make him out to be. "To hear some people say, 'Ken Starr parachuted in here and started witch hunting,'" Hickman Ewing said, "well, no." The Tennessee prosecutor noted that the investigations on Starr's plate were almost entirely continuations of work that Fiske had begun with the blessing of Clinton's own Justice Department, none of which had been seriously questioned.

For instance, on December 6, 1994, when Independent Counsel Starr announced to a cold gathering of camera crews that Webster Hubbell had pleaded guilty to two felony counts, this was merely the culmination of Fiske's work. Hubbell had confessed to engaging in a scheme to defraud the Rose Law Firm and its clients, as well as to filing fraudulent tax returns. The six-foot-five Hubbell wept as he promised to cooperate fully with Starr's prosecutors or to face a sentence of five years in prison and a fine of $250,000 on each count.

Robert Fiske's final report, filed under seal shortly after his departure, confirms that the Hubbell matter was largely complete even before Ken Starr entered the picture. From the start, Fiske's team had viewed Hubbell as a top priority. He had worked closely with Hillary Clinton and Vince Foster on Whitewater matters. If anyone held the key to information that might unlock the door to OIC's broader investigation, Hubbell seemed a likely candidate.

And this prosecution was regarded as a slam dunk. As Rusty Hardin, the

Texas lawyer who was scheduled to try the case, put it, "I mean a chimpanzee could have tried it. . . . I'll guarantee you, an Arkansas jury of twelve of his tried and truest friends, once they were exposed to the evidence against him, would have turned on him in a New York minute."

If anything, Starr's prosecutors came to believe that their boss had gone too easy on Hubbell. They would forever regret that their office had signed off on a weak plea deal (Hickman Ewing had been the principal negotiator) without ever demanding a *proffer,* or a detailed preview of Hubbell's testimony. Ken Starr had felt sympathy for Hubbell. He had taken the former assistant attorney general's word as a fellow public servant that he would cooperate fully. In the end, the prosecutors believed that they had gotten nothing but "a pig in a poke." They had been trusting and conciliatory; in return, they got nothing of value. Hubbell was shedding tears, they cursed among themselves, yet he told them nothing of any substance about the Clintons or any other major player.

Hubbell himself would express bafflement at the Starr prosecutors' growing certainty that he was stiffing them. He would later say, seated at a breakfast table at the Mayflower Hotel, "If they say I got some benefit out of the plea, I still don't know what that was. My understanding of the deal was that if I cooperated with the investigation, they would consider recommending a downward departure. . . . And in the end, they took no position on downward departure. And I got no downward departure. So I don't know what more they thought they could have gotten."

OIC delayed sentencing until late June, during which time, Hubbell later pointed out, "I met with congressional committees, I met with the FDIC [Federal Deposit Insurance Corporation], I met with everybody and anybody who wanted me. Including the other independent counsels by that time. They wanted me as well."

Hubbell insisted he was an open book. But OIC believed there were a few pages stuck together. "They clearly were wanting something on the president or First Lady," Hubbell said. "They asked everything from who was having affairs, to what was Hillary's involvement in Whitewater—what was Bill's involvement? They even asked, Did I have an affair with Hillary?" This was fueled, Hubbell surmised, by Jim McDougal's running around telling the press, "Webb knows where the bodies are buried." Hubbell put his coffee cup down and said, his eyes widening, "I mean, what's he talking about? I think the disappointment in their regard is that—probably Jackie Bennett's view is that I still know something. And I just don't know what it is. I mean, I'm being honest—it was never clear what they wanted me to say."

Ironically, the same Ken Starr whom the Clinton White House viewed as an overly zealous extremist, was getting a reputation within his own office as someone too trusting and who was not being aggressive enough. Hardin felt that the botched plea deal was directly attributable to Starr's naive expectation that people would "keep their word." Many OIC prosecutors agreed. "I mean, Ken Starr hadn't spent a life with people sitting there lying to his face," said Hardin. "They don't do that in appellate arguments."

Overall, Ken Starr's team of prosecutors felt that their boss was too weak and accommodating rather than too tough in his role as independent counsel. The Hubbell episode was a prime example.

Later, sipping iced tea in the cool comfort of his Texas law office, Hardin offered his opinion: "I don't have any doubt that Webb Hubbell held back. What he held back I don't know. I mean, did he have anything that could have changed the nature of the case? I don't know that. I'm not suggesting that. All I'm saying is that Webb Hubbell was not forthcoming.

"I think the judgment of history will be—we don't know what Webb Hubbell knew. I don't think we ever will."

THE Hubbell investigation, which later triggered charges that Starr's operation had strayed too far afield, was not the only piece of work that Ken Starr had inherited from Robert Fiske. The efforts to shore up David Hale as a witness and to see what goods this disgraced former municipal judge might have on President Bill Clinton had likewise begun well before Starr appeared on the scene.

Even before Starr took over, prosecutor Rusty Hardin had pulled Hale's lawyer into a closet in the courthouse and negotiated a deal by which Hale pledged to "truthfully disclose all information" relating to OIC's investigation. In return, OIC would seek leniency when it came time for sentencing.

What followed was an unusual series of secret meetings "in the woods of Arkansas" between FBI agents, Hardin, and Hale. During these long sessions, Hardin and his team tested the quality and quantity of the information Hale could supply. Years later, Hardin described the sessions: "We went off to a cabin. Okay? And literally, he [Hale] would be brought down by the FBI to meet with us from the undisclosed location he was being kept at, which I never knew where it was. And he'd be brought down for the meeting, and the debriefings would last six, seven hours. And then we would leave and go back to Little Rock, and he'd go back to his location."

Hardin and his FBI agents used time-tested techniques to determine if Hale was telling the truth: They would take events out of sequence, jumping back and forth from one period to another, so that Hale could not weave a false story without tripping himself up. Explained Hardin: "It's really not very different than the CIA getting somebody and taking them off into the woods in western Virginia for a while to try to find out whether they actually are a mole or whether they really are telling the truth."

There was no illusion that Hale, by himself, would enable OIC to land a big conviction. He was an admitted felon—a former public servant who had embezzled federal funds as part of a shameless "pyramid scheme." Prosecutors in the Sixth Judicial District of Arkansas were already investigating Hale for his burial-insurance fraud scheme. Evidence had also surfaced recently that Hale had engaged in a protracted extramarital affair with his secretary, and in the process swindled her grandparents out of $486,000. David Hale came with an enormous pile of baggage. If his testimony was to stick, there would have to be other witnesses corroborating it.

One prime candidate was James B. McDougal. The first failed prosecution of McDougal had left him penniless, without a wife, suffering from manic depression, and living in a trailer-cottage in Arkadelphia. Hale was now singing like a songbird, trilling away to OIC that he, Jim and Susan McDougal, then-Governor Jim Guy Tucker, and others had plotted to illegally divert $825,000 worth of Madison Guaranty Savings and Loan funds into various shady enterprises.

Emerging briefly from his nook in Arkadelphia, McDougal had spoken to *USA Today* and scoffed at Hale's agreement to "cooperate" with OIC. "They're going to let that filthy scumbag sit there and tell his story against the president of the United States?" McDougal asked. "That is one thing in life that I will do for Bill. I will flush [Hale] out."

Susan McDougal was living in Nashville with her now fiancé, Pat Harris, flying back and forth to California, where she had been charged with embezzling $150,000 from Nancy Mehta, the eccentric wife of renowned symphony conductor Zubin Mehta. Susan had been working for the couple during a two-year period in which she was attempting to pull her life back together. She was now accused of setting up a secret credit card account in the woman's name and using it for personal extravagances. Layered atop this mess was the bizarre relationship that had developed between Susan and her employer, by which (according to Susan's therapist) "Nancy had made me her husband in every sense except sexual." The embezzlement charges and the "unhealthy" nature of her personal association with Nancy Mehta had turned her life topsy-turvy again. In the midst of this chaos in her personal life, Susan was contacted by Ken Starr's office in March 1995 and was asked to pay a visit to the OIC offices in Little Rock.

According to Susan McDougal's account of that meeting, she arrived at Two Financial Center without any worries. Her ex-husband, Jim, had already been cleared of similar S&L charges—that was yesterday's news. A group of OIC prosecutors and FBI agents sat down at the table and told Susan that they would grant her "global immunity" if she gave them a complete, candid admission of everything she knew. According to Susan's account, one of the prosecutors said, "We want to know about the Clintons' role in Whitewater."

In response to the OIC prosecutors' request for information, Susan offered her cooperation: "I'll tell you everything I know about Bill and Hillary's role, from beginning to end." She saw smiles around the table. She continued: "There's one thing you should know, though. I don't know of anything wrong that either the president or the First Lady has done." According to McDougal's version of events, "the smiles disappeared."

On August 17, 1995, just one year after he was appointed independent counsel, Ken Starr indicted Jim McDougal, Susan McDougal, and Governor Jim Guy Tucker on multiple counts of defrauding the federal government. These charges involved different transactions from the failed 1990 prosecution of Jim McDougal and Susan's brothers involving Madison Guaranty and Castle Grande; there was no double-jeopardy problem (the defendants were not being retried for the same offense). The clock was ticking on the statute of limitations—OIC felt the need to move. Once again, this new action represented the culmination of an investigation begun by Robert Fiske.

Despite later accounts advanced by pro-Clinton advocates, suggesting that Ken Starr, in his role as Whitewater special prosecutor, was a partisan zealot from start to finish, the record fails to support this portrayal. Rather, Starr tended to be deliberate and cautious (at least initially), following closely in the footsteps of his predecessor Fiske.

The ingredients were the same; the principal difference was in how the soup was cooked. And for how long it simmered.

PAULA JONES ON FILM

One detail that is often overlooked, in assessments of the train wreck that came to be known as the Clinton scandal, relates to causation: With or without Ken Starr, the *Paula Jones* case was barreling down the track, headed toward President Bill Clinton.

Part of the path that the *Jones* litigation took was as foreseeable as a tornado touching down in Arkansas. Journalist Michael Isikoff had quit the *Washington Post* after a standoff with his editors, jumping over to *Newsweek*. Here, the determined reporter was drilling into the facts of the Jones story with renewed vigor. From the start, it was easy to predict that the suit would eventually lead to the questioning of Bill Clinton, under oath, about "other women." Yet the White House somehow missed that clue.

President Clinton would struggle, years later, to sort out the myriad acts of God that converged to humiliate him in the *Jones* lawsuit. Sitting in his study in Chappaqua, squinting against the sun that streamed through the window, the former president weighed his response carefully. In terms of his own view of what motivated Paula Corbin Jones, he answered slowly: "It couldn't have been what she [Jones] said." He paused. "Why do I say that? Because she said she wanted to clear her name. I didn't besmirch her name. The *American Spectator* besmirched her name." Besides, Clinton added, "Nobody reads the *American Spectator* in Arkansas, and if they did, they wouldn't know who she was. And when I was asked about it, after she became public, I said it wasn't true. I said exactly what she wanted me to say." The former president squeezed his fist and reiterated, "So, it wasn't a desire to clear her name."

Paula Jones, on the other hand, would later insist that all she wanted was vindication. "I was at the point where I was angry about it," she said, dipping her bread in olive oil in a cozy North Little Rock restaurant. "And I just wanted to get my good name back." It had already been floating around, thanks to the *Spectator* piece, that she had gone to Governor Clinton's hotel room. Moreover, Jones refused to back down from her charge that Bill Clinton's conduct constituted sexual harassment. "The reason why I felt it is," she said, "is because he was my boss, first of all. Ultimately my boss, because he was the governor for the office that I was working for. And Anita Hill claimed that a pubic hair on a Coke can was sexual harassment, and [that] had nothing to do with it [her work]. Well, this man took me up to a room and exposed himself to me. And that is sexual harassment in the worst way, I would think. That is pathetic."

Jones emphasized that this was quite different from a female employee alleging "Oh, somebody said a lewd comment to me." She explained, "He exposed himself. . . . I think mine was sexual harassment in the worst way." Staring firmly ahead, she concluded, "And he knew what was on his mind."

As the case got under way, Gil Davis and Joe Cammarata were taking creative, even unorthodox steps to force the president to pay their client big money damages. Cammarata, a thin and energetic young attorney who combed his black hair straight back—leading some to compare him to the wisecracking Italian lawyer in the film *My Cousin Vinny*—loved inventing ingenious litigation maneuvers. He would later become a successful personal-injury lawyer favoring snazzy suits and gold cuff links. Already he was honing his craft, figuring ways to box President Bill Clinton into a corner so that it would be difficult for him to breathe.

Cammarata had already drawn up a sworn affidavit memorializing Paula Jones's allegations about the "distinguishing characteristic." In a bold maneuver, he now attempted to file that affidavit under seal in federal court, without turning over a copy to defense counsel as required. When Judge Susan Webber Wright disallowed this move, Cammarata placed a copy in a sealed envelope and delivered it to himself, with a piece of initialed Scotch tape on the back, so that there would be concrete evidence that Jones had described the anatomical characteristic first, in case the White House tried to leak it and claim that Paula was parroting the media.

Ten years later, Cammarata still kept the controversial "distinguishing characteristic" affidavit, its seal unbroken, inside a file placed in an undisclosed location. A copy of that affidavit, obtained from a different source, revealed that it contained Jones's sworn statement that when then-Governor Clinton had exposed himself, she observed that his male organ "was bent or 'crooked' from Mr. Clinton's right to left, or from an observer's left to right if the observer is facing Mr. Clinton."

The distinguishing-characteristic affidavit was not the only trick up the sleeve of the Jones lawyers. Gil Davis, in a memo to Cammarata dated May 16, 1994, had already advised his younger associate: "An investigative team needs to locate Gennifer Flowers who has seen the matter 'up close and personal.' She needs to be interviewed for her description."

As the Virginia lawyers went in search of Flowers, Cammarata simultaneously contacted the Washington office of the American Civil Liberties Union

(ACLU), pressing the liberal organization to take a stand on behalf of his client. This move was designed to demonstrate that the *Jones* lawsuit was not a "Republican hatchet job." It was also aimed at shaming liberal feminist groups into siding with Jones. (A similar letter also was sent to the National Organization for Women.) In forwarding Cammarata's request to the ACLU's New York and Arkansas offices, the chief legal director of the Washington office penned a whimsical note: "Happy decision-making!"

In one of his most audacious moves, Cammarata went as far as to draft a resolution for Congress to pass. He faxed and delivered copies to prominent Republicans on Capitol Hill, including Senator Don Nickles (R-Okla.), in an effort to prod that body into taking action favorable to Paula's case. In a draft document preserved in the attorneys' files and dated July 1995, Cammarata proposed a resolution that almost certainly would have violated the U.S. Constitution's command against bills of attainder and ex post facto laws. After a few "whereas" clauses stating that "sexual harassment is degrading to the victim and can cause great lasting personal distress," Cammarata proposed self-serving language by which Congress would declare that a private citizen like Jones could sue a president like Bill Clinton in a civil case.

Many of these litigation moves were simply a "wing and a prayer," as Cammarata later admitted with a grin. Yet they began to create a sense of discomfort within the White House, like a terrible stomach cramp. When combined with the Whitewater and McDougal mess, this state of perpetual unease was something that the Virginia lawyers used to their advantage.

Still, Clinton's team had some major factors working in its favor. Judge Susan Webber Wright, a Republican appointee of President George H. W. Bush, had headed Bush's 1988 campaign operation in Arkansas. Yet she had a reputation as a jurist who called pitches down the middle. Wright had been a student of Clinton's when he was a law professor at University of Arkansas at Fayetteville. (Professor Clinton was so preoccupied with running for Congress that he lost her admiralty exam, requiring her to retake the test.) Wright knew of his rampant reputation as a womanizer. At the same time, the forty-five-year-old Wright was a disciplined jurist who kept politics out of her courtroom. She dressed without frills, like a schoolteacher. She won over lawyers with her direct style and her whimsical wit. This was not someone, from the viewpoint of Clinton's lawyer, Bob Bennett, who was going to butcher federal precedent dealing with sexual harassment (which, among other things, required concrete proof of adverse job consequences) simply to allow the Jones camp to inflict political damage on Clinton. The rule of law was important to Judge Wright. When it came time to do her duty, Bennett would later say, "I thought we'd get a fair shot."

In late August, Bennett filed a one-paragraph motion to dismiss, asking that Judge Wright stay the litigation until William Jefferson Clinton "is no longer President, at which time the plaintiff may refile the instant suit." Bennett attached a sixty-seven-page brief, citing precedents dating back to the founding of the nation. Solicitor General Drew S. Days III, a former Yale law professor with impeccable credentials, filed a statement of interest on behalf of the U.S. government, supporting the White House position.

In the history of the nation, presidents had only been subjected to private lawsuits three times; in each case, the suits were based on conduct that arose before the men took office. In 1904, a lawsuit against President Teddy Roosevelt and members of the New York City Board of Police—filed before Roosevelt took office—was promptly resolved in the president's favor. In 1946, a suit for monetary damages against President Harry S. Truman, flowing from his conduct as a state court judge more than a decade earlier, was decided in Truman's favor. In 1962, President John F. Kennedy had quietly settled a minor lawsuit arising out of an automobile accident that took place during the 1960 campaign, after JFK's motion to stay the case under the federal Soldiers' and Sailors' Civil Relief Act—which allowed military members to suspend or postpone certain civil actions—had been denied.

Truth be told, there was no clear precedent. In 1982, the Supreme Court in *Nixon v. Fitzgerald* had declared that a president had broad constitutional immunity from civil suit while in office, relating to his *official* duties. Civil suits related to a president's private conduct before the leader took office, however, were entirely different. The *Jones* case was now turning into a matter of constitutional importance.

Davis and Cammarata filed their own seventy-five-page brief opposing the president's motion. At a raucous press conference held in Washington, with a sobbing Paula Jones at his side, Davis told the crowd of reporters and supporters: "All Americans, now and forever, will owe a debt of gratitude to Paula Corbin Jones. We will know finally, and forever, that we are all equal before the law. This will be her legacy to us, to her child, to our children, and to our posterity to the last generation."

Despite that invocation of patriotism and apple pie, Judge Susan Webber Wright was not so easily seduced. She decided to split the loaf. On one hand, Judge Wright wrote in a brief opinion: "The rights to Plaintiff Jones as an American citizen must be protected." At the same time, some decorum had to be maintained to protect the office of the presidency. Judge Wright's solution was to permit discovery and depositions relating to all parties, "including the President." At the same time, the trial would be postponed until "shortly after the President leaves office." This would occur in 1996 or 2000, depending on whether Clinton was reelected. Jones would eventually have her day in court. She could move forward with the rest of the case, including compelling Clinton's testimony under oath. In the interim, however, the trial would have to wait.

Attorneys on both sides declared victory. Appearing on *CNN Daybreak,* Davis announced that Jones was "quite pleased" with the ruling. Bob Bennett, speaking for the president, called the judge's ruling "an important victory for Mr. Clinton."

Privately, both sides were thrown for a loop. The Jones camp had lost its most valuable leverage for exacting big money from the president—the specter of forcing Clinton to go to trial while he occupied the White House. Bob Bennett was even less thrilled. He now had to prep the president for embarrassing testimony in these god-awful depositions. No matter what steps the judge took to put the deposition "under seal," the ugly details would be leaked to the press within hours. Washington was a sieve. For both sides, Judge Wright's decision was a mixed bag of artificial sweeteners and poison pills. Both sides promptly appealed Judge Wright's decision to the U.S. Court of Appeals for the Eighth Circuit.

Politics is the art of bobbing and weaving, delaying danger in hopes that a truck might hit one's opponent in the interim. The White House prayed that by postponing the trial long enough, President Clinton could shake free of his ultimate day of reckoning until after he left office. Among other things, this would deflate much of the "collateral value" out of the case. Its high monetary price tag was directly linked to the ability of the plaintiff's lawyers to put the screws on a sitting president. After Clinton was out of office, the Jones lawyers' golden ticket would vanish. They would be stuck with exactly what their client had started with: a weak case against a nonpresident.

Yet legal appeals, like high-stakes games of craps, often take unexpected rolls. The Eighth Circuit Court of Appeals swiftly overturned Judge Wright's Solomonic ruling, declaring that she had given the president too much slack.

Why Bill Clinton failed to settle the *Jones* case at this stage, before it moved to the Supreme Court, is one of the great riddles of the Clinton scandal. One source close to the White House later explained that the situation was much more complicated than met the eye. It would have been a simple matter to settle the case, said the source, "if it weren't for Paula Jones, Stephen Jones, Bill Clinton, and Hillary Clinton." The clear sense around the West Wing was that "Hillary was adamantly opposed to settling." President Clinton himself seemed to be gun-shy of cutting a check if it meant incurring the wrath of his wife. One source close to the First Family said, "I can imagine the [following] scenario. Hillary would say, 'Bill, did you do it?' referring to the alleged lewd advance on Paula Corbin Jones. The president would answer, 'No, no, no!' The First Lady would step closer and glare at him. 'Then *why* would you settle the case?' "

Another presidential adviser analyzed the predicament differently: "If you wound up paying Paula Jones money, how many other women would come out of the woodwork? Do you have any doubt that other people wouldn't come forward for their million? Instead of getting this behind us, [the White House] feared it might start more cases coming."

Besides, Clinton himself seemed to bristle genuinely at the notion of paying money to Paula Jones for the alleged transgression. Apart from his feeling of having a gun unfairly aimed at his head, Clinton also had a pragmatic problem: how to *pay* for any whopping settlement. "I had the lowest net worth of any president, in constant dollars, in modern history," he later pointed out. Although he did set up a legal defense fund, Clinton was loath to call up big donors and say, "Let someone bail me out here."

"In my whole life, I have been threatened a lot," he said. "And I have normally found it's a mistake to cave in to them. And I knew that there had been no sexual harassment."

At the same time, years after he left office, President Bill Clinton would concede that if he had it to do over, he would have settled the *Jones* case at this moment. "I should have done it for the same reason that I later tried to do it for seven hundred [thousand dollars], because it interferes with your work and it interferes with the headlines. It complicates the deal. But, you know . . . I wasn't going to apologize for doing something I didn't do. I didn't sexually harass her [Jones], and we were later able to prove that. And Judge Wright later found that her claims were without . . . merit."

Although the common wisdom today is that Clinton should have bitten the bullet, swallowed hard, and settled the *Jones* case immediately, a small group of trusted advisers was providing exactly the opposite advice to the White House. That minority view, in hindsight, may have been the wiser course. It boiled down to a swift and direct plan: Attack the allegations head-on; take depositions of Paula Jones and other key witnesses immediately. Then file a motion for summary judgment and have the case thrown out by Judge Wright before it gained any traction.

In a confidential memo to Clinton's inner circle during the early stages of the litigation, one unofficial adviser with experience in civil rights lawsuits counseled: "The discovery process should be used to the fullest extent in an offensive attack and with the intent to 'pin down' the plaintiff and her witnesses on a number of the facts. By locking them in early, they cannot continue with a lie or with changing facts." The writer went on: "A critical element of [Paula Jones's] case is . . . that she suffered adverse job terms and conditions." This provided the spot of vulnerability. "By quickly taking the depositions of the governmental officials in her chain of command and examining her work and employment records with a swift use of subpoenas could provide a quick and 'clean' basis for a summary judgment motion."

The basic premise of this minority plan was very simple: Judge Susan Webber Wright was a principled jurist. She would assess the *Jones* case and toss it out, like any other baseless claim in her courtroom that failed to meet the legal threshold. As a woman, she would look at the evidence with special skepticism and say to herself, "If I were in that position, I would have done things different than Paula Jones. Why go to this man's room?"

There was another fact, overlooked by the outside world, that supported this theory. Jones was not the first person to seek to turn Clinton's alleged womanizing into a federal lawsuit that yielded money damages. A number of anti–Bill Clinton suits had been bumping around the federal courthouse in Little Rock for years; in most cases, they had been swiftly dismissed as meritless. The federal judges were already on red alert for such sham lawsuits. Robert Wright, law professor and husband of Judge Wright (who was rumored to assist her in writing opinions), told reporters over drinks that his wife was not going to permit "just a parade of women coming through her court." Although he was no fan of Bill Clinton's, Professor Wright made clear that his wife would not tolerate a circus. He also quipped that, in any event, "from what I've heard, a lot of Bill Clinton's women have been satisfied customers."

This proposal to tackle Paula Jones head-on—a suggestion that never gained any traction in the White House—may have been right on the money. Yet politicians tend to ascribe political motives to others, believing that the whole world views life through a tinted political lens. In the end, the White House simply couldn't trust Judge Susan Webber Wright. They feared that given the chance, she would be unable to resist taking a shot at Clinton to help the GOP. For that reason, Clinton's advisers gave clear marching orders to presidential lawyer Bob Bennett—instead of attacking the *Jones* complaint, he was to string out the case and push it past the November 1996 presidential election. Once Clinton was safely reelected, the White House believed, Bill Clinton would be home free.

Here, the president's strategists made a fundamental miscalculation. Getting the case past the presidential election, it turned out, was precisely the factor that allowed all the pieces to click together, paving the way for *another* sex scandal that made Paula Jones's allegations blush in comparison.

———

THE elves were now busy cranking out briefs and draft pleadings for Davis and Cammarata, without a fee. They had formed (in essence) a miniature law firm, staffed by invisible partners whose names never appeared on a formal document and whose purpose was to help expose and bring down Bill Clinton.

In the normal world of civil litigation, driven by economic assessments—how much a case is worth and how much time it can justify—high-powered lawyers do not ordinarily draft letter-perfect briefs, on demand, without submitting a bill. Yet in the high-stakes world of presidential power and politics, there was no dearth of volunteers to suit up for the job. The *Paula Jones* case ordinarily would have been settled, at best, for "nuisance value." With President Bill Clinton injected into the equation as a defendant, however, the *Jones* case took on a special gleam, like valuable treasure. If played right, this case could return the Republicans to power in the White House. It lured to the treasure hunt some of the finest conservative legal talent in America.

Gil Davis was perfectly aware that the elves might have a "political agenda" in providing assistance. This did not render their work "objectionable" in his mind. Davis preferred to think of it as similar to a "third party writing a check to make a financial contribution to Paula's cause." The fact that elves were writing briefs to which he was signing his name was no different than "if you're a Supreme Court justice and you have a law clerk and the law clerk does work for you and gives you some drafts, but it's your work, so you read it carefully and you correct it."

Joe Cammarata had no trouble sleeping at night when it came to using the elves' work. "What do I care?" he asked later with a chuckle. "I mean, you know, a guy wants to send you a brief? Okay. I don't care if he's got [an angle]." Even if the person "doesn't like the president, just as long as it's accurate, it's helpful, you know, fine."

The files in the basement of the Virginia lawyers' office disclose a regular, active interchange between Jones's attorneys and elves Jerome Marcus and George Conway. The draft briefs and pleadings supplied by these two lawyers were first-rate and sophisticated—the sort of 14-karat legal work that a small two-man office like Davis's could never have cranked out on its own.

The elves also played a role as conduits of information. Davis and Cammarata began picking up all sorts of information about Bill Clinton and "other women," which they viewed as Clinton's Achilles' heel. Tucked away in their files was a report about Clinton's "coming on" to the lead baton twirler for the University of Arkansas football squad. One tip that Davis scribbled down from a Las Vegas caller on a radio talk show suggested that a woman "who had been a student of Bill Clinton's perhaps in law school, had been a girlfriend of his and had gotten pregnant by him and thereafter committed suicide." Davis filed these notes away under the heading "Similar Conduct."

Another internal memo indicated that Joe Cammarata had received a tip from a Ph.D. in Nevada who "claims to know a number of people w/photos of Clinton & [Susan] McDougal on the hood of car having sex." It added a parenthetical "Them, not the car!" There was also a note in the files, from a journalist source in Arkansas, that indicated: "Will be receiving list of 14 or 17 children who are supposedly Clinton's." Another widespread rumor, recorded in multiple notes to the file, was that a woman whose father had worked for the British Secret Service "got pregnant" by Clinton and was now in hiding in Australia. An even darker tip, supplied by a retired preacher from Arkansas, suggested that Clinton "killed 2 boys: on railroad tracks. There were two other witnesses."

There were stories galore about Bill Clinton's purported affair with former Miss Arkansas Sally Perdue, who had gone public by telling London's *Sunday Telegraph* that she had engaged in numerous clandestine liaisons with Clinton during his governorship. (According to Perdue, state troopers would drop off the governor in a wooded area near her home and wait for Clinton to flick her patio light on and off as a signal that it was time to retrieve him.) Perdue told the press: "I want this affair wrapped up and dropped in the garbage can." There were also stories about an affair between Clinton and Dolly Kyle Browning, one of his classmates from Hot Springs High, who had recently published a book about her "affair with a Southern pol who happens to be Bill Clinton."

Gil Davis wrote a note to himself in the Paula Jones file, as a reminder: "Take the deposition of Gennifer Flowers and the troopers regarding Clinton's use of troopers as goons, in addition to use as pimps [and whatever else they were used for]." Interestingly, in an undated notation that Davis scribbled on a piece of paper some time before 1997, the lawyer wrote that he had received a call from a private investigator who "has info that Clinton made unwanted sexual advances to an intern."

In sketching out legal arguments that he hoped to make at trial, Davis wrote out numerous memos to himself. One such memo stated: "What makes [this conduct] so outrageous is the unequal power between the Governor and some little State employee." What Clinton did, scribbled Davis, was "he took advantage of a weaker person. This is despicable and outrageous."

There is no question that from the start, the Jones team believed that if it could show Bill Clinton was taking advantage of female government employees in *other* situations, this would convince a jury to buy Jones's story. Davis's personal notes to his file now confirm that he was planning to pursue aggressively the subject of "other women" from the moment he entered the case. One piece of dictation shows Davis formulating questions to ask Trooper Danny Ferguson under oath, the first of which was, "Were you given assignments, as part of Governor Clinton's Security Detail, by the Governor or anyone else, to play any role in the Governor's sexual liaisons with women?"

Appearing as a guest on CNN during the early stages of the *Jones* case, Davis was asked if he intended to "speak to other women who possibly would be able to support Mrs. Jones' claims." He replied openly, on national television, that he would do that in a heartbeat if it furthered "the welfare and vindication of the rights of our client."

So there was never any serious question that the Jones lawyers would try to get Bill Clinton under oath and force him to answer questions about "other women," assuming the case wasn't thrown out first. As early as June 13, 1994, on his to-do list, Davis's first priority was: "Supoena [sic] to President Clinton to give deposition in this case." Numerous clues were dropped that any more recent episodes of hanky-panky with female subordinates in the White House ultimately would be sniffed out—since anti-Clinton lawyers were busily searching for such evidence.

Every litigation strategy brings with it unexpected pitfalls. Davis and Cammarata were faced with their own problems if they kicked open the door on the subject of Bill Clinton's sexual exploits. *Penthouse* magazine had obtained partially nude photos of Jones from an ex-boyfriend named Mike Turner, publishing them in a slick issue appearing in January 1995. In an article provocatively titled "The Devil in Paula Jones," *Penthouse* writer Rudy Maxa turned the tables, giving readers an eyeful of this supposedly traumatized plaintiff who had posed seminude at age nineteen, cavorting for (and with) her thirty-one-year-old boyfriend, wearing only panties and posing in extremely suggestive positions. Maxa also interviewed acquaintances and family members of Paula's, most of whom painted an unflattering picture of the plaintiff. Her older sister and brother-in-law, Charlotte and Mark Brown, flatly contradicted Jones's story. They told *Penthouse* that Paula had stopped by their house the night after the alleged meeting with Governor Clinton and that his advance had thrilled her. "She just said he'd invited her up to the hotel room and that while she was up there, he asked her to do oral sex and she refused," Charlotte Corbin Brown told the magazine. "She was excited; she was in no way upset."

Brother-in-law Mark Brown also raised the subject of Paula's own sexual habits, saying he had been "shocked at the number of men" Paula had taken as lovers before she turned seventeen. Brown told *Penthouse* that he counseled her: "Paula . . . you need to take it easy about going with one guy right after another because there's venereal diseases that are very, very bad." She favored older men and purposely dressed in "provocative" fashions, he said, and added: "If I hadn't been married, I'd probably have propositioned her myself."

Charlotte chimed in that she had been "horrified" when Paula brought home the partially nude photos that now appeared in *Penthouse* and spread them out for the family to see. "She was proud of them," said the older sister. Charlotte also asserted that Paula told her excitedly before she filed the lawsuit that "there could be a lot of money" in this deal, if she decided to sue Clinton and sell her story for a sweet book deal.

In contemplating how to blunt the impact of these stories, Davis dictated several possible rebuttals to his file: "Paula Jones' consent to have these pictures taken was at a time when she was 19 years old, dating a 31 year old boyfriend, whom she wanted to please, and probably was a substitute father figure for a father who had died within the past six months. . . . Thus, this is a matter of trust which was abused." Davis tried out an additional argument: "The reaction is [always] to 'blame the victim.' In this case, Paula has been exploited twice: once when she trusted her boyfriend . . . and secondly she was subject to the Penthouse display."

To deflect the insinuations that Jones was a gold digger, Davis issued a press release declaring that any money his client received in excess of attorneys' fees would go to a charitable cause rather than to line Jones's own pockets. Jones herself told CNN that she would give any settlement funds away. "I am *not* in it for the money," she declared in an offended, high-pitched voice.

In mulling over a possible theme that might win over the American public and bolster his client's sagging case, Davis dictated these six sentences to his file: "What kind of country do we live in? What will we tolerate? Is character an issue? Is honesty an issue? Is a person who assaults women worthy of public office? Is a President above the law?"

———

PRESIDENTIAL lawyer Bob Bennett, during this time, was busy gathering evidence that would blow Paula Jones's case out of the water. Already, the media were digging up unflattering information on Paula and Steve Jones. *People* magazine reported that the Joneses, holed up in their rented condo in California, were rude and loud tenants. One condo worker said that Paula at times had "the mouth of a truck driver." Another tenant told *People* that Steve and Paula "had loud, raucous fights, recently over money and Paula's lack of employment." An eyewitness said that Paula had become belligerent with a neighbor during an argument, shouting, "I hate all you people in California! All you do is complain and sue each other!"

Steve Jones, the vociferous husband of the plaintiff, had his own set of issues that could be rolled out at trial. Former colleagues described him as someone "whose own sexual attitudes sometimes made co-workers uncomfortable," a person who enjoyed prying into others' "personal sexual habits." His propensity for showing fellow workers "photos of Paula in sexy underwear" prompted "complaints about him from women he worked with."

Bob Bennett was also sitting atop a box full of surprise evidence that would create massive problems for Paula Jones if her case ever made it to a jury. Chief among these was a forty-five-minute piece of raw film footage, capturing Paula and Steve discussing her allegations against Clinton before her case had attracted national attention. Shot some time in 1994, the footage was obtained by Bob Bennett—unbeknownst to his opponents—amid a pile of material turned over by a fundamentalist Christian film company in response to a subpoena.

Director Pat Matrisciana and Jeremiah Films had teamed up with the Reverend Jerry Falwell to produce the anti-Clinton video *The Clinton Chronicles* (subtitled *An Investigation into the Alleged Criminal Activities of Bill Clinton*), and this raw footage had survived that project. According to those close to Bennett, this uncensored interview with Paula and Steve Jones would have been Exhibit A at trial.

This remarkable footage, shot in California with the Pacific Ocean roaring in the background, would have provided an eye-opening snapshot of the plaintiff for jurors. In the lengthy segment, Paula Jones appeared more like an irreverent cabaret dancer than a traumatized victim of sexual harassment. Dressed in a low-cut blue-flowered dress that repeatedly slipped down from her shoulders and wearing long dangly earrings, bright red lipstick, and a huge purple bow in her hair (she had been nicknamed "Minnie Mouse" by security guards at the state capitol), Jones was captured recounting her not-yet-famous story with a mixture of tentativeness, sarcasm, and ribald humor. As the wind whipped her hair around, requiring Jones to clutch it against her bosom while securing the straps of her dress, she preserved her true story for posterity.

At times giggling, at times wrestling down her hair, Jones repeatedly tried to describe the alleged incident with Clinton inside the Excelsior Hotel, stumbling over her sentences and waving at the director to do numerous takes and retakes. At one point, she stopped and spoke directly into the camera: "Am I doing okay, Stephen?"

"Oh, you're doing great," her husband chimed in from the sidelines, like an acting coach.

On film, Paula described the meeting in Clinton's hotel room as if she had been captured in a revolving door—she was moving around the room as the governor tried to touch her leg, kiss her neck, and pull her toward him. When it came to the ultimate act, Jones recounted Clinton's advance with annoyance: "Before I knew it he had pulled his pants down and he had set down beside me *nude*," she said with disgust. Jones adjusted her hair and stared into the camera: "And he asked me to 'kiss it. . . .'"

"I was so shocked. I said, 'I'm not that type of girl.'"

With a mixture of sarcasm and triumph, the would-be plaintiff told the camera that she had gotten the last word on Clinton: "I turned around, I was very, very angry and I asked him, 'Does *Hillary* ever give [you] any?'"

Referring to Trooper Danny Ferguson's version of the story and sounding particularly defensive, Jones went on: "He said that I wanted to be Clinton's full-time girlfriend, which is definitely a big *lie*." At that point, Paula looked up at Steve: "Isn't that what happened?"

Her husband, apparently none too happy with this segment of the epic drama, replied off camera, "Yeh, honey."

If Paula Jones's lawyers had hoped to portray their client as a sympathetic, aggrieved plaintiff, this film segment was likely to accomplish just the opposite. Paula called out "cut" to the cameraman repeatedly; fixed her dress as it blew off her shoulders; and, at one point, flubbed a line in which she alleged Clinton had told her that he "liked the way my curves are." This caused Paula to begin laughing loudly. She looked up and blew loud raspberries into the camera.

Next, Paula was given a cue to introduce her husband. From here, a bad scene got even worse. She looked into the camera and stated dramatically that Steve "has been very, very angry with the President." She asked, "What has it done, honey?"

Paula then looked off camera and burst out laughing, saying, "It has *pissed you off*."

Steve Jones now swaggered on camera, wearing tight jeans with no belt and a tapered dress shirt with thick blue stripes. His beard was neatly trimmed, his hair combed back to perfection. The husband of the plaintiff slid one arm around Paula, with one thumb stuck in his pocket, appearing much like a B movie actor, precisely what he aspired to be. As he kissed Paula, Steve tugged at the top of his wife's dress to straighten it.

"I'm showing *naked* here," Paula giggled. "He's trying to undress me on TV!"

After five attempts to film this scene, with repeated calls of "Action!" the silver-haired producer stepped onto his own set, helping to choreograph Steve kissing Paula on the top of her head. Finally, Steve executed the kiss, commenting in a macho-sounding voice: "I'd like to take this a few steps further." Now he scowled into the camera: "I think Bill Clinton is perverted, I think he needs some deep psychological help, I really do." After railing at the *Washington Post* for printing nothing even after he and Paula had given an "exclusive" to Michael Isikoff, Paula's husband ranted: "It really infuriates me. I thought they only censored things in third world countries, I can't understand it. It's very flustrating [sic]."

Steve Jones flexed his muscles like a bodybuilder before launching into an attack on the editors of the *Washington Post* and the entire women's rights movement. "I'll tell you what their position is." He jabbed a finger toward the camera, like a man who was going off the deep end: "Their position is under the left foot of Bill Clinton, that's where they are. And every once in a while they'll creep their hands out from under his foot and give it a spit shine, that's how I feel about it. Only . . ." At this point, Steve Jones appeared as if he had been overcome by wild emotions and was ready for a physical brawl. He growled, "I'm sorry, that's about all I have to say about it."

With that, the film session came to a close.

Every lawsuit contains black, white, and shades of gray. Whatever the truth of the events involving Paula Jones and then-Governor Bill Clinton in the Excelsior Hotel, this raw film footage in the hands of the president's lawyer, if it had been shown to a jury, would have made an already tough case much tougher. The Matrisciana footage was disastrous, especially because it represented Paula's own account, captured vividly on film, close in time to the actual events, that did little to advance her cause. It revealed a woman who was actively trying to sell her story to the national press. It also displayed a Paula Jones who was decidedly irreverent and did not appear traumatized. Equally as damaging, the role of her husband, Steve—who was captured on film nudging and prodding his wife forward—which made him appear like an angry would-be actor who wanted to punch the president's lights out, in part because Clinton had made a pass at his then fiancée and in part because he simply hated Clinton's guts.

Bob Bennett put this film under lock and key, preserving it as a surprise piece of evidence. He knew that it would have the effect of lighting a stink bomb in front of any judge and jurors. As Bennett later explained: "When the jury watched her doing this, what would they see? A troubled person? Someone traumatized? I didn't see that at all. I saw someone reading a script. Someone who's had an opportunity to earn some dough. Her husband, Steve, looked like someone trying to get a Hollywood movie job."

Danny Traylor, Paula's first attorney, would later admit that he was initially unaware of the damaging footage. He had seen only one brief snippet of *The Clinton Chronicles,* the far-out film that featured allegations that Clinton had ordered people killed in Arkansas and had run drugs to fund his political addiction. "I was shocked," said Traylor. "Jesus, that really pissed me off and really motivated me to get away from these people." He took a long gulp of coffee and pushed his glasses up on his nose. "It wasn't the kind of forum that I would have picked. Money changed hands, which was a no-no. . . . I learned about it after the fact." As far as Traylor was concerned, Paula and Steve "quite frankly, misled me on that. . . . And I didn't like that."

Bob Bennett was also busy amassing evidence to prove that Paula Jones had actively sought out Governor Clinton in the state capitol on multiple occasions *after* the alleged incident in the Excelsior Hotel. He had information indicating that she made inquiries about Clinton at the governor's office after the alleged episode and referred to him as "a nice-looking man" and as "nice" and "sweet." Carol Phillips, the head switchboard operator at the governor's office, had already signed an affidavit swearing that—after the AIDC conference—Paula Corbin "asked me for a picture of the Governor" and described having met Clinton at the Excelsior Hotel in a "happy and excited manner," even checking the governor's parking space, hoping to "see and speak with Mr. Clinton." Pam Hood, who worked with Paula at AIDC, likewise would testify—if served a subpoena—that Jones displayed "bubbly enthusiasm" after having met Governor Clinton, similar to when she had caught a glimpse of movie star Arnold Schwarzenegger in Little Rock. All of this would certainly cause jurors to take Jones's story with a shaker's worth of salt.

Finally, there was the Steve Jones factor. Although this important element had largely been overlooked in the press, Paula had been wearing an engagement ring at the time of the alleged incident with Clinton. To put it more bluntly, when the woman named "Paula" had voluntarily gone to the governor's room—as reported in the *American Spectator* piece—she was already engaged to marry Steve Jones. (They married in December 1991, just seven months after the Excelsior Hotel encounter.) Bennett was prepared to argue forcefully that this gave Paula a strong motive to lie.

"The issue of Steve Jones being engaged to Paula was very much on my mind," Bennett later divulged. If he was forced to go to trial, he would argue vigorously that Paula's engagement to Steve at the time provided a powerful motive for "making up the whole story," or at least making up "key facts," in order to "avoid the damning truth that she had gone up to Clinton's room and perhaps flirted with him, at the time she was an engaged woman."

There were big surprises in store for plaintiff and defendant alike, if the case went to trial. No matter how it played out, it was unlikely that either side would escape unscathed.

CHAPTER

15

ARKANSAS FELONS

President Clinton would later say that he was "a hundred percent" sure that the prosecution against the McDougals and Governor Jim Guy Tucker was designed to "ratchet up" the investigation to do anything possible to nail him and the First Lady. He believed the facts spoke for themselves: "You know, Jim had already been prosecuted and acquitted once on all this S&L stuff in the nineties." Although it was possible McDougal was guilty as charged, said Clinton, Madison Guaranty was one of the smallest S&L failures in America. "McDougal never would have been tried again after having been acquitted once if he hadn't been seen as key to getting me."

Bill Clinton had no doubt that McDougal's business conduct had been un- orthodox. But he also knew that McDougal was suffering from a "deteriorating mental condition." "I was worried about him," Clinton recalled. "I didn't know what the facts were in his case, but I had known him when he was younger and when he was well. I thought he was a good man, and I was [hoping] that given his mental condition, he wasn't going to prison. Because I thought it would probably break him, given the disintegration of his sense of stability."

President Clinton felt that the reason Ken Starr's office was pursuing a bro- ken man like McDougal so vigorously was obvious. "When they got into that Whitewater thing," Clinton stated, shaking his head disapprovingly, "they knew that I hadn't done anything wrong and Hillary hadn't done anything wrong. So they had to go after somebody."

——

On Sunday, April 29, 1996, Jim and Susan McDougal—legally divorced since 1988—made their first and last road trip together to the White House. Their onetime friend, Bill Clinton, was slated to give testimony, hopefully beating back the effort by the Starr prosecutors to convict them in Little Rock.

Pausing to chat with the throng of reporters, Jim arrived in advance of the 1:15 P.M. start time to stake out a front-row seat. He was sporting a new straw hat purchased at a Georgetown shop Hats in the Belfry, along with a band- collared shirt with a gold pin and a navy suit. As he answered questions, Mc- Dougal leaned thoughtfully against a brass eagle cane. Pointing to a fray in the hat, he proudly told reporters that he had picked it up "at a bargain for a hun- dred dollars."

President Clinton had jogged that morning and then attended church with the First Lady. He looked rested and fit as he entered the Map Room. Clinton understood that this videotaped testimony would be shown to the jury back home in Arkansas in the Tucker-McDougal trial; he was in perfect presidential form for the occasion.

The Map Room, on the ground floor of the White House, had been trans- formed into a makeshift courtroom. President Franklin D. Roosevelt had used this room to monitor events during World War II after the Japanese attacked Pearl Harbor. Now it had been selected as the site for the president's filmed tes- timony, a neutral zone because it lacked White House artifacts that jurors might recognize. A different war was being fought between the White House and the Office of Independent Counsel; the Map Room was the new field of battle.

President Bill Clinton, dressed in a dark suit befitting the chief executive, shook hands with the defense lawyers and prosecutors. Clinton gave a bear hug to Jim McDougal and a quick embrace to Susan. Whatever past ill feelings had existed between Jim McDougal and Bill Clinton were forgotten. They were now on the same team, united in disdain for David Hale and the Starr prosecutors. The president took a seat in the center of the room, facing a lectern set up for the questioner.

It was not unprecedented that a sitting president would testify in such a case. President Gerald Ford had testified via videotape in the criminal trial of Lynette "Squeaky" Fromme, the woman who had attempted to assassinate him. President Jimmy Carter had testified in the criminal trial of a Georgia legislator accused of misconduct. In the case of President Bill Clinton, this was the fourth time that he had been called to give testimony under oath in Whitewater-related matters. For an investigation that related to events that were so distant in time, and seemed so peripheral to the Clintons, Whitewater and its related scandals had a way of bringing a perpetual sense of unease to this White House and its occupants.

U.S. District Judge George Howard, Jr., presided from Little Rock, via a satellite hookup that was scrambled to prevent interception. He disliked flying and opted to stay anchored on terra firma in Arkansas. From his safe judicial command post, Judge Howard swore in the president at 1:15 P.M. Washington time; the testimony would last for nearly five hours.

Attorney Sam Heuer, who had been appointed by the court (twice) to represent the indigent Jim McDougal, led off the questioning. He moved directly to the heart of the allegations against the McDougals, asking the president:

HEUER: Did you ever, in any shape, form, or fashion, put any pressure on David Hale for the purpose of obtaining a loan or for the purpose of causing him to make loans through his S.B.I.C.?

CLINTON: I did not put any pressure on David Hale.

HEUER: Do you have any idea what he is talking about in regard to these loans that he has come up with?

CLINTON: No, sir. He has told two or three different versions of this, and I've tried to keep up with these different stories, but all I know . . . these things are simply not true, they didn't happen.

When it came to Hale's allegations that Governor Bill Clinton had secretly jogged to Jim McDougal's satellite office located in a trailer on the Castle Grande property, where he had pressured Hale to make a loan to benefit the Mc-Dougals and Jim Guy Tucker, the president dismissed this story as a bunch of bull. During his years as governor, the president said smoothly, he did enjoy jogging around Little Rock—he still took an occasional run at the White House. But he was never in good enough shape (the president smiled and straightened his suit coat) to jog the ten or twelve miles from the governor's mansion to

McDougal's trailer-office on 145th Street. The only time he had visited McDougal's Castle Grande location to say hello, he said, he was dressed in a suit and tie, on his way to tour the Siemens-Allison plant nearby.

On cross-examination, when OIC prosecutor Ray Jahn sought to establish that President Clinton could have jogged to McDougal's office from the governor's mansion, then *hitched a ride* to McDougal's trailer-office on the Castle Grande site, wearing his jogging clothes (as alleged by David Hale), the exchange grew testy. Jahn tried to establish every which way that there was "no physical prevention, no moral prevention, no logical prevention that would have prevented you from having done it." Clinton finally threw up his hands: "I wasn't in handcuffs and chains, if that's what you are asking." The jurors nodded their heads, apparently sharing the president's frustrations.

Judge Howard adjourned the proceedings at 5:58 P.M., just in time for Sunday dinner, Arkansas time. Most participants in the Map Room appeared weary from the day's workout. President Clinton, in contrast, looked strong and unruffled. His lawyer David Kendall had not uttered a single objection during the entire five-hour testimony. It had been a virtuoso performance by Clinton. He took a few minutes to show his former business partner around the Map Room, walking Jim McDougal across the floor that FDR had once maneuvered in his wheelchair. Here, the president pointed out where Roosevelt had stuck pins on maps depicting the Atlantic Theater on the east wall and the Pacific Theater on the west wall, to trace military movements and ship positions during the war. "We're both great admirers of Franklin Delano Roosevelt," McDougal later told the press, beaming. He was pleased that Bill Clinton had carved out time to show some true Southern hospitality toward old friends.

With respect to later speculation that President Clinton had made a secret deal to pardon Jim or Susan McDougal, during their five-minute stroll around the Map Room, both Susan McDougal and Bill Clinton would dismiss that as silly. "There was no such conversation," Susan later said. "For heaven's sake, Jim would have told me." At the time, Susan pointed out, few observers expected her to be convicted; she was a peripheral figure in the trial. The idea that Clinton had promised her a deal during a fleeting conversation with her manic husband (who was certain he would be acquitted) seemed "far-fetched" at best. Clinton himself called it bunk: "I always had somebody with me, and they were always together the whole time they were there," said the president. With respect to Jim McDougal's later story that there were promises made of a pardon if he and Susan protected the president, Clinton would shake his head and disregard it as the fabrication of a desperate man: "He didn't say any of this until they nailed him and he didn't want to go to jail."

On that day, McDougal seemed perfectly fine with the proceedings in the

White House. There was a sense that Bill Clinton and his erstwhile Arkansas friends "had hit a home run." As the Whitewater defendant greeted a cavalcade of journalists outside the White House gate, he declared himself "satisfied" with the president's testimony, stating: "I did not see that he made any inconsistent statements."

When asked by one reporter what he and the president had discussed during their brief tour around the Map Room, McDougal straightened his straw hat and leaned against his cane. "I said we'd probably whip the Republicans this fall," he quipped. McDougal added, referring to Clinton's likely Republican challenger, Senator Bob Dole of Kansas: "He's the world's only living mummy."

After commenting on his possible 105-year prison sentence and answering the last of the reporters' questions, McDougal now turned to one engaged journalist and popped the question: "How would you like," he asked with his most charming Southern gentleman's smile, "to buy us a sandwich?"

THE same Sunday as Clinton's testimony, *Newsweek* reported that FBI analysts had identified First Lady Hillary Clinton's fingerprints on Rose Law Firm billing records that had appeared mysteriously in the White House residence back in January. This new development added more question marks to an already-baffling whodunit.

The "disappearance" and "reappearance" of the Rose Law Firm billing records remains one of the true mysteries of the prolonged Clinton scandals. The missing sheaf of computer printouts had been generated on February 12, 1992, by an unknown law firm employee, detailing Hillary Rodham Clinton's work there for the McDougals and Madison Guaranty. This period corresponded to the beginning of Bill Clinton's race for the presidency; the Whitewater- and McDougal-related issues were well known as potential bumps in the road to victory.

The 116 pages of newly materialized records were relevant for a host of reasons. The Senate Whitewater Committee, predominated by Republicans and guided in its investigation by hard-charging Special Counsel Michael Chertoff, saw the billing records as the Holy Grail. They hoped the records would answer the question, Had the First Lady and her closest advisers lied to federal investigators in describing her role vis-à-vis Jim McDougal's corrupt business enterprises?

There were also issues about whether Mrs. Clinton had a conflict of interest in appearing before the Arkansas Securities Department and its top commissioner, Beverly Bassett (whom Hillary's husband had appointed), in doing work for Madison Guaranty. There were issues about to what extent Mrs. Clinton was involved in the Castle Grande project for Madison—a deal that now appeared to be riddled with fraud and built atop an unlawful pyramid scheme. There were questions about whether Mrs. Clinton had lied to authorities about how the Rose Law Firm came to represent Madison, and her role as billing attorney (she had tried to place much of the responsibility for initiating and handling this account in the hands of Rick Massey, a young junior associate at the firm, but he contradicted her).

In prior sworn testimony before the Resolution Trust Corporation, the First Lady had minimized her involvement in the Madison account. Specifically, she had claimed to have "little or no" involvement with McDougal in the Castle Grande project, which was now awash in criminal sewage. The hunt was on to find out what Mrs. Clinton knew and when.

There was no dispute that Vince Foster, Webb Hubbell, and Hillary Clinton had all handled copies of the billing records during the 1992 campaign in an effort to protect Hillary's flank. Hubbell, earning a temporary reprieve from federal prison to testify in front of the Senate Whitewater Committee, had acknowledged that Vince Foster was the last person he had seen handling the records. The Senate committee had issued multiple subpoenas to obtain the records; in each case, the documents were reported missing in action.

Now, this one-inch stack of papers had suddenly "appeared" in clear view on a table in the Book Room on the third floor of the White House residence in August—discovered there by Carolyn Huber, a White House aide who handled the Clintons' personal correspondence. Huber, the former office manager at the Rose Law Firm who now worked for Mrs. Clinton in the White House, identified the documents as those relevant to Ken Starr's investigation. They contained notations, in red ink, in Foster's handwriting. These documents, Huber later told Senate investigators under oath, "were not on the table a week or two earlier" when she had been in the room.

Huber had placed the records in a box without studying them in detail and relocated them to the floor of her office. In January, when she was having new furniture placed in her office in the East Wing, she noticed the box of billing records that had been stashed under a table, and examined them more carefully. Immediately, Huber recognized that these were the Madison records for which the Senate investigators were so desperately searching. "Horrified," she contacted the Clintons' private lawyer, David Kendall, and White House Special Counsel Jane Sherburne; the attorneys immediately copied the documents before surrendering them to OIC and the Senate Whitewater Committee the next day. Hubbell, when asked by Senate investigators about the miraculous finding, said that when he learned that the records had appeared, "I just smiled." Crisis management expert Jane Sherburne told Senate investigators that, on the day of the discovery, Carolyn Huber "was very confused and . . . her recollections were very imprecise."

It was as if this story had been crafted by a mystery writer. Nobody on earth seemed to know exactly how the missing billing records appeared on a table in Room 319A of the First Family's private residence, a room used to store gifts, photos, newspaper clippings, magazine articles, and other items that needed to be catalogued. During this period, Hillary Clinton had been working regularly in Room 323, writing her book *It Takes a Village*, approximately eight feet away. A confidential witness told the FBI that he or she had observed Mrs. Clinton "comfortably" carrying a brown cardboard box in her arms, in July 1995; the box contained a stack of papers that were "coiled or rolled up" like the Madison billing records. Mrs. Clinton, however, denied seeing the documents after moving to Washington and testified that she had "no idea" how the papers suddenly reappeared in Room 319A.

The documents revealed that Mrs. Clinton had billed around 59.8 hours on Madison Guaranty matters, between April 1985 and July 1986. The longest portion of that time—24.45 hours—was spent working on the Castle Grande venture. Mrs. Clinton's fingerprints were on the documents. Tellingly, the FBI identified one fingerprint on the front upper right corner of a page near an entry showing a twelve-minute telephone conference between Mrs. Clinton and a key Madison Guaranty official on the Castle Grande deal (also known as the International Development Corp. project). Someone, apparently Vince Foster, had circled the name of the attorney on the entry: "HRC." Something smelled rotten in the state of Denmark.

To add to the aura of mystery surrounding the billing records, there were reports that Foster had removed the same documents from the Rose firm in 1992, while doing Whitewater damage control during the campaign. Deputy Chief of Staff Harold Ickes, who helped manage damage control relating to Whitewater, stated candidly: "It is what it is." Presidential aide John Podesta acknowledged that the discovery certainly added "spice to the gumbo."

The *New York Post* ran a bold front-page headline: "Hillary Did It." Senate Whitewater Committee Chairman Alfonse D'Amato (R-N.Y.) declared that the billing records "raise volumes of questions, serious questions as it relates to the first lady."

Outwardly, the White House did its best to treat this newest revelation with a yawn, pointing out that Mrs. Clinton had acknowledged from the start that she had handled the documents during the 1992 presidential campaign, and that the billing records showed only a modest amount of work on McDougal-related matters. They also stated that she did not know the Castle Grande project as such, because it had been referred to as the Industrial Development Company, or "IDC," property rather than by that name. Yet the First Lady's fingerprints fueled whispers that she was involved—in some fashion—in the documents' disappearance and reappearance. Were these the same records spirited away after Foster's death and ones that the White House was trying to hide?

Ken Starr's office, in a shot across the bow, summoned Hillary Clinton before the grand jury, making her the first First Lady in the nation's history to suffer that ignominy. Although Mrs. Clinton denied having knowledge of how the billing records had surfaced, she appeared rattled. Numerous sources inside the White House identified this as a "real affront" and a "turning point" in the Clinton-Starr imbroglio. Said Deputy Chief of Staff Harold Ickes, Whitewater had now "metastasized" into so many areas that it created a "f—— you" attitude by those encamped around the Clintons.

Behind closed doors, the White House crisis team was preparing for nuclear warfare. Jane Sherburne was secretly constructing a plan in the event that Hillary Clinton was indicted. "A good crisis manager prepares for all of the contingencies," she later confirmed. "And that was one of them." An assault on the First Lady, in the eyes of the disaster-prevention team, was tantamount to "an assault on the presidency." They were prepared to launch a political counterattack aimed directly at Ken Starr and his underlings, far more ferocious than OIC had ever imagined.

In the meantime, public skepticism relating to the Clintons continued to rise to new heights. A Washington Post/ABC News poll reported that nearly half of the respondents believed that the First Lady was "not telling the truth about Whitewater." Said one chemist from Kentucky, who responded to the random poll, "It just doesn't add up." To worsen the situation for the president and First Lady, David Hale was now popping out of his hole. The former Little Rock municipal judge, who had been held in protective custody by Starr's office for nearly two years, was reportedly ready to take the witness stand. There was rampant speculation that he was going to spill his guts about the McDougals and Governor Jim Guy Tucker and that he might even point his pudgy finger directly at President Bill Clinton.

———

On April Fools' Day of 1996, David Hale finally took the stand, testifying inside a packed federal courtroom. Now a confessed felon, he offered up a sitting governor, a sitting president, two McDougals, and others in his alleged scheme to defraud the federal government.

Hale was a "short, flabby guy with a round face" who "wore a rug" (a wig), according to one observer. He "desperately wanted to be liked," and so he poured it on for the jury.

On the first day, he testified that he had gone for a drive one night in the fall of 1985 with Jim Guy Tucker and Jim McDougal in McDougal's Jaguar, to check out a piece of property south of Little Rock, later dubbed Castle Grande. When Hale inspected the swampy land in the twilight, asking how McDougal "pawned that turkey off" on Tucker, Tucker had chuckled that McDougal "made me an offer I couldn't refuse."

Later that night, Hale testified, the three men drove back to Tucker's home and "visited" in the kitchen. (In an earlier version of the story, Hale had stated this meeting took place at the Black-eyed Pea restaurant.) Hale alleged that Mc-Dougal confided that they were going to have to take care of "some members of the political family," in arranging financing for the deal. When asked by OIC's prosecutor Ray Jahn what he understood McDougal to mean by that phrase, Hale stated that he believed "it involved Bill Clinton and maybe some of his aides and political associates, and Jim Guy Tucker."

Hale next testified that—while seated at Tucker's kitchen table—they had hatched a plan to have Madison Guaranty make an $825,000 loan to Hale's company, Capital Management Services. They would sell off the real estate to a straw buyer at an inflated price and then use the profits to obtain $2 million in Small Business Association (SBA) funds that they could illegally loan to Tucker, the McDougals, and other members of the "political family."

Prosecutor Ray Jahn pressed Hale to tell the jury why it was so important to cook up new deals to pay off the questionable loans.

"Well," Hale drawled, "if we didn't pay it, then you would have regulators coming in and investigators coming in and we'd all go to jail."

After Hale's first day of testimony, Jim McDougal told the press that Hale was "a recreational liar." Leaning on his cane, McDougal predicted to a *USA Today* reporter: "I think he'll be exposed as a liar, thief and con artist."

That night, the host of CNN's *Inside Politics* declared that the dormant Whitewater saga had suddenly been brought back to life and that "Mr. Clinton's exact ties to the matter could come into sharp focus this week." David Hale quickly made good on that prediction. On the second day of his testimony, he placed Bill Clinton at the epicenter of a key fraudulent deal.

In early 1986, Hale told the jury, he had received a call from Jim McDougal summoning him to meet with McDougal and Governor Clinton at the Castle Grande property. When he had arrived at the remote location, Hale testified, the only vehicle there was McDougal's Jaguar. Governor Clinton, he seemed to recall, was dressed in jogging clothes. McDougal and Clinton were stand-ing around "cussing" and "talking politics and this sort of thing." Small talk turned to business. According to Hale, the group discussed obtaining a loan for McDougal and Governor Clinton in the amount of $150,000, which would be put in the name of Susan McDougal's advertising firm. Clinton offered to secure the loan through "raw land" in Marion County—that is, the Whitewater property. But McDougal said that wasn't necessary: "Susan's financial statement was strong enough to handle it."

Hale's testimony was murky on specifics. Yet he recalled enough to tell the jury that—at Jim's request—he eventually doubled the amount and agreed to loan Susan McDougal's company $300,000. Governor Clinton allegedly insisted: "My name can't show up on this." Jim McDougal said not to worry—the $300,000 loan would be made in Susan McDougal's name alone.

When asked by lead prosecutor Ray Jahn, "Who did you look to as far as this loan is concerned, who were you looking to as far as repayment?" Hale replied soberly, "I was looking at Jim McDougal and Bill Clinton."

Susan McDougal's attorney, Bobby McDaniel, expressed disgust after the judge adjourned the jury for the night. "What you heard from David Hale today," he said, "is a different story than what he's said before. It's a fabrication, period. Bill Clinton is his meal ticket to a lighter sentence." Jim McDougal, toting his cane and briefcase across Capitol Avenue to the pink Legacy Hotel where he had rented a cheap room, ridiculed Hale's testimony. "I sort of wanted to kick his butt," McDougal told the *Arkansas Democrat-Gazette*. "But then I saw what poor condition he appears to be in physically, and then I couldn't work myself up to want to beat up on the guy."

Ken Starr, who happened to be working in OIC's secret office in the bowels of the federal courthouse, emerged to tell reporters that he was taking the trial "one day at a time" and that Hale's testimony did not necessarily mean that the president was a target. Prosecutor Jahn clarified that there were no plans to name the president an unindicted co-conspirator, "as of now."

———

GOVERNOR Jim Guy Tucker was attempting to use his ties with the media to paint Ken Starr as a zealot and a partisan who was manufacturing criminal charges to weaken the Democratic administrations in Washington and Arkansas. Although stories were creeping into the papers about Starr's private legal practice—especially his participation in the Wisconsin school voucher case financed by the ultraconservative Bradley Foundation and his representation of two large tobacco companies directly at odds with the Clinton Justice Department—for the most part, these charges were not sticking.

President Clinton, watching the trial of Governor Tucker and the McDougals unfold from inside the White House, still thought it reeked of politics. Clinton suspected OIC's ultimate goal was to "get [Tucker] to say something adverse about me in return for some sort of deal. At worst, if they could convict him of something, they'd get rid of him and have a Republican governor in Arkansas." When it came to Jim McDougal, if there was any truth to the Starr

prosecutors' case against him, the president felt that "it was the product of Mc-
Dougal's mental deterioration and increasing desperation."

Clinton remained optimistic that the jury would see through Starr's political motives and acquit the defendants. Then something happened to abruptly
change that assessment. Said President Clinton, sitting back in his chair and remembering, "I don't think he [Starr] would have ever convicted Susan or Jim
Guy if McDougal hadn't insisted on testifying."

———

THE day Jim McDougal took the stand in his own defense, Tuesday, May 7,
1996, was the day the prosecution won its case, in the eyes of the stunned defense
team. The plan among the defendants' lawyers, from the start, had been to show
President Clinton's filmed testimony to the jurors and immediately rest their
case. OIC's case rested heavily on the testimony of David Hale. Hale had been
badly damaged on cross-examination; the jurors wouldn't have sympathy for
this shifty-looking former municipal judge who had defrauded the federal government of nearly a million dollars and then received a light sentence in return
for pointing a finger at the defendants. There was no denying that certain documents signed by the McDougals and Tucker were problematic—not all funds
had been used for the purposes listed on the loan papers. Yet the *intent* to commit wrongdoing still had to be proven; the defense lawyers intended to hammer
home that point in closing to the jury. According to George Collins, a veteran
trial attorney from Chicago representing Governor Tucker, the defense team's
strategy was simple: "I'm from the school of criminal law that says 'nobody
talks, everybody walks,'" said Collins later. "The best successes I've had in my life,
my defendant didn't say anything."

As Governor Tucker sat at defense counsel table each day, scribbling notes
on a yellow legal pad, it was obvious that his health problems were wearing him
down. Two years earlier, Tucker had almost died from esophageal varices related to a debilitating liver disease. Now, the ordinarily handsome and robust
governor—who was often compared to Robert Redford—had begun to appear
grayish.

Tucker would later say that by this point in the trial, he had felt like an
animal with a target on his back. He believed that he had become the Starr
team's "coonskin cap." The former governor, who later pled guilty to tax fraud
with respect to various cable television deals (yet continued to proclaim his
innocence), survived this Whitewater ordeal to become a successful international businessman with cable television companies in the United States and
Indonesia. The ex-governor would later confess that this was the low point of his

life. "I was within months of a liver transplant, and I was in dreadful shape, so you had two fairly crippled defendants sitting there. Jim [McDougal] certainly was, and I certainly was."

Tucker said, his blue eyes flashing with contempt, "The motivation to protect Hale to support his allegations was very, very high for that prosecutorial team."

Tucker desperately wanted to make his case directly to the jury. He and his lawyer had "one hell of a blowup" about his desire to testify. Collins worried that Tucker was so "precisely honest and precisely truthful" that he would correct some of the flagrant mistakes Hale had made on the witness stand, unwittingly helping his accuser. The government had the burden of proof; Collins thought there was no reason to put Tucker on the stand to help clean up their case.

"So finally, we had an awful argument, and I told him, 'You're not testifying, God damn it. If you do, I'll go home.'"

Up until this point, Susan McDougal had appeared as nothing more than a minor figure in the trial. The government had a duty to prove "intent to commit fraud" on the part of Susan McDougal. Her lawyer believed with "one hundred percent" certainty that such intent was absent. So he also prohibited her from testifying.

Now all of the defense team's careful plans came unglued when Jim McDougal announced, as the Whitewater trial entered its homestretch, "I'm going to get up there and kick their ass." Sam Heuer, who had represented McDougal since the first Whitewater prosecution seven years earlier, said he begged his client not to do it. In Jim's case, "there were no pros. There were all cons. He was going to get slaughtered on cross-examination."

There is no sound explanation of why Jim McDougal made this sudden reversal. Of late, he had certainly developed a deep "distrust" of Governor Tucker, whom he had accused of cheating his mother in a recent business deal. It may have been that he was swayed, in part, by new celebrity friends like ABC's Chris Vlasto, who were encouraging him to tell his side of the story to the world.

As Susan McDougal psychoanalyzed her former husband, Jim was in a manic phase and had simply gone over the edge. Both McDougals had taken up temporary residence in the tacky pink Legacy Hotel across Capitol Avenue from the courthouse. Susan and Claudia Riley, who were sharing a single room, checked in on Jim daily. It was not, they recalled, a pretty scene. "He was taking so many drugs," Susan McDougal said, "he was smoking marijuana, he had little girls, you know, nineteen, twenty years old, bringing him, you know, uppers, downers, walking around Little Rock with him, driving him back and forth. You know, I'd go by his room, and it would just be heavy with marijuana smoke." Jim had been swept away with his new role as media darling, holding impromptu sessions outside the Legacy Hotel, where he spoke to the assembled journalists, waxing eloquent and quoting Shakespeare. "And loving it," said Susan, "because this was his time. You know, he hadn't been anything in quite a few years. He had lost everything, and now everyone's looking to Jim. It was his moment. And he was going to take it."

When Susan learned that Jim planned to testify, she marched down to his room and pounded on the door. "Jim, we agreed! . . ." Susan stood up to her ex-husband eye-to-eye. "None of us is going to testify! This could mess up everything."

Calmly, Jim replied, "My people expect to hear from me, Susan. They've heard the allegations, and now the people expect me to respond."

On the appointed day at the appointed hour, the fifty-five-year-old James B. McDougal was "looking paler than usual." He leaned on the arm of one of Susan's brothers as he entered the federal courthouse, rather than using his walking cane. His physician, Nolan Hagood of Arkadelphia, had just run tests and determined that at least one carotid artery that fed blood to McDougal's brain had become reblocked. He wrote to McDougal's lawyer that his client needed "prompt and thorough" medical attention and that he absolutely "should not testify." The doctor stated pointedly: "I believe Jim is taking a calculated risk in doing this."

Jim McDougal waded through reporters and joked: "He [Hagood] gave me some 12-hour nitroglycerin, which just blows your head off because it speeds your heart up." Smiling, he told his media friends: "So it could get interesting today."

Until this time, the momentum seemed to be moving strongly in the direction of the defendants. Judge Howard had just thrown out four counts against both Governor Tucker and Susan McDougal. These included a key ruling that Susan had not participated in the "825 loan." Still, none of the nineteen counts relating to Jim McDougal had been dismissed. As he entered the courtroom flashing his best Southern-gentleman smile, McDougal appeared to be a man walking toward his destiny.

Within minutes of swearing on the Bible to tell the whole truth, Jim Mc-Dougal began digging a hole from which he and his codefendants would never be extricated. The first casualty was his ex-wife. McDougal introduced Susan as a savvy businesswoman who worked side-by-side with him on every facet of the questionable business ventures. He told the jury with gallantry: "It was the exact model of what I had been raised on. Mother and Daddy always worked together every minute, and that's what she did and was much better than me in many, many areas."

At the end of each day, Susan McDougal had been telephoning her parents to report: "Another day. No one said my name." A female reporter from the *Los Angeles Times* had recently asked, "How's it feel to be the one person who will walk out of this unscathed?" Now, Susan's estranged husband was placing her at the epicenter of Madison's unorthodox business dealings.

In no time, prosecutor Ray Jahn was chewing Jim up on cross-examination. Jahn was a "kind of a cowboy guy, big old guy with cowboy boots." To Susan McDougal, he looked like "Porky Pig with a cowboy hat." Yet the San Antonio prosecutor was a master in the courtroom. At one point, Jahn confronted Jim McDougal with incriminating documents, forcing him to hem and haw, and then to accuse Starr's office of forging his signature.

When it came to questioning about Jim Guy Tucker, with whom McDougal had maintained an often-stormy relationship, McDougal had cheerfully told the jury that despite a few spats, "I have nothing but warmest personal feelings for Jim Guy today." On cross-examination, Jahn pulled out a transcript of an FBI interview and asked pointedly, "Mr. McDougal, isn't it a fact on June 30, 1995, you told Special Agent Norris that Mr. Tucker was a, quote, 'thief who would steal anything that wasn't nailed down'?"

McDougal peered up at Jahn with a crooked grin. "I don't think that's exactly what I said," he replied. He looked helplessly at the judge and jury. "I think I said 'like most lawyers, he would steal anything that wasn't nailed down.'" There were twitters in the jury box. Nobody on the defense team was laughing.

With their prospects for acquittal swirling down the drain, Susan McDougal waited for the next break. She made her way shakily to the elevators in the hallway, rode down to an empty witness room, closed the door behind her, and broke down sobbing. Her attorney, Bobby McDaniel, described the feeling in the courtroom as "kind of like in a football game when a coach can feel the momentum switching to [the other] team."

George Collins, trying to appear calm as the ailing Governor Jim Guy Tucker scribbled desperate notes to him, understood that the entire defense team's ship was going down. "Oh, Jesus Christ. Yes," Collins said, remembering. "It was absolutely the longest hours I've spent in a courtroom in my life. It was absolutely horrible. And Jim hated Susan. He wanted to bring her down. He deliberately did so, I think."

As Collins saw it, there was a sea of anger churning inside Jim McDougal. "He really hated Jim Guy as you hate a friend that didn't help you. He also hated Bill Clinton, because Clinton had not helped him." McDougal had even confessed to his lawyer, Sam Heuer, that he had hoped to get some sort of federal job in the Clinton administration, but like everything he wished for, this had never materialized. At one point, McDougal had been in the men's room with Governor Tucker's attorney during a break. The developer turned to the lawyer and said, his eyes turning cold, "You're the only SOB in the courtroom that never screwed me, and the only reason you didn't is because you didn't have a chance."

As the defense team watched in horror, McDougal kept marching to his death, "and it was just the knife plunging into [his codefendants'] back over and over again." Bobby McDaniel told Susan that he was going to have to "rip [Jim's] heart out" in cross-examination. Susan turned to her lawyer and said, "He's a sick old man, leave him alone."

McDaniel begged Susan to try to talk sense to her ex-husband. "Tell him I'll only ask two questions," McDaniel said. " 'When did Susan leave for Dallas?' And 'Was she involved in the business affairs [at Madison] after that?' "

So Susan walked over to Jim before court resumed. Struggling to maintain her composure, she touched Jim's shoulder and said, "Bobby McDaniel wants to ask you two simple questions, just to help me." Jim glared back at Susan and snapped, "If that hick lawyer of yours asks me even one question, it will be the biggest mistake of his career."

McDaniel would later say, still distressed over the experience, "She did not believe in attacking people that she loved, and she did love Jim. So she didn't [let] me go after him."

Jahn and his fellow OIC prosecutors at counsel table—Jackie Bennett and Amy St. Eve—were feeling bullish about their chances of conviction. They did not exactly "trust" David Hale. Yet in over a year's worth of meetings in the woods, Hale had supplied valuable information. Much of this was then authenticated with documents, because "we had a lot of his records, we had checks, we had checkbooks."

OIC had also hired a jury consultant to run several mock jury trials. Each time, the hypothetical jurors "wanted to physically lay their hands on something other than Hale's testimony. They wanted to see documents; they wanted to see Jim Guy's signature." So that's what OIC had produced, in superabundance, linking both Jim McDougal and Governor Tucker to the fraudulent Castle Grande deal. As Jahn told the jury in opening and closing arguments, it was a case of "lies told and truths concealed."

Susan had been involved in many of the "hiring and firing decisions" at Madison Guaranty. She had been named Businesswoman of the Year by the local Chamber of Commerce. There was no glossing over the fact that portions of the $300,000 loan were not used for Susan's advertising business, as stated on the loan papers, but for purchasing health-club memberships, home furnishings, and other personal expenses. As Jahn would put it, her only defense to the charge that she had misapplied $300,000 of funds was "I didn't read it. You know, I just came in and signed it, and giggled a little bit and skipped out the door." In Jahn's professional judgment, the chances of her being acquitted were "slim to none."

Although Susan McDougal and her attorney would forever believe that Jim McDougal "dropped Susan in the grease," this was not the full extent of her problems. OIC prosecutors later revealed that during their mock trial exercises, the jurors had not bought Susan's "innocent bystander" story. Hale's testimony and the documents bearing Susan's signature were just as responsible for her hopeless situation. "In every instance," Jahn later stated, "Susan McDougal was the first person they convicted."

Moreover, as much as the defendants and their lawyers were sure that they were victims of a political persecution, the suspicions and distrust were a two-way street. Starr's prosecutors were convinced that the Clinton White House had been in cahoots with the Arkansas defendants from the start. The White House (in the person of Clinton aide Bruce Lindsey) was receiving a copy of the daily transcript of the proceedings from an inside source.

There was also evidence that the Clinton team was providing a "steady stream of assistance" to the alleged felons. Ken Starr would later say, not trying to hide his suspicions: "Why would the president of the United States have his lawyers working with the defense team openly? Isn't that interesting? Wow. Some might call that a conflict of interest."

The files of Jim McDougal's own lawyer do reveal an exchange of faxes and information with the Clinton forces, including newspaper clippings, press kits, and talking points prepared by the White House. Before President Clinton's testimony at the White House, for instance, documents show that Heuer faxed a summary of his direct examination to Clinton's lawyer, David Kendall, to prepare the president for his questioning.

Starr's prosecution team was increasingly frustrated by this unholy alliance. So prosecutor Ray Jahn turned the tables on his opponents, by casting President Clinton as a victim in the case.

During closing arguments, Jahn strolled up and down in front of the jury, telling them, "The President of the United States is not on trial. Why isn't the President on trial? . . . Because he didn't set up any phony corporations to get employees to sign for loans that were basically worthless. He didn't get $300,000 from Capital Management Services like Jim and Susan McDougal did by falsely claiming their use. . . . The President didn't backdate any leases."

To shift the jury's attention from the issue of David Hale's trustworthiness, Jahn declared, "The defendants are trying to drag the President of the United States into this courtroom and set up a defense, hide behind the President by claiming that you must in some way make a bad judgment concerning the President to convict them. I submit to you that's not true."

Staring each juror directly in the eye as he allowed his gaze to move down the jury box, Jahn concluded, "Ladies and gentlemen, who is contradicting the President of the United States? It's not David Hale. It's Jim McDougal."

———

THE courtroom of Judge George Howard, Jr., was packed with reporters and onlookers. After two weeks of deliberations, the jury was ready to announce its verdict. Outside, on this Tuesday in late May, the heat had soared to 102 degrees. Inside, the temperature felt equally unbearable.

As the jurors entered the courtroom and brushed past Governor Tucker and Jim McDougal, their eyes seemed to steer clear of the codefendants. It had been a long and arduous two weeks in the locked jury room, one juror later confided. Local courtroom rules permitted jurors to take notes during the testimony, so the twelve men and women had pored over their handwritten notes, considering every angle. Laura E. Malat, a payroll specialist for the state ("Juror No. 2"), recalled: "The main thing in deliberating was dealing with the fact that Jim Guy Tucker was our governor. We wanted to make sure he had actually played a part. We didn't want to sell him down the river." Another juror concurred: "This was a very cohesive jury. The length of time it took to deliberate was not because we were bickering. It was because we were being very careful."

The jury foreperson, Sandra Wood, a nurse and homemaker from Russellville, Arkansas, rose, doing her best to remain composed. She told Judge Howard that the jury had reached a unanimous verdict: As to defendant James B. McDougal, they had found him guilty on eighteen of nineteen felony counts.

An audible gasp rose up from the courtroom. Governor Tucker, his jaw tensing, held out his hands in prayer.

That prayer, however, was not answered. Wood next told the judge that the jury had found Jim Guy Tucker guilty of conspiracy and mail fraud, two of the seven counts. When it came to the controversial $825,000 loan that had been the centerpiece of OIC's case against Tucker, the jurors registered a "not guilty" verdict. Governor Tucker had already dropped his head into his hands; he had ceased listening.

The jury foreperson turned to the charges against Susan McDougal, announcing that the jurors had found this defendant guilty on four counts—dealing with misuse of federal SBA funds and making false statements on the $300,000 Master Marketing loan. Susan McDougal smiled faintly as the jurors affirmed, one by one, their verdict.

As the jury filed out, the foreperson handed a note to the U.S. Marshal for Judge Howard. It stated simply: "We have prayed each day for wisdom and guidance."

President Clinton later observed of Jim McDougal's seemingly incomprehensible decision to take the witness stand, "He had no awareness, as people typically don't, about how much he had deteriorated mentally. And most people, most observers who watched the trial, believed that his testimony was instrumental in convicting all three of them."

Outside the courthouse, the media swarmed in a hive around the defendants. Jim McDougal, now facing eighty-four years in prison and $4.5 million in fines, whistled faintly as he walked back to the Legacy Hotel, leaning on his cane. When asked by reporters how he felt, McDougal tried to sound upbeat: "Well, I feel glad to be out of the courtroom. Nothing could be more excruciating than that."

Susan McDougal pushed her way through the crowd and rushed back to the hotel, where she collapsed.

Governor Tucker, barely able to speak to the swarm of journalists engulfing him, continued to maintain his innocence. In a faltering voice, he announced that he would abide by the Arkansas constitution and resign his office, pending appeal. Already, Lieutenant Governor Mike Huckabee, a Baptist minister and a Republican, was preparing to take over the reins of state.

The conservative *Washington Times* readied the next day's front-page story, declaring that the guilty verdicts might boost the sagging presidential campaign of Republican Senator Bob Dole. A spokesperson for the American Conservative Union declared: "It really is going to drive home to people the doubts they already have about Clinton's integrity."

Yet it was unclear that the Tucker and McDougal convictions had anything to do with President William Jefferson Clinton. Several jurors who granted interviews immediately after the verdicts made clear that they had disregarded Hale's testimony entirely. Moreover, they had found no wrongdoing whatsoever on the part of the president. One juror described Hale as "sneaky" and added: "He could slide under the door with the door closed." Juror Colin Capp told the *New York Times* that Hale was "an unmitigated liar," not to mention a perjurer. Capp, the son of popular *L'il Abner* cartoonist Al Capp, told one reporter that "it was an absolute travesty that Hale got sentenced to [only] 24 months." He went on: "David Hale invoked the President's name for one reason: to save his butt. We all felt that way."

Foreperson Sandra Wood told ABC's *Nightline* that "the president's credibility was never an issue. . . . I just felt like he was telling us to the best of his knowledge what he knew."

The exhausted defense lawyers were certain that Jim McDougal had unilaterally sunk their case. The jurors later revealed, however, that there was a consensus that all three defendants were guilty, with or without Jim McDougal's damning performance. When it came to Susan McDougal, one juror said she didn't buy Susan's message of, "Who me? I'm innocent." As a woman, Laura Malat wasn't prepared to swallow this excuse. "Your common sense tells you 'No. You can't be around it that much and not have a clue.'"

The most difficult decision concerned Governor Jim Guy Tucker. In the end, the jurors could not chalk up his conduct to "stupid mistakes." Many believed that Governor Tucker was up to his elbows in McDougal's bogus business deals. One juror said, "I think he knew what was going on. It was a case of the ends justifying the means."

President Clinton later shook his head and said of the three convictions: "I thought he [McDougal] might well have been guilty. But of diminished capacity. And I wondered whether somebody that was as troubled as he was, in his need of constant medication, was either competent to be judged to have known what he was doing when he did it, or competent to stand trial."

With respect to Susan McDougal and Jim Guy Tucker, Clinton questioned whether they were truly guilty of criminal conduct. Although Tucker had once been his political rival in Arkansas, Clinton did not wish this sort of persecution on anybody. "I worried about it . . . because I thought Starr and Jackie Bennett and Hick Ewing, and all those guys, would do anything they could to anybody they could if they thought they could break them and get them to change their story to lie about Hillary and me."

In the days and nights after the verdict, President Clinton recalled, "I just felt sick at what was going to happen to them all."

CHAPTER

16

THE "COOPERATING WITNESS"

From inside the White House, President Bill Clinton observed with sadness the metamorphosis of Jim McDougal from convicted felon to Kenneth Starr's cooperating witness. "He was a brilliant, delightful, and fundamentally a decent person," Clinton later said. "He always had demons that he wrestled with. And eventually he had, you know, a disintegration. And Starr used his morbid fear of going to prison to get him to change his story."

Clinton concluded: "Ironically, he got the worst of all worlds. He lied for him [Starr]. And he still died in jail."

Bill Clinton's top advisers buckled their seat belts, not knowing where this would lead. As John Podesta would explain, Clinton's home state was a "strange environment" filled with inscrutable political characters and dots that did not connect. Once an issue floated across the border into Ozark Mountain territory, Clinton's White House team held its breath, placing this into the category of "mysterious Arkansas stuff."

Just before the sentencing of Jim and Susan McDougal, which was scheduled to take place in August 1996, Jim McDougal called the Office of Independent Counsel and said he was ready to talk. Associate Independent Counsel Amy St. Eve, an attractive, crackerjack lawyer from Chicago who had assisted Ray Jahn at trial, quickly wrote to Sam Heuer and pressed for a meeting with McDougal: "We are interested in meeting with Mr. McDougal. Your client has called me several times asking about such a meeting. . . . Please contact me as soon as you can so we can discuss this issue."

Heuer was floored by his client's sudden desire to cast his lots with OIC. He called Jahn and ripped into him, reminding Jahn that the prosecutors had "no business corresponding in any shape, form or fashion" with a defendant represented by counsel. Heuer was suspicious of who had contacted whom first. He had observed that OIC and St. Eve had worked to develop a "friendly relationship" with McDougal before and during trial. It was no secret that Jim "thought of himself as quite a woman's man." The defense team saw the cute, button-nosed St. Eve as "flirtatious" in her dealings with McDougal. Now Heuer felt as if the Starr prosecutors, via St. Eve, were doing an end run around him.

Jim McDougal, meanwhile, was getting belligerent. He demanded to know why Heuer hadn't already "made a deal with the Independent Counsel." Heuer replied, "Well, Jim, I don't know what kind of deal you want me to make. . . . They want you to hang a lot of things on the Clintons that you have consistently told me was not possible."

OIC seemed particularly interested in an August 1, 1983, check for $5,081.82 paid out of one of Jim McDougal's business accounts, signed by Susan McDougal, with a scrawled notation at the bottom that said, "Payoff Clinton." Had Bill Clinton been paid funds, illicitly, from the Madison account? Jim McDougal had repeatedly told Heuer that there was "nothing there" on that check. Jim had also denied, under oath and in private discussions with his lawyer, that Bill Clinton had played any role in discussions with Hale on the $300,000 loan to Susan McDougal. Throughout the protracted second trial, Jim McDougal had never said a word to Heuer implicating Bill or Hillary Clinton in any wrong-doing. "No," Heuer later insisted. "Just to the contrary."

Sam Heuer now faced an ethical quandary. He had serious doubts that the story McDougal was gearing up to tell OIC—whatever that was—would be true. He said, "Jim, here's what we'll do. If that's what you want to do, I'll go ahead and prepare the proper papers." Yet he also informed McDougal that he, Heuer, would have to cease representing him, "because I can't in good conscience allow you to tell things that I have a very strong sense are not true."

On July 30, Ray Jahn advised Sam Heuer that OIC would conduct "preliminary interviews" with McDougal to determine if he might wish to cooperate. Meanwhile, the Whitewater felon began ranting that Heuer was "more interested in Bill Clinton's welfare" than Jim's own interests. McDougal decided to deal with OIC himself.

With Susan McDougal's court date still scheduled for August 20, Jim McDougal arranged for a personal audience with Independent Counsel Ken Starr, inside his tiny trailer-cottage at the bottom of Claudia Riley's driveway in Arkadelphia. Said Susan, thinking back on this period when Ken Starr's prosecutors began to court Jim as a cooperating witness, "That's when I began to hate them."

———

AMONG the numerous bizarre aspects of Jim and Susan McDougal's lives after their becoming convicted felons was the fact that both of them took up residence at Claudia Riley's home, near the Ouachita Baptist campus in Arkadelphia.

Jim was in the trailer-cottage; Susan was living in the main house in a spare bedroom. Claudia played the role of the mediator, making sure that the former husband and wife didn't go for each other's throats. She recalled, "I would sometimes go to the door when Jim would come up, and I'd say 'Jim, . . . if we're going to have any bad words, don't come in.'" McDougal would tell her, "Oh, no, baby, I'm going to be nice tonight." Claudia would then turn to Susan and warn her, "This goes for you, too."

There was more to it than just the ordinary friction between a split couple. "Jim could swing [in moods]," explained Claudia. "That's what bipolarism is, and he could go from manic to depressive in very short order. So—we were always walking carefully around him."

As he began traveling out of town for surreptitious meetings with OIC, McDougal increasingly made dark predictions that "this is going to be so much bigger than Watergate." He would refuse to share details with Claudia, stating, "What you don't know you will never have to attest to." Claudia would laugh it off, but she secretly worried. One of the last things Bob Riley had said to his wife, before he died, was, "Take care of Jim and Susan. They're going to need you." She was sticking to her promise, but it was a complex task.

One day, Jim came up from the guesthouse and excitedly announced, "Oh, Amy St. Eve called. She wants to come over and have me autograph this book, *Blood Sport.*" It was a best-selling account of Whitewater and featured McDougal prominently. Susan told him, "My God, I don't know how you go to lunch and sign a book for someone that's just convicted you. But, you know, more power to you if you can do that."

After Jim's rendezvous with St. Eve at the Western Sizzlin down the road, he told Susan triumphantly that St. Eve was prepared to get him "the best possible deal" if he gave OIC useful information. He was now visualizing writing a money-making book, and having St. Eve provide guidance to his nineteen-year-old "girlfriend" Tamara, a Ouachita undergraduate who "was just dating Jim at the time and helping him, you know, stay medicated." Jim danced around the Riley house telling Susan that "Amy is going to be a role model to Tamara and teach her how to dress and teach her how to maybe get to law school."

St. Eve, after being appointed to the federal bench in Chicago by President George W. Bush, dismissed these stories as colorful embroidery. "Jim and I never talked about a book deal," she said, correcting the record. Even though McDougal did talk about Tamara, she was "one of many" young college females who surrounded him at the time; there were never any serious discussions about assisting her. "Jim liked to tell stories and embellish," St. Eve said. "That was certainly his personality."

The only part of McDougal's story that was based on fact, Judge St. Eve acknowledged during a break in her courtroom work, was that Jim McDougal did autograph her copy of *Blood Sport* during that visit to Western Sizzlin. "I still have that," she said with a sigh, recalling her peculiar dealings with defendant Jim McDougal, who—while a likable fellow—had evident problems when it came to distinguishing truth from fiction.

Susan and Claudia observed the transformation of Jim McDougal into an OIC witness with increasing alarm. They heard more of Jim's schemes and strategies than they cared to hear, from Jim and his latest "girlfriend." "They would come up here and drink and get totally . . . he wasn't drinking," said Susan. "She was drinking. He was doing medication. Smoking [marijuana] and stuff. Claudia wouldn't allow it in the house, but they would go out on the deck or whatever, and so we knew everything."

Susan couldn't imagine how Jim could give Starr's office evidence against Bill Clinton when he had "just testified in front of God and humanity that none of these things are true." According to her version of events, Jim told her, "I don't want to die in prison, you know, and this is the only way I know to assure that I can get a deal. Because Judge Howard hates me and he is going to send me away for a really long time."

So Susan "put her arms around Jim" and told him "I absolutely understand." She consoled him: "If you can get a good deal, don't let me stop you."

Susan vividly recalled Jim's shambling up to Claudia's house one day and watching as he dialed OIC on the telephone. She remembered Jim going through a checklist of demands out loud with one of the Starr prosecutors: "I will be able to wait to be sentenced for six months" and "I will be assigned to a [lower-security] medical facility." Jim marked a check next to each item, smiling and giving Susan "the thumbs-up," as he said, "Yes, yes, yes" into the phone. Next he told the OIC prosecutor, "And one thing, you know, Judge Howard's a Christian, he's a Baptist minister on the weekends. I think it would really be good for Starr to come and say, you know, that I've had this Christian conversion, that I've become a Christian man and that, you know, I've seen the light and I'm going to tell the truth now and, you know, that really goes over with those Baptists, ha-ha, ha-ha!"

Susan cringed at the memory. "And he's laughing about it, you know. And I'm just . . . sitting there."

Jim hung up the telephone and proudly announced, "Starr's coming. He's gonna speak for me at my sentencing." Susan replied, "Well, let me just tell you something. This is great. This is terrific news." She turned her back on her ex-husband, telling Jim to add another demand to his list, now that he was such a buddy with Ken Starr. "Tell him my ex-wife gets probation . . ." she said sarcastically. Jim answered, "Oh, yeah, baby. Oh, yeah, baby, I'm—let me feel it out. And let me go see some of these people and feel them out, see who the best person is to talk to about that."

Recalled Susan, "I knew when he started his little shucking and jiving thing, that it was never going to happen."

———

SUSAN McDougal's memory of Ken Starr's visit to Claudia Riley's home was forever burned in her memory. It was a hot day in August. She was out on the deck with Claudia, aware that the independent counsel himself was coming to give McDougal "the papal hug." Susan had, by this time, developed a personal hatred of Starr, which (she acknowledged) may have clouded her recollection. Yet she would insist that this piece of the memory was crystal clear. "Three black cars, five black cars drive up. You see, I always minimize, you have to remember that. I'm not an exaggerator. Five cars drive up, black cars, and doors open and they get out like the Magi carrying gifts, you know." As the OIC prosecutors stepped out onto the dusty driveway, Susan recalled, "I want to throw insults and to yell from the deck up here, but Claudia, always being the lady, won't let me. I think there are certain times when you have to hurl insults, but she wouldn't let me. And Starr gets out. And he has on this checked shirt and these [polyester] Sansabelt slacks."

Seething, Susan watched Ken Starr and his entourage proceed into Jim's trailer-cottage at the bottom of the driveway. She recalled, "I just, you know, just made horrible remarks to Claudia and said all kinds of things about them."

Starr himself did not recall the details of the trip to Arkadelphia. At the time, he said, "I drove a little red compact, you know, a GSA [U.S. General Services Administration] rental." So he was skeptical that he had arrived in a motorcade of black cars. He did acknowledge, however, that he might have been driven to Arkadelphia in an FBI vehicle. Prosecutor Amy St. Eve was present that day. She remembered only being struck by the dwarfish dimensions of McDougal's trailer-cottage; a large framed portrait of FDR and assorted clutter gave McDougal's home an even more claustrophobic feel. "He had such a big personality," recalled Judge St. Eve, "it was kind of counter to his personality, the smallness."

Neither Starr nor St. Eve recalled having any significant discussion with McDougal during this first courtesy call. Rather, the purpose was simply to get acquainted with him and to open lines of communication. Those watching from the Riley house, however, saw it differently.

After the OIC prosecutors left, Susan McDougal marched down to the trailer to interrogate Jim; she was revolted when she saw cheap gifts on the counter. "And they had brought Jim his favorite candies. He had these kinds of mints that he liked and he had M&M's. They had brought him these presents and Starr told him, you know, how glad he was that Jim was cooperating."

McDougal's codefendants and their lawyers were certain they understood what was driving the Starr prosecutors' sudden interest in a mentally troubled man like James B. McDougal. George Collins, who watched his client Governor Jim Guy Tucker get convicted, expressed admiration for Starr on a professional level. "I mean, I like Kenny Starr in a way," said Collins. "He was always polite to me; he's a magnificent lawyer. I don't rank with him, not within a thousand miles. But he always treated me courteously and as an equal, which I am not."

Despite this profound professional respect, Collins felt that the Starr prosecutorial machine was noticeably different from his predecessor's. The Fiske people, he said, were "doing a criminal investigation." Ken Starr's team, he felt in his gut, was "doing a president hunt."

Collins had told his client bluntly at one point, "They want Bill Clinton. If you can give them Bill Clinton, it's all over." Tucker's response, according to his lawyer, was that the only incriminating information he possessed about Clinton was that "when he moved out of the governor's mansion, he left Chelsea's goldfish behind and didn't try to take care of that goldfish." Said Collins, "Jim Guy would not lie to save his own self."

Prosecutor Ray Jahn defended Ken Starr and his lawyers by saying that such attempts to "demonize" them after the Whitewater convictions constituted a serious "injustice." It was true, he said, that some people on the OIC team "obviously had a great deal of personal animosity for the Clintons." But Starr himself was not one of those persons. "He never, never targeted the Clintons," said Jahn.

Hearing a recounting of Jahn's comments, Collins cleared his throat and said, "Well, fine. And if you put your tooth in your shoes, the fairy will bring a dime."

Seated in his Chicago law office and having seen a great deal during his half-century career as a litigator, Collins did not feel bitterness toward Ken Starr or his OIC prosecutors. Yet he suffered no delusions when it came to where OIC was headed with its unusual investigation. Reflected Collins, "It was a strange time and the purpose was to hunt the great bull elephant and they never quite brought him down."

———

MANY of those who observed Jim McDougal after he became a cooperating witness for OIC saw a man who was prepared to bend and stretch in any direction necessary to escape jail time. James Stewart, the Harvard Law School graduate and award-winning author of *Blood Sport*, spent considerable time with McDougal during this period. Although Stewart's book was not particularly sympathetic toward the Clintons, he still maintained a healthy skepticism when it came to McDougal's postconviction epiphany.

Stewart's first meeting with Jim McDougal, well before the trial, said a great deal about this eccentric interviewee. McDougal had arranged to meet the author at a Total 66 gas station in Arkadelphia, just off the interstate. "It was kind of a cloak-and-dagger thing," Stewart recalled, "where I was supposed to sit there in the car reading the *Wall Street Journal*, and that's how he would know who I was." After this meeting befitting two international spies, the pair proceeded to lunch at the Western Sizzlin, a "dreadful" experience for Stewart because "he [McDougal] was talking about his heart attack and he was . . . eating so much saturated fat that I thought he would, you know, drop over right during our meal." Stewart recalled with clarity that McDougal "flirted with the waitresses in there. All of them knew him by name . . . fawned over him. He loved them. All these young girls. So he still had a flair."

Part of McDougal's special flair, in Stewart's estimation, was for manipulating facts to wriggle out of danger. As soon as McDougal was convicted of multiple felonies, he began to change his tune, telling versions of his tragic story that directly implicated Bill Clinton. Stewart had trouble buying it. "That was really his ace in the hole, that testimony," Stewart explained later, leaning his elbows on the desk in his Manhattan writer's office. "That's what kept him relevant, you know, and Jim would have been shrewdly aware of that. And just as Jim may have told story A the first time, because that was in his interest, he would have told story B the second time, and the truth may be neither one of them."

Stewart analyzed this complicated Arkansan who dressed nattily and flirted with college girls at the Western Sizzlin: "In some ways, I think he would be *more* willing to lie under oath than if he wasn't under oath. . . . Jim would see it as a game, as something to be manipulated, as something—as another system that he could, you know, operate in."

Although Stewart was no apologist for the Clintons, he had spent enough time with McDougal to know that the felon-turned-informant was going to pose numerous problems for OIC. "I would say that he was never going to be a particularly credible witness on the stand. First, because he had made so many falsehoods before, and second, because he was fully capable of, again, lying under oath at any moment."

Susan McDougal and Claudia Riley saw manifestations of those same qualities at an escalating rate. Both women recalled Jim's wandering up from his trailer-cottage and sharing his thoughts about his debriefing sessions with Starr's lawyers. He had settled back in a comfortable chair in Claudia's living room and begun "weaving these tales": "How does this sound—you know, remember that day I went to the capitol to talk to Bill [Clinton] about that water system? How about if I say that was about that Hale loan and I'm even going to tell them details about it? . . ."

After listening to Jim spin out various scenarios that would "help him at his sentencing," Susan finally interrupted: "Jim, what makes you think you can make these up, these stories, just weave them up, and that the president of the United States, with all of his power and all the people helping him, are not just going to cream you?"

Jim replied that he now had access to documents, courtesy of OIC, that would allow him to construct a plausible paper trail. Hadn't it worked for David Hale after he became a cooperating witness for Starr's office? "All I have to do is make it all fit," McDougal proclaimed.

On one occasion, Susan recalled, Jim rocked forward in his chair and said, "I'll tell you what. If you don't want to say something about Bill, let's just think up something we can say about Hillary. I mean, what did Hillary ever do for us? We could just, you know, get you in there, and you could be against Hillary, and I'll do all the stuff against Bill, and we'll be a tag team."

Susan replied to her ex-husband, "Jim, they will *kill* us. We do not have the truth here. And when you get up there and they start breaking all this down, you know, this is going to be exposed for what it is, and we're going to be looking awful. I can't do that."

At this, Jim became enraged. "F—— the Clintons!" he shouted. "What'd they ever do for us? I'll make them sorry they ever went to Washington." Pounding his cane against the floor, he hollered, "This will be the hardest presidency anyone ever had to endure."

During this period, before Jim went to prison, both Claudia and Susan also observed worsening substance abuse problems. Susan recalled a "terrible episode at Claudia's, where Jim almost overdosed. Some girls, too. They were vomiting. They had come up [to the house]."

Claudia later assessed Jim's situation candidly: "To my knowledge, Jim used whatever he needed and wanted to give him relief." Increasingly, McDougal was associating with "dubious" people who appeared at the trailer to "supply" him. Claudia was a widow trying to do right by a fifty-five-year-old family friend, but she had no power to stop McDougal.

Claudia recalled that Jim once "threw around furniture" after coming to see Susan. Increasingly, he became agitated and verbally abusive. Claudia summed up this period of erratic behavior: "Jim was two people. He was Bob Riley's close friend. He protected me. But he was eruptive."

She put down her glass of iced tea, sadness dimming her eyes. "I just felt that Jim was overmedicated and that he was fighting for survival," she said. "Jim did have a terrible, terrible fear of going to prison and dying in prison. That was his fear."

———

As the date for Susan McDougal's sentencing approached, OIC invited her to discuss a possible deal. Susan's feeling at this point was, "I wanted to talk to them. . . . I wanted to go forward, really." She and Claudia Riley drove to the office of her lawyer, Bobby McDaniel, in Jonesboro. He placed his boots up on the desk and dialed Ray Jahn, getting the Starr prosecutor on a speakerphone. McDaniel said, "I got two questions for you. One is, what do you want from her? And the second is, what are you going to give her?"

Susan recalled that Jahn said something like, "You know who this investigation is about, and we are willing to propose to the judge that Susan get probation." The conviction and jail time "could disappear." This would include the California charges involving Nancy Mehta. "With a snap of the fingers, that will just be gone."

The gist of the conversation, according to McDaniel, was that OIC was "willing to make Susan substantial accommodations in exchange for testimony helpful to the Clintons' prosecution. Claudia Riley heard the same thing: "We almost fainted. And he [Jahn] said, . . . 'She will walk, she will never serve one day in jail.'" Claudia remembered praying, "Let her do this. Let her do this."

Jahn rejected this account as a gross exaggeration. "I just basically said, 'Look, you know what our job is. All we want from you is the truth.'" The Texas prosecutor would say of Susan McDougal: "She overdramatizes things to begin with, if you want to be polite about it. Otherwise she lies about them. . . . So that would be my reaction."

Whatever precise words were transmitted over the speakerphone that day, it is clear that McDaniel eventually told Jahn, "My client's overcome." He was forced to discontinue the conversation.

Susan recalled her state of mind: "I am penniless. My family is absolutely traumatized. I am facing sentencing in three days for this conviction. I have a trial to go [to in California], where my insane, crazy boss, Nancy Mehta, is alleging things. I have no money, and I have a grand jury that is about to be impaneled to investigate me for income tax evasion, of which Jim McDougal has done all my taxes. So I am totally, totally without any defenses . . . I am beside myself."

One option that Claudia and Susan discussed, taking a break to collect themselves, was for Susan to give the OIC lawyers what they wanted. She could say, "David Hale told the truth—Bill Clinton asked me to borrow three hundred thousand dollars from Hale, and we had that conversation, and I went down there and got that money, and Bill Clinton was supposed to have gotten [some of] it." If she did that, Susan was fairly certain, "it would just be probation for me and they will have talked to the D.A. [in California] . . . and everything can go back to being somewhat normal."

Claudia and Susan sat in Bobby McDaniel's office, discombobulated. Claudia said, "If it were my daughter, I would advise her to do *anything* not to go to jail." She began weeping and blurted out, "Susan, *please* don't leave me. Please don't go to prison for this."

Susan looked at Claudia and said, "What would Bob say?" invoking the name of Claudia's late husband. At that point, "we both cried a bunch more because her husband was, you know—he would be burned at the stake before he would have done anything that he considered to be without integrity." Finally, Susan told McDaniel not to call Jahn back. No deal was possible.

The minute Susan returned to her parents' home in rural Camden that night, the phone rang. It was Jim McDougal. He shouted into the receiver, "What's going on? I just talked with OIC, and they said you never called them back." Susan told her ex-husband that she couldn't cooperate with Starr's prosecutors. Jim rattled off a string of expletives and growled: "Susan, they're going to make sure that you spend time in jail. They're going to make sure they get you. If you don't do this,

Susan, I'm never going to speak to you again." With that, he slammed down the phone.

As Susan McDougal finished the story years later, sitting on Claudia Riley's couch, squeezing Claudia's hand, and reliving that traumatic day, she said, "That was the last time I ever spoke to him, because I went to jail not long after that, and Jim died in jail, so . . ."

———

At 9:30 a.m., on August 20, 1996, the heat and humidity were settling in a thick, heavy haze over Little Rock. On this day, Susan McDougal had returned to the courtroom of Judge George Howard, Jr., to be sentenced.

Although Susan faced up to seventeen years in prison, she and her lawyer had been praying that she might get probation, as a minor figure in this elaborate criminal scheme. Now her prayers were melting away. Ken Starr, dressed in a dark suit, had personally made an appearance alongside his prosecutors to communicate the seriousness of this sentencing proceeding. The independent counsel's office viewed this as a watershed in its investigation: Susan McDougal, they believed, held the key to other information vital to their criminal probe.

Governor Jim Guy Tucker, just a day earlier, had been sentenced to eighteen months under house arrest and four years' probation, because he was slated to undergo an emergency liver transplant. Judge Howard, mulling over the fourteen-page recommendation of the Office of Independent Counsel, was in a less magnanimous mood when it came to Susan McDougal. The OIC presentence report described her as a person who had played "an active role" in obtaining the fraudulent loan from David Hale. Moreover, the report recited, she had "attempted to camouflage her criminal acts" and refused to cooperate with OIC. Gazing sternly down from the bench, Judge Howard hammered his gavel and imposed a sentence of two years in federal prison plus more than 300 hours of community service and $305,000 in fines and restitution. Howard told the defendant that she had exactly forty days to get her affairs in order before reporting to the custody of the U.S. Marshal.

As McDougal left the courtroom, an FBI agent walked up and handed her a subpoena to appear in front of Ken Starr's grand jury.

———

The battle between Senator Bob Dole and President Bill Clinton for the right to occupy the White House was in full swing. In late August 1996, as Bill Clinton boarded a railroad car dubbed the 21st Century Express en route from Virginia to the Democratic National Convention in Chicago, his prospects of reelection were looking bright. The *Paula Jones* case was now on the back burner. The

Whitewater case, following the convictions of the McDougals and Governor Tucker, seemed to be in remission, unless an andiron swung out of nowhere and knocked Bill Clinton off his perch on the flag-draped presidential train.

While Clinton was steaming toward reelection, Susan McDougal was weighing her options and deciding whether to strike a deal with OIC. She agreed to appear on ABC's *Primetime Live* with Diane Sawyer and talk about her quandary. "It is tempting every time they put the carrot before my eyes," Susan said. "It's very tempting. It's tempting when I see my mother crying. When I see my family hurting. . . ." At the same time, the convicted Whitewater defendant fixed her jaw and declared, "The Clintons didn't do this to me. . . . This is something that Kenneth Starr and the independent counsel have done to me because they have an agenda, and I am the roadblock to what they want."

The show's producers had promised Susan that certain topics would be off limits during the interview. As soon as the cameras began to roll, however, McDougal found herself being peppered with uncomfortable questions—specifically about whether she had had an affair with Bill Clinton and about whether she was withholding other dark secrets about the president. A raw transcript of that unedited interview session, turned over to OIC investigators and later obtained under the Freedom of Information Act, revealed Susan McDougal caught in an extremely uncomfortable position:

> DIANE SAWYER: There have been some stories . . . implications, reports that one of the things [causing your rift with Hillary Clinton] would have been that she thought that you and Mr. Clinton were involved.
>
> SUSAN McDOUGAL: I . . . I really don't know how to respond to that except to say that again, that is such a personal question and I really don't think I want to talk about things like that.
>
> SAWYER: You won't answer yes or no that you were or weren't . . .
>
> McDOUGAL: It's too personal for me right now to even begin to talk about things like that. It's so hurtful to so many people that it's just not a question I want to answer.

Susan McDougal, waving her hands in frustration, called timeout: The producers had agreed she wouldn't be forced to answer these questions—that had been the deal. She won the debate: the offending segments were edited out. But when the show was broadcast on national television, Susan knew that the clear implication for viewers would be "that I was hiding something about the Clintons."

Flying back to Arkansas that night, she concluded that no matter what ground rules were established, the Starr prosecutors would take liberties like these television producers had taken, casting her story in the worst possible light. She now reached a decision about how she needed to deal with the grand jury.

On September 4, Susan McDougal was ushered into the grand jury room by prosecutor Ray Jahn. Twenty-three citizens of Arkansas sat on rickety wooden chairs. McDougal clutched a prepared statement in her hands. The moment she was sworn in, OIC prosecutor Jahn began the questioning:

JAHN: Can you tell us, ma'am, where you were born?
McDOUGAL: I'd like to read a statement before we begin, if that would be okay.
JAHN: You can read it at the end of the appearance.
McDOUGAL: I would like to read it before we begin. I think the foreman can let me do that, if he will.
JAHN: Ma'am, ma'am, ma'am, you will be given ample opportunity.
McDOUGAL: May I ask the foreman if he'll let me read this statement before I begin?
JAHN: No, ma'am. No, ma'am. You are here to answer questions . . .
McDOUGAL: I'd like to read the statement. The foreman has the right to let me read the statement.
JAHN: Ma'am, where were you born?
McDOUGAL: [No response]
JAHN: Ma'am, where were you born?
McDOUGAL: [No response].

Years later, McDougal would recall standing alone in front of Starr's grand jury: "I was shaking. I was scared to death. I knew that everybody there was smarter than me. I knew there was no way that I could ever hold my own with them."

Jahn asked her to step out of the room, so that he could consult with his fellow OIC prosecutors and the grand jurors. He now called her back into the room and switched to a series of questions dealing with Bill Clinton. "To your knowledge," Jahn asked, "did William Jefferson Clinton testify truthfully during the course of your trial?"

When McDougal again refused to respond and reverted to her prepared statement, federal marshals took her away, leading her to the courtroom of Judge Susan Webber Wright, who (by sheer happenstance) was in charge of miscellaneous matters that day.

Judge Wright peered over her owlish glasses, appearing displeased. She was tired of the hubbub surrounding the *Paula Jones* litigation; it was diverting time from a huge docket of important cases. Now she was faced with another Clinton-related distraction.

After rereading her statement to Judge Wright in full, Susan McDougal told the judge in a pleading tone that even if she answered these "private and personal" questions truthfully, Starr's prosecutors would find some excuse to charge her with perjury, because her testimony "clashed with their theory of the case." If the U.S. Supreme Court directed her to testify, McDougal told the judge, she would answer. Short of that, she would not cooperate with these biased prosecutors.

Judge Wright, her hair pulled back in a pragmatic bun, allowed that McDougal's argument was "novel," but there was no legal basis for refusing to testify simply because one didn't trust a prosecutor. Judge Wright tapped her gavel—she was giving McDougal five days to reconsider. Otherwise, the judge stated matter-of-factly, the Whitewater defendant should pack her toothbrush, because she would be heading to jail for contempt.

In explaining, years later, why she chose prison over answering OIC's questions in the grand jury, McDougal narrowed her eyes and said, "An abiding, unrelenting hatred and distrust of the independent counsel." She continued, "They believed that they could manipulate anything I had to say." Already Starr's prosecutors had succeeded in getting David Hale and Jim McDougal to say that Clinton was involved with the three-hundred-thousand-dollar loan, which she knew was false. It also sickened her that "Starr was spouting his Christianity night and day," while OIC was busy turning Jim into a "craven liar." She went on: "Jim McDougal was making up stories about innocent people and laughing about it, and this man [Starr] was aiding and abetting . . . [Jim] had been on drugs, marijuana, acting absolutely outlandishly during the trial. He was making up these stories, and yet they were willing to use him as a witness against the president of the United States."

Susan understood that Judge Wright viewed her refusal to testify as irrational. In theory, if she just "told the truth" she would be spared incarceration. Yet Susan's mind saw it differently. She posed a rhetorical question: "Was I protecting Bill Clinton? If I'd known that Bill Clinton did something illegal, would I have gone to jail? And hurt my mom and dad? And all my brothers and sisters, who were crying day and night? And would I have left Claudia, who's begging me not to go?" Her answer was, "No, I'd have said everything I knew that he'd done. If I had known anything Hillary had done after she had acted so crazy, I'd have told everything I knew about her, too. I had no trouble telling anything that I knew."

Susan paused to take a breath. "And what I knew beyond a shadow of a doubt was that Bill and Hillary did not ask me to get that loan. That is not negotiable; it's not something I might have forgotten. It never happened. And so . . . the fact they're believing David Hale, who had stolen so much money from the SBA—he's lied, cheated, and stolen, and Jim McDougal . . ." she inhaled and said, "I'm going to go in there? No way . . . There's no way."

Her eyes becoming puffy, Susan McDougal said that she had not taken the stand at trial to rebut Jim's testimony "because I had no self-confidence that I could speak for myself, no self-confidence. Jim had always taken care of everything for me. And I didn't think I could talk."

Standing in front of Judge Wright on that day in the Little Rock federal courthouse, Susan felt that she needed to get her voice back. "It was time," she concluded, "for me to say no."

———

YEARS later, having spent time in federal and state prisons stretching from Arkansas to California and having recovered from the trauma of Jim McDougal's dying in solitary confinement in Fort Worth, Texas, Susan McDougal would settle herself on Claudia Riley's couch. McDougal now directly answered the questions that she had refused to answer for the Office of Independent Counsel in the grand jury.

First, when it came to OIC's question "Did you ever discuss your loan from David Hale with William Jefferson Clinton?" she replied firmly, "No. It is absolutely untrue that it was ever discussed."

In response to OIC's related question, "To your knowledge, did William Jefferson Clinton testify truthfully during the course of your trial?" Susan McDougal weighed the words carefully. "Yes," she said. "To my knowledge, he did. I don't remember every word he said. But I think if I'd heard him lie that I would have said something. . . . In my mind, I probably would have said, 'That didn't happen.' So I think basically everything he said was the truth." Specifically, with respect to President Clinton's testimony that he did not know about the $300,000 loan made by David Hale to Susan McDougal, she said firmly, "I believe that."

When it came to OIC's inquiry whether Hillary Clinton had been retained by Madison to do legal work, and if so, the extent of that work, McDougal said she had no knowledge. By this time, she said, her involvement with Madison was "very little. Hardly at all. Involved with Madison as far as picking the paint colors and the carpet? Yeah. Involved as far as retaining attorneys? No." It was true that Jim had mentioned to her in passing, "Would you mind if I put Hillary on retainer?" knowing that Susan and Hillary might not be on best terms. Otherwise, she said, "I have no idea."

Similarly, with respect to OIC's question about a microfilmed copy of a 1983 check for $5,081.82 with the notation "Payoff Clinton," which she had signed from the Madison Guaranty accounts, Susan had no recollection. She speculated it might have involved a payment relating to land that she and Jim had purchased in the town of Clinton, Arkansas; whatever it was, she was certain she had never knowingly made a payment to Bill Clinton. Nor did she know anything about a $27,600 check payable to "Bill Clinton"—a check that had been found in the trunk of an abandoned car after a tornado. Jim moved money around as if it were his own personal piggy bank, Susan noted, so it was anybody's guess what tangled web Jim had woven. "I don't know of any loan that Clinton ever got there," she said. "Jim would have told me, I think." (The FBI's own analysis confirmed that Clinton never endorsed either check, and his fingerprints were on neither one.)

Addressing the most sensitive question of all, relating to the issue of whether she had engaged in an extramarital relationship with Bill Clinton during the Arkansas years, which might have affected her willingness to answer the grand jury's questions truthfully, Susan McDougal pushed the hair out of her eyes and answered with a mixture of emotion and anger: "No. No. I was in love with my husband. Who was a totally different man from Bill Clinton. Absolutely in love with him until he got terribly sick and then I had a relationship with Pat Harris that was very strong and daily and living with him, and so, no, that never happened." Susan bristled at the notion that she refused to talk to Starr's prosecutors because of some prior amorous affair with Clinton. "Believe it or not, someone might not be attracted to a guy that, you know, is Bill Clinton." She paused. "I mean I hate to say that, but . . ."

She took another breath. "He is very needy," she said. "Very, you know, constantly needs to be told, you know, 'you're great, you're doing great,' you know. My amorous affections tend to go toward men who are more giving to me, who are taking care of me and who are giving to me." She laughed self-consciously. "You know, two needy people don't make a good couple. Bill Clinton and I are way too much alike to be together."

In response to the scenario seemingly endorsed by the independent counsel's office that she was refusing to talk because she was hiding a past extramarital relationship with Bill Clinton, Susan McDougal's voice became loud and insistent: "Yes. Oh, let me just give you this scenario. I had an affair with Clinton and then, after not speaking to him for years, literally years, of living in California with Pat Harris, going to law school with Pat Harris, helping Pat Harris through law school, planning our marriage, I then do not testify against someone that maybe five years before I had had some kind of 'sexual congress' with. It boggles my mind. It really does. I mean that's a hell of a man, is all I've got to say."

McDougal sat forward on the couch, becoming red in the face as she pondered this image. "That's a Hickman Ewing, sex-demented, circus-crazed, you know, woman-with-three-breasts kind of mentality, that would think up that a woman would put herself into jail, into prison, for a man she hadn't spoken to in years because once upon a time she had a sexual relationship with him." For Susan, it didn't even make sense. "I mean, I know women who are married to men [whom] they really love, that they rat on. You know what I mean? I know women who try to get out of jail by testifying against men they love. It makes no sense. It's that dinosaur, right-wing Christian conspiracy, Republican, crazy thing that makes me hate them."

———

KEN Starr's prosecutors would continue to insist that they just wanted straight answers, not a litany of excuses. If Susan McDougal had said, "I didn't tell him anything, I just took the records over to the governor's mansion, and that was it," OIC would have played the cards dealt to them. Ray Jahn later insisted that they were not targeting Bill Clinton or anyone else. "We're not that kind of prosecutors."

Some OIC lawyers, who preferred to speak off the record, were personally convinced that Bill Clinton had attended the meeting at the Castle Grande trailer with McDougal and Hale. They figured Clinton needed money to pay off the Whitewater debt, and that Susan intentionally decided *not* to testify, because "she might slip up and tell the truth about how much knowledge he [Clinton] had about this whole transaction." Of course, this was all speculation behind closed doors. All the Starr prosecutors knew for sure was they needed to hear Susan McDougal's testimony, and to get certain questions answered, under oath.

On the morning of September 9, Susan McDougal surrendered herself to the U.S. Marshal's office in Little Rock. She was placed in a five-by-ten-foot concrete holding cell for processing. Then the Whitewater defendant was constrained in shackles and leg irons, an unusual measure, and led outside, where a line of media people snapped pictures and shouted questions at her.

McDougal threw back her head, jutted out her chin, and walked defiantly toward the awaiting prison van, which drove her to a jail cell in the women's pod of the Faulkner County Detention Center, an overcrowded facility in the dead center of Arkansas.

In the White House residence, President Clinton watched the television intently as the evening news showed these photos of Susan McDougal in shackles. Aides recalled that ordinarily, Whitewater events did little to faze Clinton—he did not get "emotionally involved" in Whitewater distractions. This night, however, was a notable exception. One individual present recalled that Clinton "blew his stack." It was as if he had a "serious personal reaction" to this particular event—one that aides had never witnessed before. Some of those in the room suspected they knew why.

———

PAULA JONES GOES TO WASHINGTON

When the U.S. Supreme Court issued its one-sentence order granting certiorari (agreeing to hear the appeal) in the case of *Clinton v. Jones* in the summer of 1996, the White House popped open champagne bottles. Lawyer Bob Bennett had accomplished his job: the Democratic National Convention would soon be convening amid balloon and fanfare in Chicago. "Getting it past the election was humongous," one adviser close to the president later said. Even the conservative *Washington Times* observed that Clinton had won a victory in getting this "reprieve." Paula Jones's embarrassing sexual harassment suit now had been put "on ice." Oral arguments in the Supreme Court were not scheduled until well after the November election between President Clinton and Senator Dole. Once entrenched for a second term, White House advisers were confident, Clinton would be safe from this bear trap.

Their plan might have been successful, if it were not for the appearance of Susan Carpenter-McMillan, who signed on as the new spokesperson for Paula Jones. Carpenter-McMillan was the embodiment of everything that made lawyers Gil Davis and Joe Cammarata cringe, as they worried about outside factors that might destabilize Jones's case. The spokeswoman was loud, unabashedly conservative, and unabashedly Republican, and she loathed Bill Clinton.

A forty-nine-year-old California native with platinum blond hair, she was a self-styled PR expert who specialized in "high-profile controversial causes" under the banner of "The Woman's Coalition." Carpenter-McMillan had dabbled in conservative issues for years, receiving a nomination for an Emmy Award in 1991 for television news commentaries defending Clarence Thomas's nomination to the Supreme Court. She had launched a campaign to ensure that the California legislature passed a mandatory "chemical castration" bill, the only law in the country that mandated the neutering of adult males who had sexually abused children. In the early 1990s, Carpenter-McMillan had begun writing conservative commentaries for an ABC affiliate in California. One of these championed Paula Jones and her lawsuit against the president. Thus began a beautiful relationship. "Susie" and Paula met for lunch in Long Beach, becoming fast friends. As Carpenter-McMillan would summarize her impressions of the young Arkansas transplant, Jones was "very, very sweet," and "became like a kid sister. I felt the need to protect her. She was very naive."

There was plenty from which Jones needed to be protected, she felt, especially when it came to the likes of William Jefferson Clinton. "I truly believed that he [Clinton] was just . . . a slimeball," Carpenter-McMillan said later. "I mean, he was a trailer-park boy with a brain, a very brilliant brain, but still a trailer-park boy."

Carpenter-McMillan signed on to become Jones's official spokesperson and personal coach, turning the cause into an "eighteen-hour-a-day job." In previous lawsuits, for which she acted as PR consultant, she would "come in and hire the lawyers, plan the wardrobe, look at the strategy, decide, 'Is this [case] going to a jury?'" But in the *Jones* case, Carpenter-McMillan aspired toward a bigger role, and she found an immediate ally in Paula's husband. Although Steve Jones was a "very controlling figure," he clearly was itching for a confrontation with Bill Clinton. On that score, he and Carpenter-McMillan were of one mind. "I'm not sure that Paula would have been able to do this on her own," Carpenter-McMillan said later. "I will give Steve credit. It was really a lot of his strength that propelled this lawsuit, promoted it and kept it [going]."

As Carpenter-McMillan sized up the situation from a PR perspective, this case was eventually heading to a jury. "Did Steve Jones want the money? I'm sure he did," she explained. "But that is not what drove them in the beginning." Carpenter-McMillan saw a bigger incentive to go after Clinton: "The way you discipline big corporations is to hit them in the pocketbook. That's how our system works. I suppose if Clinton would have said, 'Well, instead of paying you money, I'll take thirty lashes on the front of the White House lawn,' maybe [Paula and Steve] would have opted for that."

For Paula's Virginia lawyers, the injection of Susan Carpenter-McMillan into the case was a massive headache. Where she came from and how she got hired, said Joe Cammarata, was a "mystery of life." She was constantly disrupting the lawyers' work with her PR meddling and other activities behind their backs, which caused them to have "lack of confidence in her." However it happened, Carpenter-McMillan was soon joined at the hip with Paula. As Cammarata said, exhaling loudly: "They became friends. Susie and Paula."

BESIDES Susan Carpenter-McMillan, the White House also had to deal with the fact that two leading conservative Republican lawyers had quietly stepped up to assist Gil Davis in the preparations for his Supreme Court argument.

Davis, who had no experience in the rarefied atmosphere of the nation's highest court, was doing his best to ready himself. In one random note dictated to his file, he recorded: "What Clinton is asking for is a license to be a law breaker. In other words, once he becomes President he can do no wrong, at least he can't be held accountable for any wrong that he does." In another note, he recorded: "The immunity goes to the office not to the person. . . . For the President to cowardly hide behind the office to shelter himself from answering for private wrongs, is very demeaning to the office." As the Supreme Court oral argument drew closer, Davis dictated again into his machine, reminding himself: "Use the analogy of the civil tax audit. Is the President immune from *that* while he is President?"

Davis was ready to go it alone, preparing for this Supreme Court appearance as he would any important personal injury case. Yet certain influential Republicans were worried. Only a select group of attorneys appeared in the highest court of the United States—this was no occasion for someone to get his training wheels. Davis was pitted against Bob Bennett, a veteran of high-profile cases, and Acting Solicitor General Walter Dellinger. One of the premier constitutional lawyers in the country, Dellinger had filed an amicus brief in support of the president.

Robert Bork and Theodore Olson, two of the most respected appellate lawyers in the United States, therefore volunteered to help. Bork, former solicitor general and attorney general under President Nixon, had become an icon within the conservative movement when Democrats blocked President Reagan's effort to appoint him to the Supreme Court because of his unabashedly conservative philosophy. The bearded Bork, now associated with a Washington think tank, was a major legal figure in America.

Ted Olson, former assistant attorney general in the Reagan administration, had been the plaintiff in *Morrison v. Olson,* the 1988 landmark case that sought to topple the independent counsel law when it was used to investigate President Reagan and Vice President George H. W. Bush during the Iran-Contra affair. Olson had failed in that mission. Now, with the shoe on the other foot, and with Democrats occupying the White House, he had slipped in—beneath the radar—to do his part. He had represented David Hale to keep him out of congressional Whitewater hearings that could further undermine Hale's credibility as a witness against Bill Clinton. Olson had also quietly stoked the *Paula Jones* case, serving on the board of *American Spectator,* which had launched David Brock's article. Olson and Ken Starr were close friends. Bork was a mentor to both Starr and Olson. When it came to the constitutional issue presented in the *Jones* case, all three men were of one mind.

During mock arguments at the Army-Navy Club in Washington, Bork and

Olson tried to prep Gil Davis, readying him for his appearance in the imposing Supreme Court chambers. Davis found this expert tutoring only mildly useful. His personal goal was to get one simple point across, before the justices jumped down his throat. He wanted to say: "The president has confused the office of the presidency with the person of the president." The *office* of the president was entitled to the utmost respect. But the *person* of the president, he wanted to emphasize, had "no privileges or immunity beyond that of every other citizen of this country." If he got that much out of his mouth, Davis believed, he could walk out of the argument with an even chance of winning.

In the meantime, the elves were supplying glittering briefs to the Virginia lawyers, so that their submissions in the Supreme Court would be pristine. As Davis would admit, he could snap his fingers and receive letter-perfect draft briefs "quickly, almost overnight." The Paula Jones operation, with scant funding, had moved into the major leagues.

Acting Solicitor General Walter Dellinger, as he prepared for his own argument in *Clinton v. Jones,* was getting nervous. Dellinger had clerked for Supreme Court Justice Hugo Black and taught at Duke School of Law, where Ken Starr was among his notable students. In later years, he had occupied prestigious posts in the Justice Department, becoming one of the leading Supreme Court lawyers in the country.

Dellinger was a lawyer's lawyer. He subscribed to the lesson of *U.S. v. Nixon*—the 1974 Watergate tapes case—that "not even the president should be above the law." But to extend that principle to every slip-and-fall case, and every two-bit lawsuit would paralyze the country. He believed the president should be immune from civil suit until he left office.

Many Court-watchers agreed with Dellinger, giving odds to President Clinton in *Clinton v. Jones.* After one mock argument held at the Institute for the Bill of Rights in Williamsburg, a group of prominent law professors and journalists took a straw poll, voting two-to-one that the president would prevail in the *Jones* case. But there were conflicting signals that were starting to make Dellinger uncomfortable. By 1997, the notion of presidential supremacy was on a downhill slide. In part due to the end of the Cold War, the idea that the president needed to be freed of all distractions and given absolute deference in order to guard against nuclear attacks and enemies abroad seemed passé. The days of chief executives reigning supreme in Washington were slowly vanishing. Ironically, the Whitewater scandal itself had contributed to the president's diminution of power. Bill Clinton had already answered questions from Independent Counsels Fiske and Starr on multiple occasions; he had testified under oath in the Tucker-McDougal trial. What was one more distraction in a scandal-ridden presidency?

Several weeks before the oral argument, Dellinger spent nearly three hours in a grueling moot-court exercise with top lawyers at the Justice Department. "I argued until I was drenched with sweat," he recalled, "and did not believe that I had persuaded them." Dellinger was so troubled that he immediately went back to his office "and asked my assistant to have a car come take me to the White House." He first met with White House Counsel Jack Quinn, informing Quinn that he felt that the case should be settled.

The fact that Robert Bork and Ted Olson were prepping Paula Jones's lawyer for battle made the situation even more worrisome. These were not men who ordinarily handled sex discrimination cases pro bono. This confirmed Dellinger's suspicions that "the normal incentive structures that we have to keep civil litigation in check don't apply when the litigation is against the president." Busily at work were powerful forces and individuals who "would like to destabilize, who would have enormous amounts to gain by destabilizing his presidency."

If Clinton lost this battle in the High Court, depositions and subpoenas would start to fly. "The normal incentive is *not* to do excessive discovery," explained Dellinger. In an ordinary case, the costs alone would prevent this. In the current situation, however, where a sitting political leader could be crippled and another political party could gain power, "those constraints simply don't operate." Dellinger implored the president's top White House advisers to settle quickly and cut Bill Clinton's losses.

"That just didn't happen," Dellinger later said, with a quiet sigh.

———

JUST days before the oral argument in the Supreme Court, the Jones lawyers received a huge boost, without even knowing it. Joe Cammarata sat in his office staring at a phone message slip that seemed particularly odd. As Cammarata remembered it: "The receptionist says, 'Some woman wants to talk to you. It's important.' I said, 'Tell her I'll call her back.'" The receptionist said that the woman would not leave her name and number but she insisted she 'really needs to talk to you.'" The same woman had called repeatedly. Finally, Cammarata took the call to rid himself of the nuisance.

The mystery caller on the other end spoke in a soft voice. She told Cammarata, "I had a similar thing happen to me that happened to Paula Jones." There was silence. The unidentified woman proceeded to tell a story about "how she was groped, grabbed in the little room adjoining the Oval Office." Cammarata asked, "Well, how come the Secret Service weren't around?" He additionally pressed the caller: "Tell me your name." The woman refused to go down that path. But she gave him enough details that Cammarata concluded that her story might be legitimate. The woman also provided an important clue: "My husband's death was noted as a suspicious death in the *Clinton Chronicles*."

Cammarata's contemporaneous handwritten notes of the telephone call indicated he received detailed information from this anonymous source. The woman on the other end, "age 50," stated that the event in question had occurred in 1993. She had been working a part-time job at the White House, having been a "party activist" during Clinton's successful presidential campaign of 1992. The woman stated that she had made an appointment with the president to request a full-time job because her "marriage was not going well." Her husband, a lawyer, had been charged with misappropriation of client escrow funds.

According to Cammarata's notes, the woman said that she "went to talk to BC [Bill Clinton]" in a private room adjoining the Oval Office, to ask for help. The door was closed—there were no Secret Service agents in view. She told the president that she was "afraid of things in her personal life" and she needed his assistance in securing a full-time job. President Clinton said "yes," he would gladly assist her. Then, according to her account, "it got physical." The unidentified woman told Cammarata that Clinton pulled her to him, kissed her several times, and whispered that he "always wanted to do that."

The woman also told Cammarata that she was "shocked" by the president's advance. She did not indicate, however, whether she resisted. As the kissing progressed, she said, Clinton touched her breasts. He next took the woman's hand and placed it "on his genital area—over his pants." The woman admitted that she "kissed him back." She said she was simultaneously "frightened" and "excited," and halted the encounter to tell the president that she feared "someone might walk in." She was also concerned because this interlude was holding up his cabinet meeting—wouldn't the secretary of state or some other important official put two and two together? After reiterating that she "wanted a job," the woman abruptly pushed her hair into place and stated that she had to leave. As she walked out of the president's private office, according to Cammarata's notes, she "saw 3 cabinet members." The mystery woman walked past them, smiled obliquely, and returned to her work station. She eventually told a coworker about the incident—although she declined to tell Cammarata who that coworker was.

The notes of the conversation revealed a final startling twist: The woman told Cammarata that when she got home, she "couldn't locate her husband." She went on to say, "He was found dead that night. SUICIDE."

Cammarata was in the midst of helping Gil Davis prep for the Supreme Court argument and did not have time to establish whether the story told by this unidentified caller checked out. Still, before he threw the notes of the conversation into his drawer, he decided to call Michael Isikoff at *Newsweek*. Cammarata felt that Isikoff, who had been covering the *Jones* case from the beginning, was "friendly to us and seemed to be supportive of our position." "Mike," he said, "let me give you this information. Maybe you could track it down. Let me know what you find out." After listening to the bizarre story and scribbling down notes, Isikoff played his cards close to his vest. "Okay. Fine," was all he said.

With that hurried exchange, the existence of a potentially crucial witness was about to reveal itself. Her name, Cammarata would learn soon enough, was Kathleen Willey (pronounced "Willie"). The person with whom Kathleen Willey had shared the details of her bizarre encounter with the president, it turned out, was another woman who worked in the same area of the White House.

That woman's name was Linda Tripp.

————

THE night before the oral argument in the Supreme Court, Acting Solicitor General Walter Dellinger was pulling into his driveway after another grueling night of preparation, when his beeper sounded. The text message read: "Urgent, urgent, urgent." When Dellinger called the Justice Department Command Center, an officer told him, "The president wants to talk to you. Immediately." From inside his home, the solicitor general dialed the secret land-line number. He was instantly connected with President Clinton, who began discussing cases he had been reading concerning a governor's immunity from civil suit—he wanted to make sure that Dellinger had every possible argument at his command. The president and his solicitor general spoke long into the night.

Dellinger later fell into bed, dreaming about the moment when he would stand up at the lectern to argue the historic *Clinton v. Jones* case, and wishing he could shout out to the justices: "You think this stuff isn't distracting? You know what the president was doing last night into the late hours? He's worrying about this litigation!"

————

ON Monday, January 13, 1997, demonstrators paraded in front of the Supreme Court. Some were dressed as "flashers" in trench coats, to mock President Bill Clinton. Others chanted out denunciations of Paula Jones as a publicity seeker and money grubber. Gil Davis, the advocate for Jones, had just announced his intention to run for attorney general of Virginia. As he walked up the marble steps, he now paused to gaze at the words chiseled into the stone of the marble edifice: EQUAL JUSTICE UNDER LAW. The self-described country lawyer, butterflies fluttering in his stomach, felt that he was ready.

The front page of *USA Today,* beside its top story that Green Bay and New England would clash in Super Bowl XXXI, contained a full-page spread about *Clinton v. Jones.* "Neither Paula Jones nor President Clinton will be at the Supreme Court today," the article noted. It would be up to the lawyers and the nine justices to determine whether this "steamy litigation" should go forward. One commentator told the paper that this case, more than any other on the Court's docket, had captured the public's attention. "It has sex and all the elements."

Inside the stately velvet-draped courtroom, Chief Justice William H. Rehnquist rocked backward in his chair, which was upholstered with a special padding to ease the pain for his bad back. Rehnquist checked the clock, then nodded toward the counsel table. Bob Bennett was first to step up to the ancient wooden lectern.

"Mr. Chief Justice and may it please the Court," Bennett began, straightening his notes. "I am here this morning on behalf of the President of the United States, who has asked this Court to defer a private civil damage suit for money damages against him until he leaves office . . ." Those were the only two sentences of prepared text that Bennett would get out of his mouth. He was immediately peppered with questions: What was the scope of this immunity the president was requesting? Should it cover the president even for acts that he had committed that had nothing to do with official duties? Wasn't such an immunity from civil suit unprecedented?

Acting Solicitor General Dellinger, dressed in his de rigueur swallowtail coat, was likewise met with skepticism when he walked to the lectern, arguing that the president's time should not be wasted on civil lawsuits. Justice Antonin Scalia cut in: "But we see Presidents riding horseback, chopping firewood, fishing for stick fish . . ." He was interrupted by a burst of laughter from the gallery. Justice Scalia added that if President Clinton was prepared to swear "that he'll never be seen playing golf for the rest of his administration," perhaps Dellinger's position could be taken more seriously.

Gil Davis, as he took his turn to argue on behalf of Paula Jones, deftly reached down and raised the lectern using its ancient hand-crank. The noise of the gears caused Chief Justice Rehnquist to stop, cocking his ear. This gave Davis enough time to deliver his single opening line that he had resolved to get out: "President William Jefferson Clinton," the Virginia lawyer told the justices, "[has] confused the office of presidency, which has privileges and immunities which protect its institutional duties, with the person who holds that office."

With that, Davis recalled, "we were off to the races."

Justice Stevens, a liberal Republican appointed by President Ford, was one of the few justices who seemed concerned with how long the trial might take. Davis replied: "Depending on stipulations, Justice Stevens, I would say 4 or 5 days perhaps, but that's just a guess." Justice Stevens asked whether Jones's lawyers planned to go into "collateral matters," such as the matter of "other women."

Davis told the Court that if probing into "other women" would "tend to show a fact that we need to prove," he would have no choice. "I think I would be duty bound as counsel to pursue that," he said.

At precisely 11:03 A.M., Chief Justice Rehnquist rapped his gavel and declared that the Court would take the case under advisement.

———

GIL Davis and Joe Cammarata headed for a private room at La Brasserie restaurant on Capitol Hill. Here, hidden from the media, they were joined by Steve Jones's father, who had traveled to Washington to observe the argument, and George Conway, the elf who had worked hard on preparing for this day. Conway presented the Virginia lawyers with clear plastic paperweights that contained miniature versions of the front cover of their Supreme Court brief—much of which the elf had written—as mementos of this historic day.

As Davis chatted with Steve Jones's father, sipping wine over an excellent lunch, he recalled feeling as if the planets were finally aligned to produce a settlement. Unlike his son, the father did not appear volatile or hotheaded. He seemed supportive of the Virginia lawyers' plan to seize this moment, and to sit down with the president's lawyers—before the Court rendered a decision—to resolve Paula's claim for the good of all.

Said Davis years later, thinking back on this sparkling moment of opportunity that somehow slipped away, "His efforts were as vain as ours."

———

ONE of the first things that Joe Cammarata did after the oral argument was to return to the subject of the mystery woman who had telephoned his office. Cammarata picked up the phone and called Mike Isikoff to determine whether the *Newsweek* reporter had tracked down the unknown caller. Cammarata reminded Isikoff about the conversation, in which he asked Isikoff, "What have you got?" The lawyer was aghast when the reporter now responded, "I can't tell you. I got information, but it's off the record."

Cammarata exploded, "You son of a bitch! You kidding me? I gave you that information. Now you're telling me you can't give it back to me?" Isikoff didn't flinch. "I can't," he replied coolly. Cammarata screamed back into the phone, "Well, if *you* can find it, *I* can find it."

Within twenty minutes, using the same clues that he had provided to the *Newsweek* reporter, Cammarata figured out the mystery caller's name. "And then I found out where she lived and I served a subpoena on her," he said.

But the mystery did not end there. Kathleen Willey later insisted that she was not the person who had called Paula Jones's lawyer that day. The substance of the facts relayed to Cammarata were true. Yet Willey, assuming an unusually defensive posture, would deny calling the *Jones* lawyer, stating that it must have been one of her coworkers in the White House with whom she had confided after the incident with Clinton. That caller, she said, obviously posed as her (Willey), in order to lead Jones's lawyers to this new and explosive evidence.

That person, she said, must have been Linda Tripp.

PART THREE

THE MONICA
THREAD

chapter 18

Monica S. Lewinsky

One person whose life seemed to grow infinitely more complicated in early 1997, as the Supreme Court mulled over the *Clinton v. Jones* case, was a young woman who had recently placed an anonymous Valentine's Day note in the *Washington Post* addressed to "Handsome," intending it for President Bill Clinton.

Monica Lewinsky was trying desperately to regain her job in the East Wing of the White House after having been banished to the Pentagon. Some Clinton aides, particularly Deputy Chief of Staff Evelyn Lieberman, had believed the young intern was spending far too much time around the commander in chief. These protectors of the president resolved the problem, or so they thought, by sending Monica packing to become confidential assistant to the assistant secretary of defense, in the austere surroundings of the Pentagon, just prior to the 1996 election. For Monica, it had meant a pay raise and important foreign travel assignments—much more prestigious than the jobs that most recent college graduates could dream of attaining. But this particular former intern was bouncing on an emotional seesaw. She wanted desperately to be back near President Bill Clinton. The election was over now. Why had "Handsome" not yet made good on his promise to "bring me back"?

There were additional reasons the former intern felt on edge: Monica had recently received a heads-up from a Pentagon colleague, Linda Tripp, that the president was in danger. The husky-voiced Tripp, who (like Monica) had worked in the White House until recently, confided that *Newsweek* reporter Michael Isikoff was working on a story alleging that the president had groped a woman named Kathleen Willey in the White House. This development—not a good thing under any circumstances—was an especially bad one, given the precarious status of the *Jones* case in the Supreme Court. Monica had taken it upon herself to warn the president about this problem. The last thing the president needed was another flap in the media about his alleged extramarital affairs. The young woman felt that she could help avert a disaster. She always had a magic touch, she told herself, when it came to dealing with people.

Monica Samille Lewinsky had been born at the Children's Hospital in San Francisco in the eventful month of July 1973. It was the same hot summer that the Watergate scandal had reached a boiling point during the presidency of Richard M. Nixon, with Judiciary Committee hearings chaired by Senator Sam Ervin capturing the nation's attention. Marcia Lewinsky, Monica's mother, watched snippets of the Watergate hearings on television that summer. Like most Americans, she harbored serious questions about the ethical propriety of President Nixon's behavior. Yet her focus was on bringing home her new baby, not on the dark drama of Watergate. Bernie Lewinsky, the proud father, was just finishing his medical internship at the Royal Marsden Hospital in London. The couple's plan was to move to Beverly Hills, where Bernie would build a practice specializing in oncology. Marcia's singular goal was to give their daughter all the best things Southern California could offer, plus more.

Bernie and Marcia Lewinsky understood the importance of financial success and the need for security. Bernie's family had fled Nazi Germany in the 1920s, having settled in a Jewish enclave in El Salvador, before moving to California during Bernie's teen years. Marcia's family, likewise Jewish immigrants, had left Lithuania to escape the ethnic purges of Joseph Stalin. Their backgrounds allowed them to understand both success and pain. The birth of the couple's first child, Monica Samille (her middle name was a French derivative of "Samuel," in honor of Marcia's late father), was a hopeful beginning in a country that promised unbounded success for those who worked tirelessly for it. Bernie settled into the busy life of a doctor starting a new practice; Marcia and Monica quickly grew accustomed to the finer things that a Southern California lifestyle could offer.

Twenty years later, in 1995, with her marriage fallen apart and her fashionable home on Hillcrest Road in Beverly Hills sold as part of the settlement agreement, Marcia Lewinsky (who by this time went by the nom de plume Marcia Lewis, writing for *Hollywood Reporter* and other glitzy publications) was ready for a change of scenery. Later stories in the tabloid press suggested that Monica had consciously plotted to move to the nation's capital to get a job in the White House and to ensnare the president of the United States. The path that had led Monica Lewinsky to an internship in the executive mansion, however, and to her fateful meeting with Bill Clinton, was far less conspiratorial than that.

As Monica herself would explain in the fall of 2002, having moved to New York City with her family after barely surviving the trauma of the Clinton years: "I was already planning to take the GRE [Graduate Record Exam] that fall, which I did do. My plan was probably to work, to find a job." After college, Monica was wrapping up in Portland; during school, she had worked at a tie shop, selling neckwear and chatting away with customers. It was a fun job but not the stuff of a glamorous career. Marcia Lewis had divorced Monica's father in 1988; now she told her daughter that she planned to leave the palm trees of Beverly Hills for the marble and glass of Washington. Marcia had found an apartment in the Watergate complex, close to her sister Debra's dwelling in Virginia; Monica's grandmother hoped to find a place in the same complex. It was a family migration.

So it was a natural decision for Monica Lewinsky, having earned her college degree in psychology from Lewis & Clark College in Oregon, to see what opportunities the nation's capital might offer. She could attend graduate school the next fall—the goal, she told her mother, was to get a Ph.D. in psychology or an advanced degree in forensic science.

As far as the notion, later fueled by the tabloids, that she moved to Washington with a conscious plan to have an affair with the president, Monica viewed this as preposterous. "Not at all," she stated, laughing. "In fact, I didn't find him [Clinton] attractive [at first]. I don't think he looks good on TV. And I didn't think he was attractive until I saw him in person." Nor was the allure of a high-powered government job a magnet. "I was not at all that interested in politics," Monica said. She had only been to Washington twice before the summer of 1995, both times as a tourist. What caused her to pack her boxes and move to the nation's capital, pure and simple, was the migration of the female wing of the Lewinsky family. This was a chance to get some job experience, save some money, take a breather, and then climb the next step on the educational ladder.

Yet, several extant copies of a forgotten magazine reveal that the allure of moving to the epicenter of government and politics, and the buzz associated with the youthful Clinton administration, created a sense of excitement for many Americans, including Monica Lewinsky and her mother. Although few people would ever see copies of the soon-defunct *Beverly Hills Magazine,* edited by Marcia Lewis and her sister Debra Finerman, one of the few surviving copies confirms that the two sisters viewed the newly overhauled Washington with a sense of glamor and adventure. In one 1992 issue, the editors ran a glossy story, "Hillary's Inaugural Ball Makeover," which included sketches of what a made-over Hillary Clinton would look like as she attended the Washington inaugural galas. Dressed in a dazzling green outfit, with her hairstyle redone in a carefree fashion, the incoming First Lady appeared like a modern-day princess. The caption, effusing over the arrival of Hillary Clinton and Tipper Gore, two youthful power spouses in the capital, read: "It's definitely going to be the years of Hillary and Tipper!" In an apparent reference to outgoing First Lady Barbara Bush, the editors of the publication added tongue-in-cheek: "Say good-bye to size 14 electric blue suits and faux Majorca pearls."

The magazine's masthead listed sisters Marcia Lewis and Debra Finerman as the coeditors. The publication's associate editor, at the time still a college student, was identified as Monica Lewinsky.

The same man who helped finance the short-lived *Beverly Hills Magazine*, millionaire insurance executive Walter Kaye, assisted Monica in obtaining an unpaid White House internship. Kaye, a friend of her mother and her aunt Debra through casual California contacts, had earlier recommended his own grandson for one of these plum internships. Kaye told the FBI with evident embarrassment, in an interview shortly after the scandal involving Monica and the president erupted in early 1998, that it was simply a matter of a friend helping a friend. The FBI notes summarized the agent's interview with Kaye in detail: "It was sometime after LEWIS moved to Washington, D.C. that LEWIS contacted him and asked him to assist in getting an intern job at the White House for her daughter, Monica Lewinsky. KAYE does not recall the specifics of meeting LEWINSKY, but it is reasonably certain that he did meet with her at some point in the process."

According to the FBI transcript, Kaye did not recall ever seeing Monica's résumé. At the time, he had a friendly relationship with Monica's mother and her aunt Debra. He made an informal inquiry, calling high-up contacts at the Democratic National Committee (DNC) to see if they could "help in the placement of Lewinsky." He later told the federal grand jury convened by Ken Starr that he had no doubt that his recommendation had an "important impact" on the White House decision to hire Lewinsky in light of his history of large contributions to Clinton and to the DNC. "You know," Kaye admitted to the grand jury, "I was giving them a lot of money."

Bernie Lewinsky, the pragmatist, could not understand why his daughter would want to fly off to an unpaid job in Washington when it was unrelated to her chosen field of psychology. Still, he recognized that it was a form of public service. He therefore gave his blessing to the decision. "I was born in El Salvador," Bernie would later say. "I came to this country, became a citizen, and we always looked at the White House as the top of the pyramid, you know. So, to think that my daughter was going to be working there was a tremendous honor, and I was very proud of her being there, although I didn't really understand how it was going to help her." He added, "If she was going to be a lawyer or go into government, then I could see it." Still, like any good divorced dad who tried to maintain a complicated relationship with his daughter, he kept his mouth shut.

The twenty-one-year-old Monica Lewinsky reported to duty in Washington during the summer of 1995 and found herself awed by the experience. Of her first day walking the halls of the executive complex, Monica recalled, "I just remember thinking there was so much energy there. There was so much movement and action. And you knew that it was proactive. And that it was resulting in things happening and affecting people. And I think that was something I didn't expect. The first time I was in the West Wing proper or White House proper, I was completely amazed. Everything is so pristine. The hallowed halls. There is just something very magical about it."

Monica had been assigned to work in the office of Chief of Staff Leon Panetta, helping to draft correspondence replying to citizen letters. Monica's mother recalled that her daughter "came home happy, excited." All in all, "her reports were positive." Marcia, initially apprehensive about the move east, was pleased to see that her daughter was "happy that she'd made this decision and happy to be there."

Monica saw President Bill Clinton for the first time in early July 1995, at an arrival ceremony on the South Lawn of the White House; she and her mother were attending as guests of Walter Kaye. On this occasion, she did not remember anything "clicking." Nothing made her think that she was destined to have a relationship with this man. Her feeling was, "Oh sure, it would be fun to meet him . . . but everybody has an interest in meeting the president." She later admitted, "And I think it was probably increased because I thought he was cute. But there was not a sense of, 'Oh I want to meet him so I can flirt with him. And maybe he'll like me.' Never thought [that] in a million years." In fact, she asked rhetorically, "Why would he like me?"

At a departure ceremony on August 9, just after her twenty-second birthday, Lewinsky first made direct eye contact with the president. She was wearing a sage green suit that she had bought specially from J. Crew for her internship. As the president moved down the rope line shaking hands, he spotted her. At that moment, Monica recalled, "He gave me the full Bill Clinton. . . . He undressed me with his eyes."

The next day, all interns were invited to a surprise forty-ninth birthday party for the president on the South Lawn. Monica worked her way to the front of the greeting line, wearing her "lucky green suit." Here, like many others, she held up a sign that said "Happy Birthday, Mr. President." Clinton was dressed casually, wearing a pink short-sleeved shirt and blue jeans. As he moved down the row of young well-wishers, Clinton stopped and fixed his eyes on Monica. A photographer captured them briefly on film as they squeezed hands. She would later tell a writer that the president's arm brushed up against her breast; as he walked forward, Bill Clinton did a double take as if to memorize the specifics of her face. Monica would later elaborate for the Office of Independent Counsel, in the presence of the grand jury, that this was the beginning of a "flirtation that went on at a distance." At this brief birthday-party encounter, it was clear that a scattering of sparks had transferred themselves from one person to the other during the fleeting physical contact. Monica told the grand jury, "I mean, he's a charismatic person and so—just when he shook my hand—there was an intense connection."

That night, Monica rushed home and told her mother and aunt Debra about the day's excitement. She also went to a bookstore and purchased a copy of Gennifer Flowers's autobiography—the life story of the blond-haired woman with whom Clinton had confessed to having a long-term affair during the governor years in Arkansas. Monica spent the night reading.

Yet Monica Lewinsky later insisted that there was no sense of destiny that she would meet Clinton personally or that she would follow in Flowers's footsteps. "No. Not at all," she said. "I think it was a changing experience for me. But there was no point where it was sort of inevitable that something was going to happen." In fact, as Monica saw it, the relationship evolved as the result of unplanned chemistry. As painful as it would be to analyze these events after the relationship had fallen apart, she asserted that she connected with President Bill Clinton, and they began their secret affair, simply because they were attracted to each other. "I think that's [true] in any situation between two people. You have to always re-member that. That as much as—yes, he's the president—and yes, I was an intern, it's also two people. And this is something that happens all the time."

Monica sent letters back to California, enclosing pictures and reporting on the remarkable events transpiring in Washington. After the president's birthday party, she sent a photo snapped by a White House photographer to her father and her stepmother, Barbara. The image showed her shaking hands with Bill Clinton as the president stared deeply into Monica's beaming face. Bernie Lewinsky, who devoted much spare time to photography and was a near professional at the art, recalled experiencing a strange feeling when he opened the envelope and saw that photo. "I, as a father and as a photographer, was really taken aback at the look in his eyes," said Bernie. "And what I did is I took a crop, I cropped the picture like a photographer, and just cropped it down to him looking at her. And I said to Bar-bara, 'He has lascivious eyes.' He looked at my daughter in a weird way." Bernie later admitted, "That was, you know, just an impression that I kept and I never ex-pressed it until this thing broke."

In November 1995, Clinton's nemesis, Republican House Speaker Newt Gingrich, staged a shutdown of all federal government offices in an effort to force the president to approve huge budget cuts in Medicare, education and other items to push through Gingrich's aggressive Contract with America. Gingrich ultimately lost the showdown. Yet during this episode, a brief moment in the darkened White House provided an opportunity that would forever haunt the Clinton presidency. It was during that brief lull in the normal operations of the federal government that the stars aligned to permit Bill Clinton and Mon-ica Lewinsky to begin their clandestine relationship.

Having just been promoted to a paid position in the Office of Legislative

Affairs located in the East Wing, Monica was happy to report to work during the shutdown. The date was November 15. As a small group of workers hung around the chief of staff's office in the West Wing, answering phones as a way of pitching in, the president sauntered into the room. Monica looked up; she noticed that the president was smiling at her. There was "continued flirtation," she later told the grand jury, as the informal workday continued. In fact, as Monica would later point out, the president was doing as much (or more) flirting with her as she was doing with him. He was wandering down the hallway toward her desk so frequently that a fellow intern started joking "he must have a crush on Monica" or words to that effect. During one defining moment in the evolution of the scandal, Monica happened to pass by the door to the inner office of the West Wing and spotted Clinton standing by himself. She playfully lifted the jacket of her blue pantsuit and revealed her thong underwear, visible just above the waistline of her pants. The president, she recalled, gave her "an appreciative look."

Later that night, when most of the staffers had gone home, the opportunity finally arrived. Monica recounted the events to the Office of Independent Counsel during her first grand jury appearance:

LEWINSKY: Around 8:00 in the evening or so I was in the hallway going to the restroom, passing Mr. Stephanopoulos' office, and he [President Clinton] was in the hall and invited me into Mr. Stephanopoulos' office and then from there invited me back into his study.

PROSECUTOR: Okay. And what happened there?

LEWINSKY: We talked briefly and sort of acknowledged that there had been a chemistry that was there before and that we were both attracted to each other and then he asked me if he could kiss me.

PROSECUTOR: And what did you say?

LEWINSKY: Yes.

PROSECUTOR: And did you kiss on that occasion?

LEWINSKY: Yes.

Monica recalled that there was "a softness and tenderness about him [Clinton], his eyes were very soul-searching, very wanting, very needing and very loving. There was, too, a sadness about him that I hadn't expected to see." Several hours later, at approximately 10:00 P.M., the president returned to Leon Panetta's office and asked Monica if she was free to meet again in five minutes. They arranged a rendezvous in the study area behind George Stephanopoulos's darkened office. This time, both Clinton and the intern partially disrobed. As Monica later acknowledged to the federal grand jury, one thing led to another, and "we were more physically intimate."

> PROSECUTOR: With respect to physical intimacy, other than oral sex, was there other physical intimacy performed?
> LEWINSKY: Yes. Everything up until oral sex.

That night, Monica awakened her mother and Aunt Debra to tell them that the president had kissed her. They groaned and went back to sleep. Monica, both women told themselves in a dreamlike state, had such a heightened sense of imagination.

Two nights later—with the government shutdown still in effect—Monica volunteered to work late again. This time, at the president's suggestion, she delivered two slices of vegetarian pizza to the commander in chief in the inner sanctum of the Oval Office. Following Clinton's instructions, she checked in with the president's personal secretary, Betty Currie, and used her as a passkey. Currie opened the door and said, "Sir, the girl's here with the pizza." Currie left, and Monica followed the president into the back study area, where they were "physically intimate again."

Over the next few months, Monica carried brown envelopes under the pretext of making deliveries to the president, with Currie acting as the gatekeeper. She and the president also arranged to "bump into" each other in the West Wing, setting up clandestine meetings in the bathroom and hallway behind the Oval Office.

President Clinton also began making phone calls to Monica's home phone at night. To her surprise, Monica's caller ID would light up with "POTUS," shorthand for "President of the United States." At times, these conversations would escalate into sexually playful banter. On weekends (especially Sundays), the president would invite her to sneak into the White House when only a skeleton crew and a few Secret Service agents were present. She would enter one door of the Oval Office and then exit a different door, so that the rotating shifts of Secret Service agents would never know "exactly how long I had been in there."

Two misconceptions that media accounts later propagated, that Monica would be quick to correct, related to the nature and location of their intimate activities. First, she insisted, there was never any sexual activity, of any kind, in the Oval Office. The liaisons always took place in the president's back study, in the bathroom off the main office, or in the hallway between rooms. Monica emphatically told the grand jury, correcting the inaccurate reports of the media: "No, no, we were never physically intimate in the Oval Office."

Second, Monica never believed that the relationship was purely physical. She made this clear to Ken Starr's attorneys in front of the grand jury:

PROSECUTOR: Did the relationship with the President develop into or also have a non-sexual component to it?

LEWINSKY: Yes, it did.

PROSECUTOR: Could you describe sort of that aspect of the relationship for the grand jury?

LEWINSKY: We enjoyed talking to each other and being with each other. We were very affectionate.

PROSECUTOR: What sorts of things would you talk about?

LEWINSKY: We would tell jokes. We would talk about our childhoods. Talk about current events. I was always giving him my stupid ideas about what I thought should be done in the administration or different views on things. I think back on it and he always made me smile when I was with him . . . he was sunshine.

PROSECUTOR: Okay. And would you describe sort of the affectionate but non-sexual contact?

LEWINSKY: A lot of hugging, holding hands sometimes. He always used to push the hair out of my face.

As her relationship with the president moved to these new levels, Monica enthusiastically relayed stories back to California about her job in the White House. In doing so, she conveniently omitted the fact that she was having a sexual affair with the commander in chief. Her father and stepmother considered it incredible that Monica had gained such access to the president. At the same time, this was classic Monica. Recalled Bernie Lewinsky, "She told us how one night during the lockout or during the government shutdown, they were all working late and they all ordered in pizza and she went and asked the president whether he'd like a piece of pizza, and she was able to take it to the Oval Office for him. And I said 'Wow, you know, that's amazing.'"

Her stepmother, Barbara Lewinsky, who had married Bernie in 1991, interjected, "Those who know Monica know she endears herself to everybody around her, and so the scene she was describing—while it would be outrageous for somebody to think, 'Your kid is having pizza with the president?' Knowing Monica, you'd think, 'Well, that's certainly possible.'"

Nor did it seem out of the ordinary, when Bernie and Barbara flew east to attend son Michael's high school graduation in June 1996, that they would be treated as VIPs in Washington. When the Lewinsky family gathered early for an arrival ceremony for Clinton who was greeting Ireland's president, Mary Robinson, they were incredulous that Monica had pushed her way up to the front of the rope line and that President Clinton had actually stopped in his tracks and said, "I like your hat, Monica." Recalled Barbara, "Monica insisted that we had to be there at seven in the morning or six in the morning, something like that. And I said, 'Why?' And so we got there, and the parade grounds were totally empty except for the Secret Service people, and they all came up and greeted Monica, and they all knew Monica. And I said to myself, 'Gee, I guess if you work at the White House, everybody knows you.'"

When Monica received clearance the following day to bring the entire family to the president's weekly radio address, which was held in the Roosevelt Room of the White House, it seemed like one more perk of the job. The Lewinsky family had a group photo taken with the president in the Oval Office, the whole lineup beaming. Monica was wearing a stunning, light pink suit, picked out specially for the occasion. The photo showed her looking directly into the camera with a knowing smile.

Despite all of these clues, including the "lascivious eyes" photo and this extraordinary access to the inner sanctum of the White House, Bernie Lewinsky would later confess that he did not put two and two together. He would fault nobody but himself for his naïveté. "In other words, you go back and you say, 'Oh, my God, look at this,'" Monica's father said, shaking his head disconsolately. "There was the telltale sign . . . but I sort of missed it."

Barbara Lewinsky's intuition certainly told her that something was afoot. After the radio address and tour of the White House, Barbara nudged her stepdaughter and said, "Girly, the President sure has your number—he just keeps looking at you!" Yet there was much disagreement within the Lewinsky family as to who knew what specifics, and when, struggling to find an explanation as to why nothing was done to stop it. Marcia would describe this early period that followed the first "innocent" months of Monica's internship as "a confusing picture for me." Asked whether she believed Monica might be having a physical affair with the president, Marcia would only say, "There were days that I thought— there's something wrong here. And there were days I thought no, this is just a schoolgirl crush." Bernie later questioned this equivocation by his ex-wife, saying that he believed both Marcia and her sister, Debra, had direct knowledge that Monica was having an affair with Clinton. "I think that they knew," he said, "and thought that it was cute and wonderful. That's what I think. But I'm not sure."

What cannot be disputed, however, is that the relationship between Bill Clinton and Monica Lewinsky soon developed into something that was an emotional roller coaster for the intern and a messy problem for the president. Several times, as their relationship entered its second year, the president met with Monica to say that he had been behaving badly and that he needed to terminate their liaisons. Even so, the affair continued with on-again-off-again weekend visits, risqué phone calls, exchanges of gifts (books, ties, T-shirts, cards), declarations that the relationship had to end, crying (by Monica), and occasional amorous reconciliations.

Just as rumors were flying that the Supreme Court was preparing to hand down its decision in the *Paula Jones* case in May 1997, President Clinton was meeting with Lewinsky in the pantry outside the Oval Office, repeating firmly that he needed to end the affair. During this emotional encounter, which Monica later referred to as "D-day" or "Dump day," President Clinton confessed error, saying that he really just wanted "to do the right thing in God's eyes and do the right thing for his family and he just—he didn't feel right about it."

Paula Jones's attorneys later expressed incredulity that President Clinton continued to engage in such high-risk behavior, when he knew that he was under intense scrutiny in the *Jones* litigation. "We had not hidden that thought under a bushel," explained Gil Davis, seated in his Virginia law office. "Showing a pattern or a habit of sexual advances to women, particularly in private circumstances of some related nature, would be a method of showing that this was a characteristic of the president. So, yes, we were announcing that. Made no bones about it."

For that reason, Davis could never fathom why President Bill Clinton, as they were all awaiting a decision by the Supreme Court, would continue to engage in a fresh series of sexual liaisons in the White House.

This was not, Davis believed, a man caught by surprise. "Reflection has convinced me that the president knew all along, for two years, that he was going to lie about this eventually in deposition," said Davis. "Because we had talked about the 'other women,' and there had been press reporting about this."

Jones's lawyers had waved a red flag at the president. For whatever reason, Clinton had decided to make a running charge at the bullfighters.

As President Clinton ushered Monica Lewinsky out of the pantry outside the Oval Office, in May 1997, giving her a quick hug to express his penitence for allowing this sinful affair to continue so long, he looked at the young former intern with deep remorse in his eyes. Of course, if Bill Clinton had known what was waiting for them around the corner, he would have wanted to end the relationship far more decisively and, undoubtedly, much more quickly.

19

INSIDE A TEXAS PRISON

I n the winter of 1997, just as his criminal investigation was shifting into wrap-up mode, Ken Starr made two decisions that would alter his legacy as Whitewater/Madison independent counsel: He announced that he was leaving for Pepperdine University, and (after that blew up in his face) he authorized his team to interview Arkansas women about past sexual liaisons with Bill Clinton.

Jim McDougal, now a cooperating witness for the Office of the Independent Counsel (OIC), helped prime the pump. In an article by James Stewart published in February 1997 by *The New Yorker*, McDougal said that he believed that his then-wife, Susan, was having an affair with Governor Bill Clinton during the Whitewater/Madison follies, intimating that she was refusing to answer questions of the Starr prosecutors because she was trying to protect her paramour Clinton. The article quoted McDougal as saying that he had innocently picked up his telephone one day in 1982, while working at Madison Guaranty, dialed his home number, and found himself patched into the middle of an "intimate" call between Susan and Governor Bill Clinton.

Jim McDougal told his interviewer, "It was just a country phone line. I don't know what happened, but I dialed the number and it didn't ring and I was in the middle of their conversation." An article in the *Arkansas Democrat-Gazette* cast doubt on this latest McDougal tale, reporting that an expert associated with the United States Telephone Association in that region found McDougal's claim "highly *im*probable." Yet now there existed a stronger motive that might explain Susan McDougal's refusal to testify against President Bill Clinton: a long-hidden extramarital affair. Speculation along these lines only whetted the media's thirst for details and made Jim McDougal (once again) a sought-after interviewee.

Ken Starr's prosecutors were paying regular visits to McDougal. They continued to debrief him in a tidy Little Rock apartment paid for by OIC, as he prepared to serve time in federal prison. The prosecutors took McDougal's stories with a grain of salt, as he rocked back and forth in his favorite new recliner. Yet Hickman Ewing, Ray Jahn, Amy St. Eve, and a young member of the OIC team named Bob Bittman found that much of the information their witness was providing checked out.

A remarkable FBI document summarizing OIC's meetings with McDougal, later obtained through a Freedom of Information Act request, revealed that OIC agents and prosecutors met with McDougal for nearly a hundred hours before he left for prison. These meetings in Arkadelphia and in McDougal's new Little Rock pad covered wide-ranging topics, including the ill-fated Whitewater deal; Governor Clinton's jogging by McDougal's Madison Guaranty office and drumming up legal work for Hillary and the Rose Law Firm; McDougal's nervous breakdown when his business empire began collapsing; Susan's frequent calls to Clinton and McDougal's suspicions that they were having an affair; and McDougal's alleged meeting with David Hale and Clinton at his Castle Grande trailer-office, which led to Hale's $300,000 loan to Susan McDougal. (Prior to these sessions, McDougal had told the FBI that he had "no recollection of having any meeting with both HALE and CLINTON.")

Ray Jahn, who had convicted McDougal, recalled McDougal being physically "weak" but cooperative during these debriefing sessions. On occasion, McDougal's "coloring" didn't look good, causing Jahn and his fellow prosecutors to worry that McDougal might be "overdosing himself on nitroglycerine in dealing with his heart condition." At times, McDougal's mind seemed to be acting like a shorted-out computer, lacking "the ability to isolate [a fact] and withdraw it."

Yet Jahn did ascertain one valuable new tidbit from McDougal: The bald-headed felon told Jahn, "Susan's going to be pardoned." He went on to say, "Remember we had that deposition in the White House? Did you see Bill Clinton take me over to the maps [used by FDR during World War II]? That's when he said, 'Tell Susan—hold on. I'll take care of you when I leave office.'" It was hard to tell where fact ended and fiction began, but OIC's job was to get the witness to cough up as much information as possible.

Another defining moment in the sessions came when Jim McDougal rested his head on his cane and sighed—Clinton's testimony in the Whitewater trial, he told the Starr prosecutors despondently, had been "at variance with the truth." McDougal expressed particular dismay that Clinton had uttered these bold-faced lies in the Map Room, where McDougal's hero FDR had spent so much time defending the country during the dark days of World War II. McDougal seemed believable, at least on this point.

Bob Bittman, the young prosecutor enlisted to help debrief McDougal, was warned before meeting with his witness that "the medication wears off, and he gets ornery." For the most part, however, McDougal was not a problem. He would sit on his "cheap La-Z-Boy," proud of his little apartment not far from OIC headquarters. The discussions seemed oddly "therapeutic for him." When it came to discussing his ex-wife, McDougal was generally "very protective of [Susan]." In contrast, Bittman quickly discerned that McDougal "hated Hillary." As for the president, "I don't think he liked him anymore," even though they had once been friends. Overall, Bittman's prosecutorial instincts told him that McDougal "was holding back on some important information." What it was, the young prosecutor had no idea.

Hickman Ewing, the overseer of OIC's outpost in Arkansas, complimented Bittman on his persistence and patience during the long sessions with Jim McDougal. This might turn out to be, Ewing told the young Maryland prosecutor, the most important case he would ever work on. Neither man, of course, could have ever guessed what new assignment was just around the corner for Bittman.

———

THE day Ken Starr made the unexpected announcement—in February 1997—that he was stepping down as independent counsel to move to the deanship at Pepperdine University School of Law in California, the gods of opportunity seemed to be smiling down on him. The *National Law Journal* had recently named Starr Lawyer of the Year, saluting the Whitewater prosecutor for his multifaceted talents. While juggling his independent counsel duties (which paid $115,000 per year), Starr had earned nearly $1 million in 1996 from his firm, Kirkland & Ellis. He had represented the National Football League's players' union in the Supreme Court; defended Wisconsin's school voucher program, which permitted students with vouchers to attend religious schools; and handled massive litigation on behalf of major tobacco companies. It was, as the *National Law Journal* pronounced, "a year that any lawyer would envy."

Ken Starr had long been tempted by the allure of university administration. At heart he was very much an academic. Pepperdine University, a beautiful and affluent new campus built along the beaches of Malibu with glorious views of the Pacific Ocean, had established a niche as a conservative Christian school with enviable fiscal resources. As a beaming Starr told a writer for the *Arkansas Democrat-Gazette*, it was "a wonderful and right opportunity for me and my family."

The timing seemed propitious on many levels. OIC was putting the finishing touches on a report dealing with the Vince Foster matter, and the report would be made public in less than a week. It would put to rest the theories that Foster had been murdered and that the White House had engaged in a cover-up. It would confirm, point by point, Robert Fiske's conclusion that Foster had committed suicide in Fort Marcy Park, reaffirming the original report filed by Fiske in 1994. The rest of the Whitewater/Madison investigation seemed to be moving along smoothly. A second prosecution of former Governor Jim Guy Tucker, relating to alleged tax fraud in his cable television business, was slowly gearing up for trial but that was a year away. It was a perfect time, Starr cheerfully concluded, for a professional change of life.

The whole Starr family supported the move. At a meeting at the dinner table, the Starrs voted that Ken should go for it. He called the president of Pepperdine, David Davenport, and gratefully accepted.

Starr expected this would be a nonevent. Since the investigation was still centered in Little Rock, he believed the logical choice to succeed him would be his chief Arkansas deputy, Hickman Ewing. This would make for a seamless transition.

President Bill Clinton later commented: "I thought that he had had a moment of insightful sanity and he realized that, you know, he was beating a dead horse. And that it was hurting him and hurting his reputation. And he was offered a way out, and he took it. I thought it was an entirely sensible thing. And then the right-wingers and the establishment press . . . pitched a hissy fit, and he caved in. He should have gone in 1997. And I would have wished him well."

Many Republicans interpreted Starr's decision to surf off to Malibu as a sign of weakness, indicating that the investigation against the president and First Lady was sputtering to a close. Former Independent Counsel Joseph DiGenova, a frequent Washington commentator on matters dealing with special prosecutors, declared that Starr's departure for Pepperdine signaled "the big stuff is over." A White House source concurred, asking the rhetorical question, "Is Starr going to indict the First Lady and then leave for the West Coast?" Susan McDougal's lawyer, who was watching his client languish in jail for contempt, saw Starr's bon voyage notice as heartening news. "This is a signal to me that Mr. Starr has decided against further prosecution, and it is a great sign to Susan that her incarceration will come to an end soon," Bobby McDaniel told the press. Even Ken Starr's closest allies read the tea leaves as a requiem for the Whitewater/Madison investigation. Ted Olson, a longtime friend and colleague of Starr's who had represented David Hale in congressional Whitewater matters, told reporters that the prosecution was "all but dead."

Rumors began sweeping through the media that OIC had staged four mock trials and that in none of these dry runs had Bill or Hillary Clinton been convicted by a jury of peers. The momentum was gathering to usher Ken Starr out the door; his adversaries were declaring a complete victory.

Ken Starr later said of his bungled decision: "It was like the proverbial donkey. You've got to get the attention of the donkey, so you hit the donkey with a two-by-four over the head."

Sam Dash, the OIC's ethics counsel, was delivering a speech in Naples, Florida, when a member of the audience asked him, "What do you think of the independent counsel leaving to become a dean?" Dash nearly fell over—he tried to recover by saying, "Well, I don't know about that. But maybe that's good news. Maybe he's finished." As soon as Dash located a phone, he called Starr and angrily demanded, "*How can you possibly* make that decision? First of all, without consulting [anyone]. Second, you are a court-appointed federal independent counsel under a statute. You can't pick up and quit without leave of court."

Starr's own staff was in rebellion, especially those working on the Jim Guy Tucker cable case and the Susan McDougal contempt matter, fearing their prosecutions would fall apart. The conservative pundits did their own part by calling Starr a traitor. William Safire, in a *New York Times* piece titled "The Big Flinch," referred to Starr as a "wimp" who had brought "shame on the legal profession." The *Arkansas Democrat-Gazette,* no fan of Bill Clinton's, called Starr's departure "puzzling and inappropriate." The paper declared sourly: "At the least, Starr should issue a definitive Whitewater report before leaving for academe. The job of an independent counsel is to clear up mysteries, not create them."

With his office under siege and his character under attack, Starr beat a hasty retreat. He arranged a hurried press conference in his Washington office and announced that he had changed his mind. Quoting the onetime New York Mayor Fiorello H. LaGuardia, Starr commented in a characteristic old-fashioned—some would say corny—manner: "When I make a mistake, it's a beaut."

President Clinton later went a step further: "You know, the first rule of living a sane life is when you get into a hole, stop digging," said Clinton. "So I thought Starr decided to stop digging. But ideologues and out-of-control people, when they get in a hole, they ask for a bigger shovel. And so the bigger-shovel crowd got ahold of him." The problem, Clinton insisted, was that a group of influential conservative Republicans was now chanting in unison: "If we just keep this going . . . we can break this guy [Clinton] or break somebody. Surely, we can do something. Gosh, there had to be something."

With a dismissive wave of his hand, President Clinton concluded that Ken Starr had listened to that loud chorus and taken a leap over a cliff that took him straight downward like a man in free fall.

———

IF one could trace on graph paper the trajectory of the independent counsel investigation headed by Ken Starr, one would certainly mark his abrupt nonretirement in February 1997 as a crucial turning point. Until that turnabout, his tenure as independent counsel had earned relatively high marks, at least among neutral observers who made a point of watching and judging special prosecutors.

Subsequent events would allow Starr's critics to portray his entire operation as an investigation run amok. Yet, until his botched Pepperdine decision in early

1997, there were scant facts to bear that out. He was deferential to the president far more than some on his staff would have liked (for instance, he never tolerated prosecutors speaking ill of the Clintons—he always insisted on displaying respect for the president and First Lady). Although he plodded along, he was still doing little more than carrying out the investigations begun by Robert Fiske.

As of this juncture in early 1997, Ken Starr was not even a darling of the right wing. He endured a heap of criticism from the far right when he filed his report on the Vince Foster suicide and refused to validate the conspiracy theories that had been spun by those who remained convinced that Foster had been murdered. One right-wing newsletter accused Starr of taking illicit fees from Chinese military weapons-exporters, declaring: "Starr can now kiss goodbye his widely-reported, widely-supported dream of being appointed to the Supreme Court by a Republican president." Every night, when Ken Starr returned to his home on a quiet cul-de-sac in McLean, his mailbox was stuffed with postcards and letters from groups accusing him of participating in a "cover-up" in the murder of Vince Foster. Even Richard Mellon Scaife, the conservative multimillionaire whose foundations helped to finance Pepperdine University, where Starr still aspired to move when this flap died down, took potshots at Starr for his perceived lack of fortitude.

Scaife, seated in the neatly appointed office of his family's philanthropic foundation on the thirty-ninth floor of the sparkling Oxford Center in Pittsburgh, later said that Starr was "unproductive" and "wasn't bright enough," both in political terms and as an investigator. "I've never met Ken Starr," stated Scaife to correct a misconception. "At that time, I had no idea that he was trying to become the dean of the law school [at Pepperdine]."

As Scaife had told John F. Kennedy, Jr., for a story in *George* magazine shortly before JFK Jr.'s death: "Maybe Ken Starr's a mole working for the Democrats, because he didn't get much accomplished, in this investigation."

Scaife now added, "There [were] a lot of funny things going on. I still don't know what happened to Vince Foster, and I don't think we've ever had a clear answer on that."

Nothing in the historical record would suggest that Ken Starr was extreme or over the top during the early stages of his tenure as independent counsel. Indeed, he was receiving ample criticism from the Republican party's far-right wing for his timidity and ineffectiveness. That is, until he started shifting the focus of the investigation, in the spring of 1997, in a slightly new direction.

———

SHORTLY after Starr's aborted attempt to leave his post, Bob Woodward and Sue Schmidt of the *Washington Post* reported that Starr's prosecutors were beginning to question Arkansas State Troopers on the subject of Bill Clinton and "women." The months leading up to this had been so calm that the president's lawyer David Kendall had declared Whitewater to be in "remission."

Soon enough, however, that diagnosis proved to be premature. In a June 25 front-page article, "Starr Probes Clinton Personal Life," Woodward and Schmidt revealed that FBI agents, private investigators, and Starr prosecutors had been questioning troopers about twelve to fifteen women, seeking to determine the troopers' "knowledge of any extramarital relationships Bill Clinton may have had while he was Arkansas governor." In what the article described as a "sharp departure from previous avenues of inquiry," the Whitewater prosecutors and their investigators had begun probing into Clinton's affairs with a myriad of women, including—but certainly not limited to—Gennifer Flowers. One Arkansas trooper, Roger Perry, stated that the OIC's investigators had specifically asked him "if I had ever seen Bill Clinton perform a sexual act." The trooper commented, "I was left with the impression that they wanted to show he was a womanizer." Perry also volunteered other information: "They asked me about Paula Jones, all kinds of questions about Paula Jones, whether I saw Clinton and Paula together and how many times."

It was the first linkage, however brief and ill fitting, between Starr's Whitewater/Madison investigation and the previously unconnected *Paula Jones* case. Jackie Bennett viewed the Woodward and Schmidt article as a "cheap shot." He later defended OIC's investigative tactics: "The story was false; the point had been to go out and to try to identify people who had interacted with Clinton, who were close to him, and in a position to have observed things or to hear him say things."

Despite such benign explanations, the shift in the investigative tactics appeared (to those inside the White House) to be proof of escalating, covert political warfare. The normally tight-lipped David Kendall held a press conference decrying the tactic as dirty pool. Kendall spoke into a microphone, grim-faced: "The report in today's *Washington Post,* if true, is indicative of an investigation that has lost its way. It is out of control. No one's personal life should be subjected to a desperate dragnet by a prosecutor with unlimited resources. No amount of pious rationalization can justify such conduct. It is intolerable, and it is wrong."

Starr would resent the White House's insinuations that he was punching Bill Clinton below the belt. His investigators were simply following time-honored investigative techniques, he later told the House Judiciary Committee. He harkened back to his prosecutors' first gathering with ethics adviser Sam Dash in the fall of 1994. Dash had laid out the history of the Watergate investigation and had drawn circles on the blackboard, saying, "You need to continually draw concentric circles," and reminding the prosecutors that the only reason the Watergate Senate Committee had located Nixon's aide Alexander Butterfield—who revealed the existence of the White House tapes and blew open the Watergate investigation—had been through turning over every rock. "The course of history might have changed but for our approach and our concentric circles," Dash stated dramatically. As Starr interpreted the message, it was like the story of the *Titanic*. The moral was, "In the waters of the North Atlantic, truth will find its way." For Starr, searching the depths of the ocean to see if any females with close contacts to Governor Bill Clinton knew secrets about Whitewater or Madison Guaranty was merely part of the truth-seeking process.

President Clinton later pointed to this as another example of unmitigated excess. "If you're conducting a Stalinist show trial and you've got to have something to produce, it made a lot of sense," said Clinton. "You know, it was an unconscionable waste of the FBI's assets, who could have been working on crime, drugs, terror, things that might actually make a difference to people's lives." Growing red in the face, Clinton concluded: "And I knew I couldn't prevent him from looking into my personal life, because that's what [overzealous prosecutors] do. I mean, he was into my destruction, not finding the truth about Whitewater."

The precise impetus for Starr's switching gears in the Whitewater/Madison investigation, directly zeroing in on Bill Clinton's extramarital sexual liaisons, remains a puzzle within a puzzle. Journalist Bob Woodward, who broke the story, said later, "I always had the feeling there was more to it than we actually [knew]." Woodward recalled that Hickman Ewing and other OIC prosecutors had indicated to him that they were looking for "pillow talk" that might reveal a stray comment by Clinton about Whitewater-related matters and that might have slipped out during an amorous affair. Yet this explanation seemed to be a stretch: What Bill Clinton might have revealed to a person like Paula Jones or even a paramour like Gennifer Flowers about secret Whitewater matters was almost impossible to fathom. "It struck me," Woodward said, "if they [OIC] could find anything on any subject—not even related to Whitewater—they were going to do it." For Woodward, having broken the Watergate story and having watched the shadow of scandal engulf subsequent presidents, his instinct told him that OIC's sudden desire to probe Clinton's extramarital affairs "took [the Starr investigation] into a new realm." That, as Woodward saw it, was one of the things that made the independent counsel law so pernicious. "It was just—'have at somebody.'"

The summer of 1997 thus turned into a period of unusually aggressive activity, on the part of both the independent counsel's office and the White House. The fragile civility between the two sides was finally shattering into a thousand pieces.

JIM McDougal, wearing loose-fitting prison garb and sucking on a pepper-mint, arrived at the Federal Medical Center in Fort Worth, Texas, in fair spirits. At least this was one of the less terrifying institutions among the grim selection within the Federal Bureau of Prisons system. The date was August 26, 1997; the air was hot and sticky. McDougal climbed out of the prison van and inspected his new home. Built in the 1930s as a federal hospital, the white, red-roofed facility, originally constructed to accommodate heroin addicts at the turn of the century, now housed inmates with chronic health conditions. (McDougal's arteriosclerosis had earned him this privilege.) He was wearing khaki pants, khaki shirt, khaki belt, "khaki everything," standard garb for general population prisoners.

McDougal received a spot in the Fort Worth Unit, a good location because it was not cluttered with inmates in wheelchairs crying out from pain and terminal illness. Because of his history of mental health issues, including treatment for alcoholism and bipolar disorder, McDougal was flagged as an inmate who should attend regular sessions with doctors to monitor his progress. Additionally, because he was already well known within the prison walls as the famous Whitewater convict, the psychology team wanted to keep an eye on him.

The new prisoner attended his first meeting with the prison's psychology department, which would evaluate his mental health status, on October 2 at 10:00 A.M. Here, in the basement of Building 4, James B. McDougal entered a small room where he encountered a thirty-four-year-old clinical psychology intern named Richard Clark. A thin, balding soft-spoken man, Clark had done his doctoral work after having obtained a master's in counseling from the Denver Seminary. His specialty was the integration of psychology and theology—a brand of psychotherapy that was particularly useful in a prison environment.

The records of Clark's first meeting with McDougal, obtained with permission of McDougal's legal representatives after his death, indicated that the inmate was taking sixty milligrams of Prozac per day for depression as well as twenty milligrams of BuSpar to treat anxiety. The report further recorded that McDougal, dressed in shorts and a T-shirt, was "polite and cooperative." The report went on: "He stated his mood was 'generally positive to upbeat.' His thinking was clear and easy to follow. He denied having any suicidal ideation. No homicidal or delusional thinking was elicited."

From his review of the central file, the doctor noted that McDougal had arrived late at Fort Worth, due to an anonymous death threat against him. A prosecutor from the Office of Independent Counsel in Little Rock, Hickman Ewing, had contacted the Fort Worth prison on McDougal's behalf and expressed concern that there might be "forces at work" trying to make McDougal's life more difficult than it already was.

McDougal's criminal and psychiatric history revealed that he had been deemed mentally competent to stand trial during his first S&L prosecution in 1990. McDougal quipped that he was "the only Whitewater figure declared certifiably *sane* by the United States Government," a comment that brought a smile to the young psychologist's lips.

When it came to McDougal's day-to-day activities in the prison, Clark was pleased to hear that McDougal had volunteered to pick up trash in the Fort Worth Unit. "And he told me he had done that for two reasons," Clark recalled. Although trash pickup was "one of the lousiest jobs" in the prison community, McDougal saw a tactical advantage to the chore. "One, was that it gave him an opportunity early in the mornings to get some exercise. But also to be able to try to communicate to the other inmates that he did not view himself as being in any way above them."

McDougal also confided in Clark that his book project was one of the few positive aspects of his new life as a convict. Each morning he would telephone his coauthor, Curtis Wilkie, a journalist from Mississippi, to discuss material for the book. The doctor recorded that McDougal told him that it was "therapeutic for him to do the book, much like the step in AA [Alcoholics Anonymous] wherein a person takes a moral inventory."

With respect to his ex-wife, Susan, Jim McDougal spoke in positive and protective terms, leaving the clear impression that he still cared about her. Even when it came to Bill Clinton, Clark noted, McDougal did not communicate hostility. This was true even though McDougal clearly believed that his incarceration was due to the fact that Clinton was president and that he was a victim of Clinton's powerful political enemies. Clark summarized his initial impressions of the prisoner: "I found him to be highly cooperative with the process. He was very much a gentleman, very much in the Southern tradition of men being gentlemen."

Moreover, being eligible for parole on April 29 of the following year clearly buoyed McDougal's spirits. This date, Clark noted, seemed to be etched in McDougal's mind, as if it constituted a glittering ray of hope.

Neither doctor nor patient, of course, could have foreseen the events that would prevent McDougal from leaving those stark buildings inside the Fort Worth prison. Jim McDougal would never be given parole. Nor would he see the outside of the prison walls or realize his dream of retiring to Claudia Riley's trailer-house in Arkadelphia to teach a final political science course at Ouachita Baptist University.

Instead, James Bert McDougal would die in solitary confinement, in a dark section of the sprawling complex he had not yet laid his eyes on, an unwelcome place that he would soon visit and that was known as "the hole."

THE SETTLEMENT THAT NEVER HAPPENED

Those seated in the Supreme Court gallery awaiting the day's regularly scheduled cases on May 27, 1997, were caught off guard when the Court handed down its historic decision in *Clinton v. Jones*. The white-haired Justice John Paul Stevens, considered a liberal who might have been sympathetic to Bill Clinton's plight, read the unanimous opinion in a steady voice. Straightening the trademark bow tie beneath his robe, Justice Stevens treated this like any case against any ordinary defendant. In more than two hundred years, he stated, "only three sitting Presidents have been subjected to suits for their private actions. If the past is any indicator, it seems unlikely that a deluge of such litigation will ever engulf the Presidency." Justice Stevens organized his papers and concluded, "As for the case at hand, if properly managed by the District Court, it appears to us highly unlikely to occupy any substantial amount of petitioner's time."

Solicitor General Walter Dellinger happened to be present in the courtroom that day, preparing to argue another case. Although the result did not surprise him, he viewed the majority's reasoning as overly simplistic. Dellinger worried that whatever the merits of the ruling as a matter of constitutional law, it was bad news for all future presidents at the mercy of a legion of lawyers and litigants with a "partisan incentive to go after a president." ·

The *New York Post* blared, "Grin & Bare It," declaring in a front-page story that Jones had won an unqualified victory. The tabloid stated that Paula Jones, who was still sitting on an affidavit swearing that she had observed "distinguishing characteristics" on the president's private parts, could now "go into a deposition and ask the president to drop his pants."

As President Clinton posed with Russian President Boris Yeltsin at a NATO signing ceremony in Paris, the American press was already predicting that the Court's decision would constitute a major setback for Clinton, resurrecting "doubts about [Clinton's] honesty and integrity."

Joe Cammarata dialed Paula and Steve Jones in California, sharing the happy news with his client, who was just waking up on West Coast time. "She was ecstatic," Cammarata recalled. "You know, she cried and [Steve] cried." For the whole plaintiff's team, it was "a touching moment." Susan Carpenter-McMillan also called Paula, remembering with a flicker of nostalgia, "The two of us just screamed and yelled and cried. In her cute little way, she [Jones] said, 'Susie, can you believe it? Can you believe it?' "

President Clinton later admitted that it took him years to get over the *Jones* decision. For him, the biggest shocker was that it was unanimous. He had braced himself for the likelihood that five justices—the same five who would later put George W. Bush in the White House during the "stolen" election of 2000—would vote along party lines. But he had hoped that at least *some* of the other justices would have stood up for his presidency under attack, understanding what it meant to have this sort of "a politically motivated lawsuit, the main purpose of which is to drag the president through a series of depositions which could later be used in a criminal case," while there was "a politically motivated special prosecutor out there." Clinton stated: "For the [justices] who did it on politics, it's a very candid decision. They knew what they were doing." For the rest of the justices, he concluded with a frown, it was "one of the most naive decisions in the history of the Supreme Court."

Justice Stevens, however, would express no regret about his ruling. Seated in his Supreme Court chambers several years later, the eighty-year-old justice said, "The opinion was just part of a day's work." Stevens had been assigned the job of authoring the majority opinion by Chief Justice Rehnquist, who undoubtedly selected him with political considerations in mind (Stevens said, eyes twinkling) because he was viewed as a reliable liberal, which meant that Rehnquist could shield himself from criticism "if the opinion was written by me rather than him."

Stevens did not anguish in drafting the opinion in his Florida condominium during the Court's winter break. In his small office facing the Intracoastal Waterway, surrounded by blue waters and clear skies, he had tapped away at his home computer. "When I wrote it, I had no sense that it would have a dramatic effect on anything," Justice Stevens said candidly. "It has been criticized as being naive. That is quite misguided, I think. The likelihood that *any* decision would have let him [President Clinton] get off without even a deposition being taken was about one chance in one million." Even if the trial had been postponed until the president left office, Justice Stevens underscored, discovery would still have gone forward. No matter how one sliced it, Bill Clinton was going to be forced to testify under oath. "If anything," Stevens pointed out, "the plaintiff's lawyers would have had to take a deposition *faster* to preserve testimony, if the trial was delayed." One way or another, said the senior justice, regardless of the constitutional nuances, President Clinton was going to have to give sworn testimony in the *Jones* case and face the consequences.

Justice Stevens also stressed, folding his hands patiently, that the problems that resulted from the *Jones* decision were of President Bill Clinton's own making. The Court had no way of predicting that this president would eventually be caught having an affair with a young intern and fibbing about it—this was not something that even Clinton's most ardent enemies could have dreamed up. "The possibility that this man would have done something so unwise and let himself get caught," said the eighty-year-old jurist, "was extremely remote."

In the end, Justice Stevens would stand behind the soundness of the Court's decision in the *Jones* case. Congress was perfectly free to create immunity from civil suits for presidents; it had not yet chosen to do so. It was simply not the Court's job to invent constitutional privileges out of whole cloth.

Stevens sat back on the small sofa under his chambers, having just returned from a brisk match of tennis that had energized him. When it came to the national scandal that eventually engulfed the Clinton presidency, Justice Stevens made clear that he had not even a smidgen of guilt that his opinion had caused it. "I never had that thought for a second. I never had the slightest regret about a single word of the opinion. I wouldn't change a word."

"The only thing that came out of our case," Stevens said firmly, placing a copy of the U.S. Reports on the coffee table in front of him, indicating that it was time to get back to work, "was that President Clinton had to give a deposition."

———

On August 11, 1997, Michael Isikoff published a piece in *Newsweek* titled "A Twist in Jones v. Clinton," sending a shiver through the White House. A week earlier, a gossipy new Internet publication called the "Drudge Report"—hosted by quirky California introvert Matt Drudge—had scooped the Isikoff story and dumped an advance version onto the internet. Now the lurid account was all over the world. It included the grotesque particulars of Kathleen Willey's allegations, down to Clinton's alleged kissing and fondling of her the day before her husband committed suicide. Now there was a new twist: Both publications revealed that a coworker named Linda Tripp, who had since been transferred to the Pentagon, had told Isikoff that she had spoken to Willey immediately after the incident and that Willey—an attractive reddish-haired woman who spoke freely with Tripp—was not at all "appalled" by Clinton's advance. In fact, said Tripp, her coworker seemed "happy and joyful."

Willey's lawyer, Daniel A. Gecker of Richmond, expressed "outrage" that Willey was being dragged into the case; he denied that his client had any information whatsoever "relevant to the Paula Jones case." Simultaneously, *Newsweek* revealed that a close friend of Willey's named Julie Hiatt Steele had initially told the publication that she had spoken to Willey the night after the incident, and that Willey was "distraught." Now Steele had recanted, telling *Newsweek* that Willey had asked her to "lie" about the incident to cover for her.

Presidential lawyer Bob Bennett stood before a group of wire service reporters, shaking his head with disgust at all of this spy-versus-spy skulduggery. "I really smell a rat here," said Bennett. "I'm sure this is a *Jones* team effort to humiliate the president."

———

ONE aspect of the *Paula Jones* story largely lost to history is that President Clinton's lawyer and Paula Jones's lawyers believed that they had reached a final settlement during the late summer of 1997. That deal, giving Jones everything she had requested in her original complaint—and more—ultimately collapsed because the plaintiff herself rejected it, ignoring her lawyers' pleas to honor the deal. Jones's abrupt decision to turn down the very recovery she had asked for, the record now makes clear, was tied to two people: Steve Jones (whom she would soon divorce) and Susan Carpenter McMillan, her PR guru, who detested Bill Clinton.

President Clinton endured endless criticism for failing to settle the *Jones* case expeditiously. He would express frustration, however, that the public never became fully aware that Paula Jones's own lawyers resigned because she walked away from an exceedingly generous (and fair) settlement deal. Clinton later said of Ms. Jones's two Virginia lawyers who were trying to strike a fair deal: "They weren't crazy. They knew that she'd be getting money she wasn't entitled to and I'd be getting embarrassed if I settled it. And they thought that ought to be enough."

The Supreme Court's unanimous decision was not the only reason that the case was ripe for settlement. In late August, Judge Susan Webber Wright had dismissed a defamation claim and a due process allegation in Jones's complaint, trimming down her lawsuit. Judge Wright had also held both sides' feet to the fire by setting a quick May 1998 trial date. At a status conference in her Little Rock courtroom, she lectured the parties: "What I would hope we could do is try this case in five or six days. It doesn't look like a case that's worth any more than that to me." The judge also set a tight discovery deadline of January 30, ordering all depositions and evidence gathering to be completed by that date.

With these forces bearing down on the parties, the case seemed ready for a final resolution. In fact, Bob Bennett had a specific end game in mind as he negotiated on behalf of the president: "The goal was to try to settle for under one million dollars," he recalled. "It was generally a consensus that if we paid more than that—people in the White House felt that it would be [viewed as] an admission." To sweeten the deal for Paula Jones's camp, Bennett had received authority from President Clinton to promise that Clinton would personally "make a statement that Paula was not involved in improper conduct of any kind." Wrapping that package together, Bennett believed, was a deal that no sane lawyer could reject.

Proof that the parties meant business was evident in the spirited, final round of negotiations. During one late-night session in Bennett's office, Bennett tossed out a stink bomb: "If this thing doesn't settle, we've got stuff on Paula. We're just going to lay it out." Davis and Cammarata returned the volley, announcing that they were lining up a "parade of women" to prove that the president had exhibited a pattern of "hitting on" young women like Paula.

Bennett scoffed, "Ahh, nobody cares about women anymore."

The Virginia lawyers called his bluff, stating that they could "prepare a stipulation" listing all the women with whom Bill Clinton had engaged in extramarital affairs, and both parties could sign it. "Then it won't be an issue anymore," they said, smiling at the rich humor of this proposal.

Now it was Bennett's turn: He reminded his opponents that their client had issued a press release stating that she was not interested in money and promising to "donate all amounts above payment of expenses to a charity of her choice." Since Jones had no interest in financial remuneration, Bennett deadpanned, establishing a modest amount of cash to resolve the case should be a simple matter.

With the scent of settlement in the air, the Jones lawyers turned up the heat by playing the "distinguishing characteristic" card. Talk had been raging on conservative talk radio that President Clinton suffered from a condition known as Peyronie's disease, which causes plaque or hard lumps to form in the genitalia and produces the bent shape that Paula Jones had allegedly observed. The talkshow chatter soon escalated into rampant rumors that Clinton had undergone surgery to hide the problem, after Paula Jones had tipped her hand in the complaint. Gil Davis later revealed that he did consult, confidentially, with several experts in the field. He had then delivered a subpoena to the White House, demanding evidence concerning "any treatment or advice sought or obtained by William Jefferson Clinton for any suspected or actual genital or urological problem, condition, disability, disease or disorder."

Cammarata also took a precautionary step by shooting off a confidential fax to Danny Traylor in Arkansas, firing him. Traylor, who had remained as "local counsel" in Arkansas, had recently given a wide-ranging interview to the *Legal Times*, in which he said that Paula Jones had never mentioned the infamous "distinguishing characteristic" during their extensive conversations before he agreed to take the case. Cammarata now sent Traylor a "Dear Danny" letter, stating that Traylor had engaged in "an improper disclosure of confidential case information" and had caused a "weakening of Paula Jones' bargaining position." The Virginia lawyers therefore terminated him "effective immediately." Davis and Cammarata were steering their settlement ship into port, so that they (and Jones) could go home with the spoils.

On NBC's *Meet the Press* show in June, both sides exchanged jabs, sensing that they were close to a final deal. Cammarata smiled into the camera and said he only wanted Bill Clinton to answer three questions: "Mr. President, were you in the room? . . . Mr. President, did you grab and grope Paula Jones? Mr. President, did you drop your pants and solicit oral sex?"

Bennett, for his part, tried to take the high road, issuing clear signals that the president might consider a sizable "contribution to charity" to put the case to rest. He reminded moderator Tim Russert: "The President of the United States, you know, had one heck of a week last week. We're not at war. The economy is fantastic. NATO has been expanded. Things are going well on the budget." Bennett suggested that it might be a time to seriously discuss resolving the case for the good of the nation. "I don't think it's appropriate for the President of the United States to get down in the gutter where Ms. Jones wants to drag him," he said with a tone of lawyerly gravitas. "And I'm not going to let that happen."

A deal was finally cut. President Clinton would pay $700,000, the full amount Paula Jones had demanded in her original complaint. This far exceeded, all of the lawyers knew, any likely verdict if the case went to trial. Clinton would also give the Jones lawyers a statement making clear that Paula had done nothing inappropriate in the Excelsior Hotel room, and declaring for the whole world that the *American Spectator* story was patently false. In return, the Jones lawyers would turn over to Bob Bennett their sealed affidavit concerning the "distinguishing characteristic information," so that the White House could nip that allegation in the bud, issuing a press release stating that Clinton's doctors had examined the president and found no such medical condition.

Word around the White House suggested that First Lady Hillary Clinton—who had been adamantly opposed to her husband's paying money to Jones—was now prepared to accept this settlement deal. With everything in place, President Clinton gave the go-ahead to his lawyer. Clinton would later acknowledge, "Yes. I mean, once they [the Supreme Court] decided it, I was willing to settle. Even if it cost, you know, half of all the money we had saved for thirty years." It still made him angry to think about paying this exorbitant amount of money to the likes of Paula Jones, who he believed was making an industry out of "clearing her name." But his advisers convinced him that it was time to end this gargantuan diversion. "I decided I had to do it," Clinton said, "because I didn't want to take the time away from the job to deal with it."

Because this was civil litigation, insurance questions had to be thrashed out. Chubb and State Farm both had issued policies that covered Bill Clinton at various stages: Chubb seemed eager to settle this unseemly claim; State Farm resisted putting money on the table. Ultimately, a compromise was ironed out, with the Clintons personally on the hook for a portion of the settlement dollars. The lawyers had reached a meeting of the minds. The most significant civil lawsuit ever filed against a sitting president was resolved—or so both sides' lawyers thought—with a handshake inside a windowless conference room at the Skadden Arps law firm.

Getting the final approval from Paula Jones, the Virginia lawyers believed, was simply a pro forma step. Their client was getting everything she had asked for in the complaint. It was a grand slam by any litigator's measure. As Gil Davis said candidly, "Yes, we had a deal. I mean if she [Paula] accepted it, there was a deal."

There were several impediments, it soon became apparent, to clinching the agreement. One was Paula's husband, who was becoming increasingly bellicose. More and more, Steve Jones was playing the part of a "tough guy," at times threatening to "beat up" Bob Bennett and Bill Clinton. Paula's husband would say words like "let me at that guy," requiring the lawyers to calm him down. After one gathering in a hotel room, the lawyers had nearly duked it out with him. Steve got up on his high horse and declared, "I don't care if we have to live in a pup tent . . . this case is going forward." Hearing this, Joe Cammarata moved up close to Steve Jones and said: "Let me tell you something. If you want to live in a pup tent, you can live in a pup tent. But I'm not living in any pup tent. Do you understand me? You haven't put dime one into this case." It was not helping their settlement efforts, the Virginia lawyers worried, to have Steve Jones whispering in their client's ear every day and night.

There was also Susan Carpenter-McMillan. The California PR coordinator was increasingly steering Paula Jones away from settlement, persuading her client "that she could get *more* money by squeezing Clinton." Additionally, Carpenter-McMillan was complaining that the lawyers would walk away with most of the money in fees, and Paula would get "nothing except a dirty, muddy name." Both Steve Jones and Carpenter-McMillan were advising Paula that she needed to fight to the death until she "got an apology" from Clinton, even though there was no such remedy available under Arkansas or federal law. Carpenter-McMillan later acknowledged her own position: "Twenty-million-dollar settlement, *no* apologies. Two-hundred-thousand-dollar settlement, a *big* apology. My motive always was the victimization of Paula," she said. "Now, were there fringe benefits on the side like hurting the Dems? Absolutely." Steve Jones was even more adamant. He wanted public groveling and an apology from Clinton, "no matter what—twenty million, forty million, or two dollars."

Behind the scenes, other Washington operatives were jumping into the act. Conservative activist-lawyer Ann Coulter, who was lending moral support to the elves, was aghast that the *Jones* case might be settled. In a burst of candor, she told journalist Michael Isikoff that settlement "was contrary to our purpose of bringing down the President."

The proposed stipulation of settlement that Bob Bennett agreed to have the president sign was even stronger than Davis and Cammarata had hoped for. It read: "The parties agree that Paula Corbin Jones did not engage in any improper or sexual conduct on May 8, 1991, and that the allegations and the inferences about her published in January 1994 in the American Spectator are false and their adverse effects upon her character and reputation regrettable."

For two days, the Virginia lawyers made frantic telephone calls and faxed messages to Paula, who remained holed up in her Long Beach condo. Increasingly, Davis and Cammarata felt that they were losing a grip over their client. Paula was not returning their phone calls. There were rumors that she was shopping around for new lawyers. Susan Carpenter-McMillan was reportedly horrified that the case might settle; she was making a full-court press to replace the Virginia lawyers. In a confidential letter recapping numerous phone conversations, faxed to Paula in California on August 19, the lawyers literally begged their client to accept the deal: *"It is a complete victory for the interests you seek which are the redemption of your character and reputation."*

Not only would she be receiving everything that she had asked for in her complaint, but the lawyers reminded Jones that she would be concluding the litigation in a strong position in terms of restoring her good name: "Your reputation is now at its highest peak because of your victory in the Supreme Court." The money and language "fully redeems your reputation for character and truthfulness." If she scotched the deal, on the other hand, her reputation "will suffer serious deterioration in the course of litigation, and therefore, failure to accept this settlement will, in effect, 'snatch defeat from the jaws of victory.'"

The Virginia lawyers were baffled that their client was suddenly insisting on an "explicit apology" by Clinton and "an admission of wrongdoing." The latter had never been on the table—not ever. Nor was such a remedy permitted by law. "Your focus has thus changed from proving that you are a good person, to proving Clinton is a bad person. That was never before your objective in filing suit."

Davis and Cammarata also warned Jones that their professional reputations were being compromised. Demanding x set forth in the complaint, grinding down one's opponent until that opponent agreed to pay x, then demanding y, was not how the legal system worked. They wrote: "There are serious ethical problems for lawyers who continue litigation after all the client's interests can be reached by settlement."

In a last-ditch effort to save the agreement, Davis and Cammarata offered to slash their own fees to get the case resolved. They ended the twelve-page letter by making an emotional plea: "We have given our heart and soul to your case for over three years. Paula, we believe you and we believe in you. You are a good person. You have become like family to us. When you asked if we would recommend this [settlement] to our family [or to a daughter] we told you we would."

Ten days later, Paula Jones still was not budging. The Virginia attorneys sent a second confidential communication to their client in California. It was one of the most remarkable documents ever to emerge from Gil Davis's basement files.

In a startling admission of what they believed the case was actually worth, Davis and Cammarata underscored that the settlement amount of $700,000 was already a sky-high number. Judge Wright had recently thrown out several counts, meaning that the *maximum* Jones could recover at trial had dropped to $525,000. In a blunt assessment of what Jones could *realistically* expect to recover at trial, if anything, Davis and Cammarata predicted a minuscule number: "We estimated a maximum verdict of $50,000 and now likely it will be much less, *if* the jury gives you any judgment at all."

The lawyers gave their client until 12:00 noon Washington time on Tuesday September 2, 1997, to change her mind. Otherwise, they said, they would be forced to quit. In part, according to sources, Davis and Cammarata sensed they were being forced out and wanted to jump ship before that happened; in equal part, they felt a professional obligation to sever ties with Paula if she insisted on taking an unreasonable, intractable position. "Serious differences of opinion have arisen between us," they wrote. "We believe these differences are so basic as to make it necessary for us to seek the court's permission to withdraw as your counsel as a consequence of your refusal to agree to a settlement."

As the final settlement appeared headed for collapse, Judge Susan Webber Wright convened an extraordinary powwow of all the parties, including Paula Jones herself, via conference call. The judge threatened stiff sanctions if any participant leaked the details of this conference to the press. During this highly unusual colloquy, Judge Wright reviewed the motion of Davis and Cammarata to withdraw, concluding that their reasons were well founded. One person on the call recalled that at one point, Judge Wright came within a hair of telling Paula that she was abusing the processes of the federal courts by turning down a settlement that gave her everything that her complaint had demanded. At this dressing-down, Paula began to cry. Still, she did not alter her position. Judge Wright, having led the horse to water, could not make her drink it.

The following day, Judge Wright issued a terse order granting the Virginia attorneys' motion to withdraw. She added: "Mr. Davis and Mr. Cammarata are both entitled to a reasonable attorney's fee for their zealous and effective representation of plaintiff to date." The judge also kept the case on a fast track for trial, ordering Jones to adhere to the existing tight deadlines. It was a game of chicken; now, the federal judge was establishing the rules.

Danny Traylor, Paula's original lawyer in Arkansas, who had never formally quit as local counsel, took this opportunity to bail out. He called Jones in California and informed her that he could no longer represent her. As Traylor explained his logic, he had a real problem with "that right-wing element out in Los Angeles," in the person of Susan Carpenter-McMillan, who he felt had "caused the case to go off the track." He was also miffed that seminude photos of Jones had appeared in *Penthouse* magazine, after she had assured him that "there was nothing out there." Traylor felt he had been duped and "misled."

Jones began to cry some more. Traylor said years later, shaking his head, "You know, I don't know what was motivating Paula at that time. She was getting hairdos and limousines and new clothes and getting [her nose fixed]."

Years later, President Clinton expressed dismay bordering on disbelief that the plaintiff had brought this lawsuit and then refused to settle it at full value. He concluded that the woman who sued him was no longer driving her own case, if she ever had been. "She was the front," Clinton said with evident anger. "And they desperately wanted this thing to go on. I have no idea what they said to her or what else they offered her or what representations they made to her or what role her husband, or her ex-husband had in it. I don't know any of that." From the moment the settlement fell through, however, Clinton sensed that a new group of lawyers would emerge who would fight this case as fiery political warfare rather than as an ordinary civil matter.

While this premonition may have been accurate, President Clinton himself, it turned out, was adding a potent weapon to his enemy's arsenal. Even while the *Jones* case blinked danger, Clinton was still engaged in an on-again, off-again sexual affair inside the White House with a young woman his daughter's age. This high-risk behavior would supply the new Jones lawyers with everything they needed to use as grenades, bombs, and flamethrowers.

TRAPPED OUTSIDE THE WHITE HOUSE

By July 1997, her relationship with President Clinton on the rocks, Monica Lewinsky had become overwhelmed and depressed. The prospect of returning to the White House now seemed dim. Ever since the move to the Pentagon, Monica's mother had observed that her daughter was, "very, very upset." Marcia Lewis recalled, "The early sort of halcyon days, where she was a happy intern working in the White House . . . had totally changed. She was often in her room crying, and it was awful. It was terrible. Just dreadful." Marcia would never address, head-on, whether she knew that President Clinton was the cause of her daughter's distress. Nor would she state, categorically, whether she knew that Bill Clinton had broken off an affair with Monica. Yet she was prepared to admit this much: "I definitely knew that something was wrong."

Meanwhile, in a July 3 "Dear Sir" letter that she wrote directly to President Clinton, Monica vented her growing frustration. She later described this breaking point to the grand jury:

> The President wasn't responding to me and wasn't returning my calls and wasn't responding to my notes. And I got very upset so I sat down that morning actually and scribbled out a long letter to him that talked about my frustrations and that he had promised to bring me back; if he wasn't going to bring me back . . . then could he help me find a job? At that point I said "in New York at the United Nations," and that I sort of dangled in front of him to remind him that if I wasn't coming back to the White House I was going to need to explain to my parents exactly why that wasn't happening.

Monica felt there were several reasons to commit her grievances to paper. As she explained to the rapt grand jurors, "Towards the end of the letter I softened up again and was back to my mushy self, but—one of the purposes, I think was to kind of remind him that I had left the White House like a good girl in April of '96. A lot of other people might have made a really big stink and said that they weren't going to lose their job and they didn't want to do that and would have talked [publicly] about what kind of relationship they had with the President."

Monica, on the other hand, "had been patient and waited." Yet her patience had worn thin. She was now "frustrated and angry."

So Monica delivered her letter, addressed simply to "Mr. P," to Betty Currie that same day, after meeting Currie at the Northwest Gate of the White House. Within hours Currie called Monica to tell her to arrive at 9:00 the next morning, on the Fourth of July, to meet privately with the president.

As Washington prepared for the rockets and fireworks of Independence Day, both parties prepared for their own version of a pyrotechnics display. Each assumed his or her traditional spot: The president sat in his usual rocking chair; Monica sat in the black swivel chair behind his desk. Soon the meeting erupted into "a fight." Clinton began by saying: "It is illegal to threaten the President of the United States." He told Monica that he had destroyed the letter; she should not be putting these sorts of things in writing. He also "lectured" her that she was "ungrateful"; he was doing his very best to help her.

Monica in turn launched into a laundry list of her own grievances. She accused Clinton of using her and casting her aside, at which point she broke down crying loudly. The president hurried over and hugged her. He stroked her hair, whispering, "Please don't cry." By the end of the conversation, they were talking about being together again—*someday*—in the future. The young woman was reassured that there was still a tender spot that joined them.

Before they parted company, Monica raised another subject, wishing to protect Clinton. According to a "friend" (she did not yet identify Linda Tripp), *Newsweek*'s Michael Isikoff had been digging around for information to buttress a story alleging that the president had made an unwanted pass at a woman named Kathleen Willey in the White House. That friend "did *not* corroborate Kathleen Willey's story," because she had seen Willey after the encounter and observed no sign that she had been subjected to "sexual harassment." But this friend would be forced to acknowledge, if pressed, that *some* encounter between Willey and the president had taken place on the date in question. Monica was worried that Willey "was going to be another Paula Jones," expressing concern that the president "didn't really need that."

Although she had come to the White House to read Clinton the riot act, Monica was again feeling mushy toward him. She wanted to help Clinton get out of this bind. She was thinking, "Well, gee . . . maybe there is something he could do to fix it." Maybe the president could even get this Willey woman a job, she suggested, to make the problem go away. Clinton told her, with an abbreviated hug, that he appreciated her help and friendship.

Ten days later, after Monica had flown to Madrid for a Pentagon project and returned home, the president summoned her back to the Oval Office. This time the atmosphere in the room was noticeably chillier. The president asked, Was the woman whom Monica had mentioned during their last conversation (the one who had talked to Isikoff about Kathleen Willey) a person named Linda Tripp? Lewinsky balked momentarily, then admitted, "Yes." Clinton looked "distant and very cold," she recalled. He said that there was a story on the "Sludge Report," referring derogatorily to the Internet political gossip publication, indicating that Linda Tripp had been the source of the Willey information. The president posed the question delicately: Could Monica ask this Linda Tripp person to call his adviser Bruce Lindsey in the White House? Maybe they could see if this *Newsweek* story could be nipped in the bud. Monica nodded her head; she could certainly try. The president asked one more favor: Could she call Betty Currie and let her know "mission accomplished" as soon as she had spoken to Tripp?

Clinton ended their meeting by posing two more questions to Monica. One of them, the young woman answered truthfully; the other, she did not.

The first question was, "Do you trust Linda Tripp?"

Monica answered, "Yes."

The second question was, "Have you told anything to Linda Tripp about our relationship?"

She turned to Bill Clinton, as he sat in his rocking chair, and responded firmly to the question. "No," she said.

———

As Jim McDougal grew accustomed to his new surroundings at the federal penitentiary in Forth Worth, Susan McDougal was being moved from a minimum-security facility in Texas to solitary confinement in Los Angeles, at a dank county jail designed for hardened criminals.

Flamboyant talk-show host Geraldo Rivera engaged in a lively discussion about whether the continued incarceration of this noncooperative witness, for the better part of a year, constituted an abuse of the civil contempt process. Susan's new attorney, celebrity lawyer Mark Geragos from Los Angeles, told the television audience that holding Susan behind bars for this extended period, after it became clear she would never change her mind, was an illegal form of "punishment." Prominent Washington lawyer Joseph DiGenova, who had served as an independent counsel himself, shot back that as long as Judge Susan Webber Wright believed jail time was "appropriate" to deal with this recalcitrant witness, federal law permitted the judge to keep McDougal incarcerated to gain truthful testimony and to "break [Susan's] will."

There was much speculation as to whether Ken Starr and the Office of Independent Counsel were somehow involved in the abrupt move of Susan McDougal from the "soft" Carswell Medical Prison in Texas to the "county jail hell-hole" in Los Angeles. Susan was facing embezzlement charges in the county courts of Los Angeles for the 1992 allegations that she had swiped $150,000 from conductor Zubin Mehta and his wife, while working as a "bookkeeper" for the eccentric couple. The charges themselves smelled of a payback.

Geragos now openly charged that Ken Starr and his prosecutors had manipulated the local district attorney's office, causing it to transport Susan to the decrepit Sybil Brand Institute for Women, where she was placed in lockdown status and classified "K-10," a status reserved for murderers, child molesters, and the most dangerous reprobates who flowed through the prison system. This was done, Susan's lawyer declared, as a naked form of coercion. Susan was issued a red jumpsuit and locked in a cell up to twenty-three hours a day, not "for her own safety," but because Starr's office was trying to make life as intolerable as possible for her. Although OIC denied playing any role in Susan's transfer to the California prison as she awaited trial, and an internal Bureau of Prisons investigation supported OIC's assertion, many observers were skeptical.

On NBC's *Dateline,* Susan's family weighed in, charging that this was a "deliberate" form of psychological torment "aimed at breaking Susan's silence." Her mother, Laurette Henley, had grown up in Nazi-occupied Belgium, where her family had harbored resistance fighters in their basement. She now spoke of her daughter's refusal to cave in. Mrs. Henley said that she had begged Susan to reconsider her plan not to testify in front of Starr's grand jury. When Susan refused to budge, Laurette Henley took a deep breath and told her daughter, "If I could stand up to them [the Nazis] you can stand up to them [Starr's prosecutors]."

Susan herself, granting her first television interview from inside the prison in California, appeared coolly defiant. Dressed in a simple peach-colored top, she said that the tactics used by Starr and his henchmen would never cause her to buckle. Although she felt as if "my life was run over [by] a Mack truck," she had made a solemn vow "never to have anything to do with this corrupt investigation."

When asked if she expected a pardon from President Bill Clinton when she was released, Susan replied, "No. In fact, I don't want a pardon. I didn't do anything wrong." The show's host pointed out that with two simple phone calls, Susan could be "free and wealthy." She simply needed to call the OIC prosecutors, give them a ginned-up story about the Clintons, and then place a call to a major book publisher and wait for her royalty checks to roll in. "Are those phone calls you'll ever make?"

Susan replied, her tone adamant, "No. I've put in [nearly] a year of my life, about something I believe so strongly in, that this man [Starr] is really wrong in what he's doing." She looked into the camera before being escorted back to her prison cell. "And I will never, ever be sorry for what I've done," she declared.

Jim McDougal, for his part, had settled in tolerably well at the federal facility in Fort Worth. He was enjoying working on his autobiography and hoped to call it *The Promoter,* after a series of editorials in the Little Rock papers referring to his penchant for engaging in daring business deals. He liked the sound of that title.

Yet some aspects of prison life were wearing him down. On Halloween Day 1997, Jim McDougal reported for his monthly mental status meeting at 8:00 A.M., taking his usual chair across from his doctor, Dr. Richard Clark. McDougal complained of "increased feelings of depression and anxiety due to stressors he experienced last week." The principal stressor, he told the doctor, was his inability to provide a urine sample when ordered to perform by prison guards. His inability to urinate had led to a "shot," or an incident report, being filed against him. According to Dr. Clark's notes of the meeting, McDougal said that "he did not know at this point how it was that his name had come about on a list for drug testing." This incident was particularly strange because "his crimes had nothing to do with drugs." Second, McDougal told Clark, the whole episode was mortifying. "And he told me that he tried and tried and tried, but was unable to provide a sample. He talked about how he was quite embarrassed, and was concerned about what would happen with regard to this whole event."

On a scale of one to ten, McDougal rated his anxiety level at a seven, and his depression at a six. Mainly, he was worried that this failure to "pee on demand" might count against his parole eligibility in some way. He was still scheduled to come up for parole in April of 1998. A drug-testing rap could ruin that opportunity. Clark's report noted that McDougal's "affect was slightly restricted" but that "no homicidal or delusional ideation was elicited." The psychologist made a note to meet with McDougal again "in a month's time, to check his progress."

The next meeting came much more quickly. On Thursday, November 6, the Psychology Department was alerted that McDougal had been thrown into the SHU—the segregated housing unit or "hole"—the most restricted, maximum-security area of the prison. This had occurred, the warden informed the psychology team, because of a disciplinary violation. In the SHU, prisoners were stripped of clothing, subjected to full body searches for possible contraband, and then dressed in reddish orange jumpsuits to indicate that they had been banned from the general population. In the world of the Fort Worth prison system, it was the equivalent of being condemned to the hot fires of purgatory, one stop short of hell.

Clark entered the sally port through the electronically operated doors and walked to Cell B-26, a tiny, vaultlike room. Everything was "bolted to the walls or the floor so there is nothing loose that an inmate could use [as a weapon] within the cell." A thick steel door separated the doctor from his patient. There McDougal could only communicate with his doctor through a three-inch mesh-covered hole in the thick steel door.

According to Clark's notes of the visit, McDougal was "very irritated." Through the peephole, he complained that he had been summoned to the prison's disciplinary hearing board that morning and had been found guilty of a "110" violation for "failure to pee on demand." He went on to charge that he was being "unjustly punished," and whispered that he had "managed to get a phone call out before being placed into the hole," letting the media know that he was being persecuted by the Bureau of Prisons.

His mistreatment by the prison was not a coincidence, McDougal said. On the very day he was placed in the SHU, he told Dr. Clark, the newspapers had reported that a freak act of God had recently unearthed a scrap of paper that (McDougal asserted) now conclusively proved that then-Governor Bill Clinton had played a role in some of the unorthodox business dealings at Madison Guaranty. A tornado had swept through southwestern Arkansas back in March, smashing windows and destroying an abandoned 1979 Mercury Marquis that was sitting in the lot of Johnny's Transmission Shop on the outskirts of Little Rock. Records now indicated that the car had belonged to one Henry Floyd, a former Madison Guaranty employee who had been dispatched to drive boxes of Madison papers to a warehouse for storage, but had dropped the Mercury off for repairs during a business trip, never returning to pay the bill. As the abandoned car was getting readied for the compactor, the owner opened the trunk and found long-lost Madison Guaranty documents, including a 1982 cashier's check for $27,600 payable to "Bill Clinton." The check bore no endorsement by Clinton; it was unclear whether the money had actually been paid to the governor. But McDougal insisted that this was the smoking gun that would blow Clinton's denials to pieces.

Before being placed in the hole, McDougal had called the Associated Press and told the writer—for the first time—that Bill Clinton had taken a loan from McDougal's failed savings and loan, used those proceeds to pay off his Whitewater debt, and then lied about it in his sworn testimony. McDougal had told the AP reporter: "They're going to hang them [the Clintons] with the documents that they got." He added: "It certainly proves the chief executive perjured himself when he said he never obtained a loan from Madison Guaranty."

Inside the White House, presidential lawyer David Kendall quickly dismissed McDougal's allegations as spurious. "Mr. McDougal has never told this story before, no loan documents support it, and it is flatly contradicted by the contemporary bookkeeping entry of his own accountant," Kendall told the Associated Press in response to the jailed felon. He added, "Mr. McDougal is hardly a paragon of credibility."

Dr. Clark's supervisor, Dr. James Womack, convened his entire team of six psychologists to decide how to deal with McDougal's odd situation. They discussed in hushed tones whether this was "paranoia on the part of Mr. McDougal." It was not uncommon, after all, for an inmate to make a claim that he was being incarcerated "because of some secret dealing that he had with the president." Yet in this case, "the consensus was that this was not a matter of Mr. McDougal being delusional; it was not a matter of Mr. McDougal being paranoid. . . . The fact of the matter was he *did* have associations with the president and with the First Lady." Moreover, the patient was a "chief witness now cooperating with the Office of Independent Counsel in regard to ongoing criminal investigations of the Clintons." So the team determined, "again from a clinical perspective, from a psychological perspective, that these claims were certainly not evidence of paranoia on Mr. McDougal's part."

Womack deemed it prudent to evaluate McDougal further, as soon as he was released from solitary confinement, to determine whether he might have a "possible psychological basis for [his] inability to provide a urine sample." He assigned Dr. Clark to complete this task and to determine the best course of action.

This meeting took place on Thursday, November 13. It was a session that the young doctor would never forget.

Jim McDougal, seated in the psychology department, looked more wary than usual. Someone in this prison, he told Dr. Clark, was out to get him. The young, balding doctor told his patient that he would try to help if McDougal trusted him to do that. After a long silence, McDougal reached into his pocket and pulled out something that crinkled with the sound of cellophane. He leaned over toward the young medical intern and asked, "Would you like a peppermint?"

Clark was not aware that peppermints held a special significance for McDougal—over the years, McDougal carried them around to dispense as treats for deserving children and friends. The psychologist did recognize, however, that this was a ripe opportunity. From a medical perspective, it was "one of those moments that occurs in therapy when my interpretation was that this was one final test on Mr. McDougal's part of me to see if he could trust me."

A second time, the patient reached out his hand containing the peppermint. As Clark would recall: "I did view it as an opportunity, a little therapeutic opportunity to further build trust with him. And so I reached out my hand and I said, 'Thank you,' and I took the peppermint." McDougal then reached into his pocket for another mint, unwrapped it, and placed the candy in his mouth. Clark put his own treat aside, as if to save it until after his questioning was done. At this point, McDougal settled back and began talking freely about the events of the urinalysis that had landed him in solitary confinement.

According to the report summarizing that meeting, Jim McDougal stated that "he had never before had anyone stand beside him and watch him as he tried to urinate." He described the experience as one of "embarrassment" and confided: "It just locked up."

The humiliation had continued for three hours. McDougal had tried drinking water, consuming so much that he "threw up." Still he was unable to produce a sample. Clark's notes reveal that his patient expressed utter frustration and "a sense of being powerless." Several things worried him, he told the psychologist, about being singled out for a drug-alcohol test and failing to perform. One was: "What will the press think?" He told Clark that "people would assume that he must be in prison drinking alcohol again, and that that would further then bring into question his credibility, the credibility of his testimony." This would completely undermine his new revelations about the president and First Lady.

As well, alcoholism "had been the one demon in his life that he had been able to defeat." He didn't want anyone to question his sobriety. McDougal confided that he had been raised by "two very modest Victorian ladies," in the persons of his mother and his great-aunt. He didn't think that he would *ever* be able to "pee on command," no matter how many times these prison officials tried to make him do it. All of this worried McDougal, because it might wreck his chances for parole.

McDougal then scooted his chair closer to the young doctor and said that he wanted to reiterate what he had said about the Madison Guaranty documents found in the trunk of the car after the freak tornado in South Little Rock. "The documents that they found corroborate everything I've been saying to the independent counsel." With a furtive look toward the door, McDougal added that "it was evidence of perjury on the president's part."

McDougal went on to insist that his being thrown in the hole and the drug screening "was a setup, from the get-go." According to Clark's notes, "setup was a word that he repeated several times." The last thing McDougal said, with a sardonic smile, was, "I'd do the same thing if I were on the other side. It's the nature of politics."

Immediately after his meeting, Clark sent a memo to Captain Bruce Corbett, the prison official in charge of drug screening. Clark concluded that McDougal suffered from a medical condition called *paruresis*, otherwise known as a "shy bladder" or "bashful bladder." It was a social phobia inhibiting certain individuals from urinating when others were present, or when they were in foreign places. Because Clark believed that McDougal's "performance anxiety" would "likely recur should he be placed in a similar situation," he recommended that McDougal be granted "dry cell status." In lay terms, McDougal should be permitted to take future urinalysis tests in the privacy of a cell without someone "standing right there watching." The integrity of the test could be safeguarded by using a cell without access to water, so that the prisoner could not "compromise the urine sample."

Clark's evaluation and recommendation was cosigned by Womack, as head of the psychology team. A carbon copy was sent to the Fort Worth housing unit, to be kept in McDougal's prison file.

That memo, however, inexplicably vanished.

CHAPTER

22

THE HUNDRED-PAGE REFERRAL

The Office of Independent Counsel, as it headed into late 1997, was pushing the pedal to see if there was any gas left in its investigation. Ken Starr's aborted departure for Pepperdine had blown up in his face. Nor had his office's image been helped by the Bob Woodward story about the OIC's interviewing women and acting like sex police. The top lawyers on Starr's staff wanted to regain the moral high ground so that the public would again view their investigation with respect.

In late September, OIC filed a fat 114-page report on the death of Vince Foster, but that document made virtually no splash. In ten words at the end of the report, Starr's office reached the same conclusion that Robert Fiske had reached in 1994: "Mr. Foster committed suicide by gunshot in Fort Marcy Park." Rod Lankler, the Fiske prosecutor who had headed up the initial Foster investigation, saw nothing new. "They went through the whole thing from A to Z," Lankler said. "And spent a hell of a lot more time on it than we had." Lankler believed that Starr's office had spent three years retracing their steps simply to placate loudmouthed fringe conspiracy theorists who were shouting that Fiske's office had "whitewashed [some] horrible crime." Although Lankler was a registered Republican and had no political bones to pick with Starr's office, he still considered it a huge waste of time and resources.

The Starr report on Vince Foster—albeit long and protracted—was thorough and balanced. There was no effort to cast aspersions on the Clintons or to fuel rumors that Foster had been murdered. It was as if Starr welcomed the chance to reclaim his reputation as a neutral truth-seeker, using the Foster report as an opportunity to give himself a shot of credibility. He was trying to choose his fields of battle more carefully.

One important step taken at Starr's direction remains a little-known piece of history—that OIC tried its hand at drafting an "impeachment referral" to Congress, long before Starr's prosecutors ever heard the name Monica Lewinsky. This draft impeachment report dealt exclusively with the thin body of evidence related to President Clinton's alleged criminal conduct linked to Whitewater and Madison Guaranty.

The independent counsel law, enacted in the aftermath of Watergate, contained a short, quirky provision directing the special prosecutor to turn over to Congress any "substantial and credible" information of impeachable offenses. There was virtually no legislative history indicating what Congress meant here. What was "substantial and credible"? Was the provision mandatory? (It used the word "shall," which seemed to indicate a duty.) If so, in what form was a special prosecutor supposed to hand over such information, once it was discovered? Much of the evidence gathered up by any prosecutor was raw grand jury material protected by the Federal Rules of Criminal Procedure. Disclosing it without court authorization could expose prosecutors themselves to criminal sanctions. The odd impeachment referral provision was fraught with complications.

Ken Starr, a former federal judge and constitutional expert, was well aware of these pitfalls. At the same time, he believed that the impeachment referral provision contained in the statute should be read literally. As part of his effort to push the Whitewater/Madison case to its outer boundaries and to determine if it was time to pack up and conclude the investigation, Starr quietly assigned lawyers to begin drafting an impeachment referral relating to President Clinton's alleged Whitewater offenses to see how it wrote.

As Starr later explained this well-kept secret of his investigation, the chief impetus for taking this extraordinary step was that it was now time to fish or cut bait. Jim McDougal had gone off to prison. No new leads seemed likely. "McDougal had given us everything he could," said Starr. "Susan McDougal had gone into contempt. We had exhausted everything . . . in terms of leads." Now the prosecutors had to assess the evidence and decide what to do with it. There were enough facts that potentially incriminated the president, Starr believed, that he had an obligation to determine if he should refer the matter to Congress. "Jim McDougal was quite clear with us [during debriefing sessions] that at the trial deposition, the president knowingly lied," Starr explained. "And at this point, we were crediting Jim McDougal." The Madison documents comprised millions of pieces of paper; confirming whether McDougal was telling the truth, on any particular point, was like searching for a needle in the proverbial haystack. Yet Starr believed he needed to assemble the evidence and see if it added up.

"So I initiated the drafting of a report," recalled Starr. He hired Stephen Bates, who had served as literary editor of the prestigious *Wilson Quarterly* at the Woodrow Wilson Center in Washington, to head up the project. Starr immediately dispatched Bates to Little Rock to sit down with Hickman Ewing, the person who felt most strongly that the government could make out a valid case against Bill Clinton. Together, the two men began summarizing the evidence, creating a draft report to Congress. Starr's marching orders to Bates were "I don't want this to be rushed. I want it to be perfect. . . . You take your time. You do it right."

Starr also hired a young, offbeat, and likable libertarian lawyer named Paul Rosenzweig to help produce the hush-hush impeachment referral. Rosenzweig, the only prosecutor on the OIC staff with a master's degree in oceanography, was a curly-haired, balding intellectual who favored bow ties and brewed his own beer. He had worked for the House Transportation and Infrastructure Committee for three years and then applied for a job in Ken Starr's office, knowing "that it [the Starr investigation] was winding down." He felt that taking this job for a limited duration "would burnish my résumé a little, make me a little more salable, and maybe [let me] work my way back into the federal government somewhere."

One thing that appealed to Rosenzweig about working for OIC was that Ken Starr seemed committed to keeping politics out of his investigation. From his perch inside the House Transportation Committee, he had watched the congressional Whitewater hearings taking place across the hallway and felt that the Republicans "were kind of wasting their time." When Rosenzweig applied for the job, Starr required him "to prepare a memo listing all the projects I had worked on [in the House]" and then to disclose whether any of them "were characterizable as partisan in any fashion. So I wrote them about a six- or seven-page memo about why I wasn't a raving right-wing lunatic and he could hire me," Rosenzweig said, chuckling. "That was a very comforting thing, that he asked me to approve my bona fides."

The second day Rosenzweig reported to work at the OIC offices in Washington, in early November 1997, he was handed an initial copy of the hundred-page draft referral that Stephen Bates had just finished, relating to possible impeachable offenses committed by President Clinton in the Whitewater/Madison matters. The curly-headed lawyer nearly fell over. When Rosenzweig had been hired, he had been told he was going to work on a different question: whether Hillary Clinton should be indicted for her Whitewater/Madison-related conduct. Now this? He recalled his reaction: "I must say it kind of floored the crap out of me. I mean, I knew I was being hired to think about indicting the First Lady, so I wasn't exactly an ingenue, but I walked in and then the second day they say, 'Oh, and let's think about impeaching the president, too.' And I'm like, okay. 'Okay. Where are we here?' "

The principal evidence against Bill Clinton, spelled out in this initial draft referral that remains locked in the OIC archives, boiled down to three major allegations. None of them was remotely conclusive, as confidential sources later acknowledged.

First, there was the assertion that President Clinton had lied in his videotaped testimony during the Tucker-McDougal trial, in denying that he had ever borrowed money from Madison Guaranty. OIC now had the infamous cashier's check dated November 15, 1982, in the amount of $27,600, made payable to "Bill Clinton," which had been found in the trunk of Henry Floyd's junked car. Was this a loan directly to Bill Clinton from Madison, perhaps flowing from some other shady McDougal-Hale deal? There was another check dated August 1, 1983, from James B. McDougal Trustee account to Madison, signed by Susan McDougal, in the precise amount of $5,081.82, which matched the amount outstanding on the previous Clinton loan. The notation on the check indicated "Payoff Clinton." OIC prosecutors could now establish that proceeds from both of these checks had been used for the benefit of the Whitewater project.

On one hand, the evidence found in the car's trunk seemed to corroborate Jim McDougal's story. On the other, "neither his [Clinton's] signature nor his fingerprints were on either check." That raised the question, Who was conning whom? "We know from experience that Jim McDougal often created phony companies, phony accounts and moved money around in other people's names without their ever knowing about it," Rosenzweig acknowledged. "So it sure wouldn't surpass my belief that McDougal, you know, was making it up." Did Bill Clinton himself know that the McDougals were making this payment? Rosenzweig concluded, "I don't know . . . because Susan McDougal wouldn't tell me."

The draft impeachment report, on this key issue, remained inconclusive.

The second allegation related to President Clinton's statement under oath that he knew nothing about the $300,000 fraudulent loan from David Hale to Susan McDougal's company in April 1986. Hale had testified at trial—and now Jim McDougal joined in the same refrain—alleging that both men had spoken to then-Governor Clinton about the loan at McDougal's office at Castle Grande, and that he had urged them to make it for the benefit of the "political family." There was at least a plausible basis for concluding that Clinton may have lied under oath on this one.

OIC also asserted that Clinton was untruthful when he testified in his April 1995 deposition that he had no recollection of stopping by the Madison Guaranty offices, while going on a jog from the governor's mansion, and asking Jim McDougal to throw some legal work to Hillary and the Rose Law Firm. Although there was nothing illegal per se about having the Arkansas First Lady do work for Madison, it created a potential "conflict." The more important question for OIC prosecutors was whether Clinton had lied under oath (once again) when he testified that he did not recall that conversation. Rosenzweig recognized that trying to construct a criminal case (or an impeachment referral) based upon such nebulous information was like trying to catch a cloud in a jar. He sized it up candidly: "I think Jim's a puffer, but, you know, he [Clinton] probably asked if they could throw Hillary some business." At the same time, President Clinton had insisted that he had no recollection of whether such a conversation took place. Rosenzweig "believed that lack of recall."

Stephen Bates completed the draft referral around Thanksgiving of 1997. The top-secret document was then routed to the principal legal staffers for debate, during the month of December. As Ken Starr himself would recall, "We were all of one accord—that it did not reach the level of 'substantial and credible information.'"

Even Hickman Ewing voted against sending the impeachment referral to Congress, at least for the moment. He reluctantly conceded to his fellow prosecutors, "We're one witness short."

So the Starr prosecutors put the Whitewater impeachment referral on ice, for the time being. Yet one witness was still at large, whom Ewing hoped might come around. OIC had learned from interviewing *Blood Sport* author James Stewart that Susan McDougal came from a deeply religious family and that she might be particularly loath to put her right hand on the Bible and lie under oath. Susan had gone to jail, she had defied OIC, but she had never yet perjured herself. So Starr and Ewing kept the faith. "I kept hoping against hope that she would see the light," Starr admitted.

Susan McDougal had been moved from the deplorable Sybil Brand facility to the newer "twin towers" high-tech jail in Los Angeles, where she was placed in isolation. Her cell was outfitted with Plexiglas from ceiling to floor, so that she could not communicate with any person outside the cell or hear the sound of another human voice. After a lawsuit was filed by the American Civil Liberties Union, Susan was moved to a federal prison three blocks away, a facility that was more habitable. Here, in the Metropolitan Detention Center, female inmates could at least communicate with males on the floors below through toilet pipes; some women sent tortillas and other food wrapped in paper to friends through the toilet system.

Judge Susan Webber Wright was receiving piles of mail daily pleading for Susan's release from prison. One citizen from New Mexico wrote in longhand: "Please let Susan McDougal out of jail! It is unconscionable to treat this young woman so cruelly! She is not an ax murderer or a serial killer! She simply doesn't want to say things that Kenneth Starr *wants* her to say, which are simply not true!" Another gentleman wrote: "You did the right thing recently in regard to Paula Jones. Now do the right thing and free Susan McDougal WHO IS A TRUE POLITICAL PRISONER. What is happening to Susan McDougal should not be happening in America."

Not only did Starr have a recalcitrant witness on his hands, but she was now developing a fan club. And she held the key, potentially, to filling in the missing pieces with respect to their case against Bill and Hillary Clinton.

The OIC prosecutors kept racking their brains, asking themselves, "How do we break through this logjam?" They even considered a new strategy—perhaps Susan could be brought out of jail for a deposition conducted by a respected lawyer who had no connection to OIC. One candidate was former Attorney General Griffin Bell, a mentor of Starr's and a giant in American government. He could question Susan McDougal in front of the grand jury to assuage her concerns that this was a witch hunt. After all, Bell would be perceived as a "neutral person." Starr's prosecutors felt certain that Susan McDougal "holds the key." If she started talking, Webb Hubbell might follow suit. Each of those two defendants "was likely quite knowledgeable in some important areas of the inquiry," with regard to Bill and Hillary Clinton.

Starr's hundred-page draft referral was never made public. Yet there was an inexplicable bubble of conversation within the Washington Republican elite suggesting that something big might be brewing. Whether the fact of the draft referral had been quietly leaked, or whether Starr's prominent friends simply intuited its existence from conversations with OIC's top brass, is still not clear. But this odd coincidence cannot be disputed: A "test-run" impeachment drive to remove Bill Clinton from the presidency was launched in late 1997 by highly placed Republicans in Washington, at the same time that Starr's secret draft referral was being considered internally within OIC. This was months before the affair involving Monica Lewinsky was known to anyone inside the circle of Clinton detractors in Washington.

As early as October 1997, Congressman Bob Barr (R-Ga.), who would later play a lead role for the House managers in the actual effort to impeach President Clinton, appeared as the guest speaker at a Saturday Evening Club dinner hosted by the *American Spectator*. The theme of Barr's talk, which he delivered to a select group of conservative writers and editors as they dined on poached salmon, was that impeaching Bill Clinton was a desirable "political strategy." Muckraker David Brock, seated in the audience, listened to the speech in amazement. Although Brock was still employed by the *Spectator*, he had decided to abandon the conservative movement. Now he felt like a spy planted behind enemy lines. Barr was on a rant about removing Clinton from office on the basis of the thinnest wisps of evidence. As Brock would later recall: "Basically, Barr was trying to drum up support in the world of conservative pundits. . . . And so there was this whole conversation about how to move the impeachment forward." Most of Barr's theories related to imprecise Whitewater charges and to other peripheral accusations that were "incredibly flimsy." But there was no question that a push to tangle Bill Clinton up in impeachment proceedings was under way as early as the autumn of 1997.

Within the leadership of the Republican conservative elite, there seemed to be a coordinated effort to promote the impeachment concept. Conservative writer Mark Helprin published a piece in the October 10 issue of the *Wall Street Journal*, titled simply: "Impeach." Helprin wrote: "At the very least the president, before he became president, was at the heart of criminal financial dealings and bribery involving his wife and various felons who were his close associates." Helprin argued that American citizens had to decide if Clinton was still fit for office "in light of the many crimes, petty and otherwise, that surround, imbue and color his tenure. The president must be made subject to the law." The journalist concluded with a dramatic flourish: "One word that will do justice. One word. Impeach."

In issuing a rallying cry to conservatives and Republicans, *American Spectator* editor R. Emmett Tyrrell, Jr., published a book that October titled *The Impeachment of William Jefferson Clinton*. This unflattering account, coauthored with a ghostwriter identified only as "Anonymous"—who was widely believed to be Ted Olson—left little to the imagination. A mixture of fact and fantasy, the book described a lifelike impeachment trial of President Bill Clinton that took place one year in the future (in 1998), presided over by House Judiciary Committee Chairman Henry Hyde, in which the reader was left to imagine that Clinton was ultimately convicted. The foreword to the impeachment book was written by none other than Congressman Barr, who effused that "every American who is concerned with the survival of our cherished system of government . . . must read this book." Tyrrell, dropping a hint for readers about the identity of his coauthor, revealed that "Anonymous" was a person who "has been close to the center of politics for as long as I have known him/her." He added, "Between the two of us we know most of the key players in this book."

Judge Robert Bork, an icon of the conservative legal movement who served as resident-scholar at the American Enterprise Institute, did his part by publishing a review of the impeachment docudrama for the December issue of the *American Spectator*. Bork heaped praise on the anti-Clinton tome, stating that the authors had made out a "powerful case" for removing Bill Clinton and describing the Clinton presidency as the "sleaziest" administration in the nation's history. Bork gave two thumbs up to the book's plot development, which began with Whitewater crimes and ended with a suspenseful Senate trial of Bill Clinton led by the lionlike House manager, Henry Hyde. Judge Bork hinted that the authors may have gained some inside information from the Office of Independent Counsel concerning the draft referral, telling readers provocatively: "All of the scenery is not in place . . . because a major factor, the Report of Independent Counsel Kenneth Starr, has not yet been submitted. The authors assume that it will be [released] by mid-1998, though they can say only that the report concerns 'the Whitewater cover-up.' "

Looking back at the pieces of evidence buried in the archives from late 1997, it is hard to escape the conclusion that there was some loose communication or coordination between these giants within the conservative Republican movement when it came to the now-forgotten impeachment drive that predated the Monica Lewinsky investigation. Robert Bork and Ted Olson were both close to Starr; they moved in circles that would enable them to learn discreetly what OIC might be working on. That all these men seemed to be floating trial balloons, simultaneously, with respect to an impeachment based on the Whitewater evidence, does not appear to be coincidental. As David Brock would sum it up: "The timing of it is all just extremely interesting."

At the same time, Ken Starr never received sufficient credit for keeping his draft report to Congress largely under wraps. By December 1997, the independent counsel had essentially concluded that a Whitewater-related impeachment referral to Congress would not fly. In a responsible fashion, he took pains to make sure that the specifics of the possible charges against President Clinton were not leaked to the media. Starr himself would later underscore that the draft referral was not made public until much later. "You will not find a single suggestion that any such thing was in preparation," he said, "until I revealed it in November of 1998 in my testimony before the House Judiciary Committee." Starr added, in defense of himself and his OIC team, that they could have used this to damage Clinton if that had been the singular endgame. "Look, we've been accused of every kind of wrongdoing and unprofessionalism and [being] out to get the president and so forth," Starr said. "We had information that is very unflattering to [Clinton]—that he committed perjury in [McDougal's] May 1996 trial, not over sex but over his financial arrangements in the 1980s. And we safeguarded it. We guarded it very zealously."

Ken Starr and his staff, particularly Hickman Ewing, still hoped that there might be a break in the case if Susan McDougal or Webb Hubbell found religion and disgorged new information. By Christmas of 1997, however, the odds of such a breakthrough occurring seemed low. Unless there was a legitimate basis for bringing an indictment against First Lady Hillary Clinton—a matter that was still being debated internally—the investigation appeared to be sputtering out of gas.

The most that can be said about the short-lived movement to impeach Bill Clinton as 1997 ended was this: There existed a seemingly choreographed effort to push that idea on multiple fronts, before OIC abandoned its investigation. Ken Starr's office took a stab at it; the *American Spectator* promoted it; intellectual leaders like Robert Bork added their firepower to it. Although the draft referral fizzled out within several months, it was safe to say that a collection of anti-Clinton cohorts was beginning to formulate an impeachment state of mind. So, when the chance unexpectedly presented itself, in January 1998, to "get ahead of the curve," as Jackie Bennett would put it, the OIC lawyers pounced at that opportunity with arms outstretched.

CHAPTER

23

AN UNEXPECTED CALLER

In reflecting on this period with the benefit of hindsight, President Clinton would later admit that he never imagined, in his most distressing nightmares, that Ken Starr and the Office of Independent Counsel would weave the *Paula Jones* case and his relationship with Monica Lewinsky into a single criminal investigation. The Lewinsky affair was something that the president had kept closed up in a box, where he thought it would remain locked forever.

Monica Lewinsky, after moving to New York and thereafter relocating overseas to the London School of Economics, would likewise express astonishment that the *Paula Jones* case had somehow morphed into an investigation by Ken Starr. After all, the relationship between herself and the president had become less physical by late May 1997 at Clinton's insistence. On Christmas Eve of that year, Monica had worked her final day at the Pentagon, moving out of government work and raising a stink that the president had reneged on his promise to bring her back to the White House. The *least* he could do, Monica had stated in a raised voice, was to help her find a job in New York.

President Clinton leaped at the chance to bring closure to his ill-considered affair. His friend and Washington power broker, Vernon Jordan, agreed to contact the former intern and provide assistance. It was understandable that Monica would want to move to Manhattan, where her mother had already settled into a new apartment and where she could free herself of the emotionally ruinous relationship with the president.

In Monica's mind, her affair with Bill Clinton had no bearing on the *Paula Jones* case, even if one assumed the allegations of Paula Jones to be true, which she did not. Her own sexual intimacy with Clinton had been consensual; it had no legal or logical connection to whether he had exposed himself to a young, female state worker in Arkansas in 1991. One was conduct between consenting adults; the other was potentially sexual harassment. Moreover, during Monica's ample time with Clinton, he had never exhibited any predatory behavior of the sort that Paula Jones had alleged in her lawsuit. It sounded far-fetched, like a story concocted by a gold digger.

Yet, in this strange world driven by presidential power politics, the Jones and Lewinsky matters found a way to unite. It began with a phone call to Jackie Bennett at OIC's Washington office on January 12, from a woman who said that she had proof that a young White House intern was having an affair with President Clinton and that the intern had been coached to lie about it in the *Jones* deposition. She had *tapes,* the woman whispered in a husky voice, that would confirm everything that she was telling Bennett.

Several factors came together to allow this strange phone call to propel the Starr investigation to a new level. For one, Ken Starr's offices in both cities were being run by prosecutors almost entirely different from those who, four years earlier, had initiated the OIC Whitewater/Madison investigation. Nearly all of the lawyers hired by Robert Fiske were gone. Many of Starr's early top recruits (including Mark Tuohey and John Bates) had eased back into private practice or government positions. There was a different feel within the office.

Interviews with Starr's own prosecutors now confirm that—as of early January 1998—his operation was in wrap-it-up mode. Although there was still plenty of work to be finished, especially the tax fraud case against Governor Tucker slated for trial in February, the prosecutors knew that Starr was champing at the bit to get to Malibu (where the president was still holding the deanship open) before the new academic year. In fact, he seemed "disillusioned and outright angry with the pace" of their investigation. The normally mild-mannered Starr "was pushing on people to try and get the reports written and the matters closed out." The grand jury in Arkansas already had been extended six months. The judges supervising the various pieces of the Whitewater/Madison investigation were becoming impatient.

OIC's Washington office, originally built to handle the Vince Foster case and the Rose Law Firm billing records matter, was running out of reasons to exist. Starr moved Jackie Bennett from Little Rock to the smaller Washington office, charging him with bringing that segment of OIC's work to a conclusion.

In Arkansas, Starr appointed a young state prosecutor from Maryland, Bob Bittman, to take over administrative duties. Hickman Ewing had gotten himself bogged down in minutiae. The Arkansas phase of the case seemed to be running in circles. Bittman was a tough, organized, orderly fellow who could free up Ewing to do what he did best—slugging through evidence, lining up facts, and trying to finalize his case. Ewing's sights, for some time, had been focused on Hillary Clinton. Now, he had to nail down an indictment or pack up and go home. Thus was born in both cities a new OIC apparatus that would transform the face of Ken Starr's investigation.

Hickman Ewing was personally convinced that the First Lady was culpable in the Whitewater/Madison debacle. "Her answers and her demeanor were such that I felt strongly that she was holding back," he would say. The Memphis lawyer had also come to believe that the president was "not being candid" when it came to his feigned lack of recollection [under oath] about a host of Whitewater-related events. Ewing had six more months before the Little Rock grand jury expired. He wanted to prove, with conclusive evidence, that he was right.

Jackie Bennett, too, was prepared to bet the farm that the First Lady had dirtied her hands in the Whitewater/Madison deals. He also believed that both Clintons had stonewalled OIC and intentionally withheld information by "forgetting" key facts. Tightening his jaw, Bennett later expressed his view that "a mafia-like code of silence" had come to pervade the Clinton White House. Bennett and Ewing were both prepared to crack this code before time ran out.

Another key factor nudging the dominoes into place was the appearance of a new group of Dallas lawyers willing to represent Paula Jones. Judge Susan Webber Wright, perturbed at Paula for scotching the settlement deal, had kept the case on a very short leash. A spring trial date was looming. Susan Carpenter-McMillan had now located a Dallas law firm eager to take over the *Jones* case, a new group of lawyers who made clear they intended to take no prisoners.

As part of the final trial preparation, Judge Susan Webber Wright had ruled that Jones's lawyers could ask questions about extramarital relationships between Bill Clinton and other female state or federal employees within reason—that is, during the past ten years. That would cover females working in the White House and also a five-year period during Clinton's governorship. In Judge Wright's estimation, that pool was more than big enough for the new Jones lawyers to explore.

———

JACKIE Bennett had been tipped off in advance, by Paul Rosenzweig, that an important call might be coming. Rosenzweig told Bennett that while he had

been dining with friends in Philadelphia, he had received an unusual piece of information that might be relevant to their investigation. The precise details of
Rosenzweig's trip to Philadelphia would later cause accusations to fly between
Starr's office and the Reno Justice Department. However it went down, Rosenzweig's jaunt to Philly made it possible for Starr's office to link the new, blockbuster Monica Lewinsky matter to the floundering *Paula Jones* case.

Rosenzweig later insisted that he had no suspicion that anything unusual
would happen on this trip, as he stepped off the Metroliner in Philadelphia.
Jerome Marcus, his good friend from University of Chicago Law School, had
suggested that they get together with Richard Porter (another law school buddy)
for a nice meal in the City of Brotherly Love. Marcus suggested that Rosenzweig
take the train to Philly, then stop by his law office before heading to the restaurant
because "I have some stuff to chat with you about." Rosenzweig knew that
Jerome and his wife had just adopted a child from Romania. Maybe, he thought
as he climbed the steps of the train station, this was the subject Jerome was itching to talk about

"In retrospect," Rosenzweig said with a sigh, "he was plainly alluding to the
fact that he was looking forward to telling me all about Monica and Linda,
which, if he told me he was going to do that, I'd have never gone to the meal."

Paul Rosenzweig arrived at the firm of Berger & Montague in Philadelphia, an
old brownstone that reminded him of the stockbrokers' office in Eddie Murphy's
movie *Trading Places*. A gold chandelier hanging in the lobby gave it a look of conspicuous opulence. Here, the two friends exchanged bear hugs and settled into
wingbacked chairs. They had a half hour before dinner—there was no need to
rush. Lounging comfortably in this quiet setting, Jerome Marcus broached the
subject that he had been itching to convey to Rosenzweig. Marcus said that in
assisting informally with the *Paula Jones* case, he had become privy to some incredible news that he wanted to share just between friends. Rosenzweig recalled
the gist of the information passed along in whispers: "There was an allegation of
lying by the president in the *Paula Jones* case. It was about a woman that he [Clin-
ton] was sleeping with, and that she was lying, too; there were tapes to prove that.
And the reason she was lying was because Vernon Jordan was getting her a job."

The question Jerome Marcus posed to his friend from OIC, in a confidential
tone, was, "Is that within your jurisdiction?"

The conversation lasted only ten or fifteen minutes. Rosenzweig started to say,
"No, there's no link here to OIC's jurisdiction." But something caused him to stop.
He chewed on the question for a moment. The part about Jordan's involvement
caught his attention. "Because I knew that we were undertaking an investigation of
Vernon Jordan buying Webster Hubbell's silence—amongst others—by getting
him a job as a consultant."

Rosenzweig realized that Marcus was speaking in code, posing the question "as one of those phony hypotheticals that lawyers do." Neither attorney wanted to wade directly into forbidden territory by overtly linking the *Jones* case with the Lewinsky matter. It was clear that such a fusion of atoms could turn into a radioactive bomb.

This was not idle predinner banter, Rosenzweig quickly deduced. The curly-headed lawyer knew that as early as 1994—before he had joined OIC—his classmates Jerome Marcus and Richard Porter had begun playing a behind-the-scenes role in the *Jones* case. Gil Davis's records confirmed that Davis had reached out to Rosenzweig that spring, seeking help on whether the president could be sued civilly while in office, at the suggestion of Marcus. Although Rosenzweig had provided only minimal input to the Jones lawyers, the young OIC prosecutor was clearly aware that his friends were playing silent roles in this explosive lawsuit against the president.

Rosenzweig and Marcus walked three blocks to the Deux Chemineés restaurant, shaking off the chilly rain to settle in for an excellent French dinner. They were joined by classmate Richard Porter and New York lawyer George Conway, two more elves who had come to town specially for the occasion. As they popped champagne corks to toast a $300 million corporate deal that Porter had just closed, the conversation steered far wide of the radioactive topic. Marcus believed that his goal had already been accomplished. Indeed, Rosenzweig had processed five "highlights" of inside information. These key points were, as Rosenzweig himself recalled, "president, sex, *Jones* trial, lying, jobs for silence." He had agreed to take that cryptic information back to Washington and see if it was within OIC's bailiwick. "I'll ask," he had told Marcus.

In the private room with a fireplace, as Porter poured fresh glasses of champagne, the four men enjoyed their bubbly along with the warm fire and congenial conversation. At some point that evening, while Rosenzweig was visiting the restroom, Marcus pulled Conway aside and whispered, "I told him about Lewinsky." Conway's jaw dropped open.

Rosenzweig took the 11:00 P.M. Metroliner back to D.C., sleeping soundly. It had been good wine and a pleasing meal. Years later, reflecting upon this night, he expressed dismay, on several levels, at what had transpired. First, he would kick himself for not paying more attention to the warning signals. His chat with Jerome Marcus in the law firm's lobby would turn into "probably the single most significant moment in my life." Yet Rosenzweig had missed the clue and treated it like no "big deal." He would later do his best to explain: "It wasn't like I thought this was some grave issue that was going to magnify itself into national significance. It was my friend telling me an interesting story that I had, you know, fairly substantial doubts as to, but it was like any other lead or tip." He had misread that signal. "I mean, it will follow me forever," Rosenzweig said.

The other disappointment was that his own friends had put him in this position of peril. Jerome and Richard were "good people." But how could they justify this maneuver? "I feel a bit like they took advantage of our relationship," admitted Rosenzweig. "And I feel a little hurt by it. They both had nice law firm jobs, didn't run much risk . . . so I feel a little aggrieved." He would never know for sure if his friends had "conspired" beforehand, to pop the question to him. But that question was indeed popped. Rosenzweig dutifully brought back the radioactive information to the OIC offices the next day. His former classmates had used him as a carrier. "This was a play they were making," Rosenzweig concluded.

With a sigh, he added, "And it was a fairly effective one."

———

THE next morning, Paul Rosenzweig rolled into work late. His mini-road trip to Philadelphia had been his first break from OIC labors in months. When Rosenzweig finally sauntered into Jackie Bennett's office to pass along the intelligence he had picked up in predinner chat, it was already afternoon. "It wasn't a burning thing," Rosenzweig recalled. "I didn't bolt into the office and rush to him to pass along the tip."

Bennett's fourth-floor office was the largest in the OIC suite, even bigger than Ken Starr's, with expansive windows that provided a first-rate view of the capital. To the east, one could see the Ford Theater and the Hard Rock Café, with buses unloading tourists at regular intervals. In another direction, one could see men and women walking briskly into the FBI building and the monolithic Justice Department center. Four years' worth of black binders containing Vince Foster reports, and reams of other documents filled the bookcases in Bennett's office. On the wall were a picture of his wife and three boys, and a framed copy of the front page of the *Arkansas Democrat-Gazette* with the headline "Governor to Resign"—a trophy of the Tucker-McDougal trial. Otherwise, there were few knickknacks or other decorations. Bennett was not one for mushy sentimentality.

When Bennett motioned for Rosenzweig to enter, the younger lawyer plopped down on a chair. He recounted the story that Jerome Marcus had passed along the previous afternoon, repeating the key points of "president, sex, *Jones* trial, lying, jobs for silence." Somehow, it sounded less believable as he summarized the intelligence. "I don't play telephone very well," Rosenzweig admitted later. He was skeptical, himself, about the whole account. Still, he didn't dismiss it outright. "To be honest with you, yes, I guess I was a little intrigued."

Bennett seemed captivated by the story. He was particularly "interested and intrigued by the Vernon Jordan connection." The deputy independent counsel immediately told Rosenzweig that "he would have to talk to Ken about it," a task that was complicated because Starr was in Colorado at an American Bar Association conference.

Years later, stung by the criticism his entire office had endured, Rosenzweig emphasized that Jackie Bennett did not process the information as a crazed partisan might. "It's not like he started foaming at the mouth and [giving] high fives, saying, 'We got the bastard now,'" Rosenzweig said. "He didn't do anything like that. He asked me some questions about whether or not I trusted my friend and whether I thought it was a good tip." Rosenzweig told the burly deputy, "I'm sure my friend believes it. He wouldn't be bringing me something that he thought was untrue." Rosenzweig added that, like the substance of any tip, "it could be mistaken."

Bennett remained focused on Rosenzweig's mention that Vernon Jordan had allegedly been involved in buying the intern's silence. He noted that this sounded strikingly similar to another lead OIC was investigating—that Jordan had been funneling consulting work to Webster Hubbell to keep him silent on Whitewater/Madison matters. OIC was even looking at evidence that Hillary Clinton herself and other prominent players in the White House had been involved in lining up "consulting work" for Hubbell, helping to "take care" of him financially just as he was about to go to prison. There seemed to be a discernible pattern.

The senior deputy finally said, "Well, it will have to come in the front door."

Bennett knew very little about the *Paula Jones* case, other than what he had read in the newspapers. He certainly understood that "it wasn't our deal." He also was aware, from press accounts, that in several days, the president would be testifying in the *Jones* case. A front-page article in the *Washington Post* had just reported that Judge Susan Webber Wright had scheduled Clinton's deposition for Saturday, January 17—barely a week away. Bennett put two and two together: Rosenzweig's friends were somehow knee-deep in the Jones skirmishing—it didn't take a Ph.D. to figure that out. Still, that was a secondary issue. The bigger news was that Vernon Jordan was potentially trading jobs for silence. "We were convinced that Webb Hubbell had gotten hush money at that point in time," said Bennett. "And we thought he had concealed it from us." Now here was Jordan, one of the president's closest friends in Washington, potentially aiding and abetting a former White House intern so that she would lie in the *Jones* case, and securing her a job in return. The "same fact pattern" seemed to be repeating itself.

Bennett called John Bates, his predecessor in the D.C. office, and asked if they could meet immediately. Bates had recently left Starr's team to join the Miller & Chevalier firm in Washington. Bennett considered Bates a lawyer with "great judgment" and somebody he could trust. They met for Cokes in a little restaurant halfway between their offices. Bates, a clear-eyed man with chiseled features and a thoughtful face, listened to Bennett's whispered summary of the information. "Be careful, because of the sex angle," Bates immediately warned Bennett. He had been the prosecutor stuck with answering a blizzard of media questions after Bob Woodward's article in the *Washington Post*, reporting that Starr's office had interviewed Arkansas troopers about Clinton's sexual dalliances. The "negative fall-out" from that publicity had nearly crushed OIC. Bates didn't want Bennett to be flattened by the same wrecking ball.

Years later, having been appointed by President George W. Bush to serve on the federal bench in Washington, Bates would remain close-lipped about the details of this controversial OIC case. Yet he did make clear that Jackie Bennett was not acting like a partisan lunatic in weighing his options. "He was being very deliberate and cautious," recalled Bates. "I shared the perspective that there was a need for caution." At the same time, both men agreed if there was a link to their existing investigation, OIC "couldn't simply close the door on it."

Bates gave one final piece of advice to Bennett before they left a few dollars on the table to pay for their sodas. "Watch it," he told his friend.

When Jackie Bennett finally received a return call from Ken Starr in Colorado, he closed his office door and spoke cautiously into the receiver. "Listen, something's come up," Bennett told his boss. "When are you coming back? What are your flight times?" Starr asked his deputy if there was a problem. "Information has come to us," Bennett stated cryptically. The phone line was not secure; the Indiana prosecutor was not taking any chances. Starr could discern from the tone of Bennett's voice that something was up. He told his deputy, "Fine. We'll assess it." Starr was planning to return home on Sunday afternoon. They would meet first thing Monday morning, to discuss the matter in a confidential setting.

Paul Rosenzweig spent much of the weekend putting the finishing touches on a fifty-page memorandum summarizing OIC's potential criminal case against Bill and Hillary Clinton in the Whitewater/Madison Guaranty matter. After signing his initials "p.s.r." to the memo and placing it on Starr's desk, he spent a pleasant Sunday attending his regular Tai Chi class and relaxing with his wife. It would be the last day of rest he would have for a year, as a result of events that he himself had set into motion.

"I had absolutely no idea what was coming on Monday," Rosenzweig said later. "It's amazing from what a small acorn what a large tree grew."

On Monday morning, Ken Starr was briefed on Rosenzweig's unusual tip from Philadelphia. All of the prosecutors seated around the conference table agreed that the information was directly relevant to their investigation. First, there was the smell of "hush money." There was also the presence of Vernon Jordan, meaning that "the same people were involved." The only stumbling block related to PR issues. The OIC prosecutors had been burned, big-time, by Bob Woodward's story a year ago portraying them as rabid sex police. If they followed this lead, would it be viewed as another effort to "look into the president's sex life"? There was a general feeling in the room, like, "Well, geez, if Vernon's buying other people's silence, that's something that's relevant." In the end, the Starr prosecutors voted to tell the mystery witness to come forward. They should see where the evidence led them.

Jackie Bennett reiterated that Paul Rosenzweig would have to "bring it in the front door." The unseen witness would have to contact OIC directly. She would have to lay out the facts herself so that the prosecutors could evaluate them. There would be no more shadowy friends in Philadelphia acting as go-betweens, no more "back-door stuff."

Rosenzweig shuffled down the hall to his office, where he telephoned Jerome Marcus in Philadelphia and conveyed the message from the top brass: "It may be in our jurisdiction; I still don't know. If the witness wants to, she's got to come in the front door." Marcus replied excitedly, "Who should she call?" Rosenzweig told his friend, "She should call Jackie Bennett directly." He gave Marcus a direct-dial telephone number. With that, Rosenzweig hung up the phone and went back to work, happy to have discharged his modest assignment.

He never suspected that Jerome Marcus, after hanging up, would call Richard Porter in Chicago, who would call the gossipy literary agent Lucianne Goldberg in New York, who would contact Linda Tripp in Maryland (Tripp and Goldberg had been strategizing together on the Monica Lewinsky matter for months) and pass along Jackie Bennett's direct-dial number to Tripp. Through this roundabout messenger service, Linda Tripp learned that the deputy independent counsel was awaiting her call.

Bennett stayed in the office late that night, preparing for an important deposition of the First Lady, scheduled to take place at the White House on the following Wednesday. FBI agent Steve Irons was moping around the office, feeling guilty that he had missed his son's basketball game back in Little Rock, again, the ongoing curse of an absentee father with an FBI badge. He was lamenting to Bennett about his shortcomings as a parent when Bennett's phone rang. It was unusual for calls to ring through directly this time of night. The woman on the other end asked for Bennett by name. She spoke in a halting voice. "It's me," she said.

Bennett frantically waved lawyers and FBI agents into his office. He mouthed the words "This is her!" Bennett, a big man with a deep, booming voice, towered over his colleagues like a defensive tackle in the huddle. He spoke into the phone: "Tell me how you got my name." He wanted to make sure she was the real deal.

The woman sounded miffed. "If you don't understand *that*," she said, "I'm not sure I want to meet with you." Bennett sized up the tone of the person on the other end: "She was kind of defensive or paranoid."

At first, the woman did not disclose her name. She began spinning out third-person hypotheticals, saying, "Let's say I've got a friend who is in this situation. And she is a witness—this has to do with the *Paula Jones* litigation. And she knows about a [young] person who had an affair with the president who is a witness in that. And the White House is encouraging her to lie about it."

The mystery caller then launched into a monologue about Vernon Jordan driving off with the young former intern in a limousine so that she could meet with another lawyer. This impressionable intern, she said, was supposed to sign a document and "lie about the truth of her relationship with the president." The caller added, with an abundance of caution, "This friend of mine has tapes with her." She continued her third-person game: "However, she would need immunity for that act."

As Bennett deciphered the odd soliloquy, the woman on the other end had illegally tape-recorded conversations in which the former intern had discussed a sexual affair with the president and admitted that she was being coached to lie in her upcoming *Paula Jones* deposition. As long as the woman's tape recording did not involve a *federal* offense, Bennett thought, quickly ticking through a legal analysis in his mind, there was no downside to providing immunity for these nonconsensual recordings. The likelihood of this witness being prosecuted under state law, if OIC granted her federal immunity, would be extremely low. So he said, "Well, I'm sure that immunity could be given."

The woman blurted out in a raspy voice, "Well, it's me." By the way, she stated, exhaling as if relieved to end the third-person game, the intern's name was Monica.

Next the woman revealed something that made Bennett's head swim: She had arranged to have lunch with Monica the following day. The caller didn't trust her own lawyer—the White House had lined up this person to "assist" her as a witness in the *Jones* case. The lawyer was "a personal-injury guy" named Kirby Behre, who seemed to be in cahoots with the president's people. So the mystery woman planned to take matters into her own hands. She was going to get information from Monica her own way.

The woman dropped another bombshell: "I've talked to you guys before," she said. Bennett was flabbergasted at the news. "I talked to your office before and gave grand jury testimony, and I didn't tell you everything," she said breathlessly. "You guys didn't ask the right questions."

Bennett paced around his desk. There was no indication that this woman was "a nut case." She did not "come off as somebody who was so off the wall that . . . we can dismiss out of hand this person." Rather, "she seemed pretty articulate, pretty intelligent."

Bennett pressed the woman—what was her name? After a long silence, the caller relented. "I'm Linda Tripp," she said. She had previously worked in the White House; she had been the last person to see Vince Foster alive. She had also been a minor witness in the Travel Office flap. She had never dealt with Bennett directly, but she had worked with OIC and knew his name and reputation. She trusted him.

Bennett cupped his hand over the receiver and waved more lawyers and FBI agents into the office. He spoke directly into the receiver: "We're coming out." By this time, it was 10:15 at night. There were only a few hours before Tripp's lunch date with this "Monica person."

Linda Tripp croaked, "Okay." There was no point, she said, in avoiding the inevitable. She gave Bennett directions to her home in Columbia, Maryland, a forty-five-minute drive from Washington. The prosecutor scrawled down the information, hung up the phone, and stared incredulously at the roomful of law enforcement people. This was not, he concluded, likely to be a normal night.

———

JACKIE Bennett never felt that he needed Ken Starr's approval before embarking on this mission. He later explained how his prosecutorial gears clicked: "I mean, that was not the kind of thing you needed to fill out a form to do. That's the kind of decision that I felt I had the authority to do, and certainly I had made that sort of decision from time to time in my career. Your job is to enforce the law, and that occasionally means in a proactive fashion." Bennett elaborated: "The guys who really do that are drug prosecutors. I hadn't done that kind of work very much in my career, but I'd done it a little bit." He had spent enough time with street-crime prosecutors, who had taught him the importance of making snap judgments. "So I was comfortable with the decision," he said firmly.

Before grabbing his notepad and heading out the door, Bennett did place a call to Ken Starr at home, to update him. Bennett told his boss about the call from the mystery woman and gave this synopsis: "It sounds real, and we're going to go out and meet with her now and get a briefing." Although events were moving fast and might involve wiring Linda Tripp the next day, he promised to take it one step at a time. His team would regroup in the morning. Bennett told his boss, "I won't call you at three A.M. with the briefing unless I really, really have to."

Starr himself considered this call "informational" rather than an action item. "This was not really a decision for me to make," he explained. His view was that his prosecutors and deputies had ample experience; he routinely deferred to them on these sorts of judgments in the investigative trenches. "My general position was that I was blessed to have remarkably gifted, highly experienced lawyers," Starr said. "Jackie Bennett had won the John Marshall Award from Janet Reno. He was the 'can do' guy." This was no time, Starr felt, to second-guess his top men.

So Bennett and a group of lawyers and FBI agents sped off in a white government minivan. It was driven by recently hired prosecutor Sol Wisenberg, who was eager to see some action.

Wisenberg, age forty-three, was an enigma even within the eclectic OIC office. The product of a wealthy Jewish, Democratic family in Houston, he had attended law school at the University of Texas, clerked for a pair of federal judges, worked in the Justice Department under Attorney General Edwin Meese in the Reagan administration, and prosecuted criminals for the U.S. attorney's office in San Antonio. Over time, he had become so conservative that he now termed himself a "paleoconservative." Wisenberg had worked behind the scenes to help the Bush administration get Clarence Thomas confirmed for the Supreme Court—a fact that he feared the Clinton White House might discover once he was hired by Ken Starr; somehow it had avoided detection. The other thing that was not publicly known about Wisenberg was his feeling about Bill Clinton. That sentiment, he would freely admit, was, "I didn't like him at all."

This was not a partisan thing, in Wisenberg's estimation. He disliked politicians across the board. One of his favorite books, an obscure manifesto written by Albert J. Nock in 1943 and titled *Memoirs of a Superfluous Man,* took the position that "politicians are a professional, criminal class, so we shouldn't be surprised when they commit criminal behavior or engage in criminal behavior." Wisenberg thus started with this jaded view of politicians, including presidents. Even within that suspect universe, he felt that Clinton was especially "pernicious." He would say of the forty-second president: "I thought he was, even for the American political system, unusually mendacious."

As Wisenberg sped along empty roads in the white Plymouth van, he cranked up a tape of Ralph Stanley and the Clinch Mountain Boys. With his short, black hair and pinstriped suit, he didn't look like a man who would appreciate loud bluegrass music. But Wisenberg was an iconoclast, even when it came to his musical taste. Jackie Bennett squinted at his notepad, trying to decipher the directions in the dark. The group in the traveling OIC road show also included FBI agent Steve Irons and another prosecutor named Steve Binhak. Bennett turned down the volume of the bluegrass tape so that the four men could discuss strategy. They all agreed on this much: "There's something going on that's very unholy here, involving either the White House or close aides of the White House." The mood in the van was one of being "excited by the prospect of developing this evidence."

Bennett believed that this might be one of those rare moments in a criminal investigation when all the suspicions that the prosecutors had developed over a period of years were proven true. Specifically, Bennett thought to himself, "Gosh, this might be something that confirms our suspicions about the manner in which this administration does business." He later acknowledged that by this time, "I was as skeptical of Clinton and the people he surrounded himself with." He hoped that this trip to Maryland might prove that OIC had been right all along.

The neighborhood where Linda Tripp lived was falling asleep when the OIC van pulled up, at nearly 11:00 P.M. Tripp's house on Cricket Pass in Columbia, part of a neat planned community about fifteen years old, was identified by a single light burning on the front porch. When Tripp cracked open the door, the OIC team produced identification badges and trooped inside. The house, Bennett immediately noted, was filled with expensive-looking antiques and vintage furniture. Linda Tripp, a biggish woman with a tangle of blond hair that appeared as if it had been dyed, led the men into the living room. Tripp sat in a chair and lit one of many cigarettes she would chain-smoke that night. Sol Wisenberg would remember Tripp as "dumpy, unattractive." She was wearing a blouse and a pantsuit—most likely the same clothes that she had worn to work that day. A teenage son bolted down the steps and laughed, "I guess the feds aren't coming. . . ." As soon as he peered into the room, he hustled back up stairs.

Bennett took a seat to Tripp's immediate right. He asked the fifty-one-year-old informant to repeat the story that she had relayed over the phone. Looking nervous and sounding almost paranoiac, Tripp explained that she had worked at the White House during the early Clinton period and added, "I know what these people are capable of." She then began recounting the story of Monica Lewinsky and her own love-hate relationship with the young intern, stating that she had tape-recorded the conversations with Monica (even after her lawyer informed her it was illegal) in order to "protect" herself.

One prosecutor interrupted Tripp so that he could state, for the record, that OIC had no intention of interfering with Tripp's attorney-client relationship and that OIC did not represent her in any fashion. Tripp replied sarcastically, "Well, you all can just leave, if you want." The other OIC lawyers glowered at their colleague. They coaxed Tripp to resume her story, which she did as she chain-smoked a dozen more cigarettes. By now, some of the Starr prosecutors viewed her as "smart-alecky" and "manipulative." Yet the information she was sharing was so incredible, they consumed it like an intoxicating drink and ignored her offensive attitude. Among other things, Tripp was telling them that she possessed a tape recording that would prove "Vernon Jordan had flat-out told the former intern, Monica, to lie in the deposition, and that the president had told her to lie."

The OIC prosecutors would recall that Tripp was at "her dramatic best." She also seemed "very credible." This was not a woman, they concluded, who was "dreaming it." Now the prosecutors blurted out a question that they couldn't hold back: Could they listen to the tapes, to verify that these were "legit"?

Tripp took a long drag of her cigarette. "Impossible," she answered. The prosecutors' faces turned forlorn. Tripp assured them it was nothing personal—she was in the process of firing her lawyer, Kirby Behre, because he was a White House plant. Her new lawyer, Jim Moody, would not gain custody of the tapes until Behre "cataloged" them. She was stuck with this situation; the tapes were being held hostage.

It was clear to the prosecutors, even without hearing the recordings, that they were likely made in violation of state law. Bennett told her, "Turn over the tapes to us, and we'll immunize the act of producing those tapes." That would make it "virtually impossible" for any law enforcement agency to prosecute her for such conduct.

This suggestion seemed to comfort Tripp. She now proposed a different plan to give OIC what it wanted—she had arranged for her new lawyer, Moody, to "wire her up" the next day, to tape-record a lunchtime conversation with Monica. Her goal was to get a fresh recording that contained the "greatest hits" of her myriad phone conversations with the former intern. Bennett quickly interrupted: "*You're* not going to do that. . . . We'll have the FBI do it."

As the deputy independent counsel later acknowledged, his decision to have the FBI wire Tripp "was pretty much made on the spot in her living room." OIC could not afford to have "amateurs" taking this crucial step. If Tripp and her lawyer wanted to record this former intern, Bennett wanted to enlist professionals to do it.

It was nearly 1:30 in the morning when the OIC team piled into the van and headed back toward the darkened District of Columbia, the sound of Wisenberg's Ralph Stanley tape vibrating the speakers. Wisenberg recalled the mood in the van: "We were incredibly excited. . . . The ramifications of her story were staggering." Tripp had seemed credible; what she told them could blow their investigation wide open. It was not every day that a person dished out evidence that the president of the United States was about to perjure himself and was encouraging others to do the same.

There was a shared sense of urgency among the Starr prosecutors. The allegations being leveled by Linda Tripp were "perfectly consistent with the worldview" of many OIC prosecutors; namely, that "the White House would be willing to impede investigations." Now, for once, the gods seemed to be smiling down on the downtrodden independent counsel's office. As Bennett would explain, "This was the first time we were ahead of the curve, rather than being behind the curve and having to rely on Clinton loyalists, who were exceedingly dishonest in answering questions. And so, for the first time, we were ahead of it. We could see the thing unfolding a little bit. And there was this very short window. And so what we did was we focused our energies and attentions and our analysis and our judgments on capturing that."

———

WHEN the OIC team reentered the office, it was past 2:00 in the morning. Steve Irons, a senior FBI official, contacted headquarters and arranged for a handful of the agency's best undercover people to be in place by noon. Bennett had told Irons to do whatever was necessary to get this task accomplished: "I knew we had the capacity to do this and to do it very quickly. This is what the FBI does. If it had been a bank robbery that they had gotten a tip on at this meeting, they would have had the bank surrounded with videocams and that kind of thing. It's just what you do. And so I knew it was within our ability to get it done within that very short time frame." Bennett told Irons that he should call FBI Director Louis Freeh and wake him up, if that step was needed to execute the plan. That phone call, however, was not necessary. By the time the sun came up over the Capitol, the equipment, manpower, and action plan were all in place.

One of the principal worries of the FBI was the potential for equipment failure. For these types of "wire" operations, the FBI typically used Nagra subminiature recorders, tiny devices no bigger than Walkmans that utilized small reel-to-reel mechanisms that could record hours of conversation. Occasionally, the Nagras malfunctioned and popped open during the middle of a recording, creating a mess of "spaghetti." Bennett fretted that a malfunction, as Tripp was sitting in a booth with their target, could wreck the entire covert operation.

To be safe, the FBI switched to a different, top-secret, state-of-the-art recording device that utilized digital technology. The undercover FBI agents arranged to meet with Linda Tripp the next day, at the Ritz-Carlton Hotel at the Pentagon City Mall, just after 1:00 P.M. Her lunch date with Monica Lewinsky was scheduled for 2:30 at a restaurant downstairs. It was a tight deadline. After years of waiting for a big break, however, they had only one shot at getting it right.

Bennett, groggy from lack of sleep but alert from the combined sense of excitement and danger, arrived in the office at dawn. He briefed Ken Starr on the conversation at Tripp's home and informed his boss, "We're going to surreptitiously record this arranged lunch." There was no extensive discussion about whether to go forward. The options seemed clear-cut. As Bennett later summarized his conversation, there was no exclamation of "Gosh, I think we might get challenged by Congress someday on whether this is within our jurisdiction." Rather, once Starr heard from his lawyers concerning the visit to Linda Tripp's home, he concurred that wiring Tripp was "the next logical investigative step." All of his prosecutors and agents "were of like mind that this needed to be done." And so Starr "agreed with that."

Nor was the issue of the legality of Tripp's tape recordings, or the question of "where might this wire of Tripp lead?" one that Ken Starr labored over. Starr would later put it in perspective: "That was Jackie's issue, not my issue. You have to remember that I was consumed with other serious issues—I was focused on the trial of Jim Guy Tucker. Plus the issue 'What do we do with Susan McDougal?' We had just concluded a careful evaluation of a hundred-page draft referral to the House of Representatives, referring possible impeachable offenses by the president regarding Whitewater. This had taken up my time. The decision was made in September of 1997 that we needed more information—from Susan McDougal, Jim Guy Tucker [and others]." When it came to this unexpected tip from a woman named Linda Tripp, Starr was counting on his trained professionals to take charge.

Back at the Ritz-Carlton, Tripp was being tucked back in and prepared for her lunch with Monica Lewinsky. Jackie Bennett would remember the scene: "Linda . . . is being high maintenance at this point. She's a bit of a diva. And she's the center of attention. She's gotten the FBI's attention; she's gotten the OIC's attention." Tripp seemed nervous but eager to get the job done.

In a dimly lit room on the ninth floor of the hotel, a female agent secured the recording device to Tripp's "inner thigh" and another transmitter inside her blouse. Tripp recorded in a "Steno Notebook" later turned over to the FBI that this was a "horrifying" and "Grisham-like experience." Although she was "drenched w/perspiration" and "feeling low—guilt—fear—overriding emotion," she nonetheless wrote in her mini ruled notebook: "Well, it is still the right thing to do."

Monica Lewinsky was running late; lunch had been delayed by an hour. FBI agents were "rushing around trying to get everything in place." Tripp finally took the elevator down to the piano bar inside the restaurant, where she smoked a cigarette, waiting for her date with destiny. When Monica appeared, Tripp greeted the effervescent woman by gushing, "Oh, my god. How are you?"

During the course of their four-hour lunch, Tripp coaxed Monica to talk about a host of hot topics involving Clinton, the *Paula Jones* affidavit, Vernon Jordan's role in arranging for her to meet with lawyer Frank Carter, and other matters. Among other things, Monica told Tripp that if she signed an affidavit denying any knowledge of Monica's affair with Clinton, "I would be indebted to you for life. I would write you a check for [expletive deleted in describing the amount]." After both women laughed, Monica turned serious: "Because even though [Clinton] despises me right now, I know [in] my inner mind I love him."

As incriminating stories came spilling out of Monica's lips—some of which were purposely untrue because she distrusted Tripp—the FBI agents monitoring the conversation were horrified to discover that the microphone inside Linda Tripp's blouse had slipped into an inconvenient position; they couldn't track what the subjects were saying. Nor could they be sure that the conversation was being recorded. FBI agents quickly contacted Jackie Bennett, informing him that they had "a problem." Steve Irons announced, "We're flying blind," comparing the situation to that of a spacecraft passing behind the moon.

Several plainclothes FBI agents slid into a table beside their subjects, "eavesdropping" on the conversation in old-fashioned spy mode. Tripp's preview seemed to be right on the money. Assuming technology didn't fail them, they reported back upstairs, they should be sitting pretty. An hour later, Irons called Bennett to announce that the microphone was working fine. OIC was "going to be very happy with the report," he stated, suppressing his excitement. The information Tripp had provided the previous night "is being corroborated."

It was nearly dinnertime when the two women hugged good-bye and Monica Lewinsky headed off to her apartment in the Watergate complex. (Unbeknownst to her, FBI agents were following her.) Linda Tripp, her heart pounding with adrenaline, returned to the FBI's command center to be debriefed by Starr's team. Irons, in the meantime, wasted no time in transporting the miniature tape recorder to an off-site FBI annex, where it was immediately processed. Irons called Bennett with a quick update. "We got it." The agent reported that by morning, he would drop off a perfect dub of the recording on a cassette.

Bennett, for the first time in this protracted investigation that had consumed nearly four years, finally felt that OIC was a step ahead of Bill and Hillary Clinton.

—◆—

A CUBICLE IN THE PENTAGON

Linda Tripp made no apologies, even after having been portrayed around the world as a traitor and a villainess, about her decision to expose President Bill Clinton's unseemly sexual affair with Monica Lewinsky. As Tripp would later say, having retreated from the spotlight to a quiet town in Virginia: "I felt that it was something that the country needed to know, and I felt that it had to do with not so much his [Clinton's] adolescent behavior or his completely poor judgment in partaking in a sexual relationship with a kid close in age to his daughter; it was more the recklessness and the arrogance. And that was something I thought the country needed to be aware of."

Linda Tripp—born Linda Rose Carotenuto—grew up in Morris County, New Jersey, spending summers in Germany and Austria with her maternal grandparents. The Carotenuto household was strict; her father abandoned mother and offspring when Linda was a teenager, leaving scars on the entire family's psyche. After high school, Linda commuted to Katharine Gibbs Secretarial School in Montclair, then married her first boyfriend, Bruce M. Tripp, an army operations training officer. The couple moved around from post to post in the Netherlands and Germany, then to Fort Meade, Maryland, and Fort Bragg, North Carolina. Linda searched out government jobs along the way, working and raising two children as an obliging army wife.

During the Reagan years, Linda Tripp had passed up a job in the White House working as a personal assistant for Vice President George Bush; with small children at home, she just "couldn't do the hours." By 1990, her children were more self-sufficient. After earning a civil service position in the Pentagon and moving up the ladder with top-notch reviews, she was asked to serve as a "senior executive secretary" in the West Wing of the White House during the presidency of George H. W. Bush. Tripp took the $45,000-a-year position, filled with "reverence for the White House and history in general." She also admired what she perceived to be President Bush's high personal, professional, and moral standards. When Bush lost the 1992 election to Arkansas Governor Bill Clinton, Linda Tripp (a registered Independent) was permitted to stay in the

White House as a nonpolitical, career civil servant. Seated outside the office of George Stephanopoulos, occupying a station just beside the Oval Office, Tripp had a bird's-eye view of the new president. "Initially, my impression was that he was incredibly charismatic, amazingly outgoing, and friendly, completely approachable," she said of Clinton. Most of all, he was "a fun guy."

Tripp had been divorced in 1992—she preferred not to discuss the details. She was now a single forty-three-year-old mother. After a brief post outside the Oval Office, she found herself moved upstairs in the West Wing, where she was assigned to the White House counsel's office. Tripp would say, years later, that she was convinced First Lady Hillary Clinton played a role in engineering that move. The First Lady, Tripp explained, was extremely wary of attractive females working in such proximity to the president. "In 1993," Tripp said, "I looked significantly different than you've ever seen me. . . . I was very tiny. I had long blond hair." Tripp was fairly certain that "Hillary approached Vince Foster and said, 'Don't you need her upstairs?' " pointing to Tripp. In Tripp's view, it was part of a pattern of moving temptation away from the president. To put it bluntly, Tripp believed she had been "whisked upstairs to the Office of Counsel for the President" in an office adjoining Hillary's so that the president did not hit on her.

Linda Tripp enjoyed working for White House Counsel Bernie Nussbaum and his associates Vince Foster and Bill Kennedy. Yet Foster's death in July 1993 and the questions surrounding the removal of documents from his office all left Tripp feeling wary and vulnerable. (She had been the last person to see Foster alive.) By early 1994, when Robert Fiske's Office of Independent Counsel began interviewing staff members, Tripp made no bones about telling investigators that the White House's handling of the matter had been a "debacle." She also felt that those surrounding the president were indirectly encouraging her and West Wing coworkers to "evade and avoid any forthcoming answers."

It was in this context that Linda Tripp first contacted the gossip-loving Manhattan literary agent, Lucianne Goldberg, to discuss writing a tell-all book. Tripp had made a connection with Goldberg through Tony Snow, who was a former speechwriter for President Bush, a friend of Goldberg's from the good old days, and then a television correspondent for Fox News. Snow had listened to Tripp's account and declared, "You should write a book!" Snow even volunteered to reach out to Goldberg, a "dear friend," who could help bring the story about the dark side of the Clinton White House to gestation.

Goldberg was not just any literary agent. A former gossip columnist who specialized in sex scandals, she had spied for the Nixon dirty-tricks operation against George McGovern in 1972. Goldberg wore short blond hair and dressed with a flair. Tripp herself later described the flamboyant Manhattan agent: "She was sort of the Tallulah Bankhead of literary agents. You just wanted to picture her with a long cigarette holder kind of thing. And I thought, 'Okay, this is what an agent looks like and this is how an agent behaves.'"

With Goldberg's assistance, Tripp was hooked up with a "conservative" ghostwriter who began cranking out a book proposal covering the Vince Foster affair, the Travel Office scandal, and Bill Clinton's frisky behavior with women other than Hillary. When Tripp saw the first installment of the draft, she got jittery. The draft chapters were "extremely over the top" and "very sensational," so she pulled the plug on the project.

In this never-published draft, which would surface years later, Tripp declared darkly through her ghostwriter: "I don't know who killed Vince Foster. I don't know why he committed suicide. I just know that everything that happened after his death was strange and suspicious. President Clinton's senior staff kept saying it was a straightforward suicide, an open-and-shut case. But they didn't act that way. They acted like they had something to hide."

Linda Tripp's view of the Clinton White House overall had become extremely suspicious. "I *never* hated Bill Clinton," she said later. "I was never out to get Bill Clinton." But she believed that he was built with "a moral compass that's somewhat askew." She didn't like how Clinton's followers from Arkansas, like lemmings, blindly fell in line behind the president and First Lady. Nor did Tripp like the monkey business that she believed was taking place between the president and a stable of females (other than Hillary) in the White House. These extracurricular frolics, she later insisted, were "common knowledge. There is no doubt it was occurring with multiple partners. Yes, no doubt." Although she did not disagree "that these sorts of personal exploits were [Clinton's] business," she also thought "it was completely off base for a president to behave this way." Said Tripp, "I also started to question my own value system, thinking that 'I am sort of straightlaced.'" She was especially disgusted that Clinton was engaging in these liaisons in the White House.

Lucianne Goldberg, speaking from her literary agency in Manhattan, would later say of Tripp: "She had enormous patriotism, enormous sense of duty, enormous sense of right and wrong. It was not political, and I think outrage is what motivated her."

Those who worked around Tripp in the West Wing, however, viewed her as a frustrated and irritable "woman with an attitude."

It was obvious that the situation had deteriorated. In May 1994, Linda Tripp was informed by her supervisors that she would "have to leave" the White House and that she "had no choice."

So Tripp accepted a position in the Pentagon, where she had previous experience. She received a substantial pay hike to $69,427 and was given duties in Public Affairs. Yet her new colleagues looked at her sideways, as if she had been "foisted upon them at an elevated position." Tripp was shuffled around until she was placed in charge of organizing a conference for the secretary of defense. Her office was a windowless cubicle in the basement of the Pentagon. It was here that, in April 1996, Tripp met a young former intern who had also been moved from the White House to the Pentagon, reporting directly to Assistant Secretary of Defense (for Public Affairs) Ken Bacon. This young, chatty woman, whose job involved worldwide travel and regular trips with the secretary of defense and handling highly classified information, was named Monica Lewinsky.

As Tripp surmised the situation, in observing the bubbly Lewinsky: "So one day, here comes twenty-three-year-old Monica Lewinsky into this position. It didn't take a rocket scientist to figure out that there was a reason." Tripp knew, and she believed Ken Bacon knew, "that there had to be a very strong reason to put this young lady in that position," leapfrogging out of an entry-level position in the White House. This "immediately put my antenna up and immediately told me, 'tread carefully . . . this young lady is going to be dynamite.' And I knew that from day one, because I knew the tooth fairy didn't bring her. She got this amazing opportunity because they wanted her taken care of."

Lewinsky's assigned space was a stone's throw away from Linda Tripp's, as if destiny had placed them in such proximity. Here, Tripp observed that the attractive, dark-haired Lewinsky was getting shunned by other workers "probably ten times more severely than I had, because I think there was a lot of resentment that this young gal sort of achieved this plum, excuse the pun, position."

The chatty, chain-smoking Tripp quickly became a workplace mother figure for Lewinsky. Monica loved to hang out in Tripp's office; she did so routinely. When Tripp was relocated during renovations, she moved into a suite containing jumbo posters of President Clinton on aircraft carriers and posing with troops—props for large Pentagon events. As Tripp recalled with a sardonic smile, "And, of course, this immediately created an interest on her [Monica's] part." When Monica asked for one of the jumbo posters, Tripp just shrugged her shoulders. "And I gave her one."

Tripp liked the ebullient Lewinsky. "She was such a groupie. I felt sorry for her," the older woman said. Yet it soon became too much. "The Department of Defense was not anything she was prepared for," said Tripp. "The acronyms were Greek to her. She made no real effort to educate herself to make her position more viable." Instead Lewinsky "just chatted and chatted and chatted" while Tripp tried to produce work. What baffled Tripp most was that the banter always seemed to revolve around Bill Clinton. "I didn't have time for her stories and her 'groupieness' and her 'I'm going to Radio City to see the president on his birthday,' and 'What should I wear and blah, blah, blah.' I mean, it was just so bizarre."

Although Monica did not reveal the true details at first, facts soon dribbled out hinting at the true nature of her relationship with "Handsome." As Tripp would recall: "And then it started, and it started and it started and it started, and it was sort of like watching a train wreck." Linda Tripp considered herself to be "an extremely intuitive person." In fact, she was convinced she had a sixth sense. "Anyone who knows me well will tell you that I [have that gift]—my grandmother had it as well." Although Lewinsky tried to hide the precise nature of her relationship with the president, "I knew. And she hadn't even told me."

At first, Tripp assumed that Lewinsky had engaged in only mildly inappropriate conduct with Clinton. "I really gave him more credit. . . . I had never known him to go that young," she later said, taking a puff of a cigarette. In the fall of 1996, however, while they were in the Pentagon cafeteria and Tripp was encouraging Lewinsky to return to the White House because she "was the kind of girl the president would like," Monica blurted out that she had a fling with Clinton. Tripp was "stunned" and "shocked." Hearing that the emotionally fragile Lewinsky had engaged in oral sex with President Clinton, and that they did it in the White House, was a jolt—even for a born pessimist like Tripp.

As Monica spent more time in their daily chats describing "the next note she was going to write, or her next letter she was going to write" to Clinton, Tripp tried to maintain a distance. She explained, "I had just sort of been thrown there [into the Pentagon]. And while I worked my fanny off and got incredible performance ratings, I always felt that I could be gone with a flick of the switch." As a single mother, Tripp felt "lucky to have the job, lucky I had been promoted, but I also knew I could be axed at any second."

Linda Tripp later admitted that she had conflicting feelings about the young former intern who was pouring out her life story over coffee and cigarettes: "She's extremely likable. I knew her at a time when she was also completely nuts, so . . ." On one hand, Monica portrayed herself as a "poor little rich girl," which didn't resonate with Tripp, since Monica led a queen's life compared to her own youth. On the other hand, Tripp's children were close to Monica's age, so she felt a motherly sympathy for her. Here was a young woman with profound psychological issues that were only exacerbated by her dysfunctional relationship with the president. "So she was not happy on her personal groupie side, and she was not happy on her other side, where there were all sorts of dynamics going on."

Tripp hastily added, sneaking in puffs of a cigarette, "So there was a maternal side that sort of felt sorry for her as a young girl. And there was a side that got a huge kick out of her because she was funny and witty and completely uninhibited. By that I mean—I was raised a very strict Catholic . . . and she was raised so completely differently that she was completely—her body language even was relaxed and carefree almost in a way that was interesting to watch and something that was completely foreign to me. I tend to be far more uptight. So yeah, I did like her. I felt sorry for her probably more than I liked her. And I was horrified as things were relayed over time."

By now, e-mail was beginning to catch on as a new way to communicate within the workplace, so Tripp and Lewinsky supplemented their in-person meetings with electronic banter. The e-mail records from their computer hard drives, later turned over to the FBI, revealed Monica's growing emotional dependency on Tripp, especially when it came to discussing Bill Clinton. In one exchange during the workday at the Pentagon, in late winter of 1997, Monica referred to herself as "your loyal freak" and added, "The highlight of my appearance today [is] the volcano zit I have on my cheek. Hmmm . . . attractive! I'm bored. Would you like to go for coffee later? I know you're busy these days so I won't be offended if you can't. Buh-bye. msl."

The e-mails also show that Tripp was indeed intrigued by gaining new information about Monica's relationship with Clinton. This exchange occurred in early 1997:

> I think I saw the tie briefly on a clip last night—is it
> predominantly blue from a distance? What's going on? How's
> the mood? **LRT**
>
> [Expletive deleted, referring to Clinton] is wearing the
> secret tie I gave him—the bright, blue and white one.
> I hope he chokes wearing it. Love. **msl**
>
> Wonder if this was an associative choice—i.e. Betty
> [checking in], phone call, tie today . . . whaddya think?
> I think a strong possibility . . . which may mean some
> action. **LRT**

On Valentine's Day 1997, before Monica left on a Pentagon trip to London, she sent Tripp her contact information abroad and wrote hopefully:

> I will [be] checking my messages in the hopes that the
> creep will call and say "Thank you for my love note. I love
> you. Will you run away with me?" What do ya think the
> likelihood of that happening is? . . . xoxoxo . . . **msl**

Tripp replied:

> Ah, but that has already transpired, says my omnipotent
> crystal ball.

Despite the fact that Tripp frequently egged Lewinsky on, the older woman felt her anger growing toward Bill Clinton. She was disgusted by what she viewed as the corruption of the White House and its chief occupant. "I'd had it up to my eyeballs," she said later.

In the late summer of 1997, Tripp consulted anew with Lucianne Goldberg. The feisty agent recalled that Linda's voice indicated that she felt jittery, but she had no idea that she was walking into a buzz saw. "I don't think she had a clue as to the vehemence that was going to be visited on her," Goldberg said. "I think she [expected] it would kind of be a Beltway thing, kind of wouldn't matter that much, or she just didn't have a concept of how horrendous it was going to be. . . . I don't think she was prepared in any way."

Although the call was ostensibly about writing a new tell-all book, Goldberg understood it involved more. She explained: "It makes for a human conversation to use the focus of a book because how many times can you say, 'I want this man [Clinton] to die, I want this man to suffer, I want this man to be impeached and go to prison?' You can't say that. You have to, you know, put up an umbrella of a book so you can have an intelligent dialogue with somebody."

Goldberg would not dispute that Tripp was a complex, mixed-up woman by that summer; there was no way to sort out the bundle of motives that had prompted this call. "Oh, I think at this point she was so emotionally conflicted and terrified," said Goldberg, "and that's when it really started, I think, to dawn on her how big this thing was going to be."

Tripp sensed, by this time, that Bruce Lindsey and President Clinton had likely figured out that she knew about Lewinsky. Michael Isikoff had quoted her in his story about Kathleen Willey that had appeared in *Newsweek*. She was beginning to feel like a marked woman. So Tripp asked the literary agent for "advice and protection." Unbeknownst to Tripp, Goldberg had decided to tape their juicy conversations so that she could stash them away for future reference (she was later offered $750,000 for the tapes, but instead accepted a subpoena to turn them over to OIC). The tape of the September 18 telephone chat, which took place at 10:23 P.M., reveals Tripp's plan to go public with her story. Tripp told the glitzy gossip agent, "This is so explosive. It makes [the previous book proposal], which was nothing, you know, pale."

Goldberg warned Tripp of the potential consequences this action would have for the young intern. "You realize the press will destroy her," Goldberg declared. Clinton's people would chew up both Tripp and the intern and spit them out without blinking an eye. "I mean, I love the idea; I would run with it in a second," Goldberg fessed up. But did Tripp really want to be the "instrument" of this kid's demise?

Tripp dismissed this worry—the intern (she still had not revealed Monica's name) came from a "privileged" background in Southern California and didn't deserve much sympathy. "She was not a victim," said Tripp. This was a young, sexually active woman who was "every bit a player." Tripp also revealed to Goldberg that the intern had saved incriminating phone messages from the president on her answering machine. Tripp could chart out the dates and times of these conversations and had started doing so in a notebook.

Goldberg next asked Tripp a question that nearly knocked her out of her chair: Had she considered arranging for the young intern to be "reached by the Paula Jones people?" Tripp paused, taking a long drag on a cigarette: That might be *too* dangerous. It would essentially pour gasoline on that case and might result in a wild conflagration, she thought aloud. So Goldberg offered a revised plan: Why not take the story to Michael Isikoff at *Newsweek*? After all, she had a track record with him on the Kathleen Willey piece.

Tripp replied, "Oh, I could do that in a minute, but then *he'd* write the book. Or he'd write the whole thing."

Goldberg tossed out a compromise—why didn't Tripp cut a *deal* with Isikoff? He would get the exclusive scoop to write the initial story exposing the relationship. "But the rest of it belongs to Linda because she's doing a book. He would have to honor that if he wanted the story." This proposal "protects you totally, that gets the surface of this out, and then you stand back to fill in the pieces and I get you a publisher." Tripp chewed at a finger. Finally, she conceded that she liked the idea. Goldberg proclaimed in a throaty voice, "My tabloid heart beats loud!"

Linda Tripp would later adamantly dispute the notion that she was a Judas Iscariot bent on betraying her friend Monica to earn cash for herself. Having found peace and quietude in a rehabilitated farmhouse outside of Middleburg, Virginia, with rolling hills in the distance and champion horses graying in the pastures outside, Linda Tripp was nothing if not a survivor. She had survived being pilloried in the press and being terminated from the Pentagon. She had endured a serious bout of breast cancer and a prosecution by the state of Maryland for illegally tape-recording her conversations with Monica. She had cut her hair, dyed it black, undergone cosmetic surgery to fix her nose and to sharpen her facial features. A big-boned woman who maintained a close relationship with her two grown children, Tripp had done her best to leave this period of her past behind. In this remote enclave of horse farms and antique shops, she had hidden from the outside world. She had married her former sweetheart (an architect from Germany named Dieter Rausch) from youthful summers visiting grandparents in Europe and now worked in the quaint business district of historic Middleburg in a tiny specialty shop. Of all the horrible aspects of the Clinton-Starr-Lewinsky debacle, the one that most disturbed Linda Tripp—as she reflected upon it—was the notion that she set out to profit by publishing a book on this tawdry subject.

Tripp leaned forward in a wingback chair and defended herself: "Monica Lewinsky had been talking to me for a year and three months, and I had never written a thing down, I had never documented anything, I had never taken a note." It was only after her head was on the chopping block, Tripp said, correcting the record, that she took action to protect herself. "So this notion that this was about a book, or about self-aggrandizement or self-enrichment, it was just silly. It wasn't about any of that."

Tripp's biggest fear was that she was now at the top of the White House enemies' list. "I'm now dangerous to the Clintons, and I knew that," she recalled. "I also know how they operate, and having seen how they operate, I knew I was in some physical danger. And you may think that's just a complete hysterical comment with no basis in fact. Whether or not that is true, I felt that I was in danger."

In terms of her decision to seek advice from Lucianne Goldberg, Tripp asked rhetorically, "When did writing a book become, you know, a mortal sin? Particularly when you're a civil servant and can't exactly call a press conference to share what you know." Going to Goldberg and then constructing a plan to deliver the story to Michael Isikoff, Tripp insisted, was her best insurance policy to make sure that she was not run over by a truck in the middle of the night. Going public, she believed, was her only hope.

Tripp did not deny that she recognized the potential harm to Monica. Still, she felt that a little tough love might be needed to snap the young woman out of her delusional world. "Monica Lewinsky is a bright young gal, but she can be one thousand percent tunnel-visioned," Tripp explained. In this case, "the tunnel was Bill Clinton." There were times, Tripp said, when "I wanted to shake her until her teeth would rattle just to shake some sense into her." Yet Tripp knew that would do no good. "This is a girl who thonged the president of the United States," she noted sarcastically. "She's not going to stop because you say, 'It's probably not a good idea.'"

As far as the insinuation that her own actions were driven by the lust for a juicy book deal, Tripp shook her head. "To this day, I'm still the only one that's never taken a penny ever," she said. "And, you know . . . years have gone by, I should get some credit."

Yet the tapes of Tripp's conversations with Lucianne Goldberg in the fall of 1997 seem to undermine her protestations. In another taped conversation, later turned over to the FBI and at odds (somewhat) with Tripp's own grand jury testimony, the discussion between the two is laced with references to book deals, tabloids, and not-so-nice jabs at Monica Lewinsky. Lucianne Goldberg is captured on tape stating: "What is good for you . . . in the fullness of time, is a book." The agent told Tripp to "maintain [her] virginity" by letting Isikoff write the first account with sketchy details, then "stand back and wait until the moment is right" to publish her own account.

Tripp quickly agreed: "I would have absolutely no qualms going that way. The tabloid stuff. . . . There is a definite advantage to going that way. It gets it out, it gets it out quick." Tripp also pooh-poohed Isikoff's assertion that he alone knew how to write a book like this. "It's not exactly brain surgery," Tripp told her agent.

In suggesting that Tripp should go to Manhattan to meet with Isikoff, the agent counseled her to insist that "Newsweek's got to pay for you to come to New York," perhaps putting her up at the Plaza or some other five-star hotel. Tripp seemed to like the idea.

She also joked about Monica, reminding her agent that the former intern had told her on the first day at the Pentagon: "I don't even know how I got this job. I don't even know how to type." Tripp next drifted into an account of how Clinton and Monica would totally disrobe in the bathroom outside the Oval Office and he would "press it to the—almost penetration." Lucianne Goldberg interrupted: "This poor woman. She must be going out of her mind." Tripp corrected her: "This is a girl. This isn't a woman."

Linda Tripp sought to explain the attraction to Clinton by comparing Monica to another of Clinton's would-be conquests: "She has lots of hair of the color of Paula Jones." The two women burst out laughing, as if tickled pink by the absurdity of the comment. Tripp, meanwhile, was wading deeper and deeper into a plan from which there was no exit.

————

WHEN it came to her decision to tape-record her conversations with Monica Lewinsky, Linda Tripp later insisted that this idea came about naturally. "It was Lucianne who suggested it to me, and I immediately thought it was a fantastic idea because I had no other way to document [Monica's statements]. And, for the record, I would do it again."

A number of things caused Tripp to reach this conclusion. First, "I had been called essentially an untruthful person in a national publication by the president's attorney [Bob Bennett]," after the Newsweek story relating to Kathleen Willey. So "I knew that my word against the machine that is the White House public relations center would be completely annihilated. I knew that I would have absolutely no voice." Additionally, Tripp sensed "that Monica was in jeopardy. I knew that she would be destroyed through this if there was no documentation, if there were no evidence." She concluded that tape-recording Monica's verbal gushings was her best option. "My primary focus was in being able to prove that I was a truth teller," explained Tripp. "That this was not a figment of my imagination or, worse, a gossip-mongering reach for some sort of fame on my own part. I'm the last person who would want fame. I'm the last person who would want notoriety. I like the private life, peaceful life. And I think I've shown it over the years."

There was also a motivation, confessed Tripp, linked to raw fear. "I was fearful on an 'out-there' level that a truck would hit me on purpose. I was fearful on an 'out-there' level that something would happen to my children. I knew I'd lose my job, and that was an enormous fear because I was a single parent. And I also knew that my name would be destroyed, and the one thing I did have going for me until the Clinton saga was a sterling reputation for professionalism and integrity. And I knew that they would take that away, and they did."

Additionally, Tripp was keenly aware that the *Paula Jones* litigation was heading into the discovery phase, on a fast track toward trial. It was now or never.

"*Aber . . .*" Tripp said, slipping into German, the preferred language these days when she was hanging around the home with her husband. Yet Tripp admitted that she felt, inexplicably, that fate had selected her for this mission. "I need to be clear on one thing. I *wanted* this to come out," she said with eyes fixed forward. "I was going to do anything I could to help facilitate that. I felt that it was something that the country needed to know. . . . I always wondered 'Why, why do I have this information? What serendipitous thing put me, the only nonpolitical [appointee] in the West Wing of the White House and exposed to all the things I witnessed. Why? Why was I there?' I had no answer for you or me. But I did know I wanted it exposed. And I felt it was my obligation to expose it."

Tripp also emphasized that she had telegraphed her intentions loud and clear to Monica. She had told the young coworker that, if deposed in the *Paula Jones* case, she would be forced to tell the truth about Clinton's sexual misadventures with the young woman. In her view, by passing along that message to Monica, she had given Bill Clinton every possible chance to save his own neck. "Had he told the truth, he would have walked into no perjury trap," she said, gazing out the window at horses lolling in the pasture.

"I mean, could I have done it better? Sure. I suppose I could have, but I had no one to turn to. I had no guidance. I mean, who do you go to when you're up against the president of the United States?"

So Linda Tripp had driven to a Radio Shack in Columbia, Maryland. For a hundred dollars, she had purchased a gadget that she could hook up to her home phone to begin tape-recording her conversations with Monica Lewinsky. According to the salesman's later deposition, he had explicitly warned Tripp that it was illegal to engage in nonconsensual recordings of telephone conversations in Maryland, after she blurted out that she wanted to tape phone calls. According to Tripp's version, however, she had simply communicated to the salesman her budget and told him, "I just need it to really work."

With the little black box hooked up to the phone in her study, Tripp would lie back on her sofa, chain-smoke cigarettes, and record conversations as Monica poured out her soul. The young coworker had begun calling Tripp more often—sometimes dozens of times each evening—so there were ample opportunities. After each conversation, Tripp would throw the finished tapes into a basket that she kept nearby on the floor. The basket filled quickly.

In order to get the goods on audiotape, Tripp had to coax Monica to "recap" the highlights of their most juicy past discussions by saying, "Wait—I don't remember how this happened. . . ." Employing this sneak tactic was nothing to be proud of. "Yes," she later admitted. "It felt disingenuous."

On the other hand, Tripp justified these surreptitious recordings by telling herself it was the "right thing to do" for both herself *and* Monica. As soon as depositions were taken in the *Jones* case and the truth spilled out, she told herself, Clinton's spinmeisters would brand Monica "a stalker, a maniac, and a woman of loose morals." Of Tripp, they would say, "She's ugly, she's fat, she's a gossip." Tripp described her predicament, her eyes narrowing with anger, "Well, you can't disprove a negative; you can't say 'Well, I'm not a gossip, excuse me.' And the pictures [of me] did the job for them. I looked like a villain, and they were able to make me a villain."

For that same reason—mutual self-preservation—when Tripp learned that Monica had a blue dress from the Gap stained with Clinton's semen from one of their final sexual encounters, she took action. Tripp counseled Monica not to dispose of the dress, which was still lying in a heap on the floor of her closet in the Watergate apartment, because it was critical evidence. "I encouraged her to keep the dress," Tripp admitted. In fact, she had also advised the young woman not to have it cleaned. "Why? Because it was her only tangible proof that this had occurred. That it wasn't a figment of her sordid imagination, that she wasn't a kook."

By December 1997, with Monica's deposition in the *Jones* case approaching, Tripp began experiencing a sensation akin to suffocation. One day when she arrived for work at the Pentagon, someone had dropped on her chair a list of people associated with the Clinton administration who had met "violent and questionable deaths," along with a note: "Linda, thought you might find this of interest." Tripp took this not-so-subtle warning "very seriously." There were people "very close to the Clintons working in the Pentagon." Now Tripp felt as if she was in personal jeopardy.

So Tripp contacted the Dallas lawyers handling the *Paula Jones* suit. "I wanted to guarantee that I would be subpoenaed and *soon*," she explained. Whether it was paranoia or justifiable fear, she wanted to get "outed" and spill her guts under oath—sooner rather than later. "I was very, very concerned for my safety and the safety of my children, and I very much wanted to make it to the subpoena table," said Tripp.

She made her own wish come true. Tripp received a subpoena from the Jones lawyers on November 24—her birthday.

Linda Tripp also decided to follow Lucianne Goldberg's suggestion and to contact the Office of Independent Counsel. Looking back on it, Tripp remained convinced that there were few other options. As she would later frame the question: "Tell me—you're an intelligent human being, you're up against the president of the United States, who owns the FBI, who owns the Department of Justice—he's got every police auxiliary in the country on his side. Do you think I could go to the Howard County Police and say, 'Hi, I'm after the president, I've got all this evidence, what are you going to do?'"

Tripp had been stuck with a lawyer, Kirby Behre, who had been steered in her direction by Clinton forces. (The White House was even paying his bill; she distrusted him thoroughly.) Goldberg had recommended a new lawyer, Jim Moody—a friend of the elves—but how could she afford to pay Moody's legal bills? Her whole income was going toward "raising my kids and paying my mortgage and commuting. . . . I had refinanced my house to make improvements. I mean, I was living on my salary." So Tripp decided that calling Ken Starr's office was the perfect solution. "At the time, my impression of the Office of the Independent Counsel was that of a professional truth-finder," she said. In Tripp's mind, there were "white hats and black hats" in this production. She saw "Ken Starr and his people as the white hats and the Clinton protectors and facilitators [including the Clintons themselves] as the black hats."

Tripp later editorialized: "I since have come to realize that there were shades of gray."

Linda Tripp had vaguely recalled hearing the name Jackie Bennett during her brief stint as an OIC witness. She had played only a minor role in the Vince Foster and Travel Office investigations. Yet it had been a generally positive experience. When Goldberg passed along Bennett's number, Tripp said, "Okay, he's professional, he's a good guy in the OIC, and yeah, okay, I'll call him."

At home that evening Tripp paced around, trying to get the nerve to make the call. Holding the same phone that she had used to record Monica, she felt conflicted feelings wash over her. For one, "I knew I was betraying Monica in the truest sense of the word," she admitted. No matter how much this tough love might be good for her, she knew that Monica would never see it that way. Oddly enough, Tripp also felt a vague sense of "disloyalty to Clinton." She had always respected the presidency; she worked for the Clinton administration. This was akin to insubordination. Of course, she told herself, if she did nothing, she might end up at the bottom of the Potomac River. Tripp almost felt paralyzed. "My heart was throbbing and I was in a cold sweat and I felt as though the world was coming to an end. . . . I had gotten myself into something that was so much bigger than I had anticipated."

For three hours, Linda Tripp paced around the room, smoking cigarettes and putting off the call. Her teenage son, Ryan, sensed something was amiss—he asked his mother if she was feeling okay. At approximately nine o'clock that night, Tripp finally dialed Bennett's number, "hoping against hope that he wouldn't answer."

Two hours later, Sol Wisenberg's white minivan was pulling into her driveway, a single light blazing on her porch as a beacon to a fast-walking group of Ken Starr's prosecutors.

On and off since the time when she had been yanked out of the White House, Monica Lewinsky had "toyed with the idea of leaving Washington." As her relationship with the president further deteriorated, she finally decided. "I put my foot down, I'm leaving. That's it." Ironically, it had been Linda Tripp who passed along gossip from friends back in the West Wing that Monica "was never going to go back to the White House." Tripp offered her own advice: Monica should "get out of town." She should enlist presidential friend and high-powered lawyer Vernon Jordan to help with her relocation. Monica's mother, soon to be remarried, had already moved to an apartment on Fifth Avenue in New York. Why not join her and start a new life? So Lewinsky took Tripp's advice and decided that it was time to hit the road; she told "the Big Creep" that the least he could do was offer some help.

The president's efforts to secure Monica a job in the Big Apple had begun as early as October 1997. At that time, there was no reason to suspect that she would be known to the Dallas lawyers or called as a witness in the *Paula Jones* case. Instead, Clinton's assistance to Monica seemed designed to calm an emotionally volatile young woman with whom he had just begun severing a relationship. On October 7, Monica wrote an angry letter to the president, demanding help in finding a job at the United Nations or elsewhere in New York. Within weeks, through the intercession of Clinton aide John Podesta, Monica was scheduled for an interview with U.N. Ambassador Bill Richardson at the chic Aquarelle restaurant in the Watergate complex. (Unbeknownst to Monica, a *Newsweek* reporter acting as a plant for Michael Isikoff—who had been tipped off about the meeting by Linda Tripp—was posted in the dining room. It was only because the meeting was switched to Richardson's room that the reporter walked away without a story.) The following week, Ambassador Richardson personally called Monica, offering her an entry-level position in the

PR department of the United Nations. Monica remained thoroughly undecided. As she confided in Tripp, her mother and Aunt Deb had scoped out the United Nations and found that there were "a lot of Arabs" working there. Her mother thought it was "no place for a Jewish girl."

Monica spoke again with the president, asking if Vernon Jordan might assist in finding a job in the private sector. Betty Currie arranged for her to meet with Jordan in early November. At that get-together, the dapper Jordan assured Monica that she came "highly recommended" by Bill Clinton, and that he would be pleased to help.

It was not until December 5 that Monica Lewinsky's name appeared on the plaintiff's witness list in the *Paula Jones* case, a list that was faxed to the president's lawyer. By this time, Monica's plan to move to New York was already in place. She made a few pestering calls to the president; in turn, Clinton prodded Jordan, reminding him that the young woman needed help.

On December 11, Monica met with Vernon Jordan a second time, joining him for a luncheon of turkey sandwiches. He wrote down contact names at three major corporations in New York City. Monica followed up by making arrangements to visit Manhattan the week before Christmas, setting up interview dates with American Express, MacAndrews & Forbes (the parent corporation of Revlon), and the public relations firm Burson-Marsteller.

Monica later admitted that she had no way of knowing whether there was an "increased effort" by the White House to find her a job once her name appeared on the witness list in early December. Yet she was adamant about one thing: "There certainly was never any quid pro quo—'Hey, you know, you sign this. You go to this lawyer. You be a good girl. You sign an affidavit, and we'll get you a nice sweet job in New York.'" That was simply not how it happened.

The day Monica was actually served a subpoena to testify in the *Jones* case— December 19, 1997—was the start of a long, emotional roller-coaster ride. "I was just tense and hyperventilating and freaking out," she later told her biographer, Andrew Morton. It was, she said, the start of "my waking nightmare."

Two nights earlier, Clinton had telephoned Lewinsky at 2:30 A.M. and mentioned that she was on the witness list and that if she was ever subpoenaed, she might be able to sign an affidavit to avoid testifying. Clinton had added that if that came to pass, Monica should contact Betty Currie. Currie's brother, tragically, had just been killed in a car accident—Monica couldn't impose on Currie. So she called Vernon Jordan again, sobbing over the phone.

At 5:00, she was sitting in Jordan's office, clutching the subpoena. He asked Monica bluntly whether she had ever engaged in sex with the president, or had the president ever "ask[ed] for it?" The young woman bit her lower lip and replied, "No." Jordan next reviewed the subpoena. It appeared to be a standard legal document. It could be dealt with, he said. The best approach was for him to refer her to a first-rate lawyer.

Days later, Monica drove with Vernon Jordan to the law offices of Francis D. Carter, a former public defender with an impeccable reputation. In the car, Monica divulged a tiny sliver of the truth—she confessed to Jordan that she had delivered documents to the president several times in the White House and struck up a little friendship with him, and they had engaged in "phone sex." Jordan raised his eyebrow—phone sex? She replied, turning red, that it involved arousing the other person with sexual banter over the telephone. Jordan raised his hand—"Enough." He brushed this off as too much immaterial information. In his view, the Jones lawyers were embarking on a "fishing expedition here."

Monica would forever stick up for Vernon Jordan, emphasizing that she had intentionally denied any affair with Clinton in conversations with him. Yet Monica would later say, in the interest of full disclosure, "I thought he [Jordan] might know. With a wink and a nod."

Together, Jordan and his young friend walked into Frank Carter's law office at 1341 G Street NW, a small suite with pieces of colorful African art adorning the walls. Monica later reconstructed her feelings: "I was terrified. Can you imagine? You're twenty-four years old. I guess it was equivalent, in a way, [to] going in for your first surgery. I've never been involved in any sort of legal matter. So it was very overwhelming to me."

Not only was Monica "nervous" about the prospect of signing a false affidavit, but she was also growing suspicious of Linda Tripp, who seemed to be acting unusually strange these days. First, Tripp had recently made a bizarre proclamation that she had drafted a written summary of everything Monica had told her about her relationship with President Clinton, and placed it in a sealed envelope addressed to her attorney, "to be opened in the event of [my] death." Tripp had also blurted out—in an agitated state—that she was going to reveal the "truth" and blow Monica's cover, when she gave her own testimony in the *Jones* case. Monica could not figure out how Jones's lawyers had even known about Tripp or why they would want to ask her questions. At best, Tripp seemed to be a potential witness in the peripheral Kathleen Willey matter—where was the connection? Her friend's strange behavior was starting to creep Monica out.

———

FRANK Carter, former public defender of the District of Columbia, one of *Washingtonian* magazine's top fifty lawyers who was experienced in both civil and criminal matters, considered it an ordinary day. The date was December 22. Seated in his office on G Street NW, surrounded by carved wooden faces and African tapestries, he was doing the work of any busy small-firm practitioner. It was not the first time Vernon Jordan had asked him to take on a client. The two men knew each other from the close-knit circle of African American attorneys in the district. They were not close social friends; it was all business, especially for Jordan, a man of high stature and grand formalities. He now walked into Carter's office, leaving Lewinsky seated in the waiting room, and said, "Mr. Carter, this is a straight referral. You reach whatever financial arrangement you want or can get. This lady, she needs a good lawyer, and I referred her to you because you are a good lawyer." As Carter recalled that day, Jordan was asking for no favors or "accommodations." He did not discuss the nature of the case or try to steer Carter in one direction or another. He did not even request a reduced fee. The two men returned to the waiting room, where Jordan said to Monica: "I'm putting you in capable hands." With that, he strode out of the office and drove away.

The young woman whom Carter observed that day was strikingly pretty, with long black hair, lively eyes, and a disarming openness. He perceived her to be pleasant, bright, articulate, and an easy conversationalist. As they talked about her situation, "she didn't appear particularly excited or anxious."

The story the potential new client told the lawyer was innocuous enough— a large number of former interns at the White House, Lewinsky said, were being subpoenaed in the *Paula Jones* case. She had been swept into this dragnet. Monica slid a copy of the subpoena across the table. Carter examined it, scratching his short, trimmed beard. With Christmas coming at the end of the week, there was only a small window of time in which to get this job accomplished. He asked Monica, "Well, what are your vacation plans?" She said that she was going to New York to visit her mother for the holiday. Carter swept his finger across the legal document, giving it a quick read. Besides compelling Monica to give her deposition in January, the subpoena also required her to produce tangible items, most of them connected in some way to President Bill Clinton. Carter said, "Okay, I want you to go around your house . . . see if you can gather up as many things as you think are described in that list that's attached to it, and bring those to our [next] meeting."

Two days later, Monica returned to Carter's office with items responsive to the subpoena: several White House Christmas cards signed by the president and First lady; a photo of interns standing at the South Portico of the White House with Bill Clinton (the photo appeared to be machine-signed with the president's autograph); and a photo of Bill and Hillary Clinton standing with Monica and her date in front of a Christmas tree at a White House holiday party. There were several short, innocuous notes from the president, such as "Thanks for the tie," "Hillary and I send best regards," and "Thanks for the poem for Boss's day." Carter surmised that these, too, were machine-signed. The material that Monica had dumped onto the table of his conference room appeared to be the sort of standard mementos that any intern working in the White House might save for her scrapbook.

Carter now delved into specifics: Did Monica know why she had been subpoenaed? Had she ever been with the president alone? Did she know of others whose names were on the witness list?

Monica replied with a poker face, "I don't know." (She never breathed the name of Linda Tripp.) She had delivered mail to the president once or twice during the government shutdown, she said. She had no clue why anyone might be spreading this gossip about her; it was a bunch of hooey.

The client's responses were persuasive to Carter. She told him, "I mean, I'm a woman just starting my employment career and I just would not like to be associated with this Paula Jones craziness." Monica explained that she was in the process of seeking new employment in New York, where her mother had relocated—being dragged back to testify in the *Jones* case was not a good thing for *any* young woman in her position. Carter nodded his head. "I can understand that," he said, scratching his beard thoughtfully.

By the end of the meeting, Frank Carter was satisfied. His lawyerly instincts told him that there was "no danger whatsoever here." He tapped his pen on the conference table; he proposed that he draft a motion to quash the subpoena. He would argue to the *Paula Jones* judge that having to testify was an unnecessary embarrassment for any young woman seeking to get on her feet, whose only sin was having worked as an intern within physical proximity of President Bill Clinton. Carter would also draft an affidavit for Lewinsky to sign, so that Judge Wright would "get a flavor for who she is" and that would explain why this was so disruptive and far-fetched. Such an affidavit, he said, would "add a little bit more *oomph*" to her motion.

Over Christmas break, while Monica took a break in New York City, Frank Carter contacted one of the Jones lawyers in Dallas, recounting the story of "this poor young girl" and asking, "Why are you going to sweep her up in this and tag her with this stuff?" The Dallas lawyer listened politely, then replied, "We're casting a wide net to try to get as much information as we can, and we're not inclined to withdraw a subpoena." He did inform Carter, lawyer to lawyer, that "there have been other women who have been subpoenaed who have filed motions to quash so we're used to this happening." The Dallas lawyer even gave Carter the phone number for Barry Ward, Judge Wright's law clerk in Little Rock, to cut through the red tape so that Carter could file his motion and affidavit expeditiously. The Washington criminal defense attorney felt that he was making good progress.

As part of his due diligence, Carter also contacted the president's attorney of record, Bob Bennett. He and Bennett had known each other for years as members of the criminal defense bar in D.C. He asked—did Bennett know why Monica Lewinsky might be on the witness list? Bennett replied that he had no clue: "I've done some asking around, and I don't have any information that would be of assistance to you. Or about your lady." As far as he could tell, Bennett said, this was a classic fishing expedition. For Carter, this response confirmed what he had already concluded—that Monica was "a client who was nothing more than a speck on the horizon."

After Christmas, Monica Lewinsky returned to Carter's office, where he reviewed the draft affidavit. The lawyer closed the door of his conference room and talked through each point, scribbling with a red pen and typing changes directly onto his computer. He and Monica went through the document "paragraph by paragraph" until the young woman indicated that she "felt very comfortable with the finished product."

There was a notary located in the building, so they walked down the hall to have it signed and duly notarized. Carter ran off a copy and handed it to Monica, keeping the original. Carter said that he would complete his research on the motion to quash, then FedEx the motion and affidavit directly to Judge Susan Webber Wright in Arkansas, hopefully within a week.

As attorney and client parted company, on Wednesday, January 7, they were the only two people in the world who possessed copies of the affidavit. Carter said later, still wondering how it got into the hands of Ken Starr's prosecutors, "No one else, absolutely positively no one else got a copy of that."

———

MONICA Lewinsky, as she climbed into a cab, knew that the affidavit she was carrying was likely false. In paragraph 8 of the document, she had stated: "I have never had a sexual relationship with the President." The affidavit also averred that in the period after she ceased working in the White House, the only times she had seen the president were during "official receptions, formal functions or events." She made all these false statements "under the penalty of perjury."

Thinking back on it, Monica admitted that she knew that she had done something wrong. Yet there were plenty of ways that she could justify this fibbing. When it came to the "no sex" statement, she remembered thinking, "Okay, I can argue to myself that this is true, because we didn't actually have intercourse." As she arrived at her Watergate apartment, stepping out of the cab with the document safely stashed in a folder in her handbag, she felt more and more comfortable that there were plausible arguments she could pull out of her hat if Paula Jones's lawyers ever tried to prove she had committed perjury. "I could parse that affidavit probably as well as anyone else, I guess," Monica explained. "Could you find a way to make it true? Yes. Was it actually true? No."

In any event, both of the participants in the affair had agreed to deny it. The president had already answered his written interrogatories in the *Jones* case before Christmas, denying having sexual relations with *any* state or federal employee during the relevant time period. The only other person who knew about her affair with Clinton—aside from a few close friends (and maybe her mother)—was Linda Tripp. Monica decided, shutting the door of her Watergate apartment, that she would not tell Tripp that she had signed the affidavit, until she could map out a strategy of her own.

Perhaps in a week or so.

In the meantime, Monica's interviews in Manhattan had paid off. On January 9, she was offered an entry-level position in Revlon's public relations department at a salary of forty thousand dollars. It represented a sizable pay cut from her job in the Pentagon—but desperate times called for lower salaries. With a quick phone call of thanks, Monica accepted the position and began packing up a dozen boxes in her Watergate condo. Finally, she told herself, she was free from the shackles of Washington and the destructive relationship with a man, twice her age, who also happened to be president of the United States.

Monica later described her last encounters with Bill Clinton: "We had exchanged gifts at Christmas, and I sent him a book and a warm, heartfelt note on the 5th of January. The last time we spoke was around then and it was a strained call." Monica fully expected that in another month she would have moved to New York, begun a new life working at Revlon, and "heard from him every now and again."

CHAPTER

25

PINNING THE TAIL ON CLINTON

Paula Jones had a fresh batch of lawyers from Dallas who were tackling the litigation with newfound fervor. Attorney Donovan Campbell, Jr., and his team had just taken over the reins of the *Jones* litigation; now Campbell called Jones with encouraging news: His investigators had uncovered information that Clinton had engaged in a sexual affair with a young intern in the White House, a discovery that might help their cause. "I'll never forget the call,"

Jones said. The Dallas lawyer had told her, " 'And he's still doing it, Paula. I mean, he's still doing it. In the White House, in the Oval Office.' "

Susan Carpenter-McMillan was especially excited about the report. "I knew we had something," she recalled. "I knew we had some goods."

Carpenter-McMillan herself had played a role in bringing the hard-charging Dallas lawyers together with Jones. Over a hundred law firms had volunteered to pursue the president after the Virginia lawyers had bowed out. Carpenter-McMillan had turned to the Rutherford Institute, a conservative public interest group in Virginia. Within days, founder John Whitehead had recommended a small Texas firm headed by a hard-nosed Rutherford board member. It seemed like a match made in heaven. Donovan Campbell, age forty-six, had won tough battles for conservative principles. He had written a brief defending a Texas anti-sodomy law that punished homosexuality as a mental disorder. He had defended the right of a high school girls' basketball team in Duncanville, Texas, to recite the Lord's Prayer in huddles. He had led the picketing of performances of the gay-themed *Torch Song Trilogy* at the Dallas Theater Center. Campbell was an indomitable conservative Christian who would not buckle to pressure from the Clinton White House. This was a "David-and-Goliath-type situation," Susan Carpenter-McMillan said. The Dallas firm was tough enough to bring the immoral Clinton to his knees.

Campbell was primarily a tax lawyer. Two of his partners, Jim Fisher and Wesley Holmes, were top-notch litigators with experience in sexual discrimination cases. Holmes, born in Arkansas, would present a perfect Southern face for the jury. Fisher was an intellectual and could speak the language of appellate judges. The Rutherford Institute would pay out-of-pocket expenses. In Carpenter-McMillan's eyes, it was a beautiful match. "And I think it stayed a match," she said.

Campbell's partners were enthused about handling this case. "Well, to state the incredibly obvious, the defendant was the president of the United States," Jim Fisher later explained. Wes Holmes was even more fired up. A Republican from Arkansas, he had long known of Clinton's reputation as a party boy and womanizer. Here was a chance to knock the president down a peg while gaining exposure for the firm. "Don, we gotta get that case," he said to Campbell. "I mean, this is a once-in-a-lifetime opportunity. We've got to get that case."

The Dallas lawyers concluded that the *Jones* litigation could be handled with a relatively modest investment of time. There would probably be five or ten witnesses, tops. "They'll file a motion for summary judgment; we'll do a response," they told each other. "How hard can it really be?" Wes Holmes would later reflect, looking back on the case that nearly ate up their lives and stretched the small firm to its breaking point, "How naive we were."

The Dallas lawyers first met with Paula and Steve Jones in the picturesque hills of San Marino, California, at the home of Susan Carpenter-McMillan and her husband, Bill (a prosperous trial attorney from whom she would soon be divorced). The group gathered for iced tea on the patio, instantly hitting it off. Paula struck the Dallas lawyers as "clean and well-dressed and presentable." Her general theme was, "I just want my life back. I'm just a mom, and I just want to go back to being a mom." She told the prospective lawyers, "I felt like my reputation had been hurt, and I just want everybody to know that I didn't do the things that some of those troopers are saying I was doing."

The Dallas team explained to Paula that an apology from Clinton probably wouldn't be in the cards. The best they could hope for, under the law, was a watered-down statement of "regret." Still, the lawyers explained, settlement might not be a bad thing. "Most of the time, both parties are better off if there's a settlement," they advised her.

Paula seemed receptive to some form of resolution. "Oh, that's what I want," she told the Dallas attorneys. "I want my life back."

Jim Fisher later noted that he liked Paula from the start—although they parted company on less-than-rosy terms. "Among her good qualities are the fact that she really, really wants to be a good mother to her sons and really tries to the best of her ability," he said, shedding the best possible light on the situation. "She's got some problems she was dealing with. I mean, she grew up in a strange environment, extreme poverty, and she had a poor education. And I think her parents were extremely repressive in the name of religion. As so often happens, that makes people overreact in the other direction. She boomeranged out into some pretty wild behavior and has never quite found her moral bearings. But I think she's got a good heart and she wants to do what's right."

"That's not true of her [ex-]husband," Fisher quickly added.

Steve Jones soon became a sharp nail in the shoe of the Dallas litigators, just as he had become a pain for Davis and Cammarata. He proposed plenty of "bad ideas," such as demanding that First Lady Hillary Clinton and the president's stepbrother, Roger Clinton, be put under oath and asked questions about Clinton's sexual proclivities. Steve also insisted that Paula's lawyers should join forces with Kathleen Willey to wage "some sort of parallel litigation," an idea that caused Holmes and Fisher to shudder.

At first, the Dallas lawyers gave Paula's overly aggressive, needy husband some slack. They knew that the couple "had been treated badly" since Paula had first made the accusation against Clinton. They also knew the pair had endured the humiliating publication of seminude pictures of Paula, after she went public with her story. Fisher understood that Paula and Steve believed that Clinton "orchestrated" this slime attack, probably "paying off" Paula's ex-boyfriend to go to *Penthouse.*

Fisher, Holmes, and Campbell were all devout Christians. Smut peddling repulsed them. They accepted Paula's word that the photo array had occurred without her consent. Sipping tea on the patio in Southern California, they delicately posed the question of whether she intended to pose for men's magazines in the future. As a purely personal matter, they were not interested in devoting their talents to such a misguided cause. "And she promised us she would not do that," recalled Fisher, emitting a loud sigh.

The Dallas lawyers returned to their hotel, downed some beers, and mulled over their decision. Their impression was that Paula Jones "was telling the truth." Frankly, they agreed that Paula didn't seem "intelligent enough to hold a lie together." Clearly, Bill Clinton had lured Paula up to his hotel room. The only question for a jury was "whether she *wanted* some sort of sexual encounter." They believed that twelve ordinary jurors would side with Paula, rather than the womanizing president. Campbell told his younger partners, "Go back to your room and think about this and pray and make sure—let's don't go into this half-cocked." An hour later, the Dallas lawyers regrouped in the lobby. "Yes, let's do this," they declared, gripping hands in solidarity.

Campbell did not pretend to be neutral when it came to Bill Clinton. As one former partner would explain, "Don is a very conservative guy and really sees the world in black-and-white." Campbell clearly disliked Clinton and did not consider him "a very good president." Also, it was part of Campbell's psychological makeup to believe that every opponent "is truly, truly evil and that his client is truly, truly good." Said another former partner, "He's a little bit of a scorched-earth litigator, and just his psychological makeup, he's got to believe that the person that he's suing is just incredibly black-hearted." That was the approach Campbell took into the *Paula Jones* case.

Yet the Dallas lawyers did not view themselves as biased or politically inspired. Jim Fisher, occupying the chair as lead trial attorney, was slated to handle the president's deposition. Fisher did not personally harbor any ill will toward Clinton. He was a devout Christian and believed in forgiveness. "My own faith requires me to love the sinner but hate the sin," he later explained. "We worked real hard not to build up enmity at the man [Clinton]. We abhorred what he did. But I went on national TV and told people to pray for President Clinton, and I'm not saying it was easy or that I did it successfully. But I don't think that I ever got to the point that I despised him."

Fisher's dominant emotion was one of pity. "I think he [Clinton] did some really despicable things. But I don't think I ever built up a good hate for the guy. In fact, I kind of think he's pathetic in a lot of ways. He can't control himself. He has a serious problem that has brought him a great deal of shame. And I think that's the right light in which to view him."

The Dallas lawyers quickly filed an amended complaint, beefing up certain counts and jettisoning others that Judge Susan Webber Wright had already tossed out. Since there was increased chatter on radio talk shows about the "distinguishing characteristic," the attorneys also filed new interrogatories requesting that President Clinton provide information regarding "each and every medical doctor who has performed any surgery or medical procedure on your genitalia." The president seemed to be acting unusually "defensive" on the topic of the "distinguishing characteristic," so the Dallas lawyers poked and jabbed into that sore spot, testing for telltale grimaces.

In the meantime, they had their own sources of discomfort. One big problem was that Judge Wright seemed to be hardening her position against the plaintiff's case. At a secret status conference held on January 12 in the federal courthouse in Pine Bluff, away from the Little Rock spotlight, Judge Wright had reviewed the parties' briefs and furrowed her eyebrows. On this day, the Republican judge had broken her usual rules and allowed counsel to drink coffee in the courtroom, to ease the stress. "And I have candy," she added magnanimously, "if you would like some of my hard candy."

The judge went on: "Let the record reflect that we're in the courtroom in Pine Bluff and that the windows have been pasted over."

The purpose of this in-camera gathering, convened far away from the media, was to allow the judge to decide how to handle the upcoming deposition of Bill Clinton. This was the first time in American history that a president would be forced to testify as a defendant in a civil case. The judge stated, as a court reporter typed away, that she wanted to get the ground rules straight, so nobody could cry foul later.

Judge Susan Webber Wright embodied a new age in American law. She was born in 1948 as the country was rebuilding itself after World War II. Now, for the first time in history, women occupied a place of prominence among the bench and bar. Judge Wright typefied this transformation. She was bookish yet attractive. Her brownish hair, pulled back in a pragmatic bunch, was streaked with gray, but she had resisted the urge to dye it, since vanity had no place in a federal courtroom. She wore spectacles from a steady diet of reading law books. Her voice was youthful, with a lively, high pitch that made it animated rather than flat and dull. She pursed her lips as she spoke, occasionally using facial expressions to indicate happiness or severity.

Judge Wright's first order of business was to chide both sides for constant leaks to the media in open violation of her gag order. The judge noted that Internet gossip columnist Matt Drudge seemed to have a direct pipeline to information from his home office in Southern California. She also noted that this happened to be "where Ms. Jones is and, unfortunately, where Ms. McMillan is."

Presidential Counsel Bob Bennett interjected in a booming voice, "[Paula Jones], undoubtedly, tells her husband. Ms. Carpenter-McMillan picks this stuff up, and then the world knows about it."

Judge Wright, staring down sternly from the bench, agreed that Carpenter-McMillan seemed to be the culprit and possessed an obvious "political agenda in this case." The judge did not have concrete evidence to "hold [anyone] in contempt." But, she warned, "Once I find out who is responsible, there's a whole lot I can do."

Judge Wright next announced that she would schedule the president's deposition for January 17. It would take place at Bob Bennett's office in Washington, only a block and a half from the White House, making it a convenient location for President Clinton. There was an "added security risk" with any such proceeding involving the leader of the free world. The judge would issue a statement that the deposition would take place "at an undisclosed location" and woe to anyone who leaked this information to the press.

Judge Wright put down her pen. She leaned over the bench, as if she were reading the parties the riot act: "I want you to get the thing settled," she told the lawyers with evident frustration. "This case needs—it just *screams* for settlement."

Bob Bennett stood in front of the court, sturdy and bearlike. He had made a career working eighteen-hour days and handling important cases. He had served as counsel to former Defense Secretary Caspar Weinberger after Weinberger had been indicted for lying to Congress in the Iran-Contra affair. Bennett also had handled the "Keating Five" case, in which John McCain and four other U.S. senators were charged with trying to influence federal bank regulators on behalf of prominent campaign contributors. This Washington lawyer thrived on tough situations and high stakes. He now reminded Judge Wright that the previous pair of lawyers—Davis and Cammarata—had essentially settled the case only to have Jones *herself* scotch the deal. The Dallas lawyers were now doubling their client's demand to $1.5 million plus adding an $800,000 lien to cover the previous attorneys' fees—an obscene amount. How was any lawyer supposed to deal with this attempted extortion?

Judge Wright sighed. "I regret, personally," she said, "that [Ms. Jones] was not willing to accept what was being talked about last summer. . . . I would have almost *forced* her to take it." It was only because Davis and Cammarata had already withdrawn, she said, that she felt her hands were tied. She couldn't make Ms. Jones settle, as much as she would have liked to have waved a wooden spoon at her.

Now that Jones had new lawyers, however, Judge Wright wasn't going to allow any more monkey business: "I'll say quite candidly that with respect to Paula Jones's case . . . I think it's unlikely that a jury will find for her if this matter goes to trial." Judge Wright took a sip of water and gave an even clearer clue about her intentions. "I'm going to look *very* carefully at the defendants' motion for summary judgment," she said, staring knowingly at plaintiff's counsel. "The way it looks now, more likely than not, she will fail. And she's going to be kicking herself in a couple of years, or in another year, if she goes to trial and loses and she had $700,000 right under her nose."

Wes Holmes, seated at counsel table, felt a tightening around his neck. "That's never a good thing to have a federal judge tell you," he would admit. "It's hard to put a happy face on that one."

As an equal-opportunity bearer of bad news, however, Judge Wright turned to the president's lawyer, reminding him, "I'm also aware of Bill Clinton's reputation for womanizing." She had lived in Arkansas her whole life; the entire state knew about Clinton's proclivities when it came to females. One reason she wasn't bowled over by plaintiff's case, the judge quipped, was that Clinton's reputation did not extend beyond "just chasing skirts. You know, just having a good time, harmless activity." Although Bill Clinton's behavior left plenty to be desired, it would take considerable evidence to convince a jury from Arkansas that he was a sexual predator. "Certainly, he's an extremely popular president, a lot of people like his policies. And . . . the country is in good economic shape right now. I mean, they're talking about what to do with the surplus." Moreover, Jones's evidence concerning adverse job consequences was virtually nil. It was necessary to prove damages under federal law. It was tough to imagine how her lawyers would pull that bunny out of the hat.

In light of these extraordinary circumstances, the judge was prepared to take the unusual step of sitting down with the president and with Paula Jones, individually, if that's what it took. She would say to Jones: "I don't think it's right for you to pursue a case when you don't think you can win it." Her message to Clinton would be: "People are going to be embarrassed as a result of this trial. Friends of [yours] will be [embarrassed]." Moreover, the president had more important things to do than to get down in the gutter and sling mud around. "He's my president, for example, and I want him to be able to tend to business."

The judge's rebuke was sobering to both sides. Yet the Dallas lawyers were holding back some explosive information, related to "other women," that they thought would give them a fighting chance. All along, Fisher had tried to create the impression that he had embarked on a harmless fishing expedition when it came to the topic of the other females. The court papers he filed had listed all these potential witnesses as Jane Does, redacting their names to protect their identities. Now, when Judge Wright asked for more details, Fisher spoke nonchalantly, careful not to tip his hand. The mystery women on the witness list, he said, included Kathleen Willey, who had already been prominently mentioned in Michael Isikoff's *Newsweek* story; Judge Beth Coulson (whom Clinton had appointed to the Arkansas Court of Appeals) (Jane Doe No. 2); Sheila Lawrence (whose husband, a wealthy real estate developer in San Diego, was ambassador to Switzerland) (Jane Doe No. 7); Gennifer Flowers (with whom Clinton had admitted to having an affair); Juanita Broaddrick (who had allegedly been raped by Clinton while she worked at a nursing home twenty years earlier, although she continued to refuse to confirm this story with private investigators) (Jane Doe No. 5); Dolly Kyle Browning (a former high school classmate who insisted that Clinton had engaged in a longtime love affair with her); Marilyn Jo Jenkins (one of the women with whom the troopers allegedly arranged visits for Governor Clinton) (Jane Doe No. 1); and Cyd Dunlap (a casual acquaintance from Mississippi to whom Clinton had allegedly made unwanted advances).

There was also a young woman named Monica Lewinsky (Jane Doe No. 6), Fisher mentioned in a quick breath. Judge Wright looked up. "Can you tell me who she is? . . ." the judge asked. "I never heard of her."

Fisher replied, without flinching, "She's the young woman who worked in the White House for a period of time and was later transferred to a job in the Pentagon."

Judge Wright jotted a note. "All right," she said. "Thanks."

The Dallas lawyers were confident that Judge Wright grossly underestimated the potential strength of their case, at least the god-awful pressure they could bring to bear on Bill Clinton once they unleashed this Jane Doe information. Their private investigators, the husband-wife team of Rick and Beverly Lambert, had unearthed evidence of a host of dalliances that were potentially embarrassing for the president. "We had hit pay dirt in so many areas," said Fisher, that the Jones team could not even "superficially address each of them." The latest piece of information had come from a woman named Linda Tripp—who had contacted the Dallas lawyers of her own accord. Tripp had reported that Clinton was engaged in sexual relations in the White House—fairly recently—with a young, vulnerable former intern named Monica Lewinsky. This tip was particularly "intriguing" to the Dallas lawyers, "because there seemed to be more and more corroboration for it" and "because of the similarities with Paula Jones—the age, the vulnerability of the person, the request for oral sex."

The presumably consensual nature of Lewinsky's affair with the president did not, in Jim Fisher's mind, render it irrelevant. His theory was this: "When the president of the United States is asking for a favor of a twenty-one-year-old whose entire career could be destroyed by a word from him, there are coercive elements there." Also, Lewinsky had a history of psychological counseling dating back to her teenage years. Fisher believed that he could make a strong argument to a jury that any consent given by this young woman was illusory. Fisher was prepared to argue that "he [Clinton] took advantage of his position and exploited her."

Bob Bennett again spoke up loudly, urging the judge to keep out the entire list of Jane Does. This ploy was designed solely "to embarrass the president." Most of the allegations relating to these women involved consensual relations—even if one believed the allegations, which Bennett did not—and had nothing to do with sexual harassment. Additionally, in most cases, there was "no employment nexus at all."

The Dallas lawyers, waiting for this moment, sprung to their feet and announced that they intended to call a psychiatrist to testify that Bill Clinton was a "sex addict." At this, the judge's jaw tightened with displeasure. "I think, really, Gennifer Flowers and the troopers and Paula Jones is bad enough," she chastised. She had no intention of allowing plaintiffs to use her federal courtroom to "throw dirt at the President." This litigation was not a free pass to say, "Let's ask how many other women did he pat on the fanny." The sex topic could be explored within reason, said the judge—but she planned to watch it like a hawk. Anything that occurred more than "five years before the event," or with nonemployees, was automatically out of bounds. Also, she was going to put the Jones lawyers on the clock. This case only deserved five days, six days at most. If they wanted to waste their limited time getting into titillating stories involving "other women," they could do so at their own peril.

Bob Bennett was disappointed that the "other women" topic was permitted at all. He later said: "I felt she didn't like Bill Clinton, particularly. She had views about him." But at least Wright seemed unwilling to countenance blatant political attacks in her courtroom. "I felt we had a fair, good shot," Bennett concluded.

With the early winter skies growing darker and chillier in Pine Bluff, Judge Susan Webber Wright shook the sleeves of her robe, flipping closed a file of pleadings and motions. She stared down at the lawyers on both sides, a look of judicial despair creeping over her face as if she was staring into a dark, dangerous black hole. "We're going forward," the judge said with an involuntary grimace.

———•———

W ES Holmes quietly caught a plane to Washington several days before the deposition. Over the past week, he and his Dallas partners had been in communication with Linda Tripp and her new lawyer, Jim Moody. The Dallas lawyers were now convinced that the information from Tripp—if they could get it—might be their ace in the hole. For one thing, if Holmes could get his hands on the tapes that Tripp had been rambling about, these might be used to catch Clinton by surprise. They could actually *play* the tapes at Clinton's deposition—that would certainly blow the president's mind.

Holmes would recall, of his voyage across the United States during this unusual week, that it was as if he had been thrust into a madcap adventure movie: "We were very clearly led to believe that they would get us a tape. So my job was to get up there, to try to interview Linda, and to get those tapes, and prepare for the deposition in that way."

In the White House, Bob Bennett seemed satisfied that he had done his due diligence. Those close to him observed that he had checked out the *Jones* witness list for any possible land mines, and had concluded that the Clinton team was safe. Specifically, when it came to Jane Doe No. 6, aka Monica "Lewisky" (her last name was misspelled on the typed witness list), sources inside the White House apparently told Bennett that this young lady posed no problem. "She was a receptionist. Sort of a gopher. She was no longer there," is what sources had conveyed to Bennett. "We should not even be remotely concerned about her."

As part of his preparation, Bennett had even gone looking for the elusive Ms. "Lewisky," discovering, in the process, that her name was Lewinsky and that Frank Carter represented her. When Bennett called Carter, a professional acquaintance for many years, Carter reported that as best as he could tell, this young woman had done nothing more than drop off a few slices of pizza for the president. He had drafted an affidavit to that effect, and his client had confirmed it point by point. Carter told Bennett, "Bob, I've been through this twice with her."

Bennett interrupted: "Frank, whenever I get an affidavit, I like to know what *wasn't* put in the affidavit." Bennett probed directly: "Was there a kiss or a hug?" Carter dismissed this with a laugh. "Bob," he said, "there is *nothing* there."

If Carter had said, "Bob, I can't disclose anything to you—*but be careful,*" it might have prodded Bennett to take a different course in handling the Lewinsky allegations. However, Carter's professional integrity was unassailable. His strong assurances provided a solid basis for Bennett to conclude that the Jones lawyers were barking up the wrong tree.

Bennett had additional reasons to feel confident. He had just taken Paula Jones's deposition in Arkansas on November 12, finally getting a crack at the plaintiff and wading into the subject of her own sex life. Jones had repeatedly claimed that she "wasn't that kind of girl," going as far as to assert in her complaint that Clinton's conduct had caused her trauma and emotional distress. She had put the issue into play. At the deposition, Bennett swiftly had drawn blood by getting into Jones's sexual activities—including oral sex—with older men from a very young age. "If someone has done these things for years," he had conveyed to the judge, "it is hard to see how it could cause emotional distress, the single incident she was talking about, even if you assumed it happened."

Judge Wright agreed that what was good for the goose was good for the gander. "Don't tell me, counselor," she had told the Jones lawyers during a closed-door session, "that she's some blushing magnolia."

Bennett had also taken steps to blow the Jones lawyers out of the water when it came to the "distinguishing characteristic" allegation. The president's lawyer had learned that the president was scheduled for a physical exam that included a checkup by a urologist. He communicated to the physician: "Now that you know about this issue, could you focus on it as part of your exam?" It was an unseemly task, but a necessary one. Unbeknownst to the Dallas lawyers, Bennett now had his own affidavit unequivocally stating that the president "was perfectly normal" in this regard and that the alleged "distinguishing characteristic" on which Paula Jones's credibility rested simply did not exist.

If the president's deposition went smoothly, as he expected, Bob Bennett had reason to believe that he would walk away with a complete victory.

CHAPTER

26

PANIC IN THE JUSTICE DEPARTMENT

The day after Jackie Bennett arranged for the FBI to wire Linda Tripp, he and Ken Starr arrived at the White House to take a quick deposition of First Lady Hillary Clinton. If Mrs. Clinton had known what the Starr team knew, this meeting on Wednesday, January 14, would have been even more uncomfortable than it already was.

FBI agents and OIC prosecutors had stayed up all night with dubs of the Ritz-Carlton tapes and a pair of headphones. Straining to hear each word on an old boom box, they had nearly fallen out of their chairs. If the conversation between Monica Lewinsky and Linda Tripp was even half true, they now whispered, within days—after the *Paula Jones* deposition on Saturday—they would be able to establish multiple criminal counts against President Bill Clinton, including obstruction of justice, perjury, suborning perjury, and other crimes sufficient to end his presidency.

Even before this meeting, there was never any love lost between the OIC prosecutors and the First Lady. They had hauled her before the grand jury when the missing Rose Law Firm documents popped up, insulting Mrs. Clinton and solidifying her disdain for Ken Starr and his minions. The OIC, for its part, was deeply skeptical of everything that came out of Mrs. Clinton's mouth. Unbeknownst to the First Lady, Hickman Ewing was still busily working away in Arkansas, hoping to amass sufficient evidence to indict her.

Inside the White House, the two groups went through the ritual of greeting each other, like animals whose neck hair bristled at the sight of each other. Jackie Bennett later recalled that Mrs. Clinton appeared "well-coifed" and impressive looking. She seemed, as a court reporter commented to him on the ride home, "comfortable and at ease with herself" as First Lady. Yet there was an unmistakable flicker of unpleasantness on her face this day.

Mrs. Clinton asked Jackie Bennett, who towered over her like a giant, "Have we met before? You look familiar."

Starr chimed in exuberantly: "Jackie was on the Whitewater trial team in Arkansas." Bennett blanched, understanding that this was like saying to Mrs. Clinton: "This man tried to dismember you and your husband and destroy your friends with a meat ax, we're so proud of him!" The First Lady looked as if she had just heard "fingernails on a chalkboard." Bennett thought to himself, "My gosh, Ken—what were you thinking of?" Later, Bennett asked Starr about the incident and his boss simply smiled and "sort of acknowledged that it was deliberate." Bennett thought, "Oh, that shows me something. I like that." Now that the relationship between the White House and OIC had disintegrated, even a consummate gentleman like Ken Starr was prepared to play psychological war games.

The deposition was uneventful, lasting no more than fifteen minutes. The Starr prosecutors questioned Mrs. Clinton with respect to whether the White House had improperly ordered confidential FBI background files on Republican appointees. They watched the witness and duly recorded her answers. What etched itself into Jackie Bennett's mind, however, was the picture of the First Lady, seated calmly next to her lawyer David Kendall and White House Counsel Chuck Ruff, who was belted into his wheelchair. None of these three individuals, Bennett knew, could have possibly suspected that a locomotive was barreling down the track headed toward them. He later reflected: "I'm sitting there fully conscious that something's going to come of all this evidence [relating to Monica Lewinsky] someday. And I'm looking at the First Lady and her lawyers . . . and Chuck Ruff, and they don't have a clue about this." Bennett was certain that at some point when the Lewinsky matter became public, they would think back on this moment and say, "Oh, Jackie Bennett was sitting there, and Ken Starr—they were sitting there smirking about this." So he was extra careful not to allow anything resembling a smile of satisfaction to cross his lips.

That evening, Ken Starr and his team huddled in their conference room to discuss whether OIC should pursue the lead from Linda Tripp or punt it to the Justice Department. Should they urge Janet Reno to appoint a *new* independent counsel to investigate the blockbuster or take it themselves? Starr was well aware that he had been appointed to investigate a narrow range of subjects spelled out in his charter. His jurisdiction had been expanded by the attorney general from time to time, but he knew that this did not give him a blank check. There would be hell to pay if he overstepped the bounds of his authority on something this explosive. It was, he realized, a defining moment in his assignment as independent counsel.

It was an odd setting for such a monumental meeting. The Little Rock office was winding down; the small D.C. office was remodeling to accommodate the last remnants of OIC forces from Arkansas. Walls were being knocked down. An adjoining vacant office was being painted to handle the influx of Little Rock staffers. This dark little conference room, situated in the midst of the work zone, which was covered with plastic sheets, was now stuffed with fifteen chairs around a table and another half-dozen seats crowded against the walls to accommodate FBI agents.

Starr sat back listening pensively. Jackie Bennett occupied the head seat, presiding over the discussion.

Bennett's preference, considering the fast-moving situation, was for OIC to "grab and preserve the evidence." His fear was that "if we went to the Justice Department, which was managed by political appointees," Clinton apologists in the department would silently tip off their commander in chief before the *Jones* deposition ever took place. If that happened, the opportunity to nail Clinton would be lost forever. In Bennett's view, "if the president wanted to attend this deposition and tell the *truth*, as he was required to do, he was certainly entitled to do that." On the flip side, "why was he entitled to learn that there was evidence" that might prove that he had committed perjury? Given the strange Vernon Jordan connection to Monica Lewinsky—which looked suspiciously like the "jobs-for-silence" deal that OIC was investigating between Jordan and Webb Hubbell—Bennett believed they already had jurisdiction under the section of the independent counsel law that allowed them to probe matters "related to" their existing investigation. If OIC acted swiftly and decisively, it could gain the element of surprise.

Mike Emmick, an easygoing assistant U.S. attorney from Los Angeles who had just joined the Starr team, voiced a different view. He told the assembled group, in words that would become famous within the office: "I think we need to *run*, not walk, to the Justice Department and tell them about this." Nothing good would come, Emmick said firmly, if they did not get explicit authorization from the mothership in DOJ (the Department of Justice).

A newly hired prosecutor from the vice squad in Miami, Bruce Udolf, voiced an even deeper concern: Udolf had driven Linda Tripp home to Columbia the previous night, after her debriefing. He was thoroughly unimpressed by this paranoid, blond-haired informant. Udolf told his new colleagues that he had done plenty of undercover work with all manner of cooperating witnesses, and that Tripp "was vile." OIC, he said, should be extremely wary of getting into bed with this loudmouthed informant.

Udolf, a registered Democrat, had already begun rubbing many OIC prosecutors the wrong way. He had been "carping" about the poor quality of the tapes and how the FBI had handled the wiring of Tripp. Both he and prosecutor Mary Anne Wirth, who had spent considerable time with Tripp the previous night, had reported that they didn't trust her worth a nickel. Now, Udolf's words sounded like heresy to many of his colleagues: "What if Monica is fantasizing this?" he asked. "We can be the *hero*." OIC could "rebut" the allegations being spun out by Tripp, expose her anti-Clinton paranoiac plot, and come out looking like the truth-seeking white hats.

Jackie Bennett and other hard-chargers in the room, like Sol Wisenberg, were becoming agitated. "Nothing we were ever going to do in any scenario, *ever*, was going to put us into hero status in the Clinton White House," Bennett would later say. "And it's not something that we should have wanted, anyway. I mean, that wasn't our job."

From Little Rock, Hickman Ewing and Bob Bittman chimed in by speakerphone. They counseled strongly in favor of taking the case and running with it. The Clintons, after all, had been skating on the edge of lawlessness for years. Why cut them any slack now? "We have a duty to investigate ongoing crimes," said Bittman, who had prosecuted sex offenses in Maryland before joining OIC.

Mary Ann Wirth, with years' worth of experience as a federal prosecutor in New York, expressed serious concern about delving into the president's sex life. Wasn't there a high likelihood that this would blow up in their faces, just like the Bob Woodward story had caused them grief when they began interviewing women in Arkansas the previous spring? Why not deputize *another* prosecutor to take on this undignified, sex-laden investigation? The hard-liners seated at the table rolled their eyes.

Starr made sure everyone had a chance to weigh in. He told his prosecutors: "We want to do it the right way."

After absorbing the give-and-take for two hours and after consulting with FBI agents who had listened to the Tripp-Lewinsky tapes with their own ears, Starr reached his own conclusion. "This is serious stuff," he declared. In Starr's mind, the single most important factor was the "connection between Vernon Jordan and Monica Lewinsky," which was "strangely similar to what we saw with [Webb] Hubbell." The evidence they had unearthed to date indicated that

Hubbell had received lucrative consulting deals, including one hundred thousand dollars in cash from the Riady Corporation for work that was "at best ambiguous." It was Vernon Jordan who had arranged for Hubbell to receive "consulting" jobs from this parent company of Revlon while Hubbell was under criminal investigation. Now, it appeared "he was doing the same for Monica Lewinsky."

Ken Starr did not agree with Jackie Bennett that they already possessed "related-to" jurisdiction. Yet he concurred that OIC needed to take the case. In Starr's mind, it was especially significant that Linda Tripp was "well known to us." She had "been a witness in both the Foster death case, the Foster documents case, and in the Travel Office case." Now, here was their own witness telling OIC that she had held back information in the Travel Office matter "because the right questions were not asked." Even worse, their own witness "was being asked to participate in activity that certainly was potentially criminal," to wit, "[filing] a perjurious affidavit." This was starting to look and smell like witness tampering. OIC couldn't sit idly by, Starr declared, while the White House coached government witnesses to lie.

Linda Tripp had made clear that she didn't trust the Justice Department. A majority of Starr's team shared Tripp's distrust. If they tipped off Attorney General Reno (or worse yet, Deputy Attorney General Eric Holder) about this new evidence, "they'd tell Clinton. And then he would bail on the deposition that was scheduled for Saturday." As prosecutor Paul Rosenzweig, who was present for the top-secret discussion that day, would later note: "That kind of [reflected] how dim a view we already had of the attorney general at that point."

Inside the Washington Beltway, independent counsels were generally viewed as illegitimate outsiders. Starr himself, ironically, had opposed the whole concept of the independent counsel law, going back to the Reagan and Bush years. Yet the law had been reauthorized; Clinton himself had signed it back into law. Now—whether one liked the statute or not—Starr felt that the White House had a "moral obligation" to cooperate with his investigation. That, in his view, was not happening. Instead, there was perpetual "hostility directed at us," even though his prosecutors had acted "professionally" and "play[ed] by the rules" at every step.

Still, Ken Starr believed in following the rule book. As he often reminded his prosecutors, "We repair frequently to the mothership," referring to the Justice Department. Even if the department might give a surreptitious warning to the president, Starr still felt it was his duty to inform the attorney general. They would follow procedures, Starr said, rubbing his eyes, which stung with tiredness. They would take the high road.

Starr asked Jackie Bennett to follow protocol by meeting with Eric Holder, who could then brief the attorney general. This meant his conversation with Holder would have to be tightly constructed. As Bennett retired to his office to type up a carefully worded script, his secretary handed him a message from Michael Isikoff at *Newsweek*, making his day even more complicated—the reporter wanted Bennett to call him ASAP.

Bennett didn't like the timing of this call from a big-time investigative reporter. He stuck the message in his pocket, deciding to hold Isikoff at bay. Instead, he dialed the after-hours switchboard at the Justice Department, where he reached Agent McNally at the Command Center at 9:45 P.M. Bennett asked to speak with the deputy attorney general. The agent replied that Mr. Holder had gone home for the night, adding: "We've got a pager. We'll page him." At 10:18 P.M., after receiving no response, Bennett called the switchboard a second time, emphasizing that the matter was urgent. Twelve minutes later, Eric Holder rang through to Bennett's direct line, shouting over background noise, "What's up?" He was at a Washington Wizards' basketball game. He had needed to find a pay phone with a semblance of privacy.

Bennett read from his purposely nebulous script. His typed notes, later turned over to the House Judiciary Committee, revealed that he stated: "We are sort of into a sensitive matter." It involved "people at and associated with White House." The matter was still "breaking." Starr's office was "working with FBI." The whole topic was "highly sensitive." Could they meet the following day so that he could give the deputy attorney general more details?

The roar of the basketball crowd drowned out Holder's puzzled response. He asked whether he should call Attorney General Reno and alert her to the situation. Bennett replied cryptically, "I don't want to tell you not to." Holder found this to be a "strange answer." The two lawyers had played basketball together for years in the DOJ league; they had always treated each other as friends. Holder was becoming impatient with this cloak-and-dagger business. "Jackie, this is Eric," he said in a loud whisper. Bennett answered, "I know that, but this is dicey enough."

Bennett ended his one-way conversation by saying that he would call back in the morning. When they arranged a time to sit down in private, he said, he could divulge specifics.

Ken Starr himself, years later, would concede that it was probably a mistake for OIC to expand into the Lewinsky matter. After viewing the wreckage left in the wake of that decision, he concluded that the cost to himself and his prosecutors likely outweighed any benefit to the greater good. Although Starr reiterated that his office had acted honorably at every turn, he regretted that OIC itself had become a victim of the man-eating Lewinsky matter. If he could replay this decision that wreaked havoc on his life and on his professional career, he said, he would have declared "that it had to be investigated, but I was a poor choice to do it."

Some observers would take a stronger (and less charitable) position, contending that Starr was the *last* person in the world who should have taken over the Monica Lewinsky investigation. It was problematic enough that Starr had played a role, albeit limited, in the Paula Jones saga, prior to his appointment as independent counsel. He had appeared on national television arguing that Jones could sue the president; he had consulted directly with Jones's lawyer Gil Davis; he had planned to file an amicus brief in the *Jones* case on behalf of the conservative Independent Women's Forum. When it came to the Whitewater case, Starr had been clean as a hound's tooth at the time of his appointment. Not so with the Lewinsky matter, which was inextricably intertwined with the *Paula Jones* case. The three-judge panel, when it had replaced Robert Fiske with Ken Starr, had done so on the grounds that Fiske (because he had been appointed by Clinton's attorney general) was no longer perceived to be entirely neutral. Now, some whispered, the court should have heeded its own warning. The independent counsel law was all about appearances. Whatever his glittering credentials and whatever the unfairness of prior attacks on him as Whitewater prosecutor, Ken Starr was arguably the last person in the world suited for this explosive new Lewinsky assignment. By January 1998, when Linda Tripp came knocking on OIC's door, a significant portion of the American public—rightly or wrongly—viewed Starr as a zealot on a mission to bring down the president and First Lady. Even if those assessments were unfair and unfounded, the perception of neutrality—on which the whole concept of the independent counsel law rested—was wholly lacking when it came to this particular assignment.

Earlier that same day, when Starr and Bennett had watched the First Lady and her lawyers seated at the deposition, feeling almost sorry for them, they had been able to see only half the picture. Mrs. Clinton and the White House lawyers, Starr and Bennett had correctly observed, were totally unaware that a train bearing the name Monica Lewinsky was barreling down the track, ready to plow into them with full force. What Starr and Bennett did not appreciate until much later, however, was that a second locomotive was heading down the same track at full speed, with their own names puffing out of its smokestack in bold, black letters.

MONICA Lewinsky was busy finalizing a set of "Talking Points" for Linda Tripp, hoping to keep Tripp from blowing her cover. By this point, Tripp and Lewinsky thoroughly distrusted each other. Their e-mails, previously playful and laden with ribald humor, were now stark and accusatory.

In one exchange before Christmas, after Monica forwarded her erstwhile friend a joke about "sexual morality," Tripp had lashed into the young former intern: "From now on, leave me alone," Tripp wrote. "Don't bother me with all your ranting and raving and analyzing of the situation [with Clinton]. And don't accuse me of somehow 'skewing' the truth. . . . Share this sick situation with one of your other friends, because, frankly, I'm past nauseated about the whole thing. LRT."

Lewinsky shot back a response of her own: "That's fine with me, Linda. I will respect that. I would only like to ask that I have your assurance everything I have shared with you remains between us. You have given me your word before, but that was when we were on good terms. Can I still trust that?"

The precise origin of the infamous Talking Points, which Monica handed to Linda Tripp during their car ride on Wednesday, January 14, remains shrouded in mystery. What is now evident, however, is that the written Talking Points were part of a broader series of deceptions carried out by the two women, to throw each other off the track. For one, Monica told Tripp that she had not yet signed her affidavit and that she was "holding out" for a plum job from Vernon Jordan before she did so. (In fact, Monica had already signed the affidavit in Frank Carter's office on January 7; it was unrelated to her discussions with Jordan about finding new employment; the job that she had accepted at Revlon in New York was hardly a "plum," as it paid a pittance compared with her position at the Pentagon.) Tripp, for her part, had told Monica that morning that she was thinking of firing her lawyer Kirby Behre and replacing him with attorney Jim Moody at the suggestion of a "family friend." She wanted Monica to drive her to Behre's office "for moral support" because canning Behre would be an unpleasant task. (In fact, Tripp had already terminated Behre and had replaced him with attorney Jim Moody at the suggestion—not of a family friend—but of literary agent Lucianne Goldberg, who had met Moody through the "elves.")

With these mutual deceptions in play, Monica picked up Tripp after work and handed her a typed, three-page document. The young woman described it as a way for Tripp to get through this ordeal of the *Paula Jones* deposition with minimum hassle. The concept was beautifully simple: Tripp could sign an affidavit—as Monica had done—file it with the federal judge in Little Rock, and get out of Dodge.

Captioned "points to make in affidavit," the three-page Talking Points were surprisingly innocuous for all the hoopla they later generated. The first paragraph suggested that Tripp should begin her signed statement by describing "what you do now, what you did at the White House and for how many years you were there." The Talking Points then regurgitated Tripp's position with respect to the Kathleen Willey incident—as already reported in *Newsweek*—highlighting that Willey had not seemed upset by her encounter with President Clinton. The document concluded by stating that Tripp "never observed the

President behave inappropriately with anybody." The puzzling three-page document never directly addressed Monica's affair with the president, other than an odd reference in the last paragraph, where the writer switched to first person and added: "By the way, remember how I [Tripp] said there was someone else that I knew about? Well, she turned out to be this huge liar. I found out she left the WH because she was stalking the P or something like that. Well, at least that gets me out of another scandal I know about."

Years later, Monica stared at a copy of the Talking Points and emphasized that they never directly advocated that Tripp lie about anything. She insisted that the document was nothing more than a typed synopsis of ideas Tripp had already shared with her. After presidential lawyer Bob Bennett had replied to the initial *Newsweek* story about Willey, attacking Tripp's credibility, Monica had helped Tripp draft a strong letter to the editor of *Newsweek,* defending her comments. That letter was never published. Still, its contents remained fresh in the younger woman's mind. She explained: "The genesis of a lot of the ideas [in the Talking Points] came from various things that Linda had actually said or written."

Lewinsky insisted (and the FBI later confirmed) that she typed the document on her own home computer. Indeed, several prior drafts of the document retrieved from her computer confirmed that fact. According to Monica's story, she typed the final Talking Points in a rush, over a period of a day or so, as she discussed the subject with Tripp, in anticipation of handing the short summary over to her older friend.

Linda Tripp, however, scoffed at this explanation. She remained convinced that someone inside the White House, most likely Bruce Lindsey or Vernon Jordan or even President Clinton himself, had dictated the document to Monica in order to coax Tripp to provide false testimony in the *Jones* case. Tripp later acknowledged, jiggling one foot as she spoke, that the Talking Points did accurately summarize their prior conversations. "The verbiage was similar. I'll give you that," said Tripp.

Yet Tripp never wavered from her belief that the Talking Points did not originate with the twenty-three-year-old former intern. "I've spent a great deal of time with Monica," Tripp explained. "Monica's résumés, Monica's letters to prospective employers, Monica's work product in the Office of Public Affairs. I edited it on a daily basis. I was aware of her writing. I was aware of her capability. And I took one look at this and knew she hadn't written them."

Monica defended herself by pointing out that she had received a plaque from her boss, Ken Bacon, for her diligent efforts at the Pentagon, and that she consistently received solid work performance reviews. She admitted that she allowed Linda Tripp to review some of her personal letters to Bill Clinton as a sort of "talisman," yet she countered that Tripp knew nothing about her work product.

Seated on a folding chair in a stark storage facility in Greenwich Village and digging through documents that she had forced out of her mind since the trauma of 1998, Monica Lewinsky insisted that this was another example of Linda Tripp's sick, conspiratorial thinking. Throwing into a box a lengthy scholarly article that questioned her authorship of the Talking Points, Monica blurted out, "Can you believe some Ph.D. wrote a whole paper about this? . . . Didn't he ever stop to think the versions were different because someone (Tripp) was talking to me over the telephone and I was typing some of these things as we talked?" For Lewinsky, the notion that she was incapable of writing the Talking Points was "insulting."

Yet the point made by this professor with a Ph.D., suggesting that as many as "three separate authors" wrote the three-page Talking Points, could not be dismissed as implausible. Even to the naked eye, the document seemed to shift radically in style and clarity, as if some third person (perhaps a family member or a friend) had reviewed a draft or made suggestions to Monica as she typed the words on the computer keyboard.

Whatever the actual process by which Monica finalized the Talking Points on her home computer, neither her own nor Tripp's explanation seemed fully satisfactory. Yet this much could not be disputed: Linda Tripp promptly handed over the three-page document to OIC that same night.

How the purported friendship between Tripp and Lewinsky had devolved into a relationship of such mutual dishonesty is a question that would stump even Monica Lewinsky. Years later, the former intern would say that she could never figure out what caused Linda Tripp to betray her so thoroughly. "I'm probably not a good person to answer that," Monica said, her voice turning humorless. "Because I clearly did not have a good sense of this woman." One theory, of course, was that Tripp simply wished to advance the conservative Republican agenda. There was no doubt that Tripp "was very happy when she worked for the Bush administration" and that she longed for the halcyon days of the Bush White House. Yet Lewinsky didn't subscribe to the theory that Tripp was simply a "political kook," pointing out, "I never really heard her [Tripp] say disparaging things about [Clinton] per se, except when it came to when he was being a jerk to me."

Consequently, Monica could only offer her own alternative theory: Linda Tripp was a false friend and a devious manipulator who had decided it was acceptable to hurt her, as part of the loftier mission of trying to bring down a morally corrupt president.

Tripp, for her part, expressed no regrets about her actions. The president, she concluded, was not in love with Monica Lewinsky. "Absolutely was not," she said. "He would give her ten minutes after their little sessions, and I think—against his own will, I think he found her somewhat endearing." Over time, Tripp came to believe that Monica had become like an addictive drug for the president. Tripp leaned forward in her antique chair, a faint smile overtaking her face. "Monica will grow on you in a huge way," she said. "She can be the biggest pill, the biggest pest. She jeopardized his [Clinton's] livelihood, she jeopardized his life and his marriage and his family. Yet he [Clinton] took these enormous risks."

In the end, Tripp declared that she would go to her grave satisfied that she had delivered Monica to OIC for the sake of a higher good. "I know that Monica feels she hates me, and that makes me sad because I don't hate her, in fact, at all," she said, shaking her head. "I'm completely disappointed in her choices and completely horrified that she chose the path she did after the affair . . . but, no, I don't hate her."

———

ERIC Holder was bedeviled by the call from Jackie Bennett. It certainly put a damper on his evening at the Wizards' game, not to mention the fact that the Wizards lost 89–79 in the final three minutes. Holder was a veteran of the American criminal justice system. He was not ordinarily rattled by calls like this. After graduating from Columbia Law School in 1976, he had worked his way up from trial lawyer in the Public Integrity Section of the Justice Department, to judge on the D.C. Superior Court, to U.S. attorney in Washington, and now to deputy attorney general. A tall, handsome African American man with an easy manner that neutralized opponents, Holder had entered the Justice Department with a positive view of special prosecutors. He had admired the work of Archibald Cox and Leon Jaworski during the tumult of Watergate; he respected the special prosecutor concept as a healthy one. Thus far, the relationship between the Justice Department and Ken Starr's Office of Independent Counsel had been positive enough. There was no reason to think that it would change.

The next afternoon, Holder and Jackie Bennett swapped phone calls, with Bennett continuing to delay as long as possible, telling the deputy attorney general, "Late afternoon or early evening—after 6—would be better for us." The two men finally agreed to meet in Holder's office at 6:15 P.M.

As the clock ticked away, Jackie Bennett received a second urgent phone call from Michael Isikoff. This time Bennett closed his door and took the call. The *Newsweek* reporter cut to the chase. "I know what you guys have been doing," Isikoff said. "I know everything. We need to talk." There was something "sort of threatening" about his tone. The prosecutor told Isikoff, "Come on over. We've got to talk face-to-face." Bennett hung up and immediately dialed Linda Tripp at the Pentagon. How in God's name had Isikoff learned all of these details? he thundered. Where was the journalist's information coming from? Tripp replied innocently, "Oh well, the only person I talked to was Lucianne Goldberg."

Bennett nearly blew a gasket. Lucianne Goldberg, the queen of literary gossip? Hadn't they made it clear that Tripp was to "keep all this secret"?

By the time Bennett slammed down the phone, Isikoff had arrived in a cab. The two men took seats in the small OIC conference room. Bennett slumped down, narrowed his eyes, and stared at the tenacious reporter, who was a foot shorter than him. Isikoff was an intense man with dark, slightly graying hair, in his midforties, who wore intellectual-looking wire-rimmed glasses. As usual, he was "all business." The journalist slapped his cards on the table: He knew about *everything*—about Tripp, about Vernon Jordan, about the FBI body wire, about Starr's involvement in the case, about Monica Lewinsky's sexual relationship with the president; about all of the "salacious stuff." It was a blockbuster story— maybe even *the* story of the century. He, Isikoff, was prepared to print it soon, whether or not OIC chose to corroborate any details. Now came the kicker: Isikoff's deadline was Saturday. Before he could run the story, protocol required that he contact Vernon Jordan, Monica Lewinsky, and the president's lawyer Bob Bennett, to give them a chance to rebut the explosive allegations.

"So if there's some reason you don't want me to do that right now," Isikoff said, "I need to know it."

Bennett pleaded with the reporter: Couldn't he "keep a lid" on the story for a couple of days? Isikoff was used to games of "blink." His foot jiggled with nervous energy. "As a matter of journalistic ethics," he said, he would have to "elicit a quote from somebody on behalf of the president." Very soon.

Bennett sank back into his chair, beginning to feel outraged. Isikoff knew an alarming number of accurate details. All fingers pointed to Linda Tripp as the snitch. Bennett's problem, however, was much more immediate than a loose-lipped informant. "We just were utterly unprepared for the notion that *Newsweek* was in the middle of this," Bennett would recall. Bennett told Isikoff, "You've got us over the barrel." Perhaps they could reach some accommodation. Wasn't there some way to hold off the story, temporarily, so that they didn't tip off individuals involved in ongoing criminal conduct?

The journalist tapped his pen against his head: He *might* be willing to wait until four o'clock Friday afternoon. The magazine hit the newsstands on Monday morning. Advance copies were transmitted to the national media on Sunday. He could wait that long—perhaps—before contacting the "interested parties." Bennett, in return, would have to promise to give him key information, including OIC's "basis for starting this investigation in the first place." That way, Bennett would keep the lid on his explosive case and Isikoff would be guaranteed an exclusive story.

Each man, as he shook hands to consummate the deal, felt as if he had just struck a bargain with the devil.

—————

At 6:15 p.m., Jackie Bennett and a group of OIC prosecutors—joined by Josh Hochberg, on special assignment from the Justice Department—arrived at the deputy attorney general's office. Given the supersensitive nature of the meeting and the roving eye of the Washington press corps who patrolled the halls of DOJ, Bennett had insisted that they limit the group to a small number of the most trusted, highest-ranking lawyers. With its high ceiling and ornate decor, the deputy attorney general's office had been the site of many important meetings over the years. Although Eric Holder was braced for the worst, he was totally unprepared for what he actually heard. Bennett began, according to notes of the gathering, by stating: "We have unhappily come across a very sensitive matter."

According to verbatim notes maintained by OIC lawyer Stephen Bates, who served as scrivener for the meeting, Bennett delivered a blunt summary: "We were called Monday evening by Linda Tripp, a witness in a number of matters that we have investigated." He went on: "She told us that a friend and former colleague of hers, a witness in *Jones*, has been contacting Tripp and urging her to commit perjury. The efforts seem to go back to the President and a close associate of his, Vernon Jordan. The friend's name is Monica Lewinsky."

Holder clutched the side of the table. He would later say, reliving that moment, "I mean, I was shocked." Holder had gone into the meeting "prepared to hear something very serious." But this news made his head spin. "This was not what I expected to hear," he said later, "you know, the intern and all that stuff."

In the modern, suspicion-laden world of Washington, government lawyers rarely committed anything to paper for fear it might come back to haunt them in a congressional hearing or in some vicious legal battle. At this gathering, however, Holder slid out a tablet of paper and began writing. His handwritten notes of that meeting, which escaped translation even during the massive congressional dragnet leading up to President Clinton's impeachment trial, provide a sharp picture of the information exchanged between OIC and the attorney general's lawyers.

The first words scribbled onto the lined pages were "Isikoff is on to this, getting info from Tripp's friends, far along." Holder next recorded that OIC was affirmatively seeking permission to move forward on this case. "They want to continue to investigate—want jurisdictional call from us," either determining that the investigation was already within their jurisdiction "or expanding jurisdiction to cover it." Holder hurriedly scribbled: "Goes into the White House and to the President."

The notes confirm that there was a brief discussion of the concept of OIC's and DOJ's working *together* on the investigation. Vernon Jordan, because he held no position in the executive branch, was probably *not* a "covered person" under the independent counsel law, so DOJ was free to handle the matter itself. One idea the prosecutors kicked around was having Reno's people collaborate with Starr's people. If the DOJ lawyers determined that President Clinton was involved, the whole case could be kicked over to OIC. This hybrid plan, however, was quickly junked because Michael Isikoff and *Newsweek* were breathing down OIC's neck. Holder's notes indicate: "Case will be shut down within 36 hours. Somebody has to work the case."

Holder and his colleagues did express concern that Ken Starr's office had already wired Linda Tripp without seeking the attorney general's permission. "We thought," recalled Holder, "that maybe they had acted a little precipitously in that they were getting into areas where it wasn't clear they had the jurisdiction to act yet." The fact, however, was that OIC "had done it." The question now was: How should the AG's office play the cards dealt to them?

Holder's notes confirm that Starr's office essentially communicated Linda Tripp's version of the story. For instance, OIC told its Justice Department brethren that Vernon Jordan "picked [Lewinsky] up in a limousine" and instructed her, "you can't answer questions truthfully, [you] should lie." In return, Jordan would "get her a job in private sector." Based on this quid pro quo, the notes recorded, "she signed a false declaration." (This recitation of events, it turned out, was not supported by the facts, but the Starr prosecutors had hitched their wagon to Linda Tripp's account.)

Jackie Bennett next blurted out that his office "had no contact with [Jones's] attorneys." Holder later recalled that this comment "seemed a little odd." Why would OIC's lawyers even mention the *Paula Jones* case? That disclaimer passed like a bad stomach cramp. Bennett took the opportunity to return to the issue of Starr's office needing to move quickly. Holder wrote: "Concerned about Tripp. Don't want her to sign anything that would impeach her credibility." OIC also reemphasized the Jordan link: "Jordan, Hubbell under investigation. Hush money from Jordan. This is similar."

Bennett next veered to a new startling topic, stating that the tape recordings made by Linda Tripp might be "violation of the law in Maryland." This could be problematic, Bennett noted, because these tapes would be necessary for OIC to make its case. Holder paused momentarily, wondering if this meeting could get any worse.

In fact, it might have. One topic that did *not* come up, at least according to Holder's notes, was President Clinton's pending deposition in the *Jones* case.

Even though that deposition was scheduled to take place in a matter of days, Jackie Bennett steered clear of the topic, either intentionally or through an unplanned omission.

Some members of the attorney general's team later concluded that Starr's prosecutors had hornswoggled them. The feeling grew widespread within DOJ that Jackie Bennett and his band of OIC people had intentionally shaded the facts to seduce the Justice Department into granting OIC permission to expand into the Lewinsky case. It was particularly infuriating to DOJ lawyers that Starr's office was soon telling the world that OIC had no choice but to expand into the controversial Clinton-Lewinsky investigations because Attorney General Reno had "requested" that it do so, intimating that Starr had accepted the job with great reluctance. This was not true, in the attorney general's team's view. Eric Holder later held up his notes and said firmly, "No, they were advocating—I left that meeting with the impression and the understanding that that's what they wanted to do. They wanted to expand their jurisdiction, or have us consider whether it was within their jurisdiction to handle the matter." Moreover, the fleeting discussion about DOJ's and OIC's working on the Lewinsky case together had been abandoned almost instantly. Holder's clear impression was, "They certainly wanted to remain, you know, involved, in charge." Other DOJ lawyers present at the meeting concurred.

Jackie Bennett stood up. Before leaving the meeting, he gave Holder a firm, serious handshake, telling his old Public Integrity basketball buddy, "I'm sorry to leave you with this."

———

THAT evening, Ken Starr huddled with his prosecutors around a computer terminal as Stephen Bates typed. Within hours, Starr had completed a two-page letter to Attorney General Reno, switching his position to favor the more hardline prosecutors in his office. In this revealing document, Starr argued (perhaps to cover himself when the letter became public) that OIC already possessed related-to jurisdiction and did not need, as a legal matter, the attorney general's permission to continue the Lewinsky investigation. He emphasized that Linda Tripp "is already an important witness in our investigation." Starr interjected: "Should she in fact perjure herself" in the *Jones* case, "her usefulness as a potential witness in any trial would be greatly reduced." He also reiterated the purported link involving Vernon Jordan and stressed the "nexus" with the Webster Hubbell case already under OIC's jurisdiction. Starr ended the confidential letter by expressing his strong view that his office alone was in the best position to handle this highly sensitive new investigation that might reach into the Oval Office. Unlike the Justice Department, Starr emphasized, OIC was already up and running in this investigation. Additionally, his prosecutors could bring an element of independence to this assignment that would instill public confidence in this difficult yet necessary criminal probe—something Janet Reno's Justice Department could never do.

With that, Ken Starr signed the letter and dispatched a messenger to deliver it to the attorney general's office posthaste.

CHAPTER

27

VANITY TO PRAYER

Eric Holder had resisted interrupting Attorney General Janet Reno in the midst of her weekly Thursday night excursion to a Kennedy Center symphony, in part because the press had a habit of tailing her. Pacing the floor of his home in Northwest D.C., Holder couldn't wait another minute.

At 11:00 P.M., the DOJ Command Center alerted Reno's security detail that Holder had an urgent matter to discuss with his boss. Reno had just returned to her apartment on Eighth Street a few blocks from the Justice Department. The no-nonsense attorney general asked Holder directly, was there a problem? Holder had a good relationship with Reno; he didn't attempt to sugarcoat this news. Holder put the phone down and retrieved his three pages of scribbled notes so that he could convey Jackie Bennett's statements verbatim.

Still dressed in a long dress from the symphony, Janet Reno stood in her two-bedroom unit in the Lansburgh Apartments, frozen in her tracks. She did not ordinarily experience fear. The only time FBI Director Louis Freeh had insisted she permit agents to post themselves around her apartment building—for security purposes—was following the Oklahoma City bombing, when safety concerns trumped her insistence on privacy. Tonight, however, the attorney general was feeling unusually vulnerable. In the modest living area of her apartment, knickknacks and decorations from the Florida Everglades were the only reminder of her Miami home. Here in Washington, so distant from that world, political eruptions seemed to batter the landscape more fiercely than hurricanes that ravaged the Florida coastline. Janet Reno, a tall woman at six feet one, would remember taking a deep breath. All she could summon up in her mind was a quote from the mid-twentieth-century statesman Adlai Stevenson: "The burdens of office stagger the imagination and convert vanity to prayer."

Reno paused a minute, then said, "Let me call you back, Eric." As Holder interpreted it, the attorney general "wanted to basically regroup and kind of think about the enormity of what I had told her."

Sitting down in a chair, Reno sorted out her options. "I was trying to think of what I should do," she later recalled with characteristic terseness. Specifically, the attorney general was thinking, "How should it be handled? What were my legal options? What could produce an expansion [of Starr's jurisdiction]? Was it sufficiently connected?"

A hodgepodge of other concerns swam around in her head. First, what about the fact that OIC had already wired Linda Tripp before requesting an expansion of jurisdiction? This meant there would be immediate questions about whether Starr's group had overreached. Second, Reno had secretly harbored misgivings about the appointment of Ken Starr from the start. When she had served as Dade County district attorney, she had worked closely with "specially appointed state attorneys" named by the governor. She knew how the system of special prosecutors was supposed to work, and she respected it.

From the moment the three-judge panel named Starr to replace Robert Fiske, though, the attorney general had experienced serious misgivings. She liked Starr, personally. He was a brilliant lawyer and judge. He had been an impressive solicitor general. He was an affable enough fellow, even though (she told herself) he tended to wear his emotions on his sleeve. Reno's biggest problem was on the practical side of things: "To my knowledge," she would later say, "he had limited experience in investigating and pursuing allegations. That was my concern."

When Starr had announced in the spring of 1997 that he was quitting and moving to Pepperdine, Reno had heaved a sigh of relief: "There was a faint glimmer of hope on my part that the court might appoint someone who would organize and work through it. Take what action was necessary, and get it done." On the other hand, she said, "I was very surprised that someone would undertake that assignment and then leave it, or try to leave it, midstream."

As attorney general, Reno had scrupulously avoided commenting on Starr's investigation. Now, years after leaving that post, Reno would for the first time reflect on the Starr dilemma. She sat on the back porch of her country home, a modest structure that her parents had built in the 1940s, stuffed baby alligators and fossils adorning the ledge of her screened porch. Here, in late 2001, Reno confessed that the entire Starr operation had underwhelmed her. Even before it spiraled into the Lewinsky affair, Reno acknowledged, she had felt that the Starr investigation lacked focus. Dressed in a colorful gardening shirt that matched the bright Florida peacocks strutting around her backyard, the former attorney general voiced her overall opinion: "I thought that if all of us had the opportunity to pursue matters with the kind of resources or dollars that he [Starr] had, we would have concluded it and taken whatever action was necessary in a more timely manner."

These days, Reno's hands trembled from Parkinson's disease. A collection of framed badges from a dozen federal government agencies—a gift when she had left the Justice Department—hung from the wall of her screened porch, bearing witness to the vast responsibility that she once shouldered as the nation's top law enforcement official. Her mind was still as sharp as the day she drove home from Washington in her red Ford pickup truck, a vehicle that allowed her to navigate the swampiest roads of South Florida. Reno was a prosecutor who had been reared on tough decisions and sought out pragmatic solutions. From the start, she confessed, the OIC investigation led by Ken Starr had given her dyspepsia.

Yet Reno also admitted that the circumstances presented in January 1998 placed everyone, including the top deputies in her own office, in a tough spot. She had dealt frequently with Michael Isikoff; she understood that he was "a very, very aggressive reporter." That he had drawn a line in the sand, setting a deadline by which Jackie Bennett had to act, came as no great surprise. Reno's assessment was, "That was Isikoff."

Despite her lack of confidence in Ken Starr, there was a competing sense that "time was of the essence." Reno did weigh the option of finding a *different* special prosecutor. At the time, she had asked herself as she sat in her empty Washington apartment, "Do you let Ken Starr do it?" Or was someone else a better choice? With the Isikoff deadline ticking away, however, that question had become almost academic. "Trying to get that person up to speed in the context of the whole investigation with the time line," Reno later explained, seemed futile.

There was another concern that gnawed at the attorney general. By this point in early 1998, she knew that Starr was distrusted (and even reviled) by a large segment of the American public. Correctly or incorrectly, many citizens believed that he was carrying out a costly, drawn-out, politically motivated witch hunt of the president and First Lady. "Under the ideal circumstances," she said, later analyzing the situation, it was clear that this new, controversial Lewinsky investigation "should be [done] by a person in whom everybody had confidence, who was independent and who could make the call so that it was a clear objective call." Starr was the antithesis of that person, but this was not a perfect world. A superaggressive journalist in the person of Michael Isikoff was pushing to get facts *now,* or he was going to spill the beans *before* Clinton's deposition and make a mess. Ken Starr—however imperfect a selection—was already in place, ready to take action. In light of "the nature of the allegations," Reno's prosecutorial gut told her, this unfolding criminal situation "should be handled now."

Reno remembered that the only other thought that had flashed into her head as she worried that night in her D.C. apartment had to do with turning back the clock: "I kept wishing that Fiske were there," she said.

————

In Little Rock, the young sex-crimes prosecutor Bob Bittman had driven to Best Buy and purchased several audiocassette players and sets of headphones. With dubs of Linda Tripp's tapes having been overnighted from Washington, he and FBI agent Pat Fallon, Jr., reviewed a few of these in disbelief. Bittman paged Pam Craig, a loyal office manager–secretary who had been working for Hickman Ewing since 1995, and asked her to begin transcribing the Ritz-Carlton undercover meeting along with Tripp's own tapes. Once Ken Starr was informed that Pam had been assigned the project, he protested to Bittman: "What do you mean Pam's typing it? I didn't want Pam hearing that." Bittman reassured his boss: "It's okay, Ken. We've never seen her type so fast."

Agents and prosecutors huddled around the secretary, asking, "What's she [Monica] saying? What's she saying?" attempting to catch snippets of conversation from the earphones. Craig looked up from the keyboard and offered her initial impression: "Who cares what she [Lewinsky] is saying? She's lying." Two hours later, the secretary slumped back in her chair and reached a different conclusion. She recalled a sick feeling sweeping over her and thinking, "You know, I didn't vote for the guy [Clinton]. I don't like him, but he's still president of my country and this is kind of disgusting, you know."

Craig, a single mother, had brought her nine-year-old daughter with her to the office while she worked on this emergency assignment. The little girl slept in a chair in the OIC conference room as her mother transcribed tapes long into the night.

Craig took a break long enough to teach a Sunday school class in the morning, then returned to the OIC offices to wrap up the job. The whole experience distressed her. "I mean, it was a real wake-up call for me about how our kids can turn out if you don't do the right thing," the secretary said. After packing up her equipment and her daughter and carrying them both to the car, she stared sternly at her sleepy child. Suddenly, the woman grasped her daughter by the arm and blurted out: "Look, let me tell you something. When some guy calls you at two in the morning and wants you to wait out in the rain so he can come have sex with you, it's *not* love, okay?"

Her daughter inspected her cross-eyed as if she had gone mad. "She just looked at me like, 'What in the world are you talking about?' " Craig recalled.

THE next morning at 8:30, Janet Reno convened a meeting of her own top brass. Chairs creaked; a dozen of the Justice Department's top lawyers sat back apprehensively. Only a small group within the department had been invited to this highly sensitive briefing. Reno and Holder knew that if the story leaked, DOJ would be accused of "trying to tip off the White House." Their own reputations were on the line.

Kevin Ohlson, who served as chief of staff to Eric Holder, recalled the mood inside the gathering: "It was excitement in terms of elevated blood pressure and heart rate and so forth. Just wondering what this was going to mean—not to sound melodramatic—but for the country."

Never one for small talk, Reno launched directly into her analysis of DOJ's options. She folded her arms soberly and stated: "All right, Starr's people have asked that we permit him to pursue this matter. How should we proceed?" One of the Justice Department lawyers, Josh Hochberg, had already visited Starr's office to listen to the tapes. The recordings were "of pretty good quality." The startling Lewinsky-Tripp banter confirmed the gist of what Jackie Bennett had conveyed to DOJ the previous night. Michael Isikoff was going to run with the story in thirty-six hours. Even if that didn't happen, the story could easily leak out from Matt Drudge—the young Internet gossip columnist who was scooping stories from the mainstream media and printing rumors, if necessary, to make a name for himself. Linda Tripp was on the loose and was talking to a loud-mouthed literary agent in New York. This story could blow at any moment.

Those seated around the table agreed that if the Justice Department dragged its feet, they would all be accused of "obstructing the investigation in order to benefit the president." There was also a view that DOJ "didn't have any ability to get our own investigation up and running in such short order."

One lawyer present recalled feeling as if "the ghost of John Mitchell was floating around." Mitchell had been President Nixon's attorney general who was convicted of participating in the Watergate cover-up and became the first U.S. attorney general to serve a prison term. Nobody in the room wanted to suffer Mitchell's fate once the Lewinsky bomb dropped. This new Lewinsky matter was radioactive. The underlying *Paula Jones* case was totally unrelated to DOJ's jurisdiction. Why not let someone *else* handle it?

Ohlson, seated beside the deputy attorney general, recalled feeling, "Oh, my God . . ." this could "lead to the president's resignation." Although his mind did not conjure up the word "impeachment," he felt that if the allegations were true, "out of sheer and utter embarrassment [President Clinton] would end up resigning." Ohlson was also ticking through a dozen questions in his mind: "Are they [OIC] going to wire up Lewinsky? What exactly are they going to do to her in terms of the investigative steps, and just how ugly is this about to become?"

Ohlson recalled, foremost, feeling that danger had crept into the equation. "There really was the sense of the world being turned upside down in very short order here."

Eric Holder was thinking in much more pragmatic terms. "From my perspective, the question was not *whether* we [gave the case to Starr]," he later explained. "But *how.*" The biggest worry, for Holder, was an institutional one. For the good of the two-hundred-year-old Justice Department, how did DOJ hand this hot potato off to OIC without getting its own hands singed in the process?

Janet Reno ducked out of the room to beat out a fire on a different matter. When she returned, she did not retake her seat. As Holder would explain, "She's a pretty cool character. And she's not a person who exhibits emotion, though she feels it." With one hand on the chair, Reno said, "This is what we need to do." She ticked off an action plan: DOJ would give the case to Starr, rather than seeking the appointment of a different independent counsel, because the latter was not feasible under the existing time constraints. DOJ would accomplish this by requesting expansion of Starr's jurisdiction, rather than agreeing with Starr's argument that this was "related to" his jurisdiction—that was bunk. The DOJ people would hand off the investigation and keep their fingers out of the case, so they could not be accused of steering it into a ditch. There was zero time for horsing around, so they would contact the three-judge panel by telephone *immediately,* and seek authority for Starr to do the job he had so forcefully requested.

Holder would later comment, "You know, it didn't make us very popular, I'm sure, at the White House." Yet at the time, all of the top brass in the Justice Department were convinced "it was the right thing to do."

Years later, as she sat back in a wicker chair on the screened porch of her Miami home, Reno herself recalled the unwinnable dilemma that had confronted her. Just one month before the Lewinsky-Tripp tape-recording incident, she had taken a drubbing in the national media for refusing to appoint an independent counsel to investigate alleged unlawful fund-raising telephone calls made by President Bill Clinton and Vice President Al Gore initiated from the White House during the reelection campaign of 1996. Reno had concluded these allegations were too flimsy. Now, here were new politically charged allegations, and the ordinarily unflappable attorney general felt that she was "damned if I did, damned if I didn't." No matter what course she took, half the country would accuse her of being a no-good traitor. Still, she could not slough off the responsibilities of her office. The Lewinsky-Clinton-Jordan allegations, if true, were serious ones. Looking back at the events, Reno straightened her large, aviator-style glasses and boiled the situation down to its essence: "The general consensus was that we had no choice."

In hindsight, there were few compelling reasons for Starr's office to jump into the Lewinsky case. Isikoff's deadline, in reality, was artificial. Just as OIC prosecutors rightly concluded that they had no duty to warn the president to keep him from lying at his upcoming deposition, they also had no duty to stop a journalist from printing a story that might cause Clinton or Monica Lewinsky to tell the truth. If Starr's prosecutors and Justice Department lawyers had resisted the urge to act precipitously—refusing to allow Isikoff's "deadline" to dictate the course of their investigation—many of their own problems would have dissolved.

Ben Bradlee, former editor of the *Washington Post,* where Isikoff first broke the Paula Jones story, kicked a foot up on his desk and defended his former reporter: "I loved a guy like [Isikoff]." When a tenacious investigative journalist like this latched onto a story, "you knew they were going to bring all the firepower to bear that they could, and they'd give the story a good run." Bradlee pushed up his shirtsleeves, rocked backward, and added, "Hell, he was never proved wrong, was he?"

The legendary *Washington Post* editor had been a personal friend of President John F. Kennedy's; he knew of JFK's reputation as a world-class "girler"; he understood the arguments that reporters were supposed to stay away from these "personal" matters. Still, Bradlee saw a big difference between JFK's sexual "indiscretions" and Bill Clinton's, which had produced an actual civil lawsuit. The latter, he believed, gave reporters like Isikoff license to dig deeper. Bradlee, who had overseen Bob Woodward and Carl Bernstein when they blew open the Watergate scandal story, viewed Isikoff as being cut from the same cloth. "It is in his genes to go after something aggressively," said Bradlee, "which is one of his great virtues."

Many journalists who had cut their teeth during the Watergate era were now editors or publishers of major newspapers, Bradlee noted, which made them even more aggressive in covering the Clinton scandal. Why not? Every newshound in the business hungered to be part of history, as Woodward and Bernstein had been in Watergate. Bradlee made no apologies for his colleagues' zeal. Alternative "news" purveyors like Matt Drudge, who were beginning to use the Internet to scoop the mainstream press, were constantly cutting corners. Oldfashioned bulldogs like Isikoff, he felt, should not be handicapped when they latched onto the news and brought it to readers in a responsible fashion. As

Bradlee saw it, the American public was well served by such tenacity. "We didn't make any news in Watergate," the white-haired editor said, sliding his thumbs under his suspenders. "President [Richard Nixon] made the news. And I think that's certainly true in the Clinton incidents. . . . I mean, we didn't take up with Monica Lewinsky."

Bradlee sat back and said resolutely, "Where do I draw the line? I draw the line at the truth."

Michael Isikoff would later acknowledge that he faced a difficult situation as a journalist. "Given that I knew what Starr's team had done in taking over the Lewinsky investigation," he said, "I had to move quickly and aggressively. But I also didn't want my reporting to influence what decisions any of the principals made—which in retrospect may have been impossible. It didn't make me popular with the OIC prosecutors when I told them that I had a deadline, and that I was prepared to report their still secret investigation one way or another. But the fact remained that Starr's involvement in this was blockbuster news. I wasn't going to sit on it."

Not everyone agreed that Isikoff deserved an award. Some OIC prosecutors felt that he had been too "aggressive." Lucianne Goldberg, Tripp's literary agent friend, grumbled that "Spikey" had manipulated the situation, and injected himself into events in a way that made him both reporter and subject of the saga. "All along, Michael Isikoff was a player in this story," she complained in a *Slate* piece titled "Spikey's Hypocrisy." "He guarded the story with the ferocity of a mother tiger hovering over the last shard of an impala's bloody haunch."

A number of federal prosecutors and judges, of both political stripes, would privately concur that letting a reporter establish ground rules and set deadlines was a major blunder for both OIC and the Justice Department. The job of federal law enforcement was to fight crime—not to prevent *Newsweek* reporters from contacting sources simply because they might prod Bill Clinton or any other witness to tell the truth.

One federal judge who had a strong Republican résumé and who had served as a state court prosecutor before ascending to the bench said that OIC's decision to allow Isikoff to establish the ground rules backfired terribly. Even if Starr's prosecutors had secretly hoped to punish Clinton for his exploits with the intern and for his lack of truthfulness, it would have been much better to allow Isikoff to publish his story and then permit the national media to have a field day with the scandalous facts. The judge explained: "He [Clinton] would have still faced political heat. But the process would not have been initiated by Starr." Starr was already a political lightning rod; once he planted himself in the middle of this electrical storm, "*he* became the issue as much as Clinton."

Moreover, other observers noted that the reasons that were so urgently presented by Starr's prosecutors to the Reno Justice Department for taking over the

Lewinsky case turned out to be flimsy. The argument that Linda Tripp held great significance as a witness for OIC and, further, that her testimony would be tainted if she were convinced to perjure herself was dramatically overblown. By this point in 1998, the Vince Foster matter had been put to rest. The Travel Office matter was nearly wrapped up; at any rate, Tripp was a minor player in that saga. Tripp herself would later acknowledge that she never had any serious "kinsmanship" with Starr's office. Indeed, she later admitted that when Goldberg suggested that she call OIC, she wasn't even sure if Starr and his office "were still in existence."

Likewise, the argument that Tripp was somehow in danger of being compromised as a government witness was a whopping exaggeration. Tripp had no intention of perjuring herself in the *Jones* case. She had contacted the Jones attorneys in Dallas, personally, to make sure that she disgorged every damning detail of the story about Monica Lewinsky and Bill Clinton the moment she was deposed. Even Paul Rosenzweig, one of Ken Starr's most loyal prosecutors, later admitted that this justification was "something more of an afterthought."

Finally, the concern about the Vernon Jordan connection, while valid on the surface, proved to be a colossal overstatement. OIC had embraced the Jordan story (as told by Linda Tripp) with open arms—largely because the Starr prosecutors wanted to believe it. Tripp herself would admit years later, "I made that a big deal. I mean I did, because to me that was the link to prove the obstruction, to prove the subornation of perjury. . . . I highlighted it as an enormous deal to me." Tripp would profess that it was only because she was a "mechanical midget" that Jordan had escaped his deserved day of reckoning. She explained that she had failed to record a key phone conversation, in which Lewinsky had confessed that Jordan played a role in creating the false affidavit and promised her a job as her payoff, because of a technical screwup. It turned out, said Tripp, that her little black box from RadioShack was only capable of recording calls on the phone to which it was physically attached. When it came to the Jordan conversation, she had taken the call from Lewinsky on an upstairs phone. "Had I recorded or documented what I believed I had," she insisted, "they would have had Vernon Jordan. But I didn't. And they didn't."

Yet the purported Jordan connection turned out to be much ado about nothing, as demonstrated by the scant mention of it in OIC's final report. Even during Lewinsky's extended lunch conversation with Tripp, each word of which was taped by the FBI, nothing implicated Jordan in any wrongdoing.

Finally, Justice Department lawyers felt hoodwinked, if not betrayed, when they learned about OIC's extensive contacts with the Paula Jones camp. Especially alarming was the discovery that Tripp had initially contacted Starr's office after the elves had used one of OIC's own prosecutors (Paul Rosenzweig) as the conduit to gain her access to the office. Why had Jackie Bennett failed to reveal *that* connection during their "urgent" discussions? If more facts had been put on the table, Holder and others felt, they would have asked "some searching questions and likely reached a different decision."

It was on this topic, more than any, that a lack of trust came to infect the relationship between the Justice Department and Starr's operation. The hawks on the OIC team, to the end, would make no apologies about the office's loose association with actors in the *Jones* litigation. "I never had [any] problem with getting stuff from the Jones people," Sol Wisenberg later retorted. "I have no problem if Paula Jones calls up and says, 'Guess what's happening in my case.' I mean, I have no f——ing problem with that as long as it's all revealed." Yet Justice Department officials had several big problems with it. Among other things, if they had been informed about the unholy connection between Starr's team and the Paula Jones forces, they said, this certainly could have tipped the scales in favor of selecting a different independent counsel, regardless of Michael Isikoff's artificial deadline. As one senior DOJ lawyer stated: "We were told the sky would fall." After the dust had settled, "it turned into a tawdry investigation involving oral sex."

Looking back on these events, Deputy Attorney General Holder concluded, recognizing that it was a supreme understatement: "If I knew everything [I know today], and if you could remove that time pressure, I think we would have asked somebody else to look at the case."

Ironically, the Justice Department lawyers ended up walking away from this ugly presidential sex scandal unscathed, while Ken Starr and his prosecutors marched directly into the jaws of the crocodile.

CHAPTER

28

"THE BRACE"

Jackie Bennett would have preferred to chill out for a few days. "Monica didn't know that we had recorded her," he explained. "The White House didn't know any of this." In an ideal world, OIC would have liked to "[sit] back and see what happens. Not do anything that would tip anybody off."

Yet time seemed to be moving in strange directions these days. *Newsweek* didn't hit the newsstands until Monday morning, but rough copies got faxed out over the weekend for use on Sunday morning television shows. Bennett later concluded that Isikoff's "actual deadline" given modern typesetting technology was "probably an awful lot later than he had let on." At the time, though, Bennett was operating on the assumption that the trigger would be pulled on Friday afternoon.

Early Friday morning, Ken Starr "hastened in" to work. The head of DOJ's Public Integrity section, Lee Radek, had walked over to Starr's office accompanied by his deputy, Josh Hochberg.

The group sat around a speakerphone and placed an emergency call to Judge David Sentelle, the federal judge whose three-judge panel had appointed Starr and presided over independent counsel investigations. At approximately 9:30, they reached Sentelle at home—his daughter was having jaw surgery and he had been awaiting a call from the hospital. After hearing a synopsis of the new developments, Sentelle seemed too flabbergasted to frame a question. Starr assured his former judicial colleague that OIC was prepared to accept jurisdiction over the new matter: "We agree with this, and we're willing to take this on." Sentelle finally declared in a thick North Carolina drawl, "I'll need to vet this with my colleagues. Based on what you've told me, I don't know of any impediment."

Initially, the order that Starr's team drafted would have given OIC power to investigate all criminal matters relating to "Monica Lewinsky, Vernon Jordan, and others." They even had kicked around listing President William Jefferson Clinton by name. Lee Radek, however, cautioned against naming the president or *anyone* directly identified with him, insisting that they do this in the "least inflammatory" fashion possible. The final order faxed to Judge Sentelle simply gave Kenneth Starr permission to investigate possible wrongdoing by "Monica Lewinsky or others."

Later that day, Judge Sentelle called back to say that although the order was being kept tightly under seal, Starr's jurisdiction had been expanded. As Jackie Bennett would recall: "By this time, we were well into our preparations for meeting with Monica and confronting her. And trying to enlist her cooperation."

THE so-called planning stage leading up to the sting of Monica Lewinsky—the biggest moment in the history of the Starr investigation—in fact involved little planning at all. Jackie Bennett, in making his pitch to DOJ, had downplayed the significance of President Clinton's upcoming deposition in the *Jones* case. Yet he was acutely aware of that Saturday deadline.

Inside the OIC offices, every lawyer understood that something big was brewing. Bruce Udolf and Mike Emmick, two of the newer additions to the OIC team, volunteered to help "take the president's deposition on this, or put him in the grand jury." Jackie Bennett, large and immovable like a house, replied, "Well, get in line. Because *everyone* around here thinks they should be the one to do it."

Ironically, Mike Emmick was one of the last OIC prosecutors to find out about Linda Tripp's astounding story. A graduate of the University of California at Santa Barbara (a school known for its beautiful beaches and sand volleyball), Emmick had come to OIC from the U.S. attorney's office in Los Angeles, where he was chief of its Public Corruption Section. At Bennett's request, Emmick had left the sun and surf of the West Coast for a year, to assist OIC in its wrap-up mode.

As others were holding secret meetings about the Tripp revelations, Emmick was turning over the last remaining rocks in the Whitewater case and pondering "how to bring Susan McDougal around." He was one of the architects of a last-ditch plan dubbed "The Creative Proposal," which was designed to do the un-thinkable and to give Susan McDougal everything she wanted. Before OIC packed up and shut down its operations, the plan was to throw away the rule book and cave in on all the witness's demands, to see what incriminating evidence she might cough up. OIC hoped to surprise Susan and her lawyer by saying, "We will promise that even if you lie in the grand jury, we won't prosecute you. We'll promise that the questioning will be done by persons outside the Independent Counsel's office." Emmick, the smooth and handsome prosecutor from California, was viewed as the best person to crack through the walls of resistance that Susan had set up, to give it one last shot.

Emmick had only been drawn into the Lewinsky matter out of sheer curiosity. The whole thing, he recalled, had a "gossipy" feel to it. Even by California standards, the notion of catching the president with a young intern was somewhat far-out. "You don't really hear of things like that very often in the real world," he said.

On Thursday night, Emmick had been drifting around the hallway participating in a "migratory meeting" that moved from one doorway to the next. During this bull session, the group concluded that "we really ought to have some sort of an 'approach' where we ask her [Lewinsky] if she would be willing to cooperate in the investigation." Such a function was typically carried out by FBI agents. Yet in Starr's office, prosecutors often performed tasks traditionally performed by the FBI, since OIC was short on agents in Washington. What they needed, Jackie Bennett mused, was a prosecutor who could employ a light, "softballish kind of an approach." Bennett himself was too gruff and intimidating for that.

Mike Emmick was a handsome, blue-eyed, laid-back Californian, who was viewed within the office as a ladies' man. Who better to seduce the presidential seductress? Although Bennett in hindsight concluded that it was "probably a mistake" to lead off with Emmick, Bennett had become distracted by all this jockeying for lead roles. His feeling was, "Work needs to get done." A number of the OIC prosecutors seemed to be staring at Emmick. The California lawyer finally said, "Well, I'll [volunteer]."

Jackie Bennett waved his hand and said, "Go do it." Bennett scratched his chin and added, "Let's do it tomorrow."

It was already pitch-dark outside. If they were going to "brace" or "confront" Monica Lewinsky on Friday, the whole script needed to be written and played out in less than a day—that didn't leave much time for sleep. So Emmick "went into [his] office and closed the door and just sort of thought through, 'Well, what am I going to say? How am I going to say it?' " He put on his "FBI agent hat," trying to figure out what the most experienced, sophisticated agent would do in his shoes.

The California lawyer soon began "plunking away" at his computer, "trying out different approaches, things to say, things not to say." Emmick had never executed this kind of brace. So he decided to sketch out a written plan, to give himself a detailed road map.

"The approach that we were envisioning," he recalled, "was a discussion that would last, I guess, fifteen to twenty minutes." The plan was to "explain to her [Lewinsky] what the situation was." Emmick intended to sit down calmly with the young woman and say, " 'We've spoken to Tripp. We understand that you and the president had some kind of an affair, that you filed something in which you denied that there was such an affair, that the president was planning to do the same thing, that there was some sort of agreement between you to continue to deny this, and we would like to speak with you about it.' "

After the young woman had time to digest the seriousness of the situation, Emmick would calmly explain that their investigation "has been approved by the Department of Justice." Lewinsky would then have to decide whether or not to cooperate. The California prosecutor would make sure that Lewinsky understood she would receive "credit" for any information she provided. Emmick was thinking, as he typed up his plan, "She could either just give us a debriefing about the situation. Or she could affirmatively go out and act, be wired on telephone calls, things like that, if she wanted to."

The more Monica Lewinsky did to assist OIC in catching the bigger fish, the more "credit" she would receive. "But that was going to be left in her hands."

Emmick's fingers were becoming tired and hitting incorrect keys as he typed. When he squeezed his eyes shut for a brief rest, Emmick had trouble envisioning exactly how the brace would begin and end. "I had a great deal of apprehension," he later admitted. He knew that this was "something that would come under great scrutiny later." Consequently, he "wanted to make very sure that nothing was done that was done inappropriately."

As Emmick fiddled with his script, Jackie Bennett stuck his head into the office. According to the information they had received from Linda Tripp, he told Emmick, a lawyer named Frank Carter had represented Monica Lewinsky in drafting the *Paula Jones* affidavit. Bennett asked, "Does this raise any issues relating to 'contacts' with represented persons?"

Emmick was the resident expert on this subject; he had made presentations for DOJ on the issue of "contacting" witnesses who were already represented by counsel. Emmick chewed over Bennett's question for "five or ten seconds" as if responding to a pop quiz in law school. Then he gave a quickie analysis: "No," Emmick said. "This is preindictment, and under the DOJ regulations relating to contacts, preindictment contacts are okay." More importantly, he stated, Frank Carter had nothing to do with this particular criminal case. Carter had drafted an affidavit for Lewinsky in the *Jones* case. "Carter's not our opposing counsel," Emmick said, chewing on his pen. "He only represents her in the civil case."

Bennett nodded and sauntered back to his office.

In that thirty-second exchange, OIC had made one of its most crucial decisions in the sting of Monica Lewinsky. It was almost certainly a legal assessment that was ill advised.

Emmick later pieced together how events transpired that night: "I don't actually have very much recollection of Ken [Starr] being involved at all. I also don't have much recollection of anybody being in charge. I know that Jackie was the head of the office, and I had some meetings with Jackie, but the office at that time was more or less not a traditionally organized kind of place." Each person had his or her own projects, which evolved in a fluid way. It was not, Emmick said frankly, "a top-down sort of organizational structure."

For the rest of the night, as grogginess and dreams of a long, leisurely sleep competed for his attention, Mike Emmick sat alone in his office, typing away and asking himself, as another part of his brain reassured him there was no reason to be nervous: "Well, what am I going to say? How am I going to say it?"

———

On Friday morning, clusters of OIC prosecutors and FBI agents buzzed around the office. Josh Hochberg from DOJ stopped by Emmick's office and raised, for a second time, a concern that Monica Lewinsky "has an attorney. What's your thinking on that?" Emmick ticked through his analysis of the previous night. Hochberg did not overrule or countermand OIC. He just listened.

In hindsight, Emmick would come to admit that the entire plan "wasn't gamed out nearly as much as we might have hoped." Among other things, it was a gross miscalculation to assume that this "was going to be a very brief kind of a presentation," after which Lewinsky would simply roll over and cooperate fully with OIC. Looking back on it, Emmick would marvel at his own naïveté in believing that this confrontation with Monica Lewinsky, over an affair with Bill

Clinton that could destroy Clinton's presidency, would be wrapped up neatly in a fifteen-minute exchange.

As events played out, he confessed, it took considerably longer. "Oh, it did," Emmick repeated with an exhausted sigh.

As Emmick was getting ready to depart for the Pentagon City Mall—where Linda Tripp had arranged to meet with Monica Lewinsky—he peered down the hallway and saw a group of prosecutors congregating around Ken Starr's office. Feeling somewhat cranky, Emmick thought to himself, "Gosh, here I am about to go talk with this person, and I'm not even at the meetings." So Emmick strode down the hall, his mind still ticking through the possible complications that could arise once he confronted his quarry. One thing that he had been worrying about was that Ms. Lewinsky might know enough to say, "Gosh, am I going to get prosecuted? Shouldn't I get immunity?" What was his response going to be to that simple question? Emmick decided to put it directly to his boss. He pulled Ken Starr aside and spoke in a confidential tone: "One of the things that may happen is that she may insist on immunity," he said. "So what should we do? Do we have the authority to try to handle this on an ad hoc basis, based on what the views of the people there are?" According to Emmick's distinct recollection, Starr said, "Yes, I'll just have to leave it to the people who are there." Emmick thought to himself, "Oh, that's good." One of the things that the office had become known for was its "long, protracted discussions about everything under the sun, and it was nice to have that preauthorization."

With that loose end tied up, Emmick gathered his notes and swung by Bruce Udolf's office. Udolf had volunteered to ride over with him to the Ritz-Carlton Hotel in the Pentagon City complex, where the FBI had set up its base of operations. The two lawyers took their time summoning an elevator and hailing a cab on the street level. As the cab pulled away, Emmick stared out the window, feeling as if he had been dropped into a fish tank. He told his partner that they needed to be "really, really, really, *really*" careful that they did everything by the book. They couldn't be accused of any ethical impropriety "because this is going to be scrutinized out the wazoo by everybody under the sun." They would have to act like two well-scrubbed altar boys. "We have to be the nicest people in town," Emmick said to his partner, laughing uncomfortably.

As the cab sped toward the Pentagon City Mall, the two prosecutors settled back into their seats and nodded to each other. On this point, they were in "complete agreement."

———

LINDA Tripp had called Monica Lewinsky on her cell phone that morning with news that sounded too good to be true. She had told her young former coworker that she planned to meet with her new attorney later that day to draft an affidavit for the *Jones* case and that this would resolve all their problems. Tripp said that she would like to meet with Monica to talk about specifics—what should she say in this affidavit to be most effective? Monica had become "somewhat distrustful" of Tripp. Yet now there seemed to be a ray of hope; maybe her older friend would actually keep mum about her affair with Clinton—finally, a break! Monica had just finished working out at the gym and was "doing errands." Tripp had called to say she was running late; the meeting time had been pushed back to 12:45. As Tripp rode down the escalator and the two women walked toward one another, each displayed a smile hiding an ongoing plan to deceive the other.

Tripp, dressed in a sober brown business suit, glanced nervously over her shoulder as she greeted Monica. Two men wearing dark suits immediately appeared and flashed badges, identifying themselves as FBI agents. One agent told the former intern in a firm voice that they had been authorized by the attorney general "to investigate crimes committed in relation to the *Paula Jones* lawsuit." The other agent added, according to Lewinsky's account, "Ma'am, you are in serious trouble."

Linda Tripp tried to give Monica a half-hug. She said in a throaty voice, "Monica, this is for your own good. Just listen to them. They did the same thing to me."

Monica burst into tears. The agents—Steve Irons and Pat Fallon—said something like, "We just want to talk to you. You are free to leave when you want." There was a brief exchange in which Monica uttered something about talking to her attorney. To this, the agents replied, "That's fine. But if you do that, you may not be able to help yourself so much." They suggested that Lewinsky accompany them upstairs. They had secured a quiet room in the Ritz-Carlton Hotel, where she could evaluate whether to cooperate with OIC before doing anything rash.

Years later, although discussing this topic "opened the wound up" again, Monica explained why she went along with the FBI. First, she recalled, she did not feel that she had any options: "When I said that I wasn't going to talk to them without my attorney they said that was fine . . . [but] I wouldn't be able to help myself as much. To somebody who doesn't know very much about the law, the implication there is that it's not a good idea to have a lawyer there."

Additionally, Lewinsky concluded that she might be able to *protect* the president, if she heard these people out and reasoned with them. She later acknowledged, with a hitch of reluctance, "For me, who was also crazy in love, trying to protect somebody, I had this unrealistic notion of, well, 'Okay, I have to go in there and I have to find out what's going on. I have to fix this.' Which somehow, of course, was impossible."

The FBI had set up its operations inside two adjoining rooms in the Ritz-Carlton. Mike Emmick stood waiting in Room 1012, a standard hotel room with a queen-sized bed and matching dresser. He recalled that "there were a lot more people in the room than I expected." According to the plan that Emmick thought he had mapped out, he would be the "talker" or "presenter." He placed his little sheet of notes on a dresser and "sort of went through in my mind what I was going to say and how I was going to say it, and just tried to be careful with my words, because I just wanted to make sure that everything went right."

The agents began whispering, "They're coming, they're coming!" Peering through the doorway, Emmick could see several dark-suited FBI agents huddled around a young woman, approximately five feet six and wearing black spandex pants. He purposely had reviewed grainy surveillance pictures of Lewinsky that the FBI had taken during her lunch with Tripp, so that he would not look surprised when he met her.

The FBI agents escorted the young woman inside, sitting her down on a chair. Emmick noticed that among the entourage that had entered was Linda Tripp. He cursed to himself: What in God's name was Tripp doing here? This wasn't part of the plan *he* had mapped out. The prosecutor did some "deep-breathing exercises." He wanted to make sure that he set "the right tone, the right mood." Dressed in a trim blue suit, Emmick strode into the adjoining room. He remembered sensing that the scene felt wrong. FBI agents were flanking the black-haired young woman, as if "somebody has been brought in for an audience with the king." This was not, he recalled thinking, "the perception that I wanted, at all."

The immediate reaction of the OIC prosecutor, as he walked up to the twenty-three-year-old woman, was one of astonishment. She appeared, in her black spandex exercise pants and oversized fleece sweatshirt, as if she had just finished "working out" at the gym. She wore no makeup, her jet black hair was untidy, and "she looked a little disheveled." Most of all, it struck Emmick that Lewinsky "looked quite young." He had certainly been aware of her age, but he wasn't prepared to see someone who reminded him of a fresh-faced college student. On all counts, the pieces didn't appear to fit together.

Emmick later would recall, "And one of my reactions was, 'Gosh, this just doesn't seem right. How could it be that this is a person who had an affair with the president of the United States?' " In fact, that reaction was so strong that the California prosecutor began to suspect "that she had made it all up."

Monica Lewinsky, on the other hand, knew the truth and understood that this was a potentially disastrous situation. As Emmick was assessing whether the young woman had fantasized the entire story, Monica was staring at the large sliding glass windows of the tenth-floor hotel room and debating whether to throw herself out onto the pavement below. She opened and closed her fist, trying to assess her options.

It was now time for Emmick to give the speech that he had been preparing for eighteen hours. He sat in the chair across from Lewinsky and began: "My name's Mike Emmick. . . . I'm with the Office of Independent Counsel. We've been authorized to conduct an investigation of suspected perjury and obstruction of justice in connection with the *Paula Jones* lawsuit."

The FBI agents began cutting in with their own commentary. Emmick was floored. He thought the agents would bring the young woman up and leave the speech-making to him. He would "ask for her [Lewinsky's] cooperation, she was going to say yea or nay, and it was going to be done." It soon became clear that the FBI agents had a different conception, said Emmick. "They thought it was going to be more agent-centric," while Emmick believed "it was going to be more attorney-centric." That, he confessed, "is a sign of bad planning."

Linda Tripp was still in the room, which was driving Emmick crazy. Monica kept glowering at Tripp as if she were Judas Iscariot, who had betrayed her for a fistful of silver. At one point, Monica stared at Tripp and hissed, "Make her stay and watch. I want that treacherous bitch to see what she has done to me." Monica would later tell her biographer, Andrew Morton, "I wanted to hurt her. I felt like an animal wanting to claw at her skin." Since witnesses clawing at each other's skin would certainly distract from the mission at hand, Emmick motioned for the FBI to remove Tripp to the adjoining room. He then continued his speech as rehearsed: "Your conduct could constitute one of several different kinds of crimes," he said. "The crimes are felonies; felonies have five-year maximums."

According to Monica's account, the prosecutor also stated more than once: "You could spend up to twenty-seven years in jail."

At some point in the speech, Monica completely broke down. "In fact, 'wailing' is not too strong [a word] I don't think," said Emmick. "I mean, my impression was she was just completely overwhelmed by everything that was happening." The young woman began crying out, "My life is ruined. Who's going to marry me after this?" At one point, Monica stared at the window and gasped, "All this will go away if I just kill myself." She had spent the past months worrying about her broken relationship with Clinton and desperately assessing whether anything could be salvaged of it. Next, the *Paula Jones* subpoena had arrived to knock her deeper into a black hole. Now this?

Monica would recall a host of disjointed thoughts crowding her mind. Foremost among these was, "I can't believe this has happened." How could she be sitting in this hotel room, surrounded by all these FBI agents with badges and weapons and so many prosecutors from Ken Starr's office? She had always assumed that by having an affair with a married man who happened to be the president of the United States, she always faced the possibility that something would go wrong—she might one day wake up and see her picture on the cover of a tabloid magazine, humiliating her family and hurting Hillary and Chelsea

Clinton. But even during the craziest moments obsessing about the dysfunctional relationship in which she had entangled herself, she never dreamed that she might end up with *this*—a group of federal prosecutors and FBI agents telling her she might go to jail for a quarter century. For Lewinsky, the balloon had popped and "all the air was coming out. . . . I was flipped out and in shock and somewhat suicidal. And at the same time, trying to figure out how to get myself out of this. And knowing that what they were saying they wanted me to do, I couldn't do."

As Mike Emmick clasped his hands together, trying to figure out how to deal with this emotionally overwrought young woman, he felt completely stymied. "She just cried and cried and cried," recalled Emmick. "And I admit, we should have anticipated this much more. We were completely floored by that. I mean, she was very loud, and people were even concerned that people walking down the hall would hear and wouldn't know how to interpret it. She didn't seem to be able to stop herself from crying." Emmick remembered feeling absolutely helpless, "sort of like a bunch of men standing around with a baby that needs changing. We just looked around at each other and, 'What do we do? This is not part of the game plan.'"

One FBI agent fetched Monica a glass of water. Another appeared with tissues from the bathroom. "And we tried to calm her down as best we could," recalled the California prosecutor.

Monica lost it again when the FBI pulled out a copy of her affidavit in the *Jones* case—an affidavit that had not yet been filed. In addressing one of the great riddles of that day—where did the affidavit come from?—Emmick would later reply, "We don't know. It came across a fax machine." The prosecutors were able to reconstruct that the fax originated in the building where Jim Moody, Linda Tripp's new attorney, maintained his offices. Said Emmick: "As odd as it seems, I don't think I saw it before confronting Ms. Lewinsky with it in the Ritz-Carlton." Nor was he aware that the document had not yet been filed: "We assumed that it had been filed because when you see something that has come across the fax machine, it looks legit."

Monica alternately cried and composed herself. Emmick tried to use his best college psychology, telling the woman that she was free to get up and walk out "any time she wanted to." To this, Monica replied, "No, no, I'll be okay. I want to hear more. . . . I have some questions." Although at times she looked as if an eighteen-wheeler had just run over her, Emmick noticed that Monica was capable of "completely composing herself, and then asking rational, sensible questions and having some interaction with us."

In reconstructing that difficult day, Monica admitted that Mike Emmick had "laid out the options" and told her that she could "leave at any time."

Nonetheless, the former intern said, "In my book, he lied. They were all liars in there. And they were manipulators."

For one, Lewinsky believed that leaving was not a realistic option. Agent Fallon had "accidentally" shown her his set of handcuffs. He had also flashed his gun. When she asked if the gun was loaded, Monica recalled vividly, "[Fallon] replied 'yes' and asked me if it made me uncomfortable. . . . So I don't know why somebody would think that they were really free to leave without there being consequences."

Monica would later explain: "If you're in a castle and there's a moat around you with sharks and someone says 'You're free to go whenever you want'—well, that's great, but 'How the hell do I get out of here?' "

Moreover, Starr's team seemed bent on getting her to do their dirty work. The former intern would insist that Emmick told her that if she cooperated, they would expect her to make some phone calls that they would tape-record, and maybe "put on a body wire and go and talk to Betty Currie, Vernon Jordan, and possibly even the president." She was adamant that she would not be a stool pigeon. "Nobody was going to get me to wear a wire," she later said. "I can tell you that. If threatening my mom and ultimately a few days later threatening my dad, too, wasn't going to get me to do that, nobody was going to get me to do that." Surreptitiously recording phone calls, as far as she was concerned, simply was "not in my being." She added sarcastically, "Nothing against Linda Tripp."

Indeed, Monica said that she had a sharp recollection of the discussion about wearing a body wire, because it caused her to concoct a crazy plan: What if she agreed to wire herself and visit Vernon Jordan's office, then "tried to mess it up on purpose" by blurting out something that would tip off Jordan? She thought to herself: "Well, maybe I should do that and then I won't get in trouble." Monica even tested out this idea with one of the agents, asking innocently: "Well what if I mess up . . . because I'm so nervous?"

Emmick, for his part, would insist that—whatever might have been said of wiring Monica—there was never any mention of trying to get her to tape-record President Clinton. This option had been openly discussed during their planning stage, and OIC prosecutors had agreed "that's an awfully big step. It wasn't even clear that the president was even speaking to Monica at this point, so sending her into the Oval Office wired wasn't practical." Even when it came to taping Jordan, the OIC prosecutors felt that he was likely "too cagey a fellow for anything like that to work," said Emmick. "The only real possibility we thought was maybe something with Betty Currie."

There was also the ongoing dispute as to whether OIC and the FBI were actively dissuading their witness from contacting her attorney. Early in the colloquy, Monica had asked, "Should I have a lawyer?" She specifically mentioned to

Starr's team that she had retained Frank Carter to draft her affidavit in the *Jones* case. Emmick said to her, "If you want a lawyer, you can get a lawyer." But he added, "Obviously, it's better that the fewer people know [the better] if you're going to decide to go the undercover route." Emmick was thinking, first, that it would jeopardize Monica's ability to get wired and cooperate if Carter was reporting to Vernon Jordan. The word might ricochet back to the White House within hours, and any plan to use Monica as a cooperating informant would be foiled. Second, the thought crossed Emmick's mind that Monica might even try "to hire Vernon Jordan as her [own] lawyer" as a subterfuge. One way or another, if Jordan or Carter was in the mix, Monica could telegraph to the president that he had been caught red-handed, allowing Clinton to wriggle out of danger.

Yet Monica would dismiss this as prosecutorial double-talk. She later insisted that she "continually asked for my attorney." Her proof was simple: "So if I was allowed to call a lawyer, why didn't I? Period. End of story. I'm not that stupid."

She continued, starting to become agitated: "I said, 'I want to call my attorney.' And Frank Carter was the only attorney who represented me—for anything. I was twenty-four; I had never had an attorney before." Monica also noted that OIC was threatening to prosecute her on the basis of the very "affidavit that I signed that he [Frank Carter] wrote." How could Carter *not* be her lawyer for this purpose?

These same questions concerning OIC's brace of Monica Lewinsky at the Ritz-Carlton would later prompt concerns about the conduct of OIC itself, sparking an internal Justice Department investigation of Ken Starr's office, that in turn produced some surprising conclusions that were never made public.

At the time, Monica simply knew that all of this pressure was causing her to crack. As she burst into a jag of "crying and consoling," plowing through Kleenex tissues to wipe her eyes and face, she received a page on her cell phone from her mother. Given her predicament, Monica ignored it. Instead, she excused herself to use the bathroom in the hotel room because [she told the Starr team] she was "having stomach problems." The FBI asked her to empty her pockets and remove her phone before she used the lavatory.

Some colleagues at OIC, during this intermission, suggested to Emmick that he needed to tell Lewinsky that they were "prepared to arrest her." Yet Emmick still didn't think that was "an advisable approach." Instead, when Monica returned from the bathroom he handed her fresh Kleenex tissues and waited for divine inspiration.

Ken Starr, in the meantime, was ensconced in the OIC office getting regular updates from Jackie Bennett. As Starr viewed the field operation, "it was a law enforcement activity, investigation procedure under way, and we would be advised when there were material matters to report. But we weren't in radio contact or open telephone line contact or anything of the sort." Emmick, to the extent that he was going to "flip" this key witness in a single encounter, would have to do it through his own prosecutorial ingenuity.

Monica sat down on the bed, demanded her phone back, and declared, "I just can't make a decision like this on my own. I need to talk to my mom." She and her mother, she told her inquisitors, spoke several times daily. If she didn't return the pages, her mother would suspect something was amiss. The OIC lawyers and FBI agents caucused; it was now time to bring in the reserves. They needed a "sort of a gray-haired-looking guy to turn things around." If Jackie Bennett appeared on the scene, Emmick decided, "maybe that will force her— not force, 'force' is too strong—but sort of break the logjam."

So Starr's chief deputy was summoned to the Ritz-Carlton to take a more direct approach. "She's digging in," Bruce Udolf told Bennett as he entered the suite. "It's not going well," Irons told the burly deputy, pulling him aside. Bennett felt that the OIC prosecutors "were being much too gentle with her. Much too solicitous, and that was sending the wrong signal. And she was starting to play us a little bit."

Bennett was six foot three and weighed 235 pounds. He looked the part of a tough prosecutor. The moment he arrived, Monica said, "the energy in the room changed." As she looked at this large man hulking over her, she perceived someone who was "gruff-looking," who reminded her of a villain "from the Bugs Bunny cartoons." Everything now seemed "stern and heavy." Monica felt the plan was a transparent one: "Emmick was the good cop. So they sent the good cop in, until they sent Jackie Bennett (the bad cop) in. And he lied, too."

Bennett sat down and looked over this young woman—her spandex workout pants, her unkempt hair, her legs akimbo as she sat on the chair beside the bed. The top prosecutor raised an eyebrow. His candid opinion was that "she was a mess." It was now nearly five o'clock in the afternoon. OIC still hadn't "signed her up," which troubled Bennett. He told Monica, "We just need to make a decision here." When the woman began another round of crying and again asked to talk to her mother, Bennett's face grew dark. "We're not going to sugarcoat it, Monica," he said in a deep voice. "This is serious." Monica later asserted that Bennett added gruffly, "Look, Monica, you're smart, you're twenty-four years old—you don't need to call your mommy." She also contended the prosecutor threatened to prosecute her mother "for actions you [described] on the tapes." Bennett disagreed: "I don't remember it that way. But I did say words to the effect, 'Look, you're an adult. You're a grown-up. You did this. Your mother didn't do this. You've got to deal with this. . . .'" Bennett would add, "What has been referred to in portraying me as this bully is still substantively correct. I mean, that is the gist of what I said. 'You did this; you're going to have to deal with this.' "

Monica found Bennett to be "condescending." She was so rattled by his insinuations that her whole family might be in jeopardy that she became even more insistent that she be permitted to call her mother. "I promise I won't blurt anything. I promise I won't do anything to compromise [your investigation]," she told Bennett. "But please let me call." Bennett finally threw up his hands and relented—on condition that the former intern make the call *very* short. She could let her mother know that she was fine—but that was it. As Monica dialed the number, Agent Fallon sat on the edge of the bed with his hand hovering above the phone, ready to hang up if she tried anything improper. Bennett would later say, "It was silly, but we didn't trust her. And we were right not to trust her."

The young woman spoke hurriedly into the receiver. "I can't talk," she told her mother. "I'll call you later." With that temporary bandage applied, Monica sat back in a chair and crossed her arms. Bennett concluded, "She's stringing us out at this point." He got up, shooting a disapproving look at the young woman in purple workout clothes, and walked out the door.

Bennett was not the only one losing his patience. Most of the OIC lawyers and FBI agents had come to the conclusion that Lewinsky was "purposely dragging this out." She was "stalling for time." Lewinsky would later respond angrily: "That is absolutely despicable to me. That is so disgusting. I can't even tell you." She composed herself as she remembered these events before lashing out further: "It's appalling to me because I was sitting there and I was thinking about trying to jump out the f——ing window. And it's like, what's happening has just changed my life and ruined my life." She continued for the record: "I wasn't stalling for time. You have to remember *they're* the ones [the OIC prosecutors] who were saying there was a time limit. I had no idea about Michael Isikoff." On top of that, it was preposterous that she would drag her feet so that she could "stay in the room any longer than necessary."

Emmick was running out of ideas. He whispered to his fellow prosecutors and FBI agents, "What do we do now?" Monica was getting more insistent, proclaiming, "If you're not going to let me call my mom [for a longer conversation], I guess I just have to be leaning toward not cooperating." Finally, Emmick surrendered. He told the young woman that she could go downstairs to make the call on a pay phone (she was positive the hotel phone was bugged) to put an end to this standoff.

Down in the Pentagon City Mall, which was filled with end-of-the-workweek shoppers, Lewinsky searched for a phone as far away from the common bank of telephones as possible, fearful that they were all being tapped by the feds.

As she prowled the halls of the glitzy mall, Lewinsky ran into Linda Tripp, who was carrying a pile of shopping bags. Monica kept a distance and snarled at her former friend, "Thanks a lot!" Tripp replied, "They did the same thing to me."

Monica later admitted that if the opportunity had presented itself, "I would have tried to kill her."

Indeed, the young woman might have done even worse if she had known that after finishing her shopping at the mall, Tripp was headed home on an express bus to Maryland to meet with Paula Jones's Dallas lawyer, to supply him with ammunition for the president's deposition the following day. At the time, Tripp feigned total ignorance as to what was going on.

When Monica found a phone that she deemed safe, she dialed her mother's number, her hands trembling. Marcia Lewis would remember: "She [Monica] was crying and gasping for breath and I just couldn't understand, and I obviously knew something terrible had happened. I thought it was an accident . . . that's what I thought."

Monica finally choked out the words: "The FBI has me; it has to do with the affidavit and Linda Tripp." She later admitted, "I was hysterical."

The bracing of Monica Lewinsky, and the complications that sprung from it, was one monkey that OIC would never get off its back. As much as the events of this day and night would haunt Monica Lewinsky and her family, they would also haunt OIC, leaving unanswered questions about its handling of the Lewinsky sting on which its whole case against Bill Clinton was built. These uncomfortable secrets about OIC's conduct would be locked in a government archive for a decade. But they would not be lost altogether.

CHAPTER

29

THE AVUNCULAR MR. GINSBURG

Upstairs in Room 1012, the prosecutors and FBI agents were taking bets on whether Lewinsky "was really going to come back." To their surprise, the former intern reappeared, reporting that she had made contact with her mother, who was "freaked out" when she learned of this god-awful predicament. Her mother, Monica said with tears welling, wanted to speak with the feds directly. By this point, Emmick was starting to feel punch-drunk from tiredness. He concluded that if the mother was going to help get a decision made, what the hell?

So he dialed Marcia Lewis's number and spoke into the phone: "We have your daughter, and she's in trouble and we need her to cooperate." Monica's mother recalled feeling as if she had received an injection of some crazy, mind-altering drug. She could discern that Monica's situation had something to do with the *Paula Jones* case and that Kenneth Starr and the FBI were involved. Other than that, the words were a blur of indistinguishable vowels and consonants. From the tone of the man's voice and from the sound of her daughter sobbing in the background, all Marcia could tell was that this "was not a joke."

Monica's mother told the prosecutor, "Please don't do anything; I'm coming." There was a train leaving New York for Washington at 5:00, she said. She would be on it. In response to later assertions that she was intentionally taking the slowest means of transportation in order to buy time, Marcia Lewis would react with incredulity: "I had an absolute sort of primeval mother response." Her only thought was, "They have my child; I'm going to go get her. It was that basic. I had no sophisticated understanding of why this would even be happening. Couldn't have told you at that time. Couldn't have begun to understand." Monica's mother dismissed the notion that she had *any* plan whatsoever. "No, I wish that I had been that sophisticated or that clever. I was very fearful, and my goal was to rescue my child, and I couldn't have begun to imagine where I was going and what I would find there."

With her mother en route, Monica now revisited the topic of calling Frank Carter. Mike Emmick, pacing the floor, was still not enthusiastic about the notion. "We thought that his allegiance to Jordan might be very substantial," he later explained, "and we didn't know that he had any criminal background at all." Still, he didn't want to "disparage" Carter in any way. So when Irons began talking down Carter in front of Monica, Emmick "shot a look" at Irons, telegraphing that he should "shut up."

The FBI finally called Carter's office at 5:23 P.M. The OIC lawyers were still not sure what they would say if Carter got on the phone—fortunately for them, the answering service reported that he had left for the evening. Without identifying who he was, Fallon asked how they might reach Mr. Carter if the need arose. The operator reported that the service could reach him at any time if there was an emergency. Jackie Bennett, still in the adjoining room, felt encouraged that his agents had reached out to this problematic attorney; now, this duty was discharged. With that, Starr's team offered Monica the phone number for the public defender and Legal Aid Society in case she felt compelled to contact a new lawyer.

Monica was fearful—not just about what might happen to her, but also about what the Starr prosecutors might do to her mother. From snippets of conversation, she could discern that Linda Tripp must have told OIC that Monica's mother had offered her a piece of her condo in Australia if Tripp would vanish before the *Paula Jones* deposition. The agents and prosecutors were clearly suspicious that her mother was "not only knowledgeable about the affair, but was somehow involved in the whole process of trying to keep this secret and to try to keep Tripp quiet." The young woman began pressing Emmick: If she "cooperated," what benefit would she and her family gain? The prosecutor perked up and said that OIC would ask the judge to "give her a lesser sentence." Monica responded, "That's not a guarantee. I could still go to jail. I could still be a felon and my life could still be ruined."

Emmick now excused himself to talk it over with Bruce Udolf and the other OIC lawyers. He said, "Gosh, maybe the way to break through this logjam is just offer her immunity." The consensus was, "Why not?" Emmick recalled that he was "looking down at [his own] feet" and thinking to himself, "Here I am, looking at the feet of these people and the feet are looking at me, and we're talking about these big, humongous events and it just seems really bizarre."

Udolf would later reveal that, although Monica may not have known it, she was holding the trump card. In 2007, Udolf broke his nine-year silence. He had returned to law practice in Miami after having been ostracized from Starr's prosecutors because he was viewed as an apostate. "I never viewed her as a realistic target for indictment," Udolf said. "She [Monica] was in the catbird seat and didn't know it. We needed her cooperation and that could easily be obtained by granting her immunity. The only reason to indict her would be to have a show trial or to tee the case up for an impeachment trial—neither of which would be an appropriate use of the grand jury process. It just wasn't going to happen if we had any say in the matter."

Emmick later acknowledged that the decision to offer Monica immunity was made rather impulsively, after their original plan unraveled. He and Udolf believed Ken Starr had expressly given them the go-ahead to make this decision. "So we just decided 'okay,' and shrugged our shoulders and I went off and offered her a nonprosecution," said Emmick.

Monica Lewinsky sat in her chair and chewed on her lip, mulling over the offer. She finally asked, "What about my mom?" Without further deliberation, Emmick volunteered, "Yes, we'll promise not to prosecute your mother as well." His logic was simple: "Frankly, we're not that interested in Mom, anyway, but also, we just wanted her to make up her mind."

Monica said that the offer sounded attractive. But, she added, "I still have to talk to my mom." Emmick did not write this off as a bluff: "My impression was that the house of cards had fallen down and her world was coming apart." He was reassured by the fact that when Monica was not crying, she was able to compose herself, ask "sensible questions," and "she seemed very smart." He remained hopeful that if they waited her out, she might conclude that it was in her best interest (and that of her family) to cooperate.

Evidence now reveals that the FBI did take steps to prepare to wire Monica if that option presented itself. Back at the office, Jackie Bennett received a call from Agent Irons, directing him to locate a gray briefcase under a table. The case contained recording equipment. Bennett recalled thinking to himself, "Oh, we've made some headway. . . . Maybe she [Monica] is going to call Betty [Currie]." He asked Irons, "Is she going to come around?" The agent replied, "We want to have that on hand." The signs appeared hopeful.

Yet Bennett had new problems, as he dug around looking for the recording equipment. Michael Isikoff was calling repeatedly and asking, "What's going on?" Bennett had held the reporter off by giving him little driblets of information without spilling the whole pot of soup. He told Isikoff that Monica "hasn't ruled out cooperating, but she needs to consult with somebody." The reporter parried, "Who is that person?" When Bennett refused to answer, Isikoff pressed, "It's her mother, right?" Starr's deputy thundered, "Mike, I can't say. But it's going to take some time and we know now to a certainty that she's going to talk to somebody. And that conversation cannot take place really until late this evening. And so you have got to pledge you're not going to [leak] this. Okay?"

Bennett knew that he was allowing himself to become engaged in a "very unholy alliance." Yet at this late stage there was no turning back. Isikoff grudgingly agreed to leave the prosecutor alone. But he wanted details *soon*. "First thing in the morning," the *Newsweek* reporter warned Bennett.

The weary group in the hotel room passed the time by watching television reruns. Monica tried to ease her own tension by telling "some kind of [mildly] dirty joke." Emmick screwed up his face and said, "You know, maybe under the circumstances we shouldn't be getting into areas like that."

Finally, Monica said that she was feeling claustrophobic. She gulped down air and asked, "Can't we just go out and take a walk somewhere?" She would later say that she was overcome by a "suffocating feeling," knowing that her mother was on a train and "knowing I had three more hours with these people." Her sense of panic also flowed from "knowing I had screwed up. I had caused all this trouble." So she convinced Emmick and Fallon to take her down to the Pentagon City Mall, to get some fresh mall air.

At the Crate and Barrel store, Monica tried to act friendly and to "humanize" herself so that her captors would like her. She began examining household goods as Emmick shuffled his feet because he was "not much of a shopper." The young woman then veered in the direction of Macy's, saying that she needed to use the bathroom. Agent Fallon whispered to Emmick that they needed to follow her. The prosecutor shook his head: "No, no, no. It's unnecessary. We told her she can leave any time she wants, anyway." Emmick worried about treating the former intern as if she were in custody—that would trigger additional messy legal issues. So the two men hovered near the entrance while Monica hustled up to Macy's and disappeared. Twenty minutes later, she returned.

In that time, it turned out that Monica had made a frantic call to Betty Currie, but had been unable to reach the president's secretary. Jackie Bennett later chastised Monica for this breach of trust. Monica, on the other hand, pointed out that she owned up to this from the start and expressed no remorse for trying to thwart OIC's plans to nail the president. She admitted, without compunction, that she called Currie knowing *full* well what she was doing. "Betty was the only one that I knew that I could call for two seconds," she explained, "and say something cryptically that I knew would get to him [President Clinton]." Her only regret was that Currie did not answer the phone so that OIC's plan would be foiled.

The threesome went to Mozzarella's American Grill for a light dinner, having "pretty much exhausted all the small talk." As they got up to leave, Emmick and Fallon offered to pay the check, but Monica pulled out her wallet and covered her own tab. Emmick thought to himself, "This does not bode well for the ultimate cooperation decision. She certainly is not viewing herself as one of us."

Back at the hotel room, the prosecutors learned that Marcia Lewis had called to report that her train had been delayed. Now Starr's office was losing its cool—both mother and daughter, they were convinced, were playing them for dupes. Starr himself, who had repaired to his home, where he was receiving periodic briefings from Bennett, was skeptical of the whole mother-daughter sob story. Monica Lewinsky "was playing Hamlet," he felt. She was also getting "extension after extension after extension." They were extremely leery of her mother's convenient excuse: " 'I never fly. I only take trains.' " Starr would state bluntly: "I find it difficult to believe that she [Marcia Lewis] travels from Los Angeles to New York by train or Greyhound or Oldsmobile Aurora. I think it was all buying time. She was buying time. The FBI viewed us as being soft. She was playing us like a fiddle."

Monica responded to this charge with a swift counter-jab: "They should have gone to look at the records of how many times my mom had flown from New York to D.C. They would see that she normally took the train. Because she doesn't like to fly. She has a bad back." For Lewinsky, this sort of paranoid thinking only confirmed that Starr's office was predisposed to assume the worst, demonstrating that these prosecutors were on a mission to nail Clinton, whatever it took.

Bennett had become famished. He rounded up a few other prosecutors from the OIC offices and located a pizza joint across from the Ritz-Carlton, where they could have dinner and wait in vigil. The group, by this point, was consumed with wildly conflicting emotions. "We all had high hopes going into this that we would be able to enlist [Lewinsky]," Bennett explained. "And it was kind of—your head tells you one thing, your heart tells you another." If the prosecutors had taken a dose of truth serum, they would have admitted they had a strong sense that "it wasn't going to happen." On the other hand, said Bennett, "you really, really wanted it to happen. And you invested so much in preparing your best approach to try to make it happen."

These clashing emotions led to "increasing frustration" within the OIC ranks, accompanied by "a little bit of backbiting." Bennett learned during his pepperoni-pizza dinner that Emmick "had essentially agreed not to prosecute [Lewinsky]," something that added to his heartburn. Bennett would later say, "I was angry about that. Because we hadn't vetted it."

Among the hard-liners, which included Bennett and most of the Starr team who had started out together in Arkansas, there was a creeping sense that the new "Democrats" in the office were trying to sabotage their operation. It was clear that Emmick, Udolf, and Mary Anne Wirth were hostile toward Linda Tripp from the start. The day the FBI had wired Tripp, Udolf had driven her home and reported that she was "rude," "mistrustful," and "paranoid." Tripp, for her part, had called Wirth a "big-haired witch." At one meeting with his fellow prosecutors, Udolf had blurted out, "Do you think Clinton is a bad president? Do you think he ought to lose his office over a piece of ass?" All of these pieces of evidence were starting to add up in the minds of Bennett and others. The "hawks" had tried to put aside their distrust and display good faith by putting the "doves" in charge of the brace of Lewinsky. Now, they felt Udolf and Emmick were intentionally tanking the investigation.

Back in the room, the OIC prosecutors and agents stationed with Emmick lounged on the bed watching a Monty Python movie. As one prosecutor recalled, "It did feel a bit like a time lock in a movie where the clock is ticking down and the bomb's about to go off." There was also a sense that as each minute passed, Lewinsky was less likely to cooperate.

At 10:16, Monica's mother arrived at the Ritz-Carlton carrying a travel bag and wearing a fur coat over her black business suit. Marcia Lewis later recalled that moment when she reunited with her daughter in the room: "She was standing by the window, and her face was red and swollen from crying and she was holding a Bible, and she was shaking, just uncontrollably, just shaking so hard." Monica's mother also recalled that "one of the men, whom I later found out was Mike Emmick, was lounging on the bed," which she found "distasteful." No sooner had

Marcia "hugged Monica" than Starr's team asked the mother to step into the adjoining room. According to Marcia's recollection, they said, "Your daughter's in trouble. She could go to jail for twenty-seven years for witness tampering and filing of false affidavit and obstruction of justice." That doomlike scenario could be erased, but only if Lewinsky was willing to "cooperate."

Marcia Lewis answered, "Of course she'll cooperate." She wasn't sure what that meant, legally speaking. The most baffling thing, for Monica's mother, was that all of this had happened "because she lied . . . *about* this?" Adultery was a bad thing, she knew. But it usually didn't result in a horde of prosecutors and FBI agents swooping down on the young woman and threatening to send her to jail for twenty-seven years.

The OIC group agreed to give mother and daughter "some private time to talk" in the hallway, since the women were thoroughly convinced that "the room was bugged." Even from a distance, the prosecutors could hear Monica and her mother "yelling amongst themselves." Marcia Lewis kept telling her daughter, "It's okay, it will be all right." Monica, in turn, was whispering so loudly she half shouted, "I'm not going to be the one who brings down the *f——ing* President."

It was during this heated caucus that Marcia Lewis recalled her daughter saying, "They want me to wear a wire, and they want me to tape-record people, and they want me to tape-record conversations with Betty Currie, and they want me to wear a wire and tape President Clinton and Vernon Jordan." Marcia Lewis clearly remembered her daughter communicating, "I can't do that; I *won't* do that."

Truth be told, in recent months Marcia Lewis had grown downright distressed about her daughter's infatuation with Bill Clinton. She had repeatedly encouraged Monica "to find single men her own age." Still, wasn't the punishment being bandied about by the Starr prosecutors a bit extreme? Monica's mother raised the idea with the Starr troupe: Could her daughter receive immunity without having to tape-record anyone? Emmick shook his head; they needed evidence that could be used in court. Marcia next asked if the Starr prosecutors could put the offer of immunity in writing? Emmick left the room for another powwow and then returned to say he couldn't do that, because they "didn't have a typewriter."

It was at that point that Marcia Lewis concluded that she and her daughter were in a lose-lose situation. Seated in her New York condo years later, remarried to a wealthy newspaper owner, Peter Straus, and having attempted to put this trauma behind her, Monica's mother would say, "I'm afraid of them still." She felt that she was dealing with "a frightening, frightening situation." All she could say to Mike Emmick that night, as he pressed for an immunity agreement while declining to put anything in writing, was, "I don't see how I can make this decision, either. We really ought to talk with [Monica's] dad."

It turned out that Marcia Lewis had *already* contacted her ex-husband, Bernie Lewinsky, giving him a hurried call on the train using her cell phone. Even though the signal kept fading in and out as the train roared through tunnels, Bernie had processed the basic facts. Marcia now made her confession to the OIC team—Mr. Lewinsky *had* been notified and *he* wanted to talk to Starr's prosecutors, too.

Agent Fallon threw a pencil against the desk. It landed on its eraser and bounced across the room. He cursed, "You called her father?"

———

BERNIE Lewinsky had been sitting in the lounge at the Biltmore Hotel in Los Angeles, attending the annual meeting of the Southern California Radiation Oncology Society (of which he was president), when his beeper went off. His receptionist informed him, "Marcia, your wife, called, she wants you to call her immediately." She added, "Monica is in deep trouble." Bernie knew that this weekend, Monica was scheduled to move from Washington to New York City to begin a new job; there had already been a discussion about moving expenses. Bernie had joked with the receptionist, "Oh, she probably needs more money."

When he dialed his ex-wife's cell phone, however, the subject had nothing to do with cash. Marcia was on a train. She spoke in whispers, something about the federal authorities scooping up their daughter. "Bernard?" Marcia said breathlessly. "Bernard, Monica's in trouble. The FBI has her in a hotel. Do you know anything about her having a relationship with the president?" Bernie nearly dropped the phone. This was definitely Marcia. She was the only person in the world who called him "Bernard." "What are you talking about?" he demanded. Marcia continued: "Well, she's in deep trouble, and she needs a lawyer." The phone kept cutting on and off, as the train climbed hills and barreled through tunnels. Bernie thought quickly. He said, "I know that Bill Ginsburg has a secondary office in Washington, D.C., and Bill is going to be talking here. I'm going to call him and see if he can give me the name of his office over there. I'll call you back."

Bill Ginsburg was one of Bernie Lewinsky's closest friends, until this case extinguished their friendship. At that moment, he was in court arguing a case when his pager went off. The text message read: "Call me immediately, it's an emergency, Bernie." Ginsburg was scheduled to speak at the oncologist's convention later that day, where he was to discuss "emerging HMO ethics," including important issues like, "Should we bombard prostates, as opposed to doing urethral ultrasounds and just hitting the tumor?" Ginsburg was one of the best attorneys in the business when it came to defending hospitals and physicians in nasty, high-stakes medical malpractice litigation. Bernie Lewinsky was a regular client and a faithful friend. When Ginsburg finally reached Bernie, his friend sounded worried and even desperate. Bernie told Ginsburg, "You've got to come down here. I can't talk over the phone." He added in a hushed voice, "It involves Monica."

Ginsburg requested an emergency recess of his case, drove at a high speed to the Biltmore, and sought out his friend in need. The bearded lawyer entered the room and gave Bernie a bear hug, asking, "What's the trouble?" Bernie Lewinsky gulped down some air, then recounted the incredible story, saying that Monica "was being held at the Pentagon City Ritz by the FBI. And they were questioning her and said that she was under arrest or words to that effect." Ginsburg would recall that his friend Bernie "was beside himself as any father would be." So Ginsburg took immediate action. "The first thing I did was prescribe a vodka and, opening the minibar, took one out," he later said. "That was the extent of my license to prescribe."

After several failed attempts, Bernie finally got through to Mike Emmick. He held the phone to his ear as Emmick told him that "Monica was involved in a cover-up, and she and her mother were going to go to jail unless they cooperated. And they wanted Monica to wire herself and make some phone calls to some key people before midnight." Bernie Lewinsky recalled saying to Emmick, "Isn't Monica entitled to an attorney?" The prosecutor answered, "Attorney? Well, yes, I guess she is entitled. Does she have an attorney?" Bernie replied, "Yes, she does."

At that point, he handed the phone to Bill Ginsburg.

Emmick would later say, "We just were happy to be speaking to anybody, although, in retrospect, perhaps not."

From the moment of this initial phone call, Emmick would confess, his interaction with Bill Ginsburg was a strange and bedeviling experience. Whether Ginsburg was an expert at getting under opponents' skin, or whether he was simply an obnoxious person who possessed a law license, was a determination that history would have to make. All Emmick knew was that Ginsburg made a bad night even worse.

Bernie Lewinsky, clearly distraught, got on the line and told his daughter, "Bill Ginsburg is going to be your lawyer."

Monica would recall that she responded, "Bill Ginsburg? The malpractice lawyer?" Although it was unknown to anyone else in the world, she had called Ginsburg after Thanksgiving to sound him out on "the definition of perjury"— she had never imagined that this garrulous personal-injury defense lawyer soon would represent her.

Bernie Lewinsky said to his daughter, "Do what Ginsburg says."

In Monica's own mind, Frank Carter was still her lawyer. But it was 11:30 at night and something had to be done. "It was fine," she said. "I trusted my dad. So if my dad's telling me to do something, I did it."

William Ginsburg took charge, administering a tongue lashing to the OIC prosecutors. Mike Emmick would later say, struggling to sound diplomatic, "So Ginsburg was kind of bombastic, an odd sort of fellow. He said a lot of rude stuff to me on the phone, which is an odd thing when you're, you know, trying to represent someone in a cooperation mode." The OIC prosecutors quickly realized that Bill Ginsburg was no Perry Mason. When Emmick began talking about possible immunity for Monica, Ginsburg cut in sarcastically: "Oh, I didn't know you were a judge!" Emmick was flabbergasted. "He [Ginsburg] said a couple of other things like that, that suggested that he really didn't know what the heck he was talking about."

Ginsburg also began pestering Emmick to reduce some kind of immunity agreement to writing and fax it to him. Emmick answered, "If we have to put this in writing, I gotta go drive back to the office. It's already eleven o'clock at night. Why don't you just make up your mind?" Ginsburg snapped back that this was impossible, because "I haven't even talked to my client yet." So Emmick handed the phone to Monica and let her communicate with her new attorney, for better or worse.

After this brief consultation, Emmick next made an offer that—if it had been accepted on the spot—might have led to a completely different outcome in this prolonged saga. In one of the greatest lost opportunities for both sides, Emmick retrieved the phone and told Ginsburg, "We'll give you a pass." This was prosecutorial lingo for "we'll give you complete immunity." Although Ken Starr's office would later back-pedal and argue that Emmick did not have the authority to make a binding immunity agreement on that night, Emmick would insist that if Ginsburg had accepted the deal at that moment, it would have been virtually impossible for OIC's top brass to undo it. "Yes, absolutely," Emmick said later. If Monica had accepted the immunity deal, then and there, he was "prepared to make it stick."

Bruce Udolf concurred that there was "absolutely" a deal that he considered legally and morally binding. He added, "If the OIC had honored the deal, seven months of parading people in front of the grand jury would have ended. Monica said in the end what she said in the beginning. If she had been given incentive to cooperate right away, we would have known if we had a prosecutable case right away. If not, the country could have been spared much of what took place over the next year."

On the other end of the phone, Bill Ginsburg was conferring loudly with Bernie Lewinsky. Word circulated in whispers among OIC lawyers that it sounded as if Ginsburg had been drinking—more than just a friendly cocktail. Emmick would sum up his impressions of Bill Ginsburg that night: "His mood was very, I don't know, 'bombastic' is the word that keeps coming to mind, but very sort of dismissive. I don't think he really was taking any of this seriously."

Udolf, who had no reason to stick up for OIC after later being shunned as a traitor, nonetheless concurred: "He [Ginsburg] had no apparent experience in this kind of case. He knew nothing."

The FBI agents and prosecutors dropped the bombshell that they already possessed a copy of Monica Lewinsky's affidavit in the *Paula Jones* case. Even though Frank Carter had not formally filed that document with the court in Little Rock—the package was still en route to Judge Susan Webber Wright's chambers and would arrive the next day—they had somehow put their hands on a copy. Ginsburg said to Emmick, "Can you fax me this affidavit?" Emmick replied, "Yes, we can fax it to you." Fallon made a face indicating, "I can't believe you just said that." After another time-out, during which the prosecutor engaged in a heated conversation with his FBI agents, Emmick returned to the phone and said that he could *not* fax a copy of the affidavit, because there was "no fax machine in the hotel room."

In fact, the FBI agents had reminded Emmick that this crucial document on which OIC was premising its criminal pursuit of Lewinsky had not even been docketed in the federal courthouse. Once again, OIC was trying to stay "ahead of the curve."

During the course of their whispered conversations in the hotel room, Emmick and the FBI agents had repeatedly suggested that the situation with Lewinsky was "time sensitive." Marcia Lewis remembered looking at the clock and being puzzled by their perceived urgency. "I couldn't understand what they meant by 'time sensitive,' " she said. Ginsburg decided to call the question; he couldn't deal with prosecutors like this from three thousand miles away. "We can't say that she's going to cooperate now," he boomed loudly over the telephone. "I'll catch the red-eye, and I'll get there and this thing will move along as quickly as it can."

For the life of her, Monica's mother could not remember meeting Bill Ginsburg, although he kept telling the prosecutors that he was an intimate family friend. She knew that he was an acquaintance of Bernie's, but she could not recall his ever setting foot in their home. Still, she was grateful that someone was prepared to come to Monica's rescue. She had asked Starr's lawyers as gingerly as possible whether she and Monica could "take a room in the hotel so that we could sleep." So far, there was no sense that walking out the door was an option. As Marcia Lewis would describe it, "They never said, 'We'll shoot you if you leave.' But it was very clear to me we weren't supposed to leave. So yes, they can technically say that we weren't 'held' there. I mean, that's ludicrous."

Ginsburg got back on the line with Emmick. "Look," he said, using his tough voice, "you've got a young lady there who is my client. . . . You've held her for in excess of several hours, and you have no right to speak with her whatsoever without having given her the right to call an attorney." As Ginsburg would reconstruct it years later, "So I basically gave him *Miranda* in the teeth and told him, you know, this was out of line."

Ginsburg demanded to speak with Monica again, now ordering her, "Just leave. Don't say another word to them, but leave." Emmick turned to Monica and her mother and said, "Well, he says there's no deal, so I guess we're done." The two women looked at each other. Did this mean they could return to Monica's apartment? Emmick shrugged his shoulders. "Fine, you can go home." Emmick remembered this moment as "a little bit touching." All of them "had actually been through quite a lot." Monica and her mother, as they gathered up their belongings, said a lot of "really nice things," including "Thank you for being so nice to us and for being so professional and for explaining all these things and letting me [Marcia] come down and all the delays—you've really just been wonderful." Emmick, who hadn't slept in over twenty-four hours, was thoroughly burned out. He was feeling good, in one way, about the way things had gone down. "We thought we had done everything right in some very, very difficult circumstances," he would say, recalling that night with weariness.

On their way out, the FBI agents handed Monica and her mother a pair of subpoenas. They were now legally required to turn over tangible items relating to Monica's relationship with the president—a grand jury would doubtless want to hear from them, too. Carrying these official summonses, mother and daughter headed for the elevator to retrieve Monica's car in the garage, as prosecutors and FBI agents slumped in their chairs.

"I was completely exhausted," recalled Emmick, "just because it had been very intense and very trying in lots of ways. I was also a little bit disappointed. Disappointed because we had tried and tried and tried . . . and it still just didn't work out." Some of his fellow prosecutors, still in the room, would recall Emmick's pacing back and forth and asking himself, "What else could we have done?" Nobody had an obvious answer.

At least he felt they had handled the situation in an admirable and professional manner, Emmick recalled with a forced laugh. "As we looked back on the day, one of the things that we said to ourselves was, 'At least we did everything right.'" He was confident that when the American public inevitably learned about the events that had transpired in Room 1012 of the Ritz-Carlton that day—a public airing was inevitable—people would conclude the OIC prosecutors had lived up to the highest professional standards. He expected the morning-after assessment would be this: "They let her leave; they gave her [phone] numbers of lawyers; they had Mom come down; they talked to Dad; they talked to everybody."

Emmick concluded, a tinge of sadness in his voice, "We just thought we were going to look golden."

In reality, the sting of Monica Lewinsky at the Ritz-Carlton would turn into the single event in OIC's thoroughly controversial handling of the Lewinsky case from which Ken Starr and his team would never fully recover. As several FBI agents escorted Monica Lewinsky and Marcia Lewis to the parking garage in the dark January night, Emmick returned to OIC's office to give Jackie Bennett a quick briefing before going home and collapsing into bed.

Jackie Bennett stayed up, pacing the floor of his office. Michael Isikoff had continued his badgering calls from *Newsweek*'s Washington offices, digging around for more information. At one point, Bennett blurted out, "Okay, you've got to knock this off. It's not going to happen tonight. You just got to sit on this." Isikoff reluctantly agreed, saying, "Okay, but keep me informed." Both sides understood that they had placed their souls in hock.

Bennett knew that the president's deposition was scheduled to take place the next morning. As long as they kept Monica and her mother from making any phone calls to tip off the principals, the bullet in the game of Russian roulette would spin into the proper chamber. Bennett sized it up: "Once he [President Clinton] got into that deposition, it was going to be very hard for them to get word to him." The moment Clinton strode into that proceeding at Bob Bennett's law firm to give his testimony under oath, the next morning at 10:30 A.M., OIC would be home free.

"That was kind of the drop-dead event," said Bennett.

———

In Los Angeles, Bernie Lewinsky downed another vodka for medicinal purposes. Bill Ginsburg, out of a sense of loyalty to his friend and because it seemed like an interesting professional adventure, volunteered to take the first red-eye to Washington. The bearded lawyer drove home, packed a minimal bag—expecting to return in a day or two—and caught the early-morning flight from LAX to Washington via Pittsburgh (a maneuver designed to throw off reporters) to "see what the hell [was] going on."

In Washington, Monica Lewinsky was so hysterical that Marcia Lewis drove the SUV, navigating it back to the Watergate. Monica said that she needed to take a shower, feeling dirty after this confrontation with the Starr prosecutors. What she didn't tell her mother, in the darkness of the apartment (she kept the lights off so that they wouldn't be watched), was that she was still contemplating the logistics of suicide. As she attempted to shower away the horrible images of the past twelve hours, she began hatching "crazy plans." Even if she was going to kill herself, she thought, she needed to warn Bill Clinton first. One immediate idea was, "I'm going to get into a taxi and go to Betty Currie's house, because she has to tell him he can't testify." The other side of her brain told her, "Okay, I won't do that. I'm sure they have someone at Betty Currie's house. I'll go to Bruce Lindsey's house. No. Bruce Lindsey doesn't even know who the hell I am. He'll call the police on me." As traumatized as she was, Monica kept telling herself, "He [Clinton] has to know what's going on."

Neither Monica nor her mother was able to sleep. Instead, they crept back into the SUV and drove, out of pure impulse, to the Four Seasons Hotel in Georgetown, figuring that the phones there would be safe. One possible candidate for a late-night call was Betty Currie. Monica also wanted to call her dad in California just to hear his voice. As they entered the lobby at around 2:30 A.M., a couple trailed behind them. The two women looked at each other in panic, as if to communicate: "Oh my God, they're agents!" In desperation, mother and daughter discussed whether they should flee the country. Monica concluded, "They probably have all the borders covered," and "my name's on the list at the airport." She later realized that her thought processes were impaired, yet there was no stopping the flood of doomsday scenarios. "Your mind sort of goes to the things that happen in the movies and on TV," she would later say, "because that's the only point of reference." Assuming the worst, Monica and her mother turned around and headed for the hotel exit.

The last time Monica had seen Bill Clinton was on December 28 when he had given her "all those Christmas presents and we had a nice Christmas kiss." After New Year's, Monica had sent the president "a book and this mushy note." They had also had a "weird discussion" about a mishmash of topics the day before she signed the affidavit. Other than that, the relationship with "Handsome" was virtually dead, without a pulse or a heartbeat. All of a sudden, Bill Clinton was again looming front and center in her mind. As she and her mother pulled out of the Four Seasons parking lot and drove back into the cold night, Monica was thinking about three things: Bill Clinton, her family, and whether everyone would be spared this nightmare if she could figure out an efficient way to kill herself.

Marcia Lewis could intuit that her daughter was teetering on the brink of mental collapse. When they were safely inside the Watergate condo, Marcia waited for Monica to use the bathroom, listening for any unusual sounds that might indicate she was trying to harm herself. "And then I had her lie down and I just sat there next to the bed," Marcia recalled. "I was really afraid."

During the night, the phone rang. Bernie Lewinsky had taken the risk and called his daughter directly. Marcia said, "We're home now. Monica is not doing well. She's very shaken up." Bernie told his ex-wife, "Don't leave her alone. Just stay with her and be sure if you hear anything that you go in there immediately." Both parents recognized that Monica was extremely "unstable." They might need to seek intervention.

Marcia later acknowledged that in hindsight, it sounded paranoiac that she would worry about who might be watching them inside Monica's apartment. Still, she couldn't escape these terrible, racing thoughts. "My thinking was that they were going to come and get us. I figured if they didn't come that night, they would come the next day. . . . It was that simple."

All Marcia could remember of the next few days and nights, as Monica lay on her bed sobbing as if consumed with fever and drifting in and out of a troubled sleep, was that it turned into "a very strange sort of twilight zone time."

CHAPTER

30

CLINTON TAKES AN OATH

President Bill Clinton, heading into the deposition that would forever change his presidency, did not take kindly to Paula Jones's allegations. Nor was he pleased that she had turned down what he perceived to be an overly generous settlement offer. Clinton would reconstruct his thoughts going into the *Jones* deposition as follows: "I wasn't going to apologize for something I didn't do. She said she wanted her name cleared. I did that from the moment the thing surfaced. I said she didn't do anything wrong, and I didn't sexually harass her. The whole story's not true. If she was worried about the lies of the *American Spectator,* she would have gone after the *American Spectator* instead of getting in bed with them. So that was never what this was about."

An unfair twist to this civil deposition, as Clinton saw it, was that the Supreme Court's precedent and the decision in *Clinton v. Jones* itself only permitted him to be sued as "Bill Clinton, private citizen." The Constitution and age-old concepts relating to executive privilege protected a president from being sued in his official capacity. Now, his opponents were trying to have their cake and eat it, too. They were going after him as a private citizen, yet holding him to a higher standard. "The only reason I *was* sued is because I was president," Clinton would explain. In an ordinary civil case, he stressed, a judge would have tossed out this entire lawsuit early on as "lacking merit." Clinton felt he was being subjected to a double standard; he believed this proceeding was all about shaming him and doing political damage.

"They would leak it if it were embarrassing, and I would be hurt that way," he explained. "Or they could, you know, bludgeon me into paying everything I'd worked to save and Hillary had worked to save and apologizing for something I didn't do. . . . That was what this is about."

Paula Jones arrived at the deposition, in the capital city of Washington, with a Pollyannaish view that Bill Clinton would be forced to fess up. "I did," Jones would later acknowledge, "only because of how the law works. You're supposed to go under oath. . . . I thought, 'Okay, he sure wouldn't commit perjury.' But he did, anyway." Jones added, having lost the sparkle of optimism after that deposition, "I guess I'm at the point now I think he could do anything. I think he didn't care. He'd lie, cheat, steal, anything. He stole the furniture from the White House. So he's lied, he's cheated, he stole, he's committed adultery. Let's see, what else. There's a lot of confessing to do."

Jim Fisher, the soft-spoken litigator from Dallas who would conduct the deposition, had arrived at the Hyatt Regency in Washington a day early, framing questions that he would pose to the president. Fisher had handled hundreds of depositions as a litigator. But this was different from others. "I had the strong sense," Fisher said, "that this was going to be a deposition that people were going to read and comb through and look at line for line." He had to make the questions "extremely simple and clear and plain."

"To win the case, the thing I had to do was to destroy [Clinton's] credibility," explained Fisher. "We were going to provide ample evidence that he had done many times exactly what Paula Jones said he did to her."

Fisher was not enthralled with the prospect of digging into the sexual predilections of the president of the United States. At the same time, he said, "I felt that there needed to be some recognition of how low our standards had fallen. As a Christian, it bothered me that this man who purports to be a Christian would so sully our faith by his hypocrisy and his pretext. I believed at the time and still believe that he used his alleged faith as a mere tool for political gain. And that bothered me."

Fisher also spent time in his hotel room tinkering with a definition of "sexual relations." He planned to spring this definition on the president so that there was no room for the Arkansas two-step. Fisher had extracted this language from the Violence Against Women's Act, a federal law that Clinton himself had signed into existence. "And I thought that at trial, I could exploit the fact that it was his law. He signed it. And if he said he didn't know what it meant or it's not clear, then he'd look pretty damned silly. I could see that playing out well in front of a jury."

Fisher's law partner, meanwhile, was hitting pay dirt. Less than twenty-four hours before the Saturday deposition, Linda Tripp's new attorney, Jim Moody, finally contacted Wes Holmes and said, "Okay, come pick me up at five. We're going to drive out to her house."

The trip to Columbia, Maryland, was a long one. Moody, it turned out, was blind. As Holmes recalled, "And so I'm literally getting directions from a blind man, and we get lost in Washington, D.C., for forty-five minutes trying to find the loop, because I hadn't gotten the level of detail of directions that I ended up needing. So we managed to finally stumble and bumble and get out to her house. And I met with her."

Holmes sat at Linda Tripp's kitchen table, as the frazzled-looking blond-haired woman stared at him. Unbeknownst to him, Tripp had just been dropped off by FBI agents after having assisted in the sting of Monica Lewinsky. "I remember she was extremely agitated and chain-smoking and acting as if she had been, you know, living on coffee for a couple of days," Holmes recalled.

The informant began rambling, and "it was hard to keep her on a subject." Holmes told Tripp, "Look . . . we got very limited time. What I need is detailed, factual recitals of things that Monica Lewinsky said on the tapes that she and Bill Clinton had done and said together, and gifts that he had given her, or that she had given him." He needed "specific, factual" information before the sun came up.

Tripp continued to chain-smoke. She seemed unable to focus. At one point, she blurted out, "He gave her a book."

"Okay," Holmes pressed. "What was the name of the book?"

"I think that she also said that he gave her candy," Tripp declared.

"Okay, well, let's run this book to the ground," Holmes interrupted. "Then we'll talk about the candy."

Little by little, Holmes was able to extract useful nuggets. In the middle of the debriefing, one of Tripp's colleagues from the Pentagon rang the doorbell, bearing a box of her personal effects "just in case she got fired." The meeting now began to unravel. Holmes finally blurted out, "Okay, you know, can I have my tape so I can go back and listen to it?"

"Well," answered Tripp, glaring at him, "we're not going to give you the tape. I can tell you everything, but I can't give you the tape." It was clear Tripp and her lawyer were worried because she had recorded them illegally.

Holmes stared at Moody, who nodded somberly from behind his dark glasses. The Dallas lawyer threw up his hands and groaned. "Well, that's extremely disappointing," he said. "I've been out here for four days; you've been telling me you'd give me a tape, and now you won't give me a tape." Yet Holmes was still armed with valuable information.

On the drive back to the district, Moody used his cell phone to call George Conway, one of the elves who was in town to monitor the deposition. Conway had booked a room at the Four Seasons, where he and conservative lawyer-writer Ann Coulter (who had provided occasional assistance to the elves) were enjoying room service and a few drinks. Conway invited Moody and Holmes to join them. In a remarkable gathering of anti-Clinton brain power, the group compared notes. Holmes nearly dropped his glass when he learned of the latest development: "The FBI had picked up Monica Lewinsky"—the sting had occurred that very day. Somehow, Ken Starr was now involved in the case. This was nothing short of astounding. The group hoisted their beers and toasted the wonderful news, saying to Holmes, "Oh, my God, you're going to depose the president tomorrow. Can you believe it, you know, don't you wonder what Monica Lewinsky is saying [to the FBI and OIC]? I mean, what if she gives him up? This could be it. He could have to resign over this. Can you believe it?"

At six o'clock the next morning, Wes Holmes rapped lightly on Jim Fisher's door. Holmes had barely slept. He now awakened his law partner and shared the rich information that Linda Tripp had passed along the previous night during her rambling session, and the new intelligence from the elves. The normally low-key Fisher nearly fell over with disbelief. The information from Tripp, he understood—especially the unexpected details about gifts and Betty Currie's smuggling Monica into and out of the White House—was probably enough to hang the president. Additionally, Starr's presence in the case meant that Clinton was walking into a buzz saw without knowing it. Fisher took copious notes; he would have time to fashion a dozen new questions that would enable him to take Clinton by surprise.

Holmes received a fresh adrenaline rush when he met George Conway for breakfast, and the elf informed him that Moody had "played one of the [Tripp] tapes for the editors of *Newsweek.*" The specific tape was potentially the most damning of the bunch: the recording dated December 22. On this cassette, Lewinsky had supposedly spoken openly about her affair with Clinton and even outlined a plan to have Tripp fake a "foot accident" in order to avoid being deposed. Moody had reportedly played the tape for Michael Isikoff and several editors at *Newsweek,* a day or two earlier, which meant that the story could break at any time.

What Conway did not tell Holmes, however, was that he himself had heard the December 22 tape at Coulter's apartment—Tripp's lawyer had given the elves a sneak preview before turning it over to the FBI. Conway had been elated to hear the titillating sexual detail involving Monica Lewinsky's relationship with Bill Clinton. What was noticeably missing, however, was any reference to the president telling Monica to lie, or Vernon Jordan telling her to lie or linking his assistance in finding her a job with the false affidavit. Although Tripp had bragged that this tape contained the "smoking gun," Conway had noted with alarm that the key admission was missing. That meant that the sex angle might be the only viable path, if they wanted a perjury charge to stick.

Conway wished Holmes luck. Assuming the Dallas lawyers' questions were framed carefully at this morning's deposition, the elf noted encouragingly as he dabbed a napkin to his mouth, President Bill Clinton might finally run out of wiggle room.

———

JUDGE Susan Webber Wright and her law clerk, Barry Ward, exited their airplane on the tarmac at Washington National Airport, looking like cold Southern birds who had migrated in the wrong direction. Originally, Judge Wright was scheduled to preside over the Saturday deposition from her home in Little Rock. During a conference call with the lawyers, she had broken down and agreed to fly to Washington. It seemed to be the wisest course, she had concluded, if she wanted to keep a firm hand over the questioning. Her only other alternative was to rule on objections via her daughter Robin's teddy bear phone, the only phone in her house with a speaker function that would free up her hands to take notes. Now the chilly Washington air and gray winter skies seemed to suggest that the teddy bear phone might have been a better option.

Judge Wright was wearing a red wool winter coat; that was the extent of her preparation for this wintry trip north. Under one arm, she carried a paperback novel, a prop designed to make her appear like an ordinary Washington tourist. A detail of U.S. Marshals was waiting inside the airport. When a gaggle of reporters in the baggage claim area recognized the Arkansas judge, they immediately started chasing her, trying to snap pictures. Judge Wright and her law clerk began running in the direction of the U.S. Marshal's car, their suitcases banging off the curb as they attempted to outrun the Washington press corps. It was the first of many endurance tests in a case that had morphed from a barely tenable civil lawsuit into a national media event.

———

THE Paula Jones caravan over to the Skadden Arps law firm was a sight to behold. Jones herself was "excited." She told her lawyers, "I want him [Clinton] to be called to account for what he did." As the group piled into cabs, Susan Carpenter-McMillan hustled around like a wedding coordinator, preparing for the big event. She had surprised Paula by purchasing matching upscale suits of different colors, so that they would be dressed like sisters. (Carpenter-McMillan had been shopping for suits at the Pentagon City Mall while Monica was getting braced by Starr's prosecutors in the same shopping complex.) "That was my way of really kind of sharing an historical day," Carpenter-McMillan would say. "I always dressed her in pants. She had on the same outfit and nobody knew it but me." Paula was wearing a cream jacket and pants; Suzie was sporting a black jacket and skirt. "It's a woman's thing," Carpenter-McMillan later explained.

Jones had told Carpenter-McMillan just before leaving for the deposition, "Suzie, I'm so anxious for this to happen. I'm going to be right there looking at him, and he's going to have to tell the truth." The PR consultant remembered wanting to say, "You naive little person. If you think for one minute that lying sleazebag is going to come up and tell the truth, you're wrong." In the interest of keeping Jones's morale up, Carpenter-McMillan instead smiled and told the young woman that she looked great.

At the glittering Skadden Arps offices, the Dallas lawyers hustled Jones past a throng of reporters into a waiting area where Secret Service agents tapped their earpieces, preparing for the arrival of the president. Carpenter-McMillan and Steve Jones were not permitted to enter the deposition room; Susan stayed outside in the cold answering media questions in her short designer skirt. Steve Jones paced the floor of a holding room inside the building, becoming angrier.

Bob Bennett had parked his car and rode over in the presidential limousine with his client. As the limo rolled several blocks to his office, Bennett had no particular reason to worry about today's deposition. He had run through a dress rehearsal of the questioning with the president multiple times, as recently as that morning. If the Jones lawyers launched into the subject of this new woman his opponents had identified—named Monica Lewinsky—Bennett had an ace up his sleeve: He was carrying an affidavit that would douse that fire.

President Clinton entered the glass double doors of the Skadden Arps conference room, looking sharp and even luminous. On this day, several observers noted, he appeared exceptionally presidential. Clinton worked the crowd, shaking hands and welcoming Judge Susan Webber Wright, his former law student. Next he moved down the line to greet the lawyers, video crew members, and even the stenographer. The president and his lawyer had already decided that he should not shake hands with Paula Jones—this would appear "phony." When he reached Jim Fisher, who would be posing the questions, Clinton managed to brush right past him. Neither man extended a hand.

Judge Wright looked out of place in her presiding chair. Rather than a robe, she was wearing a navy blue Austin Reed business suit with pleated skirt. Her law clerk chatted briefly with the videographer to make sure that only two copies of the filmed deposition were created—one for each side. These videocassettes were to be delivered to Judge Wright as "bailee" and placed in her briefcase for safekeeping at the conclusion of the proceedings. There would be no spare copies made; in that fashion, nothing could be leaked.

The president took a seat at one end of the table. On the other side of the court reporter sat Jim Fisher, positioned to look directly into the deponent's eyes. Fisher would recall—in describing a scene that had previously been illegal to discuss, under Judge Wright's protective order—that the president looked incredibly "buffed and polished." The Dallas lawyer would add: "I mean, he looked like he'd been groomed for hours before he came in, and I guess that's how the president probably always looks."

Fisher expected Clinton to treat him with "contempt." To his surprise, the president did not seem to "intimidate me or give me the hairy eyeball or do anything to sort of upset me. I didn't get that sense at all."

Yet others present sensed a palpable tension inside the room. It was clear that Bill Clinton "would have preferred to be somewhere else." Still, he seemed remarkably composed for someone occupying the hot seat.

The eleventh-floor conference room—which served as Skadden's boardroom—glittered with recessed lighting. The participants sat at a huge marble table that was shaped like a gem polished into a perfect oval. The entire wall of the boardroom, to the president's right, was filled with windows that provided a breathtaking view of the Treasury Building and the White House along Fifteenth Street and Pennsylvania Avenue. Today, the shades were drawn and heavy drapes pulled over so that news cameras and swooping helicopters could not discern that this room of the tall office building was the site of this historic proceeding.

The deposition commenced at 10:30 A.M. sharp. Bob Bennett made a brief opening statement imploring Judge Wright to keep a tight rein over the questioning—especially relating to tawdry sexual topics. Information in this case had been leaking like a sieve, he said, and that had to cease. "A lie gets around faster than [the truth]," Bennett stated with a booming New York accent that echoed in the small conference room. "The Presidency is an important institution, Your Honor," he declared. "And it is very important that it not be held in disrespect or it be held up to the laughingstock of the world."

Judge Wright nodded as she told the parties, "I have agonized over this case and the very embarrassing nature of some of the issues in this case, and it does not give me pleasure even to be here today." Turning to the president's lawyer, she continued: "However, we're here, I've done it before, I've gotten tougher. . . . What was initially very shocking and embarrassing to the Court is not quite as shocking and embarrassing anymore." Judge Wright waved a finger in the air and made clear that if anyone violated her gag order and disgorged *any* details of this deposition, there would be hell to pay. The guilty party would be sanctioned and even locked up in jail. After nodding their heads in response to this stern warning, the assembled lawyers picked up their pens and readied their notepads.

Jim Fisher, counsel for the plaintiff, began his direct examination by reminding the president that he was under oath and that his testimony "is subject to the penalty of perjury." He then pulled out a typed definition of "sexual relations" and placed it on the table. "Sir, I'd like to hand you what has been marked Deposition Exhibit 1." Fisher slid the paper in front of the president. "So that the record is clear today, and that we know that we are communicating, this is a definition of a term that will be used in the course of my questioning, and the term is 'sexual relations.'"

Immediately, the defense team erupted into objections. Bob Bennett declared that the definition was confusing, overbroad, and a "political trick." Bennett turned to Judge Wright and demanded, "They have got the President of the United States in this room for several hours. Why don't they ask him questions about what happened or didn't happen?" This kind of grandstanding filled with sexual innuendo, Bennett said, had only one purpose—to get the salacious details leaked to the media.

Judge Wright scratched her head; she hadn't been expecting to make major rulings within the first three minutes. The judge inspected the proposed definition and immediately crossed out two subsections that potentially dealt with *non*-intentional conduct. These, she said, could include something as innocent as a slap on the rear end. Plaintiff's counsel could use only that portion of the definition of "sexual relations" that dealt with "knowingly" engaging in or causing "contact with the genitalia, anus, groin, breast, inner thigh, or buttocks of any person with an intent to arouse or gratify the sexual desire of any person."

"I'll permit that," Judge Wright said, sliding the definition back onto the table. "Go ahead."

Fisher flipped over a new page of notes. "Mr. Clinton," he asked, "do you know a woman named Kathleen Willey?"

The president and his attorneys were fully prepared for this line of questioning. Clinton had already denied—in response to written interrogatories—"groping" or inappropriately touching Willey outside the Oval Office. Now, he addressed the questions effortlessly. When asked why Willey would invent such a grotesque story, the president reminded counsel that her husband had been caught up in an embezzlement scheme and committed suicide that very night: "When she came to see me she was clearly upset. I did to her what I have done to scores and scores of men and women who have worked for me or been my friends over the years. I embraced her, I put my arms around her, I may have even kissed her on the forehead. There was nothing sexual about it."

In terms of his own motivation, the president said, "I was trying to help her calm down and trying to reassure her. She was in [an extremely] difficult condition. But I have no idea why she said what she did. . . . She's been through a terrible, terrible time in her life, and I have nothing else to say. I don't want to speculate about it." Those in the room, even the president's opponents, marveled at the fluidity of his responses. As one observer said, "It was all flowing."

Next, Fisher digressed into an examination of the Sexual Harassment Policy that Clinton had signed as governor of Arkansas in 1987. Bob Bennett, his eyes baggy from long nights of preparation and his jowls showing the weight of middle age, waved a pencil. "Your Honor," he cut in, "if Mr. Fisher wants to use his time with the President of the United States to ask these kinds of questions, I personally have no objection. But at three o'clock, I don't want to hear that we have ten major integral areas that you haven't gone into."

Fisher rearranged himself in his chair and asked the president, "Now, do you know a woman named Monica Lewinsky?"

The room fell silent. The president answered, "I do."

Jim Fisher would later reveal that the timing of the Lewinsky questioning was carefully choreographed. He had led off with Kathleen Willey to lull the president into complacency; he knew Clinton had already thoroughly rehearsed that topic. Now, Fisher had switched abruptly to Lewinsky, in order to catch the president off guard. The Dallas lawyer later explained, "This was naive on my part—but I thought that it might actually prompt him to give more candid, complete, truthful answers if he was uncertain about what we knew and what we could prove."

Fisher now continued his questioning relating to Lewinsky: "How did you know her?"

The president replied, "She worked in the White House for a while, first as an intern, and then in, as the, in the legislative affairs office."

The cat-and-mouse game continued for nearly a half-hour:

> FISHER: Is it true that when she worked at the White House she met with you several times?

Clinton bobbed and weaved, talking about the government shutdown and the fact that Ms. Lewinsky may have brought him documents once or twice.

> FISHER: So I understand, your testimony is that it was possible, then, that you were alone with her, but you have no specific recollection of that ever happening?
>
> CLINTON: Yes, that's correct. It's possible that [Lewinsky], while [she] was working there, brought something to me and at the time she brought it to me, she was the only person there. That's possible.

Now Bob Bennett jumped in, trying to rescue his client: "Your Honor, excuse me, Mr. President, I need some guidance from the Court at this point. I'm going to object to the innuendo. I'm afraid, as I say, that this will leak." He continued in a commanding voice: "Counsel is fully aware that Ms. Lewinsky has filed, has an affidavit which they are in possession of saying that there is absolutely no sex of any kind in any manner, shape or form, with President Clinton."

With the Lewinsky affidavit now in front of him on the table, the president took the opportunity to mimic Monica's version of the story, telling Fisher that the intern had probably brought him pizza one night during the government shutdown. Clinton added, "I do not believe she was there alone, however . . . on a couple of occasions after that she was there but my secretary, Betty Currie, was there with her. She and Betty are friends. That's my, that's my recollection. And I have no other recollection of that."

A final time, Jim Fisher sought to pin the president to the wall, asking point-blank: "At any time have you and Monica Lewinsky ever been alone together in any room in the White House?" Again, the president avoided, evaded, and denied.

Suddenly, the questioning veered into a direction that was totally unexpected. It was at this moment, according to those in the room, that President Clinton momentarily lost his balance and faltered like a man losing his grip on a climbing wall, before regaining his footing and hoisting his way back up the dangerous incline.

Jim Fisher looked directly at the president and asked, "Well, have you ever given any gifts to Monica Lewinsky?"

There was an inordinately long pause. One witness would later reveal that the president's face turned an unhealthy shade of crimson. He began: "I don't recall . . ." After taking a good minute to scratch his head and think—a painfully obvious measure designed to buy time—the president asked his inquisitor with boyish impishness, "Do you know what they were?"

FISHER: A hat pin?
CLINTON: I don't, I don't remember. But I certainly, I could have.
FISHER: A book about Walt Whitman?

Wes Holmes, who was taking notes and watching the president carefully as he answered these questions, was surprised at Clinton's facial reactions: "He typically has fairly light skin. . . . But it's extremely expressive; it's almost like a mood ring. I mean, you can just see his emotions going through different stages, which I hadn't expected. I mean, somebody who's as brilliant as he is, I would have thought that he could have played poker with his emotions better than that."

Not only did Clinton seem "a bit surprised" by the detailed nature of Fisher's questions, but he also seemed to be searching for a lifeline. He turned and looked at Bob Bennett, one of the few clues that there might be problems roiling under the surface of this otherwise smooth deposition.

CLINTON: I give—let me just say, I give people a lot of gifts, and when people are around I give a lot of things I have at the White House away, so I could have given her a gift, but I don't remember a specific gift.

FISHER: Do you remember giving her a gold brooch?

CLINTON: No.

FISHER: Do you remember giving her an item that had been purchased from The Black Dog store at Martha's Vineyard?

At this point, a light seemed to go off in Clinton's head: There was a mole—somebody had fed specific, incriminating information to these Dallas lawyers! The look on his face now revealed anger.

CLINTON: I do remember that, because when I went on vacation, Betty [Currie] . . . asked me if I was going to bring some stuff back from The Black Dog, and she said Monica loved, liked that stuff and would like to have a piece of it . . . and I gave Betty a couple of the pieces, and she gave I think something to Monica and something to some of the other girls who worked in the office.

Those seated around the conference table were totally surprised that Fisher had landed such a solid blow relating to Jane Doe No. 6, a person about whom they knew nothing. Although there seemed to be little or no connection between this young intern and the allegations of sexual harassment being lodged by Paula Jones, the name of this game (as in an ugly divorce or custody case) was to bloody the opponent with any weapon available.

FISHER: Has Monica Lewinsky ever given you any gifts?

CLINTON: Once or twice. I think she's given me a book or two.

The president attempted to neutralize his answer by suggesting that many well-wishers gave him gifts; he had piles of them in the White House.

FISHER: Did she [Lewinsky] give you a tie?

CLINTON: Yes, she has given me a tie before. I believe that's right. Now, as I said, let me remind you, normally when I get these ties, I get ties, you know, together, and then they're given to me later but I believe that she has given me a tie.

Now Fisher attempted to move in for the kill, asking the question as he looked directly at the president:

FISHER: Did you have an extramarital sexual affair with Monica Lewinsky?

CLINTON: No . . .

FISHER: If she told someone that she had a sexual affair with you beginning in November of 1995, would that be a lie?

CLINTON: It's certainly not the truth. It would not be the truth.

FISHER: I think I used the term "sexual affair." And so the record is completely clear, have you ever had sexual relations with Monica Lewinsky, as that term is defined in Deposition Exhibit 1, as modified by the Court?

Bennett waved his hand, bringing the questioning to a halt. "I object!" he bellowed. Judge Susan Webber Wright, watching the legal jousting from her side of the oval table, glanced down at her copy of Exhibit 1. She ruled: "Well, it's real short. . . . I will permit the question and you may show the witness definition number one."

After studying the typed definition, the president pushed the piece of paper away and answered, with a tone of adamancy, "I have never had sexual relations with Monica Lewinsky. I've never had an affair with her."

President Clinton himself would later protest that the questions about "other women" propounded by the Dallas lawyers were grossly unfair, because they had absolutely nothing to do with obtaining discoverable evidence relating to Paula Jones's claim. Rather, he said, the questions were clearly designed to embarrass him and to place his head in a meat grinder. "You know," Clinton later explained, recalling that uncomfortable day, "[if] you're really trying to find out 'Is there some sort of pattern of sexual harassment here?' you ask a whole different set of questions than you do if you're trying to get something that you can smear someone in public with."

The proper line of inquiry, President Clinton insisted, would have been to ask him "whether I was alone with certain people and what was the nature of my relationship and did I ever sexually harass them? Then they would have gone and asked the women that. But, you know, that was not what it was about. It was about trying to elicit some admission from me that they could then leak."

Jim Fisher, however, believed that the line of questioning was perfectly proper. The federal judge presiding over the *Jones* case had specifically authorized him to ask questions about the nature of Clinton's relationship with other women. Now, President Clinton had chosen not to answer these questions truthfully. As to the assertion that this was a perjury trap, Fisher would say, "I've been amused by this term 'perjury trap.' Well, I'm sorry, but that's what just about every deposition is. That's what it's all about, if you're deposing your client's adversary." Said Fisher, in a quiet but firm voice, "Yes, I was hoping he'd commit perjury and I'd catch him."

To the extent that some would later criticize the Dallas lawyers, saying that *any* married man put in Clinton's position would deny having an extramarital sexual affair, Fisher would express no sympathy. "Well, I guess my response to that is [Clinton] forfeited the right to have people feel bad for him when he told the American people he was done doing that sort of thing, but continued to do it under circumstances that to me are really disappointing as a citizen." Fisher added, his voice unwavering, "No, I didn't feel bad. I'm an advocate, and I was trying to win. That's my job."

Yet Fisher was up against a master. To the extent he avoided asking sexually explicit questions to show respect for the presidency, instead relying upon the murky "sexual relations" definition to corner Clinton, he may have committed a major strategic blunder. "You could visually see Clinton in the deposition, locking into the deposition," said one observer. "He could see that he had running room. He had an out." That observer concluded: "The lack of specificity of questions probably saved Bill Clinton."

Before the lunch recess, President Clinton volunteered a question of his own, which certainly caused his legal team to experience indigestion. As if fishing for clues as to what evidence the Dallas lawyers might have squirreled away to ensnare him, the president piped up, "Mr. Fisher, is there something, let me just—you asked that with such conviction and I answered with such conviction, is there something you want to ask me about this [the Lewinsky matter]. I don't, I don't even know what you're talking about, I don't think."

The president would later suggest that in blurting out this question, he was giving Fisher a wide-open opportunity to ask questions that were more specific if he wished to nail down the truth about the Lewinsky relationship. That argument, however, had a hollow ring to it. The president's entire testimony concerning Lewinsky, from start to finish, was programmed to deny any form of romantic or sexual contact, no matter how the Jones lawyers phrased it.

Fisher declined to take the bait. He replied soberly, "Sir, I think this will come to light shortly, and you'll understand."

BACK at the White House, a frantic *Time* magazine reporter was calling John Podesta (now Clinton's deputy chief of staff), "freaking out" as he explained that *Newsweek* was preparing to drop a "bombshell." Michael Isikoff, the *Time* reporter said, was jealousy guarding a story that had "something to do with Ken Starr and perjury." What did the White House know about it? Podesta was totally in the dark. He responded: "They're just chasing a rumor." The minute he hung up, however, Podesta picked up the phone and called Isikoff, summarizing the tip that he had received from the *Time* reporter and asking: "Mike, what's going on?" Isikoff responded hastily, as if rushing out the door: "I don't think we're going with anything. I'll get back to you if we are." Isikoff paused, then asked Podesta a single question before concluding the conversation: "Do you know somebody named Monica Lewinsky?"

———

AFTER lunch, when the deposition reconvened, the Dallas lawyers drilled directly into the subject of Paula Jones's allegations. On cross-examination, Bob Bennett neatly summarized his client's testimony, with the following exchange:

> BENNETT: Now you're aware, are you not, of the allegations against you by Paula Corbin Jones in this lawsuit; is that correct?
>
> CLINTON: Yes, sir, I am.
>
> BENNETT: Mr. President, did you ever make any sexual advances towards Paula Jones?
>
> CLINTON: No, I did not.
>
> BENNETT: Did you ever expose yourself to Paula Jones?
>
> CLINTON: No, I did not.
>
> BENNETT: Did you ever ask Paula Jones to kiss your penis?
>
> CLINTON: No, I did not.
>
> BENNETT: Now, Mr. President, you've stated earlier in your testimony that you do not recall with any specificity the May 8th, 1991 conference at the Excelsior; is that correct?
>
> CLINTON: That's correct.
>
> BENNETT: If that is true, sir, how can you be sure that you did not do these things which are alleged in Ms. Jones' complaint?
>
> CLINTON: Because, Mr. Bennett, in my lifetime I've never sexually harassed a woman, and I've never done what she accused me of doing. I didn't do it then, because I never have, and I wouldn't.

Bennett himself now returned his client to the topic of maximum danger. Having performed his own due diligence and having satisfied himself that the allegations of a sexual tryst between the president and Monica Lewinsky were poppycock, Bennett held up the Lewinsky affidavit and read it for the benefit of Judge Wright. Lewinsky had stated in paragraph eight of that document: "I have never had a sexual relationship with the President, he did not propose that we have a sexual relationship, he did not offer me employment or other benefits in exchange for a sexual relationship, he did not deny me employment or other benefits for rejecting a sexual relationship." Bennett now asked Bill Clinton, "Is that a true and accurate statement as far as you know it?"

The president seemed to listen carefully, according to those in the room. He nodded his head. "That is absolutely true," he stated.

One of the great ironies of this daring deposition was that the information concerning Lewinsky—in all likelihood—never would have been admissible in the *Jones* proceedings. The existence of this affair was wholly peripheral to Paula Jones's complaint. Judge Wright, a stickler for procedure, in all probability would have excluded this evidence at trial. Additionally, the Linda Tripp tapes were likely inadmissible, because of serious hearsay objections along with the fact that they had been recorded illegally.

The Dallas lawyers understood that their chances of surmounting these hurdles at trial were slim. But they also knew something that President Clinton and his lawyers didn't know: Ken Starr—through some divine intervention—had just launched a criminal investigation linked to Clinton's testimony in this case. Now the lies themselves on the subject of Monica Lewinsky could mortally wound this president.

At the conclusion of the deposition, all parties stared at the black VHS tapes that the videographers had removed from two separate cameras anchored to tripods. These constituted the only visual record of one of the most important pieces of legal testimony in American history. Judge Wright had agreed to take custody of the tapes as a "bailee" for both parties. Sliding them into her briefcase, the judge now shook hands with the president and his lawyers and told Paula Jones and the Dallas attorneys, "You all have a safe flight." With that, the deposition of the century was concluded.

Bennett and Secret Service agent Larry Cockell escorted the president to his limousine. Overall, the White House team was feeling upbeat. "I don't think they laid a glove on him" was the team's assessment of Bill Clinton's smooth performance. Although Clinton had been thrown off stride here and there, he had bounced back and shifted the burden to the plaintiff's lawyers to prove their outlandish allegations. There had been those odd questions about Monica Lewinsky. Yet the White House team was satisfied that Lewinsky's affidavit had mooted that point. By all indications, they were now home free.

Outside, the Skadden building cast a winter shadow in the direction of the White House. On the sidewalk, Paula Jones huddled with her lawyers and burst into tears. She felt that the afternoon's testimony had been disastrous. Dressed in her new cream suit and sporting a special hairstyle for the occasion, Jones was visibly "distraught." She told her lawyers, "He's lying. I can't believe he's lying."

Wes Holmes put one arm around his client. "Well, of course, he's lying," he said. "I mean, everybody knew he was going to lie when we asked him some of these questions." Jones wiped a tear from her face. "I know, I know," she said. "But it's just so hard to sit here and listen to that."

Susan Carpenter-McMillan, who had been locked outside in the cold, hugged Paula Jones for warmth. She told her young client that no matter what happened in the deposition, they needed to put on a happy face for the media. There was a gag order in place, issued by Judge Wright, which meant they couldn't say a word. But this didn't mean that the Jones team couldn't be *seen* having a rip-roaring celebration after the proceedings were over. It was, as Wes Holmes said, "one of the very few useful bits of advice that she gave."

So the Jones troupe headed to the Old Ebbitt Grill, one of the most popular restaurants in Washington and one that Carpenter-McMillan had scoped out earlier in the day. It featured a large window facing the street, with a big table visible to passersby. When she had called the restaurant to request that table, the maître d' had replied, "We're really sorry, but that's been booked for six months for a birthday party." Carpenter-McMillan had expressed dismay, explaining that she was the publicist for Paula Jones and that the deposition was in town today and that they needed a highly visible spot, where they could "be seen." The maître d' called back a few minutes later and informed her, "Well, you're in luck. These wonderful people are Republicans; they love what you're doing, they're going to give up that table, and we're going to seat them someplace else."

Carpenter-McMillan had proclaimed, "Oh, thank you, Lord."

That night, as a horde of reporters stood outside in the winter's night, snapping pictures and filming video footage to their hearts' content, the Jones team drank glass after glass of bubbly. Susan Carpenter-McMillan would laugh, "Unbeknownst to us, Clinton went back to the White House and canceled his dinner reservations. So you know what the headlines were the next day, 'Jones camp popped champagne bottle, Clinton's camp canceled dinner reservations.' I mean, it just couldn't have been any better."

Dressed in her red wool coat to fend off the cold Washington weather, Judge Susan Webber Wright avoided any fuss and exited the law firm. She nodded politely to a few straggling reporters and walked briskly toward an awaiting car. The journalists knew that she would not comment—she had become an almost irrelevant figure in their story. What the journalists did not know was that the only two existing copies of the videotaped deposition of President William Jefferson Clinton—one set of three tapes for each side—were stuffed inside the judge's black leather briefcase. She had arranged for herself and law clerk Barry Ward to meet a family friend for dinner, since they had only one night free for relaxation in the nation's capital. A source close to Judge Wright later disclosed that she had another pressing concern besides getting the Clinton tapes home safely: The judge's ten-year-old daughter, Robin, had asked for a "Spice Girl" Barbie doll, because it was nearly impossible to find those special dolls in the noncosmopolitan environs of Little Rock. The judge's friend had made some calls and had eventually located a store in a tough Maryland neighborhood that still had a few left on the shelf after Christmas.

With the videotapes crammed into the judge's briefcase, the group drove to an unsafe-looking neighborhood over the Maryland border, ventured out of the car long enough to purchase one Spice Girl Barbie doll in a box, and then drove quickly back into the district for dinner.

As Paula Jones and her team popped champagne corks in the window of the Old Ebbitt Grill, Judge Wright and her tiny entourage enjoyed a quiet dinner at a small restaurant, undetected by the media. Inside the judge's black briefcase, stashed safely at her feet under the table, were the only two sets of Clinton videotapes in the world, along with one equally valuable Spice Girl Barbie doll.

CHAPTER

31

———

SCANDAL IN WASHINGTON

Bernie Lewinsky and his second wife, Barbara, were soaking up rays in Hawaii, beginning a long-planned vacation, when the story of Clinton's alleged affair with Monica first leaked into the national media. Bernie and Barbara were working out in the exercise room of the Grand Wailea hotel in Maui, on this day in late January, when "all of a sudden we saw our daughter's ID photo, which was horrible, flashed up, and we just felt like crawling under the blanket and didn't want anybody to see us."

Bernie placed a call to Bill Ginsburg's wife back in California. She said, "Do you know your house is on TV? I see your van." Bernie's license plates on his car spelled out LWNSKY, a cute advertisement for his medical practice. Now the camera was zooming in on that vanity plate, so there was no mistaking whose daughter was involved in this sex scandal. Bernie Lewinsky would later recall of that horrifying day: "And all of a sudden, we just felt our life was being invaded."

As Bernie and Barbara regrouped poolside, the couple with whom they were vacationing flip-flopped outside to find Bernie. The Internet was just coming into vogue; the husband-friend fancied himself a real "computer-nick." He told Bernie that he had seen something called the Drudge Report, a gossipy Internet news site, implicating Monica in some crazy tryst with President Bill Clinton. Bill Ginsburg, meanwhile, called on Bernie's cell phone; the malpractice lawyer had just arrived in Washington and met with Monica. The picture he painted was staggering. "This is big," Ginsburg said, filling him in. "Apparently, Monica has had an affair with Clinton, and she was taped by [a woman] Linda Tripp. There are tape recordings. Apparently, Marcia is implicated in the tape recordings. And this is going to become a huge scandal, and there may be legal action." Ginsburg paused and added dramatically, "This can go to where Clinton may be kicked out of office."

Bernie's first question was, "Bill, how much is this going to cost? What do we need?" Ginsburg answered, "Bernie, it can go from hundreds of thousands to millions, especially if there is a trial, because they're going to indict Monica for perjury and there's going to be a trial . . . We're probably going to have to file a suit against the president." At this point, Ginsburg lowered his voice a notch. "To tell you the truth, Bernie," Ginsburg whispered, "I'm scared. Can you imagine *me* trying the president of the United States of America?" Bernie answered candidly, "No, Bill Ginsburg, I can't believe it." He thought for a minute and asked, "Are you an expert in this area? You're a malpractice attorney." Ginsburg reassured his friend, "Look, Bernie, you've seen me in trial. This is no different than a medical malpractice case where you put your issues [in] and carry on the trial." Ginsburg added, by way of comfort, that he had contacted a Washington, D.C., criminal attorney named Nate Speights to assist him on the case.

At that moment, Bernie Lewinsky was nearly overcome. *Two* lawyers? This was going to cost a *lot* of money. It was also going to do untold damage to the family name: "Lewinsky" would become a synonym for "presidential sex scandal." Toward President Clinton, at that moment, Bernie felt only a numb uncertainty. After all, he still did not know the true story. Toward Monica, Bernie's overwhelming feeling was, "God, what have you done? What have you been doing?" He was seeing flashbacks of a little girl splashing in the pool at their first home in Los Angeles—a radiant little girl he called "my little *Farfel*," a Jewish term meaning "noodle"—and thinking, "Oh, my God, you're in trouble, we've got to protect you."

———

Monica Lewinsky had crept out of her apartment and had driven away in her brother's Ford Explorer SUV—it was being stored at her Watergate parking garage while he attended college—heading for Dulles Airport. She worried that if she didn't watch carefully over her shoulder, "a van would zoom up, swoop me in and they'd arrest me." Yet she met her arriving passenger without a hitch. As Bill Ginsburg walked out into the cold Washington air wearing a gray crewneck sweater, a cameraman appeared and asked, "Are you William Ginsburg?" The California lawyer answered, "That's me." He was surprised that someone on one side or the other had already leaked his identity to the press, allowing this lone cameraman to follow his movements from Los Angeles via Pittsburgh—most likely by obtaining the planes' manifests. As the camera rolled, the television journalist asked, "What's going on?" Ginsburg smiled into the camera and stated genially, "I don't know what's going on," walking away with a polite bow. From that point forward, the California malpractice lawyer became known to the American media as "the avuncular Mr. Ginsburg."

For sure, he was an anomaly in Washington: a bearded, laid-back-looking medical malpractice lawyer from Los Angeles; a graduate of University of California–Berkeley with a major in theater arts and literature who spoke and moved with a dramatic flair. He was a highly successful Jewish lawyer who had begun his practice in Los Angeles at a time when Jewish lawyers were still a distinct minority. An irreverent, funny, sarcastic, smart, occasionally kamikaze-like civil defense lawyer, he felt comfortable wearing gold chains around his neck and had little time for uptight, Brooks Brothers Washington lawyers who appeared to him more like lobotomized human beings than inspired counselors at law, fighting with passion for their clients.

Bill Ginsburg was, above all, a lawyer who marched to his own drum. In early years of practice, he had defended swimming pool manufacturers in horrible death and accident cases, racking up an astounding won-loss record. He relished jury trials and feared nobody in the courtroom. Nor was he intimidated by new challenges—which is why he was willing to take this case for Bernie Lewinsky's daughter, without a background in the field of criminal law or, much less, presidential sex scandals.

When Ginsburg slid into the passenger seat of Monica's SUV, he observed an attractive young woman who was older than when he last saw her, but still too young to be in this sort of mess. Ginsburg sized up his new client: "She was calm, but nervous. She was glad to see me. She was wearing slacks and an appropriate top. . . . It was conservative. It was dark-colored. And she was nervous, happy to see me and anxious to talk."

Saturday afternoons were usually safe in the district—the odds of running into reporters were slim. So Ginsburg sought out a table at the Hay Adams Hotel, before the late-afternoon cocktail crowd arrived, ordering two drinks by the fireplace. Ginsburg's thought was, "It was a little darker, and I thought maybe I could get a little more information out of her in a less public, more closed-place-type situation." Monica was open and painfully candid. From this first meeting to the last, Ginsburg would recall that the facts that Bernie's daughter laid out were remarkably consistent "all the way down the line." Although lawyer and client would have their differences over time, Ginsburg would later concede, "One thing Monica has never done, I mean with all of her foibles, she has never told me an untruth. She's manipulated me, and has done her thing, but she's never told me an untruth."

Seated beside the crackling fire in the basement of the Hay Adams, just about the time President Clinton's deposition was winding up nearby at the Skadden Arps firm, Monica recounted the general story of her involvement with the president. Among other things, she told Ginsburg that she "did not have sexual relations with him [Clinton]," elaborating that her "understanding of sexual relations was intercourse." This was consistent, the California attorney would later point out, with Monica's surreptitiously taped conversations with Linda Tripp. In these conversations, she told Tripp that she never had "sex" with Clinton, explaining that she did not think of "oral sex" as "sex." Although one could debate the meaning of these terms forever, Ginsburg would say—and the written definition presented to President Clinton at the *Jones* deposition was another matter altogether—Monica never departed from the facts as she saw them. "You know," said Ginsburg years later, "everything that she said was always the truth."

Late that afternoon, Ginsburg returned with Monica to her Watergate residence, so that he could make sure all was okay. He walked into a small, not particularly well-kept apartment, where Marcia Lewis was guarding the door. Monica had already begun packing her belongings for the move to New York to begin her new job at Revlon. Boxes were piled up. The apartment was cold and near empty. The doors were bolted and the shades were drawn, to shut out stray FBI agents who might be watching. Both mother and daughter were mentally strung out. As Ginsburg recalled, "Mom was a wreck, she [Monica] was a wreck, and Mom was asking me, 'What to do, what to do?'" Although the substance of their conversations remained privileged, Ginsburg would acknowledge—as would his clients—that a principal topic of their discussion was immunity: how to get it, and under what terms.

The puzzle was complicated by the fact that Monica Lewinsky still seemed to be very much in love with Bill Clinton. This part of the story would often be ignored or trivialized, particularly after the titillating details of the sexual relationship printed in the Starr Report eclipsed it. Yet the facts were the facts. Ginsburg, who spent as much time with Monica during this time as anyone, acknowledged, "I had a sense that she was in love with him and really was enamored of him. I wasn't sure what that meant or how deep it went or what was going on. I knew that she cared for him. And that to her, anyway, this was more than casual sex."

So Ginsburg was aware that he was not simply dealing with a woman whom Starr's office wanted to indict because of a false affidavit in the *Jones* case; he was also dealing with an emotionally fragile young woman who had recently been dumped by the president and was attempting to come to grips with it. "She was serious about the relationship," Ginsburg confirmed.

That evening, Ginsburg joined Monica and her mother for dinner at the Oval Room, a chic, contemporary restaurant not far from the White House.

Ginsburg permitted Monica to call her father on a pay phone. Moments into this conversation, Monica "just totally fell apart." On the other end, Bernie "started to howl," unable to believe that life had dealt him this set of cards in the Old Maid deck. Monica began sobbing into the phone, "I'm sorry, I don't know what's happening," which caused Bernie to become even more emotional, demanding that Monica promise that she would not hurt herself in any way and declaring "that bastard [Clinton] is not worth it." When Monica lost her composure a second time, Ginsburg yanked the phone away. He whispered gruffly to Bernie, "I can't have her breaking down." Ginsburg instructed the emotionally unglued father, "You just tell Monica that she needs to tell me everything that's happened." Otherwise, he wanted his client's parents to butt out.

———————

As the Lewinsky saga unfolded, the American media's fixation with all things Monica intensified. Reporters asked: How much did Monica's parents *themselves* contribute to the dysfunction that caused their daughter to have an affair with the president and to get ensnared in this web of political intrigue? Not every young woman, after all, would find herself in this mess.

By the late 1980s, as Bernie and Marcia Lewinsky were nearing their twentieth anniversary, their marriage had virtually collapsed. Bernie had established a successful radiation oncology practice that netted him nearly a half million dollars a year in income; he had accomplished this by working two full-time jobs that kept him out of the house most days and nights. This allowed the family to move into a $1.6 million Mediterranean-style home with a red-tiled roof in Beverly Hills, in one of the most exclusive neighborhoods of an exclusive town.

Bernie Lewinsky would later admit, "We had big aspirations, bigger than we needed to have." Marcia's own statement in the court papers relating to the couple's rancorous divorce in 1998 declared: "I and my children have maintained an affluent lifestyle and have traveled first class extensively. We have always provided the children with expensive extracurricular lessons and tutoring to satisfy any desires that either they or we may have."

There was no question that money was a central issue in the irreconcilable differences that arose in the couple's marriage. Further adding to the discord, there were unrebutted allegations that Bernie had strayed from his marital vows by engaging in a relationship with a nurse at his practice, a fact that stung Marcia. There were also charges and countercharges by husband and wife that the other spouse did not have a firm grip on parenting responsibilities. Bernie Lewinsky, years later, admitted that "we had a total disagreement on how to bring Monica up from the day that she was born." As Bernie described it, Marcia's "value systems" were quite different from his own; she allowed Monica to do "whatever she wanted in order to have Monica be happy." For instance, he said, as part of a high school project, Marcia had allowed Monica to "do some filming in a construction site in a not-so-good neighborhood of LA at two or three in the morning." Bernie raised his usually calm voice as he remembered it. "I mean, what mother would allow a thirteen-, fourteen-year-old girl to be out at night in dangerous areas without knowing where she was?" Admittedly, he was a father who was missing in action for much of his children's lives and had little standing to cast the first stone. Yet, Bernie Lewinsky concluded, "I think that there were a lot of things that were left for Monica to decide that were adult decisions that she shouldn't have made as a child, that she couldn't make as a child."

Yet broken marriages and families with skeletons rattling in their closets and young men and women with complications were not unique to the Lewinskys of Beverly Hills. Marcia Lewis, who slept in the empty Watergate apartment to provide support for her daughter and to make sure Monica did not harm herself during this horrendous ordeal, felt particularly "defensive" because of "the public nature" of this scandal.

When it came to insinuations that she, as the mother, was responsible for Monica's predicament, Marcia Lewis insisted that this was too simplistic an analysis: "Young women have made very poor choices, have fallen in love with the wrong men, sometimes married, sometimes a boss or a supervisor, for centuries. Forever, really. From the dawn of time. So, to treat this or to talk about this as such an anomaly and such an out-of-the-mainstream sort of thing to happen, I think it's wrong. That doesn't mean it wasn't a mistake. It just means that people seem to have ascribed so much beyond the normal to it, when in fact, sadly, I think it happens. It does happen."

Although Marcia and her ex-husband may have been imperfect parents, she pointed out, it was unfair for the media to latch onto this family and treat it as a freak of nature. After all, "any young woman who makes a foolish choice, her parents, whoever they might be, you could say, made a mistake somewhere." At the same time, said the mother, "In the same way that I can't take full credit for all the wonderful things Monica has done—I can't take credit for her sparkling, wonderful personality, for how bright she is, for how creative she is, she has many talents I don't have—I don't think I can take full responsibility, either, for mistakes that she's made. So I wish more than anything that this had never happened. And to the extent that, well, that I am responsible for it, I so deeply, deeply regret that."

When it came to the million-dollar question, whether Marcia Lewis had known about the extramarital affair between her daughter and President Clinton—and indeed, whether she had encouraged it—Marcia would reply guardedly that she had a *general* sense that something more than friendship had crept into the relationship between her daughter and the chief executive. Yet she insisted that she did not know the precise details, and further emphasized that she and her daughter did not have the sort of relationship in which they shared such private details. Although Linda Tripp and Bernie Lewinsky, among others, would lay bets that Marcia was completely "in the know" about Monica's hanky-panky with Clinton, she dismissed their theories as the product of watching too many soap operas.

Marcia was willing to make a partial admission, despite her abiding fear—even years later—that Starr's prosecutors might still come after her if she uttered some fact at odds with her testimony under oath. She had discerned that *some* sort of romantic link had developed between Monica and the president and that it had gone haywire. (Monica herself would later tell the grand jury that she had admitted to her mother she "fooled" around with the president—she had disclosed a few facts but not the whole picture.) For this reason, Marcia "had been begging [Monica] to get away from this situation for months and months and months." Indeed, the mother would confess that she had "concerns about [Monica's] safety," and even mentioned (in worried conversations with her daughter) the tragic story of Mary Jo Kopechne and Chappaquiddick in 1969—when a young woman accompanying Senator Edward M. Kennedy was killed in a car crash late at night, plummeting over a remote bridge off Martha's Vineyard.

With respect to the precise nature of the relationship with Clinton, however, and the details that eventually spilled out in bound copies of the Starr Report, Marcia Lewis still denied knowing the graphic details. "You know, most people don't tell their mothers those things," she said slowly. "That is something nobody seemed to get." Although some media accounts tried to portray Monica and her mother as "roommates," because they shared an apartment for a time, Marcia would take offense at this characterization. "It is very common nowadays for children to move back home right after they graduate from college. Very common. That doesn't make her my 'roommate,' " she said emphatically. "We had a loving mother-daughter relationship. We were *not* roommates." Moreover, Marcia would underscore that Monica was not in the habit of discussing her sex life with her mother. "It's very safe to say that. That's correct."

The first time Marcia heard anything about the possibility of Monica being subpoenaed as a witness in the *Paula Jones* case, she later divulged, was during one of Monica's visits to New York on a job interview trip. Monica had leaned over in a taxi and whispered cryptic words to her mother indicating that she was "going to be subpoenaed," and that "Linda Tripp posed some kind of a threat or some kind of danger." It was only after the Ritz-Carlton sting, as mother and daughter spent time in the dark apartment together, that Monica began to share additional information. Marcia would acknowledge that her daughter did "explain to me that this had to do with the *Paula Jones* affidavit." Monica also hinted that there was some connection to President Clinton's upcoming testimony. Other than that, the mother said, she was largely in the dark.

In Marcia's eyes, what seemed particularly unfair was that Monica was doing what *any* sane person would do if confronted with allegations of an extramarital affair: Whether it involved the president or the local milkman, the natural thing to do was to deny it. It may have been wrong for Monica to engage in this conduct, Marcia understood, but what in God's name were her options? And why were the Jones lawyers asking these questions of her daughter in the first place, when her affair with Bill Clinton had nothing to do with the *Paula Jones* case? If Monica fessed up and said, "Yes, we had consensual oral sex," not only would it create embarrassment and wreak havoc on her own family, but it would also hurt Clinton's family (especially Hillary and Chelsea) and potentially wreck the Clintons' marriage and lead to problems for all concerned. Monica may have told a white lie. But Marcia believed with every fiber in her body that her daughter was not involved in some grand conspiracy to thwart justice in the *Paula Jones* case. It was much less villainous than that: Monica had *always* planned that if confronted about her relationship with President Clinton, "she intended to deny it."

"Paula Jones had voluntarily come forward," Monica's mother said, spelling out her position. "Paula Jones had chosen to make a public statement about this. That was her choice. Her free will." On the other hand, "just because Paula Jones may have thought it was her right to make a public spectacle of this, I think Monica felt it was her right to keep it private. And not to tell anyone about it, and to deny it, which is exactly what she did.

"And I think innocently, not really understanding how serious that was at the time."

———

THE OIC prosecutors had been "waiting on pins and needles," wondering where this Bill Ginsburg character was. Jackie Bennett was becoming ticked off that Ginsburg didn't seem to appreciate the urgency of OIC's efforts. Starr's lawyers had been monitoring President Clinton's deposition via news reports. Bennett assumed that if Jones's attorneys asked a few pointed questions about Monica, the president most likely would not answer truthfully. "I remember certainly thinking and expecting that he [Clinton] would lie," Bennett recalled years later, "because he's a liar after all."

So the OIC team was becoming angry that Ginsburg was treating this like some sort of joke. "The time to do something proactive is just running down the drain," Bennett later explained. "And we've got multiple felonies at that point in time against Monica. And if she wants to help herself and ameliorate them and come to some terms, she's blowing it by not coming in and talking to us." To make matters worse, said Bennett, "We've got this jackass coming in from California."

It was not until Sunday morning that Ginsburg finally strolled into their office as if he were on vacation. The California lawyer was wearing a pair of slacks, a charcoal gray V-neck sweater, and a bright pink dress shirt underneath. The OIC lawyers instantly discerned that Ginsburg was a bird of a different feather. "His real specialty is broken necks from [swimming pool and] diving board accidents," Bennett would later comment. It was clear from the get-go that this lawyer was far removed from the elite world of Washington defense attorneys, and he didn't "understand the lexicon of criminal law."

Seated at the small OIC conference table, Bennett and his fellow prosecutors produced a document verifying that the three-judge panel had expanded Ken Starr's jurisdiction. They also flashed a copy of Lewinsky's false affidavit.

Ginsburg, appearing like a frisky prizefighter psyching himself up for a big fight, made clear that he viewed Clinton as a "misogynist" and perhaps as a "child molester." Yet he did not believe that the Starr prosecutors had any business sticking their noses into the affair. Ginsburg told them, "If the president had a sexual relationship with a young lady, however morally wrong that might be and whatever you think of him, so what?" He glared at the prosecutors across the table. "What has this got to do with national security? Unless you're investigating Monica for espionage or something. Or the president for espionage." This didn't involve selling secrets to the Chinese or Russians. Ginsburg nearly shouted, "What are you looking for with little Monica? I mean, what is it that you want?"

Baffled, the OIC prosecutors explained that Lewinsky was on the hook for perjury arising out of the *Jones* case and that the president might be involved in "a conspiracy to obstruct justice." They wanted the truth, not a lot of blustering from a swimming-pool lawyer about whether Monica was in cahoots with the Chinese.

When the subject turned to possible immunity, the mood in the room grew even uglier. Jackie Bennett was annoyed that Mike Emmick had offered Lewinsky immunity in the Ritz-Carlton. The OIC lawyers had now decided that there would be no more free passes; the "fire sale" was over. Bennett leaned over to Ginsburg and growled, "You rejected the offer of immunity. And so, now if she wants to get it, she's got to earn it." Bennett was actually thinking, "Thank God you were stupid enough to [reject the deal]. Now you're going to have to work for it."

Bennett felt strongly that federal prosecutors should never take "a pig in a poke." They should never cut a deal to grant a cooperating witness immunity, until that person spelled out what he or she was prepared to say in a written "proffer." OIC had already been burned once, in the botched Webster Hubbell deal. Bennett was not going to allow his office to do that again. He wanted a *written* proffer from Lewinsky, whether this loopy lawyer from California understood federal criminal procedure or not. If OIC did not insist on this precautionary measure, Lewinsky could sign the immunity deal and then say, "I fantasized all of this. I made it up and I consciously lied to Linda Tripp." If that happened, the government would be stuck with a "tainted evidence."

The avuncular Mr. Ginsburg didn't seem moved. He was beginning to appear oddly demonic to the OIC team, with his pointed, salt-and-pepper beard. "I feel this is like a Gestapo Nazi technique," Ginsburg now said, blasting his adversaries. "It just doesn't make any sense to me unless you can demonstrate to me that there is an issue of national security involved." He next threw the prosecutors a curveball. "I need to see Mr. Starr," declared Ginsburg. "Why isn't he here? Why are you guys giving me the alternatives? Why isn't *he* giving me the alternatives?"

The OIC prosecutors shot back, "He's not involved at this point. It's not your business."

When Ginsburg excused himself to use the restroom, he stood at the urinal and was surprised to find Ken Starr standing beside him. The two men exchanged pleasantries. Ginsburg washed his hands, told Starr to have a pleasant day, and returned to the field of battle. The California lawyer recalled with a smile, "Starr has a good work ethic, too. He was there [on Sunday]. The only time I met Ken Starr was in the bathroom."

The OIC lawyers now slid a draft "proffer" agreement across the table. Prosecutors routinely did this, allowing the defense lawyer to propose changes until they reached a workable deal. Instead, Ginsburg "didn't even look at [the paper] at all." He slid it aside, glared at his two opponents, and declared, "My girl isn't going down for you." Ginsburg repeated that he would not allow his client "to get involved in something un-American like wiring and taping to catch the president of the United States unless there was a really good reason," such as if "the president was involved in espionage," giving away secrets to a foreign enemy.

Jackie Bennett was seething. He would later say of Ginsburg: "He's viewing this as, 'Oh, you want $850,000 for this swimming pool settlement? No, no. You're going to give me $1.2 million.' He's viewing it as 'all is negotiable.' " Bennett leaned close to his bearded opponent and snarled, "Look, you're blowing this." Bennett raised his voice louder, almost shouting: "We've got you. We've got felonies against your client. She has got to cooperate, or else she can be prosecuted for serious offenses." Ginsburg unloaded his own salvo: "I just don't see why I should cooperate here, because I'm not that interested in catching the president *en dasha belle* [undressed with his rear end exposed]."

As this nuttiness was unfolding, one of his prosecutors handed Bennett a fax. His face darkened as he read it. In the wee hours of Sunday morning, at 2:32 A.M., tenacious Internet publisher Matt Drudge had scooped Michael Isikoff. *Newsweek* had "spiked" the story for the moment, nervous about printing still-unsubstantiated details. Drudge had no such compunction. The banner on his news site read:

NEWSWEEK *KILLS STORY ON WHITE HOUSE INTERN*
BLOCKBUSTER REPORT: 23-YEAR-OLD, FORMER WHITE HOUSE INTERN,
SEX RELATIONS WITH PRESIDENT
WORLD EXCLUSIVE
MUST CREDIT THE DRUDGE REPORT

As Bennett absorbed the news flash, he concluded, "The cat was out of the bag. And it was going to get farther out of the bag very quickly." Although Lewinsky's name still had not been revealed and Drudge apparently did not know that Starr was involved in the case, it was just a matter of time. Bennett turned and whispered to Emmick, "I don't know how long I can contain this." Ginsburg cut in: "Contain what? What the hell are you talking about?"

Bennett engaged in a quick aside with Emmick, muttering something about Matt Drudge.

"Who is Matt Drudge?" Ginsburg demanded.

Bennett answered angrily, "He is an Internet gossip columnist, he's an anti-Washington guy, he's Walter Winchell on the Internet." He turned back to Emmick: "We gotta get something done: we're losing time." He pounded his fist against the table and glared at Ginsburg. "We're not going to be able to do it," he said.

Ginsburg was thoroughly puzzled. He gathered up his papers, even more suspicious of Starr's team than when he'd arrived.

The OIC prosecutors, for their part, felt as if they were being dragged into a dark, swirling river and that Ginsburg had emerged from the mud like a creature from the deep, pulling them downward into an underwater madhouse.

———

OUTSIDE the OIC offices, an SUV pulled up and Bill Ginsburg climbed in. Monica Lewinsky was driving; her mother was buckled into the backseat. As they sped away, Ginsburg's mind was turning over a number of questions. Among them was, "Why hadn't Clinton just defaulted on the *Paula Jones* case? You know, some judge would have hit him up for a hundred thousand dollars in default damages, and that would have been over." It seemed odd to Ginsburg, as a lawyer accustomed to the finer points of hardball civil litigation, that this whole thing had been allowed to spiral out of control.

He shared some of these musings with Monica and her mother as they reluctantly followed him into a conference room at the Ritz-Carlton—the two women were aghast that Ginsburg had decided to stay at the same hotel where OIC prosecutors had braced Monica. It wasn't the most comfortable environment for them. Yet Ginsburg seemed oblivious to the location. First, the lawyer declared that his meeting with the OIC prosecutors had been a waste of time. He believed Monica should "hold out": "When the grand jury in Washington, D.C., gets ahold of this, they are going to laugh. They hate the government. They hate the cops. They hate the FBI."

Monica immediately questioned her lawyer's analysis: "I've heard that the grand jury will indict a ham sandwich, if the prosecutor asks for it."

Ginsburg allowed that this might be true in *some* parts of the country. But not in the nation's capital, from what he had heard. "They're not going to prosecute you for protecting a confidential relationship," he said, sharing his gut instincts. "They're just not going to do it."

As the subject turned to other matters, Monica revealed that Betty Currie had been trying to page her all day. The messages, appearing in code, were obviously designed to prompt a return call. They read: "Family emergency, please call," or "Good news, please call!" Ginsburg instructed his client not to respond; the White House would have to prepare for Armageddon on its own.

With her situation becoming more impossible by the minute, Monica asked the lawyer if she should consider checking herself into a psychiatric hospital. "It was all too much for one person to handle," she would later say. "I just felt I was having a nervous breakdown." Moreover, Monica thought that going to a psychiatric hospital might be the best way to avoid appearing in public. Her lawyer quickly threw a wet blanket on the idea. "That may create more problems than it solves," he told the ashen-faced young woman. It was better to evaluate Monica's options. Was there any way for her to *cooperate* with Starr's office and get out of this jam? Ginsburg asked. He, like Lewinsky, opposed the idea of her wearing a wire. Neither of them wanted her to be a wired snitch, no matter what OIC threatened to do to her. As Monica herself later explained, "Coming forward and telling the truth, that's one thing. But doing something that dirty, I just felt that was so wrong." She understood that plenty of people would look at her cross-eyed and say, "Oh, what you did [with Clinton] is so wrong." She took a breath and concluded, "But we all have our own standards."

Ginsburg next sobered up his clients by informing mother and daughter that if a grand jury *did* indict Monica and they went to trial, it might cost upward of a half-million dollars, ruining her father's medical practice. Both Monica and Marcia cried for a few minutes, then indulged themselves in an angry outburst, telling Ginsburg that he was offering them insufficient options.

It was already evident that Ginsburg harbored a strong dislike for Marcia

Lewis—she had been on the bad end of a divorce with his good friend, Bernie, which made her the enemy. Yet Monica's mother would still give Ginsburg credit for assisting them during this time of need, when they were incapable of formulating their own legal strategy.

Marcia Lewis would not disclose this fact until years later, but she had a special reason for valuing Ginsburg's willingness to suit up and march into battle for her daughter. The truth was that she had attempted to find a *different* lawyer to represent Monica, a sobering experience that made her more fully appreciate Ginsburg's fiery defense of her family. A day or two after OIC had confronted her daughter, Marcia had sneaked out of the Watergate without even telling Monica, flagging down a cab and riding to a high-powered law firm in downtown Washington. As she recalled, "I was just shaking uncontrollably. I could hardly speak, and I spoke to a lawyer there and asked him to help her, and gave him my phone number. And then afterwards, he called. I'll never forget his kindness. He called and he said that it wouldn't be appropriate for him to take this case, because his firm represented the Democratic National Committee. And that's when I understood that there would be no one ever to help us, because each side had too much to gain and too much to lose, ever to care what happened to Monica."

BILL Ginsburg, at heart, was an unfulfilled civil rights lawyer. Born on the East Coast, he had obtained his law degree at University of Southern California Law School in 1967 during the height of the civil rights movement. Ginsburg had represented doctors who wanted to receive "02" exemptions during the Vietnam War, winning "conscientious objector" status for physicians who were morally opposed to the conflict. He had helped file a lawsuit against the Los Angeles County Bar Association, because it would not allow blacks to join, ultimately forcing that bar association to change its policy.

So in deciding how to handle the blockbuster Lewinsky matter, Ginsburg had picked up the phone and called Nate Speights, an African American criminal defense attorney, "a good lawyer and pal" whom he knew from D.C. work over the years. Although the Washington, D.C., bar was still highly segregated through a silent network dominated by the white establishment, Ginsburg planned to do things L.A.-style.

Ginsburg believed that he and Speights could strike a quick deal with Starr's prosecutors. If OIC promised her "nonrecourse immunity," they would advise Lewinsky to "tell all." This would include "every meeting she ever had with Vernon Jordan, and it included Betty Currie, and it included the White House visits, and it included her relationship with the president. I mean, I couldn't squeeze the rag any drier," Ginsburg said later. He would ensure that Lewinsky disclosed "every ax murder she ever committed." The only condition that he would insist upon was that OIC could not force her to become a wired government snitch.

Unfortunately for all concerned, no such deal was ever consummated.

On Monday, as the rest of the district celebrated Martin Luther King Day, Ginsburg and Speights walked into Suite 490 of the obscure Pennsylvania Avenue building that housed the OIC headquarters. Monica herself attended the meeting to signal, "I'm here just to be available, depending upon what transpires in the discussions between the attorneys." The plan was to hammer out an agreement on the spot.

Ginsburg and Speights volunteered to act as the "post office." They would convey OIC's questions to their client and report her answers, giving the Starr prosecutors a taste of her testimony. The Starr team was encouraged—it wasn't a full proffer, but it seemed to be a reasonable compromise.

In short order, however, OIC's optimism faded. Ginsburg and Speights would leave the conference room carrying basic questions from the Starr team to Monica—questions such as "Did you have sexual relations with the president?" or "Did President Clinton or Vernon Jordan encourage you to lie about the nature of your relationship?" There would be long waits, sometimes as long as an hour, before Lewinsky's lawyers returned with ambiguous, worthless answers. Monica seemed unwilling even to admit that she had engaged in sexual relations with Clinton, a basic starting point. All these things were causing the Starr prosecutors "to have greater and greater anxiety" about Monica's "believability and candor." It also was solidifying their distrust of Bill Ginsburg.

Bob Bittman, the young prosecutor who was overseeing OIC's scaled-down operations in Arkansas, had flown to Washington to lend a hand. He was now "babysitting" Monica in the reception area, chatting about movies, California, and trendy hangout spots. Before long, Bittman could hear loud noises coming from the conference room. Tempers had begun boiling like overheated pots. Inside the room, Ginsburg was taunting the OIC lawyers: "We'd like to talk to Mr. Starr; he's the man." Ginsburg demanded to know if Starr's continued absence meant that the hotshot Whitewater independent counsel "was not running the show."

Those present discerned that a fissure was also developing within the ranks of the OIC prosecutors. Mike Emmick and Bruce Udolf were content to take whatever they could get from Lewinsky—for them, a written or oral proffer was unnecessary. As these two soft-liners saw it, Lewinsky was a small fish whom they had no real interest in prosecuting. On a scale of one to ten, she was a "one." Giving this young woman an immunity bath without detailed assurances seemed like a low-risk proposition. "So how much would we be giving up?" Emmick asked, discussing the question years later. "So to speak, how much are you paying for the pig? Whether it's hidden in the poke or not."

Jackie Bennett, however, was not budging. He did not suffer fools lightly, and he now viewed Ginsburg as Bozo the Clown disguised in lawyer's clothing. Bennett was in charge of the biggest case of his career; he wasn't going to let some "crap proceedings" directed by a swimming-pool lawyer from Beverly Hills foul it up. If Lewinsky had to be charged by a grand jury and prosecuted so that OIC could extract the truth from her, so be it.

The OIC prosecutors relocated down the hallway to Bennett's office to have it out. Ken Starr was summoned to join them. Quickly the meeting degenerated into "a very heated shouting match." Bennett slammed his fist on his desk and thundered, "It smells bad to me. It smells like they're trying to get us to take a pig in a poke without a good understanding. And she's not really answering questions." Udolf repeated, in an equally loud voice, that he knew a good polygraph person in Miami. They could fly this guy up in a matter of hours to hook up a quick lie-detector test on Lewinsky if Bennett was worried that the information the former intern was providing might be bogus.

Starr, who always favored putting civility first, suggested getting Hickman Ewing on the speakerphone so that he could weigh in from Little Rock. "This is a process," he stated cheerfully. "We're supposed to be colleagues."

Bennett shouted, "There's no way! We don't have time to brief Hickman on this issue. Ginsburg is right down the hall. The answer is 'no.' We need a decision."

Just then, the OIC team heard a "stage whisper." Emmick stuck his head outside the door, only to find Ginsburg conversing with Speights, apparently eavesdropping. Recalled Bennett, still angry at the memory, "He had been standing outside listening to us." To Bennett, the California lawyer appeared "like the cat that's eaten the canary." He had now seen that Starr's team was deeply divided; he was eager to use this to his advantage.

In the conference room, with Ginsburg and Speights back at the negotiating table, Jackie Bennett slapped a printout of the latest Drudge Report on the table. It gave extensive details relating to the emerging presidential sex scandal, mentioning Monica Lewinsky by name. Ginsburg's client, declared Bennett, was now "radioactive." This genie could not be put back in the bottle. The chance for "undercover work or taped phone calls" quickly was going up in smoke. The value of Lewinsky's cooperation "was [becoming] diminished."

The climate in the conference room had changed from lukewarm to chilly. Bennett now leaned forward and told Ginsburg that if he wanted a deal, Lewinsky would have to make a complete oral proffer—known in prosecutors' parlance as a "Queen for a Day" arrangement. If the information she provided was useful enough, Starr's prosecutors would consider giving her limited "use immunity." The sweeping sort of transactional immunity that Ginsburg and Speights had wanted was officially off the table.

Ginsburg unloaded a string of expletives at Bennett, accusing him of changing the deal midstream.

Bennett, for his part, had endured enough of these outbursts by the swimming-pool lawyer. It was time to pull rank. He shouted across the table, "This isn't working. Let's just stop." Bruce Udolf stood up and handed Ginsburg a subpoena for Bernie Lewinsky, asking, "Will you accept service for the father?"

With this, according to those present, Ginsburg "went berserk." He whipped Bernie's subpoena across the conference table, knocking over a cup of coffee, causing it to shower the area like a small bomb. After hurling out a dozen more expletives, Ginsburg snarled at Jackie Bennett, "You've just made the worst enemy you've ever had. You want trouble, now you're going to see trouble." As Mike Emmick would later say of Ginsburg's blowup, "It was a good act, if it was an act."

Ginsburg marched into the reception room and collected Lewinsky. "Let's go, Monica," he shouted, "we're out of here." Monica had come to this meeting expecting the ordeal to be over. Now, the negotiations seemed to be suffering a meltdown.

Walking toward the elevator, Ginsburg informed her that Starr's prosecutors had "threatened" to serve a subpoena on him for Bernie Lewinsky. They were obviously going after Dr. Lewinsky's tax records in an effort to ruin him. At that news, Monica collapsed to the floor. The Starr prosecutors could hear their would-be witness sobbing all the way down the hallway, as Ginsburg pulled the young woman up and propped her against his shoulders. They could also hear the elevator doors slam shut as Bill Ginsburg, still cursing Ken Starr and the Office of Independent Counsel, removed his client from the building.

PART FOUR

THE GRAND
CONFESSIONAL

A PRESIDENCY IN PERIL

On Wednesday, January 21, 1998, the *Washington Post,* the *Los Angeles Times,* and ABC News dropped the bombshell, finally catching up with Matt Drudge and his salacious Drudge Report. The *Post* first posted the story on its Web site at 12:32 in the morning. Six minutes later, news anchor Jackie Judd reported it on ABC Radio. On the West Coast, the *Los Angeles Times* quickly followed suit. The dam had broken open.

The story was unlike any that the nation's capital had seen in decades, not since President Richard M. Nixon had been caught with the smoking-gun tapes during the Watergate scandal, forcing him to resign in disgrace during the summer of 1974.

Early editions of the major newspapers were already printed and bundled by the time the Lewinsky story broke. This meant some readers opened their morning papers to see an innocuous headline about President Clinton's summit with Israeli Prime Minister Benjamin Netanyahu. It was not until after midnight that the printing presses were retooled in record time. Later versions of newspapers delivered to the doorsteps of millions of American homes contained the shocking headlines: CLINTON ACCUSED OF URGING AIDE TO LIE; STARR PROBES WHETHER PRESIDENT TOLD WOMAN TO DENY ALLEGED AFFAIR TO JONES LAWYERS.

One paragraph of the *Washington Post* story surprised even Michael Isikoff, who had been covering the Lewinsky-Tripp saga from day one. It read: "In some of the conversations—including one in recent days—Lewinsky described Clinton and Jordan directing her to testify falsely in the Paula Jones sexual harassment case against the president, according to sources." Isikoff already had heard key tapes; he knew that this crucial piece of evidence involving Vernon Jordan— evidence that Linda Tripp had bragged about to him and OIC prosecutors—was nowhere corroborated on those tapes. Yet the Jordan story somehow had been pumped into the media and the rumor had shot around the world like a rocket.

John Podesta, inside the West Wing, recalled that the first full blast of the Lewinsky story felt like "a shotgun shot in the head." The notion that the president may have engaged in a sexual dalliance of any kind with a young intern inside the

White House nauseated him. "What's the strategy, after you're done vomiting?" he asked. Podesta assembled some of the president's top advisers and announced: "Houston, we've got a problem." The potential problem was not only Bill Clinton; it was also Ken Starr. The whole story that connected Paula Jones with Monica Lewinsky with Starr seemed mind-boggling. "These are like parallel lines," explained Podesta. "They're not supposed to be crossing."

President Clinton appeared "rocked" by events. As he huddled with his closest aides, he insisted that the story was false but provided scant explanation. Recalled Podesta, the president met with him personally and gave him "a strong denial" that left him "with the feeling that something funky was going on, but that he hadn't had sex with [the intern]." Clinton had planned to spend the day giving interviews to generate support for his State of the Union initiatives the following week. Instead, the chief executive faced a barrage of questions about "adultery and obstruction of justice" from reporters. In a prescheduled interview with Jim Lehrer for PBS's *NewsHour,* from which he could not extricate himself, a defensive president (accompanied for moral support by his chocolate Labrador retriever, Buddy) told Lehrer emphatically: "There is no improper relationship" with Lewinsky. The low-key but persistent Lehrer pressed the president to define what he meant by "no improper relationship." Clinton tensed up, then responded: "Well, I think you know what it means. It means that there is not a sexual relationship, an improper sexual relationship, or any other kind of improper relationship."

In an interview with National Public Radio later that day, radio journalists Mara Liasson and Robert Siegel pressed for additional answers. Liasson asked with a tone of bewilderment: "Mr. President, where do you think this comes from? Did you have any kind of relationship with her [Lewinsky] that could have been misconstrued?" Clinton did his best to deflect the question: "Mara, I'm going to do my best to cooperate with the investigation. . . . I think it's more important for me to tell the American people that there wasn't improper relations, I didn't ask anyone to lie, and I intend to cooperate. And I think that's all I should say right now so I can get back to the work of the country."

In a third scheduled telephone interview with the Capitol Hill publication *Roll Call,* the "I-word" was finally uttered by a reporter, which brought terror to the souls of White House advisers. The questioner asked President Clinton: "Some Republicans have been talking about impeachment for months now. And even your former adviser, George Stephanopoulos [of ABC News], mentioned it this morning. . . . What is your reaction to the suggestion that this may lead to impeachment?" The president tried to squelch this talk immediately: "Well, I don't believe it will. I'm going to cooperate with this investigation. And

I made it very clear that the allegations are not true. I didn't ask anybody not to tell the truth. And I'll cooperate."

The *Roll Call* journalist next pressed for more details concerning the nature of the president's relationship with Monica Lewinsky, asking bluntly: "Was it in any way sexual?" Clinton paused, then gave his most definitive answer of the day, careful to use the past tense: "The relationship was not sexual," he said. "And I know what you mean, and the answer is no."

White House aides hunkered down, trying to calculate what bombshell might drop next. The president himself, in between horrific interviews, placed an urgent call to his erstwhile consultant Dick Morris, who could sympathize with the president's dilemma: He himself had been outed for having an affair with a high-priced hooker that involved a foot fetish. "I just slipped up with that girl," Clinton told his former pollster, almost in tears. The two men talked over the options—should the president come clean in public? Ask forgiveness? Fight Starr to the death? As Morris later recalled, he was struck with a brilliant idea: "Let's poll it!" he said. By late that night, Morris had called Clinton in the private residence with preliminary results. On the questions dealing purely with adultery, the public was prepared to forgive and forget. But on the perjury and related questions, the numbers were scary. One poll question asked: "If President Clinton lied, he committed the crime of perjury. If he encouraged Monica to lie he committed the crime of obstruction of justice. In view of these facts, do you think President Clinton should be removed from office?" A whopping 60 percent of the respondents answered "yes." Dick Morris told his former client: "If you get anywhere near lying under oath, you're cooked." The president slumped back in his chair.

The *Washington Post* ran a story titled "Clinton Denies Affair, Says He Never Asked Former Aide to Lie," while another headline blared "Former Intern Refers to Relationship with President." The American public was treated to its first pictures of the blond, frizzy-haired Linda Tripp, along with a Defense Department file photo of a beaming Monica Lewinsky with black hair bouncing off her shoulders and pearls strung around her neck. News accounts were beginning to describe former civil rights lawyer Vernon Jordan as a "key figure in the Starr probe," stating that Jordan had arranged for Lewinsky to get a job interview in New York with a big corporation and allegedly "was enlisted to persuade Lewinsky to deny having had an affair with the president."

The *Post* declared: "President Imperiled As Never Before."

Friends and family of President Bill Clinton reacted with a mixture of shock and disbelief. Supporters of Independent Counsel Ken Starr immediately rose to his defense. Already, dividing lines were beginning to split the country in two.

Joe Purvis, who had grown up with Clinton and who had barely gotten over the trauma of Vince Foster's death, remembered thinking, "For the love of God, if the son of a bitch was so stupid to do something like that, he deserves what he gets." As Purvis watched the photos flash on the television of this young former intern named Monica, he could only assume that this was "the latest in one of these slime attacks of Clinton."

Betsey Wright, Clinton's chief of staff during his years as governor and the person who had handled the "bimbo eruptions" during the presidential election of 1992, was living in seclusion on Beaver Lake in the northwest mountains of Arkansas. Although she had long since relinquished her role as guardian of Bill Clinton's virtue, she still had plenty of friends in the White House. For some time, she had been worried about the stories she was hearing from secondhand sources: "I remember getting rumors about Bill alone in the Oval Office with a woman. And I would call people I knew on the staff and say 'Just don't ever let him in there by himself with anybody.' " Her principal fear, after decades of knowing Bill Clinton, was that *this* time, he might really cook his own goose and in the process deeply hurt Hillary and Chelsea. "Yes," Wright said, choking back emotion. When she saw the Lewinsky allegations reported in the paper, she was overcome by an instant fear that they might be true.

Susan McDougal, still imprisoned for contempt, was convinced that the story was false. During her first stay in an Arkansas prison after she refused to answer the questions propounded by the Starr grand jury, a deputy sheriff had whispered to her: "Just tell those Starr people what they want. You think the Clintons care about you? They're having dinner in the White House right now while you're in this God-awful place. Think about it."

Now Susan was in yet another God-awful jail cell; the president knew that one question the Starr prosecutors likely wanted to ask her related to whether she had engaged in an extramarital affair with him during the governor years, because it might explain why she wouldn't talk. It seemed utterly implausible, McDougal told herself, that Bill Clinton would risk having a frolic with a young intern under these circumstances. Certainly the president knew that the longer Starr's investigation kept grinding forward, the longer she would remain in prison for contempt, continuing to endure cockroaches and inhumane conditions. "I didn't believe he would be so reckless," Susan later confessed. "I believed Monica Lewinsky's story was imagined—a fake."

On Ken Starr's side of the divide, friends and family were confident that the independent counsel would adhere to his strong principles and follow the evidence wherever it took him. His sister, Billie Jeayne Reynolds, who lived in Kingwood, Texas, saw support for her brother running high. The retired fourth-grade teacher would steadfastly decline interviews during the scandal, but later say of Ken, "He was looking for the truth. And we knew that they felt that if he could do this additional thing [investigating the Monica Lewinsky case], he would do a good job." Her son, Gary, added a nephew's perspective: "I don't think any of us were terribly happy about it or pleased, but we knew that Ken was doing a good job."

Alice Starr, the independent counsel's wife of twenty-seven years and his most ardent supporter, had sensed something unusual was up. Ken never talked about his OIC travails, in large part to protect his family. Yet Alice saw her husband's patterns changing. During this period in mid-January, Ken had been coming home regularly after midnight. All she knew was that he was "working [hard] on a project" and that "things were very tense in the office." Like most Americans, she was totally shocked when she opened her newspaper on January 21 and read that her husband had moved from investigating the Whitewater/Madison deal to investigating perjury and obstruction of justice in the *Paula Jones* case. Yet Alice could see "a connection with what [Ken] had been working on." She saw the link between the Webster Hubbell jobs-for-silence investigation and Vernon Jordan. "So I don't think he was really looking at Monica Lewinsky's love life," Alice said, "but that's what it turned out that the press thought."

During this period of stress, Alice saw deep creases developing on her husband's face. "If you know Ken," she said, seated at a wooden conference table at her corporate real estate office, "he's just not someone who's ever read a magazine that even hints at that kind of [sexual] thing. He's just a very proper person and does not discuss people's personal lives or want to know about them. I am sure it had to be very hard on him." Ken's workdays now seemed to last eighteen hours, regularly. There was little time for dinner or relaxation of any sort. When her husband did come home, he could not speak to his spouse about the case that was consuming his life and turning him into a pariah in the eyes of many Americans. "He just worked very, very hard on it," Alice recalled, "trying to get the facts out."

———

THE final weeks of January, after the Lewinsky story erupted in the media, were among the most fast-moving in American political history. On the same day that "Unabomber" Theodore J. Kaczynski earned life in prison by pleading guilty to a spree of mail bombings that killed three victims and maimed others, Vernon Jordan issued his first public comment in the Clinton-Lewinsky scandal. Dressed in a gray suit and speaking into a bank of microphones, the six-foot-four Jordan told journalists at the Park Hyatt Hotel that he was prepared to speak the truth. "I want to say absolutely and unequivocally that Ms. Lewinsky told me in no uncertain terms that she did not have a sexual relationship with the President,"

Jordan stated with his classic smooth delivery. "At no time did I ever say, suggest or intimate to her that she should lie."

Judge Susan Webber Wright postponed Monica Lewinsky's *Jones* deposition, to keep the beleaguered young woman away from the salivating media. Starr and his staff used the time to issue a spray of subpoenas to the president's personal secretary, Betty Currie, and other potential witnesses in the White House. They also filed a subpoena duces tecum requesting entry logs that would show how often, and when, Lewinsky visited the White House after her employment in the executive mansion ceased in April 1996.

The American public, if ever it was glued to a story involving the personal life of a president, was stuck fast to this one. By Sunday, the *Washington Post* was already recapping "Washington's Extraordinary Week." One article called the twenty-four-year-old Lewinsky "an ebullient, vulnerable 'child' infatuated with the president," and a "despairing, ravaged woman who in tape-recorded conversations describes him as 'the creep' and 'Dear Schmucko.' " A group of Bill and Hillary Clinton's close friends, including high-ranking White House aides, offered the baffling explanation to reporters that the president had become "emotionally close" with Lewinsky during the time she worked in the West Wing, but that their relationship "never became sexual." The spin machine now began weaving stories on "deep-background" that Lewinsky's prattle about a sexual relationship with the leader of the free world was either "fantasy or untruthful boasting."

As photographers captured the president and the First Lady leaving Sunday services at the Foundry United Methodist Church in Washington, with psalm books clasped firmly in their hands, a series of weekend polls revealed wildly fluctuating numbers for the president, swinging from enthusiastic approval to outrage. Public opinion was bouncing around like unstable atoms in a nuclear reactor. A survey conducted by ABC News/Washington Post found that 63 percent of Americans believed that Clinton "should voluntarily resign if he lied in sworn testimony" or if he "suggested [Lewinsky] lie." At the same time, the president's job approval remained solid, with 56 percent of those polled saying that the alleged affair with the former intern "was not an important issue." As one journalist wrote, this was "a crisis with no parallel." The news media previously had given presidents a "free pass" when it came to their personal lives. "For whatever reason," observed Republican pollster Robert Teeter, "the worms are out of the can here."

Democratic allies of the Clintons kept their mouths shut or issued "tepid statements" of support for the embattled president. Senate Democratic Leader Tom Daschle declared, as if trying to avoid a pool of quicksand: "These are serious allegations which the president has denied, and which deserve an investigation that should be conducted quickly and fairly." Even the president's own teammates knew that the "other shoe" could drop at any moment.

To add to the precarious situation, reports were surfacing that Ken Starr was seeking interviews with Secret Service agents in the White House to determine if they had observed any untoward behavior between Clinton and Lewinsky. Rumors were flying around the Internet that several Secret Service agents had witnessed illicit liaisons in the private study off the Oval Office and in the White House movie theater in the East Wing. The Starr team was taking steps to piggyback onto the work of Paula Jones's lawyers, who had already sought to depose Secret Service agents posted in the White House, to drill into the topic of "other women."

Panicked congressional Democrats were privately expressing concern that President Bill Clinton—like Harry Houdini tied upside down in a water tank with his arms and legs chained together—"might be unable to recover" from this latest impossible situation into which he had submerged himself. Longtime Clinton friends Harry and Linda Thomason, Hollywood filmmakers who produced the popular television sitcom *Designing Women,* flew to Washington to offer public relations help. As Bill Clinton and dog Buddy sloshed around the White House grounds through the rain, Harry Thomason advised the president that it was time to take charge, before this intern debacle spun further out of control. The State of the Union address was just days away. Instead of letting the scandal overshadow his ambitious agenda for the country, said Thomason, why not take bold steps to correct the situation *now?* Another trusted adviser, Harold Ickes, in whose office Monica Lewinsky had worked during the government shutdown, told Clinton bluntly that his comments on radio and television "would not lead one to conclude you were totally innocent here." It was time to take action; it was time for the president to clear up this misunderstanding.

On Monday morning, January 26, as First Lady Hillary Clinton was welcoming a group of special guests to the White House for a program on education and child care, Vice President Al Gore stepped to the microphone and told the audience that he was honored to introduce "America's true education president." The crowd sprung to its feet and applauded, unsure how to deal with this unexpected appearance. Bill Clinton, wearing a blue suit and "red power tie," strode to the podium and delivered an extemporaneous locution on after-school programs, Internet-accessible classrooms, and other forward-thinking education initiatives.

Then, before returning to the White House theater, where he was rehearsing his State of the Union speech, the president grabbed the lectern with one hand, raising his index finger threateningly with the other. His jaw suddenly became clenched like that of a fighter. His eyes were baggy from lack of sleep but possessed the kind of fire that indicated fierce determination. Bill Clinton glared directly into the camera and growled in a tired but combative voice: "I want to say one thing to the American people. I want you to listen to me. I'm [not] going to say this again." He wagged his finger. "I did not have sexual relations with that woman . . ." Clinton momentarily blanked out, forgetting the woman's name. Then he recovered: ". . . Ms. Lewinsky." He continued: "I never told anybody to lie, not a single time, never."

The president thumped the wooden lectern, narrowing his eyes and looking around the Roosevelt Room. "These allegations are false. And I need to go back to work for the American people." As Clinton swiveled to depart, reporters shouted questions about the true nature of his relationship with Lewinsky. The First Lady, still on the dais, stared blankly into space as her husband waved these questions off with an angry gesture, moving swiftly toward the door flanked by his Secret Service agents.

The White House later tried to smooth over this bad day, telling the *New York Times* that the president had become "distracted by events."

Bernie Lewinsky, father of the presidential intern now known round the world, had watched Clinton's remarks about "that woman" and felt like spitting at the TV screen. "I was offended with the cowardliness that he depicted with that phrase," said Dr. Lewinsky, "and that's when I began to feel that he was a really disgusting person. I'm not condoning anything, but if you're going to have an affair, you gotta be prepared to have the consequences and face up to it."

The day after the president's impromptu, finger-wagging denial, First Lady Hillary Clinton launched a surprise counteroffensive of her own. Sitting in an easy chair with ferns adorning the background and giving a wide-ranging interview to Matt Lauer on NBC's *Today* show, Mrs. Clinton suddenly rose to the defense of her husband. Dressed in a black suit with a chic necklace, she responded to Lauer's question concerning the truth of the president's relationship with Monica Lewinsky, insisting that she had talked with her husband "at great length" and she believed his story. "I think as this matter unfolds," Mrs. Clinton stated, her voice growing tight as if she needed a sip of water, "the entire country will have more information. But we're right in the middle of a rather vigorous feeding frenzy right now."

When Mrs. Clinton alluded to abuses by the "independent counsel," Lauer interrupted: "We're talking about Kenneth Starr, so let's use his name because he is the independent counsel." At the mention of Starr's name, the First Lady seemed stirred to arms. "I do believe that this is a battle," she said, her voice punctuated by anger. "I mean, look at the very people who are involved in this. . . . The great story here, for anybody who is willing to find it and write about it and explain it, is this *vast right-wing conspiracy* that has been conspiring against my husband since the day he announced [he was running] for president."

Hillary Rodham Clinton was standing by her husband, alleging that a broad, black-hearted conspiracy of political enemies was seeking to do him in. The national television audience—or at least a portion of it—loved it.

That same night, President Bill Clinton gave a masterful State of the Union address. He made no mention of adultery or Monica Lewinsky or the scandal that was threatening to wreck his presidency. Instead, the embattled chief executive spoke of the importance of safeguarding budget surpluses, and of the dangers posed by Iraq, where a military strike by American forces might be necessary if Iraqi President Saddam Hussein continued to defy United Nations weapons inspectors. It was a virtuoso performance, one of the most dazzling of his career, bumping Clinton's finicky poll numbers upward.

Yet there were ominous signs that not everyone was buying the president's slick salesmanship, even among his most loyal supporters. Justice David Newbern, longtime "Friend of Bill," or FOB, watched the finger-wagging speech from his living room in Little Rock and reached an unpleasant conclusion: "I thought it was probably not the truth," he would recall. As someone who had known Bill Clinton for years, Newbern detected something in his face and mannerisms that disturbed him. "It seemed to me that there was something wrong there, that we were headed for a downhill slide."

Betsey Wright felt almost sickened by all the signs. "I know his body language too well," she said as if in a trance. "I knew he wasn't telling the truth." She still felt a large measure of responsibility for allowing Bill Clinton to rise to this position of power, knowing the dirty secrets of select "sexual escapades" in the past. "God, was I angry with him," she said, recalling this low point in her own life. "Because he knew that he was under a microscope. I guess I have felt for some time that the dalliances that Bill Clinton had, had nothing to do with sex. They had to do with some kind of inferiority complex that he inexplicably had. And that it was a sickness that he as president of the United States wasn't free to go get help on it. I didn't want him to run for president. And I remember telling him that I didn't think he could control [his desire for women]. And that he would end up nationally embarrassing and humiliating Hillary and Chelsea. And he told me that he had it all under control now."

John Brummett, a Little Rock journalist who had worked the state capital beat for the *Arkansas Gazette* and had followed Bill Clinton since he ran for attorney general, was attending a party with a group of Arkansas friends at the conclusion of this incredible week and reached a three-part conclusion: "One, he did it. Two, he lied under oath about it. Three, he's gotta go." Brummett now predicted that Clinton would resign: "Only because he would *have to*."

Even among folks from home, Brummett detected, an irreparable split was developing. "By that point, I don't think Arkansas had any view of Clinton that was discernibly different from the rest of the country," he explained, "except we'd had ours longer. . . . I mean, all the things the nation was going through, we'd been going through that before. We'd just been doing it longer."

As one journalist acquaintance of Brummett's who was an avowed FOB put it, "You know Bill just kind of eats you up. You give and give and give to him. And then, when you're done giving to him, he moves on to somebody else who's got some more to give. I think that's kind of the nature of this all-consuming politician that he is."

When Clinton was first elected president, many Arkansans had believed that capturing this high office would bring a treasure trove of glorious prizes to Arkansas. Instead, many were muttering that they were getting "nothing except a bad name" out of this deal. The rest of the country was making jokes as if Arkansas was a haven for hillbillies who intermarried and cheated on each other for amusement. Now, critics were snickering louder than ever: "This is what you get when you elect a guy from Arkansas, someone with shady business dealings who can't keep his pants zipped, can't tell the truth. That's just Arkansas!"

Many Arkansans now gathered together, after this staggering week, and gasped to each other in horror: "Oh God, now this?"

CHAPTER

33

"OF TRUST AND CONFIDENCE"

One of the fiercest battles that erupted between Ken Starr's office and the Justice Department, to which he theoretically was appended, related to the question of whether United States Secret Service (USSS) agents could be forced to testify.

Within days of the Lewinsky story's erupting in the mainstream press, news reports swept over the Internet and wire services, declaring that Secret Service agents posted in the White House had walked in on President Clinton and Monica Lewinsky in various compromising positions. The first media outlet to break the story was the *Dallas Morning News;* it posted a late-night report on its Web site, slaking the public's thirst for more salacious news about the Lewinsky affair. Under the byline of David Jackson, the Dallas paper reported that a specific Secret Service agent had stepped forward "Ready to Testify." A person identified as a Washington lawyer familiar with the FBI and Starr's office was quoted as saying: "Starr has this person in his hand. This person is now a government witness." The source added: "This person is real."

Web sites, newspapers, and the worldwide media piled onto the story. The *New York Post* featured a front-page sizzler with the banner: "*Sexgate Stunner*, Secret Service Agent to Testify: I SAW THEM DO IT." An inside story promised "G-Man Who 'Saw Tryst' Will Tell." The media also reported that Monica Lewinsky had dictated a "complete proffer" of her testimony over the phone to Starr's prosecutors, and that she was prepared to walk into the grand jury and "spill the beans."

No sooner had the Secret Service story swept around the world than the *Dallas Morning News* retracted it. A day after its publication, editor Ralph Langer made the embarrassing admission that "a primary source was now claiming that he had provided incorrect information." Yet there was no way to put the genie back in its bottle. With rumors abounding that Secret Service agents held the key to proving the illicit affair, Ken Starr's office swung into action. The best way to find out what ordinarily mum Secret Service agents had seen, OIC decided, was to question them under oath.

The person most incensed and troubled by this decision was Lewis C. Merletti, director of the Secret Service. The short, agile Italian American with jet black hair had grown up in Pittsburgh and looked more like an athlete than a member of a counterassault team trained to kill. In 1998, at age fifty, Lew Merletti had risen to the top of his profession. He had accomplished this by remaining low-key, by maintaining an intense ability to focus, and through grueling preparation. Awarded a Green Beret at age twenty, Merletti had completed a tour of duty in Vietnam on the Special Forces A-Team, returned to pursue a career in the Secret Service (he was assigned to the Washington, D.C., counterassault team), and then received an appointment to one of the most coveted but stressful jobs in the agency: serving in the Presidential Protection Division, or PPD.

The PPD stressed attention to detail, disciplined focus, and a work ethic that treated each moment of each day as "strictly business." When he first arrived, the Secret Service had just dealt with an assassination attempt on President Reagan in March 1981—sixty-nine days after Reagan's inauguration. Consequently, Merletti and his fellow PPD agents worked relentlessly on drills involving AOPs (attacks on principals). He followed a strict regimen that included weight-lifting, running, and monthly shooting requalifications to gain every advantage in case of an attack. Merletti practiced "evacuating" from burning motorcades and fleeing from fiery buildings created by exploding pyrotechnics at the Secret Service's undisclosed training center, preparing for any dark scenario that might present itself.

For much of the term of President George H. W. Bush, Lew Merletti and his fellow PPD agents walked close by the president's side. They were dressed as hospital technicians, as major league baseball coaches, as priests, as students in caps and gowns, as Arab sheiks, and in an array of other disguises that allowed them to stick next to President Bush like alter egos. On his wall—beside a photo of himself exiting a burning building with a submachine gun as part of an antiterrorism maneuver—Merletti kept a framed copy of the cover of the *Washington Post* dated January 17, 1991. On that day, President Bush, wearing a trench coat and walking somberly through the rain with the Washington Monument in the background, was flanked by a single, slight man in a dark suit. The caption read: "U.S., Allies Launch Massive Attack Against Targets in Iraq and Kuwait." On that walk, President Bush had leaned over and confided to Agent Merletti, "Thousands of our pilots are in the air right now. God bring them back safely."

Every day of this job, Merletti would later say softly, he knew that he was engaged in the most "serious business imaginable."

When President William Jefferson Clinton moved into the White House in January 1993, Merletti told his director, Eljay Bowron, that he would prefer not to return to the PPD. Besides the job's being an unusually stressful assignment—he had already done his time under two presidents—Merletti feared that Clinton's people would view him as a "Reagan-Bush" loyalist, which would prevent him from carrying out his job effectively. "Although in the Secret Service, we are apolitical," Merletti explained, "the politicians don't necessarily see it that way. And if they have seen you with a prior president from a different party, they think that your loyalties may lie with that president or with that party." His greatest fear was that the new president would lack trust in him, pushing him away when sensitive matters were discussed, creating unacceptable risks for the new commander in chief.

Yet Director Bowron promoted Merletti to head the protective detail for President Clinton. In 1997, when Bowron retired unexpectedly, Merletti was elevated to the agency's top position, becoming the nineteenth director of the Secret Service. Now, barely a half-year into his tenure, Merletti was confronted with one of the greatest challenges ever to face that agency in its 132-year history. If Secret Service agents were forced to testify by Independent Counsel Ken Starr, Director Merletti believed strongly, the agency would be irreparably harmed.

Truth be told, when the Lewinsky story made headlines worldwide, Merletti was stunned "because the events, if they had happened, had happened when I was agent in charge of the president's detail, and I did not know who Monica Lewinsky was." A review of the archives would later reveal that "Monica Samille Lewinsky" had sent Merletti at least one letter in October 1996, thanking him for doing such a great job "of protecting the 'Big Guy.'" Yet Merletti had no recollection of this note. It was common to receive pieces of mail as head of PPD from unknown "fans" of all kinds, sane or otherwise. The Lewinsky name rang no bells. But this problem was arising under Merletti's watch, and he had to deal with it. As head of an agency whose motto was "Worthy of Trust and Confidence," he could not allow federal prosecutors—from Starr's office or anywhere else—to interrogate his agents about things they had seen and heard while protecting the chief executive.

Merletti immediately convened a briefing session at the Old Executive Office Building with the Secret Service's chief counsel, John Kelleher. A veteran of the Justice Department, Kelleher assured Merletti there was nothing to worry about. The attorney had dealt with Starr when Starr was solicitor general, and again on Whitewater-related matters; he had always found Starr to be agreeable and accommodating. As Merletti recalled, Kelleher "felt that from past experience with Starr, that once we went over and explained to him our concerns—Secret Service concerns—that it would be a nonissue and that the subpoenas would go away."

Merletti next requested an audience with Attorney General Janet Reno and Deputy Attorney General Eric Holder. In high-level meetings attended by a slew of Justice Department lawyers, Merletti dimmed the lights and gave a highly classified PowerPoint presentation about the dangers presented if Secret Service agents were pushed away from a president for any reason—including lack of trust. Over three thousand threats were directed at the president of the United States each year; the Secret Service had to investigate and guard against them all. Ten of the last eleven presidents had been the subjects of assassination attempts. In each case, *proximity* of the agents was critical.

The most powerful aspect of Merletti's presentation, according to those in attendance, was rarely seen footage regarding the assassination of President Kennedy in Dallas, and Kennedy's trip the previous week to Tampa. In photos of the Florida trip, dated November 18, 1963, one could observe sharp images of Secret Service agents kneeling on the rear bumper of the president's limousine, scanning the crowd and buildings, maintaining a location within an arm's length of President Kennedy's position in the backseat.

In the haunting film clips that Merletti now showed of President Kennedy being shot in Dallas, the Secret Service agents were missing from the car's bumper. Only Agent Clint Hill knew all of the tragic details, and he since had gone into seclusion and did not speak publicly about that day.

Yet the story was well known within the Secret Service. Lew Merletti took a chance and reached out to Hill, who had settled in Northern Virginia, seeking Hill's guidance on the Starr matter. Agent Hill, a handsome man with deep furrows of mental stress on his face, had retired early from the service as a result of neurological and psychological problems. The former agent did not hesitate to share his views with the director; he still remembered those events of November 1963 too vividly.

Hill technically had been assigned to protect First Lady Jacqueline Kennedy, who was riding in the left rear seat of the presidential limousine. The crowds were so large that spectators were "swarming up on top of the car." To deal with the cluster around the motorcade, the driver "ran the [limo] closer to the left-hand side of the street . . . to keep the people away from the president." Agent Hill's sixth sense was telegraphing that something was wrong. Yet just after the Tampa trip, President Kennedy had directed all Secret Service agents to stay off the running board on the rear bumper, complaining that it created the appearance to the public that there was "somebody or something between them and him."

Disobeying the president's orders, Agent Hill had climbed onto the left side of the bumper, scanning the crowds and buildings, and then jumped off, returning to the follow-up car. The motorcade turned left. In an instant that would forever haunt him, Hill heard a shot ring out from behind, followed by the echo of two more gunshots.

By the time Agent Hill could scramble onto the back of the limousine, Mrs. Kennedy was crawling onto the trunk in her pink suit. Even as she hoisted Hill up, the agent knew it was too late. "It was a bloody mess," he recalled decades later, his voice cracking. "I mean—the president's head, the third shot hit him in the head just above the right ear, kind of. Took out a piece of his skull about the size of my palm and scooped out a whole mass of brain matter. Now, that stuff was all over the car, inside the car. Blood, white brain matter, portions of bone and skull. And everybody was covered with it." The former agent, becoming unglued as he recounted the story even forty years later, took a deep breath and continued: "What I meant by telling Lew [Merletti] about that scene . . . Here was the president of the United States, who we were sworn to protect. And we failed. At least those of us who were assigned that day to that mission were not able to fulfill our responsibility."

What continued to torment Agent Hill as he replayed these images in his head, decades later, was the fact that he had been pushed away. "If we had been in proximity, where we should have been," he explained, ". . . the event would not have happened as it did." Had Hill been allowed to do his job, a human shield would have been formed between the unseen shooter and President Kennedy, creating a near-impossible shot. As Hill would summarize it, "Either the guy would have been faced with, 'Well, I can't do it . . . I'll do it again some other time.' Or he would have made the attempt, but he would have had to have shot *through* an agent."

Regardless of which of those scenarios would have confronted the assassin, one of the great tragedies in American history would have been undone.

Merletti's PowerPoint presentation clicked forward to a blowup of the key frame of the famous Zapruder film, with a red circle around the empty space on the limousine behind President Kennedy, showing a clear shot for the assassin.

With the lights in the conference room still dimmed, Merletti cut to a rarely seen television interview with Clint Hill by Mike Wallace, filmed in the 1970s, after Hill's premature retirement from the Secret Service. The forty-three-year-old Hill chain-smoked cigarettes and choked up with emotion as he spoke of failing to protect the president that day in Dallas and of allowing himself to be pushed away by the president. "It was my fault," said Hill, crying as he stared into the camera. "I'll live with that till my grave."

Said Merletti, as the film clip ended and the room fell absolutely silent: "The sound of a gunshot is what every Secret Service agent prepares for his whole life. That takes place in a second." Allowing agents to be subpoenaed and forcing them to reveal the intimate details of a president's activities and conversations, said Merletti, his voice becoming emotional as he concluded his presentation, would cause presidents to push away any time that sensitive matters were being discussed. If this happened, the trust between agent and chief executive would dissolve and the protective function of the agency would be destroyed.

Janet Reno shook Merletti's hand, telling him that his presentation had moved her deeply. That night, Eric Holder called him and said, "Listen, I don't know how you did this, but you now have the vast majority of the Department of Justice that believes you are right." Merletti replied, "Eric, I mean it's logic. There's nothing secret here. There's nothing that's a trick here. This is the truth."

Merletti next paid a visit to the Office of Independent Counsel on Pennsylvania Avenue, determined to make a similar impression on Ken Starr and his prosecutors. Merletti knew that this was his only shot at persuading the special prosecutor. He first handed Starr a booklet—his PowerPoint presentation in printed form—to vividly illustrate the danger of presidents pushing away. He also gave Starr a 1910 memorandum written by USSS chief John E. Wilkie, who explained the critical importance of the presidential protective function. "So far as the actions of the President and his family and his social or official callers are concerned the men [of the USSS] are deaf, dumb and blind," Wilkie wrote. "In all the years this service has been maintained at the White House and the freedom with which many important public matters have been discussed in the presence, there never has been a leak or betrayal of trust."

Merletti also presented Starr with a letter from John W. Magaw, USSS director during the Bush administration, written to Senator John F. Kerry, then chairman of the Select Committee on POW/MIA Affairs. That committee had subpoenaed a retired agent who had served in the PPD for President Reagan and Vice President Bush, seeking to "compel his testimony" regarding a conversation he reportedly heard involving the president. Director Magaw had written to Senator Kerry to oppose this directive, insisting that such a subpoena would undermine the Secret Service, whether or not Congress technically possessed the power to issue it: "To compel an employee or former employee of the Secret

Service to reveal such a conversation would violate the trust and confidence which is the foundation of our ability to perform our mission," he wrote. In response to that letter, the committee had withdrawn its subpoena.

Despite these seemingly compelling pieces of precedent, Merletti described his reception by Independent Counsel Ken Starr as one of chilly disinterest. "And I mean he [Starr] couldn't have cared less. I didn't even think he was really paying attention to what I was saying." As Merletti recalled the scene, Starr seemed downright impatient for him to finish the assassination presentation. They sat in the OIC conference room, staring at each other. "I perceived him as very aloof, very detached from what I was saying," Merletti recalled. His impression of the special prosecutor was: "He's not listening—he's not going to be objective toward us at all."

Starr would later defend himself, saying that he viewed this as a clear-cut constitutional issue. As sympathetic as he might have been to the Secret Service's plight, he said, there was nothing in the Constitution that shielded these agents from answering questions, under oath, in front of his grand jury, if they possessed evidence of possible criminal wrongdoing by the president. The notion that Secret Service agents were entitled to some amorphous "protective function privilege," which was spelled out nowhere in the Constitution or in the laws of Congress, Starr felt, "bordered on a frivolous position." The independent counsel held no ill feelings toward Merletti. The presidential scandal of the century had blown up on Merletti's watch, and it was understandable that Merletti would try to defuse it. Yet Starr believed that—as both a constitutional and legal matter—Merletti's "praetorian guard approach" lacked merit.

Lew Merletti, on the other hand, did not discern that he was dealing with a neutral, dispassionate special prosecutor. "He could not have been more dismissive of what I had to say," Merletti would counter.

It seemed that Starr had a motive—namely, to extract certain sensational information that he believed Director Merletti was holding back. Merletti recalled, "When I finished, he [Starr] immediately wanted to know if agents were at the family theater in the White House. If they were posted there, and the president was inside, could they see inside?" Merletti instantly deduced that someone had given OIC a tip "that the president was in the family theater and the First Lady walked in on him and Monica Lewinsky." Merletti added, "It turned out to be false—[like] the vast majority of information he was given."

"It was their little version of Deep Throat—that's what they were hoping for," concluded Merletti as he walked out the door. "That they were getting Deep Throat information and that the Secret Service was witness to all this stuff."

So Merletti called every former USSS director who was still alive and able to travel, as well as every former special agent in charge of the PPD, and convened an extraordinary meeting at his offices in Washington. The purpose of the meeting was to communicate: "I seek your advice. Tell me what to do."

This remarkable assemblage took place within days of new reports trickling into the media that Secret Service agents had witnessed other salacious events and might be called soon to testify. With directors and heads of the PPD dating back to the Eisenhower administration seated around him at the conference room table in Secret Service headquarters at 1800 G Street, Merletti asked for guidance.

From every former USSS official on every side of Lew Merletti, the advice was the same. As one former director told Merletti, pointing to the chair at the head of the table, "You are the one who sits in that chair. When we sat there, we stood on these exact same principles. We were just never challenged on it."

"You'd better fight this," another said. "That is your responsibility—to fight this to the fullest. You take it as far as you can go."

Eljay Bowron, who had preceded Merletti as director, raised his hand and made a painful confession. Several years earlier, Starr's office had pressed him, when the missing Rose Law Firm billing records had mysteriously appeared in the White House, to have Secret Service agents testify about things they had seen and heard in the First Family's living quarters. Eventually, Bowron had capitulated and agreed to have his agents *voluntarily* submit to interviews by OIC prosecutors, to avoid having them testify in front of the grand jury. Now, Bowron was plagued by guilt that he had allowed Starr to open the door by permitting even this incursion into the confidentiality of the Secret Service's protective web. "The only regret I have in my entire time as director," he told Merletti, "is that I did not resign right then."

When the next hand rose, the room fell silent; all eyes were focused on former special agent Clint Hill. A rugged, tough-looking man with a deep look of sadness and concern in his eyes, Hill had experienced many personal difficulties after that fateful day in Dallas, when he had been instructed to protect the First Family and watched President Kennedy murdered in cold blood just feet away from him. "He was only recently coming back into the family of the Secret Service, coming back into the fold," Merletti recalled, "because he had felt for years that he failed." Merletti quickly added: "He didn't realize we held him as a hero. But we did. He did everything right that day in Dallas. He was prevented from doing his job by the president."

Seated at the table, Hill strongly urged Director Merletti to resist Starr's strong-arm tactics. Allowing this sort of outside force to disrupt the Secret Service's essential duty when it came to protecting the life of the president, said the retired agent, would be potentially disastrous.

When the meeting broke up, Merletti took Hill aside and thanked him for his support. What happened next was a moment that burned itself into Merletti's memory: Clint Hill stood close to the director and confided "how every night the demons come and visit him—and how he relives that."

As he finished recounting Agent Hill's private confession, Merletti became choked up. "And he begged me—and I don't even know if the word 'beg' is wrong, I mean he told me in no uncertain terms, 'You will fight this.' " The former agent, dark circles still engulfing his eyes, had told Merletti, clamping a hand on the director's shoulder, "I will be by your side."

———

During this dark period, Merletti could not avoid thinking back to the middle of the Persian Gulf War. He had frequently sat in the room with George H. W. Bush as the president was being briefed on highly sensitive matters, including strategy and military movements. Generals and intelligence officials would glance uncomfortably at Merletti and say, "Mr. President, . . ." allowing their eyes to linger on the unknown Secret Service agent. President Bush would say, "They repeat nothing. Continue the briefing."

As Merletti saw it: "The fight is what's going to be important." If the Secret Service lost this battle, future presidents would never again allow them into their private spheres.

This didn't mean, however, that if agents witnessed criminal conduct like murder or theft, they would remain mum. "If there's a crime, you're not going to have to ask us about it," Merletti would later say. "We're going to come forward and *tell* you about it. But if you have an investigation, then you're going to have to investigate it otherwise. Because it's compromising Secret Service trust and confidence, which then compromises proximity, and it's all over."

Deputy Attorney General Holder asked Merletti to make his presentation to Ken Starr a second time, just to "make sure that he [Starr] is hearing the same things that we heard." On this occasion, Merletti felt that Starr was even more dismissive.

The special prosecutor began lecturing Merletti on 28 United States Code Section 535(b), which required officers of the executive branch—including Secret Service agents—to report any wrongdoing they observed to the attorney general. "So Congress has already spoken on this issue," Starr lectured Merletti. While others continued to insist that Starr was a prince of a fellow, Merletti saw no manifestations of this trait. In their private meetings, the special prosecutor seemed humorless and unyielding. As far as the jovial, gracious Southern gentleman whom so many others had spoken about so glowingly, Merletti would say, "I never had the pleasure of witnessing that side of [Starr]."

After their second meeting, Merletti walked out of the OIC conference room and concluded, "It was a total waste of time. And I had the sense he just didn't want me there. He didn't want to hear anything I had to say."

On February 4, the friction between Starr's office and the Secret Service reached a new level. A retired uniformed USSS officer assigned to the White House, Lew Fox, granted an interview to a local paper in rural Western Pennsylvania, telling the paper that he "saw the President and Lewinsky alone together" for approximately forty minutes. Although the actual news story noted that Fox admittedly had no knowledge of what went on inside the Oval Office while Lewinsky was present, and that the retired officer said that he could not "imagine" an affair taking place, those details quickly got lost in the maw of the media. Within a week, the *Washington Post* was announcing: "Clinton, Lewinsky Met Alone, Guard Says." The story reported: "Former uniformed Secret Service officer Lewis C. Fox said in an interview yesterday that Lewinsky, then a White House intern, spent at least 40 minutes alone with Clinton while Fox was posted outside the Oval Office door. She had arrived with papers for the President, he said, and Clinton instructed Fox to usher her into his office."

Merletti hit the roof when Fox's comments became national news. If anyone knew about the elaborate protective clockwork that made the White House tick, it was Merletti. To him it was utter nonsense, that Fox or any other uniformed officer could use his or her x-ray vision to determine what was going on inside the Oval Office. He also found the idea that a former Secret Service officer would blab to the press nothing short of a breach of the time-honored Secret Service code of silence and honor. Merletti would later say of the Fox episode: "It was inappropriate behavior."

Fox also had suggested to the media that he had enjoyed an almost breezy relationship with Monica Lewinsky, who reportedly chatted with him periodically at his post outside the Oval Office door. Some of the security personnel even took to referring to Lewinsky as "your girl," razzing Fox whenever they saw the young intern. Merletti had trouble digesting any of this. "What was that about? I mean we're talking about security, so he was obviously preoccupied with other issues than security. It was very unprofessional. He's not [supposed] to be involved in *anyone's* social life."

Merletti's second objection was that if Fox or any other officer actually saw something that caused him to believe there was inappropriate behavior going on inside the Oval Office, he was duty-bound to report it to his superiors. "If he was so concerned about this," Merletti said, "why didn't he come to me or—he had his other supervisors that he could have gone to. Why keep it to yourself? Why sit on this information?" The proper procedure, if there was any serious question at all, was to tell the head of the PPD, who could then go to the president's chief of staff and resolve the problem.

Moreover, the facts did not add up. A uniformed officer like Fox, the equivalent of a security guard within the White House, performed a wholly different role from that of the agents on the PPD who were assigned to protect the president. On a purely practical level, Merletti did not believe such an officer could have any clue as what was going on behind the closed doors of the president's office. Speculation and gossip were a cheap commodity in these high-level governmental posts; he did not want his agents participating in it. Merletti had no intention of telling Ken Starr or anyone else the precise details of how the Secret Service agents and uniformed officers rotated around the White House. "This is all tactical information that any terrorist would love to have," he said, shutting the door on that subject. Yet, it was public knowledge (from published accounts of the Secret Service operation) that the agents and officers moved around the White House at frequent intervals. As soon as the president entered the Oval Office, a Secret Service agent relieved the uniformed officer who moved down the hall. In regular rhythms, they engaged in rotations, or "pushes." This meant that all Secret Service personnel were constantly moving. It would be virtually impossible—especially for a uniformed officer—to know how long any individual was present in the Oval Office.

There was another important fact to which the media seemed oblivious: The White House operated on a pass system, with codes indicating where individuals had security clearance to move about. Once an individual had obtained clearance to walk around the White House, no further questions were asked. The Oval Office was a working office with as many as four hundred or five hundred individuals flowing in and out on any given day. There was simply no way for Fox or any other officer to look inside the walls of the Oval Office, and to know what—if anything—was going on with Lewinsky or any other visitor.

FBI interviews later confirmed that Lew Fox knew no damning details. He admitted to the FBI that he had never walked in on the president and Lewinsky, and made clear that if he had ever barged into the Oval Office or the presidential study without knocking and being invited to enter by the president, "I would have probably been transferred immediately." The FBI report reached an unambiguous conclusion: "FOX never observed any physical contact between MONICA and the President."

Still, the stories of Fox observing "his girl" Monica Lewinsky as she entered the Oval Office tickled the interest of the national media. They also piqued the interest of the Office of Independent Counsel.

ONE NATION DIVIDED

K en Starr would later conclude that it was a mistake for him to expand into the Monica Lewinsky matter, largely because of the disastrous impact it would have on his Whitewater/Madison investigation and in sullying his otherwise sterling professional reputation. His view in hindsight about the Lewinsky case was that "it had to be investigated. But I was a poor choice to do it."

If he had this decision to do over again, Starr would later muse, he would have gathered up the evidence from Linda Tripp prior to the president's deposition in the *Jones* case and dropped it on the doorstep of Attorney General Janet Reno. In this revised scenario, as he later daydreamed about the Lewinsky matter minus Ken Starr, Attorney General Reno would have said, "Thank you very much, and I have another independent counsel ready to go." The case then would have been assigned "within twenty-four hours" to a different lawyer with an impeccable reputation, someone who had not been tarred with a negative image, however unfair it had been in this case. Sadly, however, life did not allow such replays of fumbled handoffs.

Former President Bill Clinton, on the other hand, would see Starr's expansion into the Lewinsky morass not as an error in judgment, but as conclusive proof that the special prosecutor's motives were impure. "What should *never* happen," Clinton insisted, "is that someone [like Starr] should be appointed a prosecutor with unlimited powers, unlimited access to law enforcement personnel, unlimited access to budget, an unlimited time frame in which to operate, and their main purpose becomes using the criminal law and its ability to indict, to bankrupt and to destroy, to dig up things on someone's personal life. That's wrong." Clinton added, "It's wrong for me; it would be wrong for any person [investigating] a Republican president."

Clinton found the whole notion appalling that Starr and his Republican co-conspirators should have been given the green light to leapfrog from Whitewater to the Lewinsky affair. "Otherwise, we should have a special prosecutor on every president," explained Clinton. "And we should have the FBI looking into the past of every president. And every time they don't get an answer they like about, you know, sexual matters, past drug use, past treatment for drug use, any kind of this kind of stuff, we should just start indicting people like crazy. That's what was wrong. And everybody knows it was wrong." The former president paused for emphasis, before adding, "I think they did it because they could."

Looking back on the tidal wave of events that nearly sank him during his second term in the White House, the former president made no effort to disguise his anger. In Clinton's view, Ken Starr was the last human being on earth who should have been deputized to spearhead an investigation into his sexual sins, because Starr "had a stackful of conflicts of interest." Granted, Clinton's own attorney general, Janet Reno, had been cajoled into permitting Starr's team to jump from Whitewater to this sex scandal. Yet the president forgave his top law enforcement official. First, he concluded that she hadn't been "told the truth" by Starr about OIC's reasons for the expansion. Second, Clinton recognized that there was enormous pressure on Reno to give "Kenny Starr" the green light. "I think the baying at the moon of the conservative Republicans in the Congress, and in the media, and those that had a vested interest in salvaging something out of Whitewater—which by then we knew was nothing—put her in a difficult position," Clinton conceded.

In fact, the president came to agree wholeheartedly with First Lady Hillary Clinton's assessment of this episode as a "vast right-wing conspiracy," with one caveat. "The only thing that I thought was questionable about her characterization," Clinton said, sitting back in his chair and pursing his lips, "was the word 'conspiracy.' Because most of it wasn't a secret at all. A conspiracy is a secret, and people try to keep it a secret. Most of this stuff was right out in the open."

Yet the alleged right-wing conspirators themselves considered this an absurd outburst of self-pity on the part of Bill Clinton. Richard Mellon Scaife, Clinton's purported nemesis, insisted that the so-called Arkansas Project—by which right-wing extremists set out to ensnare Clinton from the start—was entirely a figment of the Clinton White House's imagination. The Scaife foundations, he pointed out, had contributed to the *American Spectator*'s "Editorial Improvement Project" only after Vince Foster's death and Troopergate had created issues worth exploring. "He was POTUS," said Scaife. "President of the United States. What he and his wife had been doing pre-POTUS, I think, reflected a lot on their ethics." The Pittsburgh multimillionaire had long been an advocate of "transparency in government." For him, it was the job of responsible investigative journalists to ferret out misbehavior by those occupying high office.

R. Emmett Tyrrell, Jr., founder and editor of the *American Spectator*, likewise expressed amusement at the Clintons' screeches of indignation. Tyrrell's cousin had gone to high school with Hillary Rodham; this cousin had alerted the publisher as early as 1991, during Clinton's first run for the presidency, that this story was worth pursuing because Clinton was "tarnished with sex scandals" for years.

Around the *Spectator* offices, said Tyrrell, there was a running joke about the White House's protestations concerning the "Arkansas Project" and vast conspiracies. "There was no conspiracy," said Tyrrell. "It was a legitimate news story. There was nothing secret about it. This was no different than *Frontline* getting special funding to do an investigation."

—— —— ——

As each side cast blame on the other, one person who was especially peeved that this new scandal had burst like a supernova over Washington was Starr's ethics adviser, Sam Dash. Dash would later admit, "I was angry that on such an important matter . . . that they [OIC] went ahead and exposed themselves to that kind of criticism without getting my advice."

Dash did not think that he was intentionally left in the dark by the special prosecutor. Still, he was upset and embarrassed that he, the highly touted ethics adviser of Watergate fame, had been left out of the loop on the all-important Lewinsky decision. His colleagues at Georgetown Law School were encircling him like riled coyotes demanding to know whether he agreed with this new, unseemly course charted by the independent counsel to whom he reported. Dash therefore threw on his winter coat and walked briskly from his Georgetown office to the OIC command center, ten blocks away, to confront Starr about the latest turn of events.

Dash's exclusion had been only partly unintentional. Behind closed doors in Starr's office, Dash was considered "high maintenance" and "a real pain." The OIC prosecutors felt they didn't have time to stroke the egos of self-important academics—so when the Lewinsky story broke, Jackie Bennett had blocked Dash out of his mind, consciously or subconsciously. Bennett later accepted the blame: "Somebody probably should have called Sam. And that was me. And I didn't do it. With predictable results."

The moment the bald ethics adviser marched into the office, he told Starr: "I've got to talk to everybody. I've got to see what the basis of all this was." He started with Jackie Bennett and quizzed every prosecutor who had played a role in expanding OIC's jurisdiction, including Ken Starr himself.

Before he died in 2004, Dash declared—in a remarkable defense of the Starr operation, from which he ultimately resigned—that he was satisfied that OIC had acted properly in taking on the distasteful Lewinsky case. From the facts he had gathered from Starr and his staff, including OIC's notes of the meeting with Eric Holder, he had determined they "were not salivating for this, or aggressively seeking it." Starr's lawyers had simply presented the facts to the attorney general's lawyers, who in turn had requested an expansion of jurisdiction for Starr. As Dash saw it, "If she [Janet Reno] thought that she was being pressured by Ken, or that Ken wasn't the appropriate guy to do it, there's nothing that would have prevented her from asking for the appointment of another independent counsel."

Yet Dash still emphasized that he would have strongly counseled against expanding into the Lewinsky investigation if he had been given the chance. Given the "whirlwind of attacks on Ken" that the White House had already set into motion, nothing could be gained by delving into Clinton's alleged sexual dalliances with a young intern. Now, Dash concluded with dismay, "It was too late."

———

ONE unexpected consequence of switching gears so abruptly from the dried-up Whitewater investigation to the red-hot Lewinsky matter was the appointment of the young, previously untested Bob Bittman to run the Washington office. Precisely how a thirty-five-year-old neophyte federal prosecutor who had worked as an assistant state's attorney in Annapolis and who had been practicing law for not quite ten years could wind up managing the most important criminal case in the United States was the subject of some mystery, even within the office. Bittman had come to OIC early in Starr's tenure and had impressed his boss with his orderly mind and diligence. A solid, clear-thinking, button-down son of a well-known Washington criminal defense attorney, Bittman displayed all the signs of a quick study and a good administrator. Nicknamed "Bulldog" or "Maximum Bob" for his no-nonsense style, Bittman knew how to buckle down and get assignments done. Hickman Ewing, whom Bittman was assisting in Little Rock, was a brilliant courtroom advocate, but got bogged down in the minutiae of the sprawling Whitewater/Madison case. In contrast, Bob Bittman could sit behind a desk and bull forward to a conclusion.

When the Lewinsky case broke open, Bittman was in Arkansas helping Ewing wrap up before the grand jury expired. Now, with the Lewinsky investigation falling out of the sky "like a bolt out of the blue," Jackie Bennett concluded that it was necessary to make some adjustments. Things were moving at warp speed; it was "all hands on deck in Washington." Bittman, it turned out, was perfectly positioned to play a key role. While others were bracing Monica Lewinsky at the Ritz-Carlton, he sat in an office a thousand miles away, alongside an FBI agent, listening to taped conversations between Monica Lewinsky and Linda Tripp. He had also drafted an "investigative plan," which included action items such as subpoenaing telephone logs and other documents from the White House and drafting subpoenas—for Lewinsky, for her mother, for Betty Currie, and for other key witnesses.

Most prosecutors in D.C. were too busy to focus on this kind of careful lawyer work. So it had seemed natural for young Bob Bittman to fly to Washington to lend a hand, the week after the Lewinsky case broke open. Soon, he was functioning as the deputy in charge of that operation.

Jackie Bennett, who had run the D.C. office during the previous year, had no particular experience, or interest, in managing a massive new prosecution from the ground up. The Lewinsky case was Whitewater times ten. The roller-coaster speed of the Lewinsky investigation required Starr to reconfigure his Washington office overnight. Prosecutors like Mike Emmick and Bruce Udolf had far more experience than Bittman did. But they were viewed with increasing suspicion by their hard-line colleagues. As Bennett would say, in recalling how Bittman came to be selected to run this massive new investigation with such little experience: "There just weren't many candidates."

Bittman's first order of business was to implement the investigative plan that he had mapped out. He would recall, "It was not the Holy Grail—much was obvious. Debriefing Linda Tripp. Issuing subpoenas. Getting traces on calls, DNRs [dialed number recorders]. Listing people involved. Issuing a subpoena to the mother and Monica and the dad."

Bittman prided himself in being a cautious prosecutor. During the initial bracing of Lewinsky at the Ritz-Carlton, some OIC lawyers had sounded the war cry, declaring, "We have probable cause to believe she's involved in a crime. Let's arrest and charge her!" Bittman's advice from Little Rock was, "No. That's preposterous." The Lewinsky investigation was potentially explosive. The slower they moved, the better. OIC needed to put pressure on the avuncular Mr. Ginsburg to see if he could be brought around. If that failed, only then should they move to Plan B. The best course would be to bring charges against Lewinsky in Northern Virginia, he thought, rather than in Washington, where the Lewinsky lawyers would be expecting it. The heavily African American juries in D.C. would be far too sympathetic to President Bill Clinton and to the young former intern. In contrast, the federal courts in Northern Virginia were an excellent place to prosecute, because judges and juries there "didn't mess around." Said Bittman, in laying out OIC's strategy years later, "We decided it would be in Virginia. If we hadn't worked out a deal, we would have [indicted her]. She would have been charged in mid-August in Virginia."

OIC had one important ally in FBI Director Louis Freeh, who was a big fan of Starr's work and did not particularly like or respect Bill Clinton. He immediately called to pledge whatever resources OIC needed to deal with the Lewinsky morass. Bittman spoke up directly: "I want twenty FBI agents and ten FAs [financial analysts]." He recalled that Director Freeh did not waste a minute: "We had them the next day."

One person who was not pleased with the whole turn of events in Washington was Hickman Ewing, Jr., still camped out in Little Rock. In that Southern locale, the OIC offices were beginning to resemble a sheriff's office covered with cobwebs in a ghost town. Ewing felt as if Bittman had been called by a trumpet blast and transported to the heavens of Washington with other true believers, never to return. "It was like he was raptured," Ewing said. "My main guy that knows about Hillary is gone." He knew that the Lewinsky allegations were far more sexy than the tired old Whitewater case. "And look, I understand. . . . We have a present perjury obstruction of justice going on, as opposed to trying to prove beyond a reasonable doubt, 'Did people lie about something that happened between 1984 and 1986?' "

Ewing understood the shift in priorities, now that the president had been caught with his pants down in the Lewinsky/Paula Jones soap opera. Yet he was not prepared to let the case against First Lady Hillary Clinton die before the grand jury expired. He wanted to give it every ounce of Tennessee grit at his command. Former Arkansas Governor Jim Guy Tucker was still scheduled for trial on tax fraud charges on February 23. If they were able to strike a plea deal on the eve of trial, Tucker might finally cough up information that was helpful—"especially as to Mrs. Clinton." So as the rest of the office was going great guns on the Monica Lewinsky case, which had fallen into their laps like manna from heaven, Ewing was still cobbling together his dwindling resources to take one final shot at Hillary.

With these two efforts moving ahead on wholly disconnected east-west tracks, the Office of Independent Counsel steamed forward, entering a winter like no other.

——————

If a single event convinced the Starr prosecutors that they were dealing with obstruction of justice, it was the unexpected visit from a lawyer named Lawrence Wechsler, just two days after the Lewinsky story blew open in the media. Wechsler, a respected Washington criminal defense attorney, appeared at the OIC office carrying a flat box. The bespectacled lawyer asked to meet privately with Ken Starr. Inside a small conference room, with Starr and Jackie Bennett listening with astonishment, Wechsler informed them that he represented Betty Currie. "This is not going to look good for the president," he stated. The lawyer quietly unpacked a collection of gifts—T-shirts, photos, and assorted baubles—that President Clinton had given to Monica Lewinsky. These gifts had been kept inside a box under Currie's bed, Wechsler said, at Ms. Lewinsky's request.

As Starr and Bennett did their best to camouflage their disbelief, the heavy-set criminal attorney explained that Currie was being pressured heavily by the White House to protect the president. Around the time of the *Paula Jones* deposition, Clinton had called his secretary into the White House to rehearse a series of facts about his relationship with Monica that simply weren't true. Consequently, Betty and her husband had gone into hiding. The poised, discreet African American woman knew plenty about the Clinton-Lewinsky affair, but her loyalty to the president was causing her to feel conflicted. Starr's office would have to handle this matter delicately to extract the full story from her, but she was prepared to cooperate.

This surprise visit, Ken Starr recalled, was a defining moment in his investigation. He was now certain that the president was lying, and engaging in blatant obstruction by pressuring others to cover up for him.

Ken Starr viewed his role as that of a "minesweeper." He always needed to be on the alert for explosives that might blow up in OIC's face. Betty Currie's lawyer assured him that his client was an "honorable, loyal, God-fearing, church-attending lady who felt just terribly about all of this." Betty was being barraged by "increasingly urgent overtures from the White House . . . pages and so forth," transmitting messages such as "we love you, please call us." The president's secretary was prepared to meet with OIC to have an honest discussion. But this meeting needed to occur "off campus."

The next day, Sunday, Starr's new deputy Bob Bittman sat alongside two FBI agents in a room at the Bethesda Marriott Residence Inn, attending a secret meeting with Betty Currie and her lawyers. Although Currie appeared uncomfortable seated on a couch facing the prosecutor, she was forthcoming—at least up to a point. The president's secretary acknowledged that her boss and Monica Lewinsky had been alone nearly a dozen times in the Oval Office or in the private study outside that office. Ms. Lewinsky seemed lovestruck; President Clinton had returned the flirtatious attention with phone calls and occasional gifts (many of which were kept in the box just turned over by her lawyer). Currie next described being "summoned" into the White House by her boss on the Saturday just after Clinton's testimony in the *Paula Jones* deposition, and being led through a series of questions purportedly designed to refresh her boss's recollection. The president had posed leading questions such as: "You do remember I was never alone with Monica, right?" and "You were always here when she was here, right?" and "You could see and hear everything, right?"

Currie had answered "Right" to these statements; yet she knew they were inaccurate.

Although the president's secretary seemed wary and tentative as she spoke to Bittman and the FBI agents, she was "quite sharp in her recollection." After debriefing with his prosecutors that afternoon, Starr concluded that this re-markable confession by the president's secretary, and the delivery of the box of evidence by her lawyer, were "extremely promising."

More than any other information they had gleaned to date, this new evi-dence solidified the feeling among Starr's team that Bill Clinton was capable of all manner of deceit and misconduct in his quest to escape the clutches of Lady Justice.

———

KEN Starr and his top prosecutors were prepared to wager all their golden poker chips that future events—such as the conviction or resignation of President Clinton—would eventually justify their aggressive approach in the Lewinsky matter. Yet not everyone shared their optimism that history would vindicate them.

Archibald Cox, the legendary Watergate special prosecutor who had be-come a national hero a quarter century earlier, watched the Starr expansion with deep concern. Cox, then eighty-six years old, lived on a secluded farm in Maine and made it a point of staying out of politics. The retired Harvard law professor—one of the great constitutional lawyers of the twentieth century and a man who had helped secure the passage of the independent counsel law—was scrupulously closemouthed when television film crews tramped up to his re-mote property looking for sound bites about this new twist in the investigation. When asked by reporters whether the morphing of Starr's investigation from Whitewater into the Lewinsky matter was justified, the crew-cutted Cox stood erect and declared that he possessed insufficient facts to pass judgment on the matter. He was loath to second-guess Kenneth Starr, a fellow special prosecutor and former solicitor general.

In private, however, Cox was plagued by increasing doubts about the wis-dom of this prosecutorial decision. Before his death in 2004, Cox broke his si-lence and said that the first question that he would have asked himself if he were Ken Starr would have been "whether I had been given jurisdiction in that area." Since the answer to that question, according to Starr's narrow charter dealing with Whitewater, was likely "no," Cox believed Starr should have avoided this case like a deadly plague.

Cox's chief worry was that Starr's detour into the Lewinsky sex scandal could damage the public perception of the entire independent counsel investi-gation, regardless of any good that it might accomplish. The ramrod-straight Watergate prosecutor had spent his whole life concerned about protecting the institutions of government. Explained Cox, "I would have been awfully reluctant to do it—whoever the president was—simply on the ground that I wasn't comfortable, and I don't think the country would be comfortable, in exploring sexual fault, weaknesses. I'm not saying that it was wrong. I just personally would have been disgusted."

Moreover, Cox was concerned that both the White House and Starr's office had lost their objectivity. They were now treating this investigation like a boxing match in which the pugilists had thrown off their gloves and had begun punching below the belt. Confidential information (from the grand jury and elsewhere) seemed to be leaked to the media daily, from both camps. For Cox, who had refused to tolerate any amount of leaking to the press as Watergate special prosecutor, both the White House and OIC deserved to be faulted for the "fighting of a war in the media aggressively all the way."

Cox was so troubled by the unexpected direction Starr's investigation was taking into the Lewinsky mess that he privately told his wife that he feared the whole independent counsel law might have to be scrapped.

Robert Fiske, the first Whitewater independent counsel, who had been replaced by Ken Starr, also avoided taking sides. He declined to speculate on whether he would have gone down the Lewinsky path if he had still been in Starr's position. Because he understood the significance of the Vernon Jordan connection, assuming it was real and not exaggerated, Fiske was not prepared to condemn Starr's decision to get into the case. All the silver-haired former prosecutor could say, with certainty, was that he was "grateful" that he was not in Starr's shoes.

Most prosecutors who had worked closely with Fiske, however, were far less diplomatic. In private discussions among themselves, they agreed that Robert Fiske never would have ended up in this Lewinsky jackpot, in a million years. Julie O'Sullivan, who had since moved to the law faculty at Georgetown, summarized the sentiment of many of her former colleagues by saying that Fiske would have wrapped up and gone home much earlier, mooting this issue. "We'd have been long since done," she insisted.

William Duffey, Jr., who had returned to practice in Atlanta after having served as Fiske's top deputy heading up the investigation in Little Rock, believed that Starr's insistence on working part-time rather than devoting twenty-four hours a day to the independent counsel job had finally caught up with him. "I have always said that if he had done it full time, [Starr] would have been at the point of [wrapping up the case] when the Monica Lewinsky thing came up," said Duffey. "And at that time, it would have made more sense to appoint a different independent counsel to investigate that."

He added with a note of regret, "Which I think would have had a totally different result."

THE VILIFICATION OF KEN STARR

In the midst of the hubbub involving the newly launched Lewinsky investigation, Ken Starr was in San Antonio, speaking at an American Bar Association conference and visiting with his ninety-year-old mother. "She was not in good health, so I made it down to San Antonio as frequently as I could to be with her," Starr recalled. "She lived by her own choice alone, so I had stayed with her the night before, and I knew it was going to break that next day."

Immediately after the conference session, the special prosecutor took his mother to lunch at her favorite eatery—Luby's, a cafeteria chain that specialized in Southern fare—and then drove Vannie back home to get her settled in. Before kissing the most important woman in his life good-bye, Ken knelt down and said, "Mother, there may be some press; you may be reading about some things . . . but just don't worry about it, and if there's any issue, just call me and we'll take care of it."

With that, Ken Starr drove to the airport, where he was greeted by a phalanx of cameramen and journalists. No sooner had he returned home to Virginia than the FBI and U.S. Marshal's office were compiling "death threat assessments," assigning Starr "round-the-clock security." The Monica Lewinsky matter had transformed him from a low-key figure to a reviled prosecutor wearing a target on his chest.

The vilification of Ken Starr, among Clinton fans and Starr-bashers around the globe, had become increasingly distressing to Ken and Alice, who were struggling to shield their family from this unexpected backlash.

Seated in the TV room of his home in McLean, Ken would later observe that the impugning of his character seemed to reach a crescendo shortly after the eruption of Mount Lewinsky. Why had he even accepted the Lewinsky inquiry and opened himself up to this vicious abuse? Starr would later make the following confession: When Monica Lewinsky came along, he was still smarting from the public rebuke that he had endured from the Pepperdine fiasco in the winter of 1997. The Pepperdine blunder—and his decision to abruptly reverse course on it—was a bruising personal experience. Now he was gun-shy about appearing weak or indecisive when it came to *any* major decision linked to the investigation of President Clinton. So when pressed to expand into the Lewinsky matter, he was afraid to say no. It was, Starr later conceded, a grand "miscalculation on my part."

It hadn't helped, he hastened to add, that the White House ruffians had piled atop him during the Pepperdine debacle and rubbed dirt in his face. They were trying to "spin" the story that Starr's criminal probe was dead; they were openly "declaring victory." They were bragging that he had turned tail and returned to his post as independent counsel only because "the master right-wing conspiracy wouldn't allow [Starr] to leave." As Starr saw it, the White House PR hit squad had not helped its cause by taunting him and demeaning his investigation, shortly before the Lewinsky case was dropped on his doorstep.

Starr also had become convinced that the Justice Department (particularly Deputy Attorney General Eric Holder) was engaged in a smear campaign, dishing out dirt to the press "on background," and "trying to poison the well" in order to besmirch Starr and his dedicated prosecutors.

Starr wasn't about to be intimidated. He and his prosecutors had "come through the perfect storm, and we were still afloat." With the White House engaged in a "coordinated effort to kill me politically and at the national level," the independent counsel felt his only choice was to march forward and to deploy all troops at his command.

Alice Starr sat for interviews with *Ladies' Home Journal* and several other publications, doing her best to help her husband. Unfortunately, each glossy article seemed to give her comments an unflattering slant, so she canceled the rest of her media appointments. "I didn't want to start a political war of my own," Alice later explained. Their son, Randy, was in college at Duke. Daughter Carolyn was a senior in high school. Their youngest, Cynthia, was only thirteen; they could not risk allowing this scandal to scar the children. Alice instead remained "very, very busy" at work, keeping her chin up.

Years later, Alice Starr confessed that the most maddening aspect of this post-Monica vilification of her husband was that *Bill Clinton* was the person who had acted immorally and lied about it. Yet Ken somehow was being painted as the evildoer. From the moment Clinton had shaken his finger and adamantly denied a relationship with "that woman," Alice said, she "knew that Bill was lying." At the same time, "I expected him to lie about it. . . . Wouldn't you expect someone who's having an affair with a young intern to lie about it?"

The real tragedy, Alice thought, was that Bill Clinton could have headed off his day of reckoning by doing the right thing and confessing guilt. "If people are honest, people are so forgiving," she said. "Had Bill Clinton been honest to begin with, I just know he would not have been in any trouble at all. That's the motto in our family: 'Please be truthful.' That's the best way."

With respect to the First Lady who had rushed to the president's defense, Alice Starr felt a certain amount of sympathy—but not much. "I probably reacted more to Hillary than I did to Bill," she said. Chalking it up to "women's intuition," Alice did not buy the story that Hillary was totally in the dark about Bill's indiscretions. "I mean, almost every book you have ever read about their relationship, she is [certainly aware] that he's had many, many other affairs," said Alice. "And that's their marriage. That's fine if she wants to accept that. But to deny it, to me, meant that she was covering up."

It was especially unacceptable to Alice that Hillary Clinton would accuse Ken of engaging in a "vast right-wing conspiracy" to bring down the president. In fact, Alice found it downright insulting. Ken had hired Democrats for top posts in his office. He had spent his career trying to act professionally and without partisanship. "We don't run around in a circle of any vast right-wing conspirators," Alice insisted, struggling to keep her voice measured. "We have dear friends [including both Democrats and Republicans] from the children's school or from church or whatever. But neither of us are into a right-wing conspiracy and never have been. And Ken never, ever met with people who conspired about anything."

At their split-level home on a cul-de-sac in McLean, in a neighborhood that did not flaunt its affluence, the Starr family did its best to maintain its equilibrium. At night, during the height of the Lewinsky hubbub, the whole family waited for Ken to come home (if it wasn't past bedtime) so they could sit down for dinner together. Ken's favorite dish was "Mexican Mess," something Alice whipped up "where I sort of combined everything including the kitchen sink. It's actually Barbara Bush's recipe . . . you know, guacamole and Tostitos and cheese and lettuce and tomato and all. That's what Ken really loves."

Ken would put down his briefcase wearily and tell his family, "This is not pleasant, this is going to be a rough patch, but we've just got to maintain our spirits and keep on trucking." Happily for the Starrs, they had an enormous amount of support from the community and from their church. Friends would call and say "telephone hugs," which for Ken was "a very nice term and apt."

The besieged independent counsel generally avoided watching television so that he was not demoralized by the round-the-clock attacks on him. Alice would sneak into the family room to watch *Geraldo*, a talk show on which host Geraldo Rivera constantly "castigated" Starr. The minute she even mentioned the latest scandal-related news, her husband would raise his hand and say, "I don't want to hear about it." The television would be turned off, and the discussion would cease. Alice said, "And that was about as impatient as [Ken] gets."

Although Ken was being skewered in the media and savaged by the White House, Alice accepted this burden with silent resignation. Her husband's job, she told the children, was "basically to get the truth out and the facts, wherever that led him." If it led into the White House, she said, that was not their father's cross to bear. Rather, the responsibility had to be borne by the president sworn to uphold the law, who had set these destructive events into motion.

———

On January 29, Judge Susan Webber Wright ruled that all evidence related to the Lewinsky matter was inadmissible in the *Paula Jones* case. Any "probative" value of the Lewinsky-related evidence, Judge Wright ruled, was outweighed by the "possibility of prejudice."

A Republican from Arkansas, Judge Wright was no great fan of Bill Clinton, but she thought this new Monica Lewinsky investigation smelled to high heaven of politics. The Lewinsky testimony represented a barely relevant speck of evidence in a sexual harassment lawsuit that was already on shaky ground. The president may have lied in his deposition—and if he did, she would need to deal with that appropriately. But the *Jones* litigation had nothing to do with Clinton's consensual fling with an intern in the White House. The judge was having no part of it.

When Monica Lewinsky learned of Judge Wright's ruling while watching television inside her darkened Watergate condo, she remembered feeling a jolt of hope. "I was elated," she recalled. "Elated! I just thought 'Oh, does this mean it's all over?' "

But Ken Starr's prosecution steamed forward, even after Monica's situation was disentangled from the *Paula Jones* litigation. And Monica, in the following weeks, sank into a deep depression.

Although this part of the story would remain a carefully guarded secret, interviews now reveal that the young woman had slowly unraveled until she had become, as one confidential source described it, a "mental basket case." After seeking the advice of a psychiatrist in Washington, Lewinsky's lawyers had secluded her for several days in a room at the Cosmos Club, where Bill Ginsburg was temporarily residing. Here, hidden away on the dark, wood-paneled guest floors of the exclusive D.C. social club, Ginsburg and Nate Speights and their private investigator took turns, seated on chairs in the hallway or in the suite adjacent to Monica's room, staying up all night, watching over the young woman to make sure she did not harm herself. When they returned to her apartment at the Watergate complex, she walked the halls because she was convinced that her unit was bugged.

The black cloud hanging over Lewinsky, as the weeks passed, only seemed to grow darker. Rumors now swirled that the president had engaged in a relationship with another intern, a report that almost "blew Monica away." She had already been thrown for a loop when she had learned that Clinton was alone in the White House with Eleanor Mondale—the free-spirited and beautiful daughter of former Vice President Walter Mondale—to whom the president was rumored to be romantically attracted. The notion that Bill Clinton might have cheated on *her* while she engaged in an extramarital affair with *him*—combined with the humiliation of being the subject of round-the-clock news coverage and sex jokes—was too much for Monica to process. Although the "other intern" story proved to be apocryphal, Monica began bottoming out. She slowly slipped into a state of "catatonia." One individual described her appearance during this period as "frozen," displaying absolutely "no affect."

The psychiatrist treating Lewinsky in Washington raised the question as to whether the young woman should be hospitalized, to remove her from the toxic situation. Monica's lawyers worried, though, that the media and tabloids would have a field day if they discovered her whereabouts. In the end, the doctor agreed that such a move might actually worsen Monica's state. As a rule, the psychiatrist warned, it was better for a patient to develop coping skills to deal with this kind of emotional trauma. It didn't take a shrink to understand that a person in Monica's situation might suffer a massive jolt to her mental equilibrium. Unlike other sorts of psychological tailspins, this one would not correct itself simply by checking her into a hospital. Even after she was released, she would still have to deal with the facts involving her affair with Clinton—most likely for the rest of her life.

There were disturbing signs that Monica might be coming unhinged. She spent much of the time hidden in her grandmother's apartment, upstairs in the Watergate, sleeping in a twin bed next to her mother and grandmother who shared a sofabed to keep watch. Her doctor feared that Monica could slip into "suicidal ideations." Her lawyers arranged for the psychiatrist to visit; other times an investigator transported Monica in a nondescript, "soccer mom" van to her doctor's office, where she received doses of selective serotonin reuptake inhibitors (SSRIs), potent antidepressants. During this time, the lawyers took turns keeping watch over their client, assigning a young female assistant to sit with Monica in her room, holding her hand and trying to soothe her. As one observer noted, "Remember, this was a twenty-one-year-old girl in love with a fifty-year-old man. It may not have meant anything to him, but it meant everything to her. She thought it was true romance."

Monica herself later confessed that these early weeks of the scandal were like being thrown into the mouth of hell. "I was pretty bad," she admitted, still struggling years later to maintain her composure. "I think that I had a certain level of denial for some things. . . . I don't know what kept me going. I really don't."

During those winter months of 1998, at the ripe age of twenty-four, Monica

Lewinsky had become a prisoner of a national scandal in which, to her horror, she was the leading lady. All she could do was watch the round-the-clock coverage of Ken Starr's ramped-up investigation and the president's denials and her own staggering situation on the television. Lewinsky later said, "I watched all of those shows, because that was the [only] way that I would get information."

On February 1, Monica was shuttled to the Cosmos Club. Here, she sat down, at Bill Ginsburg's instruction, and wrote out a handwritten proffer designed to strike a deal with the Office of Independent Counsel. This straightforward ten-page account, printed neatly on ruled paper, spelled out Monica's own version of her wrecked relationship with President Clinton, giving Starr's prosecutors (Ginsburg thought) everything they could possibly want. "Ms. Lewinsky had an intimate and emotional relationship with President Clinton beginning in 1995," she wrote. "At various times between 1995 and 1997, Ms. Lewinsky and the President had physically intimate contact. This included oral sex, but excluded intercourse."

Monica explained how Betty Currie served as the chief go-between for her meetings with the president, and how Vernon Jordan helped steer her toward attorney Frank Carter after she was subpoenaed in the *Jones* case. All of this was precisely what the Starr prosecutors wanted. It probably would have assured Monica a swift immunity deal—were it not for Monica's disclaimer, which wrecked the deal as far as OIC was concerned. "Neither the Pres. nor Mr. Jordan (or anyone on their behalf) asked or encouraged Ms. L to lie," she wrote. "Ms. L was comfortable signing the affidavit with regard to the 'sexual relationship' because she could justify to herself that she and the Pres. did not have sexual intercourse."

Mike Emmick and Bruce Udolf, the leading doves in the OIC hawk-nest, were still heading up negotiations with Ginsburg. In an effort to salvage the immunity deal, they asked Monica to address directly the issue of the president's encouraging her to lie about the relationship. The former intern thus added language that was at least mildly damaging to Bill Clinton: "At some point in the relationship between Ms. L and the President, the President told Ms. L to deny a relationship, if ever asked about it. He also said something to the effect of if the two people who are involved say it didn't happen, it didn't happen." Yet Monica cut the legs out from under any possible obstruction of justice charge by adding that the president had urged her to deny the relationship *before* she was a potential witness in the *Jones* case. By implication, she was declaring that Clinton's motives had nothing to do with causing her to lie in the legal proceedings.

Many prosecutors in Starr's office remained certain that the former intern was hiding key facts. People like Jackie Bennett and Bob Bittman, it seemed, had convinced themselves that Clinton and Jordan had said to her, " 'Look, kid. If you shut up and you sign this affidavit, we'll get you a job.' ' " "The proffer didn't say that," Monica later emphasized, because it hadn't happened.

Udolf and Emmick agreed that "there does not seem to be any purpose in prosecuting this woman." So they telephoned Bill Ginsburg and told him, "I think we have a deal." They asked Bob Bittman to fax a three-page immunity agreement to Ginsburg, which he did on February 2. Ginsburg promptly signed the document, obtained Monica's signature, and returned it forty-eight hours later. There were two final signature lines that needed to be filled in: one for Emmick and one for Udolf.

The avuncular Mr. Ginsburg called his client and declared triumphantly, "You have a deal." Hearing those words, Monica packed her bags and flew to Beverly Hills, to be with her father. "So yes," she recalled later, "I went to California thinking I had a deal." Both Emmick and Udolf would later confirm that they, too, believed they had entered into a binding agreement with Lewinsky. Back at the office, however, there was a growing sentiment that OIC was being sold down the river by two Democratic-leaning, weak-willed turncoats.

Monica Lewinsky's own lawyer, ironically, helped to unravel the deal. The bearded California attorney took to the national airwaves and became a sudden media darling, rubbing the prosecutors' noses in the immunity deal as if he had won the jackpot. Ginsburg set a new record by appearing, in one day, on all five major Sunday television shows reserved for the political power hitters of Washington. During his *Meet the Press* debut, Ginsburg—who was alternately philosophical and in-your-face—told host Tim Russert that his client would provide her immunized testimony to the Starr prosecutors and the nation would be saved. "The president will remain in office," the malpractice lawyer predicted, smiling with humility into the television camera. "He'll do a good job. We'll all hopefully have a sound economy, keep our jobs, and I think everything's going to be fine."

Ginsburg seemed to be crowing from every rooftop about beating the big bad Kenneth Starr. With Monica's written proffer in hand, he proclaimed that the Starr prosecutors would only be able to prove that Clinton had lied in the *Jones* deposition about one thing—a consensual fling with a White House intern that had zero connection to the allegations by Paula Jones. First Lady Hillary Clinton might be justified in taking a rolling pin to her husband, Ginsburg now chuckled, and that might not be a pretty sight. But he did not expect that a jury would convict Bill Clinton any time soon. Monica Lewinsky could go on with her life, and the president could go on running the country, having (hopefully) learned his lesson that he needed to keep his bounding sex drive on a leash.

Ginsburg had initially felt contempt toward Clinton for soiling his hands in a sexual escapade with a young lady half his age. At one point he had even threatened to go on national TV and call Clinton a "pedophile." Now, those feelings had melted into a sense of revulsion for the Starr prosecutors, who had insisted on turning this into a federal case. The California lawyer had a newfound pity for Clinton. "I felt sorry for the poor bastard," Ginsburg said later. "That's exactly what I thought to myself. I said, 'I understand what's going on. He's a human being. Even though he's president of the United States, he is clearly a human being.' "

Around the time he was riding high as a national lawyer-celebrity, with a deal nearly consummated, Ginsburg arranged a clandestine meeting at the Cosmos Club with the president's lawyer, David Kendall. Ginsburg made clear that "we were completely on the president's side and that we really care about what happens here." To his credit, he also made clear that he would not allow Monica to deny the relationship under oath, because "I don't suborn perjury." Kendall seemed genuinely surprised at Ginsburg's intimation that a relationship existed; he sat quietly and listened. The LA lawyer went on to communicate that if Clinton's hit squad tried to "trash Monica in any way, shape, or form," or suggest that "she was a crazy fool, a stalker, a prostitute, anything else," they were in for a big surprise. Ginsburg told Kendall, "In the final analysis, you'll be sorry, because I have the dirty laundry."

Kendall seemed startled—if not baffled—by this cryptic threat.

Starr's office, in the meantime, was developing a deep suspicion that the grinning, bombastic fifty-four-year-old California medical malpractice lawyer had crawled fully into bed with the Clinton White House. The "written proffer," OIC hawks feared, was simply a ploy to skate around the truth in order to save Bill Clinton's hide.

The more they saw of Ginsburg, the more the OIC prosecutors distrusted him. Ginsburg was captured in print telling one journalist: "I'm the most famous person in the world." He quipped that *he*—rather than Monica—might accept *Penthouse* magazine's two-million-dollar offer to pose partially nude. As journalists Ruth Marcus and Bob Woodward noted, the bearded Southern California lawyer "look[s] for all the world like he is having the time of his life."

At a meeting convened on February 3, Jackie Bennett and the hard-liners voted to stick it in Ginsburg's ear. "It's just not going to come together," Bennett declared. Bennett and fellow skeptics remained convinced that Monica was holding back crucial information. She should be forced to sit down with them as "Queen for the Day," they declared, and give an extensive oral proffer, at which time they could evaluate her trustworthiness while staring the witness straight in the eyes. After all, this young, bubbly woman had won over the president. They needed to make sure that she was not sweet-talking *them*. As well, the hard-liners were aghast that Emmick and Udolf were willing to grant Monica immunity without getting a full proffer—wasn't that exactly what had caused them to be burned in the Webb Hubbell deal?

Sol Wisenberg, one of Starr's prosecutors who argued most strenuously to squash the immunity deal, was convinced that a little tough love was necessary: "I really think Monica is the kind of person that you simply cannot treat nicely," he later explained. In Wisenberg's view, this investigation had to be handled like a case against the mob: "There is a certain kind of person who is common, and it's a female, in these investigations," Wisenberg said. "You see them in white collar, and you see them in drug investigations. Basically, if you want to think of the Clinton White House as an organized-crime ring, and Clinton is the head of it, [Lewinsky] is the kind of person who, in a drug or white-collar crime ring, is a female and a relatively minor person substantively, but maybe has a relationship with a top person. They are incredibly loyal to the leader of the gang, and they only understand force. . . . They only understand harsh treatment. Sometimes, even that's not enough."

Wisenberg concluded, "Monica just happened to be the type who, if we had ever early on arrested her ass, I think she would have broken and told us everything, which she never really [did]. And that was the problem. We displayed incredible weakness that night [at the Ritz-Carlton], and we let ourselves be manipulated."

Accepting this weak immunity deal crafted by Emmick and Udolf, the hardliners believed, would make OIC a laughingstock and allow Lewinsky (and Bill Clinton) to skate away like free birds. Wisenberg, who was famous for sprinkling expletives throughout his everyday vocabulary, concluded that Ginsburg had gone "batsh——t crazy" with his media blitz. "And that's when the White House starts declaring war and we go f——ing crazy," he said, recalling the sequence of events. "We just f——ing wet our pants. I couldn't f——ing believe it. We're having staff meetings every f——ing minute." At one such meeting, Wisenberg finally stood up and quoted Stonewall Jackson: "Never take counsel of your fears," he said, sprinkling in his own modern vernacular: "What the f—— are we doing?"

Wisenberg next threw around his briefcase and promised to resign if Ken Starr capitulated on this point. If Monica Lewinsky was not required to give them the full story as Queen for a Day, he declared, then "[I want] to keep a deal from going down."

Emmick and Udolf were aghast. They had given their word. Starr had authorized them to cut a deal. In the world of criminal lawyering, one's word meant everything. Monica was already in California preparing for OIC's first interview session. Even if she was giving them "ninety percent of the truth," their reaction was, "So what?" That's what witnesses did. Witnesses hid facts, and skillful prosecutors extracted more of the truth. "Sometimes, cooperators will only give you sixty percent and you try to pull teeth and get it up to seventy,"

Emmick said, summarizing his logic. "We were pretty sure we could get it up to ninety."

If any battle within his office caused Starr to be tugged in opposite directions, it was this one. Emmick was on leave as chief of the Public Corruption Section in the U.S. Attorney's office in Los Angeles. Udolf was legendary in Miami "for locking up corrupt mayors." Both of these lawyers were highly experienced. Starr worried to himself, "My goodness, these aren't rookies." At the same time, most of his top deputies were literally shouting at him, "This is just wrong! This is weak negotiation! How can you do this?" After chewing over the pros and cons, Starr made a decision: He was scotching the entire deal.

In a short letter dated February 4, Bob Bittman thanked the Lewinsky lawyers for their "proposed modifications to the draft agreement," informing them that "we must respectfully decline to enter into an agreement on the proposed terms." Bittman went on to instruct Ginsburg to deliver his client to the OIC offices in Washington on February 9, so that she could be interviewed, at length, in person.

Ginsburg, having already returned to Los Angeles, fired back an angry response at 4:18 P.M., charging the Starr prosecutors with "blatantly reneging on your . . . grant of immunity." He gave them a tongue-lashing: "It seems clear that your continued bad faith negotiating techniques represent an effort designed to force Ms. Lewinsky to make false statements implicating the President and others in high crimes and misdemeanors."

Monica Lewinsky, when Ginsburg called to tell her that OIC had pulled the rug out from under the immunity deal, broke down crying hysterically.

The young Maryland sex-crimes prosecutor used this opportunity to solidify his standing among the hawks in the office. Besides serving a subpoena on Lewinsky to appear before the grand jury in Washington, Bittman also drafted a subpoena to Monica Lewinsky's mother and a motion to compel her testimony; along with a string of letters to David Kendall, requesting that the president himself appear to give testimony. On February 9 he wrote to Kendall: "Let me make our request specific and clear: the grand jury deserves to know whether the President will respond, favorably, to the invitation." Kendall hand-delivered a reply on February 13, in which he refused to yield an inch: "The President has the greatest respect for the grand jury. However, under the circumstances, it is impossible to accept this invitation. The situation in Iraq continues to be dangerously volatile, and this has demanded much of the President's time and attention." Kendall threw in another zinger, telling the young prosecutor that he had been unable to respond the previous week, because "I was in the process of dealing with prejudicial and false leaks of information" by the Office of Independent Counsel.

———

AROUND the world, the reaction to the ongoing Monica Lewinsky story was a mixture of surprise that Bill Clinton had become ensnared in such a tawdry episode, and amazement that Americans were reacting with such righteous indignation. Anne-Elisabeth Moutet, working in a cramped newspaper office in the heart of Paris, had served as the bureau chief for *European* newspaper in London and also covered the Clinton presidency from New York. From Moutet's perspective, Ken Starr's never-ending investigation amounted to a form of entertainment for most European audiences. The Paula Jones story, as she saw it, possessed a "fantastic sort of trailer-park ethos that permeated the whole thing." The Lewinsky affair, dubbed "Le Zippergate" in France, seemed even crazier than fiction. "It looked pretty ridiculous," said Moutet. Men and women in Europe would repeatedly ask with amusement, "Why doesn't he have a normal relationship, with a nice, elegant, clever mistress who won't talk? Can't he find [a mature woman] who worked with the Democratic National Committee. . . . Why a twenty-one-year-old intern?"

In France, said Moutet, this sort of event simply wasn't newsworthy: "We do not talk about politicians' private lives. President François Mitterrand had lots of mistresses and two regular mistresses, and every journalist in town, myself included, knew all about them, and we had the telephone numbers and we knew about the kids and everything. And we never wrote it. It was perfectly understood that 'nobody will back you up. The public will hate you to kingdom come. Do not talk about politicians' private lives.' "

Far-out theories began circulating in Europe concerning the true nature of the relationship between Bill Clinton and Monica Lewinsky. "Some people concentrated on her being Jewish," said one journalist, "and some lunatics, unfortunately, gave some credence to that tenet that she might be an Israeli spy." For the most part, however, the reaction was one of puzzlement as to why this had been allowed to turn into a raging scandal. The almighty American media, many Europeans concluded, "had gotten too big for its britches."

One of the most interesting side effects of this latest outbreak of scandal, however, was that First Lady Hillary Clinton began rising in the esteem of observers abroad. Said Moutet, "The French like, you know, well groomed, tough-as-nails women who have got a brain." Hillary Clinton's appearance on the *Today* show to fight back against Ken Starr's prosecutors, in defense of her husband, only enhanced her reputation among many Europeans. "They felt a bit sorry for her, and they thought she was impeccable," said Moutet. "She fought for her man; she kept her own counsel. They thought that she was great because she immediately said, 'This is a vast right-wing conspiracy against us,' and she moved. The French always suspect that there are conspiracies. And therefore, the worldview from start to finish was that they thought that she had dignity, which is something that the French appreciate, and that she was behaving very well throughout."

Starr, on the other hand, was increasingly perceived on the other side of the Atlantic as an "inquisitor," even as a "sort of repressed, frustrated figure," who was leading a crusade against President Bill Clinton because he was taking perverse delight in it. Michel Gurfinkiel, editor of *Valeur actuelles,* the leading conservative newsweekly in France, noted: "Most people understood Starr as a disgusting, sex-obsessed puritan or as an equally disgusting arch conservative using any available means to undermine the Democratic president." Although Gurfinkiel did not necessarily share that view and was appalled that Clinton likely uttered falsehoods with impunity in the *Jones* case, the whole issue of Clinton's "lying under oath" as a violation of Anglo-American law simply did not resonate with most Europeans. Nor could they fathom that this particular scandal would, or should, lead to the ousting of Clinton from office. Noted Gurfinkiel with a faint smile, "The only way we know of getting rid of a leader is to behead him."

At Oxford University in England, George Cawkwell, a retired Fellow who specialized in ancient history, had interacted regularly with Bill Clinton when the future American president was a young Rhodes Scholar in the late 1960s. Now, the eighty-five-year-old scholar expressed deep dismay that this Lewinsky matter had gotten so thoroughly out of control. Living in a quaint retirement community in North Oxford with colorful flower gardens and plenty of time for reading, Cawkwell had watched the Lewinsky story on the "telly" with increased frustration. The Bill Clinton whom he had known was a likable, engaging graduate student who had come to meals at Cawkwell's home several times and was appropriate in every way. Seated at his desk in his second-floor study, Cawkwell pulled out a small red notebook, flipping to the entry dated June 19, 1969. "Yes, Bill came to lunch that day," he said, reviewing the notations that he kept of all graduate students whom he and his wife had entertained. "He had asparagus soup. Cold pork with ham sauce. New potatoes. Salad. And a strawberry almond meringue . . . bloody good meringue, that was."

Cawkwell saw nothing in the aspiring young politician that was negative in any way. "There was no suggestion that he was a romping 'sexo' then," insisted Cawkwell. "He was a fine fellow."

Regardless of whether Bill had strayed from his marital vows, Cawkwell believed that the effort to discredit an international leader in this fashion was "low-level." As he and many of his fellow Brits saw it, this dogged investigation by Independent Counsel Starr was producing nothing but a black eye for the United States. "If Clinton did it, I'm sorry for his reputation. But that's his business," explained Cawkwell. Even if Clinton had lied in his deposition about

Ms. Lewinsky, Cawkwell believed, the context was important. "I think the truth is that people behave in sex matters in a way they'd never behave in anything else," the Oxford professor declared, standing up for his former student. "I'd like to keep sex out of politics entirely. This was discrediting to America."

Cawkwell went on: "As head of state, it is damaging to portray someone as a fallible human being. We [in Great Britain] don't attack our monarchs all the time. It wouldn't have been good for people to have known every bit about Henry the Eighth. All of these personal things damage us terribly."

As far as Cawkwell was concerned, Ken Starr had gone round the bend. Most observers across the Atlantic, he said, could not fathom why this battle between Clinton and Starr had become so bloody, and so bloody personal.

CHAPTER

36

A MOTHER'S COLLAPSE

I f anything hardened Monica Lewinsky against Starr's prosecutors, it was their pulling the plug on the immunity deal and simultaneously dragging her family into the ring of criminal jeopardy.

Monica was holed up at her home in Beverly Hills, conversing in whispers with her father and stepmother in the bathroom for fear the house was bugged, completely "stressed out" and mistrustful of the Starr prosecutors. One image on television continued to haunt the whole Lewinsky family: Susan McDougal had appeared on the news dressed in a bright prison jumpsuit, being led in chains from the jail on her way to a court appearance. Unexpectedly, the convicted Whitewater defendant had looked into the camera and said: "Monica, it's not so bad in jail." Monica's mother would later whisper: "I'll never forget that. . . . I was very taken aback by that."

Then OIC pushed the envelope, calling Monica's mother in front of the grand jury. For Marcia Lewis, that day in February was forever fixed in her memory. She was driven to the federal courthouse in Washington by her attorney, Billy Martin. "And I remember driving up there in an SUV and looking out the window and seeing, you know, masses and masses of people. . . ." Monica's mother felt as if she were being forced to do the unthinkable: "You are there because they are hoping that you will say something unknowingly that will hurt your own child. That is why you are there. . . . My daughter was the target."

She would fall silent, then end her statement in a challenging voice: "And it's my position that if a prosecutor does not have enough evidence without the testimony of a parent, then he does not have enough evidence. . . . That's how I feel."

Much of the questioning in Grand Jury Room 4, conducted by Mike Emmick and Bruce Udolf on February 10, was aimed at pinning down a single fact: that Monica's mother knew her daughter was engaged in a sexual affair with President Clinton. This would corroborate, for the first time, that Linda Tripp's secret recordings did not capture a flight of fantasy. It was not the most direct evidence, but it would finally confirm that Clinton had lied in his *Jones* deposition.

"And there are half a dozen (prosecutors) lined up against you, all by yourself," Monica's mother would recall, "and you have no legal experience and no legal training. So it is very, very possible that unknowingly and unwittingly, you could say or do something that could be catastrophic and not even know it. It's a terrifying, terrifying situation, and it's barbaric."

Emmick proceeded gingerly during the questioning. He established first that Monica's mother had *suspected,* while her daughter was interning in the White House, that Monica might be developing a romantic interest in the president. She further acknowledged that this had caused her to be "very concerned and not happy." When the prosecutor asked why, Monica's mother looked at him quizzically. "Because I would like my daughter to find a nice young man and get married and I would like grandchildren," she responded.

The grand jurors, seated in stiff wooden chairs, listened attentively. The California prosecutor next coaxed Monica's mother to admit that she *suspected* that there had been some level of sexual activity, combined with some measure of love, at least flowing in one direction. The tall OIC prosecutor fixed his eyes on the grand jurors, to make sure they were catching the drift. He asked, "On some occasion, did she ever say that she was in love with the president?"

Marcia Lewis answered, "Yes. I think she did, but I can't say when."

After the first day of testimony, the two OIC soft-liners—Emmick and Udolf—felt that they had accomplished their mission. Monica's mother had substantiated the likelihood of *some* physical relationship. In their view, this was good enough—they couldn't expect the moon. Yet the OIC hard-liners had a different view. On the second day of Marcia Lewis's testimony, Sol Wisenberg took over. As Monica's mother would recall: "I could feel that the atmosphere had changed."

Wisenberg, striding in front of the grand jurors, demanded to know if Monica had an "affair" with the president. He hammered away, refusing to accept "no" for an answer. Marcia Lewis replied, "She talked about a relationship. She talked about she thought she was in love with him."

Next, Wisenberg demanded to know if Monica had referred to Hillary Clinton as "Bubba"—a term of endearment for Jewish grandmothers—as a way of suggesting that Clinton's wife was sexually unattractive like an old lady wearing a babushka. When Wisenberg did not elicit the clear response he wanted, the prosecutor stepped down from the questioner's platform "and started questioning [Marcia] about whether Jewish people call their mothers Bubba."

After ten minutes of such interrogation, which included questions about her own family and whether she had used the nickname "Bubba" for her own grandmother, Marcia Lewis turned pale. She dropped her head into her hands. Mike Emmick asked his witness, "Would you like—do you need a few minutes?" Udolf stood up and motioned to the grand jury foreperson: "Time out." Monica's mother began gulping for air.

As she would later explain, several things caused her to become unglued. Marcia Lewis was seeing in her head images of Susan McDougal in shackles for refusing to testify. Her own situation, she felt, was even more hopeless. "If a parent doesn't testify and they put the parent in jail, well, then the child or the young adult in this case [Monica], doesn't have a parent to help, so it's absolutely a horrible situation to be in." What's more, she feared the consequences if she refused to cooperate. "I know this sounds ridiculous," Monica's mother said later, "but I thought if I got up and left, that would be contempt and they'd put me in jail."

But the final straw that caused her to collapse related to the relentless questioning about "Bubba." That had been the family term of respect and love for her grandmother—Wisenberg's refusal to let the subject drop had finally caused her to become unhinged. Monica's mother recalled, "I was very embarrassed that I was becoming too emotional, you know, but my grandmother was dead and she had raised us." Marcia Lewis paused and collected herself: "And it's too much that this man . . . this Jewish man had been chosen to come down and ask me questions . . . 'What do I call my Jewish grandmother?' It was just—it was just really too much for me. So I just put my head down and started to cry. And so they called Billy Martin, and he just came and took me away."

An anonymous observer outside Grand Jury Room 4 would later tell the FBI that he or she had observed Marcia Lewis emerging from the room "crying loudly and exclaiming, 'I can't take it, I can't take any more, I can't stand it.'" Her lawyer, Billy Martin, an African American criminal defense attorney with a cool presence, instructed the U.S. Marshals to "summon medical aid." Within several minutes, the courthouse nurse arrived with a blood pressure cuff, but Marcia Lewis waved her away. Instead, Lewis was escorted out of the courthouse by her lawyer, tears streaming down her face, clutching onto Martin's arm. As photographers and cameramen captured an emotionally overwrought Marcia Lewis on that night's evening news, the grand jury testimony of Monica's mother came to an abrupt end.

Some members of the OIC team were certain that Marcia Lewis's breakdown was simply a theatrical performance designed to pull at the heartstrings of the grand jury. "I don't think her angst was legitimate," Jackie Bennett said. "I think it was all kind of putting on a show." Sol Wisenberg added, "Certainly, Billy [Martin] milked it for all it was worth."

Moreover, Wisenberg would insist that there was nothing legally or ethically improper about calling the young woman's mother to testify. "It's not done often, but it's certainly done," he said, defending the decision. "You can make an argument that it was dumb for us to do it and alienate her. . . . You can make that argument. I can certainly understand why somebody wouldn't like it. But she certainly had evidence. We thought she had evidence that we needed."

To the extent that anyone in Starr's office thought that her collapse might have been contrived, Marcia Lewis's first reaction was, "I have no response." She would quickly add, "Why should I care what they think? They think it's a show? That's outrageous. That is outrageous. How dare they. Maybe that's how they salve their conscience."

Her daughter jumped in: "I think anybody who would allow that to come out of their mouth is a disgusting human being." She took a deep breath and added, "They should be subpoenaed to testify against their child. Period. End of story."

Ken Starr himself would decline to take a position as to whether Marcia Lewis's breakdown had been real or feigned. Yet he emphasized that OIC was between a rock and a hard place: "Here we are as prosecutors under assault, having to establish that the president of the United States—and a very popular and pretty successful [president]—had lied to the American people. And had lied under oath. This was a very daunting, challenging assignment." One important slice of facts, Starr noted in defense of OIC's decision, was known only to Monica's mother. "So, part of the unfortunate thing about all of this," explained the independent counsel, "is there were any number of individuals who suffered through this process. And that process could have been much more abbreviated, had the president been forthcoming and truthful in the first instance."

For Starr, there was a "certain perversity" connected to the accusation that his office was being "too tough" on witnesses. All this was happening, he underscored, because of "the president's continued unwillingness to face up to the truth."

Monica Lewinsky, still at home in California, tuned in to a minitelevision in the kitchen, where she saw footage of her mother leaving the courthouse in a state of emotional distress. Monica recalled becoming sick to her stomach. "I had never seen my mother like that," Monica said later. "You have to know my mom. . . . She's one of those people who has this sort of warm spirit and is sort of very effervescent." Witnessing this breakdown and seeing what the Starr prosecutors had done to her mother was too much for Monica to bear. "She was just an empty body," she recalled thinking. "There was no soul."

So Monica turned off the television, packed her clothes, and booked a flight to Washington. "I came home straightaway," she recalled.

In a misguided strategic decision it would come to regret, the White House decided to launch an attack on Mike Emmick and Bruce Udolf, assuming (incorrectly) that these two prosecutors would be leading OIC's offensive against President Clinton. The Clinton forces began disseminating "opposition research" over fax machines and in sealed envelopes, spreading the word to its vast network of media contacts about purported skeletons in the closets of these two Starr prosecutors. This effort was coordinated, OIC believed, by Sidney Blumenthal (known as "Sid Vicious" and "Sid the Squid" within Starr's office), a superaggressive political journalist who was now one of Clinton's top advisers. Ironically, the two Starr prosecutors who were being raked over the coals in the media were likely the president's best hope of escaping the noose.

In Emmick's case, one newspaper story trumpeted: "STARR AIDE NOT STRANGER TO SEX TAPE INQUIRIES," suggesting that the Southern California prosecutor had been involved in sleazy sex crime prosecutions for the past decade. The media simultaneously clobbered Udolf, proclaiming that the Miami vice squad prosecutor had once been forced to flee his position as district attorney in an Atlanta suburb, because he had wrongfully jailed a man for possession of a stolen gun, requiring taxpayers to ante up fifty thousand dollars to correct his misfeasance. An *Atlanta Constitution* editorial, widely circulated by the White House in brown envelopes and faxes, referred to Udolf as "a man who trampled a citizen's rights; now he's investigating the President."

Emmick and Udolf were being squeezed from both ends. The hard-liners inside OIC, led by Sol Wisenberg, saw them as Clinton apologists. It was time to stand up and to be strong, they felt, or succumb to the weak defectors in the office. Wisenberg feared that Emmick and Udolf were positioning themselves to take over the Lewinsky investigation. "So I approached Jackie to f——ing do something about it," he later recounted. Wisenberg shouted at Bennett, "Goddam it, you can't let something like this happen. You can't let them f——ing call meetings like they're running the f——ing meetings."

As a result of this power play, Emmick and Udolf were pushed out of meaningful roles. Instead, the more aggressive, less experienced Bob Bittman solidified his position as leader of the Lewinsky investigation. Wisenberg, whose tour of duty with OIC was set to expire, agreed to stay on as deputy in charge of Lewinsky grand jury matters.

One former OIC prosecutor who generally admired Ken Starr (and thus asked not to be identified) worried that a "B team" quality had crept into the new management structure. None of the new prosecutors running the show in Starr's office had developed those key Washington connections that were necessary to "keep a perspective and make things run smoothly." None of them had a positive working relationship with the Justice Department or with the White House Counsel's Office, or with David Kendall, who stood between OIC and extracting information from the president and First Lady. Inside the Beltway, personal relationships and private telephone numbers and feelings of mutual trust meant everything. The new leadership team that had locked down control of the OIC operation in Washington, virtually overnight, possessed none of these assets.

The newly constituted Starr office quickly flexed its muscles by going after Clinton adviser Sidney Blumenthal, a former journalist for the *Washington Post* and the *New Yorker,* who was believed to be spreading "vicious, false information" about OIC to the media. Starr's prosecutors were itching to get Blumenthal under oath. As Starr himself would explain: "We viewed it as possibly bearing on obstruction. Why would the White House, through a very senior adviser who has all of these friendships in the press . . . be disseminating sewage?"

Yet the moment OIC issued a subpoena to Blumenthal, this triggered a new uproar. In news reports, Starr's office was suddenly being accused of thumbing its nose at First Amendment freedoms and the prerogatives of the press, in its wrongheaded quest to get Bill Clinton. Starr himself, taking out the garbage at his home in suburban Virginia, paused long enough to lecture reporters at the curbside: "It isn't in the interest of the First Amendment for distortions, lies about career civil servants [or OIC prosecutors] to be spread. . . . Lies and distortions have no place in our First Amendment universe."

As the OIC prosecutorial team poured its energy and resources into the Monica Lewinsky investigation, fighting feverishly on a dozen new fronts, one lone prosecutor took a different path, filled with hope that it would pay dividends.

That prosecutor was Hickman Ewing, Jr.

———

WHILE the rest of the world was focused on the Lewinsky story, Ewing was debating whether he could indict Hillary Rodham Clinton before May, when the Little Rock grand jury expired. One piece of his strategy, as Ewing raced against the clock, was to push harder on Webb Hubbell to see if he would crack. Ewing also wanted to tighten the screws on Susan McDougal, who was now in prison in

Los Angeles. If he could force these witnesses to corroborate the information provided by Jim McDougal—still locked up in Texas but scheduled to be paroled soon—he might be able to ensnare both the president and the First Lady while their attention was diverted by the Lewinsky pandemonium.

Most of Ewing's colleagues in the swelling OIC Washington offices now viewed Hillary and Whitewater as moot issues. The prevailing sentiment was, "Forget about that. We have the president in the sights. We got him."

Ewing saw it differently. Jim Guy Tucker had just pleaded guilty on February 20. Ewing had conducted nearly fifteen sessions with the former governor, who had produced smidgens of information that were "helpful on some of the Hillary issues." As Ewing sized it up, Tucker "pretty much agreed with [Jim] McDougal" when it came to confirming that "she [Hillary] is unethical" and that she had "used her status" improperly in carrying out certain legal work for Madison Guaranty and others. Ewing was confident that the fallen governor, however recalcitrant, would add a sprinkling of detail in building a case against the ever-evasive Mrs. Clinton.

The most important witness, however, was still Jim McDougal. Inside the walls of the federal prison in Forth Worth, McDougal had found religion and had directly contradicted President Clinton on key points crucial to the Whitewater and Madison Guaranty investigations. Among other things, McDougal now insisted that Clinton was lying when the president denied meeting with him and David Hale at McDougal's office-trailer to discuss a loan designed to benefit the "political family." He also told Starr's prosecutors that Clinton had lied in denying knowledge of the Madison Guaranty check that was marked "Payoff Clinton" and was found in the trunk of an abandoned car. McDougal was equally helpful when it came to Mrs. Clinton, particularly relating to her legal work on the Castle Grande development. McDougal didn't flinch when it came to serving up the First Lady to OIC. He seemed eager to prove her a liar, Ewing felt, with respect to "what she did and [how] she had denied things."

Ewing understood that McDougal had serious "credibility problems." He was a convicted felon who had ripped off the federal government and lied compulsively under oath. OIC's own prosecutor, Ray Jahn, had torn McDougal to shreds when he took the stand in the Whitewater trial. Yet Ewing was spending more time on the phone with McDougal in prison these days; the two men were starting to bond. Ewing had come to trust the great S&L con artist, at least when it came to his account of the myriad sins committed by Bill and Hillary Clinton.

Ewing was actively assisting McDougal in his bid to be paroled in the spring. If all went well, the Memphis prosecutor hoped the pieces might finally come together like a spectacular jigsaw puzzle that finally locks into place. Assuming Jim McDougal was released in April as planned, just as his book hit the bookstores

and McDougal became a national TV celebrity, the eccentric former businessman would be able to rehabilitate his image and speak the truth about those
long-ago days in Arkansas. In the process, he might also provide the final key to
indicting the First Lady, just as the world collapsed around Bill and Hillary
Clinton in the peripheral Lewinsky probe.

CHAPTER

37

LAST NIGHT IN SOLITARY CONFINEMENT

Richard Clark, during his psychological evaluation meetings with Jim
McDougal in early 1998, observed that the Arkansas prisoner was
increasingly tormented with thoughts that powerful people were
out to destroy him. At first, McDougal attributed these suspicions to his physical
environment. The psychologist's notes revealed that his patient "was indicating
that his mood had been slightly down of late and he attributed that to the
cloudy weather of the winter season. He talked about how he was a true Southerner and enjoyed sunshine and how cloudy weather had always made him feel
somewhat down."

McDougal's book was in galley form and ready for its national release. The
publishers were stretching out the publication date until April, so that McDougal
could hit the speaking circuit the moment he was paroled and make a big splash.
To the extent that a silver lining existed on Jim McDougal's horizon, the anticipated release of the book was it. As Clark recounted, "The idea was that he'd be
paroled in late April of 1998, that the book would come out, that he would spend
some time promoting the book and then would settle back down in Arkadelphia
near the college. He was telling me about how he really enjoyed having university
students come by, and he was hoping that he would just be living a quiet life in
Arkadelphia with occasional opportunities to be able to lecture at the university."

Although McDougal's conviction on nineteen counts of fraud and conspiracy could have led to eighty-three years in prison, his cooperation with OIC had
shaved that sentence down to three years with eligibility for parole based on "good
behavior" in a third of that time. Starr's deputy, Hickman Ewing, Jr., had written
a glowing letter for him, in which Ewing had recommended that McDougal "be

paroled due to his acceptance of responsibility for his crimes and his cooperation with authorities in the investigative process." The magic April day was not far off.

On February 2, prison medical records indicate that McDougal requested a special counseling session, or a "cop-out," with the Psychology Unit. In this meeting, the prisoner questioned the right of guards to make him "pee on demand." In early January, officers had rounded up the entire wing of his unit in a maneuver called "saturation," requiring inmates to provide urine samples for drug testing. Once again, McDougal had "locked up," unable to perform. After protesting that the psychologists had placed in his file a document recommending that he be given "dry cell status" for urinalysis, he had been told by Philip Shanks, the caseworker assigned to assembling materials for his parole hearing, that his "central file does not contain a copy of the evaluation report recommending dry cell status."

Clark found the situation extremely odd. First, it had always troubled Clark that McDougal's name had been placed on the suspect list for drug screenings in the first place, since nothing in his file (evidence of drug use, etc.) would justify such a step under the prison's procedures. Even more perplexing, Clark knew that he had directed, personally, that the "dry status" report be placed in McDougal's central file. The unit manager had confirmed that they had "received the report."

To correct this problem, Clark arranged for a new copy of the report to be sent out immediately. Scribbling notes in longhand, the young doctor assured Jim McDougal that his "request would be honored." This problem would not occur again.

ON the afternoon of Sunday, March 8, Clark was at home celebrating his wife's birthday when the phone rang. His supervisor, Jim Womack, was on the other end. Womack's voice sounded subdued. "Have you heard the news?" he asked.

Clark sank into a kitchen chair. His boss continued in a tentative voice: "I just heard about it on television. They're saying that he died at a local hospital today." Womack added that he wanted the young psychologist to have some time "to process all of this before going back into the institution."

A single thought immediately lodged itself in Richard Clark's mind. "They killed him," he told himself. It was the only conclusion he could reach, looking at everything that had occurred since October, including Jim McDougal's "placement in the hole, and all the controversy about the suspect list . . . [and then] the evaluation report was missing from his file." Years later, Clark recalled, "My spirit just knew something was wrong about all of this."

The prison had released a carefully worded statement indicating that James B.

McDougal had died that morning of natural causes. But Clark wasn't buying it. As he reconstructed the facts over the next few days, from his own sources inside the prison, they simply didn't jibe with the official accounts. He managed to gather up additional information from reporters who had gained access to the prison's internal report of McDougal's death, a report that was still being kept under lock and key. The true story, as Clark pieced it together, was deeply troublesome.

On Saturday, March 7, at approximately 4:30 P.M.—just hours before his death—Jim McDougal had been summoned to the correctional office for yet another urine sample. Although he had again requested dry-cell status, that request had been denied without explanation. McDougal was unable to urinate. This time, McDougal began to get testy—he demanded to know "why he was on the UA [list for urinalysis]." He added sarcastically that "the only person involved in [the Whitewater] case who had anything to do with drugs was the president." After McDougal complained to the guards of dizziness, they grabbed him by the arms and informed the prisoner that he was being taken to the segregated housing unit (SHU), or the "hole."

In a freak onset of weather for Texas, it had begun snowing that evening. While McDougal was being led across the compound to the SHU at approximately 10:30 P.M., snowflakes left watery splotches on his khaki prison jumpsuit. McDougal appeared to have difficulty breathing: The guard escorting the prisoner stopped long enough to give him an opportunity to catch his breath. As they entered the jail unit, they passed a large, official, smiling portrait of President Bill Clinton hung on the wall alongside portraits of other top government officials, including Attorney General Janet Reno. McDougal glanced at the photo of his former friend and then marched into a holding area, where he was stripped naked and issued a reddish orange jumpsuit. This was the badge of shame for inmates condemned to the hole.

As McDougal was processed in the shower area of the SHU, he vomited. The bald-headed inmate was then placed in solitary confinement in cell B-24, a fourteen-by-eight-foot space in the prison's most isolated unit.

Clark later pieced together additional facts from off-the-record conversations with guards in the SHU: Somewhere in this time frame, McDougal would have been required to participate in a "stand-up count." This was a routine followed each night in the hole. One by one, each inmate was required to stand up in his cell to be accounted for, to ensure that dummies could not be stuffed into bunks, which would allow prisoners to escape undetected. Clark surmised that McDougal "raised a ruckus about his having been placed in the hole and also raised the issue about his medication."

At approximately 1:30 A.M., an internal prison report noted that McDougal shouted out to the guard that he thought he could now provide a urine sample.

The guard, who was ten feet away and reportedly playing cards with a fellow officer, replied dismissively, "It's too late."

At 10:55 the next morning, Sunday, another guard reported hearing "a loud sighing from within the cell." Although this relevant fact appeared in none of the official reports, the guard confided to Clark that he heard a "thud" noise, as if something had fallen over. "That's what they said," Clark recalled. "It sounded as if [something] had fallen." Clark added, "In the isolated cell, there's just the bed there, so I don't know how you fall down." Yet the sound of a person collapsing and a loud sigh attracted the attention of the guard, who found McDougal lying on the floor "unresponsive."

Immediately, the guard shouted, "Man down!" The officers in the hole hurriedly called for assistance from the medical unit that dispatched men carrying a portable defibrillator. However, as Clark calculated it, "at the quickest, it would have been fifteen minutes to get that equipment over from the Health Services Unit into segregation." According to officers present, the medical unit personnel "worked on McDougal for about 25 minutes." One inmate in an adjacent cell later told a reporter that a guard went around "taping newspaper over the windows" so that the other prisoners could not see what was transpiring. A MedStar ambulance arrived at the prison, its red light flashing noiselessly as it crept into the compound. A team of paramedics received clearance to enter the prison facility, wheeling a gurney that clattered against iron bars as they rolled the equipment into the dark SHU. McDougal's body was then transported to a hospital in Fort Worth, where he was pronounced dead at 12:01 P.M.

Notwithstanding news reports that McDougal had died of a heart attack at a hospital off prison grounds, Clark's sources in the SHU confirmed that he was likely "dead before the portable defibrillator ever arrived."

The autopsy report issued by the Office of Chief Medical Examiner of Tarrant County certified that James B. McDougal, a white male "appearing somewhat older than the given age of 57 years," had arrived in a body bag clad only in red coveralls, a white T-shirt, and white socks. The decedent, according to this report, had died of natural causes. Specifically, the autopsy listed the cause of death as "sudden cardiac death due to hypertensive atherosclerotic cardiovascular disease."

Ironically, McDougal's death occurred exactly six years to the day after Jeff Gerth's story first appeared in the New York Times, linking Bill and Hillary Clinton to McDougal's misdeeds in the Whitewater scandal.

As news of Jim McDougal's death swept through the cells at Fort Worth prison, numerous "wild rumors" gained traction. One was that a Blackhawk helicopter had landed at the facility shortly before McDougal was taken to the hole, and that he had been "injected with some sort of a substance" by mysterious men in dark suits. Inmates also whispered that McDougal's cell in the hole was roped off and repainted once the body was removed, to whitewash over clues concerning the true cause of his death.

Claudia Riley was the person listed on prison records as the sole next of kin. She had just returned from Chicago when her daughter delivered the news at the Little Rock airport. Claudia let loose an "animalistic cry." She later recalled that moment: "Jim was going up for parole, and it was assured pretty much that he was going to get out. His book was being finished and he was going on a book tour. That's what he was living for. It was one of those things that you find very hard to believe."

Although the sky was dark and the air was cold with the remnants of winter, Claudia exited her car in the middle of her driveway in Arkadelphia, giving a spontaneous eulogy to the man who had occupied her little trailer-cottage after he had become a destitute, convicted Whitewater felon. The rest of the night, Claudia remembered, "messages were pouring in, and the warden from the prison was calling . . . so I spent most of the night taking telephone calls from these people."

As prison officials scrambled to explain the sudden death of its celebrity Whitewater inmate, Claudia Riley undertook the more basic task of figuring out how to get McDougal's body released for shipment back to Arkansas. Despite her general revulsion with the Office of Independent Counsel, she contacted Hickman Ewing, knowing that he had worked closely with McDougal in recent months. Ewing seemed shaken up; he was heartsick that McDougal had died so ignominiously in the hole. He seemed equally distraught that death had now sealed the lips of the only man who might have been able to prove the criminal complicity of Bill and Hillary Clinton in the Whitewater/Madison Guaranty misdeeds. Ewing would later say, "I didn't think that they [the prison guards] did him right. I think they were negligent at the very least in the way that they handled him. I was very [upset]—it was like a relative died."

As a general matter, Claudia Riley was spooked by corpses. "I don't view bodies," she explained. "It's not necessary; they're gone." But there were so many "wild" rumors circulating about Jim McDougal's death, she called her daughter and said, "We're going to the funeral home." They entered the Murry-Ruggles Funeral Home on Clay Street in Arkadelphia, where she directed the undertaker to open the casket so that she could peer inside. "It was obviously Jim," Claudia said. "None of us wanted to do this, but we did."

Just before he had left for prison, McDougal had sat at a table in Claudia's living room and announced that he wanted to "write out a few things." Claudia now opened the sealed envelope and discovered a handwritten will, naming her as the sole executor. Jim had expected (or hoped for) money from the sale of his book. In his last will and testament, he asked Claudia to handle all arrangements and to take care of two people: an elderly aunt, who was his only surviving relative, and his ex-wife, Susan. Said Claudia softly, "He cared about Susan to the end."

Susan McDougal was in the federal Metropolitan Detention Center in Los Angeles, a facility that primarily housed the poor and destitute. It was here that she received the news from a Catholic chaplain.

Susan's overwhelming feeling was one of numbness. She would later reconstruct her thoughts: "I wasn't sure how I felt about Jim's death. The Jim I'd known had died years earlier, and I had already mourned that passing." The ultimate irony, she felt, was that Jim was so terrified of dying in prison, that he was willing to tell Starr's prosecutors anything they wanted to hear. "Jim had made his deal with the devil," she said, clasping her hands together, "and then he died in prison, anyway."

As she sat in her own dark jail cell trying to make sense of Jim's bizarre demise, Susan's dominant thought was, "Oh my God, Jim, you can never take this back." She had always thought there would come a day when Jim would be freed from jail and he would confess to her face-to-face that he had cooperated with OIC because he was "scared" and wanted desperately to "save himself." When that day came, she had been prepared to forgive her ex-husband, who had ruined her life. Now, they would never have that conversation. Susan concluded: "We were left with that."

This complex and tragic man who had once been her chivalrous husband, Susan McDougal told herself as she stared blankly at the walls of her cell, "was capable of unbelievable acts of generosity." Yet the same man could engage in "unbelievable acts of perversity and deceit." She had come to loathe that second Jim McDougal, "the man who threw away every principle he believed in . . . the man who cared about no one but himself and who seemed to take pleasure in hurting others." Another feeling kept sneaking in and made her even more confused: Despite the anger, Susan could not shut out a feeling that approximated love. "For every bad thought I had about Jim, there were also numerous good memories of the Jim I'd married, the man who so effortlessly gave whatever he had to [others]," she said, recalling that strange period of mourning in prison.

But her thoughts toward Ken Starr and Hickman Ewing and the whole crew from OIC remained unwavering: These sentiments were so un-Christian and filled with hate that she preferred not to repeat them. Susan would later reflect, "Whatever sins Jim committed—and he certainly committed his share—he didn't deserve to die lying on a concrete prison floor, pleading for help."

When Claudia Riley called Susan in prison to discuss funeral services, Susan sobbed into the phone and reminded Claudia that Jim "always wanted a jazz band." Susan seemed distraught and was feeling helpless because she was locked up a thousand miles away. As Claudia recalled, "And I simply talked her through it, because I was sort of a mother figure and a friend figure and I love her very much. She's like a beloved daughter to me."

Claudia finally said, "Susan, leave this one with me. I'll handle it. I'll do exactly what you and Jim would have wanted if you were here." She added, "We're going to make a party. It's going to be like an Irish wake."

Claudia had no intention of turning this into a sideshow, especially with the national media swarming around. Still, when it came to the likes of McDougal—whether in life or in death—it seemed pointless to follow a normal path.

On a chilly Friday in Arkadelphia, a small congregation of friends and curious onlookers assembled at a hilly grave site to pay their final respects to James Bert McDougal, the onetime Whitewater mastermind. Reporters and a half-dozen camera crews huddled together as a Dixieland band marched up the hill playing, "When the Saints Go Marching In," a selection that Jim had told his minister he would appreciate as a final send-off. Along with the jazzy sound of brass horns, a note of irony hung in the March air. Ewing delivered a passionate eulogy that seemed both bizarre and fitting for the occasion. The OIC lawyer who had helped put McDougal in prison was an evangelical Christian and had personally requested to speak at the burial service. He stood at the grave as flags rippled, extolling the virtues of the felon convicted on nineteen counts of fraud and conspiracy. With gray clouds blocking out the sun, Ewing offered thanks "for the life of Jim McDougal," praying aloud, "Lord, you created him as a very unique person. You knit him together in his mother's womb those many years ago. Now he's gone. Lord, we thank you for the joy that he brought to people's lives."

The Starr prosecutor went on to tell the small congregation of mourners that Jim McDougal had been a defendant, an adversary, and later a cooperating witness. In the end, Ewing told those assembled, he had also become a friend.

As the musicians raised their glinting horns and played "Just a Closer Walk with Thee," McDougal's inexpensive casket was lowered into the Riley family plot beside his former mentor, the late Lieutenant Governor Bob Riley. McDougal's minister placed a single stone on the coffin to symbolize his fervent prayer that there would be "an end to throwing stones" in American government and politics. Claudia Riley likewise placed a stone on the casket, tapping it gently. One distant relative of McDougal's left the grave site in disgust, telling a reporter that Ewing should have never been permitted to speak at the service. "The pressure of being put in jail," said Shirley Davis of Jackson County, Arkansas, "the confinement and the humiliation of being put in prison—it killed Jim."

Yet Claudia didn't worry about such things. "I don't think that anybody thought that anything dealing with [Jim] would be inappropriate," she said. "Because Jim was off-the-wall most of the time."

After the funeral service, Ken Starr's chief prosecutor wandered up to the Riley home. Here, Ewing sipped iced tea and munched on cookies, telling Claudia before he left, "You know, I genuinely loved Jim McDougal." Claudia Riley would later reflect, "And it really was, it was like a black comedy. Jim would have liked it." She hastened to conclude, "But his death, his death was strange. There will never be any answer. . . . It [just] wasn't right."

OIC had its own doubts. Although Hickman Ewing would never go so far as to suggest that the White House was involved in McDougal's death, he certainly felt the Clinton people had welcomed it. "People in the Federal Bureau of Prisons were putting him in places he shouldn't have been put," Ewing said. "Once he cooperated, in the spring of 1998, we were full-court pressing on Hillary. . . . There's a grand jury in Little Rock that could indict Hillary. And they [the Clinton White House] are trashing me. I'm sure they were glad that Jim was dead. Could it be that people in the Bureau of Prisons sympathetic to the Clintons said, 'Don't cut him any slack?' They knew who he was. They weren't going to do anything to bend over backward to help us. It was just very unfortunate the way he died."

Those inside the White House disavowed any connection to McDougal's death in a Texas prison. As one adviser stated: "Christ Almighty, we had a hard enough time staying alive ourselves." Indeed, there is no evidence that Bill Clinton or his surrogates played any role in McDougal's sudden demise in solitary confinement. Rogue prison officials, on the other hand, could easily have taken it upon themselves to get McDougal—many clues gathered by Richard Clark pointed toward mischief inside the prison walls.

Neither the president nor the First Lady was able to attend the funeral services in Arkadelphia. President Clinton, however, would later say that he was deeply saddened by the circumstances surrounding Jim's death in solitary confinement. In terms of rumors that the Clinton White House or his Justice Department had something to do with McDougal's strange demise, the president would dismiss this as cruel and patently false. Bill Clinton had watched McDougal's mental and physical decline over the years; this deterioration of a sick man had provided no cause for rejoicing or celebration. "You know, I never did nor could I have done anything to adversely affect his circumstances," Clinton said later. "He was sent to prison because he got convicted. And, you know, Starr and those guys kept trying to work on him, getting him to say more stuff."

Indeed, it was the independent counsel's office, Clinton pointed out, that was watching over McDougal in the Texas prison. It was both absurd and wrong-headed to suggest that anyone associated with the White House had contributed, even one iota, to McDougal's tragic death.

President Clinton rocked back in his chair and closed his eyes, recalling the Jim McDougal who had once been a friend and a fellow aspiring Arkansas politician. "They [Ken Starr's office] played him, they squeezed him, they broke him," said Clinton. "And there was nothing for them to be proud of, because he was an easy target. He needed his medication; he needed to be in a supportive, not in a difficult environment." Clinton shook his head and observed that even if McDougal was guilty of committing crimes, "I don't know that the interests of justice were served by spending all that amount of money to incarcerate a guy who was in the kind of shape he was in. . . . How can you get angry at a person who's basically not in control of their life? Not even in control of their mind anymore?"

Clinton concluded, his voice becoming softer, "Nobody on my account would have done anything to make his life any worse." Whatever Jim McDougal had said or done to implicate Clinton in order to save his own neck, the president had completely forgiven him. "I didn't blame him," said the former president. "He was just a vulnerable, weak reed in a strong wind."

The Federal Bureau of Prisons scrambled to tamp down ugly speculation, issuing a statement that McDougal's placement in the hole "had no adverse impact on Mr. McDougal's medical condition." Richard Clark and others, in the meantime, questioned this official line. What concerned Clark most was that the autopsy revealed a high level of Prozac in McDougal's blood at the time of his death, indicating (most likely) that he had recently ingested that drug. Yet an internal prison report confirmed that "there is no evidence that inmate McDougal had access to his other self-administered medications," specifically those related to his heart problems.

Clark was particularly concerned that McDougal had been placed in the hole without access to his nitroglycerin, which he normally had within reach to "take as needed." Prison regulations required that inmates be given access to their meds at all times. Since the autopsy confirmed that McDougal had died from a sudden heart-related incident, Clark noted, "the nitroglycerin well could have bought some very necessary time." He added, "The question at that point is, 'Why weren't his other medications given? Why weren't those brought over?' "

In Clark's professional opinion, the autopsy's notation that McDougal had died from "sudden cardiac death" was particularly telling. This medical term referred to a specific type of cardiac event requiring "a precipitating acute stressor" similar to the type of stressor that would cause an individual to drop dead "during an electrical blackout or in the midst of a stampede at a football game." Here, the facts all pointed toward a single "acute stressor"—namely, "an interaction between Mr. McDougal and the officer or guards in segregation." On the night before McDougal's death, not only had he been subjected to humiliation during another six-hour ordeal involving the demand for urine samples, but he had also been thrown into the hole and separated from his meds, all of which would have caused him to make a ruckus when the guard came to his cell for "stand-up count" between 10:00 and 11:00 P.M. During this time, McDougal undoubtedly acted up and complained that the guards were retaliating against him because he was blowing the whistle on Bill and Hillary Clinton—a theme he had repeatedly sounded during his final weeks.

Clark was convinced that some "interaction between Mr. McDougal and the officer in segregation . . . would have been enough of an agitation within Mr. McDougal's system to trigger sudden cardiac death."

The young psychologist, in the weeks after McDougal's death, continued to gather information. While snooping around the hole, Clark checked the green-bound SHU visitors log that listed all individuals—including prison staff—who had entered and exited the unit. When he checked the book for the dates in question, the visitors' log through March 9, 1998, was "missing." It had been replaced with a brand-new logbook, beginning with the date of March 10—just after McDougal's death. Clark said, "So the visitors log [for the key date] was taken."

What thoroughly convinced Clark that the prison was hiding relevant facts, however, was a strange episode that the psychologist was reluctant to share until years later, in 2003, after he had left the employ of the prison. Shortly after McDougal's funeral, Clark revealed, he had received a phone call from one of his supervisors indicating that "there is an investigator who's going to come down to the Psychology Department" to discuss McDougal's death. The moment Clark raised concerns about doctor-patient confidentiality, his supervisor cut him off: "Confidentiality no longer applies, . . ." he explained. "They've already confiscated the entire psychology file for Mr. McDougal." The chief psychiatrist added hesitantly, "This is an official investigation; answer all of their questions."

As Clark headed down the corridor toward his office, he was followed by a tall man dressed in a dark suit. The man said that he needed to speak with Clark in private, so the young doctor led him into his cramped office, with room only for one chair beside his desk. The man sat down and closed the door. According to Clark's account, the serious-looking man got right to the point: "You know why I'm here. The information you have is of interest to the White House, the Office of Independent Counsel, and the Federal Bureau of Prisons," he said. The man disclosed that he worked with the bureau's legal staff, and that he had been appointed as special agent in charge of investigating James B. McDougal's death.

For three hours, the light-haired agent with a stern face questioned Clark in areas that made the young doctor feel extremely uncomfortable. The man probed into Clark's credentials, challenging "the appropriateness of conducting the evaluation" that had led to a recommendation of dry-cell status for McDougal. Increasingly, the man's tone became "adversarial." The agent suggested that McDougal had been "faking" his inability to produce a urine sample, to which Clark rejoined that this was highly unlikely, because McDougal had "offered to have blood drawn as a way of testing for substances." He had even "volunteered to be catheterized so that the sample could be provided." All of this, noted the young psychologist, indicated "this was not a case of malingering. Someone who would go to the extent of volunteering to be catheterized." The man, however, did not seem appeased.

He returned to the subject of the "ill-advised nature" of Clark's recommendation that McDougal be given dry-cell status, opening a black leather satchel and throwing a stack of papers onto the desk, stating coldly, "You might want to refer to these." The young doctor observed that the papers were copies of the entire psychology file regarding McDougal—a file that was normally off-limits to anyone other than the medical staff. In a calm voice, Clark tried to explain the basis for his handling of McDougal's case. The agent's face turned severe when Clark told him that McDougal had repeatedly questioned why he was on the "suspect list" in the first place, when there was no "triggering event" involving drug use that would have justified receiving a "shot" (or a charge of wrongdoing). The agent replied angrily, "That's *another* issue that does not concern Psychology." The man demanded to know if McDougal had ever "seen in writing that he was on the suspect list." When Clark responded that he had no knowledge on this score, the agent's face seemed to indicate relief.

The dark-suited man then began a line of questioning that was especially troublesome to the young psychologist. He told Clark that prison officials had known nothing about his dry-cell memo until after McDougal's death. The man narrowed his eyes and said, "No one outside of Psychology had ever seen your memo. It was a surprise to everyone." The doctor shot a look of disbelief at his interrogator and countered, "That's ridiculous." Not only had he sent the memo to the captain at the Fort Worth Unit, but he had also sent a *second* copy to the case manager, Philip Shanks, to be placed in McDougal's file so that there was no chance it would be forgotten during his parole hearing.

The agent's face tightened and he reiterated, "I'm telling you, the story is, no one had ever seen your memo."

Clark objected again, explaining how McDougal had specifically requested that the dry-cell memo and the letter from Hickman Ewing be placed in his packet for the parole hearing so that nothing happened to them. At this, the agent screwed up his face and said, "Mr. McDougal was never going to be paroled." Clark was stunned. He tried to correct the record by interrupting: "What do you mean he was never going to be paroled? . . . He was eligible for parole in late April."

The agent repeated firmly, according to Clark's handwritten notes of the meeting: "I'm just telling you—Mr. McDougal was never going to be paroled."

Clark glanced at his watch. It was now nearly five o'clock. The meeting suddenly "went from bad to worse." The stern-faced special agent flipped through the stack of documents from McDougal's file, holding up Clark's original dry-cell memo in which he had questioned the urinalysis procedure that had been repeated the night before McDougal had died. The federal agent now looked up and said to the young doctor, "Will you recant your statement?"

This moment was frozen forever in Clark's mind. He would later say, "And what stuck out to me was the word 'recant,' in that I had never been asked to 're-cant' before, and that's one of those words I was just thinking, 'Okay, what an odd word.' It's a word that's not used very often. With my theological training, I thought of 'recant' in terms of having real significance regarding 'denying one's faith,' so that word was one that stuck out for me."

The young psychologist stared at the man and said, "No, I will not. I will not recant."

The agent stood up stiffly. He assumed an especially unpleasant demeanor. "This meeting is over," he said. The man in the suit then gathered up the pile of documents and placed them in his satchel. He instructed Clark that the doctor should "speak to no one about the meeting."

Then, as the man turned to open the door of the cramped office to leave, he issued his parting words with a dark look crossing his face: "It's getting extremely hot in your office, Dr. Clark."

CHAPTER

38

THE INDICTMENT OF HILLARY CLINTON

One piece of the investigation headed by Ken Starr that has remained locked in a secret vault—despite the airing of dirty laundry and intimate details concerning virtually every other aspect of the Whitewater and Lewinsky probes—involved the final-hour effort by OIC to indict First Lady Hillary Clinton.

Documents unearthed from OIC now reveal that the attempt by Hickman Ewing to bring a formal indictment against Mrs. Clinton reached a crescendo in April 1998. Although the details of this effort have largely been kept from the public, the proposed indictment was designed to encompass not only the First Lady, but also one other alleged "co-conspirator."

A hushed-up meeting was held at OIC's Washington offices on April 27, just before the Whitewater/Madison grand jury was scheduled to expire. In preparation, a thick draft indictment was reviewed by top prosecutors in Starr's office. It was a defining moment for the Starr investigation. On April 25, Ken Starr and his prosecutors had visited the White House to question the First Lady under oath for the sixth time—on this occasion for nearly five hours—about her business dealings with the McDougals and her legal work for Madison Guaranty. Many remained skeptical of the truthfulness of the First Lady's account, especially relating to the troublesome billing records issues. Yet the consensus was that any effort to prosecute Mrs. Clinton would be extremely risky.

It was only Hickman Ewing, unshakable in his belief that Hillary Clinton had perjured herself, who clung to the hope that OIC might bring formal criminal charges against her before his investigation came to a close. Never before had a First Lady of the United States been indicted. That was no reason, in Ewing's mind, to resist taking this historic plunge.

The Tennessee prosecutor still burned with frustration as he watched his fellow prosecutors trip over themselves pursuing the matter involving Monica Lewinsky; he believed far too much emphasis was being placed on this Johnny-come-lately investigation. Lewinsky had never been part of Starr's original jurisdiction as independent counsel. In contrast, the office had spent four grueling years tracking down the facts relating to the Whitewater/Madison Guaranty irregularities involving the McDougals, Jim Guy Tucker, the Clintons, and other bad actors. Now, if it proceeded boldly, OIC could finally justify its existence. Ewing believed as passionately as he had ever believed anything in his career that Hillary Rodham Clinton needed to be brought to justice and tried in criminal court before a jury of her peers.

Yet Starr's other top prosecutors, in private, worried that this would amount to whistling in the wind. Although they were thoroughly distrustful of Mrs. Clinton and leery of her testimony, getting an Arkansas or a Washington grand jury to indict the First Lady seemed like a long shot. The better course, they opined as they poured coffee and took seats at the conference table, was to funnel all of OIC's resources into stalking the great bull elephant and bringing down Bill Clinton with one great blast relating to his perjured testimony in the *Jones* deposition. They repeated their mantra: "Forget about [Hillary]. We have the president in [our] sights."

And so, Ewing later asserted, only half facetiously, "Monica saved Hillary."

THE spring of 1998 was a busy time for OIC, as Starr's prosecutors sought to tighten the noose around Bill Clinton's neck. The president had lapsed into a state of evasive denial, continuing to disavow a sexual relationship with Monica Lewinsky but deferring to his lawyers whenever questions became uncomfortably specific.

The president's secretary, Betty Currie, had turned out to be far less helpful than Starr's team had hoped. After Currie had allowed herself to be swept back into the White House's fold, she suddenly displayed signs of "amnesia." As Jackie Bennett recalled, OIC had left the initial meetings with Currie and her attorney thinking: "Betty is the occasional rare person who is not going to lie. We haven't seen many such people in our dealings with the Arkansas crowd." After Currie appeared in the grand jury and gave testimony that was oblique and included plenty of "I don't remembers," the Starr prosecutors threw up their hands. "In a very short period of time she was backpedaling and forgetting," said Bennett. "And so the view very quickly became in the office, you know, 'they've gotten to her.' And I think that's probably what happened."

So Starr's office decided to summon a parade of its own witnesses to Washington who could not be reached by the White House's tentacles. On St. Patrick's Day, OIC subpoenaed Catherine "Cat" Allday Davis to supply sworn testimony. Davis, who had been flown in from Tokyo, where she and her husband were now residing, was Monica's closest friend and confidante since their days as psychology majors at Lewis and Clark College. Monica had been a bridesmaid in Davis's wedding the previous year. Davis now paid for that friendship by spending a day in Grand Jury Room 3, facing Sol Wisenberg and Mary Anne Wirth, the latter of whom was added to provide a woman's touch to the grilling.

If OIC had hoped to strengthen its hand in this first round of Blind Man's Bluff poker, it succeeded in spades with Catherine Davis's testimony. A poised young woman whose husband was employed by a Japanese corporation, Davis was openly defensive of Monica and hostile toward Ken Starr. By the end of her testimony, however, Davis had corroborated Monica's initial story to the Starr prosecutors and then some.

In response to questioning by the hard-driving Wisenberg, Davis confirmed that she had chatted by phone and by e-mail regularly during Monica's tenure in the White House, and that she knew that her friend had developed a relationship with the president. Monica had told Davis that she and President Clinton spent time in the Oval Office chatting about politics, life, and "emotional matters." They had talked tearfully about the death of Clinton's mother, Virginia, after that period of grieving for the president. Monica and Bill Clinton had even spoken, frankly and openly, about the state of the president's marriage to First Lady Hillary Clinton. According to Monica's accounts passed along to Davis in their regular discussions in the confessional, the president had freely admitted to marital difficulties but had expressed a desire to reform his rocky relationship with Hillary, declaring that "he was committed to it over time."

Davis was under oath and therefore could not deny that there was a "physical" dimension to the relationship between Monica Lewinsky and the president. Beginning in late 1995 and lasting through late 1997, Monica had told Davis, the young intern had met with Clinton in a small room adjacent to the Oval Office and described "giving the President oral sex on numerous occasions." There had also been "kissing, hugging, him touching her breasts," according to Monica's love-struck accounts. Monica had even called Davis and played her recordings of the president that she had kept on her answering machine, in which the president could be heard drawling in his smooth Arkansas voice, "Ah, shucks, you're not there," or lamenting "Oh, I wanted to talk to you." It also turned out that Monica and the president frequently spoke by phone after midnight, and the conversations often turned risqué. The light-haired Davis took a sip of water and told the grand jurors, "It was described to me as phone sex."

OIC also hit the jackpot by confirming a tantalizing fact that had popped up in the Linda Tripp tapes: Monica had indeed worn a dark blue dress that she had bought at the Gap, "short-sleeve, sort of around the knee-ish," during one of her later encounters with the president. She had confessed to Davis that she believed it was stained with Clinton's semen. Monica had asked Davis joshingly, "I wonder if he's going to pay for the dry cleaning?" Davis paused for another sip of water and told the grand jury that she believed the Gap dress was still hanging in a closet, although she wasn't sure where. This revelation caused Wisenberg's eyebrows to jump with excitement. It meant physical evidence existed that, if found and tested, could scientifically prove that Bill Clinton had lied through his teeth.

One of the most startling facts that was confirmed by Catherine Davis's testimony related to the universe of people who knew that Monica was engaging in hanky-panky with the president. It turned out to be larger than expected. Davis rattled off names of others whom she believed Monica had taken into her "confidence" about the affair. They included Monica's mother; her aunt Debra Finerman; Linda Tripp; mutual friends Ashley Raines, Natalie Ungavari, Neasa Erbland; and several others. When Monica had sworn Davis to secrecy about the presidential fling, she had instructed her friend to tell nobody "other than your husband." So Davis's husband, too, had been brought into the web of "secrecy." This extramarital presidential affair, it turned out, had not been the most carefully guarded secret in the Beltway.

There were a number of other surprises awaiting the grand jury. Much of Catherine Davis's day-long session in the grand jury turned out to be unexpectedly touching. She read from cards and e-mails swapped between herself and

Monica, chronicling the ups and downs of Monica's romance with Clinton, and Davis's own efforts to protect her friend from an emotional train wreck. Even though OIC may not have intended to generate sympathy for Monica by calling this witness, the grand jury soon learned that Monica, barely over twenty, had been hopelessly love-struck.

In one card mailed in May 1997, Lewinsky had written to her friend: "Dear Catherine: I miss you so much. It was wonderful to hear your voice the other day." She continued half hopefully: "Well, it's Sunday. I might get to see the Big Creep today. He called yesterday and said he's going to see if Betty can come in so I can go there. It seems that he is really trying to get me back there. Who knows?"

In another e-mail sent to Japan in late summer, Monica had divulged that she had given "the Creep" a "mushy romance" novel titled *The Notebook* before he left for vacation to Martha's Vineyard. It had been a gesture of sentiment because the president had given her a copy of *Leaves of Grass* by Walt Whitman— it was referenced in this novel. Monica told her friend that "Handsome" seemed to appreciate this "neat and sweet" present. The intern had only offhandedly asked the president "if he could bring me a Black Dog T-shirt" from a trendy tavern in Martha's Vineyard. The e-mail went on to tell Davis: "Well, I found out from Betty yesterday that he not only bought me a T-shirt, he got me two T-shirts, a hat, and a dress. Even though he's a big schmuck, that is surprisingly sweet, even that he remembered."

Davis occasionally joined in the electronic gossip, telling her pal in Washington: "The President is looking pretty good on the telly lately, quite fit and slim." Yet Davis was a pragmatist when it came to matters of men and happily-ever-after relationships; she was increasingly worried that this emotional roller coaster might fly off the track and hurt Monica. After one e-mail in which Monica had despaired that "the Creep" was becoming more distant and removed, Davis shot back a response, telling her college friend bluntly:

> *I cannot say I am surprised that this whole situation has taken its toll on you. I'm sure it has for a while now. If I may be so bold to state my unequivocal opinion, I think your "situation" is a lose-lose situation with him. He cannot ever totally be yours, Monica, ever.*
>
> *I'm sorry any of this has or will hurt you, but I think you are really better off emotionally and professionally getting out now. I hope your experience with him will not jade you to other men. I know you thought he was pretty awesome, and he sure holds a damn successful position [understatement], but he is still human and still flawed like all the rest of them.*

Personally, I think the best guys in the world are the low-key kind who
care more about watching a movie at home and taking care of you than of
going to expensive sushi bars and showing you off.

Not only did Catherine Davis's testimony build sympathy for Monica among the attentive grand jurors, but it also partially undermined the Starr prosecutors' cause. Under tag-team questioning by Wirth and Wisenberg, Davis insisted that Monica had said very little about being subpoenaed in the *Paula Jones* case and even less about drafting the affidavit denying an affair with Clinton. Nor was Davis aware of any grand plan by the White House to suborn perjury. She knew that Monica and the president had agreed, as a general matter, that they "wouldn't expose the relationship." Monica had told her friend something like, "We would be the only two witnesses. If we both denied it, there would be no evidence." At the same time, Davis had cautioned Monica against going out on a limb for "the Big Creep" and had actively discouraged her from getting dragged into the Paula Jones mess. As the grand jurors listened carefully, Davis explained: "My thought was I didn't want her to lie to protect the President." She had no knowledge of any "quid pro quo" for Monica's disavowing the affair.

For OIC, Catherine Davis still turned out to be worth her plane fare from Tokyo, many times over. In one day, the witness had put to rest any lingering theory that Monica was a stalker who had fantasized a sexual relationship with the president. Now, a half-dozen other witnesses could be hauled before the grand jury to confirm the affair. Additionally, OIC had received highly credible confirmation that a blue Gap dress existed—at one point—and could be subpoenaed for DNA testing.

Ken Starr's prosecutors finally felt that they had gathered up the goods on Bill Clinton.

—·—

ADDITIONAL evidence had also surfaced in the *Paula Jones* case, threatening to throw that litigation into a fresh state of pandemonium. Kathleen Willey had finally broken her silence on *60 Minutes,* telling a national television audience that President Bill Clinton, for whom she had once volunteered as a Democratic fund-raiser, had groped her in the White House in 1993, the day before her husband had killed himself. "It was kind of like I was watching it in slow motion and thinking surely this is not happening," she said, adding in a subdued voice: "I thought, 'Well, maybe I should give him a good slap across the face.' And then I thought, 'Well, I don't think you can slap the President of the United States like that.'" President Clinton had flatly denied the Willey accusation while testifying in the *Paula Jones* deposition. This might constitute a *second* potential count of perjury, if Willey's story could be proven.

Clinton's political team launched a swift counterattack, releasing a dozen letters written by Willey to the president *after* the alleged assault. In these letters, Willey had gushed about her admiration for Clinton and described herself as the president's "number one fan." Still, the drums were beating louder for Clinton's scalp.

The Paula Jones lawyers from Dallas also filed court papers alleging that Clinton had raped a nursing-home owner named Juanita Broaddrick in the late 1970s, during his stint as Arkansas attorney general. Although this story had bounced around for years and Broaddrick had denied it, Ken Starr's office had dispatched FBI agents to Van Buren, Arkansas, where the wary blond-haired woman finally confirmed her view that Clinton had decades ago assaulted her.

With the White House reeling from this series of body blows, something astounding occurred that caused some Clinton defenders to have renewed faith in the existence of God: On April Fool's Day of 1998, Judge Susan Webber Wright granted summary judgment in favor of President Bill Clinton, throwing the *Jones* case out—lock, stock, and barrel.

In a thirty-nine-page opinion stamped with the seal of the clerk of courts, Judge Wright addressed each of Jones's claims and rejected them as a matter of law. Acknowledging that the governor's alleged conduct "may certainly be characterized as boorish and offensive," the judge went on to conclude that "even a most charitable reading of the record in this case fails to reveal a basis for a [legal] claim." One of the biggest problems was a lack of any "tangible job detriment." Judge Wright pointed out that Jones "received every merit increase and cost-of-living allowance for which she was eligible" while employed by the State of Arkansas. In fact, the plaintiff's job had been upgraded from Grade 9 to Grade 11, meaning a boost in salary. Additionally, Jones had been permitted to return from a maternity leave after her first child was born, further proof that she had not received adverse treatment at work. Indeed, the judge noted that Jones "continued to go on a daily basis to the Governor's Office to deliver items and never asked to be relieved of that duty." There was not a shred of evidence that her alleged encounter with Clinton, if it ever occurred, had led to any "materially significant disadvantage" in her employment status, an essential element of proving the case under federal law.

In a final blow, the Republican judge had turned to the issue of "other women"—including the former intern Monica Lewinsky—and declared that the entire body of evidence relating to other females was irrelevant in this federal lawsuit. Judge Wright wrote tersely: "Whether other women may have been subject to workplace harassment, and whether such evidence has allegedly been suppressed, does not change the fact that plaintiff has failed to demonstrate that *she* (Paula Jones) has a case worthy of submitting to a jury."

President Clinton, on a six-nation diplomatic tour of Africa, received word of the judge's decision from his lawyer Bob Bennett. At first, Bennett had worried this might be an April Fool's joke—he had gone as far as to call Judge Wright's chambers to confirm that the opinion was genuine. Shortly after the order was verified, a worldwide broadcast showed President Clinton in Senegal, smoking a cigar and beating an African drum in celebration. (Accompanying the president on the Africa trip were First Lady Hillary Clinton and secretary Betty Currie; skeptical Starr prosecutors called it the "ten-million-dollar-witness tampering trip.")

A teary-eyed Paula Jones, meanwhile, vowed to appeal, sobbing to reporters, "I believe what Mr. Clinton did to me was wrong, and the law protects women who are subjected to that kind of abuse of power."

Ken Starr told reporters that this major setback in the *Jones* case did not mean an end to his own investigation. "You cannot defile the temple of justice," Starr stated with his lips pursed. The real question that he needed to resolve in his investigation, said the independent counsel, was, "Were crimes committed?"

Although a casual observer might have assumed that the death of the *Jones* case would mean the extinguishment of any criminal actions relating to Bill Clinton's testimony in that proceeding, the lawyers on both sides understood that Judge Wright had deftly left that issue in play. In an earlier decision in which she had excluded all evidence relating to Monica Lewinsky, Judge Wright had dropped a footnote stressing that her ruling "should [not] be construed as indicating how the Court would rule on such matters were the Lewinsky evidence being considered for admission at any trial." Even though the media failed to pick up this clue, the lawyers understood that the judge had not eliminated the possibility that Clinton's testimony still might constitute a "material misstatement" that constituted perjury.

President Clinton would later admit that he was neither surprised, nor particularly reassured, by Judge Wright's ruling. "She knew from the get-go—she's a smart person—that there was nothing in this lawsuit. And I was relieved that she did it," he explained. "I was glad, you know, but not particularly surprised. Because the most important thing from the Republican point of view was the deposition and their leaking it. And then getting Starr involved in it."

Mail poured into the federal courthouse in Little Rock, as citizens expressed radically different views concerning Judge Wright's decision. Vivian Van Cura from Ohio wrote: "I actually prayed that you'd dismiss that suit. Any decent woman would not go to a hotel room of a man by herself. Sleep well!!" Donna Korbel of Florida chimed in: "I want to applaud your just decision in the Paula

Jones case. Now what can be done about Ken Starr? Enough is enough—wasted time and wasted money!"

Other letters took Judge Wright to task for her decision. Howard Shoemaker of Nebraska declared that if Clinton had made this sort of inappropriate advance toward his wife or daughters, "I'd have busted the Governor's nose!" Ron Christian of Umatilla, Florida, was even less restrained: "You are a God-Damned disgrace," he wrote to Judge Wright. "If you have any respect for America you will take your pay-off and retire."

———

In the wake of this unexpected April Fools' Day development in the *Jones* case, Hickman Ewing convened his secret meeting at the OIC headquarters in Washington, to decide, once and for all, whether it was time to indict First Lady Hillary Clinton.

On Monday, April 27, the entire prosecution team—including Starr himself—was present in the large OIC conference room at 8:30 in the morning. This was Hick Ewing's baby; he would be given the floor for three full hours to lay out the case against Mrs. Clinton. Just weeks earlier, Ewing had proposed notifying Hillary Clinton that she was a "target" of the investigation. That idea had been scuttled as potentially suicidal. Instead, Ewing was given a chance to persuade his fellow prosecutors that OIC should go directly to the grand jury and indict the First Lady.

Each of the lawyers in the room was flipping through a black binder approximately four inches thick, marked in bold letters on the exterior: "HRC Meeting," referring to Hillary Rodham Clinton. Inside that binder was a memo dated April 22, 1998, directed to "All OIC attorneys" from the "HRC Team," summarizing the criminal case against Mrs. Clinton. Following this were four documents for their review: a memo, dated April 10, that spelled out the "Theory of the Case"; an overview of the evidence against Mrs. Clinton; a draft indictment against Mrs. Clinton and her alleged co-conspirator; and a draft order of proof that listed all the witnesses the Starr prosecutors would call against the First Lady in a criminal trial.

Although nobody outside the room would ever know the details of the proposed indictment against the First Lady, it was captioned *United States of America v. Hillary Rodham Clinton and Webster Lee Hubbell*. It was to be filed in the United States District Court for the Eastern District of Arkansas.

The Starr prosecutors, as they flipped through the voluminous materials, were already up to speed. The "Theory of the Case" memo recited: "The object of the conspiracy was to conceal, by unlawful means, the true facts relating to Hillary Rodham Clinton's and Webster Lee Hubbell's relationship with Seth

Ward [Hubbell's father-in-law], Madison Guaranty Savings and Loan and Madison Financial Corporation . . . [to] avoid and evade political, criminal and civil liability, fraudulently secure additional income for the Rose Law Firm and safeguard the political campaigns of William Jefferson Clinton."

Hickman Ewing, according to those present, delivered a virtuoso performance. He strolled back and forth in the conference room, weaving together facts, holding up documents, discussing the potential criminal charges against the First Lady. The allegations—as compiled in the "Summary of Crimes" and the 206-page evidentiary summary contained in the black binder—fell into several groupings. First and foremost, Ewing pointed to Mrs. Clinton's work as an attorney for the Rose Law Firm, where she billed hours on the questionable Castle Grande project orchestrated by Jim McDougal. These entries, circled on the billing records in red with notations in Vince Foster's handwriting, included phone calls and meetings with Seth Ward, who turned out to be the straw man in the sham Castle Grande transaction. The First Lady had denied being involved in the Castle Grande deal. When her billing records mysteriously appeared in the White House living quarters, however, the numbers revealed that she had worked approximately sixty hours on Madison Guaranty projects over a period of fifteen months, including a portion on the Castle Grande matter—a relatively small chunk of time in the life of a busy attorney, but enough to suggest that she had been untruthful in her Resolution Trust Corporation interrogatories and Whitewater depositions.

Mrs. Clinton had tried to dig her way out of this inconsistency by testifying that she knew the Castle Grande project by the name "IDC," since the property had been purchased by McDougal from the Industrial Development Company and that was how she identified it in her billing. She also emphasized that the minuscule number of hours billed confirmed that it was a mere blip on her professional radar screen. Yet this argument was dubious, Ewing argued as he paced back and forth in front of his fellow prosecutors. There was plenty of evidence that Hillary Clinton was up to her ears in Madison Guaranty work.

Also, Mrs. Clinton's demeanor in testifying about the missing Rose Law Firm billing records, and her protestations that she had "no idea" how they ended up on a table in the living quarters of the White House, indicated that her nose was growing longer each time she spoke about that topic. Ewing was prepared to tell the grand jury: "There is a circumstantial case that the records were left on the table by Hillary Clinton. She is the only individual in the White House who had a significant interest in them and she is one of only three people known to have had them in her possession since their creation in February 1992." These records did not simply get up and walk into that room. Hillary Clinton had the motive to remove them from Vince Foster's office after his death, because they revealed inconsistencies with her prior statements and sworn testimony. She also had an opportunity to cause them to "reappear" in the Book Room when the heat generated by the Senate Whitewater Committee began toasting her feet after the documents were subpoenaed.

Ewing would later say, making clear the depth of his skepticism concerning the First Lady's testimony under oath, "When the records popped up on January fourth—I don't believe it was an accident; I don't believe it happened like they say it happened." He knew that Mrs. Clinton had insisted, "I found them in the Book Room," and "I didn't know what they were. . . . I found these things and I called my lawyer and Kendall and they came over." But Ewing delivered his own verdict: "I don't think it happened like that."

To further add to Ewing's suspicions, OIC had come into possession of a *second* copy of the Madison Guaranty billing records (the originals had never materialized) when Vince Foster's widow, Lisa, found them stashed inside a dusty briefcase in the attic of her Arkansas home in July 1997. This newly discovered set contained a document that was conspicuously missing from the version the White House had produced: namely, an old Rose Law Firm bill issued to the Bank of Kingston in July 1982 and marked "paid." This single piece of paper flatly contradicted Hillary Clinton's earlier story that she had not initiated the representation of Madison Guaranty and that her husband the governor had not solicited Madison work on her behalf. Although the conduct at issue might be more an ethical problem than a legal problem, her falsehoods in sworn statements were still potentially criminal.

The fifth count of the draft indictment, Ewing said as he flipped through the binder, averred that Mrs. Clinton "knowingly made a false material declaration" in 1995, when she asserted that she did not initiate Madison legal business from Jim McDougal and that a younger associate at the Rose Law Firm, Rick Massey, had secured the client. Said Ewing, "Whether she didn't remember, obviously that's another question. But [the "paid" document] certainly showed that her story that she promulgated was incorrect."

Ewing believed that this long-lost document also confirmed that Vince Foster knew of the falsity of that story when it was first unveiled during the 1992 campaign—perhaps Foster or Hillary, or both, had intentionally "jerked" that bill out of the set contained in the White House. "And I don't know what all was on his mind," Ewing conceded later, "but I know this: Had he [Foster] been alive, he would have either been a key witness for us, or he'd have been a defendant, as far as I'm concerned." In Ewing's eyes, Mrs. Clinton had lied to OIC, had lied to the grand jury, and would keep lying till the cows came home if she was not brought to justice.

Another important document found in Vince Foster's attic along with the second set of billing records, Ewing pointed out, was a summary memo prepared by Foster during the 1992 campaign and a cover note from Hillary's friend Diane Blair, making clear that Hillary had reviewed this summary. It seemed to confirm that the First Lady had lied when she denied that she had no memory of her legal work for McDougal on Castle Grande and other projects, during the course of her sworn RTC interrogatory answers and grand jury testimony. This document, Ewing said, would be his exhibit 1 at trial.

He also ticked through a list titled "Other Rose Law Firm work for Madison Guaranty Savings and Loan and before state Agencies," evidence that pointed to abundant conflicts of interest in work handled by Hillary Clinton while her husband was governor. The effort to whitewash over Hillary's involvement, the Tennessee prosecutor said as he pounded away, "began in earnest" during the 1992 presidential campaign. Although her initial conduct may not have been criminal, she had constructed a pyramid of lies in responding to the Jeff Gerth exposé during the 1992 campaign. Thereafter, Hillary's own hubris and unwillingness to confess error caused her to repeat those untruths when placed under oath during the RTC investigation and when summoned before the grand jury. Mrs. Clinton's lies, originally uttered for the sake of political expediency, had turned into lies that violated the law. For two straight hours, Ewing paced back and forth, as if he was closing to a jury in the biggest case of his career.

The other Starr prosecutors who gathered in the room viewed it as a masterful performance. But they felt that OIC had a snowball's chance in hell of convicting the First Lady. It was one thing to believe a witness was pathologically dishonest—that was their shared assessment when it came to Hillary Clinton. It was another to convince a grand jury to indict that person, and even more difficult to get a jury to agree that a crime had been committed—especially when that person was First Lady of the United States and the wife of an enormously popular president.

After lunch, Ken Starr called on each person seated around the conference table, asking for initial impressions. Sam Dash, the self-appointed "conscience of the office," piped up that the evidence amounted to "a bunch of nothing." Ewing's face turned red with anger; here was Dash, an unabashed Democrat, "overstat[ing] in favor of the Clintons." Why didn't Dash take a hike off a short pier, if he was going to repeatedly flip-flop and undermine OIC's work?

The faces of Ewing's fellow prosecutors, however, were beginning to reveal growing impatience. Time was growing short. OIC's future, they felt, rested with the Monica Lewinsky investigation. The independent counsel team was now expending twenty-four hours a day, seven days a week, keying in on her. Assuming Judge Wright's dismissal of the *Jones* case did not sink their otherwise seaworthy ship, Bill Clinton seemed to be dead in the water.

Several months earlier, one colleague in Arkansas had predicted that if they indicted Hillary Clinton that moment and tried the case in Little Rock, "we'd have a sixty-forty chance of winning." Now, almost overnight, the wind was blowing in the reverse direction. A secret memo written to the file by one prosecutor predicted that the chances of the First Lady being acquitted were approximately 20 percent; the odds of a hung jury were a whopping 70 percent; and the chances of Mrs. Clinton being convicted a slight 10 percent. Wrote that prosecutor: "Not enough in my view." The strong consensus, suddenly, was that the Hillary case was a loser. Ewing later explained, "I don't think they wanted anything to distract from what was considered a sure thing. Because you've got the president in your sights."

The order of proof that Ewing reviewed with the Starr prosecutors was an eye-opener. It set forth a "rough outline" of what a trial against Hillary Clinton and Webb Hubbell would look like. Remarkable in its scope and providing a window into the thought processes of OIC never before seen, this thirty-two-page document listed witnesses roughly in order of their anticipated appearance. Some of them would be pro-prosecution witnesses; others would be hostile to OIC's cause, but essential to making a case. Ewing had hoped and prayed that when the time came, Jim McDougal would take the stand and directly contradict the First Lady on crucial points. The Arkansas developer had been slated to be Ewing's star witness. These hopes were now dashed with McDougal buried in a pauper's grave in Arkadelphia. Ewing expressed his frustration: "It's like your key witness. If what he's saying is true, then the president and the First Lady of the United States had both committed perjury. And I believed him. And he's dead."

So the leadoff witness for Starr's office would have to be FBI agent Steve Irons, who had worked on all aspects of the Arkansas investigation. He would lend the credibility of that law enforcement agency to the prosecution. He would give the jury an overview. Next would be Chris Wade, the Whitewater real estate broker and Jim McDougal's "business partner," who had pleaded guilty to bankruptcy fraud and submitting false loan applications—Wade would dump Hillary Clinton in the soup, by dint of her dealings in the failed Whitewater venture. Following Wade would come a group dubbed "Principals in Investments," an all-star lineup that included David Hale, Susan McDougal, and former governor Jim Guy Tucker. Other planned witnesses included William Kennedy III, Hillary's erstwhile law partner who had worked alongside Vince Foster at the White House; Carolyn Huber, who had discovered the missing billing records in the White House; Jane Sherburne, of the White House Counsel's office, who had conducted a search of the living quarters when the Rose Law Firm documents had appeared; and Lisa Foster Moody, Vince Foster's widow, who would be questioned about the mysterious briefcase that had turned up in her attic years after Vince's death. The final witness for OIC would be FBI Agent Pat Fallon, a stalwart member of the Starr team, who would weave together a spellbinding summary for the jury.

By midnight, Starr's prosecutors had heard all they needed. Ken Starr asked each member of the OIC team to cast a vote. The group was tired, but the consensus was unanimous. Even those who had worked closely with Hickman on the Arkansas phase of the case, including Jackie Bennett and Bob Bittman, voted against indicting Hillary Clinton. To Ewing's ears, it sounded like the same old tune: "We had the president. We had him cold committing perjury." So why "muddy it up" by indicting the First Lady? David Kendall, who represented both the president and First Lady, would undoubtedly move for a change of venue from Arkansas to Washington, arguing that the First Lady of the United States "can't be involved in a four- to six-week trial in Little Rock." If that move succeeded—which was likely, because Kendall was a master at litigation maneuvers—the prosecutors knew that Bill Clinton "carried ninety-seven percent of the vote" in the heavily African American District of Columbia, all of which dramatically lessened the chances of convicting Mrs. Clinton, assuming a grand jury even found sufficient cause to indict.

Paul Rosenzweig, who had spent months working on the Hillary matter, agreed that this was "one of Hick's bravura performances." Yet, it was evident that even Hickman Ewing at his dramatic best couldn't make this cow fly.

"In some ways, it was kind of like Moses on Mt. Nebo," recalled Rosenzweig. "He could see the promised land, but he wasn't going to enter."

Rosenzweig, like many of his colleagues, listened to all of the evidence and assessed the prospective criminal prosecution of Hillary Clinton like this: "The same set of facts, if tied to an indictment of a Mafia figure who comes to the table with a presumption of guilt that most criminal defendants have, would have been sufficient circumstantial evidence to establish guilt. The pattern was, you know, fairly damning in a lot of ways. But she [Mrs. Clinton] wasn't a Mafia figure; she was a sympathetic figure. We were going to have to do it in Washington or Arkansas, where the juries didn't like us." Rosenzweig concluded with absolute candor, "So we were going to get our asses kicked."

At the conclusion of the voice votes, Ewing told his fellow prosecutors in a thick Memphis drawl, "As far as I'm concerned, she [Hillary Clinton] did it." Yet Hickman conceded that they might be missing certain key ingredients necessary to convict. Given that death had sealed Jim McDougal's lips and that neither Susan McDougal nor Webb Hubbell seemed ready to cooperate—at least not yet—Ewing surprised his fellow prosecutors by concurring. "We shouldn't go," he said, shaking his head in exhaustion. Ewing himself cast the final vote against going forward with the indictment of Hillary Rodham Clinton—at least for now.

For the rest of the night, the worn-out Starr prosecutors shifted to the next essential topic: Should they take further action against Susan McDougal or

Webb Hubbell, to tighten the screws so that Hickman could make one final push to extract the "real" story from these intractable witnesses?

Instead of indicting Hubbell anew, on the basis of his business dealings with Mrs. Clinton, as set forth in the existing draft indictment, several prosecutors suggested resurrecting an earlier plan: Why not indict him in Washington on tax evasion? That might be a quick and easy way to apply pressure on the hulking former associate attorney general to force him to cooperate. As for Susan McDougal, she had already spent eighteen months in prison on civil contempt charges; now she was beginning her two-year sentence for bank fraud on the Whitewater/Madison Guaranty conviction. OIC needed to ratchet up the discomfort level for her, too. Brett Kavanaugh and other prosecutors proposed indicting McDougal for criminal contempt, a much more serious charge, and then giving her additional jail time until she was ready to talk.

The nervous energy sapped from his body, Ewing headed home to catch a few hours of sleep. As he drove off into the Washington night, he resigned himself to the fact that the Office of Independent Counsel would not "charge her [Mrs. Clinton] *now*." At the same time, the Tennessee prosecutor would admit, "I was hopeful, of course, that perhaps [after exerting pressure on] Hubbell or Susan McDougal, we would have information from them that might change things."

He knew the odds of that happening were not great, especially given the enormous amount of prosecutorial time and resources being plowed into the Monica Lewinsky investigation that had eclipsed his Arkansas case overnight.

"On the other hand," Ewing told himself, "I've been a prosecutor a long time, and very seldom do I ever say, 'That's [over] forever.' "

CHAPTER

39

—⋄—

OUT-GUNNING THE SECRET SERVICE

Although the Whitewater grand jury in Arkansas had expired without charging Mrs. Clinton, the White House didn't crack open any champagne bottles. One unnamed adviser told the *New York Times:* "Until they announce they will not empanel another grand jury, I'm not even going to break out a Diet Coke." Sources in Starr's office made clear that they still viewed the Whitewater and Lewinsky probes as "parallel investigations." Both sides understood this meant escalated warfare.

On April 30, the Office of Independent Counsel filed surprise new tax evasion and fraud charges against Webb Hubbell. The indictment, dubbed "Hubbell II," featured highly unusual criminal charges against Hubbell and his wife, Suzy (as well as their Little Rock accountant and attorney, both of whom had assisted Hubbell while he was in jail) for failing to pay delinquent taxes after he had run out of money. In part, the indictment focused on taxes still owing on $700,000 paid to Hubbell in "consulting fees" by companies friendly to the White House, just as Hubbell was facing prison time. Hubbell stood at the door of his home next to his wife and told a reporter for the *Washington Post*, nearly choking up, "I want you to know the Office of Independent Counsel can indict my dog, they can indict my cat, but I'm not going to lie about the President, I'm not going to lie about the First Lady or anyone else. My wife and I are innocent of the charges brought today."

Hubbell's lawyer John Nields later commented that the charges were particularly unfair to his client. "People normally don't get prosecuted for not paying taxes," Nields would emphasize. "They get prosecuted for lying about how much they earn or not filing returns. Failure to pay taxes is not prosecuted as a crime: debtor's prison was abolished a long time ago." As well, there was a serious Fifth Amendment self-incrimination issue, because OIC was building its case using records that it had compelled Hubbell to produce pursuant to subpoena.

To add to the ignominy, Starr's office also hauled Hubbell's wife (a political appointee employed in the Department of Interior) and the Hubbells' college-aged son before the grand jury, sifting through their financial records and making life a living hell for the whole family. It was as if Hubbell was being squeezed from all directions. His lawyer observed: "If there was supposed to be some crime he knew about, I can't tell you what it was."

The House committee investigating Whitewater-related matters meanwhile released tape recordings of conversations from inside federal prison between Hubbell and his wife, his lawyer, and others close to him. Republican Chairman Dan Burton of Indiana—a Clinton detractor who had once fired a rifle at a watermelon to re-create the shooting of Vince Foster to "prove" it was murder—handed over transcribed recordings to the media, suggesting that Hubbell was hiding information to protect the First Lady.

Democrats on the House Committee, however, smelling rotten politics, quickly discovered that the Hubbell prison tapes, as released, were riddled with "alterations and omissions," and that Representative Burton had "systematically edited [them] to delete references to exculpatory information." Burton's top aide, avowed Clinton enemy David Bossie, was forced to resign for his role in the episode. Yet the message was clear—the congressional Whitewater committee was joining forces with Starr's office to exert maximum pressure on Hubbell, until he became more cooperative.

OIC also got tough with Susan McDougal. The recalcitrant Whitewater witness had just defied Starr's office a second time, again refusing to answer its questions. On May 4, just days before the Arkansas grand jury was set to shut down, Starr's prosecutors took the unusual step of indicting Susan McDougal for *criminal* contempt and obstruction of justice. Starr urged President Clinton to intervene and to convince McDougal to cooperate. The White House shot back that it would be "entirely inappropriate" for the president to badger a putative witness whom Starr's office had already put through the wringer.

Susan McDougal, still incarcerated in a federal facility in Los Angeles, had spent eighteen months locked up for civil contempt—the maximum ordinarily permitted by law because it equaled the duration of the grand jury's term. In a rare interview granted to *BBC Tonight* inside the prison walls, she rejected the notion that Ken Starr could make her talk, no matter what scheme he cooked up. Seated in a space bedecked with an American flag, with a narrow window behind her to let in a sliver of light, McDougal appeared worn out. Her ex-husband was now dead; creeping cold sores were visible below her bottom lip. Yet the prisoner, dressed in a brown V-necked prison shirt, looked surprisingly composed. Susan stared into the camera with eyes alert and told the interviewer, "Kenneth Starr is a dangerous man. He is a man with an agenda. . . . And that's why I have decided not to deal with him." McDougal added, looking straight into the camera, "It's a battle to the death."

———

YET the luck of special prosecutors, like the fortunes of politicians, can change as swiftly as the color of a chameleon. Ken Starr's strong suit was writing dazzling briefs and arguing high-level cases in the appellate courts. Now, his expertise as a former solicitor general and federal judge began to yield dividends.

In early May, Chief Judge Norma Holloway Johnson handed the independent counsel an important win, rejecting the White House's efforts to invoke "executive privilege" to shield key Clinton aides from appearing in front of the Lewinsky grand jury. The White House had worked frantically to keep two of its gatekeepers, Deputy Counsel Bruce Lindsey and Senior Adviser Sidney Blumenthal, from testifying about their conversations with the president and First Lady around the time of the *Paula Jones* deposition. Both of these Clintonites were on OIC's "most wanted" list. Blumenthal, a former journalist who maintained strong ties to the media, had tried to make a monkey out of Starr's office by howling that OIC was violating his First Amendment rights. Now Starr got the last word: In a sealed ruling that was swiftly leaked to the press, Judge Johnson ordered the presidential advisers to appear before the grand jury and to tell what they knew.

With OIC appearing to be on a roll, Bob Bittman wrote a *seventh* letter to David Kendall, demanding that President Clinton appear before the grand jury and ending with a touch of sarcasm: "Having tried and tried, I will now try once again. Please give me a straightforward yes or no answer to the following question: Will the President ever agree to testify voluntarily about the matters involving Ms. Lewinsky?"

In a blistering seven-page reply, Kendall told Bittman, in essence, to pound sand. He also took his younger opponent to task for his insolent tone, upbraiding him for the "Alice-in-Wonderland nature of this whole enterprise."

Kendall had his own surprise up his sleeve: In a move that nearly blew Starr's lawyers off their feet, Kendall on May 6 filed a "rule to show cause" against OIC, his second in a series of frontal assaults. After again accusing the special prosecutor of leaking grand jury information to the media (he had filed an initial "show cause" motion in February), he demanded that Starr appear before Judge Johnson and "show cause why your office and/or persons therein should not be held in contempt of court for these latest flagrant leaks." Kendall cited dozens of examples, including the leak of Judge Johnson's opinion just days earlier. *Fox News* seemed to know every detail about that sealed opinion—Starr himself had appeared on *Fox News* and proclaimed the ruling "magnificent." How blatant could one get? demanded Kendall. Starr had already pledged to conduct an "internal investigation" to find the person or persons in his office responsible for smuggling out information to the media. How long would the judge permit the fox to guard the henhouse?

With OIC under siege from all directions, Starr's team took a bold step by initiating a showdown with the U.S. Secret Service, hoping that the testimony of a few closemouthed agents would allow OIC to salvage its investigation and repair its badly damaged reputation.

———

THE Secret Service issue had been brewing even before the Lewinsky story broke. In January, Paula Jones's lawyers had tried to subpoena four Secret Service agents in close proximity to the president, hoping to unearth evidence of Clinton's extramarital affairs. Judge Susan Webber Wright had slammed the door shut on this inquiry, ruling that U.S. Secret Service agents' observations had no bearing on "the core issues in this case." Moreover, the judge wrote, there existed a real possibility that interrogating these agents could "provide critical information at the core of how the Secret Service actually functions," which could create an "unacceptable" risk to the president and others if disclosed.

So the Office of Independent Counsel moved to a different playing field. Ken Starr personally appeared in the courtroom of Judge Norma Holloway Johnson on May 14, seeking to force the agents to testify. OIC had continued to gather up nuggets of "anecdotal" information suggesting that Secret Service agents had witnessed Bill Clinton and Monica Lewinsky in compromising positions. Now, the prosecutors needed to overpower the Justice Department in seeking to shoot down the notion that Secret Service agents were cloaked with a special "protective function" privilege.

Starr, a scholar of the Constitution, felt that this so-called privilege was "totally groundless in law" and bordered on "frivolous." Congress had already spoken on the subject, when it enacted a criminal law that required officers of the Executive Branch to report to the attorney general "evidence of wrongdoing." There was no exception in this law for Secret Service or any other agents. As a matter of history, Secret Service agents had assisted law enforcement officials on plenty of occasions. Starr himself had represented the Secret Service during his Justice Department days, when agents had been "very helpful during Iran-Contra in disproving Oliver North's alleged access to President Reagan."

Granted, the shoe was now on the other foot, and the Secret Service was being asked to provide information *damaging* to the president, whom they were sworn to protect. Still, Starr felt it was irresponsible for the Secret Service and Justice Department to rebuff OIC's "very carefully calibrated request" for information. Off the record, Starr knew that FBI Director Louis Freeh was unsupportive of his Secret Service brethren; Freeh had informed the attorney general "personally" that he opposed this privilege. So it was a double affront to Starr that Janet Reno would side with the renegade agency.

Seated in the front row behind counsel table in Judge Johnson's courtroom, Secret Service Director Lew Merletti was accompanied by an intense-looking man who sat impassively beside him. Although the press did not know his identity, this man was former agent Clint Hill, who, at age thirty-one, had witnessed the assassination of a president.

Now sixty-six years old and living in Northern Virginia, Agent Hill was determined to keep others from being pursued by the demons that still haunted him. When it came to these stories suggesting that Secret Service agents had seen Monica Lewinsky and President Clinton engaged in nebulous forms of hanky-panky, Hill was incensed. It reminded him of the irresponsible reports about President Kennedy's extramarital adventures published after JFK's death, some of which were purportedly based on authors' "off-the-record" conversations with Secret Service agents. (Seymour Hersh's book on JFK, *The Dark Side of Camelot*, especially stuck in Hill's craw.) Hill considered it poppycock for agents to assert that they knew what was going on behind closed doors in the Oval Office or inside the president's private residence. "We provide a protective umbrella or envelope," Hill explained. "We know who is going in and who is there. . . . That doesn't mean we're in the Oval Office all the time." The job of a Secret Service agent was not to be a snoop or tattler. "We don't know what the conversation is, and we don't *want* to know."

Hill's response to Officer Lew Fox and others who gossiped about Monica Lewinsky was the same as it had been when loose-lipped agents speculated about President Kennedy's activities: "Well, if you really thought that that was a violation of security," Hill would give them a dressing-down, "you should have stepped up at that time and done something about it." He had no patience for retired Secret Service agents or "uniformed officers" who tried to get "fifteen minutes of fame" by circulating White House gossip. These individuals were sworn to protect the president. "So, they either should keep their mouths shut," said Hill, "or do something."

Ken Starr now stood before Judge Johnson and told her that inventing a privilege for the Secret Service would create a "Praetorian guard," allowing the president to "engage in criminal activity" at will. His twelve-page brief had already laid out these points in chapter and verse: No "protective function privilege" had ever been recognized in American law, and this was no time to invent one.

Norma Holloway Johnson, an African American judge born "Normalie" Holloway in Lake Charles, Louisiana, was a former schoolteacher who ran her courtroom like a mathematics classroom. A Carter appointee with a Democratic registration, she had a reputation for being tough on criminals and even tougher on elected officials who violated their oaths of office. In sending one former Reagan administration official to prison for lying to Congress, the judge had tongue-lashed the defendant from the bench: "You violated the public trust and your perjury offends and strikes at the very core of the trust." Recently elevated to Chief Judge of the federal district court in Washington, Johnson meted out punishment to criminal defendants regardless of political affiliation.

Starr now stood before the judge and posed this hypothetical: What if the president was "actually engaged in an act of treason"? Would Secret Service agents be immune from testifying, even when it threatened to bring down the nation? As the arguments droned on, Lew Merletti was concerned that "all of [Judge Johnson's] body language was negative towards us." Starr's oratory, to Merletti's ears, seemed like a bunch of "legalistic mumbo-jumbo." After all, this highly confidential, close-lipped group of professional agents wasn't called the "*Secret* Service" for nothing.

Merletti leaned over, staring at Clint Hill. The former agent's eyes were sunken; he looked like a man with demons still climbing across his back encumbered by chains and shackles. Agent Hill shook his head slowly, agreeing with Director Merletti's quiet message. "They just don't get it," Merletti thought.

One of the things that especially angered Merletti was that Starr and his prosecutors were creating the false impression that his Secret Service agents had facilitated inappropriate womanizing by Bill Clinton. With stories still swirling in the air about Arkansas state troopers arranging "dates" for then-Governor Clinton as part of the Paula Jones saga, Starr's zealous prosecutors were now insinuating that Secret Service agents might have been playing a similar role inside the White House. The notion that he or his agents might have been "sneaking Monica Lewinsky" or any other female into the West Wing was an insult to a highly trained professional like Merletti.

"I'm going to tell you right now," he said later, struggling to keep his voice restrained, "that would not have been going on. Not under my watch. That would not have happened. I can't imagine any Secret Service person who would have allowed that."

To the extent some former uniformed officers were now telling Starr's investigators that they had "placed bets on how long it took for POTUS to move to the West Wing once Monica came into the gates," this sort of after-the-fact gossip infuriated Merletti. Although the agents in the PPD did not talk about this subject publicly, they knew how to take care of business if there was even a hint that a female subordinate might be getting too close to the president. Evelyn Lieberman, who had risen in the ranks within the Clinton White House to deputy chief of staff under the president, was a no-nonsense task-mistress who watched the Oval Office like a hawk. Lieberman supervised females' dress code in the White House. She spoke sternly to young women if she did not approve of their attire. It was Lieberman who was instrumental in transferring Monica Lewinsky from the White House into the Pentagon after she detected that the young intern was "spending too much time around the West Wing." If agents had even the faintest suspicion that inappropriate conduct was going on within the confines of the White House, their job was to report it to their superiors, who would take it to Evelyn. Said one high-level Secret Service official: "It would have ended."

It was also maddening to Merletti that people like Starr and Judge Johnson had no idea what it meant to wake up each morning before dawn, as a member of the elite Presidential Protection Division (PPD), mentally preparing oneself to "step in the line of fire" and to die, if necessary, to safeguard the president. Those who imagined that Secret Service agents would do the president's bidding when they disagreed with his instructions had no clue what the agents were built of.

One incident that Merletti kept locked in his mental file and that was unknown to the rest of the world related to a disagreement he had with President Clinton in November 1996. In this episode, Merletti had overruled Clinton and, in doing so, saved the president's life. Merletti had been traveling with the president to Manila in the Philippines, when a snap decision confronted him as head of the presidential protective detail. Clinton was scheduled to attend a late-afternoon appointment with a senior member of the Philippine government. As was common for the gregarious Clinton, he was running late. The motorcade route from the hotel, where Clinton was wrapping up his meeting, to the government official's office would take approximately fifteen minutes. President Clinton instructed Merletti, "You gotta get me there fast. I'm really late."

One of the jobs of the Secret Service was to "make the president's schedule work." Merletti understood that. As they climbed into their long, black car, however, Merletti received a crackly message in one earpiece: Intelligence operators in the field had picked up a radio transmission in which the unknown speakers used the words "bridge" and "wedding" in close proximity. The latter word, he knew, was a code word once used by terrorists to mean a hit, or an assassination. On the motorcade route that had been mapped out, the president's car was scheduled to cross a bridge.

Merletti urgently requested if intelligence could get "more information." After a momentary buzz in his earpiece, the response came back: "Negative." In the meantime, the president was still pushing Merletti, "Let's go, let's go. We're late!" As head of the PPD, Merletti had to take a stand. His paramount job was to protect the chief executive, regardless of what the president wanted. Merletti climbed into the car and looked directly at Clinton: "Mr. President, I have bad news for you," he said. "We're going to be *real* late, because we're taking a different route."

There followed a "strong discussion" between the president and Agent Merletti. It was "professional" in every way, Merletti recalled, but the conversation involved "strong language" on each side. In the end, Merletti directed the motorcade to travel the direction he wanted, and the president sunk back in his seat, unhappy but overruled.

As the presidential entourage wound forward along its altered route, a U.S. intelligence team was dispatched to the bridge. The structure was a white concrete span in a busy downtown area of Manila and was flanked by picturesque palm trees and neat pedestrian sidewalks. Underneath the bridge, explosives specialists uncovered a bomb powerful enough to blow up the entire presidential motorcade.

This thwarted assassination attempt was never made public; it remained top secret except to select members of the U.S. intelligence community. The

American government's subsequent investigation of this plot to kill Clinton, however, revealed that it had been masterminded by a Saudi terrorist living in Afghanistan—a man named Osama bin Laden. Intelligence reports revealed that this bearded criminal's nascent terrorist organization, known as al Qaeda, had engineered the effort to murder the American president. The Secret Service was already watching bin Laden—he had been involved in at least one earlier attempt to assassinate Clinton in the Philippines in 1994. The plot to kill Clinton in Manila had failed only because members of the PPD were trained to put the safety of the president first, regardless of conflicting instructions, even from the chief executive himself. In Merletti's view, "If you're not capable of making decisions like this, you don't belong in that position."

It was therefore infuriating and insulting to Merletti that Ken Starr and his gung-ho prosecutors would insinuate that Secret Service personnel might "cover up" for the president, in the Lewinsky matter or anything else. When it came to the notion that Secret Service agents would countenance liaisons between the president and females other than the president's wife, Merletti declared, his voice beginning to shake, "It's not going to happen. I mean, let me tell you this."

Agent Clint Hill was distressed by Ken Starr's decision to force testimony from Secret Service agents, for a different reason. Perhaps the Kennedy murder seemed inapposite, but the key issue in both situations was maintaining proximity. "If agents have to testify" in circumstances like the Lewinsky case, worried Hill, "then 'Katie bar the door.'" Presidents would push away, and agents would be nudged out. He added, "Once the precedent's been established, it's like squeezing toothpaste out of a tube. It's out." Announcing that agents were available to testify was like placing "an informant or spy" in the midst of the president's inner circle, which would "inevitably cause a lack of proximity." Consciously or unconsciously, future presidents would find excuses to distance themselves from their protective detail.

As he sat in the courtroom beside Lew Merletti, shutting his eyes to chase away ghosts that still haunted him long after that horrible day in November 1963, Hill whispered to himself, "And if they start pushing you back, look out."

———

PRESIDENT George H. W. Bush had written an extraordinary last-minute letter in support of the Secret Service's position. Surely, Merletti hoped, this submission by a former Republican president would have some impact on the judge. President Bush was no big fan of President Bill Clinton. By all accounts, he was appalled by the Lewinsky escapades that had come to light. Nonetheless, Bush had shown great fortitude in publicly supporting the agency during this time of crisis, writing: "I can assure you that had I felt [Secret Service agents] would be compelled to testify as to what they had seen or heard, no matter what the subject, I would not have felt comfortable having them close in."

As Judge Johnson gathered up her papers and waved the arguments to a close, Merletti felt like standing up and screaming, "You just don't get it!!!" As a matter of hypertechnical legal citations, maybe Kenneth Starr was right that no formal privilege existed in the Constitution to safeguard Secret Service agents who guarded the president. But there was an equally important question here: "What was sane public policy?" There was a reason that agents protecting presidents in the White House had not been dragged into grand juries to testify for the past 123 years. Didn't Independent Counsel Starr, who professed to be an American patriot, understand that the U.S. Secret Service could only do its job if other branches of government cooperated?

Numerous retired agents in the field had sent e-mails of encouragement to Merletti during this period. One stated emphatically: "STAY THE COURSE TO THE END. YOU ARE DOING EXACTLY WHAT IS RIGHT FOR THIS AGENCY." Another retired agent wrote to Merletti's secure e-mail address: "THERE IS NO DOUBT HERE, AS FAR AS THE WIDE RANGING IMPLICATIONS FOR FUTURE PROTECTIVE DETAILS AND THE POTENTIALLY TRAGIC CONSEQUENCES, SHOULD A FINAL DECISION GO AGAINST US."

Merletti and Hill stood respectfully as Judge Johnson adjourned the proceedings, stepping down from the bench and retiring to her chambers. These two men, who had guarded most modern-day presidents throughout their combined careers, waited quietly for the courtroom to clear. Once the members of the press had dispersed, they walked with silent footfalls down the hallway of the federal courthouse, wondering what this day would mean for presidents who succeeded Bill Clinton, and for Secret Service agents who would put their lives at risk, long after the name Monica Lewinsky meant anything to those who dispensed justice in this majestic building.

GINSBURG'S FINAL PHOTO SHOOT

The Starr prosecutors, now tasting blood, became even more confident of proving their case against Clinton in early June, when Monica Lewinsky canned the avuncular Bill Ginsburg as her lawyer. Ginsburg had become a media celebrity and a darling of talk-show hosts, yet he had been driving OIC lawyers berserk. He was also pushing his own client over the brink.

The bearded California lawyer would defend himself, in an op-ed piece published in the *Washington Post* days after he was replaced, in which he proclaimed: "I Didn't Get 'Dumped.' " The accounts from every source other than Ginsburg, however, indicate that he was canned unceremoniously after his handling of Lewinsky's case became intolerable.

Bernie Lewinsky, father of the former intern who was responsible for paying Monica's legal bills—until she could pay him back—had become distressed with Ginsburg's inability to cut a deal for his daughter. The senior Lewinsky had dispatched his medical-malpractice lawyer friend to Washington with the goal of "putting a team together" to save his daughter from the clutches of Ken Starr. In his then-fragile state of mind, Bernie had viewed Ginsburg as "a God-sent rescuer." Maybe the California attorney wasn't a criminal lawyer with expertise in this area, Bernie had rationalized, but Ginsburg was a practicing lawyer, who had been thoughtful enough to prescribe vodkas for Bernie on that terrible night when OIC prosecutors had swooped in and grabbed Monica. Ginsburg seemed to be the best available option at that moment. "The way I would equate it," Monica's father later explained, "if I was in the middle of Africa and I got appendicitis, I wouldn't have time to look for a good surgeon."

Unfortunately, Bernie concluded, Ginsburg now was acting like a control freak and substitute parent, making decisions for Monica that were none of his business. The lawyer was also employing a "divide and conquer" tactic, playing Monica against members of her own family. "He can't become the father and try to deal with her and treat her as his daughter," Bernie said, seated on a couch in his fashionable Brentwood home and summarizing his grievances.

Bernie also felt that his former friend had milked the media attention for all he could, often to the family's detriment. On the first night that Monica had returned to California, for instance, Bernie had selected a "hidden restaurant" and reserved "a special room where we could all sit privately." As they exited the eatery, hundreds of reporters and photographers "mauled" them, appearing out of the woodwork like cockroaches. Said Dr. Lewinsky, sitting upright: "It turned out Ginsburg called the media to tell them where we were going to be. And he was supposed to be protecting us."

Bernie was also distressed that, although Bill Ginsburg claimed he had everything under control, Monica was soon being summoned to FBI headquarters in Los Angeles to be fingerprinted like a common criminal. Bernie had driven to the federal building at six A.M.; this experience had rattled him to the core. "I was exposed to a side of the FBI that I had never seen," he recounted. "I mean, these humungous metal bars that pop up from the ground in the garage (as a security measure) to just block entry, and I got really scared." Fifty or sixty media trucks were surrounding the perimeter of the building, with hundreds of reporters creating a human wall through which he and Monica had to pass. A wave of anger overcame Bernie and he shouted out, "This is totally un-American; this is not fair! My daughter is not a criminal. This is not right!"

For Bernie, it was especially galling that Monica was being subjected to such treatment when she "had the highest clearance in the Pentagon." "You don't work at the Pentagon without a fingerprint," he declared loudly. "What the hell did Starr need fingerprints for? It was the most intimidating, unreal thing I have ever done." Agent Fallon of the FBI, assigned to Starr's detail, had greeted him by saying, "Oh, Doctor Lewinsky, nice to meet you." Said Bernie, "And I felt like spitting on him."

After passing through an area with rows of "huge metal gates" and jail cells, Monica was taken to a room where she was welcomed by FBI agents who had been present at the initial sting at the Ritz-Carlton, a ploy that Bernie viewed as "an intimidation tactic again." The agents "took each finger, three sides—I mean, it took forever—the palms, the hands, the digits, the sides, right hand, left hand." Next, Monica was taken upstairs to write numerous handwriting exemplars, at which point Bernie stormed out of the office shouting, "I can't take this!" His blood pressure soaring, he drove off to work to settle himself.

Bernie viewed this whole episode as proof positive that the Starr operation had run amok. "When the kids were young, little toddlers," he explained sarcastically, "there were a lot of kidnappings here in L.A. I had my kids fingerprinted. I [still] had their fingerprints and their footprints in my safe. I still have them. I could have given them to Starr. He didn't need anything. This was a tactic to scare the sh—— out of Monica. That's all it was about."

Although the traumatic fingerprinting incident could not be attributed to

Bill Ginsburg, and the FBI likely had no choice but to fingerprint Monica because prints were not transferable among government agencies, the experience drained Bernie of every last drop of confidence in Ginsburg. At a minimum, Bernie believed that Monica's lawyer had leaked the time and place of the ordeal to CNN anchor Wolf Blitzer, his new media pal, in advance. This had led to the appearance of every camera crew west of the Mississippi, heightening the indignity.

Monica, too, had steadily lost faith in Ginsburg. Although she understood that no lawyer could control the "crazy" behavior of the OIC attack dogs, Ginsburg seemed to be waltzing into their trap. The act of entering the stark interior of the FBI building that day, Monica recalled, "was pretty close to knowing what it was going to feel like going to jail." Years later, those images still tormented her: "There are bars, turnstiles. It was scary. And they fingerprinted me like I had just murdered somebody." Her complaint about Ginsburg was, "Why isn't he questioning this?" Increasingly, Ginsburg seemed to rely on Nate Speights for legal decision-making, while the California lawyer gallivanted around and appeared on TV shows. "I just didn't feel secure," concluded Monica.

The Lewinsky family was also horrified by the inappropriate comments coming out of Ginsburg's mouth. In one instance, Ginsburg gave a magazine a supposedly humorous blurb in which he quipped that Monica "was caged up like a dog in heat," or words to that effect. Bernie's wife, Barbara, recalled, "When Monica read this, she became completely unglued," telling Ginsburg, "How could you say something like that about me, given the nature of the case?" Although Ginsburg maintained that he had been "misquoted" and that the line had been "taken out of context," the Lewinskys viewed this as one more Ginsburgian comment that was "completely outrageous."

On another occasion in Philadelphia, Monica and her attorney were walking down the street when Ginsburg "stopped at a newsstand and pulled out the *Playboy* magazine to look at." Monica froze in her tracks and said, "Bill, you can't look at that while you're here [with me]." It was, she felt, a "total disconnect."

There was also a much-quoted interview in which Ginsburg had declared that he had known Monica since birth and that as a baby he had kissed her "little pulkes"—a cute Yiddish term for inner thighs. The normally calm Bernie Lewinsky would become enraged even at the recollection of this episode. "This is a total fabrication," he said. "I told him [Ginsburg] he was lying." Monica's father pointed out that he did not even meet Ginsburg until the late 1970s. "He did not know her [Monica] . . . when she was two years old," Bernie said angrily. "He met her in nineteen seventy-eight, seventy-nine perhaps, when she was six years old. And a six-year-old of mine would never have sat on his lap for anything. She barely sat on my lap. I mean, that was totally false."

There was also the *Vanity Fair* photo shoot, which was orchestrated by Ginsburg and turned into a full-blown disaster. Ginsburg had told Monica's parents that "the kid should have some fun and *Vanity Fair* wants to do this, and it would do her ego a lot of good." The lawyer further enticed Bernie by saying that the famous photographer Herb Ritts—an international star who had photographed rock star Madonna in Mickey Mouse ears and made millions shooting Calvin Klein ads—would be doing the shoot of Monica. Ginsburg told Bernie, a camera bug himself, "You may be interested in seeing how Herb Ritts does these things, and so if you want, you can come out to the shoot." Bernie asked nervously, "Bill, is this a good thing?"

The bespectacled attorney answered, "Oh, it will be great. *Vanity Fair* has assured me that it will be in the utmost of taste."

Bernie and Barbara Lewinsky drove to the beach in Malibu for the shoot, where everything seemed over the top. Bernie recalled, "We got there when she [Monica] was all dolled up, and she looked like Marilyn Monroe with a pink poodle in her arms. . . . And I said, 'Oh, my God, this is my daughter?' " One provocative photo snapped of Monica behind a fan of pink feathers made Bernie and Barbara shuffle in the sand with discomfort. Later in the day, when the photographers and wardrobe people moved down the beach to photograph Monica "vamping" barefoot in a "little black dress" and wrapped in an antique American flag, radiating "coy seductiveness," Bernie finally popped his cork. He told Ginsburg, "I think this is really going a little too far." The lawyer waved the crew to a halt, shouting, "Stop, stop, stop the photographing! I do *not* give permission for this photograph to be published." Yet the paperwork was already signed; the picture with the American flag appeared in *Vanity Fair,* another traumatic experience for the Lewinsky family.

Ginsburg later defended the photo shoot, telling a reporter that Monica's "libido" was suffering, and that this experience was designed to say, "Honey, you're beautiful and sweet and we want the world to know." Moreover, the photo with the American flag, Ginsburg felt, was "a very uplifting piece" designed to "lift her [Monica's] ego." He later explained, "It wasn't time to take pictures of her, you know, washing dishes."

There was also a hint that the lawyers had signed up Monica for the *Vanity Fair* experience on the advice of her psychiatrist, who feared that Monica was potentially suicidal and desperately needed to "assist her self-esteem." This photo spread in a chic magazine, the theory went, would portray her as a "sophisticated, beautiful woman" who was "maturing and able to attract a president." For the sake of Monica's "mental health," the suggestion was, her lawyers did the right thing by providing their client with an "exhilarating emotional high experience."

Bernie, however, didn't buy that explanation. He was shelling out piles of money to pay for airfare and other costs that seemed to be mounting by the minute, and it all seemed aimed at satisfying Ginsburg's own thirst for a media buzz. "A psychiatrist suggested this?" Bernie later asked skeptically. "I never heard of it."

By all accounts within the Lewinsky family circle, the straw that broke the camel's back was Ginsburg's infamous "Open Letter to Kenneth Starr," published in the June issue of *California Lawyer* magazine. In this eloquent yet provocative piece, Ginsburg poured out his soul, expressing his love for the American Constitution and his abhorrence of Ken Starr's guerrilla tactics: "Your investigation into President Clinton's sexual conduct threatens to tear a giant hole in the fabric of our democracy," Ginsburg wrote. He castigated Starr for "subpoenaing practically everyone in the Washington, D.C., phone book."

And in the most startling paragraph of the article, the acerbic-tongued California lawyer seemed to concede that hanky-panky had probably occurred between Monica Lewinsky and President Bill Clinton: "Congratulations, Mr. Starr!" he taunted. "As a result of your callous disregard for cherished constitutional rights, you *may* have succeeded in unmasking a sexual relationship between two consenting adults." As soon as Bernie Lewinsky saw a copy of Ginsburg's remarks, reprinted in the *Washington Post* for the world to read, he phoned Ginsburg and shouted, "As our attorney, you cannot publish something without us knowing what it is that you're going to publish!"

Monica herself completely "flipped out." Ginsburg had shown Monica and her father a first draft of the article—they had made clear that "he was not supposed to publish it." She later recalled: "I was with my dad and we were beside ourselves."

Around this time, prominent Harvard law professor Alan Dershowitz spoke on television, his entire face filling up the screen: "Lewinsky family, listen to me. Get rid of Ginsburg." As Bernie would recall, "And that's pretty much what put us over the edge."

Several high-level advisers in the Clinton White House later defended Bill Ginsburg's legacy, saying that he did exactly what an aggressive criminal defense lawyer was supposed to do: He confused the opposition and tangled up the prosecution in knots. One White House insider noted, "Ginsburg deserves a lot of credit for driving them nuts. He protected his client through his egomania. He did a good job for his client."

Ginsburg himself, sipping coffee in the trendy Jerry's Diner nestled in the picturesque hills of Encino, California, later reflected on this unusual detour in his career, maintaining that he always tried to act in the best interests of his client. A prosperous medical-malpractice attorney with offices in multiple states, Ginsburg defended his handling of the Lewinsky matter: "[I] kept Monica out of the grand jury and away from indictment for nearly six months." The "Open Letter to Kenneth Starr," he said, was a last-ditch effort to grab his attention because Starr "wouldn't communicate with me personally." After their brief meeting in the OIC lavatory, Ginsburg had run into Starr only once, while arguing a motion in front of Judge Johnson. Ginsburg had sidled up to him and said in a friendly tone, "Ken, you and me and Sam [Dash] ought to sit down sometime, you know, in a deli somewhere and figure this all out." Starr had smiled, but he had never gotten back to him.

So Ginsburg decided, "Okay, if this is where we're at, I've got to destroy this man because he represents the worst [in government]—not only the position he holds, but the way he handles the position that he holds. He won't even [negotiate]. It is *his* way or the highway." Ginsburg had planned to send the independent counsel a copy of the "Open Letter to Kenneth Starr" with a note: "Dear Ken, what are we doing here? Why are we killing ourselves?"

He never sent that note, Ginsburg later explained, because his piece was reprinted in the *Washington Post* "before I could address the envelope."

With respect to the comment that he had kissed Monica's "little pulkes" as a baby, Ginsburg felt the media had made a big deal out of nothing, unduly upsetting the Lewinsky family. "I'm kind of a Dutch uncle," he explained. "So what the hell are they talking about? They're trying to make everything be a sexual thing. And that's ridiculous. It would be like saying that [someone] had a newborn baby and I kissed him, and that I was, you know, a pervert." Ginsburg believed that he had been caught in the middle of a "typhoon," becoming a victim of the media's unhealthy obsession with the Lewinsky scandal.

Moreover, Ginsburg insisted that he had talked about stepping down as counsel *before* his services were terminated, because he had reached a philosophical impasse with his client. According to Ginsburg's version of how the relationship ended, Monica Lewinsky was now prepared to negotiate immunity "at any cost." In Ginsburg's view, it would be an "indignity" to both Monica and President Clinton to disclose the sordid details of their relationship to this drooling band of Starr's prosecutors. He knew about the blue Gap dress; he feared it would open up a can of worms if its existence were disclosed. Ginsburg had come to believe that "no grand jury would indict [Monica]." He also believed that the most the Starr prosecutors could prove was "a sexual misadventure." The president would tell the American public, "I admit that we had an inappropriate relationship," but "no further comment." His client would do the same. If OIC was foolish enough to take Monica Lewinsky to trial, Ginsburg would subpoena the Tripp tapes and play them in open court, throwing the proceedings into pandemonium and validating everything that Lewinsky had already written in her draft proffer. Ginsburg would once and for all prove that

Lewinsky's white lie in the affidavit had nothing to do with the *Jones* case and did not involve a quid pro quo. The California lawyer would plan to tell the jury with a laugh, "This is some conspiracy to obstruct justice, sending her approximately 150 miles away for a $29,000-a-year job in Manhattan? She'd have to be pretty god-damned stupid, and she's not. I mean, to be bribed for a job that you can't support yourself on in Manhattan?" Furthermore, he would lecture the jury, there was absolutely no evidence that President Clinton had encouraged Lewinsky to lie under oath or to obstruct justice. She was acting out of "deep feelings for him at that time, [such] that she would have done anything to protect him." In the end, Ginsburg believed that he would beat the pants off Starr's prosecutors if they were foolish enough to make a federal case out of his client's sexual fling with the president. The game would be over, and Monica would walk away relatively unscathed.

Ginsburg's standard line, in warning Monica not to buckle under to OIC's threats, was, "What do Jim McDougal, Webb Hubbell, and David Hale have in common? They all had been granted immunity by Starr and they all went to jail!"

Yet Monica was not feeling in the mood to roll the dice, wagering her whole life on the outcome. The same week as the disastrous photo shoot for *Vanity Fair*, Judge Norma Holloway Johnson had allowed Ken Starr's office to nullify the immunity deal that Emmick and Udolf had promised her. Letting Starr take her to trial, Lewinsky felt, was a "last choice option": "I did not want to go to trial, for a million reasons—for emotional reasons, for the risk of [going to jail], for the cost of it." Already, her father was paying astronomical legal bills. She feared there would come a day when Ginsburg geared up for trial and mailed her family "a bill for a million dollars." Although she was admittedly unstable at this moment, what Monica had decided in her own mind was, "I wanted immunity if they were going to accept the truth from me." She desperately needed a lawyer who would work out that deal with Starr.

Monica's mother still gave Ginsburg credit for the work he did. Marcia Lewis had never seen eye-to-eye with Bernie's bearded friend, a man who still viewed her as the enemy. Yet, she said firmly, "I think he had [Monica's] best interest at heart, and while he exercised poor judgment, I don't think he ever meant her any harm, and my God, compared to what other people had done to her, you know [it was minor]." It had become painfully clear to all concerned that Monica needed to have "different representation." Yet Marcia Lewis preferred to go easy on Bill Ginsburg: "I just saw this as her mother. She needed an attorney. And then it became clear she needed a different attorney."

Monica had flown back to Washington disguised in a blond wig. She and her mother were trying to remain hidden from view, staying under assumed names in the Washington Court Hotel near Capitol Hill. In a letter faxed to Bill

Ginsburg's Los Angeles law office, Monica wrote that she "hereby rescind[ed] and terminat[ed]" his services.

Ginsburg later scratched his beard, and his eyes grew sad as he explained the pain he suffered from his break with the Lewinsky family: "Bernie is one of the sweetest men I have ever met in my entire life," he said. "He doesn't have a hostile bone in his body. It is so easy to take advantage of Bernie, and he is so bighearted, loving, and good, that the thought of anybody hurting Bernie bothers me to this day." Ginsburg understood that Bernie felt that he "had betrayed him in some way." The lawyer also comprehended that when things got messy, his friend "took the side, as I would expect him to, of his daughter." Ginsburg was crushed that his friendship with Bernie Lewinsky had been snuffed out by these misunderstandings, one of the first casualties of the Clinton-Starr disaster. "And I haven't had contact with him for many years," he said, staring at his empty cup of coffee.

As he cleared out his room at the Cosmos Club and headed back to California, Ginsburg voiced only one regret about being terminated by Monica Lewinsky. "Since we parted company," the ordinarily loud lawyer would say softly, "I have not seen or heard from Bernie Lewinsky."

Monica and her mother immediately scheduled a meeting with Plato Cacheris and Jake Stein, two leading Washington attorneys with decades' worth of experience in highly sophisticated criminal cases. The Lewinsky ladies liked what they saw.

Stein had served as an independent counsel during the Reagan administration, investigating alleged financial improprieties by Attorney General Edwin Meese III, finding insufficient evidence to indict Meese, and wrapping up his probe quickly. With his silver hair and tight-lipped smile, the seventy-three-year-old trial lawyer was the picture of professionalism. A large bluefish mounted on the wall of Stein's law office bore the inscription "If I'd kept my big mouth shut, I wouldn't be here." That was his credo.

The other half of the team was Plato Cacheris, a suspender-wearing son of a Greek immigrant from Pittsburgh who had represented former Attorney General John Mitchell in Watergate and Colonel Oliver North's secretary in the Iran-Contra scandal. More recently, Cacheris had defended convicted CIA traitor Aldrich Ames in a spy thriller that had attracted international attention. At sixty-nine, the solid and formidable lawyer was at the top of his game. If Monica Lewinsky had prayed for divine intervention (which she did), it would have been hard to beat the Cacheris/Stein team.

On June 2, in the late afternoon, the two lawyers arranged for a press conference to announce their joint representation of Monica Lewinsky. Facing the press corps in front of Cacheris's law office building on Connecticut Avenue, they flanked Monica Lewinsky like an impenetrable wall. The two Washington attorneys smiled politely for the cameras, announced matter-of-factly that they had taken over Ms. Lewinsky's case, and then swiveled and escorted Monica back into the building. Said Cacheris: "We were drawing an immediate distinction, if you will, from the prior representation."

The Lewinsky investigation had entered a new phase. For both sides, it promised both danger and opportunity.

———

JUST as Monica Lewinsky appeared ready to flip, OIC's investigation took a nosedive.

Ken Starr was en route from teaching a seminar in New York when he received the heart-stopping news: He was directed to appear in the courtroom of Chief Judge Norma Holloway Johnson immediately—his office was accused of engaging in criminal conduct by leaking grand jury information. Starr's train was already late; he would never make the courtroom proceeding in time. The independent counsel scrambled to contact Bob Bittman and Paul Rosenzweig to cover the emergency 6:00 P.M. hearing.

The precipitating event was an article titled "Pressgate," appearing on the cover of Steven Brill's slick new "media watchdog" magazine dubbed *Brill's Content,* for which Starr had granted a lengthy interview. The article laid out in chapter and verse alleged leaks by Starr's office. It gave page after page of damning detail, suggesting that Starr himself and his top deputies, including Jackie Bennett, were leaking grand jury information like a sieve in connection with the Clinton-Lewinsky investigation. David Kendall had swiftly filed another rule-to-show-cause motion, demanding to know why the Office of Independent Counsel should not be held in contempt for violating the federal rules of criminal procedure.

Until now, Judge Johnson had seemed to be in OIC's corner. When Bittman and Rosenzweig arrived at her courtroom on this night, however, everything about the judge's face, manner, and voice indicated that she felt betrayed by these prosecutors who had repeatedly denied leaking to the press. Kendall seemed to be on fire with righteous indignation, demanding that the judge give him authority to take the depositions of Starr's entire office to get to the bottom of this lawbreaking.

Having rushed back from Union Station, his eyes filled with shame, Ken Starr quietly gathered with his prosecutors in the OIC conference room. Wet and rain-soaked after returning from the train station, he began: "Let me apologize to each of you personally for the damage I've done to the office and the investigation." Within minutes, Starr's team was drafting a nineteen-page response to Steven Brill, trying to dig its way out of this frightful new hole.

Chief Judge Johnson wasted no time, declaring that the president's lawyers had "presented a prima facie case" to move forward. She pointed to specific broadcasts on major news networks and published accounts in the *New York Daily News* and the recent *Brill's Content* article, all of which identified "sources in Starr's office" as the conduit for sensitive grand jury information. If proven, she declared, this breach could constitute criminal conduct. The judge would permit the president's lawyer to depose Ken Starr, personally, and to dig into OIC's internal records to determine if the prosecutors had violated federal rule 6(e). She was giving Kendall the green light to drill into the heart of the Starr operation.

If any decision threatened to blow Starr's investigation out of the water, this was it. Starr would later acknowledge, "It was the nadir, as far as I'm concerned, of the investigation." He removed his spectacles and rubbed his eyes. "We had many travails, but there was no worse day than that day when the chief judge [rendered her decision]."

Suddenly, Starr's office was transformed from the hunter into the hunted animal. Although he shared this decision with no one but his most trusted deputies, Starr resolved to fight to the death. Empowering President Clinton's lawyers to dig into the most confidential aspects of OIC's investigation would plunge a knife into the heart of OIC's operation. Starr filed an emergency appeal with the Court of Appeals. He also confided in his inner circle that he was ready to defy Judge Johnson's order. He would stand tough and refuse to give Kendall access to OIC's evidence vault, to save his office from ruination, even if this act of disobedience led to his removal.

Starr's investigation seemed to be unraveling in every direction. To the surprise of everyone, including Susan McDougal herself, the usually hard-nosed Judge George Howard in Little Rock released McDougal from prison for ninety days— out of concern for serious back problems (scoliosis) that had caused the inmate's health to deteriorate such that doctors warned that her medical problems could become permanent. Newspapers showed Susan McDougal enjoying a celebratory dinner with family and friends at the Capital Hotel in Little Rock, with well-wishers flocking into the grand hotel lobby to show their support for the defiant OIC witness.

In a swift one-two punch, U.S. District Judge James Robertson in Washington threw out OIC's newly filed tax evasion case against Webster Hubbell and his wife in "Hubbell II." Judge Robertson declared sternly that the tax-evasion charges filed against the Hubbells were "six degrees of relationship" away from anything Starr was authorized to investigate in his charter and violated Hubbell's Fifth Amendment rights against self-incrimination, because they were premised upon documents extracted from Hubbell as part of his immunity deal with OIC.

The hulking Webb Hubbell, speaking at the doorstep of his home in Washington, expressed relief. "It's a good day," he told reporters in a weary Arkansas drawl.

OIC was even hitting a brick wall on the Secret Service issue, despite its initial high hopes. Judge Johnson had issued a ten-page ruling denying the Secret Service's request for protection, declaring that the so-called protective function privilege lacked any basis "in the Constitution, Congressional intent, history, or . . . common sense." Yet even after calling a parade of agents to the grand jury, OIC had obtained no evidence of value. One OIC prosecutor declared: "The Secret Service is a dry hole; there's nothing there."

Starr personally telephoned Director Lew Merletti to vent his frustration: "You guys knew nothing that was of any substance whatsoever," the special prosecutor protested. "Why didn't you tell me? You've wasted my time fighting on all of this."

Merletti was tempted to slam the phone down. Instead, he set his jaw and stared at a poster hanging in his office. It displayed an unfurling American flag with the agency's motto blazoned across it: "Worthy of Trust and Confidence." The head of the Secret Service replied, "You didn't understand. We were standing on principle."

Now, as the walls seemed to be crumbling down in every direction, Starr received a fax from Eric Holder at the Justice Department and was nearly knocked out of his chair. Holder had faxed a draft pleading that the attorney general planned to file with Judge Johnson, proposing that the Justice Department investigate a laundry list of allegations involving prosecutorial misconduct by Starr's office—accusations that had been lodged by an assortment of complainants.

"I think he [Holder] meant to do us harm," Starr said later, sharing his most private thoughts. "I felt that he was a Rasputin who was pulling the strings and controlling the department's tactics. And felt that he was being very clever, when in fact, it was becoming increasingly known throughout the city what he was up to. 'He was too clever by half,' as Churchill would say."

Starr called Holder and lashed out, admonishing the deputy attorney general that if he filed this pleading in the context of the current hostile climate, it could destroy OIC's investigation. If that happened, Starr warned, the blood of his entire prosecutorial staff would be on Janet Reno's hands. Holder backed off, agreeing to postpone any investigation of Starr's office—for the moment.

By mid-summer of 1998, Starr's operation seemed to be hanging by a thread. Although Starr was prepared to defy Judge Johnson's rule-to-show-cause order, he understood that such an act of defiance could give Attorney General Reno the excuse she needed to "fire him immediately." With both Starr's job and his investigation in serious jeopardy, his prosecutors determined that there were only two people who could pull OIC out of the fire by conclusively making the case against the president.

These two people, they agreed behind closed doors, were Monica Lewinsky and William Jefferson Clinton.

CHAPTER

41

—•—

MONICA'S TRUTH

Linda Tripp, reporting to the grand jury room on the last day of June, provided the best hope to Ken Starr's prosecutors that, finally, they might emerge victorious at the conclusion of their draining investigation.

Literary agent/gossip queen Lucianne Goldberg appeared on *Larry King Live,* exuding confidence that Tripp would provide the missing evidence necessary to show that President Bill Clinton had lied with impunity. Goldberg, who proudly took credit for coaxing Tripp to tape her conversations with Monica Lewinsky, told the talk-show host that twenty or so cassette tapes would confirm everything Tripp had told Starr's prosecutors. When King asked the flamboyant literary agent how she knew that this wasn't simply a case of "a young girl living out a fantasy, lying to a friend," Goldberg replied with a cagey smile, "You can't lie contemporaneously for 20 hours. . . . Remember, these tapes were made after the president basically ditched this girl."

Larry King, jutting a thumb under his trademark suspenders, asked whether taping a friend constituted an act of betrayal: "[Doesn't] twenty hours seem a bit much? It seems like someone was enjoying this." Nine out of ten Americans viewed Tripp negatively, King pointed out. Didn't that statistic suggest that the blond-haired woman's story had an unpleasant stench as far as most average citizens were concerned? Goldberg glared into the camera. She retorted that the White House spin machine was leaking false and twisted information about Tripp. "They can spin and spin and spin, and eventually, the truth will come out," she said, "and then this awful mess that has us all screaming at each other is going to be over."

Displaying the flair that made her one of New York's premiere literary divas, Goldberg added that she was paying a steep price herself. Already, the White House had sicced a bunch of photographers on her trail, following her day and night. "I would like to have gotten my roots done," Goldberg said. "They caught me on the day I was headed for the hairdresser. You know, that's hell for a woman." When asked whether she had any regrets about assisting Tripp in making public this scandal, the Manhattan literary agent told the show's host in a throaty voice, "[This] is going to save [Tripp] in the end."

Tripp's journey to the grand jury room seemed more like a visit to purgatory than a ticket to salvation. Tripp had abandoned her home in Columbia, Maryland; she had walked away from her desk at the Pentagon, as if leaving her job in suspended animation. The woman who had delivered over the Lewinsky story to OIC now moved around like a fugitive, staying with her mother in New Jersey, finding rooms at friends' homes, staying at undisclosed hotel rooms paid for by the FBI. Tripp herself had even come under criminal scrutiny as the Pentagon announced it was investigating whether she had lied on government forms to obtain "top secret" clearance in 1987. On those official documents, Tripp had claimed that she had never been arrested. Now officials in Greenwood Lake, New York, released a police report indicating that Linda Carotenuto (her maiden name) had been arrested back in 1969 at Inn on the Lake, at the age of nineteen, in connection with the theft of $263 and a watch valued at $600. The case against her had been dismissed after a friend was found guilty of stealing and stashing the items in Tripp's purse. Yet the Pentagon was still weighing whether to charge Tripp for making a "knowing and willful false statement" on her security clearance forms, a felony under federal law.

As Tripp showed up for her date with the grand jury, she issued an official statement: "The vicious personal attacks against me . . . and the general climate of threats, intimidation, McCarthyistic tactics, and guilt by association can only serve to deter those who in the future may dare to bring information to law enforcement officials." Hoping to adjust her public image, Tripp did her best to portray herself as a woman deeply concerned with Lewinsky's plight. "As a parent of children close to Monica's age, I felt and continue to feel horror at the abuse of power and emotional anguish she has endured over a two-year period," she stated. "I am disturbed by the smear campaign that maligns Monica. She is a bright, caring, generous soul—one who has made poor choices. She was not a stalker, she was invited. . . . Monica's moral compass is her own. She, as anyone else, should not be forced to defend her private life as a fully orchestrated campaign is launched to discredit her."

With her frizzy blond hair pulled back in a dignified style, and wearing white pearls to provide a classy accent to her blue business suit, Linda Tripp now arrived at the courthouse flanked by her son, Ryan (age twenty-three), and her daughter, Allison (age nineteen). The image she conveyed was that of a concerned mother and hardworking government employee who was caught in the cross fire, enduring this ignominious treatment for doing what was right. As the doors slammed shut behind her and she walked before the assembled grand jurors, however, Tripp was greeted with a healthy dose of skepticism.

The first order of business was for Tripp to give a disclaimer about her own immunity deal with Ken Starr's office—which included blanket federal immunity to prevent prosecution by the State of Maryland for violations of its wiretap law. Without further ado, Tripp jumped into a "greatest hits" sketch of Lewinsky's X-rated affair with Bill Clinton, triggering a push-back from the grand jurors. One asked if this whole saga might amount to a replay of the movie *Fatal Attraction,* in which a dangerously obsessed woman stalked a married man with whom she had a brief affair. "Is it possible that she [Lewinsky] wasn't living in reality, that she was fantasizing and you were part of this fantasy? . . ." Tripp quickly took the defensive: "No. I promise you on my mother's soul and on the lives of my children, this is not a fantasy." The grand juror pressed on, asking whether a "professional" might reach a different opinion: "You know, somebody who's really trained to deal with people with emotional problems more so than you are?" Tripp insisted that the "level of detail" Lewinsky had provided—including her description of the president's study inside the West Wing of the White House, which few people in the world (even with the highest security clearances) had ever seen—made it impossible for the intern to be concocting these stories.

As Tripp continued her lengthy account of the Bill-Monica soap opera, the grand jurors listened in stunned silence. The witness described one scene in which Clinton broke down and confessed to the young intern that he had engaged in affairs with "literally hundreds of women over the time of his marriage." The president had tearfully admitted that "it was his fault, that he has a compulsion, he would never be able to recall all of their names, some he didn't even know." On official road trips, Clinton had even begun keeping a calendar "marking down all of the days he had been good," meaning "the days that he overcame the compulsion to be with someone sexually other than his wife."

Tripp offered her own psychological assessment that Bill Clinton and Monica Lewinsky had become "soul friends," largely because the young woman reminded Clinton of his mother by virtue of her spunk and irreverence. Monica was an "up-front, direct, in-your-face kind of person" who would have been "equally kind and respectful to a head of state as she would be to whoever rang up her groceries." She also held an allure for Bill Clinton, Tripp told the grand jurors, because she treated Clinton "very much as a human being."

As the relationship took root, Tripp went on, it became hot and cold, especially after Lewinsky had been "banished" to the Pentagon. Tripp confided that Monica and Bill would get into verbal fights like a quarrelsome couple. "She would use obscenities, she would scream and yell. He would do the same thing back. It was volatile—" For instance, when Lewinsky first learned of Kathleen Willey's allegations and other stories suggesting that she (Lewinsky) was not the only female with whom the president might be engaging in adultery, Tripp recalled that the intern began shouting, "I hate his [expletive deleted] guts," and "I never want to see him again."

One grand juror finally interjected, "May I ask, *why* did you continue to have these conversations with Ms. Lewinsky?" Tripp fumbled to formulate an answer. She blurted out that she initially felt sorry for Monica, especially because the former intern's mother had moved to New York and left her without a parent nearby. Tripp had assumed the role of mother hen, she said, until she could no longer condone this dysfunctional relationship.

The grand juror searched for a better answer: "Why did you continue the relationship if you didn't feel as if you were supportive of her?" Tripp replied, "I thought it was in her best interests at the time to be a little harsher [given] the reality of the situation."

Tripp regrouped by getting back to her narrative. It was Clinton's personal secretary, Betty Currie, Tripp explained, who facilitated Lewinsky's meetings and other communications with the president. At first, Tripp told the grand jurors, Currie only had a vague suspicion about the nature of the relationship. Then, Monica and Betty had scheduled a "sit-down" at the restaurant in the swanky Hay-Adams Hotel, and Monica had "laid [it all] on the table." From that point forward, Monica was able to use Betty as a conduit to pass gifts (ties, sunglasses, a jigsaw puzzle) and notes to Clinton. Betty also helped Monica "clean up" after several sessions of hanky-panky with Clinton, said Tripp, so that the intern looked presentable when she scurried out of the Oval Office.

Asked whether First Lady Hillary Clinton knew of these goings-on, Tripp hedged her bets. She admitted that it was unclear if Mrs. Clinton "*personally*" knew about her husband's extramarital flings. However, it was clear that "her *people* knew." Also, said Tripp, it was "well known in the White House and respected and understood that Mrs. Clinton didn't much care what he did as long as it wasn't discovered." As the grand jurors listened with puzzlement, Tripp recounted how she believed that she herself (Tripp) had been moved out of her position in the West Wing early in the Clinton administration because Hillary Clinton viewed her as "threatening" and a possible temptation to Bill. Tripp quickly added that this suspicion was unfounded because "I was [not] at all romantically interested in the President."

Tripp next knocked the grand jurors back in their chairs when she related that even when Monica and the president were physically separated and unable to "mess around" in the White House, they shifted to having "phone sex." The president, on these occasions, would typically call from his private quarters and announce that he was wearing his usual outfit—"a T-shirt and blue underwear." Since the calls came late at night, Monica would chat in her bedroom and tell Clinton that she was wearing something sexy—"underwear that he liked" or some provocative outfit—even though usually she was really wearing "sweatpants and a sweatshirt."

Telephonically, there were no bounds to the "sexual activity" in which Clinton and Monica would partake, said Tripp, spinning out her titillating tale. In contrast, when they messed around in the flesh, the president always stopped short of the final act. Monica would demand to know the reason: "Why won't you have intercourse with me?" she would ask, sexually aroused, confused, and upset. Clinton would heave a sigh of regret: "When you get to be a certain age," he would say, "you realize that every action you take . . . has a consequence."

Tripp also acknowledged that Monica herself repeatedly made clear that she did not consider oral sex to constitute "having sex." As Lewinsky told her older friend in one conversation captured on tape and played to the grand jury, "having sex is having intercourse." In Monica's sexual dictionary, engaging in oral sex just amounted to "fooling around."

As Linda Tripp's testimony entered its second and third days, filled with more and more hair-curling details, a number of grand jurors openly questioned her motives in exposing this deeply personal information. After all, Tripp had professed to be worried about Monica's "mistreatment" at the hands of Bill Clinton. One grand juror asked: "Did you feel by continuing the relationship [with Monica] that you would be able to take some sort of action or help her do something to correct that mistreatment?" Tripp replied that she had given Monica "the same guidance I'd give my own daughter" until the situation had become "too dangerous" to handle. The grand juror shot back: "But some of that was self-inflicted." Another juror jumped in: "Why didn't you just cut her off? Just say, 'Look. I've had enough. Don't ever call me again. Period. I'm going to end this right now.' "

A third grand juror noted that Tripp's odious portrait of the Clinton-Lewinsky relationship was based solely on Monica's version of events: "Have you thought about [the fact that] you've only heard one side of the story? Have you talked to Betty yourself? . . . Have you talked to the President himself?" Duly chastened, Tripp replied, "That's a good point."

The grand jurors were both intrigued and baffled when Tripp revealed that she had maintained a steno notebook, at Monica's urging, listing the chronology of the young woman's self-destructive affair with the president. This odd record in Tripp's own handwriting listed specific dates and code words for each sexual encounter. As OIC prosecutors read from the notebook, grand jurors leaned forward, all ears. One entry for Sunday, August 4, recorded: "HRC [Hillary Rodham Clinton] away. Afternoon 45 minutes—" followed by "kinky phone sex." Another entry, dated August 19, corresponded to the president's birthday party at Radio City Music Hall, which Monica had attended by paying $250 for a ticket: "New York. Juicy. Touched. Grabbed his [crotch area]. Sent tie for birthday."

After an extensive review of material contained in the spiral notebook, a juror piped up: "Ms. Tripp, *why* were you documenting?" In a response that bordered on paranoiac, the witness explained exactly why she had decided to keep such careful records. She told the men and women, "I am afraid of this [Clinton] administration. I have what I consider to be well founded fears of what they are capable of." When asked by a grand juror to explain those fears, Tripp replied, "I had reason to believe that the Vince Foster tragedy was not depicted accurately under oath by members of the administration." She was particularly spooked by "the list of 40 bodies . . . that were associated with the Clinton administration," including a man named Jerry Parks, who had worked on Clinton's security detail in Arkansas during the 1992 election and was gunned down in his car in Little Rock under mysterious circumstances.

A juror interrupted: "So you felt that making this information public would sort of rectify the situation?" Tripp replied, "I thought he [Clinton] would be accountable." Another grand juror turned the tables by asking whether Tripp took into consideration the well-being of Lewinsky. Tripp countered: "I have always felt that if it became public she wouldn't be in danger at all." These steps, she said, were an "insurance policy" for both herself and Monica, if the huge Clinton machine tried to mow them down to protect the president.

Toward the end of this startling grand jury session, one juror asked bluntly whether Tripp had taped Monica in furtherance of "a book proposal." Linda Tripp snapped back, "The book proposal died a year prior to that." The grand juror continued: "I'm trying to understand, then, why this was so exciting to you." Another grand juror noted that if one reviewed the tape transcripts, it seemed that Tripp sounded positively "gleeful" at catching Clinton in this wrongdoing. Linda Tripp became adamant: "I reiterate that there was no book proposal at that time, there is no book proposal now and this had nothing to do with a book proposal."

In a final remarkable confession, Tripp admitted that in November 1997, she had ceased taping Monica, on the advice of her lawyer and a Paula Jones attorney from Dallas, both of whom had warned her that it was illegal to do so under Maryland law. Nonetheless, on a subsequent occasion when Monica called and began pouring out her soul, Tripp glanced down and noticed the self-activating tape recorder was spinning—it had been left on by mistake. She hesitated a few seconds and then made a conscious decision to let the machine keep running. "I decided to continue to tape," she confessed to the grand jurors in a raspy voice. "I realized I was probably going to go to jail anyway and [I decided to] just go ahead and do it."

At the end of her grueling seven-day testimony, one thoroughly perplexed juror asked the witness, "What really was the catalyst that made you realize that you had to go to OIC? . . ." Tripp responded tersely, "Fear. Outrage. A line in the sand that was crossed. I was no longer going to be motivated by fear. I made a decision that this was something I had to do."

———

THE debate inside the Office of Independent Counsel as to whether to force President Clinton himself into the grand jury, now that the group had secured the damning testimony of Linda Tripp, was fiercer than the public ever knew. In early July, Starr's office had won a big victory from the federal court of appeals when it blocked Chief Judge Johnson's order that would have permitted David Kendall to paw through Starr's internal files to determine if OIC had unlawfully leaked grand jury information. This win in the court of appeals relieved a huge amount of pressure from the Starr prosecutors. Now they could refocus on more pressing issues—such as extracting the truth from Bill Clinton.

Ken Starr himself was firmly opposed to subpoenaing the president—at least not yet. Despite the general perception that Starr was a zealous Clinton hater, he was extremely reluctant to do anything that might appear to be an affront to this or any other president. His overriding concern, as a former federal judge and solicitor general, related to "our duty to be respectful of the presidency."

During one staff meeting over which Bob Bittman presided, the young former Maryland sex-crimes prosecutor had begun by telling his colleagues that "our information is that Clinton did this" and "Clinton did that." At the conclusion of the meeting, Starr took his young deputy aside and corrected him: "Bob, you referred to the president as 'Clinton.' He is the president. Please refer to him as 'the president' or 'President Clinton.' " Starr insisted that nobody on OIC's staff should act disrespectfully toward the president, no matter how intense the hatred toward Bill Clinton might be growing.

Starr repeatedly hammered this point home in meetings with his prosecutors, reminding them of Chief Justice John Marshall's 1805 opinion in U.S. v. Burr and other cases suggesting that issuing subpoenas to the president was a measure of last resort. Starr's theme was, "We've got to be very respectful. We've got to really go the extra mile." The independent counsel did not claim to be optimistic that President Clinton would voluntarily show up in the grand jury room. Yet he felt that

OIC needed to continue to "reach out and encourage" because "lightning might strike." Starr also believed that Chief Judge Norma Holloway Johnson needed to see "that we have done everything [possible]" before taking the final step of serving a subpoena on the chief executive.

Increasingly, Starr dropped comments indicating that he favored a "dump-truck" approach—a notion that horrified most of his legal team. The independent counsel wanted to assemble all their evidence and just "send it up there to the Congress and let them take it over." After all, OIC was a puny operation with no biceps to flex. It was "ill equipped" to take on the entire executive branch in order to prove that the president had committed impeachable offenses. Starr would whisper to his staff, behind closed doors, that they were now squarely in "593c territory," referring to the provision of the independent counsel law mandating that they pass along "substantial and credible" information to Congress if they determined that the president may have committed impeachable offenses. Wasn't it *Congress's* job to take over from here?

As Starr debated this point with his doubting prosecutors, he invoked "the image of [an] island that suddenly appears out on the ocean and is buffeted by the winds and the waves and storms at sea." OIC was now this little island. It had no support from the executive branch, even from the Justice Department, to which it was theoretically appended. Through his own horrible blunder in the *Brill's Content* mess, OIC prosecutors had lost the respect of Judge Johnson, who oversaw their case. At this point, he and his staff were a band of truth seekers adrift in dark, choppy waters.

Starr removed his glasses, rubbed his eyes, and sat back in his chair pensively. He asked his staff to indulge him in one more analogy. Back in his days of appellate practice, Starr recalled, he had handled a satellite technology case that seemed to offer an apt parallel. Their position was now akin to that of a communications satellite that had moved into its final, transitional orbit—a dangerous stage in which scientists on earth lost touch with the ship and crossed their fingers, hoping that the ship didn't explode in a fiery farewell in outer space. Starr told his faithful prosecutors, "We are in transitional orbit right now. We are here. The world is waiting for us, and we are under assault [on] this little island. The Justice Department hates us. The American people are disliking us intensely. We're lost, and we're not even out on the field of play. We've lost in the battle of public opinion, which we never entered, by virtue of the sense that [the Lewinsky case] was terribly invasive of privacy and it was a runaway investigation."

Starr's advice to his troops, as he struggled to maintain a steady voice, was, "We need to get it up there [to Congress]." It was time to soar past the moon, jettison the evidence of Clinton's grotesque law violations so that another branch of government could deal with it, activate their parachutes, and hope that the OIC starship might come down safely without further explosions that threatened to burn them beyond recognition.

In one of the great tragedies of this saga filled with many catastrophic moments, Ken Starr was overwhelmingly outvoted by his staff.

Had Starr's view prevailed—had the case gone to Congress at this early stage—the House of Representatives would have had to gather up its own evidence relating to possible impeachable offenses by the president, and Starr and his team might have extricated themselves from the worst predicament of their rough and bloodying tenure. Starr was becoming half federal prosecutor, half impeachment deputy for a politically charged Congress. At this moment, if OIC had backed off gracefully, Starr might have removed himself from the political bloodbath that followed. Yet his penchant for deferring to his prosecutors and seeking consensus like a wise judge finally led to his own professional meltdown, no different from that experienced by the ill-fated satellite in transitional orbit.

Given their bruising experiences with the Clintons since 1994, most members of Starr's team were vehemently opposed to surrendering this case to Congress at such an early stage. They wanted to push over every rock until the vipers in the Clinton White House were captured with forked sticks. Even Bob Bittman, whom Starr himself had appointed to oversee the Washington operation, took issue with his boss's "pass it off to Congress" approach. The harsh reality was that Clinton was making a monkey of their operation. Most of the witnesses in the grand jury were taking their oaths, providing testimony, then running back to provide information to the White House. "He was mirroring our investigation," Bittman would later say. "He would only tell us, and admit to us, as much as we knew." The only way to beat the president at this game, Bittman told his boss in front of his fellow prosecutors, was to haul Clinton's rear end in front of the grand jury and pin him down under oath. In light of the "vituperative" correspondence from David Kendall, Clinton was likely to stall indefinitely, until OIC called his bluff.

Starr recognized that he had lost the battle with his staff; so he reluctantly agreed to allow them to issue a subpoena to the president. As Starr himself would later explain, the choices had narrowed themselves down to one. "Well, what was it that remained? You've only got a circumstantial case. You've got to nail it down. We knew that meant the two participants: Lewinsky and the president."

With that, Bittman drafted a new letter to Kendall on July 17, attaching a subpoena for William Jefferson Clinton to appear before the grand jury in eleven days. Bittman stated that the grand jury "simply can wait no longer." This extraordinary subpoena was signed and sealed by the clerk of the U.S. District Court. Bittman also attached an advice-of-rights form, reciting that the president had a right to retain counsel and that "anything that you do or say may be used against you. . . ."

"If the President agrees to comply with the subpoena and testify," Starr's young deputy wrote, "we and the grand jury—as we have previously stated—will accommodate his schedule." Otherwise, President Clinton would have to face the consequences.

As soon as Clinton's lawyers filed an emergency motion to quash the subpoena, and Chief Judge Johnson denied that motion, the president suddenly found some time in his schedule.

———

PLATO Cacheris and Jake Stein sat across a conference table from Ken Starr. A new era had dawned in Monica Lewinsky's representation; these new lawyers were not willing to negotiate with middlemen. After being driven by the FBI to the underbelly of OIC's building and whisked up an elevator to the secure fourth floor, the lawyers now confronted Starr and laid it on the line: "She does not trust you," they told the independent counsel. "She is willing to be tried rather [than] be demeaned by repeated threats." For that reason, OIC needed to fish or cut bait. "The truth of what happened is unpleasant for her, unpleasant for the president and unpleasant for the state of the union," they told Starr, according to notes of the meeting. Stein added, "Plato and I have at least one good trial left in us and we are happy to devote it to [this] case."

Cacheris and Stein, both of whom had represented defendants in the fabled Watergate trial, were feeling bullish about their odds. As Cacheris would later explain, "Here was a young lady that I think everybody would sympathize with. Here was the president who said, 'We didn't do anything. We didn't have sex.' " Vernon Jordan was going to confirm there was a denial of sex. Cacheris concluded, "And I said to myself, 'This could be a very interesting case.' "

Jackie Bennett's mantra was that there could be no deal unless there was an "in-person" proffer from Ms. Lewinsky—they could not accept "a pig in a poke." They wanted to be able to look Lewinsky in the eye before deciding whether to offer her a plea deal. In response to this, Cacheris and Stein halted the conversation: "You want a witness, we'll give you a witness," they said. But they weren't about to allow Lewinsky to spill her guts and have OIC decide it wanted her to "plead to a felony." In-person proffers and one-sided plea deals might be fine in Justice Department training sessions, but this case had progressed too far. "We weren't going to play that game," Cacheris later explained. "We were doing it differently."

Cacheris was no great fan of Bill Clinton. "I thought his conduct was abominable, and I thought he was a disingenuous person," he recalled. "I had admired his talent and intelligence, but I didn't admire his personal style." Still, Cacheris told the Starr prosecutors that this meeting was not about Clinton—it was about Ms. Lewinsky. "I [have] no interest in protecting anybody except her," he stated firmly.

After the meeting, ethics adviser Sam Dash pulled Ken Starr aside. Dash fancied himself as an ombudsman, as well as the resident OIC "fussbudget." He knew both Stein and Cacheris from the Washington legal community—he believed he might be able to facilitate a resolution.

The timing was propitious. Inside Starr's office, there was a growing sentiment that striking a new immunity deal with Monica's lawyers was the preferred solution. It was true that the OIC prosecutors were prepared to indict Monica. However, even if they went to federal court in eastern Virginia, as planned, and placed the case on the "rocket docket," it would take months before a criminal trial could be scheduled. It was better to fashion a workable immunity deal with two levelheaded lawyers, the OIC prosecutors agreed privately, than to indict Monica and suffer further delays in pinning down the truth.

As promised, Dash arranged to host a private breakfast at his home in Chevy Chase, days later. On the Dashes' glassed-in back porch, overlooking their brightly colored flower garden and far from the eye of photographers' cameras, the men partook of ample coffee and bagels. Ken Starr settled himself into a comfortable chair and reopened the dialogue with Lewinsky's lawyers by proposing an intriguing compromise: OIC would make their client "Queen for a Day," prosecutorial lingo for giving her a onetime free pass. Nothing Lewinsky said during this session with OIC lawyers could be used against her. If the former intern's statements were "truthful and sufficiently complete," Starr said, he would give her a full immunity bath. If her story turned out to be false, OIC would be free to prosecute the young woman, but they would be precluded from using her "queenly" statements against her.

Cacheris and Stein took long sips of coffee. They dabbed their mouths and sat back, nodding slowly. They could be persuaded to recommend this proposal to their client, they allowed.

Documents contained in the defense lawyers' files, released with permission of their client, now reveal that Cacheris and Stein recognized that—however unfair this full-blown criminal investigation of their client was—Lewinsky was at serious risk if her lawyers did not broker a swift deal. One memo prepared solely for the eyes of her lawyers concluded that two federal statutes relating to "obstruction of justice" provided ample grounds to charge and prosecute Lewinsky. One of these provisions, set forth in Section 1503 of the crimes code, permitted conviction of any person who "corruptly endeavors" to hinder the administration of justice—a broad umbrella. A related provision dealt with "witness tampering" and allowed a defendant to be prosecuted even for "non-threatening persuasion and advising" of potential witnesses. The fact that Monica had signed a false affidavit and coaxed Linda Tripp to do the same was a big problem. Even though it seemed unfair to apply these rules to a twenty-four-year-old love-struck young woman, the lawyers understood that their client could get jail time for her actions.

Plato Cacheris later confirmed, "Her exposure was the affidavit . . . and possible obstruction of justice with Tripp."

Another memo in the files of Lewinsky's attorneys, marked in bold letters STRICTLY CONFIDENTIAL, emphasized that the magic window to cut a deal might be ajar only fleetingly: "This may be the time, rather than to jump on OIC while they have their problems, to resume a negotiation. ML must agree and must understand that she is experimenting with a way out that has its perils for her. The perils include an indictment for grand jury perjury and there may be few defenses to such a charge."

Surveying the Dashes' flower garden, which was bathed in sunlight that seemed auspicious, the group moved to the next logical step: *Where* would OIC conduct such a "conversation" with Monica Lewinsky? Was there an out-of-the-way place where the media would never sniff them out? Starr piped up that he knew a perfect location—his mother-in-law's apartment on East Fifty-sixth Street in New York, otherwise known as "Grandma's house." It was a cozy spot, Starr said, beaming. The media would never suspect *this* locale in Manhattan as the venue for a high-level meeting to resolve the biggest criminal investigation in America. Cacheris and Stein shrugged their shoulders: Why not? "Grandma's house" seemed as good as any. The bald-headed Dash chuckled, noting that they could dub the mission Red Riding Hood, a joke that produced polite twitters around the table.

The defense lawyers asked, "When do you want to do it?" Starr replied, "Like, now."

As the opposing lawyers strode to their cars under the shade trees of Newlands Street, departing this leafy section of Chevy Chase, there was a mixture of victory and apprehension in the warm summer air. Back at the office, Plato Cacheris telephoned Monica, who had just turned twenty-five on that day, July 23. Cacheris told his client, allowing her to savor, finally, something resembling good news, "I've got a birthday present for you."

———————

THE meeting at "Grandma's house" in New York City was a moment of truth for all concerned. Monica Lewinsky's lawyers had debriefed their client extensively, using a female attorney in the office to conduct interviews when it came to "personal" details. Plato Cacheris stated with a grimace: "We didn't want to get into all the 'who did this and what and how?' " From those sessions, the lawyers concluded that their client could give OIC all it needed. Lewinsky was "extremely intelligent and focused and had a great recall of events," Cacheris felt. If she simply laid out the facts, she could give Starr everything necessary and lock down her immunity.

Although some later accounts would mangle this point, Cacheris emphasized that he and his partners never believed that Lewinsky might be fantasizing her affair with Clinton. The defense team had consulted a psychiatrist about "de Clerambault's syndrome" (otherwise known as *erotomania*)—a rare condition with which the afflicted, usually young females, can delude themselves into believing a famous or powerful person has fallen in love with them. Yet the lawyers slammed the door shut on this theory immediately. "She didn't fantasize [an affair]," Cacheris said. "She *had* one." This presented its own set of problems.

The defense lawyers quickly discerned that Monica Lewinsky still had a "soft spot" for Clinton. Fortunately, they could tell that her fear for life and liberty was beginning to trump her lingering love for the president. "She did not want to be charged with any criminal offense or certainly convicted of one or face the possibility of incarceration," said Cacheris. "All of those things preyed very heavily on her." Moreover, Cacheris and Stein knew that they were holding an ace card that they could play at any moment: The blue dress would provide the single incontrovertible piece of evidence that Starr's office needed for a checkmate. "We knew that she had it," said Cacheris. "And we told her to keep it, retain it."

The blue Gap dress was a mystery that seemed to elude everyone who sought its whereabouts, like an intriguing yet repulsive relic. Linda Tripp had tried to get the keys to Monica's apartment, on one occasion, to swipe it. Tripp had also encouraged Lewinsky to swab the semen-stained area with a cotton swab to preserve the evidence or to seal the dress in a plastic bag and hide it for safekeeping.

Bill Ginsburg had known about the blue dress "[almost] from day one," but he had deftly managed to avoid revealing its whereabouts. If OIC had formally subpoenaed the garment, he would later admit, "I would have been in a pickle." Fortunately for Ginsburg, "nobody ever asked me for it."

Ironically, the FBI and OIC had made a big kerfuffle early on, calling Ginsburg and saying they wanted to "search [Lewinsky's] apartment." When the government agents asked Ginsburg if a search warrant was necessary, he responded genially, "Not at all." The bearded lawyer told Monica's mother to "have a pot of coffee, both decaf and regular, and bear claws, donuts, pastries." He added with a wry smile, "Make it easy for these guys, because they promised me they weren't going to tear the place apart and break down the walls." On the appointed day and with the coffeepots bubbling away, Monica's mother had waited apprehensively. Not a single G-man arrived. When Ginsburg called OIC, Mike Emmick told him, "Oh, we forgot."

After a new date was arranged, more coffee and pastries were delivered. "It wasn't stale; it was new stuff," Ginsburg later vouched. The FBI this time searched Monica's Watergate apartment, seizing any dark dress in sight. "It didn't matter if it was blue, black, purple—any dress," Ginsburg recalled. All the dresses were apprehended.

Three days later, Emmick called back, openly disappointed that the only blue dress bearing stains had come back negative for semen residue. Emmick was also miffed that his agents had found none of the "gifts" that Clinton supposedly had given Lewinsky, as spelled out on the Tripp tapes. The prosecutor said to Ginsburg, "Okay, where is the stuff we were looking for?" He added sternly, "We know for a fact that she got *Leaves of Grass*." Ginsburg replied politely, "Do your people have eyes?" Monica and her mother were moving to New York; there were four large boxes piled up in the living room of their Watergate apartment. "Did your guys ever search the boxes?" he asked. "If you had searched the boxes, you would have found . . . a lot of other presents." (In fact, the copy of *Leaves of Grass* from Clinton was sitting on a bookshelf in the room.)

"Oh," Emmick replied. With that, he hung up.

Said Ginsburg, "And I never heard from him again."

As for the blue dress, Ginsburg felt secure in knowing that it was "stored in a safe place." Beyond that, his lips remained sealed.

When Plato Cacheris and Jake Stein took over, Lewinsky initially acted coy, giving them conflicting stories about the mysterious, never-seen dress. One version was that "it was stained by Clinton." The second was, "Maybe I spilled something on it, like clam chowder." In light of these conflicting accounts, Cacheris and Stein had debated whether to have the fabric tested themselves for DNA matter. They decided that such a course was dangerous. The last thing they needed was to be charged with "tampering with evidence." Over time, as their client came to trust them and to speak more candidly to them, they became convinced that she possessed the real item. So they told Lewinsky to "keep the dress," wherever it was. She was not to wash it; she was not to give it away to Goodwill. As reluctant as their client might be to help OIC capture the president, the blue dress was her best chance of keeping *herself* out of one of those frightful-looking jails the FBI had shown her in Los Angeles.

KEN Starr arrived by plane the night before the meeting at "Grandma's house," wearing a baseball cap tipped over his eyes as a disguise. Starr needed to arrange the furniture and tidy up his mother-in-law's pied-à-terre on the East Side of Manhattan. After all, this was the biggest meeting he would ever convene as independent counsel—even though he himself would not be attending.

Finally, everything seemed to be looking up for Starr. Of late, his prosecutors "were really of one cheerful accord," he felt. Bruce Udolf had left the investigation, supposedly because of health concerns, but in truth he had been driven out by his own colleagues. The rest of the nonbelievers, that is, the moderates in the office, had now found religion. Everyone agreed that pinning down Monica Lewinsky was the proper fix to repair their stalled investigation.

After Starr spent a restful night in his parents-in-law's cozy apartment, getting up at dawn to purchase plenty of orange juice and breakfast treats, he scooted out and walked several blocks to the Fitzpatrick Manhattan Hotel. Here, the independent counsel and a backup team of prosecutors were establishing a second base of operations. Starr was fully aware that Monica detested him—he did not want to "make her feel more uncomfortable." Also, he told himself that as head of the OIC operation—much like the attorney general in charge of the Justice Department—the appropriate role of "yours truly" was to stay out of the fray.

Ken Starr was not the only person traveling in disguise for this gathering. Monica Lewinsky had flown in from California wearing a "platinum blond wig . . . long hair, bangs" along with "a baseball cap and sunglasses." Cacheris and Stein had met with Lewinsky the night before at her mother's apartment in Manhattan, noting that his client was unusually "apprehensive." She had become thoroughly skeptical of the motives of the independent counsel. She was especially leery since her mother had been hauled before the grand jury and had suffered a public "breakdown."

Marcia Lewis would remember that her daughter was "conflicted": "I think in a perfect world, she could have stood her ground and never cooperated. And yet, what was the end going to be then? That she would risk going to jail while everybody else sat back and had a happy life ever after? It was just a very difficult period for her. She did all of this with a very heavy heart."

Monica herself recalled that her principal emotion at this time was fear. She had waited eight months for the president to admit the truth and put a stop to this—that had not happened. Now, fearing prosecution for herself and her family, she needed immunity. But nobody, she worried, would understand that.

Monica felt that she had somehow become a player in a strange tragicomic production, the absurdity of which was beginning to overwhelm her. She would say, years later, "I'm sorry, you just have to stop and laugh for a second when you kind of look at the whole scope of this thing. And you stop and say, 'What is probably one of the most bizarre things that's going to happen?' And you say, 'Okay, let's go to Starr's grandmother's apartment.' I'm sorry. That's kind of funny. Sidebar."

That muggy Monday morning, July 27, Monica and her attorneys arrived by cab. FBI agents escorted them up to the thirty-third floor. It was a nicely furnished getaway with a breathtaking view of the Chrysler Building, of the Empire State Building, and, in a third direction, of the East River.

Cacheris and Stein began by making clear that they were only interested in going forward if the final deal involved immunity for Monica's whole family. "The joke," Cacheris later deadpanned, "was that anybody named Lewinsky got immunity." With that understanding reached, the parties gathered at the dining room table. OIC was represented by Bob Bittman, Sol Wisenberg, Mary Anne Wirth (added to supply a woman's touch), and several FBI agents. Sam Dash lounged in an easy chair in an adjoining room, out of sight, like the Wizard of Oz.

Monica began by disclosing that she had been taking two antidepressants—Effexor and Serzone—since early February 1995, and that these medications sometimes created "an inability to think of certain words during conversation." With that disclaimer on the table, her lawyers led her through a vivid account of her extramarital involvement with the president, including precise times and dates of their clandestine encounters and specific events taking place in the White House. OIC's official summary of the meeting recorded: "The relationship [between the president and Lewinsky] then blossomed and eventually included 14 sexual encounters. Sexual encounters included one or more of the following: kissing, hugging, touch, and oral sex on the person of the President." The transcription of Monica's extraordinary session also revealed that there were "about 50 telephone calls, with the majority of them being between 10:00 p.m. and 6:00 a.m.," about fifteen of which turned into a form of "phone sex."

OIC was intrigued but not sold. As Bob Bittman would recall, "Monica was pretty open, but emotionally fragile. She broke down or was on the cusp of breaking down several times." He and his fellow prosecutors wondered how much of this might be playacting. "We did not believe she was totally forthcoming with everything she knew," Bittman said.

Monica's lawyers were surprised that Bittman and Wisenberg seemed to be vying for control as if they were in some rough competition. One prosecutor would ask a question; the other would cut in brusquely and ask, "Are you through now?" Although Cacheris had a great deal of respect for Starr, he was not particularly impressed with his underlings. At one point when Bittman tried to quiz Monica about the blue dress, Cacheris decided to cut the young deputy off at the knees: "Look, when we have a deal, we'll talk about dresses. But we're not talking about it now."

After a lunch of tuna fish sandwiches and sparkling water, questioning resumed for two hours, until Cacheris announced with an abrupt wave of the hand that it was time for his group to catch a four o'clock flight home. He declared that the OIC prosecutors had interrogated Monica long enough. Now it was time for them to decide if they wanted to play ball.

The OIC lawyers hurriedly caucused. Bittman straightened his tie, reporting that they were generally pleased—but he would like to have Monica return for one more session. At this, Cacheris motioned for his group to stand up. He announced, "If you don't have it now, you'll never have it. We're getting out of here."

Truth be told, Starr's team had concluded that Monica's story, although a bizarre assortment of puzzle pieces, was generally credible. Bittman recalled, "Some of the stuff we had doubts about—[like] the stuff she was telling us about Vernon Jordan. Also, the truthfulness regarding some of her conversations with the president." On the other hand, it was a question of playing the odds. "Overall," he said, "we felt she was truthful."

As Monica and her lawyers headed for the airport, the OIC prosecutors joined Starr's hidden hotel encampment, where they got the Washington office on a speakerphone. Sam Dash declared in a booming voice that Monica's credibility quotient was high. If she indeed had the dress, Dash and others agreed, why worry about minor details? The dress alone would supply the goods necessary to nail Clinton. OIC had already forced him to agree to appear before the grand jury—a fact that was still not public. Monica's testimony, even if imperfect, would choke the last false denial from the president's lips.

That evening, shortly after Monica's lawyers had driven home from the airport after a long day, Starr called Stein and stated cheerfully, "You have a deal."

Monica would later note that if Starr's lawyers had come to her initially in a way that was "appropriate" and "sounded normal to me," allowing her to call a lawyer and without threatening that she needed to "wear a wire," she would have probably agreed to the same deal six months earlier.

———

INSIDE Plato Cacheris's office the next day—on July 28—Monica Lewinsky signed an immunity agreement with OIC, her hand shaking as she affixed her signature to the document. Under the terms of this deal, Lewinsky agreed to cooperate fully and to allow OIC lawyers to debrief her. She also agreed to testify truthfully in the grand jury and in other "judicial or congressional proceedings." Assuming Monica stuck to her end of the bargain, OIC pledged not to prosecute her *or* her parents "for any crimes committed prior to the date of this Agreement arising out of the investigations within the jurisdiction of the OIC." To avoid a repeat of the previous debacle involving the questionable "authority" of Emmick and Udolf to consummate a binding immunity deal, this document was signed personally by "Kenneth W. Starr."

Monica Lewinsky recalled that as she put down the pen, she was overcome by a wave of unsettling emotions. "I had mixed feelings about even getting immunity when I got it," she said. "It was hard. It was difficult. It's like I had to put myself and my family [first]—I had to do what was best for me. But it was hard to know that I was betraying somebody. It was hard to do. Even after I knew this person had trashed me and abandoned me and everything else."

Lewinsky now asked to be excused, walked into the bathroom in her attorney's office, and broke down crying. As Cacheris recalled, "I think it was all just emotion, but bottom line, she was happy. I mean after all this time . . . eight months' anxiety over what was going to happen to her. Basically, you can understand her being emotional."

Cacheris instructed his client, before she left: "Just bring everything that you have [relating to Bill Clinton], *including* the dress, and bring it to my office."

So Monica arrived at her lawyer's building the next day carrying a shopping bag filled with items. These were immediately handed over to Mike Emmick and an FBI agent, who were present for the exchange. In a handwritten inventory marked "Federal Bureau of Investigation," Monica listed approximately thirteen articles that bore some connection to her relationship with Bill Clinton. These included "stuffed animal from black dog," "white canvas bag w/ black dog on it," "Book: *Leaves of Grass*," "brown marble bear sculpture," "Rockettes Christmas blanket (1997)," and "GAP dress size 12, dark blue." The latter item was wrapped in plastic and folded neatly in the bag, as if on its way to the cleaners.

The whereabouts of the dress had been one of the great puzzles of OIC's half-year chase of Lewinsky. Sources now confirm that the garment had been quietly moved to the New York apartment rented by Monica's mother and then transported back to Washington shortly before the immunity deal was struck, after Marcia Lewis had married media executive Peter Straus and given up her Fifth Avenue apartment.

Some sources later indicated that the dress was "sequestered in a vault" inside Marcia Lewis's apartment. Monica's mother herself later stated cautiously that the garment was "on the floor of the closet"—at least initially—but declined to go into further detail.

How the dress got to New York, however, is no longer a secret. "I took it there," Monica Lewinsky disclosed years later. At the time, since she was getting ready to move to Manhattan anyway, Monica had decided to "get it out of my apartment." She was worrying to herself, "I don't know what I'm going to do with it," and "Maybe I'll throw it away; maybe I'll keep it." If Starr's people or the FBI asked her for the dress, she could always reply, "Well, it's not in my house; it's not in my possession. So I'm not lying. I don't have [it]." But when her new lawyers had confirmed the existence of the garment that might hold the key to immunity, they had made clear that if OIC served "legitimate process" on Monica, she would have to give it up. For the time being, Cacheris had simply advised his client, "Keep the damn thing. Just hold on to it."

Monica had been tormented over what to do about the dress until this final, unavoidable moment when she handed over the bag to OIC. While she had been moving her possessions from her mother's apartment in Manhattan, during the cleaning-out process, she had exclaimed to herself, "Oh, my God, now's my chance! I could wash this dress. Nobody knows about it. . . . It's not public; it's just speculated about. I could just throw it in a washing machine."

She later recalled, "And I just started to freak out, because I didn't know [to what extent] I was being watched. And I thought, 'This is completely obstruction. This is knowingly doing this.' "

One voice whispering inside her head told Monica, "You're already in a lot of trouble. What's one more charge?" The louder voice, however, was shouting, "You're already in a lot of trouble; you don't need to make it worse!"

Now, as Monica handed over the blue Gap dress to federal authorities, the mystery was finally mooted.

Cacheris would later say, puzzled by OIC's handling of the interminable search for the single piece of incontrovertible evidence that was sitting right under its nose, "Why they just didn't subpoena her and the dress, give her immunity way back in February [I don't know]. They'd have had the whole case then."

As Cacheris ushered Starr's representatives out the door with the much-sought-after bag of evidence, he instructed Mike Emmick to keep the fruits of his work to himself. "I do not want to know," said Monica's lawyer, "the results of the DNA until it's made public."

A newspaper photographer already had managed to capture Monica carrying the shopping bag filled with evidence en route to her lawyer's office. Within hours, that photo was transmitted across the wire services, enabling President Clinton's advisers to huddle in the White House, enlarging that same photo and "trying to figure out what was in the bag. Could there be a dress in there?"

In the OIC offices, Bittman personally took custody of the bag of evidence, whisking it into a locked conference room so that his technician team could photograph and label each item—just in case an earthquake struck Washington or a burglar broke into OIC headquarters in the dead of night. Bittman was one of the few people to lay eyes on the infamous dress before it was handed over to the FBI and placed under lock and key. The deputy prosecutor recalled, "I remember it was large. I'm large now, too. And I remember seeing some stains on it. It was hanging up, on a hanger. An agent pointed out to me without touching—there were visible whitish stains on the dress, in the crotch area." Bittman authorized the FBI to take the dress to its lab for analysis, after being assured that only "several top people would work on it."

In less than twenty-four hours, the FBI had determined that the stain on the dress was "positive for human semen."

———

Bob Bittman walked into Ken Starr's office and closed the door. The president's appearance before the grand jury was now confirmed for August 17. There were two options: OIC could take a blood sample from Clinton in order to conduct a DNA test, and risk tipping off the president before he perjured himself further. Or Starr's prosecutors could hold back on the DNA test until *after* Clinton had committed himself to a story under oath, maximizing their chances to catch him in another lie. Starr asked Bittman, "What is normally done?" Bittman, a former sex crimes prosecutor, replied, "It is normal to do the test. You do DNA analysis if it will assist in the investigation of the crime. You don't wait." Starr scratched his head and said, "We're not going to play games." Even though it might give Clinton a warning signal and allow him to avoid compounding his criminal problems, Starr opted to follow the rule book. They would take the sample immediately. True to his professional creed, Starr wanted to err on the side of showing respect for the chief executive. He directed Bittman, rather than subpoenaing Clinton for the blood sample, to see if the president would surrender his blood voluntarily.

It was as a result of this sequence of events that Bittman sent a letter to David Kendall via hand delivery, unknown even to other lawyers in OIC. "Investigative demands," Bittman wrote, now required OIC to draw a blood sample from the president. Out of respect for the presidency, the independent counsel was willing to do this quietly. Within hours, Kendall fired back a reply: "We want to know what reason you have for the test. I don't believe you have any basis . . ." Bittman called his bluff, citing chapter and verse of legal precedent and stating that OIC had a "powerful predication" for its request. Bittman wrote to the president's lawyer: "If you want to challenge it, let me know and we will issue a subpoena."

On Monday, Kendall sent an envelope marked "to be opened by Mr. Bittman only," following up with a phone call communicating the same message. "Okay, we'll do it," he said. "The president has agreed to do it. It must be done tonight, at the White House, by a White House physician at ten o'clock."

As the early August sun was slipping behind the Capitol, Bittman drove his green Dodge Stealth over to the White House, accompanied by a female FBI agent. They pulled up to the Northeast Gate, where a Secret Service agent led the pair into a darkened waiting area, then ushered them into the Map Room. It was the same room where the president had given his testimony in the Whitewater case for Jim and Susan McDougal, during his first brush with Starr's office. Bill Clinton now stepped forward—he was already in the Map Room, awaiting them.

The president was dressed in a black tux, having ducked out of a formal dinner party for youth-violence experts. On this night, he didn't want his guests—among them, Attorney General Reno—to know where he was headed. Extending his hand to greet his adversaries, the president chatted with the FBI agent, who produced two vials. Clinton said, "Okay, let's get this going." He sat down in a stiff chair and rolled up his sleeve, holding out his right arm. The White House physician, Eleanor Maricino, tightened a rubber strap around the president's arm and felt gingerly for a vein. David Kendall, ill at ease, tried to make a joke: "Usually, it's the lawyer who bleeds for the client," he said. Clinton shot a sizzling glance at his lawyer. He then focused on the needle being inserted into his vein. Four milliliters of deep red blood were extracted.

The White House physician filled two vials. Recalled Bittman: "I watched very closely, to make sure there was no switch. It was given immediately to the FBI agent. The only people who touched it were the White House physician and the FBI agent." As they were escorted out of the Map Room through the darkened corridor to the exit, Bittman whispered, "I watched closely, but for one moment, ever so slightly, I couldn't tell." The FBI agent assured him: "They're his. It's very warm."

Bittman noted that the president's neck and face appeared unusually red, as if sunburned; he wondered if the president had just returned from vacation. The agent, who held a Ph.D. in the field of science, commented as they exited the northeast gate. "That was not sunburn," she said, offering her expert opinion. "He was angry."

Although OIC would never know it, the White House physician took a *third* vial of blood from the president's arm, the moment the Starr representatives left the building. The president's private lawyers, still not knowing the truth about the Lewinsky puzzle, feared that Starr's office might "hoke up the sample." The only safe option, they concluded, was to extract their own specimen and lock it in a refrigerated repository in case OIC tried to pull a trick. David Kendall, feeling that he was obligated to maintain a strict dividing line between himself (as private counsel), the president's White House counsel, and his political team, kept this second sample a secret even from Clinton's highest-level advisers. Said one member of Kendall's team: "We had to assume, whatever the facts were, the dress would reflect those facts. It was physical evidence." DNA tests, the president's lawyers knew, were "precise and powerful." Like everyone else in the world interested in this drama, the president's own counselors remained "totally in the dark."

As speculation concerning President Clinton's upcoming grand jury appearance intensified in the national media, the games of spy-versus-spy escalated. During this time, the friction between the Secret Service and the FBI reached a new level of intensity. One group was sworn to protect the life of the president; the other was fiercely loyal to the investigation headed by Ken Starr. This tension finally sent sparks flying by early August, as the nation held its breath waiting to see what President Bill Clinton would say once Starr's prosecutors got him under oath.

Secret Service Director Lew Merletti was attending a conference in Atlantic City, trying to conduct business as usual. Merletti was making the rounds at a reception when a "very high level" official in the FBI's Criminal Investigative Division sidled up to him quietly. This official, whom Merletti had known for years, leaned over and whispered, "Boy, what a mess with this whole thing."

As Merletti recalled the startling sidebar discussion, his compatriot from the FBI began wading into forbidden waters, talking about the pending Starr investigation as if they were engaging in the most natural conversation in the world. "Now, certainly only a fool would go ask him about anything about the Monica Lewinsky case," Merletti said later. "I mean, I hope I'm not a fool. At least not that big a one." Already, the Secret Service had been accused of covering up for Bill Clinton and funneling sensitive information to the president. Director Merletti was not about to take the bait, yet the FBI official kept talking.

"Listen," the man said in confidence. "I'm going to tell you something right now. The president has nothing to worry about."

Merletti stared at him. The man continued: "I'm in charge of that at the lab. We've gone over that whole dress. There's nothing there. There's no DNA on it. That thing's clean."

Merletti thought to himself, "Why is he telling me this?" With that, the FBI official walked away as quickly as he had appeared.

The director of the Secret Service remained frozen in his tracks. He thought, "I've been told this for a reason. I mean, I believe they're either trying to set me up, or they're trying to set the president up, or they're setting both of us up." Obviously, the endgame was to see "if I would take this [information] back." Merletti later concluded, raising his hands in angry exclamation, "Well, regardless, I wouldn't take it back [to the White House], anyway. So I didn't say a word. Not a word. And I'm thinking to myself, 'Well, if he [President Clinton] knew what I knew, he would be able to testify a certain way.' "

Regardless of the possible consequences, the director of the Secret Service resolved not to share this information with another soul. He did not share it with the White House, with President Clinton, with his fellow agents, or with anyone else. Instead, Lew Merletti returned to Washington, wondering what this high-level FBI official knew, and what kind of trap Louis Freeh's unfriendly lieutenants might be trying to set.

CHAPTER

42

—————

THE DRUDGE REVOLUTION

On the last day of July, Paula Jones appealed Judge Susan Webber Wright's summary judgment order, asking a federal appeals court to reverse the Arkansas judge and to permit Jones to get in front of a jury of her peers. To further strengthen Starr's hand, the U.S. Court of Appeals in Washington granted OIC a reprieve on the "leaks" issue, adopting OIC's position that the independent council's office should be allowed to prove that it had acted "in full compliance with the rule of law," before David Kendall could take Starr's deposition or sift through OIC's documents.

As both sides awaited the grand jury testimony of Monica Lewinsky and President Bill Clinton, the whole world seemed to have its eyes glued to the Clinton-Starr showdown. The story had turned into a form of twenty-four-hour news that had merged with high-tech drama to produce an unprecedented form of titillating entertainment. It was as if American journalism had slipped into a new groove, rivaling even the era of yellow journalism in the late 1800s, when the invention of photography and mass-circulation newspapers had turned the press into an implement of scandalmongering. Throughout the summer of 1998, the advent of Internet news and round-the-clock cable television had caused many time-honored journalistic standards to be tossed out the window in the scramble for viewers and Web site hits. The thirst for coverage kept stories coming. By August, the result was near journalistic hysteria.

Stories concerning the infamous blue dress, which had first appeared in the Drudge Report in late January, had turned into a search for the unholy Grail. *Time* magazine ran an article headlined "The Press and the Dress: The Anatomy of a Salacious Leak, . . ." noting that the story about the blue dress "chang[es] slightly each time it is repeated." By August, even after the FBI had the dress in its custody, television host Geraldo Rivera had declared indignantly to a national audience, "There is, ladies and gentlemen, absolutely no possibility that a so-called semen stained dress exists."

Stories had also bounced around the media and the Internet concerning the so-called Talking Points that Monica Lewinsky had given to Linda Tripp. Many of these accounts asserted that presidential assistant Bruce Lindsey or President Clinton himself probably had written the Talking Points; some called this document the "smoking gun" for Starr's prosecutors. Chris Matthews declared on CNBC, "If the President gave her [Lewinsky] the Talking Points, she can't give him away without bringing down this administration." Matthews congratulated Starr, noting, "If every prosecutor in this country were as tough as Ken Starr, the streets would be swept of criminals right now."

New rumors about Secret Service agents witnessing the president and Monica Lewinsky in "compromising positions" proliferated like frisky gerbils, even as agents denied such accounts in sworn testimony before the grand jury. One story that gained traction was that a White House steward, Bayani Nelvis, had told Secret Service Agent Gary Byrne that he "found lipstick-stained towels in the Oval Office study after a Clinton-Lewinsky meeting." Agent Byrne denied the account; Nelvis himself appeared before the grand jury, calling the story about Monica's lipstick utter nonsense. When questioned persistently by OIC prosecutor Sol Wisenberg, who cited a tabloid publication as his source, the steward declared under oath: "There's nothing true in that magazine."

There were even stories bouncing around the Internet and cable news shows intimating that "four other interns" besides Monica had been sexually "servicing" Clinton. In August, *Fox News* reported that the Beltway was abuzz with a story that "there's a second intern who was sexually involved with the President." The *Fox* report added provocatively, "If there is, that will certainly be dynamite." In no time, Internet news king Matt Drudge had proclaimed that "there is talk all over this town another White House staffer is going to come out from behind the curtains . . . there are hundreds, hundreds, according to Miss Lewinsky."

A study conducted by a group of prominent journalists, looking back on this train wreck, concluded that the media repeatedly "got ahead of the facts in its basic reporting."

For veteran journalists who had grown up in an era when accuracy was paramount and facts had to be scrupulously double-checked before stories went to print, the new world ushered in by the Clinton-Starr reporting frenzy was unlike anything in history. Walter Cronkite, the retired anchor of *CBS Evening News* who had spent six decades in the business, felt that many rules of professionalism were being tossed out overnight as journalists scrambled to cover the Clinton scandal. Cronkite had grown up in Missouri and Texas, working his way up from copy boy to reporter to radio sports announcer to war correspondent for the United Press syndicate during World War II. As anchor for *CBS Evening News*, he had covered the U.S. space program, President Kennedy's assassination, the Vietnam War, the Watergate scandal, and news around the world. His rock-solid reporting had earned him the title "the most trusted man in America."

The dapper, mustachioed Cronkite—by this time doing work as a commentator and film producer—watched the Clinton saga unfold with bedevilment. He did not dispute that the Lewinsky story was fair game for coverage. "This is the president of the United States involved," Cronkite acknowledged. "And therefore, the people are entitled to know peccadilloes that might have influenced the course of affairs" since these might be relevant as to "whether the president was trustworthy or not in other matters."

Yet, as he followed the Clinton-Starr media frenzy from his summer home on Martha's Vineyard, Cronkite detected something he had never seen in journalism before. "Far too much material was being leaked from the grand jury," he said, "which kept the story, of course, very much alive." The introduction of Internet news sources, fax machines, e-mails, and round-the-clock cable coverage had oversaturated the market. Moreover, the rush by journalists to post stories led to sloppy reporting. "Simply the volume of material being put out by the cable news, twenty-four-hour news organizations, and the Internet helped feed the frenzy," Cronkite explained.

Back when Cronkite had cut his teeth in the business, under mentors like the legendary editor Gordon Kent Shearer and the famed broadcaster Edward R. Murrow, there was a journalistic credo: "Get it first, but get it right." Now, a free-for-all in media coverage had been unleashed, composed of hundreds of cable news programs that required constant feeding and Internet gossip columnists like Matt Drudge, who trolled day and night looking for rumors and news tips that could be dumped onto the World Wide Web in raw, uncut form. The obsession with publishing stories "first" had led to the disembowelment of once-sacred journalistic tenets, in Cronkite's view.

This was particularly ironic, he said, because the need to be first had become dramatically *less* important with the advent of new technology. "The rush to print was essential in the days when street sales were critical to the circulation of newspapers," explained the veteran journalist. Cronkite began his career in the 1930s when television was nonexistent and newspaper boys still hawked papers on street corners. "And you could sell thousands of extra papers if your boys were on the street first with that big headline. So the rush to print was important." By the end of the twentieth century, street sales were largely irrelevant in most locations in America. Yet journalists and broadcasters were still obsessed with "you've got to be first!" As Cronkite saw it, the result was ruinous for the profession. "Nobody's going to remember who was first by a few minutes," he said, reflecting on this unpleasant saga before his death in 2009. "The minute you broadcast the story, the other [networks and papers] are going to pick it up and swipe it, anyway. So it has become meaningless. And I think all journalism could slow down and think things through before rushing to print or to broadcast."

Instead, responding to the public fascination with the Lewinsky story during the summer of 1998, the media had turned up its jets. Cronkite would later say, shaking his head, "That story could have been broadcast *without* the details that would have awakened the curiosity of every five-year-old."

Part of the willingness of journalists to go out on such a big limb on the Lewinsky matter, Cronkite believed, related to the fact that many of the editors and publishers who were calling the shots relating to this story had cut their teeth during Watergate. Tenacious investigative reporters like Bob Woodward and Carl Bernstein had been their heroes. Now, here was a chance for a new generation of editors and writers to help deliver a story that, like Watergate, might change the course of American history. The result, Cronkite feared, was the proliferation of "lazy journalism."

Yet the king of the Internet gossip web, Matt Drudge, viewed this transformation in a far more positive light; he saw it as a shining moment for a new brand of reporting. The quirky and semireclusive thirty-one-year-old publisher of the Drudge Report had beaten *Newsweek* to its own scoop relating to the Lewinsky story, yet he drove a cheap Metro Geo and lived in a $600-a-month apartment in Hollywood with a six-toed cat as his roommate. Drudge's Internet "news site" had soared from attracting a hundred stray readers to six million visitors per month during that wild summer of 1998. The Lewinsky scoop had made him internationally famous. Many conservatives, especially, flocked to Drudge's easy-to-navigate site believing that the national print media could not be trusted to cover the Clinton scandal fairly. Now, as the world awaited a conclusion to his astounding story, Drudge rode that crest of celebrity to deliver a keynote speech at the National Press Club, where Doug Harbrecht, president of that institution and an editor at *BusinessWeek*, observed in introducing the Internet gossip king: "Like a channel catfish, he mucks through the hoaxes, conspiracies and half-truths posted on-line in pursuit of fodder for his website."

With the Lewinsky thriller in full bloom, Drudge now stood before the crowd of Washington writers, declaring that journalism was undergoing a metamorphosis and that he was proud to be in the middle of it. The public maintained a "hunger for unedited information," he told the group. "We have entered an era vibrating with the din of small voices. Every citizen can be a reporter. The Net gives as much voice to a . . . computer geek like me as to a CEO or speaker of the House. We all become equal."

The self-made gossip hound, who referred to himself as a "modern-day Walter Winchell," had skipped college and worked in a CBS gift shop before launching the Drudge Report in 1995. A skeptic and cynic who thrived on exposing contradictions and hypocrisies, Drudge saw a brave new world in gestation. "Now, with a modem, anyone can follow the world and report on the world—no middle man, no big brother," proclaimed Drudge.

He reveled in the fact that the biggest story of the century, involving the president of the United States and an "obscure intern," had been *his* story, exclusively, for four days. "Everyone was afraid of it . . . and then everyone jumped on it."

Rather than viewing the dissemination of raw information in the Lewinsky saga as a negative, Drudge saw it as a high point in an ongoing revolution. "The Internet is going to save the news business," predicted Drudge. "I envision a future where there'll be 300 million reporters, where anyone from anywhere can report for any reason. It's freedom of participation absolutely realized."

The Internet had allowed an ordinary person like him—a person equipped with nothing more than a local phone connection—to catch a mendacious president in the act. It allowed everyday citizens sitting at PCs in their homes to help reshape America, for the better. Said Drudge, before stepping down from the Press Club microphone to return to his apartment, where he would troll for new scandals and sensationalistic stories, "Let the future begin!"

———

WITHOUT the Internet, it is doubtful that the Clinton-Lewinsky scandal would have launched itself in the national media and seized the public's attention. Plato Cacheris was receiving so many letters and e-mails addressed to Monica Lewinsky that he bundled them up and dumped them in boxes so that his client would not read them. Some messages were supportive, yet many were downright disturbing. Cacheris was especially shocked that individuals could sit at their computer keyboards and type out obscene messages to a twentysomething young woman whose world had just collapsed. "I didn't think it was necessary for her to receive these messages," Cacheris said in a stern monotone. One relatively mild posting on Lewinsky's "Fan Club" Web site ranted: "Monica is nothing but a 2 bit BIMBO. . . . Anyone who puts a valentine message in a news paper [sic] on her own free will for a married man has got tom [sic] be a sicko stalking bimbo. That's Monica, her and her mother belong together, like 2 peas in a pod."

On the "Hillary Rodham Clinton Defense Forum" Web site, commentators blustered and offered prophecies about the likely ending to this sordid drama.

John Potts wrote from an unidentified location to Mrs. Clinton: "I am amazed that you are still with Bill. He has rubbed your face in the dirt and all you do is smile. . . . Well Little Lady, you are getting exactly as you deserve. Have a great time at the impeachment."

Another unnamed author posted a message on the Web, declaring that Hillary and Bill "are the most corrupt couple ever to hold power in our nation's history." The writer predicted ominously: "Impeachment is right around the corner."

CHAPTER

43

A WALK IN THE WOODS

As Monica Lewinsky suffered the mortification of being "debriefed" by OIC prosecutors before her date with the grand jury, she found herself eating peanut M&M's and feeling stressed out. It was a period of growing apprehension. Her greatest fear, as she recalled, was that "I would misstep and I would lose my immunity. And then I would be extra screwed. Because I had given them this information, so they could then use it against me." Monica understood—in theory—that providing truthful testimony to the grand jury would be her ticket to freedom. Still, from her candid perspective, "nothing else in the process had been fair."

Mike Emmick, the man who had coordinated the "sting" at the Ritz-Carlton, was the lead questioner at the grand jury. Karen Immergut, one of the few women on the OIC team, was selected to handle the more personal aspects of the sessions. The Starr lawyers sought to convey a tone of reasonable accommodation, as a panel of twenty-three men and women of mixed racial and ethnic backgrounds, designated Grand Jury 97-2, assembled in the federal courthouse on Constitution Avenue.

Each grand juror was handed a copy of the same typed definition of *sexual relations* that had been used in the *Paula Jones* deposition. Karen Immergut quickly got to the nitty-gritty. "When you described that you had other physical intimacy during your contact with the President on November 15, 1995," she asked Lewinsky, "did that include sexual relations within the definition that I've just read to you?"

"Yes, it does," Monica replied. Within minutes, the witness had just confirmed that as she interpreted it, the president of the United States had lied under oath.

OIC proceeded to coax out of Lewinsky the most complete picture she would ever share about her relationship with Bill Clinton. The former intern told the grand jurors of numerous gifts she had given to, and received from, Bill Clinton. Some of these (a "wooden frog letter opener," an "antique paperweight," a book of Jewish jokes titled *Oy Vey*, a "standing cigar holder"), the president had displayed openly in the White House. Monica recounted that in December, after she was subpoenaed as a witness in the *Jones* case, she suggested to the president that maybe she should "put the gifts [from him] away outside my house somewhere or give them to someone, maybe Betty." Shortly after that, Betty Currie had stopped by the Watergate apartment to pick up a Gap box into which Monica had stashed many of her treasures from Clinton. Monica had scribbled "do not throw away" on the box, as a reminder that these were special keepsakes. Mike Emmick interjected: "Is there any other way Betty would have known to call and pick up this box of gifts except for the President asking her to?"

Monica replied that she could think of no other explanation.

As the grand jurors sat in rapt attention, Monica recounted the full story of the infamous blue dress, emphasizing [contrary to grotesque press accounts] that she had never kept it as a "souvenir." Rather, the dress had remained on a heap in her closet because, like many other young women, she was a bit sloppy. "I gained weight so I couldn't wear the dress and it didn't fit," she told the jurors with evident embarrassment. "And I'm not a very organized person. I don't clean my clothes until I'm going to wear them again." Monica had noticed the splotches on the material when she had pulled the dress out of the closet to wear it for a family gathering at Thanksgiving. She had looked at the front and said, "Oh, no"—she recognized that she had worn this dress during her last romantic encounter with the president, one of only two times Clinton had engaged in oral sex "to completion." On that occasion, Monica had insisted that the president continue to a climax, despite his protestations that he "didn't want to get addicted to me and he didn't want me to get addicted to him." After Clinton ejaculated, a tender moment had followed—he embraced Monica, leaving two tiny spots on the intern's dress: one in the lower hip area and one in the chest area. When she later showed the dress to Linda Tripp, Monica had joked about the splotches as a "funny, gross thing." Tripp had become dead serious and insisted that Monica not wear the garment or clean it. The older woman had promised to bring her friend an outfit from her own closet to replace it, so she did not wash away any evidence. So Monica had left the dress on the floor. Explained the witness: "And so it wasn't a souvenir. I was going to clean it. I was going to wear it again."

The questioning became more graphic when prosecutor Immergut prodded the witness to admit that she and the president had engaged in "brief direct genital contact at least once." As Immergut pressed for more details, Monica stopped in midsentence and told the grand jurors, "Oh, my gosh. This is so embarrassing."

One juror interjected, trying to be helpful, "You could close your eyes and talk." Another juror, expressing sympathy for the young woman's plight, added, "We won't look at you." Monica asked the grand jurors: "Can I hide under the table?"

Next, the Starr prosecutors extracted a direct admission from the witness that her sworn affidavit in the *Paula Jones* case was false. There was never any question in her mind, Monica told the grand jurors bluntly, that she and President Clinton planned to deny the affair. Frankly, she didn't think it was "anybody's business." Monica's principal worry when she had seen her name on the witness list for the *Jones* case wasn't that she would have to deny the affair—that had always been expected. She was more concerned that there were ten *other* women on the list. She immediately had confronted the president about these names, and Clinton reassured her that there was nothing to fret about—they were "all women from the old days in Arkansas." That had been a relief. There was no further discussion about her being called as a witness in the *Jones* case. There had been no great conspiracy between her and the president to lie, Monica told the grand jurors. She had simply followed the plan that was established from the first day they had engaged in sexual foreplay outside the Oval Office.

The OIC prosecutors next pounced on a question that was generating oodles of speculation in the media: Was President Clinton wearing ties from Monica as a "signal" to her, in recent weeks, to telegraph some message in secret code? The witness sat back with a shrug and acknowledged that ties had always held a special significance for her. She had worked in a men's necktie store in Southern California before moving to Washington. For Monica, picking out ties was like selecting colorful greeting cards. She had given at least six ties to the president as gifts. "I used to bug him about wearing one of my ties," she told the grand jurors, "because then I knew I was close to his heart."

So it couldn't have been a coincidence that Clinton recently had appeared on the television news wearing these special ties, Monica concurred. Yet she was not prepared to say that the president had worn them "to tug on my emotional strings" or to sway her testimony. Rather, the ties seemed to be incorporated in Clinton's wardrobe—for instance, on the day after her first appearance in the grand jury—to communicate, "Hey, you had to do what you had to do." For Monica, it was simply a symbol of an emotional bond.

The more time Monica spent baring her soul, the more the grand jurors opened up and began asking questions of their own. One juror asked directly why the former intern had persisted in this dead-end relationship.

WITNESS: I fell in love. . . .

JUROR: When you look at it now, was it love or a sexual obsession?

WITNESS: More love with a little bit of obsession. But definitely love.

JUROR: Did you think that the President was in love with you also?

WITNESS: There was an occasion when I left the White House [that] I did think that. . . .

Monica confessed that she was aware that Bill and Hillary Clinton were experiencing complications with their marriage. Clearly, "something was not right." This gave her hope that there might be a future for her with the president. The grand juror kept pressing, trying to figure out what made this attractive but obviously confused young woman tick:

JUROR: You said the relationship was more than oral sex. I mean, it wasn't like you went out on dates or anything like that like normal people, so what more was it?

WITNESS: Oh, we spent hours on the phone talking. It was emotional. . . . I thought he [Clinton] had a beautiful soul. I just thought he was just this incredible person and when I looked at him I saw a little boy and . . .

The grand juror expressed bafflement, countering: "The only part I know is that he was a married man with a wife and a family." Monica, who had been seduced into an affair with a married man (a former drama teacher named Andy Bleiler) during high school, took a sip of water and blurted out, "Obviously there's . . . there's work that I need to do on myself . . . you know, a single young woman doesn't have an affair with a married man because she's normal, quote-unquote." She took a breath and forged ahead: "But I think most people have issues and that's just how mine manifested themselves. It's something I need to work on and I don't think it's right. . . . I never expected to fall in love with the President. I was surprised that I did. My intention had really been to come to Washington and start over and I didn't want to have another affair with a married man because it was really painful. It was horrible. And I feel even worse about it now."

A second grand juror jumped in to throw Monica a lifeline: "I want to let you know that we're not here to judge you in any way, I think many of us feel that way."

Now, in a surprise twist, several grand jurors insisted that Monica tell them about the day OIC had confronted her at the Ritz-Carlton. Prosecutor Mike Emmick immediately tried to steer the inquiry away from that topic, interjecting, "This was a long day. There were a lot of things that—" Yet the grand jurors directed Monica to continue. They also asked Emmick and his team to excuse themselves so that Monica could speak freely—not exactly what OIC had bargained for. The grand jurors, it turned out, had their own questions about Lewinsky's treatment on that night:

JUROR: During this time in the hotel with them, did you feel threatened?
WITNESS: Yes.
JUROR: Did you feel that they had set a trap?
WITNESS: I didn't understand why they had to trap me into coming there, why they had to trick me into coming there. I mean, this had all been a set-up and—I mean, that was just so frightening. It was so incredibly frightening.

Toward the end of the session, as Monica was nearing an emotional breakdown, the jurors rallied around her. One gave an impromptu pep talk: "Monica, none of us in this room are perfect. We all fall and we fall several times a day. The only difference between my age and when I was your age is now I get up faster."

Another juror delivered a soft pitch down the middle: "Monica, is there anything that you would like to add to your prior testimony, either today or the last time you were here, or anything that you think needs to be amplified on or clarified? I just want to give you the fullest opportunity."

Monica, her voice becoming shaky with emotion, replied, "I think because of the public nature of how this investigation has been and what the charges are, that I would just like to say that no one ever asked me to lie and I was never promised a job for my silence. And that I'm sorry. I'm really sorry for everything that's happened." She broke down sobbing. Monica took a final breath and blurted out, "And I hate Linda Tripp. . . ."

With this, multiple jurors rushed to Monica's defense, circling around the fallen witness like protective mothers.

JUROR: Right now you feel a lot of hate for Linda Tripp, but you need to move on and leave her where she is because whatever goes around comes around.
JUROR: It comes around.
JUROR: It does.
JUROR: And she is definitely going to have to give an account for what she did, so you need just to go past her . . . [because that's] going to keep you from moving on.

———

As David Kendall was busy negotiating the ground rules for the president's own grand jury testimony, President Clinton was privately meeting with top military advisers, planning a rocket strike on Afghanistan. The move was based on intelligence reports that terrorists would be gathering at a hidden camp in that mountainous country to plot their next attack.

One person who knew about the complicated world in which Bill Clinton found himself operating during that summer of 1998 was Secret Service Director Lew Merletti. He was increasingly incensed that Starr's office and the FBI were wasting manpower and resources chasing after evidence of the president's sexual misadventures when true threats to the country's well-being were darting around in shadowy corners of the United States and elsewhere around the globe. Merletti was also angry that the FBI had questioned his predecessor, Eljay Bowron, insinuating that there was some quid pro quo by which President Clinton had appointed Merletti director in return for protecting the president in the *Jones* case—an insulting notion. Although Merletti had forced Starr to apologize via the Justice Department, that didn't remove the burr from under his saddle.

Merletti was keenly aware of the growing problem of terrorists encamped in Afghanistan; he had engaged in confidential briefings with Richard Clarke, Clinton's chief counterterrorism adviser and member of the U.S. National Security Council who had served under Presidents Reagan and Bush. In February 1998, there had been another aborted plot to assassinate Clinton in Pakistan. Osama bin Laden's al-Qaeda group had hoped to carry out the plan in Islamabad, until it was thwarted by American intelligence officials, who abruptly canceled the president's trip. Bin Laden was also suspected in a plot to kill Clinton in Indonesia and in masterminding the bombings of the U.S. embassies in Kenya and Tanzania on August 7.

Now, ten days before the president's scheduled grand jury testimony, this whole scene enraged Merletti. The FBI had somehow become attached at the hip to Starr's operation, when "what they should have been investigating was terrorism." That agency's obsession with Monica Lewinsky and Paula Jones and "Jane Does" in Arkansas was "diverting us terribly," Merletti felt. To add insult to injury, Starr's office was fueling accusations that the Secret Service was covering up for Clinton in the Lewinsky matter. "I couldn't even travel internationally with the president," the Secret Service director said. Agent Larry Cockell, who headed the elite Presidential Protection Division, had gone as far as to remove himself from his duties in the White House. Now that his identity had been leaked as one of the agents Starr's office was pursuing, his face was being splashed across newspapers and television screens all over America. Cockell's job depended upon anonymity. Starr's quest to get him under oath had put him, and those he guarded, at risk.

BOB Bittman was frustrated. President Clinton seemed to be "mirroring our investigation." Clinton knew, before the next morning's breakfast, what his witnesses were saying in the grand jury. So the young OIC deputy decided to set a definite date for Clinton to appear in front of the grand jury, "earlier rather than later." The only way to corner a greased pig, the stocky deputy concluded, was to back him into the pen.

Ideally, Bittman wanted Clinton to testify for two days; yet Kendall shaved him down to four hours. The Starr deputy also capitulated by allowing the testimony to take place in the White House, with Clinton's lawyer present, rather than inside the unfriendly grand jury room—another big win for the president. The grand jurors would watch via live feed from a remote location; this was ideal for the Clinton team. Finally, Kendall convinced Bittman to withdraw the subpoena so that the president's appearance would be purely "voluntary." The White House had pressed hard for this last concession: It meant that if Clinton refused to answer any questions, Starr's prosecutors would be required to go to court for a formal subpoena, allowing the president's defenders to buy more time.

Bittman had hung tough on at least one issue—that he would be permitted to videotape the testimony. The White House feared that if it allowed Starr's rogue team to film the "voluntary" appearance by the president, the prosecutors "were going to screw us" by "giving it to Congress and releasing it." Kendall tried a dozen maneuvers to abort the videotaping, even inviting the grand jurors to come to the White House to observe the questioning in person. Yet Bittman wouldn't budge. He knew that if the grand jurors traipsed into the executive mansion, Clinton would end up giving them a tour of the White House and handing out boxes of presidential M&M's until they were thoroughly charmed. So Bittman used his only piece of leverage: One grand juror, it turned out, was unavailable on the date in question. Bittman *insisted* that Kendall permit him to preserve the testimony on film, for the benefit of that absent juror. This demand was nonnegotiable.

In this type of high-stakes negotiation, one took what one could get. Kendall surrendered.

Interviews now reveal that a number of advisers had counseled President Clinton not to appear at all. They had urged him to "take the Fifth," invoking his constitutional right against self-incrimination. The law required Starr to prove his case. If Monica Lewinsky's blue dress had no DNA matter on it, they argued, OIC would be up the creek without a paddle.

One plan was for Clinton to "reluctantly" invoke the Fifth Amendment and then lay the blame at the feet of his attorneys by saying, "I have no choice but to follow the advice of my lawyers." Clinton would take a beating in the media for a few weeks, but the American public would gradually grow weary of the tussle and it would blow over.

As a legal matter, this was a sensible plan. As a practical matter, however, Clinton's political advisers told him that it was like placing a loaded gun to his head. Invoking the Fifth Amendment sounded like admitting guilt, which seemed like a perfect recipe for impeachment and removal.

Ultimately, David Kendall's team counseled the president that if he was determined to go to the grand jury, he needed to run out the clock. A neophyte like Bob Bittman, the lawyers argued, would grossly underestimate Bill Clinton's prowess as a world-class witness. Answering questions for four hours was a piece of cake for a nimble politician like Clinton. He could talk his way out of a tied rucksack in that short time. A group of ten of Ken Starr's prosecutors was no match for a star orator like Bill Clinton.

In the end, the president accepted this advice; he also rejected the Fifth Amendment approach. Appearing in the grand jury and running out the clock provided the greatest odds of survival. To implement this bold plan on behalf of their client, Clinton's legal team crafted twelve or fourteen "blocks of testimony" or "set pieces" that the president could roll out in response to questions, allowing him to talk away long stretches of time. Clinton was primed to begin each answer with "Well, let me think," or "Please don't interrupt me," or "Can't you let me answer it fully?" The White House team knew that OIC would be bending over backward to appear respectful. So the president's job was to "roll over their questions, like a steam-roller."

One of the greatest concerns of the White House lawyers was that they had not yet heard the Linda Tripp tapes; the team had nothing but thirdhand knowledge of what was on them. To compensate for this handicap, the president's lawyers created their own mock tapes. On these tapes, they pretended that Tripp was saying various "outrageous things," and then played them for Clinton to get him to "react." The president would get agitated and say, "What—she's saying *that*?" The team would have to calm him down, reminding the president "that these were exaggerations." By going through these practice drills, which provoked Clinton and caused his blood to boil, the president was prepared to deal with "some rather extreme situations."

Clinton's friend Harry Thomason—an award-winning Hollywood producer—also contributed his expertise by advising the White House lawyers to conduct the filming so that Clinton's face dominated the screen. None of the Starr prosecutors, he said, should appear on the live feed at all. The viewers would see the president at all times and be forced to "imagine" his disembodied interrogators as if they were invisible gremlins. "We wanted nobody else but Clinton on that film," one presidential counselor would later divulge. Yet these plans, like all preparations involving grand jury testimony, were kept strictly secret so that they could be sprung on OIC as a fait accompli at the final hour.

Starr's prosecutors, in the meantime, were holding their own secretive "moot court" sessions, prepping for their date with destiny. Hickman Ewing, Jr., feeling lonesome in Arkansas now that Whitewater had dried up, flew to Washington to play the role of Bill Clinton for OIC's practice sessions. By all accounts, Ewing turned in a masterful performance. Adopting a perfect Southern accent and "aw shucks" charm, he danced around his colleagues' questions and tied them in knots, giving them a taste of what to expect with a pro like "the Comeback Kid." Already, the *New York Times* and *Washington Post* were reporting that Clinton might walk into the grand jury session and confess to some minor sexual indiscretion, while denying perjury in the *Jones* deposition.

OIC struggled to agree on a master strategy. Bittman's overall philosophy, in sync with that of Starr, was, "We should treat [Clinton] with dignity and let him tell his story." For one, he was president of the United States. Besides, "no matter what he said, it was going to be helpful to us."

Yet within the hard-line OIC faction there were rumblings that Bill Clinton needed to be handled much more like a recidivist felon. Ewing, during the moot court sessions, had pulled a few maneuvers as Clinton's stand-in, admitting "petting" but "no perjury," or confessing to some "physical relationship" with Lewinsky but refusing to give details. These "partial admissions" were tough to handle. A number of OIC prosecutors believed the only antidote to such slick maneuvers was to "pop Clinton in the nose" immediately, by confronting him with his lies: Why had he said he was never alone with Monica Lewinsky except when she was delivering pizza? Wasn't this patently false? Why had the president called Betty Currie into his office, immediately after his *Paula Jones* testimony, and recited out loud to Currie that she could "see and hear everything" during his meetings with Lewinsky? Wasn't this designed to taint Currie's testimony and to make her lie? Didn't this also constitute proof that Clinton possessed a guilty mind and wrongful intent when he coached Betty Currie, hoping to create a sham witness to buttress his false story? The hard-liners believed that if they hit Clinton between the eyes early on, no matter how "Slick Willie" answered, he would dig himself into a deeper hole.

But the less experienced Bittman continued to express trepidation about going down that path. As one OIC lawyer later confessed, "Bob did not want to cross him. He just kept saying, 'We don't need to do that.' . . . He was petrified by the idea of handling this as a cross." Most of Bittman's experience as a state prosecutor had been in "dope cases and sex cases." This sort of complex cross-examination involving slippery topics and a world-class witness seemed to be outside his comfort zone.

OIC files now reveal that prosecutor Brett Kavanaugh, who had clerked for Supreme Court Justice Anthony Kennedy and was considered one of Starr's intellectual heavy-lifters, pushed hardest to confront Clinton with some of the dirtiest facts linked to his sexual indiscretions with Lewinsky. In a memo to "Judge Starr" (with a copy to "All Attorneys"), dated just two days before the grand jury showdown, Kavanaugh disclosed a stark division within OIC over how to handle this slippery president. He wrote:

> After reflecting this evening, I am strongly opposed to giving the President any "break" . . . unless before his questioning on Monday, he either i) resigns or ii) confesses perjury and issues a public apology to you. I have tried hard to bend over backwards and to be fair to him. . . . In the end, I am convinced that there really are [no reasonable defenses]. The idea of going easy on him at the questioning is thus abhorrent to me. . . .
>
> [T]he President has disgraced his Office, the legal system, and the American people by having sex with a 22-year-old intern and turning her life into a shambles—callous and disgusting behavior that has somehow gotten lost in the shuffle. He has committed perjury (at least) in the Jones case. . . . He has tried to disgrace [Ken Starr] and this Office with a sustained propaganda campaign that would make Nixon blush.

So Kavanaugh listed ten sample questions, however explicit and unsavory, that he believed Starr and his questioners should ask. They included the following:

> *If Monica Lewinsky says that you ejaculated into her mouth on two occasions in the Oval Office area, would she be lying?*
>
> *If Monica Lewinsky says that on several occasions you had her give [you] oral sex, made her stop, and then ejaculated into the sink in the bathroom off the Oval Office, would she be lying?*
>
> *If Monica Lewinsky says that you masturbated into a trashcan in your secretary's office, would she [be] lying?*

The tension within OIC was only growing thicker as the clock ticked away. Bittman had insisted that they take Clinton to the grand jury immediately—rather than waiting until September, as the White House had repeatedly requested. Now, Bittman's own team members whispered that they may have given themselves insufficient time to prepare.

To add to the pressure-cooker environment, the results of the DNA tests came back just one day before Clinton was scheduled to testify. The FBI now confirmed that the DNA on the dress matched that of President Bill Clinton, with the chance of error being only one in 7.8 trillion.

As the team of Starr prosecutors climbed into their dark sedans accompanied by a detail of U.S. Marshals, setting off for the White House at 12:15 P.M. on August 17 to elicit the sworn testimony of President Bill Clinton, Ken Starr tried to remain calm and reflective. To his prosecutors, he quoted a passage from the King James version of the Bible as a reminder that they should stay focused on their responsibilities and duties, rather than fret about matters beyond their control. "Sufficient unto the day," Starr recited, "is the evil thereof."

———

TOP military and national security advisers were competing with President Clinton's lawyers and political advisers for his time, huddling in West Wing conference rooms to address the worsening situation in Afghanistan, in the wake of deadly American embassy bombings in Tanzania and Kenya. Osama bin Laden, who was taking credit for those attacks, was only part of their problem. The White House staff was equally skittish about the president's raising his right hand, with Ken Starr in the room, and testifying under oath. "One was we don't know what the real facts were," said one adviser. "And two, we thought there was probably more going on there [with Monica Lewinsky] than what [the president] had indicated."

David Kendall was in an especially awkward position. As a lawyer, he represented both Bill and Hillary Clinton in a personal capacity. He was duty-bound to use his professional skills for both husband and wife with equal vigor. It was conceivable that the couple could split as a result of this trauma to their marriage. He could not allow *either* client to be hurt under his watch.

So Kendall enlisted his law partner Bob Barnett, who had handled business matters for the Clintons, to prepare Hillary for the bad news on the Friday before the testimony: "What if there's more to this than you know?" Barnett had asked gently. The next morning, with nowhere left to hide, Bill Clinton woke up his wife and—pacing back and forth beside their bed in the family quarters of the White House—confessed that "the situation was much more serious" than he had admitted previously. When he appeared before the grand jury, he intended to testify "that there had been an inappropriate intimacy." According to Hillary Clinton's later account, she could "hardly breathe." She began crying and yelling, "What do you mean? What are you saying? Why did you lie to me?"

The only thing that Bill Clinton, penitent husband, could keep repeating, like a mortal sinner who had finally been caught and now begged for absolution, was, "I'm sorry. I'm so sorry. I was trying to protect you and Chelsea." Hillary Clinton would later describe her emotional turmoil: "I was dumbfounded, heartbroken and outraged."

Despite rampant speculation in the press that the First Lady must have known about, and condoned, Bill's sexual flings with Monica Lewinsky and others, there is no direct evidence to support this theory. One close friend of the Clintons would later say that it was "absolutely, unequivocally" true that Hillary did not know of her husband's sexual affair with Lewinsky until the weekend before the grand jury testimony. The First Lady certainly knew that "there was an intern who was smitten by the president," and that her roving-eyed husband "may have indulged" this young woman by flirting inappropriately. Yet Bill Clinton was famous for putting his arm around women and exuding a warmth that "gets misread by people." It was potentially harmless.

Still, nobody was suggesting that Bill Clinton was an altar boy. One high-level adviser who asked not to be identified recalled riding with both Clintons in the presidential limousine during an official trip, and Bill "ogling" a busty young woman in her early thirties who was standing on the sidewalk. Hillary observed her husband's line of vision and interrupted: "Oh, Bill, you always liked those trashy types." Stated the observer: "He luxuriated in women. Hillary probably knew in her heart of hearts (at least during certain periods of their marriage) that on occasion he had an affair or a quickie."

Those closest to the Clintons, however, felt certain that the First Lady did not believe that her husband's relationship with this young intern had escalated into a full-scale sexual dalliance under the roof of the White House. Hillary had come to believe—whether rationally or not—that Bill's major lapses were a thing of the past. "I don't think she knew," said one adviser. Another observer added, "Hillary didn't want to know."

As rocky and volatile as the Clintons' marriage had been over the years, the people surrounding the First Couple perceived that Bill and Hillary had become closer, rather than more distant, in the years since the Gennifer Flowers revelation had almost blown their marriage apart during the first campaign. Going back to the early political days in Arkansas, there had been "rumors about hundreds of women." Like a Hollywood celebrity wife who was regularly confronted with sensational headlines about her spouse in tabloid magazines at the supermarket checkout counter, Hillary "was dealing with rumors all the time." Friends of Hillary would insist that she had assumed—after moving into the "fishbowl" of the White House, where Bill's movements were under constant scrutiny—that her husband had reformed himself, in part out of necessity.

Even Betsey Wright, who had managed the "bimbo eruptions" during the 1992 campaign and knew some of Bill Clinton's darkest secrets, concurred that Hillary never in a million years would have countenanced this extramarital fling. "Well, there was no agreement," Wright said in assessing the situation. "There was a constant forgiveness." As Wright saw the pattern repeat itself, Hillary "loved him very, very deeply." Bill was "constantly wanting another chance and really believing that he would never do it again." And Hillary, for better or worse, was "giving him that chance." Wright added, "I mean, they both believed that they were better people with each other."

This time, Bill's straying from his marital vows was especially painful for Hillary. The "feeling of betrayal" was combined with the shock and ignominy of "how public it all was."

OIC's blue Crown Victoria and two vans pulled up at the White House gate. On the sidewalk, tourists had gathered, hoping to catch a glimpse of history in the making. Some held pictures of Monica Lewinsky lashed to sticks. Others waved signs attacking Starr. Vendors sold Clinton memorabilia, including large blue T-shirts with splotches on them, parodying the infamous blue dress. Ken Starr and his prosecutors climbed out of their vehicles and blinked as two dozen pocket-sized cameras flashed. On this day, the independent counsel appeared unusually grim. With swift steps, Secret Service agents ushered the OIC team through the diplomatic entrance into the Red Room, where the prosecutors sat in chairs, waiting.

This day, Monday, August 17, also happened to be Ken Starr's mother's ninety-first birthday. Vannie Starr had been sick recently; Alice Starr and the girls had flown to Texas that weekend to be with the family matriarch. As he situated himself in the Red Room and took a sip of tepid water to wet his lips, the independent counsel was hoping that things might wrap up quickly so that he could catch a plane to Houston that night. It was an unfortunate fact of life, Starr thought to himself, that the happiest occasions were marred with such unpleasant duties.

On the opposite side of the West Wing, a group of the president's political advisers began sprinting down the hallway in a state of panic. The small electronic device that identified where the First Family was at all times, within the White House, indicated that "President" was in the "Medical Unit." In two minutes, the advisers had raced to the nurses' station. Here, they found President Clinton huddled with David Kendall, talking strategy one last time, a grave look on his face, as if understanding that this was the most important legal proceeding in his life. Clinton and Kendall had simply wandered into the Medical Unit because it was the closest available space to speak in absolute privacy. The political advisers smiled weakly; they apologized and walked out—at least the president hadn't fallen dead of a heart attack.

Kendall, before escorting his client to this unprecedented grand jury appearance, strode down to the Red Room, where Ken Starr and his team were waiting. Short, compact, and exuding energy that nearly crackled with intensity, the president's lawyer walked up to Starr and looked him in the eye. Kendall asked if the independent counsel would take a stroll with him—it was time to discuss a few matters. Together, the two men walked down the hall into the library, where they sat in chairs that seemed uncomfortably close.

Kendall had planned this "walk in the woods" for days. He leaned close to Starr and said in a serious tone, "You know all those nice things I was quoted saying about you in the *Washington Post* yesterday?" referring to a piece suggesting that the two opposing lawyers had much in common. "I didn't say them," Kendall stated. "I didn't think you did," Starr replied with an awkward laugh.

According to Starr's recollection of this encounter, Kendall continued: "I want to tell you what we're going to do. I don't want there to be surprises. The president is going to acknowledge an improper relationship with Ms. Lewinsky. He will give you what you need. But I am very concerned about the dignity of the president and the presidency and the privacy of these matters to the family. He [the president] will have an opening statement, comment to make. He has it prepared, and he will read it."

Kendall obviously had planned this last-minute talk so that the special prosecutor would have virtually no time to react. Starr blinked his eyes and said, "After he reads it, I think we should take a break." Kendall replied, "Fine." He, too, was operating on little sleep and large amounts of caffeine. The president's lawyer continued, "We are going to give you what you need. We're not going to play around with words. But if you try to humiliate or embarrass him—I will fight you to the knife."

Starr was puzzled by Kendall's phrase—"fight to the knife." What did the lawyer mean by this threat? What rough-and-tumble brawl was awaiting OIC now?

In fact, Kendall would later confess that he was borrowing a line from an action movie that had been one of his favorites as a boy—*The Iron Mistress*, a 1951 film starring tough-guy Alan Ladd in which Ladd played Jim Bowie, the famed inventor of the Bowie knife. The motto of this rugged frontiersman, an idol to Midwest boys like Kendall, was, "When you lose your spare sword, you still have your knife. You fight to the last weapon." The message Kendall was trying to deliver to Starr was, "The president is making a big admission here. You are filming this session, and you had better not try to bully him like you've bullied other witnesses. If your people start getting out of hand, we will fight back to the bitter end." No judge, Kendall was prepared to wager, would force the president to answer explicit and lewd questions about sex acts after Clinton had made a confession, however generic and murky. The president's lawyers were prepared to fight to the death on this point, if necessary.

Upon returning to the Red Room, the independent counsel grimly reported the news to his prosecutorial team. The hard-liners were outraged—they wanted to "walk out" the moment the president gave his canned speech if he refused to answer their detailed questions. Bob Bittman, however, cautioned that they should not be alarmists. His vote was, "Let's see what he has to say. We have a subpoena. If he in fact refuses to testify, we can serve it and ask him more questions later." Bittman's point was, "Let's see what questions he *does* answer."

Starr stood up, smoothing the wrinkles out of his suit. Bittman's approach, he said, was most consistent with obtaining the maximum amount of information, while showing respect for the presidency. With that, Starr picked up his briefcase and followed a White House aide down the hallway.

A diagram of the Map Room contained in OIC's files would later reveal the layout of this historic proceeding: The president was seated in the front right corner at a small table. In the back of the room, there was a podium for the OIC lawyers. Beside them was an electronically operated camera. On the opposite side of the room, the official court reporter, Elizabeth A. Eastman, recorded the proceedings, tapping away on a transcribing machine.

President Clinton, dressed in a dark suit and handsome gold-black tie, did his best to assume a presidential posture as he took a seat at the witness table. Starr recalled thinking as the chief executive settled into his chair that Clinton was "physically quite large" and surprisingly "imposing."

Just as Bittman began the questioning for OIC, President Clinton took a long sip of water and then interrupted: "Mr. Bittman, I think maybe I can save you and the grand jurors a lot of time if I read a statement, which I think will make it clear what the nature of my relationship with Ms. Lewinsky was and how it related to the testimony I gave."

The president removed a single sheet of paper from his jacket pocket and smoothed it out, extracting his reading glasses and affixing them to his nose, as if every moment that ticked away on the clock was worth a shimmering gold piece. The sheet had been typed with an antiquated IBM Selectric typewriter that David Kendall kept in his office so that certain highly sensitive documents were kept under wraps no matter how secure the firm's computer system. Kendall could not risk that anyone other than he and Bill Clinton saw this folded sheet of paper in advance. The president commenced in a steady voice: "When I was alone with Ms. Lewinsky on certain occasions in early 1996 and once in early 1997, I engaged in conduct that was wrong. These encounters did not consist of sexual intercourse. They did not constitute 'sexual relations' as I understood that term to be defined at my January 17th, 1998 deposition. But they did involve inappropriate intimate contact."

After expressing deep regret and insisting that he took "full responsibility for my actions," the president looked deep into the camera as if searching for the eyes of each grand juror. Clinton said that he was prepared to answer questions from the Starr prosecutors. Yet, he continued in a firm voice, "Because of privacy considerations" and in an effort "to preserve the dignity of the office I hold," this written statement was "all I will say about the specifics of these particular matters."

Starr's prosecutors instantly called for a recess and halted the proceedings. They had expected some slick maneuver like this, even before Kendall's "walk in the woods." During Hickman Ewing's moot court playacting, they had referred to this as the "modified limited hangout" approach, by which Clinton would admit to oral sex with Monica, in some obtuse fashion, then declare innocently, "But I didn't think it was sex!" So Clinton's "admission was not a shock." What *was* surprising was that they had never formulated a precise plan as to how to handle it.

Wisenberg wanted to "hit [Clinton] right there with a new subpoena." Starr and Bittman vetoed that idea—as slippery and shameless as Clinton's tactic might be, it was best to give him enough rope to hang himself. They could always come back with a subpoena later, if they needed to finish him off.

Wisenberg would later lament, "I think that was a mistake."

When the OIC lawyers walked back into the Map Room and resumed their questioning, President Clinton seemed to be more in control than ever. Several blocks away in a secure room of the federal courthouse, grand jurors were watching by live video feed. Observers in the room with the grand jury noted that the Starr prosecutors' questions were barely audible. Like children trying to communicate through tin cans tied together with string, the questioners seemed to murmur and mumble off camera. Clinton's image, on the other hand, filled the screen in a commanding, presidential fashion. The White House had successfully controlled the medium of communication.

During the extraordinary four-hour session that ensued, President Bill Clinton gave a detailed account of his affair with Monica Lewinsky—the only time, for the rest of his public career, that he would speak candidly about his relationship with the former intern. Clinton admitted that he met with Lewinsky approximately fourteen times in the White House—five before she was transferred to the Pentagon and then nine or ten times thereafter. He confessed to "phone sex" banter during isolated evenings in the family quarters of the White House. He acknowledged that in December 1997, Lewinsky had arrived at the White House gate, angry after learning that Eleanor Mondale had been visiting Clinton earlier in the day. When pressed to explain how Lewinsky had learned what was going on within the top-secret confines of the Oval Office, the president replied with a nostalgic smile: "Ms. Lewinsky has a way of getting information out of people when she's either charming or determined."

The president, several times, displayed unmistakable affection for Lewinsky.

He confessed to the grand jury: "She's basically a good girl. She's a good young woman with a good heart and a good mind. I think she is burdened by some unfortunate conditions of her, her upbringing. But she's basically a good person." He added: "It breaks my heart that she was ever involved in this."

Even as he confessed his sins, Clinton artfully turned the tables. He told the grand jurors, in a spontaneous burst of candor, "Did I want this to come out? No. Was I embarrassed about this? Yes. Did I ask her [Lewinsky] to lie about it? No."

The president next turned his attention to the "strange" definition of "sexual relations" that the lawyers had handed him during the *Jones* deposition, insisting that he never intended to lie under oath, because he believed this tortured language referred (generally) to "sexual intercourse." He sought his best to dance around a slew of questions by the prosecutors: "I understood the definition to be limited to—to physical contact with those areas of the bodies with the specific intent to arouse or gratify."

President Bill Clinton was dominating the proceedings so thoroughly that the Starr prosecutors were getting exasperated. Wisenberg cursed to himself that the deputy in charge of this make-it-or-break-it proceeding, Bob Bittman, still hadn't asked any of the hard-hitting "sex" questions that they had directed him to ask. Indeed, the overall report from those OIC lawyers inside the grand jury room, when they sneaked out periodically to use a phone in the hallway, was that they were getting pummeled. It was so bad that some prosecutors watching the faces of the grand jurors communicated that "the referral is in danger," meaning that OIC might ruin its chance to send anything resembling a credible impeachment report to Congress.

With their chance to corner Clinton swirling down the drain, Wisenberg took over, throwing off the gloves. He asked the president bluntly: Would *receiving* oral sex constitute engaging in "sexual relations" under the definition he had been handed?

President Clinton replied that "if performed on the deponent," his reading was that it was not covered. "As I understood it, it was not, no."

Wisenberg pressed forward, making the president concede that if he had touched or kissed Ms. Lewinsky's breasts with the "purpose to arouse or gratify," *that* would fit the definition.

"That's correct, sir."

And "touching her genitalia" with the desire to gratify sexually would also fall within that definition.

"That's correct," said Clinton. Sensing danger from this line of questioning, the president shifted to his previous defense: "My recollection is that I did not have sexual relations with Ms. Lewinsky and I'm staying on my former statement about that," he repeated, clearing his throat.

No matter how close Clinton came to falling over the perilous cliff, he seemed to skate back from the edge. In animated fashion, the president waved his hands and implored the OIC prosecutors to listen: "Now, I'm trying to be honest with you, and it hurts me," he proclaimed, intending his speech for the grand jurors. "And I'm trying to tell you the truth about what happened between Ms. Lewinsky and me. But that does not change the fact that the real reason [the Jones lawyers] were zeroing in on [me] was to . . . hurt me politically."

It was perhaps the most genuine explanation the president would ever give of his untruthful answers in the *Jones* deposition. As Paul Rosenzweig said later, "I mean, a lot of what he said was true. His anger. The fact that he thought he was being 'set up' probably. He felt like he was entitled to lie." Unfortunately, from the perspective of Rosenzweig and his law enforcement colleagues, President Clinton had forgotten what it meant to take an oath as a citizen and as an officer of the court. Regardless of perceived "traps" and "trick questions," one was not permitted to slide out of political danger by uttering falsehoods under oath. Watching Clinton's face on the screen, Rosenzweig was most troubled that the president still seemed to lack remorse, except for the fact that he had been caught. Said Rosenzweig, "I mean, I saw no contrition, and I thought that was very unfortunate."

Yet Bill Clinton continued to sprint around the field in all-star form. He was now using the grand jury proceedings to clean up the record from the *Jones* deposition, reducing rather than broadening his criminal exposure. At the same time, Wisenberg was methodically scoring his own points. By delving into the nasty "sex" questions that nobody else was willing to touch, he was slowly making a case.

In fact, the president was digging himself into a hole that was not yet visible. In response to a new flurry of questions posed by the tenacious Wisenberg, Clinton repeated that touching Monica's breasts, kissing her breasts, or touching her genitalia with intent to arouse or gratify would constitute "sexual relations" under the typed definition. He then continued to deny engaging in such activity. This was particularly significant because, unbeknownst to Clinton, Monica Lewinsky had already confessed to the grand jury that the president had sexually gratified her, in that fashion, on numerous occasions.

A number of grand jurors "hooted" or guffawed when it came to some of Clinton's word dances, particularly when the president tried to get cute with the "sex" definition. When Starr's prosecutors reminded the president that his own lawyer, Bob Bennett, had assured Judge Wright during the deposition "there is absolutely no sex of any kind in any manner, shape or form," Clinton tried to pirouette around this point by taking advantage of verb tenses, stating with a straight face, "It depends on what the meaning of the word *is*, is." A number of grand jurors audibly "snorted" at this blatant use of wordplay.

But the clock was running out. Ken Starr took his turn posing several perfunctory questions, asking the president whether he had improperly invoked his "executive privilege" on certain subjects, including the Secret Service matter. As if swatting away a fly, Clinton replied that there was "an honest difference" between the White House and OIC on these issues.

Wisenberg jumped in again, trying to salvage the proceedings. After producing a photo of the president wearing a bright tie on August 6—the first day of Lewinsky's grand jury testimony—Wisenberg asked, "My question to you on that is . . . Were you sending some kind of a signal to her by wearing a tie she had given you on the day that she appeared in front of the grand jury?"

The president appeared genuinely baffled. He drawled, "No, sir. I don't believe she gave me this tie. And if I was sending a signal, I'm about to send a terrible signal, and maybe you ought to invite her to talk again. I don't want to make light about this. I don't believe she gave me this tie. . . . And I had absolutely no thought of this in my mind when I wore it. If she did, I don't remember it, and this is the very first I've ever heard of it."

In a final flurry of oratory, as the proceedings continued to deteriorate, Bill Clinton stared into the camera and spoke from the heart: "I would say to the grand jury, 'put yourself in my position.' This is not a typical grand jury testimony. . . . I'm doing my best to cooperate with the grand jury and still protect myself, my family, and my office." President Clinton emphasized that he was downright skeptical about OIC's insistence on filming these proceedings. After all, grand juries routinely functioned with grand jurors absent. As long as sixteen of the total panel of twenty-three grand jurors were present, they were permitted to conduct business. Typically, an FBI agent or a federal prosecutor simply read or orally summarized the testimony in the next session, if a juror was missing. Filming witnesses, especially potential targets, was almost unheard-of.

As each side openly accused the other of abusing the grand jury process, the clock finally ticked out. At 6:25 P.M., with both sides appearing worn out and filled with hatred, the proceedings came to an abrupt ending.

Bill Clinton's defense team, as they hustled the president out of the Map Room, felt that it had been one of his most dazzling performances. Despite the rancorous exchanges, the Starr team had barely laid a glove on him. "He bulldozed them," one adviser said later. Not only had the president rolled over the questions of the Starr prosecutors, but he had also "given a gloss to the original Paula Jones deposition testimony that would make it [even] hard[er] to prosecute." The tortured definition of "sexual relations" used in the *Jones* deposition, the Clinton team felt, had left enough room to drive a Mack truck through it. The president had taken full advantage of this opening. Already, his lawyers had been compiling a thick file containing articles affirming the view that "oral sex" did not amount to "sex" in the minds of many Americans. A 1991 Kinsey Institute Report recently republished in the *Journal of the American Medical Association* reported that nearly 60 percent of all college students surveyed indicated that they "don't consider oral sex to constitute having 'had sex.'" Some members of religious groups viewed oral sex as a form of abstinence to preserve a person's virginity. The White House team was confident that there was enough wiggle room in the "sex" definition to make it nearly impossible for OIC to prosecute on this basis. Clinton had succeeded in using his grand jury performance to "clean up" his prior testimony and to "fill in the blanks," actually strengthening his hand.

As he walked out of the room, Ken Starr felt "heartsick." He had arrived at these historic proceedings agreeing with Senator Orrin Hatch and other prominent Republicans who were admonishing President Clinton on the Sunday talk shows: "Please don't lie before the grand jury. Everything else will be forgiven." The independent counsel thought that this had been the time for "plain speaking and telling the truth." Instead, Clinton had "crossed the Rubicon," marching in the opposite direction. Yet Clinton's performance had been so brilliantly deceitful, Starr feared, that the truth might be obscured forever in the minds of the American public.

As Starr was gathering up his papers, Bill Clinton walked into the Red Room. The president's face was deeply serious. As if hesitating for a moment, he extended his hand to Independent Counsel Ken Starr. Starr's instinct was to shake it and to say something like, "I'm sorry that we're in all this." No words, however, came out of his mouth. Bill Clinton seemed to be afflicted by the same paralysis. Neither man, mortal enemies in a war bigger than themselves, was able to utter a single word. Instead they shook hands perfunctorily, turned away, and exited the room in separate directions.

Jackie Bennett, whose sole contribution was to lob out a few wrap-up questions concerning Kathleen Willey at the end of the proceeding, felt absolutely deflated. Carrying his briefcase alongside his boss, he felt as if he had just participated in "trying to nail Jell-O to the wall." As the Starr prosecutors climbed into their cars, driving around the circular driveway at the South Lawn and exiting the White House gates onto Pennsylvania Avenue, Bennett recalled staring out the window at the overcast day and feeling that there was a "pall over the [whole] city."

Back at the OIC offices, Starr's prosecutors gathered for a somber "postmortem." The general consensus was, "As a whole, it was not a winner." Those who had been in the room with the grand jury gave an especially gloomy report. As Sol Wisenberg expressed it in rather vivid terms, "We had gotten the everliving sh—— beat out of us."

Still, as the demoralized lawyers went their separate ways, Brett Kavanaugh patted Wisenberg on the back and quietly congratulated him for asking the "sex questions." Kavanaugh reassured him, "You got what you needed to get."

Starr, thoroughly exhausted, had trouble imagining what the next week would bring, or the week after that. The independent counsel was not just angry that things had gone so poorly; he was also upset because "it was my mother's ninety-first birthday. I was missing that birthday, my family was now away." What could be more distressing? His life was in shambles, thanks to a hellish sex scandal caused by a president who seemed to slide out of trouble, no matter how shameless his behavior. Starr dragged himself home to McLean, walking tiredly past his security detail and feeling an overwhelming "sense of gloom." He paced the floor of his empty house, called his ill mother in Texas for her birthday, and then collapsed into bed.

The question that kept churning over in his mind, as he fell into a troubled sleep, was, "How could a sensible and sane government come to this?"

CHAPTER

44

———

MAXIMUM PERIL

President Clinton, holed up in the White House solarium, was slashing his pen through draft after draft of proposed remarks, none of which seemed right. To defuse public speculation concerning his closed-door grand jury appearance, Clinton's White House political team had arranged for the president to address the nation at ten o'clock that same night. Despite their boss's strong showing in the Map Room, his political handlers still worried: Starr's prosecutors might deem the whole session bogus and slap a subpoena on the president the next day. Those who had been with the president knew that it had been an emotionally draining day. Now Bill Clinton appeared downright "mad." The scene in the solarium had turned into one of "chaos." Political advisers and legal counselors and Arkansas friends were all offering conflicting advice. As one observer put it, "this was like halftime at an NFL game." People were shouting that he had to "do this!" or "do that!" as the president worked himself into a royal fury.

Some urged Clinton to savage his nemesis, Kenneth Starr. Other advisers, including John Podesta, felt it was important for the message to be "conciliatory" so the White House team could "pull up our socks and move on." Clinton, in the meantime, was fuming that "no one was setting the record straight here." No one was "putting in context what this out-of-control prosecutor was doing." In the middle of this hubbub, Hillary Clinton walked briskly into the room. The First Lady looked cross-eyed at her husband and then said in a chilly voice, "Bill, it's your speech. You have to decide." She added a verbal jab: "You're the President of the United States—I guess."

As one person in the room would later sum it up, "so he went off and did it."

At precisely 10:00 P.M., seated in the same chair in the Map Room where he had been questioned for four hours by the despised Starr prosecutors, President Clinton looked into a camera and told the nation that he had engaged in a relationship with Monica Lewinsky that was "not appropriate. In fact it was wrong." Looking tired and combative, he acknowledged that he was guilty of a "critical lapse in judgment and a personal failure on my part for which I am solely and completely responsible." The president then narrowed his eyes and proceeded to lash out at the independent counsel (refusing even to utter his name), reminding viewers that the investigation had started with a bogus inquiry into the Whitewater land deal and had now spiraled into intensely private matters that had "gone on too long, cost too much and hurt too many innocent people."

With a look of a puffy-eyed pugilist having survived fifteen rounds in the ring, President Clinton declared in a challenging voice, "Even presidents have private lives. It is time to stop the pursuit of personal destruction and the prying into private lives and get on with our national life."

Clinton's speech was essentially a condensed version of his effective testimony earlier that day. Punching Ken Starr and his prosecutors in the gut during four hours of adversarial jousting had been effective enough. But lashing out at the Starr bogeymen in this different setting, during a prime-time presidential address, when the whole nation was expecting an apology, appeared petty, inappropriate, and unrepentant. Clinton had lived in the protective bubble of the White House for more than five years, addressing bigger-than-life issues and never second-guessing himself. For a tired and cranky Bill Clinton, what seemed like just another sit-down in front of a camera in a familiar room in the White House was in fact one of the biggest challenges of his political career. Millions of unseen television viewers were on the other end of this lens, watching carefully for signs of remorse and contrition. Instead, President Bill Clinton served up a giant-sized bowl of sour grapes. It was, the White House quickly realized, a bad ending to a day in which Clinton could have knocked the independent counsel out of the ring.

For most of Bill Clinton's career, the stars and moon had aligned to provide cover to the "Comeback Kid." Tonight, that magical luck had been eclipsed by rotten advice and poor judgment. One political adviser said that permitting Clinton to go in front of the cameras "was a big mistake on our part." If his aides had insisted on calling a time-out until the following day, giving Clinton a chance to rest, catch his breath, and put the events into perspective, history might have played out differently. The angry draft speeches that his political people had watered down "maybe ten percent," it was now apparent, "needed to be watered down eighty percent."

Public opinion polls fluttered and remained relatively constant, still favoring the president after his bitter admission. Yet there were ominous signs that Bill Clinton's pillars of support were beginning to crack.

Senator Dianne Feinstein, a Democrat from California who had ardently defended Clinton at a time when many women were standing on the sidelines warily, was now distancing herself from him. She stated that the president had betrayed her and dragged the whole country to this ugly place: "My trust in his credibility has been badly shattered." Even some close friends of the president were having trouble forgiving and forgetting, particularly after he had looked so many of them straight in the eye and flat-out denied the affair. Betsey Wright, Clinton's chief of staff from the governor days, felt that her former boss's admission had come a day late and a dime short. "I wished that he had tried [making an honest confession] in the beginning," she said.

Alice Starr, who watched every minute of the president's speech, remembered thinking, "'Whoa, I can't believe he's taking the attack to Ken.'" Her assessment as a citizen was, "If I were him, I would have been very deferential . . . and it would have probably slid through." Instead, she was surprised to see that "he went on the attack." This was a major miscalculation, she felt, because "it looks like you're hiding something when you do something like that."

———

WHEN the First Family left for their summer vacation the next morning, heading to Martha's Vineyard via the presidential helicopter, the mood was anything but warm and sunny.

A *Washington Post* photographer captured Bill, Hillary, and daughter Chelsea Clinton walking across the White House lawn with heads lowered, eighteen-year-old Chelsea positioned between her parents, clutching their hands as if trying to hold together a broken string of paper dolls. The president's political people had spoken to Hillary's staff, extremely gingerly, about ways to handle this situation. In the end, both groups had retreated. This was a "family matter," they whispered, that was far too hot to handle. Clinton's chocolate Labrador retriever, Buddy, which he guided forward on a leash, seemed to be the only one willing to show affection toward the president. As the First Family climbed aboard *Marine One,* the president attempted to assist his wife up the stairs; Hillary shook him off and mounted the steps alone.

Both Bill and Buddy, the media now joked, would be in the doghouse as soon as they arrived at the Massachusetts coast.

Dick Kelley, the president's stepfather from Hot Springs, had witnessed a considerable amount of sin during his eighty-three years on earth. He would later scratch his head and admit, "It was just a hard thing for me to believe, you know, that Bill Clinton would be involved in that [affair with Monica Lewinsky]." His worry was that Bill's moral lapse would drive knives into the hearts of Hillary and Chelsea and do irreparable harm. "Hillary is a great woman," said Kelley. "But I know that this hurt her very much. And Chelsea also."

Another person who was not particularly pleased with the president's performance was Monica Lewinsky, the former intern who potentially held the key to his survival. She would later say of Bill Clinton's soft-shoe, by which he tried to dance away from danger by protesting that there were no "sexual relations," because this was a one-way physical relationship: "I was very hurt. I was angry. I felt that the language he chose was so discounting of me as a person. And once again, made this seem like it was a 'servicing' relationship."

Indeed, when Lewinsky arrived at the grand jury to continue her own testimony, days later, she was no longer in a forgiving mood. Starr's office had purposely called her back, looking for "flaws" in Clinton's account. When asked by one grand juror if she still felt love for the president, Lewinsky shot back, "I don't know *how* I feel right now." She was absolutely devastated by his new defense that "all I did was perform oral sex on him and that that's all that this relationship was. And it was a lot more than that to me and I thought it was a lot more than that [to him]."

She told the grand jurors, who listened with misty eyes, that she had done everything humanly possible "not to hurt him." Now this was the thanks Clinton gave her?

The former intern began to pour out her soul, telling the grand jurors that the president's people had "trashed me . . . they have smeared me and they called me stupid, they said I couldn't write, they said I was a stalker." All she wanted Bill Clinton to say was "that I was a nice, decent person and that he was sorry this had happened."

Her lip trembling, she added, "And I'm only 24 and so I felt that . . . this had been hard for me and this had been hard on my family and I just wanted him to . . . by saying something nice, he would have taken back every disgusting, horrible thing that anyone has said about me from that White House. And that was what I wanted."

None of the women in Bill Clinton's life, past or present, was happy with how he was expressing remorse for his wretched behavior.

———

AT Martha's Vineyard, a fashionable island retreat off Cape Cod, President Clinton was staring into the dark face of the Grim Reaper of politics, a specter that foretold the death of politicians who had skated too close to the edge. At the Oyster Pond compound, a choice piece of property owned by wealthy Boston developer Dick Friedman, and with dazzling views of the Atlantic Ocean, Bill Clinton looked like a man without a place to hang his swimsuit. One observer summed up the vacation: "Hillary and Chelsea spent a lot of time together." The president, it was obvious, had not been invited to hang out with the female members of the family. This same observer noted, "I would say 'palpable tension' would be an adequate description."

As Hillary and Chelsea set up their own rooms in the main bungalow, the president was exiled to the guesthouse downhill. These simple quarters contained a living room area, a kitchenette, a TV, a computer, and several telephones. In this cottage, the president was condemned to spend most of his beach days, making calls in an effort to salvage his presidency. There was little time for sun and surf. Clinton spent his days on the phone, from morning until night. In Washington, White House advisers were "taking temperatures" on the Hill, then communicating results back to the commander in chief. The thermometer readings were extra chilly.

Clinton's political people feared several possible scenarios. First, if the public started to perceive that the scandal was affecting the president's ability to govern, people could quickly decide that he was not fit "to [stay] in office." Second, if Democrats in Congress ever chose to bolt on Clinton, he was dead in the water. One political adviser later explained, "The lesson from Watergate was—it wasn't when the Democrats wanted Nixon to leave; it's when [the Senate Republicans] told him 'it's time.' So we always saw the Democrats as our biggest vulnerability."

Senate Democratic leader Tom Daschle of South Dakota would not accept Clinton's calls from the sunny Vineyard. The president was also getting the cold shoulder from powerful Democrats like Harry Reid (Nev.), Joe Lieberman (Conn.), and Bob Graham (Fla.). In the House, Minority Leader Dick Gephardt (Mo.) had cut off communication with Clinton for days. His behavior had "personally outraged" congressional leaders; his bold-faced deception had left them speechless. All congressmen and many senators were facing reelection in the fall—back home, many of their constituents were screaming for Clinton's scalp. Not only had he engaged in immoral and incredibly stupid conduct, but there was no sign of "contrition." This put members of Congress at risk with their own political bases. So Clinton and his aides set up a phone bank in the little cottage overlooking the shimmering Atlantic, divided up the names of key Democrats in Congress, and tried to "grind it out one at a time." Over and over, Clinton offered a supersized mea culpa, allowing members of Congress to shout, swear, and otherwise "let off steam." The goal was to "at least contain them until things could settle down." The greatest fear was that "a couple breakaways could really break the dam."

In January, Bill Clinton had consulted with pollster Dick Morris, who had advised the president that if he gave a "full frontal acknowledgment" of the affair, he would be "removed from office—on the spot." At that time, a "death watch" composed of journalists and photographers had assembled at the White House gate. George Stephanopoulos, Clinton's boyish adviser turned ABC correspondent, had even uttered the "I" word, suggesting that impeachment was in the wind. Under these circumstances, Clinton had decided that he "couldn't come completely clean." Instead, he had stalled for time and made personal assurances to his staff that the Starr prosecutors had grossly exaggerated the Lewinsky indiscretion. Now it was time to pay the piper.

Top staffers like Paul Begala, who had been with Clinton since his campaign of 1992, poured out their bitter feelings to the press. Begala was a devout Catholic who deplored Clinton's extramarital shenanigans; this staffer was personally devastated that Clinton had lied to his face about the Lewinsky affair. Clinton had said, "This all is not true," but insisted that "he could not tell me any details." Begala was equally heartsick about Hillary and Chelsea. He had been present in the studio for Hillary's "vast right-wing conspiracy" interview. He recalled: "She wanted to believe him. We all did." Now Begala was openly talking about resigning.

Some top Clinton advisers felt that it might be best if they cut their losses and let people like Begala quit instead of engaging in "therapy in public." On the other hand, if a few top Cabinet members or White House aides walked out and tendered their resignations, Clinton would be toast. "If two or three senior people, particularly if there's a woman or two in there, had gone to the North Lawn and resigned," said one adviser, "I think it could have in fact brought down his presidency." To prevent his administration from unraveling altogether, Clinton began contacting lower-level staff members and "checked in to see how people were doing."

Those who observed Bill Clinton during these tough days, as he worked away shielded from the sun of Martha's Vineyard, saw him at the low point of his career. Said one: "I think he was angry. He was angry at himself, and he was angry at Starr and the whole process. I would say anger more than contrition, and I think people saw that." Another adviser added, "This was the period in which he probably was in the most danger of having the whole thing unravel."

It was in the midst of this stressful period that Bill Clinton was also forced to decide whether to bomb suspected terrorist training sites in Afghanistan and Sudan. After a low-key fifty-second birthday celebration with Vernon Jordan and family at a farm on the Vineyard where Jordan was vacationing, President Clinton returned to his bungalow and consulted with military advisers on a secure phone.

Intelligence reports indicated that Osama bin Laden and his top deputies would meet at the camp in Afghanistan the next day, August 20. If the United States succeeded in its surprise attack, these top-secret reports indicated, it could wipe out the core of the al Qaeda leadership. After seeking input from National Security Adviser Sandy Berger in Washington, as well as the Joint Chiefs of Staff and CIA, a shaken Bill Clinton directed U.S. Navy destroyers in the northern Arabian Sea to prepare to launch Tomahawk missiles at targets in Afghanistan. He also readied ships in the Red Sea to fire missiles at a chemical plant in Sudan, zeroing in on targets connected with Osama bin Laden.

Military advisers, including Richard Clarke, Clinton's chief counterterrorism specialist, warned the president that there would inevitably be cries of *Wag the Dog*, referring to a movie in which a desperate president embroiled in a sex scandal concocted a fake war to save himself. Critics would surely accuse him of taking this military action abroad to divert attention from his predicament at home. Clinton replied tersely: "Do you all recommend that we strike [tomorrow]? Fine. Don't give me political advice or personal advice about the timing. That's my problem." He worried until 3:00 A.M., at which time he authorized the attack.

Dressed in a dark suit and appearing unusually grim-faced, the president appeared the next morning at an impromptu press conference held at a school gym on Martha's Vineyard, publicly announcing the military strike. Minutes later, Clinton boarded a plane to Washington to oversee this military operation from the White House, telling the American people in an afternoon televised address: "Today I ordered our armed forces to strike at terrorist-related facilities in Afghanistan and Sudan because of the threat they present to our national security." Before returning to Martha's Vineyard the president also signed Executive Order 13099, imposing economic sanctions against Osama bin Laden and the al Qaeda terrorist organization.

Although the military strikes did not kill bin Laden or his top deputies, the U.S. intelligence team reported that a group of Pakistani terrorist officers was "taken out" by the attacks. Yet the American media remained deeply skeptical.

Even some of Clinton's closest advisers worried in private, "This may be more than the country can handle. This may be more than Congress can handle."

The president returned to Martha's Vineyard to complete his purgatory-like vacation. He slept on the couch downstairs in the main bungalow, while Hillary and Chelsea occupied the bedrooms upstairs, maintaining a chilly distance.

It was during this period that Bill Clinton finally hit rock bottom. There was not much sympathy for him, even among his staffers. One member of the Clinton team who regularly traveled with the president expressed the view shared by many of his peers: Their boss had squandered his chance to become one of the greatest leaders in world history. At the start of 1998, Clinton had everything going for him that a president could want: He enjoyed unprecedented economic prosperity at home, with the Dow Jones index soaring near nine thousand going into the summer. He had made significant advances on the domestic policy front. He had won extraordinary popularity on the worldwide scene and had earned foreign affairs successes in hot spots like the Middle East and Northern Ireland, while continuing to work at defusing new crises such as the ethnic cleansing in Kosovo. Now all of these triumphs, it seemed, had been flushed down the drain—all for a reckless fling with a chubby-cheeked female who was the age of Clinton's own daughter. Said one dispirited staffer, "We had a mandate that could have affected the whole world. It was gone. The whole focus was now on Lewinsky and impeachment matters."

Overseas, Bill Clinton had always attracted throngs of adoring fans as if he were a world savior. In Northern Ireland, where he was largely credited for hammering out a peace accord with British Prime Minister Tony Blair, Clinton had nearly reached the status of sainthood. Yet all of that incredible goodwill had been squandered. Said one staffer, "The feeling among many of us was—he had thrown it all away. He was not entirely blameless." Bill Clinton had known that he was under a microscope when it came to extramarital dalliances, ever since the 1992 primaries, when the Gennifer Flowers affair nearly knocked him off his horse and out of the race. He was on notice that every time he strayed into the back alleys of carnal temptation, he was putting his whole administration at risk. Even the most lowly staff member in the White House knew that one "did not mess with interns." Yet the most powerful man in the world had been unable to resist that base, prurient enticement.

One member of the Clinton entourage would recall watching the president deliver an emotional speech about the proposed peace accord in Armagh, Northern Ireland, shortly after his controversial grand jury testimony. The staffer watched silently, tears welling up. Not only was the Lewinsky mess a maddening distraction, but now the chief executive was suffering from a "lack of credibility," a "lack of mandate," and a growing "inability to do anything in Congress." "There had been a chance to change history," the staffer thought to himself, "and he [President Clinton] blew it."

Those surrounding the embattled president also knew that Clinton had "stiff-armed the press" for years, refusing to devote much energy toward befriending the Washington press corps, even though the media would inevitably sit in judgment of his administration. Now it was payback time.

A scattering of newspapers around the country began calling for Clinton's resignation, on the theory that, whether or not he had committed an impeachable offense, he had thoroughly disgraced the office of the presidency. Public opinion polls fluttered uncertainly like flags in a chilly wind, indicating that many Americans were plagued by conflicting emotions—their distaste for Clinton's actions, on one hand, and their abhorrence of the invasions of privacy committed by Starr's office, on the other.

The *Journal Star* in Lincoln, Nebraska, editorialized: "Bill Clinton should resign as president. He has created a sordid mess. He has prolonged it with lies. The nation wants to put this tormenting distraction behind it." The *Daily Oklahoman* pronounced: "He seemed sorrier he got caught in sex acts than he was for lying about it or for damaging his office and the country." The *Sacramento Bee* echoed the advice of Republican Senator Orrin Hatch of Utah, calling for swift action by Independent Counsel Ken Starr and the U.S. Congress so that this "painful and tawdry" episode could be brought to an end. The California paper predicted: "This isn't the end, but it's at least the beginning of the end."

Key Democrats in the House and Senate appeared "ready to bolt." President Bill Clinton, his White House advisers concluded with alarm, had reached a position of "maximum danger."

In the midst of this pandemonium, another tidal wave slammed the White House. To the horror of those trying to hold the wobbly Clinton administration together, Vice President Al Gore was suddenly the subject of an investigation. In response to increased pressure to determine whether Gore had lied to Justice Department officials when he denied, the previous December, engaging in illegal fund-raising activities during the 1996 reelection campaign, Attorney General Janet Reno finally capitulated. On Wednesday, August 26, while the Clinton family was completing its somber vacation on Martha's Vineyard, Reno ordered a ninety-day preliminary investigation into whether Gore had lied to federal officials investigating the campaign allegations. Suddenly, it appeared as if the entire Clinton administration might be sunk in the wake of an independent counsel tidal wave.

On a secluded and well-appointed dude ranch outside Bozeman, Montana— a destination for world-class fly-fishing near the scenic northwest entrance to Yellowstone National Park—a group of federal judges was attending an elite conference hosted by the conservative Foundation for Research on Economics and the Environment (FREE). One of those participants, Judge David B. Sentelle, exited his cabin dressed in casual garb and cowboy boots, a mobile telephone pressed to his ear. Judge Sentelle, the court of appeals judge who presided over all independent counsel appointments, now pumped his fist into the air and held up the phone triumphantly, announcing to his colleagues in a North Carolina drawl: "They did it! They did it!" A cheer rose up from some judicial colleagues who exchanged "high fives."

Stated one judge present at the unusual dude ranch assemblage: "Every Republican knew what he was talking about. It was terribly, terribly partisan in a way I had never seen before." Said the judge, who requested anonymity: "I found it disturbing."

The *New York Times* observed that the Clinton White House, already "battered" by Ken Starr's surprise probe of the Lewinsky matter, was now reeling from the solid blow that had knocked the vice president to the ground. There was new momentum to force Reno to conduct a full-blown investigation of potential campaign law violations by both the president and vice president during the 1996 campaign. The Republican party seemed poised to complete its palace coup and to waltz back into the White House in 2000, with both Clinton and Gore emasculated.

Vice President Gore, vacationing on Hawaii, met with reporters dressed in a flowered aloha shirt, standing resolute against this latest onslaught. Gore had already issued a statement from this island retreat days earlier, when Clinton had first admitted to an inappropriate relationship with an intern nearly the same age as Gore's own daughter, Karenna. According to those close to the vice president, he had weighed his options carefully before publicly supporting the president. From Oahu, Gore now stated tersely: "I am proud of him, not only because he is a friend, but because he is a person who has the courage to acknowledge mistakes."

As stunned staffers of both Clinton and Gore hurried back to Washington to confront those dark forces that had seemingly gathered over the executive mansion, a surprise figure emerged, according to those hunkered down in the White House, who saved the Clinton presidency.

That person was Kenneth W. Starr.

PART FIVE

HIGH CRIMES AND
MISDEMEANORS

45

———

BOMBSHELL REPORT

By early September, an ominous sense hung over the Capitol that a report from the special prosecutor would arrive imminently. Senator Joe Lieberman, a centrist Democrat from Connecticut and ordinarily an ally of Bill Clinton's, took to the Senate floor on September 3 and gave the president a tongue-lashing, declaring that his "immoral" conduct was "wrong and unacceptable and should be followed by some measure of public rebuke and accountability." Still traveling abroad in Ireland, President Clinton was cornered by a reporter who asked him to comment on Senator Lieberman's rebuke. Clinton stated distractedly, "I agree with what he said. . . . I made a bad mistake, it was indefensible, and I'm sorry about it."

Monica Lewinsky, meanwhile, was appearing before the grand jury for her final session. Foreperson Freda Alexander, departing from protocol, issued a sympathetic farewell on behalf of all twenty-three grand jurors: "We wanted to offer you a bouquet of good wishes that includes luck, success, happiness and blessings."

Days later, the former intern was being dragged through the wringer again, this time being grilled by two female prosecutors from Ken Starr's office. In a "privileged and confidential" memo to his file, Plato Cacheris recorded that he had received a call from Monica's father, who had asked him to implore the OIC prosecutors not to force Monica to answer "explicit questions." The lawyer had passed along this plea, but it had been ignored. OIC "needed to get [Monica] under oath" with respect to each "sexual encounter" with the president, Starr's people had told Cacheris, no matter how awkward or intimate the questioning became.

In private, President Bill Clinton commented to an aide that he was "appalled" at how roughly the Starr prosecutors were treating Monica. He also noted "how [well] she seemed to be holding up under it" and how she "was not basically cracking."

OIC, in the meantime, was busy trying to finish its report on the Lewinsky affair while simultaneously keeping a tiny flame flickering under the Whitewater probe. It was a tricky predicament. After four years of investigating Whitewater,

Starr's office was now preparing a report for Congress that had nothing to do with the topic it was originally hired to investigate. One internal memo suggested adding language in the introduction of the report that said: "We will transmit a narrative and report to Congress (relating to Whitewater) at a *later* time." In this way, OIC could string out the nearly kaput Whitewater matter and place maximum emphasis on the red-hot Lewinsky investigation.

It seemed like an opportune time to roll out the report. Information had begun flying over the transom, suggesting that the Clinton presidency might be teetering on the edge of collapse. A confidential memo in Ken Starr's file noted that FBI agent Steve Irons had notified the office that a "source" informed him that Judge Susan Webber Wright "believes that Clinton made a fool of her" by his lying in the *Jones* deposition. The same source told the FBI that "as of 5:00 Eastern time on 9/3, there was a rumor that Al Gore's inner circle has been told to prepare for a transition."

OIC returned Lewinsky's passport, allowing her to travel beyond the U.S. borders, but only on condition that she make herself available "on a day's notice." The Starr prosecutors alluded darkly to the fact that they were finalizing a confidential report to Congress, for which they might need additional information.

The draft referral to Congress had actually been in the works since March. At that time, Ken Starr had assigned a team of his top writers to begin summarizing the evidence against the president, even before Monica Lewinsky had agreed to cooperate. The writers had scrapped OIC's earlier 100-page referral relating to Whitewater and started afresh. Their new work quickly ballooned in length to 250 pages. Stephen Bates, one of OIC's scriveners, later recalled that they were deluged with a "great fire hose flow" of incriminating grand jury interviews and FBI reports, which they began funneling into a single document encapsulating all "potentially impeachable acts."

There had always been an assumption that OIC would produce *some* report to Congress. The only question was what form the document would take, and when it was best to dump it into the House's lap. Starr, in an unusual role reversal, had become the most impatient person in his office. He wanted to "send it up [to Congress]" in the spring, even before Lewinsky had been pinned down as a cooperating witness. Most of the OIC prosecutors were aghast at their boss's impulsiveness. They were frustrated and displeased at "how little" concrete evidence they had even after "months of frenzied activity." Most of Starr's prosecutors believed it would be disastrous to send their messy collection of evidence to Capitol Hill, because "it wasn't there [yet]."

Ethics adviser Sam Dash was also horrified that Starr's lawyers were organizing the draft referral into "counts," as if it were an indictment. Dash shouted at his younger boss, "The independent counsel does not draw up an indictment of impeachment! That's the House of Representatives. All the statute calls for is referring information." If Starr did not slow down and fix his misguided report, Dash said, he would be forced to quit.

Starr backed off, for the time being. Yet he was itching to pass off this hot potato to Congress. The ordinarily passive independent counsel was now a man with a mission. He first issued an "edict" that the report had to be completed by the "end of July." After his staff pushed back, Starr modified his directive and gave them until Labor Day. This would leave a couple of months before the November elections—a safe enough cushion if they wanted to avoid being accused of seeking to manipulate the midterm elections. Paul Rosenzweig piped up that "we might as well wait until January" when the new Congress took office, since nothing would happen before then, anyway. The mild-mannered independent counsel became "livid" at that suggestion. He was insistent that his staff adhere to the new September deadline.

Starr later categorically denied that he timed the release of his report to impact the November elections. To the contrary, he said, his only goal was "to get it out as promptly as possible." Starr explained, pushing his glasses firmly onto his nose, "We were not trying to do anything in terms of stirring up public interest. The public interest was already there." Yet this much could not be disputed: Ken Starr was more insistent about getting the report to Congress in September than about almost any other deadline during his tenure as special prosecutor. He pointed to calendars on the wall and issued the command, his eyes gleaming with resolve: "Circle Labor Day!"

———

A NAGGING issue that continued to divide the Office of Independent Counsel had to do with the level of sexual detail that should be included in its still-growing report. Some of the prosecutors suggested "segregating" the nasty stuff. They could bury the extra-spicy details in a separate appendix, locking them away in a triple-X location. Other prosecutors feared that this would "draw more attention" to the juicy material, flashing red lights as if inviting readers into a lurid peep show. The "sex appendix," they warned, would be the first thing that got "leaked" by Congress. Paul Rosenzweig, one of the voices opposed to hiding the X-rated material, circulated a confidential memo titled, "Bowdlerdizing the Final Report." In this, he invoked the name of the nineteenth-century English physician, Thomas Bowdler, who was infamous for publishing a sanitized version of William Shakespeare's plays for women and children in order to protect them from smutty and offensive material. Bowdler's name had become synonymous with prudishness and literary censorship. Rosenzweig argued that if OIC tried to hide the sexual detail, the public would conclude they did so "because Ken was a puritan." Moreover, the explicit sexual details were necessary to expose and rebut "the president's utterly insane notion that [Monica] had sex with him but he hadn't had it with her."

In the end, Starr's deputies agreed with Rosenzweig: It was best to treat the steamy sexual material "in a sort of a grown-up way" by "interspersing it with everything else." Starr himself reached the unhappy conclusion that there was no alternative but to pour a healthy dose of sexual content into the body of the report, even though it personally repulsed him. After all, he agreed with his aides, the president had been the one who denied a "sexual relationship" as defined by the federal judge in the *Paula Jones* case. It was OIC's duty to prove this was false.

There was "no joy in it," Starr said later. To the contrary, there was "an enormous amount of discomfort."

As the Starr Report took shape and grew fatter, it blossomed into two parts. Initially, it had been crafted as a list of "potential impeachment allegations" with little commentary. Before long, it became so hefty that it was divided into a "charging section" that spelled out possible offenses, and a more descriptive "narrative." With two teams of authors working around the clock, the two sections took on lives of their own, with many sexual particulars repeating themselves multiple times.

Jackie Bennett later emphasized that none of this was designed to "pile on" Bill Clinton. "I think we could have made it much more embarrassing if that had been anybody's goal," he insisted. "We just kind of had to put our nose to the grindstone and go prove the case." Consciously or not, however, Starr was taking a step that would forever damage his legacy. He was permitting his prosecutors to construct a report that erred on the side of overinclusion, rather than a lean and precise document like that produced by his Watergate predecessors.

Starr was aware of the history: During the final stages of the Watergate probe, before President Nixon had resigned in disgrace, special prosecutor Leon Jaworski had written a bare-bones list of potential impeachable offenses and delivered this compact report to Congress. Jaworski's factual recitation amounted to a mere "road map," taking no position as to whether President Nixon had committed any impeachable offenses. Judge John Sirica authorized the report's transmittal to the House Judiciary Committee under seal, taking steps to ensure that it could not be leaked.

Only a few people in the world had ever seen the Jaworski road map. Scattered sources would later describe it as "a simple document, fifty-five pages long, with only a sentence or two on each of the pages." Each entry referred to some relevant piece of evidence, such as: "On March 6, 1973, E. Howard Hunt demanded $120,000" and referred to pages of grand jury transcripts and White House tape transcripts that discussed the relevant evidence. Judge Sirica himself verified that the report drew no "accusatory conclusions." Nor did it contain any "recommendations, advice or statements." The Jaworski Report left Congress to conduct its own investigation and to reach its own conclusions on the monumental impeachment question.

It should have been a telling clue, within Starr's office, that its own researcher was unable to get his hands on a copy of the Jaworski Report, even twenty-four years later. Stephen Bates had visited an archivist friend at the National Archives and had obtained "a lot of cool stuff" from the Watergate era. When he requested the Jaworski road map, however, the archivist demurred. That document was still locked up; Bates was unable to get his hands on it.

Had Starr and his deputies opted to construct even a scaled-back version of the Watergate model, this might have provided a fig leaf behind which they could have hidden when the lewd details of the Clinton-Lewinsky affair were revealed. Instead, the special prosecutor's team chose the "more rather than less" approach, the same approach Starr had taken in compiling a fulsome report in the Vince Foster matter. Starr explained to his prosecutors that he took seriously the language in the independent counsel law, which declared that a special prosecutor "shall advise the House of Representatives of any substantial and credible information which such independent counsel receives . . . that may constitute grounds for an impeachment." That language, however sparse and imprecise, seemed to mandate that an independent counsel do *something* with its information. As Starr himself deciphered it, the law "required more than a road map." He felt that his office "owed it to the Congress" to assemble the materials "in a way that's meaningful for them, in a way that would help out maximally."

An initial letter was drafted that would have forcefully directed Congress to keep the material in Starr's report under wraps. After further debate, that letter was scrapped and a more wishy-washy request made its way onto the computer screen; it said nothing explicit about Congress keeping the report under seal. Some staffers felt OIC had no business telling Congress what to do with the report and accompanying evidence; that would trigger separation of powers problems. To a certain extent, however, Stephen Bates admitted it was "just an oversight that [the stronger language] got left out." Anyway, he noted, "we assumed impeachment reports didn't get published."

Starr himself defended that omission, stating that Congress remained "on notice" that the report contained material that was "deeply, highly sensitive." His view was, "It was entrusted to Congress. And Congress could do with it as it saw fit."

DURING the final scramble to ready the Starr Report for Congress, another distressing development arose. The FBI reported to OIC that many of Linda Tripp's "original" tapes had been duplicated and/or altered to some extent.

Starr's prosecutors were outraged; they felt personally betrayed by Tripp. Among other things, this discovery obliterated Tripp's credibility as a witness, because such duplications/alterations were directly at odds with her sworn testimony about the making and handling of the tapes. Also, OIC's draft report was laden with references to the Tripp tapes as support for the allegations against Clinton. Now the entire report had to be scrubbed. Although this secret was carefully guarded by Starr's top deputies, virtually all references to the Tripp tapes were stricken from the footnotes and replaced with other backup sources, creating a major headache for the already stressed-out draftsmen of the huge referral. The relationship between the Starr prosecutors and Tripp, their chief informant, was ruptured forever as a result of this discovery. Now, OIC was marching toward the House of Representatives alone.

The day the Starr Report was delivered to Congress—Wednesday, September 9—was one that would remain etched in the minds of those working in the Office of Independent Counsel. As Ken Starr stood over a computer screen in Brett Kavanaugh's office preparing to authorize the final draft so that it could be delivered to Capitol Hill, Sam Dash entered and demanded to review the final work product. Those present recalled that the ethics adviser was "extremely agitated." A loud discussion ensued, during which Dash insisted that changes had to be made to "Ground Eleven" of the impeachment referral—the ground dealing with the president's abuse of power—or he would quit. Dash told Starr that "the whole American Bar ought to come out against you" if the independent counsel went forward with the referral as written. The report was cleaned up, and Dash withdrew his threat to resign, remaining in OIC's employ—for now.

Jackie Bennett had worked diligently to throw both Congress and the news media off the scent, dropping hints that a report would not be concluded for weeks. At approximately 3:45 P.M., Bennett phoned several contacts on the Hill and told them, "Okay, now is the time to deliver this. Where do you want us to take this thing?" OIC would be dropping off the report itself plus thirty-six boxes of evidentiary material—eighteen boxes for the Democrats, and an identical set for the Republicans. The House staffers instructed Bennett to deliver the material to the House sergeant at arms, who would meet them inside the Capitol grounds.

On the loading dock of the OIC building, workers hoisted cartons into the rear of a dark government van. Bob Bittman had assigned himself to make the historic trip, several blocks away to the Capitol. As he buckled into the front seat, the Starr deputy kept a firm grasp on two envelopes, which contained transmittal letters for both parties' leaders in the House.

As FBI agents climbed into the backseat, Jackie Bennett handed the driver, Sandy Oldham, a Sony minicam video camera to record the historic voyage. No sooner had she secured it to the van's dashboard and pulled out onto Pennsylvania Avenue than a pair of media trucks swept alongside with film crews "hanging out the window," pointing cameras at the Starr entourage. Oldham shouted, "Get away!" cutting the wheel as if to drive the paparazzi off the road. Bittman said calmly, "Sandy, the last thing we want is to get into an accident. Just drive straight and be careful."

The van sped through the streets and reached a bumpy halt on the grounds of the Capitol; here, the Capitol Police were waiting at a cordoned-off section of the driveway to accommodate the transfer. Sergeant at Arms Wilson Livingood waved the vehicle to a halt and spoke to Bittman: "I understand you have something for us."

After personally serving a copy of the transmittal letter on Speaker Newt Gingrich (who was across the street at the Library of Congress and seemed annoyed to be interrupted) and a second copy on Minority Leader Dick Gephardt, Bittman climbed back aboard his unmarked van and left, just as a horde of television film crews surrounded the Capitol.

Back in the OIC offices, Starr's troops were exhausted. More than twenty-five lawyers had pulled all-nighters for weeks to complete this report. Brett Kavanaugh started driving home but was so punch-drunk that he was forced to stop along the side of the road and hail a cab. Ken Starr slipped past the gathering horde of media trucks in the OIC parking garage and headed home to McLean, preparing to brace his family for the news. He had tried to handle his duty in a low-key way, titling the 452-page report simply "Referral to the United States House of Representatives pursuant to Title 28, United States Code, Section 595c," rather than giving it a sensationalistic name. Yet these kinds of things, Starr knew, tended to make a stir in the Beltway and would likely attract some coverage on the nightly news. On the bright side, Starr told himself, this was Congress's responsibility now. The matter "was completely out of our hands."

The president's lawyers were thrown off guard. They had known the report was coming. Yet they had expected that it would be kept strictly confidential, rather than being dropped off in boxes like a delivery from Sears or Amazon.com. Sequestered in the West Wing of the White House long into the night, the president's legal team studied news footage of Bittman stepping out of the van, and of the Capitol Police hoisting cartons out of the back. They tried to reconstruct the details: How many boxes were there? What could be in this truckload of material? Was it possible there were *multiple* reports, not just on the Lewinsky matter but also on Whitewater?

Already, David Kendall and the rest of the president's legal team had begun preparing a lengthy "prebuttal." Largely thanks to media sources who transmitted information back to the White House like carrier pigeons, Clinton's lawyers had gained remarkably accurate information concerning the planned Lewinsky referral. Now they worked furiously to address a report that they had never laid eyes on.

Congressman Henry J. Hyde of Illinois, the distinguished, white-haired chairman of the House Judiciary Committee, issued a statement pledging a nonpartisan approach to handling the Starr referral. The Republican chairman declared: "The American people deserve a competent, independent, and bipartisan review of the independent counsel's referral. They must have confidence in this process. Politics must be checked at the door."

Before the sun had even peeked its head over Washington, however, rumors were sweeping through the Capitol that Speaker Newt Gingrich and his more ardent Republican colleagues were planning to release the entire, unexpurgated Starr Report before a single member of Congress had read it. President Bill Clinton, having just returned from Ireland, exhausted yet feeling a new urge for repentance, summoned his Cabinet to the White House in hopes of heading off a mass exodus. "He sat with the Cabinet and he did his deal," recalled one observer. In the ornate Yellow Oval Room of the White House residence, with gold chairs from the Jacqueline Kennedy era arranged in amphitheater style, the president apologized for lying to his Cabinet members and to the American public. He then made an emotional plea for another chance so that he could steer his presidency back on track.

Environmental Protection Agency administrator Carol Browner tore into the president, asking Clinton how she was supposed to explain these lurid accounts of sex in the White House to her eleven-year-old son and demanding, "What do I say to him?" Secretary of Health and Human Services Donna Shalala lectured Clinton that it was one thing to profess remorse and quite another "to demonstrate it."

At the conclusion of the bloodletting session, having swallowed another healthy serving of humble pie, the president rushed up to Shalala and hugged her, expressing gratitude that she had not walked out on the administration. Each tiny victory was one more day in office.

Clinton repeated the same drill with key Democratic members of Congress. One presidential aide recalled that these meetings were "like a spy movie where you're hypnotized." Time seemed to be moving backward. It was a political exercise of the most basic sort; Bill Clinton was forced to throw himself at the mercy of his core supporters and beg forgiveness. His advisers worried that traditionalists like Senator Robert Byrd (D.-W.Va.) and Harry Reid (D.-Nev.) might consider Clinton's actions so offensive that they would take a hike. "You know, if they took a walk along with a couple others," said one aide, "we could end up with a stampede."

KEN Starr said later that he was appalled when he learned that Congress was preparing to dump his report into the public domain without ever reading it. Deputy Bittman phoned a high-ranking staffer friend on the Hill and chastised him: "This is crazy. You guys aren't even going to read the thing?" His friend replied stoically, "The train has left the station. Nobody wants to touch this thing. Even to open it to see what's in it."

There was a short-lived debate within OIC about delivering a *second* letter to Congress, instructing them not to release the report—at least not until the legislators had reviewed its contents and determined if some material was too sensitive or too explicit for public consumption. Prosecutors "ran around in the hallway" giving Starr conflicting advice. Finally, the independent counsel issued his proclamation: It was too late to change course; it would look like "a loss of confidence in our own work product" to issue an edict that the report had to stay under wraps. Rather than trying to halt its release, Starr's deputies now swung in the opposite direction, providing House staffers with an electronic version of the Starr Report, "so that they could more easily load it onto the Internet."

The next morning, Friday, President Clinton was scheduled to attend the traditional national prayer breakfast at the White House. He had stayed up all night preparing for his atonement. As a hundred clerics of mixed faiths sat silently in the East Room at this awkward fellowship gathering, the president confessed: "I don't think there is a fancy way to say that I have sinned." He had caused hurt and pain to many people—his family, his friends, his staff and Cabinet members, Monica Lewinsky, her family, and the American people. The president now begged forgiveness with tears welling up in his eyes. He confessed that he had hit the "rock-bottom truth," possessing "what my Bible calls a broken spirit: an understanding that I must have God's help to be the person that I want to be, a willingness to give the very forgiveness I seek, a renunciation of the pride and the anger which cloud judgment."

Many doubting Thomases found an element of political theater, if not hypocrisy, in Clinton's use of clerics to pull him out of his cesspool of sinfulness. Yet President Clinton himself would take issue with those who pooh-poohed the sincerity of his apology. "You know, most every Sunday when Hillary and I were in Washington, we went to Foundry Methodist Church," Clinton later said. "And when we were at Camp David, we went to the chapel to services; this was a big part of my life. The ministers that I asked to come meet with me after this whole thing broke were people that I knew well and admired enormously. And they weren't about to be used as pawns in political theater. They were going to, you know, work with me in a spirit of love, but also, you know, toughness and accountability. It's more insulting to them than it is to me. I mean, I don't care what they say about me. But it was very real. And it was a very important part of my life and my family's life for the next year or so."

Even as ministers filed out of the prayer breakfast prepared to lend absolution to Bill Clinton, the House of Representatives was debating whether to release the unexpurgated Starr Report so that the fullest details of his sins could be made public. By an overwhelming 363 to 63 vote that transcended party lines, the House decided to release the entire Starr Report—that afternoon—to be followed by the publication of the massive evidentiary record, unless the Judiciary Committee determined otherwise within seventeen days.

Representative Barney Frank, the fiery, openly gay Democrat from Massachusetts and one of the few stalwarts to defend Clinton publicly after the president admitted to an inappropriate relationship with Lewinsky, saw trouble brewing on the horizon. As Congressman Frank read the tea leaves, the lopsided vote in the House reflected the sentiment, even among Democrats, that "this guy's in trouble. He did bad things. We're angry at him and he was stupid. Starr may have more. We don't know what else Starr's got. We haven't even really fully digested this. And we think the public's going to be mad at him."

At approximately two o'clock in the afternoon, the House clerk posted the 452-page Starr Report on Congress's intranet site. With the simple click of a PC mouse, the document was made available to major media sources and millions of Americans were soon reading the startling report online, the first time a government document that might change the course of history made its debut on the Internet.

In college study carrels and law libraries from West Coast to East, students huddled around computer terminals to scroll through the Starr Report, alternately guffawing and gasping at the president's sexual exploits with an intern the same age as many of them. Web servers were crushed with so many hits that they experienced "online traffic jams." Readers cut and pasted the juiciest portions for friends and family members who might appreciate the explicit details, transmitting these via e-mail; most interest focused on the episode involving the president inserting a cigar into Monica Lewinsky's vagina and tales of kinky phone sex as the president lay alone in bed in the White House wearing blue undershorts.

The next day, newspapers printed the entire text of the Starr Report in fat inserts, simultaneously captivating and repulsing the American public. Hundreds of papers posted the voluminous document electronically on their Web sites, many including warnings like that of the *Denver Post*: "The following report contains material that readers may find offensive or objectionable. . . ."

The White House was nearly rocked off its wheels. One high-level staffer described the frenzy to obtain copies of the salacious Starr referral as similar to "giving away Rolling Stones tickets." Eager readers lined up to grab copies of the report at newsstands and at workplace computer printers which swiftly ran out of ink.

David Kendall released a seventy-eight-page "preliminary rebuttal," calling the Starr Report "an unreliable, one-sided account of sexual behavior." Yet Starr's handiwork was now gathering momentum like a rock slide; there was no telling what damage it would do when it finally crash-landed.

Those close to the president and First Lady during this period of public humiliation later described it as "dispiriting in the extreme." Because the Starr Report had been released in a vacuum, without any evidence defending Clinton to provide balance, the White House braced itself for a pummeling that weekend. Said one aide, "And we did get killed on the weekend."

The version of the Starr Report bouncing around the Web wasn't even the correct one. A bug in OIC's computer software had caused outdated text to pop up once Congress had downloaded the document onto the Internet. Much to OIC's embarrassment, the publicly released version of the Starr Report included typos and other sloppy editing errors. Now the *Washington Post* and the *Chicago Tribune* and dozens of other papers were churning out stacks of copies of that flawed version like hotcakes at a Rotary Club breakfast.

As men, women, teenagers, and curious children gazed upon pullout sections of newspapers containing the presidential sex-scandal document, there seemed to be no middle ground. Some exclaimed that they could not "fully understand" how the president could have defiled his office so egregiously. Others declared the Starr Report to be "pornography." "You got both flavors," recalled Jackie Bennett.

The Starr team members had expected some backlash. But they were shocked by the vehemence of the attacks aimed at them following the worldwide release of their referral. Bob Bittman later objected, "We had nothing to do with it. Congress released the material without even reading it. It was a hundred percent their fault. They didn't have the political guts to read it first."

In the wake of the huge stir created by the Starr Report, over sixty-five major newspapers called on President Clinton to resign before he was run out on a rail. The *Los Angeles Times*, ordinarily supportive of the Clinton administration, wrote with disgust: "The picture of Clinton that now emerges is that of a middle-aged man with a pathetic inability to control his sexual fancies." The *Philadelphia Inquirer* blasted: "Bill Clinton should resign. He should resign because his repeated, reckless deceits have dishonored his presidency beyond repair." The *Pittsburgh Post-Gazette*, reflecting the sentiment of working-class America, declared: "Character does matter, we've always known that. . . . A spontaneous and immediate resignation without histrionics is the only outcome that might salvage a measure of respect for [Mr. Clinton] and help the nation regain its moral bearings."

In the aftershock of the Starr Report's release, however, it was not clear that many high-ranking government officials were buying it. Attorney General Janet Reno later stated that she was at a loss for words after seeing a copy of Starr's handiwork. Reno's principal problem was, "I didn't know what the purpose of it was." Although any federal prosecutor had an obligation to transmit information to Congress in an "orderly" fashion if he or she believed that an impeachable offense had been committed, *how* that was accomplished was crucial. In this case, Starr certainly had a duty to "fully apprise" the House of relevant evidence. Yet Reno also felt strongly that he had "the responsibility to maintain that evidence," and to protect his investigation from being wrecked by disclosing sensitive grand jury information.

Sitting on the screened-in porch of her modest home in Miami, Attorney General Reno later summed up her dismay at the Starr Report. "I would have handled it differently," she said, her jaw locked tight.

One of Reno's top assistants would put it more bluntly: "It made me want to take a shower after reading it."

Professor Julie O'Sullivan, who had worked closely with both Robert Fiske and Ken Starr during the early stages of Whitewater, found the Starr Report "appalling." O'Sullivan was particularly aghast that Starr's office had given Congress the report and evidence "in a diskette [form] so that they could put it online." This, she felt, "certainly undermined his [Starr's] contention that he intended it to be private." It looked as if Starr was hanging out all his most sensitive evidence for the world to see, consequences be damned.

O'Sullivan was also troubled that Starr's team had intentionally lined up the case for the House to impeach Clinton. She explained: "Ken made it very easy. He organized the documents for them. Organized the evidence. Wrote an indictment. I thought the report itself was written as an advocacy piece, instead of a balanced statement of the facts."

William Duffey, Jr., a Republican who had served as one of Fiske's chief prosecutors before returning to private practice, was especially troubled by the level of sexual information. "That sort of detail wasn't necessary to inform Congress of offenses or things that might be grounds for impeachment," the Atlanta attorney said. When he and Fiske had worked on the first Vince Foster report, they had consistently deleted information that was "too private." Fiske would ask Duffey, "Is this detail really necessary to communicate our findings?" If the answer was "probably not," it would be stricken. The Starr Report seemed to do just the opposite.

Even Archibald Cox, the principled and soft-spoken Watergate special prosecutor who had scrupulously avoided reporters during the Starr investigation to avoid second-guessing a fellow independent counsel, would later confess that he was deeply disturbed by the issuance of Starr's bombshell report. Now almost ninety, Cox would fault Starr for succumbing to pressure from his younger, more aggressive prosecutors. During Watergate, Cox emphasized, he had literally sealed himself off from his own hard-charging prosecutors, sitting down in private with Attorney General Elliot Richardson in order to exercise restraint despite his staff's urge to push harder. Starr, he believed, seemed to be buckling to his staff's wishes.

Additionally, Cox believed that a simple road map of possible impeachable offenses, of the sort his successor Leon Jaworski had turned over to Congress under seal, would have been much more in keeping with the prosecutor's role of remaining divorced from politics. It was true that both sides were behaving terribly, with the White House and Starr's office taking turns leaking information and throwing mud at the opponent. Yet Cox believed that the special prosecutor had a duty to rise above such political mudslinging. "Ken Starr's investigation was carried on as an attack on the White House from beginning to end," Cox said, seated in a stiff chair at his farmhouse in Maine. "And that is a very questionable spirit in which to perform such an assignment."

THE issuance of the Starr Report, ironically, caused Clinton fans and detractors alike to lash out at Ken Starr with a newfound fervor. Particularly appalling to some readers was the report's inclusion of facts that seemed to purposely rub the affair in the face of First Lady Hillary Clinton, flagging down her whereabouts (often far away from Washington) when her husband's extramarital dalliances with Lewinsky were taking place. "Talk about something that flies in the face of family values," said Joe Purvis, a friend of Bill's since kindergarten. "It smacked of being a prurient document put out by voyeuristic sick people, if you want to know the truth." He also scoffed at the notion that Congress—not Starr himself—was responsible for releasing this material worldwide. In Purvis's estimation, Starr was merely "[doing] the Pontius Pilate number, where he washed his hands of the whole matter." Purvis mocked the independent counsel: "It was those Jews—the Congressmen—that ordered Jesus' crucifixion."

Betsey Wright, who had already sunk into a deep depression over the revelation that Bill Clinton had lied (again) about his inability to curb his sexual appetites, was blown away by the issuance of Starr's missive. Hiding in a remote area of the Ozark Mountains and humiliated by Bill Clinton's conduct that she had enabled, Wright could no longer bear it. For her, the delivery of the Starr Report was proof positive that the world had gone completely mad and that she had played a role in its becoming unhinged. "I remember watching the delivery of the boxes on TV," Wright said stoically. "And just breaking down in tears. I didn't read newspapers or watch TV ever after [that]. . . . I locked that world away from me. I couldn't watch it. So I didn't read the Starr Report. Not one word of it."

Marcia Lewis, Monica's mother, had written a personal letter to Ken Starr "begging him not to release" this private information. For the sake of her daughter's sanity and to preserve some shred of Monica's self-respect, she had pleaded for restraint. She had even written directly to Congressman Henry Hyde, imploring him not to make the Starr materials public. Monica's mother had not received a reply from either man. Now, the Starr Report, as published, was a hundred times worse than she had imagined in her worst nightmares.

"Someone had told me early on that grand jury testimony was never, ever made public. That was my understanding," Marcia Lewis said, still coming to grips with the experience years later. "I was surprised on that level. And then beyond that, on a personal level, I was mortified and I felt terrible for Monica and everyone else."

Monica Lewinsky, on that day, was in a New York hotel room with a friend of her mother's, trying to lie low. When the news channel reported that Congress had dumped the entire Starr Report onto the Internet, Monica plugged in her laptop and connected to the Web. As she scrolled through the document's introduction, she felt like curling up in a ball and disappearing. "I was in flux between being flabbergasted and being in tears and just disbelief," she recalled.

For the young woman, the psychological devastation that had been wrought over the past eight months was now compounded by sheer anger. For one, the report contained information that she intentionally had deleted from her computer and that OIC had dredged up from her hard drive. "Talk about sort of raping your mind," she said. "To write something that you not only think is not for anyone else, you then decide you don't ever want to look at it again. . . . To have the government take it out [of the e-mail trash] and then print it and disseminate it for the entire world to see" seemed Orwellian and unconscionable.

Moreover, members of Starr's staff, particularly Karen Immergut ("the only prosecutor that I [Monica] thought was a semidecent human being"), had made representations to Monica that certain extremely personal information "would not be published." Now, here was the report staring her in the face and containing truckloads of superprivate material.

Then there was the disgrace to her family: Monica could not imagine how she was going to face her father after he saw this sex-laden account. It created yet another "barrier" that would be difficult to surmount. Already, her grandmother Lewinsky and a number of other family members had shut her out, refusing to acknowledge her existence. In the midst of Monica's grand jury testimony, her eighty-seven-year-old grandmother had "stroked out" and nearly died. Lying in the hospital bed, Grandma Lewinsky had looked away from the television and asked her son Bernie in a thick German accent, "Vat's this about the [blue] dress?" Bernie had "pled the Fifth," replying, "Mom, I don't know." Not to be deterred, the elderly lady then asked, "Vat is oral sex?" Bernie was speechless. Thinking quickly, his wife, Barbara, interjected, "It's when you *talk* about it, Mom."

Even worse, someone had slid a "huge stick bomb" through the Lewinskys' mailbox in the fashionable Brentwood section of Los Angeles, blowing up their piano and nearly causing a house fire. There were "crazy people" out there who were stirred up by public drama; Starr's sexually explicit referral was bringing them out of the woodwork. At age twenty-five, Lewinsky thought in horror, the whole world knew her most intimate sexual secrets.

She summed up that day when the Starr Report was made public as one of the worst in a year filled with low points: "I was [beyond] humiliated and angry. I just felt violated."

Back in Virginia, Alice Starr did her best to defend her husband's work, letting her children and friends know that Ken was not the purveyor of smut that some accused him of being. "I talked to our kids," said Alice. "I was surprised that [Congress] would ever let that information out on the Internet. And I hoped that they knew that their dad did not intend for that to happen."

Alice was saddened for all parents who suddenly faced a hundred questions about explicit words and acts depicted in the report. "Of course, I was very upset. I have never read it, because I have no interest in it. I don't read any of those kinds of books. I don't like to watch those kinds of TV programs. And I just had no interest in it. I knew the synopsis of it. I knew generally what it was about. That's all I needed."

The publication of the Starr Report had turned the whole Starr family upside down. Ken and Alice's oldest daughter, Carolyn, was suddenly being dragged through the mud in print. A freshman at Stanford, where Chelsea Clinton was also a student, Carolyn Starr was being portrayed by tabloids as a wild woman even though she was a mature, considerate young lady. One local California rag reported that "Carolyn had punched Chelsea Clinton in the nose and she had punched her out and they had gotten into an altercation." Alice was contacted by the president and provost of Stanford, who reported that they had received "about fourteen different letters" threatening her daughter's life and "threatening to rape her." These threats were taken seriously enough that U.S. Marshals initiated round-the-clock protection for Carolyn, causing her parents further distress.

The sickest part about all this, in Alice Starr's mind, was that her daughter was the last person on earth who would ever harbor ill feelings toward the president's daughter. "She has never met Chelsea to this day," Alice said. "Had my daughter ever met her, she would have given her a hug," she added. "That's the kind of person she is. She's a very lovely, wonderful person and is very forgiving, very gracious, and never, ever would have held it against Chelsea. Nor would I hope Chelsea would have held it against Carolyn. I mean, this is something your parents were working on."

The most distressing thing for the special prosecutor's wife, however, was that so many Americans seemed to be reacting sympathetically toward Bill Clinton. "I guess I thought the public would be disgusted with our president," she admitted, "and that's not the way it happened." Instead, many citizens seemed to be saying, "Oh, naughty boy," and then taking Ken Starr to task "for releasing the information." This threw Alice for a loop. "I thought that there would be pretty much disgust and that he [Clinton] would be asked to resign. . . . I guess I thought members of his own party, the Joe Liebermans of the world, would think that Al Gore should be president and Bill Clinton should step down."

On a personal note, Alice Starr was troubled that the Starr Report was coming to be viewed as her husband's memoir rather than as a piece of work that he had been obligated to produce as part of his duties in public office. "And I'm a little embarrassed that people ask [Ken] to sign the Starr Report all the time. They want his autograph. And I think, 'What a horrible thing to have to sign.' People have it in their hand and want him to sign it. Well, he's so nice, he doesn't say no. But I am sure he's embarrassed by it."

From his increasingly lonely OIC office, Ken Starr had forwarded his son Randy a letter from a cowboy named "A.R.," who had served as their guide one year during a family vacation to a dude ranch in Wyoming. The old cowboy had been kind enough to write during this time of trouble: "Ken, Alice, you two should pack your bags and come out here and let me take you riding and driving cattle through this beautiful country. I'm sure y'all need a break from those 'city lights' and come here and there are no people and just peace and quite [sic] . . . this is a great place to 'hideout.'" In passing along this letter to his son at Duke, Ken had noted, "Even if only in the imagination, the letter reminds us all that there are other worlds out there. . . . Love, Dad." Ken Starr himself—like Bill Clinton—was now teetering between hero status and infamy.

Matters only worsened for Starr's office when Congress released the videotape of President Clinton testifying in front of the grand jury. OIC had refused to discard the tape after showing it to the absent grand juror, declaring: "We cannot and will not destroy evidence of a crime." So Clinton's political team had allowed conservative media pundits to run wild with stories that the president had misbehaved during his testimony, "lost his temper" in a fit of rage, and committed transgressions against God and humanity. As one political adviser would explain the strategy with a smile: "When the actual testimony itself was released . . . [President Clinton's] performance and the expectations set prior to people watching his performance were such that we actually did quite well."

The *Philadelphia Inquirer* called the release of the tape a major "blunder."

Paul Rosenzweig, one of the few OIC prosecutors who adamantly opposed its release, later said with an audible sigh, "We got our butts kicked."

Starr's office suffered another setback when Congress chose to release the fat evidentiary record that had accompanied his report. David Kendall swiftly purchased dozens of magnifying glasses, dispensing them to an army of lawyers and paralegals who began combing through thousands of pages of miniature print in the appendixes, in order to identify exculpatory material and details that provided a less nefarious context to many of Starr's accusations against the president. The Starr prosecutors, Kendall's team quickly announced, had "cherry-picked" the most damaging snippets of testimony. The media was beginning to reach the same conclusion, "contextualizing" the Starr Report and concluding that it was grossly one-sided.

Ken Starr did his best to put on a happy face. To the vice chancellor and dean emeritus of the Pepperdine Law School, where he had hoped to be ensconced as dean—rather than being mired in this ugly sex scandal—Starr wrote wistfully: "As the academic year begins, I cast an occasional thought westward, beyond the great spaces of our beloved Texas and out to the shores and surrounding hills that provide Pepperdine with its singularly blessed location. We genuinely wish we were with you, but duty and providence have determined otherwise. I cheerfully accept the result, seeking ever to bear in mind the admonition of all things working together for those who love our Lord."

However optimistic Starr tried to remain, his resolve was not translating itself into public support. New polls showed President Clinton's job approval ratings hovering at numbers above 60 percent. One question posed by Gallup/CNN/USA Today asked: "Based on what you know at this point, do you think that Bill Clinton should or should not be impeached and removed from office?" A whopping 66 percent of those polled answered: "Should *not* be."

The Starr Report, in a word, was backfiring.

Even First Lady Hillary Clinton, who had ample motive to allow her husband to twist in the wind, seemed galvanized to support her unfaithful spouse, largely because he was doing battle with the ever-treacherous Ken Starr. Indeed, it was Hillary who played a key role in bucking up demoralized White House staffers, telling them to stand firm against the Starr forces. Paul Begala recalled that the First Lady was visibly in "a lot of pain." Yet her willingness to demonstrate compassion and support for the shell-shocked White House troops, when she was hurt so deeply herself, caused many to say: "Well, if she can take it, I can take it."

As one friend close to the president and First Lady explained Mrs. Clinton's resolute mind-set, "Remember . . . she's been harassed; her staff has been harassed [for years], OIC has made her miserable, and she knows they are really after [Bill]." For Hillary Rodham Clinton, the Starr Report was like a call to arms. "It was almost as if the devil himself had caused this," said a close friend. Hillary was feeling, "That's *my* anger." It was galling to the First Lady that Starr's people were "using it for their own benefit." She now focused her hatred on the man who had turned Bill Clinton's marital infidelity into a worldwide spectacle.

"This was an outraged wife," said one observer. Hillary planned to deal with her husband later. For now, the principal target of the First Lady's ire was Kenneth W. Starr.

President Clinton himself later confessed with surprising candor, "Look, this was a terrible personal ordeal for me, and it was, you know, pretty dicey politically. But one of the things that I realized is that I still had sworn a duty to do my job, and that I was going to do it till the last day. And, frankly, it was a constant source of reassurance and consolation to me that I could do my job. . . . I mean, I knew I had done a bad thing personally, a terrible thing. But I also knew there was nothing about it that was impeachable, by any reasonable definition of what an impeachable offense was. And I just decided that the only way that the whole thing could go bad was if I was unable to function as the president."

Only one piece of news shook up Bill Clinton badly: He was thrown for a loop emotionally when he learned that Chelsea had read portions of the Starr Report online at Stanford. For Clinton, according to one aide, nothing was more distressing than finding out that his daughter was "reading this sh——over the Internet." But the president steeled himself and kept working. Hillary Clinton herself set up meetings with jittery White House staffers, urging them to "stay the course of what we're doing." The aggrieved wife told them, "We can't let these guys get to us."

CHAPTER

46

STARR WITNESS

The blowback from the Starr Report was so intense that Washington was thrown into a state of political turmoil. Five days after Congress released the report, the online magazine *Salon* reported that Republican Judiciary Committee leader Henry Hyde had engaged in an extramarital affair with one Cherie Snodgrass in the late 1960s, when the aspiring Illinois politician was in his forties. Blood was in the water and sharks had begun circling.

Hyde, now seventy-four, had ended the affair after five years when Snodgrass's husband had discovered the relationship. Hyde had reconciled with his wife and remained happily married for three decades, until his spouse's death of cancer in the early 1990s. Now, this frightful ghost had been let out of the closet for no reason but to intimidate and humiliate him, Hyde felt. In a statement to the press, he defended himself: "The statute of limitations has long since passed on my youthful indiscretions." Unfortunately, the congressman's four grown children had never known of these "youthful indiscretions." As hail clouds gathered over the Capitol, Hyde was forced to make four phone calls to his children, confessing that he had cheated on their dead mother so they did not hear it first on the nightly news.

Seated years later in his office in a converted brick schoolhouse in the leafy Chicago suburb of Addison, Illinois, Hyde pursed his lips, searching for words to describe this horrible turn of events. "It is the most hurtful thing that has happened to me in public life," Hyde said, not long before his death. "It was in the distant past. . . . I wanted this to go away."

Hyde lowered his voice and noted that there were certain things about his relationship with Snodgrass that he "could not talk about," certain factors that (perhaps) mitigated his own blameworthiness. He intimated that Snodgrass, whose family members were friends, suffered from emotional problems that had made it difficult for him to break off the relationship.

Said Hyde, "It was over thirty-some years before, and my wife had forgiven me . . . and I felt that should have put an end to it." The Judiciary Committee chairman added, his eyes becoming misty as he invoked the memory of his late wife: "She died in 1992. If there was any good aspect to her death—and it's hard to find one—it's the fact that she didn't have to live through this *Salon* story and be humiliated and embarrassed." To have his children and grandchildren know that he was guilty of this inexcusable misconduct, he said, was "a price I wouldn't be willing to pay for anything in the world."

Although Hyde did not directly attribute his "outing" to the White House— he believed that Cherie Snodgrass's husband probably set the *Salon* magazine story into motion—he still suspected that the Clinton forces were stoking the brush fire with whatever kindling they could gather up.

White House insiders would later disavow any involvement in the "Larry Flynting" of Chairman Hyde. The president's advisers viewed these sex stories as "a third rail." If they stirred up dirty scandals for Republicans and got caught, "it could be simply the worst thing that could ever happen to the president." Chief of Staff John Podesta made clear that if any White House employee was involved in dredging up sex stories on Republicans, "I would kick their ass right out of the gate. And I meant it." At the same time, admitted one aide, there were outside "free agents" deeply loyal to the Clinton cause, who were out there "doing their own thing." Acknowledged one adviser, "Who knows?"

—•—

By the end of September, House Democrats were floating a resolution to censure President Clinton publicly as a means to avoid impeachment. Using prominent Washington lawyer Robert F. Bauer as an intermediary, Democratic leader Dick Gephardt crafted a "censure-plus" resolution that would declare that the president "engaged in misconduct unbecoming the stature and high responsibility of the office that the President holds." Part of the proposed deal was that Bill Clinton would have to forfeit his government pension for five consecutive years after leaving office, a total hit of $760,000—a bitter pill that Clinton would be forced to swallow if he wished to survive.

Within days of the censure-plus proposal's being tested by Democrats, Majority Whip Tom DeLay wrote to Republican colleagues declaring that censuring the president was not an option. DeLay directed his troops sternly: "Any talk of censure or 'censure plus' should be stopped."

So Democrats devised a new strategy. They began drafting their own version of an impeachment resolution, hoping that their Republican colleagues would nix it. This bold approach, placed under the supervision of moderate Democrat Rick Boucher of Virginia, involved constructing a proposal that both allowed Democrats to show their constituents that they were not dodging a fair consideration of impeachment and exposed the Republicans as mean-spirited "partisans." As Representative Barney Frank would explain the Democratic strategy, "We realized they were like the Russian army. . . . We were the Chechens. They would come out with no flexibility. They would just use their massed forces and come forward."

Representative Amory "Amo" Houghton, Jr., a moderate Republican from upstate New York, watched the maneuvering of his own party leadership and saw trouble on the horizon. A World War II veteran whose great-great-grandfather had founded Corning Glass Works, and who had himself served as chairman and CEO of Corning, Houghton was wealthy enough and respected enough in his district to be largely immune from threats and intimidation by party bosses. As he witnessed the Republican strategy unfold inside the House, the impeachment march was being led by a "troika"—Speaker Newt Gingrich, Majority Leader Dick Armey, and Majority Whip Tom DeLay (a.k.a. "The Hammer"). These were the "terror guys," as Houghton saw it. They thrived on "exaggerating, dramatizing . . . making dramatic statements." Henry Hyde, in Houghton's view, was an honorable man "who really believed Clinton was morally wrong" and became a "point man" for the more aggressive House leaders. Explained Houghton: "Sometimes your emotions get in the way and you block out logic. They felt we had to be attack dogs."

The Clinton White House recognized that it was now "fighting for survival." Clinton's handlers made accommodations whenever possible to those whose support he relied upon to survive. If the president needed to suffer through extra rubber-chicken dinners to help allies in Congress, he did it. If he needed to eat crow along with the meal, so that voters could hear repentance in his voice, Bill Clinton served it up. His political advisers openly began entering into Faustian bargains with Democrats and friendly Republicans on the Hill. "Things that were important to them—that were even inside the realm of being plausibly reasonable—we would honor," explained one staffer. "If that meant five extra photos or if that meant two extra speakers or if that meant putting someone in a car [with the president], the answer was, we would try to do it rather than not do it."

In the Senate, Democratic Leader Tom Daschle was returning Bill Clinton's calls again, but the senator's reports from the trenches were guarded. Daschle told the president that a trial in the Senate easily could be fatal: "I was concerned that a number of [Democratic senators] would bolt," Daschle later explained. "Many of them came into my office to express grave concern and some doubt that they could be supportive."

It was in this highly volatile setting that *Hustler* magazine publisher Larry Flynt ran a full-page ad in the *Washington Post,* offering a bounty of a million dollars for anyone who could supply "documentary evidence of illicit sexual relations" involving any member of Congress, preferably of the Republican stripe.

Seated in his golden wheelchair inside the posh offices of his publishing empire in Beverly Hills, the self-styled "smut peddler who cares" later explained his goal. "People on Capitol Hill were trying to get Bill Clinton for the same thing they were doing," Flynt said in a slurred voice. "Hypocrisy never wins." Weeks earlier, Flynt had submitted an initial version of his advertisement to the *Washington Post,* only to have it returned as "inappropriate." Flynt immediately scribbled a note to Katharine Graham, the *Post* publisher who had become an icon during Watergate for standing behind journalists Woodward and Bernstein in defending free press. Flynt wrote: "How in the hell can you in good conscience and your newspaper—a beacon of democracy—refuse to run an ad like this? It is a matter of free speech." In short order, the *Hustler* publisher received a note back from Graham: "Mr. Flynt. Will you please resubmit?"

Flynt later made clear that he had no contact with the White House before taking this step. The *Hustler* multimillionaire, who had been paralyzed after having been shot outside a Georgia courthouse during an obscenity trial in 1978, said in a low voice, "I'm a realist. I know there is no upside to a politician rubbing elbows with me. I'm a pornographer. I didn't want to hurt Bill Clinton; I wanted to help him." Yet Flynt clucked his tongue with satisfaction at the outcome. "What I wasn't prepared for," he said in a garbled voice, "was as much information as I got out of that ad."

Republican members of Congress, meanwhile, were trekking over to the Ford Office Building to inspect secret evidence alleging that Clinton had attempted to rape a woman named Juanita Broaddrick—Jane Doe No. 5—in one of the most explosive new allegations yet unveiled. Broaddrick had initially denied any sexual involvement with Clinton when questioned by Paula Jones's lawyers. Recently, however, she had recanted to FBI agents dispatched by Starr's office, asserting that then–Attorney General Bill Clinton had sexually assaulted her in a Little Rock hotel room in the 1970s. The Broaddrick matter fell outside Ken Starr's jurisdiction; for that reason, it had languished. Yet this material had been thrown into OIC's evidence boxes that had been shuttled over to Congress. Suddenly, a steady stream of congressmen, mostly Republican, were digging into this top-secret stash and, in the cloakrooms of Congress, whispering about "rape."

Democrats were becoming increasingly fearful that the other shoe could drop at any moment. In a letter to the House Judiciary Committee, Ken Starr himself made clear that he did not rule out "further impeachment referrals." Feeling empowered and emboldened, Republicans on the Judiciary Committee defeated the moderate Democratic "Boucher plan" by a straight party-line vote of 21 to 16. Barney Frank told his skittish Democratic colleagues, "This is the Russian Army. They can't maneuver. They're just going to go straight ahead." On October 8, the full House, led by resolute Republicans, voted 258 to 176 to authorize the Judiciary Committee to commence a wide-open impeachment investigation.

———

THE president was not the only one on the ropes. On October 30, Chief Judge Norma Holloway Johnson named a "special master" to investigate Ken Starr and his prosecutors, to determine if they had illegally leaked grand jury material to the media.

The details of this piece of the Clinton-Starr saga, although significant, were largely hidden from public view. The special master appointed to handle this sensitive inquiry was Judge John W. Kern III, a senior judge on the D.C. Court of Appeals, the equivalent of a state supreme court jurist. Judge Kern was a straight-shooting, conservative Democrat who was appointed in 1968 by President Lyndon Johnson. At age sixty-nine, Kern had a caseload light enough that he was willing to accept the assignment. Kern's job was to put witnesses under oath, as an "agent" of Chief Judge Johnson, and to write a report on his findings. His office, unknown to the rest of Washington, was tucked away in the Watergate complex, sharing space with a small law firm to remain hidden from view. In the same building where Monica Lewinsky was holed up in her apartment, Judge Kern began quietly preparing to investigate the investigators. He hired a former law clerk to serve as his assistant and then secured a second room in the bowels of the John Marshall Courthouse, tiptoeing around the press and gathering evidence to determine if Starr and his team had crossed the line that separated aggressive prosecutors from criminal lawbreakers.

———

THE midterm election, scheduled for November 3, represented a test of mettle for both sides. For months, House Speaker Newt Gingrich had boasted publicly that the Republicans would pick up twenty-two seats in the House, increasing their commanding majority in that chamber while simultaneously boosting their numbers in the Senate. Indeed, Gingrich had bet the farm by allocating $10 million of Republican funds for television and radio ads that showcased the nasty Clinton scandals, pounding away at the president's moral debauchery and the disgrace he had visited upon his office. The confident Speaker went as far as to tell Clinton, during a private phone conversation, that he (Clinton) should start drafting his letter of resignation. The midterm elections, Gingrich predicted, would mark the beginning of the end of the defiled Clinton presidency.

Yet politics was an unpredictable business. As one Clinton insider would note, the Republicans' overzealousness provided Bill Clinton with just the escape hatch he needed. "If in October of 1998 Newt Gingrich had accepted the Democratic impeachment resolution," this adviser pointed out, "then all of a sudden, there would have been a unanimous inquiry." A united Democratic-Republican front, the White House understood too clearly, would have likely ended the Clinton presidency. To the relief of many top Clinton political advisers, however, the Republicans kept marching forward and went for a total victory.

Not only was Gingrich's bold prediction about the outcome of the November election wildly off the mark, but the unexpected election results proved to be the beginning of the end for Gingrich himself. Rather than picking up a dozen seats in the House, the GOP lost five, whittling down its majority from 223 to 218. It was the first time since 1934 that the party not occupying the White House had failed to gain representatives in a midterm contest. In the Senate, the results were equally staggering. Three-term Senator Alfonse D'Amato (R-N.Y.) went down in flames, defeated by Democratic Charles Schumer. In the South, powerful Republican Lauch Faircloth of North Carolina was toppled by Democratic trial lawyer John Edwards. Both D'Amato and Faircloth had led the charge against Clinton in the congressional Whitewater hearings. The voters, it seemed, were not buying what the Republicans were hawking.

For the Clinton White House, Gingrich's unexpected fall from grace was like the arrival of Christmas in November. By week's end, it was Speaker Gingrich who was tendering his resignation and surrendering his leadership post. He had wagered the Republicans' war chest and the party's credibility on a smashing victory and instead had lost the farm. In the meantime, jittery poll numbers revealed a consistent 60 percent job approval rating for Clinton.

Despite these setbacks in Washington, the Republican juggernaut was reamassing its strength, especially in states with strong conservative power bases. Jeb Bush, the young heir apparent to the Bush political dynasty, handily had won a first term as governor of Florida. His older brother, George W., easily had captured a second term as governor of Texas, producing speculation that one Bush or another might become a formidable candidate for president against Vice President Al Gore in 2000. Representative Bob Livingston (R-La.) was pictured in a *Newsweek* piece pumping his fist in the air with energy, as he prepared to replace Gingrich as Speaker. The GOP was poised to roar back with a vengeance.

The White House, meanwhile, decided to use the election results to Bill Clinton's benefit.

In a surprise move, his lawyer Bob Bennett agreed to settle the *Paula Jones* case for a whopping $850,000. Although the lawsuit had been thrown out by Judge Wright and his chance for success on appeal in federal court was likely more than fifty-fifty, President Clinton now was prepared to pay a king's ransom to make Jones go away. His lawyers' strategy was brilliantly transparent—if the underlying case no longer existed, the alleged perjury in the *Jones* lawsuit would evaporate, snatching away Congress's basis for passing impeachment articles.

Paula and Steve Jones were separating. Not only had their marriage fallen apart, but they also had messy tax problems, which meant the unhappy couple needed cash. Bob Bennett had repeatedly boasted, "Under no circumstances will we pay you another penny more than seven hundred thousand dollars." Paula Jones's Dallas lawyers now told their client that she should take the $850,000 and run. "That's powerful evidence that you whacked them hard," they argued. "You ought to declare victory and depart the field."

Each side would later claim that it possessed "inside information" that it would have won in the Eighth Circuit Court of Appeals if the plug had not been pulled on the appeal. Despite this chest thumping, court watchers familiar with Judge Susan Webber Wright's work gave the edge to Bill Clinton; Judge Wright was famous for writing tight, ironclad opinions that would be tough for any appeals court to overturn.

But such speculation about the never-written Eighth Circuit decision was largely academic. Even if they won the appeal, the Jones lawyers were keenly aware, they were a long way from cashing a check. Her Dallas lawyer, Wes Holmes, told Paula bluntly that if the Eighth Circuit reversed Judge Wright and the case went to a jury, "We're going to try a really, really good case, and you're probably going to lose." He elaborated: "I mean, [Clinton is] an extremely popular character [in Arkansas]. And I really think that there was an easy way for the jury to decide against [you]." The jurors might believe 95 percent of her story, but then conclude, "I think that she was interested in him, and that this was just a flirtatious episode gone awry."

There was either $850,000 behind the curtain, or zero.

Paula Jones herself would later say, seated in a restaurant in North Little Rock, "It was time for it to be over with. And I was ready to get on with my life. I wasn't ever going to get an apology." It drove her crazy that Bill Clinton continued to protest, "'I didn't do it. Blah, blah, blah.'" Yet she felt that the world would see this $850,000 settlement for what it was—an "admission of guilt." Said Jones, tapping a long fingernail on the table as she explained her logic, "I don't think you're going to pay anything if you're not *guilty* of it."

Up until the final moment, Susan Carpenter-McMillan tried to talk her client out of the settlement, arguing, "Paula, if it was me, I'd go all the way with this. You've come so far, you have been maligned, your character has been assassinated and raped and pillaged, so I'd go on with it." Paula replied, "Suzie, I'm too tired. I can't."

President Clinton was equally beaten up and drained of his will to fight. He later confessed that he "hated like hell" to pay a dime to Paula Jones. "I had to be dragged across the finish line," Clinton admitted. "You know, we already had a summary judgment saying that the case was without [legal] merit." He only agreed to settle the *Jones* case, Clinton insisted, because "I was not going to let any of this interfere with my being president." His eyes flashing like a fighter's, Bill Clinton concluded, "And so [Hillary and I] gave up over half our net worth in a case we had already won. And I *never* would have settled it if she [Judge Wright] hadn't given us a [victory on] summary judgment. Never. I would never have admitted to that. It was never true."

WITH the *Jones* case out of the way, Clinton's advisers made a conscious decision to "lay off the gas," hoping to "help [the House Republicans] figure out a graceful exit strategy." In retrospect, this was a serious tactical blunder.

The Clinton team was gambling that most Republicans didn't *really* want to throw Bill Clinton out of office. After all, this would hand Vice President Gore the presidency for two years, paving the way for him to run in 2000 as an incumbent. Yet the Clinton strategists underestimated the strength of the Republican Party's "Hezbollah wing," those who hated Clinton so viscerally that they believed their divine mission "was to end [his presidency] regardless of the consequences."

As the White House made peace offerings, the House Republicans regrouped, girding themselves for a bloody battle. As their first move, Henry Hyde and his congressional troops decided to call Ken Starr before the Judiciary Committee. The Republicans desperately needed a game stopper. If anyone could drive home the seriousness of the charges in the Starr Report, they reasoned, it was the man whose name was on the cover. The independent counsel, they now agreed, needed to speak directly to the American people.

Four days before Ken Starr was set to make his historic appearance before the Judiciary Committee, he scheduled an appointment to meet with Attorney General Janet Reno. Starr's ethics adviser, Sam Dash, was raising another stink, protesting that if Starr delivered his remarks to the House Committee as drafted, this would amount to advocating in favor of Clinton's impeachment—an inappropriate move for any federal prosecutor. Dash was again threatening to resign. This time, Starr decided to nip the problem in the bud; he would tell the attorney general face-to-face exactly what he planned to say in the congressional hearing room.

Starr also saw this as a chance to come clean about certain facts, so that the six-foot attorney general was not blindsided by his testimony. He had never disclosed to Reno that he had briefly been involved with the *Paula Jones* case, both in providing legal advice to Jones's lawyers and in tentatively agreeing to file two amicus briefs in that lawsuit, prior to his appointment as independent counsel. He hadn't been hiding anything: These were relatively minor events in his professional life, he felt. Besides, they were matters of public record—he hadn't outright deceived anyone. Yet prudence seemed to dictate that he should clear the air of any misunderstandings. Starr lived by the creed that honesty was the best policy.

They sat down together in Reno's stately office on the fifth floor of the Justice Department. It was the first such meeting between the independent counsel and the attorney general. It also turned out to be the last.

As soon as Starr had finished making his full disclosures, the unflappable Reno leaned forward in her chair and said, "I want to raise a point with you." With this, Reno pulled out a sheet of talking points and explained that there were a number of "charges" against OIC—ten or eleven, to be exact—that needed to be investigated. Reno insisted that she didn't want to cause Starr any embarrassment. To that end, she had asked the Office of Professional Responsibility, or OPR, to discreetly look into these accusations. She would call it a "review" rather than an "investigation" so that the media's antennae were not alerted.

The ordinarily mild-mannered Starr nearly climbed over the conference table. He glared at his nemesis—Deputy Attorney General Eric Holder, seated next to Reno—and then stated in a trembling voice, "I didn't do anything to justify removal." Reno, ever cool, replied, "I've got these complaints. . . . What would you want me to do?" Bob Bittman, who occupied the chair next to Starr, recalled that his boss was visibly "angry." When Reno tried to assure the special prosecutor "it's not that big of a deal," Starr shot back, "To do this *now* is unbelievable."

From OIC's perspective, this was a thinly veiled effort to kill the impeachment probe and to smear the special prosecutor himself. As a political matter, Janet Reno couldn't shut down his operation without having hell to pay from the Republicans and anti-Clinton forces. Moreover, federal law made it extremely difficult for the attorney general to remove an independent counsel except "for cause," a tough hurdle to surmount. So DOJ, Starr believed, was trying to snuff out his operation indirectly. After all, he was about to appear on Capitol Hill to defend his report to Congress; a public investigation of him announced by the Justice Department at this pivotal moment could derail his investigation and kill his credibility. In the past, whenever complaints about OIC had popped up, the independent counsel had addressed them himself. Now, this decision to assign the matter to OPR smelled like a setup.

Starr himself would later say, anger rising up in his voice, "I knew she [Reno] was corrupt at that stage." He set his pen on the table and explained: "It is like seventy-two hours before I'm going to go testify before the House Judiciary Committee. I'm working, you know, virtually around the clock." Suddenly, the attorney general wanted to refer nearly a dozen allegations to OPR, specifically to one Marshall Jarrett, whom Starr viewed as "a yes man to Eric Holder."

Starr tightened up his jaw as Reno went through her talking points. The whole scene, he concluded, was "pathetic." Holder seemed to have a smirk on his face as if communicating that his team was "in the catbird seat." In response, the independent counsel folded his arms and glared at Reno. "I've never acted like this towards any attorney general," he recalled, "and I've been around a lot of them." At this moment, however, such a naked effort to destroy his credibility went far "beyond the pale."

Before Attorney General Reno had finished her monologue, Starr cut in. "I have two concerns," he said. "One is the independence of the investigation. And secondly, the confidentiality of this matter, which could be quite harmful to the investigation, were it known that the Justice Department is launching a review."

The attorney general replied laconically, "You would be the second maddest person in Washington if this leaked out."

The two law enforcement officials stood up, doing their best to maintain a professional decorum as they parted company, a look of mutual distrust flashing between them. Five minutes later, Starr and Bittman were stepping out of the attorney general's private elevator when they were paged by Jackie Bennett, who delivered the jolting news: DOJ's plan to "review" Starr's office had already been leaked to *Newsweek*.

Starr located a phone and called Holder, nearly shouting, "This is obscene!" The special prosecutor's face was nearly purple; it was the angriest his staff had ever seen him. Holder replied "in his smarmy way," as Starr later described the conversation, that he was shocked the information had been leaked. Starr later shared his own theory as to how this terrible breach of confidentiality had occurred: "It was Eric Holder. *He* leaked it."

Yet Justice Department officials would insist that Starr was seeing evil villains lurking in every shadow, where none existed. Charges against Starr's office had been accumulating for an "extended period of time." Now, DOJ lawyers felt there was no alternative but to take action. Holder responded later to the charge that DOJ had orchestrated a plan to bring Starr down: "It's convenient for them to kind of take shots at [me and other DOJ lawyers]. . . . They don't want to come to grips with the fact that, you know, a lot of people were turned off by a lot of things that they did."

Although these details were not even known to Starr, H. Marshall Jarrett, a career OPR prosecutor with decades' worth of experience, had started reviewing a stack of complaints against Ken Starr as early as the summer of 1998. Jarrett's job, in conducting a preliminary investigation, had been to sift through thirty or so categories of charges filed against the independent counsel, to determine if any had merit. Most of these complaints—dealing with alleged leaks, conflicts of interest due to political bias, and so forth—Jarrett had quickly tossed out. He then wrote a lengthy preliminary report, winnowing the charges down to ten or eleven that warranted further investigation. These were the charges that Reno had placed on the table at her meeting with Starr.

Reno understood that the timing was not perfect. Yet she also worried that the impeachment process could drag on for months, even longer. Some of the complaints about Starr's office, particularly those relating to OIC's handling of the sting of Monica Lewinsky, were serious matters. Reno now felt that she had a duty to take the next step, however angry it might make Starr.

"That was the point from which the relationship between Janet Reno and Ken Starr never recovered," one DOJ official would state soberly.

THE papers of Sam Dash later revealed that OIC convened a hurried meeting on Monday, November 16, just as Starr was preparing for his do-or-die appearance before the House Judiciary Committee. The purpose of this gathering was to decide whether Starr's team should send Congress a quick "supplemental referral" concerning Kathleen Willey. In a twenty-three-page document written by Stephen Bates and circulated to "All Attorneys," the OIC scrivener began: "There Is Substantial and Credible Information That President Clinton Lied under Oath, Both in a Civil Deposition and in the Grand Jury, about an Encounter with Kathleen Willey." On September 15, the FBI had administered a polygraph test to Willey, providing fresh evidence of potentially impeachable offenses. In response to the question, "Did the president place his hand on your breast?" Willey had responded, "Yes." In response to the follow-up question, "Did President Clinton place your hand on his groin?" the witness had answered, "Yes." The FBI polygrapher concluded in his report: "It is the opinion of this examiner that Ms. Willey was truthful when responding to the above listed questions during this test."

OIC also was prepared to make public that Kathleen Willey had told a number of friends about the encounter. These confidantes included Linda Tripp and Willey's close friend Julie Hiatt Steele.

There were problems in opening this can of worms, however. The internal OIC memo itself acknowledged that Willey's story could be discredited on a half-dozen grounds. For one, Willey had taken *two* polygraph tests. The first of these, conducted on September 15 (which the OIC memo reduced to a footnote), had produced "inconclusive" results due to "a lack of consistent, specific, and significant physiological responses." To compound the problem, Willey had told many versions of the story to many friends. To some, she had asserted that Clinton had "kissed" her; "kissed and fooled around"; given her a "forced lengthy kiss and not just a peck"; touched her breast; and a wide variety of other permutations. According to OIC's own summary, friends described Willey's demeanor in describing the encounter in dramatically different ways—ranging from "shocked" to "surprised and caught off guard" to "not [particularly] upset." In another strange twist, Willey had sent glowing letters to President Clinton after the alleged incident, which seemed "incompatible" with the grotesque sexual advance she had alleged. Worst of all, Kathleen Willey had recently admitted to "giving false information to the FBI."

During the course of official interviews, Willey had denied engaging in sexual intercourse with a man named Shaun Docking and denied telling Docking that she was pregnant with their child—both denials, the FBI had determined, were patently false. Also, Willey's former friend, Julie Hiatt Steele, who had originally corroborated Willey's account in interviews with *Newsweek,* had now recanted under oath, insisting that "she had lied to *Newsweek* at the request of Ms. Willey."

After a heated internal debate, the Starr prosecutors decided to scrap the idea of sending Congress a new referral on the Willey matter because her serious credibility problems might further tarnish OIC's own standing, just as Starr was preparing for the most important testimony of his public career.

———

As he worked endless days and nights during the late fall of 1998, Ken Starr felt as if he had sunk to the lowest point of a terribly bleak year. The ordinarily cheerful public servant was becoming insecure and wary. He sent a note defending his record to his ninety-one-year-old mother in Texas, who was recovering from a recent illness: "Dear Mom. Howdy. I don't usually burden you with newspaper pieces, but the enclosed article caught Alice's eye." The dutiful son attached an article from the conservative weekly *Human Events*: "Kenneth Starr's Real Crime: He Told Truth, Not Lies, About a Perjurious, Salacious President."

In a letter to daughter Carolyn at Stanford, Starr enclosed a clipping from the *Houston Chronicle* about the still-distant race for the White House in 2000. The newspaper noted that Governor George W. Bush, from Starr's home state of Texas, was "looking forward to pushing his agenda through the Legislature and making the most momentous decision of his life—whether to run for president." Governor Bush had emphasized that he would first need to consult with his wife, Laura, and their twin sixteen-year-old daughters because this important decision affected them all. The Texas governor reminded the reporter that Iraqi President Saddam Hussein had "threatened his [Bush's] family in 1991" when his father, President George H. W. Bush, had sent troops into the Persian Gulf. This death threat had necessitated "around-the-clock Secret Service protection," an ugly time for the whole Bush family. Ken Starr now reassured his daughter, who was dealing with uncomfortable security issues of her own at Stanford: "The comments by Governor George W. Bush . . . remind us that public service sometimes carries with it the (temporary) demands of intrusive measures."

Those close to Starr could tell that he was plagued by increasing self-doubt. Sealy M. Yates, an attorney in Orange, California, who served on the Pepperdine Law School Board of Visitors with Starr, circulated a then-high-tech "E-Mail Memorandum" to family and friends around the country, alerting them that the situation for the independent counsel was worsening: "I have a friend who is going through hell right now," Yates wrote. "My friend is also my brother in

Christ. I believe that my friend and brother is in trouble with the world because he desires to represent Christ well in the task to which he has been called. My friend is Judge Kenneth Starr, the special prosecutor in the Whitewater and Monica S. Lewinsky matters, both involving the President of the United States and his advisers, and both involving the issue of lying and obstruction of justice." Yates closed by telling his list of electronic contacts: "I know that Ken Starr needs, and would very much appreciate, our prayers as he stands up for righteousness in a world which has forgotten what the word means."

———

ALICE Starr sat in the congressional hearing room two rows behind her husband. She tried to remain calm despite the bright lights aimed at Ken. "I thought it was something he had to do," she later said. "Sounds like something if he refused to do it, there would have been really bad PR press." Alice was accompanied by her parents, who sat motionless in the hearing chamber alongside OIC prosecutors Sol Wisenberg and Bob Bittman. "I saw the back of [Ken's] head the entire time," Alice recalled, replaying the scene. "So I could just listen. I couldn't see his facial expressions." She at least found comfort in the fact that Ken was carrying notes in his suit-coat pocket from their three children, who had written the messages to tell their dad that "they love him and support him and just wanted him to know that they thought he was doing the right thing."

Dressed in a dark suit and red-striped tie, Starr arranged his fifty-eight pages of remarks with supreme concentration, as if he were preparing for the Supreme Court argument of his life. In one draft of his remarks, the special prosecutor had tried his hand at explaining his mission in near-poetic terms: "The truth is sacred. The oath, both of office and of witnesses, is sacred. The law must be obeyed. There is right. There is wrong." That theme was now running through his head.

Rows of Judiciary Committee members took their seats in the ornate hearing room, leaning forward in their chairs. On the wall, a portrait of Congressman Peter Rodino (D-N.J.), famed Judiciary Committee chair who had successfully guided the difficult Nixon impeachment proceedings by appealing to the loftiest virtues of colleagues of both parties, seemed to watch over the room in silence. Today, the spirit of bipartisanship seemed to be conspicuously absent. Even before Starr delivered the first word of his typed script, Representative John Conyers, Jr., from Michigan, the ranking Democrat on the committee, claimed the microphone and called Starr a "federally paid sex policeman." This unexpected attack appeared to rattle Starr. Not until he got a few minutes into his prepared statement, which would last nearly two hours and fifteen minutes, did the independent counsel's voice become stronger and more confident.

OIC prosecutors watching on a television monitor noticed that Sol Wisenberg was falling asleep in the seat directly behind Starr, creating an impression on national television that their boss's remarks were deadly boring. They scribbled out a bold-lettered note and passed it down the row, instructing the slouching deputy to snap out of it. Wisenberg later took the blame like a man: "I was fat, out of shape; it was hot in the room, and I was hungry. It's hard to stay awake in those chairs. You basically have to be rigid and immobile. . . . So you're sitting there sweating like a pig, and you have no circulation, and I probably didn't have a lot of sleep."

The moment Ken Starr concluded his scripted remarks, Democrats on the committee pounced, forcing the fifty-two-year-old independent counsel to admit that he had no additional evidence relating to Whitewater, Travelgate, Filegate or any other aspect of his investigation, even though he had hinted that these matters were still in play. Henry Hyde himself later confessed that Starr's revelation knocked him for a loop: "We were really surprised at his testimony—that he did not have more material on any of these other matters." When Starr confessed that he had reached this conclusion months earlier, Democrats nearly went berserk—why had the independent counsel submitted nothing to Congress *exonerating* the president or the First Lady on these crucial aspects of his investigation? Here he was, rushing to deliver the Starr Report, which was filled with tawdry accusations relating to Monica Lewinsky—totally unconnected to his original charter—just weeks before the November elections. Yet the special prosecutor had done nothing to *clear* the Clintons, despite taking a solemn oath to do justice. He was obviously engaged in a political hatchet job!

For ten hours, Starr maintained his cool. It was not until twilight crept over the Capitol that David Kendall walked up to the lectern and changed the dynamic in the sleepy hearing room. The president's lawyer squared his shoulders like a reluctant parent about to administer a whipping to a child and then went after the special prosecutor, leading to the sharpest exchange of the day.

Kendall began: "Mr. Starr, good evening." Starr answered pleasantly: "Good evening. How are you, David?" Observers in the gallery chuckled nervously, knowing the true feelings the two men had for each other. Cameras zoomed in on Starr from an angle, capturing the large black mole on his face.

Within minutes, Kendall had forced Starr to admit that he had never laid eyes on Monica Lewinsky or asked her a single question to assess her credibility, even though the entire Starr Report was premised upon her veracity as a witness. When Kendall proceeded to excoriate the former judge for "massive leaking from the prosecutor's office," Starr finally lost his composure. "That's an accusation and it's an unfair accusation!" he snapped. "I completely reject it. And I would say, David, let's wait until the litigation has concluded. . . . That's not fair."

Kendall pressed forward, leading Starr into a buzz saw by cajoling the special prosecutor into denying that OIC had urged Monica Lewinsky to "wear a wire." The president's lawyer immediately produced the FBI's "302" report contained in the appendix of Starr's referral, using Starr's own documents to disprove his testimony.

Kendall next bored away on the issue of the Ritz-Carlton "sting," demanding to know why Starr's agents "held" Ms. Lewinsky against her will. Starr replied loudly: "I have to interrupt. That premise is false."

"I was not meaning to be offensive. Let me rephrase it." Kendall could tell that he was getting under his opponent's skin.

"That is false and you know it to be false," retorted Starr, becoming angrier.

"Well, I'll rephrase the question."

"She was not held."

Kendall returned fire: "Her own psychological state will speak for itself. As to how she felt, it's in the record in her testimony."

Watching the clock run out, Chairman Hyde jumped in to break up the tussle. Just as Ken Starr sighed wearily, "It's almost my bedtime," Representative Maxine Waters (D-Calif.) took a final shot at the special prosecutor, declaring that he had provided the committee with "conflicting information" that might rise to the level of "perjury." Hyde directed Waters to send in her question by mail. He then called on his chief investigator, David Schippers, to deliver a brief closing. The burly Chicago criminal lawyer stood up and lobbed Starr a few softballs, doing his best to end on a rousing note that energized Starr's supporters. He gazed at the special prosecutor admiringly and asked: "And, Judge, for . . . doing your duty, you've been pilloried and attacked from all sides. Is that right?"

Starr replied with a self-effacing shrug: "I would hope not *all* sides but I guess that's . . ." Now came the softest pitch of all:

SCHIPPERS: How long have you been an attorney, Judge Starr?

STARR: Twenty-five years.

SCHIPPERS: Well, I have been an attorney for almost forty years, and I want to say I am proud to be in the same room with you and your staff.

For a moment that provided a stark glimpse into the future, all pretense of bipartisanship was cast to the wind. The Republicans in the hearing room rose to give the independent counsel a roaring ovation, while Democrats on the committee remained bolted to their chairs, scowling. Barney Frank later summarized the Democratic view of this performance: "They were a couple of drunks trying to hold each other up."

Hyde, who rapped his gavel to conclude the proceedings, marked his own scorecard in favor of Ken Starr. "His [Starr's] testimony gave Democrats plenty of time to take shots at him. They missed on every one. Ken was our 'star witness,' if you don't mind the pun."

Ken Starr gathered up his papers, wearily kissing Alice and patting his pocket where the good-luck messages from his children were safely tucked. The long day had gone well, he felt. He had not lost his temper, except for those few flashes of pique in response to Kendall's grilling. The independent counsel had been calm and statesmanlike in explaining the need for his issuance of the unpleasant Starr Report. He had allowed the American public to see him in a proper light—not taking his garbage out or sipping Starbucks coffee—but in the arena of law and government, where he performed best.

In the adjoining anteroom, with Bittman at his side, the special prosecutor looked toward the ceiling and exhaled with evident relief: "To God be the glory."

The euphoria of that night, however, soon gave way to a bittersweet morning, when Starr was informed that his ethics adviser, Sam Dash, had resigned in protest.

Starr's deputies had known the letter was coming. Dash had huffed and puffed about Ken's draft testimony for days, complaining that it had crossed the line from summarizing OIC's report to advocating in favor of impeachment. According to Dash, who would explain the decision prior to his death, he simply couldn't continue to defend the company line. But he agreed to hold his letter until after Starr's testimony. Dash later explained: "Because if I released it right away, it would take precedence over his statement. And I felt that as a courtesy to him . . . I wouldn't issue the letter until the day after, which was Saturday morning."

Starr's prosecutors were livid. Hadn't Dash initially agreed with their decision to file the Starr Report? This resignation based on "conscience" seemed to be calculated to sabotage their operation, just like Janet Reno's stab in the back days earlier.

Journalists, too, questioned Dash's motives. It was no secret that he admired the Clintons; it was also clear that he worried that his badge of Democratic heroism earned during Watergate might be tarnished if he continued to associate with a band of prosecutors dedicated to slaying Bill Clinton. The *Washington Post* issued an editorial calling Dash's resignation "peculiar."

Yet Dash's explanation was not far-fetched, in his own mind. Cautious special prosecutors like Archibald Cox and Robert Fiske, in the past, had stayed far away from Congress to avoid the political sea creatures snapping in the waters surrounding Capitol Hill. The Starr operation, Dash had concluded, was beginning to resemble a lap pool for the House impeachment sharks. "And so I told Ken that the statute didn't authorize him to do this," Dash later commented in his Georgetown law school office. "I thought the Constitution *prevented* him from doing it."

As Starr put out the trash at home that Saturday morning, with pestering reporters demanding an explanation for the abrupt resignation of his ethics adviser, Starr replied tersely that "reasonable minds can differ." He quickly added, with a whimsical sigh, "I love Sam Dash."

Despite the flurry of bad press caused by Dash's resignation, Starr tried to remain hopeful. After all, there were some signs that his public appearance had touched a positive chord among a certain segment of Americans. The *Journal*, a small paper in Martinsburg, West Virginia, told its readers: "The country got a glimpse Thursday at something rarely seen anymore, particularly from those in the national political and media spotlight. Truthfulness." Bonnie Shea, a senior citizen from Seminole, Florida, wrote to Starr that she had watched every minute of his appearance on television. "You appeared as a knight in shining armor inspite [sic] of negative remarks. In every picture of you, sincerity reigns supreme." A seventeen-year-old from Los Angeles, Rachel Scherer, sent a note to "Judge Starr" suggesting that he should run for president of the United States. A French student named Monique Bach wrote to "Monsieur le Procureur General," telling Starr in her best English: "Please allow me to congratulate you on your political work, your action in the field of justice, to which I devote the most sincere admiration."

To Mama Starr in Texas, Ken forwarded a letter from a fourteen-year-old "Christian young man" who had sung his praises as a servant of the Lord. The independent counsel jotted a quick postscript to his mother, now fully recovered from her illness: "Sorry I haven't checked in the last two days, but we will have chatted, God willing, before you receive this little note. Hope all is well. We're all looking forward to being home in Texas after Christmas."

He also dashed off a note to Randy and Carolyn, letting them know that the family was "bubbling over with anticipatory enthusiasm" awaiting their return for Christmas. "Look homeward, angels, to coin a Wolfeian phrase," the ever-optimistic father wrote. "The fatted calf is awaiting. Or Lions Club freshly squeezed orange juice. Or whatever suits your fancy." Starr took the opportunity to enclose an article that he had clipped out of the *Wall Street Journal* titled "Clinton Has Corrupted His Party's Soul." The piece ended with a stark prediction that when the presidential election of 2000 arrived, "and if the Republicans choose a candidate who is thoughtful and ethical, Democrats and independents will rebel against a presidency that rejects individual responsibility and has no ideal higher than the lowest common denominator."

Ken Starr concluded with a hint of vindication, telling his children that the article "speaks eloquently for itself."

47

"MEN OF THE YEAR"

As if to send a strong signal to Ken Starr in Washington, a Southern California jury on November 24, 1998, acquitted Susan McDougal of all twelve felony counts in the embezzlement trial involving former Hollywood starlet Nancy Mehta. Susan hugged friends and supporters, choking out the words: "I'm overcome."

The former Whitewater defendant had gone from eighteen months in prison for civil contempt to house arrest at her parents' home in Camden, Arkansas, to a grueling eleven-week trial in *State of California v. Susan McDougal*, finally prevailing on the Nancy Mehta charges. Dressed in a striking white pantsuit, the defendant walked out the door, sobbing, "Thank you, thank you." Jurors followed Susan McDougal out of the Santa Monica courtroom and blasted the district attorney for even bringing this case. They questioned—openly— whether Kenneth Starr had fanned the flame of this baseless prosecution.

Already, Starr had filed new criminal contempt and obstruction of justice charges against McDougal, scheduling a February 1999 trial in "Whitewater II" to force her testimony. A reporter in the seaside town asked McDougal as she stepped into a car: "Are you scared of Kenneth Starr?" She replied with her "best Clint Eastwood imitation," throwing back her hair and growling contemptuously, "He had better be scared of *me*."

Back on a farm in Arkansas, where she awaited Starr's next assault, McDougal sorted through fifty thousand letters she had received since going to prison. The outpouring of support from female inmates was particularly moving, prompting her to write her own notes of thanks. "I AM A CHANGED PERSON," she penned to a local newspaper editor, "FOR THE SEVEN DIFFERENT JAILS AND PRISONS WHERE I WAS INCARCERATED, AND BECAUSE OF THE WOMEN I MET THERE . . . I THANK EVERYONE WHO PRAYED FOR ME, AND STOOD BY ME, BECAUSE I WAS ONE OF THE FEW WHO HAD ANYONE WHO CARED."

To friends and family, she reported that there was an upside to having done time as a recalcitrant witness: "Every day I sat there [in prison] the one thing that made me happy was knowing that I was a gall to him, to Kenneth Starr."

Even as Susan McDougal was publicly mocking the special prosecutor, the OIC lawyers were huddling behind closed doors, plotting strategy. Starr's office had secured a third indictment against Webb Hubbell in Washington, accusing him of lying to Congress and to federal banking officials in order to cover up work that he and Hillary Clinton had handled for Madison Guaranty. Although nobody outside the office knew it, the Hubbell III indictment was merely a modified version of OIC's draft charges against Hillary Clinton and Hubbell, which Starr's office had scrapped months earlier. Now, this new fifteen-count indictment rehashed many of the same allegations, without naming the First Lady as a target and instead giving Hubbell top billing.

The hulking former Justice Department official stood at the front door of his home, telling reporters with a mixture of puzzlement and anger, "I do not know of any wrongdoing on behalf of the First Lady and President. And nothing the independent counsel can do to me is going to make me lie about them."

Internally, OIC prosecutors were deadlocked. Confidential memos now confirm that Julie Myers had warned her boss that a third indictment of Hubbell under the federal crimes code would pose serious "double jeopardy" issues under the Fifth Amendment. Paul Rosenzweig, one of Ken Starr's most loyal prosecutors, cautioned Starr that this move would lead to another avalanche of bad publicity for OIC and (most likely) a humiliating loss in court due to "Hubbell's age, complexity [of the case], alleged overreaching against Hillary Clinton etc."

Yet the bulldogs in the office could not resist taking one more bite. A confidential OIC report titled "Hubbell Hush Money Summary" and an internal OIC memo dated October 22, 1998, now reveal that Starr's top prosecutors remained firmly convinced that Hubbell was holding back crucial information. Specifically, OIC believed that Hillary Clinton and the White House had taken steps to "take care" of Hubbell financially, setting up lucrative consulting work for him before he went to prison. They suggested a "sinister reason" for this charity work—namely, that Hubbell knew of Hillary Clinton's role in performing shaky jobs for Madison Guaranty, and in lying about it. OIC lawyers were convinced that Hubbell had been paid off.

So Starr and his deputies initiated new prosecutions against both Hubbell and Susan McDougal despite the risks, hoping that these efforts might recharge Congress's stalled-out impeachment drive and allow the House of Representatives to ensnare the embattled President.

———

In mid-November, Henry Hyde drafted eighty-one questions and shipped them to Bill Clinton. The chairman viewed these as akin to interrogatories in a civil case, which would allow Congress to pin Clinton down fair and square. Now, the day after Thanksgiving, Hyde took one look at the president's responses and concluded that they were "smart-alecky," "sarcastic" and even "smart-assed."

For instance, in one exchange, Hyde had asked the president, "Do you admit or deny that you gave false and misleading testimony under oath?" specifically pointing to Clinton's statement in his *Jones* deposition that he had received gifts from Monica Lewinsky only "once or twice." The president had fashioned his reply in double-talk, stating that he "had a chance to search my memory" and suddenly recalled a pile of additional gifts.

Hyde had hoped that Clinton would use the interrogatory answers to "apologize in a sincere way," employing this legal device as a vehicle to show his honest remorse and to "ask the forgiveness of God." If he had done that, insisted Hyde, the evasive Clinton could have "closed the book" and spared himself the ignominy of impeachment proceedings. Hyde would contend, with an open expression on his face, "Nobody lusted after his scalp. I mean really and truly."

The White House political advisers' response was, "Tell me a better joke." They viewed these written questions as a setup, designed to leapfrog over impeachment and to force Clinton to resign. Representative Barney Frank likened it to a matador in a bullfight after having wounded the animal, toying with the bull, waiting for the perfect moment to drive his sword into the beast's shoulder blades: "You know the bull is not going to move his head, so you wiggle your hips near the horns."

Ken Starr's prosecutors, in the meantime, were puzzled by the direction Hyde and company were taking. Privately, they were stunned that the House would even *consider* voting to impeach Clinton without conducting its own investigation. Many OIC prosecutors had envisioned the Starr Report as a mere "guideline" that the House would use to launch its own investigation, hold hearings, and develop its own body of evidence. Now, to OIC's horror, Congress seemed poised to use Starr's controversial report to avoid doing its own independent inquiry, transforming the beleaguered band of OIC prosecutors into the bad guys.

Some of Starr's men also perceived a motive: Rumors were abounding that Chairman Hyde wasn't the only one guilty of "youthful indiscretions"— scuttlebutt now suggested that Speaker Newt Gingrich and other prominent Republicans might be hiding their own extramarital affairs. Starr's prosecutors were beginning to feel as if the congressional leaders were throwing them under the bus, to keep from being flattened themselves.

House Republicans, for their part, were fed up with Starr's impotent investigation. Privately, they were stunned that after all this time and millions of dollars of resources, Starr didn't have "more goods" on Bill Clinton. Hyde's investigative chief, David Schippers, had all but written Starr off. Schippers had begun devising his own radical plan by which Congress would use its extraordinary impeachment-related powers to subpoena Justice Department records relating to suspected law violations by the Clinton-Gore campaign in 1996. When DOJ refused to comply, the House of Representatives would immediately hold Justice Department officials (including Attorney General Janet Reno) in contempt and lock them up in a "jail-type facility." Hyde's committee then would keep the recalcitrant officials incarcerated until they handed over evidence that Republicans believed they were hiding—the documents might then provide another footing for impeachment. Schippers intended to subpoena every record in the Justice Department if necessary. "If they won't give it to us," he told Hyde, "we'll bring them in and we'll put them in jail."

Schippers also tried to shore up the case against Clinton by driving to Fredericksburg, Virginia, to meet secretly with Kathleen Willey. If Starr couldn't deliver additional firepower, Schippers told his boss, they would build up their own arsenal of blockbuster evidence.

<hr>

THE effort by some Republicans to amass new evidence against Bill Clinton by proving criminal conduct on the part of the Clinton-Gore campaign in 1996 had largely sputtered out by early December. Attorney General Janet Reno had formally notified the three-judge panel that there existed "no reasonable grounds" that would warrant further investigation of these matters. With this avenue foreclosed, House Republicans marched forward, carrying their most potent grenades.

On December 12, Henry Hyde garnered a majority vote on four proposed impeachment articles flowing directly from the Starr Report. These were patterned closely after the Watergate counts lodged against President Nixon. From Hyde's perspective, it was time to "let the chips fall where they may." He knew that under ordinary circumstances, it might have been more appropriate to wait until the 106th Congress took over in January, rather than steaming ahead in the final weeks of the 105th Congress. But nothing about this situation was ordinary. Hyde later explained: "We had a bill of impeachment, we had the evidence already adduced, let's see it through. Let the jury take its vote."

Nearly a dozen moderate Republicans, including Jack Quinn of New York, were starting to "go South" on Bill Clinton. According to Clinton's intelligence, the Republican Whip, Tom DeLay (nicknamed "The Hammer"), was openly threatening to punish members by taking away committee assignments and chairmanships if they didn't fall in line.

Moderate Republicans looking for an out latched onto the theme that voting to impeach was not "really throwing the President out of office"; it was just "moving [the matter] on to the Senate" for a decision. "And so, you know, a lot of them folded like Dick's hatband," President Clinton would later say of the moderate Republicans who turned on him. "And they wanted to look like they did it on principle so they said, 'Well, [the president] wasn't contrite enough.'"

Representative Barney Frank, watching from the Democratic sidelines, would posit that "true believer right-wing fundamentalists" like Tom DeLay had stepped into a "vacuum" in Republican leadership and had seized control. As Frank watched the march toward an impeachment vote, these "true believers" were in control: "Their view was that Bill and Hillary Clinton were two kinds of wizards that sort of bewitched America. And they really believed that if they could get rid of the Clintons and their sort of magical powers, they'd have their country back. So to them this was not an impeachment. They wanted to drive a stake through the Clintons' hearts. This was an exorcism."

———

JUST as the full House of Representatives prepared to take a final vote, all hell broke loose in the Middle East. President Clinton was checking out of a hotel in Jerusalem on December 15, having met with Palestinian and Israeli leaders on a four-day peace mission, when political advisers informed him that Iraqi President Saddam Hussein was again defying the U.N. weapons inspectors, refusing to permit them to search suspected facilities for "weapons of mass destruction." Despite repeated promises to comply, the Iraqi dictator was thumbing his nose at the United States and the United Nations. National Security Adviser Sandy Berger and Secretary of State Madeleine Albright—who accompanied the president back to Washington on *Air Force One*—warned that if a military strike was not executed within forty-eight hours, the United States would put itself at risk and endanger security around the globe.

His eyes puffy from stress and exhaustion, made worse by allergies that some mornings caused him to remain hidden from view in the White House residence, Clinton received a final briefing early on the 16th. National Security Council advisers recommended an immediate attack aimed at Saddam's elite Republican Guard to catch the Iraqi dictator off guard. Yet there was a delicate matter of timing, recalled Clinton aide Doug Sosnik: "If you looked at the calendar and looked at the clock, the Ramadan [the Islamic holy month of fasting and prayer that commenced with the new moon] and the climate, the weather and other issues . . . we didn't have a lot of good choices." The window of opportunity for a military strike was narrowing by the hour.

The "cloud of impeachment," those surrounding President Clinton observed, was placing staggering pressures on the commander in chief at this moment in his presidency. The president's national security advisers understood that their decision to strike at Iraq had nothing to do with the impeachment situation. But they also knew that Republican flamethrowers would soon be shrieking, "Wag the Dog!"

By 8:00 in the morning, nearly a dozen U.S. Navy warships, joined by British forces, moved into position to launch missile sorties and bombing raids on nearly a hundred targets in Iraq. As soon as the news of Operation Desert Fox became public, Republican leaders in Congress went ballistic. Senator Trent Lott, Majority Leader from Mississippi, stated angrily into a bank of microphones: "I cannot support this military action in the Persian Gulf at this time." The Republican leader declared, "Both the timing and the policy are subject to question." Representative Gerald Solomon of New York, a staunch conservative who openly despised Bill Clinton, lashed out: "It's obvious they're doing everything they can to postpone the vote on this impeachment in order to try to get any kind of leverage they can, and the American people ought to be outraged about it."

The House Republican caucus crowded into a basement room in the Capitol to watch televised coverage, as tracer lights arced through the sky and bombs rained down on the Iraqi capital of Baghdad shortly after 5:00 P.M. Eastern Time. With dark bags under his eyes, President Clinton delivered a sober address to the nation, explaining the necessity of swift military strikes to disarm Iraq's "nuclear, chemical and biological weapons programs." If left unchecked, Clinton warned, "Saddam Hussein will use these terrible weapons again." The haggard-looking president declared that even the current crisis in Washington would not "distract Americans or weaken our resolve to face [our enemies] down."

Defense Secretary Bill Cohen hurried over to Capitol Hill, seeking to calm the jitters of vacillating members of Congress. In the meantime, House Speaker–designate Bob Livingston scheduled the opening of impeachment debates for Friday, December 18. He would postpone impeachment hearings one day, Livingston allowed, in deference to the troops. But Bill Clinton was not going to avoid his day of reckoning by picking fights with Iraqi dictators.

Experts in the American presidency would forever speculate on whether the stress of five years' worth of scandals and, now, an imminent impeachment vote, were finally beginning to cloud President Clinton's judgment. The party line, expressed by the president's inner circle, was that Clinton compartmentalized matters so masterfully that he was able to block out this (and any other) distraction.

A number of advisers speaking off the record, however, acknowledged that in these circumstances it was humanly impossible for Clinton or any other mortal to keep from being shaken to the core. Underneath the crisp presidential suits, Bill Clinton was hurt, angry (at himself and others), and fearful of what would happen when the House vote arrived. "There is not a way in the world that you can have all this crap going on and it's not going to affect you," one aide said. "And just the energy level, distraction, whatever the criteria . . . it's just mathematically an improbability that you can have all that going on and it doesn't have an impact."

Ordinarily, Bill Clinton had an uncanny ability to deflect distractions. "He was like a summer thunderstorm," said a high-level adviser. "He could work himself up into quite a fuss and then literally get over it and go on to the next thing." This time, however, things seemed different.

At some moments, during this period of incessant stress and upheaval, Clinton "was there, but he really wasn't there. Either he was tired or distracted." Ordinarily, William Jefferson Clinton was a "game-day player" who could "suck it up" and wrap his mind around issues even when chaos was unleashed around him. By the middle of December 1998, however, Clinton's legendary mental reserves were nearly tapped out.

Clinton's advisers were acutely aware that President Richard M. Nixon had slowly become obsessed with Watergate, lashing out daily in the media about the scandal and ultimately causing his own demise. For this reason, the Clinton team tried to keep their boss focused on his job, creating a "parallel universe" in which the impeachment maelstrom did not even exist. Recalled Paul Begala: "Almost every day in private he would vent" to force the anger "out of his system." Then his staff would hustle him off to his next presidential engagement to shift his mind to other subjects.

At a White House Christmas concert held on December 17, with the impeachment vote dangling like the sword of Damocles over the executive mansion, guests observed Bill Clinton trying valiantly to appear "in control," presiding over the receiving line with the First Lady, shaking hands and giving bear hugs to close friends. The concert, celebrating thirty years of the Special Olympics, ironically was dubbed "A Very Special Christmas from Washington D.C." A star-studded cast of well-wishers led by host Whoopi Goldberg lined up to take pictures with the president and then boarded small trolleys to the South Lawn. One Justice Department official rode over in a clanging cart with rock star Eric Clapton and David Hasselhoff from the television show *Baywatch*, thinking, "I can't believe this bizarre event is happening at the White House."

Friends remembered Bill Clinton looking much thinner than usual, appearing as if he had been unable to sleep for a decade, like an Arkansas version of Rip Van Winkle. Hillary had a bad cold and looked equally washed-out. Congressman Barney Frank would recall stepping forward in the receiving line at this Christmas event, accompanied by a male companion, and President Clinton becoming emotional, giving him a litany of thank-yous for his support. Frank reconstructed the scene: "In June of ninety-eight, the man I'd been living with for ten years and I split. And then I started dating another guy in October, and he was my date for the White House [party]. And I must say, you want to impress a date, have the president of the United States begin the conversation in the reception line by telling you how grateful he is to you, and what you've been doing [for him] and so forth. That was very nice."

Frank assured the president and First Lady that he "didn't think impeachment was going to pass." Two moderate Republicans had told Frank that very evening, he said, that they would vote against the impeachment as a way to restore sanity to the divided Congress.

Years later, President Clinton squeezed his eyes shut and said that he knew Frank's optimistic nose-count was wrong. In the "play yard" that Hyde, Starr, Schippers, and their cohorts had erected for themselves, Clinton said, the outcome was foreordained. "For the first time I think maybe in my life almost, I was dealing with a group of people for whom I had basically no regard," Clinton said, sharing his private thoughts. "I mean, I knew that they didn't care about the Constitution, the law, the personal hypocrisy. It wasn't about telling the truth . . . it was just about power."

Congressman Amory "Amo" Houghton from upstate New York, one of the few moderate Republicans who would stick with President Clinton until the very end, spoke with Clinton several times during this dark period before the impeachment vote. "He wanted to know how I thought it would go," recalled Houghton. "He never asked me for anything. Obviously, he felt that it was good to have as many friends as possible." Houghton's own unwavering view, which he had communicated to leaders within his own party, seemed to be falling on deaf ears, because a certain "mob psychology" had taken hold. He expressed frustration to Clinton—his Republican colleagues just weren't listening. "I thought [going forward with impeachment] was absolutely crazy. It wasn't going anywhere," said Houghton. "Some thought it would send a message—but I thought it would send a failed message."

Bill Clinton now understood that there were few moderate Republicans who still shared Houghton's view.

As strings of festive Christmas lights twinkled over the White House, those closest to the president felt engulfed by a sense of dark inevitability. David Kendall would later acknowledge that the legal team was braced for the worst. "We'd better just batten down the hatches and prepare for the Senate," Kendall told his colleagues bluntly. "Because we're going to lose."

———

At 4:15 p.m. on Saturday, December 19, Vice President Al Gore stepped onto the South Lawn of the White House. His job was unlike any other he had ever faced: He needed to say something reassuring to several hundred million people, because President William Jefferson Clinton had just been impeached by the House of Representatives.

Several blocks away, with a chilly drizzle enveloping the Capitol, a group of congressional Democrats had boarded a caravan of buses and arrived en masse at the White House entrance. The final vote in the House had been 228 to 206 in favor of Article One (involving perjury to a grand jury) and 221 to 212 in support of Article Three (involving obstruction of justice), with two articles failing. The vote on each count ran almost completely along party lines. In the Democrats' eyes, this amounted to a naked display of partisan politics that made a mockery of the Constitution. Not everyone, however, had climbed aboard the buses to join this parade of solidarity. Representative Barney Frank, one of Clinton's most faithful supporters, had stayed behind in his office. He told friends privately, "You know, this guy wasn't up for a commendation. He did have oral sex in the White House and lied about it." Frank's view was that this was "not a moment to be celebratory."

On the Republican side, Chairman Henry Hyde watched the events on television while puffing on a cigar, spitting a sliver of tobacco out of his mouth. As Hyde saw it, this was nothing more than a "high school pep rally."

In this thoroughly toxic environment, with nothing to win and everything to lose at a defining moment of his own political career, Vice President Al Gore stepped to the microphone and issued a rock-solid defense of the president.

Those close to the famously private and introspective vice president knew that he was inwardly seething that Bill Clinton could have been so reckless as to engage in *another* extramarital affair—let alone with a White House intern barely older than Chelsea. Al Gore, both publicly and privately, was straight as a shoelace. "Second Lady" Tipper Gore was built to match. When it came to personal moral issues, Al and Tipper Gore were conservative Tennesseans to the core. Those close to the Gores during this time confirmed that Bill Clinton's escapades with Monica Lewinsky downright repulsed the couple.

As one close adviser recalled, the vice president "was just royally pissed at Clinton." There was also the problem that Bill Clinton was screwing up Al Gore's chances to become president. Prior to the Monica Lewinsky debacle, Gore had been the presumptive heir to the White House throne. With the economy humming along sweetly and with the Clinton administration racking up successes in both foreign and domestic affairs, Al Gore had appeared to be the man to beat in the 2000 election. Now, with *another* sex story marring this scandal-worn presidency, the Republicans seemed ready to pounce and retake the White House. Because Bill Clinton could not keep his pants zipped up, Gore's advisers cursed among themselves, Gore's status as presumptive president in waiting was being shot to hell.

Charles Burson, former attorney general of Tennessee and longtime friend of Gore's who now served as White House legal counsel to the vice president, watched the nationally televised event with "consternation." For Burson and others loyal to the veep, this was like watching him walk toward a buzz saw and not knowing if and when someone would flick the switch. "Here's a guy sitting in the vice presidency," Burson recalled, "in the middle of potentially terminal events. Al's gearing up to run." The question screaming out in the minds of Burson and those closest to Gore was: "What are the implications?"

Gore took a deep breath, as if understanding that the words he was about to utter would certainly come back to haunt him very soon. Clearing his throat, he tapped the microphone and declared that the highly partisan House impeachment vote "does a great disservice to a man I believe will be regarded in the history books as one of our greatest presidents." He continued: "The verdict of history will undo the unworthy judgment rendered a short while ago in the United States Capitol."

With First Lady Hillary Clinton standing beside her husband in an unexpected show of spousal support, Gore cut a commanding figure behind the lectern embossed with a gold presidential seal. As gray clouds crowded the sky, and as the branches of a barren magnolia tree shivered in the wind behind him, the vice president introduced William Jefferson Clinton as "my friend, America's great president."

Democratic legislators broke into a spontaneous chorus of applause. Those in the crowd observed Clinton brushing away tears.

Even those within Clinton's inner circle who didn't particularly like Al Gore, or who found the veep aloof and impenetrable, were impressed with his unwavering performance on this overcast Saturday afternoon. After all, "there was a psychological dimension between the two of them," observed one aide. Over the course of six years in the White House, a "sibling resentment" had developed between the president and his running mate. Now, the bad angel on Gore's shoulder was certainly shouting, "This is your chance for a payback!"

There was also the Hillary factor. The First Lady, from the start of this administration, had been viewed as a rival of the vice president's. Now she had signaled her interest in running for a U.S. Senate seat in New York, seeking to replace Senator Daniel Patrick Moynihan when he retired in 2000. Hillary was suddenly a potential competitor of Gore's when it came to vying for campaign dollars. If there was ever a time when Gore would benefit from throwing both Clintons to the circling wolves, this was his moment.

Yet Gore walked away from all such temptations, doing what his oath as vice president required him to do.

"Al's intense sense of duty was a dominant factor," said Charles Burson. "Also, if he threw Clinton overboard [at that moment], it would have busted up the Democratic party." Gore's brother-in-law Frank Hunger, a Justice Department lawyer and one of the few people in whom the famously introspective vice president confided, confirmed that allowing Clinton to "go down" was not an option for Gore. "He wouldn't have done that," said Hunger. "It's not in his character."

President Clinton himself would later say that Al Gore's support, at a time when most politicians in Gore's shoes would have been tempted to jump ship, was essential to Clinton's political survival. The president understood that this was not a walk in the park for his vice president. "Well, I think he was angry," Clinton would say of his two-time running mate. "He *should* have been angry. Everybody should have been mad at me." As Bill Clinton gave a quick embrace to his vice president and begged the American public to help them "rise above the rancor, to overcome the pain and division," he understood that he had hurt Gore deeply. "So it was difficult for him," Clinton said.

"And he had the same reaction a lot of my Cabinet members did. You know, 'We don't want to see the guy kicked out of office. We're going to support him. We know he's been through a lot of terrible things these last six years for the way they [Starr's office and Republican enemies] treated him. But he still shouldn't have made this mistake.' "

In private, staffers for Clinton and Gore were wondering whether to begin preparing "Plan B" to move Al Gore into the Oval Office, in the event Clinton was forced out. They also agonized over whether to discuss this plan with the president. Both staffs knew that merely raising this idea was like playing with fire. For one, it would cause Clinton to go ballistic. Second, even the slightest whiff of succession planning, if it trickled into the media, could gain traction and propel Clinton out of office. Gore himself made clear through his disciplined silence that there would be no discussions concerning succession. His staff was not permitted to say or do anything that might cause the teetering Clinton administration ship of state to capsize itself.

As he stepped down from the microphone and retreated to his home in the old Naval Observatory, having given aid and comfort to a president who had just been impeached by the House of Representatives, Al Gore glanced over his shoulder out the car's rear window, watching the White House vanish behind him. He recognized that this day would most likely mean "nothing but trouble" for him, in terms of furthering his own aspirations to inhabit that magnificent white mansion.

———

A SECOND act of courage that largely went unnoticed in the public's eye was former President Gerald Ford's effort to promote a tough censure resolution in order to save the country from a bruising impeachment trial.

Ford, who had served as Republican House minority leader before becoming president, stood to lose his status as GOP elder statesman by taking a public stand that would save Clinton's neck. At age eighty-five, though, Gerald Ford had stopped worrying about shoring up his political base. He had taken plenty of criticism for pardoning President Nixon during the dark finale of Watergate. In his autobiography *A Time to Heal,* Ford had argued passionately that the pardon of Richard Nixon "was the right thing to do for the country." Now, Gerald Ford saw haunting parallels between the horrible Nixon situation and the Clinton imbroglio. For that reason, he decided to advocate publicly in favor of a censure resolution.

Former President Jimmy Carter heard of Ford's plan and asked "whether we could do something jointly." Relaxing at his home in Rancho Mirage, California, President Ford would later reveal how this unprecedented joint proposal between two former presidents of opposing parties came to be—and how President Clinton himself rejected it.

In a joint op-ed article in the *New York Times* on December 21 titled "A Time to Heal Our Nation," worked out through negotiations "on the phone and by fax," Ford and Carter argued that a Senate trial would "exacerbate the jagged divisions that are tearing at our national fabric." They instead proposed "a bipartisan resolution of censure," by which President Clinton would be forced to accept a "rebuke" and make "a public acknowledgment that he did not tell the truth under oath." In return, the House would guarantee that this admission could not "be used in any future criminal trial to which he [Clinton] may be subject." Ideally, Independent Counsel Starr would promise to "publicly forgo the option of bringing [further] charges against the President when Mr. Clinton leaves office," to put the matter to rest.

The idea of a censure resolution had been floated for months, particularly by House Democrats. Chairman Hyde and other leading Republicans had rejected it based on an argument that Congress lacked constitutional power to take such action. As Hyde himself later explained, "It's a terrible precedent to have Congress condemning presidents." In his view, this was no different from a "bill of attainder," which the Constitution flatly prohibited. More importantly, Hyde was acutely aware that as a political matter, if a censure resolution of any sort passed, "the steam would have gone out of the [impeachment] action."

Former President Ford later disclosed that White House Counsel Chuck Ruff contacted him by phone, initially, to explore his censure proposal. Soon thereafter, President Clinton himself called. Ford and Clinton had talked periodically about the North American Free Trade Agreement and other matters of state in which they shared an interest. The two men had a good working relationship (in contrast to Clinton and Jimmy Carter, who had a prickly relationship despite both being Democrats).

In a remarkable revelation, Ford additionally disclosed that Bill Clinton was eager to have him (Ford) carry the ball on the censure proposal and to contact members of Congress personally to sell the plan. That plan died, Ford said, only because Clinton himself flatly refused to accept any proposal that required him to acknowledge that he had lied under oath. In 2000, several years before his death, former President Ford revealed the impasse: "The bottom line came down to—I said I could not help individually unless he was willing to concede that he had committed perjury. And he wouldn't. He would not do that."

Ford held strong views on this point. He had pardoned Richard M. Nixon only after insisting that Ford's own White House lawyers fly to San Clemente and explain to the disgraced former president that accepting a pardon, as a legal matter, amounted to an admission of guilt. For Ford, it was all about accepting responsibility—the American people deserved that much, he told President Clinton. Speaking by phone three thousand miles apart, the two men butted heads. Recalled Ford, "He [Clinton] was very rational in his discussion. He had strong feelings that he had not committed perjury. And I tried to convince him, as I saw it, that he had."

Perhaps it was Bill Clinton's abiding distrust of Ken Starr and his fear that any censure resolution could easily be revoked by the next Congress, allowing Starr to march forward and indict him anyway, that caused Clinton to balk at this compromise. Perhaps it was his stubbornness, having convinced himself that his word dances in front of the grand jury would enable him to beat any possible perjury rap. Whatever the basis for Bill Clinton's unyielding position, he was surprisingly candid with his predecessor. Ford recalled, "There was never any rancor. Just a very pragmatic conversation." When Clinton refused to budge on the perjury issue, Ford told the younger president that he could do nothing further to help. "So our discussion ended."

President Ford would go to his grave believing that a stiff and meaningful censure resolution would have been the proper solution to the Clinton impeachment imbroglio. "I believed it was the right thing to do," Ford insisted in a strong and clear voice at age eighty-seven. Nothing good, he felt, would come of a Senate impeachment trial. "I didn't think it [would enhance] the reputation either of the President or the Congress. I greatly preferred another route."

———

JUST as *Time* magazine was going to print with its year-end issue in which it named Kenneth Starr and Bill Clinton joint "Men of the Year" for 1998, as a testament to the historic cataclysm they had wrought, the Starr family received news that dimmed any sense of achievement. Ken's mother, Vannie Mae Starr, was found dead in her San Antonio home at age ninety-one, just two days after Christmas. The Bexar County Medical Examiner's Office determined that Mrs. Starr had died of arteriosclerotic cardiovascular disease, linked to old age. The death was believed to be sudden; Mrs. Starr had failed to activate an emergency communication device she wore around her neck.

For the weary independent counsel, the fact that his mother had passed away before he could travel to Texas for the holidays, while the strain of the ugly impeachment proceedings still weighed heavily on the whole family, added a dose of special sadness that would linger for years. Becoming openly emotional at the memory of his beloved mother, Starr said that he worried that this independent counsel mess had "upset" her greatly. In his heart, Ken Starr feared that the whole Clinton-Lewinsky-impeachment ordeal was a "source of sorrow" for his mother in her final months on earth. "Yes, I was distressed for her," he admitted. "And yet I don't want to sound too—well, the words are failing me in talking about my mother due to emotion. . . ."

After taking a deep breath and collecting himself, Starr continued: "I think it was hard on her, and yet, she was a very strong person." Seeing her son dragged into the thick of a scandal like this—and watching him become demonized as special prosecutor—was certainly disturbing for a saintly, old-fashioned lady like Vannie Starr. Yet she had remained strong and had learned to "speak her mind" when journalists (including those from the *National Enquirer*) traipsed around her property looking for a quote. Ken Starr said, regaining a flicker of humor, "She was from the old school. Honor, integrity, the stuff I was brought up on. And that was mother's milk; that's Mom. That was Mother. She was very grounded in a sense of right and wrong and 'what's honorable and what is not honorable.' And 'what is excellent and what is not.' The sacred versus the profane. And 'you strive imperfectly to aim high, to aim for excellence and for the sacred. . . .' It was a very Christian perspective."

The independent counsel sat silently for a moment, before concluding: "She was a very sweet lady, and not a lady of this world, of the things of this world."

A terrible snowstorm in the East prevented the Starrs from arriving in San Antonio at the Mission Park Funeral Chapel in time for the visitation and viewing. They did make it, accompanied by a U.S. Marshals' protective detail, in time for the graveside service and burial at "the Starr Cemetery" in Elkhart, Texas, a plot originally dedicated to family members who had served in the Confederate army during the Civil War. In this dry, rural expanse of East Texas, where Ken Starr's father had grown up, Vannie Mae Starr was lowered into her final resting place, while her son the special prosecutor wept aloud.

As he bid farewell to the woman who had reared him and taught him to lead a humble and honorable life, Ken Starr found a bitter irony in the fact that his face was appearing on the covers of millions of copies of *Time* magazine—covers that his mother would never see. The *Time* article, in feting two men locked in a political fight to the death—as the country tumbled into a new year with a Senate

impeachment trial pending—amounted to a backhanded compliment to both recipients. It was as if the magazine were presenting a dubious award to two combat-
ants who had engaged in a prolonged, bloody, undignified struggle that had
stripped away the mystique of public service, thus hastening the death of American virtue.

The *Time* piece began: "For rewriting the book on crime and punishment,
for putting prices on values we didn't want to rank, for fighting past all reason a
battle whose casualties will be counted for years to come, Bill Clinton and Kenneth Starr are TIME's Men of the Year."

CHAPTER

48

THIRTEEN ANGRY MANAGERS

Senate Majority Leader Trent Lott was sitting in the den of his home on
the Gulf of Mexico in Pascagoula, Mississippi, as the House of Representatives registered its historic vote to impeach President Bill Clinton.
The handsome former cheerleader from Ole Miss, who favored an American flag
pin on his lapel to display his ardent patriotism, was not in the least pleased. As
a member of the House for sixteen years, he represented a district that abutted
that of Congressman Bob Livingston, just across the Pearl River in Louisiana.
The Livingston and Lott children had grown up together; wives Trish Lott and
Bonnie Livingston were dear friends. Watching the "staggering sequence of
events" that had forced Livingston to step down after Larry Flynt had "outed"
him was like a knife driven into Lott's own heart. This president, whom Lott
didn't especially like, had engaged in disgraceful conduct. Yet the Mississippi
senator had no desire to manage an unseemly impeachment trial. As he stared at
the television, Senator Lott's jaw fell open. He remembered thinking, "This
bomb [is] being pitched into my lap."

Lott picked up the phone and dialed the home of Senate Minority Leader
Tom Daschle, Democrat from South Dakota. The two men's relationship was at
times prickly; yet of late, they had been working together productively. Lott
calmly told his colleague, "Tom, we're going to have to deal with this thing. And
I hope we can do it with the proper decorum and dignity and fairness."

The two senators agreed on one point—the whole impeachment effort had been "mishandled in the House." It had turned into "far too politicized and far too confrontational an experience." They would now have to manage the trial "in keeping with the expectations of the American people" in a fashion that would withstand history's scrutiny. To do this, the two leaders would have to eliminate the stench of partisanship, however difficult that might be.

Quietly, the Senate had already begun printing copies of a memo called "Procedures and Guidelines for Impeachment Trials in the United States Senate." This obscure document had been authored by the Senate parliamentarian during the Watergate era; it covered the impeachment trial of President Andrew Johnson in 1868, with updates to include more recent trials of federal judges in the late 1980s. This pamphlet was all the Senate had as a road map for the Clinton impeachment trial. Using only a four-digit document number to keep reporters from catching wind of it, the Senate staffers had quietly ordered thousands of copies to be published and bound, readying themselves for an onslaught of questions concerning a trial for which they were completely unprepared.

The dubious impeachment trial of President Andrew Johnson, which had opened in the Senate in March 1868 and lasted two and a half months, provided the only precedent for structuring the Clinton proceedings. President Johnson, a Democrat, had been impeached by a House of Representatives dominated by radical Republicans who had floated dark theories that Johnson had played a role in President Lincoln's assassination and was a traitor to Lincoln's Reconstruction policies in the South. As a technical matter, Johnson had been impeached for refusing to follow the Tenure of Office Act when he fired Secretary of War Edwin M. Stanton without Congress's approval; Johnson had claimed the act was unconstitutional. As a practical matter, however, the Johnson impeachment trial was a showdown between political opponents fighting for control of the nation's agenda after the Civil War.

Seven House impeachment managers, all of them Republicans, had served as prosecutors. The chief justice of the United States, Salmon P. Chase, presided over the trial pursuant to Article I, Section 3, of the Constitution. The president did not appear at trial; nor was he required to do so. The proceedings consisted of lengthy presentations by the managers who introduced evidence; testimony from scattered witnesses; long rebuttals by President Johnson's defense team; impassioned closing arguments; and a prolonged roll call vote on three articles of impeachment (there had been eleven in total). In the end, the Senate acquitted Johnson by a razor-thin margin of one vote. The president survived the political assault—just barely—and the nation slowly put this bruising experience behind it.

Other than that long-ago history preserved in dusty boxes in the Senate's archives, little precedent was available to construct a blueprint for the trial of William Jefferson Clinton in the winter of 1999. Alexander Hamilton, in *Federalist Paper No. 65*, had suggested that impeachable offenses were limited to "offenses which proceed from the misconduct of public men," or from the abuse or violation of some public "trust." The legal scholar Joseph Story, who later occupied a seat on the Supreme Court, had described impeachment as "a proceeding purely of a political nature. It is not so much designed to punish an offender as to secure the state against gross official misdemeanors. It touches neither [the accused's] person or his property, but simply divests him of his political capacity." Yet not everyone shared such a narrow view. Then House Minority Leader Gerald R. Ford, in leading an unsuccessful impeachment effort against ultraliberal Justice William O. Douglas in 1970, had proclaimed that an impeachable offense was "whatever a majority of the House of Representatives considers it to be at a given moment in history."

Two centuries after the founding of the nation, there was scant precedent as to how—or why—William Jefferson Clinton could be convicted and removed from office.

———

THE duty fell upon Chief Justice William H. Rehnquist, seventy-four years old and a pillar of conservatism on the Court, to occupy the presiding chair in the Clinton impeachment trial. Senators Lott and Daschle now faced a hundred logistical nightmares: How would the Senate leaders, who usually ran that body's proceedings, interface with the chief justice? (They immediately dispatched their staffs to the Supreme Court, to meet with the chief.) What about space? Every member of Congress, including all 435 House members, technically had a right to a seat in the Senate chamber for the entire trial. Where in heaven's name would they fit? What about the thirteen House managers (who would serve as prosecutors) and the half-dozen lawyers for the president who needed space on the Senate floor? If witnesses were going to be called, would the Senate carpenters need to construct a witness box? The most recent impeachment proceedings— involving federal judges Henry Claiborne, Alcee Hastings, and Walter Nixon— had all been handled under Senate rules by a "Committee of Twelve," a dozen senators who heard testimony and made recommendations to the full body. The impeachment trial of a president was a totally different creature, requiring the participation of all hundred senators. How would everyone be squeezed into the tiny Senate chamber without turning this into a Ringling Brothers Circus?

Robert Dove, the nonpartisan Senate parliamentarian, was assigned to work out the details. A political scientist from Iowa who had advised senators of both parties for decades, Dove was an intellectually sharp man with the friendly manner of Burl Ives. He was viewed as a person absolutely loyal to the Senate as an institution. He understood that in sharp contrast to their colleagues in the House, senators of neither party seemed eager to detonate this impeachment bomb. Most feared that the trial would gobble up months of time that had been allocated for pressing legislative matters and that would wreck their own agendas.

Dove, who interacted daily with senators of both parties, recalled that the general sense among them, save for a few highly partisan members, was, "How does the Senate, in effect, stiff the House?" He added, "There was very much a sense of giving a payback." Senators felt as if they had "been had" by their colleagues in the lower chamber. The prevailing opinion was, "The House had done this to the Senate, and the Senate was going to do it back to the House. The president was almost an afterthought."

The senators understood that a successful trial could not possibly work from a one-sided, "partisan basis." Convicting a federal official required a vote of two-thirds of the senators; experience had shown that a divided Senate would never accomplish this feat. "The impeachments [of federal judges] that had happened in the 1980s had been overwhelmingly bipartisan," explained Dove. "The assumption was that that's how an impeachment worked."

As Christmas break vanished in a wintry blur, Trent Lott explored a proposal to wrap up the impeachment trial in as few as six days. Dubbed the "Gorton-Lieberman plan"—for Senators Slade Gorton, a Republican from Washington, and Joseph Lieberman, a Democrat from Connecticut—this proposal called for a quick trial without any witnesses or additional testimony. The record would be "reviewed, read, [and] presented" by the House managers, and a vote taken.

Strong conservative senators like Republican Whip Don Nickles of Oklahoma and Rick Santorum of Pennsylvania mocked this plan, calling it pusillanimous and saying it would let Clinton off the hook too easily. So Lott's own team scotched the idea before they had even returned from the holiday break. Lott would later express regret that it had been derailed. "Sometimes, a leader makes a decision and starts going down the trail; he looks back and the troops are not there, . . ." the Mississippi senator explained. "Do you keep going forward? No. You say, 'Okay. That was one proposal. Let's try something else.'"

A variety of censure proposals were being floated as trial balloons. Most of these were popping on impact in the chilly atmosphere. Even the White House lawyers were ambivalent. David Kendall, for one, thought it was "better to duke it out" than to agree to some "nasty censure motion" that would rebuke the president and open the door for later criminal prosecution by Starr. The feeling inside the White House was, "We had the cards. We were concerned with the historical record. Censure was a device in lieu of impeachment . . . it was too late." On the other hand, *anything* seemed better than going to trial and risking Clinton's removal from office, especially since a core group of deeply conservative Republicans seemed to view Clinton as "the Spawn of Satan" and wanted to remove him at all costs.

Kendall and White House Counsel Charles Ruff paid a courtesy call on Chairman Hyde at his Capitol Hill office, to determine if a compromise might be feasible. The chairman, famous for smoking long, odoriferous cigars, pulled out a fistful of stogies from a humidor and offered them to his guests. Kendall, a lapsed cigar smoker, accepted this as a peace offering. The group smoked and talked in pleasantries, yet they found little common ground. Hyde seemed dead set on a full-blown impeachment trial; he expressed no interest in censure or any other alternative. The meeting, in sum, was a bust. On their way back to the White House, Ruff halted his wheelchair and told Kendall, "The next time we go to a meeting together and you decide to smoke cigars, tell me, and I'll bring my gas mask." Kendall later summarized their effort at détente: "I don't think my gesture did anything necessarily to foster goodwill. But it certainly was a good cigar."

The White House team compared notes and concluded that the ordinarily reasonable Hyde had somehow gone over to the dark side. Said one White House observer, "It was almost like someone had stolen Henry Hyde's body or his brain."

On December 30, Chairman Hyde sent a blistering letter to his good friend Senator Lott, chastising him for betraying his House colleagues by telling reporters that there was no need for live witnesses at the trial. Lott immediately phoned Hyde and defended himself—he had served in the House for sixteen years; he was "one of them." Moreover, as a God-fearing Christian, Lott made clear that he was "just absolutely horrified that the president had fallen into this in the Oval Office." Yet he told Hyde bluntly, "I just did not want the United States Senate to become the scene of a loaded sex trial."

Hyde implored the conservative Senate leader to be flexible. If he and his fellow managers were permitted to put on their full complement of evidence, Hyde said, he believed the odds were high that "we would convict [Clinton]." Even if his team of managers fell short, "Boy, I thought we'd come close."

————

On January 7, 1999, at 10:00 a.m., Chairman Hyde led his twelve House managers from the south wing of the Capitol to the north, moving through the marble halls with brisk footsteps. One reporter noted: "The walk looked like a funeral procession: everyone glum, walking slowly. The House members were all in dark suits. Even their aides were in dark clothes." As cameras flashed and video cameras recorded the historic scene, Chairman Hyde arrived in the well of the Senate and stated solemnly: "With the permission of the Senate, I will now read the articles of impeachment." Web sites streamed live video of the proceedings, the first time any such historic congressional event had been broadcast live on the Internet.

Two hours later, Chief Justice William H. Rehnquist exited a black limousine at a secure entrance on the Senate side of the Capitol. Escorted by three Democratic and three Republican senators, the chief made his way down the center aisle of the chamber. Majority Leader Lott would forever remember being struck by "the seriousness of it, the historical nature of it, the constitutional aspects of [this moment]." Minority Leader Daschle would recall being jolted by the realization that for better or worse, they were "about to embark on one of the most momentous occasions in Senate history."

Ninety-six-year-old Senator Strom Thurmond of South Carolina, wearing a red paisley tie to match his slicked-back orangish hair, stooped over to read the oath to Chief Justice Rehnquist. The tall, bald-headed chief wore a distinctive black robe bearing four gold braid stripes across each sleeve. He nodded his head impassively. Even as Rehnquist was sworn in, media commentators were engaging in wild speculation that the previously unseen gold stripes on the chief's robe might amount to some secret message, in code, concerning his true feelings about President Clinton's impeachment. Justice Sandra Day O'Connor, a former law school classmate of Rehnquist's and his closest friend on the Court, "had a big laugh" over this chatter as she watched the televised proceedings in her chambers. She knew the truth: The chief had seen the Gilbert and Sullivan operetta *Iolanthe,* in which the lord chancellor, who wore a robe with glittering gold stripes, was granted magical powers to settle a dispute among a colony of fairies and sang: *"The Law is the true embodiment, of everything that's excellent!"* Rehnquist had enjoyed the performance so much that a year earlier, he had asked the Supreme Court tailors to make him a robe like the lord chancellor's. Now, media pundits hungry for intrigue were finding hidden meaning sewn on to the chief's sleeves.

Rehnquist rapped his nublike gavel, an ancient prop in the Senate, and asked all hundred senators to rise and be sworn. The blue drapery of the Senate chamber provided a rich background for this historic moment. After standing at their wooden desks to take the oath as fact finders in this solemn impeachment trial, each senator was called forward to sign the official Oath Book. Parliamentarian Robert Dove recalled this as an especially poignant moment. Typically, senators signed that book only when they were sworn in, one of the happiest occasions in their public careers. Now, the demeanor of most senators was "sardonic." Most returned to their seats, quietly clutching the ceremonial pens, not knowing whether to keep them as souvenirs or to pitch them to avoid some hidden curse. Dove recalled the feeling inside the Senate chamber as one of "apprehension and angst." The questions adrift in the room were, "How long is this going to go on? What is going to happen? Is there any reason to do this?" When the Senate recessed at 1:40 P.M., the senators were still asking themselves those questions.

That same day, Independent Counsel Ken Starr indicted Julie Hiatt Steele, onetime friend of Kathleen Willey, who had recently recanted her story supporting Willey's charges of sexual groping by President Clinton. In an effort to rehabilitate Willey as a witness and to provide fresh ammunition to the House managers if they were able to broaden the scope of their impeachment inquiry to include Willey's allegations, Starr's office charged the fifty-two-year-old Steele with obstruction of justice and uttering false statements. These criminal charges, if proven, potentially would land the single mother in prison for years. That sort of strong medicine, OIC hoped, would cause Steele to recant her recantation, paving the way for a new impeachment referral at a time when the House managers desperately needed a pick-me-up.

LATER that same evening, January 7, hidden away in the Capitol, senators of both parties gathered in an extraordinary joint session that would dramatically reshape the impeachment trial. Those in attendance at this rare joint caucus, held on the second floor of the Old Senate Chamber, remembered it as a turning point, although not a single camera or tape recorder or Washington journalist was able to make a record of it. This small, ornate room that had once been home to the Senate (1810–1859) and to the U.S. Supreme Court (1860–1935) continued to instill a sense of awe in senators, no matter how long they had served. Here, under a glittering chandelier that bathed it in soft light, the Missouri Compromise of 1820 had been fashioned, and famous statesmen like Daniel Webster and Henry Clay had given stirring orations that had preserved a fledgling nation. On the wall, a handsome porthole portrait of George Washington in military uniform, painted by Rembrandt Peale—for whom Washington had personally posed—served as a reminder that the country's richest history reposed in this tiny room, a symbol of the strength and unity of the American democratic republic. It was here, on the first day of the historic Clinton impeachment trial, that Republicans and Democrats forged a plan to save the nation (and themselves) from ruination.

One observer present in the Old Senate Chamber that night recalled two hours filled with open, eloquent, brutally frank discussion. Some younger senators, including John Edwards of North Carolina, were forced to stand. Others set up folding chairs in the back. At first, many speakers expressed anger—at the president, at the House of Representatives, at each other. Eventually, the bitter distrust yielded to an honest, near-desperate search to find common ground. Regardless of political affiliation, all the senators seemed to fear that there would be "absolute chaos" if this trial went forward without strict limitations. The senators also worried, speaking frankly among themselves, that the chief justice did not appear to be "in particularly good health." They fretted that if Rehnquist had to preside over an impeachment trial for months, nonstop, this could lead to his physical collapse. A long trial, too, would disrupt thousands of pieces of legislation and wreck their own chance to shine as elected leaders. There needed to be a beginning and an end to this trial, with a relatively narrow alley in between.

Senator Robert Byrd of West Virginia, one of the oldest and most revered members of the body at age eighty-one, told his colleagues, according to notes taken at the meeting: "The White House has sullied itself. The House has fallen into the black pit of partisan self-indulgence. The Senate is teetering on the brink of that same black pit."

Just as there seemed to be no hope of finding a way out, Senator Phil Gramm of Texas (an ardent Republican) and Senator Ted Kennedy (a die-hard Democrat) abruptly stood up "and proposed that the two of them, they thought, could work [things] out." As one observer recalled, the clear implication of their words was "this was not going to be months; this was going to be weeks and perhaps not that many weeks." Gramm was a tough-nosed Texan famous for bashing wimpy liberals. Kennedy was the poster child for left-wing Democratic causes. Suddenly senators began pounding their desks, shouting "Here! Here!" and "Seal the deal!" According to one individual who witnessed this remarkable coming-together, "the two men walked down into the middle of the Old Senate Chamber shaking hands, and the reaction was, if those two senators can get together, the rest of us could follow along."

Trent Lott later explained that the Gramm-Kennedy "compromise" was nothing more than an agreement to agree. As senators filed out of the historic room at the end of the night, they whispered to Lott, "Well, what was [the deal]?" All Lott could reply was, "Don't worry, Gramm and Kennedy are on the same page."

The next day, the offices of both sides were flooded with calls, constituents demanding to know, "How could Senator Ted Kennedy join with Phil Gramm on *anything*? . . . Obviously, this is an outrageous sellout!"

Amid the howling in their own caucuses, the senators quietly worked to clarify the terms of the ambiguous nondeal. One key aspect of the Senate pact was that there would be no additional evidence permitted. The record in the Senate would be limited to "what the record was in the House. Nothing else." Essentially, it was confined to material in the Starr Report and accompanying documents.

This would lock down the case and prevent the House managers from sneaking in any additional allegations (such as the nasty, wholly peripheral Willey or Broaddrick charges) against Clinton. It would also ensure that the Senate proceedings did not turn into a "food fight," as had occurred in the House. Second, the parties agreed that the issue of witnesses would be postponed for several weeks. If any senator wished to file a motion to dismiss the case before voting on the question of witnesses, he or she could do so. If the trial proceeded, the senators would vote on proposed witnesses as a group rather than individually, to prevent dragging out the process. Moreover, witnesses would have to be deposed first; only then would senators consider whether to permit live witnesses at trial. Implicitly, the two sides agreed that no procedural decisions would be made by the Republican leadership without the concurrence of the Democrats. "It was a resolution which effectively gave a veto power to Senator Daschle, the minority leader, about all the further proceedings in that trial," said Parliamentarian Dove, summing up the remarkable nonagreement.

Although Senator Lott emphasized that the Gramm-Kennedy deal had very few teeth as a *formal* matter, he did admit that it allowed his Democratic colleagues to feel "that they weren't being stiffed, they weren't being railroaded, they were going to be consulted, they were going to be a part of the process." Even so, both caucuses were acutely aware that President Clinton's acquittal was not "foreordained." Plenty of unforeseen factors—if the train barreled forward with faulty brakes and unstable freight cars—still could cause a massive derailment.

Lott was facing enormous problems on the Republican side. He and other senior members were being buffeted by "cross-currents" driven by a recent sea change in Senate membership. There existed one of the highest percentages ever of former House members in the upper chamber. Lott was now confronted with a potential rebellion by twenty-two conservative senators led by Nickles and Santorum, who believed that Lott was selling their party downriver and being too "accommodationist." The "House-ification" of the Senate by many senators philosophically aligned with the thirteen House managers, White House advisers observed, was making it difficult for Senate leadership to implement the Gramm-Kennedy plan, even if they knew what it was.

On the Democratic side, too, many senators were still "keeping their own counsel," worried whether they could afford to stand by this seriously damaged commander in chief once the trial moved forward.

At noon on Thursday, January 14, a clutch of spectators huddled together at the east entrance of the Capitol, moving forward under dark umbrellas, hoping to catch a glimpse of the second presidential impeachment trial in American history. A chilly drizzle fell over the public line; a thin fog hung over the Capitol's dome, resembling the backdrop of a state funeral procession.

In the Senate gallery, busts of the first twenty vice presidents, each of whom had once presided over this body, seemed to keep watch over the solemn chamber. An ancient marble clock ticked off each minute. The thirteen House managers, led by Chairman Henry Hyde, crammed together at a long table, facing each other, the victims of lack of space. White House lawyers entered from the opposite side of the well. They were led by Chuck Ruff, who deftly maneuvered in his wheelchair, and presidential lawyer David Kendall.

Just minutes before the trial was scheduled to begin, Chief Justice William H. Rehnquist had summoned the White House lawyers and the House managers to the President's Room, an ornately decorated nook off the Senate chamber. Here, the ghosts of presidents Abraham Lincoln, Woodrow Wilson, and other chief executives glided across the floor, marking the spot where these historic figures had once appeared to sign bills on the last day of Congress's sessions. Rehnquist stood tall in his judicial robe, as the opposing forces milled around him with apprehension. Finally, the chief cleared his throat and stated: "I can't assign you your seats because that is done by precedent." This was a joke: The White House lawyers had ended up on the Republican side of the aisle, while the House managers were on the hostile Democratic side. Rehnquist made a few more faint attempts at humor, then concluded his brief speech by admonishing, "Well, fight fair!" With that, the chief turned around, buttoned up his robe, and walked toward the door. Kendall whispered to Rehnquist's administrative assistant, "Is that it?" The chief's assistant replied, "Apparently."

Seated in the gallery, members of Congress and special guests clutched their yellow tickets, which had been printed according to the parliamentarian's "Procedures and Guidelines" that spelled out the protocol based upon President Johnson's impeachment trial in 1868. Capitol guards scoured the crowd for spectators who might be attempting to use a pen (writing instruments were strictly prohibited) or trying to sneak a mint (food was banned). In the press gallery, journalists hung over the marble railing, absorbing the historic scene with a mixed sense of awe and agnosticism.

As the chief justice entered from a side door, at precisely 1:05 P.M., senators scurried to their seats. The hall was packed. The Senate chamber fell into reverential silence.

Whatever the circus atmosphere that had pervaded the House of Representatives had been, it did not penetrate the walls of the U.S. Senate. Chaplain Lloyd Ogilvie offered a brief prayer, imploring Almighty God to impart "a special measure of wisdom" to those seated in judgment of President William Jefferson Clinton, and praying for "a spirit of nonpartisan patriotism."

Chairman Henry Hyde now stepped up to the narrow wooden lectern, commencing the House managers' presentations. Hyde swept his hand across the rows of senatorial desks, declaring, "We are here, Mr. Chief Justice and distinguished Senators, as advocates for the rule of law, for equal justice under the law and for the sanctity of the oath . . . You are now stewards of the oath."

Wearing a dark suit and a shimmering silver tie, Hyde introduced his fellow managers, who, for the next twenty-four hours of Senate time, would present the case for impeachment of the president. They unveiled charts and played video clips on huge television screens, largely for the benefit of the national television audience, hoping to drive public opinion polls that in turn would exert pressure on these senators to remove Bill Clinton. The managers pounded away, presenting argument upon argument to buttress the charges of perjury and obstruction of justice, reading from typed scripts prepared by staff members who had been working round the clock. In this trial, the prosecutors from the House were leaving nothing to chance.

Chief Justice Rehnquist sat in his large brown-leather chair, hands folded. His only visible movement was to stand in a dignified fashion, at periodic intervals, to stretch his bad back. At one point, Majority Leader Lott tried to exercise his leadership role by announcing a short recess for a bathroom break. Rehnquist vetoed the idea, interjecting: "I don't need to go, so thank you very much. We won't leave." The uneasy twitters subsided and the group went back to work, as the majority leader retook his seat with a polite bow. The senators were not used to a foreign creature in robes telling them how to run their business.

Parliamentarian Robert Dove, who had a bird's-eye view from beside Chief Justice Rehnquist's seat on the raised dais, observed that many senators appeared as if they had been confined to prison. All of them "had to sit without speaking, a totally unnatural act for a senator." As Dove observed it, "the longer they sat, the more unhappy they became." Six hours of listening was an eternity for this collection of extroverted public officials who liked to deliver orations to adoring audiences without restraint. As time passed, there was a palpable sense that the House prosecutors and their Senate audience "were eyeing each other increasingly in an adversarial mode." The fact that the managers were seated in a cluster on the Democratic side of the aisle only made the feeling of unease more acute. As one senator recalled, there was an unmistakable sensation of "friction" in the room.

At 6:59 P.M., when the chief justice rapped his gavel to end the first day's proceedings, nearly half the spectators in the gallery had already left. Outside, freezing rain shellacked the streets in front of the Capitol, creating hazardous driving conditions for those returning home for a night's rest. Bad weather was the least of the problems for the senators; they worried that this trial would go on for weeks, perhaps months. There was no way to tell when, or how, it would end.

THE House managers committed several major blunders as they marched forward, putting in their case. For one, the fact that all thirteen managers made presentations led to repetition that annoyed the already perturbed senators. Henry Hyde later admitted that if he had it to do differently, he would have cut the number of managers in half. "I'd have learned to say 'no' a little better," he said. Nor did it help that all the managers were white males, starkly reinforcing the lack of diversity among the group. (In contrast, the president's defense team was lean and agile and included a dynamic young African American woman in the person of Deputy White House Counsel Cheryl Mills.) Also conspicuous was that all thirteen managers were Republicans. In other modern-day impeachment trials of federal judges, the House Judiciary Committee had scrupulously included managers of both parties to avoid even a whiff of partisanship. Chairman Hyde had managed to assemble a team that looked strikingly like an appendage of the "anti-Clinton" posse in Ken Starr's office, which had whipped up this impeachment drive in the first place. To many journalists and observers in the gallery, it appeared to be more of the same.

Hyde himself later insisted that most of his managers were not "salivating" to boot President Clinton out of office. Only one manager—Bob Barr of Georgia—was "ideologically committed to [Clinton's] impeachment," because of "a particularly strong animosity towards Clinton." Just months earlier, Barr had written the foreword to a wildly anti-Clinton book depicting a hypothetical impeachment trial of Bill Clinton based on flimsy Whitewater allegations—the only grist available at the time. Now, it was as if Barr's wildest dreams were being fulfilled; the Monica Lewinsky charges were Whitewater times a thousand. Although Hyde viewed it as a fair-minded group, to many Americans watching the trial at home on their television sets, the House managers looked like a baker's dozen of bitter, conservative, partisan Clinton haters.

An even more serious misstep by the House Republicans was that they had succeeded in passing only two articles of impeachment: those relating to Clinton's purported obstruction of justice and perjury in his grand jury appearance. In a moment of weakness, they had dropped perjury charges stemming from the *Paula Jones* deposition—by far their strongest basis for a conviction, as a legal matter. Representative Lindsey Graham and other wavering Republicans had explained their logic by saying that Clinton "didn't have any warning before his deposition and therefore this amounted to a surprise attack." Privately, they were also concerned that the *Jones* lawyers had "bollixed things up," asking imprecise questions and using a definition of "sexual relations" that was so ambiguous that the managers would be knocked out of the ring if they pursued this count.

In the grand jury, Clinton had artfully dotted his i's and crossed his t's—even the best prosecutor in America would have trouble proving criminal conduct on the basis of that testimony. With the *Jones* count tossed out the window, this gave the Senate nothing but straws to grasp between its fingers.

On the second day of trial, as the senators fought off the urge to take a late-afternoon snooze, Chief Justice Rehnquist was snapped to attention by a voice that declared: "Mr. Chief Justice, I object." Senator Tom Harkin, Democrat from Iowa, had risen to his feet and interrupted the presentation of Representative Bob Barr. Fifty years old with gray hair and a dark little mustache, Barr had just finished lecturing the senators: "We urge you, the distinguished *jurors* in this case, not to be fooled."

Harkin now lodged his protest: "Mr. Chief Justice, I object to the use and the continued use of the word 'jurors' when referring to the Senate."

Senator Harkin, a distinguished-looking statesman from America's breadbasket, held in his hand a pocket copy of the Constitution. He invoked *Federalist Paper No. 65*, authored by Alexander Hamilton, in explaining why senators in an impeachment trial were far different from regular jurors: "Regular jurors, of course, are chosen, to the maximum extent possible, with no knowledge of the case," said Harkin. "Not so here. Regular jurors do not decide what evidence should be heard . . . nor do they decide what witnesses shall be called. Not so here."

The Republican side of the chamber appeared stunned. Representative Barr was not in the best position, at the moment, to beat back this Democratic assault. Just days earlier, Larry Flynt had accused him of hypocrisy, releasing transcripts of a 1985 divorce proceeding in which Barr had refused to answer whether he had been unfaithful to his second wife by engaging in a sexual affair with his soon-to-be third wife. As Barr smoldered on the sidelines, an aide to the House managers gasped, "Harkin's speaking! Stop him!"

Dove fully understood the nature of the commotion. Most in the room assumed that during these unnatural impeachment proceedings, members of the Senate "are not supposed to speak. They're supposed to be sitting there absolutely quietly." Now, the fact that a senator was daring to open his mouth—a Democrat, no less—created an "audible buzz" in the chamber. Some Republicans whispered, "Senator Harkin is getting around the rules that require senators to be silent!" If Harkin was going to talk, there were plenty of others who had something to say—a hundred senators were penned up like animals; soon they would all begin to stand up and pose objections, launching into speeches, and this trial "was going to spin out of control."

Republican Senator Judd Gregg of New Hampshire raised a parliamentary point of order: Was it appropriate for *any* member of the Senate to speak during the impeachment trial? Even under the guise of a motion? The chief justice peered downward, through his large aviator glasses.

Harkin repeated his original objection even more loudly, as if to rub the Republicans' noses in it. Chief Justice Rehnquist squared his shoulders. This was his first test. He now issued his ruling: "The Chair is of the view that the objection of the Senator from Iowa is well taken, that the Senate is not simply a jury; it is a court in this case. Therefore, counsel should refrain from referring to the Senators as jurors."

The Republicans were stunned. It was a resounding victory for the Democrats, even though it was only a tiny procedural point. It made clear that they would not be stifled or bullied by the House managers. More significantly, it underscored that the chief was not going to throw the ballgame for the home team, even though he was a philosophical soulmate of the conservative Republicans.

"There were questions, initially, whether Rehnquist would be fair in presiding over this trial," acknowledged the chief's administrative assistant, Jim Duff. "I think this made absolutely clear he would be [neutral]." For Duff, this came as no surprise. Politicians tended to see every issue in terms of whether it favored the "D's" or "R's." A disciplined jurist like Rehnquist saw only a legal question on which he had to rule fairly. Said Duff, "I'm certain it didn't enter his mind whether [Harkin] was a Democrat or a Republican."

William Hubbs Rehnquist, seated in his presiding chair, hardly looked like an American hero. With his nearly bald pate, his penchant for brusquely interrupting lawyers who appeared in his courtroom, the bland Milwaukee accent, and his oversized plastic-rimmed glasses, Rehnquist looked more like a grumpy Midwesterner. The son of a paper salesman from Wisconsin, he had established a reputation as a smart but ultraconservative government lawyer when President Nixon appointed him to the Court in 1971. Nixon had admonished the new associate justice: "Just be as mean and rough as they said you were." Indeed, Rehnquist was known as "the Lone Ranger" on the Court, for his willingness to take tough conservative positions even when he was the lone dissenter.

Yet as chief, Rehnquist had steadily turned himself into a consensus builder. Among his colleagues, he was respected as an able administrator. Among his clerks, the chief was admired as a good boss with a dry wit. Rehnquist was known to sit in his office with his feet on his desk, working tirelessly and sneaking an occasional snack of Oreo cookies and milk—one of his weaknesses in life. He also disappeared once or twice a day (especially after a good cheeseburger lunch) to catch a cigarette, a minor vice that he kept hidden from public view, but that kept him marching forward.

President Bill Clinton, from the moment Rehnquist took his seat in the Senate to preside over his impeachment trial, distrusted him. As Clinton saw it,

Rehnquist had already done a huge favor for the Republican "right-wingers" by "keeping Sentelle [on the three-judge court] and having him appoint Starr." Within the White House, the story was legendary that Chief Justice Rehnquist, after instructing President Clinton to place his hand on the Bible for the oath of office at the second inauguration, had quipped, "Good luck." The way Clinton and his team had interpreted the remark, Rehnquist was communicating, "You'll need it."

The chief's aides, however, viewed these stories as reflecting a failure to understand a genuinely private man with a dry sense of humor who was innately fair to a fault. Jim Duff, himself a distinguished Washington lawyer, later said that the notion that the chief had an ax to grind with Clinton constituted a colossal misunderstanding.

"I'd like to say that to President Clinton someday," said Duff, who served as a pallbearer in Rehnquist's funeral in 2005. Even if the chief had made an innocent joke on occasion, he said, "I can't imagine that he meant anything by it." In fact, throughout the course of the entire impeachment proceedings, said Duff, "I never heard him utter a negative thing about President Clinton whatsoever."

What drove Rehnquist more than anything in handling this assignment, those close to him concurred, was his firm grasp of history. Years earlier, the chief had authored *Grand Inquests,* a book about the great impeachment trials in American history. Rehnquist was keenly aware that Chief Justice Salmon Chase, who had presided over the trial of President Andrew Johnson a century earlier, had seriously tarnished his own reputation, along with that of the Court, by favoring the overly aggressive House managers who had utterly failed to make their case against the president. Rehnquist had no intention of repeating that mistake as his legacy to American history.

His paramount concern was to make sure this Senate trial did not disrupt his duties at the Supreme Court. "He was going to get the work of the Court done," Duff said. "Every break, he spent reading briefs. We had some brutal snowstorms during that time. He never closed the Court. He was from Wisconsin; these things didn't phase him."

Even many White House loyalists came to change their opinions of the chief justice. One Clinton adviser confessed reluctantly, "There was (initially) a presumption if Rehnquist could screw us and get away, that he would." As the trial moved forward, however, "while we weren't interested in paying him any compliments, privately or publicly, I think on balance we felt like, other than his imperialness, that he played it straight."

Still, neither Democrats nor Republicans were placing any bets. Despite later accounts that suggested that the outcome of the trial was foreordained, this was not the feeling that pervaded the Senate chamber. As it entered its second week, the Clinton impeachment trial seemed more like a game played according to "bar room rules," by which participants "sit in a bar and make rules up while they're drinking." Anything could change; any contestant could switch sides without warning; any rule in the rule book could be rewritten without notice.

Explained one White House insider, the only thing that was perfectly clear was "how inevitable nothing was."

CHAPTER

49

A SCOTTISH VOTE

Charles Ruff, representing the president of the United States, locked up his wheelchair in the middle of the Senate well. His hands were trembling. On this day, Tuesday, January 19, he was perspiring noticeably. It was one of the rare times, other than the day he learned of the president's indiscretions with Monica Lewinsky, that colleagues had seen the unflappable Ruff worked up.

Ruff appeared uncomfortable with his back facing the chief justice; as a courtroom lawyer, he was trained to show respect to the presiding judge. Glancing over his shoulder to wait for Rehnquist's nod, he finally began: "William Jefferson Clinton is not guilty of the charges that have been proffered against him. He did not commit perjury; he did not obstruct justice; he must not be removed from office." With his notes resting on his lap, his eyebrows arched to reflect the seriousness of the day, Ruff promised to rebut each charge that the House managers had leveled against the president.

Without forewarning, his lapel microphone fell to the floor. The senators fell silent as the paraplegic lawyer waved off assistance, hanging over his wheelchair to reattach himself to the sound system. Chuck Ruff was no stranger to important cases. He had represented senators John McCain and John Glenn in the "Keating Five" scandal. He had handled major criminal prosecutions as U.S. attorney in Washington. He never allowed his physical handicap to interfere with his quest for excellence. The senators now listened with attentiveness.

Ruff, who had graduated from Columbia Law School in the early 1960s and joined the Peace Corps as part of an idealistic crop of volunteers, had served in an underdeveloped area of Africa where he had contracted type 2 polio that left him paralyzed for life. After lying in a hospital bed for six months and learning that his wife, Sue, was pregnant, Chuck told her, "This is it. I'm not going to ever walk." He got fitted with braces that would allow him to stand upright and began the long process of therapy. By the time their first daughter, Carin, was born in 1965, Chuck was in the hospital room rolling back and forth like any other expectant father, using his wheelchair to do his pacing.

Chuck Ruff quickly found his professional niche in Washington, distinguishing himself in a series of government posts, working as a private attorney at the firm of Covington & Burling, and then serving as White House counsel to President Clinton in the years after Bernie Nussbaum's forced resignation. Ruff brought a steadiness to the West Wing. He knew and respected Ken Starr. He had a positive working relationship with Henry Hyde. This serious-minded lawyer, who dressed in conservative Brooks Brothers suits, settled himself into his wheelchair each morning and, with grim-faced determination, handling whatever crisis awaited him.

Sue Ruff was glued to her husband's opening remarks on television in the privacy of their living room. "Listening to Chuck argue was always an incredible turn-on," she said later. Sue feared that if she attended the Senate proceedings in person, she might stand up and shout insults at the managers, like the spectator who had been hauled away days earlier by the Capitol Police after yelling, "Good God Almighty, take the vote and get it over with!" Sue concluded, "I was much better off here, pacing and shouting at the TV."

As her husband worked day and night preparing for this grueling assignment, Sue Ruff played an all-important "chicken soup role." If Chuck was scheduled to get home at 11:00 at night, "I would be at home on the couch sleeping, with some hot chicken soup on the stove." She recalled, after her husband's untimely death in 2000, "I just tried to be supportive and keep him going."

The team of Chuck Ruff and David Kendall, representing the president, was a formidable one. Both veterans of white-collar criminal defense work in Washington, they shared "a surgeon's sense of humor" about the grim profession of pulling clients out of legal train wrecks.

Ruff was in charge of representing the "official president." Kendall represented the "private president." This meant that Ruff would give opening and closing statements at the trial. Kendall focused on "possible criminal exposure," which included the distinct likelihood that Starr might try to prosecute Clinton, before or after the president left office.

Each morning, Kendall and Ruff would get outfitted with special electronic buttons on their lapels, allowing them to enter the Capitol without setting off a hundred security alarms. Inside, they would make their way to their cramped office behind the Senate chamber, to continue the unending cycle of preparation. One day Ruff turned the corner and nearly collided with another man in a wheelchair—it was Senator Jesse Helms, the archconservative seventy-seven-year-old Republican from North Carolina. Kendall, walking alongside Ruff, knew that this senator viewed them with distrust bordering on disdain. The president's personal lawyer stopped and spoke loudly to the elderly politician, waving his hands for drama: "Senator Helms—that man was driving recklessly—do you need a lawyer? I'll represent you." At first, Helms didn't know what to make of this near collision with his adversaries. When the joke finally sunk in, the veteran senator erupted into laughter. From that point forward, whenever Senator Helms encountered the two White House lawyers, he would wheel over to Kendall and say, in a thick drawl, "How's my lawyer there? Do y'all have a settlement from Mr. Ruff for me yet? I'm very easy—but I've got to tell you, the back of my neck still hurts."

It was a relief, even for such brief moments, to have a topic to joke about.

———

THE night after Chuck Ruff's powerful opening to the senators, on January 19, President Bill Clinton delivered his State of the Union address in the Capitol. He was standing before the very representatives who, by day, were prosecuting him and before the very senators who were sitting in judgment of him. Robert Dove, who attended the president's speech that night, recalled it as a surreal scene: "I mean, the State of the Union is one of those occasions that normally everybody is relatively happy about. It's just one of the neat things that happens in Washington, and suddenly it wasn't neat. People didn't know how to act."

House Manager Bob Barr stayed away, as a showing of contempt for Clinton. Chief Justice Rehnquist declined to attend, in part because he was presiding over the impeachment trial and in part because of his back problems. Chairman Henry Hyde was absent, joking that he was skipping all such speeches on a "bipartisan basis" because health problems prevented him from getting up and down repeatedly during these political stem-winders. Hyde declared that he preferred to "sit in my shorts with a cigar and watch the television" at home.

The mood this night in the House chamber was one of supreme unease. If Clinton choked at this dicey moment in his presidency, he might finally run out of wiggle room. His best protection against removal from office was to "[show] that his personal travails were not going to affect his ability to do a good job for the American public." As aide Doug Sosnik summed it up, "Now, if he ever lost that, then we probably were going to lose the franchise."

Bill Clinton stepped into the well of the House of Representatives and

turned in one of the most brilliant performances of his career, appearing unfazed by the political chaos surrounding him. During this masterful hour-long
address, Clinton condemned the atrocities committed by Iraqi President Saddam Hussein that recently had necessitated military action. He spoke of the
booming U.S. economy and of his plan to earmark $2.7 trillion of the projected
budget surplus to shoring up social security. He tipped his hat to Chicago Cubs
home-run slugger Sammy Sosa, who was seated in the audience—prompting a
wild ovation. He mouthed the words "I love you" to First Lady Hillary Clinton,
who waved back elegantly from the gallery. Nowhere was there any mention of
the impeachment trial during this virtuoso performance, except for a subtle
plea for peace and harmony at the conclusion. "Let us lift our eyes as one nation," Clinton intoned, "and from the mountaintop of this American century,
look ahead to the next one, asking God's blessing on our endeavors and on our
beloved country."

By all accounts, Bill Clinton, like Sammy Sosa, had smashed a grand slam over
the bleachers. Senate Democratic Leader Tom Daschle, who led the standing ovation in the gallery, later described the address as "remarkable." Even Majority
Leader Trent Lott conceded that he marveled at Clinton's pluck in the face of
overwhelming adversity: "I was amazed and impressed. How in the world can he
sleep at night? How in the world can he stand up there and give this speech just
like everything's hunky-dory? I mean, it was an amazing performance."

Back in the Senate the next day, Clinton's defense team likewise batted a
thousand. Deputy White House Counsel Cheryl Mills stole the show by picking
apart the House managers' opening speeches and blasting the audacious Republicans for repeatedly referring to Paula Jones's lawsuit as a "federal civil rights"
case. Wearing a stylish beige suit and a sparkling gold necklace, the African
American deputy counsel told the senators in a firm tone, "I am not worried
about civil rights because this President's record on civil rights, on women's
rights, on all of our rights is unimpeachable."

David Kendall, one eye droopy from tiredness, rode Mills's momentum and
kept going, dissecting the charges that related to obstruction of justice and displaying a complete mastery of the record. He reminded the senators that Monica
Lewinsky had specifically told the grand jury, " 'No one ever asked me to lie and
I was never promised a job for my silence.' " Kendall surveyed the senators and
demanded, "Is there something difficult to understand here?"

Kendall had started his association with the president when Clinton arrived
in the White House; now he was closing with Clinton as strong as ever. For the
sophisticated politicos, watching Kendall maintain his "top dog" status while
other lawyers in the White House came and went was like "watching the Polit-
buro in the old days of the Soviet Union." Kendall remained the "first among

equals" within the elite inner circle of presidential lawyers. He could fight over a semicolon or a comma, rip the opposing side to shreds, and walk away unscathed. Kendall's presentation on this day showed why he was one of the foremost litigators in the country: As he wrapped up his remarks, he appeared as if he had jogged five miles, taken a nap, showered, pressed his suit, and walked into the hall totally refreshed. "The President did not commit perjury," Kendall lectured the senators, repeating the defense team's opening theme, "He did not obstruct justice, and there are no grounds to remove him from office."

BILL Clinton, by all accounts, was getting back into fighting form. His chief counterterrorism adviser, Richard A. Clarke, recalled riding over with the president to a major policy address at the National Academy of Sciences in the midst of the surreal Senate impeachment trial. Clinton was flipping through the speech Clarke had helped to draft, "On Keeping America Secure for the 21st Century"; then Clinton closed the binder and started regaling Clarke with stories about "his cousin from Arkansas and her sexual escapades." As the presidential limousine wound through neighborhoods to the Foggy Bottom area of Washington, Clinton seemed oblivious to the Senate trial aimed at removing him from office; instead, he tried to make Clarke laugh like a mischievous schoolboy. The intense-looking security adviser would later state with a mixture of astonishment and amusement: "That was Bill Clinton. That was 'Bubba.' He was being impeached and he still [wasn't ruffled]." When Clinton arrived at the National Academy of Sciences, having barely glanced at the prepared text, he gave a masterful speech on the growing threat of terrorism in the United States—far better than the one Clarke had drafted.

Bill Clinton was returning to his old battle-tested self, seemingly impervious to thrusts and body blows being aimed at him by those wielding traditional political weapons.

Just as it appeared that the Republicans' case might burst into flames, a story in the New York Times shook the foundation of the White House. The January 31 piece was headlined "Starr Is Weighing Whether to Indict Sitting President." Citing anonymous "associates" of Starr, the article reported that the special prosecutor "has concluded that he has the constitutional authority to seek a grand jury indictment of President Clinton before he leaves the White House in January 2001." The Times also revealed that two constitutional scholars serving as paid consultants to OIC—Ronald E. Rotunda from the University of Illinois and William Kelley from Notre Dame—had concluded that the Constitution permitted such action.

The White House was hurled into a new state of panic. As one adviser close to the president recalled, "I thought it was a signal that they might actually indict him. All of a sudden, there was another threat." The proposition that the president could be criminally indicted while in office was not, by any means, a settled matter. Conservative icon Robert Bork, while solicitor general to President Nixon during the Watergate showdown, had issued a categorical opinion that such a course was impermissible. The only recourse for criminal conduct by a sitting president, Bork had opined in 1973, was impeachment. Only *after* being removed from office could criminal proceedings go forward. As one Republican federal judge had warned during Watergate, allowing the government to indict, prosecute, or arrest a sitting president prior to impeachment could effectively grind the executive branch to a halt.

Yet Starr had found allies with impressive credentials and who were prepared to reach the opposite conclusion. Professor Rotunda was a leading constitutional law scholar who had been aligned with Starr's team from the start; he was highly regarded among Supreme Court justices and would get their attention. Professor Kelley, a former clerk to Judge Starr, was known for his bold conservative stripes; his endorsement added to OIC's firepower. These signals of a potential sneak attack, by which Starr might indict the president in the middle of the impeachment trial, were deeply troublesome for the White House lawyers. David Kendall later noted, "It was just a flagrantly illegal leak. It was, in my view, designed to influence the proceedings."

The Starr team members didn't know it, but they were in a race against the clock. One of the judges on the special three-judge court that oversaw the independent counsel operations—Senior Judge John D. Butzner, Jr., of Virginia—was privately mulling over whether to pull the plug on Ken Starr's operation. Seated in a wheelchair in his assisted-living home in Richmond, Judge Butzner would later answer a firm "yes" to the question whether he favored removing Starr at this juncture. Tucked away in Butzner's files was a newspaper clipping that explained that a little-known provision in the independent counsel law permitted the three-judge panel to terminate an investigation if it was "substantially completed." Each year, on the anniversary of an independent counsel's appointment (in Starr's case on August 5), the court had authority "on its own motion" to terminate an investigation. Judge Butzner, who had opposed Starr's appointment from the get-go, was watching the calendar carefully. He was prepared to cut off the lifeline to this particular investigation—if he could find a second vote.

———

IF history were to identify a watershed moment in the impeachment trial of President William Jefferson Clinton, a point when the momentum shifted dramatically in favor of the president, it would have to be the remarkable twenty-four-hour period that began when former Senator Dale Bumpers of Arkansas gave an impassioned speech in the Senate. The president's lawyer David Kendall later confirmed: "That's when I thought we were okay."

Dale Bumpers had retired the previous month after twenty-four years in the Senate. He had known Bill Clinton since the early 1970s, when he was governor of Arkansas and Bill Clinton was a young law professor itching to win a seat in Congress. A quarter century later, Bumpers lamented that the whole Whitewater scandal "stunk to high heaven [from] the very beginning," and that the Lewinsky charges were being used by Clinton's enemies to pile it on. Bumpers was unabashedly pro-Clinton. Still, he was surprised when Senator Tom Harkin of Iowa called him the Sunday before Martin Luther King Jr. Day, proposing that he deliver a "closing argument" in Clinton's impeachment trial.

The White House had learned from poring over old *Congressional Globe* volumes that a number of former attorneys general and other prominent public figures had played key roles in defending President Andrew Johnson in 1868. The president's defense team had decided they wanted an "elder statesman" to lend stature to their own case. They had first approached retired Senate Majority Leader George Mitchell (D-Maine), who declined for personal reasons. Dale Bumpers was their second choice. Bumpers told Harkin, "If you think a speech by Dale Bumpers is going to change any Republican votes, you ought to disabuse yourself of that immediately." Harkin swatted aside that concern—their sole goal was to shore up Democrats and to prevent Republicans from stealing away any new converts.

Bumpers continued to resist. Even if the speech were a "howling success," he said, he wasn't sure he could do much to slow the Republicans' momentum. "Frankly," recalled Bumpers, "I didn't feel up to it."

Three days later, Bumpers stood in the well of the Senate, delivering the most important speech of his political career, even though his career was over.

Bumpers had been told to keep the speech to twenty-five minutes. Now, as he stepped up to the lectern, holding twenty-one pages of scattered notes, White House aides whispered that Senate Majority Leader Trent Lott might introduce a motion to permit testimony from Monica Lewinsky and other witnesses. They needed to stop that train; Bumpers was instructed to keep talking and double the length of his remarks.

The retired senator looked into the sea of former associates' faces and began his oratory. "You can take some comfort, colleagues, in the fact that I am not being paid," he joked, "and when I finish, you will probably think the White House got their money's worth." Gusts of laughter swept through the room. Finally, the senators were listening to one of their own. Bumpers was folksy. He was humorous. Unlike the House managers, he didn't sound vengeful. This was music to their senatorial ears.

Paul Wellstone, Democrat from Minnesota, was suffering from back problems and was forced to listen from the cloakroom. The remaining ninety-nine senators all were seated upright in their chairs, fully attentive. "It was a really awesome time," Bumpers would later say, shaking his head. "A most memorable, historic time."

Bumpers began by admitting that he was a longtime friend of Bill Clinton. They had gone on political jaunts together in Arkansas, one time flying in a twin-engine plane that had crashed on the way to the Gillett Coon Supper (a yearly gathering in Gillett, Arkansas, at which fresh raccoons were cooked in kettles before being smoked). Bumpers noted that he and Clinton had both jumped out of their twin-engine plane on that snowy evening "and ran away unscathed, to the dismay of every politician in Arkansas." As the senators laughed appreciatively, Bumpers grew more serious: "The President and I have been together hundreds of times at parades, dedications, political events, social events. And in all of those years and all of those hundreds of times we have been together, both in public and in private, I have never one time seen the President conduct himself in a way that did not reflect the highest credit on him, his family, his state and his beloved nation."

Bumpers had soon found a rhythm, strolling back and forth in front of the lectern, nearly yanking the twenty-two-foot cord on his microphone out of the wall. There was "danger" afoot in these historic proceedings, he told his former colleagues—the United States Constitution could be horribly abused if the senators were not vigilant. Alexander Hamilton in *Federalist Paper No. 65* had made clear that the purpose of impeachment was to remove a leader who posed a threat to the state. Bumpers now waved his hands so that no senator could miss his point: After five years of *relentless* investigations of President Bill Clinton, and after $50 million spent by Ken Starr's office, there was not a single scrap of evidence of criminal wrongdoing. "*Nothing,*" Bumpers stated, shaking his fist in the air.

"We are here today"—Bumpers was now on a roll—"because the President suffered a terrible moral lapse of marital infidelity . . . a breach of his marriage vows. It was a breach of his family trust. It is a *sex* scandal." He paused and shook a finger. "H. L. Mencken one time said, 'When you hear somebody say, "This is not about money," it's about money.'"

The senators were all ears.

"And when you hear somebody say, 'This is not about sex,'" Bumpers declared, delivering the punch line, "it's about sex."

The senators erupted with laughter. Now Bumpers had them eating out of his hand. He moved in for the kill. "There is a human element in this case that has not even been mentioned. That is, the President and Hillary and Chelsea are human beings." Although Bill Clinton's conduct had been shameless and abhorrent, what the House managers were trying to do—heaping pain and ignominy on Clinton after he had been publicly disgraced—was "too much for a family that has already been about as decimated as a family can get."

Why had Bill Clinton lied? For the same reason any man or woman in his position would have done it, declared Bumpers: "Well, he knew this whole affair was about to bring unspeakable embarrassment and humiliation on himself, his wife whom he adored, and a child that he worshipped with every fiber of his body and for whom he would happily have died to spare her or to ameliorate her shame and her grief."

House Manager Henry Hyde was squirming in his seat. He would later complain that this seventy-three-year-old Arkansas populist made him grit his teeth. Hyde would say of Bumpers's closing argument: "It was sawdust in the meatloaf." Yet others in the room were listening with rapt attention.

"We are, none of us, perfect," Bumpers declared, pacing back and forth. "There is a total lack of proportionality, a total lack of balance in this thing. The charge and the punishment are totally out of sync." Bumpers reminded his colleagues, almost in a whisper, that 65 to 70 percent of the American public believed Clinton should remain in office. He concluded, his voice quivering, "They are calling on you to rise above politics, rise above partisanship. They are calling on you to do your solemn duty, and I pray you will."

A throng of senators jumped up to shake Bumpers's hand. These included dozens of Republicans, including the elderly Strom Thurmond, Kay Bailey Hutchison of Texas, and William V. Roth, Jr., of Delaware.

When Bumpers returned to his home in D.C., exhausted, his wife handed him the phone: President Clinton was on the line. Clinton had watched every minute of the speech on television. If the senators could have voted "within an hour after [Bumpers] spoke," the president told his elder Arkansas friend, he would have been acquitted on the spot.

That evening on the national news, Senator John Chafee, a moderate Republican from Rhode Island, told a national audience that every senator needed to reassess his or her position in light of the former Arkansas senator's speech. Bumpers felt a sense of quiet satisfaction with his work. Even if his remarks did not change a particular senator's views, he felt, at least maybe they "knocked [a few] off the log."

THE next day, a sheet of paper was circulated within the Senate chamber: "Statement by U.S. Senator Robert C. Byrd—a Call for Dismissal of the Charges and End of the Trial." In this brief document, which Byrd personally handed to Henry Hyde, the West Virginia senator announced that he would file a motion to dismiss all charges against President Clinton. Senator Byrd wrote: "I am convinced that the necessary two-thirds for conviction are not there and that they are not likely to develop. I have also become convinced that lengthening this trial will only prolong and deepen the divisive, bitter, and polarizing effect that this sorry affair has visited upon our nation. I see a motion to dismiss as the best way to promptly end this sad and sorry time for our country."

Byrd's announcement not only threw the House managers for a loop, but also nearly knocked the Democratic leadership out of their chairs. Byrd was the antithesis of a Clinton coddler. He seemed appalled by Clinton's behavior that had led to this impeachment mess. Not even Democratic Leader Tom Daschle had dared to approach Byrd in an effort to line up his vote. Byrd seemed to be above politics, if that was possible in this inherently political profession. There was no mistaking what this announcement from the senior Democrat meant: The field of play had shifted dramatically.

Senator Trent Lott was a master at counting votes. He understood the ramifications of Byrd's statement. He had known all along that "in order to have any chance at all of getting [sixty-seven] votes, we had to get people like Lieberman and Byrd." The case was slipping from the Republicans' grasp.

Henry Hyde and his managers, meanwhile, were beginning to feel like the "proverbial skunk at the garden party." Angry that their senatorial brethren were not doing enough to rescue their case, they decided to call Monica Lewinsky as a live witness.

At an emergency hearing in Judge Norma Holloway Johnson's chambers, just as Senator Byrd's motion was shot down along party lines, Ken Starr's office made an appearance to support the House managers. Deputy Bob Bittman told Judge Johnson that Lewinsky's immunity agreement *required* her to cooperate with government officials in *all* proceedings, including "congressional hearings."

Robert Dove would later recall: "The whole issue of Monica Lewinsky could be summed up in the phrase 'tacky.' Just something that should never happen on the Senate floor." Increasingly, senators—including Republicans—were becoming irked that Starr was still sticking his nose into their business. This did not help the senators' cause. Their cause was getting elected every six years, passing legislation, worrying about tax cuts and social security. It was not about seeking public retribution "for the sins of the president." With the reappearance of Starr on the scene, "it was like Cotton Mather was somehow abroad in the land. And his time had passed."

The House managers, as well, seemed to be going off the deep end. They had gone so far as to float the idea of hauling Bill Clinton himself into the Senate and forcing him to testify. Even Majority Leader Trent Lott whispered to fellow Republicans that this latest proposal bordered on madness: "We are not the British Parliament or the Canadian Parliament," he said. The idea of summoning the president of the United States into the well of the Senate and giving him a "tongue-lashing" seemed to be flatly inconsistent with the American system of government premised upon separation of powers.

Henry Hyde, for his part, regretted that his team did not declare all-out war on his Senate brethren. "I should have stood up, gotten the attention of the chief justice [Rehnquist], and moved that he request the president to appear and answer questions," Hyde later said.

Hyde also kicked himself for not raising holy hell and demanding that Monica Lewinsky appear in the flesh. Who was Senator Byrd to play "Stonewall Jackson," acting like a sanctimonious statesman who had never seen a lady's petticoat? What Hyde believed was a clear-cut case of perjury and obstruction of justice was being spun by the White House to make it appear as if it were a benign case of "lying about sex." He was also frosted that the senators were treating him and his fellow managers like "the [drunken] uncle who shows up at an anniversary party," keeping them at a distance as if they might act inappropriately. Hyde felt like subpoenaing the infamous blue dress and waving it around the Senate floor so that these holier-than-thou senators would be forced to confront Clinton's outright lies and gross misdeeds. Hyde's chief counsel, David Schippers, noted, "That would have killed Byrd. He would have died right on the floor."

On February 1, Monica Lewinsky faced a swarm of photographers outside the Mayflower Hotel as she arrived for her formal deposition by the House managers. It was a scene reminiscent of the early days of Monicagate. In the spirit of the initial Gramm-Kennedy deal, the Senate Democratic and Republican leadership had forbidden live testimony but permitted the House managers to take a videotaped deposition of Monica and several other witnesses, for use at trial. Now, news trucks with huge dish-shaped antennae and photojournalists wielding Sony cameras crowded the street in front of the Mayflower, engulfing Monica. It seemed like a scene from a Fellini film.

Monica herself would recall: "The whole thing was really scary. Just arriving and having everybody there and it being a mob scene." She had moved back to Los Angeles to regain her mental health; now, getting dragged back to Washington to answer questions posed by the House managers with the support of Kenneth Starr was a psychologically distressing turn of events.

The Starr investigation had been horrible enough, but impeachment sounded far worse. Monica's greatest fear was that the managers eventually would find a way to make her stand in the middle of the Senate and testify, like a woman compelled to be photographed naked against her will. The whole experience of being interrogated by the House managers seemed "overwhelming." She also considered it "a waste of taxpayers' money." Although Monica was displeased with Bill Clinton's conduct these days, she couldn't help feeling that "people did not want him to go. Enough already."

Lewinsky was not the only one experiencing extreme discomfort. The White House lawyers were alarmed that the managers were "bringing Monica back," figuring that "there's got to be something there." Clinton's team worried that the House managers had dredged up some new factual inconsistency in Bill Clinton's sworn testimony and might pull it out at the Senate trial as a smoking gun.

Dressed in a smart navy-blue outfit with a strand of pearls around her neck, the dark-haired Lewinsky looked startlingly beautiful to those who had never seen her. She also demonstrated that she was much smarter than her inquisitors had planned. Throughout six hours of testimony, the former intern took command of the Republican congressmen and never lost the upper hand. In response to questioning by the soft-spoken manager Edward G. Bryant of Tennessee, Monica carefully stuck to her grand jury testimony, refusing to offer up any sizzling new details. On the topic of whether Bill Clinton had lied under oath when he swore that he had not engaged in a "sexual relationship" with her, Lewinsky respectfully demurred: Because that definition referred to touching the body of another person with the intent to gratify or arouse sexual desire in that person, Monica said, "I'm just not comfortable commenting on someone else's intent or state of mind or what they thought."

It was clear to those inside the room that Monica was not going to color outside the lines. Inside the lines, she was carefully selecting her brushstrokes so that she did not harm Bill Clinton. Halfway into the questioning, Senator Fred Thompson of Tennessee, one of the Republican observers, began slumping back in his chair and "looking at the ceiling."

As Lewinsky wrapped up her testimony, the president's lawyers held a quick caucus. There was no need to cross-examine this witness; she had handled herself brilliantly. Deputy White House Counsel Nicole Seligman instead surprised those present by reading a touching apology from President Clinton, causing tears to well up in Monica's eyes. The former intern later said, "I appreciated the gesture at the time, but I was also skeptical. I didn't believe it was his idea or even his choice of words." Nonetheless, the words of atonement from Clinton seemed to do their magic. As Monica walked out of the deposition, she stuck out her chin resolutely, clearly aligned with the White House defense team.

Henry Hyde had warned his managers before this session with the former intern, "She will not lie. But if you give her any opening, she'll slip through it." When the junior managers reported back to Chairman Hyde's office to brief him, Hyde threw up his hands in despair: Monica had found an opening the size of the Capitol Tunnel and had driven right through it.

Hyde would blame himself for the disaster. He had allowed the mild-mannered Bryant to handle the sensitive questioning rather than unleashing a bulldog like David Schippers to rip into Lewinsky. "In retrospect, I should have pleaded, insisted, threatened—whatever we had to do—to have Dave Schippers take the questioning of Lewinsky," Hyde said. He was also steaming mad that the managers were forced to accept this sort of weak deposition testimony instead of being permitted to grill Monica on the Senate floor under the bright lights of the C-SPAN cameras.

Leaning forward at his desk, the chief House manager allowed a tinge of bitterness to slip into his voice: "[The Senate] wouldn't let us produce bodies. We had to use a [video] screen to have them testify. They did everything but put duct tape around our mouths."

Chairman Hyde had become thoroughly demoralized. "It wasn't overdramatizing to talk about 'we band of brothers,'" Hyde recalled of this deflating time. "We were alone."

———

WITH the cold weather of February gripping Washington, Chief Justice Rehnquist came down with a nasty flu. Yet he refused to call for a recess, recognizing that any break in the proceeding might cause some new crisis to bubble up, keeping him trapped in the Senate forever. Justice Sandra Day O'Connor was concerned that her friend the chief appeared tired and overworked. It was obvious that he was looking forward to the day when he would "not have to spend time over there [in the Capitol]." O'Connor concluded, lifting her steely eyes as if to express the sentiment of every justice, that Rehnquist had ample reason to want to finish his assignment in the Senate. "Good heavens . . ." she said, leaving her explanation at that.

Yet there was no easy escape hatch. To the dismay of senators of both parties, Chairman Hyde announced that all thirteen managers would make closing statements, like a bad movie that continued to play in a loop. Senator Orrin Hatch, the respected Republican from Utah, proposed adjourning the trial and issuing a stiff resolution rebuking the president in order to snatch acquittal from Bill Clinton's grasp.

As appealing as the Hatch plan was to some Republicans, the leadership viewed it as a cop-out. "I mean, if our goal was only to make a statement or to embarrass [Clinton] . . . maybe that would have been okay," Majority Leader

Lott later explained. "But I really thought we had an impeachment process that was laid out by history and precedent and we ought to [finish] it."

During the House managers' closing, Lindsey Graham of South Carolina scored points when he played a segment of Monica Lewinsky's videotaped testimony, in which she commented on a late-night call during which Clinton broke the news that the young woman was on the *Jones* case witness list. "Where I come from," said Graham, "you call somebody at two-thirty in the morning—you're up to no good." That line elicited a hearty burst of bipartisan snickers among the senators. But the video appearance of Monica Lewinsky, viewed by millions of Americans at home, did nothing to change the trial's momentum. In fact, many viewers were surprised to see how professionally and deftly the twenty-five-year-old former intern—sporting a chic new hairstyle—had bested her questioners from the U.S. Congress.

White House Counsel Charles Ruff closed for the defense team on February 8, wheeling himself into the middle of the floor and excoriating the House managers for "wanting to win too much." Ruff ended the trial with the same words he had used to open it. William Jefferson Clinton, he told the senators, "did not commit perjury. He did not commit obstruction of justice. He must not be removed from office." Parliamentarian Robert Dove, who was seated next to Chief Justice Rehnquist's chair, could sense that Ruff's tenacity and intellectual clarity was carrying the day. Dove recalled, "If you are going to acquit, it's nice to have some plausible argument as to why you should [do it]."

Majority Leader Lott had already done the mental tabulations. "Short of murder," he had calculated, the Democratic senators "weren't going to vote to remove [Clinton]." Conviction required a two-thirds vote, or sixty-six senators. Lott had concluded, "The best—if you counted, stretched it, squeezed it, pulled it, pushed it—it would never have exceeded sixty-two votes." In fact, the numbers could easily dip lower than that. Suddenly, Lott was fighting to cobble together a bare majority on a single article of impeachment, to save face.

There was still a shred of hope that a few fiercely independent Democrats might buck their party leadership. Senator Byrd, for instance, was still rumored to have moral qualms about voting to *acquit* Clinton, even following his motion to dismiss. After all, federal judge Walter L. Nixon of Mississippi had been impeached and convicted in 1989 on a charge very similar to that lodged against Clinton—making false statements to a grand jury. How did an institutional purist like Byrd ignore this precedent? In a desperate effort to shore up their numbers, the House managers turned up the heat on wavering Republican colleagues to vote yes on at least one article so that the managers were not embarrassed. The entire Republican caucus was calling in every chit available in search of a slim plurality. They were now "playing for history," trying to "justify what they had done."

On the day of the vote—Friday, February 12—word swept through the chamber that Senator Arlen Specter of Pennsylvania, a Republican known for his moderate impulses, might invoke Scottish law and vote "not proven" rather than "not guilty." Specter had sought advice in advance from Parliamentarian Robert Dove, who informed the senior senator that he could invoke language from whatever country he wished, but under the Senate rules, the clerk would be required to record the vote as "not guilty." Specter was clearly miffed. He asked Dove, "Are you a lawyer?" Dove replied respectfully, "Yes, Senator. I attended Georgetown Law School." With that, Specter swiveled and walked away, displeased that he had lost his cover.

Senator Lott now navigated through desks to the rear of the floor and collared Specter. "Arlie," he pleaded, "what are you doing here? . . . 'Guilty but not proven?' What is that?" Specter replied that he had researched Scottish law and that this accurately reflected his position. Lott was livid; the numbers in his mental tabulator had just dropped by another digit.

As a last-ditch measure, there was yet another proposed censure resolution floating around, crafted by Democratic Senator Dianne Feinstein of California along with Republican Senator Bob Bennett of Utah. Suddenly, this measure seemed as if it might be the answer to every vacillating senator's prayers. The language of the Feinstein resolution was tough and condemnatory, calling the conduct of President Clinton "shameless, reckless and indefensible." It also made clear that Clinton "deliberately misled and deceived the American people and officials in all branches of the United States Government." It even kept the door ajar by declaring that "William Jefferson Clinton remains subject to criminal and civil actions."

The White House was aghast that the Feinstein resolution might pass. Clinton's legal team felt, "We want an up or down verdict on the impeachment articles, and that's it." Now that the president had been "dragged through the mud," there was no reason to permit a bipartisan resolution condemning Clinton to add to the indignity of the House impeachment vote. Republicans would try to weave this into American history books to further besmirch Clinton's legacy.

Plenty of Democrats, however, stood to gain by latching on to this stiff censure resolution. It was now obvious that President Clinton would not be convicted. If the senators slapped Clinton with a tough-sounding censure measure, they could go home proclaiming that they took the high road and escape the wrath of their constituents in the next election cycle.

Plenty of Republicans, too, saw it as an attractive option. Even Henry Hyde, disillusioned and bitter after this exhausting fight, was prepared to give his silent nod to this tough-sounding censure resolution. "I felt we did not have the votes to convict," he later admitted. "And this would be better than having the president get off scot-free." The Feinstein resolution was particularly enticing, Hyde said, because it "called [Clinton] every name in the book." The head manager telegraphed that if a group of senators was able to broker this deal, "I didn't intend to stamp my feet and throw my books down. I would have accepted the verdict."

In one of the greatest missteps committed by both parties, the Feinstein resolution collapsed just short of the finish line.

On the Republican side of the aisle, some GOP senators viewed it as a CYA ("cover your ass") maneuver and were loath to hand Democrats the opportunity to "cover themselves by a vote to censure." Senator Phil Gramm personally announced that he would lie down on the tracks to prevent a vote on censure from reaching its destination, if it came to that. Democrats, for their part, quibbled over whether the Feinstein resolution gave them too much of a victory against Bill Clinton or too little. White House political adviser Doug Sosnik would say that neither side could agree upon the best deal, because neither could figure out "what the deal is that they wanted."

At 9:30 A.M., Chief Justice William H. Rehnquist entered the Senate chamber to preside over this historic vote. His face devoid of emotion, Rehnquist rapped the nublike gavel against his desk. "The Senate will be in order," the chief stated in a flat voice. The time had come for a roll call on Article I, relating to perjury in the grand jury.

Senators' names were announced in alphabetical order. They stood up at their mahogany desks, built by a New York cabinetmaker circa 1819 to replicate the style favored by the Founding Fathers, and registered their votes in loud voices. As the legislative clerk recorded each senator's vote seriatim, Hyde recalled two emotions hitting him like a truck. "Expectancy and disappointment," said Hyde. "Repeatedly. Repeatedly as the roll is called."

First, the clerk called the name of Senator Spencer Abraham, Republican from Michigan.

"Guilty," he declared.

Next came Senator Daniel K. Akaka of Alaska.

"Not guilty," Akaka stated.

When the clerk reached the Bs and called out the name of Senator Byrd of West Virginia, the chamber became silent.

"Not guilty," pronounced the white-haired statesman.

By the conclusion of the votes on Article I, the tally was forty-five guilty as charged, fifty-five not guilty. The article had failed by a wide margin.

On Article II dealing with obstruction of justice, the Republicans held their collective breath; the result was equally devastating. Once Senator Specter's Scottish "not proven" vote was counted as "not guilty," the final tally was fifty guilty, fifty not guilty. Not only had President Bill Clinton been acquitted, but the House managers had failed to garner a simple majority on either article.

At 12:43 P.M., Chief Justice Rehnquist formally entered judgment in favor of the defendant "William Jefferson Clinton, President of the United States." Rehnquist rapped his gavel for the final time and scooped up his papers, lingering long enough to accept a Golden Gavel Award, presented jointly by the Republican and Democratic leadership. His work done, the chief was escorted out of the chamber, the four gold stripes on his black sleeves gleaming as he walked briskly away, senators on both sides of the aisle applauding lustily. This august body of legislators seemed thrilled to reclaim their rightful places, where they could give speeches for the *Congressional Record* and tussle over proposed bills. It was a sense, said one observer, of "we're in the Senate again. Let the chief justice go back to wherever he lives."

A bomb scare, requiring the evacuation of the Capitol, capped off the afternoon. One official groaned, "Oh, this is all we need." Senator Tom Daschle wandered into the Air and Space Museum in the Smithsonian several blocks away. "It was such an eerie experience," he remembered. "I was literally walking through the Space Museum moments after the final vote was taken." The Democratic leader stood in front of John Glenn's space capsule, the first manned ship to orbit the earth. Senator Glenn, who had retired in January just as the impeachment trial had engulfed the Senate, was a close personal friend of Daschle's; the two men had worked together on many projects as colleagues. It struck the South Dakota senator, in this moment of reflection, how great certain accomplishments of mankind were, and how misguided others turned out to be. "In any case," he later concluded, "that was just an odd way to end this ordeal."

Daschle returned to his office in the Capitol in time to accept a call from President Clinton, who expressed "a sense of relief and a sense of gratitude." Mixed with this was an unmistakable note of anger in the president's voice, a sound that Daschle would detect in Bill Clinton's voice for many years to come.

Henry Hyde, leader of the House managers, packed up his papers and led his dejected troops back to the south wing of the Capitol. To the managers' surprise, as they ducked through the rotunda a group of tourists began clapping, reaching across the roped-off passageway to shake the hands of the defeated impeachment prosecutors. In this national drama that had produced fault lines down the middle of every segment of the American public, supporters of the president and defenders of Independent Counsel Ken Starr continued to occupy adjoining corridors of the same building.

The impeachment trial of William Jefferson Clinton was over, slightly more than one year after the Monica Lewinsky affair had first seized the nation's attention.

It would remain unclear to many of those who participated in the drama, on both sides of the political aisle, exactly what it had accomplished.

CHAPTER

50

CLINTON'S CONTEMPT

Those who played significant roles in the failed impeachment of President William Jefferson Clinton, during that winter of 1999, would later express a jumble of emotions about its unusual trajectory and outcome.

Majority Leader Trent Lott, sitting back in his Capitol office shortly before he retired from politics, would emphasize that he was proud that the Senate had successfully defused this bomb, even though he was "hurt and concerned that the House [managers] didn't feel like we had acted aggressively enough." The Mississippi senator also admitted that he was baffled that Bill Clinton had escaped without paying a heftier price for his misdeeds. "There are only a couple of political things in my career that I still have not been able to understand," Lott said in a firm voice that came with years of leadership positions. "One is the fact that the American people apparently continued to support Clinton throughout this whole thing, knowing what he did, knowing what he said, knowing how he had demeaned the office." Lott weighed his words, before adding, "That doesn't jibe with all the other stuff I hear about women's rights and feminism and, you know, misconduct in the office place and workplace and all that. It's one of the real anomalies, I think, of American political history."

He stood up and closed his leather senatorial folder. "I still think history needs to try to explain why the American people thought that all that was okay. Was it just the pure charm of [Clinton's] personality? Was it just that they thought Republicans were being mean? I don't know."

Minority Leader Tom Daschle, equally proud of how the Senate had handled these dicey proceedings, disagreed with Lott's history lesson. Daschle cut to the chase: "I think Henry Hyde is the one who will be judged poorly in history, and I think that the House bent the rule of law, and I really think it was one of the greatest disservices done in the last century to any president, and the country as a whole." The House managers, insisted Daschle, "had a political agenda. They were motivated by a hatred that ran so deep that I think it colored their judgment about their own deportment."

One of the chief reasons that their effort had fallen flat on its face, Daschle believed, was that Ken Starr and the House of Representatives had cajoled an impeachment vote before the courts ever had a chance to determine whether Clinton had committed perjury or some other "high crime or misdemeanor." Daschle explained: "The courts would have had the best opportunity to make [this] legal assessment. I don't think it came anywhere close to fitting or meeting the constitutional threshold for impeachment."

In terms of the lessons learned from the Clinton impeachment drive, Senator Daschle concluded soberly, "My personal view is that it's not as much a lesson learned as a suspicion confirmed, and that is, that there are those who in the name of acquiring greater power in this republic are prepared to use whatever means available to them." Daschle, who had been targeted by the Republican Party and defeated in his own bid for reelection in 2004, thereafter moving to a prominent Washington law firm, felt that the greatest injustice of the failed impeachment of President Clinton was that "the punishment exceeded the crime." He explained, "I mean, just think of the public humiliation and the extraordinary loss of stature and credibility in the image that will be forever a part of [Bill Clinton's] legacy . . . all of that [due to] this one silly experience. If that isn't punishment for a man who would otherwise know real greatness in history, I don't know what is."

Congressman Henry Hyde, leader of the failed impeachment drive, had watched several of his own men, including Jim Rogan (R-Calif.) and George Gekas (R-Pa.), suffer defeat at the polls, likely because of their roles in this controversial proceeding. Hyde said later, his voice becoming choked with emotion, "Every one of the managers in some measure was a hero." He added, "They saw their job, and embraced it."

The avuncular Hyde regained his composure and stated with a flicker of humor: "Bill Clinton is making the most of his retirement. I'm glad he has no more pardons to sell. The country is safe to that extent. Bill Clinton could have been one of our great presidents. I think he had the brains and the energy and the ambition, but he lacked the vision. And the character. And that's the sad part. What might have been."

Hyde's chief investigator David Schippers interjected, "It was damning evidence. . . . We had one hell of a case."

Ken Starr, the erstwhile independent counsel who had set the impeachment

juggernaut into motion with his risky investigation of the Monica Lewinsky affair, would later say that he felt the House and Senate "probably got it just about
right." After all, the House had adopted articles of impeachment and had determined that President Clinton had violated his oath of office. The president had
escaped conviction in the Senate largely because the American public did not
want their elected leader removed from office, whether or not he was a miscre-
ant or lawbreaker. As many of Starr's prosecutors told themselves, after the Senate voted to acquit their elusive target: "Probably, all things considered, it was a
reasonable outcome."

Former President Bill Clinton, on the other hand, found nothing reasonable
about the impeachment ordeal. "The only thing I remember is that I was grateful
they couldn't get a majority on either count," Clinton said with a forced smile.

"The hardest part of the whole process, besides, you know, kind of working
through my anger and guilt and remorse and all that personal stuff," Clinton
continued in a level voice, "was seeing the way all those guys in the House just
melted away . . . basically [succumbing to] any excuse to cave in to Tom DeLay.
But the more they caved, the more resolved I got. That [part] was difficult. The
rest of it was just more or less predictable political theater."

President Clinton believed that the American people deserved much of the
credit for bringing the God-awful impeachment trial to an end. He had been
heartened when he learned that a principal of a small Catholic grade school in
Pennsylvania had blurted out with frustration during the middle of the Senate
trial, "Why don't we just leave this guy alone and let him do his job?" Once he
had "won over" a six-foot nun, Clinton commented, it was evident that the
American public would not permit this impeachment charade to continue. The
better angels of American politics had somehow joined hands and prevailed.

In response to the claim of Hyde and other managers that they were
vindicated—because the name "William Jefferson Clinton" would always have
an asterisk next to it in American history books as the second president ever to
be impeached by the House—the former president made no effort to hide his
contempt. "*They* were disgraced, and he [Hyde] knows it," Clinton said, his
voice becoming accusatory. "They didn't stick up for the rule of law. They conducted no independent investigation. . . . They ran a partisan hit job run by a
bitter right-winger, Henry Hyde, who turned out to be a hypocrite on the personal issues. But he pleased Tom DeLay and his right-wing masters. That's what
I believe." Clinton leaned forward, resting his elbows on the table of his Chappaqua study, before unloading more thoughts: "Yeah, I will always have an asterisk after my name, but I hope I'll have two asterisks: One is 'They impeached
him,' and the other is 'He stood up to them and beat them. And he beat them like
a yard dog.' Because the way they behaved was atrocious, and [Hyde] knows it."

Politics, like professional mud-wrestling, was a strange business. Within weeks of the impeachment trial's shutting down, Senate Majority Leader Trent Lott was back in the White House dealing with President Clinton on matters relating to social security and global debt relief. As they exchanged pleasantries in the Oval Office, neither politician spoke of the past. "There was nothing to be really said," sighed Lott. "I mean—I didn't want him to thank me. And I didn't want to heckle him, so probably we were two sons of the South just putting that chapter behind us."

Bill Clinton behaved with equal civility when he met with Henry Hyde and other Republican House members who had tried to expel him from office. The president would tell world leaders like Yasir Arafat, president of the Palestinian National Authority, and others who marveled at his graciousness toward his political enemies: "These guys that impeached me, they come in and out of the White House all the time. They want to come to the Christmas parties and have their picture taken with their children." Any political leader who was incapable of blocking out personal feelings, he would tell them, needed to "quit your job and get another line of work." His mother, Virginia, had often lectured: "You must never become bitter. That's the ultimate failure in life." Bill Clinton had taken this advice to heart. He vowed that he would never display a hint of ill will, even toward those who had sought to destroy him politically, no matter how much he was boiling inside. "As far as they know, I don't remember any of it," he said of the impeachment proceedings that had nearly ended his presidency.

———

At least one governmental official sat quietly on the sidelines, waiting for the dust to settle.

Precisely two months after the Senate voted to acquit President Clinton and a full year after she had thrown out the *Paula Jones* lawsuit, Judge Susan Webber Wright surprised court watchers by holding President Bill Clinton in civil contempt for giving "intentionally false" testimony in his *Jones* deposition. In a stern thirty-two-page rebuke of the president, dated April 12, 1999, the federal judge from Arkansas reprimanded Clinton for giving "false, misleading and evasive answers that were designed to obstruct the judicial process." Judge Wright noted that it did not take a rocket scientist to figure out, in light of the vast sea of evidence that had washed ashore during the congressional impeachment proceedings, that Clinton had lied through his teeth during his deposition. He clearly had uttered falsehoods when he had denied being alone with Monica Lewinsky; he had flagrantly misled the court when he insisted that he had never engaged in *any* sort of "sexual relationship" with the former intern. The judge wrote tersely: "Sanctions must be imposed, not only to redress the president's misconduct," but also to deter other public officials and ordinary citizens from emulating the president and to prevent Bill Clinton from "undermin[ing] the integrity of the judicial system."

Judge Wright's contempt decision came at an awkward time, just as Bill Clinton was seeking to regain his footing as leader of the free world, immersing himself in a NATO-led air campaign against Yugoslavia in response to ethnic cleansing in Kosovo. As bombs were falling on Serbian military targets, the judge who had once been Bill Clinton's law student ordered him to pay $90,000 to cover "reasonable expenses, including attorneys' fees" and to repay the federal government $1,202 for her own travel costs to Washington. The no-nonsense Judge Wright also declared that she would refer this matter to the disciplinary committee of the Arkansas Supreme Court, to decide whether Clinton should be disbarred or sanctioned for violating the state's rules of professional conduct.

President Clinton later expressed vigorous disapproval of Judge Wright's postimpeachment sanctions. These, he felt, were clearly designed to heap insult atop injury like a belt-whipping after a child had already been publicly thrashed. "I thought it was wrong," Clinton said of Wright's contempt order. This was especially true because the judge had implied in a footnote in her earlier summary judgment opinion that the president would be off the hook if he settled the *Jones* case. Clinton especially felt aggrieved because the *Jones* team had "regularly and flagrantly flouted" Judge Wright's orders by leaking material to the press—yet *they* were never sanctioned for *their* overt violations of the court's directives. The political animal in Clinton believed that Judge Wright had felt pressured to wallop him one last time to save face with the "right-wingers," after tossing out the *Jones* case. The former president mused, "So I guess, you know, by zapping me a little in the aftermath, it probably helped her restore her position with the dominant wing of her party."

What President Clinton and his advisers in the White House would never fully appreciate, however, was that Judge Susan Webber Wright was the single person in the United States who could have ended his presidency with a stroke of the pen. Yet she refrained from signing that order.

One individual close to Judge Wright at the time, who would insist upon anonymity, confirmed that she weighed a number of options to deal with Bill Clinton's blatant violations of her discovery orders. One option was to exercise the court's "general contempt" powers, which were extremely broad when it came to controlling the court's proceedings. An even more direct course of action was to cite Clinton for "criminal contempt"—a move that could have ended his political career in a nanosecond.

If Judge Wright had chosen the latter route to deal with Bill Clinton's falsehoods under oath, while the congressional impeachment proceedings were still under way, she could have virtually guaranteed President Clinton's conviction in the Senate. A judicial finding of "criminal contempt" would have handed the House managers the single missing ingredient that they lacked from the start—a finding of criminal conduct by a court of law. Among other things, it would have made Clinton's case nearly indistinguishable from those of the three federal judges whom the Senate had removed from office in the late 1980s. Even a finding of civil contempt, if it had been issued by Judge Wright in the thick of the Senate impeachment trial, could have easily inflicted a mortal blow on Clinton.

It was only because Ken Starr had swept in with his investigation so early (before Clinton had even testified), and the House of Representatives had commenced impeachment action so swiftly (before there was a judicial finding of wrongdoing by Clinton) that the falsehoods uttered by Clinton in the *Jones* case had been frozen in a state of suspended animation. If Judge Wright had pushed the defrost button in the middle of Clinton's impeachment trial, she could have changed that equation instantly.

As Chief Justice Rehnquist's administrative assistant would note, such a move could have cut off Clinton's escape route. "If Judge Wright had held the president in [criminal] contempt first," posited Jim Duff, "if that had happened, along with the strong condemnation that the Democrats had drafted . . . there might have been a different outcome."

At least one source close to Judge Wright during that period confirmed that she had weighed the criminal-contempt option and then consciously chose to take a different path, after the impeachment proceedings sputtered to a conclusion, treating Bill Clinton as she would have treated any other civil defendant who had fibbed under oath.

Only after Ken Starr's office and Congress had intervened prematurely, wrecking her civil case and making hash of the judicial process, did Judge Wright return to her courtroom and take steps to restore the dignity of this case that fell within her jurisdiction. Although President Bill Clinton would forever remain miffed by Judge Susan Webber Wright's decision to impose civil contempt, which in turn set him up for disbarment in his home state of Arkansas, that decision had another unseen consequence.

It left Clinton in office for the remainder of his presidency.

———————

THE same day in mid-April that Judge Wright issued her surprise order, Susan McDougal walked out of a different federal courtroom in Little Rock a free woman, having beaten Ken Starr's latest and final effort to convict her on charges of criminal contempt and obstruction of justice. As soon as jurors found McDougal innocent on the obstruction counts and declared that they were "hopelessly deadlocked" on the criminal-contempt charges, U.S. District

Judge George Howard, Jr., had declared a mistrial, ordering federal marshals to release the Whitewater felon. Susan's attorney, California superlawyer Mark Geragos, told the press: "If anything should put a stake through the heart of Kenneth Starr, this should be it. This guy should pack up, should get out of here. I'm happy to be the one, along with Susan, to wish him a bon voyage. Get the heck out of Arkansas and do it now."

Outside the courthouse in Little Rock, Susan McDougal pushed the hair out of her eyes, declaring, "This is the first day that I haven't been indicted in years, so I'm a little numb from it."

Juror Michael Nance, a truck driver from Little Rock, shared with reporters his reasons for concluding that McDougal had not "willfully" violated Judge Wright's court order: He had based his verdict upon the testimony of Susan Mc-Dougal herself. Ending her self-imposed silence by answering all the questions originally propounded by the grand jury, Susan had disavowed any knowledge of wrongdoing by Bill or Hillary Clinton in connection with Whitewater, Madison Guaranty, or any of Jim McDougal's dubious business dealings, putting these questions to rest.

Nance paused on the courthouse steps, telling a reporter that he and other jurors had concluded that there was an "innocent reason" for Susan McDougal's eighteen months of silence, namely, her abiding fear that Independent Counsel Starr would "charge her with perjury" unless she falsely implicated Bill and Hillary in a crime. Whether or not this conclusion was rational, explained the forty-eight-year-old juror, he certainly believed it was the reason "why Susan didn't talk."

Waving to a throng of onlookers, Susan McDougal stepped into an awaiting car, wearily commencing the hundred-mile drive back to Camden, Arkansas, where she would begin the long process of forgetting about her past. She would do her best to block out memories of her dead ex-husband; of her bygone days as a failed business partner with Bill and Hillary Clinton; and of the man she detested more than any other mortal who walked the face of the earth—Independent Counsel Kenneth W. Starr.

WHITE HOUSE
EXODUS

—◆—

"WHO WILL BLINK?"

Ken Starr's decision to depart as independent counsel in October 1999, according to those close to him, was an emotionally tough one. Starr himself was confident that he could act objectively in deciding whether to bring criminal charges against Bill Clinton, even after the flopped impeachment. At the same time, he realized that he had become "so demonized" in the press that it "warped gravity" around him. "He wanted people to have a clean view on the merits of whether or not the president should be prosecuted," said Mike Emmick. "And he thought that it was only going to be possible if he left."

Jackie Bennett had already cleared out of OIC, returning to private practice in Indiana. Hickman Ewing, whose name had been submitted for the position to replace Starr, told the three-judge panel chaired by Judge Sentelle (who advocated in his favor): "My answer is 'no.' Don't appoint me." Ewing had been "trashed" by the White House, branded a "religious fanatic" and kicked around by the pro-Clinton camp. He no longer maintained an open mind on the subject. As Ewing saw it, both Bill and Hillary were "crooks" who would have to answer to a Higher Judge. The Tennessee prosecutor wanted no part in pursuing a president who continued to "thumb his nose" at the justice system. Moreover, Ewing could not ignore that Ken Starr had been treated so abhorrently. "Ken unfairly took lots of hits," said Ewing. "And Ken has got more integrity in his little finger than Clinton's got in his whole body, or ever will have."

For his own part, Ken Starr blamed much of his unfortunate situation on the dysfunctional independent counsel law. Congress had permitted that statute to die in late June 1999, with both Democrats and Republicans bidding it good riddance. The past year's events, capped off by the draining impeachment trial, had simply worn legislators out. Ironically, Starr himself had testified against renewing the law under whose banner he had marched. "All roads led to the structural defects of the independent counsel mechanism," Starr later said, sitting on the couch in his McLean home, which he and Alice would soon sell so that they could start a new chapter of their life. The independent counsel law, in Starr's view, had caused prosecutions to become "very personal, very personalized," which was "quite inimical to the idea of the administration of justice."

Some commentators were quick to point out that Starr himself had been the chief grave-digger who had buried this noble Watergate-era law, through his prosecutorial overzealousness and lack of self-restraint. They noted that the requiem for the independent counsel statute was as much about Ken Starr as it was about the statute's defects. Yet supporters and detractors of the independent counsel law, alike, agreed on one point: Starr was "simply too much of a lightning rod" to stay on the job pursuing Bill Clinton.

Alice Starr seconded that vote. "It was a relief," she said. "It wasn't necessarily a happy time, but definitely a relief."

The transition from internationally famous (or infamous) special prosecutor to ordinary citizen was a welcome but bumpy one for Ken Starr. He spent the first few months playing "Mr. Mom" for daughter Cynthia (age fourteen) and remaining sequestered at home in his jeans and plaid shirt, writing a book about the role of the U. S. Constitution in American life.

Ken and Alice next went through the tough transition of selling their home in McLean, where they had raised their family and accumulated twenty-three years' worth of happy memories, trading it in for an anonymous abode in a different section of the Northern Virginia suburbs. The former special prosecutor's wife would say, a slight hitch in her voice, "Ken was still getting letters, threatening letters." She paused and added soberly, "All you need is one person . . . I worried about my daughter and some of her friends."

Starr wrote a farewell opinion piece for the *Wall Street Journal*—a publication that consistently had stood behind OIC—admitting that it had been a "mistake" for him to expand from Whitewater into the Lewinsky case, because it "slowed our progress, increased our costs, and fostered a damaging perception of empire building." Yet he made no apologies for his team's vigorous efforts. "I do not for a moment regret my appointment or my tenure as independent counsel," he told the paper's readers. "I did not seek this responsibility, but I have done my best to uphold the public interest in each and every decision."

As fall leaves blew across the lawn of the stately Army and Navy Club in Northern Virginia, OIC lawyers and FBI agents and staff threw a "bittersweet" going-away party, paying tribute to the man who had endured a public savaging for their cause. Over two hundred guests packed the ballroom to watch a film about their boss's five-year journey, followed by toasts and Hick Ewing's presenting Ken with a red "Hog Head" hat (a popular Arkansas Razorbacks accessory). Taking a deep breath and holding Alice's hand to maintain his composure, the departing independent counsel bade farewell to those who had never lost faith in their noble mission, a cheerfully determined smile on his face, yet an unmistakable look of sadness in his eyes.

———

Robert W. Ray threw down the *Washington Post*, livid that the story had leaked. Since replacing Ken Starr and assuming the mantle of independent counsel, charged with wrapping up a six-year investigation that had already cost the public $52 million, Ray had worked scrupulously to avoid any recurrence of bad publicity. The dark-haired, no-nonsense forty-year-old from New Jersey was a career prosecutor noted for keeping a low profile. Before joining Starr's team in 1999 as senior litigation counsel, he had worked on Independent Counsel Donald Smaltz's investigation of former Agriculture Secretary Mike Espy. Up until this point, Ray had managed to avoid being splattered by mud in either investigation. Indeed, when the three-judge panel had selected Ray to replace Starr in the fall of 1999, Senior Circuit Judge Richard Cudahy, the lone Democrat on the panel, had noted with optimism: "There can be no more vital consideration than closure with all deliberate speed. Our selection of Robert Ray carries much promise."

Now, the new special prosecutor seemed to be thrown into a madhouse filled with leaks. On the night of August 17, 2000, CNN and other news sources had broken the story that Ray had empaneled a new grand jury to decide whether to indict Bill Clinton. The potential charges against Clinton involved perjuring himself in the *Paula Jones* deposition and obstructing justice to cover his tracks. The morning *Post* reported—correctly, it turned out—that Ray was weighing whether to indict Clinton as soon as the president turned in the keys to the White House.

This leak was particularly damaging because it had occurred just hours before Vice President Al Gore stepped to the podium to accept his party's nomination for president at the Democratic convention in Los Angeles. One Clinton White House official stated scornfully, "The timing of this absolutely reeks." Gore's Republican opponent, Texas Governor George W. Bush, was already capitalizing on the news about a possible indictment. While on a campaign swing along the West Coast, Governor Bush—who had pledged "to restore honor and dignity" to the White House, along with his vice presidential running mate, Dick Cheney—called upon Vice President Gore to "emphatically state his disapproval of President Clinton's sexual conduct in office." Bush declared: "If Al Gore has got differences with the president, he ought to say them loud and clear."

With a tight presidential race barreling toward the finish line, the latest "leak" was unwelcome news for Robert Ray and OIC. As Ray later conceded, sitting in his New Jersey law office, "It did some damage."

It turned out, to Ray's relief, that his office was not the culprit. Senior Judge Richard Cudahy, the token Democrat on the three-judge panel, had inadvertently let slip about the new grand jury in discussing "background" with the media.

It turned out that Cudahy, in a confidential internal memo faxed to his two Republican brethren, had earlier argued in favor of "terminating" Starr's office unless he could provide "specific evidence" to prove that his investigation was not "substantially complete." Now, in discussing this topic with an Associated Press reporter, Cudahy had let the cat out of the bag and mentioned OIC's newly constituted grand jury. As judges Cudahy and Sentelle exchanged blistering letters, Fed-Exing copies to Chief Justice Rehnquist as they feuded over whether the leak was intentionally calculated to embarrass Republicans (including Sentelle), the Office of Independent Counsel faced its own dilemma.

A month earlier, Mike Emmick—who had been quietly working on this matter during the Senate impeachment trial—convened an "all-hands" meeting that lasted a full weekend. The issues on the table related to every angle of a possible Clinton prosecution: Were crimes provable? Did it make sense to go forward after the Senate had conducted an impeachment proceeding? After Judge Wright had held Clinton in civil contempt? After the underlying *Jones* case had settled for a hefty sum of $850,000? At the conclusion of the marathon session, the group reached a consensus: "There were definitely counts that were provable . . . before a neutral jury," recalled Emmick.

The Justice Department, too, was exploring the question. In a confidential memo dated August 18, 2000, the Office of Legal Counsel submitted a fifty-page memorandum to Attorney General Janet Reno, addressing the issue of whether a president or former president found "not guilty" in an impeachment trial could nonetheless be indicted. The DOJ lawyers agreed that "the question is more complicated than it might first appear," but concluded that the Constitution did not preclude such action, so long as prosecutors waited until the president left office.

With these memos on his desk, Robert Ray quietly constructed his own plan: He would clear the decks of extraneous matters and make a final decision about indicting Clinton by January 20, 2001—the day Bill and Hillary Clinton walked out of the White House. To do this, he needed to wrap up the FBI Filegate matter, the Travel Office case, and the original Whitewater probe. In a low-key fashion, Ray accomplished his goal by mid-September, announcing that there was insufficient evidence to move forward with criminal action against the president or Mrs. Clinton in each of these matters.

The Whitewater case was particularly touchy. By this time, First Lady Hillary Clinton was in the final stretch of her quest for election to the U.S. Senate seat in New York. Ray knew that Republicans supporting Hillary's opponent might not like it, yet he concluded he had a duty to announce publicly that he had "declined to prosecute" Mrs. Clinton. Ray later explained, "I thought it was up to the voters to use this information as they deemed appropriate."

Even most of his own staff members, it turned out, were not privy to the chief prosecutor's plan. The tight-lipped Ray was laying the foundation, preparing to deal with the eight-hundred-pound gorilla.

At night, Ray sat at home reading and rereading a book written by Watergate special prosecutor Leon Jaworski, *The Right and the Power*. He was impressed that Jaworski, a consummate Texas trial lawyer, had demonstrated such strength and foresight by helping to forge a deal, entirely behind the scenes, that amounted to a masterful compromise: President Nixon resigned from office, and the special prosecutor elected not to pursue criminal charges. Ray recalled, "There were so many parallels. I thought to myself, 'Wow. The country has been through this before. A prosecutor has faced this before.'"

Ray also met with Attorney General Reno and her top deputies, signaling that he would work with them cooperatively rather than poking sticks in their eyes; he needed the assistance of the Justice Department to accomplish his plan.

The special prosecutor also took steps to instill the fear of God in the White House. He hired a fresh crop of prosecutors, telegraphing to the president's people that he was prepared to prosecute Clinton if they pushed his back up against the wall. "Did I realize that it would be perceived as a fan dance?" the New Jersey lawyer later posed the question. "Darn right I did. I wanted them [Clinton's advisers] to know that I was coming." He added, jiggling his gold wristwatch, "I was fully of the view that if I was not prepared to carry out the threat, it wasn't worth making."

———

KEN Starr had left behind a number of messy problems for Bob Ray to clean up. Judge John W. Kern III, the special master appointed to dig into alleged improprieties by OIC, had filed a report that nobody (except Judge Norma Holloway Johnson) was permitted to see. Yet those close to Kern could discern that it was not all pleasant. Confidential sources would later confirm that the Kern Report "did not paint a rosy picture" of OIC's dealings with the media. The special master was deeply troubled by the repeated "off-the-record conversations" that Jackie Bennett and other OIC deputies had engaged in with journalists. Although Judge Kern stopped short of concluding that the Starr prosecutors had violated the law or illegally disclosed grand jury information, a reliable source confirmed that the special master believed OIC had acted overaggressively—and perhaps irresponsibly—in responding to perceived attacks by the White House.

Ray also had to deal with the fallout from OIC's "bracing" of Monica

Lewinsky. Of the myriad complaints lodged against Ken Starr's office with the Justice Department, this was the only one that OIC couldn't shake. The Office of Professional Responsibility (OPR) had completed its report on this topic, raising serious concerns. Now, Ray had no choice but to investigate his own office. He appointed a neutral professional—Jo Ann Harris, the former assistant attorney general who had headed DOJ's Criminal Division in the mid-1990s—to determine whether Emmick and other Starr prosecutors had violated Justice Department regulations in conducting their "sting" of Lewinsky. Specifically, Harris was assigned to determine if Starr's prosecutors had crossed the line in discouraging Lewinsky from contacting her attorney Frank Carter, despite her repeated requests to make that call.

Harris, who was then working as a criminal defense lawyer and law professor in New York, pledged to proceed swiftly and fairly. "I would give him [Robert Ray] findings of fact, conclusions and recommendations, and he was free, as is anyone in the Department of Justice, to accept them or to not accept them," she later summarized the plan. As Harris understood it, the results of her investigation would then be made public. In this fashion, she said, the American people could judge for themselves whether Starr's office had acted appropriately.

Even as these problems were piling up on Ray's desk, another one appeared: The tax charges filed by Starr's team against Webb Hubbell in *Hubbell II* were thrown out by the U.S. Supreme Court, nullifying Hubbell's guilty plea. The Court declared that OIC's use of Hubbell's own financial documents against him—documents that he had turned over pursuant to his grant of immunity—would violate his Fifth Amendment rights.

———

WITH the Office of Independent Counsel under siege from all directions, Robert Ray summoned Monica Lewinsky to his office in downtown Washington for a meeting: He wanted to look the former intern in the eyes and assess whether she was a truthful witness. Ray intended to make clear, immediately, that he was handling things differently from Ken Starr. His strategy was to communicate to Monica: "You're hearing from the horse's mouth. This is what I expect. This is what you need to know." Indirectly, Ray also planned to send a strong message to the White House that he meant business. "I was aware that if I met with her, that word would travel to where I wanted it to travel," he later disclosed.

If Ray's goal was to shake up the former intern, he succeeded masterfully. Monica had hated Ken Starr so passionately that she assumed Robert Ray couldn't possibly be a threat. Now, in December 2000, her stomach turned somersaults as she returned to OIC's offices in Washington to meet with the new special prosecutor. "I left that meeting thinking that he [Ray] was not only going to prosecute the president," Monica recalled, "but that he was going to prosecute [Vernon] Jordan and Betty [Currie] as well. That was how I felt from the way I was being questioned [based on] the level of detail that he wanted."

This was distressing to Monica, not because she cared so much about Bill Clinton anymore, but because she would end up being put on the stand as the chief witness against Clinton. It would be an emotionally and psychologically catastrophic experience, she feared—perhaps even worse than being dragged through the muck by Ken Starr for two years. As Monica walked out of Ray's office and exited the building on Pennsylvania Avenue, she recalled thinking to herself, her heart racing with a sudden jolt of panic, "Oh my God . . . This is not good."

Robert Ray was also playing mind games with the White House. He had contacted David Kendall after Thanksgiving and communicated that he wanted an "in person" meeting with the president. "I want to have a conversation," he told Kendall. "A one-way conversation."

David Kendall had dealt briefly with Ray on the Hubbell investigation. He had also crossed swords with the young prosecutor when Ray announced his Whitewater findings during Hillary's Senate campaign. In both cases, Kendall felt that Ray was playing it straight. Now Kendall was bedeviled. He kept pressing: "What are we going to do here? What do you want to talk about?" Ray refused to tip his hand. "I want a fifteen-minute conversation with the president," he told the Williams & Connolly lawyer. If Kendall wanted to instruct his client to "stay mute" or to strap a muzzle over his mouth, that was fine. This wasn't about Bill Clinton; this was about the independent counsel's communicating a message directly to the potential target "without it being filtered through an attorney." Kendall agreed to the proposal. He had no idea where it would lead.

Ray's endgame wasn't the only mystery in December 2000. The election between Vice President Al Gore and Governor George W. Bush had erupted into a state of near pandemonium—Florida's deciding electoral votes were dangling in limbo as Florida's courts and state legislature vied for control over a surreal recount that included local judges of election trying to count "hanging chads" through magnifying glasses. Ray purposely kept mum about the Clinton situation and his negotiations with the White House. "We were concerned about having anything in the press while the election was in doubt," Ray later divulged. "I felt [the country] needed to focus on the election, not on me."

On the evening of December 27, 2000, Ray rode with Kendall in Kendall's 1995 green Toyota Camry, a vehicle chosen to keep the visit inconspicuous since it frequently came and went at the president's residence. The car was waved through the White House gates at 10:00 P.M., just as the final Christmas candlelight tour was departing the grounds. Nobody in Ray's own office, other than his deputy Keith Ausbrook who now rode in the backseat, knew anything about this secret summit. Ray's motto was, "When it comes to certain important matters, resist the temptation to inform anyone."

Robert Ray had never met President Bill Clinton, other than one day the past August when Ray had golfed with his father at the Army and Navy Club and spotted a group of men carrying black bags that he deduced did not contain golf clubs (his experience in law enforcement told him) but were packed with automatic weapons. On this afternoon, a huge crowd had gathered near the eighteenth hole. Suddenly, Ray found himself on a rope line; President Bill Clinton was walking down the fairway, greeting admirers and shaking hands. When Clinton reached him, the new special prosecutor smiled and spoke up cheerfully: "Hello, Mr. President, I'm Bob Ray. I'm pleased to meet you." Clinton did not seem to recognize Ray's name or his face. He simply shook hands and kept walking. The next day, a tiny headline appeared on an Internet news site: "*President meets and disses his prosecutor.*" Other than that fleeting encounter, Ray had never laid eyes on this or any other sitting president.

The men now entered through the diplomatic entrance and proceeded to the Map Room—the same room where, two years earlier, Ken Starr and his prosecutors had extracted a confession from President Clinton during his grand jury testimony. As the new special prosecutor inspected his target on this wintry night, the president looked intense, focused, and pumped full of nervous energy. It was as if Clinton were sprinting toward the finish line after eight years in office, determined not to succumb to heat exhaustion in the final lap. The group sat down at a small table. Ray got directly to the point, summarizing what it was going to take for him to "exercise my discretion not to prosecute the president after he left office." President Clinton and David Kendall watched and listened. Their eyes searched for signals regarding the special prosecutor's true intentions.

Ray emphasized that there would need to be "a *complete* resolution" of all matters before any deal could be struck—and he wasn't promising any deal. He first addressed the disciplinary matters pending against Clinton before the Arkansas Supreme Court's Committee on Professional Conduct, flowing from Judge Wright's contempt order. These would have to be worked out. Most likely, he said, Clinton would have to agree to "a suspension of his bar license for some period." The parties would also have to hash out a final resolution to the amorphous Monica Lewinsky investigation. For Ray to even consider resolving the case, he stated bluntly, there would have to be some "acknowledgment [by Clinton] that his testimony was false."

Kendall had already made crystal clear that there would be "no [guilty] plea, absolutely no way, never." Even pleading to some lesser crime like "uttering false statements," Kendall had emphasized, was out of the question. So the new special prosecutor proposed a different plan to change the equation: He wanted the president to admit that his testimony was "knowingly evasive and misleading." This wouldn't constitute an admission of a crime. It *would* amount, however, to an admission of wrongdoing.

It was a game of "who will blink first?" All of the players were highly skilled.

Already, Kendall was developing a strategy for crushing OIC if Ray took the risky step of indicting Clinton. The president's lawyer had prepared enormous binders of cross-examination questions for Linda Tripp, Ken Starr, Monica Lewinsky, and other likely witnesses. He had assembled evidence to demonstrate how Monica's affidavit had been obtained by Tripp's lawyer in cahoots with Paula Jones's lawyers. He would file motions to exclude the Clinton deposition in its entirety as "tainted by prosecutorial misconduct"; he would strive to select a predominantly older jury, including plenty of women, who would understand that the Jones lawyers' tortured definition of "sexual relations" left plenty of room for honest differences of interpretation.

For the most part, this was turning into an elaborate word game. Even Monica Lewinsky concluded that Bill Clinton had lied under oath. She later acknowledged in 2009: "In the *Paula Jones* case, the only way he could not have been lying was if, in his mind, he had other reasons for intimately touching me (i.e., not that he didn't touch me, but that it was not for the reasons/intentions given in the *Paula Jones* definition of sexual relations)." When it came to Clinton's grand jury testimony, however, Monica concluded that "there was no leeway on the veracity of his statements because they asked him detailed and specific questions to which he answered untruthfully." Moreover, in the *Jones* deposition Clinton had denied that *she* had engaged in a "sexual affair" or "sexual relations" with *him*, which was certainly false under the operative definition. Additionally, Clinton had stated that her affidavit denying the affair was "absolutely true," another patent falsehood. Yet the president's lawyers were confident that all of this was water under the bridge.

David Kendall had already gotten Robert Ray to concede, privately, that Bill Clinton had successfully danced through the raindrops during most of his grand jury testimony. Although the president had made several "provably false" statements during the course of that appearance—such as when he continued his word dances and tried to defend his past testimony, that he had never been "alone" with Monica and had never sexually gratified her—Ray had conceded that these statements were largely "derivative" of the falsehoods Clinton previously made in the *Jones* deposition and constituted "the criminal back-half of the same thing." The new special prosecutor already had signaled, with a quiet nod, that he was prepared to give Clinton absolution on his grand jury sins. The more serious exposure was still on the *Jones* case deposition. Yet Kendall was ready for that—the president had already been confronted with those charges in the House of Representatives; that impeachment article had failed. Kendall was prepared to bet that a jury would take this into account in deciding whether to allow prosecutors to pursue Bill Clinton again, on the basis of the same tawdry facts. Kendall absorbed every word of Ray's soliloquy, allowing his mental gears to crank through the possible pathways this poker-faced prosecutor might take.

At the conclusion of Ray's one-way conversation that lasted no longer than fifteen minutes, the special prosecutor stood up to leave. Staring Bill Clinton in the eye, the special prosecutor said, "Look, Mr. President, this is what is required. You figure out how to accomplish it."

Ray had resolved to conduct every aspect of this meeting "on my own terms." He later stated firmly, "There were only two decision makers, me and the president. The law enforcement had its moment on that evening."

As he walked toward the door, Ray heard a voice piping up from the other side of the room: "Have you been out there to play?" The young prosecutor turned around. It was the commander in chief speaking to him. Ray swiveled and stared steely-eyed at the president. Clinton continued: "You know, to play golf at the Army [and] Navy Country Club?" Ray was surprised that the president had been quick enough to remember the incident, or astute enough to have his aides locate this one-inch story among the news reports. The new special prosecutor replied with a faint smile, before walking out of the Map Room, "Not since that day, Mr. President."

———

THE Florida election dispute in *Bush v. Gore* had catapulted into the Supreme Court, nearly erupting into a constitutional crisis by the second week of December. In a unanimous effort to patch together a judicious solution, the High Court first declared that there was "considerable uncertainty" as to the basis for the Florida Supreme Court's decision to order a statewide recount of ballots in the Bush-Gore contest, remanding the case back to the Florida court to clarify whether it had based its decision on Florida law, federal law, or both. After receiving a belated and murky response, the U.S. Supreme Court jumped into the fray, abandoning its effort at compromise. On December 12, the High Court splintered along ideological lines holding, five to four, that the Florida recount needed to be halted because the method in place violated the Equal Protection clause and there was no way to cure the problems within the requisite time frame. This swift intervention by the justices effectively handed the election to Texas governor George Bush by a slim margin of 271 to 266 electoral votes, even though Vice President Al Gore had won a clear majority of the popular vote.

Bill Clinton, watching his vice president go down in flames after the Supreme

Court's surprise intervention, was convinced that Gore miscalculated in distancing himself too much from the Comeback Kid. Clinton considered it "patently absurd" that Americans would vote against Gore as retribution for his own past sins. "No one thought Al Gore was going to do something improper like I had done," the former president explained. "And so to believe that he was going to lose votes over that impeachment, required you to basically believe that the American people were (a) unfair, (b) stupid, and (c) had changed their minds." Over 65 percent of the country, Clinton rattled off the statistics, thought he was doing a good job even after impeachment; an even higher percentage thought the Republicans had gone too far. As Clinton analyzed the situation, the theorem ginned up by the media that Gore's electoral prospects were wrecked by Clinton's misdeeds was preposterous.

"If you let the election become a referendum on [the question] 'Do you think Bill Clinton did a good thing or not?' that's a hundred to nothing. I mean, *I* would vote against me." Clinton chuckled at the joke. "Right? I would vote against myself." On the other hand, if the question posed to the electorate had been, "Has this administration done a good job and no matter how bad what the president did was, is what the Republicans attempted to do in impeaching him, run him out of office, worse?" Clinton believed Al Gore would have won that question "two to one."

To punish Gore for his boss's mistakes, Clinton concluded, would have been "manifestly unfair" and "manifestly against [the voters'] own interests."

Yet Gore's closest advisers didn't buy Clinton's attempt at self-absolution. Said one high-ranking adviser who requested anonymity, Bill Clinton's protestations that he didn't adversely impact the election were delusional. "There's about as much truth to that as his saying 'I didn't have sex with that woman,'" quipped that adviser. The Monica scandal and impeachment maelstrom had opened up the primary for Democratic contenders like former New Jersey senator Bill Bradley; it had paved the way for Republicans like George W. Bush to line up and begin raking in campaign dollars. It had put Al Gore on the defensive from the start, creating the impression that he was floundering and forcing him to continually reestablish his identity, even moving his campaign operation from Washington to Nashville.

Charles Burson, who served as Gore's chief of staff during the campaign, believed the facts spoke for themselves: "You have to put it in the context of the time," he explained. "The country was on a steady course. Bush was a likable guy. Gore was losing his identity. [The scandals] enhanced the feeling of exhaustion. And voters were saying to themselves 'why not? This [Bush] guy wouldn't be so bad.'"

Moreover, the scandal also constituted the principal reason that Gore felt that he had to distance himself from Clinton. "Good God, why would you want to embrace him?" said one adviser. Not only had Clinton's conduct been "un-pardonable," but it had shown a complete "lack of respect for the people of this country." Statisticians and political pundits could debate forever whether keeping Clinton at a distance helped or hurt the campaign, said Gore's defenders, yet the fact remained that the vice president felt he had no alternative. As a consequence of this decision, "Al gave up reminding people how far the country had come along and the Clinton administration's accomplishments. These were *his* accomplishments, too." Gore's advisers were convinced that—although there were many additional factors in the mix—the vice president likely would have carried Tennessee, Arkansas, Florida, and other states sufficient to win a healthy majority of the electoral votes, if it were not for the Clinton mess.

If Bill Clinton had resigned, or if the impeachment trial had never happened in the winter of 1999, the Gore camp was certain that history would have been altered. "People forget the lessons of Watergate," said one Gore confidant. "The country would have cooled off. There would have been less Clinton fatigue. Absolutely, Al Gore would have been president."

Independent Counsel Robert Ray stayed safely away from all of this political debate and finger-pointing. Yet he couldn't help agreeing that the vice president had gotten a raw deal: If Bill Clinton had been forced to resign or been removed by impeachment, Gore would have been president for a year. "And then his chances of election would have gone up dramatically," Ray acknowledged.

Instead, as inauguration day approached, it was George W. Bush who was getting suited up for the gala balls in Washington rather than Vice President Gore. That, however, was none of Ray's concern. As the special prosecutor counted down Clinton's final days in office, waiting to make a move with respect to the outgoing president, his sole focus was on whether to indict Bill Clinton the moment he vacated the executive mansion.

In a final twist never known to the Justice Department or the White House, the FBI and OIC made a last-ditch effort to bring down Bill Clinton during the concluding days of his presidency. In early January, Special Agent Jennifer D. Gant contacted former Secret Service Director Lew Merletti, who had recently retired and moved to Cleveland. Agent Gant "invited" the former USSS director to meet with her and OIC representatives in Washington to discuss the topic of Monica Lewinsky.

Agent Gant formalized her invitation by delivering a subpoena, directing Merletti to appear before the grand jury on January 18, just two days before President Clinton was scheduled to vacate his office. Thoroughly baffled, Merletti returned to D.C., reporting to FBI headquarters where he walked into a conference room occupied by two associate independent counsels, an investigator, and the agent who convened this gathering.

Gant cut to the chase. She told Merletti: "There's only one person left who can give us the president of the United States. And that's you. And we know that you were involved in a conspiracy with him, and we want to hear it today."

Merletti would later say that he was insulted and appalled by this effort to have him confess to a nonexistent conspiracy. "I've been in the Secret Service for close to twenty-five years," he said later. "I was a polygraph examiner for five years. . . . I'd interviewed no less than a thousand criminal suspects." As Merletti sat and listened to Special Agent Gant engage in "child's play" in an effort to ensnare him, his blood slowly began to boil. "I mean, I listened to her questioning and she knew nothing of basic interview techniques. I mean she knew nothing."

As Merletti recalled these events, Gant went as far as to insinuate that Merletti had been involved in a cover-up with President Clinton. Merletti stared back across the table; the FBI agent proceeded to spell out her theory, suggesting that Merletti "was protecting the president because I wanted to become the director," and that "the president was getting me women and that that was part of the bargain." As the retired Secret Service director tightened his jaw to contain his anger, Agent Gant next intimated "that I put [Monica Lewinsky and Bill Clinton] together" for trysts, and that "I knew the whole story and that I was going to stonewall Ken Starr on this entire issue."

Jennifer Gant recalled making no such accusation. She had been a street agent with the FBI for ten years; her specialty was handling major white-collar crime investigations. As she saw it, her job was to "wrap up loose ends" before President Clinton left office. She later stated: "My overall feeling was, 'I'm an FBI agent. I'm law enforcement. We both have badges. You know why I'm asking the questions. If you answer truthfully, we're done.' "

Gant finally proposed a deal for the former director: If he would "admit that the president was involved in this conspiracy," according to Merletti's version of the conversation, Clinton alone would be charged criminally; Merletti would be permitted to walk away scot-free.

Years later, Merletti remembered the unpleasant session, a vein in his neck starting to bulge as he spoke: "She had a preconceived story, and she was trying to get my answers to fit her preconceived story." It was apparent to Merletti that his "colleagues" in the FBI had decided that he was their final hope of hanging Bill Clinton. "I will tell you this," he stated, "I have absolutely no respect for [Agent Gant] whatsoever. I mean, it was offensive the way she spoke to me and what she said to me." Moreover, he was "insulted" by the FBI's final squeeze play designed to bait him into incriminating the president whom he was sworn to protect. "Starr had an agenda," said Merletti. "But so did the FBI.

"What they should have been doing was investigating terrorism," Merletti concluded, looking around his office at mementos of his quarter-century career with the U.S. Secret Service. "Chasing down Monica Lewinsky. A lot of good that did for us."

———

On Friday, January 19, President Bill Clinton was preparing to sign a final batch of orders as chief executive and packing up boxes for his new home in Chappaqua, New York, where he and his wife, Senator-elect Hillary Clinton, would be making their new home. As a house-warming gift, a deal had been struck that would give the former president a new lease on life.

Over the past ten days, David Kendall had been fighting off a nasty flu while flying to and from Arkansas. He had been secretly meeting with members of the Supreme Court of Arkansas's Committee on Professional Conduct, the group weighing disbarment proceedings against its once-favorite son. Most of the Democrats and "Friends of Bill" on that committee had recused themselves, leaving Kendall with tough sledding. Its lead prosecutor was a former nun and hard-nosed lawyer, Marie-Bernarde Miller, who seemed unforgiving of Bill Clinton's sins. Ordinarily, lawyers were only sanctioned for professional misconduct when they misrepresented clients or abused drugs or alcohol—indiscretions that impaired their functioning as attorneys. In this case, however, Kendall could read the tea leaves. Legal precedent seemed irrelevant to the Arkansas committee. Clinton was about to be slapped with a sanction based on a generic offense: "You've brought disrespect to the profession."

With this likelihood floating in the wind, the president agreed to have his law license suspended for five years and to pay a $25,000 fine to the Arkansas Supreme Court's Committee on Professional Conduct, to cover that group's costs. Clinton also surrendered the right to seek even a penny's worth of legal fees from OIC. In return, Ray agreed to close the books on all criminal investigations against the departing president. With one big caveat: Clinton was required to admit that he "knowingly gave evasive and misleading answers" in his *Paula Jones* deposition. Clinton reluctantly complied with that final condition. That same day, he issued a terse but painful statement: "I tried to walk a fine line between acting lawfully and testifying falsely, but I now recognize that I did not fully accomplish this goal and that certain of my responses to questions about Ms. Lewinsky were false."

Minutes after David Kendall released the president's *apologia* to reporters, Robert Ray issued his own brief statement. "This matter is now concluded," he stated. "May history and the American people judge that it has been concluded justly."

President Bill Clinton later admitted that he was sickened by the final deal struck between his lawyer and Robert Ray. "Yes, I had reservations about accepting it, and no, I didn't think it was fair," Clinton said. "I took it because I thought the country ought to be able to get over this. I thought, you know, we were starting a new administration and I wanted to start a new life. And I took it. I don't think there was anything fair about it."

The former president further unburdened himself by confessing that he was especially "outraged" by the suspension of his bar license. This occurred, he insisted, only because the *Arkansas Democrat-Gazette* had "succeeded in intimidating every person off the Bar Committee who wasn't anti-Clinton." He didn't mind swallowing some nasty-tasting medicine to remedy this malady that he had contracted from his own heedlessness. But the whole bottle seemed a bit much.

"So they did something totally without precedent, which I still think was disgusting," the former president said. "But I did it because my cooler heads advised me that, you know, there was no point in continuing to fight this."

Yet President Clinton would never fully grasp how close he came to being indicted and having to face the ordeal of a criminal trial. Interviews with sources close to Robert Ray, who requested anonymity, now confirm that Ray was ready to "pull the trigger" if the conditions he imposed were not satisfied. "This wasn't a bluff," stated one source. "He was prepared to seek an indictment." Indeed, Ray had to be "cajoled" by his deputy, Julie Thomas, to sign off on the final deal. The new special prosecutor had misgivings up until the final moment about signing a document that let Clinton off the hook. "He agreed after talking with his deputy that the time was right and the conditions he had set had been adequately met," said the source.

———

Ray's secretary tracked down Ken Starr on the morning of January 19, 2001—the day before George W. Bush's inauguration—and asked if he could come immediately to the OIC offices. At first Starr begged off, requesting, "Can we make it another time?" and explaining that he was busy with household chores. Ray's secretary replied, "It's important to be here." So the former special prosecutor drove into the district, joining the reconstituted prosecution team and staff in the OIC conference room, where he had presided over hundreds of meetings linked to the Clinton scandals. Here, Starr was among the first to learn that a deal had been struck that would allow Bill Clinton to go free; the seven-year battle, Ray told Starr personally, was now over.

Ray observed that Starr and his original prosecutors "had a difficult time at first—it took them some time to get their arms around the fact that I had resolved this short of bringing charges." Quickly enough, however, Starr came around. "Both outwardly and inwardly, he came to feel that it was the best decision," recalled Ray. "It was good for him, too. It allowed him to have closure, like the rest of the country."

Among OIC prosecutors and staffers, generally, the announcement produced a snarl of conflicted emotions. Ray received one fax, which he surmised was from a member of his own staff, telling him: "You'll rot in hell. Allowing Bill Clinton to get off is terrible for the country." Yet most OIC prosecutors softened as they realized that a new chapter of the nation's history would begin the next day with the inauguration of President-elect George W. Bush. Forcing the new president to deal with the criminal trial of his predecessor, the hard-liners whispered among themselves, would vastly complicate the new Bush administration's important agenda. Some compromises, they reluctantly conceded, had their virtues.

As Ken Starr stood silently in the conference room where he had presided over one of the longest and most divisive investigations of a sitting president in American history, he thought to himself, "This is right. This is the right disposition, and we were finally closing the matter."

———

In the White House, during his last frenetic twenty-four-hour blitz in office, President William Jefferson Clinton agonized over the towering stack of pardon applications on his desk, a pile that included requests on behalf of Susan McDougal and Webb Hubbell. In a decision that he would forever regret, the sleep-deprived Clinton signed one of those pardon applications but not the other. The outgoing president also scribbled out signatures on a final blizzard of paperwork dealing with miscellaneous executive matters, then penned a note of good wishes to incoming President George W. Bush, a modern-day tradition for departing chief executives.

His final act on Saturday, January 20, however, dealt neither with pardons nor executive orders nor transmitting perfunctory greetings to a new president.

Bill Clinton's last piece of presidential correspondence was a handwritten note addressed to Marge Mitchell in Arkansas, his mother's close friend of fifty years, the woman whose home had always been open to him as a boy in Hot Springs while Virginia Clinton worked endless shifts as a nurse-anesthetist to keep her family afloat. The departing president wrote to his mother's Birthday Club friend, just as he had promised, in a steady hand:

"Marge—I am on the way out the door! . . . How I wish Mother could have seen this whole ride. Best, Bill."

AFTERMATH

The legacy of the Clinton-Starr scandal, in all of its broken pieces, was interpreted different ways by different witnesses using their own field glasses to view the wreckage.

Ken Starr and his deputies had hoped that they would clean up corruption in Arkansas and return home as unsung heroes, having achieved justice. Instead, Bill Clinton's escape act had left them frustrated and foiled, with a large swath of Americans now viewing the OIC prosecutors as dangerously unbalanced zealots.

Ken Starr himself, having been appointed dean at his beloved Pepperdine Law School in Malibu after a false start, did his best to reflect calmly upon his Clinton-related investigations. His neat hair turning white, his spectacles gleaming to give him the look of an academic, Starr made no apologies about the work of his dedicated team of prosecutors. "We just had a nasty, unpleasant task to do, and we simply had to do it," he said. "It was being portrayed for political reasons as essentially some sort of religious-inspired jihad, as part of the culture wars and an assault on individual privacy and autonomy." Starr shook his head and lamented: "I understood that there was literally nothing I could do about it."

Despite the notion—fueled by the White House and hostile media sources—that his pursuit of President Bill Clinton was driven by his fundamentalist Christian beliefs, Dean Starr set the record straight by noting that his own staff would have rebelled if he had pursued this investigation like a Bible-thumping preacher. "If [my prosecutors] felt that I was on some sort of messianic holy war, people would have resigned and I should have been fired," he said. His faith was admittedly "a great source of strength and comfort in a time of adversity." Yet Starr quickly added that his Christian moorings had nothing to do with his indefatigable pursuit of Bill Clinton: "My sense of duty was a professional sense of duty."

For Starr, the worst part of looking back on this unsettling experience related to Bill Clinton's attitude. "He's been treating the whole thing very smugly," the former special prosecutor said. As Starr perceived it, the former president took every opportunity to belittle OIC's efforts by saying "there was nothing to Whitewater. The whole investigation was bogus and everybody knows it." Said

Starr, removing his gold-rimmed glasses and blinking, "I mean, it's the most un-repenting kind of [behavior]."

Starr himself believed that the proper way for Clinton to have brought clo-sure to this national scandal was for him to fess up by saying, " 'I recognize that I have made some pretty serious mistakes.' " Starr added with a grimace, "And that's never been forthcoming." Even in Clinton's bestselling memoir, which Starr had delayed reading for some time, partly due to new duties at Pepperdine, the president had resorted to blaming the special prosecutor and OIC for all his downfalls rather than taking a good look in the mirror. The independent coun-sel remarked, "And everybody's been saying, 'Stop it, stop it. Admit it. Get it be-hind you.' And he will not do it."

Starr paused before adding: "It is shocking that the president of the United States would conduct himself as a witness in such a way to essentially 'lie till he dies.' We all know the truth. And yet here he is [still] mocking the system."

In 2002, Starr's successor, Robert Ray, issued a multivolume final report that vindicated many aspects of Starr's exhaustive six-year probe. Yet there was little joy in OIC-ville, even after copies of this thick document were shelved in library repositories. The report raised serious questions about the testimony provided by both Bill and Hillary Clinton linked to Whitewater, Madison Guar-anty, and other subjects. Nonetheless, it concluded in each case that the evidence was "of insufficient weight and insufficiently corroborated to obtain and sustain a criminal prosecution beyond a reasonable doubt." The inability to demon-strate wrongdoing on matters at the heart of this long-running investigation was deflating for members of the original Starr team who had sacrificed years of their careers to prove that the Clintons had flouted the law.

In terms of his own role in these events, Starr expressed conflicted feelings. If he were to run into Bill Clinton at an out-of-the-way barbecue joint, where he could speak freely without microphones recording each word, he would probably say to the former president, " 'I'm sorry that it all happened.' " Starr quickly clarified: "Not in the form of an apology, but really as a reflection." He certainly would express deep sorrow that "the country was put through this. And then our respective families and those around us. Living in rancor is just a hor-rible way to live." But Starr also would be forced to tell Clinton, for his own sake, "It's so much better to deal candidly and forthrightly with the truth. And then make matters right. . . . Don't engage in a cover-up. Don't engage in these of-fenses against the integrity of our system."

Starr prayed that a hundred years in the future, when scholars and ordinary citizens studied these events, history would view him in a kind and forgiving light. He would be satisfied, he said, if accounts of the Clinton-Starr imbroglio in American textbooks simply recorded that "I was a lawyer and former judge who was called upon to do a very unpleasant duty under very difficult circumstances, and who did it honorably." He lifted his eyes and concluded in a quiet voice, "That's about all I can hope for."

Alice Starr, Ken's bride of over thirty years, expressed pure relief that her husband's work was over. She was thrilled when Clinton finally struck a deal with Robert Ray and ended this long national nightmare. "There was no sense in sending [Clinton] to jail," Alice said, analyzing the options. "He never would go to jail anyway, and what more needs to be said? To rehash all these details again in a court of law would be miserable for the country."

To those who remained convinced that her husband had plotted to bring down the president on account of some black-hearted loathing of Bill Clinton, Alice would correct the record: "His job wasn't to hate [Clinton] or to try to convict him. His job was to bring out the facts. He did do that." She added, "And he didn't relish his job at all."

In the end, Alice Starr took solace in Ken's proving himself, once again, to be a man of absolute honesty and integrity. Once her husband was able to resume a normal life—giving speeches, attending conferences, and mingling with regular folks at church socials—she was heartened to see that most Americans, of all political persuasions, were duly impressed. "Pretty much everywhere we go," Alice said, "people who meet him can't believe that he doesn't have horns, you know, growing out of his head."

As the Starr family relocated to the sun-sprayed Pacific coast to begin life anew at Pepperdine, Alice summarized the five-year Clinton "unpleasantness" by saying that her husband accepted the post as independent counsel out of a sense of duty, yet he did so at a huge personal cost. "It's really the worst job he's ever, ever had," she said, folding her hands and ending her comments on that polite note rather than sharing her unadulterated opinions.

———

KEN Starr's team of prosecutors did its best to shut down the Washington office with an element of dignity. Yet there remained an unpleasant little secret that continued to dog OIC, no matter how hard it struggled to cling to the moral high ground. That secret related to OIC's handling of Monica Lewinsky.

The Starr Report had disgorged tens of thousands of pages of the most intimate details about Ms. Lewinsky's sex life and her emotionally disastrous relationship with Bill Clinton. That policy of full disclosure, it turned out, had been a one-way street.

Although Ken Starr's office launched a successful blitz to bury the hundred-page report filed by former Justice Department lawyer Jo Ann Harris—the person charged with investigating OIC's handling of Lewinsky—new evidence now reveals that Harris found serious problems with OIC's January 1998 brace of Lewinsky, particularly OIC's repeated efforts to dissuade the former intern from contacting attorney Frank Carter.

Speaking for the first time about her lengthy report that remains locked in a government archive, Harris—a former assistant attorney general who headed the Criminal Division of the Justice Department and then worked as a trial attorney and scholar in residence at Pace Law School in New York—expressed deep dismay that her findings had been shielded from public view.

As part of her exhaustive investigation, Harris had interviewed Ken Starr and "virtually everybody in Starr's office," including key FBI agents and the Justice Department officials who had interacted with OIC during their brace of Lewinsky. The initial, internal OPR report had been "none too kind" in assessing the conduct of Starr's team. At the end of Harris's investigation, she had reached the same regrettable conclusion, with additional evidence to buttress her findings. On the million-dollar question of whether Starr's lawyers had acted appropriately in plowing forward with the brace after Monica had pleaded to speak with attorney Frank Carter, Harris said, "I wouldn't have touched her with a ten-foot pole. I really wouldn't have. I mean, Frank Carter was representing her, as far as I am concerned, on a matter that really fell 'within the scope of their investigation,' and that's applying almost verbatim the Department's language."

Explained Harris, "The minute she says, 'Can I call my lawyer?' you stop. And when she says it for the sixth or seventh time, you *really* stop. It won't be the first time that an investigator's lead hasn't quite played out the way prosecutors think it should. I mean, there are limits."

Had Monica been permitted to call Frank Carter as she had repeatedly requested, Harris believed that Carter—a first-class criminal defense lawyer—would have swiftly worked out a sensible deal and likely avoided the year-long national ordeal. "It could probably have been done in a week with Carter," Harris said matter-of-factly. "And it would all have been done quietly and in a dignified way, and there wouldn't have been all this [damaging] press."

It was also troublesome to the federal investigator that Monica "had not [necessarily] committed a crime yet" when Starr's prosecutors confronted her. At the time of the sting, Monica's affidavit—smuggled to OIC by Linda Tripp's lawyer—had not yet been filed in the Arkansas federal court. "It's one thing to sign an affidavit, and I suppose if the notary stamps it, then you have already committed whatever [offense] you have committed," explained Harris. "But I start looking at it more seriously when it gets filed with the court." If Frank Carter had spoken with Monica that afternoon and learned that the affidavit contained false information, Harris noted, the lawyer could have easily instructed his secretary: " 'Call the clerk in Little Rock and say, "Hold that thing, we don't want to file it." ' "

Furthermore, Harris was troubled that Starr was out of the picture while much of the decision making was made. "The thing was run by committee, and whatever guys happened to have the aggressive personalities were the ones who prevailed on everything," she said. "I don't think I'm talking out of school when I say they really didn't have a strategy about Lewinsky until about two hours before they went to the hotel, because everyone was doing everything, and no one was in charge."

From Harris's perspective, the brace of Monica was ill fated from the start. "Ken Starr was over his head," she said, "and I don't mean that in a denigrating way at all. For heaven's sake, he's one of the most outstanding lawyers we've got in the country, but he was in the wrong job. And then he made some wrong decisions about who he was going to rely on." The result was that Starr simply "ratified stuff after it was done," including the botched handling of Lewinsky.

Moreover, Harris concluded from her investigation that OIC had constructed a conscious plan to expand into the Lewinsky matter come hell or high water, maneuvering the situation so that it was "difficult for the [Justice] Department to say no." Her interviews with OIC prosecutors and FBI agents convinced Harris that the Starr team wanted desperately to land this new investigation of Clinton. "Very badly," she said. "I think everyone I talked to . . . was absolutely persuaded, including Ken Starr, that Bill Clinton was a low life who would lie about anything. And this happens to prosecutors—but fortunately not very often—that they would have done virtually anything to get him." Nor was Harris buying the argument that Starr's office had no alternative because DOJ was untrustworthy and they feared Janet Reno would tip off the president. Harris, who had worked closely with Attorney General Reno for years, countered: "Frankly, she wouldn't take that crap from Clinton."

The final section of Harris's report made two recommendations to Robert Ray. First, she acknowledged that DOJ rules were "all over the place" on the subject of confronting persons already represented by attorneys, prior to any criminal charges being filed. For this reason, she concluded that Starr's prosecutors had not committed a "clear violation" of any established DOJ policy. Second, however, Harris determined that at least one OIC lawyer had exercised "poor judgment" in confronting Monica and handling this investigative step "by the seat of their pants."

Harris's report also had determined that Starr's office had been "less than cooperative and less than 'accurate' in its submissions to OPR." For all these reasons, she felt strongly that the public needed to learn the truth about the Starr prosecutors' conduct.

Ray had accepted her first finding, but rejected her second finding that any OIC prosecutor had exercised poor judgment in his or her handling of Lewinsky at the Ritz-Carlton. As Harris deciphered it, Ray wanted to take the easy way out, by latching onto the observation that DOJ rules were murky and ending matters there. "That's where his analysis stopped," she said. "That's where ours started."

Yet Harris was a coolheaded professional. She was satisfied that the American public would read her report and reach its own conclusion.

So she was "stunned" when Judge David Sentelle and the three-judge panel overseeing Ray's investigation slapped a "sealed" sticker on her detailed findings, burying her report from public view indefinitely. Harris was doubly perturbed that Ken Starr's former prosecutors aggressively fought to keep her report under wraps, on the theory that it would disclose "personal" information protected by the Privacy Act that might harm the professional reputation of OIC lawyers. How Starr's prosecutors could invoke "privacy" to prevent the American public from knowing *all* the facts relating to OIC's treatment of Monica Lewinsky—when the prosecutors had disgorged a mountain of private information relating to scores of people whom they were investigating—was difficult for Harris to fathom.

Years later, having anguished over the matter, Jo Ann Harris made her own decision to lift the veil of secrecy with respect to her report. "Federal prosecutors got a really bum rap from the criticism of the way OIC conducted themselves," she explained. Starr had repeatedly defended his actions by proclaiming in public venues, "That's how prosecutors act," and "We did nothing wrong." The only way to reassure citizens that the system of justice worked, Harris believed, was to address such matters openly and honestly. "You do investigate, and you let it hang out when you find that there's been bad judgment. That just makes so much sense to me in a context like this, where it's so public to begin with."

Robert Ray understood Harris's strong desire to air her findings, given the public nature of the Monica Lewinsky investigation. Although this fact was not generally known, Ray even proposed attaching the Harris report to his own final report to Congress, allowing it to become public in this fashion. One of his own OIC prosecutors hired an attorney to block this release. In the end, Ray concluded there was no "perfect solution" to the dilemma. OPR reports involving alleged professional misconduct were not typically dumped into the public domain—especially if there was no finding of wrongdoing. Prosecutors' reputations were at stake, and there were privacy concerns to worry about. This situation was even more sticky because only one OIC prosecutor involved in the sting still worked for the Justice Department and was subject to its regulations; it seemed unfair to tar this person alone with the brush of the Harris report findings when many other OIC prosecutors, including Ken Starr himself, deserved to shoulder some of the responsibility for the office's poor decision-making. Ray concluded that "reasonable minds can disagree" on the appropriate way to deal with such a sensitive situation. "I wasn't going to make the call whether [the Harris report] should be released or not released," he said. "The way to handle it was to put it in the court's hands."

Harris, on the other hand, reached a professional and moral judgment that this information should not be hidden any longer. "I feel pretty free talking about this," she concluded, taking a break from her teaching and trial work. The "final bottom line" of Harris's extensive investigation was crystal clear, and she felt strongly that American citizens were entitled to know about it. "There was one person who was senior and in charge and ought to have shown better judgment," Harris said, "[and] the office itself did not cover itself with glory."

———

THE Monica Lewinsky saga was not the only aspect of the Clinton-Starr drama that produced recriminations long after the bucking bronco of history had thrown its riders from its saddle.

The failed effort by the House managers to impeach and remove President Clinton led to plenty of finger-pointing. Like the impeachment trial of President Andrew Johnson more than a century earlier, the unsuccessful drive to remove Clinton had left the House managers looking unduly partisan and lacking sound judgment to many; yet the managers themselves did not see it that way.

Henry Hyde, sitting back in his suburban Illinois office looking relaxed and eager to begin his retirement from public office, shortly before his unexpected death in 2007, defended the work of his House managers till the very end. This dedicated "band of brothers," Hyde insisted, had done the right thing by ignoring the fickle winds of popular sentiment. The former lead House manager even expressed sympathy for Monica Lewinsky, who was denied attorney's fees under the independent counsel law after cooperating with Ken Starr and who ended up being stung badly as a result of entrusting her heart to Bill Clinton. "She got into a hornet's nest and could be carrying this around the rest of her life," said Hyde. "I think to some extent, she was victimized."

Jutting a thumb under his suspenders, Hyde went on: "This whole saga ends up with Mr. Clinton still making all kinds of dough, being idolized by his clique, but the man has an asterisk after his name in every history book that he was impeached." He added: "[Clinton has had] his lawyer's license suspended. Not only that, but he was fined by a federal judge. Not only that, but he settled the case with Paula Jones for no small amount of money . . . all of that is on his side of the ledger."

On the House managers' side of the ledger, Hyde felt, there was nothing to record for posterity except that they had acted honorably and out of a patriotic sense of duty. Hyde stood up, tugging on his suspenders to hide his weight problem, which was expertly hidden by his tailor. He walked toward a special spot on the wall and removed a framed citation signed by Chief Justice Rehnquist and issued on behalf of the Judicial Conference of the United States. This proclamation recognized Hyde's distinguished service as chairman of the House Judiciary Committee and his "unwavering respect for the Constitution of the United States and an abiding belief in the rule of law." Said Hyde, a look of emotion swamping his eyes, "I'll take that trade-off any day."

He placed the framed document down and concluded, "I take consolation in comments [by political experts] that George W. Bush would not have been elected if we had not impeached President Clinton. The core Republican support would have walked away and said, 'Nobody believes in anything anymore.' At least these guys [the managers] believed in something and did their duty."

Henry Hyde recalled with pride that shortly after losing the vote in the impeachment trial, he had attended an event at an elegant Washington hotel at which Justice Antonin Scalia was among the distinguished guests. The conservative intellectual leader of the Supreme Court had draped his arm around Chairman Hyde and said, "You guys covered yourselves with glory."

Said Hyde, looking back on that moment with satisfaction and closing his eyes to savor it, "I accept that."

———

PRESIDENT Bill Clinton would see nothing heroic in the efforts of the House managers who had pursued him doggedly until they ran out of steam. "I understood them," he later said. "They're both ideological and very focused on concentrating power. And they believed they're supposed to hurt their enemies by whatever means they have at their disposal." The House managers and Ken Starr, said the former president, had deluded themselves into believing that they were on a divine mission to stage a coup d'état and to replace his unholy administration with one of their own making. "And because they talk in these righteous terms, they get a lot of people to defend whatever they do. Because if they're righteous . . . obviously, whatever they do to me is whatever I deserve."

Even years later, having commenced a new life in New York with a wife who had become a national political figure in her own right, Bill Clinton refused to talk about his amorous relationship with Monica Lewinsky despite his willingness to grant interviews to discuss almost every other aspect of the Starr investigation that had nearly toppled his presidency. Yet Clinton occasionally let down his guard and spoke frankly about the personal impact of this scandal upon him and his family.

Dressed in a brown vest perfect for tramping around his backyard in Chappaqua and appearing rested and fit, Clinton lifted his eyes upward. "There were some really positive aspects," he reflected. "I mean, you know, if you live a busy life, you risk the fact that a lot of your life goes unexamined, both the good and the bad parts of it. And then all of us have secrets, and we're entitled to them. But once you've been publicly humiliated like I was, you really don't think you have anything to hide anymore. It doesn't really much matter what people ever say about you again for the rest of your life. And it's kind of liberating."

Clinton took a moment to chew on an unlit cigar (his doctors advised him against smoking after his heart surgery), before adding that the nasty battles with Henry Hyde and Ken Starr had turned out to be oddly therapeutic for him. "And the fact that, you know, my family stayed together and Hillary stayed with me and my daughter got through this, it was all pretty wonderful in a certain way. I mean, the overall thing was terrible, [but] the American people got [it].

"I'd give anything if I hadn't done it and anything if it hadn't happened—but there were some unbelievably touching moments. As well as the larger fact that my family came through it and the public stayed with me."

For Susan McDougal, the whole experience of becoming an internationally known Whitewater convict still seemed unreal.

She didn't blame Bill Clinton for her tribulations. The entire time she was in prison, she had never reached out to Clinton or called collect to the White House. "Although I probably would have if I'd had the number," she said with a laugh. "I called everybody else in Christendom."

Susan "didn't have a clue" if Clinton would grant her a pardon, despite rumors (initiated by her ex-husband, Jim, while he was trying to get himself sprung from prison) that the president had made a secret deal to absolve her. The extent of Susan's lobbying effort consisted of Claudia Riley's calling the White House and speaking into an answering machine, stating in a firm voice, "Bill, this is Claudia. I just want to call and say, 'Do the right thing.'" For the most part, Susan was leaving the final decision in God's hands. "If anyone in the world knew I was innocent, it was Bill Clinton," she said, re-creating her thinking. "My God . . . No, I didn't ask for [a pardon]; I got it. And I deserved it because I was innocent. And he knew it."

In the midst of the televised coverage of George W. Bush's inauguration, Susan and Claudia had been watching CNN when the news anchor broke in to announce that Clinton's pardons had been issued. Susan had expected the newsman to go down the list alphabetically starting with the A's. "And they said straightaway, the very first name, 'Susan McDougal has been pardoned.'"

After checking another channel to make sure she wasn't dreaming, Susan grabbed her coat and the two ladies jumped into Claudia's car. "And we went and had greasy eggs and bacon at the Steak and Egg," Susan said, recalling that day. "We ate everything we could eat. We ate and ate and ate . . . I hadn't even combed my hair, and we got back to the house from Steak and Egg, and there were like twenty trucks with big satellite dishes on them at the foot of the driveway." Claudia interjected: "It was kind of an Arkansas celebration of getting a pardon. We prayed and we drank."

Vanity Fair ran a story about Susan McDougal titled "Joan of Arkansas," while the *Los Angeles Times Magazine* dubbed her the "Steel Magnolia." Such tributes only infuriated Ken Starr, who felt that it was "profoundly wrong" that Susan McDougal should be "lifted up and honored" when she was a "felon" who had defied a federal judge's orders. Starr later posed the rhetorical question: "She [and Jim McDougal] were looting a savings and loan, and now she's a great hero or heroine?"

When it came to one of the great mysteries that had stumped Starr and his prosecutors during their long-running Clinton investigation—namely, the true nature of the past relationship between Governor Bill Clinton and Susan McDougal—interviews with confidential sources and additional evidence now confirm that some intimate involvement did occur between Susan McDougal and Governor Clinton years earlier, during the period when Jim and Susan's marriage first deteriorated, before she divorced Jim. Ken Starr had spent five years and untold resources trying to extract the truth concerning the relationship between Susan McDougal and Bill Clinton, never succeeding. Now this much can be substantiated: There was a romantic affair, albeit brief in duration.

Nonetheless, it is also clear that the brief period of intimacy between Bill Clinton and Susan McDougal, whenever it took place during Clinton's tenure as governor, was not the reason for Susan's refusal to answer the Starr prosecutors' questions in the grand jury. Sources confirm that she did not wish to hurt her husband, Jim, or Hillary Clinton. However, her principal motivation had nothing to do with protecting Bill Clinton. One source expressed it by stating that Susan did not endure two years of incarceration in prison, watch her parents suffer strokes and heart-bypasses, and risk further criminal convictions in order to avoid confessing the truth about an age-old fling with then-Governor Clinton, however great his supposed prowess as a ladies' man. In the end, this source made clear, Susan McDougal refused to testify out of an abiding hatred and distrust of Ken Starr and his OIC prosecutors, whom she believed would pursue her—regardless of the testimony she gave under oath—if her account did not suit their need.

Once she was cleared of criminal charges and freed to return home to Camden, Arkansas, however, Susan no longer worried about Ken Starr or his prosecutorial minions. She spent most of her time giving speeches on topics relating to issues facing women in prison. She also cleaned out her storage shed and dumped boxes of papers relating to Whitewater and Madison Guaranty in the trash, taking steps to erase memories of Jim McDougal and the events that had wrecked their lives.

Susan had received several phone calls from Richard Clark, Jim's prison psychologist, and struggled with remnants of her strange feelings of grief. When she finally learned the truth about the events leading to Jim's death in solitary confinement, she wept like a child. "I had no idea he was going to be denied parole," she said of her dead ex-husband, still shaken emotionally. "That's what killed him. Seven days before he died? He thought he was going on a book tour. It killed him."

Susan waited more than a year after she was released from jail before mustering up the courage to visit Jim's grave at the Rest Haven Memorial Gardens, on the hilly plot where Jim was buried next to his mentor, war hero Bob Riley. She arrived at Jim's resting place accompanied by Claudia, squeezing her friend's hand, not knowing how she would react. When she finally lowered her eyes toward the nondescript plot, Susan almost shouted, pointing at the simple bronze marker on the ground that identified Jim's eternal resting place: "Claudia," she cried out, "they've got him as a Vietnam veteran, for God's sake!" With that, Susan began laughing and crying in a mixed outpouring of emotion. It seemed too rich to be true: Jim fleetingly had served in the U.S. Air Force Reserve in his twenties; during his youthful drinking days, he had made a sport of going to bars with a coat draped over his arm, telling wide-eyed patrons that he had lost his arm in Vietnam and spinning tales about his imaginary acts of valor, thus earning himself free drinks. Jim had probably prodded someone at the Fort Worth prison to make sure he was buried with military honors, Susan said, no doubt repeating his apocryphal stories and insisting that the paperwork be filed for his grave marker from the Veteran's Administration. "Jim's down there laughing," Susan told Claudia, sweeping the leaves off the bronze marker. "He always wanted to be a veteran, a wounded soldier." In death, she said, her deceased ex-husband Jim had pulled off his final con job.

"It's entirely Jim McDougal," Susan said laughing, her eyes sparkling with a distant flicker of nostalgia that resembled a remnant of love.

———

PRESIDENT Bill Clinton's principal regret about his final days in office was that he had not pardoned Webb Hubbell at the same time he had pardoned Susan McDougal. That forty-eight-hour period now seemed like a blur. He had made several unfortunate decisions that he wished he could undo—such as pardoning billionaire fugitive Marc Rich, whose ex-wife Denise Rich had donated nearly a half million dollars to his nascent Clinton Presidential Library, and whose pardon for tax fraud had sparked Senate hearings and another big controversy. Clinton said, looking back on that sleep-deprived time, "I'd have pardoned

[Webb] and I wouldn't pardon [Marc] Rich." He confided, "I woke up in the middle of the night several times in the first two months I was out of the White House, not worried about Rich, but full of regret that I hadn't pardoned Hubbell and [Governor Jim Guy] Tucker."

Webb Hubbell himself admitted that he was deeply hurt by the nonpardon. But he eventually concluded, as a philosophical matter, that it was probably meant to be. "I don't hold any regret or grudge," he said. "Or animosity whatsoever. That was a decision he made. We all make decisions . . . [some] we wish we had back." Hubbell lifted his head and added, in a subdued drawl, "If I had been pardoned, it might have taken away from the rehabilitation that I've gone through from having served my time and dealt with the issue and come face to face with it. So in a lot of ways . . . it was probably a good thing."

Despite his fall from grace, plummeting from number three lawyer in the U.S. Justice Department to former convict, Hubbell had concluded that it was pointless to do anything rash. Suicide had entered his mind, on and off, during this horrible period. But he had decided that it was counterproductive to take the path that his friend Vince Foster had taken. "I'd be lying to you if I said [I didn't] get depressed," he admitted. "Especially bearing the shame of what I did and having to confront it. Having to admit to your kids that you'd done something wrong. To your wife. Face all that I faced—you know, in prison." Making the transition to a new life and a new career—selling insurance in Washington—was hardly a cakewalk. At the same time, said Hubbell, "anybody who's been around somebody who committed suicide realizes that it doesn't solve any problems. It doesn't leave your family better off."

Hubbell remembered first arriving in Washington after having been nominated to serve as associate attorney general and meeting with Senator Joe Biden, who chaired the Judiciary Committee. Biden had said to him, half-facetiously, "Are you sure you want this job? The president's best friend always gets indicted." Now, Biden's remark had proven to be prescient, like an ugly nightmare come alive. But Webb did not allow himself to consider what-ifs, such as whether he would have ended up in prison if he had never been a close personal friend of Bill and Hillary's. Hubbell bit his thick lower lip and said, "I don't even think about that. I did something wrong, and I've paid for it and that's behind me. To get into would-haves and should-haves is not healthy."

Similarly, Bill Clinton's decision not to grant him a pardon was now cordoned off in a remote corner of his mind. Hubbell's only regret, after disgracing himself and cobbling the pieces of his life back together, was that he had never spoken to Bill or Hillary again. "I mean, I miss them as friends," he said, folding his napkin after indulging in an infrequent breakfast at the Mayflower Hotel. "They're wonderful people. We had wonderful friendships. I cannot deny that's a loss in my life. But it was brought on by my own actions. So I can regret it. But I don't blame them for anything."

Putting on a worn corduroy jacket, Webb Hubbell paused before lumbering off to his Washington office to sell insurance, long enough to formulate a final question that still bedeviled him. Although he liked Ken Starr as a Southern gentleman and as a former colleague in the law, and had long ago forgiven Starr for the treatment he and his family had endured in the wake of his admitted crimes, Hubbell couldn't discern, for the life of him, what else Starr's lawyers were trying to extract from him. The fact that Bill Clinton had not pardoned him seemed to be proof positive that he had not hidden any deep, dark secrets. After all—Hubbell pointed out, shrugging his shoulders in bewilderment—if this had been a grand conspiracy designed to protect the Clintons, surely Bill would have been *forced* to pardon him to keep him from spilling his guts.

"I'd love to know what they were really after," Hubbell mused, before stepping into the overcast Washington morning to continue his rehabilitation, one day at a time. "It's never been clear to me—what did they think the Clintons had done that they couldn't prove? That led them to spend this much money? Or was it merely the belief that they had to go down every alley and every pathway? . . ."

Monica Lewinsky had done her best to move on with her life, securing an apartment in New York City. It was an awkward place to call home, since Hillary Clinton was now her U.S. senator and Bill Clinton had set up his office nearby in Harlem. Yet she did her best to carve out her own space. She had designed and sold her own line of handbags as a temporary business venture, then enrolled at the London School of Economics to complete a master's degree in social psychology.

But the former White House intern would never quite outgrow the scars of her relationship with President Bill Clinton or shake the memories of the massive criminal investigation that it had unleashed.

In a spontaneous moment of reflection during an interview in 2008, Monica posed the question: "I wonder did he feel any responsibility to make sure I was okay? He certainly hasn't [taken any steps to do that]." She took a breath and continued: "As I've gotten older, I think about that."

Despite Bill Clinton's repeated protestations to the grand jury, to Congress, and to the American people that he recognized the misguided nature of his actions, Monica remained unconvinced. "I think if he really felt these things— especially given the age difference and where I was in life, so young—at the very least, he would have apologized. Then he would have done something [to rectify the situation]." Unfortunately, she said, that had never happened. With Hillary Clinton having entered the national political scene in her own right and former President Clinton doing quite well as the retired leader of the world's greatest superpower, there had been no effort by "the Big Creep" to make amends in any meaningful way. Monica Samille Lewinsky had written this off as an unpleasant lesson in life that she had learned the hard way.

She pushed the hair out of her face and said of Clinton with a note of sadness, "I guess my biggest disappointment was that he just turned out not to be the person that I thought he was, that I thought I knew."

Monica still had the blue dress, packed away in storage. As her mother would say, "What do you do with it?" There had been offers to buy the soiled garment at generous prices to sell it at memorabilia auctions, but Monica had turned them all down, feeling it was unseemly to profit from this grotesque souvenir of a hurtful, long-ago affair.

In looking back on one of the most highly publicized political/sexual scandals of the twentieth century, which she would have given anything to make vanish from her life's story, Monica would say in 2009: "I have contemplated moving to a remote country or changing my name. However, when you tease [that] out . . . you realize in another country there are still safety issues to consider. It would also mean not living near friends and family, who have been incredibly supportive." Monica continued: "As for changing my name, I can't imagine, even if I tried to file the legal paperwork under seal, that it wouldn't leak. And then, what would be the point? Also, on principle, I don't think I should have to change my name. Anyway, it will change when I get married."

Bernie Lewinsky, who had watched his daughter suffer for years as a result of her affair with Clinton, had much more blunt, uncensored words for the man who had managed to transform the name "Lewinsky" into a synonym for "presidential sex scandal." If he were to run into Bill Clinton on the street, Bernie Lewinsky said, he would share a piece of his mind; he would tell Clinton flat out "that I respected him as a president, but I don't respect him as a man." He felt that Clinton "was cowardly in his behavior towards Monica, and that if he had been forthright and spoke the truth in the beginning, the whole country and the world could have been spared the spectacle."

Monica's father sipped some bottled water to relieve the dryness in his throat and then finished: "He had an opportunity to put this whole thing to rest. And instead of saying, 'I did not have sex with that woman,' he should have just come out and said, 'My fault. I'm sorry. It is true. I regret it. And that's the end of that.' "

"He's never apologized to her. And as far as I'm concerned, the only apology he can give her is to say 'I'm sorry for what I put you through and here's my check for two million dollars to pay for your legal fees.' He got her into it just as much as she did, and he certainly had responsibilities he should have fessed up to. And I don't think he's going to do that. He certainly hasn't apologized to us in any form."

Of course, Bernie Lewinsky would reserve even harsher words for the independent counsel who set this criminal investigation into motion. If he could meet up with the former special prosecutor who had pursued his daughter so tenaciously and published a graphic account of her sex life, Bernie would unload every insult he could muster. "You're a pervert, Ken Starr," he wanted to tell the former independent counsel. "There was absolutely no reason to make this public."

———

LINDA Tripp, the older "friend" who had tossed Monica into Starr's net, had endured her own travails after the Clinton-Starr scandal had receded into history. Following a bout with breast cancer (which required a lumpectomy, chemotherapy, and radiation) and after assuming a new identity, settling amid the quiet horse farms of Middleburg Virginia, Tripp would do her best not to revisit the disastrous Lewinsky chapter of her life. Happily married to Dieter Rausch, a former teenage sweetheart from Germany, Tripp saw no benefit in wallowing in Monicagate.

The healing process was made easier after she received a $595,000 settlement from the Bush Defense Department, under the federal Privacy Act, to compensate her for the Pentagon's improper leak of her teenage arrest record—relating to a crime she had never committed. Linda Tripp had traded in the lunacy of the Washington Beltway for peace and tranquility. As she cooked spaghetti and meatballs, using a favorite recipe from the Italian side of her family, Tripp concluded that she had handled an ugly situation as best she could. Glancing out the window at the horse pasture, the now dark-haired Tripp said, "I just look out there and [think], 'How in the hell did I ever get myself into all of this?'"

With respect to the media's portrayal of her as an evil villainess who had betrayed a young and vulnerable friend, Tripp offered her own defense: "I know [Monica] will never see this and never understand it, and it would be futile to try to convince her otherwise, but she, in her tunnel [vision], was suicidal. She was contemplating and threatening suicide almost daily. She was in the most fragile state of mental health I've ever seen a functioning human being in. So did I think [exposing her relationship with Clinton] would help her? No, I didn't think it would help her. Did I think ultimately it might help her in the end and that she'd survive it? Yeah, I did." Tripp added a postscript: "It had nothing to do with trying to hurt Monica. I never wanted to hurt Monica."

Tripp insisted, however, that the former White House intern was not blameless. "I can tell you this, and I swear on my children's lives, I haven't lied throughout all this. You may not like my motivation. You may think my motivation's shady, but I've tried to be as truthful as I can. And I've never been a liar." Tripp insisted that she was incapable of committing such a mortal sin. "I grew up as a Catholic with the notion that God's going to get me on the meat rack for eating baloney on Friday. And I also believe God is going to get me if I lie, and cause others pain. So I'm not lying here . . . someone [else] is." Specifically, Tripp would point to Monica's grand jury testimony in which the former intern swore that Vernon Jordan had never known of her affair with Clinton and did not arrange a job in return for her signing a false affidavit in the *Paula Jones* case. Said Tripp, her face darkening with the reappearance of a ghost from the past, "When I saw her testimony, and saw her lie, and there was no way to prove otherwise, because of conversations that were not recorded that I thought had been, I knew she would get away with it. And she did."

Tripp concluded, a look of pain overtaking her face, "I think the most hurtful thing throughout this whole thing has been the notion that I was motivated by money or by any sort of self-enrichment, because to this day, I'm still the only one that's never taken a penny, ever—and, you know, several years have gone by; I should get some credit."

Yet Tripp's precise role in these events—and her motives—remained a puzzle in a story laced with unanswered riddles. Among other things, her steadfast denial that a book deal was ever a major motivating factor in her own conduct seemed to be undercut by the hard facts. Interviews later revealed that Tripp actively pursued a book contract even after the Clinton-Starr saga had begun fading out. Indeed, Tripp had arranged numerous clandestine meetings with a New York author—whom she referred to by the fictitious name "Pamela," for fear that the Clinton hit-squad would learn of her project and stop it by brute force. Tripp and "Pamela" wore pillows under their blouses (to appear pregnant) and donned wigs to throw off would-be pursuers.

In the end, Tripp had abandoned the book project only because she could not negotiate a satisfactory percentage split of royalties. As one acquaintance said, it was as if Linda Tripp could not decide if she was going to make a name (and a small fortune) for herself by standing up to her enemies and declaring, "I have the truth on my side!" or crawl into a hole and die from fear and self-doubt. Said a source who worked with Tripp on the book deal until it collapsed, "Was this about writing a book and making money? Or something else? It was a combination. . . . She was thinking about a rainy day [fund]. But she also wanted to set the record straight."

The source paused and delivered a frank assessment: "She's never come clean—I hate to say that." For whatever reason, this smart, complicated woman with a slight disposition toward paranoia had been eaten alive by a vast scandal that she herself had helped conceive. "When you're up against the most power-ful [figures] in the world," stated Tripp's acquaintance, "people can act like moths. They go toward where the light is. Sometimes, that impacts the truth."

Concluded the source: "She was conflicted to the end—she thought the American public had a right to know what was going on in the White House. But she chickened out. I think she's still chickening out."

Tripp's former literary agent friend, Lucianne Goldberg, added her own un-varnished postscript. "She was over her head," said Goldberg. "I don't think Linda had a clue about the vehemence that was going to be visited on her. If you strike the king, you must kill the king."

———

PAULA Jones, the woman whose lawsuit against Bill Clinton had commenced the scandal train a-rolling, had returned to a slower-paced life in Cabot, Arkansas, liking it just fine. Here, Paula had remarried a construction worker named Steven Mark McFadden and had found a new vocation selling real estate while raising her two boys, free from the likes of Steve Jones and Bill Clinton. She had also found time to dabble in money-making ventures that capitalized on her fleeting notoriety, such as appearing in a boxing match against disgraced Olympic skater Tonya Harding (Paula was billed as "the Arkansas Pounder," Harding was dubbed "TNT") on television's short-lived *Celebrity Boxing* show.

When it came to tabloid reports that she had raked in the big bucks from her lawsuit, Paula quickly objected, pointing out that lawyers had to be paid and expenses had to be covered. "A hundred and fifty-one thousand dollars. That's all I got out of $850,000," Paula said, tapping a painted fingernail against the table. "And I had to pay taxes on that money."

In the end, Paula Jones McFadden insisted that her lawsuit wasn't about money; it was about some loftier principle. "All the crap I'd been through, the mud they'd drug me through," she said. "And talking about 'trailer park trash.' I never lived in a trailer in my life. And discrediting me and saying I'm a bimbo. Just name it, and they called it to me. That's why they have money judgments. It's for—what's it called?" Her friend Debbie Ballentine interjected, "Pain and suf-fering." "Yes," Paula said emphatically, taking a quick sip of her Diet Coke. "The trauma."

At the end of the day, despite all the jokes and cartoon artists making fun of her nose and all the "negativity," Paula said, she was pleased that plenty of every-day people in Arkansas continued to treat her as a hero, of sorts: "They're just ex-cited and want autographs and [say], 'We're so proud of you. We knew how he [Bill Clinton] was.'"

Nor did Paula feel any guilt for the long-running scandal that had ensnared

Bill Clinton. She believed in her heart that Clinton himself deserved all the blame. "He's the one that made the United States of America look bad because of his actions and stuff," she said, swirling the ice in her soft drink. "If someone would have done this in another country, they would have probably been hung or thrown out of office.

"I have a right just like anybody has a right to get justice, be heard, and stuff like that," Paula insisted. "So, it wasn't *my* fault. And I don't feel guilty a bit about it."

Paula's media guru, Susan Carpenter-McMillan, echoed that sentiment: "I can tell you with every fiber of my body I believe one hundred and ten percent of what [Paula] said. Now, could she have been a little flirtatious and rolled her eyes when she was down in the lobby and [Clinton] came by? Absolutely. Who wouldn't? But did she go up there with any intention of any sexual behavior? Absolutely not."

Carpenter-McMillan felt that Bill Clinton had acted like a roving dog who couldn't be kept on the porch, and he deserved to answer to God and the legal system for that. It was understandable that Clinton might try to hit on Paula, she observed, because she was a "sexy, provocative gal" who was "pure enough to take home to mommy." Nonetheless, his behavior was thoroughly boorish and discriminatory. "How appealing do you think a man's going to be if he says, 'Hi, honey, nice to meet you, my name's Bill,' pulls his pants down, whips it out? . . . That is the biggest turnoff for anyone, unless you're a prostitute and getting paid five thousand dollars for it. I mean, it just doesn't play well."

In terms of considering her own role in the saga, Susan Carpenter-McMillan responded like any good PR spokesperson: "I smile, and I'm so humbled that I feel like I played a little part of history. But I believed that she [Paula] showed us that the Constitution is truly what it is, and that when our—being of British descent—Founding Fathers left the motherland, they came here because they didn't believe there was a king, and I think that Paula just proved it."

———

Not all of those involved in the Paula Jones saga, however, bought into these lofty invocations of motherhood and constitutional history. For one, there were nagging factual issues that the passage of time had not resolved. Indeed, evidence from confidential sources now establishes with near certainty that the alleged "distinguishing characteristic" described by Paula Jones at the time of her encounter with then-Governor Clinton in 1991 did not exist, as an anatomical matter. Thus, at least one key aspect of Ms. Jones's account is not corroborated by medical sources or individuals who would have had an ample opportunity to observe that trait if it had existed.

More important, the wrapping-up of the *Jones* case had left a sense of dismay and nonfulfillment in the minds of many who had played key roles in it. Danny Traylor, the small-time Little Rock lawyer who had initially handled Paula's suit against the president, admitted that he had never fully recovered from the ordeal. "I feel bad for the country," Traylor said. "I feel bad about the whole thing." He was turned off by the fact that his former client had turned to *Celebrity Boxing* and other low-level endeavors to make money. He was especially displeased that Paula had gone on to pose for *Penthouse* and had told the magazine that Clinton's enemies on the far right had "used" and "manipulated" her. "I think that's pretty tacky," said Traylor. "She'd expressly told me that she wasn't interested in any of that kind of trash, garbage. She fought to keep some of her [bootleg] photos out of *Penthouse,* and then she goes and [poses for money]. It just doesn't seem too consistent, I guess."

Wes Holmes, one of the Dallas lawyers whose law firm was nearly obliterated as a result of handling the *Jones* litigation, likewise felt unfulfilled. Paula's posing for *Penthouse,* Holmes said, was a disappointment if not a double cross. After all of their efforts, the firm had little to show for its massive investment of time, legal talent, and emotional energy other than this grotesque trophy that proved their client had appeared nude in a skin magazine.

Holmes had one other cheap memento: After the case was over, Paula had sent him and the other Dallas lawyers a small FTD floral arrangement in a coffee cup with a picture of a duck on it. Now that the historic *Clinton v. Jones* case was over, Holmes kept that cup in his office as his final souvenir of his efforts. Lifting the chipped ceramic mug by its handle to inspect it, he concluded, "We hadn't gotten paid for nine months; we hadn't seen our wives; it was financial Armageddon for us to take that case, and at the very end of the deal, she sends us a little FTD thing."

"So I still have [this] coffee cup with a duck on it; that's all I have." He sighed. "It's just so perfect."

———

RICHARD Clark, the prison psychologist who had worked closely with James Bert McDougal at the federal facility in Fort Worth, Texas, had never fully gotten over the tragic death of Jim McDougal in solitary confinement. A year after Jim's funeral, Clark pulled into the driveway of Claudia Riley's house in Arkadelphia, past the little trailer-cottage that had served as Jim's last home before he was jailed. The doctor had decided it was time to pay a visit and show his respects. Here, the balding young psychologist sipped iced tea with Claudia, sharing stories about the kindly Southern gentleman–convict whom they both missed.

Claudia took Clark around the house. She pointed out the chair where Jim liked to sit; various knickknacks from Jim's career as an aspiring politician and a real estate visionary before he became a felon; and a collection of family photos of Jim—as a child, standing proudly alongside his parents, and as an adult posing with an aspiring young politician named Bill Clinton. "Jim just always appeared to be so very different than his family was," Dr. Clark remarked softly as he flipped through the photos. Claudia answered, "That's right. Jim was a diamond in a patch of cabbages."

On this day of Clark's visit, thermometers recorded new highs for mid-September, sweltering even by southern Arkansas standards. Dabbing a bead of sweat off his forehead, Clark drove into town, located the Murray-Ruggles Funeral Home, and then exited with a map of the cemetery that identified where the Riley family plot was situated.

He shooed away flies as he tramped up the hill, finally reaching the plot where Bob Riley was buried, and, beside him, James Bert McDougal.

Over the hillside, a pond shimmered green in the sunlight. Tall, spindly pines huddled around the secluded patch of grave markers. The former prison psychologist knelt down, reached into his pocket, and removed a pink and white peppermint—the same peppermint Jim McDougal had given him during one of their last meetings in his prison office as an offering of trust and friendship.

Here at the peak of the hilly graveyard, Clark remained motionless on one knee, said a quiet prayer, placed the wrapped peppermint on the grave, stood up, then tramped down to his car and drove silently away, taking the long, flat expanse of I-30 from Arkansas, down through Hope (where Bill Clinton had been born) and back into Texas (where Ken Starr's family had established its roots), relieved that he had fulfilled this final important mission.

In this private fashion, the epic scandal ended—a scandal that had spanned twenty years and thousands of miles, from the cool Ozark Mountains of Arkansas, where Jim and Susan McDougal had once imagined success and prosperity awaiting them in the sparkling waters of Whitewater, to the stark marble edifices of Washington, where the conflicts involving President William Jefferson Clinton had played out, one by one.

Clark's silent prayer, as he had gazed on the tall pines casting shadows over Jim McDougal's grave, stirred by a gentle Southern wind that bathed the cemetery in a rejuvenating air that permitted temporal wounds to heal, had been a simple one: However this had happened, Clark had prayed silently to God, this story could not be permitted to repeat itself—ever again—in the yet unborn cycles of American history.

Notes

Chapter 1: The Impeachment Vote

3: Article I accused William Jefferson Clinton: House, *Impeachment of President William Jefferson Clinton,* Debate of the House on H. Res. 611, 614 (18–19 Dec. 1998), H11774-75; C-SPAN videotape, impeachment proceedings, 19 Dec. 1998.

3: Chairman Hyde would remember: Henry J. Hyde, interview by author.

3: Pornographer Larry Flynt: Peter Baker, *The Breach: Inside the Impeachment and Trial of William Jefferson Clinton,* 120.

4: Flynt had dubbed: Larry Flynt, *Sex, Lies and Politics: The Naked Truth,* 15, 20–21.

4: Now, thirty-three years later: Henry J. Hyde, interview by author; Baker, *The Breach,* 98.

4: Capitol Hill's *Roll Call*: Flynt, *Sex, Lies and Politics,* 16.

4: "Well, that's right": Larry Flynt, interview by author.

4: "You know," Hyde whispered to Livingston: Robert L. Livingston, interview by author.

5: Those who knew: Larry Flynt, who was watching these events seated in a wheelchair in his glittering *Hustler* offices in Beverly Hills, understood what was causing Livingston's nervousness. "You could have stuck a fork in him at that time," Flynt said, smiling. "He was *done*" (Larry Flynt, interview by author).

5: "It just needs a kicker": Robert L. Livingston, interview by author.

6: "I hope to God": David Schippers, remarks made while author was interviewing Henry J. Hyde.

6: Two counts passed: Amy Keller, "House Impeaches President: Two of Four Articles Go to Senate for Trial," *Roll Call,* 21 Dec. 1998, 1, 26.

7: "This has not been": Ed Henry, "Overwhelming Events Overwhelm Everyone," *Roll Call,* 21 Dec. 1998, 1.

7: "I knew nothing about it": William Jefferson Clinton, interview by author (hereinafter cited as Bill Clinton).

8: A cold front: *Arkansas Democrat-Gazette,* 19 Dec. 1998, D6.

8: "Impeached": *Arkansas Democrat-Gazette,* 20 Dec. 1998, A1.

8: He watched: Skip Rutherford, interview by author.

9: "My God": Joe Purvis, interview by author.

9: Sitting with his wife: David Newbern, interview by author.

10: Marge Mitchell had known Bill: Marge Mitchell, interview by author.

10: Marge and some of Virginia's: Nancy Adkins, interview by author.

11: "I was a basket case": Betsey Wright, interview by author.

12: "I just believe": Liz Green, interview by author.

12: "I mean, it was proven": Kathleen Cavoli, interview by author.

12: "I think the House gets": Alice Starr, interview by author.

12: "I had very little to say": Kenneth W. Starr, interview by author (hereinafter cited as Ken Starr).

13: Holed up in an apartment: Monica Lewinsky, interview by author.

13: "I was so numb": Paula Jones, interview by author.

14: "I started watching": Susan McDougal, interview by author.

15: "I think he [President Clinton] is tired": "A 'Sober Moment' Then Up and at 'Em at the White House," *Democrat-Gazette Press Services,* 20 Dec. 1998, A1.

Chapter 2: Bill Clinton and Ken Starr

15: "I always thought I understood him": Bill Clinton, interview by author.

15: The Church of Christ believed: Ken Starr, interview by author; Sue Anne Pressley, "The

Roots of Ken Starr's Morality Plays," *Washington Post*, 2 Mar. 1998, C1.

16: The name recorded: Bill Clinton, *My Life*, 4; David Maraniss, *First in His Class: The Biography of Bill Clinton*, 28–29.

17: Virginia Clinton Kelley would marry: Maraniss, *First in His Class*, 41.

17: Kenneth Winston Starr was born: Ken Starr, interview by author.

17: The elder Starr passed along: Ibid.; Billie Jeayne (Starr) Reynolds, interview by author.

17: Vannie worked tirelessly: Billie Jeayne (Starr) Reynolds, interview by author.

18: Vannie Starr would live: Pressley, "Ken Starr's Morality Plays."

18: He was elected: Maraniss, *First in His Class*, 69–73, 96–121.

18: Ken Starr likewise entered: Ken Starr, interview by author.

18: He was haunted: Bill Clinton to Marge Mitchell, air letter, 13 May 1969, Marge Mitchell papers.

20: "He was an avid reader": Marge Mitchell, interview by author.

20: "I always knew him to be": Elizabeth Buck, interview by author.

21: "He liked world history": Paul Root, interview by author.

21: Leopoulos would never forget: David Paul Leopoulos, interview by author.

21: "old-time speaking affair": Ernie Dumas, interview by author.

22: Newbern recalled attending: David Newbern, interview by author.

22: "wonderboy Clinton": L. T. Simes II, interview by author.

23: "I've never said I hated": Nancy Adkins, interview by author.

23: "You can't put in there": Dick Kelley, interview by author.

24: "Ken was never pushed": Billie Jeayne (Starr) Reynolds, interview by author.

24: purchased a barbering license: Pressley, "Ken Starr's Morality Plays."

24: "He polished his shoes": Bennett Roth, "Starr's Road to Political Center Stage Began in San Antonio," *Houston Chronicle*, 8 Feb. 1998, A23.

24: "Oh, it played a very important role": Billie Jeayne (Starr) Reynolds, interview by author.

24: a cherubic boy who: Roberta Mahan, interview by author.

24: "He was one of those guys": James Castillo, "Special Prosecutor Was a Star at Sam Houston High," *San Antonio Express-News*, 2 Feb. 1998, A5.

24: "Ken himself thought": Roberta Mahan, interview by author.

25: "probably the most conservative": Alan Reaves, interview by author.

25: Starr was devastated: Roberta Mahan, interview by author; Billie Jeayne (Starr) Reynolds, interview by author.

25: "To think that it all happened": Alan Reaves, interview by author.

25: "Now, as we begin to pick up": Castillo, "Special Prosecutor."

25: "had the manners of a country gentleman": Lou Butterfield, interview by author.

25: His freshman yearbook included: *1965 Harding University Yearbook*.

26: "In my life, I have never": Lou Butterfield, interview by author.

26: "Starr Dust": Ken Starr, "Starr Dust: Crowded Cities, Plentiful Problems," *Harding (University, Searcy, AR) Bison*, 12 Jan. 1966, 2.

26: "Record players blaring": Ken Starr, "From the Editor's Desk: Golden Rule Is Often Forgotten in Every Day Activities on Campus," *Harding (University, Searcy, AR) Bison* 15 Apr. 1965, 2.

26: Together they drove: Lou Butterfield, interview by author; Ken Starr, interview by author.

26: "Country selling was nice": Lou Butterfield, interview by author. Starr later liked to tell the story about writing an editorial for the school paper sharply criticizing the construction of the alumni facility, which led to a confrontation with President Ganus (Ken Starr, interview by author). However, a search of the issues of the *Harding Bison* during the two years he was a student there revealed no such editorial. What is clear, though, is that this issue caused great discomfort for Starr, who had some conversation with President Ganus about it.

27: "I had never met a Texan": Alice Starr, interview by author.

27: "This was genuinely great living": Ken Starr, interview by author.

28: After discussing: Ibid. Regarding the insinuation that Starr would be on the short list for the Supreme Court, see Jan Crawford Greenburg, *Supreme Conflict*, 89.

28: "We don't run around": Alice Starr, interview by author.

Chapter 3: Breathtaking "Whitewater"

33: "who has served": Psychology Services Intake Screening Summary, James McDougal, 4 Sept. 1997, Federal Medical Center, Bureau of Prisons, Fort Worth, Texas, obtained through written permission of the executors of the McDougal estate.

33: McDougal was on a regular diet: Psychology Services Intake Screening Summary, 2 Oct. 1997.

34: "the original American Gothic couple": Claudia Riley, remarks made while author was interviewing Susan McDougal.

34: This propelled: Jim McDougal and Curtis Wilkie, *Arkansas Mischief: The Birth of a National Scandal*, 47–56, 63, 70.

34: "The very first time I tried": Jim McDougal ["Bert," pseud.], Alcoholics Anonymous Memo, "MCAA 9-25-90," Heuer papers.

34: McDougal was running: Susan McDougal, interview by author; George Wells, "McDougal's Life: Highs and Lows," *Arkansas Gazette*, 14 Jan. 1990, A1–A6; Bob Lancaster, "Newsmaker," *Arkansas Times*, 8 Sept. 1995, 11; "Whitewater's Inventor Has Seen a Lot Pass Under the Bridge," *Arkansas Times*, 8 Sept. 1995, 10.

34: McDougal fell: Susan McDougal and Pat Harris, *The Woman Who Wouldn't Talk*, 21.

35: He also taught: McDougal, Alcoholics Anonymous Memo; McDougal, *The Woman Who Wouldn't Talk*, 21; McDougal and Wilkie, *Arkansas Mischief*, 133–35.

35: trademark black patch: Claudia Riley, interview by author; McDougal, *The Woman Who Wouldn't Talk*, 19–20.

35: Riley had surmounted: Claudia Riley, interview by author.

35: a Latin scholarship student: Susan McDougal, interview by author; James B. Stewart, *Blood Sport: The Truth Behind the Scandals in the Clinton White House*, 46.

35: "I don't think they even sold": Susan McDougal, interview by author.

35: Jim kicked open: Stewart, *Blood Sport*, 46; McDougal and Harris, *The Woman Who Wouldn't Talk*, 17–18; McDougal and Wilkie, *Arkansas Mischief*, 136.

36: "shy" and "private" person: Claudia Riley, interview by author.

36: "They just showed up": McDougal and Wilkie, *Arkansas Mischief*, 136.

36: "He seemed to admire": Claudia Riley, interview by author.

36: had served as an intern: Stewart, *Blood Sport*, 47.

36: "a big, raw-boned hammy kind": Susan McDougal, interview by author.

38: In attendance: McDougal and Wilkie, *Arkansas Mischief*, 120, 185–86; Lancaster, "Newsmaker"; McDougal and Harris, *The Woman Who Wouldn't Talk*, 41.

39: "I made a little money": Bill Clinton, interview by author.

40: obtained her real estate: OIC/FBI interview of Susan McDougal, 23 June 1995, Heuer papers; Lancaster, "Newsmaker."

40: "There were people who would go": Susan McDougal, interview by author.

40: he had splurged: McDougal and Wilkie, *Arkansas Mischief*, 135.

40: "looked like a cigar shop": Susan McDougal, interview by author.

40: "almost see-through": Ibid.; Stephen A. Smith, interview by author.

40: In McDougal's master plan: Susan McDougal, interview by author.

41: the project hauled: McDougal and Wilkie, *Arkansas Mischief*, 149.

41: "We must have been there": Susan McDougal, interview by author.

42: They had already entrusted: McDougal and Wilkie, *Arkansas Mischief*, 148; Stewart, *Blood Sport*, 56–57.

42: "As a native Arkansan": Interrogatory Responses of William Jefferson Clinton to RTC, 24 May 1995, 45, 53.

42: Jim and Susan McDougal had slid: McDougal and Harris, *The Woman Who Wouldn't Talk*, 48–49; McDougal and Wilkie, *Arkansas Mischief*, 150–51.

42: "You'll want to go": Stewart, *Blood Sport*, 60.

42: "it was just like": Susan McDougal, interview by author.

43: the Clintons shook hands: Stewart, *Blood Sport*, 61–62.

43: A simple two-page: Deed, 2 Aug. 1978, Heuer papers.

43: the Clintons became co-owners: George J. Church, "Investigations: Raw Nerves and Tax Returns," *Time*, 14 Feb. 1994, 26–27; Stewart, *Blood Sport*, 61–63.

43: Real estate was: Stephen A. Smith, interview by author.

44: "Talk about beautiful sights": Whitewater brochure, Susan McDougal papers.

44: Bill Clinton won: Maraniss, *First in His Class*, 357.

Chapter 4: McDougal Paints the Town

44: "in the middle of nowhere": Gene Lyons, interview with author; Gene Lyons, *Fools for Scandal: How the Media Invented Whitewater*, 32 n.1.

45: usury laws in Arkansas: Susan McDougal, interview by author; McDougal and Harris, *The Woman Who Wouldn't Talk*, 96; Susan Wesson, "A Cost-Benefit Analysis of the Arkansas Usury Law and Its Effect on Arkansas Residents and Institutions," *Academic Forum Online* 18 (2000–2001), Henderson State University, Arkadelphia, AR.

45: as the nation sunk: Interrogatory Responses of Hillary Rodham Clinton, In the Matter of: Madison Guaranty Savings & Loan Association (7236) McCrory, Arkansas, United States of America, Resolution Trust Corporation, Washington, D.C. (hereinafter Hillary Clinton, "RTC Interrogatory Responses"), 24 May 1995, no. 10, pp. 15–16.

45: "We were selling": Susan McDougal, interview by author.

45: McDougal accepted a position: McDougal and Wilkie, *Arkansas Mischief*, 153–55; Stewart, *Blood Sport*, 85. McDougal's formal title was Liaison for Industrial Development, Banking, Insurance and the Highway Department.

45: The day Jim walked: Susan McDougal, interview by author.

46: "Don't worry, baby": McDougal and Harris, *The Woman Who Wouldn't Talk*, 51.

46: "And we let the business go": Susan McDougal, interview by author.

46: a failed effort to organize: George Wells, "McDougal's Life: Highs and Lows," *Arkansas Gazette*, 14 Jan. 1990, A1–A6.

46: Already tired: Stewart, *Blood Sport*, 93; McDougal and Harris, *The Woman Who Wouldn't Talk*, 61; McDougal and Wilkie, *Arkansas Mischief*, 171.

46: He purchased 42 percent: Jim McDougal to Sam Heuer, 10 July 1990, Heuer papers.

47: "Dear Jim": J. William Fulbright to Jim McDougal, 11 Jan. 1982, Heuer papers.

47: "We went into Kingston": Susan McDougal, interview by author.

47: "Jim did not give a damn": Susan McDougal, interview by author, comments of Claudia Riley.

47: Hippies growing marijuana: McDougal and Wilkie, *Arkansas Mischief*, 174.

48: The loan McDougal had finagled: Stewart, *Blood Sport*, 94–95.

48: "We had to keep taking": Susan McDougal, interview by author; McDougal and Wilkie, *Arkansas Mischief*, 74–75.

48: "There were many years": Hillary Clinton, "RTC Interrogatory Responses," no. 26, p. 67.

48: "Whitewater will pay": Susan McDougal, interview by author; Hillary Clinton, "RTC Interrogatory Responses," no. 10, pp. 15–16; McDougal and Wilkie, *Arkansas Mischief*, 211.

48: "McDougal believed that the placement": Hillary Clinton, "RTC Interrogatory Responses," no. 10, pp. 15–16.

48: When Bill Clinton lost: McDougal and Wilkie, *Arkansas Mischief*, 197–98; Stewart, *Blood Sport*, 98.

48: "Dear Jim: How is business": J. William Fulbright to Jim McDougal, 16 Feb. 1982, Heuer papers.

48: "It's gone bankrupt": McDougal and Harris, *The Woman Who Wouldn't Talk*, 67. See also McDougal and Wilkie, *Arkansas Mischief*, 179–80.

49: "Neither she [n]or her husband": McDougal, "OIC/FBI Interview," 95, with attached FBI Report from 1989.

49: Now McDougal stumped: John Brummett, "Democratic Meeting Turns into Pep Rally for Party's Nominees," *Arkansas Gazette*, 20 June 1982; descriptions contained in Wells, "McDougal's Life," A1.

49: he energized audiences: McDougal and Harris, *The Woman Who Wouldn't Talk*, 70; McDougal and Wilkie, *Arkansas Mischief*, 189.

49: "Isn't it time": Wells, "McDougal's Life."

50: "I fell in love": McDougal and Harris, *The Woman Who Wouldn't Talk*, 66, 71; Susan McDougal, interview by author.

50: with an array of sixteen-year-old: Terry Ford, "It's Rodeo Time Again! Parade Friday," *Montgomery County (AR) News*, 29 July 1982.

50: He delivered a "fiery" speech: John Brummett, "Report Delights Democrats: Party Leader Suggests White's Resignation," *Arkansas Democrat-Gazette*, 18 Sept. 1982.

50: McDougal also shared: "Democrats Open Office," *Russellville (AR) Daily Courier-Democrat*, 14 Oct. 1982, 16; McDougal and Wilkie, *Arkansas Mischief*, 187.

50: Mrs. Mondale was pictured: Ginger Shiras, "Mrs. Mondale Sees Eureka Arts, Attacks Republicans," *Harrison (AR) Daily Times*, 10 Sept. 1982.

50: McDougal was trounced: McDougal and Wilkie, *Arkansas Mischief*, 191.

50: a big loan went bad: McDougal and Harris, *The Woman Who Wouldn't Talk,* 73.

50: "In October at the crucial time": Jim McDougal to Sam Heuer, 10 July 1990, Heuer papers.

50: "Oh, I loved": Bill Clinton, interview by author.

51: McDougal transferred: Jim Guy Tucker, interview by author; Stewart, *Blood Sport,* 102–106; McDougal and Wilkie, *Arkansas Mischief,* 197.

51: "winos and porn houses": Hickman Ewing, Jr., interview by author.

51: "That's where they were grinding": Bill Simmons, Jim McDougal, and Sam Heuer, transcript of conversation, circa 1993, 75, Heuer papers.

51: The location was also ideal: Stewart, *Blood Sport,* 106–107.

51: He built himself: McDougal and Harris, *The Woman Who Wouldn't Talk,* 83; McDougal and Wilkie, *Arkansas Mischief,* 197; Jim Guy Tucker, interview by author.

51: McDougal used "creative financing": McDougal and Wilkie, *Arkansas Mischief,* 200.

51: Susan took charge: Susan McDougal, interview in Borod & Huggins Report, 81, attached to McDougal, "OIC/FBI Interview," 95.

51: "Just a twelve-minute drive": McDougal and Harris, *The Woman Who Wouldn't Talk,* 80.

52: "We were selling lots": Simmons, McDougal, and Heuer, transcript of conversation, 43.

52: Governor Clinton one day jogged: McDougal and Wilkie, *Arkansas Mischief,* 208–10.

52: McDougal claimed: For Mrs. Clinton's explanation concerning this work, see Hillary Clinton, "RTC Interrogatory Responses," no. 30, pp. 74–75.

52: Jim was now hiring: McDougal and Harris, *The Woman Who Wouldn't Talk,* 94.

52: A former armed guard was promoted: Stewart, *Blood Sport,* 107.

52: *Arkansas* magazine listed: McDougal and Wilkie, *Arkansas Mischief,* 93, 98, 199.

52: "I don't like [these] people": Susan McDougal, interview by author.

53: "Dear Jim: You do move fast": J. W. Fulbright to Jim McDougal, 15 Apr. 1983, Heuer papers.

53: he came to believe: McDougal and Wilkie, *Arkansas Mischief,* 220.

53: "close the Savings and Loan": McDougal to Heuer, 10 July 1990, Heuer papers.

53: Susan McDougal had begun: McDougal and Wilkie, *Arkansas Mischief,* 216–17; McDougal and Harris, *The Woman Who Wouldn't Talk,* 88–92.

53: "Jim helped me pack": Susan McDougal, interview by author; McDougal and Harris, *The Woman Who Wouldn't Talk,* 91–92.

53: Clinton personally called: Susan McDougal, interview by author.

53: He wanted to take: Simmons, McDougal, and Heuer, transcript of conversation, 89–94.

53: Susan dutifully drove: Susan McDougal, interview by author.

54: "All these years of our paying": Stewart, *Blood Sport,* 133.

54: "has been for isolated": Hillary Rodham Clinton to Jim McDougal and John Latham, 14 July 1986, Gene Lyons papers.

54: "Baby, I've found a piece of land": McDougal and Harris, *The Woman Who Wouldn't Talk,* 100; McDougal and Wilkie, *Arkansas Mischief,* 320–21.

54: "It's obvious that our marriage": Susan McDougal, interview by author.

54: McDougal said he knew: McDougal and Wilkie, *Arkansas Mischief,* 218; McDougal and Harris, *The Woman Who Wouldn't Talk,* 100–101.

54: "Sure, of course": Susan McDougal, interview by author.

55: She engaged: Robert W. Ray, *Final Report of the Independent Counsel, In Re: Madison Guaranty Savings & Loan Association,* vol. 1, filed 2 Mar. 2001, 74, 101 (hereinafter cited as Final Report/Ray).

55: the Federal Home Loan Bank Board examiners announced: McDougal and Harris, *The Woman Who Wouldn't Talk,* 93.

55: Jim McDougal would later rant: Simmons, McDougal, and Heuer, transcript of conversation, 30, Heuer papers.

55: Yet there was now: McDougal, Borod & Huggins Report, 2.

55: The *Arkansas Gazette* ran: "Madison Has Shakeup," *Arkansas Gazette,* 16 Sept. 1986; Stewart, *Blood Sport,* 146.

55: Jim McDougal was suffering: Transcript of Proceedings Before the Hon. George Howard, Jr., vol. 1, 16 Jan. 1996, 107, Heuer papers; McDougal and Wilkie, *Arkansas Mischief,* 222, 226.

55: "very, very sick": Susan McDougal, interview by author.

55: Jim jumped up: Jim Guy Tucker, interview by author.

55: McDougal was taken: McDougal and Wilkie, *Arkansas Mischief*, 226; Stewart, *Blood Sport*, 139–40.

55: "I got him out": Susan McDougal, interview by author.

55: Susan had begun seeing: McDougal and Harris, *The Woman Who Wouldn't Talk*, 86, 89.

56: "It was in this climate": Jim McDougal to Sam Heuer, 10 July 1990, Heuer papers.

56: "I was so scared": Susan McDougal, interview by author.

56: Hillary began "cross-examining": Stewart, *Blood Sport*, 150.

56: So Susan "packed up": Susan McDougal, interview by author.

56: "get all that behind us": Hillary Clinton to Jim McDougal, 28 Nov. 1988, Gene Lyons papers.

56: "Well, I did the power of attorney": Susan McDougal, interview by author.

57: gave Jim McDougal: For Jim McDougal's account of this incident, see McDougal and Wilkie, *Arkansas Mischief*, 239.

Chapter 5: Seeds of Scandal

57: The first was born: "Indictment," 20 Nov. 1989, Heuer papers; George Wells, "Ex-Banker: No Assets: Court Names Attorney for Fraud Charge Defense," *Arkansas Gazette*, 1 Dec 1989, B1.

57: McDougal had picked: The Castle Grande property was necessary to gain access to the highway, making the development attractive for commuters. It was thus a puzzle piece in McDougal's grander scheme. Final Report/Ray, vol. 1, 39–48; Borod & Huggins Report, 22–35; Hickman Ewing, Jr., interview by author; Susan McDougal, interview by author.

58: Castle Grande and its companion deals: Final Report/Ray, vol. 1, 39–48. Prominent investors included Jim Guy Tucker, David Hale, and the elderly Senator Fulbright. Another key figure turned out to be Seth Ward, retired businessman and father-in-law of Webster Hubbell, Hillary's partner at the Rose Law Firm. Ward served as a "straw man" to purchase the Castle Grande property, so that it would not appear on Madison Guaranty's books, earning a handsome $300,000 commission in the process. Hubbell himself handled some of the legal work for his father-in-law, which eventually formed the basis for a draft indictment against Hillary and Hubbell by Ken Starr's Office of Independent Counsel.

58: For now, in the fall of 1989: "Indictment," 20 Nov. 1989, Heuer papers; Wells, "Ex-Banker: No Assets." Jim McDougal and Susan's two brothers were indicted for setting up "sham transactions" totaling about $950,000, filing "false statements relating to Madison Guaranty financing the transactions," and paying themselves royal commissions.

58: "numerous tracts of land": Borod & Huggins Report, 4–6.

58: "So it is a sad tale": Transcript of Proceedings Before the Hon. George Howard, Jr., vol. 1, 16 Jan. 1996, 23, 30, Heuer papers.

58: McDougal still insisted: McDougal to Heuer, 10 July 1990, Heuer papers.

58: "[It was] the documents": Sam Heuer, interview by author.

58: Banks was a no-nonsense prosecutor: Charles Banks, interview by author.

59: took a stab at pleading: Transcript of Proceedings Before the Hon. George Howard, Jr., vol. 1, 16 Jan. 1996, 104, Heuer papers.

59: "spellbinding effect": Joe Conason and Gene Lyons, *The Hunting of the President: The Ten-Year Campaign to Destroy Bill and Hillary Clinton*, 31.

59: "had left 'em alone": Simmons, McDougal and Heuer, transcript of conversation, 16.

59: Jim McDougal and Susan's brothers were: Stewart, *Blood Sport,* 177.

59: Charles Banks was sure beyond: Charles Banks, interview by author.

59: "Do you have peppermints?": McDougal and Wilkie, *Arkansas Mischief*, 240.

59: "He was taking lithium": Susan McDougal, interview by author.

60: "Would you get": Ibid.; Stewart, *Blood Sport*, 178–79; McDougal and Wilkie, *Arkansas Mischief*, 242–43.

60: "Jim was living in the house": Claudia Riley, interview by author.

60: Jim listened as Clinton: McDougal, *Arkansas Mischief*, 240.

60: "Jim visibly crumbled": Claudia Riley, remarks made while author was interviewing Susan McDougal.

60: "Jim could never forgive": Susan McDougal, interview by author.

61: "Jim McDougal was a friend": Betsey Wright, interview by author.

61: Although the essence of the Whitewater story: John Reed, "Clinton Tops List of Gift Receivers," *Arkansas Democrat-Gazette*, 1 Feb. 1990. See also James Merriweather, "Governor,

Wife List Salaries, Plane Trips," *Arkansas Democrat-Gazette*, 4 May 1990.

61: "I mean, you really got to hand": Bill Clinton, interview by author.

61: "The Whitewater case unfolded": McDougal and Wilkie, *Arkansas Mischief*, 236–38.

62: Nelson had lost: Lyons, *Fools for Scandal*, 47–50.

62: Nichols had been: *Larry Nichols v. Bill Clinton et al.*, LR-C-90-746, U.S. District Court, Eastern District of Arkansas, filed 25 Oct. 1990; Larry Nichols, interview by author. Nichols was terminated, according to an Associated Press report, after using state-owned telephones to make hundreds of calls in support of Nicaragua Contra rebels. Nichols's case was dismissed with prejudice in February 1992.

62: convening a press conference: Larry Nichols, interview by author; McDougal and Wilkie, *Arkansas Mischief*, 244; Conason and Lyons, *The Hunting of the President*, 16–17.

62: Records contained in the files: Sheffield Nelson, Janet Lawrence, and Jim McDougal, transcription of recorded conversation, Mar. 1992, Heuer papers. It is unclear whether McDougal knew the conversation was being recorded.

62: Soon afterward, McDougal: McDougal and Wilkie, *Arkansas Mischief*, 244–45.

62: Jeff Gerth's article appeared: Lyons, *Fools for Scandal*, 31.

62: Gerth became the first journalist: Jeff Gerth, "The 1992 Campaign: Personal Finances; Clintons Joined S&L Operator in an Ozark Real-Estate Venture," *New York Times*, 8 Mar. 1992, 1.

62: (McDougal later admitted): McDougal and Wilkie, *Arkansas Mischief*, 245.

63: Even in that context: The nature of the alleged wrongdoing by the Clintons would change over time. However, the original Gerth story focused on the facts that (a) the Clintons contributed little to the failed Whitewater venture and took little risk financially, but stood to "cash in" and reap a windfall if the venture succeeded; (b) the Clintons improperly deducted $5,000 on their tax returns in 1984 and 1985 for interest paid on Whitewater loans, saving themselves about $1,000 in taxes; (c) once federal regulators discovered that Madison Guaranty was insolvent and might be closed by the state, Governor Clinton appointed a new state securities commissioner (Beverly Bassett Schaffer), who allegedly gave the struggling S&L preferential treatment, in part at the urging of First Lady Hillary

Rodham Clinton in her capacity as a lawyer for the Rose Law Firm representing Madison; and (d) the Clintons and the McDougals could not account for the whereabouts of all the Whitewater records, some of which were allegedly "delivered to the Governor's mansion," but were now missing in action. Concluded Gerth: "Many questions about the enterprise cannot be fully answered without the records" (Gerth, "The 1992 Campaign," 1).

63: It related to Madison Guaranty: Charles Banks, interview by author.

64: Later accounts confirm: McDougal and Wilkie, *Arkansas Mischief*, 248.

64: Moreover, records establish: Final Report/Ray, vol. 4, 15–17, 19; see also David Kendall to Hon. Mark J. Langer, Clerk of Court, Final Report/Ray, 24 Oct. 2001.

65: "combined with Mr. McDougal's previous acquittal": Charles A. Banks to Don Pettus, 16 Oct. 1992, Heuer papers.

65: "the alleged involvement": Final Report/Ray, vol. 4, 25; David Kendall to Hon. Mark J. Langer, 24 Oct. 2001.

65: Indeed, Banks made it clear: Charles Banks, interview by author.

65: "He played it straight": Bill Clinton, interview by author.

65: In an odd twist: Simmons, McDougal and Heuer, transcript of conversation, 55–56, 115.

66: so he "loaned" McDougal: Sam Heuer, check for $1,000, 24 Dec. 1992, Gene Lyons papers. Author James Stewart later reported that Clinton attorney Jim Blair supplied the funds for the "loan" to McDougal (Stewart, *Blood Sport*, 233–34).

66: In a gesture designed: Ibid.

66: "closed for good": Vincent Foster, Jr., to Whitewater Development Corporation File, 30 Dec. 1992; ibid.

Chapter 6: Death Song in the West Wing

67: Vince Foster had assembled: William Kennedy III, interview by author.

67: Webb Hubbell had joined: Webster Hubbell, interview by author.

67: "McDougal was losing it": William Kennedy III, interview by author.

68: "the last four [elected] presidents": Bernard Nussbaum, interview by author.

69: Vince Foster described him: Office of the Independent Counsel, *Report of the Independent*

Counsel In Re: Vincent W. Foster, Jr., 30 June 1994, 8 (hereinafter cited as Fiske Report/Foster).

70: Foster "came in on a high": Peter J. Boyer, "Life After Vince," *New Yorker,* 11 Sept. 1995, 57–58; Stewart, *Blood Sport,* 245–50; Bob Woodward, *Shadow: Five Presidents and the Legacy of Watergate,* 229–30.

70: He knew that Clinton: Bernard Nussbaum, interview by author.

70: Some of the ugliest stories involved: Fiske Report/Foster, 10–12.

70: After ordering: Ibid., 11; Woodward, *Shadow,* 230; Boyer, "Life After Vince," 58; Toni Locy, "For White House Travel Office, a Two-Year Trip of Trouble," *Washington Post,* 27 Feb. 1995, A4. Former Travel Office Director Billy Dale was later acquitted of charges.

71: Assertions now began flying: Fiske Report/Foster, 11; Woodward, *Shadow,* 230. An extensive discussion of the Travel Office matter is contained in Office of Independent Counsel, *Final Report of the Independent Counsel (In Re: Madison Guaranty Savings & Loan Association) In Re: William David Watkins and In Re: Hillary Rodham Clinton,* 18 Oct. 2000.

71: "People in the Travel Office": Bernard Nussbaum, interview by author.

71: Bill Kennedy, who led: William Kennedy III, interview by author.

72: Foster was a handsome man: Joe Purvis, interview by author.

73: "Does it take a $50,000-a-day fine": "Who Is Vincent Foster?" *Wall Street Journal,* 17 June 1993, A10.

73: "because Vince read": Joe Purvis, interview by author.

73: a follow-up editorial: "What's the Rush?" *Wall Street Journal,* 19 July 1993.

73: Yet those present would recall: Fiske Report/Foster, 17.

73: "There is no victory": Vince W. Foster, Jr., "Roads We Should Travel," commencement address, University of Arkansas, Fayetteville, 8 May 1993, 3, Fiske Report/Foster, exhibit 7.

73: One faculty member: Jan Levine, interview by author.

74: "He felt like there": Joe Purvis, interview by author.

74: "the best day we had [ever] had": Bernard Nussbaum, interview by author.

74: Foster's assistant had noticed: Fiske Report/Foster, 23–24. The letter to Foster's mother, it later turned out, contained oil leases

that were left to her upon his father's death in 1991, and instructions as to how to handle them. The letter to the insurance company contained a payment for an insurance premium (Fiske Report/Foster, 24). The policy in question included a suicide clause that permitted recovery for a beneficiary even if the premium holder died by his own hand, as long as the insured party held the policy for a specified period (Boyer, "Life After Vince," 62).

74: He noticed that Foster: Fiske Report/Foster, 26.

74: "I'm going out": Ibid.; Bernard Nussbaum, interview by author.

75: Tripp brought Foster: Office of the Independent Counsel, *Report on the Death of Vincent W. Foster, Jr. by the Office of Independent Counsel, In Re: Madison Guaranty Savings & Loan Association,* 10 Oct. 1997, 1–4, 18–23 (hereinafter cited as Starr Report/Foster).

75: he had traded phone calls: William Kennedy III, interview by author.

75: "I'll be back": Starr Report/Foster; Boyer, "Life After Vince," 54, 61, 66; Stewart, *Blood Sport,* 288–89.

76: On the front passenger seat: Starr Report/Foster, 1–4, 18–23, 28–30; Fiske Report/Foster, 30–34; Boyer, "Life After Vince," 54, 61, 66; *60 Minutes,* CBS News, transcript, 8 Oct. 1995, 1–9; Stewart, *Blood Sport,* 25–27.

76: Inside Foster's wallet: Fiske Report/Foster, 22, 36; Starr Report/Foster, 35.

76: The official autopsy report: The autopsy stated: "The wound track in the head continues backward and upward with an entrance wound just left of the foramen magnum with tissue damage to the brain stem and left cerebral hemisphere with an irregular exit scalp and skull defect near the midline in the occipital region. No metallic fragments recovered" (Starr Report/Foster, 1–4, 18–23, 28–30).

76: Beyer declared: Ibid., 28–34.

76: The Secret Service was notified: Final Report/Ray, vol. 1, 101.

76: As soon as McLarty got: Stewart, *Blood Sport,* 27–30.

77: "First of all": Bill Clinton, interview by author.

77: Thunderstorms had knocked out: Joe Purvis, interview by author.

77: "Every man has his breaking": Woodward, *Shadow,* 232.

77: He lived only a few blocks away from: Skip Rutherford, interview by author.

78: First, he had just realized: Bill Clinton, interview by author.

79: "When he came down": Bernard Nussbaum, interview by author.

79: The president set out: Stewart, *Blood Sport*, 30.

79: Lisa Foster already had been notified: Final Report/Ray, vol. 1, 101.

79: Bill Kennedy undertook: William Kennedy III, interview by author.

79: The medical examiner's personnel: Ibid.

Chapter 7: Conspiracy Theories

81: Advisers and staff arrived: Stewart, *Blood Sport*, 294.

82: "They looked in the trash": U.S. Senate, *Statement of Bernard W. Nussbaum Before the Special Committee to Investigate Whitewater Development Corporation and Related Matters, United States Senate, 104th Cong., First Session,* 9 Aug. 1995, 6 (hereinafter cited as Nussbaum Statement/Foster); Bernard Nussbaum, interview by author.

82: White House records indicate: Final Report/Ray, vol. 1, 101.

82: After waking up: Nussbaum Statement/Foster, 6.

82: "spoke in a sweet, calm": Bernard Nussbaum, interview by author.

82: had gone into Foster's office: Nussbaum Statement/Foster, 6; Final Report/Ray, 103.

82: Pond denied: Final Report/Ray, vol. 1, 102.

82: "It was not a crime": Ibid., 6. For a full examination of the events involving the handling of documents in Vince Foster's office following his death, see U.S. Senate, Special Committee to Investigate Whitewater Development Corporation and Related Matters, *Investigation of Whitewater Development Corporation and Related Matters, Final Report of the Special Committee to Investigate Whitewater Development Corporation and Related Matters,* Senate Report 104-280, 17 June 1996, 36–118 (hereinafter cited as Final Senate Report/Whitewater).

83: "Nothing else was removed": Nussbaum Statement/Foster, 7; Stewart, *Blood Sport*, 296–97.

83: Nussbaum personally examined: Nussbaum Statement/Foster, 9–10.

84: The files included: Stewart, *Blood Sport*, 304.

84: the cardboard boxes were: Final Report/Ray, vol. 1, 104–105.

84: "Bernie, are you hiding": Stewart, *Blood Sport*, 304.

85: Although Vince had been raised: Joe Purvis, interview by author.

85: "No one ever knows why": William Kennedy III, interview by author.

85: "You hypocritical jerk": Joe Purvis, interview by author.

86: As this assistant had packed up: Assistant White House Counsel Steve Neuwirth had picked up Vince's briefcase, the same one from which Nussbaum had removed files during the July 22 search. When he turned it upside down to pack it into a box, "scraps of paper fell out of the bottom of the case" (Bernard Nussbaum, interview by author; Nussbaum Statement/Foster, 15).

86: "I made mistakes": Fiske Report/Foster, appendix 5.

86: "we found [some] scraps": Bernard Nussbaum, interview by author.

87: "Why did you wait": Stewart, *Blood Sport*, 307.

87: telephone records later turned over: Final Senate Report/Whitewater, 46–48.

88: Phone records and sworn testimony: Ibid., 101–105; see also Final Report/Ray, vol. 3, 156–235.

88: Officer Henry P. O'Neill: Final Report/Ray, vol. 3, 156–235; Final Senate Report/Whitewater, 53–54.

88: "It brought it all": James Stewart, interview by author.

89: had jumped out: Bernard Nussbaum, interview by author.

89: the *Wall Street Journal* published: "A Washington Death," *Wall Street Journal*, 22 July 1993.

89: Self-appointed experts began questioning: For a discussion of these questions that seemed to haunt the Foster investigation from beginning to end, see Fiske Report/Foster, 53–57.

89: Rumors being disseminated: Boyer, "Life After Vince," 63.

89: "I heard a lot of": Bill Clinton, interview by author.

90: The ornery McDougal almost defied: Joel Williams, "Wanted Clintons Out of Whitewater, McDougal Says," *Associated Press*, 10 Jan. 1994.

90: "All of a sudden": Bernard Nussbaum, interview by author.

Chapter 8: The Special Prosecutor

91: Dick Kelley, her fourth: Dick and Virginia met in the early 1970s at a horse race, a fitting beginning to any Hot Springs romance. He had gone to the nurse's office at the Oak Lawn racetrack, with his friend Marge Mitchell, for an aspirin. As soon as he met the on-duty nurse Virginia Clinton, his headache went away. A decade later, after Virginia's third husband, Jeff Dwire, had passed away and Dick had divorced, they met again at a dinner hosted by friends. Dick and Virginia left together, went to the local drive-in "for a Coca-Cola," talked all night, and fell in love. He and Virginia were married in 1982 in Marge Mitchell's living room, just up the street from the lake house where they would settle (Dick Kelley, interview by author).

91: "Oh, my goodness": Dick Kelley, interview by author.

92: Virginia had just returned: Clinton, *My Life*, 564, 567.

92: "She drinks Scotch": Dick Kelley, interview by author.

92: Virginia called her son: Clinton, *My Life*, 567.

92: "Well, I got up": Dick Kelley, interview by author.

93: "Virginia was like a": Clinton, *My Life*, 568.

93: "cries out more than": Woodward, *Shadow*, 236. Years later, Clinton would say: "I liked and respected Dole and I knew he wanted to be president. But I thought it was wrong and, to his everlasting credit, he apologized to me [later] for it" (Bill Clinton, interview by author).

93: "You had your two": Stewart, *Blood Sport*, 373.

93: "If we allow": Bernard Nussbaum, interview by author.

94: How was the administration: Woodward, *Shadow*, 237; Stewart, *Blood Sport*, 373.

94: "You could appoint": Bernard Nussbaum, interview by author.

94: "I'll sleep on it": Stewart, *Blood Sport*, 239.

94: "He feels he has no choice": Bernard Nussbaum, interview by author.

94: President Clinton would describe: Bill Clinton, interview by author.

95: "At that time, Monica Lewinsky was": Bernard Nussbaum, interview by author.

96: Attorney General Reno, wary: Janet Reno, interview by author; Philip Heymann, interview by author.

96: The New York prosecutor: Robert B. Fiske, interview by author; Department of Justice, press release, 20 Jan. 1994, Fiske papers; Eleanor Randolph, "Fiske Seen as No 'Publicity Hound,' and as Totally, Totally Thorough," *Washington Post*, 21 Jan. 1994, A20.

96: assembled a list: Philip Heymann, interview by author.

96: A number of accounts would: Woodward, *Shadow*, 265.

96: Heymann did include: Ken Starr, interview by author.

96: "I was told that": Philip Heymann, interview by author.

97: "As much as I like": Jo Ann Harris, interview by author.

97: "as highly regarded": Philip Heymann, interview by author.

97: frosting on the cake: Philip Heymann, interview by author; Woodward, *Shadow*, 242.

97: Upstairs, Janet Reno's top advisers: Robert B. Fiske, interview by author.

97: Fiske sat alone: David Johnston, "Counsel Granted a Broad Mandate in Clinton Inquiry," *New York Times*, 20 Jan. 1994, A1. For all practical purposes, Fiske possessed the same power as did the attorney general to investigate this particular matter. The charter gave him broad power to investigate "President William Jefferson Clinton's or Mrs. Hillary Rodham Clinton's relationships" with (1) Madison Guaranty Savings & Loan Association; (2) Whitewater Development Corporation; and (3) David Hale's Capital Management Services Company. The jurisdictional charter also gave Fiske the authority to investigate obstruction of justice, perjury, and conspiracy with respect to any of these matters, a provision Fiske had added to give himself breathing room. The broad "related to" provision also gave the independent counsel authority to probe other matters "connected with or arising out of" the principal Whitewater and Madison investigations (Code of Federal Regulations, title 28, sec. 603.1).

97: "Are you satisfied": Robert B. Fiske, interview by author; Woodward, *Shadow*, 240–42.

97: "the epitome of what": Michael Isikoff, "Whitewater Special Counsel Promises Thorough Probe," *Washington Post*, 21 Jan. 1994, A1; Woodward, *Shadow*, 242.

97: "All I wanted was": Bill Clinton, interview by author.

97: Fiske's appointment prompted: Bill Clinton, interview by author. See also Randolph, "Fiske Seen as No 'Publicity Hound.'"

97: "The Attorney General has made": Johnston, "Counsel Granted."

98: Robert Fiske took: U.S. Senate, Testimony of Robert B. Fiske, Jr., 206.

98: Julie O'Sullivan, who had worked: Julie O'Sullivan, interview by author.

98: this case created "a question": Robert B. Fiske, interview by author.

98: "It really wasn't": Rusty Hardin, interview by author.

Chapter 9: David Hale Visits Justice Jim

99: "a paranoid liar": Max Brantley, interview by author.

99: "He is a grifter": Larry Jegley, interview by author.

99: The FBI had raided Hale's office: Ultimately, the evidence indicated that Hale had extracted $3.4 million in federal funds, distributed it to dummy corporations, defaulted on the loans, and then kept the proceeds for himself (Sidney Blumenthal, *The Clinton Wars,* 75; Lyons, *Fools for Scandal,* 110; Office of the Independent Counsel, *Final Report of Robert B. Fiske, Jr., Independent Counsel: In Re Madison Guaranty Savings & Loan Association* (under seal), 6 Oct. 1994 (hereinafter cited as Fiske Final Report/Madison), 31–32; Indictment, 23 Sept. 1993, Heuer papers.

99: (Some conspiracy theorists): James Ring Adams and R. Emmett Tyrrell, Jr., "The Case Against Hillary," *American Spectator,* February 1996, 22. Among the items specified in the search warrant for Hale's office were the files relating to Susan McDougal's Master Marketing loan (ibid., 26).

100: Some of the proceeds: Fiske Final Report/Madison, 14–15; Murray Waas, "False Witness: Part I," *Salon,* 12 Aug. 1998; Woodward, *Shadow,* 242.

100: the McDougals allegedly would loan: Blumenthal, *The Clinton Wars,* 76; Conason and Lyons, *The Hunting of the President,* 91.

100: In footage: David Hale, interview by NBC, unedited video, 6 Nov. 1993, segment 3, Sam Heuer files.

100: Hale's early appearances: Woodward, *Shadow,* 242; Blumenthal, *The Clinton Wars,* 75; Jeffrey Toobin, *A Vast Conspiracy: The Real Story of the Sex Scandal That Nearly Brought Down a President,* 65; Robert L. Bartley, ed., *Whitewater: A Journal Briefing from the Editorial Pages of the Wall Street Journal,* 1:89–90.

100: Johnson rose: interview by author.

101: In one issue, he penned: Jim Johnson, *Arkansas Faith,* March 1956, 14 (courtesy of Arkansas History Commission).

101: "mongrelization": Ibid., April 1956, 13, and June 1956, 5.

101: "This will please": Ibid., April 1956, 20.

101: Johnson went on to win: Jim Johnson, interview by author.

102: Hale was also a financier: Conason and Lyons, *The Hunting of the President,* 87–88; Toobin, *A Vast Conspiracy,* 64.

102: Hale scratched: Jim Johnson, interview by author.

103: Johnson had pounced: Clinton, *My Life,* 159–60.

103: "queer-mongering": Blumenthal, *The Clinton Wars,* 75.

103: asking the colonel to write: Clinton, *My Life,* 388; Jim Johnson, interview by author.

104: Johnson passed along: Jim Johnson, interview by author.

104: As usual, Johnson hit: Jim Johnson, follow-up interview by author. Justice Johnson also contacted Floyd Brown and David Bossie, with whom he had worked on the "Slick Willie" publication, and they saturated the media with phone calls and press packets (Blumenthal, *The Clinton Wars,* 78–80).

104: The Hale story was swiftly picked: Ibid., 75; Toobin, *A Vast Conspiracy,* 66.

104: Even if Hale: Jim Johnson, interview by author.

104: "I've got a back": Jim Johnson, follow-up interview by author; Conason and Lyons, *The Hunting of the President,* 90.

104: "Oh, he was trying": Bill Clinton, interview by author.

105: Their first line of attack: Paula Casey, interview by author.

105: It was through: Ibid. Initially, the case was assigned to Don MacKay, a career DOJ prosecutor in the Frauds Section. It was then passed off to Robert Fiske (ibid.).

105: Fiske's book: Fiske Final Report/Madison, 4, 15, 49. Governor Tucker's cable company had merged with a Texas shell corporation.

105: Prosecutor Bill Duffey: William S. Duffey, Jr., interview by author.

106: The Hubbell scandal had blown: Marie Brenner, "The Price of Loyalty," *Vanity Fair,* June 2001, 182.

106: Now Hubbell had been caught: Fiske Final Report/Madison, 41–43. Hubbell had written out checks drawn on the law firm's bank accounts and then used these funds for personal spending sprees. Hubbell's law partners, it turned out, had confronted him about these billing irregularities even before he was confirmed as associate attorney general. They had given him the chance to "just write a check [for thirty thousand dollars or so] and resolve it." Again, in the winter of 1994, a group of partners went to see Hubbell and threatened to report the misconduct to the state bar association for disciplinary action if he did not make restitution. Hubbell denied the charges, shaking his index finger at his accusers as if he was untouchable. (Brenner, "The Price of Loyalty," 229).

106: "I can give you": Brenner, "The Price of Loyalty," 228; Webster Hubbell, interview by author.

106: "the distractions on me": Jane Fullerton and Terry Lemons, "Distractions Drive Hubbell to Quit," *Arkansas Democrat-Gazette*, 15 Mar. 1994, A1.

106: As new evidence trickled: Newspaper reports had indicated that the firm was investigating such irregularities in early March, and in April a confidential witness informed Fiske's office about such overbilling in connection with OIC's routine investigation of work that Hubbell had performed for Madison Guaranty. See Fiske Final Report/Madison, 41, 43.

106: The *Arkansas Democrat-Gazette* reported: Noel Oman, "Law Partners Plan Action on Hubbell," *Arkansas Democrat-Gazette*, 16 Mar. 1994, A1.

106: a "personal setback": David Johnston, "Clinton Associate Quits Justice Post as Pressure Rises," *New York Times*, 15 Mar. 1994, A1. Regarding the poor timing because of other attacks on the Clintons, see Letter of Resignation of Bernard W. Nussbaum to President Bill Clinton and Letter Accepting Resignation by President Bill Clinton, March 5, 1994, "The Whitewater Inquiry; Text of Resignation Letter and Reply," *New York Times*, 6 Mar. 1994. Regarding the alleged improper contacts with the Treasury Department, see Woodward, *Shadow*, 243–47.

106: reports surfaced: Brenner, "The Price of Loyalty," 229. According to Fiske's Final Report/Madison, two Rose Law Firm couriers gave interviews stating that they had each shredded a portion of a box of documents that had belonged to Vince Foster, with the initials "VWF" on the boxes, in January 1994. However, neither of these individuals recalled seeing or destroying anything relating to Whitewater. After conducting thirty-nine interviews and bringing twelve witnesses before the grand jury, Fiske's office concluded there was "an insufficient evidentiary basis to support a prosecution based on the destruction of Whitewater-related materials at the Rose Law Firm" (ibid., 16, 32–34).

107: "it was a sad day": Bill Clinton, interview by author.

107: "absolutely devastated": William Kennedy III, interview by author.

107: But the Office of the Independent: One confidential witness indicated that Hubbell had overbilled the Federal Deposit Insurance Corporation and the Resolution Trust Corporation in a matter involving Madison Savings & Loan, providing grist for those who speculated that there was some linkage to the now-resurrected Whitewater controversy (Robert B. Fiske, interview by author).

108: "little blood loss": Russell Watson, "Vince Foster's Suicide: The Rumor Mill Churns," *Newsweek*, 21 Mar. 1994, 32–33.

108: Christopher Ruddy, a journalist who wrote: Richard Brookhiser, review of *The Strange Death of Vincent Foster: An Investigation,* by Christopher Ruddy, *New York Times*, 28 Sept. 1997, 13; *60 Minutes,* CBS, 8 Oct. 1995, transcript, 4–8.

108: "claims that Vince Foster was": Watson, "Vince Foster's Suicide," 32–33.

108: "It was absolutely": Joe Purvis, interview by author.

108: Contributing to the incessant rumors: Peter Baker, "One Death Altered Path of Presidency," *Washington Post*, 20 July 1998, A1. Ultimately, the Supreme Court supported Hamilton's position, concluding that the attorney-client privilege survived Foster's death and that Foster likely would never have consulted with his attorney if he had not been assured that the conversations were privileged. Walter Pincus, "Starr Says Dead Men Should Tell Tales," *Washington Post*, 24 May 1998, C2.

108: pledging to complete: Fiske Final Report/Madison, 12, 19–20, 21–26.

108: The questioning would take: Robert B. Fiske, interview by author; Woodward, *Shadow*, 261–62.

109: "He could have me there": Bill Clinton, interview by author.

109: "I don't think": Robert B. Fiske, interview by author.

109: "would pose a severe risk": James A. Leach, "A Chilling Effect," *Wall Street Journal*, 14 Mar. 1994, in *Whitewater: A Journal Briefing,* ed. Robert L. Bartley, 253, 254.

109: "I am concerned": Leach, "A Chilling Effect," 254; Ann Devroy, "Leach Urges Keeping Focus in Whitewater Inquiry," *Los Angeles Times*, 28 Mar. 1994, 16.

110: likewise chastised: Helen Dewar and Ann Devroy, "Senate Leaders Make Whitewater Hearings Deal," *Washington Post*, 18 Mar. 1994, A1.

110: "congressional hearings on *any*": Helen Dewar, "Fiske, Hill Negotiate on Hearings:

Whitewater Counsel Gets GOP Senators to Adjust Time Line," *Washington Post*, 10 Mar. 1994, 1 (emphasis added).

110: **special prosecutor Archibald Cox had fought:** Ken Gormley, *Archibald Cox: Conscience of a Nation*, 269–74; Ken Gormley, "Impeachment and the Independent Counsel: A Dysfunctional Union," *Stanford Law Review* 51 (1999): 309, 338–39.

110: **Cox had gone:** Gormley, *Archibald Cox*, 339. The usual dangers posed by intermingling federal prosecutions with congressional inquiries—pretrial publicity, leaks of grand jury information, and other problems that could sink a prosecution—had prompted Cox to avoid this trap. The fact that Congress had granted Dean "use immunity" made it doubly important for Cox to segregate his own evidence to keep the matters separate. Cox's successor Leon Jaworski, in limiting his interaction with Congress, worried primarily about the danger of pretrial publicity and securing a fair trial for President Nixon if the embattled Nixon was ever criminally prosecuted (Gormley, "Impeachment and the Independent Counsel," 339).

110: **Fiske rode:** Stephen Brill, "Anonymity and Dignity," *American Lawyer*, Sept. 1994, 5.

110: **"committed suicide by firing":** Woodward, *Shadow*, 262.

110: **"We hope these rumor":** Statement by Special Counsel to the President Lloyd Cutler on the Independent Counsel Report, 30 June 1994.

110: **took to the Senate floor:** Toni Locy, "Lunch Among 'Old Friends' Causes Latest Whitewater Ripple," *Washington Post*, 24 Aug. 1994.

110: **Faircloth also publicly rebuked:** Howard Schneider, "Judge Met Sen. Faircloth Before Fiske Was Ousted; Sentelle Says Special Counsel Wasn't Discussed," *Washington Post*, 12 Aug. 1994, A1.

111: **"It wasn't like":** Bill Clinton, interview by author.

111: **Congress marched:** Woodward, *Shadow*, 263.

111: **"No court would ever":** Bill Clinton, interview by author.

111: **Attorney General Janet Reno wrote:** Janet Reno, interview by author.

111: **"reputation for integrity":** Jo Ann Harris, interview by author.

Chapter 10: Paula Corbin Jones

115: **"His Cheatin' Heart":** David Brock, "Living with the Clintons: Bill's Arkansas Bodyguards

Tell the Story the Press Missed," *American Spectator*, Jan. 1994, 18.

115: **"We keep dishing":** Jane Fullerton, "Mainstream Media in Tug of War Over Play of Troopers' Allegations," *Arkansas Democrat-Gazette*, 20 Jan. 1994, A10.

116: **"Their motivation, I mean":** David Brock, interview by author.

116: **Indeed, Brock later disclosed:** David Brock, *Blinded by the Right: The Conscience of an Ex-Conservative*, 154.

116: **Tyrrell recalled:** R. Emmett Tyrrell, Jr., interview by author.

117: **"He'd embarrassed hisself":** Paula Jones, interview by author.

118: **Traylor was hardly known:** Daniel M. Traylor, interview by author.

118: **"Never talk about it":** Paula Jones, interview by author.

119: **Ballentine briefed her:** Daniel M. Traylor, interview by author.

119: **"But the world's made up":** David Ellis, "The Perils of Paula," *People*, 23 May 1994, 88, 90, 92.

119: **During this period of experimenting:** Ibid., 90–91.

120: **"So what do you":** Daniel M. Traylor, interview by author.

121: **"a nice Christian girl":** Ibid.

121: **At this time, her name was Paula Corbin:** Conservative Political Action Conference, Washington, D.C., 11 Feb. 1994, transcript, 4 (hereinafter cited as CPAC Transcript); Michael Isikoff, "Clinton Hires Lawyer as Sexual Harassment Suit Is Threatened; Bennett Opens an Aggressive Campaign on Public Relations and Legal Fronts," *Washington Post*, 4 May 1994, A4.

121: **Her employment file indicated:** Ellis, "The Perils of Paula," 90.

121: **She had worked:** Rudy Maxa, "The Devil in Paula Jones," *Penthouse*, Jan. 1995, 107, 112.

121: **Although her handwritten application listed:** Paula Corbin, application for employment, 21 Jan. 1991, State of Arkansas employment file; State of Arkansas Office of Personnel Management, memorandum, 23 Jan. 1991.

121: **Paula Corbin received marginal:** State of Arkansas, Performance Evaluation Plan Rating Form, Mar. 1991 to Mar. 1992.

121: **Her employment records reveal:** Paula Corbin, State of Arkansas employment file.

122: **At the time that she was asked:** Clydine Pennington to Paula Corbin, Re: Six-Month

Probationary Period, 28 Aug. 1991, Paula Corbin, State of Arkansas employment file.

122: "come over just to chat": Isikoff, "Clinton Hires Lawyer," 4; Paula Corbin Jones Deposition, *Jones v. Clinton*, vol. 1, 101–102. Most accounts suggested these events took place in the morning. Paula herself would later maintain that they occurred at 2:30 in the afternoon (CPAC Transcript, 4), which now seems unlikely, given documentary evidence.

123: "I love your curves": Declaration of Paula Jones, 11 Mar. 1998, 2.

123: "come over there": Paula Corbin Jones Deposition, 106–108.

124: "Well, I don't want": Declaration of Paula Jones, 11 Mar. 1992, 3.

124: This account of her quick exit: Danny Ferguson Deposition, 49–52.

124: The entire sequence: Pamela Blackard Deposition, 67.

124: "From far off I could tell": Ibid., 68.

125: "I'm just going": Debbie Ballentine Deposition, 50. Emphasis in original.

125: "She cried most": Lydia Cathey Deposition, 53–54.

126: Ferguson meandered: Danny Ferguson Deposition, 49–50.

126: "asked for a piece": Answer to Complaint, *Jones v. Clinton*, para. 16.

127: "She came up": Danny Ferguson Deposition, 63–64.

127: "Mr. President, did you ever make": Bill Clinton Deposition, 17 Jan. 1998, 204–205. Years later, while scrupulously avoiding a flat-out denial of the facts outlined by Paula Jones in her testimony, President Clinton would instead emphasize: "I didn't sexually harass her." (Bill Clinton, interview by author).

127: 'fessed up, apologized: Bill Clinton, interview by author.

Chapter 11: Danny Traylor: "Can We Settle for Five Thousand Dollars?"

128: His research papers reveal: Daniel M. Traylor legal files.

129: "So I laid it out": Daniel M. Traylor, interview by author.

129: Although later accounts: Toobin, *A Vast Conspiracy*, 13.

129: "My recollection is": Daniel M. Traylor, interview by author.

129: George Cook would later sign: George L. Cook, Affidavit, 3 May 1994, Gilbert Davis files; Toobin, *A Vast Conspiracy*, 13.

129: "She's gone": Daniel M. Traylor, interview by author.

130: "It was a preposterous": George Cook Affidavit, 3 May 1994, Gilbert Davis files.

130: "Once this genie got out": Daniel M. Traylor, interview by author.

130: To further complicate: Ibid.

131: This group had gone to work: Cliff Jackson, interview by author; Noel Oman and Kevin Freking, "Ad Attacks Clinton, Pokes Fun at 'Arkansas Miracle,' " *Arkansas Democrat-Gazette*, 3 Oct. 1991; "Good Luck, Governor Clinton," advertisement in *Arkansas Democrat-Gazette*, 3 Oct. 1991; Laura Blumenfeld, "Bill Clinton's Worst Friend," *Washington Post*, 30 Dec. 1993, C1.

131: "It is much more fundamental": Cliff Jackson to Bill Clinton, 29 Dec. 1993.

132: It also contained: Agreement for Legal Services, 7 Feb. 1994, Daniel M. Traylor legal files.

132: Dear Sir: Daniel M. Traylor to President Clinton, 11 Feb. 1994, Daniel M. Traylor legal files.

132: "I started feeling": Daniel M. Traylor, interview by author.

133: "I'm not a political animal": CPAC Transcript, 11 Feb. 1994, 2, 4.

134: "Being seen as allied": Daniel M. Traylor, interview by author.

134: Most of the national papers: Julia Malone, "Critics Say Media Buried Sex Harassment Charge Against Clinton," *Arkansas Democrat-Gazette*, 7 Apr. 1994, A9; Randy Lilleston, "Clinton Made Advances, Woman Says," *Arkansas Democrat-Gazette*, 12 Feb. 1994, A1; Lloyd Grove, "It Isn't Easy Being Right: At the Conservative Confab, Out of Sorts About Who's in Power," *Washington Post*, 14 Feb. 1994, D1.

134: "They butchered": Daniel M. Traylor, interview by author.

134: The conservative media watchdog: "Censored by the Post," advertisement, Daniel M. Traylor legal files; Malone, "Critics Say Media Buried," 9A.

134: "amazed that journalists": Malone, "Critics Say Media Buried."

134: he had the gut feeling: Michael Isikoff, *Uncovering Clinton: A Reporter's Story*, 72.

134: At Jackson's urging: Daniel M. Traylor, interview by author.

135: Neither famous lawyer ever answered: Daniel M. Traylor, interview by author; Noel Oman, "Paula Jones' Attorney Mulls Suit Against

Clinton," *Arkansas Democrat-Gazette,* 17 Apr. 1994, A16.

135: Among these were: Daniel M. Traylor, interview by author.

135: "Whitewater was": "Whitewater: The Politics of a Second Watergate?" *American Political Report* 24, no. 13 (11 Mar. 1994): 1.

135: A letter dated: Anonymous to Paula Jones, 7 Apr. 1994, Daniel M. Traylor legal files.

135: Several events helped: Michael Isikoff, Charles E. Shepard, and Sharon La Franiere, "Clinton Hires Lawyer as Sexual Harassment Suit Is Threatened: Former State Employee in Arkansas Alleges Improper Advance in 1991," *Washington* Post, 4 May 1994, A1. Isikoff faxed a published copy of his piece to Traylor on May 4 at 4:03 P.M. (Michael Isikoff to Dan Traylor, 4 May 1994, Daniel M. Traylor legal files).

135: "Then the whole damn thing busted": Daniel M. Traylor, interview by author.

136: faxed him a more polished: Isikoff, *Uncovering Clinton,* 84.

136: Traylor was still: Daniel M. Traylor, interview by author.

136: He also drafted: Daniel M. Traylor, press release, 4 May 1994, Daniel M. Traylor legal files.

136: Traylor's telephone records show: Traylor telephone records, 3–5 May 1994.

136: "FYI, Review, Comment": Daniel M. Traylor, complaint and press release, 4 May 1994, Daniel M. Traylor legal files.

136: "We're still headed": Daniel M. Traylor, interview by author.

136: "Don't you feel": Joseph Cammarata, interview by author.

136: Gil Davis was: Gilbert Davis, interview by author.

137: Joe Cammarata, a young: Joseph Cammarata, interview by author.

137: God-fearing woman: Gilbert Davis, interview by author.

137: "Well, if there's enough": Ibid.; Noel Oman, "Ex–State Employee to Sue Clinton," *Arkansas Democrat-Gazette,* 4 May 1994, 1–16.

137: So the next day: Joseph Cammarata, interview by author.

137: "Oh, that's too bad": Gilbert Davis, interview by author.

138: she had volunteered: Joseph Cammarata, interview by author; Isikoff, *Uncovering Clinton,* 89. Although Danny Traylor would later tell Jane Mayer of *The New Yorker* that "in my many hours of interviews [with Paula]," she had never

mentioned anything about a "distinguishing characteristic," he also admitted that maybe he "never asked the right question" (Jane Mayer, "Distinguishing Characteristics," *The New Yorker,* 7 July 1997, 36).

138: pop star Michael Jackson: Joseph Cammarata, interview by author; Isikoff, *Uncovering Clinton,* 89.

138: "Goddamn it!": Gilbert Davis, interview by author; Joseph Cammarata interview by author.

139: The Jones lawyers next insisted: Joseph Cammarata, interview by author; Toobin, *A Vast Conspiracy,* 45.

139: Charlotte stated: Isikoff, *Uncovering Clinton,* 92.

139: "White House sources?": Joseph Cammarata, interview by author; Gilbert Davis, interview by author.

139: Bob Bennett and the rest: Robert Bennett, interview by author.

140: Paula remained silent: Joseph Cammarata, interview by author.

140: The twenty-page complaint against: Complaint, 6 May 1994, Daniel M. Traylor legal files. The complaint included a count alleging deprivation of federal constitutional rights under 42 U.S.C. Section 1983; one for conspiracy to deprive the plaintiff of civil rights under 42 U.S.C. Section 1985(3); one for intentional infliction of emotional distress under Arkansas law; and one for defamation under Arkansas law.

140: they had piggybacked: Joseph Cammarata, interview by author. A Title VII action would have required filing an administrative complaint within 180 days of the incident. The claim under Section 1983—part of the old Ku Klux Klan Act from the period after the Civil War—was creative, but an uphill battle. Claims under Section 1983 for sexual harassment required concrete proof of adverse job consequences, which the Jones lawyers knew was a challenge at best. The federal claim under Section 1985(3) was almost a throwaway; that statute dealt with private conspiracies to deprive constitutional rights. It was used primarily to deal with conspiracies against African American civil rights workers and other such situations; its application here was dubious.

141: "I do not seek": Paula Corbin Jones, public statement, 5 May 1994, distributed and read 6 May 1994, Gilbert Davis papers.

142: "Elf" Jerome Marcus had faxed: Jerome Marcus to Gilbert Davis, 10 June 1994, Gilbert Davis papers.

142: Davis and Cammarata had ordered: Ken Starr, interviewed on *MacNeil/Lehrer NewsHour,* PBS, transcript 4934, "Presidential Immunity," 24 May 1994.

142: So they left: Gilbert Davis, interview by author; Joseph Cammarata, interview by author.

142: "And I think": Gilbert Davis, interview by author; Gilbert Davis, record of phone conversation with Ken Starr, 10 June 1994, Gilbert Davis papers.

142: Starr, it turned out: Ken Starr, interview by author; Robert B. Fiske, interview by author.

143: Davis's billing records reveal: Isikoff, *Uncovering Clinton,* 109; Gilbert Davis, interview by author.

143: young lawyer named Paul Rosenzweig: Memo: Immunity Question, 16 June 1994, Gilbert Davis papers; Gilbert Davis, follow-up interview by author, 28 April 2006.

143: "as a person who can do": GKD to file, memorandum, 16 June 1994, Gilbert Davis papers.

Chapter 12: Three Judges in Black

143: "whether we [OIC] should do": Ken Starr, interview by author.

144: Fiske and Starr quietly agreed: Robert B. Fiske, interview by author.

144: "something was wrong": Dennis McInerny, interview by author.

144: "a really decent": Julie O'Sullivan, interview by author.

144: "I was in an alien landscape": Gabrielle Wolohojian, interview by author.

144: "We needed to close": Ibid. See also Jerry Seper, "In Limbo, Fiske Team Continues Probe," *Washington Times,* 9 Aug. 1994, A1.

145: "It certainly never crossed": Jo Ann Harris, interview by author.

145: "To my knowledge, he had limited": Janet Reno, interview by author.

145: "We're going to": Julie O'Sullivan, interview by author.

145: "No one really knew": Gabrielle Wolohojian, interview by author.

145: MacKinnon felt: John D. Butzner, Jr., interview by author; Viola "Pete" Butzner, interview by author.

146: The lone Democrat: John D. Butzner, interview by author; William H. Rehnquist to John D. Butzner, Jr., 26 Oct. 1992, the papers of John D. Butzner, Jr., Special Collections, University of

Virginia Law Library, MSS 00-1, box 1 (hereinafter cited as Butzner papers).

146: Judge Sentelle had circulated: David B. Sentelle to John D. Butzner, Jr., and Joseph T. Sneed, 20 Nov. 1992, Butzner papers, box 1, folder 1992–1997, Candidates for Independent Counsel.

146: Sentelle also circulated: "Independent Counsel List," undated, ibid.

146: "It was a huge looseleaf": David B. Sentelle to author, 19 Dec. 2002.

146: As judges suggested: David B. Sentelle, testimony to Senate Governmental Affairs Committee, Federal News Service, 14 Apr. 1999, 3.

146: "anyone who wished": David B. Sentelle to author, 19 Dec. 2002.

146: this list included: David B. Sentelle to John D. Butzner, Jr., and Joseph T. Sneed, 18 July 1994, Butzner Papers, In re: Madison Guaranty Savings & Loan Association (Whitewater): Appointment of Independent Counsel. Interestingly, the list also included Washington lawyers Plato Cacheris and Jacob Stein, who later represented Monica Lewinsky.

147: By July 20: David B. Sentelle to John D. Butzner, Jr., and Joseph T. Sneed, 20 July 1994, Butzner papers. Besides Starr, this short list included Robert C. Bonner (former federal judge and U.S. attorney from central California); John M. Dowd (a prominent Washington, D.C., lawyer with experience in corruption and ethics cases); John Van De Kamp (former attorney general of California); and Warren B. Rudman (former U.S. senator and state attorney general from New Hampshire).

147: "Looking over": John D. Butzner, Jr., to David B. Sentelle and Joseph T. Sneed, 25 July, 1994, Butzner papers, box 12, folder 1994–1999, In Re Madison Guaranty Savings & Loan Association (Whitewater), Candidates for Appointment of Independent Counsel in Whitewater Investigation.

147: First, he worried that Starr was: John D. Butzner, Jr., interview by author.

147: "He was opposed": Viola "Pete" Butzner, interview by author.

147: Judge Sentelle transmitted: David B. Sentelle to John D Butzner, Jr., and Joseph T. Sneed, 18 July 1994, Butzner papers. The attached list, which noted Ken Starr as a "maybe," then included the footnote: "During preparation [of this memo], Judge Starr called to say 'YES.' "

148: "I have arranged": David B. Sentelle to John D. Butzner, Jr., and Joseph T. Sneed, 29 July 1994, Butzner papers, box 12, folder 1994–1999.

148: railing against Fiske: Floyd G. Brown to John D. Butzner, Jr., 3 Aug. 1994, Butzner papers, box 11, folder 1994, In Re: Madison Guaranty Savings & Loan Association (Whitewater) Appointment of Independent Counsel.

148: "The report released": ClintonWatch, Aug. 1994, Butzner papers, box 11, folder 1994.

148: Certainly, Sentelle was a fan: David B. Sentelle to author, 19 Dec. 2002.

148: A strong conservative: Joseph T. Sneed, interview by author.

149: "the importance and sensitivity of": David B. Sentelle to author, 19 Dec. 2002.

149: They also inquired: David B. Sentelle, testimony to Senate Governmental Affairs Committee, Federal News Service, 14 Apr. 1999, 10.

149: "We actually cross-examined": Ibid.; Sixty-Seventh Judicial Conference of the Fourth Circuit, "The Independent Counsel Process: Is It Broken and How Should It Be Fixed?" *Wash. & Lee L. Rev.* 54 (1997): 1515, 1539 (remarks of Judge Butzner).

149: He knew little about: Ken Starr, interview by author.

149: "Ken is so fair": Alice Starr, interview by author.

150: "I will have it ready": David B. Sentelle to John D. Butzner, Jr., and Joseph T. Sneed, 4 Aug. 1994, Butzner papers, box 11, folder 1994.

150: it was better for the special court: U.S. Court of Appeals for the District of Columbia Circuit, Special Division, In Re: Madison Guaranty Savings & Loan Association, Order Appointing Independent Counsel, 5 Aug. 1994, 4; Richard Whittle, "Judges Appoint New Whitewater Counsel," *Dallas Morning News,* 6 Aug. 1994, A7.

150: This was not meant to be: David B. Sentelle to author, 19 Dec. 2002.

150: agreed to join the opinion: John D. Butzner, Jr., interview by author.

150: a reporter asked him: Michael J. Sniffen, "Ex–Bush Official Replaces Whitewater Investigator," *Fort Worth Star-Telegram,* 6 Aug. 1994, A7.

150: "You know": Bill Clinton, interview by author.

151: "Oddly, but perhaps not": David B. Sentelle to author, 19 Dec. 2002.

151: Judge Sentelle also later insisted: Ibid.

151: "I think we differed": John D. Butzner, Jr., to David B. Sentelle, 21 Oct. 1998, Butzner papers, box 12, folder 1994–95.

151: "You know," he said: Bill Clinton, interview by author.

151: "I wanted there to be": Robert B. Fiske, interview by author.

151: As Fiske introduced: Julie O'Sullivan, interview by author.

151: "I love this": William S. Duffey, Jr., interview by author.

152: Now Starr had been: Julie O'Sullivan, interview by author.

152: said the scene resembled: Rusty Hardin, interview by author.

152: Before Ken Starr caught: Dennis Cauchon, "Starr Easing into Whitewater, May Signal a Long Investigation," *USA Today,* 10 Aug. 1994.

152: "He agreed": Robert B. Fiske, interview by author.

153: had been friendly: Locy, "Lunch Among 'Old Friends' "; David B. Sentelle to author.

153: An unidentified witness now told: Schneider, "Judge Met Sen. Faircloth," 1.

153: most of the conversation had revolved: Howard Schneider, "Judge Met Senator Faircloth Before Fiske Was Ousted; Sentelle Says Special Counsel Wasn't Discussed," *Washington Post,* 12 Aug. 1994, A1.

153: "[gave] rise to the appearance": Robert Toricelli, "It's Time to Reconsider Independent Counsel Statute's Effectiveness," *Roll Call,* 20 Mar. 1997.

153: Thirty-six Democratic members of Congress wrote: U.S. Congress, letter to David B. Sentelle, 17 Aug. 1994.

153: "Neither Faircloth nor Helms ever attempted": David B. Sentelle to author, 19 Dec. 2002.

153: "We did not discuss": Ibid.

154: "There is no vast right-wing conspiracy": Senate Government Affairs Committee, Testimony of Judge Sentelle, questions by Senator Lieberman, 14. Apr. 1999.

154: Among other things: Carl Levin to David B. Sentelle, 12 Aug. 1994, Butzner papers, box 11, folder 1994.

154: "Mr. Starr did not mention": "Presidential Immunity; Fertility Rights; America's Values," *MacNeil/Lehrer NewsHour,* PBS, transcript 4,934, 24 May 1994. In response to the argument that the president should enjoy some special immunity from civil suit, Starr replied forcefully: "I think the President is one of us and should be treated like one of us, except with respect and with accommodating the President's schedule. . . . [W]e don't say to the President, 'don't bother to file your tax returns because we know that you're busy with very compelling issues of state.' We ask the President to obey the law and to be like other citizens, except with respect to protecting his actions as the President of the United States" (ibid., 4).

154: ill considered: Judge Sneed fired off a confidential fax from San Francisco, cautioning Sentelle not to be drawn "into the arena of public discourse" and urging the special court to stand strong in defense of Starr. "Let me say emphatically I would vote to designate Starr Independent Counsel [again] tomorrow were that before us," he wrote. "My confidence is not shaken." Sneed went on to conclude: "I certainly hope Starr does not cut and run from his assignment." Joseph T. Sneed to David B. Sentelle and John D. Butzner, Jr., 16 Aug. 1994.

154: "I was against Starr": John D. Butzner, Jr., interview by author.

Chapter 13: Ken Starr: Special Prosecutor

155: President Clinton blamed himself: Bill Clinton, interview by author.

156: Starr noted: Ken Starr, interview by author.

156: two decades' worth: Hickman Ewing, Jr., interview by author.

156: He had served for eight years: Joan I. Duffy, "Prosecutor Ewing Up and At 'Em Again, Whitewater Job Returns Him to Legal Specialty," *Memphis Commercial Appeal*, 10 July 1996, A1. For an excellent discussion of Ewing's background, see John Branston, "More Power Than a Good Man Ought to Want," in *Rowdy Memphis: The South Unscripted*, 13–23; John Branston, "Toppling the Good Old Boys" *The Making of Modern Memphis: 1976–1996* (July 1996), 60.

156: "rendered infamous": Ibid.; Glenn R. Simpson, "Southern Edge: A Veteran Prosecutor of Political Corruption Steers Whitewater Case," *Wall Street Journal*, 31 July 1996, A1.

156: The family's home was: Duffy, "Prosecutor Ewing."

156: It was also what: Simpson, "Southern Edge."

156: Ewing came to embrace: Hickman Ewing, Jr., "Combating Official Corruption by All Available Means," *Memphis State University Law Review* 10 (1980): 423.

157: A state senator: Lewis Lord and Julian Barnes, "Whitewater Mind Games," *U.S. News & World Report*, 3 Mar. 1997.

157: "We had lots of chicken": Hickman Ewing, Jr., interview by author. When Ewing arrived on September 14, 1994, Bill Duffey, a Fiske holdover, was deputy independent counsel in charge of the Little Rock office. However, it was clear Duffey would not be staying indefinitely. Ewing gradually took over the role of overseeing that office (Hickman Ewing, Jr., interview by author).

158: Bennett played tight end: Jackie Bennett, interview by author.

158: Bennett had prosecuted: Jackie Bennett, interview by author; Maria Recio, "Starr's Lieutenant Built His Reputation on Texas Court Cases," *Fort Worth Star-Telegram*, 16 May 1991, 1.

158: "We prided ourselves": Jackie Bennett, interview by author.

159: Starr drove: Ibid. Starr himself recalled crossing over the Arkansas River into Little Rock, and assuring Bennett that the job could be completed expeditiously. "I tend to be the eternal optimist," Starr said. "A year or two struck me as a reasonable amount of time" (Ken Starr, interview by author).

160: For Fiske it "was an all-consuming job": Robert B. Fiske, interview by author.

160: "The whole structure": Ken Starr, interview by author.

160: "deep academic interest": William S. Duffey, Jr., interview by author.

161: "wasn't physically present": Gabrielle Wolohojian, interview by author.

161: Prosecutors needed to arrange: Julie O'Sullivan, interview by author; William S. Duffey, Jr., interview by author.

161: "It was just harder to get": William S. Duffey, Jr., interview by author.

162: gave Ken Starr high marks: Mark Tuohey, interview by author.

162: "I had no idea how": Gabrielle Wolohojian, interview by author.

162: Picking up their families and moving: William S. Duffey, Jr., interview by author.

163: If Starr wanted: Dash was not the only Democratic figure from Watergate to whom Starr and his staff reached out. OIC lawyers also met with James Doyle, press secretary and spokesman for the legendary Archibald Cox, and asked if he was interested in joining the team. Doyle made several discreet phone calls and was advised to "stay away from it." He therefore declined (James Doyle, interview by author).

163: "There was criticism": Sam Dash, interview by author.

164: "a very collegial": Mark Tuohey, interview by author.

164: "We never did": Hickman Ewing, Jr., interview by author.

164: "I can't think": Jackie Bennett, interview by author.

165: "Ken worked almost": Sam Dash, interview by author.

165: "To hear some people say": Hickman Ewing, Jr., interview by author.

165: Hubbell had confessed to engaging: Plea Agreement, 6 Dec. 1994.

166: "I mean a chimpanzee could": Rusty Hardin, interview by author.

166: They would forever regret: Jackie Bennett, interview by author.

166: Hubbell himself: Webster Hubbell, interview by author.

167: Starr's naive expectation: Rusty Hardin, interview by author.

167: The Hubbell investigation: Starr's office eventually evolved into teams, most of them working on familiar assignments. One handled the Hale plea and the transactions involving Capital Management Services, debriefing Hale in an attempt to flush out the truth. Another team dealt with the Hubbell case, attempting to recover ground despite the botched plea agreement. The "825 team" dealt with Hale's bogus loan from Madison Guaranty in the amount of $825,000, which in turn encompassed the $300,000 loan from Hale to Susan McDougal; a $25,000 loan allegedly designed to pay off a Whitewater obligation for the McDougals (and the Clintons); and a loan of $150,000 that allegedly went to a corporation called Castle Sewer and Water, which was incorporated by Jim Guy Tucker. There were also separate teams devoted to the Whitewater investment and to Madison irregularities. And there was a team putting together the tax fraud case involving Jim Guy Tucker's cable company (Hickman Ewing, Jr., interview by author). In Washington, none of the principal matters under investigation—dealing with Vince Foster, Treasury Office contacts, the Travel Office, or other sundry investigations—related to the original Whitewater matter.

167: into a closet: Rusty Hardin, interview by author; Robert Fiske to Randy Coleman, Re: Hale plea agreement, 19 Mar. 1994, Heuer papers.

168: a former public servant: Conason and Lyons, *The Hunting of the President*, 87.

168: Prosecutors in the Sixth Judicial: Larry Jegley, interview by author; Conason and Lyons, *The Hunting of the President*, 221.

168: Evidence had also surfaced: Joe Conason and Gene Lyons, "Nabbing David Hale," *Salon*,

3 March 2000; Conason and Lyons, *The Hunting of the President*, 88. A judgment was eventually entered against Hale, in this scheme, in the amount of $486,000.

168: Hale was now singing: Robert B. Fiske, interview by author.

168: McDougal had spoken: Bill Nichols, "McDougal: No S&L Funds in Whitewater," *USA Today*, 29 Mar. 1994, A4.

168: "Nancy had made me her husband": McDougal and Harris, *The Woman Who Wouldn't Talk*, 132–146, 160–65.

169: According to Susan: Ibid.; Robert McDaniel, interview by author.

169: Ken Starr indicted: Indictment, 17 Aug. 1995, Heuer papers.

Chapter 14: Paula Jones on Film

170: Journalist Michael Isikoff had quit: Isikoff, *Uncovering Clinton*, 72–77, 96–97.

170: "It couldn't have been": Bill Clinton, interview by author.

170: "I was at the point where": Paula Jones, interview by author.

171: Cammarata had already drawn: For Cammarata, this was no different from a car accident case, in which a lawyer sends a private investigator to "videotape the [alleged victim]." The lawyer can then use this as leverage, telling the other side: "I've got this surveillance tape of you, but I'm not going to show it to you until after your deposition" (Joseph Cammarata, interview by author; Motion to Permit Filing of Affidavit of Paula Corbin Jones, under seal, *Jones v. Clinton*, 3 Oct. 1994).

171: When Judge Susan Webber Wright disallowed: Order, *Jones v. Clinton*, 23 Oct. 1994.

171: Cammarata placed a copy: Joseph Cammarata, interview by author.

171: A copy of that affidavit: Distinguishing Characteristic Affidavit, 26 May 1994, Gilbert Davis papers.

171: "An investigative team needs": GKD to Joseph Cammarata, 16 May 1994, Gilbert Davis papers.

172: This move was designed: Joseph Cammarata, interview by author.

172: It was also aimed at shaming: Joseph Cammarata to Arthur B. Spitzer, 8 May 1994, Cammarata papers; Joseph Cammarata, interview by author.

172: "Happy decision-making": Arthur B. Spitzer to Steven R. Shapiro and Rita Sillinger, 10 May 1994, Cammarata papers.

172: After a few "whereas": Joseph Cammarata to Office of Senator Nickles, 28 July 1995, Cammarata papers.

172: Wright had been a student: Jeffrey Toobin, "Presiding Over the President," *The New Yorker,* 9 Mar. 1998, 45.

172: "I thought we'd get": Robert Bennett, interview by author.

173: Bennett filed: President Clinton's Motion to Dismiss, *Jones v. Clinton,* 10 Aug. 1994; Memorandum in Support of President Clinton's Motion to Dismiss, *Jones v. Clinton,* 10 Aug. 1994; Statement of Interest of the United States, *Jones v. Clinton,* 19 Aug. 1994, 2–3.

173: a lawsuit against President Teddy Roosevelt: *People ex rel. Hurley v. Roosevelt,* 71 N.E. 1137 (N.Y. 1904); *Devault v. Truman,* 194 S.W.2d 29 (Mo. 1946); *Bailey v. Kennedy,* No. 757, 200 (Cal. Super. Ct., 5 July 1962). See also Statement of Interest of the United States, *Jones v. Clinton,* 19 Aug. 1994, 2–3, for a discussion of these cases.

173: there was no clear precedent: 457 U.S. 731 (1982).

173: with a sobbing Paula Jones: Thomas Galvin, "Paula: I'll Put Prez's Privates on Parade," *New York Post,* 26 Oct. 1994, 18; press release, re: Press Conference, 25 Oct. 1994, Gilbert Davis papers.

173: "The rights to": Memorandum Opinion and Order, *Jones v. Clinton,* 28 Dec. 1994, 20.

174: Attorneys on both sides: Patricia Manson, "Clinton Wins Trial Deferral in Jones Sex Suit," *Arkansas Democrat-Gazette,* 29 Dec. 1994, A1.

174: Davis announced: Gilbert Davis, interview, *Daybreak,* CNN, transcript, 29 Dec. 1994, Gilbert Davis papers.

174: swiftly overturned: *Jones v. Clinton,* 72 F.3d 1354 (8th Cir. 1996). Judge Pasco Middleton Bowman II, a Reagan appointee, wrote that President Clinton was *not* immune from suit, particularly where "only personal, private conduct by a President is at issue."

175: Clinton himself seemed to bristle: Bill Clinton, interview by author.

176: A number of anti–Bill Clinton suits: Two of the most prominent of these pre-*Jones* lawsuits were *Larry Nichols v. Bill Clinton et al.,* first filed in 1990 and dismissed in 1992 at docket number 9-746 (in which Nichols alleged wrongful termination against then-Governor Clinton and in the process asserted that Clinton had extramarital affairs with numerous women, including Gennifer Flowers), and *Benita T. Jones v. William "Bill" Clinton et al.,* at docket no. 92-352, originally

filed in 1991 but refiled in 1992 to include Clinton as a defendant (alleging a conspiracy to engage in a variety of conduct, including sexual harassment). Both cases were dismissed.

176: He also quipped: Lois Romano, "U.S. Judge's Husband Talks About Jones Case," *Washington Post,* 9 Feb. 1998. From the earliest stages of the *Jones* litigation, Judge Wright's husband was known for speaking to journalists on these topics, often off-the-record.

177: Davis preferred to think: Gilbert Davis, interview by author.

177: Joe Cammarata had no: Joseph Cammarata, interview by author.

177: Tucked away: All these documents are contained in Gilbert Davis papers: GKD to File, 16 May 1994, and Memo from Lady in Arkansas to GKD, undated, "Other Women" file [baton twirler]; GKD to File, 28 Nov. 1995 [girlfriend commits suicide]; Undated notes, 1994–97 [Bill Clinton and Susan McDougal]; 14 June 1995 notes [woman in Australia]; Alleged witnesses to Jones incident, undated [killed two boys].

178: "I want this affair wrapped": Ambrose Evans-Pritchard, "I Was Threatened After Clinton Affair," *Sunday Telegraph,* undated, Gilbert Davis papers.

178: There were also stories: "Affair of State," *Texas Monthly,* July 1997, 19, Gilbert Davis papers.

178: "Take the deposition": GKD to file, 16 Oct. 1995, Gilbert Davis papers.

178: "has info that Clinton made": Notes, 30 Aug., year unknown, Gilbert Davis papers.

178: "What makes [this conduct] so outrageous": GKD to File, 16 May 1994, Gilbert Davis papers.

178: "Were you given": Memo, "Interrogatories to Ferguson," undated, "Open Matters" file, Gilbert Davis papers.

178: "speak to other women who": Gilbert Davis, interview, *Daybreak,* CNN, transcript, 29 Dec. 1994, Gilbert Davis papers.

179: "She just said he'd invited": Maxa, "The Devil in Paula Jones," 107–109.

179: "Paula Jones' consent": GKD to File, 20 Dec. 1994, Gilbert Davis papers.

180: Davis issued: Statement of Gilbert K. Davis and Joseph Cammarata, 17 May 1994, Gilbert Davis papers.

180: "I am *not* in it": Paula Jones, interview, CNN, transcript, 17 June 1994, Gilbert Davis papers (emphasis added).

180: "What kind of country do we live": GKD to File, undated, "Speeches," Gilbert Davis papers.

180: **rude and loud:** David Ellis, "The Perils of Paula," *People*, 23 May 1994, 88–94.

181: **this raw footage:** Robert Bennett, interview by author.

181: **Dressed in a low-cut:** Jeremiah films, raw film footage, Paula Jones interview, 1994.

183: **"When the jury watched":** Robert Bennett, follow-up interview by author.

183: **"I was shocked":** Daniel M. Traylor, interview by author.

183: **Bob Bennett was also busy:** Affidavit of Carol Phillips, 27 June 1994. Paula Jones herself later filed a sworn declaration alleging that on one occasion, Governor Clinton had run into her in the Rotunda of the Arkansas State Capitol, "accosted" her, and then draped his arm around her and said to his bodyguard, "Don't we make a beautiful couple: Beauty and the Beast?" (Declaration of Paula Jones, 11 Mar. 1998). This encounter, if it occurred, arguably cut both ways. Bennett was in a position to argue that Jones repeatedly sought out opportunities to run into the governor and enjoyed the attention.

183: **Pam Hood:** Jane Mayer, "Distinguishing Characteristic," *The New Yorker*, 7 July 1997, 36.

184: **"The issue of Steve Jones being engaged":** Robert Bennett, interview by author.

Chapter 15: Arkansas Felons

184: **"You know, Jim had already been":** Bill Clinton, interview by author.

185: **He was sporting:** Paul Bedard, "Old Friends Reunited for Clinton's Whitewater Testimony," *Washington Times*, 29 Apr. 1996, A6; Lloyd Grove, "Steamed by Whitewater," *Washington Post*, 29 Apr. 1994, B1.

185: **He looked rested:** Ruth Marcus, "President Testifies in Fraud Case," The *Washington Post*, 29 Apr. 1996, A1; Warren E. Leary, "Clinton Tapes His Testimony in Fraud Trial of Ex-Partners," *New York Times*, 29 Apr. 1996, A18; Bedard, "Old Friends"; Sara Fritz, "Clinton Testifies, Denies Role in Alleged Fraud," *Los Angeles Times*, 29 Apr. 1996, A1; Paul Bedard, "In Video Testimony, Clinton Denies Loan Pressure," *Washington Times*, 29 Apr. 1996, A1.

185: **A different war was being fought:** Marcus, "President Testifies"; Bedard, "In Video Testimony."

186: **He moved directly:** "Clinton: 'I Never Pressured David Hale to Make a Loan,' " *Arkansas Democrat-Gazette*, part 1, 10 Sept. 1996, A14 (hereinafter cited as Clinton Trial Testimony).

186: **"Did you ever":** Clinton Trial Testimony, part 2, p. 14.

186: **During his years as governor:** Clinton Trial Testimony, part 9, p. 14.

187: **Here, the president pointed:** "The Map Room," Office of Curator, Nov. 1995, Susan McDougal papers.

187: **"We're both great admirers":** Bedard, "Old Friends."

187: **"There was no such":** Susan McDougal, interview with author.

187: **"I always had somebody with me":** Bill Clinton, interview by author.

188: **"had hit a home run":** Bedard, "Old Friends."

188: **"I did not see":** Marcus, "President Testifies."

188: **'He's the world's only living":** Grove, "Steamed."

188: **The missing sheaf:** The most detailed account of the missing billing records can be found in Final Senate Report/Whitewater, 240–264; 660–668 (minority view).

189: **In prior sworn testimony:** *Newsweek*, 6 May 1996, 6; Susan Schmidt, "First Lady's Prints on Document, Magazine Says," *Washington Post*, 29 Apr. 1996, A14; Jerry Seper, "FBI Finds Hillary's Fingerprints on Rediscovered S&L Papers," *Washington Times*, 29 Apr. 1996, A1.

189: **There was no dispute:** Final Senate Report/Whitewater, 258.

189: **Hubbell, when asked:** Ibid., 242.

189: **Crisis management expert:** Ibid., 666; Jane Sherburne, interview by author.

190: **Nobody on earth:** Final Report/Ray, vol. 1, 138–39; "Once Upon a Time in Arkansas: Rose Law Firm Billing Records," *Frontline*, PBS, Oct. 1997.

190: **During this period:** Final Report/Ray, vol. 3, 141.

190: **The documents revealed:** Final Senate Report/Whitewater, 662 (minority view).

190: **Tellingly, the FBI:** Ibid., at 262.

190: **"It is what it is":** Harold Ickes, interview by author.

190: **"spice to the gumbo":** John Podesta, interview by author.

190: **The *New York Post* ran:** Terry Lemons and Jane Fullerton, "Closing In on the First Lady," *Arkansas Democrat-Gazette*, 7 Jan. 1996, A1.

190: **Yet the First Lady's fingerprints fueled:** Fritz, "Clinton Testifies, Denies"; Schmidt, "First Lady's Prints."

191: Numerous sources: Paul Begala, interview by author; Harold Ickes, interview by author.

191: "A good crisis manager": Jane Sherburne, interview by author.

191: A Washington Post/ABC News poll reported: R. H. Melton, "First Lady Bears the Brunt of Unfavorable Opinion on Whitewater," *Washington Post,* 24 Mar. 1996, A16.

191: "short, flabby guy": George Collins, interview by author.

191: he testified that he had gone: David Hale Testimony, Transcript of Proceedings Before the Hon. George Howard, Jr., 1 Apr. 1996, vol: 16, 3083–3118 (hereinafter cited as Hale Testimony); Susan Schmidt, "Hale Describes Arkansas Fraud Scheme," *Washington Post,* 2 Apr. 1996, A4; Hugh Aynesworth, "Hale Details Plans Behind Illegal Loans," *Washington Times,* 2 Apr. 1996, A1.

192: Later that night, Hale testified: Jim Guy Tucker, interview by author.

192: they were going to have to take care of: Hale Testimony, vol. 16, 3095–3106; Schmidt, "Hale Describes Arkansas."

192: Hale next testified that: Schmidt, "Hale Describes Arkansas"; Aynesworth, "Hale Details Plans." See also Hale Testimony, vol. 16, 3083–3123, and vol. 17, 3221–3315. The straw purchaser was Dean Paul.

192: "if we didn't pay": Hale Testimony, vol. 17, 3128–3129.

192: Jim McDougal told the press: Aynesworth, "Hale Details Plans."

192: "I think he'll be exposed": Leslie Phillips, "Mystery Man's Allegations Central to Bank Fraud Case," *USA Today,* 2 April 1996, A6.

192: "Mr. Clinton's exact ties": Noel Oman, "Media Turn Out in Full Force for Hale Testimony," *Arkansas Democrat-Gazette,* 3 Apr. 1996, A8.

193: Hale's testimony was murky: Hale Testimony, vol. 17, 3221–3315; Joe Stumpe and Patricia Manson, "Clinton In on Deal, Hale Testifies," *Arkansas Democrat-Gazette,* 3 Apr. 1996, A1. See also Conason and Lyons, *The Hunting of the President,* 227–29.

193: "My name can't show": Hale Testimony, vol. 17, 3224–28; Hugh Aynesworth, "Hale Says Clinton Got Money from Illegal Loan," *Washington Times,* 3 Apr. 1996, A1.

193: "Who did you look": Aynesworth, "Hale Says Clinton Got Money"; Hale Transcript, vol. 17, 3314–3315.

193: "What you heard": Phillips, "Mystery Man's Allegations."

193: "I sort of wanted": "McDougal, Sorry for Hale, Forgoes Fisticuffs," *Arkansas Democrat-Gazette,* 3 Apr. 1996, A8.

193: Prosecutor Jahn clarified: Joe Stumpe, "For Now, Clinton Not Named as Co-Conspirator," *Arkansas Democrat-Gazette,* 4 Apr. 1996, A1.

193: Governor Jim Guy Tucker was attempting: Jim Guy Tucker, interview by author. See also Noel Oman, "Governor Takes Aim at Starr," *Arkansas Democrat-Gazette,* 2 May 1995, A3. For another early story reflecting such attacks on Starr, see Daniel Klaidman, "Branded, Besieged, and Battling Back," *Legal Times,* 5 June 1995, 1.

193: Although stories were creeping: Frank J. Murray, "Starr's Billings Prompt Unease," *Washington Times,* 27 Mar. 1996, A4; "On Another Case," photo, *Arkansas Democrat-Gazette,* 4 Apr. 1996, A5.

193: "get [Tucker] to say": Bill Clinton, interview by author.

194: "I'm from the school of criminal law that says": George Collins, interview by author.

194: As Governor Tucker sat: Michael Haddigan, "Trial Is Taking Its Toll on Tucker," *Washington Post,* 24 Mar. 1996, A17; Jim Guy Tucker, interview by author.

195: "The motivation to protect": Jim Guy Tucker, interview by author.

195: Collins worried that Tucker: George Collins, interview by author.

195: nothing more than a minor figure: Robert McDaniel, interview by author.

195: "I'm going to get up": George Collins, interview by author.

195: "there were no pros": Sam Heuer, interview by author.

195: "He was taking": Susan McDougal, interview by author.

196: "My people expect": McDougal and Harris, *The Woman Who Wouldn't Talk,* 192.

196: He wrote to McDougal's lawyer: Grant Tennile, "James McDougal Pale in Court, but Vows to Continue," *Arkansas Democrat-Gazette,* 8 May 1996, A12.

196: "It was the exact model": *United States v. James B. McDougal, Jim Guy Tucker, Susan McDougal,* James McDougal Testimony, 7 May 1996, vol. 39, 6973–74.

197: "Another day": Susan McDougal, interview by author.

197: **Jahn confronted Jim:** Conason and Lyons, *The Hunting of the President*, 238.

197: **Susan McDougal waited:** Ibid.; for a slightly different account, see McDougal and Harris, *The Woman Who Wouldn't Talk*, 195.

197: **"kind of like in a football game":** Robert McDaniel, interview by author.

197: **"Oh, Jesus Christ":** George Collins, interview by author.

197: **McDougal had even confessed:** Sam Heuer, interview by author.

198: **"rip [Jim's] heart out":** Robert McDaniel, interview by author.

198: **"If that hick lawyer of yours asks":** McDougal and Harris, *The Woman Who Wouldn't Talk*, 195.

198: **"She did not believe":** Robert McDaniel, interview by author.

198: **They did not exactly "trust":** Ray Jahn, interview by author.

199: **"innocent bystander":** Ibid. Susan McDougal's attorney, Bobby McDaniel, later replied to this assertion by prosecutor Jahn: "A mock jury, and I've done many of them, is not better than the fairness by which you present the evidence. So I put zero stock in that" (Robert McDaniel, interview by author).

199: **Starr's prosecutors were convinced:** Ray Jahn, interview by author.

199: **"Why would the president of the United States have":** Ken Starr, interview by author.

199: **Before President Clinton's testimony:** Sam Heuer to David Kendall, 18 Apr. 1996, Sam Heuer papers. Attorney Heuer's files relating to the Tucker-McDougal trial contain numerous exchanges of information with the president's lawyers.

199: **prosecutor Ray Jahn turned:** It is worth noting that when David Hale had attempted to testify about conversations he allegedly engaged in directly with Clinton, Governor Tucker's attorney George Collins had objected forcefully. Collins argued that such testimony was inadmissible "unless they say Clinton is a co-conspirator, and they have never said that" (Stumpe, "For Now, Clinton Not Named"). Prosecutor Ray Jahn did not contest the objection; Judge Howard had ruled the testimony inadmissible. Thus, Jahn was incapable of arguing that Clinton was a wrongdoer.

200: **The courtroom of Judge George Howard:** Hugh Aynesworth, "Tucker Felt Heat Waiting for Jury," *Washington Times*, 29 May 1996, A9.

200: **"The main thing in deliberating":** Laura E. Malat, interview by author.

200: **The jury foreperson turned:** Aynesworth, "Tucker Felt Heat Waiting"; Conason and Lyons, *The Hunting of the President*, 244.

200: **"We have prayed":** Hugh Aynesworth, "Tucker Will Step Down, but Says He's Innocent," *Washington Times*, 29 Apr. 1996, A9.

201: **barely able to speak:** Ibid. Tucker briefly attempted to switch his position, indicating that he would only step aside temporarily, considering this a "disability" under the state constitution, which could be extinguished by a successful appeal. However, after a flurry of activity in the state capitol, Tucker finally tendered his resignation on July 16, as originally planned (Jerry Seper, "Tucker Flip-Flops Way Out of Office," *Washington Times*, 16 July 1996, A1).

201: **Lieutenant Governor Mike Huckabee:** Conason and Lyons, *The Hunting of the President*, 245.

201: **"It really is going to drive":** Laurie Kellman, "Verdicts Give Morale Boost to Flagging Dole Campaign," *Washington Times*, 29 May 1996, A8.

201: **One juror described:** Laura E. Malat, interview by author.

201: **"an unmitigated liar":** Conason and Lyons, *The Hunting of the President*, 245.

202: **"Who me? I'm innocent":** Laura E. Malat, interview by author.

202: **One juror said:** Risa Briggs, interview by author; Laura E. Malat, interview by author. Some jurors, requesting anonymity, even intimated that they believed that Governor Tucker had tried to engineer some "dirty tricks" during the trial, to orchestrate a mistrial.

202: **"I thought he [McDougal] might well have":** Bill Clinton, interview by author.

Chapter 16: The "Cooperating Witness"

202: **"He was a brilliant, delightful":** Bill Clinton, interview by author.

203: **"We are interested":** Amy J. St. Eve to Sam Heuer, 25 July 1996, Heuer papers.

203: **"no business corresponding":** Sam Heuer, interview by author.

203: **It was no secret that:** Robert McDaniel, interview by author; Sam Heuer, interview by author.

203: Jim had also denied: United States McDougal et al., James McDougal testimony, trial transcript, 6988.

204: "preliminary interviews": Ray Jahn to Sam Heuer, 30 July 1996, Susan McDougal papers. See also W. Ray Jahn and Amy J. St. Eve to Sam Heuer, 8 Aug. 1996, Susan McDougal papers.

204: "more interested": Susan McDougal, interview by author.

204: Among the numerous: Claudia Riley, interview by author.

205: Jim came up from: Susan McDougal, interview by author.

205: St. Eve was prepared to get: ibid.

205: "Jim and I never talked": Amy J. St. Eve, interview by author.

206: "I knew when he started": Susan McDougal, interview by author. In *The Woman Who Wouldn't Talk*, 201–202, McDougal and Harris described this phone conversation as occurring immediately after Starr's visit. In interviews with the author, however, Susan McDougal placed the call immediately before Starr's visit to the Riley property to see Jim.

206: She was out: Susan McDougal, interview by author.

207: "I drove": Ken Starr, interview by author.

207: "He had such a big": Amy J. St. Eve, interview by author.

207: "And they had brought": Susan McDougal, interview by author; McDougal and Harris, *The Woman Who Wouldn't Talk*, 201.

207: "doing a criminal": George Collins, interview by author. The same point was made by Jim McDougal's lawyer (Sam Heuer, interview by author).

208: attempts to "demonize" them: Ray Jahn, interview by author.

208: "It was kind of a cloak-and-dagger": James Stewart, interview by author.

209: "How does this sound": Susan McDougal, interview by author.

210: "terrible episode at Claudia's, where": Susan McDougal, follow-up interview by author.

210: "To my knowledge": Claudia Riley, follow-up interview by author.

210: "I wanted to talk": Susan McDougal, interview by author.

210: "willing to make": Robert McDaniel, interview by author.

211: "We almost fainted": Claudia Riley, remarks made while author was interviewing Susan McDougal.

211: "I just basically said": Ray Jahn, interview by author.

211: "I am penniless": Susan McDougal, interview by author.

211: "If it were my daughter, I would": Claudia Riley, remarks made while author was interviewing Susan McDougal.

211: "we both cried": Susan McDougal, interview by author. For Susan McDougal's written account of these events, which is similar but not identical, see McDougal and Harris, *The Woman Who Wouldn't Talk,* 206–207.

211: "Susan, they're going": Susan McDougal, interview by author; McDougal and Harris, *The Woman Who Wouldn't Talk,* 209.

212: Susan McDougal had returned: "Sentencing Date Altered for Susan McDougal," *Arkansas Democrat-Gazette,* 7 Aug. 1996, B12.

212: had been sentenced: Howard also ordered Tucker to pay a fine of $25,000 and restitution to the Small Business Administration of $293,951 (Joe Stumpe, "Susan McDougal Used to Breathing Society's Rarefied Air," *Arkansas Democrat-Gazette,* 21 Aug. 1996, A7).

212: "attempted to camouflage": Memo of the United States Regarding the Sentencing of Susan McDougal, 19 Aug. 1996, Susan McDougal papers; Stumpe, "Susan McDougal Used to Breathing."

212: Judge Howard hammered: Ibid.; McDougal and Harris, *The Woman Who Wouldn't Talk,* 212.

212: as Bill Clinton boarded: "Le Grande Show Démocrate va Faire la fête à Clinton," *Soir,* 26 Aug. 1996, Susan McDougal papers.

213: "It is tempting": "McDougal" clipping, *Arkansas Democrat-Gazette*, 3 Sept. 1996, A7, Susan McDougal papers.

213: A raw transcript: Susan McDougal, interview by Diane Sawyer, *Prime Time Live,* ABC News, 30 Aug. 1996, unedited transcript, tape 4, pages 4–18, 4–19 (obtained from Office of Independent Counsel through Freedom of Information Act request).

213: "that I was hiding something": McDougal and Harris, *The Woman Who Wouldn't Talk,* 218.

214: Can you tell us, ma'am: Susan McDougal and Ray Jahn, Grand Jury Testimony, 4 Sept. 1996, transcript, contained in OIC indictment of Susan McDougal, 4 May 1998.

214: "I was shaking": Susan McDougal, interview by author.

215: "clashed with their theory": "McDougal" clipping, *Arkansas Democrat-Gazette,* 3 Sept. 1996, A7, Susan McDougal papers.

215: Judge Wright tapped: Stumpe, Supra; McDougal and Harris, *The Woman Who Wouldn't Talk*, 227.

215: "An abiding, unrelenting": Susan McDougal, interview by author.

217: (The FBI's own analysis): Final Report/Ray, vol. 2, 42–44, 61–63.

217: "No. No. I was in love": Susan McDougal, interview by author.

218: "We're not that kind": Ray Jahn, interview by author.

218: McDougal threw: McDougal and Harris, *The Woman Who Wouldn't Talk,* 233–34.

Chapter 17: Paula Jones Goes to Washington

219: Even the conservative *Washington Times* observed: Frank J. Murray, "Clinton Won't Face Jones Suit Before Election," *Washington Times,* 25 June 1996, A1.

219: "high-profile controversial": Susan Carpenter-McMillan, interview by author.

219: She had launched: Ibid. Carpenter-McMillan would later say, "Thank God—glory goes to God—it succeeded."

220: Where she came: Joseph Cammarata, interview by author.

221: "What Clinton is asking": Memo to File, 2 Nov. 1994. See also these documents from Gilbert Davis papers: Memo to File, "Demeaning the Integrity," undated; Memo to File, "Oral Argument on Immunity," undated.

221: Davis was ready to go it alone: Gilbert Davis, interview by author.

221: Robert Bork and Theodore Olson: Isikoff, *Uncovering Clinton*, 110.

222: "The president has confused": Gilbert Davis, interview by author.

222: Dellinger had clerked: Walter Dellinger, interview by author. Dellinger had served as assistant attorney general and headed the Office of Legal Counsel before becoming acting solicitor general.

223: "The receptionist says": Joseph Cammarata, interview by author.

224: stated that the event in question: Joseph Cammarata, "Telephone Call with Woman," handwritten notes, undated, Joseph Cammarata papers; Affidavit of Joseph Cammarata, 5 Sept. 1997, Cammarata papers.

224: As she walked out: One was later identified as Treasury Secretary Lloyd Bentsen, whose calendar confirmed that he met with Clinton at 3 P.M. that afternoon (Matt Drudge, "Tripp

Turns on Clinton, Tells of Willey Episode," *Drudge Report,* 3 Feb. 1997).

224: "couldn't locate her husband": Cammarata, "Telephone Call with Woman"; Affidavit of Joseph Cammarata, 5 Sept. 1997, Cammarata papers; Mark Johnson, "Willey Death Likely Suicide," *Richmond Times,* undated, Cammarata papers. In fact, the body of Willey's husband was discovered the following day. His death came just a week before the Virginia State Bar was set to investigate his handling of a quarter-million-dollar payout on a land deal in Richmond.

225: "Okay. Fine": Joseph Cammarata, interview by author.

225: "Urgent, urgent": Walter Dellinger, interview by author.

225: Some were dressed: Gilbert Davis, interview by author.

225: "Neither Paula Jones nor President Clinton will": Tom Squitieri and Tony Maura, "Issue Has Little to Do with Sex Harassment," *USA Today,* 13 Jan. 1997, A1.

226: "Mr. Chief Justice and may it please": Official Transcript of Proceedings Before the Supreme Court of the United States, *Clinton v. Jones,* 3, Gilbert Davis papers.

226: "we were off": Gilbert Davis, interview by author.

226: "other women" would "tend": Official Transcript of Proceedings, 53–54.

227: "His efforts were": Gilbert Davis, interview by author.

227: Cammarata picked: Joseph Cammarata, interview by author.

227: But the mystery: Kathleen Willey, interview by author. Willey further stated that her phone records proved that she had not called from her home or work, and she insisted that she took a lie detector test administered by OIC to confirm that she had not placed the call. Where the truth of the story lies remains unclear.

Chapter 18: Monica S. Lewinsky

231: These protectors: Andrew Morton, *Monica's Story,* 84.

231: But this particular former intern was: Monica Lewinsky, Grand Jury Testimony, 6 Aug. 1998, 60–65; U.S. Senate, *Impeachment of President William Jefferson Clinton, Evidentiary Record,* vol. 3, part 1, 780–85 (hereinafter cited as Evidentiary Record).

231: Monica had taken: Tripp, another former White House employee, had been one of the

only witnesses immediately after Kathleen
Willey's encounter with the president.

232: Yet her focus was: Marcia Lewis Straus,
interview by author.

232: Bernie and Marcia Lewinsky understood:
Morton, *Monica's Story*, 19–20.

232: Their backgrounds allowed: Marcia Lewis
Straus, interview by author.

232: "I was already planning": Monica Lewinsky, interview by author.

232: It was a fun job: Bernie Lewinsky, interview
by author.

232: Marcia Lewis had divorced: M. J. Firestone,
"Unsinkable Marcia," *Georgetown & Country* 5
(1998): A1–A7; Morton, *Monica's Story*, 22, 32.

233: Marcia had found: Marcia Lewis Straus,
follow-up interview by author.

233: She could attend: Ibid.; Monica Lewinsky,
interview by author.

233: As far as the notion: Monica Lewinsky, interview by author.

233: "It's definitely going": "Hillary's Inaugural
Ball Makeover," *Beverly Hills Magazine* 1, no. 2
(1992). Monica later stated that she had little to
do with the magazine.

234: recommended his own grandson: Walter
Kaye, Grand Jury Testimony, 21 May 1998,
60.

234: "It was sometime after": Walter Kaye, FBI
interview, transcript, Office of Independent
Counsel, 1 Apr. 1998, 1–2.

234: "I was born": Bernie Lewinsky, interview
by author.

234: "I just remember": Monica Lewinsky,
interview by author.

235: "came home happy": Marcia Lewis Straus,
interview by author.

235: "Oh sure, it would be": Monica Lewinsky,
interview by author. President Clinton, during
the course of his interviews for this book, declined to discuss his relationship with Ms.
Lewinsky.

235: "He gave me the full": Morton, *Monica's
Story*, 58–59.

235: "flirtation that went": Monica Lewinsky,
Grand Jury Testimony, 6 Aug. 1998, 9; Evidentiary Record, vol. 3, part 1, 729.

236: Monica rushed home: Morton, *Monica's
Story*, 59.

236: "No. Not at": Monica Lewinsky, interview
by author.

236: "I, as a father": Bernie Lewinsky, interview
by author.

**236: shutdown of all federal government offices
in an effort:** Blumenthal, *The Clinton Wars*, 135.

236: Having just been promoted: Morton,
Monica's Story, 60.

237: "continued flirtation": Monica Lewinsky,
Grand Jury Testimony, 6 Aug. 1998, 10–11;
Evidentiary Record, vol. 3, part 1, 730–31.

237: He was wandering: Monica Lewinsky to
author, January 26, 2009.

237: She playfully lifted: Morton, *Monica's
Story*, 63.

237: "a softness and tenderness": Morton,
Monica's Story, 63.

237: Several hours later: Lewinsky, Grand Jury
Testimony, 12; Evidentiary Record, vol. 3, part 1,
732.

238: Monica awakened: Morton, *Monica's Story*, 65.

238: Two nights later: Lewinsky, Grand Jury
Testimony, 16; Evidentiary Record, vol. 3, part 1,
736.

238: She would enter: Lewinsky, Grand Jury
Testimony, 57; Evidentiary Record, vol. 3, part 1,
777; Morton, *Monica's Story*, 66–71.

238: there was never: Lewinsky, Grand Jury
Testimony, 36; Evidentiary Record, vol. 3, part 1,
756.

239: Did the relationship with: Lewinsky, Grand
Jury Testimony, 17–18; Evidentiary Record, vol. 3,
part 1, 737–38.

239: "She told us how": Bernie Lewinsky, interview by author.

239: "Those who know": Barbara Lewinsky,
remarks made while author was interviewing
Bernie Lewinsky.

239: When the Lewinsky family gathered:
Morton, *Monica's Story*, 86.

239: "Monica insisted": Barbara Lewinsky,
comments made while author was interviewing
Bernie Lewinsky.

240: "Girly, the President sure": Morton,
Monica's Story, 86.

240: Marcia would describe: Marcia Lewis
Straus, interview by author.

241: President Clinton confessed: Lewinsky,
Grand Jury Testimony, 25; Evidentiary Record,
vol. 3, part 1, 745.

241: "We had not hidden": Gilbert Davis, interview by author.

Chapter 19: Inside a Texas Prison

242: In an article: "McDougal Changes
Story," *Arkansas Democrat-Gazette*, 16 Feb.
1997, 12.

242: "It was just a country": Joe Stumpe and Jim Brooks, "McDougal's Claim of Intercepted Call Highly Improbable," *Arkansas Democrat-Gazette*, 15 Feb. 1997, A10 (emphasis added). McDougal's lawyer, Sam Heuer, would later recall no mention by McDougal of a purported affair between Susan and Clinton (Sam Heuer, interview by author).

243: A remarkable FBI document: Office of the Independent Counsel, "Dates of Interviews with James McDougal," 9 June 1997.

243: On occasion, McDougal's "coloring": Ray Jahn, interview by author.

243: Yet Jahn did ascertain: Ray Jahn, follow-up interview with author, 2 Dec. 2008.

243: Another defining moment: Ken Starr, interview by author.

243: Bob Bittman, the young prosecutor: Robert J. Bittman, interview by author.

244: The *National Law Journal*: "His Reach Knows No Bounds," *National Law Journal*, 6 Jan. 1997, B12.

244: "a wonderful and right": Joe Stumpe, "Starr Has New Job in August," *Arkansas Democrat-Gazette*, 18 Feb. 1997, A1.

244: It would put to rest: Jack Nelson, "Starr Report Rules Out Foul Play in Foster Death," *Los Angeles Times*, 23 Feb. 1997, A1.

245: Since the investigation was still centered: Ken Starr, interview by author.

245: "I thought that he had": Bill Clinton, interview by author.

245: Former Independent Counsel: Stumpe, "Starr Has New Job."

245: Ted Olson: "Investigation of Clintons Is Far from Completed, Starr Insists," *Commercial Appeal*, 19 Feb. 1997, A1. See also Glenn R. Simpson, "Whitewater Counsel Takes University Post," *Wall Street Journal*, 18 Feb. 1997, A3.

245: Rumors began sweeping through: Rodney Bowers, "Juries in 4 Mock Trials Let Clintons Off, Source Says," *Arkansas Democrat-Gazette*, 15 Feb. 1997, A1.

245: "It was like": Ken Starr, interview by author.

245: "What do you think": Sam Dash, interview by author.

246: William Safire, in a *New York Times* piece: William Safire, "The Big Flinch," *New York Times*, 20 Jan. 1997; Blumenthal, *The Clinton Wars*, 330.

246: called Starr's departure: "A Waning Starr," *Arkansas Democrat-Gazette*, 19 Feb. 1997, A10.

246: He arranged: "Investigation of Clintons Is Far from Completed, Starr Insists," Memphis *Commercial Appeal*, 19 Feb. 1997, A1; Jackie Bennett, interview by author.

246: "When I make": Craig S. Karpel, "Conflict of Interest," *Strategic Weekly Briefings*, Agora Financial Publishing, 28 Jan. 1997, 2.

246: "You know, the first rule": Bill Clinton, interview by author.

247: "Starr can now kiss": Karpel, "Conflict of Interest," 1.

247: Richard Mellon Scaife, the conservative: Nelson, "Starr Report Rules Out Foul Play."

247: Starr was "unproductive": Richard Mellon Scaife, interview by author.

247: "Maybe Ken Starr's a mole": John F. Kennedy, Jr., "Who's Afraid of Richard Mellon Scaife?" *George*, January 1999, 54, 57; Richard Mellon Scaife, interview by author.

247: Nothing in the historical: Sam Dash, interview by author.

248: The months leading: Bob Woodward, interview by author.

248: Woodward and Schmidt revealed: Bob Woodward and Susan Schmidt, "Starr Probes Clinton Personal Life," *Washington Post*, 25 June 1997, A1.

248: "The story was": Jackie Bennett, interview by author.

248: "The report in today's": David E. Kendall, press conference statement, 25 June 1997.

248: Starr would resent: Kenneth W. Starr to Honorable Henry J. Hyde and Honorable John Conyers, Jr., 11 Dec. 1998. Starr insisted that the questions directed at the troopers were designed to elicit information "whom then-Governor Clinton and Mrs. Clinton might have been close to and confided in." However, Starr respectfully declined to turn over rough notes of the interviews, "because the troopers interviewed were explicitly promised confidentiality" (ibid.).

248: Dash had laid out: Ken Starr, interview by author.

249: "a Stalinist show trial": Bill Clinton, interview by author.

249: "I always had": Bob Woodward, interview by author.

250: The new prisoner attended: Richard Clark, interview by author.

250: From his review: Federal Bureau of Prisons, Monthly Mental Status Report, 2 Oct. 1997, Richard Clark papers.

251: Clark summarized: Richard Clark, interview by author.

Chapter 20: The Settlement That Never Happened

252: The white-haired Justice John Paul Stevens, considered: Joan Biskupic, "Legal Setback for Clinton," *The (Bergen County, N.J.) Record,* 28 May 1997, A1.

252: "only three sitting Presidents": *Clinton v. Jones,* 520 U.S. 681, 684 (1997). The only justice to distance himself from the opinion was Clinton appointee Stephen Breyer, who concurred and noted that he was "less sanguine" than his brethren about the practical ramifications of this ruling (ibid., 722).

252: Dellinger worried: Walter Dellinger, interview by author.

252: The *New York Post* blared: Rita Delfiner, "Paula's Lawyer Wants 'Private' Peek at Prez," *New York Post,* 28 May 1997, 20.

252: As President Clinton posed: Clinton, *My Life,* 756.

252: the American press was already predicting: Biskupic, "Legal Setback."

252: "She was ecstatic": Joseph Cammarata, interview by author.

253: "The two of us just screamed": Biskupic, "Legal Setback."

253: "one of the most naive": Bill Clinton, interview by author.

253: "The opinion was just part": Justice John Paul Stevens, interview by author.

254: Michael Isikoff published: Michael Isikoff, "A Twist in Jones v. Clinton," *Newsweek,* 11 Aug. 1997, 30.

254: A week earlier: Matt Drudge, "Tripp Turns on Clinton, Tells of Willey Episode," *Drudge Report,* 3 Aug. 1997, www.drudgereport.com/2.txt.

254: Both publications revealed: According to Isikoff, "A Twist," 30, Tripp said that she had bumped into Willey in the West Wing immediately after she left the Oval Office, and Willey looked "disheveled. Her face was red and her lipstick was off." Willey then confided that the president had taken her into a small, private office, where he "kissed and fondled her."

255: Now Steele had recanted: Steele's revised story was that Willey had not (in fact) told her about the brush with Clinton until weeks after it happened; Willey had stated only that Clinton "made a pass at her," and Willey had not appeared upset when she conveyed the story (Isikoff, "A Twist," 30).

255: "I really smell": Drudge, "Tripp Turns on Clinton."

255: "They weren't crazy": Bill Clinton, interview by author.

255: Judge Susan Webber Wright had: Opinion and Order, *Jones v. Clinton,* 520 U.S. 681, 22 Aug. 1997.

255: "What I would hope": Status Conference, *Jones v. Clinton,* 520 U.S. 681, 22 Aug. 1994, 7, 28–30.

255: "The goal was to try": Robert Bennett, interview by author; Robert S. Bennett, *In the Ring: The Trials of a Washington Lawyer,* 237–38.

256: called his bluff: Joseph Cammarata, interview by author.

256: "donate all amounts": Paula Jones, press statement, 1 June 1997, Gilbert Davis papers.

256: The talk-show chatter: Charles D. Willis to Joseph Cammarata, 8 Aug. 1997, Gilbert Davis papers.

256: "any treatment or advice sought": Subpoena, *Jones v. Clinton,* 520 U.S. 681, 25 July 1997.

256: Cammarata also took: Joseph Cammarata to Daniel M. Traylor, 23 June 1997, Gilbert Davis papers.

256: in which he said: Stuart Taylor, Jr., and Timothy J. Burger, "Jones' Credibility," *Legal Times,* 23 June 1997, 20.

257: "effective immediately": Joseph Cammarata to Daniel M. Traylor, 23 June 1997.

257: both sides exchanged: Joseph Cammarata and Robert Bennett, interview, transcript, *Meet the Press,* NBC, 1 June 1997, 9.

257: "The President of the": Ibid., 17–18.

257: Clinton would also give: Gilbert Davis, interview by author.

257: "Yes. I mean": Bill Clinton, interview by author.

258: Chubb seemed eager: Gilbert Davis, interview by author. The Clintons had two umbrella policies that they had purchased for $120 and $130 respectively. One happened to cover claims for "false imprisonment" and the *Jones* complaint contained one count that alleged then-Governor Clinton had falsely detained Paula Corbin in the hotel room, allowing Clinton to receive several hundred thousand dollars' worth of coverage.

258: "that she could get *more*": Gilbert Davis, interview by author.

258: *"Twenty-million-dollar settlement"*: Susan Carpenter-McMillan, interview by author.

259: **Conservative activist-lawyer:** Isikoff, *Uncovering Clinton*, 182–84.

259: *"The parties agree"*: "Stipulation of Settlement," undated, attached to Gilbert Davis and Joseph Cammarata to Paula Jones, 29 Aug. 1997, Gilbert Davis papers.

259: *"It is a complete victory"*: Gilbert Davis and Joseph Cammarata to Paula Jones, 19 Aug. 1997, 1, Gilbert Davis papers (emphasis added).

260: **Davis and Cammarata offered:** Isikoff, *Uncovering Clinton*, 182.

260: *"Serious differences of opinion"*: Gilbert Davis and Joseph Cammarata to Paula Jones, 29 Aug. 1997, 1, Gilbert Davis papers.

261: *"Mr. Davis and Mr. Cammarata are"*: Order, *Jones v. Clinton*, 520 U.S. 681, 9 Sept. 1997, 58.

261: **He called Jones;** Daniel M. Traylor, interview by author.

261: *"She was the front"*: Bill Clinton, interview by author.

Chapter 21: Trapped Outside the White House

262: *"The early sort of halcyon"*: Marcia Lewis Straus, interview by author.

262: **The President wasn't responding:** Descriptions of the end of the relationship between Monica Lewinsky and Bill Clinton and their discussion of Kathleen Willey and Linda Tripp in July 1997 are from Lewinsky, Grand Jury Testimony, 68–71 and 75–79; Evidentiary Record, vol. 3, part 1, 788–91 and 795–97; and Morton, *Monica's Story*, 121 and 123.

264: **an illegal form of "punishment":** Mark Geragos, interview by Geraldo Rivera, *Rivera Live*, CNBC, 20 May 1997.

265: **Susan was facing:** "Susan McDougal's Ordeal," *Dateline with Stone Phillips*, NBC, 5 Oct. 1997. Nancy Mehta was a somewhat different plaintiff, on top of her wealth and her own status as a former Hollywood celebrity. She was former actress Nancy Kovack, a tall, long-legged beauty who had starred with Elvis Presley in *Frankie and Johnny* and then appeared in episodes of *Star Trek*, *Bewitched*, and a Tarzan film. The embezzlement charges against Susan related to a heap of credit card bills, most traceable to a single charge card in Nancy Mehta's name with bills sent to a different address accessed only by Susan. The eccentric conductor's wife insisted that the money had been stolen; Susan McDougal countered that she was given "permission" to use the credit card—the funds were voluntarily given to her as a bonus for "spending time" with Mrs. Mehta. That Susan virtually moved in with Nancy Mehta and became a housemate during her famous husband's prolonged absences added to the odd factual circumstances.

265: **Geragos now openly charged:** *Dateline,* 5 Oct. 1997; McDougal and Harris, *The Woman Who Wouldn't Talk*, 261–64.

265: **locked in a cell:** Alexander Cockburn, "The Torture of Susan McDougal," *Nation,* July 14, 1997, 9. This syndicated column appeared in papers across the country, detailing the allegedly inhumane nature of her incarceration.

265: **Susan's family weighed:** Susan McDougal family, interviewed on *Dateline with Stone Phillips,* NBC, 5 Oct. 1997.

266: *The Promoter*: Richard Clark, interview by author; Curtis Wilkie, interview by author.

266: *"increased feelings of depression"*: Monthly Mental Status Report, 31 Oct. 1997, Richard Clark papers.

266: *"he did not know"*: Richard Clark, interview by author.

267: *"very irritated"*: Ibid.; Notes of Counseling Session, Dr. Clark, 6 Nov. 1997.

267: **As the abandoned car was getting:** Dan Sewell, "McDougal Now Claims Clinton Took Loan from S&L," Associated Press, 12 Nov. 1997; "McDougal: Mystery Check a Secret Loan to Clinton," *Arkansas Democrat-Gazette,* 12 Nov. 1997; John Bridges, "Floyd Reluctant Figure in Whitewater," *Arkansas Democrat-Gazette,* 12 Nov. 1997, A12; Richard Clark, interview by author; Mental Status Check, Dr. James Womack, 11 Nov. 1997.

268: **convened his entire team:** Richard Clark, interview by author.

268: *"possible psychological basis"*: Richard Clark to Captain Corbett, memo, 13 Nov. 1997, Richard Clark papers.

268: **peppermints held:** McDougal and Wilkie, *Arkansas Mischief,* 240.

268: *"one of those moments"*: Richard Clark, interview by author.

269: *"he had never before"*: Clark to Corbett, memo, 13 Nov. 1997.

269: *"people would assume"*: Richard Clark, interview by author.

269: *"performance anxiety"*: Clark to Corbett, memo, 13 Nov. 1997.

270: **A carbon copy was sent:** Richard Clark, interview by author.

Chapter 22: The Hundred-Page Referral

270: In late September: Starr Report/Foster.

270: Rod Lankler, the Fiske prosecutor: Rod Lankler, interview by author.

271: The independent counsel law, enacted: Ethics in Government Act of 1978, 28 U.S.C. Section 595(c) (Independent Counsel Law).

271: There was virtually no: Gormley, "Impeachment and the Independent Counsel," 310–72.

271: "McDougal had given": Ken Starr, interview by author.

272: He had worked: Paul Rosenzweig, interview by author.

273: "Payoff Clinton": Final Report/Ray, vol. 1, 149–50.

273: Hale had testified: Ibid.; Final Report/Ray, vol. 1, 150–51.

273: OIC also asserted: Ibid.

274: "We're one witness": Ken Starr, interview by author.

274: Her cell was outfitted: McDougal and Harris, *The Woman Who Wouldn't Talk*, 279–88.

274: One citizen from New Mexico: Evelyn Post to Judge Wright, 3 Feb. 1998, and Fohn Farst to Judge Wright, 24 Apr. 1998, Judge Wright papers, U.S. District Court for the Eastern District of Arkansas.

275: They even considered: Ken Starr, interview by author; Hickman Ewing, Jr., interview by author.

275: which he delivered: Brock, *Blinded by the Right*, 299–300.

276: "Basically, Barr was trying": David Brock, interview by author.

276: Conservative writer Mark Helprin published: Mark Helprin, "Impeach," *Wall Street Journal*, 10 Oct. 1997, A22.

276: *American Spectator* editor: R. Emmett Tyrrell and Anonymous, *The Impeachment of William Jefferson Clinton*.

276: coauthored with a ghostwriter: Brock, *Blinded by the Right*, xviii, 301. Tyrell later stated that the coauthor was not Ted Olson, although he declined to identify the person or persons (R. Emmett Tyrell, interview by author).

276: Bork heaped praise: Robert H. Bork, "Should He Be Impeached?" *American Spectator*, Dec. 1997, 74–78.

277: impeachment drive that predated: David Brock, interview by author.

277: "You will not find": Ken Starr, interview by author.

Chapter 23: An Unexpected Caller

278: It was understandable: Isikoff, *Uncovering Clinton*, 261, 265.

279: originally built: John Bates, interview by author.

280: "Her answers and her demeanor": Hickman Ewing, Jr., interview by author.

280: "a mafia-like code of silence": Jackie Bennett, interview by author.

281: "In retrospect": Paul Rosenzweig, interview by author.

282: Gil Davis's records confirmed: Gilbert Davis, interview by author.

282: the four men enjoyed: Paul Rosenzweig, interview by author.

282: "I told him about": Isikoff, *Uncovering Clinton*, 267.

283: a picture of his wife: Jackie Bennett, interview by author.

283: "I don't play telephone": Paul Rosenzweig, interview by author.

284: Bennett remained focused: Jackie Bennett, interview by author.

284: OIC was even looking: Jerry Seper, "Once-Secret Memos Question Clinton's Honesty," *Washington Times*, 8 May 2006.

284: "it wasn't our deal": Jackie Bennett, interview by author.

284: A front-page article: Isikoff, *Uncovering Clinton*, 268.

284: it didn't take: Jackie Bennett, interview by author.

285: They met for Cokes: John Bates, interview by author.

285: "Listen, something's come up": Ken Starr, interview by author.

285: "I had absolutely no idea": Paul Rosenzweig, interview by author.

286: the presence of Vernon Jordan: Jackie Bennett, interview by author.

286: There was a general feeling: Paul Rosenzweig, interview by author.

286: He never suspected: Isikoff, *Uncovering Clinton*, 272.

286: Bennett stayed: Paul Rosenzweig, interview by author; Jackie Bennett, interview by author.

286: "This is her!": Jackie Bennett, interview by author.

288: "This was not": Ken Starr, interview by author.

289: become so conservative: Sol Wisenberg, interview by author.

289: **Wisenberg had worked:** Sol Wisenberg, follow-up interview by author.

289: **"There's something going on":** Jackie Bennett, interview by author.

290: **"dumpy, unattractive":** Sol Wisenberg, interview by author.

290: **She was wearing:** Jackie Bennett, interview by author.

290: **Tripp explained:** Sol Wisenberg, interview by author.

291: **"dreaming it":** Jackie Bennett, interview by author.

291: **"We were incredibly":** Sol Wisenberg, interview by author.

292: **Steve Irons, a senior FBI official:** Isikoff, *Uncovering Clinton*, 280.

292: **"If it had been":** Jackie Bennett, interview by author.

292: **Bennett told Irons:** Susan Schmidt and Michael Weisskopf, *The Truth at Any Cost: Ken Starr and the Unmaking of Bill Clinton*, 23.

292: **One of the principal worries:** Jackie Bennett, interview by author.

292: **Her lunch date with Monica Lewinsky was:** Isikoff, *Uncovering Clinton*, 281–82; Schmidt and Weisskopf, *Truth at Any Cost*, 24.

292: **"We're going to":** Jackie Bennett, interview by author.

293: **"where might this wire":** Ken Starr, interview by author.

293: **"Linda . . . is being":** Jackie Bennett, interview by author.

293: **Tripp recorded in a "Steno Notebook":** Tripp notes, in Evidentiary Record, vol. 4, part 3, 3797–3843. See also Isikoff, *Uncovering Clinton*, 281–82; Schmidt and Weisskopf, *Truth at Any Cost*, 24.

293: **"Oh, my god":** Isikoff, *Uncovering Clinton*, 283.

294: **As incriminating stories:** Tripp-Lewinsky conversation, 13 Jan. 1998; "From the Evidence: Tripp's Story," *Washington Post*, 3 Oct. 1998, A 24.

294: **FBI agents quickly contacted:** Jackie Bennett, interview by author.

Chapter 24: A Cubicle in the Pentagon

295: **"I felt that it was":** Linda Tripp, interview by author.

295: **The Carotenuto household was:** Linda Tripp, interview by author; Elaine Sciolino and Don Van Natta, Jr., "Testing of a President: The

Confidant; Linda Tripp, Elusive Keeper of Secrets, Mainly Her Own," *New York Times*, 15 Mar. 1998, 1.

295: **Linda Tripp had passed up:** Linda Tripp, interview by author.

297: **"I don't know who killed":** Sciolino and Van Natta, "Testing of a President," 1.

297: **"I *never* hated":** Linda Tripp, interview by author.

297: **"She had enormous":** Lucianne Goldberg, interview by author.

298: **Her office was:** Sciolino and Van Natta, "Testing of a President"; Linda Tripp, interview by author.

298: **"So one day, here comes":** Linda Tripp, interview by author. Kenneth Bacon, assistant secretary of defense for Public Affairs, later told the FBI that he had no discussions with anyone in the White House about hiring Ms. Lewinsky (Evidentiary Record, vol. 4, part 1, 5–12). He did receive complaints from some employees that Lewinsky's work was "less than satisfactory," but Bacon stated that she improved after he raised these concerns. Finally, Bacon stressed that Lewinsky did not discuss any relationship with the president, although "she bragged about a tie she had given the President as a gift and would bring this to his attention when he was wearing it on television."

299: **"She's extremely likable":** Linda Tripp, interview by author.

300: **In one exchange:** Linda Tripp and Monica Lewinsky e-mails, 5 Mar. 1997, in Evidentiary Record, vol. 4, part 1, 915–16.

300: **The e-mails also show:** Ibid., 1007–1008.

300: **On Valentine's Day:** Ibid., 923–24.

301: **The feisty agent:** Lucianne Goldberg, interview by author.

301: **"advice and protection":** Linda Tripp and Lucianne Goldberg, telephone conversations, in Evidentiary Record, vol. 14, 160–71. See also Isikoff, *Uncovering Clinton*, 175, 190–97.

301: **"This is so":** Linda Tripp and Lucianne Goldberg, telephone conversations, in Evidentiary Record, vol. 14, 160–71; Isikoff, *Uncovering Clinton*, 189. See also Lucianne Steinberger Goldberg, FD 302 of interview (FBI form for notes of interviews), 17 July 1998, in Evidentiary Record, vol. 4, part 1, 1227 (discussing 18 Sept. 1997 tape).

302: **"Monica Lewinsky had been talking":** Linda Tripp, interview by author.

303: In another taped conversation: Linda Tripp and Lucianne Goldberg, telephone conversation, in Evidentiary Record, vol. 14, 166–71. Isikoff had already located Tripp and extracted the essence of her story.

304: "It was Lucianne who suggested": Linda Tripp, interview by author.

306: One day when she arrived: Ibid.

307: Tripp received: Ibid.; Morton, *Monica's Story*, 155.

308: "toyed with the idea": Monica Lewinsky, interview by author. See also Isikoff, *Uncovering Clinton*, 200–201, 207–209.

308: time to hit the road: Monica Lewinsky, interview by author.

308: On October 7: Isikoff, *Uncovering Clinton*, 201, 207, 212.

308: Monica was scheduled: Ibid., 215–16; Morton, *Monica's Story*, 138–39.

309: Betty Currie arranged: Isikoff, *Uncovering Clinton*, 219–20.

309: "There certainly was": Monica Lewinsky, interview by author.

309: Clinton had added: Morton, *Monica's Story*, 156–58.

310: Monica would forever: Monica did tell her biographer, years later, that she had confessed to Jordan that she and Clinton had engaged in *some* form of hanky-panky, but that "it had stopped just short of full sex" (ibid., 165).

310: "I thought": Monica Lewinsky, interview by author.

310: Tripp had recently made a bizarre proclamation: Morton, *Monica's Story*, 155–56.

310: Her friend's strange behavior: Monica Lewinsky, interview by author.

311: "Mr. Carter, this is": Frank Carter, interview by author.

313: Carter ran off: Ibid.; Monica Lewinsky, interview by author.

313: Wednesday, January 7: Jane Doe No. 6 (Monica Lewinsky), Affidavit, 7 Jan. 1998, in Evidentiary Record, vol. 3, part 1, 1235; Morton, *Monica's Story*, 166; Isikoff, *Uncovering Clinton*, 265.

313: "No one else": Frank Carter, interview by author.

313: "I have never had": Morton, *Monica's Story*, 166–67.

313: "Okay, I can argue": Monica Lewinsky, interview by author.

314: The president had already answered: Isikoff, *Uncovering Clinton*, 225.

314: she was offered: Morton, *Monica's Story*, 168; Toobin, *A Vast Conspiracy*, 195.

314: "We had exchanged": Monica Lewinsky to author, January 26, 2009.

Chapter 25: Pinning the Tail on Clinton

314: "I'll never forget": Paula Jones, interview by author.

315: "I knew we had": Susan Carpenter-McMillan, interview by author.

315: after the Virginia lawyers had bowed: Carla Hall and David G. Savage, "Dallas Lawyers Take On Paula Jones' Case," *Los Angeles Times*, 2 Oct. 1997, 14.

315: Within days, founder: For a thorough discussion of the role of John Whitehead and the Rutherford Institute, see Lindsay Barnes, "Suing the President: Charlottesville Lawyer John Whitehead Reflects on How Paula Jones Changed Him, the Lives of the Clintons and the Course of History," (*Richmond, VA*) *Style Weekly*, 13 Feb. 2008, 14.

315: He had led the picketing: Thomas G. Watts, "Dallas Firm to Represent Paula Jones," *Dallas Morning News*, 2 Oct. 1997, A1.

315: Two of his partners: Wesley Holmes, interview by author.

315: "Well, to state": Jim Fisher, interview by author.

315: Here was a chance: Wesley Holmes, interview by author.

316: "Among her good qualities are": Jim Fisher, interview by author.

316: "some sort of parallel": Wesley Holmes, interview by author.

318: The Dallas lawyers quickly filed: First Amended Complaint, *Jones v. Clinton*, 27 Oct. 1997.

318: the attorneys also filed: This was actually filed on October 1, in the interim before the Dallas lawyers were officially hired to take over the case. Plaintiff's Second Set of Interrogatories, *Jones v. Clinton*, 1 Oct. 1997, No. 8.

318: At a secret status conference: Wesley Holmes, interview by author; Toobin, *A Vast Conspiracy*, 207.

318: "And I have candy": *Jones v. Clinton*, in-camera hearing, 12 Jan. 1997, 3.

319: agreed that Carpenter-McMillan: *Jones v. Clinton*, in-camera hearing, 12 Jan. 1997, 10, 32.

319: He had served as counsel: Claude R. Marx, "Lawyer Robert Bennett," *Investor's Business Daily*, circa 1995.

319: "I regret": Pine Bluff Transcript, 27, 30–31; Toobin, *A Vast Conspiracy*, 209; Wesley Holmes, interview by author; Jim Fisher, interview by author.

320: "I'm also aware": Wesley Holmes, interview by author.

320: Fisher spoke nonchalantly: Pine Bluff Transcript, 35–39. See also Jim Fisher, interview by author; Wesley Holmes, interview by author.

321: "All right": Pine Bluff Transcript, 37–38.

321: "We had hit pay dirt": Jim Fisher, interview by author.

322: Bob Bennett again spoke: Pine Bluff Transcript, 45.

322: "I think, really": Ibid., 47, 53.

322: "I felt she": Robert Bennett, interview by author.

323: Holmes would recall: Wesley Holmes, interview by author.

323: "Frank, whenever I get": See, generally, Robert S. Bennett, *In the Ring,* 250–51. A variety of sources confirmed this account.

Chapter 26: Panic in the Justice Department

324: the conversation between: Jackie Bennett, interview by author; Schmidt and Weisskopf, *Truth at Any Cost,* 25.

325: Jackie Bennett later recalled: Jackie Bennett, interview by author.

325: lasting no more than: Ibid.; Schmidt and Weisskopf, *Truth at Any Cost,* 58.

325: "I'm sitting there fully conscious that": Jackie Bennett, interview by author.

326: The Little Rock office: Ibid.

326: In Bennett's view: Jackie Bennett, interview by author; Paul Rosenzweig, interview by author.

326: "I think we need": Mike Emmick, quoted by Jackie Bennett, interview by author.

327: He was thoroughly unimpressed: Jackie Bennett, interview by author.

327: Jackie Bennett and other hard-chargers: Sol Wisenberg, interview by author.

327: "Nothing we were ever going to do": Jackie Bennett, interview by author.

327: "We have a duty": Schmidt and Weisskopf, *Truth at Any Cost,* 27.

327: Starr made sure: Sol Wisenberg, interview by author.

327: In Starr's mind: Ken Starr, interview by author.

328: Linda Tripp had made clear: Ibid.

328: "That kind of [reflected] how": Paul Rosenzweig, interview by author.

328: "moral obligation": Ken Starr, interview by author.

328: "We repair frequently": Paul Rosenzweig, interview by author.

328: Starr asked Jackie: Jackie Bennett, interview by author.

329: "We are sort of into": Jackie Bennett's side of phone conversation with Eric Holder, 14 Jan. 1998, attached to Robert J. Bittman to David P. Schippers and Abbe D. Lowell, Committee on the Judiciary, 18 Nov. 1998; Jackie Bennett, interview by author.

329: "I don't want": Eric Holder, interview by author.

329: Bennett ended his one-way conversation by: Jackie Bennett, interview by author.

329: If he could replay: Ken Starr, interview by author.

329: Some observers: See, generally, Ken Gormley, "Impeachment and the Independent Counsel: A Dysfunctional Union," *Stanford Law Review* 51 (1999): 309.

330: The three-judge panel: In Re: Madison Guaranty Savings & Loan, Order Appointing Independent Counsel, 5 Aug. 1994. The court wrote: "It is not our intent to impugn the integrity of the Attorney General's appointee, but rather to reflect the intent of the Act that the actor be protected against perceptions of conflict."

330: In one exchange: Linda Tripp and Monica Lewinsky e-mails, 27 Oct. 1997, in Evidentiary Record, vol. 4, part 1, 980.

331: She wanted Monica to drive: Morton, *Monica's Story,* 172–74; Linda Tripp, interview by author.

331: The first paragraph suggested: "Points to Make in Affidavit" (three-page document), Evidentiary Record, vol. 3, part 1, 1241–43.

332: Lewinsky insisted: Monica Lewinsky, interview by author, and follow-up interview by author.

332: "The verbiage was": Linda Tripp, interview by author.

332: Yet Tripp never wavered: Ibid. Tripp later revealed that she had confirmed that the Talking Points had been physically typed on Monica's computer. She discovered this fact "inadvertently" one day, cooling her heels in the OIC offices waiting to meet with Starr's lawyers. On the desk in front of her were "little pieces of typed stuff" that turned out to be "extractions" from Monica's computer. Tripp had stretched her neck far enough to see that one document was a copy of the Talking Points. A notation from the FBI on the sheet indicated that it had come from Monica's computer. Said Tripp: "I didn't move from my chair, but I could see." In Tripp's mind, this only buttressed her theory that the document "was dictated." Tripp concluded, "She can tell you that [she wrote them] until she's blue in the face. And if you'd spent a year and a half doing the editing for her writing, you would know that [she is not telling the truth]."

333: a lengthy scholarly article: Monica Lewinsky, interview by author. The paper to which Lewinsky was referring had been sent to her lawyer and kept in storage. See Willard Fox and John F. X. Gillis, Point "Talking Points" Abstract, June 5, 1998, Monica Lewinsky papers. Under oath, Monica repeated her assertion that she was the sole author of the Talking Points (Evidentiary Record, vol. 3, part 1, 944–47).

333: shift radically in style and clarity: The first page is grammatically and organizationally the cleanest. The second page switches from second to first person. The third page is a mishmash and is the least polished in style. Although Monica Lewinsky, through her autobiographer, later insisted that she prepared two different versions—one for Tripp herself and one for Tripp to give her lawyer—this still fails to explain the puzzling (and obvious) difference in writing styles (cf. Morton, *Monica's Story*, 173, 256).

333: Linda Tripp promptly handed: Schmidt and Weisskopf, *Truth at Any Cost*, 37; Toobin, *A Vast Conspiracy*, 199.

333: "I'm probably not a good person to answer": Monica Lewinsky, interview by author.

333: "Absolutely was not": Linda Tripp, interview by author.

334: Eric Holder was bedeviled: Jackie Bennett, interview by author.

334: He had admired: Eric Holder, interview by author.

334: "Late afternoon": Jackie Bennett's side of phone conversation with Eric Holder, 15 Jan. 1998, attached to Robert J. Bittman to David P. Schippers and Abbe D. Lowell, Committee on the Judiciary, 18 Nov. 1998.

334: The two men finally agreed: Jackie Bennett, interview by author.

334: "I know what you guys have": Isikoff, *Uncovering Clinton*, 297.

334: "sort of threatening": Jackie Bennett, interview by author.

335: The journalist slapped his cards: Ibid.

335: "So if there's some reason": Michael Isikoff, quoted by Jackie Bennett, interview by author.

335: "basis for starting": Isikoff, *Uncovering Clinton*, 298–300.

336: "We have unhappily come": Stephen Bates to OIC File, "DOJ meeting 1-15-98," 22 Apr. 1998.

336: "I mean, I was": Eric Holder, interview by author.

336: "Isikoff is on to": Notes, undated, attached to L. Anthony Sutin, Acting Assistant Attorney General, to Honorable John Conyers, Jr., Committee on the Judiciary, 16 Nov. 1998; Eric Holder, interview by author.

337: One idea the prosecutors kicked: Eric Holder, interview by author.

337: "picked [Lewinsky] up": Eric Holder, interview by author; Eric Holder notes, OIC meeting, 15 Jan. 1998.

337: "had no contact": Eric Holder, interview by author.

337: OIC also reemphasized: Ibid. Notes of the meeting indicate OIC's assessment of Jordan: "Jordan's involvement in obstruction not clear on tape but supposed to be in prior conversations." Linda Tripp would forever insist that Monica Lewinsky had explicitly told her that Jordan was a knowing participant in the plan to cover up the affair with Clinton, and that she (Tripp) had simply flubbed up by failing to turn on her Radio Shack recording device to capture that conversation on tape.

337: "violation of the law": Eric Holder, interview by author.

337: One topic that did *not* come: Ibid. Holder later stated that he surely would have included this crucial fact in his notes if the topic had come up. See also Summary of Meeting with IC on 15 Jan. 1998, attached to L. Anthony Sutin to Honorable John Conyers, Jr., Committee on the Judiciary, 16 Nov. 1998; Isikoff, *Uncovering Clinton*, 300.

338: "No, they were advocating": Eric Holder, interview by author.

338: Other DOJ lawyers: Not only was Eric Holder clear in his recollection on this point, but others concurred. For instance, Kevin Ohlson (interview by author) said, "They were very much the advocates for gaining jurisdiction over this issue." Although Jackie Bennett would later say, "We weren't lobbying for it," and would point to portions of the notes of the meeting indicating that OIC was open to someone else's handling of the case, that was not the dominant thrust of the meeting. Indeed, Bennett himself said that "this is something we're invested in" and that he believed Starr's office was entitled to expand into it (Jackie Bennett, interview by author). Moreover, the letter Starr sent to Janet Reno that night clearly indicated that OIC believed it had a right and duty to handle the case, and even spelled out proposed language by which the attorney general could formally expand OIC's jurisdiction to eliminate any issue about its ability to proceed. See Kenneth W. Starr to Janet Reno, 15 Jan. 1998, attached to L. Anthony Sutin, Acting Assistant Attorney General, to Honorable John Conyers, Jr., Committee on the Judiciary, 16 Nov. 1998.

338: "I'm sorry to leave": Stephen Bates to OIC File, 15 Jan. 1998, 3.

338: Ken Starr huddled: Ken Starr, interview by author.

338: Starr argued: Kenneth W. Starr to Janet Reno, 15 Jan. 1998, attached to L. Anthony Sutin, Acting Assistant Attorney General, to Honorable John Conyers, Jr., Committee on the Judiciary, 16 Nov. 1998.

Chapter 27: Vanity to Prayer

339: Eric Holder had resisted: Eric Holder, interview by author; Janet Reno, interview by author.

339: Reno had just returned: Janet Reno, interview by author.

340: "The burdens of office": The precise quote from Stevenson, delivered on July 26, 1952, in accepting the Democratic nomination for president in 1952, was: "The burdens [of the presidency] stagger the imagination. Its potential for good or evil now and in the years of our lives smothers exultation and converts vanity to prayer" (Richard Dowis, *The Lost Art of the Great Speech,* 192).

342: Bittman paged Pam Craig: Pam Roller Craig, interview by author.

343: Janet Reno convened: Kevin Ohlson, interview by author.

343: She folded her arms: Eric Holder, interview by author.

343: This story could blow: Kevin Ohlson, interview by author.

344: Eric Holder was thinking: Eric Holder, interview by author.

344: Just one month before the Lewinsky-Tripp: "The Decision Is Mine," *NewsHour with Jim Lehrer,* PBS, 2 Dec. 1997; Robert Suro, "Reno Decides Against Independent Counsel to Probe Clinton, Gore," *Washington Post,* 3 Dec. 1997, A1.

344: "damned if I did": Janet Reno, interview by author.

345: Just as OIC prosecutors rightly concluded: Kevin Ohlson, interview by author.

345: "I loved a guy like": Ben Bradlee, interview by author.

346: Michael Isikoff would later: Michael Isikoff, interview by author, December 29, 2009. For a fuller account of Isikoff's complicated position as a journalist, see *Uncovering Clinton,* 356–58.

346: Lucianne Goldberg: Lucianne Goldberg, interview by author; Lucianne Goldberg, "Spikey's Hypocrisy," *Slate,* 31 Mar. 1999. Isikoff himself has expressed ambivalence about his own role, once he was "sucked into the story," and acknowledged that "legitimate journalistic issues linger" in that regard (*Uncovering Clinton,* 356).

347: The argument that Linda Tripp: Starr later reiterated this argument: "She [Linda Tripp] had a record with us. We knew her. We felt she was highly intelligent, extremely knowledgeable, quite well informed, and was, from all that appeared, trying to be helpful. . . . And she was very much in our minds because we spent a lot of time worrying about the state of mind of Vincent Foster, Jr." (Ken Starr, interview by author).

347: Tripp herself would later acknowledge: Linda Tripp, interview by author.

347: "something more of": Paul Rosenzweig, interview by author.

347: "I made that a big deal": Linda Tripp, interview by author.

347: as demonstrated by: For information on the Vernon Jordan issue, *Final Report In Re: Madison Guaranty Savings & Loan Association, Regarding Monica Lewinsky and Others, Robert W. Ray, Independent Counsel.* Washington DC: U.S. Government Printing Office, 2002, 28–29, 34 n. 113.

347: Especially alarming: Ken Starr, interview by author. Although Starr did not know about this link, Jackie Bennett certainly did.

348: Holder and others felt: Eric Holder, interview by author.

348: "I never had": Sol Wisenberg, interview by author.

348: As one senior DOJ lawyer: A number of Justice Department lawyers, commenting off the record on this moment when the Starr investigation slid off the track, would express their views that a little prosecutorial diplomacy also might have gone a long way. Some government attorneys, speaking anonymously, said that a seasoned prosecutor might have quietly conveyed the message to White House counsel: "There are rumors flying around that certain witnesses might give untruthful testimony at the *Paula Jones* depositions concerning the nature of the relationship between the president and a former intern named Monica Lewinsky. We certainly hope that doesn't happen." That sort of gentle slap upside the head, not uncommon in the world of civil litigation, might have prompted a reevaluation by both the president and Monica Lewinsky as to the proper course to take. It also may have forced President Clinton to deal with the political and legal consequences of his conduct up front, rather than dragging the country through a year-long criminal investigation and impeachment trial as he worked his way up to a public confession.

348: "If I knew everything": Eric Holder, interview by author.

Chapter 28: "The Brace"

348: "Monica didn't know": Jackie Bennett, interview by author.

349: Ken Starr "hastened in": Ken Starr, interview by author.

349: "I'll need to vet": Jackie Bennett, interview by author. See also Isikoff, *Uncovering Clinton*, 312–13.

349: Initially, the order that Starr's team drafted: Jackie Bennett, interview by author.

349: The final order faxed: Isikoff, *Uncovering Clinton*, 312–13; Jackie Bennett, interview by author. Jackie Bennett, however, was convinced that no matter how one sliced it, Bill Clinton was a "target" of this investigation. In fact, Bennett made sure to clarify this point with his Justice Department overseer, asking Radek whether this language "was broad enough to cover Vernon Jordan and Bill Clinton." Radek responded, "Yes, sure."

349: Judge Sentelle called back to say: The order stated in part: "The Independent Counsel shall have jurisdiction and authority to investigate to the maximum extent authorized by the Independent Counsel [law] whether Monica Lewinsky or others suborned perjury, obstructed justice, intimidated witnesses, or otherwise violated federal law . . . in dealing with witnesses, potential witnesses, attorneys, or others concerning the civil case *Jones v. Clinton*" (Order, In Re: Madison Guaranty Savings & Loan Association, 16 Jan. 1998).

350: "get in line": Jackie Bennett, interview by author.

350: Ironically, Mike Emmick was one: Michael Emmick, interview by author.

350: "The Creative Proposal": One name kicked around, again, was that of former Attorney General Griffin Bell (ibid.).

351: "brace": Paul Rosenzweig, interview by author. The word *brace* is a term of art sometimes used in law enforcement to mean "to confront" or "to brace a person up," indicating that the person must cooperate or face going to jail.

352: Josh Hochberg from DOJ stopped: Ibid.

354: "somewhat distrustful": Monica Lewinsky, interview by author.

354: Tripp had called to say she was running late: Morton, *Monica's Story*, 16.

354: "Monica, this is for": Ibid., 18; Monica Lewinsky, interview by author.

354: "opened the wound": Monica Lewinsky, interview by author.

355: "there were a lot more people in": Michael Emmick, interview by author.

355: Monica was staring: Morton, *Monica's Story*, 177.

356: "My name's Mike": Michael Emmick, interview by author.

356: "Make her stay": Morton, *Monica's Story*, 175; Toobin, *A Vast Conspiracy*, 205; Monica Lewinsky, interview by author.

356: Emmick motioned: Michael Emmick, interview by author.

356: "You could spend": Morton, *Monica's Story*, 176, 179.

356: "In fact, 'wailing'": Michael Emmick, interview by author.

356: "My life is": Schmidt and Weisskopf, *Truth at Any Cost*, 40.

356: "I can't believe": Monica Lewinsky, interview by author.

357: "She just cried and cried": Michael Emmick, interview by author.

357: The prosecutors were able: Ken Starr would later tell the House Judiciary Committee that the fax originated in the "business center" of the building from which Moody routinely sent faxes, and that "we understood it had been provided to us by Mr. Moody, who had received it in his capacity as Mrs. Tripp's attorney" (Kenneth W. Starr to Honorable Henry J. Hyde and Honorable John Conyers, Jr., 11 Dec. 1998, Evidentiary Record, vol. 12, 717–45).

357: "laid out the options": Monica Lewinsky, interview by author.

358: Lewinsky believed that leaving: Morton, *Monica's Story*, 177; Monica Lewinsky, interview by author.

358: She was adamant: Monica Lewinsky, interview by author.

358: This option had been openly discussed: Michael Emmick, interview by author. Ken Starr reiterated this position in a letter to the House Judiciary Committee in December (Kenneth W. Starr to Honorable Henry J. Hyde and Honorable John Conyers, Jr., 11 Dec. 1998, Evidentiary Record, vol. 12, 717–45).

358: "Should I have a lawyer?": Lewinsky did not, according to Emmick, say, "I want to talk to my lawyer." Nor did she indicate whether she viewed Carter as her lawyer for any purpose other than having drafted the affidavit (Michael Emmick, interview by author).

359: "If you want": Monica Lewinsky, interview by author.

359: "to hire Vernon Jordan as": Michael Emmick, interview by author.

359: Her proof was simple: Monica Lewinsky, interview by author; Monica Lewinsky to author, 26 Jan. 2009.

359: she received a page on her cell phone: Morton, *Monica's Story*, 179.

359: Some colleagues: Michael Emmick, interview by author; Schmidt and Weisskopf, *Truth at Any Cost*, 37.

359: "it was a law enforcement": Ken Starr, interview by author.

360: Monica sat down on the bed: Michael Emmick, interview by author.

360: She and her mother: Marcia Lewis Straus, interview by author.

360: If she didn't return: Jackie Bennett, interview by author.

360: it was now time to bring: Michael Emmick, interview by author.

360: So Starr's chief deputy was summoned: Jackie Bennett, interview by author.

360: "the energy in the room": Monica Lewinsky, interview by author.

360: "she was a mess": Jackie Bennett, interview by author.

360: "We're not going to sugarcoat": Schmidt and Weisskopf, *Truth at Any Cost*, 41.

360: "Look, Monica, you're smart": Monica Lewinsky, interview by author; Morton, *Monica's Story*, 179.

360: "I don't remember": Jackie Bennett, interview by author.

360: "What has been referred": Jackie Bennett, interview by author; Michael Emmick, interview by author.

361: Monica found Bennett to be "condescending": Monica Lewinsky, interview by author, and follow-up interview by author; Morton, *Monica's Story*, 180.

361: "I promise I won't blurt": Jackie Bennett, interview by author.

361: Agent Fallon sat: Jackie Bennett, interview by author; Morton, *Monica's Story*, 179.

361: "It was silly": Jackie Bennett, interview by author.

361: "I can't talk": Monica Lewinsky, interview by author; Marcia Lewis Straus, interview by author.

361: "She's stringing us out": Jackie Bennett, interview by author.

361: "It's appalling to me": Monica Lewinsky, interview by author.

361: "What do we do": Michael Emmick, interview by author.

361: "If you're not going to let": Monica Lewinsky, interview by author.

362: "I would have tried": Morton, *Monica's Story*, 181; Monica Lewinsky, interview by author. Ironically, at the same time these events were occurring, Susan Carpenter-McMillan—who was picking out a new suit in the same mall for Paula Jones to wear at the next day's deposition of the president.

362: "She [Monica] was crying": Marcia Lewis Straus, interview by author.

362: "I was hysterical": Monica Lewinsky, interview by author.

Chapter 29: The Avuncular Mr. Ginsburg

363: "We have your daughter": Marcia Lewis Straus, interview by author; Michael Emmick, interview by author.

363: So when Irons began talking down: Michael Emmick, interview by author. Emmick later conceded, "And 'talk to my lawyer' is awfully darn close to 'I want to talk to my lawyer.'" Even Emmick himself, after evaluating all the facts, later concluded, "I was a little troubled by that," ibid.; Morton, *Monica's Story*, 17–18.

363: Fallon asked how they might reach: Morton, *Monica's Story*, 183; Schmidt and Weisskopf, *Truth at Any Cost*, 42; Isikoff, *Uncovering Clinton*, 315; Michael Emmick, interview by author.

363: Jackie Bennett, still in the adjoining room: Jackie Bennett, interview by author.

363: Starr's team offered: Schmidt and Weisskopf, *Truth at Any Cost*, 41; Monica Lewinsky, interview by author.

364: The agents and prosecutors were clearly suspicious: Michael Emmick, interview by author.

364: "I never viewed her": Bruce Udolf, interview by author.

364: "What about my mom?": Michael Emmick, interview by author.

365: "Oh, we've made": Jackie Bennett, interview by author.

365: she began examining household goods: Michael Emmick, interview by author; Monica Lewinsky to author, 26 Jan. 2009.

366: Jackie Bennett later chastised: Jackie Bennett, interview by author. In fact, Monica Lewinsky did recount this story in her book. Her biographer wrote that she went to the restroom on the third floor of Macy's, where "she saw a pay phone, and she tried to call Betty Currie to warn her, but there was no answer and Monica slammed down the handset in frustration" (Morton, *Monica's Story*, 184).

366: "Betty was the only one that I knew": Monica Lewinsky, interview by author.

366: "was playing Hamlet": Ken Starr, interview by author; Michael Emmick, interview by author.

366: "They should have gone": Monica Lewinsky, interview by author.

367: "We all had high hopes going": Jackie Bennett, interview by author.

367: there was a creeping sense that: Bruce Udolf, interview by author.

367: "It did feel": Michael Emmick, interview by author.

367: "She was standing": Marcia Lewis Straus, interview by author. The OIC lawyers and FBI agents, according to later accounts, had put a copy of a book written by Marcia Lewis Straus, *The Private Lives of the Three Tenors,* on the table to make her feel uncomfortable. In that book about Placido Domingo, Luciano Pavarotti, and José Carreras, she strongly hinted that she had engaged in an affair with the world-famous tenor Domingo while he was artistic director of the Washington National Opera (Jeff Lean, "Role Puts Spotlight on Lewinsky's Mother," *Washington Post,* 4 Feb. 1998, A1).

368: "Your daughter's in": Marcia Lewis Straus, interview by author. Monica, her mother, and attorney Bill Ginsburg all gave some version of the story that the OIC prosecutors talked about the potential of Monica's going to jail for twenty-seven or twenty-eight years (depending on the version of the story). Ken Starr later dismissed that as exaggeration, telling the House Judiciary Committee that his prosecutors at no time told Monica Lewinsky "what her actual sentence would be" and emphasized that "no

possible combination of charges could carry a 27-year maximum penalty" (Kenneth W. Starr to Honorable Henry J. Hyde and Honorable John Conyers, Jr., 11 Dec. 1998, House Evidentiary Record, vol. 12, 726).

368: "Of course she'll cooperate": Marcia Lewis Straus, interview by author.

368: "some private time to talk": Michael Emmick, interview by author.

368: the prosecutors could hear: Marcia Lewis Straus, interview by author.

368: "I'm not going to be": Michael Emmick, interview by author; Schmidt and Weisskopf, *Truth at Any Cost*, 43.

368: "They want me to wear": Marcia Lewis Straus, interview by author.

368: encouraged Monica "to find": Schmidt and Weisskopf, *Truth at Any Cost*, 43.

368: "I'm afraid": Marcia Lewis Straus, interview by author.

368: "I don't see how I can make": Michael Emmick, interview by author.

369: "Marcia, your wife, called": Bernie Lewinsky, interview by author.

369: "Call me immediately": William Ginsburg, interview by author.

370: Bernie Lewinsky gulped down some air: Ibid.

370: "Monica was involved": Bernie Lewinsky, interview by author.

370: "Bill Ginsburg is going to be": Monica Lewinsky, interview by author.

371: "So Ginsburg was kind of bombastic": Michael Emmick, interview by author.

371: "If the OIC had": Bruce Udolf, interview by author.

371: "His mood was": Michael Emmick, interview by author.

372: "He [Ginsburg] had no apparent experience": Bruce Udolf, interview by author.

372: "Can you fax": Monica Lewinsky, interview by author.

372: "I couldn't understand": Marcia Lewis Straus, interview by author.

372: "We can't say": Michael Emmick, interview by author.

372: Monica's mother could not remember: Marcia Lewis Straus, interview by author.

372: Ginsburg got back on the line: William Ginsburg, interview by author.

373: "Just leave": Monica Lewinsky, interview by author.

373: Emmick remembered: Michael Emmick, interview by author.

373: the FBI agents handed: Monica Lewinsky, interview by author.

373: "I was completely exhausted": Michael Emmick, interview by author.

374: "Okay, you've got to knock": Jackie Bennett, interview by author.

374: The bearded lawyer drove home: William Ginsburg, interview by author; Bernie Lewinsky, interview by author; Morton, *Monica's Story*, 195.

374: As she attempted to shower: Monica Lewinsky, interview by author.

375: One possible candidate: Ibid.; Marcia Lewis Straus, interview by author.

375: "They probably have": Monica Lewinsky, interview by author.

375: "And then I had her lie": Marcia Lewis Straus, interview by author.

375: "Don't leave": Bernie Lewinsky, interview by author.

376: All Marcia could remember: Marcia Lewis Straus, interview by author.

Chapter 30: Clinton Takes an Oath

376: "I wasn't going to apologize": Bill Clinton, interview by author.

377: "I did," Jones would later acknowledge: Paula Jones, interview by author.

377: "I had the strong sense": Jim Fisher, interview by author.

378: "Okay, come pick": Wesley Holmes, interview by author.

378: Moody used his cell phone: The outspoken Coulter would later express her views about the *Jones* case and her disdain for Bill Clinton: "If only the mastermind of the ingenious 'kiss it' line had been a Republican, Paula would have been represented by some white-shoe law firm—openly, proudly, and free" (Ann Coulter, "Spikey & Me," *George*, May 1999, 48).

379: "The FBI had picked": Wesley Holmes, interview by author.

379: What was noticeably missing: Isikoff, *Uncovering Clinton*, 305–306, 321–322.

380: "I want him [Clinton] to be called": Wesley Holmes, interview by author

380: She had surprised Paula: Susan Carpenter-McMillan, interview by author; Toobin, *A Vast Conspiracy*, 215.

381: the Dallas lawyers hustled: Wesley Holmes, interview by author; Jim Fisher, interview by author.

381: Susan stayed outside: Susan Carpenter-McMillan, interview by author.

381: The president and his lawyer: Robert Bennett, interview by author.

382: "I mean, he looked": Jim Fisher, interview by author.

382: "A lie gets around": Robert Bennett, *Transcript of Videotaped Oral Deposition of William Jefferson Clinton*, 17 Jan. 1998, 5–6 (hereinafter cited as Transcript/Clinton Deposition).

383: Plaintiff's counsel could: Ibid., exhibit 1.

383: "I'll permit": Ibid., 27, 35–36.

384: "This was naive on my part": Jim Fisher, interview by author.

384: "She worked": Transcript/Clinton Deposition, 48.

385: "He typically has": Wesley Holmes, interview by author.

386: "I give—let me just say": Transcript/Clinton Deposition, 75–78.

387: "You know": Bill Clinton, interview by author.

387: "I've been amused": Jim Fisher, interview by author.

388: "Sir, I think this will": Transcript/Clinton Deposition, 85.

388: Back at the White House: John Podesta, interview by author.

389: "That is absolutely": Ibid., 204. Wesley Holmes (interview by author) later said, "When Bennett was going on and on about Lewinsky's affidavit, it's baloney for him [Clinton] to say that he wasn't paying attention. He was sitting there reading it, looking at Bennett, listening to what Bennett said, very involved. You know, it's just a lie to say he wasn't paying attention to what Bennett said." Judge Wright's law clerk, Barry Ward, later signed an affidavit stating that President Clinton seemed totally engaged when his lawyer made the statement that Ms. Lewinsky had declared there was "absolutely no sex of any kind in any manner, shape or form with President Clinton." Ward stated under oath: "From my position at the conference table, I observed President Clinton looking directly at Mr. Bennett while this statement was being made" (Barry W. Ward, Affidavit, 25 Jan. 1999). Ward would later make clear, however, that he had no idea what was in Clinton's mind.

390: the Linda Tripp tapes were: Jim Fisher, interview by author.

390: These constituted the only visual: Wesley Holmes, interview by author.

390: "I know, I know": Paula Jones, quoted by ibid.

Chapter 31: Scandal in Washington

392: Bernie and Barbara were: Bernie Lewinsky, interview by author.

393: She worried: Monica Lewinsky to author, 26 Jan. 2009.

393: As Bill Ginsburg walked: William Ginsburg, interview by author. OIC prosecutors later made clear that they did not leak Ginsburg's identity. Indeed, they were trying desperately to keep the media from learning that they had expanded into this matter (Paul Rosenzweig, interview by author).

396: Monica "just totally fell": Bernie Lewinsky, interview by author.

396: demanding that Monica promise: Morton, *Monica's Story*, 195.

396: "I can't have her breaking": Bernie Lewinsky, interview by author.

396: This allowed the family to move: Jeff Leen, "Role Puts Spotlight on Lewinsky's Mother," *Washington Post*, 4 Feb. 1998, A1.

396: "We had big aspirations": Bernie Lewinsky, interview by author.

396: there were unrebutted allegations: Morton, *Monica's Story*, 30.

396: There were also charges: Leen, "Role Puts Spotlight," A1.

396: "we had a total disagreement": Bernie Lewinsky, interview by author.

397: felt particularly "defensive": Marcia Lewis Straus, interview by author.

398: Although Linda Tripp and Bernie: Among other things, Bernie Lewinsky would point out that his ex-wife called him months before the "sting" of Monica by Starr's office, seeking to seal their divorce records. He later concluded this was likely because she knew Monica's affair with Clinton might be exposed. Bernie Lewinsky, interview by author.

398: (Monica herself): Monica Lewinsky, Grand Jury Testimony, 1138.

398: "had been begging [Monica]": Marcia Lewis, Grand Jury Testimony, 1 Feb. 1998. 60–65.

399: "waiting on pins and needles": Michael Emmick, interview by author.

399: "I remember certainly thinking": Jackie Bennett, interview by author.

400: "If the president had": Ginsburg would later describe it as expanding "from a real estate matter into a sexual witch hunt." William Ginsburg, interview by author.

400: the "fire sale" was: Michael Emmick, interview by author.

400: "You rejected": Jackie Bennett, interview by author.

401: "a Gestapo Nazi technique": William Ginsburg, interview by author.

401: Ginsburg "didn't even look": Michael Emmick, interview by author.

401: "My girl isn't going down": William Ginsburg, interview by author.

401: Jackie Bennett was seething: Jackie Bennett, interview by author.

402: "*NEWSWEEK* KILLS": Isikoff, *Uncovering Clinton*, 339–40.

402: "The cat was out": Jackie Bennett, interview by author.

402: "Why hadn't Clinton just defaulted": William Ginsburg, interview by author.

403: "It was all too much": Monica Lewinsky, interview by author.

403: Ginsburg next sobered up his: Morton, *Monica's Story*, 196; Toobin, *A Vast Conspiracy*, 265–66.

403: Both Monica and Marcia cried: Marcia Lewis Straus, interview by author.

404: He had helped file: William Ginsburg, interview by author.

405: "I'm here just to be": Michael Emmick, interview by author.

405: Ginsburg and Speights would leave: Schmidt and Weisskopf, *Truth at Any Cost*, 50–51; Michael Emmick, interview by author.

405: All these things were causing: Michael Emmick, interview by author.

405: He was now "babysitting": interview by author; Monica Lewinsky, interview by author.

405: Mike Emmick and Bruce: Michael Emmick, interview by author.

406: He did not suffer: Jackie Bennett, interview by author.

406: If Lewinsky had to be charged: Michael Emmick, interview by author.

406: "There's no way!": Jackie Bennett, interview by author; Schmidt, *The Truth at Any Cost*, 52.

406: "He had been standing": Jackie Bennett, interview by author.

406: Jackie Bennett slapped: Toobin, *A Vast Conspiracy*, 267.

406: The chance for "undercover": Michael Emmick, interview by author.

406: Lewinsky would have to make: Toobin, *A Vast Conspiracy*, 267–68.

407: "This isn't working": Jackie Bennett, interview by author.

407: "Will you accept service": William Ginsburg, interview by author. OIC prosecutors, on the other hand, insisted that they were simply taking necessary steps to "make sure that if the father had any documents that were pertinent," Ginsburg would hand these over (Michael Emmick, interview by author).

407: **"went berserk"**: Jackie Bennett, interview by author.

407: **"Let's go, Monica"**: Robert J. Bittman, interview by author.

407: **Ginsburg informed her that Starr's prosecutors**: William Ginsburg, interview by author; Morton, *Monica's Story*, 197; Jackie Bennett, interview by author; Schmidt and Weisskopf, *Truth at Any Cost*, 53; Toobin, *A Vast Conspiracy*, 268.

407: **The Starr prosecutors could hear**: Robert J. Bittman, interview by author.

Chapter 32: A Presidency in Peril

411: **innocuous headline**: "Clinton Gives Netanyahu Plan to Aid Peace Process," *Washington Post*, 21 Jan. 1998.

411: **Later versions of newspapers delivered**: Isikoff, *Uncovering Clinton*, 344.

411: **"a shotgun shot"**: John Podesta, interview by author.

412: **Clinton had planned**: John F. Harris, "Clinton Denies Affair, Says He Never Asked Former Aide to Lie," *Washington Post*, 22 Jan. 1998, A1.

412: **"There is no improper"**: Federal News Services, "Clinton: 'There Is No Improper Relationship,'" *Washington Post*, 22 Jan. 1998, A13.

413: **"I just slipped up:"**: Dick Morris, "Here's What I Told the Grand Jury About My Pal—the President," *New York Post*, 19 Aug. 1998.

413: **"Clinton Denies"**: Harris, "Clinton Denies"; Peter Baker and Sue Schmidt, "Former Intern Refers to Relationship with President, Pressure," *Washington Post*, 22 Jan. 1998, A1.

413: **The American public was treated**: Dana Priest and Rene Sanchez, "Kindred Spirits' Pentagon Bond," *Washington Post*, 22 Jan. 1998, A1.

413: **News accounts were beginning to describe**: Thomas B. Edsall, "Jordan: Power Broker and 'FOB' Without Peer," *Washington Post*, 22 Jan. 1998, A12.

413: **"President Imperiled"**: Dan Balz, "President Imperiled As Never Before," *Washington Post*, 22 Jan. 1998, A13.

414: **"For the love of God"**: Joe Purvis, interview by author.

414: **Betsey Wright, Clinton's chief of staff**: Betsey Wright, interview by author.

414: **"Just tell those Starr"**: Susan McDougal, interview with author.

415: **"He was looking"**: Billie Jeayne (Starr) Reynolds, interview by author.

415: **Ken never talked**: Ken Starr, interview by author; Alice Starr, interview by author.

415: **"I want to say"**: Ruth Marcus and Thomas B. Edsall, "Jordan Gives Beleaguered President His Presence," *Washington Post*, 23 Jan. 1998, A1, A20.

416: **Judge Susan Webber Wright postponed**: Susan Schmidt and Peter Baker, "Judge Delays Lewinsky Deposition," *Washington Post*, 23 Jan. 1998, A1.

416: **"an ebullient, vulnerable 'child'"**: Jeff Leen, "Two Coasts, Two Lives, Many Images," *Washington Post*, 24 Jan. 1998, A1.

416: **A group of Bill and Hillary Clinton's close friends**: John F. Harris, "Aide, Clinton Were Close, Friends Told," *Washington Post*, 25 Jan. 1998, A1.

416: **ABC News/Washington Post found**: Richard Morin and Claudia Deane, "For Public, the Issue Is Trust, Poll Shows," *Washington Post*, 26 Jan. 1998, A1.

416: **As one journalist wrote**: Dan Balz, "A Crisis with No Parallel," *Washington Post*, 26 Jan. 1998, A1, A10.

416: **"These are serious allegations"**: Thomas B. Edsall, "President's Supporters on Hill Offering Mostly Tepid Statements—If Any," *Washington Post*, 26 Jan. 1998, A11.

417: **The Starr team**: Peter Baker and Susan Schmidt, "Starr Seeks to Confirm Allegations," *Washington Post*, 26 Jan. 1998, A1, A8.

417: **Panicked congressional Democrats**: Richard L. Berke, "White House Acts to Contain Furor As Concern Grows," *New York Times*, 26 Jan. 1998, A1.

417: **Harry Thomason advised**: Toobin, *A Vast Conspiracy*, 246–50.

417: **Another trusted adviser, Harold Ickes**: Harold Ickes, interview by author.

418: **"These allegations are"**: John F. Harris and Dan Balz, "Clinton More Forcefully Denies Having Had Affair or Urging Lies," *Washington Post*, 27 Jan. 1998, A1; Stephen Labaton and Jeff Gerth, "Clinton Emphatically Denies an Affair with Ex-Intern," *New York Times*, 27 Jan. 1998, A1.

418: **"distracted by events"**: James Bennet, "Lawyers Say He Is Distracted by Events," *New York Times*, 27 Jan. 1998, A1.

418: **"I was offended"**: Bernie Lewinsky, interview by author.

418: "I think as this matter unfolds": Howard Kurtz, "For Clintons, No Lack of Attackers," *Washington Post,* 28 Jan. 1998, A1.

418: "I do believe": Kurtz, "For Clintons"; Toobin, *A Vast Conspiracy,* 256 (emphasis added).

419: the embattled chief executive spoke: John F. Harris, "Clinton Pledges Activist Agenda," *Washington Post,* 28 Jan. 1998, A1.

419: It was a virtuoso: John F. Harris, "Clinton Tries to Sell Agenda in Heartland," *Washington Post,* 29 Jan. 1998, A1.

419: "I thought it was": Justice David Newbern, interview by author.

419: "I know his body language too": Betsey Wright, interview by author.

419: "One, he did it": John Brummett, interview by author.

420: As one journalist: Max Brantley, interview by author.

420: "This is what you get": John Brummett, interview by author.

Chapter 33: "Of Trust and Confidence"

420: that a specific Secret Service agent had stepped: See Howard Kurtz, "Dallas Paper's Story: A Scoop That Wasn't," *Washington Post,* 28 Jan. 1998, D1.

421: The *New York Post* featured: Marilyn Rauber and Denise Buffa, "G-Man Who 'Saw Tryst' Will Tell," *New York Post,* 27 Jan. 1998, 1.

421: editor Ralph Langer made: Kurtz, "Dallas Paper's Story."

422: "U.S., Allies Launch": *Washington Post,* 17 Jan. 1991.

422: Merletti would later say: Lew Merletti, follow-up interview by author.

422: A review of the archives: Monica Lewinsky to Agent Lewis Merletti, 28, Oct. 1996, Lew Merletti papers.

423: Kelleher "felt that from past experience": Lew Merletti, interview by author.

423: Merletti dimmed the lights: Lew Merletti, interview by author; Merletti Power Point presentation, Lew Merletti papers.

423: *proximity* of the agents was critical: President William McKinley, while visiting Buffalo in 1901, had been shot fatally in the stomach by a gunman named Leon Czolgosz, because the Secret Service agent posted next to McKinley had been moved aside at the request of a dignitary who wanted a spot close to the president. Merletti next showed classified photos of the shooting of President Reagan by

John W. Hinckley, Jr., in March 1981; followed by haunting photos of that same would-be assassin stalking President Carter five months earlier in Dayton.

424: "swarming up on top": Clint Hill, interview by author.

424: Merletti cut to: Clint Hill, interview by Mike Wallace, *60 Minutes, CBS,* 8 Dec. 1975.

425: "the men of [the USSS]": John E. Wilkie to Charles D. Norton, 1910, 7, Merletti papers.

425: That committee had subpoenaed: John W. Magaw to John F. Kerry, 24 July 1992, Merletti papers.

426: "And I mean": Lew Merletti, interview by author.

426: Starr would later defend himself: Ken Starr, interview by author.

426: "He could not have been more dismissive": Lew Merletti, interview by author.

427: "You'd better fight this": Lew Merletti, interview by author.

428: "Mr. President, . . .": Ibid.

429: A retired uniformed USSS officer assigned: Bob Niedbala, "Greene Man Witnessed Lewinsky Visits," *Washington (PA) Observer-Reporter,* 4 Feb. 1998.

429: the *Washington Post* was announcing: Susan Schmidt, "Clinton, Lewinsky Met Alone, Guard Says," *Washington Post,* 11 Feb. 1998, A1.

429: "It was inappropriate": Lew Merletti, interview by author.

430: Lew Fox knew no damning details: OIC interview with Lewis C. Fox, 9 Feb. 1998, Evidentiary Record, vol. 4, part 3, 1171. See also Grand Jury Testimony of Lewis Fox, 17 Feb. 1998, Evidentiary Record, vol. 4, part 3, 1175–88.

Chapter 34: One Nation Divided

431: "it had to be investigated": Ken Starr, interview by author.

431: "What should *never*": Bill Clinton, interview by author.

432: The Scaife foundations: Richard Mellon Scaife, interview by author. For a fuller discussion of the so-called Arkansas Project, see Joe Conason and Gene Lyons, *The Hunting of the President,* chapters 7 and 10; David Brock, *Blinded by the Right,* chapter 10.

432: Tyrell's cousin: R. Emmett Tyrrell, Jr., interview by author.

433: "I was angry": Sam Dash, interview by author.

433: Dash's exclusion: Jackie Bennett, interview by author.

433: "I've got to talk to everybody": Sam Dash, interview by author.

434: "like a bolt out of the blue": Jackie Bennett, interview by author.

434: He had also drafted: Robert J. Bittman, interview by author.

436: "It was like he was raptured": Hickman Ewing, Jr., interview by author.

436: Tucker might finally cough up information: Hickman Ewing, Jr., interview by author. Tucker pleaded guilty soon thereafter, giving Ewing a proffer that included some statements that Ewing believed helped to accomplish his goal.

436: Ewing was still cobbling: Hickman Ewing, Jr., interview by author. Paul Rosenzweig was summoned back to Little Rock to help Ewing "put together a possible indictment" with respect to the First Lady.

436: "This is not going to look good": Ken Starr, interview with author; Jackie Bennett, interview with author. See also Schmidt and Weisskopf, *Truth at Any Cost,* 63–65.

437:"Increasingly urgent overtures": Ken Starr, interview with author; Schmidt and Weisskopf, *Truth at Any Cost,* 67–71.

438: the first question that he would have asked: Archibald Cox, interview by author.

439: avoided taking sides: Robert B. Fiske, interview by author.

439: "We'd have been long since done": Julie O'Sullivan, interview by author.

439: "I have always said that": William S. Duffey, Jr., interview by author.

Chapter 35: The Vilification of Ken Starr

440: "She was not in good health": Ken Starr, interview by author.

441: "I didn't want to start": Alice Starr, interview by author.

442: Ken would put down his briefcase: Ken Starr, interview by author.

443: evidence related to the Lewinsky: Toobin, *A Vast Conspiracy,* 271. Judge Wright fell short of declaring that the Lewinsky evidence was totally irrelevant and immaterial in the *Jones* case. Instead, she took a more nuanced approach, ruling that any "probative" value of the evidence was outweighed by "the possibility of prejudice" vis-à-vis a potential jury. Ironically, Starr's office had forced Judge Wright's hand on this issue. OIC had filed a motion demanding that the Arkansas judge suspend discovery in the parallel *Jones* litigation to stop the Dallas lawyers from shadow-ing Starr's investigation and subpoenaing witnesses OIC called to the grand jury. Judge Wright had chosen to deal with the problem in a different way—she had issued a succinct order declaring that "evidence concerning Monica Lewinsky should be excluded [entirely] from the trial of this matter."

443: "I was elated": Monica Lewinsky, interview by author.

443: Rumors now swirled: Author's interviews with confidential sources.

444: "I was pretty bad": Monica Lewinsky interview by author.

445: "Ms. Lewinsky had an intimate": Monica Lewinsky, handwritten proffer, 1 Feb. 1998, Evidentiary Record, vol. 3, part 1, 709.

446: "Look, kid'": Monica Lewinsky, interview by author.

446: Ginsburg promptly signed: Bruce L. Udolf and Mike Emmick to William Ginsburg and Nathaniel H. Speights, 2 Feb. 1998, and signed fax, 4 Feb. 1998, Lewinsky papers.

446: "You have a deal": Monica Lewinsky, interview by author.

446: "The president will remain in office": Toobin, *A Vast Conspiracy,* 276.

446: At one point: Monica Lewinsky to author, 26 Jan. 2009.

447: "I felt sorry for": William Ginsburg, interview by author.

447: that "we were completely on the president's side": William Ginsburg, interview by author (Vernon Jordan's lawyer, William Hundley, was also present at this meeting).

447: Starr's office, in the meantime: Ruth Marcus and Bob Woodward, "As Ginsburg Broadcasts, Colleagues Air Disbelief; With Lewinsky's Jeopardy Still Uncertain, Many Attorneys Are Amazed by Lawyer's TV Gambit," *Washington Post,* 2 Feb. 1998, A-1; Toobin, *A Vast Conspiracy,* 276–77.

447: "I'm the most famous person in the world": Marcus and Woodward, "As Ginsburg Broadcasts."

447: "It's just not going to": Jackie Bennett, interview by author.

448: "I really think Monica": Sol Wisenberg, interview by author.

448: Starr had authorized them: Toobin, *A Vast Conspiracy,* 278.

448: "Sometimes, cooperators will only": Michael Emmick, interview by author.

449: Bittman thanked the Lewinsky: Robert Bittman to William Ginsburg and Nathaniel Speights, 4 Feb. 1998, Lewinsky papers.

449: Ginsburg, having already returned: William Ginsburg to Kenneth Starr, 4 Feb. 1998, Lewinsky papers.

449: when Ginsburg called to tell: Monica Lewinsky, interview by author.

449: to solidify his standing: See correspondence between Bittman and Ginsburg, Lewinsky papers.

449: Besides serving a subpoena: Subpoena to Monica Lewinsky, 6 Feb. 1998, Lewinsky papers.

449: "Let me make our request specific": Bittman to Kendall, 9 Feb. 1998, Kendall papers.

449: "I was in the process": Kendall to Bittman, 13 Feb. 1998, Kendall papers.

450: "fantastic sort of trailer-park ethos": Anne-Elisabeth Moutet, interview by author.

450: "Some people concentrated": Michel Gurfenkiel, interview by author.

451: "Most people understood": Ibid.

451: Seated at his desk: George Cawkwell, interview by author.

Chapter 36: A Mother's Collapse

452: If anything hardened: Monica Lewinsky, interview by author.

452: "Monica, it's not so bad": Marcia Lewis Straus, interview by author.

453: "Because I would like": Marcia Lewis, testimony, 10 Feb. 1998, Evidentiary Record, vol. 4, 2270.

453: "On some occasion, did she ever": Ibid.; Marcia Lewis Straus, interview by author.

454: "Would you like": Marcia Lewis, testimony, 10 Feb. 1998, Evidentiary Record, vol. 4, 2299.

454: "If a parent doesn't testify": Marcia Lewis Straus, interview by author.

454: An anonymous observer outside: Statement, 11 Feb. 1998, Evidentiary Record, vol. 4, 2301; see also Peter Baker and Amy Goldstein, "Lewinsky's Mother Overcome by Emotion During Testimony," *Washington Post*, 12 Feb. 1998, A1.

455: "I don't think her angst": Jackie Bennett, interview by author.

455: "Certainly, Billy [Martin] milked it": Sol Wisenberg, interview by author.

455: "I have no response": Marcia Lewis Straus, interview by author.

455: "I think anybody who would allow": Monica Lewinsky, interview by author.

455: "Here we are as prosecutors": Ken Starr, interview by author.

455: Monica Lewinsky, still at home: Monica Lewinsky, interview by author.

456: one newspaper story trumpeted: Jonathan Broder, "Prosecuting—or persecuting—the prosecutors," *Salon*, 24 Feb. 1998. See also Martin Berg, "Starr Aide No Stranger to Sex Tapes Inquiries," *Los Angeles Daily Journal*, 6 Feb. 1998; Martha Ezzard, "Starr's Tainted Lieutenant," *Atlanta Constitution*, 14 Feb. 1998.

456: Sol Wisenberg, saw them: Sol Wisenberg, interview by author.

456: As a result of this power play: Ibid.; Jackie Bennett, interview by author.

457: Starr's prosecutors were itching: Ken Starr, interview by author.

457: Starr's office was suddenly: Blumenthal, *The Clinton Wars*, 410–11. See also Howard Kurtz, "Prosecutor Lobs a Grenade: Blumenthal's Subpoena Sends Press Corps a Shock," *Washington Post*, 25 Feb. 1998. With respect to the more germane topic—what President Clinton had told Blumenthal in the days after the Monica Lewinsky affair became public—Blumenthal quietly invoked "executive privilege." Yet this fact quickly got lost in the clamor over the Clinton adviser's First Amendment rights.

457: Starr himself, taking out the garbage: "White House Prepares to Assert Executive Privilege," CNN AllPolitics, 25 Feb. 1998.

458: "Forget about that": Hickman Ewing, Jr., interview by author.

458: He also told Starr's prosecutors: Ibid. For instance, Ewing had come to believe that the mysterious Madison Guaranty check for $27,600, marked "Payoff Clinton"—in Susan McDougal's handwriting—found in the trunk of a junked car after a tornado, represented a payoff of the Clintons' Whitewater loan. If this was true, as McDougal now alleged, Bill Clinton had committed perjury during the Whitewater trial when he denied ever receiving a loan from Madison Guaranty. The other possibility, as Ewing himself would admit, was that McDougal moved around money, paid off the loan with Madison funds, and didn't even tell Clinton.

Chapter 37: Last Night in Solitary Confinement

459: "was indicating that his mood": Richard Clark, interview by author.

459: Although McDougal's conviction: Monthly Mental Status Reports, 15 Jan. 1998, Clark papers.

460: prison medical records indicate: Brief Counseling Session, 2 Feb. 1998, Clark papers.

460: Clark found the situation extremely odd: Richard Clark, interview by author.

461: After McDougal complained to the guards: Richard Clark, interview by author; Jack Douglas, Jr., "Doctors Ignored McDougal, Report Says," *Fort Worth Star-Telegram*, 13 Sept. 1998, B1.

462: the guard confided to Clark: Richard Clark, interview by author.

462: "unresponsive": Autopsy Report of Jim McDougal, Office of Chief Medical Examiner, Tarrant County, Texas, 8 Mar. 1998.

462: "at the quickest, it would have": Richard Clark, interview by author.

462: One inmate: Jack Douglas, Jr., "The Mysterious Death of Jim McDougal," *George*, Oct. 1998.

462: The autopsy report issued: Autopsy Report of Jim McDougal, 8 Mar. 1998, 3.

462: numerous "wild rumors": Richard Clark, interview by author; Claudia Riley, interview by author.

463: an "animalistic cry": Claudia Riley, interview by author.

463: Ewing seemed shaken up: Richard Clark, interview by author.

463: "I didn't think that they": Hickman Ewing, Jr., interview by author.

463: "It was obviously Jim": Claudia Riley, interview by author.

464: As she sat: Susan McDougal, follow-up interview by author.

464: This complex and tragic man: McDougal, *The Woman Who Wouldn't Talk*, 302–303; Susan McDougal, interview by author.

464: "always wanted a jazz band": Claudia Riley, interview by author.

465: had personally requested: Bill Simmons, "Starr Deputy Eulogizes Jim McDougal," *Arkansas Democrat-Gazette*, 14 Mar. 1998, A1.

466: "But his death": Claudia Riley, interview by author.

466: Although Hickman Ewing: Hickman Ewing, Jr., interview by author.

466: "Christ Almighty": Harold Ickes, interview by author.

466: he was deeply saddened: Bill Clinton, interview by author.

467: The Federal Bureau of Prisons scrambled: Statement of the Federal Bureau of Prisons, September 1998, Clark papers.

467: Richard Clark and others: Richard Clark, interview by author.

467: "there is no evidence": Douglas, "Doctors Ignored."

467: Clark was particularly concerned: Richard Clark, interview by author.

468: "You know why I'm here": Ibid. While Clark identified the name of the agent, it is not repeated in this account for security reasons. However, the individual was indeed employed by the Federal Bureau of Prisons.

470: "No, I will not": Richard Clark, interview by author.

470: "It's getting extremely hot": Ibid.

Chapter 38: The Indictment of Hillary Clinton

471: On April 25, Ken Starr: Peter Baker and Susan Schmidt, "Prosecutors Question First Lady at Length; Starr Prepares to End Ark. Phase of Probe," *Washington Post*, 26 Apr. 1998, A1.

471: "Forget about [Hillary]": Hickman Ewing, Jr., interview by author.

472: After Currie had allowed: Jackie Bennett, interview by author.

472: In response to questioning: Catherine Allday Davis, Grand Jury Testimony, 17 Mar. 1998, Evidentiary Record, vol. 4, 842.

473: Davis was under oath: Catherine Allday Davis, OIC summary of testimony, 20 Mar. 1998, Evidentiary Record, vol. 4, 829, 842, 844, 845.

473: One of the most startling: Ibid., 831, 833.

474: "The President is looking": Ibid., 866.

475: "It was kind of like I": Kathleen Willey, transcript of interview by *Sixty Minutes*, CBS News, 15 Mar. 1998; "Kathleen Willey: 'I Just Thought It Was Extremely Reckless,'" Federal Document Clearing House, 16 Mar. 1998, A8.

476: "number one fan": Schmidt and Weisskopf, *Truth At Any Cost*, 120–21.

476: Juanita Broaddrick: Ibid., 121; Toobin, *A Vast Conspiracy*, 140–41. The unwanted assault, allegedly, had taken place in a Little Rock hotel room.

476: Judge Susan Webber Wright granted: Memorandum Opinion and Order, *Jones v. Clinton*, No. LR-C-94-290, 1 Apr. 1998, J. Wright. The court also granted summary judgment with respect to Clinton's co-defendant, Trooper Danny Ferguson.

476: "even a most charitable": Ibid., 13, 30. One of the only attempts by the plaintiff to show that she suffered at work, due to her refusal to succumb to Governor Clinton's alleged sexual advances, was that she did not receive flowers from her boss on Secretary's Day. The judge was also unimpressed by a last-ditch declaration from a purported expert in education and counseling, Patrick J. Carnes, Ph.D., who had met briefly with Paula and Steve Jones and rendered an opinion that Ms. Jones's alleged encounter with Governor Clinton in 1991 had caused plaintiff to suffer "severe emotional distress" and "consequent sexual aversion." Judge Wright found these eleventh-hour assertions to be "vague and conclusory," as well as legally uncompelling (ibid., 27, 37–38).

476: In a final blow: Ibid., 39.

477: At first, Bennett had worried: Robert S. Bennett, *In the Ring: The Trials of a Washington Lawyer*, 256.

477: A teary-eyed Paula Jones: "Jones Says She Will Appeal," CNN AllPolitics, 16 Apr. 1998.

477: "You cannot defile the temple": Andrew Philips, "Clinton Harassment Suit Dismissed," *Maclean's Magazine*, 13 Apr. 1998; "Ken Starr Discusses His Investigation," CNN AllPolitics, 2 Apr. 1998.

477: In an earlier decision in which she had excluded: Memorandum and Order, *Jones v. Clinton*, 9 Mar. 1998, 9 nn. 2, 7, 8; Order, *Jones v. Clinton*, 29 Jan. 1998, 2.

477: President Clinton would later admit: Bill Clinton, interview by author.

477: Mail poured into: Misc. 1998 letters approving Judge Wright's decision to dismiss the *Jones* case, Federal District Court Papers.

478: Just weeks earlier, Ewing: Schmidt and Weisskopf, *Truth at Any Cost*, 156.

478: Following this were four documents: Memo, 22 Apr. 1998, "HRC Meeting" binder, confidential source. Redacted versions of some of these documents were obtained through an FOIA request from the Records of Independent Counsel Starr/Ray, National Archives and Records Administration, College Park, Maryland.

478: Although nobody outside the room: Draft Indictment, "HRC Meeting" binder, confidential source.

478: "Theory of the Case" memo: Memo, 10 Apr. 1998, "HRC Meeting" binder, confidential source.

479: These entries, circled on the billings records: "Once Upon a Time in Arkansas: Rose Law Firm Billing Records," *Frontline*, PBS, October 1997; Final Report/Ray, vol. 2, 468–72.

479: There was plenty of evidence: Among other things, the Senate Whitewater Committee had obtained the handwritten notes of New York

lawyer Susan Thomases, one of Mrs. Clinton's closest advisers. The notes indicated that Mrs. Clinton had numerous conferences with officials at Madison and that "she did all the billing" (Jerry Seper, "Once-Secret Memos Question Clinton's Honesty," *Washington Times*, 8 May 2008).

479: "There is a circumstantial case": "Summary of Crimes," "HRC Meeting" binder, confidential source; Hickman Ewing, Jr., interview by author.

479: Hillary Clinton had the motive: These points regarding the motive and opportunity for Mrs. Clinton to lie are set forth in detail in Final Report/Ray, vol. 3, 140–44; Final Senate Report/Whitewater, 240–61. Mrs. Clinton, however, insisted that she was pleased that the billing records turned up because they had confirmed what she had said all along: that her involvement in Madison Guaranty work was minimal by the standards of any busy lawyer. A summary of Mrs. Clinton's position can be found in Final Senate Report/Whitewater, 659–68 (minority view).

480: Ewing would later say: Hickman Ewing, Jr., interview by author.

480: To further add: Final Report/Ray, vol. 1, 140–41. See also "Second Set of First Lady's Billing Records Found," CNN AllPolitics, 26 Mar. 1998.

480: This single piece of paper: Hickman Ewing, Jr., interview by author. Hillary Clinton's story had always been that she was brought into the case to collect an old bill from McDougal that was due on Bank of Kingston work. Ewing would say: "That document right there proved that certain statements she made were not so. They definitely were not true."

480: that Mrs. Clinton "knowingly made": Draft Indictment, "HRC Meeting" binder, confidential source. For a discussion of these events, see Stewart, *Blood Sport*, 123–25 and n.

481: For two straight hours: Hickman Ewing, Jr., interview by author; Schmidt and Weisskopf, *Truth at Any Cost*, 155.

481: "a bunch of nothing": Schmidt and Weisskopf, *Truth at Any Cost*, 156.

481: "overstat[ing] in favor of the Clintons": Hickman Ewing, Jr., interview by author.

482: A secret memo written: Memo, Paul Rosenzweig to File, 24 Apr. 1998, Records of Independent Counsel Starr/Ray, National Archives, obtained through FOIA request.

482: The final witness for OIC would: Order of Proof, "4-22-98, HRC meeting" binder, confidential source.

483: By midnight, Starr's: Hickman Ewing, Jr., interview by author.

483: "like Moses on Mt. Nebo": Paul Rosenzweig, interview by author.

483: "As far as I'm concerned": Hickman Ewing, Jr., interview by author.

484: Instead of indicting Hubbell: Hickman Ewing, Jr., interview by author; Schmidt and Weisskopf, *Truth at Any Cost*, 156–57. OIC files now reveal that in June 1998, OIC also tried its hand at drafting an indictment against Hubbell based on the Madison Guaranty–related charges, simply removing Hillary Clinton's name from the indictment and leaving her, in essence, as an unindicted co-conspirator. See Seper, "Once-Secret Memos."

484: "On the other hand, I've been": Hickman Ewing, Jr., interview by author.

Chapter 39: Out-Gunning the Secret Service

484: "Until they announce they will not": Stephen Labaton, "Testing of a President: The Grand Jury; On Last Day, No Indictment of First Lady," *New York Times*, 6 May 1998, A20.

485: "parallel investigations": John Crudele, "The Jury's Still Out on Hillary," *New York Post*, 6 May 1998.

485: Hubbell stood at the door: Susan Schmidt, "Indictment Claims Hubbell Lived Lavishly," *Washington Post*, 1 May 1998.

485: the charges were particularly unfair: John Nields, interview by author; John Nields to author, 3 Aug. 2009.

485: The House committee investigating: House Committee on Government Reform and Oversight, "Hubbell Master Tape Log," 30 Apr. 1998.

485: Republican Chairman: In one conversation recorded on the Master Tape Log in March 1996, in which Hubbell ruminated about pursuing a lawsuit against the Rose Law Firm, he told his wife, Suzy, "I will not raise those allegations that might open it up to Hillary. And you know that. I told you that." Suzy replied that she had heard from Marsha Scott, one of Hillary's closest aides at the White House, and that Marsha "is ratcheting it up and making it sound like if Webb goes ahead and sues the firm, then any support [the Hubbells] have at the White House is gone. I'm hearing the squeeze play." Hubbell answered with a sigh, "So I need to roll over one more time" (ibid., tapes 4A and 5B).

485: Democrats on the House Committee: House Committee on Government Reform and Oversight, Memorandum Re: Analysis of Hubbell Master Tape Log (by Minority Staff), 4 May 1998. In the actual tape recording of the above conversations, for instance, Hubbell went on to tell his wife that the First Lady was totally blameless: "OK. Hillary's not. Hillary isn't . . . She just had no idea what was going on," he said. "She didn't participate in any of this."

485: Burton's top aide: Jackie Koszczyk, "Hubbell Tapes Imbroglio Puts GOP Finance Probe on the Defensive," *Congressional Quarterly*, 9 May 1998.

486: Starr's prosecutors took the unusual step: Labaton, "Testing of a President: The Grand Jury," A20.

486: The White House: Schmidt and Weisskopf, *Truth at Any Cost*, 157.

486: In a rare interview granted to *BBC Tonight*: (*BBC Tonight*) 3 April 1998, Peter Marshall Interview with Susan McDougal in Jail, Susan McDougal film clips.

486: OIC's "most wanted" list: Labaton, "Testing of a President: The Grand Jury"; "Excerpts from Ruling on Compelling Testimony of 3 in the Lewinsky Case," *New York Times*, 28 May 1998, A24.

486: In a sealed ruling that was swiftly leaked: Stephen Labaton, "Testing of a President: The Prosecutor; Starr Asks Supreme Court to Speed Process for Ruling on President's Privilege Claims," *New York Times*, 29 May 1998, A14.

487: "Having tried and tried, I will": Robert J. Bittman to David E. Kendall, 3 Apr. 1998, Kendall papers.

487: "Alice-in-Wonderland nature": David E. Kendall to Robert J. Bittman, 17 Apr. 1998, Kendall papers.

487: "show cause why your office": David Kendall to Kenneth Starr, 6 May 1998, Kendall papers. Jackie Bennett, on behalf of OIC, issued a sizzling reply to Kendall that same day, writing that Kendall's latest accusations against OIC were "not only wrong, but reckless. . . . Although we understand your keen desire to once again change the subject when you receive bad news [from the judge], we demand that you withdraw the motion forthwith" (Jackie Bennett to David Kendall, 6 May 1998, Kendall papers). Of course, the president's lawyer did no such thing.

487: Judge Susan Webber Wright had slammed: Order relating to Secret Service Motion for a Protective Order, *Jones v. Clinton,* 30 Jan. 1998.

488: OIC had continued to gather up: Jackie Bennett, interview by author.

488: Starr, a scholar of the Constitution: Ken Starr, interview by author. Through information and "movement logs" within the White House, the Secret Service had shown that Colonel North was not someone "who was so intimate with the president that he could walk into the Oval Office."

488: Although the press: Clint Hill, interview by author; Lew Merletti, interview by author.

489: "We provide a protective umbrella": Clint Hill, interview by author.

489: "Praetorian guard": Woodward, *Shadow,* 137.

489: No "protective function privilege" had: Brief in Support of Motion to Compel, In Re: Grand Jury Proceedings, May 1998.

489: In sending one former: Ruth Marcus, "Johnson Strict with Officials and About Her Privacy," *Washington Post,* 20 Mar. 1998, A20.

489: "all of [Judge Johnson's] body language": Lew Merletti, interview by author. See also Lewis C. Merletti, declaration, In Re: Grand Jury Proceedings, May 1998.

489: this highly confidential: Manning J. O'Connor, interview by author.

490: "spending too much time": Starr Report, 62–66.

491: As the presidential entourage wound: Photo of Manila bridge, Merletti papers.

491: This thwarted assassination attempt was never: Lew Merletti, interview by author, and follow-up interview by author, 30 June 2006.

492: The Secret Service was already watching: Knut Royce, "Death Mission: Plots to Kill Clinton Linked to Bin Laden," *Newsday,* 25 Aug. 1998, A3; Lew Merletti, follow-up interview by author, 30 June 2006.

492: "If you're not capable of": Lew Merletti, interview by author.

493: "I can assure you": President George H. W. Bush to Lew Merletti, 1 Apr. 1998, Merletti papers.

493: "You just don't get it!!!": Lew Merletti, interview by author.

493: "STAY THE COURSE": E-mail to Lew Merletti, name redacted, 26 May 1998, Merletti papers.

493: "THERE IS NO DOUBT HERE": E-mail to Merletti, name redacted, 4 June 1998, Merletti papers.

493: wondering what this day would mean: Lew Merletti, interview by author. See also John M. Broder and Stephen Labaton, "Shaped by a Painful Past, Secret Service Director Fights Required Testimony," *New York Times,* 29 May 1998, A7.

Chapter 40: Ginsburg's Final Photo Shoot

494: in an op-ed piece: William H. Ginsburg, "I Didn't Get 'Dumped,' " *Washington Post,* 4 June 1998, A23.

494: The senior Lewinsky had dispatched his: Bernie Lewinsky, interview by author.

496: Monica, too, had steadily lost: Monica Lewinsky, interview by author.

496: The Lewinsky family was also horrified: Barbara Lewinsky, remarks made while author was interviewing Bernie Lewinsky. The actual quote that Ginsburg had given to *Time* magazine was, "She's been imprisoned like a dog for four months" (Nancy Gibbs, "No Deal," *Time,* 11 May 1998).

496: her "little pulkes": Monica Lewinsky, interview by author; John Cloud, "Monica's Makeover," *Time,* 8 Mar. 1999.

496: "This is a total fabrication": Bernie Lewinsky, interview by author.

497: There was also the *Vanity Fair*: Ibid.

497: "Oh, my God, this is": Ibid.; Gibbs, "No Deal"; Laura Pulfer, "One Last Brief from Monica's Lawyer—Flack," *Cincinnati Enquirer,* 11 June 1998, and *Salon News Reel,* 11 June 1998.

497: "Honey, you're beautiful": Gibbs, "No Deal."

497: "It wasn't time to": William Ginsburg, interview by author.

498: "A psychiatrist suggested this?": Bernie Lewinsky, interview by author.

498: Ginsburg poured out his soul: William H. Ginsburg, "An Open Letter to Kenneth Starr," *California Lawyer,* June 1998.

498: "As our attorney, you cannot": Bernie Lewinsky, interview by author.

498: "he was not supposed to publish it": Monica Lewinsky, interview by author; Monica Lewinsky to author, 26 Jan. 2009.

498: Ginsburg defended his: William H. Ginsburg, "I Didn't Get 'Dumped,' " *Washington Post*; William Ginsburg, interview by author.

500: Yet Monica was not feeling: Gibbs, "No Deal."

500: "I did not want to go to trial": Monica Lewinsky, interview by author.

500: "I think he had [Monica's] best interest": Marcia Lewis Straus, interview by author.

500: Monica had flown back: Plato Cacheris, interview by author.

501: "hereby rescind[ed] and terminate[d]": Monica Lewinsky to William H. Ginsburg, 5 June 1998, Lewinsky papers.

501: "Since we parted company": William Ginsburg, interview by author.

501: "If I'd kept my big mouth shut": Pierre Thomas, "Who Are Plato Cacheris and Jacob Stein?" CNN AllPolitics, 3 June 1998.

501: the two lawyers arranged: Plato Cacheris, interview by author. Stein and Cacheris were initially contacted by Billy Martin, lawyer for Marcia Lewis, who was a "hero" to Monica and her mother, making it possible to change lawyers (Monica Lewinsky to author, December 31, 2009).

502: Starr was en route: Ken Starr, interview by author.

502: It gave page after page: Steven Brill, "Pressgate," *Brill's Content,* Aug. 1998. Ken Starr knew lawyer-publisher Steven Brill, who launched this new magazine, as the respected publisher of *American Lawyer* magazine. Starr trusted him as an earnest young lawyer who wanted to better the world through his writing.

502: David Kendall had swiftly filed: Ken Starr, interview by author.

502: Judge Johnson had seemed: Schmidt and Weisskopf, *Truth at Any Cost,* 177.

502: Within minutes, Starr's team: Kenneth W. Starr to Editor, *Brill's Content,* 16 May 1998; Statement by Steven Brill, 16 May 1998, Kendall papers. Among other things, Starr accused Brill of unprofessionalism and libelous inaccuracy.

502: "presented a prima facie case" to move: Order, In Re: Grand Jury Proceedings, 6 June 1998; "Testing of a President: Excerpts from Order Regarding Leaked Grand Jury Information," *New York Times,* 8 Aug. 1998.

503: "It was the nadir, as far": Ken Starr, interview by author.

503: He would stand tough: Ken Starr, interview by author.

503: Judge George Howard in Little Rock: McDougal and Harris, *The Woman Who Wouldn't Talk,* 305–14, 323, 326.

503: In a swift one-two punch: Memorandum Opinion, *United States v. Hubbell et al.,* Criminal Action No. 98-0151 (Robertson, J.), 1 July 1998; "The Hubbell Case: Excerpts from a Federal Court's Dismissal of the Hubbell Tax Evasion Case," *New York Times,* 2 July 1998; Stephen Labaton, "The Hubbell Case: The Overview; In Slap at Starr a Judge Dismisses Hubbell Tax Case," *New York Times,* 2 July 1998.

504: "It's a good day": Stephen Labaton, "The Hubbell Case."

504: the Secret Service issue: James Bennett, "Testing of a President: The Ruling; Judge Rejects Bid to Cite 'Privilege' in Clinton Inquiry," *New York Times,* 23 May 1998, A1; Order, in Re: Grand Jury Proceedings, 22 May 1998.

504: "The Secret Service is a dry hole": Lew Merletti, interview by author.

504: Now, as the walls seemed to be crumbling down: Ken Starr, interview by author; Jackie Bennett, interview by author; Schmidt and Weisskopf, *Truth at Any Cost,* 140–41.

504: "I think he [Holder] meant to": Ken Starr, interview by author.

504: "fire him immediately": Jackie Bennett, interview by author.

Chapter 41: Monica's Truth

505: "You can't lie contemporaneously for 20 hours": CNN Transcript, *Larry King Live,* Lucianne Goldberg, "Investigating the President: Lucianne Goldberg Talks About Linda Tripp and the Tapes," *Larry King Live,* CNN, 30 June 1998, transcript, 6–7.

506: Tripp's journey to: Elaine Scolino and Don Van Natta, Jr., "Testing of a President: The Confidant; Linda Tripp, Elusive Keeper of Secrets, Mainly Her Own," *New York Times,* 15 Mar. 1998.

506: "The vicious personal attacks against me": Linda R. Tripp, statement, issued by James A. Moody, 30 Jan. 1998.

506: With her frizzy blond hair pulled back: Evan Thomas and Michael Isikoff, "The Tripp Trap?" *Newsweek,* 13 July 1998, 22.

507: The first order of business: Evidentiary Record, vol. 4, part 3, 4033–34.

508: Tripp hedged her bets: Ibid., 4168.

509: Telephonically, there were no bounds to: Ibid., 4099.

510: These steps, she said, were an "insurance policy": Ibid., 4286–87.

510: In a final remarkable confession, Tripp admitted: Ibid., 4335–36.

511: His overriding concern, as a former federal judge: Ken Starr, interview by author.

513: Even Bob Bittman, whom Starr himself had: Robert J. Bittman, interview by author.

513: Starr recognized that he had lost the battle with: Ken Starr, interview by author.

513: the grand jury "simply can wait no": Robert J. Bittman to David E. Kendall, 17 July 1998, Kendall papers.

513: Bittman also attached an advice-of-rights form: Subpoena to: William Jefferson Clinton, U.S. District Court, District of Columbia, 17 July 1998, Kendall papers; Robert J. Bittman, interview by author.

514: After being driven by the FBI: Plato Cacheris, interview by author.

514: "Plato and I have at least one": Outline for Meeting, 9 June 1998, Plato Cacheris papers.

514: Cacheris and Stein, both of whom: Plato Cacheris, interview by author.

514: they could not accept "a pig in a poke": Jackie Bennett, interview by author. See also Robert Bittman to Jacob Stein and Plato Cacheris, 15 June 1998, Plato Cacheris papers.

514: "We weren't going to play that game": Plato Cacheris, interview by author.

515: Dash fancied himself as an ombudsman: Ibid.; Sam Dash, interview by author; Schmidt and Weisskopf, *Truth at Any Cost*, 203–204.

515: It was true: Paul Rosenzweig, interview by author.

515: One memo prepared solely for the eyes: Matthew Umhofer to Lewinsky File, 7 July 1998, Lewinsky papers.

516: "Her exposure was the affidavit": Plato Cacheris, interview by author.

516: "This may be the time": "Memo Concerning Present Status," undated, Lewinsky papers.

516: Surveying the Dashes' flower garden: Sam Dash, interview by author.

516: As the opposing lawyers strode to their cars: Notes, author's visit to Sara Dash home; Schmidt and Weisskopf, *Truth at Any Cost*, 204.

516: The meeting at "Grandma's house": Plato Cacheris, interview by author.

517: Linda Tripp had tried: Monica Lewinsky, interview by author; Morton, *Monica's Story*, 144–45.

517: Tripp had also encouraged: Morton, *Monica's Story*, 144–45; Schmidt and Weisskopf, *Truth at Any Cost*, 221.

517: If OIC had formally: William Ginsburg, interview by author.

518: Three days later: Ibid.; Plato Cacheris, interview by author.

518: The prosecutor said to Ginsburg: William Ginsburg, interview by author.

518: the copy of *Leaves of Grass*: Monica Lewinsky to author, January 26, 2009. Of course, the gifts that Monica had given to Betty Currie were no longer in Monica's apartment. Ibid.

519: Starr was fully aware: Ken Starr, interview by author.

519: wearing a "platinum blond wig": Monica Lewinsky, interview by author.

519: thoroughly skeptical of the motives of: Plato Cacheris, interview by author.

519: "I think in a perfect world, she could": Marcia Lewis Straus, interview by author.

519: Monica herself recalled: Monica Lewinsky, interview by author.

520: That muggy Monday morning: Ken Starr, interview by author.

520: "anybody named Lewinsky got immunity": Plato Cacheris, interview by author.

520: OIC was represented by: OIC Interview with Monica Lewinsky, 28 July 1998, Evidentiary Record, vol. 3, part 1, 1389.

520: OIC was intrigued but: Robert J. Bittman, interview by author.

520: seemed to be vying for control: Plato Cacheris, interview by author.

521: "Overall," he said, "we felt she was truthful": Robert J. Bittman, interview by author.

521: That evening, shortly after Monica's lawyers: Plato Cacheris, interview by author.

521: Monica would later note: Monica Lewinsky, interview by author.

521: Monica Lewinsky signed an immunity agreement: Immunity Agreement, 28 July 1998, Lewinsky papers.

522: "I had mixed feelings about even getting": Monica Lewinsky, interview by author.

522: "I think it was all just emotion, but bottom line": Plato Cacheris, interview by author.

522: Monica arrived at her lawyer's building: Inventory, 29 July 1998, Plato Cacheris papers.

522: Monica's mother herself: Marcia Lewis Straus, interview by author.

522: "I took it there": Monica Lewinsky, interview by author.

523: But when her new lawyers: Plato Cacheris, interview by author.

523: "Oh, my God, now's my chance!": Monica Lewinsky, interview by author.

523: As Cacheris ushered Starr's representatives: Plato Cacheris, interview by author.

524: assured that only "several top people": Robert J. Bittman, interview by author.

524: "Investigative demands," Bittman wrote, now required: Robert J. Bittman, interview by author; Schmidt and Weisskopf, *Truth at Any Cost*, 217–18.

525: As the early August sun: Robert J. Bittman, interview by author; David Kendall, interview by author.

526: As Merletti recalled the startling sidebar discussion: Lew Merletti, interview by author. The FBI official would later acknowledge, in a confidential interview with the author, that he had attended the conference in Atlantic City. He also confirmed that he was directly involved, at the request of Director Louis Freeh, in the lab examination of the blue dress and the DNA analysis. However, the official did not recall engaging in this conversation concerning the blue dress with Merletti.

Chapter 42: The Drudge Revolution

527: To further strengthen Starr's hand: "Statement of Independent Counsel Kenneth W. Starr," 7 Aug. 1998, Starr personal papers, F7, July 1998.

527: Stories concerning the infamous blue dress: Committee of Concerned Journalists, "The Clinton/Lewinsky Story: How Accurate? How Fair?" 20 Oct. 1998, 7–11. This study was conducted under the supervision of journalist Jim Doyle, former special assistant to the Watergate Special Prosecutors Cox and Jaworski. The project was chaired by Bill Kovach, curator of the Nieman Foundation, and Tom Rosenstiel, director of the Project for Excellence in Journalism.

528: Stories had also bounced around the media: Committee of Concerned Journalists, "The Clinton/Lewinsky Story," 12–17.

528: Nelvis himself appeared before: Bayani Nelvis, Grand Jury Testimony, 12 Mar. 1998, 16–19, Evidentiary Record, vol. 4, part 2, 3077–78.

528: "four other interns": Committee of Concerned Journalists, "The Clinton/Lewinsky Story," 34–35.

528: looking back on this train wreck: Ibid., 1.

528: Walter Cronkite, the retired anchor of *CBS Evening News*: "Walter Cronkite: Witness to History," *American Masters*, PBS, 26 July 2006, http://www.pbs.org/wnet/americanmasters/database/cronkite_w.html.

529: "the people are entitled to know peccadilloes": Walter Cronkite, interview by author.

530: The quirky and semireclusive thirty-one-year-old publisher: Matt Drudge, "Anyone with a Modem Can Report on the World," address before the National Press Club, 2 June 1998.

531: "I didn't think": Plato Cacheris, follow-up interview by author, 3 Oct. 2008.

531: "Monica is nothing but": Jared Hohlt, "Where on the Web Is Monica Lewinsky?" *Slate*, 31 Jan. 1998.

531: "Hillary Rodham Clinton Defense Forum": These e-mails were found on the Hillary Rodham Clinton Defense Forum site for the months of January through July 1998, http://www.kwik-link.com/e/hillary.clinton.jan.feb.1998.html, site visited 14 Oct. 2003. This site, like many on the World Wide Web during the Clinton-Starr matter, provided a window into the reactions of the American public to the scandal that no longer exists. See also "More Lewinsky Letters," http://www.cnn.com?ALLPOLITICS/1998/03/03/voters.voice/, site visited 12 Oct. 2003.

Chapter 43: A Walk in the Woods

532: As Monica Lewinsky suffered: Monica Lewinsky, interview by author.

533: the witness had just confirmed that: Evidentiary Record, vol. 3, part 1, 732–33.

533: in December, after she was subpoenaed: Ibid., 871–83; Monica Lewinsky, OIC interview, 28 July 1998, ibid., 1396.

533: Monica recounted the full story of the infamous blue dress: Evidentiary Record, vol. 3, 758–61.

534: There was never any question: Ibid., 924. Monica also confessed that she had intentionally deleted from her computer's hard drive all e-mails related to her affair with Clinton, and had asked Linda Tripp to do the same, so that written evidence of the relationship would be destroyed.

534: For Monica, it was simply a symbol: Ibid., 959; Monica Lewinsky, interview by author.

535: "we spent hours on the phone": Monica later clarified by stating: "This was a relationship. Everything was not calculated. It may not have been some cinematic grand love affair, but it was a relationship. When we talked on the phone, we talked like normal people. Every call did not have an intimate aspect to it" (Monica Lewinsky to author, 26 Jan. 2009).

536: President Clinton was privately meeting: Clinton, *My Life*, 799.

537: One person who knew about the complicated: Lew Merletti, interview by author.

537: In February 1998, there had been another aborted plot: Knut Royce, "Death Mission: Plots to Kill Clinton Linked to Bin Laden," *Newsday*, 25 Aug. 1998, A3.

537: Now, ten days before: Lew Merletti, interview by author; "Osama Bin Laden," "Wanted" poster, Merletti papers.

537: Agent Larry Cockell, who headed: Lew Merletti, interview by author; Larry Cockell, interview by author.

538: Bob Bittman was frustrated: Robert J. Bittman, interview by author.

538: Kendall tried a dozen maneuvers: Schmidt and Weisskopf, *Truth at Any Cost*, 23.

540: Starr's prosecutors, in the meantime: Robert J. Bittman, interview by author.

540: Already, the New York Times: Schmidt and Weisskopf, *Truth at Any Cost*, 230. OIC assumed that this trial balloon was being floated by the White House itself.

540: "We should treat [Clinton] with dignity and let him tell": Robert J. Bittman, interview by author.

540: Ewing, during the moot court sessions: "WJC Testimony Outline," attached to "Questions for the President: from Hickman," Starr papers, KWS outbox F8, August 1998.

541: "I am strongly opposed to giving the President any 'break'": Brett M. Kavanaugh to Judge Starr, 15 Aug. 1998, Ken Starr personal papers, KWS Outbox, F8, Aug. 1998.

541: The tension within OIC: Sol Wisenberg, interview by author.

541: To add to the pressure-cooker environment: Robert J. Bittman, interview by author.

542: "Sufficient unto the day": Ken Starr, interview by author.

542: Top military and national security advisers: Clinton, *My Life*, 797.

542: Bill Clinton woke up his wife: Hillary Clinton, *Living History*, 465–66.

542: The only thing that Bill Clinton: Ibid., 466. See also Clinton, *My Life*, 800; Carl Bernstein, *A Woman in Charge*, 512–13.

543: One close friend of the Clintons would later say: Confidential source, interview by author; Schmidt and Weisskopf, *Truth at Any Cost*, 233. One account suggests that it was late Thursday night when Bill Clinton actually broke the news that he had "strayed," when Chelsea was out with friends. However, that timing is inconsistent with the Clintons' own accounts, and those of close friends, who say that Bill did not confess to Hillary until Saturday morning.

543: Those closest to the Clintons: Betsey Wright, interview by author.

544: OIC's blue Crown Victoria and two vans pulled up: Robert J. Bittman, interview by author; Jackie Bennett, interview by author; itinerary, Starr personal papers, KWS Outbox, F8, Aug. 1998.

545: Kendall replied, "Fine": Ken Starr, interview by author; Robert J. Bittman, interview by author.

545: the independent counsel grimly reported: Robert J. Bittman, interview by author.

546: A diagram of the Map Room: Ibid.; diagram of Map Room, Starr personal papers, KWS Outbox, F8, Aug. 1998.

546: "physically quite large": Ken Starr, interview by author.

546: "When I was alone with Ms. Lewinsky": "Testimony of William Jefferson Clinton Before the Grand Jury Empaneled for Independent Counsel Kenneth Starr," 17 Aug. 1998, transcript published by Jurist, University of Pittsburgh, at www.jurist.law.pitt.edu/transcr.htm, 5 (hereinafter cited as Transcript).

547: Starr's prosecutors instantly called for: Paul Rosenzweig, interview by author.

547: "admission was not a shock": Robert J. Bittman, interview by author.

547: Wisenberg wanted to "hit [Clinton]": Sol Wisenberg, interview by author.

547: President Clinton seemed to be more in control: Ibid.

548: "She's basically a good girl": Transcript, 60–61.

548: in a spontaneous burst of candor: Transcript, 38–39.

548: the Starr prosecutors were getting exasperated: Sol Wisenberg, interview by author.

548: they were getting pummeled: Paul Rosenzweig, interview by author.

548: some prosecutors watching the faces: Ken Starr, interview by author; Paul Rosenzweig, interview by author.

548: Wisenberg took over, throwing off the gloves: Transcript, 45.

549: It was perhaps the most genuine explanation: Paul Rosenzweig, interview by author.

549: By delving into: The president's principal defense was that his conduct did not fall within the definition of "sexual relations," because he was on the *receiving* end of oral sex. Yet this defense was a real stretch, given the context of the *Jones* litigation, which specifically revolved around allegations that he had requested oral sex from Paula Jones. Even if one was able to accept that argument, Clinton could no longer dance around the fact that this sexual relationship with Monica Lewinsky had been a two-way street. There was now ample evidence—from Monica herself—that the president had been on the *giving* and *receiving* end of sexual activity with Lewinsky.

549: In response to: Transcript, 46–47, 54. To the extent that the president or his lawyers would try to revert to the argument that he had engaged in such conduct, but that he had lacked the intent to "arouse or gratify" Monica Lewinsky, such a technical argument would almost rise to the level of the absurd. Under such a defense, every male charged with sexual misconduct under the federal statute from which the definition was derived would simply protest: "I did it for self-gratification—I had no intent to gratify my female partner!" That, of course, would render the criminal laws meaningless.

549: "It depends on what the meaning of": Transcript, 29.

549: A number of grand jurors audibly "snorted": Paul Rosenzweig, interview by author.

550: But the clock was running: Ken Starr, interview by author.

550: Already, his lawyers had been compiling: "AMA Fires Journal Editor: Oral Sex Triggers Action," ABCNews.com, 15 Jan. 1999, Kendall papers. The *JAMA* editor who republished these findings in the midst of the Clinton scandal was fired because of the awkward "timing" of publishing the article.

551: Some members of religious groups: Alan Guttmacher Institute, "Scattered Evidence Indicates Oral Sex Becoming Increasingly Common Among Teens," news release, no date, Kendall papers.

551: Ken Starr felt "heartsick": Ken Starr, interview by author.

551: As Starr was gathering up: Ibid.

551: Jackie Bennett, whose sole contribution: Jackie Bennett, interview by author.

551: a somber "postmortem": Paul Rosenzweig, interview by author.

551: As Sol Wisenberg expressed it: Sol Wisenberg, interview by author.

552: Starr, thoroughly exhausted: Ken Starr, interview by author.

Chapter 44: Maximum Peril

553: Other advisers: John Podesta, interview by Chris Bury, "The Clinton Years," *Frontline,* PBS, Sept. 2000.

553: President Clinton looked into a camera and told: Transcript, televised address, 17 Aug. 1998.

554: Senator Dianne Feinstein: Richard L. Berke, "Democrats Distancing Themselves," *New York Times,* 19 Aug.1998; Todd S. Purdham, "The Nation: In Washington, Breaking the Rules of Hypocrisy," *New York Times,* 23 Aug. 1998.

554: Betsey Wright, Clinton's chief of staff: Betsey Wright, interview by author.

554: Alice Starr, who watched every minute: Alice Starr, interview by author.

554: A *Washington Post* photographer: Robert A. Reeder, *Washington Post,* 18 Aug. 1998, photo; Baker, *The Breach,* 46, photo at 224 insert.

555: Dick Kelley, the president's stepfather: Dick Kelley, interview by author.

555: Another person who was not particularly pleased: Monica Lewinsky, interview by author.

555: Starr's office had purposely called her back: James Bennett and Don Van Natta, Jr., "Starr Summons Lewinsky Again, Seeking Flaws in Clinton Account," *New York Times,* 19 Aug. 1998, A1.

555: When asked by one grand juror: Evidentiary Record, vol. 3, part 1, 1110.

556: At Martha's Vineyard: author's interviews with confidential sources.

557:Begala was a devout: Paul Begala, interview by author.

558: Intelligence reports indicated that Osama bin Laden: Clinton, *My Life,* 799.

558: After seeking input from National Security Adviser: Ibid.; Richard Clarke, *Against All Enemies,* 188–89; Baker, *The Breach,* 48–50.

558: "Don't give me political advice": Clarke, *Against All Enemies,* 186.

558: "Today I ordered our armed forces to strike at": Baker, *The Breach,* 50.

558: the president also signed Executive Order 13099: Clarke, *Against All Enemies,* 190.

558: Although the military strikes did not kill: Ibid.; Clinton, *My Life,* 803.

558: "This may be more than the country can handle": Paul Begala, interview by Chris Bury, "The Clinton Years," *Frontline,* PBS, June 2000.

559: The president returned to Martha's Vineyard: Clinton, *My Life,* 803; Hillary Clinton, *Living History,* 469.

559: It was during this period that Bill Clinton finally hit rock bottom: Hillary Clinton, *Living History,* 464. Relating to Kosovo, see Clinton, *My Life,* 787, 796, 848–51. See also "Albania Accuses Serbia of Ethnic Cleansing," BBC, 2 June 1998.

560: Those surrounding the embattled: Harold Ickes, interview by author.

560: A scattering of newspapers: *Lincoln Journal Star,* editorial, 19 Aug. 1998. This and other editorial pieces on the subject can be found in the publication *Editorials on File* 29, no. 16 (16–31 Aug. 1998).

560: "He seemed sorrier he got caught in sex acts": *Daily Oklahoman,* editorial, 19 Aug. 1998. The *Tampa Tribune* announced: "The president's moral authority is damaged, perhaps beyond repair"(*Tampa Tribune*, editorial, 21 Aug. 1998).

560: "This isn't the end": *Sacramento Bee*, editorial, 19 Aug. 1998.

560: Reno ordered a ninety-day: Roberto Suro and Michael Grunwald, "Reno Orders 90-Day Investigation of Gore," *Washington Post*, 27 Aug. 1998, A1; David Johnson, "Reno Is Extending Inquiry into Gore and Fund-Raising," *New York Times*, 27 Aug. 1998, A1.

561: Stated one judge: Two different federal judges in attendance confirmed these events. Both requested not to be identified. Moreover, newspaper reports confirm that the three-judge panel was notified of Reno's decision (ibid.).

561: Gore now stated: B. Drummond Ayres, Jr., "Testing of a President: The Vice President; Long a Defender of the Boss, Gore Praises Clinton Courage," *New York Times,* 18 Aug. 1998; Charles Burson, interview by author.

Chapter 45: Bombshell Report

565: Senator Joe Lieberman, a centrist Democrat: Woodward, *Shadow*, 454.

565: "I agree with what he said": Clinton, *My Life*, 808.

565: "a bouquet of good wishes": Evidentiary Record, vol. 3, part 1, 1163.

565: dragged through the wringer again: Monica S. Lewinsky, Deposition, 26 Aug. 1998, Evidentiary Record, vol. 3, part 1, 1281.

565: OIC, in the meantime, was busy: H. Ewing to K. Starr et al., "Some reasons for length of investigation," memo, 2 Sept. 1998, Starr personal papers, KWS Outbox, F8, Aug. 1998.

566: "We will transmit a narrative": Ronald D. Rotunda to Kenneth W. Starr, 3 Sept. 1998, Starr personal papers, KWS Outbox, F9, Sept.–Oct. 1998, italics added.

566: "believes that Clinton": Memo to Ken Starr, undated, Starr personal papers, KSW Outbox, F9, Sept.–Oct. 1998.

566: OIC returned Lewinsky's passport: Plato Cacheris to "Monica Lewinsky file," 26 Aug. 1998, Cacheris papers.

566: "a great fire hose flow": Stephen Bates, interview by author.

566: Ethics adviser Sam Dash was also horrified: Sam Dash, interview by author.

567: Yet he was itching to pass off: Stephen Bates, interview by author.

567: Starr later categorically denied: Ken Starr, interview by author.

567: A nagging issue that continued: Paul Rosenzweig, interview by author.

568: In the end, Starr's deputies agreed: Stephen Bates, interview by author.

568: there was no alternative but to pour: Ken Starr, interview by author.

568: "potential impeachment allegations": Stephen Bates, interview by author.

568: "I think we could have": Jackie Bennett, interview by author.

568: Leon Jaworski had written a bare-bones list: See Ken Gormley, "Impeachment and the Independent Counsel: A Dysfunctional Union," *Stanford Law Review* 51 (1999): 309, 345. See also Leon Jaworski, *The Right and the Power: The Prosecution of Watergate*, 101–102.

568: "a simple document, fifty-five pages long": James Doyle, *Not Above the Law: The Battles of Watergate Prosecutors Cox and Jaworski*, 290–91.

568: Judge Sirica himself verified: In Re: Report and Recommendation of June 5, 1972 Grand Jury Concerning Transmission of Evidence to House of Representatives, 370 F. Supp. 1219, 1226 (D.D.C. 1974) (Sirica, J.).

569: its own researcher was unable: Stephen Bates, interview by author.

569: "shall advise the House of Representatives": 28 U.S.C. Section 595c (1994).

569: That language, however sparse: Jackie Bennett, interview by author; Michael Emmick, interview by author.

569: An initial letter: Ken Starr, interview by author.

569: To a certain extent: Stephen Bates, interview by author. The final letter of transmittal stated, ambiguously: "The contents of the referral may not be publicly disclosed unless and until authorized by the House of Representatives. Many of the supporting materials contain information of a personal nature that I respectfully urge the House to treat as confidential."

569: Starr himself defended that omission: Ken Starr, interview by author.

570: Although this secret: For details concerning this little-known controversy involving the Tripp tapes, that permanently ruptured the relationship between Starr's prosecutors and Tripp, see Starr Report, 268, n. 125 (stating that these duplications/alterations "raise questions about the accuracy" of Ms. Tripp's testimony). See, also, Impeachment of President William Jefferson Clinton, Evidentiary Record, vol. 3, part 1, 225–27 (stating that nine tapes exhibited signs of duplication and were not consistent with being recorded on Tripp's RadioShack tape recorder; one tape exhibited signs of being produced by a recorder "that was stopped during the recording process").

570: As Ken Starr stood over a computer screen: Starr had taken the precaution of getting permission from the special three-judge panel before turning over this radioactive material. Although he believed that he had authority to disgorge "6(e)" material to Congress, he did not want OIC to be "charged with a violation of law" (Ken Starr, interview by author; Robert J. Bittman, interview by author).

570: A loud discussion ensued: As Ken Starr recalled the confrontation, Dash felt "very strongly" that Ground Eleven of the impeachment referral "had to be strengthened," to make even clearer that President Clinton's conduct "in using the powers of the presidency and invoking executive privilege and the like were unlawful" (Ken Starr, interview by author). Sam Dash, before his death, insisted that Starr and his prosecutors misconstrued his position. Dash's sharp recollection was that he had *opposed* language that suggested the president's assertion of "executive privilege" and "attorney-client" privilege were impeachable offenses. Dash explained, "[My position] was that the president had a right to assert these, even though he'd lose them after asserting them. And that they were *not* the kind of acts which would be impeachable acts" (Sam Dash, interview by author). What the ethics counsel *did* want to strengthen, he said, was the notion that the president had arguably conspired to obstruct justice, a theme that ran throughout a number of the counts. If proven, such conduct violated the president's constitutional duty to "faithfully execute the laws."

570: Dash told Starr: Sam Dash, interview by author.

570: The report was cleaned up: The final version of Ground Eleven in the Starr Report did include this allegation: "The President Repeatedly and Unlawfully Invoked the Executive Privilege to Conceal Evidence of His Personal Misconduct from the Grand Jury." Thus, this general point survived.

570: Jackie Bennett had worked diligently: Jackie Bennett, interview by author.

570: The House staffers: Jackie Bennett, interview by author; Schmidt and Weisskopf, *Truth at Any Cost*, 258.

570: No sooner had she secured it: Robert J. Bittman, interview by author.

571: "I understand you have": Ibid.; Schmidt and Weisskopf, *Truth at Any Cost*, 258.

571: More than twenty-five lawyers had pulled all-nighters: Jackie Bennett, interview by author.

571: "completely out of our hands": Ken Starr, interview by author.

572: "The American people deserve": Press release, "Hyde Statement to House Rules Committee," United States House of Representatives Committee on the Judiciary, 10 Sept. 1998.

572: In the ornate Yellow Oval Room: CNN, AllPolitics, 11 Sept. 1998; John Harris, "White House Rushing to Prepare Response," *Washington Post*, 11 Sept. 1998, A33; Woodward, *Shadow*, 461.

573: he was appalled when he learned: Ken Starr, interview by author.

573: Deputy Bittman phoned a high-ranking staffer: Robert J. Bittman, interview by author.

573: a short-lived debate within OIC: Stephen Bates, interview by author.

573: Prosecutors "ran around in the hallway": Jackie Bennett, interview by author.

573: Rather than trying to halt: Bob Bittman, e-mail to author, 3 Oct. 2008.

573: The next morning, Friday, President Clinton was scheduled: Bill Clinton, National Prayer Breakfast speech, White House, 11 Sept. 1998; John F. Harris, "For Clinton, a Day to Atone but Not Retreat," *Washington Post*, 12 Sept. 1998, A1.

573: Yet President Clinton himself would take issue: Bill Clinton, interview by author.

574: saw trouble brewing on the horizon: Barney Frank, interview by author.

574: "online traffic jams": Howard Kurtz, "Newspapers Weigh In," *Washington Post*, 13 Sept. 1998, A31.

574: David Kendall released: "White House Lawyers Prepare a Second Rebuttal," CNN AllPolitics, 12 Sept. 1998.

575: Those close to the president: David Kendall, interview by author.

575: A bug in OIC's: Jackie Bennett, interview by author; Michael Emmick, interview by author.

575: "You got both flavors": Jackie Bennett, interview by author.

575: "We had nothing to do with it": Robert J. Bittman, interview by author.

575: In the wake of the huge stir: See Kurtz, "Newspapers Weigh In"; "Time to Resign,"

Philadelphia Inquirer, 13 Sept. 1998, 56; *Pittsburgh Post-Gazette,* editorial, 13 Sept. 1998.

575: at a loss for words: Janet Reno, interview by author.

576: O'Sullivan was particularly aghast: Julie O'Sullivan, interview by author.

576: "That sort of detail wasn't necessary": William S. Duffey, Jr., interview by author.

576: Even Archibald Cox, the principled: Archibald Cox, interview by author.

577: "Talk about something that flies": Joe Purvis, interview by author.

577: Betsey Wright, who had already sunk: Betsey Wright, interview by author.

577: had written a personal letter to Ken Starr: Marcia Lewis Straus, interview by author.

578: Monica Lewinsky, on that day: Monica Lewinsky, interview by author.

578: Lying in the hospital bed: Bernie Lewinsky, interview by author.

579: Even worse, someone had slid: Ibid.

579: Back in Virginia, Alice Starr: Alice Starr, interview by author.

580: From his increasingly lonely: Kenneth Starr to Randy Starr, 28 Sept. 1998, Starr personal papers.

580: Matters only worsened: *Editorials on File* 29, no. 18 (16–30 Sept. 1998).

580: OIC had refused: Office of Independent Counsel, press release, 17 Sept. 1998.

580: a major "blunder": *Philadelphia Inquirer,* 22 Sept. 1998.

581: "We got our butts kicked": Paul Rosenzweig, interview by author.

581: dozens of magnifying glasses: David Kendall, interview by author.

581: "As the academic year begins": Kenneth Starr to Ronald F. Phillips, 25 Aug. 1998, Starr personal papers, Sept. 1998.

581: New polls showed: Democratic National Committee, collection of public opinion polls, 14 Sept. 1998, Starr personal papers, KWS Outbox, Sept.–Oct. 1998.

581: "Well, if she": Paul Begala, interview by author.

582: "Look, this was a terrible personal ordeal": Bill Clinton, interview by author.

Chapter 46: Starr Witness

582: Henry Hyde had engaged in: Woodward, *Shadow,* 471; Baker, *The Breach,* 98–99.

583: "It is the most hurtful thing": Henry J. Hyde, interview by author.

584: "I would kick": John Podesta, interview by author.

584: "engaged in misconduct unbecoming": Baker, *The Breach,* 112–13. The resolution further stated that Clinton had "failed to provide completely truthful and forthcoming testimony" in the *Jones* deposition and in his subsequent grand jury testimony.

584: Part of the proposed deal: As Gephardt and Bauer constructed the final plan, Ken Starr and President Clinton would have to work out their differences by the date of the president's State of the Union address in January. If the parties could not put the matter to rest, Congress could go forward with impeachment proceedings if warranted, or cut off funds to the independent counsel if that was in order (ibid.).

584: DeLay directed his troops: Ibid., 114.

584: So Democrats devised: The Boucher plan would have created tight deadlines, required a determination of what constituted an impeachable offense before considering the merits of the Clinton case, and required that the whole process be wrapped up by November 25, at which time the House would have to vote to impeach, dismiss the charges, or settle on a third option (ibid., 115–16).

584: "We realized they were like": Barney Frank, interview by author.

584: As he witnessed: Amory Houghton, interview by author.

585: Daschle told the president: Tom Daschle, interview by author.

585: Seated in his golden wheelchair: Larry Flynt, interview by author.

586: Democrats were becoming: Baker, *The Breach,* 108–109, 137–39.

586: "further impeachment referrals": "Independent Counsel Responds to Hyde-Conyers Letter; Starr Does Not Rule Out Further Impeachment Referrals," 7 Oct. 1998, House Judiciary Committee Web site.

586: Feeling empowered and emboldened: Editorial, *Chicago Sun Times,* 6 Oct. 1998; Baker, *The Breach,* 123. House Republicans snuffed out the Democratic-sponsored "censure plus" concept. They additionally rejected a compromise plan by Congressman Howard Berman of California. His plan would have permitted the Judiciary Committee to take its time studying whether the Starr Report established a proper basis for a formal impeachment inquiry, before the committee would delve into it.

586: "This is the Russian Army": Barney Frank, interview by author.

586: On October 8: "White House Scandals: House Votes for Impeachment Inquiry to Clinton's Conduct with Lewinsky," *Editorials on File* 29, no. 19 (1–15 October 1998); Editorial, *San Diego Union Tribune,* 9 Oct. 1998.

586: On October 30, Chief Judge Norma Holloway Johnson: Order, 25 Sept. 1998, in Re-Grand Jury Proceedings, Misc. No. 98-228, 1998 U.S. Dist. LEXIS 17290, 32; David Kendall to Honorable Mark J. Langer, Clerk of Court, 11 Jan. 2002, Kendall papers. The federal judge found a *prima facie* violation of Rule 6(e), stating that the twenty-four alleged violations were "serious and repetitive."

587: For months, House Speaker Newt Gingrich: Baker, *The Breach,* 132–33; Schmidt and Weisskopf, *Truth at Any Cost,* 260–61.

588: Gingrich's unexpected fall from grace: Howard Fineman and Matthew Cooper, "The Loser," *Newsweek,* 16 Nov. 1998, 30.

588: His lawyers' strategy was: Although in theory a "material misstatement" under oath could still be established, most judges would consider it imprudent to make such a finding if the case itself had settled.

588: Paula and Steve Jones were separating: Wesley Holmes, interview by author.

588: Each side would later claim: The Jones team had contact with certain court personnel who hinted that Judge Wright's opinion was about to be overturned (Wesley Holmes, interview by author). Bob Bennett, on the other hand, ran into an unidentified law clerk who intimated that the Eighth Circuit was prepared to rule two to one in the president's favor (Robert Bennett, interview by author).

588: Judge Wright was famous for: Judge Wright had essentially assumed the truth of the conduct alleged by Paula Jones, but found that it did not meet the legal standard for a sexual harassment claim. The Eighth Circuit had upheld other summary judgment findings in discrimination cases of a similar ilk.

589: Wes Holmes, told Paula bluntly: Wesley Holmes, interview by author.

589: "It was time for it to be over with": Paula Jones, interview by author.

589: "Paula, if it was me": Susan Carpenter-McMillan, interview by author. Carpenter-McMillan, although displeased with the decision, still volunteered to help out her "younger baby sister" Paula by enlisting her own husband, Bill, a successful personal injury lawyer (from whom she would soon divorce), to haggle out a deal with Bob Bennett. It was unclear who outfoxed who, but the two Irishmen got together and came up with a settlement number that allowed both sides to declare victory (ibid.).

589: "hated like hell": Bill Clinton, interview by author.

590: Starr also saw this as a chance: Ken Starr, interview by author; Schmidt and Weisskopf, *Truth at Any Cost,* 263–64.

590: "I want to raise a point with you": Janet Reno, interview by author.

591: visibly "angry": Robert J. Bittman, interview by author.

591: Starr himself would later say: Ken Starr, interview by author.

592: "It's convenient for them": Eric Holder, interview by author.

593: "There Is Substantial and Credible Information": Memo, Stephen Bates to "All Attorneys," 15 Nov. 1998, Samuel Dash papers, box 62, Library of Congress (hereinafter cited as Dash papers).

593: The internal OIC memo: Memo, 15 Oct. 1998, 20, Dash papers. See also Florence Graves and Jacqueline E. Sharkey, "Starr and Willey: The Untold Story," *The Nation,* 17 May 1999.

594: "Dear Mom. Howdy": Ken Starr to Vannie Starr, 5 Nov. 1998, and Thomas Sowell, "Kenneth Starr's Real Crime," *Human Events,* 6 Nov. 1998, Starr personal papers.

594: In a letter to daughter Carolyn: Ken Starr to Carolyn Starr, 4 Nov. 1998, and clipping from *Houston Chronicle,* 4 Nov. 1998, Starr personal papers.

594: "I have a friend who is going through hell": Sealy M. Yates to Ken Starr, 5 Oct. 1998, Starr personal papers.

595: "I thought it was something": Alice Starr, interview by author.

595: "The truth is sacred": Draft comments, marked "not used," Nov. 1998, Starr personal papers, KWS Outbox, Sept.–Oct. 1998.

595: Rows of Judiciary Committee members: Nancy Gibbs, "Men of the Year," photograph, *Time,* 28 Dec. 1998/4 Jan. 1999, 78–79; "Impeachment Hearings, Opening Remarks of Ranking Democratic Rep. John Conyers," *Federal News Service,* 19 Nov. 1998.

595: This unexpected attack: Statement of Independent Kenneth Starr Before the Committee on the Judiciary, U.S. House of Representatives, 19 Nov. 1998, OIC papers.

596: "I was fat, out of shape": Sol Wisenberg, interview by author.

596: "We were really surprised": Henry J. Hyde, interview by author.

596: The president's lawyer squared his shoulders: Gibbs, "Men of the Year," photograph, 84–85.

596: Observers in the gallery: "Impeachment Hearings, Clinton Lawyer David Kendall Questions Starr," *Federal News Service*, 19 Nov. 1998.

596: Within minutes, Kendall had forced: Fred Hiatt, "Kendall's Theatre," *Washington Post*, 22 Nov. 1998.

597: The burly Chicago criminal lawyer: "The Impeachment Hearings, Republican Counsel David Schippers Questions Starr," *Federal News Service*, 18 Nov. 1998.

597: "They were a couple of drunks": Barney Frank, interview by author.

598: "His [Starr's] testimony gave Democrats": Henry J. Hyde, interview by author.

598: Ken Starr gathered up his papers: Schmidt and Weisskopf, *Truth at Any Cost*, 271.

598: he simply couldn't continue to defend: Sam Dash, interview by author. According to Dash, Bob Bittman and Paul Rosenzweig urged him not to resign.

598: It was no secret: With Congress marching toward impeachment, Dash was receiving letters like one from lawyer Edward H. Weinberg of Great Neck, New York, who upbraided him for participating in Starr's "reign of terror": "I believe you have tarnished perhaps irreparably your standing with millions of Americans by reason of your connection with and role in Starr's Witch Hunt" (Edward H. Weinberg to Samuel Dash, 18 Aug. 1998, Dash papers, box 1).

598: The *Washington Post* issued an editorial: ". . . And Mr. Dash's Resignation," *Washington Post*, 22 Nov. 1998.

598: "And so I told Ken": Sam Dash, interview by author. See also Sam Dash, letter of resignation, *Salon*, 20 Nov. 1998.

599: As Starr put out the trash: "Starr Defends Testimony After Ethics Adviser Resigns," CNN AllPolitics, 20 Nov. 1998; Sam Dash, interview by author. In a two-page written reply, Ken Starr took issue with his ethics adviser's logic: "You suggest that by appearing, I harmed public confidence in the independence of the Office. With respect, I disagree with that. Indeed, had I chosen to refuse the invitation to testify, I believe that would have harmed public confidence in

the Office. A refusal to appear would have suggested that we have something to hide, or that we are unwilling to defend and stand by the written referral." Despite this disagreement, Starr concluded by telling his elder adviser: "Today's developments will not alter my deep affection for you and profound appreciation for all you have done for us" (Kenneth W. Starr to Professor Sam Dash, 20 Nov. 1998, Dash papers, box 1).

599: "The country got a glimpse": "A Real Starr," *Martinsburg (W.V.) Journal*, 22 Nov. 1998, A10, Starr personal papers.

599: "You appeared as a knight": Bonnie Shea to Kenneth Starr, 20 Nov. 1998; Ken Starr to Randy and Carolyn Starr, Nov. 30, 1998, Starr personal papers.

599: A seventeen-year-old from Los Angeles: Rachel Scherer to Judge Starr, and Ken Starr to Rachel Scherer, 30 Nov. 1998, Starr personal papers.

599: "Monsieur le Procureur General": Monique Bach to Ken Starr, and Neille Mallon Russell to Monique Bach, 17 Dec. 1998, Starr personal papers.

599: "Sorry I haven't checked in": Ken Starr to mother, 16 Dec. 1998, Ken Starr personal papers.

599: "bubbling over with anticipatory": Ken Starr to children, 8 Dec. 1998, Ken Starr personal papers.

599: "and if the Republicans choose a candidate": Henry Ruth, "Clinton Has Corrupted His Party's Soul," *Wall Street Journal*, 8 Dec. 1998. Ruth was the third of four Watergate special prosecutors. He was preceded by Archibald Cox and Leon Jaworski, then succeeded by Charles Ruff.

Chapter 47: "Men of the Year"

600: acquitted Susan McDougal: Todd S. Purdon, "Clintons' Friend Found Not Guilty of All 9 Embezzlement Charges," *New York Times*, 24 Nov. 1998. Besides embezzlement charges, there were also counts relating to failure to pay income taxes.

600: The former Whitewater defendant: McDougal and Harris, *The Woman Who Wouldn't Talk*, 329–48.

600: Already, Starr had filed: Purdon, "Clintons' Friend." See also Judy Bacharach, "Joan of Arkansas," *Vanity Fair*, January 1999, 86.

600: "I AM A CHANGED PERSON": Susan McDougal, letter to editor, undated, Susan McDougal papers.

600: "Every day I sat there": Susan McDougal, interview by author.

601: Starr's office had secured a third indictment: Indictment, *United States v. Webster Hubbell et al.,* Criminal no. 98-0394, 13 Nov. 1998; Susan Schmidt, "Starr Brings Third Indictment Against Hubbell," *Washington Post,* 14 Nov. 1998, A1.

601: The hulking former Justice Department official: Schmidt, "Starr Brings Third Indictment."

601: were deadlocked: Paul Rosenzweig to "All Attorneys," 23 Oct. 1998, Dash papers, box 62.

601: Confidential memos now confirm: Julie Myers to "All OIC Attorneys," 25 Oct. 1998, Dash papers, box 62.

601: cautioned Starr that this move: Paul Rosenzweig to "All Attorneys." Myers proposed "dropping the mail fraud count," which would at least eliminate the most egregious double-jeopardy problem.

601: A confidential OIC report: Jerry Seper, "Once-Secret Memos Question Clinton's Honesty," *Washington Times,* 8 May 2008.

601: In mid-November, Henry Hyde drafted: Henry J. Hyde, interview by author.

602: "smart-alecky," "sarcastic": Committee on the Judiciary, Requests for Admission of William J. Clinton, President of the United States, and Responses to the Requests for Admission, No. 43, Nov. 1998, David Schippers papers. See also Baker, *The Breach,* 179–81.

602: Hyde had hoped: Henry J. Hyde, interview by author.

602: Representative Barney Frank likened it: Barney Frank, interview by author; Tom Daschle, interview by author.

602: Many OIC prosecutors had envisioned: Stephen Bates, interview by author.

602: Now, to OIC's horror: Sam Dash, interview by author.

602: House Republicans, for their part, were fed up: David Schippers, comments made during author's interview with Henry J. Hyde; David Schippers, follow-up interview by author, 20 Mar. 2009. The efforts in part involved obtaining memos written by Louis Freeh, FBI director, and Charles G. LaBella, head of DOJ's campaign task force; the memos were still under seal (Baker, *The Breach,* 183–85).

603: Schippers also tried: Baker, *The Breach,* 182–85.

603: Attorney General Janet Reno: "Excerpt from Reno's Report Rejecting Independent

Counsel in Gore Case," *New York Times,* 25 Nov. 1998. Not only did Reno refuse to commence an investigation into whether Vice President Gore had lied to federal officials on this matter, she also rejected a separate inquiry relating to both Clinton and Gore. See also Ronald J. Ostrow and Robert L. Jackson, "Reno Rejects Outside Probe of '96 Campaign," *Los Angeles Times,* 8 Dec. 1998.

603: On December 12: Baker, *The Breach,* 216.

603: "We had a bill of impeachment": Henry J. Hyde, interview by author.

603: According to Clinton's intelligence: Bill Clinton, interview by author; Barney Frank, interview by author.

603: Moderate Republicans looking for an out: Barney Frank, interview by author; Baker, *The Breach,* 263. Two days after the House vote, Congressmen Gilman and Boehlert along with Mike Castle and Jim Greenwood—all Republicans who had voted for several articles of impeachment—wrote to Senator Trent Lott: "We are not convinced, and do not want our votes interpreted to mean that we viewed removal from office as the only reasonable conclusion of this case" (Baker, *The Breach,* 263; Jonathan Weisman, "GOP Faction Makes Pitch for Censure," *Baltimore Sun,* 22 Dec. 1998).

603: "folded like Dick's hatband": Bill Clinton, interview by author.

604: "true believer right-wing fundamentalists": Barney Frank, interview by author.

604: all hell broke loose in the Middle East: Woodward, *Shadow,* 490–94; Baker, *The Breach,* 226–28.

604: "If you looked": Doug Sosnik, interview by author.

605: Republican leaders in Congress went ballistic: Brian Knowlton, "Republicans Lash Out at the Timing; Gulf Action May Delay Impeachment Vote," *International Herald Tribune,* 17 Dec. 1998.

605: With dark bags under his eyes: "Clinton Announces Iraq Strikes," *BBC News,* 17 Dec. 1998.

606: "He could work himself": Harold Ickes, interview by author.

606: "Almost every day": Paul Begala, interview by author.

606: Frank reconstructed the scene: Barney Frank, interview by author.

607: he knew Frank's optimistic nose-count was wrong: Bill Clinton, interview by author.

607: "He wanted to know": Amory Houghton, Jr., interview by author.

607: "We'd better just batten down": David Kendall, interview by author.

608: The final vote: Article II, relating to perjury in the *Paula Jones* deposition, failed by a vote of 229 to 205. Article IV, relating to abuse of power, failed, 285 to 148 ("House Impeaches Clinton," CNN AllPolitics, 19 Dec. 1998). Only four Republicans had broken ranks and voted against all four articles, while only a handful of Democrats voted to impeach.

608: "You know, this guy wasn't up": Barney Frank, interview by author.

608: "high school pep rally": Henry J. Hyde, interview by author.

609: "Here's a guy": Charles Burson, interview by author.

609: Gore took a deep breath: James Bennett, "Impeachment: The President—Clinton Impeached; President Digs In," *New York Times,* 20 Dec. 1998; Baker, *The Breach,* 255.

609: the Hillary factor: Sally Bedell Smith, "White House Civil War," *Vanity Fair,* November 2007, 296, 298, 352, excerpted from Sally Bedell Smith, *For Love of Politics: Bill and Hillary Clinton—The White House Years.*

609: "Al's intense sense": Charles Burson, interview by author.

610: "He wouldn't have done that": Frank Hunger, interview by author.

610: President Clinton himself: Bill Clinton, interview by author; Bill Clinton, speech on the South Lawn of White House, 19 Dec. 1998.

610: A second act of courage: Gerald R. Ford, "The Path Back to Dignity," *New York Times,* 4 Oct. 1998. In early October, Ford had authored this op-ed for the *New York Times,* urging the Republican-dominated House to forgo impeachment for the good of the nation. The thirty-eighth president proposed that Bill Clinton should be required to appear in the well of the House—the same spot where Clinton usually appeared to thunderous applause as he delivered his State of the Union address—and be forced to endure "not an ovation from the people's representatives, but a harshly worded rebuke as rendered by members of both parties." Under Ford's plan, Clinton would be required to "accept full responsibility for his actions. . . . No spinning, no semantics, no evasiveness or blaming others for his plight." If this could be accomplished "without partisan[ship] or mean-spiritedness," Ford argued, "[it] would be the first moment of majesty in an otherwise squalid year."

611: "whether we could do something jointly": Gerald R. Ford and Jimmy Carter, "A Time to Heal Our Nation," *New York Times,* 21 Dec. 1998. President Carter, as early as September 22 at a town hall meeting in Georgia, had indicated that he had serious concerns about the House's pressing for an impeachment, particularly because he believed that conviction in the Senate was nearly impossible and that forcing impeachment proceedings would be bad for the country (Jimmy Carter, Emory University Town Hall Meeting, Atlanta, 22 Sept. 1998, transcript of comments, Starr personal papers, Sept. 1998).

611: As Hyde himself: Henry J. Hyde, interview by author. It was hard to fathom that a censure measure would amount to an unconstitutional violation of separation of powers if the president himself *consented* to it. As Ford and Carter correctly noted in their op-ed piece, history was filled with creative accommodations among the three branches of government. The Framers of the Constitution would certainly not have mandated that Congress go through a draining, divisive impeachment trial if the president himself agreed to accept a public rebuke on the floor of Congress.

611: Former President Ford later disclosed: Gerald R. Ford, interview by author.

612: Ford held strong views: Ken Gormley, "Explaining the Pardon," *Pittsburgh Post-Gazette,* 1 Jan. 2007.

612: "He [Clinton] was very rational": Gerald R. Ford, interview by author.

612: Perhaps it was Bill Clinton's: President Clinton, in a Rose Garden speech on December 11, while steering clear of any admission of perjury or lying under oath, did make clear that he would accept "rebuke and censure" from the American people and Congress, if that was what they decided was fitting (Bill Clinton, Rose Garden Statement, *Associated Press,* 11 Dec. 1998).

612: "There was never any rancor": Gerald R. Ford, interview by author.

612: Ken's mother, Vannie Mae Starr: Lisa Sandberg, "Starr's Mother Dies at Her Home," *San Antonio Express-News,* undated, Roberta Mahan papers.

613: For the weary independent counsel: Ken Starr, interview by author.

613: "the Starr Cemetery": Billie Jeayne (Starr) Reynolds, interview by author.

614: The *Time* piece began: Gibbs, "Men of the Year," 76–78.

Chapter 48: Thirteen Angry Managers

614: Senate Majority Leader Trent Lott was sitting: Trent Lott, interview by author.

615: "mishandled in the House": Tom Daschle, interview by author.

615: Quietly, the Senate had already: Robert Dove, interview by author.

615: President Johnson, a Democrat: See, generally, Gormley, *Archibald Cox*, xv–xx; Eleanore Bushnell, *Crimes, Follies, and Misfortunes: The Federal Impeachment Trials*; David Miller DeWitt, *The Impeachment Trial of Andrew Johnson*; William H. Rehnquist, *Grand Inquests: The Historic Impeachments of Justice Samuel Chase and President Andrew Johnson*; Hans L. Trefousse, *Impeachment of a President: Andrew Johnson, the Blacks, and Reconstruction*.

615: Seven House impeachment managers: "The Impeachment of Andrew Johnson: The Impeachment Managers," *Harper's Weekly*, 1868, 179.

616: Alexander Hamilton: Alexander Hamilton, "The Federalist No. 65," in *The Federalist Papers*, ed. Clinton Rossiter, 396.

616: The legal scholar Joseph Story: Joseph Story, *Commentaries on the Constitution of the United States*, 4th ed. (ed. Thomas M. Cooley), vol. 2, section 803, p. 566.

616: Yet not everyone: Gerald R. Ford, remarks, U.S. House of Representatives, 15 Apr. 1970, 6, available at http://www.ford.utexas.edu/library/speeches/700415f.htm.

617: He understood that in sharp contrast: Robert Dove, interview by author.

617: The record would be: The trial would have only moved into a second phase if two-thirds of the senators voted for it (Baker, *The Breach*, 269).

617: "Sometimes, a leader": Trent Lott, interview by author.

618: Kendall and White House Counsel Charles Ruff: David Kendall, interview by author.

618: On December 30, Chairman Hyde: Baker, *The Breach*, 270.

618: Lott immediately phoned: Trent Lott, interview by author.

618: Hyde implored: Henry J. Hyde, interview by author.

618: "The walk looked like a funeral": Carin Dessauer, "History in the Making: Clinton on Trial," CNN AllPolitics, 7 Jan. 1999.

618: As cameras flashed: *Congressional Record*, 7 Jan. 1999; "Jan. 7: The Managers Arrive," washingtonpost.com, 7 Jan. 1999.

619: Two hours later: The Senate escorts were Senators Ted Stevens (R-Alaska), Robert Byrd (D-W.V.), Orrin Hatch (R-Utah), Patrick Leahy (D-Vt.), Olympia Snowe (R-Maine), and Barbara Mikulski (D-Md.) (Trent Lott, interview by author; Tom Daschle, interview by author).

619: "had a big laugh": Justice Sandra Day O'Connor, interview by author; Linda Greenhouse, "The Trial of the President: The Chief Justice; Rehnquist, in New Arena, Appears at Home," *New York Times*, 8 Jan. 1999.

619: "sardonic": Robert Dove, interview by author.

620: indicted Julie Hiatt Steele: "Grand Jury Indicts Witness in Willey Investigation," CNN *AllPolitics* 7 Jan. 1999; Florence Graves and Jacqueline E. Sharkey, "Starr and Willey: The Untold Story," *Nation*, 17 May 1999. For a discussion of the complicated Steele-Willey charges and countercharges, see Isikoff, *Uncovering Clinton*, afterword, 366–67.

621: Senator Robert Byrd of West Virginia: Baker, *The Breach*, 289.

621: Just as there seemed: For accounts of this closed-door session in the Old Senate Chamber, see Andrew Miga, Joe Battenfield, and Ellen J. Silberman, "Senate Agrees on Trial Ground Rules; Format Postpones Vote on Witnesses," *Boston Herald*, 9 Jan. 1999, 1; Maria Recio, "Gramm Joins Kennedy to Forge Bipartisan Deal," *Fort Worth Star-Telegram*, 9 Jan. 1999, 6; Curt Anderson, "Amid Ghosts of Senate Past, Sides Seal Deal in Rare Private Session," 9 Jan. 1999. See also "Press Conference on Senate Impeachment Procedure Agreement," Federal News Services, 8 Jan. 1999.

621: "Well, what was [the deal]?": Trent Lott, interview by author.

621: One key aspect: David Kendall, interview by author.

622: "It was a resolution which effectively gave a veto power": Robert Dove, interview by author.

622: Although Senator Lott emphasized: Trent Lott, interview by author.

622: At noon on Thursday: See Ken Gormley, "Impeachment Trial, Day One," *Pittsburgh Post-Gazette*, 17 Jan. 1999.

623: "Is that it?": David Kendall, interview by author.

623: Whatever the circus atmosphere: U.S. Senate, 106th Congress, 1st sess., 14 Jan. 1999, videotape (hereinafter cited as Senate video).

624: Chairman Henry Hyde: *Congressional Record*, 14 Jan. 1999; "The Impeachment Trial,

Jan. 14: Hyde Opening Statement,"
WashingtonPost.com, 14 Jan. 1999.

624: introduced his fellow managers: The initial speakers included Representative F. James Sensenbrenner, Jr., from Wisconsin, who in 1989 had served as a manager for the impeachment trial of federal Judge Walter L. Nixon; Representative Asa Hutchinson, a former U.S. attorney from Bill Clinton's home state of Arkansas; and Representative Jim Rogan of California, a former judge and local prosecutor from Los Angeles. The other eight House managers, who would make presentations over the next two days, were Representatives Bill McCollum of Florida, George Gekas of Pennsylvania, Steve Chabot of Ohio, Bob Barr of Georgia, Chris Cannon of Utah, Charles Canady of Florida, Steve Buyer of Indiana, and Lindsey Graham of South Carolina.

624: a bathroom break: Trent Lott, interview by author.

624: "had to sit without speaking": Robert Dove, interview by author.

624: an unmistakable sensation of "friction": Tom Daschle, interview by author.

625: "I'd have learned to say 'no'": Henry J. Hyde, interview by author.

625: In contrast: The president's defense team consisted of Charles Ruff (an attorney who used a wheelchair), David Kendall, Cheryl Mills (an African American lawyer who served as deputy counsel to the president), Special White House Counsel Greg Craig (a high-ranking State Department official and friend of the Clintons), Nicole Seligman (a former *Harvard Law Review* standout and clerk to Justice Thurgood Marshall who was working at Williams & Connolly alongside Kendall), and Clinton confidente Bruce Lindsey. Kendall and Ruff worked diligently to avoid repetitious presentations so that their efficient, seven-person team would stand in stark contrast to the oversized collection of House managers.

625: In other modern-day impeachment trials: Robert Dove, interview by author.

625: "ideologically committed": Henry J. Hyde, interview by author.

625: by far their strongest basis: Jim Fisher, the Dallas lawyer who had handled President Clinton's deposition in the *Jones* case, would later say that he was frustrated as he watched the House strategy unfold: "The instances of lying were so clear in my deposition. . . . When he [Clinton] said things like he couldn't remember ever being

alone with Monica Lewinsky anywhere in the White House, or he couldn't remember giving her gifts . . . there were a half-dozen instances where it was extremely clear that he had lied. That should have been, I think, more of the focal point" (Jim Fisher, interview by author).

625: "bollixed things up": Confidential source, interview by author.

626: On the second day of trial: Senate video, 15 Jan. 1999; *Congressional Record,* 15 Jan. 1999; "The Impeachment Trial, Jan 15: Barr on Perjury and Obstruction," WashingtonPost.com, 15 Jan. 1999.

626: Just days earlier, Larry Flynt: Howard Kurtz, "Flynt Calls Rep. Barr a Hypocrite for Divorce Case Answers," 12 Jan. 1999, *Washington Post,* A7.

626: "Harkin's speaking!": Baker, *The Breach,* 310.

626: Dove fully understood: Robert Dove, interview by author.

626: Some Republicans whispered: Ibid.; James Duff, interview by author.

627: "Just be as mean": John Dean, *The Rehnquist Choice: The Untold Story of the Nixon Appointment That Redefined the Supreme Court,* 285.

627: As Clinton saw it: Bill Clinton, interview by author.

628: "I'd like to say": James Duff, interview by author. Duff considered it "a bit paranoid" to suggest that Rehnquist had plotted to get Clinton by appointing Judge Sentelle: "Quite honestly, it wasn't anything he'd sit down and calculate, 'We'll load it in favor of the Republicans this way.'" Duff typically would walk into Rehnquist's chambers with a list of the pending vacancies and the interested judges, and the chief would make rapid selections. "He would have to be extremely calculating and vindictive to figure these things out in advance," Duff said. "He would also have to be prescient. He made these decisions very quickly, without any great premeditation. I do not think the appointment of Judge Sentelle was nefarious in any way." As to the story that Rehnquist had told Clinton "good luck" after swearing him in, Duff would say that if the chief even uttered those words (Duff was nearby and heard no such comment), it was merely a droll expression of what others told him when he became chief: "It's going to be a tough job, but I wish you the best."

628: Years earlier, the chief had authored: Rehnquist, *Grand Inquests;* Trefousse, *Impeachment of a President;* Michael Les Benedict, *The Impeachment and Trial of Andrew Johnson.*

628: Rehnquist had no intention: Chief Justice Rehnquist would say very little about the Senate impeachment trial of Bill Clinton, before his death, other than to note dryly: "I was an observer like everyone else." He would rebuff requests for interviews, telling would-be historians: "My role was almost ministerial. No witnesses were called, and there were very few objections to rule upon" (William H. Rehnquist to author, 14 Feb. 2000).

628: His paramount concern: James Duff, interview by author. Rehnquist prevailed on Senate leaders to schedule impeachment sessions in the afternoon, to avoid interfering with the Court's calendar. He also refused to conduct proceedings in the Senate on Fridays, because that was the day the Court held its conferences.

Chapter 49: A Scottish Vote

629: Charles Ruff, representing the president: Senate video, 19 Jan. 1999; *Congressional Record*, 19 Jan. 1999; "The Impeachment Trial. Jan. 19: Ruff Begins the Defense," washingtonpost.com, 19 Jan. 1999.

629: Chuck Ruff was no stranger: Daniel Becker, "Legends in the Law: Charles F.C. Ruff," *Washington Lawyer*, April 2001, 31–35.

629: Ruff, who had graduated from Columbia: Susan Ruff, interview by author.

630: a series of government posts: Ruff was first a lawyer in the Criminal Division of the Justice Department. Later, he was an interim special prosecutor wrapping up the Watergate investigation, before going on to serve as U.S. attorney for Washington, D.C.

630: Sue Ruff was glued: Susan Ruff, interview by author; Danny Westneat, "Impeachment Diary—Voice of Public Rains Down on Senate: 'Get It Over With!' " *Seattle Times,* 5 Feb. 1999.

630: "a surgeon's sense": David Kendall, interview by author.

630: Each morning, Kendall and Ruff: Ibid.

631: "I mean, the State of the Union": Robert Dove, interview by author.

631: House Manager Bob Barr stayed away: Frank Bruni, "State of the Union: The No Shows," *New York Times,* 20 Jan. 1999.

631: "sit in my shorts": Henry J. Hyde, interview by author.

631: "[show] that his personal travails": Doug Sosnik, interview by author.

632: "Let us lift our eyes": "Transcript: Clinton's State of the Union Speech," cnn.com, 20 Jan. 1999; Baker, *The Breach,* 319.

632: a grand slam over the bleachers: Tom Daschle, interview by author; Trent Lott, interview by author.

632: "I am not worried": Senate video, 20 Jan. 1999; *Congressional Record,* 20 Jan. 1999; "The Impeachment Trial, Jan. 20: Mills on Obstruction of Justice Allegations," washingtonpost .com, 20 Jan. 1999.

632: David Kendall: Senate video, 21 Jan. 1999; *Congressional Record,* 21 Jan. 1999; "The Impeachment Trial, Jan. 21: Kendall Defends the President," washingtonpost.com, 21 Jan. 1999.

633: "That was Bill Clinton": Richard A. Clarke, interview with author. See, also, "Remarks by President Bill Clinton on Keeping America Secure for the 21st Century," National Academy of Sciences, 22 Jan. 1999.

633: Just as it appeared: Don Van Natta, Jr., "Starr Is Weighing Whether to Indict Sitting President," *New York Times,* 31 Jan. 1999.

634: Conservative icon Robert Bork: Memorandum for the United States Concerning the Vice President's Claim of Constitutional Immunity, 5 Oct. 1973, 20. *In re Proceedings of the Grand Jury Impaneled December 5, 1972: Application of Spiro T. Agnew, Vice President of the United States (D. Md.1973) (No. 73-965).* Then Solicitor General Bork wrote: "The Framers could not have contemplated prosecution of an incumbent President because they vested in him complete power over the execution of the laws, which includes, of course, the power to control prosecutions." The principal point of Bork's memo was that Vice President Spiro T. Agnew could be indicted and tried while in office, for alleged bribes taken as governor of Maryland, because a vice president stood in a completely different position than did the president, who was the unitary chief executive under the Constitution.

634: As one Republican: Ken Gormley, "Impeachment and the Independent Counsel," 315–24. If state officials in the South had wanted to prevent President Kennedy from enforcing federal law during the civil rights crises of the early 1960s, the argument went, they could have arrested the president during a visit to Mississippi or Georgia, held him in jail, and paralyzed the executive branch until JFK surrendered to their demands.

634: Professor Rotunda: An expert in constitutional law, Rotunda had earlier been consulted by the elves in the *Paula Jones* case (they had kicked around his name as a possible candidate to argue *Clinton v. Jones* in the Supreme Court); he also had led a team of law professors in writing a "friend of the court" brief supporting Jones's position (Memorandum *Amicus Curiae* of Law Professors, *Jones v. Clinton*, U.S. Court of Appeals for 8th Circuit, Nos. 95-1050, 95-1167 [Ronald D. Rotunda, counsel of record]; Ken Starr, interview by author). Rotunda now took the position that the Nixon situation was inapposite, since Bill Clinton had surrendered his constitutional authority to "control" this criminal prosecution by signing into law the independent counsel statute (Ronald D. Rotunda to Kenneth W. Starr ["Indictability of the President"], 20 July 1998, Starr personal papers, Outbox, F7, July 1997).

634: These signals of a potential: The *New York Times* took Ken Starr to task for again "meddling" with the impeachment proceedings and leaking sensitive information in an effort to influence the verdict. The paper declared that the Senate impeachment trial "was Mr. Starr's cue not only to shut up but to stop any activity by his office that would direct attention away from the Senate [proceedings]." OIC issued a terse press release in which Starr denied leaking the story about indicting the president (Kenneth W. Starr, statement, 1 Feb. 1999, Kendall papers). Yet the talk of a criminal indictment was now in the air ("Ken Starr's Meddling," *New York Times*, 2 Feb. 1999).

634: One of the judges: Judge John D. Butzner, Jr., interview by author.

634: Tucked away in Butzner's files: See Ken Gormley, "Court Must Do Its Duty in Starr Case," *Newsday*, 9 July 1998, Butzner papers, University of Virginia.

635: Dale Bumpers had retired: Dale Bumpers, interview by author.

636: Unlike the House managers: Robert Dove, interview by author.

636: Paul Wellstone, Democrat from Minnesota: Dale Bumpers, interview by author.

636: Bumpers began by admitting: Senate video, 21 Jan. 1999; *Congressional Record*, 21 Jan. 1999; "The Impeachment Trial, Jan. 21: Bumpers Defends the President," washingtonpost.com, 21 Jan. 1999.

637: "It was sawdust in the meatloaf": Henry J. Hyde, interview by author.

637: A throng of senators: Dale Bumpers, interview by author. One senator who was not impressed was Majority Leader Trent Lott, who did his best not to grimace as Bumpers delivered his remarks (Trent Lott, interview by author).

637: When Bumpers returned to his home: Bill Clinton, interview by author.

637: That evening on the national news: Dale Bumpers, interview by author; John Chafee, interview, *NewsHour with Jim Lehrer*, PBS, 21 Jan. 1999.

638: which Byrd personally handed: Henry J. Hyde, interview by author.

638: Senator Byrd wrote: Robert C. Byrd, transcript of statement, *NewsHour with Jim Lehrer*, PBS, 22 Jan. 1999; Baker, *The Breach*, 335–36. The initial version of Byrd's motion had included tough language condemning Clinton, almost as damning as the articles of impeachment. Many Democratic senators expressed misgivings. Byrd finally relented, amending his motion to read simply: "The Senator from West Virginia, Mr. Byrd, moves that the impeachment proceedings against William Jefferson Clinton, President of the United States, be, and the same are, duly dismissed" (Baker, *The Breach*, 351).

638: He had known all along: Trent Lott, interview by author.

638: At an emergency hearing: Baker, *The Breach*, 337–38.

638: "The whole issue": Robert Dove, interview by author.

639: "We are not the British": Trent Lott, interview by author. David Kendall, the president's lawyer (interview by author), considered it "unthinkable" that he would permit Bill Clinton to walk into the Senate well and testify.

639: "I should have stood up": Henry J. Hyde, interview by author.

639: "That would have killed": David Schippers, comments made during author's interview with Henry J. Hyde.

639: It was a scene reminiscent of: Robert Dove, interview by author.

639: "The whole thing was really scary": Monica Lewinsky, interview by author.

640: Throughout six hours of testimony: Monica Lewinsky, deposition, *Congressional Record*, 1 Feb. 1999, transcript of video; Baker, *The Breach*, 371.

640: Halfway into the questioning: David Kendall, interview by author.

640: "I appreciated the gesture": Monica Lewinsky, interview by author; Monika Lewinsky to author, 26 Jan. 2009.

641: "She will not lie": Henry J. Hyde, interview by author.

641: O'Connor concluded: Justice Sandra Day O'Connor, interview by author.

641: Senator Orrin Hatch, the respected Republican: Orrin G. Hatch, "A Precedent the Senate Shouldn't Set," *New York Times,* 2 Feb. 1999. Hatch argued that such a rebuke would constitute "the highest form of condemnation."

641: "I mean, if our goal": Trent Lott, interview by author.

642: During the House managers' closing: Senate video, 6 Feb. 1999, closing remarks of House Manager Lindsey Graham; *Congressional Record,* 6 Feb. 1999; "The Impeachment Trial, Feb. 6: White House Counsel Presentations," washingtonpost.com, 6 Feb. 1999.

642: "If you are going to acquit": Robert Dove, interview by author.

642: "Short of murder": Trent Lott, interview by author.

642: There was still a shred of hope: Tom Daschle, interview by author.

643: Specter had sought advice: Robert Dove, interview by author.

643: Senator Lott now navigated: Trent Lott, interview by author.

643: As a last-ditch measure: "The President's Acquittal; Senator Feinstein's Motion on Censure," *New York Times,* 13 Feb. 1999.

643: The White House was aghast: David Kendall, interview by author.

644: "I felt we did not have": Henry J. Hyde, interview by author.

644: In one of the greatest missteps: As a formal matter, the Feinstein motion was defeated immediately after the vote on the articles of impeachment, with Senator Gramm of Texas blocking the effort by the California senator to suspend the rules in order to vote on the censure resolution (Senate video, 12 Feb. 1999).

644: On the Republican side of the aisle: Robert Dove, interview by author.

644: Senator Phil Gramm personally: Trent Lott, interview by author.

644: White House political adviser: Doug Sosnik, interview by author.

644: At 9:30 A.M.: Senate video, 12 Feb. 1999; *Congressional Record,* 12 Feb. 1999; "The Impeachment Trial, Feb. 12: Final Votes," washingtonpost.com, 12 Feb. 1999.

644: "Expectancy and disappointment": Henry J. Hyde, interview by author.

645: "we're in the Senate again": Robert Dove, interview by author.

645: Senator Tom Daschle wandered: Tom Daschle, interview by author.

645: To the managers' surprise: Henry J. Hyde, interview by author; Schippers, *Sellout,* 281–82.

Chapter 50: Clinton's Contempt

646: "hurt and concerned": Trent Lott, interview by author.

647: "I think Henry Hyde is the one": Tom Daschle, interview by author.

647: "Every one of the managers": Henry J. Hyde, interview by author.

647: "It was damning evidence": David Schippers, comments during author's interview with Henry J. Hyde.

648: "Probably, all things considered": Stephen Bates, interview by author.

648: "The only thing I remember": Bill Clinton, interview by author.

648: He had been heartened when he learned: Bill Clinton, interview by author. The six-foot principal, Sister Mary Victor Powers, taught at Word of God Catholic School in Swissvale, Pennsylvania, and communicated those sentiments to the author, who thereafter discussed them with President Clinton.

649: Within weeks of the impeachment trial's: Trent Lott, interview by author.

649: Bill Clinton behaved with equal civility: Bill Clinton, interview by author.

649: "You must never": Paul Begala, interview by author.

649: Precisely two months after the Senate voted: Roberto Suro and Joan Biskupic, "Judge Finds Clinton in Contempt of Court," *Washington Post,* 13 Apr. 1999, A1.

650: NATO-led air campaign: "NATO: Reports Indicate Stepped Up 'Ethnic Cleansing'; Refugees Say Thousands More Kosovars Murdered," CNN.com, 17 Apr. 1999.

650: President Clinton later expressed vigorous disapproval: Bill Clinton, interview by author.

650: If Judge Wright had chosen: Criminal contempt generally relates to an act of disrespect for the court—an act that impedes the administration of justice. Typically, it has involved improper conduct committed by a defendant in the judge's presence, such as throwing the proverbial ink-pot at the judge. In this case, Judge Wright had ordered President Clinton to answer certain questions about relationships with "other women"; she had flown to Washington to preside over the deposition; and in her presence, Clinton had intentionally answered certain questions untruthfully. Although it would have been a stretch, Judge Wright could have found grounds for criminal contempt. Pursuant to Rule 42 of the Federal Rules of Criminal

Procedure, the Republican federal judge could have appointed a prosecutor to look into the charges, held a short contempt trial, and then adjudicated that Clinton had engaged in criminal contempt when he had flouted her discovery order and lied under oath.

651: "If Judge Wright had held": James Duff, interview by author.

651: Susan McDougal walked out: "McDougal Not Guilty On One Count; Mistrial Declared on Other Two Charges," cnn.com, 12 Apr. 1999.

Chapter 51: "Who Will Blink?"

655: "He wanted people to have": Michael Emmick, interview by author. In late spring, OIC had suffered a major setback in the only criminal case it had pursued during its protracted investigation of the Lewinsky matter, when a federal judge in Virginia granted a mistrial in the prosecution of Julie Hiatt Steele (Don VanNatta, Jr., "Jury Deadlocked in Case Involving Starr Investigation," *New York Times*, 8 May 1999). Steele, Kathleen Willey's former friend who had recanted her story corroborating Willey's version of events, had been charged with obstruction of justice and making false statements to federal investigators. After the Steele prosecution imploded, OIC had polled numerous jurors in Virginia and reached the worrisome conclusion that there were increasing numbers of citizens who "were not going to convict Clinton or anybody connected to Clinton on anything, no matter what" (Hickman Ewing, Jr., interview by author).

655: "My answer is 'no'": Hickman Ewing, Jr., interview by author.

655: Ironically, Starr himself: U.S. Senate, "The Future of the Independent Counsel Act," *Hearings Before the Committee on Governmental Affairs,* 106th Congress, 1st sess., 14 Apr. 1999 (testimony of Honorable Kenneth W. Starr).

655: "All roads led to": Ken Starr, interview by author.

656: Some commentators were quick: Ken Gormley, "A Post-Mortem of the Lewinsky Scandal and Clinton Impeachment," lecture at Chautauqua Institution, Chautauqua, N.Y., August 11, 1999.

656: "It was a relief": Alice Starr, interview by author.

656: Starr wrote a farewell: Kenneth Starr, "What We've Accomplished," *Wall Street Journal,* 20 Oct. 1999.

656: a "bittersweet" going-away: Alice Starr, interview by author; Hickman Ewing, Jr., interview by author; *Ken Starr: The Way We Were,* Oct. 1999, film, courtesy of Hickman Ewing, Jr.

657: Since replacing Ken Starr: Judy Keen and Kathy Kiely, "It Ain't Over, New Independent Counsel Says," *USA Today,* 10 Jan. 2000, 8A; Pete Yost, "Starr Steps Down: Successor Asked to Wrap Up Clinton Investigation," *Associated Press,* 18 Oct. 2000.

657: "The timing of this": "Grand Jury Probing Clinton-Lewinsky Scandal, Sources Reveal," CNN AllPolitics, 17 Aug. 2000.

657: Gore's Republican opponent: "A New Grand Jury Looks at Clinton's Past," *New York Times,* 18 Aug. 2000.

657: "emphatically state his disapproval": Frank Bruni, "The 2000 Campaign: The Texas Governor; Bush Calls on Gore to Denounce Clinton Affair," *New York Times,* 12 Aug. 2000.

658: had inadvertently let slip: "Lashing Out at Leaks," *Washington Post,* 22 Aug. 2000; Richard D. Cudahy, "Written Statement of Judge Richard D. Cudahy Issued August 18, 2000," U.S. Court of Appeals for the Seventh Circuit.

658: argued in favor of "terminating": Richard D. Cudahy to Judges David Sentelle and Peter Fay, Re: Starr-Madison Guaranty, 9 Aug. 1999. Nonetheless, Cudahy had voted with his brethren to continue Robert Ray's operation for another year. This was because Ray, unlike Starr, had filed an extensive report detailing his activities. Judge Cudahy felt compelled to explain his switched position to the press.

658: As judges Cudahy and Sentelle: See Judge Richard D. Cudahy to Chief Justice William H. Rehnquist, 29 Aug. 2000. A judicial misconduct complaint was filed against Judge Cudahy by two Republican congressmen. He was ultimately cleared of any wrongdoing by the Judicial Council of the Seventh Circuit, in a sweeping opinion by Judge Richard Posner, a Republican heavyweight who could not be accused of throwing the game for Cudahy (*In Re: Complaint Against Circuit Judge Richard D. Cudahy,* 294 F. 3d 947, 7th Cir. Judicial Council, 24 May 2002).

658: A month earlier: Michael Emmick, interview by author.

658: The DOJ lawyers agreed: There was a plausible argument that the Impeachment Judgment Clause in Article I, Section 3, of the Constitution "[could] be read to bar prosecutions following acquittal by the Senate." The better interpretation, the DOJ memo concluded, allowed for subsequent criminal action in order to "[make] for a sensible and fair system of responding to the misdeeds of federal officials." However, the Office of Legal Counsel prepared a separate memorandum taking a strong position that the president, under no circumstances, could be indicted or criminally prosecuted while in office. Reaffirming the legal opinion of then Solicitor General Robert Bork during the Nixon-related Watergate scandal in 1973, the Justice Department lawyers wrote to Attorney General Reno: "Our view remains that a sitting President is constitutionally immune from indictment and criminal prosecution." This immunity lasted until the president was removed from office by impeachment or had left office at the conclusion of his term (Randolph D. Moss, "A Sitting President's Amenability to Indictment and Criminal Prosecution," Memorandum for the Attorney General, Office of Legal Counsel, 16 Oct. 2000, OIC archives).

658: the Constitution did not preclude: Randolph D. Moss, "Whether a Former President May Be Indicted and Tried for the Same Offenses for Which He Was Impeached by the House and Acquitted by the Senate," Memorandum for the Attorney General, 18 Aug. 2000, OIC archives.

658: With these memos on his desk: Robert W. Ray, interview by author.

658: Ray accomplished: Ibid.; Bill Miller, "Prosecutor Clears Clintons: 6-Year Probe of Their failed Arkansas Real Estate Dealings Ends with No Charges Filed," *Pittsburgh Post-Gazette,* 21 Sept. 2000. With respect to the lengthy and expensive Whitewater probe, for instance, Ray wrote tersely: "This office determined that the evidence was insufficient to prove to a jury beyond a reasonable doubt that either President or Mrs. Clinton knowingly participated in any criminal conduct."

659: "I thought it was up to": Robert W. Ray, interview by author. At first, David Kendall fired off letters to Ray warning that there would be hell to pay if Ray released his findings before the election, because these might provide fodder for opponents who would try to suggest that Mrs. Clinton had done something wrong that simply wasn't provable. Ray released the results anyway, sticking to his plan.

659: a number of messy problems: Among other things, David Kendall's barrage of motions in court had led to the lodging of criminal charges against Starr's former press spokesper-

son, Charles Bakaly. In October 2000, Judge Norma Holloway Johnson finally cleared Bakaly of contempt charges, although Starr's own prosecutors testified against him. Bakaly was accused of leaking an earlier plan to indict Clinton during the midst of the impeachment trial (Byron York, "The Ordeal of Charles Bakaly," *American Spectator,* September 2000; David Stout, "Aide to Starr Is Acquitted of Contempt," *New York Times,* 7 Oct. 2000; David Grann, "Background Noise—Starr Wars: The Finale," *New Republic,* 28 June 1999).

659: Although Judge Kern: Reliable sources confirm that the special master had concluded that at a minimum, Starr's prosecutors had been "tone deaf to the political situation" and had flirted with risky prosecutorial practices by being "[too] outspoken with members of the press."

660: Harris was assigned: Jo Ann Harris, interview by author.

660: The tax charges filed by Starr's team: "Court Dismisses Tax Charge Against Clinton Friend Webster Hubbell," *Associated Press,* 5 June 2000.

660: Ray intended to make clear: Robert W. Ray, interview by author.

660: Monica had hated: Monica Lewinsky, interview by author.

661: "I want to have a conversation": Robert W. Ray, interview by author.

661: Kendall felt that Ray was: David Kendall, interview by author.

661: This wasn't about Bill Clinton: Robert W. Ray, interview by author.

662: "no [guilty] plea": David Kendall, interview by author.

663: "In the *Paula Jones* case": Monica Lewinsky to author, 26 Jan. 2009.

663: "the criminal back-half": Robert W. Ray, interview by author.

664: the High Court first declared: *Bush v. Palm Beach County Canvassing Board* (Bush I), 531 U.S. 70 (2000) (per curiam).

664: On December 12: *Bush v. Gore* (Bush II), 531 U.S. 98 (2000) (per curiam). Seven justices agreed that the method established by the Florida courts to recount ballots violated the Equal Protection clause. The Court split five to four, however, on the issue of whether an appropriate, alternative method could be implemented within the requisite time frame. The majority's negative ruling allowed the prior decision of Florida Secretary of State Katherine Harris (a Republican) to stand, awarding Governor George W. Bush the state's 25 electoral votes and allowing him to edge out Vice President Al Gore by obtaining one more than the number of votes (270) necessary to receive a majority in the electoral college.

665: Clinton considered it: Bill Clinton, interview by author. President Clinton pointed to a study indicating that only a small percentage of "non-right-wing, deeply religious people" voted for Bush over Gore "because they were upset about me and the impeachment." A much larger percentage of voters, the study showed, voted in *favor* of Gore "because they supported me [Clinton] so strongly and were so bitter about what happened to me," giving Gore a "net gain of about three-and-a-half percent" of those who were influenced by the scandals.

665: "You have to put it in the context": Charles Burson, interview by author.

666: Agent Gant formalized: Subpoena, from OIC to Lewis Merletti, 8 Jan. 2002, Lew Merletti papers.

666: Thoroughly baffled: Lew Merletti, interview by author; business cards, Lew Merletti papers. The associate independent counsels were Monte C. Richardson and D. Thomas Ferraro. The investigator was Coy A. Copeland.

667: "wrap up loose ends": Jennifer Gant, interview by author.

667: "admit that the president": Agent Jennifer Gant did not recall making such a statement and insisted that she did not deal in "gossip, innuendo, and rumor" (Jennifer Gant, interview by author). However, notes of the session, maintained by a source who wished to remain anonymous, confirmed that the initial questions were designed to determine if Merletti was "in collusion" with the president in carrying out his affair with Monica and other females.

667: "What they should have been doing": Looking back on these events nearly a decade later, Merletti was particularly troubled that the FBI spent so much time "investigating the foibles of the President and Monica, [while] a number of senior al-Qaeda operatives were traveling through the United States" developing funding networks and planning attacks (Lew Merletti to author, 7 Apr. 2009). Specifically, Merletti pointed to the fact that the first World Trade Center bombing had occurred in February 1993. From that time forward "the FBI had several solid opportunities to develop double agents as well as to arrest senior [al-Qaeda] op-

eratives." One major blunder involved failing to shut down the growing operation of Ayman al-Zawahiri, widely considered to be Osama bin Laden's "number two" in command, who helped to merge the radical al-jihad with al-Qaeda. See Peter Bergen, "Aman al-Zawahiri," *Time*, 30 Apr. 2006. A second significant blunder, which occurred on American soil, involved Ali Abdelsoud Mohammed, a militant Egyptian double agent who worked directly with the CIA and the FBI in the United States; he was involved in the August 1998 bombing of U.S. embassies in Kenya and Tanzania as well as other al-Qaeda terrorist activities. See Lance Williams and Erin McCormick, "Al-Qaeda Terrorist Worked with FBI; Ex–Silicon Valley Resident Plotted Embassy Attacks," *San Francisco Chronicle*, 4 Nov. 2001. Merletti concluded that the FBI's overzealous pursuit in support of Ken Starr's independent counsel investigation demonstrated that agency's utter "failure to recognize priorities."

668: a nasty flu: David Kendall, interview by author.

668: the president agreed: "Clinton Admits Misleading Testimony, Avoids Charges in Lewinsky Probe," CNN.com, 19 Jan. 2001; "Clinton Pays $25,000 Fine in Arkansas Case," *New York Times*, 8 Apr. 2001.

668: With one big caveat: In court papers closing the Arkansas disbarment proceedings, the president further admitted that he had engaged in conduct "prejudicial to the administration of justice" ("Clinton Admits Misleading Testimony").

668: sickened by the final deal: Bill Clinton, interview by author.

669: Ray's secretary tracked down: Robert W. Ray, interview by author.

670: "This is right": Ken Starr, interview by author.

670: In the White House: CNN, "Clinton's Final Day Includes Pardons, New Monument and Note for His Successor," CNN AllPolitics, 20 Jan. 2001.

670: Bill Clinton's last: Bill Clinton to Marge Mitchell, 20 Jan. 2001, Marge Mitchell papers.

Chapter 52: Aftermath

671: "We just had a nasty:" Ken Starr, interview by author.

672: Even in Clinton's bestselling: Clinton, *My Life;* see also Sonja Steptoe, "10 Questions for Kenneth Starr," *Time*, 5 July 2004, 8.

672: In 2002, Starr's successor: Neil A. Lewis, "Final Report by Prosecutor on Clinton Is Released," *New York Times,* 21 Mar. 2002; Final Report/Ray.

672: Starr expressed conflicted: Ken Starr, interview by author.

673: pure relief that her husband's work: Alice Starr, interview by author.

673: a one-way street: Monica Lewinsky, interview by author. The persistent marching orders from OIC, Monica Lewinsky recalled, boiled down to: "I was not allowed to talk about January nineteenth." Even during her much-anticipated interview with ABC's Barbara Walters in early March 1999, after the impeachment trial had concluded, the parties had been instructed to steer clear of discussing OIC's treatment of Monica at the Ritz-Carlton (CNN, "Excerpts of Lewinsky Interview," CNN AllPolitics, 4 Mar. 1999; Martin Mbugua and Thomas M. Defrank, "Monica Asks Judge to Lift Gag Order," *New York Daily News,* 26 Jan. 1999). Monica did, however, discuss OIC's treatment of her extensively in her as-told-to book written by Andrew Morton released that same month. This was possible, she later said, based on a "loophole" in the immunity agreement that permitted her to talk freely to Morton because he was an "author" rather than a "journalist." The supreme irony of OIC's decision to establish strict parameters that prevented interviewees from probing into OIC's treatment of Monica, she later pointed out, was that the entire Starr investigation and impeachment effort seemed to rest on the veracity of her testimony. On one hand, Starr's office had proclaimed to the courts, to Congress, and to the American people that she was the "most credible person in the world" with respect to its effort to prove criminal conduct on the part of Bill Clinton. When it came to her testimony about her own treatment by OIC, however, Starr's prosecutors took the contrary position that she "completely lacked credibility" on that topic (Monica Lewinsky, interview by author).

674: "I wouldn't have touched her": Jo Ann Harris, interview by author; Jo Ann Harris to author, 8 July 2006. Harris emphasized that there was a special office in DOJ designed "to advise prosecutors as to ethical issues and to give them cover." If Starr's prosecutors had contacted that office, they would have discovered, among other things, that Frank Carter was "extraordinarily respected, well known in Washington" and a "cool, clear-headed" criminal defense

lawyer who was perfectly capable of advising Monica Lewinsky.

675: Moreover, Harris concluded: Additionally, to the extent Robert Ray tried to paint a picture in his own report that OIC was off the hook because a young DOJ attorney, Josh Hochberg, had "approved" of OIC's decisions, Harris viewed this as a "cheap shot." Hochberg had been sent over as a liaison to report the facts back to his office. "He was not over there to advise the independent counsel, and in fact, they would have been offended had he tried to advise independent counsel. . . . Bennett said exactly that to me, and Starr said it to me" (Jo Ann Harris, interview by author).

675: "Very badly": Jo Ann Harris, interview by author.

675: Starr's prosecutors had not committed: Ibid.

675: "poor judgment": The identity of that lawyer was never made public. For that reason, and because most OIC lawyers had left the Justice Department, leaving only one lawyer subject to its regulations, the author has chosen not to disclose that individual's name.

675: Harris's report also: Jo Ann Harris to author, 8 July 2006; Jo Ann Harris, interview by author.

675: Ray had accepted: Robert Ray, interview by author; Mike Emmick, interview by author.

676: "That's where his analysis stopped": Jo Ann Harris to author, 26 July 2006, and 8 Sept. 2006.

676: Harris was doubly: Harris understood that Robert Ray felt there was a certain element of "unfairness" in singling out one OIC prosecutor for his or her exercise of poor judgment when the whole office was to blame. For that reason, Harris herself had not recommended any sanctions for that individual, because of his or her "long and distinguished history with the Department of Justice."

676: difficult for Harris: Harris had written a long letter to the court objecting to Robert Ray's characterization of her report in his own voluminous final report. Ordinarily, any party was given a chance to "comment" and respond to errors and mischaracterizations of that sort. However, the three-judge court had rejected her request to publish even this abbreviated comment. This was the only time that Harris felt she had been muzzled in her long career of government service (Jo Ann Harris, interview by author). Not even Monica Lewinsky was allowed to obtain a copy of the Harris findings, to allow her lawyers to comment on OIC's final report, as permitted by the independent counsel statute.

676: Robert Ray understood: Robert Ray, follow-up interview by author, 13 Mar. 2009. Ray did not specifically recall agreeing with Harris that the report would be released in its entirety. Rather, his best recollection was that the *outcome* of the report—and his decision to reverse Harris's second finding relating to "poor judgment"—would be made public. Harris, however, recalled that she did extensive research to determine the proper protocol for handling OPR reports and concluded that a detailed summary of the report was permitted to be released by the Justice Department. Her understanding was that such a summary of her report would be released. She prepared this summary, but it, too, was placed under seal (Jo Ann Harris, follow-up interview by author, 19 Mar. 2009).

677: Henry Hyde, sitting back: Henry Hyde, interview by author.

678: "unwavering respect": Resolution, Judicial Conference of the United States, 19 Sept. 2000, Henry Hyde papers.

678: The conservative intellectual leader: Henry J. Hyde, interview by author; David Schippers, follow-up interview by author, March 20, 2009. The event in question was an intimate alumni gathering hosted by Amherst College, attended by (among others) David Eisenhower, grandson of former President Dwight D. Eisenhower and son-in-law of former President Richard M. Nixon. During the course of this gathering, Hyde's chief counsel, David Schippers, described to Justice Scalia his plan, endorsed by Chairman Hyde, to issue subpoenas to Attorney General Janet Reno and other DOJ officials and to jail them if they failed to comply, pointing out that the matter would have then been ripe for the Supreme Court. Scalia commented: "David, we would have backed you" (Ibid.).

678: President Bill Clinton would see nothing heroic: Bill Clinton, interview by author.

679: For Susan McDougal, the whole experience: Susan McDougal, interview by author.

680: *Vanity Fair* ran a story: Judy Bachrach, "Joan of Arkansas," *Vanity Fair,* January 1999; Ann W. O'Neill, "Steel Magnolia," *Los Angeles Times Magazine,* 9 May 1999.

680: "profoundly wrong": Ken Starr, interview by author.

680: There was a romantic affair: A number of journalists have at various times reported pieces of evidence, never corroborated, suggesting that Susan McDougal may have had an affair with Clinton at some point, and that this might explain her refusal to testify before the grand jury. See James B. Stewart, "Susan McDougal's Silence: Why Won't She Talk?" *The New Yorker,* 17 February 1997, 62, 63–64 (reporting Jim McDougal's allegation that he had overheard Clinton and his wife talking on the phone in 1982, in an intimate fashion, and that Susan thereafter admitted to him that she was having an affair with Clinton); Michael Isikoff, *Uncovering Clinton,* 381–82 n. 1 (reporting that two White House lawyers, Jane Sherburne and Mark Fabiani, indicated that Fabiani had received a call from Harvard law professor Alan Dershowitz in September of 1996, just days before Susan McDougal refused to testify in front of Starr's grand jury. According to this account, Susan had called Dershowitz to seek advice concerning her pending grand jury appearance because she feared she would be forced to acknowledge a sexual relationship with Clinton. Dershowitz purportedly confirmed to Susan that there would be no way to avoid the subject if she testified under oath. Dershowtiz would not admit or deny the conversation to Isikoff, citing attorney-client privilege, even though he did not formally represent Susan). Susan McDougal later emphatically denied these reports and denied the existence of an affair with Clinton. Sources now confirm, however, that Dershowitz indeed placed the call to Mark Fabiani, conveying the information as a "heads up" that it might come out if Susan McDougal testified. However, it is also clear that this was not "the primary motivating factor causing Susan to question whether to testify." Rather, it was as if she wished to deliver a message to the White House, through Dershowitz, that she was mulling over her options and "this was not something that she wanted to do," but that President Clinton "needed to plan for it" because if she did testify she would have to "answer questions about [the affair]."

681: "I had no idea": Susan McDougal, follow-up interview by author, 26 Aug. 2006.

681: In death, she said: It is likely that Jim McDougal was entitled to a government grave marker, in light of his satisfactory (albeit basic) participation in the Arkansas Air National Guard. Although he fell just short of the usual six-year stint in the National Guard, official records indicate that he did serve from February 26, 1964, through March 27, 1968 (Statement of Service for James B. McDougal, State of Arkansas, Office of the Adjutant General, 6 Apr. 2009 [obtained through Freedom of Information Act]). The Veterans Administration guidelines defining which veterans are entitled to government grave markers can be found at www.va.gov/vaforms/va/pdf/va40-1330.pdf.

681: pardoning billionaire fugitive Marc Rich: Jessica Reaves, "The Marc Rich Case: A Primer," *Time,* 13 Feb. 2001.

681: Clinton said: The case of Webb Hubbell had presented a tough situation for the outgoing president and his Justice Department. Hubbell, unlike Susan McDougal, had pleaded guilty to a crime, in the form of cheating the Rose Law Firm and its clients. There were also issues under Justice Department guidelines as to whether sufficient time had passed before granting a pardon, since Hubbell had been indicted three separate times by Starr's office and five years had not passed—the usual rule of thumb before granting a pardon. On the other hand, Hubbell had clearly been targeted for prosecution "for the simple reason that [he] refused to lie about me [Bill Clinton] or Hillary"—that much seemed evident to Clinton as he wrangled with the decision. The presidential pardon power, he understood, was included in the Constitution precisely to remedy that sort of political retribution.

682: Webb Hubbell himself admitted: Webster Hubbell, interview by author.

683: "I wonder did he feel": Monica Lewinsky, follow-up interview by author, 9 Sept. 2008.

684: "I guess my biggest disappointment": Monica Lewinsky, interview by author.

684: As her mother: Marcia Lewis Straus, follow-up interview by author, 13 Aug. 2009.

684: "I have contemplated": Monica Lewinsky to author, 26 Jan. 2009.

684: "that I respected him as a president": Bernie Lewinsky, interview by author.

685: a $595,000 settlement: "Defense Department Settles with Linda Tripp," *Associated Press,* 3 Nov. 2003.

685: "I just look out there": Linda Tripp, interview by author.

687: She had also found time: "And in This Corner, . . ." *New York Times,* 8 Mar. 2002. Paula Jones lost the boxing match.

687: "A hundred and fifty-one thousand dollars": Paula Jones, interview by author.

688: at least one key aspect: Besides the affidavit obtained by lawyer Bob Bennett from Clinton's urologist that Bennett was prepared to offer at trial, Ms. Jones's own lawyers had reached out to Gennifer Flowers with whom Clinton had admittedly engaged in sexual relations during the time period in question. According to Jones's own lawyers, Ms. Flowers was unable to corroborate the existence of the distinguishing characteristic (James Fisher, interview with author). As well, other confidential sources in a position to observe such a trait stated unequivocally that it did not exist (author's interviews with confidential sources). It is true that Ms. Jones's lawyers from Virginia had insisted that she take a polygraph test concerning her alleged encounter with Clinton and that she passed that test (Gilbert Davis, interview with author). Moreover, it is true that Peyronie's disease can be corrected through a treatment regimen of vitamins and/or surgery. Nonetheless, the vast weight of the evidence failed to support Ms. Jones when it came to the existence of this condition relating to Clinton's genitalia that she had made a centerpiece of her lawsuit.

689: "I feel bad for the country": Danny Traylor, interview by author.

689: Paula had gone on to pose: Joe Conason, "The Perils of Paula Jones," *Penthouse,* December 2000, 41.

689: Penthouse: Even conservative columnist Ann Coulter condemned Paula Jones for appearing in *Penthouse,* after Jones's repeated protestations that she was a wholesome young lady uninterested in profiting from her lawsuit; Coulter wrote of Jones: "She used to have dignity and nobility and tremendous courage. Now she's just the trailer-park trash they said she was" (Ann Coulter, "Clinton Sure Can Pick 'Em," *Jewish World Review,* 30 Oct. 2000).

689: "So I still have [this] coffee cup": Wesley Holmes, interview by author.

690: Here at the peak: Richard Clark, interview by author.

BIBLIOGRAPHICAL SOURCES

Author's Interviews

An asterisk (*) denotes an interview by telephone; all other interviews set forth below were conducted in person.

*Nancy Adkins, Hot Springs, Ark., July 7, 2001.

Debra Ballentine, North Little Rock, Ark., June 18, 2001.

Charles Banks, Little Rock, Ark., August 2, 2003.

Judge John Bates, Washington, D.C., May 13, 2005.

Stephen Bates, Washington, D.C., February 5, 2003.

Paul Begala, Washington, D.C., April 14, 2009.

Jackie Bennett, Indianapolis, March 30–31, 2001; *July 20, 2001; June 11, 2002; *January 28, 2003; *May 21, 2003.

Robert Bennett, Washington, D.C., December 7, 2001; *June 18, 2002; *September 18, 2003.

Robert J. Bittman, Washington, D.C., *May 15, 2003; *May 28, 2003; *July 7, 2004; July 12, 2004.

*Susan Low Bloch, Washington, D.C., January 27, 2005.

Ben Bradlee, Washington, D.C., April 7, 2005.

Bert Brandenburg, Washington, D.C., June 9, 2004.

Max Brantley, Little Rock, Ark., June 15, 2001.

Dorothee Bringewatt, Cologne, Germany, October 16, 2002.

*Bill Bristow, Jonesboro, Ark., February 22, 2005.

David Brock, Washington, D.C., August 13, 2004.

*John Brummett, Little Rock, Ark., June 25, 2001.

Elizabeth Buck, Hot Springs, Ark., June 17, 2001.

Senator Dale Bumpers, Washington, D.C., July 8, 2004.

*Charles Burson, St. Louis, Mo., April 8, 2009.

Lou Butterfield, Searcy, Ark., June 14, 2001.

Judge John D. Butzner, Jr., Richmond, Va., November 5, 2004.

Viola "Pete" Butzner, Richmond, Va., November 5, 2004.

Plato Cacheris, Washington, D.C., November 19, 2001; *December 20, 2001; June 11, 2002.

Joseph Cammarata, Washington, D.C., February 7, 2003; July 21, 2003; January 4, 2006.

*Susan Carpenter-McMillan, Los Angeles, July 15, 2003; July 21, 2003.

Frank Carter, Washington, D.C., July 8, 2004.

*Paula Casey, Little Rock, Ark., August 6, 2004.

Kathleen Cavoli, San Antonio, July 25, 2002.

George Cawkwell, North Oxford, England, July 14, 2005.

*Dr. Richard Clark, Louisville, Tex., July 27, 2003; August 10, 2003; August 31, 2003; September 28, 2003.

Richard A. Clarke, Pittsburgh, October 25, 2007.

President William Jefferson Clinton, Philadelphia, November 10, 2004; Chappaqua, N.Y., December 17, 2004; February 9, 2005.

*Larry Cockell, New York City, May 25, 2004.

*George Collins, Chicago, August 12, 2004.

*Archibald Cox, Brooksville, Maine, December 1, 2000.

Walter Cronkite, New York City, March 9, 2001.

Senator Tom Daschle, Washington, D.C., May 15, 2005.

*Samuel Dash, Washington, D.C., January 19, 2001; February 5, 2001; February 16, 2001; February 21, 2001; February 28, 2001.

Gilbert Davis, Fairfax, Va., March 24, 2003; *Moneta, Va., April 8, 2003.

*Walter Dellinger, Chapel Hill, N.C., February 18, 2005.

Robert Dove, Falls Church, Va., June 10, 2004.

*James Doyle, Bethesda, Md., July 7, 2000.

James C. Duff, Washington, D.C., October 21, 2005.

*William S. Duffey, Jr., Atlanta, December 20, 2000.

Ernie Dumas, Little Rock, Ark., July 9, 2001.

*Michael Emmick, Los Angeles, July 1, 2002; July 8, 2002; July 16, 2002; July 17, 2002.

Hickman Ewing, Jr., Little Rock, Ark., June 17, 2001; *Germantown, Tenn., November 20, 2001; *Memphis, Tenn., November 28, 2001; *Germantown, Tenn., July 16, 2002; *Nashville, Tenn., August 5, 2003.

*James Fisher, Dallas, February 19, 2003; February 23, 2003.

*Robert B. Fiske, New York City, September 8, 2000; April 14, 2005; April 26, 2005.

*Larry Flynt, Beverly Hills, Calif., January 15, 2007.

*President Gerald R. Ford, Rancho Mirage, Calif., March 31, 2000.

Representative Barney Frank, Washington, D.C., July 18, 2000.

*Jennifer Gant, Washington, D.C., June 1, 2009.

*Justice Ruth Bader Ginsburg, Washington, D.C., August 2, 2006.

William Ginsburg, *Las Vegas, September 30, 2003; *Los Angeles, November 17–18, 2003; Encino, Calif., May 22, 2004.

*Lucianne Goldberg, New York City, September 5, 2008.

*Jamie Gorelick, Washington, D.C., November 25, 2003.

Elizabeth Green, San Antonio, Tex., July 24, 2002.

George Green, San Antonio, Tex., July 24, 2002.

Paul Greenberg, Little Rock, Ark., June 15, 2001; June 26, 2001.

*Gary Grindler, Washington, D.C., June 11, 2004.

Michel Gurfinkiel, Paris, France, October 18, 2002.

*Rusty Hardin, Houston, April 9, 2001.

*Jo Ann Harris, New York City, August 25, 2003.

Samuel Heuer, Little Rock, Ark., September 2, 2003.

*Philip Heymann, Cambridge, Mass., June 13, 2002; June 11, 2003.

*Clint Hill, Alexandria, Va., June 2, 2004.

*Eric Holder, Washington, D.C., November 27, 2001; February 24, 2003; February 27, 2003.

Richard Holiman, Little Rock, Ark., August 1, 2003.

*Wesley Holmes, Dallas, February 24, 2003; February 27, 2003.

*Amory Houghton, Jr., Cohasset, Mass., April 17, 2009.

Webster Hubbell, Chevy Chase, Md., March 16, 2001; Washington, D.C., January 4, 2006.

*Frank Hunger, Nashville, December 3, 2008.

Representative Henry J. Hyde, Washington, D.C., August 2, 2001; Addison, Ill., December 19, 2003; Addison, Ill., January 8, 2004 (with David Schippers).

*Harold Ickes, Washington, D.C., November 23, 2004.

Michael Isikoff, Washington, D.C., April 7, 2005; *December 29, 2009.

Cliff Jackson, Hot Springs, Ark., June 17, 2001.

*LeRoy Jahn, San Antonio, Tex., December 18, 2003; July 14, 2004.

*Ray Jahn, San Antonio, Tex., December 18, 2003; July 14, 2004.

*Larry Jegley, Little Rock, Ark., March 8, 2005.

*Justice Jim Johnson, Conway, Ark., February 7, 2005.

Paula Jones, North Little Rock, Ark., June 18, 2001; *Cabot, Ark., November 18, 2001.

Dick Kelley, Hot Springs, Ark., December 14, 2004.

David Kendall, Washington, D.C., October 30, 2008.

William Kennedy III, Little Rock, Ark., December 10, 2004.

Greg Kitterman, Little Rock, Ark., July 22, 2002.

*Thomas J. LaFond, Boston, September 29, 2004.

*Roderick Lankler, New York City, December 20, 2000.

David Paul Leopoulos, Little Rock, Ark., February 28, 2003.

Jan Levine, Pittsburgh, Pa., August 5, 2008.

Bernie Lewinsky, Los Angeles, May 22, 2004.

Monica Lewinsky, New York City, March 10, 2002; *July 30, 2002; *September 10, 2002; *October 22, 2002.

*Congressman Robert L. Livingston, Washington, D.C., March 9, 2005.

Senator Trent Lott, Washington, D.C., April 8, 2005.

Gene Lyons, Little Rock, Ark., June 15, 2001.

Roberta Mahan, San Antonio, Tex., July 25, 2002.

*Laura E. Malat, Jacksonville, Ark., January 10, 2006.

Carol Martineau, Hot Springs, Ark., June 17, 2001.

*May Mason, San Antonio, Tex., July 19, 2002.

*Ann Askew McCoy, Little Rock, Ark., January 5, 2007.

*Robert McDaniel, Jonesboro, Ark., August 5, 2005.

Susan McDougal, Arkadelphia, Ark., July 23, 2002; August 26, 2006.

*Gerry McDowell, Cape Cod, July 19, 2004.

*Dennis McInerney, New York City, January 26, 2001.

Lew Merletti, Cleveland, May 5, 2004; May 17, 2004.

*Abner Mikva, Chicago, September 26, 2003.

Marge Mitchell, Hot Springs, Ark., June 17, 2001; July 11, 2001.

*H. T. Moore, Paragould, Ark., July 11, 2001.

Anne-Elisabeth Moutet, Paris, France, October 17, 2002.

*Dee Dee Myers, Washington, D.C., July 29, 2003.

*Justice David Newbern, Little Rock, Ark., June 22, 2001.

*Larry Nichols, Conway, Ark., April 21, 2006.

*John Nields, Washington, D.C., April 28, 2006.

Mimi Noe, Hot Springs, Ark., June 17, 2001.

Bernard Nussbaum, New York City, October 16, 2003; November 25, 2003.

Manning J. O'Connor II, Pittsburgh, Pa., May 18, 2003.

*Justice Sandra Day O'Connor, Washington, D.C., June 16, 2003.

*Kevin Ohlson, Washington, D.C., June 24, 2002.

*Julie O'Sullivan, Washington, D.C., December 17, 2000.

Dora Phea, Cologne, Germany, October 16, 2002.

John Podesta, Washington, D.C., July 22, 2004.

Joe Purvis, Little Rock, Ark., June 17, 2001; July 9, 2001; July 24, 2002.

Robert W. Ray, Morristown, N.J., July 6, 2002; *July 11, 2002; New York City, *March 13, 2009.

Alan Reaves, San Antonio, Tex., July 25, 2002.

Janet Reno, Miami, Fla., December 2, 2001.

Billie Jeayne (Starr) Reynolds, Kingwood, Tex., July 26, 2002.

Gary Reynolds, Kingwood, Tex., July 26, 2002.

Claudia Riley, Arkadelphia, Ark., July 23, 2002.

*Pam Craig Roller, Washington, D.C., January 27, 2005.

*Paul Root, Arkadelphia, Ark., July 6, 2001.

Paul Rosenzweig, Washington, D.C., August 2, 2001; *May 22, 2002; *May 24, 2002; *June 19, 2002; *June 28, 2002.

Madelyn Ross, Pittsburgh, Pa., July 11, 2002.

Susan Ruff, Washington, D.C., February 7, 2003.

*Skip Rutherford, Little Rock, Ark., June 16, 2004.

*Judge Amy St. Eve, Chicago, June 16, 2004; June 29, 2004.

Richard Mellon Scaife, Pittsburgh, Pa., January 20, 2009.

Judge David Sentelle, Washington, D.C., December 19, 2002 (via letter); January 9, 2003.

*Jane Sherburne, Washington, D.C., March 4, 2005.

*Judge L. T. Simes II, West Helena, Ark., July 16, 2001.

*Bill Simmons, Little Rock, Ark., April 21, 2005.

*Stephen A. Smith, Fayetteville, Ark., July 18, 2004.

*Judge Joseph Sneed, San Francisco, July 15, 2003.

Douglas Sosnik, Washington, D.C., June 4, 2004; July 2, 2004.

Alice Starr, McLean, Va., August 3, 2001.

Carolyn Starr, McLean, Va., August 3, 2001.

Kenneth W. Starr, Washington, D.C., January 6, 2000; McLean, Va., March 8, 2000; Arlington, Va., May 16, 2000; June 16, 2000; July 17, 2000; August 18, 2000; Pittsburgh, Pa., November 14, 2000; *July 31, 2002.

Justice John Paul Stevens, Washington, D.C., July 18, 2000.

James Stewart, New York City, October 16, 2003.

*Marcia [Lewinsky] Lewis Straus, New York City, September 16, 2004; January 5, 2007.

Daniel M. Traylor, Little Rock, Ark., March 1, 2003.

Linda Tripp, Plains, Va., April 22, 2005.

Jim Guy Tucker, Little Rock, Ark., July 23, 2002.

*Mark Tuohey, Washington, D.C., February 23, 2001.

*R. Emmett Tyrell, Jr., Arlington, Va., March 4–5, 2009.

Greg Victor, Pittsburgh, Pa., July 11, 2002.

*Lloyd Wacaster, Hot Springs, Ark., June 11, 2001.

*Lawrence Walsh, Oklahoma City, Okla., December 7, 2000.

*Curtis Wilkie, Oxford, Miss., August 18, 2008.

*Kathleen Willey, Powhatan, Va., July 28, 2007.

Sol Wisenberg, Washington, D.C., February 4, 2003; February 10, 2003.

*Gabrielle Wolohojian, Boston, December 29, 2000.

*Bob Woodward, Washington, D.C., November 14, 2003.

*Betsey Wright, Rogers, Ark., July 19, 2001.

Manuscript Collections

Library of Congress, Washington, D.C., Samuel Dash papers.

Office of the Independent Counsel, Washington, D.C., Press releases (1994–1999).

National Archives and Records Administration, College Park, Md., Records of Independent Counsel Starr/Ray.

University of Virginia Law Library, Special Collections, Charlottesville, Va., Judge John D. Butzner, Jr., papers.

U.S. Court of Appeals for the District of Columbia, Division for the Purpose of Appointing Independent Counsels, Washington, D.C., Public papers.

U.S. House of Representatives Committee on the Judiciary, Washington, D.C., Press releases, 1998–1999 (Henry J. Hyde, Chairman).

Judge Susan Webber Wright correspondence, U.S. District Court for the Eastern District of Arkansas.

Private Collections

Plato Cacheris papers.
Dr. Richard Clark papers.
Gilbert Davis papers.
Robert B. Fiske, Jr., papers.
Samuel Heuer papers.
Representative Henry J. Hyde papers.
Monica Lewinsky papers.
Roberta Mahan papers.
Susan McDougal papers.
Lew Merletti papers.
David Schippers papers.
Kenneth W. Starr papers.
Daniel M. Traylor legal files.

Audiovisual Sources

The Clinton Chronicles: An Investigation into the Alleged Criminal Activities of Bill Clinton. Produced by Citizens for Honest Government. Citizens' Video Press, 1994. Videocassette.

"The Clinton Years." *Frontline.* PBS, Jan. 2001. Videocassettes and transcripts.

Grand Jury Testimony of President William Jefferson Clinton. MPI Home Video, 17 Aug. 1998. Videocassette.

"House Sessions." *Proceedings on the Impeachment of William Jefferson Clinton.* C-SPAN, 11–17 Dec. 1998. Videocassettes.

Impeachment Debate: U.S. House of Representatives. C-SPAN, 18–19 Dec. 1998. Videocassettes.

Impeachment Trial; U.S. Senate Sessions. C-SPAN, 7 Jan.–12 Feb. 1999. Videocassettes.

Impeachment Trial; U.S. Senate Sessions. U.S. Senate, Library of Congress, 7 Jan.–12 Feb. 1999. Videocassettes.

60 Minutes. CBS, 8 Oct. 1995. Transcript.

Government Publications

Clinton, William J. *Public Papers of the Presidents of the United States, William J. Clinton.* 8 vols. Washington, DC: U.S. Government Printing Office, 1993–2001.

Congressional Record. Washington, DC: U.S. Government Printing Office, 8 Oct. 1998–12 Feb. 1999.

Office of the Independent Counsel. *Final Report In Re: Bernard Nussbaum, Robert W. Ray, Independent Counsel.* Washington, DC: U.S. Government Printing Office, 16 Mar. 2000.

———. *Final Report In Re: Madison Guaranty Savings & Loan Association, Robert W. Ray, Independent Counsel.* 5 vols. Washington, DC: U.S. Government Printing Office, 2002 ("Final Report/Ray" in notes).

———. *Final Report In Re: Madison Guaranty Savings & Loan Association, Regarding Monica Lewinsky and Others, Robert W. Ray, Independent Counsel.* Washington DC: U.S. Government Printing Office, 2002.

———. *Report of the Independent Counsel In Re: Vincent W. Foster, Jr., Robert B. Fiske, Jr., Independent Counsel.* Washington, DC: U.S. Government Printing Office, 30 June 1994 ("Fiske Report/Foster" in notes).

———. *Report on the Death of Vincent W. Foster, Jr. by the Office of Independent Counsel, In Re: Madison Guaranty Savings & Loan Association, Kenneth W. Starr, Independent Counsel.* Washington, DC: U.S. Government Printing Office, 1997 ("Starr Report/Foster" in notes).

———. *Final Report of the Independent Counsel (In Re: Madison Guaranty Savings & Loan Association) In Re: William David Watkins and In Re: Hillary Rodham Clinton, Robert Ray, Independent Counsel.* Washington, DC: U.S. Government Printing Office, 2000.

———. *Final Report of Robert B. Fiske, Jr., Independent Counsel, In Re: Madison Guaranty Savings & Loan Association.* Washington, DC: U.S. Government Printing Office, 1994 (under seal) ("Fiske Final Report/Madison" in notes).

Starr, Kenneth W. *Communication from Kenneth W. Starr, Independent Counsel, Transmitting a Referral to the United States House of Representatives Filed in Conformity with the Requirements of Title 28, United States Code, Section 595(c), One Hundred Fifth Congress, Second Session.* Washington, DC: U.S. Government Printing Office, 1998 ("Starr Report" in notes).

U.S. House Committee on the Judiciary. *Constitutional Grounds for Presidential Impeachment: Modern Precedents—Report by the Staff of the Impeachment Inquiry, Committee on the Judiciary, House of Representatives, One Hundred Fifth Congress, Second Session.* Washington, DC: U.S. Government Printing Office, 1998.

U.S. House Committee on the Judiciary. *Impeachment Inquiry: William Jefferson Clinton, President of the United States—Consideration of Articles of Impeachment, United States House of Representatives, One Hundred Fifth Congress, Second Session.* Washington, DC: U.S. Government Printing Office, 1998.

U.S. Senate. *Impeachment of President William Jefferson Clinton: The Evidentiary Record Pursuant to S. Res. 16, United States Senate, One Hundred Sixth Congress, First Session.* 24 vols. Washington, DC: U.S. Government Printing Office, 1999 ("Evidentiary Record" in notes).

U.S. Senate. *Statement of Bernard W. Nussbaum Before the Committee on Banking, Housing, and Urban Affairs, United States Senate,* 4 Aug. 1994.

U.S. Senate Committee on Banking, Housing, and Urban Affairs. *Hearings Before the Special Committee to Investigate Whitewater Development Corporation and Related Matters Administered by the Committee on Banking, Housing, and Urban Affairs, United States Senate, One Hundred Fourth Congress, First Session.* 18 vols. Washington, DC: U.S. Government Printing Office, 1997.

U.S. Senate Committee on Governmental Affairs. *Hearings Before the Committee on Governmental Affairs, United States Senate, One Hundred Sixth Congress, First Session, on Future of Independent Counsel Act.* Washington, DC: U.S. Government Printing Office, 1999.

U.S. Senate Special Committee to Investigate Whitewater Development Corporation and Related Matters. *Investigation of Whitewater Development Corporation and Related Matters, Final Report of the Special Committee to Investigate Whitewater Development Corporation and Related Matters Together with Additional and Minority Views, United States Senate, One Hundred Fourth Congress, Second Session.* Washington, DC: U.S. Government Printing Office, 1996 ("Final Senate Report/ Whitewater" in notes).

Miscellaneous Documents

Borod & Huggins, Madison Guaranty Savings & Loan Association Special Counsel Investigative Report, 3 Mar. 1987.

"Clinton Accused." washingtonpost.com archives, Jan. 1998–May 1999, http://www .washingtonpost.com/wp-srv/politics/ special/clinton/keystories.htm (accessed 19 Apr. 2009).

Clinton v. Jones, 520 U.S. 681, 117 S.Ct. 1636 (1997). Oral argument available at 1997 WL 9248 (with streaming audio).

Facts on File News Services. *Editorials on File.* New York: Facts on File, 1998–1999.

Grand Jury Testimony of William Jefferson Clinton. August 17, 1998. Transcript of testimony, http://www.cnn.com/icreport/ report/volume3/volume373.html (accessed 19 Apr. 2009).

Office of the Independent Counsel. *Statement of Independent Counsel Kenneth W. Starr Before the Committee on the Judiciary, U.S. House of Representatives,* 19 Nov. 1998.

Paula Corbin Jones v. William Jefferson Clinton and Danny Ferguson, Docket No. LR-C-94-290 (E.D.Ark., 1994). Pleadings and discovery documents.

United States of America, Resolution Trust Corporation, In the Matter of: Madison Guaranty Savings & Loan Association (7236), McCrory, Arkansas. "Interrogatory Responses of Hillary Rodham Clinton, May 24, 1995"; and "Interrogatory Responses of William Jefferson Clinton, May 24, 1995."

United States of America v. James B. McDougal, Jim Guy Tucker, Susan McDougal, Docket No. LR-CR-95-173 (E.D.Ark., 1996). Transcript of proceedings, 16 Jan. 1996 to 28 May 1996 (multivolume).

Books

Baker, Peter. *The Breach: Inside the Impeachment and Trial of William Jefferson Clinton.* New York: Simon & Schuster, 2000.

Bartley, Robert L., ed. *Whitewater: A Journal Briefing from the Editorial Pages of the "Wall Street Journal."* 5 vols. New York: Wall Street Journal, 1994.

Benedict, Michael Les. *The Impeachment and Trial of Andrew Johnson.* New York: W. W. Norton, 1973.

Bennett, Robert S. *In the Ring: The Trials of a Washington Lawyer.* New York: Random House, 2008.

Bernstein, Carl. *A Woman in Charge: The Life of Hillary Rodham Clinton.* New York: Vintage, 2008.

Blumenthal, Sidney. *The Clinton Wars.* New York: Farrar, Straus and Giroux, 2003.

Brock, David. *Blinded by the Right: The Conscience of an Ex-Conservative.* New York: Crown Publishing, 2002.

————. *The Seduction of Hillary Rodham.* New York: Free Press, 1996.

Bumpers, Dale. *The Best Lawyer in a One-Lawyer Town.* Fayetteville: University of Arkansas Press, 2004.

Bushnell, Eleanore. *Crimes, Follies, and Misfortunes: The Federal Impeachment Trials.* Urbana: University of Illinois Press, 1992.

Clarke, Richard A. *Against All Enemies: Inside America's War on Terror.* New York: Free Press, 2004.

Clinton, Bill. *My Life.* New York: Knopf, 2004.

Clinton, Hillary Rodham. *Living History.* New York: Simon & Schuster, 2003.

Conason, Joe, and Gene Lyons. *The Hunting of the President: The Ten-Year Campaign to Destroy Bill and Hillary Clinton.* New York: St. Martin's Press, 2000.

Dean, John. *The Rehnquist Choice: The Untold Story of the Nixon Appointment That Redefined the Supreme Court.* New York: Free Press, 2002.

Dewitt, David Miller. *The Impeachment and Trial of Andrew Johnson.* New York: Macmillan, 1903.

Evans-Pritchard, Ambrose. *The Secret Life of Bill Clinton: The Unreported Stories.* Washington, D.C.: Regnery Publishing, 1997.

Flynt, Larry. *Sex, Lies and Politics: The Naked Truth.* New York: Kensington Books, 2004.

Gerth, Jeff, and Don Van Natta, Jr. *Her Way: The Hopes and Ambitions of Hillary Rodham Clinton.* New York: Back Bay Books, 2007.

Gormley, Ken. *Archibald Cox: Conscience of a Nation.* Boston: Addison-Wesley, 1997.

Greenburg, Jan Crawford. *Supreme Conflict: The Inside Story of the Struggle for Control of the United States Supreme Court.* New York: Penguin Press, 2007.

Hamilton, Alexander. "The Federalist No. 65." In *The Federalist Papers,* edited by C. Rossiter. New York: Penguin Putnam, 1961.

Harris, John F. *The Survivor: Bill Clinton in the White House.* New York: Random House, 2005.

Hunter, Nan D. *The Power of Procedure: The Litigation of Jones v. Clinton.* New York: Aspen Publishers, 2002.

Isikoff, Michael. *Uncovering Clinton: A Reporter's Story.* New York: Crown Publishing, 2000.

Jaworski, Leon. *The Right and the Power: The Prosecution of Watergate.* New York: Reader's Digest, 1976.

Johnson, Haynes. *The Best of Times: America in the Clinton Years.* New York: Harcourt, 2001.

Kalb, Marvin. *One Scandalous Story: Clinton, Lewinsky, and Thirteen Days That Tarnished American Journalism.* New York: Free Press, 2001.

Lyons, Gene. *Fools for Scandal: How the Media Invented Whitewater.* New York: Franklin Square Press, 1996.

Maraniss, David. *First in His Class: The Biography of Bill Clinton.* New York: Simon & Schuster, 1996.

McDougal, Jim, and Curtis Wilkie. *Arkansas Mischief: The Birth of a National Scandal.* New York: Henry Holt and Company, 1998.

McDougal, Susan, and Pat Harris. *The Woman Who Wouldn't Talk: How I Refused to Testify Against the Clintons and What I Learned in Jail.* New York: Carroll and Graf Publishers, 2003.

Morton, Andrew. *Monica's Story.* New York: St. Martin's Press, 1999.

National Commission on Terrorist Attacks. *The 9/11 Commission Report: Final Report of the National Commission on Terrorist Attacks Upon the United States.* New York: W. W. Norton, 2004.

Posner, Richard A. *An Affair of State: The Investigation, Impeachment, and Trial of President Clinton.* Cambridge, Mass.: Harvard University Press, 1999.

Rehnquist, William H. *Grand Inquests: The Historic Impeachments of Justice Samuel Chase and President Andrew Johnson.* New York: Holt, Rinehart and Winston, 1992.

Rozell, Mark J., and Clyde Wilcox, eds. *The Clinton Scandal and the Future of American Government.* Washington, D.C.: Georgetown University Press, 2000.

Ruddy, Christopher. *The Strange Death of Vincent Foster: An Investigation.* New York: Free Press, 1997.

Schippers, David. *Sellout: The Inside Story of President Clinton's Impeachment.* Washington, D.C.: Regnery Publishing, 2000.

Schmidt, Susan, and Michael Weisskopf. *The Truth at Any Cost: Ken Starr and the Unmaking of Bill Clinton.* New York: HarperCollins, 2000.

Smith, Sally Bedell. *For Love of Politics: Bill and Hillary Clinton—The White House Years.* New York: Random House, 2007.

Stewart, James B. *Blood Sport: The President and His Adversaries.* New York: Simon & Schuster, 1996.

Story, Joseph. *Commentaries on the Constitution of the United States.* Edited by T. M. Cooley. 4th ed. 2 vols. Boston: Little, Brown, and Company, 1873.

Toobin, Jeffrey. *A Vast Conspiracy: The Real Story of the Sex Scandal That Nearly Brought Down a President.* New York: Random House, 1999.

Trefouse, Hans L. *Impeachment of a President: Andrew Johnson, the Blacks, and Reconstruction.* Knoxville: University of Tennessee Press, 1975.

Tyrell, R. Emmett, and Anonymous. *The Impeachment of William Jefferson Clinton.* Washington, D.C.: Regnery Publishing, 1997.

Wickham, Dewayne. *Bill Clinton and Black America.* New York: One World/Ballantine, 2002.

Wittes, Benjamin. *Starr: A Reassessment.* New Haven, Conn.: Yale University Press, 2002.

Woodward, Bob. *Shadow: Five Presidents and the Legacy of Watergate.* New York: Simon & Schuster, 1999.

Scholarly Articles

Barrett, John Q. "All or Nothing, or Maybe Cooperation: Attorney General Power, Conduct, and Judgment in Relation to the Work of an Independent Counsel." *Mercer Law Review* 49 (1998): 519.

Butzner, John D. "The Independent Counsel Process: Is It Broken and How Should It Be Fixed?" *Washington and Lee Law Review* 54 (1997): 1515.

Gormley, Ken. "Impeachment and the Independent Counsel: A Dysfunctional Union." *Stanford Law Review* 51 (1999): 309.

"Whitewater: The Politics of a Second Watergate?" *American Political Report* 24, no. 13 (1994): 1.

Select Popular Articles

Adams, James Ring, and R. Emmett Tyrell, Jr. "The Case Against Hillary." *American Spectator,* Feb. 1996, 22.

Bachrach, Judy. "Joan of Arkansas." *Vanity Fair,* Jan. 1999, 86.

Becker, Daniel. "Legends in the Law: Charles F. C. Ruff." *Washington Lawyer,* Apr. 2001, 31.

Bork, Robert H. "Should He Be Impeached?" *American Spectator,* Dec. 1997, 74.

Boyer, Peter J. "Life After Vince." *The New Yorker,* 11 Sept. 1995, 54.

Brenner, Marie. "The Price of Loyalty." *Vanity Fair,* June 2001, 180.

Brill, Stephen. "Anonymity and Dignity." *American Lawyer,* Sept. 1994, 5.

Brock, David. "Living with the Clintons: Bill's Arkansas Bodyguards Tell the Story the Press Missed." *American Spectator,* Jan. 1994, 18.

Church, George J. "Investigations: Raw Nerves and Tax Returns." *Time,* 14 Feb. 1994, 26.

Conason, Joe, and Gene Lyons. "Nabbing David Hale." *Salon,* 3 Mar. 2000.

Ellis, David. "The Perils of Paula." *People,* 23 May 1994, 88.

Gibbs, Nancy R. "No Deal." *Time,* 11 May 1998, 26.

Ginsburg, William H. "An Open Letter to Kenneth Starr." *California Lawyer,* June 1998.

Grann, David. "Starr Wars: The Finale." *New Republic,* 28 June 1999, 18.

Henry, Ed. "Overwhelming Events Overwhelm Everyone." *Roll Call,* 21 Dec. 1998, 1.

"The Impeachment of Andrew Johnson: The Impeachment Managers," *Harper's Weekly,* 21 Mar. 1868, 179.

Isikoff, Michael. "A Twist in *Jones v. Clinton.*" *Newsweek,* 11 Aug. 1997, 30.

"It's Definitely Going to Be the Years of Hillary and Tipper." *Beverly Hills Magazine,* vol. 1, no. 2, 1992.

Kelly, Amy. "House Impeaches President: Two of Four Articles Go to Senate for Trial." *Roll Call,* 21 Dec. 1998, 1, 26.

Klaidman, Daniel. "Branded, Besieged, and Battling Back." *Legal Times,* 5 Dec. 1995, 1.

Maxa, Rudy. "The Devil in Paula Jones." *Penthouse,* Jan. 1995, 107.

Mayer, Jane. "Distinguishing Characteristics." *The New Yorker,* 7 July 1997, 34.

O'Neill, Ann W. "Steel Magnolia." *Los Angeles Times Magazine,* 9 May 1999.

Starr, Ken. "From the Editor's Desk: Golden Rule Is Often Forgotten in Everyday Activities on Campus." *Harding (University, Searcy, AR) Bison,* 15 Apr. 1965, 2.

———. "Star Dust: Crowded Cities, Plentiful Problems." *Harding (University, Searcy, AR) Bison,* 12 Jan. 1966, 2.

Toobin, Jeffrey. "Presiding Over the President." *The New Yorker,* 9 Mar. 1998, 45.

Waas, Murray. "False Witness: Part I." *Salon,* 12 Aug. 1998.

"Was Dash's Starr Role Ill-Fated from the Start?" *Legal Times*, 29 Apr. 1996, 1.

Watson, Russell. "Vince Foster's Suicide: The Rumor Mill Churns." *Newsweek*, 21 Mar. 1994, 32.

York, Byron. "The Ordeal of Charles Bakaly." *American Spectator*, Sept. 2000.

Magazines and Journals Consulted

American Lawyer
American Political Report
American Spectator
Beverly Hills Magazine
California Lawyer
George
Legal Times
Los Angeles Times Magazine
Maclean's (Canada)
Nation
National Law Journal
New Republic
Newsweek
New Yorker
Penthouse
People
Salon
Time
Vanity Fair
Washington Lawyer

Newspapers Consulted

Arkansas Democrat-Gazette
Arkansas Democrat-Gazette Press Services
Arkansas Times
Associated Press
BBC News (London)
Bergen (NJ) Record
Boston Globe
Boston Herald
Chicago Tribune
Cincinnati Enquirer
Dallas Morning News
Darien (CT) Times
Fort Worth Star-Telegram
Harding (University, Searcy, AR) Bison
Houston Chronicle
International Herald Tribune
Investor's Business Daily
Los Angeles Times
Martinsburg (WV) Journal
Memphis Commercial Appeal
Montgomery County (AK) News
New Jersey Star-Ledger
New York Daily News
New York Post
New York Times
Philadelphia Inquirer
Pittsburgh Post-Gazette
Richmond Times
Roll Call (Washington, DC)
Russellville (AR) Courier-Democrat
Sacramento Bee
San Antonio Express-News
San Francisco Chronicle
Seattle Times
Sunday Telegraph (London)
USA Today
Wall Street Journal
Washington (PA) Observer-Reporter
Washington Post
Washington Times

ACKNOWLEDGMENTS

Reaching the end point of a project of this magnitude requires more thanks than an author could fit in print without doubling the size of the book.

My first nonfiction book, *Archibald Cox: Conscience of a Nation*—about the principled Watergate special prosecutor who was one of the great constitutional lawyers and public servants of the twentieth century—was published just as the Monica Lewinsky affair exploded in the news in early 1998. Cox, my former professor at Harvard, was so distraught over the Clinton-Starr imbroglio that it ultimately caused him to give up on the independent counsel law that he had helped to forge after Watergate. Fortunately, he agreed to sit for an interview with his former student before his death in 2004—I am pleased that his voice appears in the pages of this work. If only America could figure out how to build new models like him.

One of the first people I contacted, when I decided to pursue this project in 1999, was Ken Starr. At the time, Starr had just stepped down as independent counsel. Despite a slew of demands on his time, he completed more than fifty hours of interviews with me at his home in McLean, Virginia, and at George Mason Law School, where he was then teaching. These interviews with Starr, along with interview sessions with his top deputies, provided a remarkable window into the thought processes of the Office of Independent Counsel at a time when these dramatic events were still fresh in their minds. Ken Starr also made available to me boxes of his personal correspondence housed in a storage facility in Northern Virginia, an invaluable resource in preserving this difficult yet historic period of his career. The entire Starr family has been open and cooperative in every way; for this I am deeply grateful.

President Bill Clinton first agreed to sit down with me to be interviewed for this book project in 2004. Weeks later, he underwent open-heart surgery. Yet he remained true to his promise: We met in Philadelphia to talk about the events of Whitewater, then met twice at his home in Chappaqua, New York, to discuss the *Paula Jones* lawsuit, the explosion of the Lewinsky affair in the media, and the draining congressional impeachment proceedings. President Clinton was charming, hospitable, and surprisingly candid when it came to reflecting on the scandal that nearly ruined his presidency. As I drove back to the airport, crossing the Hudson River on that sunny day after my final interview session with the former president, I knew I had a book unlike any other.

There are many other players in this drama who contributed to the finished story. The editors of the *Arkansas Democrat-Gazette* gave me complete access to that paper's archives, a treasure trove of news stories. Susan McDougal turned over boxes of original documents relating to Whitewater, allowing me to use them without limitation. As well, even though it was still difficult for her to revisit the past, she took me to the grave of her former husband, Jim McDougal, so that I could climb the hill and describe that scene in the final chapter of the book. The McDougals' close friend and vigilant guardian, Claudia Riley, provided a place for this author to eat and sleep during trips to Arkadelphia, even opening the doors of the little cottage at the foot of her driveway where Jim McDougal lived before going to prison. Claudia Riley also introduced me to Dr. Richard Clark, the thoughtful psychologist who treated Jim McDougal at the Fort Worth prison and who made available (with permission of the executor) never-before-released psychological records that chronicled McDougal's tragic death in the "hole" of that federal institution.

Paula Jones's first lawyer, Danny Traylor, welcomed me into his office in Little Rock and took me on a memorable boat ride on the Arkansas River, recounting the story of how a small-time real estate lawyer found himself in the midst of the most politically charged lawsuit in the United States. Greg Kitterman, another Jones attorney, helped to arrange an interview with Paula and her friend Debra Ballentine at a cozy Italian restaurant in North Little Rock; this meeting was instrumental in allowing me to understand what made Ms. Jones tick and why she felt compelled to sue the president. Ms. Jones's Virginia lawyers, Gil Davis and Joe Cammarata, were consummate professionals who provided much assistance. Davis permitted me to review file cabinets filled with documents relating to the *Jones* case in the basement of his Virginia law office—a researcher's gold mine. Two of Ms. Jones's Dallas lawyers, Jim Fisher and Wes Holmes, told their side of the story with fairness and balance. Bob Bennett, who represented President Clinton in the lawsuit, pointed me in the direction of material that shed new light on key events. And the clerk's office of the U.S. District Court for the Eastern District of Arkansas scanned thousands of pieces of correspondence from the public records of Judge Susan Webber Wright—relating to the *Jones* case—in order to assist in this historical undertaking.

Monica Lewinsky overcame her understandable skepticism of writers to sit down with this author for dozens of hours of interviews. Even though the process was clearly painful for her, she maintained enough trust that the finished product would be fair and balanced that she eventually opened up and provided a wealth of information, for which she did not receive a single cent. Ms. Lewinsky also shared documents—we sat on folding chairs inside a storage facility in Greenwich Village, reviewing personal papers that brought back disturbing memories and clearly upset her but allowed me to recount this piece of the story with rich detail that otherwise would have been lost. Monica's parents, Marcia Lewis and Bernie Lewinsky, also cooperated in this project from the start. Her lawyer, Plato Cacheris, a true son of western Pennsylvania, urged his client to contribute to this historical endeavor and reassured her that law professors from Pittsburgh were generally harmless.

In writing the impeachment chapters, President Clinton's lawyer David Kendall was instrumental in allowing me to reconstruct the pieces. Kendall's mastery of the record and his inexhaustible talents as a lawyer were humbling for this former litigation attorney. Most important, he helped to facilitate the meetings with President Clinton and to ensure that they were carried out efficiently and professionally. Finally, as I sat in the chair that Kendall had occupied during the Senate impeachment trial, Kendall recounted those events with clarity and accuracy that was invaluable in writing the final chapters.

Representative Henry Hyde, legendary chairman of the House Judiciary Committee and manager who led the prosecution of President Clinton in the Senate, met with me numerous times in Washington and Illinois, even handing over a good Dominican cigar on occasion. One of my few regrets in writing the compact impeachment chapters was that it was impossible to fully capture Hyde's disarming wit, openness, and friendly demeanor. Although I came to disagree with the course taken by Chairman Hyde during the failed impeachment effort, I never came to dislike or hold in disrespect this icon of the United States Congress. As well, Hyde's burly and scrappy chief counsel from Chicago, David Schippers, provided boxes of documents relating to the impeachment trial and treated the author to one of the best lunches in years (at Portillo's Hot Dogs in Chicago).

Senator Edward M. Kennedy, who sadly became sick and passed away before I could interview him for this book, helped at many stages—most important, he arranged for me to obtain videotapes of the entire House and Senate impeachment proceedings, which in turn allowed me to view hundreds of hours of tapes in my study at home, in order to describe the impeachment scenes with far richer detail than if I had simply read those proceedings on paper. Senators Trent Lott (Republican) and Tom Daschle (Democrat), who managed the impeachment trial for their respective parties, provided a wealth of additional information, as did Bob Dove, the Senate parliamentarian.

Friends and family of both President Clinton and Ken Starr were an enormous help in navigating the previously foreign terrain of Arkansas and Texas, where portions of the story played out. Marge Mitchell, a best friend of Bill Clinton's mother, shuttled me around Hot Springs in her Cadillac and took me to nursing homes to meet former teachers and octogenarian admirers of Bill Clinton. Joe Purvis, one of Clinton's childhood friends, took me to fish on the White River in order to see the site of the failed Whitewater investment; then we dined on rainbow trout fried in peanut oil, an unexpected perk of the project. Clinton's stepfather, Dick Kelley, welcomed me into his cottage on the lake in Hot Springs to tell the story from the perspective of his late wife, Virginia Clinton Kelley. David Matter, a world-class civic leader and businessman in Pittsburgh, who was a close friend of President Clinton's at Georgetown, helped to arrange my first meeting with the President in the William Penn Hotel; for that, I will always be grateful. As well, countless Clinton friends from every corner of the country rallied to provide support for the proposition that William Jefferson Clinton—despite Ken Starr's effort to derail him—remains one of the great presidents in American history.

Ken Starr, too, had many unwavering admirers. His high school teacher Roberta Mahan drove me down gravel-covered roads in San Antonio to point out where young Ken Starr had grown up in modest surroundings and listened to his father (a preacher and a barber) preparing sermons in the backyard next to a cow pasture. Starr's wife, Alice, overcame her wariness of writers in the wake of the bruising independent counsel period to share touching stories about her husband—adding a wife's elegant touch to the story. Starr's personal assistant, Neille Mallon Russell, was more enthused about helping to shine a light on her former boss's multitudinous good qualities than any other person on earth. Starr's top deputy in Arkansas, Hickman Ewing, Jr.—a prosecutor with boundless energy and a near photographic memory—took the author on a "scandal tour" of Little Rock to see where key events took place. Jackie Bennett, an imposing Indiana lawyer who eventually ran the Washington office for Starr, gave up many hours to speak candidly with me; for this openness in the face of known disagreements that could have led others to refuse to talk, I will always be appreciative. Finally, OIC prosecutor Paul Rosenzweig arranged for me to tour the Office of Independent Counsel in Washington before it shut down its operations, making it possible to describe crucial scenes with much more accuracy. Rosenzweig also read a draft of the manuscript and provided unvarnished comments—a hazardous task, especially because he knew that he disagreed with my perspective in many places. His suggestions made the finished manuscript much better than it would have been without his careful eye.

Lew Merletti, who served as director of the Secret Service during the Starr period, broke his silence to share his dramatic story about that agency's struggle to prevent the special prosecutor from destroying the protective envelope around the president—and about his agents' battle with the FBI that was often seeking to thwart them. Merletti agonized for months before agreeing to tell his story on the record. He and his fellow USSS agents, including Clint Hill, turned out to be living embodiments of the Secret Service's motto: "Worthy of trust and confidence."

A host of journalists shared their time and expertise to assist in this endeavor. Special thanks to Jeffrey Toobin in New York (who covered the Lewinsky affair for *The New Yorker*) and Gene Lyons in Arkansas (who wrote excellent accounts of Whitewater). They shared massive archives of raw material that they had gathered up as they covered the story on the ground. James Stewart, author of *Blood Sport*, was likewise generous in helping a fellow Harvard Law grad navigate the Arkansas environs. David Maraniss, author of *First in His Class*, still one of the best biographies of Bill Clinton, provided useful information relating to Clinton's prepresidential years.

Numerous folks read draft chapters, to the great benefit of the book. My sincere thanks to Roger Newman, a superb writer and editor; Judge Thomas Hardiman; Judge D. Brooks Smith; and the Honorable Robert J. Cindrich, my best friend and co-conspirator when it comes to all overly ambitious projects that seek to prove that even people from Swissvale and Avella can think big.

On the literary side of the house, I am indebted to my fellow *Pitt Newser* Jess Brailler, one of the most creative thinkers in the book business, who guided me in holding out for the kind of first-rate book I wanted. My artistic guru, friend, and collaborator, Matt Kambic, helped to brainstorm by creating early drafts of jacket art, providing input to the creative team at Crown until they settled on the perfect cover (many thanks to Whitney Cookman who led that creative effort). My cohort since kindergarten, Patty Boyd, did a spectacular job as copy editor, topping her Herculean effort on the Archibald Cox book and slogging through an additional two thousand notes.

Over the course of nine years, I have had a dozen stellar research assistants from Duquesne Law School, who have camped out in a dark war room in the basement and pored over documents and dug through boxes of newspapers that housed cockroaches and waterbugs. Special thanks to Linda Hernandez, who jumped in and helped to create a magnificent archive from the project's inception; David Cardone, who devoted thousands of hours to the Clinton-Starr cause and helped me tape up boxes of documents in Arkansas and ship them back before the donors changed their minds; and Beth Lamm, who threw herself into every aspect of the work and completed the daunting task of checking each note prior to publication. Additional thanks to Kate Sabatos, Susan Burkett, David Cook, Sara Restauri, Ryan Hemminger, Erin McCurdy, Sam Yamron, Marcus Graham, Glen Downey, Nichole Starr, and Catrina Rogers for their able research assistance.

This book required hundreds of trips to Washington, D.C., for interviews. On these visits I had the best lodgings possible, staying with my brother, William T. Gormley, Jr., currently the reluctant dean of the Georgetown Public Policy Institute. I will always treasure those late-night car trips to visit Bilbo, his wife, Rosie Zagari, a professor of history at George Mason, and their daughter, Angela Rose, who made sure we had time to buy penny candy at the hardware store. My other siblings—B. J. Gormley, Nancy Pfenning, and Susie Hogan—and their families have been consistent supporters of their brother who started writing stories in the St. Anselm's playground at age nine. As well, thanks to Greg and Cindy Peterson for providing a writer's haven at Chautauqua and Jamestown; and my extended family from Kentucky, New York, and New Jersey.

Some people who provided valued support did not get to see the publication of this book, one of the few sad aspects of reaching such a milestone. My father and mother, Bill and Elena Gormley, both passed away shortly after I began interviews for the project (my dad died the morning I arrived in New York for my first interview with Monica Lewinsky; it was the most difficult interview I ever completed in my career). Both of my parents were tireless supporters of my writing—I did my best to make this one perfect for you, Mom and Dad. As well, my mother-in-law, Noreen Kozler, loved all of my literary adventures and was present for my first speech about the Clinton-Starr investigation at the Chautauqua Institution in 1999; sadly, she died several years later, far too young—you would have loved the next seven years' worth of interview stories, Mom. My uncle, John Furia, Jr., was a noted writer and film producer in Hollywood, who conspired with his nephew on every writing project and was scheduled to receive galleys of the Clinton-Starr book when he passed away unexpectedly: his grace, integrity, and professionalism as a writer will always serve as my model. My aunt Laura Galdi was a perpetual optimist who took care of her nephew on my many treks to New York: I will miss those side trips to Blauvelt. My nephew, Nils Pfenning, passed away this past summer at age twenty-one after two kidney transplants; he was always interested in creative projects and would have loved to have attended the book-signing bashes in Squirrel Hill—Nils, you remain an inspiration for all of us. Finally, Chief Justice Ralph Cappy of the Pennsylvania Supreme Court was a friend and mentor for twenty years; he was so excited about this project that he threatened to stow away in my suitcase when I traveled to New York to interview Bill Clinton. If only I could give you your signed copy, Ralph.

My secretary, June Devinney, did a masterful job at editing and re-editing chapters, often thirty or forty times—June, I told you I would finish it, eventually! Thanks also to Doris Walls, who faithfully typed hundreds of interview transcripts. My agents at William Morris Agency in New York have been remarkable: Mel Berger is the ideal literary agent who inhales political writing, guides his authors with professionalism, and knows just where to place each book to maximize its success. He conceptualized a big project from the start and his grand vision was contagious. At Crown, my editor, Sean Desmond, has been the best in the business, the modern equivalent of Max Perkins. He has never sacrificed quality or historical accuracy for expedience. His calm and thoughtful approach to handling each issue that came our way made working with him one of the great privileges of this endeavor. Crown's publisher, Tina Constable, believed in the book from day one, long before the chapters were complete; for her unyielding confidence in the project, I am extremely grateful. Thanks also to editorial expert Christine Tanigawa; legal counsel Min Lee; assistant extraordinaire Stephanie Chan; and jacket designer Whitney Cookman. Each of them devoted care to the project in order to create an enduring piece of American history. And Penny Simon, the greatest publicist an author could ever hope to find, tackled the release of the book with such tenacity, professionalism, and assuredness that we exceeded every initial dream of positive reviews and media exposure many times over.

My friends and colleagues at Duquesne University and its School of Law, where I am privileged to serve as interim dean, have been a steady source of support for this endeavor. I benefited from a Faculty Development Fund grant that paid for many trips to Arkansas, Texas, and other far-flung destinations. I also benefited, at every step of the process, from the ideas and boundless enthusiasm of my students. My law school roommates, including Rex Van Middlesworth and Senator Mark Warner, offered much kibitzing throughout the project—wisely, I ignored all of their suggestions. Other partners in crime from the *Somerville Bar Review* have cheered me on in my work; I look forward to doing at least one dramatic reading at O'Henry's.

It is only fitting to begin and end this book with thanks to my wife, Laura, and our four beautiful children—Carolyn, Luke, Rebecca, and Maddy. Although I am extremely proud of this book, it pales in comparison to the pride I have for my family, who made each daily trip into the salt mines worthwhile.

INDEX

Abraham, Spencer, 644
Accuracy in Media, 134
Adkins, Nancy, 23
Afghanistan and Sudan military operations, 558
Akaka, Daniel K., 644
Albright, Madeleine, 604
Alexander, Freda, 565
Alliance for Re-Birth of the Independent America (ARIA), 131
Al-Qaeda, 492, 537, 558, 758
American Civil Liberties Union (ACLU), 171–172, 274
American Conservative Union, 201
American Spectator, 115, 116–117, 119, 170, 221, 275, 376
Anthony, Sheila, 73
Arafat, Yasir, 649
Arkansas Project, 432, 433
Armey, Dick, 584
Ausbrook, Keith, 662
Ayer, Donald B., 96

Bach, Monique, 599
Bacon, Ken, 298, 332, 721
Baird, Zoe, 70
Bakaly, Charles, 757
Ballentine, Debra, 117, 118–119, 120, 121, 125, 138, 687
Banks, Charles, 58–59, 63–65
Barnett, Bob, 542
Barr, Bob, 275–276, 625, 626, 631
Bassett, Beverly, 188
Bates, John, 279, 284–285
Bates, Stephen, 272, 274, 336, 338, 566, 569, 593
Bauer, Robert F., 584
Begala, Paul, 557, 581, 606
Behre, Kirby, 287, 291, 307, 331
Bell, Griffin, 275
Bennett, Bob, 304
  Jones case, 135, 137, 172, 176: Clinton's deposition, 127, 381, 382, 383, 384–385, 387, 389, 390; "distinguishing characteristic" allegation, 324; immunity of the president from civil liability, issue of, 173, 174, 219, 221, 226; Jones's deposition, 323; Jones's image, tarnishing of, 180, 183, 184, 711; leaking of information, 319; Lewinsky's affidavit, 312–313, 323; "other women" issue, 322; settlement agreement, 588, 747; settlement initiatives, 138–140, 255–256, 257, 258, 259, 319; summary judgment in Clinton's favor, 477; Willey's charge of sexual harassment against Clinton, 255
Bennett, Sen. Bob, 643
Bennett, Jackie, 278, 348–349, 655
  background of, 158
  Lewinsky case: Bittman's selection to manage OIC investigation, 434, 435; brace of Lewinsky, 349, 350, 351–352, 359, 360–361, 363, 365, 366, 367, 374; Clinton's grand jury testimony, 551; Currie's cooperation with OIC, 436–437, 472; ethical concerns within OIC, 433; immunity for Lewinsky, 367, 399–402, 406–407, 445, 447; Isikoff's reporting on, 334–335, 365, 374; "jobs for silence" issue, 283–285; leaking of grand jury information, 502, 737–738; Lewis's grand jury testimony, 455; OIC given jurisdiction over, 326, 327, 328–329, 334, 336–338, 724–725, 726; perjury allegations against Clinton and Lewinsky, 279, 280, 283; prosecutorial misconduct charges against OIC, 592, 659; Starr Report, 568, 570, 575; Tripp's initial meeting with OIC, 286–292, 307; Tripp's recorded conversations with Lewinsky, 279, 287, 291; Tripp's "wired" conversation with Lewinsky, 291, 292–293, 294; wiring of Lewinsky option, 365
  Whitewater/Madison case, 198: Jackie Bennett's hiring by OIC, 158–159; Clinton's extramarital relationships, investigation of, 248; Hillary Clinton's deposition in January 1998, 324, 325; Hillary Clinton's possible indictment, 280, 483; daily functioning of OIC office, 164–165; "jobs for silence" issue, 284; wrap-it-up mode of OIC in early 1998, 279
Berger, Sandy, 558, 604
Beyer, James, 76
Biden, Joe, 682
Binhak, Steve, 289
Bin Laden, Osama, 492, 537, 542, 558
Bittman, Bob, 405, 595, 598
  Lewinsky case, 502: Bittman's selection to manage OIC investigation, 434–435, 436, 456–457; Clinton's blood samples for OIC, 524–525; Clinton's grand jury testimony,

ABOUT THE AUTHOR

KEN GORMLEY is interim dean and professor at Duquesne University Law School, specializing in constitutional subjects. He is a nationally renowned expert on Watergate and special prosecutors, and the author of the critically acclaimed *Archibald Cox: Conscience of a Nation*. He lives with his wife, Laura, and their four children in Pittsburgh.

Printed in the United States
by Baker & Taylor Publisher Services